CollegeBoard

THE COLLEGE BOARD
Scholarship handbook
2005

THE COLLEGE BOARD
Scholarship
handbook
2005

With a foreword by Joseph A. Russo
Director of Student Financial Services
University of Notre Dame

Eighth Edition

The College Board, New York

The College Board: connecting students to college success™

The College Board is a not-for-profit membership association whose mission is to connect students to college success and opportunity. Founded in 1900, the association is composed of more than 4,500 schools, colleges, universities, and other educational organizations. Each year, the College Board serves over three million students and their parents, 23,000 high schools, and 3,500 colleges through major programs and services in college admissions, guidance, assessment, financial aid, enrollment, and teaching and learning. Among its best-known programs are the SAT®, the PSAT/NMSQT®, and the Advanced Placement Program® (AP®). The College Board is committed to the principles of excellence and equity, and that commitment is embodied in all of its programs, services, activities, and concerns.

For further information, visit www.collegeboard.com.

The scholarship descriptions in this book are based on information supplied by the program sponsors themselves in response to the College Board's Annual Survey of Financial Aid Programs 2004–2005. The survey was completed in the spring of 2004. A total of 974 sponsoring organizations throughout the United States participated in this effort, and the information they provided was reviewed and verified by a staff of College Board editors. While every effort was made to ensure the completeness and accuracy of the information contained in this book, sponsors' policies and programs are subject to change without notice, and the College Board cannot take responsibility for changes made by sponsoring organizations after the information was submitted. If users of this book find that any of the descriptions are inaccurate, please contact the College Board Annual Survey of Financial Aid Programs, Attn: College Planning Services, by mail at 45 Columbus Avenue, New York, NY 10023-6992, or by telephone: 212 713-8000.

Copies of this book are available from your local bookseller or may be ordered from College Board Publications, P.O. Box 869010, Plano, TX 75074-0998. The book may also be ordered online through the College Board Store at www.collegeboard.com. The price is $26.95.

Library of Congress Catalog Number: 97-76451
International Standard Book Number: 0-87447-715-8

Printed in the United States of America

Contents

Dear Friends,

The College Board is dedicated to connecting students to college success and opportunity. We believe in the principles of excellence and equity in education and try to promote them in all that we do. With the College Board's Handbook series, we hope to put an authoritative source of college information at your fingertips to help connect you to a college education.

College is a dream worth working hard to achieve. I've been a businessman, a governor, and now the president of the College Board, but nothing makes me prouder than to say that I am a college graduate. With perseverance, anyone who desires a college education can attain one. College Board publications can help you get there.

My best wishes on your journey to success.

Gaston Caperton

Gaston Caperton
President
The College Board

Foreword

A college education is understandably one of the more commonly sought-after goals of American families. The opportunities it provides are arguably the finest and most diverse in the world. Both access and wide choices are generally available to just about everyone who wants to pursue education beyond high school.

The benefits

The benefits that come with additional schooling are clearly evident to individuals as well as to our society. Most college graduates enjoy a significantly higher economic status than those without the same level of education. Median family income for bachelor's degree recipients is almost twice as much as the median income for those with only a high school diploma…and this gap is growing. Over a lifetime, the difference in earnings between these two groups exceeds $1,000,000. With this perspective in clear focus, the cost of attending college should be viewed as the lifetime investment it surely can be. In addition to the obvious financial advantages, statistics show that college-educated people often live healthier and longer lives, are more involved in their communities, and raise children who are more likely to attend college and share in the same intellectually and economically richer lifestyle. Society as a whole benefits from a more involved citizenry, less crime and unemployment, and a strong tax base. Certainly the cost of college today can present a challenge for many families. Yet the cost of not securing the further skills and training which typically are provided by a college education can often be even more expensive.

The cost factors

Steadily rising college costs have created much concern among students and parents about the affordability of this American dream. This is true both in the private and public sectors, especially in recent years as state legislatures react to budget problems. While it's true that the costs of college have been rising at a rate greater than the cost of living, media commentators have tended to exaggerate the impact of this escalation, making it appear much worse than it really is. The facts are that the vast majority (almost 70 percent) of students pay less than $8,000 a year for college tuition and fees, while only 8 percent pay more than $24,000. Almost 30 percent of undergraduates attending four-year colleges and universities full-time are at institutions charging less than $4,000 in tuition and fees. As Donald M. Stewart, former president of the College Board, pointed out in testimony before the U.S. Senate Hearing on Access and Costs, "the misinformation fosters public alarm, and discourages many students and families from even considering the option of higher education and the chance of reaping the benefits enjoyed by those with a college degree."

The challenge

Nonetheless, paying for college is a concern for most American families. While traditional need-based financial aid programs continue to help students afford the costs of higher education, those resources are limited and more than ever include troublesome levels of student loans. Current government efforts to provide additional resources lean heavily toward further borrowing opportunities. Although such programs offer generous provisions in the form of low interest rates and deferred repayment over lengthy periods of time, they leave students and families with the prospect of long-term debt. Yet, even an individual's level of student debt upon graduation needs proper perspective, as the impact of such debt against a college graduate's starting salary is actually *less* today than it was 10 years ago, further reinforcing the value of a college degree. Nonetheless, the challenge is to find ways of achieving college and graduate school goals in the face of limited financial aid resources.

The options

The good news is that there are a number of things that families can do to position themselves to meet that challenge. The most basic step is finding out what their options are in order to make informed decisions about tailoring lifestyle choices to the needs of educational priorities.

Every family makes decisions regarding lifestyle on a regular basis. Food, housing, transportation, clothing, and entertainment are fundamental expenses, but there's considerable latitude in how much income is earmarked for any of those categories. Even if there hasn't been much advance planning, as the college-going years approach, parents have the choice of reordering some of their priorities—spending less on clothing and entertainment, for example, so they can increase the amount of money they allocate for savings and investments, or take advantage of the benefits of a tuition prepayment plan. Every state in the country now offers one or more programs, commonly known as "529 plans," intended to help families prepare for college costs through college savings plans or prepaid tuition plans or both. More than ever before, these programs provide very favorable federal income tax consequences to these investments. Many also offer additional state income tax breaks. The "independent 529 plan," sponsored by over 230 private institutions nationally, is the latest program added to this special savings opportunity. Students have comparable choices—cutting back on what they spend for CDs, movies, or the latest fad in clothes; forgoing afternoons at the mall in favor of an after-school job; taking AP® courses that could reduce overall college costs by a full year's tuition and fees. Another hidden cost that families need to have on their radar screens arises from the fact that many students often require more than four years to complete their bachelor's degree. Only 36 percent of undergraduates complete their degree on time. Indeed, the wise consumer would investigate the on-time graduation rate at the institutions they are considering.

Financial aid eligibility versus availability

Prior to the 1970s, before the federal government began to provide substantial aid to cover college costs, families had to depend almost entirely on their own resources. The need to save for college was paramount.

With the advent of financial aid and formulas for expected family contribution, it seemed to some that saving was counterproductive because it reduced student aid eligibility. If that point of view ever had validity, it certainly doesn't today. As families are discovering, often the hard way, *eligibility* does not automatically translate into *availability* of funds. And the funds that are available are more likely to be in the form of loans than gift aid, so the results of not having saved are often a much more expensive set of options at best, or a very reduced set of college opportunities at worst. Recent legislation designed to help families through limited tax credits and deductions for tuition costs, although admirable, will fall far short of the resources needed by many families.

Incentives for saving

What is encouraging and very positive about some of the new tax legislation are the incentives to save for college. These incentives may not be of immediate help to families with students about to enter college, but they can have an impact on future years. So parents should certainly investigate these avenues and begin to take advantage of them. It goes without saying that the earlier a saving program begins, the better. But the type of program and the amount of money to be set aside will depend on individual family circumstances such as income, nondiscretionary expenses, number of children, number of years remaining prior to college and, of course, the choice of college and its actual cost when the time comes. There are simple ways of projecting costs, using an estimated inflation factor compounded by the number of years remaining before college.

Once you know the estimated costs, the next step is to develop a savings/investment plan that assumes a compounded rate of return and monthly amount to be saved. There are a number of educational and financial organizations that have developed methods for making those kinds of projections, among them the College Board and the National Association of Student Financial Aid Administrators (NASFAA). Information and guidelines are available on the Internet from those organizations as well as from a number of others, including most major investment companies.

Even with careful advance planning and saving, the majority of families need some financial aid, including loans, to help them cover the full annual costs of college. But that doesn't mean that the decision about where to apply should be based on cost of tuition and fees. Families should not be discouraged by the price tag, and should never rule out a college, no matter how expensive, before exploring every financial aid option available. All colleges and universities have a variety of programs to assist in paying the bill. Most of them include scholarship, grant, loan, and work opportunities, often combined in "packages" based on individual family circumstances. For families who do not receive financial aid or who, for whatever reason, may be concerned about meeting some remaining expenses even after financial aid has been considered, there are a number of alternatives. Some colleges offer other financial products and services as well, so it's important to find out what the "net cost" will be after all financial aid has been factored in before making a decision.

The role of private scholarships

The one additional source of funding that hasn't been addressed up to this point is private scholarship opportunities—and they can play a significant role in supplementing a family's personal resources. As this book demonstrates, there are substantial programs sponsored by foundations; civic, fraternal, veterans, and religious associations; corporations; the military; and other private and public sector organizations.

Eligibility for these programs often requires meeting some condition such as demonstrating special talents or skills; being a member of a particular organization or ethnic group; pursuing a specified major or career goal; or agreeing to fulfill some postgraduate obligation. Such programs can be very helpful, though their resources are not always adequate to meet the full demand. Applicants have to realize that they're competing for limited resources—identifying potential programs and applying to them as early as possible offer the best chances for success.

A few words of caution—don't let your common sense be overwhelmed by the glowing claims of some commercial scholarship search companies that offer, for hefty fees, to tap into "untold millions of scholarship dollars" that go unused each year because no one applies. The general rule is that if it sounds too good to be true, it probably is. If scholarships are guaranteed for a fee, then beware. Rely on your own search efforts using resources such as this book or one of the annually updated scholarship search software programs that may be available free of charge in your local library or high school. The Internet is also an up-to-date, accurate source of free scholarship information. You can access the College Board's online scholarship and college search programs at: www.collegeboard.com.

There is also a growing number of other free scholarship search organizations and other enterprises on the Internet, advertising to assist in the college entrance process, that provide similar information. Some will require a "registration," which includes personal data about yourself and even your family. Those using such services should be aware of the terms and options that these registrations authorize, including the potential of sharing your personal information with other "organizations" and vendors. Again, the disclosure of your personal data to third parties should not occur without your authorized permission.

Students who want to explore scholarship prospects need to be especially diligent in their schoolwork and extracurricular activities because superior academic and personal credentials often are critical factors in awarding scholarships. Moreover, colleges tend to look favorably on the awarding of outside scholarships as an indication of students' initiative and sense of responsibility, often adjusting those students' financial aid packages to reduce the loan and work study components rather than the gift aid portion. Scholarship awards clearly enhance students' credentials and, all things being equal, make them stronger candidates from the colleges' perspective.

Meeting the challenge

Even with nearly $105 billion in financial aid currently made available, paying for college is indeed a major challenge for most families. But with resources such as *The College Board Scholarship Handbook*, students and parents can expand their access to funding for college and move another step closer to their goals for the future.

Joseph A. Russo
Director of Student Financial Services
University of Notre Dame

How to use this book

General information

Searching for scholarships has often been described as looking for a needle in a haystack. There are thousands of award programs available, but the typical student can expect to qualify for only a small number of them. *The College Board Scholarship Handbook* is designed to point you toward the specific award programs that match your own personal and academic qualifications.

What's included. Compiled within this book are detailed descriptions of national and state level award programs for undergraduate students. Most are available to all undergraduates, but some are restricted to entering freshmen, and others are only for continuing students—sophomores, juniors, or seniors. Local award programs that are restricted to a single community or school are not included; these are best located through your high school guidance office or local chamber of commerce. Also not included are award programs offered by the colleges themselves to their own students. For these "inside" awards, you should consult the financial aid offices at the colleges you are considering. Detailed financial aid information for almost 3,000 colleges can also be found in *The College Board College Cost & Financial Aid Handbook*.

The award program descriptions are based on information provided by the sponsors themselves, in response to the College Board's Annual Survey of Financial Aid Programs, conducted in the spring of 2004. A staff of editors, under the direction of Andy Costello, Project Manager, and with the assistance of Stephen Jordan, verified the facts for every award program to be certain that each description is as complete and accurate as possible. While every effort was made to ensure that the information is correct and up-to-date, we urge students to confirm facts, especially deadline information, with the programs themselves. The award programs' Web sites are the best sources for current information.

Getting started. The opening sections of *The College Board Scholarship Handbook* offer advice from financial aid experts, guidance on paying for college, tips for avoiding scholarship scams, answers to some of the most frequently asked questions about funding college or graduate studies, and a glossary of terms.

You may be tempted to go directly to the program descriptions and start browsing, but to get the most out of this book, start by reading the information and advice in the opening pages. They'll help you get a realistic perspective on financial aid and give you useful guidelines for understanding and taking advantage of your college funding options.

Your next step should be to complete the Personal Characteristics Checklist on page xxvi. This will help you inventory all possible qualifications that can be used to match award program eligibility requirements. Check anything that applies to you or your family members. Even if you are undecided about a major or what career you want to pursue, check any that might be of interest. On a separate list, write down any organization, civic group, or industry that you or members of your immediate family are, or have been, involved with.

Match yourself to the programs. After your checklist is complete, use the eligibility indexes beginning on page 1 to find the award programs that correspond to your qualifications. You can also use the award-winning scholarship search program on collegeboard.com. This user-friendly program enables you to search with more criteria and with much greater speed than is possible with print indexes.

The eligibility indexes

- **Corporate/Employer:** Listed here are the many companies and businesses that offer scholarships to employees and/or their employees' dependents or relatives. You should check out any company that employs a member of your family.

- **Disabilities:** This category covers students with disabilities. Most awards in this category, as well as other categories, have additional eligibility requirements.

- **Field of Study/Intended Career:** This category, by far the longest, identifies broad major and career areas, so if you don't see your specific area of interest, look for the general area into which it might fit.

- **Gender:** Although the vast majority of awards are not gender-specific, there are nearly 100 awards in this book exclusively for women, and more than 20 for men only.

- **International Students:** This category includes awards that are open to students from outside the United States.

- **Military Participation:** Many of the awards in this category are for the children, descendants, or spouses of members of the military, including the Reserves and National Guard, going back as far as the Civil War.

- **Minority Status:** There are seven groups within this category, representing a wide range of awards.

- **National/Ethnic Background:** The national/ethnic groups in this category are determined by the sponsoring organizations that responded to our annual survey.

- **Organization/Civic Affiliation:** Many membership organizations and civic associations have generous higher education funding programs that are available for their members and/or their members' dependents or relatives. Check to see if any apply to your family.

- **Religious Affiliation:** The 10 groups in this category represent a broad range but, like the national/ethnic category, are determined by the respondents to our annual survey.

- **Returning Adult:** This category includes awards for undergraduate, graduate, and nondegree study. The age qualification varies, but most often is for students 25 years or older.

- **State of Residence:** Each state has several award programs exclusively for state residents. Be sure to examine closely all those listed under your state.

- **Study Abroad:** While most award programs for study abroad are for graduate students, a few are geared for undergraduates, and you will find them listed here.

In addition to the eligibility indexes preceding the scholarship descriptions, there are two general indexes in the back of the book, following the descriptions, which list award programs by sponsor name and program name.

What's in the program descriptions

The scholarship programs in this book are organized alphabetically by sponsor within three sections:

- **Scholarships:** This section covers public and private scholarships and research grants for undergraduates. To be included, a scholarship program must be granting a monetary award of at least $250 in the upcoming year for the purpose of financing some aspect of higher education: tuition and fees, research, study abroad, travel expenses, or other educational endeavors.

- **Internships:** This section covers public and private internships, providing opportunities either to earn money for education or to gain academic credit. To be included, paid internships must pay at least $100 per week and provide a viable path toward a future career. (The Sony Music internship is an example of this—the Oscar Mayer Wienermobile is not.)

- **Loans:** This section covers public and private educational loan programs. Many have loan forgiveness options, usually in exchange for public or community service for a certain period of time.

Each program description contains all of the information provided by the sponsor and verified for accuracy by a staff of editors at the College Board. A typical description includes:

Type of award: tells you whether the award is a scholarship, grant, internship, or loan; and whether it's renewable.

Intended use: tells you the range and limitations of the award, such as level of study, full-time or part-time, at what kind of institution, whether in the United States or abroad.

Eligibility: indicates the characteristics you must have to be considered for an award—for example, U.S. citizenship, specific state of residence, disability, membership in a particular organization, minority status.

Basis for selection: may include major or career interest; personal qualities such as seriousness of purpose, high academic achievement, depth of character; financial need.

Application requirements: outlines what you must provide in support of your application, such as recommendations, essay, transcript, interview, proof of eligibility, résumé, references.

Additional information: gives you any facts or requirements not covered in the categories above—for example, which test scores to submit, GPA level required, whether a particular type of student is given special consideration, when application forms are available, etc.

Amount of award: a single figure generally means the standard amount, but may indicate the maximum of a range of amounts; two figures indicate the range of awards from lowest to highest amounts.

Number of awards: tells you how many awards are granted by the sponsor.

Number of applicants: tells you how many students applied the previous year.

Application deadline: the date by which your application must be submitted; some scholarships have two deadlines for considering applications *Note: This information was obtained in Spring 2004. Deadlines may have passed or changed. Check the sponsor's Web site for current deadlines.*

Notification begins: the earliest date that an award notification is sent; in some cases, all go out on the same date, in others, notification is on a rolling basis; if there are two application deadlines, there are usually two notification dates.

Total amount awarded: tells you how much money is disbursed in the current award year, including renewable awards.

Contact name, address, phone, fax, and Web site: gives you all available information on where to get application forms and further information. Where the contact name and address are identical for several different scholarship programs sponsored by the same organization, this information will appear at the end of the last scholarship in that group.

While some descriptions don't include all these details because they were either not applicable or not supplied by the sponsor, in every case all essential information is provided. *Readers are urged to verify all information (the sponsor's Web site is the best source) before submitting applications.*

Ground rules for college planning

■ When it comes to planning for college, the very first rule to remember is: *Time is money!*

Experts suggest that parents start saving for college somewhere between the time they decide on a name for the baby and the start of middle school.

■ The second rule is: *It's never too early to begin saving and planning, but it's never too late to develop strategies and options if your savings aren't sufficient.*

Virtually all colleges and graduate schools have financial aid professionals on staff to help you bridge the gap between your resources and the cost of attending those institutions. Last year, almost $90 billion in financial aid enabled millions of students to continue their education beyond high school.

■ The third rule is: *The responsibility of paying for college begins with you and your family.*

While help comes from colleges and universities as well as federal and state governments, you are a partner in the effort to cover the costs of your higher education. You are expected to contribute an amount calculated by the federal government and/or the institution you're attending as a fair share based on your family financial situation.

■ The fourth rule is: *The cost of a college or graduate degree is an investment in the future.*

An investment is money spent to earn a financial return—and for most people, one of the benefits of a college education is higher lifetime earnings potential. When you add to that some of the more subjective benefits such as broadened perspectives and interests, expanded knowledge, and friendships, college begins to look like one of the best, most reliable, and high-yield investments you can make.

Advice to parents: The "five C's" of preparing for college and graduate school costs

1. **Collect** as much information as possible. Catalogs from colleges and graduate schools, federal government brochures, state education department publications, bank and credit union information and, increasingly important, Web sites on the Internet provide extensive information on college-preparatory courses, college savings strategies, college costs, financial aid programs, and private sector scholarship opportunities.

2. **Coordinate** the information and develop a timetable for getting the most out of your own resources. Understand what colleges and graduate studies cost today, anticipate that those costs will continue to increase, and at least estimate what share of those costs you might be expected to pay. If you're starting the planning process several years before that first tuition bill is due, you have a number of options to consider in terms of savings and investment strategies. You also have time to explore need and non-need scholarship opportunities to get an idea of what supplemental funds may be available.

3. **Consider** all of your options and opportunities. Time can be your most important advantage if you have even modest resources to invest in the stock market, mutual funds, prepaid tuition plans, state-sponsored Section 529 college savings programs, or "Education IRA" savings plans. Remember that, although nearly 90 billion dollars of financial aid was available to students last year, an increasing percentage of that money is in the form of education loans. Making your money work for you enables you to earn interest now rather than pay interest later.

4. **Communicate** with college or graduate school financial aid offices and with private-sector scholarship programs. Find out in advance what their requirements and application deadlines are; get a sense of what typical college financial aid packages or private scholarship awards may consist of and whether they're renewable. This book is a good place to either start or continue your efforts. The extensive listing of award programs illustrates the extent to which support is available to supplement what you are able to contribute toward college costs.

5. **Copy** all scholarship applications and financial aid documents you submit and keep them on file so that you can refer to them if any questions arise or duplicate them if necessary. No matter how reliable the postal service and electronic communications systems are, sometimes things you've sent get lost in the mail, don't arrive by fax, or disappear on their way via e-mail. Don't risk having to start over from scratch if that should happen.

Take the time to collect, coordinate, consider, communicate, and copy—you'll find that it's a wise investment of your time and your money.

Jack Joyce
Director, College Planning Services
The College Board

Important advice and information

What does college cost? How much will you be expected to pay?

Some of the best things in life may be free, but college is not one of them. The purpose of this book is to help you:

- understand the components of college costs

- get a sense of what you'll be expected to contribute toward those costs

- learn from financial aid experts about ground rules and strategies for paying for college

- find additional resources to cover the costs of your college education

The components of college costs

Whether you're an undergraduate or graduate student, part-time or full-time, commuting or living on campus, your outlay is going to include both direct educational expenses and living expenses. Typically, they fall into the following five categories:

- tuition and fees

- books and supplies

- room and board

- personal expenses

- transportation

Tuition and fees

Tuition is the charge for instruction. Fees may be charged for services such as Internet access, student activities, or the health center. The amount of tuition and fees charged by a particular college varies considerably. Public colleges, because they're funded by tax dollars, are generally less expensive than private institutions, though out-of-state (or, in the case of community colleges, out-of-district) students usually pay higher tuition, which can make a public college as costly as a private one for nonresident students.

Books and supplies

The amount you spend for books, pens, pencils, paper, and other basic supplies isn't affected by the type of college you're attending, but will vary considerably based on the courses you're taking. Science, engineering, and art courses, for example, require specialized equipment and materials.

Room and board

Whether you live in a campus dorm or in a private apartment off-campus, you have to cover the basic living expenses of food and housing. Even students who live at home have to factor in meals and snacks at school, and their parents still have the expense of providing them with living quarters and food.

Personal expenses

You're probably used to paying for some of your personal expenses—clothes, toiletries, magazines, CDs, movies. But once you're at college, you're also going to be responsible for laundry and dry cleaning bills, phone bills, accessories and supplies for your living quarters, and a lot of other little incidentals, which average more than $1,000 and can add up to a lot more than that.

Transportation

If you live on campus, you will need to consider the cost of travelling to get there at the beginning of the academic year and to return home at the end, and for as many times as you expect to go home during the year.

For financial aid purposes, colleges often factor in two round trips home per year by the lowest-cost means of transportation available. If you're a commuter student, you will need to figure the cost of your weekly commute, either by public transportation or by private car. These costs, too, are built into student expense budgets by colleges for financial aid purposes.

Estimating your expected family contribution

As Jack Joyce of the College Board's College Planning Services pointed out in the preceding section, the responsibility of paying for college begins with you and your parents. The amount that you as a family are expected to pay is the sum of what your parents can contribute from their income and assets plus what you can contribute from earnings and savings. If you're curious about what that means in terms of dollars, the table on page xix gives you a sense of what parental contribution is expected at various income and asset levels. Pick the combination of annual income and asset figures that are closest to your family's, and you'll have a very rough idea of what your parents' share might be.

Don't panic!

Although the expense of going to college or graduate school may seem like a heavy burden, the fact is that the majority of students get financial aid that covers at least a portion of the cost. Of the four basic potential sources, this book deals with the first three listed below:

1. Much of the aid comes from the federal government in the form of grants, work-study programs, and subsidized loans.

2. State governments also dispense significant amounts of financial aid in various forms to state residents.

3. In addition, there are a number of private foundations and corporations that have established scholarship programs to help qualified students pay for college.

4. Financial aid awards sponsored and administered by colleges, universities, and graduate schools are another important resource. They include scholarships, fellowships, fee waivers, internships, and teaching and research assistantships. Because criteria and application procedures vary considerably, your best source of information is the institution's own catalog or financial aid bulletin.

In this book you'll find detailed descriptions of over 2,100 scholarship, internship, and loan programs representing over 1.8 million awards, with eligibility indexes to help you zero in on the awards for which you're likely to qualify.

Frequently asked questions

Q When should I start looking for scholarships?

A It's never too early to start finding out about what kinds of scholarships are available. If you're a high school student, it's a good idea to start research in your sophomore or junior year, even if you can't apply until you're a senior. If you're in college and need financial aid for graduate school, there's no time like the present to start exploring your options.

Q Will going to college part-time lessen my chances of receiving aid?

A Depending on your personal circumstances, you could be eligible for a Pell Grant and a number of other forms of federal aid. Many of the private sector scholarships in this book make no distinction between full-time and part-time study in awarding funds.

Q Are international students eligible for financial aid?

A If you're an international student (a noncitizen from abroad), you're generally not eligible for tax-supported aid such as federal or state grants, but there are private sector awards included in this book for which international students are eligible.

Q If I get a scholarship from a foundation or corporation, will the financial aid offered by the college be affected?

A Colleges' policies on outside scholarships vary a great deal, so you'd have to check with the financial aid officer at the college itself to find out.

Q Is it true that my college financial aid package could be reduced by as much as the full amount of any outside scholarship I receive?

A Probably yes if your financial aid package meets your full need (as measured by the college); probably no if your need has been only partially met. The other factor to take into consideration is that many colleges will reduce the loan or work-study component of your aid package rather than the gift aid portion.

Q Are there scholarships that cover the whole four years or are they only awarded for one year?

A That varies from sponsor to sponsor. Many undergraduate scholarships cover a single year of study but are renewable. Some graduate and postgraduate grants and fellowships cover the entire period required to earn the degree or complete a research project.

2004–2005 Estimated Parents' Contribution (FM)

Net Assets:	$25,000				$50,000			
Family Size:	3	4	5	6	3	4	5	6
2003 Income before taxes:								
$10,000	$0	$0	$0	$0	$0	$0	$0	$0
15,000	0	0	0	0	0	0	0	0
20,000	0	0	0	0	0	0	0	0
25,000	75	0	0	0	284	0	0	0
30,000	893	78	0	0	1,102	287	0	0
35,000	1,680	896	129	0	1,888	1,105	338	0
40,000	2,442	1,661	928	88	2,651	1,870	1,136	297
45,000	3,276	2,424	1,691	865	3,518	2,632	1,899	1,074
50,000	4,249	3,255	2,453	1,628	4,548	3,494	2,662	1,837
55,000	5,405	4,224	3,289	2,391	5,778	4,519	3,533	2,599
60,000	6,805	5,376	4,263	3,218	7,250	5,744	4,565	3,455
65,000	8,435	6,765	5,422	4,181	8,880	7,211	5,798	4,468
70,000	10,064	8,395	6,828	5,325	10,510	8,840	7,274	5,684
75,000	11,692	10,025	8,458	6,695	12,137	10,470	8,904	7,140
80,000	13,086	11,560	10,088	8,324	13,532	12,006	10,533	8,770
85,000	14,481	12,955	11,532	9,912	14,927	13,401	11,977	10,357
90,000	15,963	14,437	13,014	11,394	16,409	14,883	13,460	11,839
95,000	17,504	15,978	14,554	12,934	17,949	16,423	15,000	13,380
100,000	19,044	17,518	16,095	14,475	19,490	17,964	16,540	14,920
150,000	34,206	32,723	31,343	29,765	34,651	33,168	31,788	30,211

Net Assets:	$100,000				$150,000			
Family Size:	3	4	5	6	3	4	5	6
2003 Income before taxes:								
$10,000	$0	$0	$0	$0	$291	$0	$0	$0
15,000	0	0	0	0	1,219	337	0	0
20,000	786	0	0	0	2,106	1,265	431	0
25,000	1,604	789	22	0	2,957	2,109	1,342	432
30,000	2,422	1,607	840	0	3,950	2,960	2,160	1,301
35,000	3,280	2,425	1,658	799	5,091	3,954	3,018	2,119
40,000	4,253	3,259	2,456	1,617	6,417	5,062	3,996	2,971
45,000	5,409	4,228	3,292	2,394	8,001	6,383	5,108	3,913
50,000	6,811	5,380	4,267	3,221	9,631	7,962	6,437	5,011
55,000	8,441	6,771	5,426	4,184	11,261	9,591	8,025	6,323
60,000	10,070	8,401	6,834	5,329	12,890	11,221	9,654	7,891
65,000	11,700	10,031	8,464	6,701	14,520	12,851	11,284	9,521
70,000	13,330	11,660	10,094	8,330	16,150	14,480	12,914	11,150
75,000	14,957	13,290	11,724	9,960	17,777	16,110	14,544	12,780
80,000	16,352	14,826	13,353	11,590	19,172	17,646	16,173	14,410
85,000	17,747	16,221	14,797	13,177	20,567	19,041	17,617	15,997
90,000	19,229	17,703	16,280	14,659	22,049	20,523	19,100	17,479
95,000	20,769	19,243	17,820	16,200	23,589	22,063	20,640	19,020
100,000	22,310	20,784	19,360	17,740	25,130	23,604	22,180	20,560
150,000	37,471	35,988	34,608	33,031	40,291	38,808	37,428	35,851

Note: The figures shown are parents' contribution under Federal Methodology (FM), assuming the older parent is age 45. Both parents are employed (equal wages); income is only from employment; no unusual circumstances; standard deductions on U.S. income tax; 1040 tax return filed; and one undergraduate child enrolled in college.

Source: The College Scholarship Service® (CSS®), The College Board.

How to avoid scholarship scams

As college costs continue to rise, families have begun to look beyond government and college sources of funding, which has given rise to a growing industry of scholarship search services. Some do a responsible job for a modest fee, but many make unrealistic claims and charge substantial fees. Some are outright fraudulent in their tactics.

Buyer beware!

The Federal Trade Commission (FTC) developed Project $cholar$cam to alert consumers about potential scams and how to recognize them. Here are the FTC's six basic warning signs and advice:

"The scholarship is guaranteed or your money back."
No one can guarantee that they'll get you a grant or a scholarship. Refund policies often have conditions or strings attached. Get refund policies in writing before you pay.

"You can't get this information anywhere else."
Check with your school or library before you decide to pay someone to do the work for you.

"May I have your credit card or bank account number to hold this scholarship?"
Don't give out your credit card or bank account number on the phone without getting information in writing first. It may be a setup for an unauthorized withdrawal.

"We'll do all the work for you."
Don't be fooled. There's no way around it. You must apply for scholarships or grants yourself.

"The scholarship will cost some money."
Don't pay anyone who claims to be "holding" a scholarship or grant for you. Free money shouldn't cost a thing.

"You've been selected by a national foundation to receive a scholarship" or *"You're a finalist"* in a contest you never entered.
Before you send money to apply for a scholarship, check it out. Make sure the foundation or program is legitimate.

Sources of information about state grant programs

Alabama
Alabama Commission on Higher Education
P.O. Box 302000
100 North Union Street
Montgomery, AL 36130-2000
334 242-1998; www.ache.state.al.us

Alaska
Alaska Commission on Postsecondary Education
3030 Vintage Boulevard
Juneau, AK 99801-7109
800 441-2962; www.state.ak.us/acpe

Arizona
Arizona Department of Education
1535 W. Jefferson St.
Phoenix, AZ 85007
800 352-4558; www.ade.state.az.us

Arkansas
Department of Higher Education
114 East Capitol
Little Rock, AR 72201
501 371-2000; www.arkansashighered.com

California
California Student Aid Commission
P.O. Box 419027
Rancho Cordova, CA 95741-9026
888 224-7268; www.csac.ca.gov

Colorado
Department of Education
201 East Colfax Avenue
Denver, CO 80203
303 866-6600; www.cde.state.co.us

Connecticut
Department of Higher Education
61 Woodland Street
Hartford, CT 06105
860 947-1800; www.ctdhe.org

Delaware
Delaware Higher Education Commission
820 North French Street
Fourth Floor
Wilmington, DE 19801
800 292-7935; www.doe.state.de.us/high-ed

Florida
Florida Department of Education
Office of Student Financial Assistance
325 West Gaines Street
Suite 1514
Tallahassee, FL 32399-0400
850 245-0505; www.firn.edu/doe

Georgia
Georgia Student Finance Authority
2082 East Exchange Place
Suite 100
Tucker, GA 30084
800 505-4732; www.gsfc.org

Hawaii
Hawaii Department of Education
P.O. Box 2360
Honolulu, HI 96804
808 586-3230; www.doe.k12.hi.us

Idaho
Office of the State Board of Education
P.O. Box 83720
650 West State Street
Boise, ID 83720-0027
208 332-6800; www.sde.state.id.us

Illinois
Illinois Student Assistance Commission
1755 Lake Cook Road
Deerfield, IL 60015-5209
800 899-4722; www.isac-online.org

Indiana
State Student Assistance Commission of Indiana
150 W. Market Street
Suite 500
Indianapolis, IN 46204
888 528-4719; www.ai.org/ssaci

Iowa
Iowa College Student Aid Commission
200 Tenth Street
Fourth Floor
Des Moines, IA 50309-2036
515 242-3344; www.iowacollegeaid.org

Kansas
Board of Regents
1000 SW Jackson Street
Suite 520
Topeka, KS 66612-1368
785 296-3421; www.kansasregents.org

Kentucky
KHEAA Student Aid Branch
1050 U.S. 127 South
P.O. Box 798
Frankfort, KY 40602
800 928-8926; www.kheaa.com

Louisiana
Office of Student Financial Assistance for Louisiana
Scholarship/Grant Division
P.O. Box 91202
Baton Rouge, LA 70821-9202
800 259-5626; www.osfa.state.la.us

Maine
Finance Authority of Maine
Maine Education Assistance Division
P.O. Box 949
5 Community Drive
Augusta, ME 04332
800 228-3734; www.famemaine.com

Maryland
Maryland Higher Education Commission
State Scholarship Administration
839 Bestgate Road
Suite 400
Annapolis, MD 21401-1781
800 974-0203; www.mhec.state.md.us

Massachusetts
Board of Higher Education,
Office of Student Financial Assistance
One Ashburton Place
Room 1401
Boston, MA 02108-1696
617 994-6950; www.mass.edu

Michigan
Michigan Higher Education Assistance Authority
Office of Scholarships and Grants
P.O. Box 30462
Lansing, MI 48909-7962
517 373-3394; www.michigan.gov

Minnesota
Minnesota Higher Education Services Office
1450 Energy Park Drive
Suite 350
St. Paul, MN 55108-5227
651 642-0533; www.mheso.state.mn.us

Mississippi
Mississippi Office of State Student Financial Aid
3825 Ridgewood Road
Jackson, MS 39211-6453
800 327-2980; www.mde.k12.ms.us

Missouri
Missouri Coordinating Board for Higher Education
3515 Amazonas Drive
Jefferson City, MO 65109-5717
573 751-2361; www.mocbhe.gov

Montana
Montana Board of Regents of Higher Education
P.O. Box 203101
2500 Broadway
Helena, MT 59620-3101
406 444-6570; www.montana.edu/wwwbor

Nebraska
Nebraska Department of Education
P.O. Box 95005
Lincoln, NE 68509-5005
402 471-2847; www.ccpe.state.ne.us

Nevada
Nevada Department of Education, Financial Aid
700 East 5th Street
Carson City Main Location
Carson City, NV 89701
775 687-9200; www.nde.state.nv.us

New Hampshire
New Hampshire Postsecondary Education Commission
3 Barrell Court
Suite 300
Concord, NH 03301-8543
603 271-2555; www.state.nh.us/postsecondary

New Jersey
New Jersey Higher Education Student Assistance Authority
4 Quakerbridge Plaza
P.O. Box 540
Trenton, NJ 08625
800 792-8670; www.hesaa.org

New Mexico
Commission on Higher Education
1068 Cerillos Road
Santa Fe, NM 87505
505 476-6500; www.nmche.org

New York
Higher Education Services Corporation
Student Information
99 Washington Avenue
14th Floor
Albany, NY 12255
888 697-4372; www.hesc.state.ny.us

North Carolina
North Carolina State Education Assistance Authority
P.O. Box 14103
Research Triangle Park, NC 27709-3663
919 549-8614; www.ncseaa.edu

North Dakota
North Dakota University System
600 East Boulevard
Dept. 215
Bismarck, ND 58505
701 328-2960; www.ndus.nodak.edu

Ohio
Ohio Board of Regents
30 East Broad Street, 36th floor
Columbus, OH 43215-3414
614 466-6000; www.regents.state.oh.us

Oklahoma
Oklahoma State Regents for Higher Education
Tuition Aid Grant Program
655 Research Parkway
Suite 200
Oklahoma City, OK 73104
405 225-9100; www.okhighered.org

Oregon
Oregon Student Assistance Commission
Valley River Office Park
1500 Valley River Drive
Suite 100
Eugene, OR 97401
800 452-8807; www.ossc.state.or.us

Pennsylvania
Pennsylvania Higher Education Assistance Agency
1200 N. Seventh St.
Harrisburg, PA 17102
877 603-6010; www.pheaa.org

Puerto Rico
Departmento de Educacion
P.O. Box 190759
San Juan, PR 00919-0759
787 724-7100

Rhode Island
Rhode Island Higher Education Assistance Authority
560 Jefferson Boulevard
Warwick, RI 02886
401 736-1170; www.riheaa.org

South Carolina
South Carolina Tuition Grants Commission
1333 Main Street
Suite 200
Columbia, SC 29201
803 737-2260; www.che400.state.sc.us

South Dakota
Department of Education
700 Governors Drive
Pierre, SD 57501-2291
605 773-3426; www.state.sd.us/deca

Tennessee
Tennessee Student Assistance Corporation
Parkway Towers
Suite 1900
404 James Robertson Parkway
Nashville, TN 37243-0820
615 741-3605; www.state.tn.us/thec

Texas
Texas Higher Education Coordinating Board
Division of Student Services
P.O. Box 12788, Capital Station
Austin, TX 78711
512 427-6101; www.thecb.state.tx.us

Utah

Utah Higher Education Assistance Authority
Board of Regents Building, The Gateway
60 South 400 West
Salt Lake City, UT 84101-1284
801 321-7200; www.uheaa.org

Vermont

Vermont Student Assistance Corporation
Champlain Mill, P.O. Box 2000
Winooski, VT 05404-2601
802 655-9602; www.vsac.org

Virginia

Virginia Council of Higher Education
James Monroe Building
101 North 14th Street
Richmond, VA 23219
804 225-2600; www.schev.edu

Washington

Washington State Higher Education Coordination Board
917 Lakeridge Way
P.O. Box 43430
Olympia, WA 98504-3430
360 753-7800; www.hecb.wa.gov

West Virginia

West Virginia Higher Education Policy Commission
Central Office, Higher Education Grant Program
1018 Kanawha Boulevard East
Suite 700
Charleston, WV 25301-2827
304 558-2101; www.hepc.wvnet.edu

Wisconsin

Wisconsin Higher Educational Aids Board
131 West Wilson
Suite 902
Madison, WI 53707
608 267-2206; www.heab.state.wi.us

Wyoming

Wyoming State Department of Education
2300 Capitol Avenue
Hathaway Building, Second Floor
Cheyenne, WY 82002
307 777-7673; www.k12.wy.us

Guam

Student Financial Aid Office
303 University Station
Mangilao, GU 96929
671 735-2283; www.uog.edu

Virgin Islands

Financial Aid Office, Virgin Islands Board of Education
P.O. Box 11900
St. Thomas, VI 00801
340 774-4546

Glossary

College Scholarship Service® (CSS®): A unit of the College Board that assists postsecondary institutions and scholarship programs in the equitable distribution of financial aid funds.

Credit by examination: Academic credit granted by a college to entering students who have demonstrated proficiency in college-level studies through examinations such as those sponsored by the College Board's AP and CLEP® programs. This is a means of cutting college costs by reducing the number of courses needed to earn a degree.

CSS/Financial Aid PROFILE®: A service offered by the College Board and used by some colleges, universities, and private scholarship programs to award their own financial aid funds. Students pay a fee to register and send reports to institutions and programs that use it. Students register by calling a toll-free telephone service or by connecting to the College Board Web site. CSS provides a customized application for each registrant, based on the individual's information and the requirements of the colleges and programs from which she or he is seeking aid. CSS/Financial Aid PROFILE is not a federal form and may not be used to apply for federal student aid.

Expected family contribution: The total amount that you and your family are expected to pay toward college costs from your income and assets. The amount is determined by a need analysis of your family's overall financial circumstances. A Federal Methodology is used to determine your eligibility for federal student aid. Colleges, state agencies, and private aid programs may use a different methodology in assessing eligibility for nonfederal sources of financial aid.

Federal Work-Study Program: A federally sponsored campus-based program. Participating colleges provide employment opportunities for students with demonstrated need.

Fellowship: A form of graduate financial aid that usually requires service—often in the form of time devoted to a research project.

Financial aid package: The total financial aid award offered to you. It may be made up of a combination of aid that includes both gift aid (which doesn't have to be repaid) and self-help (work-study and/or loans). Many colleges try to meet a student's full financial need, but availability of funds, the institution's aid policies, and the number of students needing aid all affect the composition of a financial aid package.

Financial need: The difference between the cost of attending college and your expected family contribution.

Free Application for Federal Student Aid (FAFSA): A form you must complete to apply for federal student aid. In many states, completing the FAFSA is the way to establish your eligibility for state-sponsored aid programs. There is no charge to you for submitting this form, which is widely available in high schools and colleges, and may be filed any time after January 1 of the year for which you're seeking aid.

Internship: A short-term, supervised work experience, usually related to your major, for which you may earn either academic credit or a stipend.

Need analysis form: The starting point in applying for financial aid. All students must file the FAFSA to apply for federal financial aid programs. Some colleges will also require CSS/Financial Aid PROFILE to determine eligibility for nonfederal financial aid. To apply for state financial aid programs, the FAFSA may be all that you'll need to file, but check to be sure.

Research grants: Some scholarships are for research and require you to describe the project for which you're requesting funds. Although most research grants are for graduate students, some in this book are available for undergraduates.

SASE: Self-addressed stamped envelope.

Scholarship or grant: A type of financial aid that doesn't have to be repaid. Grants are often based on financial need. Scholarships may be based on need, on need combined with other criteria, or solely on academic merit.

Personal characteristics checklist

Disability:
- ❐ Hearing
- ❐ Learning
- ❐ Physical
- ❐ Visual

Field of study/intended career:
- ❐ Agricultural science, business, and natural resources conservation
- ❐ Architecture and design
- ❐ Area and ethnic studies
- ❐ Arts, visual and performing
- ❐ Biological and physical sciences
- ❐ Business, management, administration
- ❐ Communications
- ❐ Computer and information sciences
- ❐ Education
- ❐ Engineering and engineering technology
- ❐ English and literature
- ❐ Foreign languages
- ❐ Health professions and allied services
- ❐ Home economics
- ❐ Law
- ❐ Liberal arts and interdisciplinary studies
- ❐ Library science
- ❐ Mathematics
- ❐ Military science
- ❐ Mortuary science
- ❐ Protective services
- ❐ Philosophy, religion, and theology
- ❐ Social sciences and history
- ❐ Trade and industry

Gender:
- ❐ Female
- ❐ Male

International student: ❐

Military participation/affiliation:
- ❐ Air Force
- ❐ Army
- ❐ Marines
- ❐ Coast Guard
- ❐ Navy
- ❐ Reserves/National Guard

Minority status:
- ❐ African American
- ❐ Alaskan Native
- ❐ American Indian
- ❐ Asian American
- ❐ Hispanic American
- ❐ Mexican American
- ❐ Puerto Rican

National/ethnic background:
- ❐ Armenian
- ❐ Chinese
- ❐ Danish
- ❐ Greek
- ❐ Italian
- ❐ Japanese
- ❐ Mongolian
- ❐ Polish
- ❐ Swiss
- ❐ Ukrainian
- ❐ Welsh

Religious affiliation:
- ❐ Christian
- ❐ Eastern Orthodox
- ❐ Episcopal
- ❐ Jewish
- ❐ Lutheran
- ❐ Presbyterian (USA)
- ❐ Protestant
- ❐ Roman Catholic
- ❐ Unitarian Universalist
- ❐ United Methodist

Returning adult: ❐

Want to study abroad: ❐

Eligibility Indexes

Field of Study/
Intended Career

Agricultural science, business, and natural resources conservation

Architecture and design

Area and ethnic studies

Arts, visual and performing

Biological and biomedical sciences

Biological and physical sciences

Business/management/administration

Communications

Computer and information sciences

Education

Engineering and engineering technology

English and literature

Foreign languages

Health professions and allied services

Home economics

Military science

Mortuary science

Multi/interdisciplinary studies

Philosophy, religion, and theology

Protective services

Social sciences and history

Trade and industry

Visual and performing arts

Gender

Female

Male

International Student

Military Participation

Air Force

Army

Coast Guard

Marines

Navy

Reserves/National Guard

Minority Status

African American

Asian American

Hispanic American

Mexican American

Puerto Rican

National/ethnic background

Arab or Jewish

Armenian

Chinese

Danish

Greek

Italian

Japanese

Jewish

Polish

Swiss

Ukrainian

Welsh

Organization/civic affiliation

1199 National Benefit Fund

25th Infantry Division Association

Slovak Gymnastic Union Sokol, USA

Slovenian Women's Union of America

Sociedad Honoraria Hispanica

Society of Automotive Engineers

Society of Manufacturing Engineers

Society of Physics Students

Society of Women Engineers

Soil and Water Conservation Society

Sons of Norway

South Dakota National Guard

Third Marine Division Association

Transportation Clubs International

Ukrainian Fraternal Association

United Food and Commerical Workers

United States Association of Blind Athletes

United Transportation Union

Wyoming Job's Daughters/DeMolay

Religious Affiliation

Christian

Eastern Orthodox

Episcopal

Jewish

Lutheran

Presbyterian

Protestant

Roman Catholic

Unitarian Universalist

United Methodist

Returning Adult

Air Traffic Control Full-Time Employee Student Scholarship, 57

A.J. "Andy" Spielman Travel Agents Scholarship, 146

B. K. Krenzer Reentry Scholarship, 433

Charles R. Ford Scholarship, 281

Connecticut Tuition Waiver for Senior Citizens, 198

Delayed Education Scholarship for Women, 135

Eight and Forty Lung and Respiratory Nursing Scholarship Fund, 112

Elizabeth Dow Internship Program, 508

Fran Johnson Non-Traditional Scholarship, 221

Friends of Oregon Students Scholarship, 387

GEICO/Golden Key Adult Scholar Awards, 235

Laywomen Scholarships, 491

Lighthouse Undergraduate Incentive Award II, 293

Missouri Minority Teaching Scholarship, 315

Montgomery GI Bill Plus Army College Fund, 473

NASA Space Grant North Carolina Consortium Undergraduate Scholarship, 328

New York State Vietnam Veteran Tuition Award/Persian Gulf Veteran Tuition Award, 371

North Carolina Community Colleges Bell South Telephone/Telegraph Scholarship, 374

Returning Student Scholarship, 205

Second Effort Scholarship, 155

Senior Citizen, 65 or Older, Free Tuition for 6 Credit Hours, 455

Slovenian Women's Union Scholarship For Returning Adults, 419

Stanfield and D'Orlando Art Scholarship, 464

West Virginia Higher Education Adult Part-time Student (HEAPS) Grant Program, 486

Women's Education Fund, 282

State of Residence

Alabama

Alabama Junior/Community College Athletic Scholarship, 63

Alabama National Guard Educational Assistance Award, 62

Alabama Robert C. Byrd Honors Scholarship, 63

Alabama Scholarship for Dependents of Blind Parents, 449

Alabama Student Assistance Program, 62

Alabama Student Grant, 62

American Legion Alabama Auxiliary Scholarship, 86

American Legion Alabama Oratorical Contest, 86

American Legion Alabama Scholarship, 86

Charles Clarke Cordle Memorial Scholarship, 159

Institutional Scholarship Waivers, 63

NASA Space Grant Undergraduate Scholarship, 322

Pickett and Hatcher Educational Loan, 568

Police/Firefighters' Survivors Educational Assistance Program, 63

Alaska

Alaska Family Education Loan, 555

Alaska Teacher Education Loan, 555

Alaska Winn Brindle Memorial Education Loan Program, 555

American Legion Alaska Auxiliary Scholarship, 87

American Legion Alaska Oratorical Contest, 87

American Legion District Postsecondary Scholarship, 487

Cady McDonnell Memorial Scholarship, 73

Mary Lou Brown Scholarship, 161

Arizona

American Legion Arizona Auxiliary Health Care Occupation Scholarship, 87

American Legion Arizona Auxiliary Nurses' Scholarship, 88

American Legion Arizona Oratorical Contest, 87

Anne Lindeman Memorial Scholarship, 447

Arizona Chapter Dependent Scholarship Fund, 147

Arizona Chapter Gold Scholarship, 147

Arizona Community College Scholarship, 447

Arizona Section Scholarship, 432

Arizona Tuition Waiver for Non-Residents, 153

Arizona Tuition Waivers for Children/Spouses of Slain Public Servants, 153

Arizona Tuition Waivers for Residents, 154

A.W. Bodine Sunkist Memorial Scholarship, 450

Burlington Northern Santa Fe Foundation Scholarship, 82

Cady McDonnell Memorial Scholarship, 73

Charles N. Fisher Memorial Scholarship, 160

Italian Catholic Federation Scholarship, 279

NASA Space Grant Arizona Undergraduate Research Internship, 526

Rocky Mountain Coal Mining Scholarship, 409

Shell Legislative Internship Program (SLIP), 528

Stephen T. Marchello Scholarship for Survivors of Childhood Cancer, 450

Walt Bartram Memorial Education Award (Region 12), 426

Wilma D. Hoyal/Maxine Chilton Memorial Scholarship, 89

Arkansas

Academic Challenge Scholarship, 154

American Legion Arkansas Auxiliary Scholarships, 88

American Legion Arkansas Oratorical Contest, 88

American Legion Arkansas Scholarship, 88

Arkansas Department of Higher Education Arkansas Student Assistance Grant, 154

Arkansas Department of Higher Education Teacher Assistance Resource (STAR) Program, 154

Arkansas Law Enforcement Officers' Dependents Scholarship, 154

Arkansas Minority Teachers Loan, 557

Arkansas Missing/Killed in Action Dependents Scholarship, 155

Fred R. McDaniel Memorial Scholarship, 51

Governor's Scholars Program, 155

NASA Space Grant Arkansas Undergraduate Scholarship, 323

National Society of Black Engineers Leroy Callendar Award Program, 355

Second Effort Scholarship, 155

California

AFCEA/Orincon IT Scholarship, 157

American Heart Association Undergraduate Student Research Program, 80

American Legion California Auxiliary Department Scholarship, 89

American Legion California Oratorical Contest, 90

Anna and Charles Stockwitz Children and Youth Fund, 561

Associated Press/APTRA-CLETE Roberts Memorial Journalism Scholarship, 167

A.W. Bodine Sunkist Memorial Scholarship, 450

BIA North County Division Scholarship, 178

Eligibility Indexes

Delaware

District of Columbia

Florida

Georgia

Hawaii

Idaho

Illinois

Indiana

Eligibility Indexes

Maryland

Massachusetts

Michigan

North Carolina

North Dakota

Ohio

Tourism Foundation Cleveland
Legacy 1 Scholarship, 358
Tourism Foundation Cleveland
Legacy 2 Scholarship, 359
University Journalism
Scholarship, 381

Oklahoma

Burlington Northern Santa Fe
Foundation Scholarship, 82
Fred R. McDaniel Memorial
Scholarship, 51
Future Teachers Scholarship, 382
Heartland Scholarship Fund, 382
Independent Living Act (Department
of Human Services Tuition
Waiver), 382
National Guard Tuition Waiver, 381
National Society of Black Engineers
Leroy Callendar Award
Program, 355
Oklahoma Engineering Foundation
Scholarship, 381
Oklahoma Higher Learning Access
Program (OHLAP), 382
Oklahoma Tuition Aid Grant, 383
Regional University Baccalaureate
Scholarship, 383
Robert C. Byrd Honors Scholarship
Program, 381
Tom and Judith Comstock
Scholarship, 162
Tourism Foundation Tulsa
Scholarship, 359

Oregon

Agricultural Women-in-Network
Scholarship, 384
Alpha Delta Kappa/Harriet Simmons
Scholarship, 384
American Ex-Prisoner of War, Peter
Connacher Memorial
Scholarship, 385
American Legion Oratorical
Contest, 121
American Legion Oregon Auxiliary
National President's
Scholarship, 121
American Legion Oregon Auxiliary
Nurses Scholarship, 121
American Legion Oregon Auxiliary
Scholarship, 122
American Legion Oregon Auxiliary
Spirit of Youth Scholarship, 122
The Audria M. Edwards Scholarship
Fund, 397
Ben Selling Scholarship, 385
Benjamin Franklin/Edith Green
Scholarship, 385
Bertha P. Singer Scholarship, 385
Burlington Northern Santa Fe
Foundation Scholarship, 82
Cady McDonnell Memorial
Scholarship, 73
Crowley Family Scholarship, 385
Danish Foundation Scholarship, 378
David Family Scholarship, 386

Dorothy Campbell Memorial
Scholarship, 386
Fashion Group International of
Portland Scholarship, 386
Ford Opportunity Program, 386
Ford Scholars Program, 387
Friends of Oregon Students
Scholarship, 387
Glenn Jackson Scholars, 387
Grange Insurance Scholarship, 238
Howard Vollum American Indian
Scholarship, 387
Ida M. Crawford Scholarship, 388
Jackson Foundation Journalism
Scholarship, 388
James Carlson Memorial
Scholarship, 388
Jerome B. Steinbach Scholarship, 388
Jose D. Garcia Migrant Education
Scholarship, 388
Kaiser-Permanente Dental Assistant
Scholarship, 389
Laurence R. Foster Memorial
Scholarship, 389
Maria C. Jackson-General George A.
White Scholarship, 389
Mark Hass Journalism
Scholarship, 389
Mary Lou Brown Scholarship, 161
Mentor Graphics Scholarship, 390
NASA Space Grant Oregon
Community College
Scholarship, 329
NASA Space Grant Oregon
Undergraduate Scholarship, 330
Oregon AeA Technology Scholarship
Program, 55
Oregon AFL-CIO Scholarship, 390
Oregon Collectors Association Bob
Hasson Memorial Scholarship Fund
Essay, 390
Oregon Dungeness Crab
Commission, 390
Oregon Education Association
Scholarship, 390
Oregon Metro Federal Credit Union
Scholarship, 391
Oregon Occupational Safety and
Health Division Workers Memorial
Scholarship, 391
Oregon Robert C. Byrd Honors
Scholarship, 391
Oregon Scholarship Fund Community
College Student Award, 391
Oregon Trucking Association, 392
Pendleton Postal Workers (APWU
Local 110) Scholarship, 392
Professional Land Surveyors of
Oregon Scholarship, 392
Richard F. Brentano Memorial
Scholarship, 392
Roger W. Emmons Memorial
Scholarship, 393
Teamsters Clyde C. Crosby/Joseph M.
Edgar Memorial Scholarship, 393
Teamsters Council #37 Federal Credit
Union Scholarship, 393

Teamsters Local 305 Scholarship, 393
Walter and Marie Schmidt
Scholarship, 393

Pennsylvania

American Legion Pennsylvania
Auxiliary Scholarship, 122
American Legion Pennsylvania
Auxiliary Scholarship for Children
of Deceased/Disabled Veterans, 123
American Legion Pennsylvania Joseph
P. Gavenonis Scholarship, 122
American Legion Pennsylvania Robert
W. Valimont Endowment Fund
Scholarship, 122
ASHRAE J. Richard Mehalick
Scholarship, 141
Congressional Black Caucus
Foundation Spouses
Scholarship, 196
Cymdeithas Gymreig (Welsh Society)
Philadelphia Scholarship, 202
Horatio Alger Association
Pennsylvania Scholarship
Program, 259
Katharine M. Grosscup
Scholarship, 230
Lighthouse College-Bound
Award, 293
Lighthouse Undergraduate Award
I, 293
Lighthouse Undergraduate Incentive
Award II, 293
Long and Foster Scholarship
Program, 293
NASA Academy Internship, 527
NASA Space Grant Pennsylvania
Undergraduate Scholarship, 330
Pennsylvania Grant Program, 398
Pennsylvania Robert C. Byrd Honors
Scholarship, 398
Pennsylvania Work-Study
Program, 540
Pittsburgh Local Section
Scholarship, 136
"You've Got a Friend in
Pennsylvania" Scholarship, 163
Shannon Scholarship, 462
Sonia Streuli Maguire Outstanding
Scholastic Achievement Award, 451
Swiss Benevolent Society Pellegrini
Scholarship, 452

Puerto Rico

American Legion Puerto Rico
Auxiliary Nursing Scholarship, 123
Ford Motor Company Fellows
Program, 528
Puerto Rico Robert C. Byrd Honors
Scholarship, 404

Rhode Island

College Bound Fund Academic
Promise Scholarship, 408
Dr. James L. Lawson Memorial
Scholarship, 160

Scholarships

1199 National Benefit Fund

Joseph Tauber Scholarship

Type of award: Scholarship, renewable.
Intended use: For full-time undergraduate or non-degree study at accredited vocational, 2-year or 4-year institution in or outside United States.
Eligibility: Applicant or parent must be employed by ECM Publishers, Inc. Applicant or parent must be member/participant of 1199 National Benefit Fund.
Basis for selection: Applicant must demonstrate financial need.
Application requirements: Transcript, proof of eligibility.
Additional information: High school graduates, postsecondary school students and previous awardees whose parents have been in Benefit Fund Wage Class One for one year at time of application are eligible. Visit Website for future updates.

Amount of award:	$750-$13,000
Number of awards:	2,037
Application deadline:	February 1
Total amount awarded:	$7,794,558

Contact:
1199 National Benefit Fund
330 West 42nd Street
New York, NY 10036
Phone: 646-473-6820 ext. 21
Fax: 646-473-6949
Web: www.1199NBF.org

25th Infantry Division Association

25th Infantry Division Educational Memorial Scholarship

Type of award: Scholarship.
Intended use: For full-time freshman study at accredited 4-year institution in United States.
Eligibility: Applicant or parent must be member/participant of 25th Infantry Division Association. Applicant must be U.S. citizen. Applicant must be in military service, veteran or disabled while on active duty; or dependent of active service person, veteran, disabled veteran or deceased veteran who serves or served in the Army. Deceased member must have died on active duty or as a result thereof. Veterans must be Association members. Applicant on active duty must be scheduled for release/retirement or discharged from division by December 31 of award year.
Basis for selection: Applicant must demonstrate financial need, high academic achievement, depth of character, leadership, seriousness of purpose and service orientation.

Application requirements: Recommendations, essay, transcript, proof of eligibility. SAT/ACT scores. Photograph. Letter of acceptance from college/university.
Additional information: Applicant must be dependent of 25th Infantry Division Association member. Applicant must be pursuing first bachelor's degree. May not be used at U.S. military academies.

Amount of award:	$1,000-$1,500
Number of awards:	30
Application deadline:	April 1
Notification begins:	June 1

Contact:
25th Infantry Division Association
c/o Lawrence Weist
3930 South Bridlewood Drive
Bountiful, UT 84010
Phone: 801-292-7354
Fax: 801-585-3350
Web: www.25thida.com

AARL Foundation, Inc.

Fred R. McDaniel Memorial Scholarship

Type of award: Scholarship.
Intended use: For undergraduate or graduate study at accredited postsecondary institution in United States. Designated institutions: Institutions in Arkansas, Louisiana, Mississippi, New Mexico, Oklahoma, and Texas.
Eligibility: Applicant must be residing in Oklahoma, Texas, Mississippi, Arkansas, New Mexico or Louisiana.
Basis for selection: Competition/talent/interest in amateur radio. Major/career interest in electronics; communications or engineering, electrical/electronic. Applicant must demonstrate financial need.
Application requirements: Recommendations, transcript.
Additional information: Preference to students with 3.0 GPA. Must be amateur radio operator holding general license. Application may be obtained from Website.

Amount of award:	$500
Number of awards:	1
Application deadline:	February 1
Total amount awarded:	$500

Contact:
ARRL Foundation Inc./Scholarship Program
225 Main Street
Newington, CT 06111
Phone: 860-594-0200
Fax: 860-594-0259
Web: www.arrl.org/arrlf/scholgen.html

Abbie Sargent Memorial Scholarship Fund

Abbie Sargent Memorial Scholarship

Type of award: Scholarship, renewable.
Intended use: For undergraduate or graduate study at accredited 2-year or 4-year institution.
Eligibility: Applicant must be residing in New Hampshire.
Basis for selection: Major/career interest in agriculture or veterinary medicine. Applicant must demonstrate financial need, high academic achievement and depth of character.
Application requirements: Transcript.
Additional information: Only New Hampshire residents should apply. Recipient may attend out-of-state university. Send SASE for application. Award amount tentatively set at $400, but may vary from year to year depending on funding.

Amount of award:	$400
Number of awards:	4
Number of applicants:	43
Application deadline:	March 15
Notification begins:	May 1

Contact:
Abbie Sargent Memorial Scholarship Fund
295 Sheep Davis Road
Concord, NH 03301
Phone: 603-224-1934

Academy of Motion Picture Arts and Sciences

Nicholl Fellowships in Screenwriting

Type of award: Scholarship.
Intended use: For undergraduate or graduate study.
Basis for selection: Major/career interest in playwriting/screen writing.
Application requirements: $30 application fee.
Additional information: Screenwriting competition with prize of $30,000 fellowship. Open to anyone who has written an original feature-length screenplay and who has never earned more than $5,000 from writing for film and television.

Amount of award:	$30,000
Number of awards:	5
Number of applicants:	5,489
Application deadline:	May 1
Total amount awarded:	$150,000

Contact:
Academy of Motion Picture Arts and Sciences
1313 N. Vine Street
Hollywood, CA 90028
Phone: 310-247-3010
Web: www.oscars.org/nicholl

Academy of Television Arts & Sciences Foundation

College Television Award

Type of award: Scholarship.
Intended use: For full-time undergraduate or graduate study in United States.
Basis for selection: Competition/talent/interest in visual arts, based on excellence of submitted film/video. Major/career interest in radio/television/film.
Application requirements: Must submit 3/4-inch cassette of original film/video made for course credit within eligibility period. Must be student producer of record. Yearly updated official entry form must be submitted.
Additional information: Award for student producer of student videos and films in categories of drama, comedy, music, documentary, news/sports/magazine shows, traditional animation and computer animation. Submissions must have been made for college course credit. First- and second-place winners also receive film stock from Kodak. First-place and second-place winners chosen for work on humanitarian concerns eligible for $4,000 Bricker Family College Award. Foreign applicants must be pursuing a degree at U.S. college or university. Visit Website for application.

Amount of award:	$500-$2,000
Number of awards:	21
Application deadline:	December 15
Notification begins:	February 1
Total amount awarded:	$24,500

Contact:
Academy of Television Arts & Sciences Foundation
Educational Programs and Services
5220 Lankershim Boulevard
North Hollywood, CA 91601-3109
Phone: 818-754-2830
Web: www.emmys.tv/foundation

The Actuarial Foundation

Wooddy Scholarship

Type of award: Scholarship.
Intended use: For full-time senior study at 4-year institution.
Eligibility: Applicant must be U.S. citizen or permanent resident.
Basis for selection: Major/career interest in insurance/actuarial science. Applicant must demonstrate high academic achievement.
Application requirements: Recommendations, essay, transcript.
Additional information: Applicant must have passed at least one actuarial examination and must rank in the top quarter of their class. Leadership judged in relation to extracurricular activities. Application is available on Website. Mail completed application form and required documentation to the Actuarial Foundation.

Amount of award:	$2,000
Number of awards:	4
Application deadline:	June 25
Notification begins:	August 31
Total amount awarded:	$8,000

Scholarships

Contact:
The Actuarial Foundation
Attn: Diane Rutherford
475 Martingale Road, Suite 800
Schaumburg, IL 60173-2226
Phone: 847-706-3500
Fax: 847-706-3599
Web: www.actuarialfoundation.org/research_edu/
prize_award.htm#wooddy

ADA Foundation

Allied Dental Health Scholarship for Dental Assisting Students

Type of award: Scholarship.
Intended use: For full-time freshman study in United States. Designated institutions: Must be accredited by Commission on Dental Accreditation.
Eligibility: Applicant must be U.S. citizen.
Basis for selection: Major/career interest in dental assistant. Applicant must demonstrate financial need and high academic achievement.
Application requirements: Completed application form, typed biographical questionnaire, two sealed references, copy of school's acceptance letter.
Additional information: Minimum 2.8 GPA. Applicants must be entering students enrolled in dental assisting program accredited by Commission on Dental Accreditation. Must demonstrate minimum financial need of $1,000. Contact school for application. Notification in fall.

   Amount of award: $1,000
   Application deadline: September 15
Contact:
ADA Foundation
Scholarship Coordinator
211 East Chicago Avenue
Chicago, IL 60611-2678
Phone: 312-440-2763
Fax: 312-440-3526
Web: www.adafoundation.org

Allied Dental Health Scholarship for Dental Hygiene Students

Type of award: Scholarship.
Intended use: For full-time sophomore study in United States. Designated institutions: Must be accredited by Commission on Dental Accreditation.
Eligibility: Applicant must be U.S. citizen.
Basis for selection: Major/career interest in dental hygiene. Applicant must demonstrate financial need and high academic achievement.
Application requirements: Completed application form, typed biographical questionnaire, two sealed references.
Additional information: Minimum 3.0 GPA. Applicant must be entering last year of study in dental hygiene program accredited by Commission on Dental Accreditation. Must demonstrate minimum financial need of $1,000. Contact school for application. Notification in fall.

   Amount of award: $1,000
   Application deadline: August 15

Contact:
ADA Foundation
Scholarship Coordinator
211 East Chicago Avenue
Chicago, IL 60611-2678
Phone: 312-440-2763
Fax: 312-440-3526
Web: www.adafoundation.org

Allied Dental Health Scholarship for Dental Laboratory Technology Students

Type of award: Scholarship, renewable.
Intended use: For full-time sophomore study in United States. Designated institutions: Must be accredited by Commission on Dental Accreditation.
Eligibility: Applicant must be U.S. citizen.
Basis for selection: Major/career interest in dental laboratory technology. Applicant must demonstrate financial need and high academic achievement.
Application requirements: Completed application form, typed biographical questionnaire, two sealed references.
Additional information: Minimum 2.8 GPA. Applicants must be entering last year of study in dental laboratory technology program accredited by Commission on Dental Accreditation. Must demonstrate minimum financial need of $1,000. Contact school for application. Notification in fall.

   Amount of award: $1,000
   Application deadline: August 15
Contact:
ADA Foundation
Scholarship Coordinator
211 East Chicago Avenue
Chicago, IL 60611-2678
Phone: 312-440-2763
Fax: 312-440-3526
Web: www.adafoundation.org

Dental Student Scholarship

Type of award: Scholarship.
Intended use: For full-time sophomore study in United States. Designated institutions: Dental schools accredited by the Commission on Dental Accreditation.
Eligibility: Applicant must be U.S. citizen.
Basis for selection: Major/career interest in dentistry. Applicant must demonstrate financial need and high academic achievement.
Application requirements: Completed application form, typed biographical questionnaire, two sealed references.
Additional information: Minimum 3.0 GPA. Applicant must be entering second-year student attending dental school accredited by Commission on Dental Accreditation. Must demonstrate a minimum financial need of $2,500. Contact school for application.

   Amount of award: $2,500
   Number of awards: 1
   Application deadline: July 31
   Notification begins: September 15

Contact:
ADA Foundation
Scholarship Coordinator
211 East Chicago Avenue
Chicago, IL 60611-2678
Phone: 312-440-2763
Fax: 312-440-3526
Web: www.adafoundation.org

Minority Dental Student Scholarship

Type of award: Scholarship.
Intended use: For full-time sophomore study in United States. Designated institutions: Dental schools accredited by the Commission on Dental Accreditation.
Eligibility: Applicant must be African American, Mexican American, Hispanic American, Puerto Rican or American Indian. Applicant must be U.S. citizen.
Basis for selection: Major/career interest in dentistry. Applicant must demonstrate financial need and high academic achievement.
Application requirements: Completed application form, typed biographical questionnaire, two sealed references.
Additional information: Minimum 3.0 GPA. Applicant must be entering second-year student attending dental school accredited by Commission on Dental Accreditation. Must demonstrate a minimum financial need of $2,500. Contact school for application.

Amount of award:	$2,500
Number of awards:	1
Application deadline:	July 31
Notification begins:	September 15

Contact:
ADA Foundation
Scholarship Coordinator
211 East Chicago Avenue
Chicago, IL 60611-2678
Phone: 312-440-2763
Fax: 312-440-3526
Web: www.adafoundation.org

ADHA Institute for Oral Health

ADHA Institute for Oral Health Minority Scholarship

Type of award: Scholarship, renewable.
Intended use: For full-time undergraduate certificate study at postsecondary institution in United States.
Eligibility: Applicant must be Asian American, African American, Mexican American, Hispanic American, Puerto Rican or American Indian. Men are considered a minority in this field and are encouraged to apply for this program.
Basis for selection: Major/career interest in dental hygiene; dentistry; dental assistant or dental laboratory technology. Applicant must demonstrate financial need, depth of character, leadership, seriousness of purpose and service orientation.
Application requirements: FAFSA. Must provide statement of professional activities related to dental hygiene.
Additional information: Download application from Website. Minimum 3.0 GPA required. Applicants must be working

toward a certificate or associate's degree. Evidence of dental hygiene licensure eligibility must be provided. Applicants must be eligible for licensure in academic year award is being made. Applicant must be member of ADHA or Student ADHA.

Amount of award:	$1,500
Number of awards:	2
Application deadline:	June 1

Contact:
ADHA Institute of Oral Health
444 N. Michigan Ave., Suite 3400
Chicago, IL 60611
Phone: 800-735-4916
Fax: 312-440-8929
Web: www.adha.org/institute

ADHA Institute for Oral Health Part-Time Scholarship

Type of award: Scholarship, renewable.
Intended use: For half-time undergraduate or master's study at 4-year or graduate institution in United States. Designated institutions: Accredited dental hygiene schools.
Basis for selection: Major/career interest in dental hygiene. Applicant must demonstrate financial need, depth of character, leadership, seriousness of purpose and service orientation.
Application requirements: FAFSA.
Additional information: Download application from Website. Minimum 3.0 GPA. Applicants must be pursuing associate/certificate, baccalaureate or graduate degree enrolled part-time in accredited dental hygiene school. Applicant must be member of ADHA or Student ADHA.

Amount of award:	$1,500
Number of awards:	1
Application deadline:	June 1

Contact:
ADHA Institute for Oral Health
444 N. Michigan Ave., Suite 3400
Chicago, IL 60611
Phone: 800-735-4916
Fax: (312) 440-8929
Web: www.adha.org/institute

Colgate "Bright Smiles, Bright Futures" Minority Scholarships

Type of award: Scholarship, renewable.
Intended use: For full-time junior, senior, master's or doctoral study at 4-year or graduate institution in United States.
Eligibility: Applicant must be Asian American, African American, Mexican American, Hispanic American, Puerto Rican or American Indian. Men are considered a minority in this field and are encouraged to apply for this program.
Basis for selection: Major/career interest in dental hygiene. Applicant must demonstrate financial need, high academic achievement, depth of character, leadership, seriousness of purpose and service orientation.
Application requirements: FAFSA. Graduate applicants must provide statement of professional activities related to dental hygiene.
Additional information: Download application from Website. Applicant must be enrolled in a dental hygiene program. Minimum 3.0 GPA. Evidence of dental hygiene licensure must be provided or applicant must be eligible for licensure in the academic year the award is being made. Graduate applicants must provide evidence of acceptance into a full-time master's or doctoral degree program. Applicant must be member of ADHA or Student ADHA.

Amount of award:	$1,250
Number of awards:	2
Application deadline:	June 1

Contact:
ADHA Institute for Oral Health
444 N. Michigan Ave., Suite 3400
Chicago, IL 60611
Phone: 800-735-4916
Fax: 312-440-8929
Web: www.adha.org/institute

Dr. Harold Hillenbrand Scholarship

Type of award: Scholarship, renewable.
Intended use: For full-time undergraduate study at 4-year institution in United States.
Basis for selection: Major/career interest in dental hygiene. Applicant must demonstrate financial need, high academic achievement, depth of character, leadership, seriousness of purpose and service orientation.
Application requirements: FAFSA. Applicant must provide statement of professional activities related to dental hygiene.
Additional information: Download application from Website. Applicant must be enrolled in a dental hygiene program. Minimum 3.5 GPA. Evidence of dental hygiene licensure eligibility must be provided. Applicants must be eligible for licensure in the academic year the award is being made. Applicant must be member of ADHA or Student ADHA.

Amount of award:	$1,500
Number of awards:	1
Application deadline:	June 1

Contact:
ADHA Institute for Oral Health
444 N. Michigan Ave., Suite 3400
Chicago, IL 60611
Phone: 800-735-4916
Fax: 312-440-8929
Web: www.adha.org/institute

Margaret E. Swanson Scholarship

Type of award: Scholarship.
Intended use: For full-time undergraduate or graduate study at 4-year or graduate institution in United States. Designated institutions: Accredited dental hygiene schools.
Basis for selection: Major/career interest in dental hygiene. Applicant must demonstrate financial need, depth of character, leadership, seriousness of purpose and service orientation.
Application requirements: FAFSA.
Additional information: Download application from Website. Minimum 3.0 GPA. Applicant must demonstrate exceptional organizational leadership potential and be pursuing an associate/certificate, baccalaureate or graduate degree while enrolled at an accredited dental hygiene school. Applicant must be member of ADHA or Student ADHA.

Amount of award:	$1,500
Number of awards:	1
Application deadline:	June 1

Contact:
ADHA Institute for Oral Health
444 N. Michigan Ave., Suite 3400
Chicago, IL 60611
Phone: 800-735-4916
Fax: 312-440-8929
Web: www.adha.org/institute

Oral-B Laboratories Dental Hygiene Scholarship

Type of award: Scholarship.
Intended use: For full-time undergraduate study at 4-year institution in United States.
Basis for selection: Major/career interest in dental hygiene. Applicant must demonstrate financial need, high academic achievement, depth of character, leadership, seriousness of purpose and service orientation.
Application requirements: FAFSA.
Additional information: Download application from Website. Applicant must be enrolled in dental hygiene program. Minimum 3.5 GPA. Evidence of dental hygiene licensure eligibility must be provided. Applicant must be eligible for licensure in the academic year the award is being made. Applicant must be member of ADHA or Student ADHA.

Amount of award:	$1,000-$1,500
Number of awards:	2
Application deadline:	June 1

Contact:
ADHA Institute for Oral Health
444 N. Michigan Ave., Suite 3400
Chicago, IL 60611
Phone: 800-735-4916
Fax: 312-440-8929
Web: www.adha.org/institute

Sigma Phi Alpha Undergraduate Scholarship

Type of award: Scholarship.
Intended use: For full-time undergraduate study at 4-year institution in United States. Designated institutions: Accredited dental hygiene schools.
Basis for selection: Major/career interest in dental hygiene. Applicant must demonstrate high academic achievement, depth of character, leadership, seriousness of purpose and service orientation.
Application requirements: FAFSA.
Additional information: Download application from Website. Minimum 3.0 GPA. Applicant must be pursuing associate/certificate or baccalaureate degree at accredited dental hygiene school with an active chapter of the Sigma Phi Alpha Dental Hygiene Honor Society. Applicant must have ADHA or Student ADHA membership.

Amount of award:	$1,000
Number of awards:	1
Application deadline:	June 1

Contact:
ADHA Institute for Oral Health
444 N. Michigan Ave., Suite 3400
Chicago, IL 60611
Phone: 800-735-4916
Fax: 312-440-8929
Web: www.adha.org/institute

AeA - Oregon Council

Oregon AeA Technology Scholarship Program

Type of award: Scholarship, renewable.

Intended use: For full-time freshman study at postsecondary institution. Designated institutions: Oregon University System (EOU, OIT, OSU, PSU, SOU, UO, WOU).
Eligibility: Applicant must be high school senior. Applicant must be residing in Oregon.
Basis for selection: Based on three categories: at-large, women, and ethnic minorities underrepresented in the technology industry. Major/career interest in engineering; computer/information sciences; chemistry or physics. Applicant must demonstrate high academic achievement, leadership, seriousness of purpose and service orientation.
Application requirements: Recommendations, essay, transcript. Applicant must complete application online. Include SAT/ACT scores.
Additional information: Women and underrepresented ethnic minorities are especially encouraged to apply. To renew, recipients must maintain 3.0 GPA, continue to make satisfactory progress toward degree and declare a major in engineering, computer science, or related technology field. Awards include assignment of a corporate mentor and, in most cases, paid internships at sponsor company. Sponsors are member companies in AeA, including Intel, Hewlett-Packard, and In Focus Systems. Award recipients notified in April. Visit Website for details and application.

Amount of award:	$2,500
Number of awards:	32
Number of applicants:	315
Application deadline:	March 1
Total amount awarded:	$277,500

Contact:
AeA Technology Scholarship Program - Oregon University System
Engineering & Computer Science
18640 NW Walker Road, #1027
Beaverton, OR 97006-1975
Phone: 503-725-2920
Fax: 503-725-2921
Web: www.ous.edu/ecs/scholarships

AGC of Maine Education Foundation

AGC of Maine Scholarship Program

Type of award: Scholarship.
Intended use: For full-time sophomore, junior or senior study at accredited 4-year institution in United States.
Eligibility: Applicant must be U.S. citizen residing in Maine.
Basis for selection: Major/career interest in construction or engineering, civil. Applicant must demonstrate financial need and high academic achievement.
Application requirements: Interview, recommendations, essay, transcript.

Amount of award:	$500-$2,000
Application deadline:	March 21
Total amount awarded:	$12,000

Contact:
AGC of Maine
P.O. Box 5519
Augusta, ME 04332
Phone: 207-622-4741
Web: www.acm-inc.org

AHEPA Educational Foundation

AHEPA Educational Foundation Scholarships

Type of award: Scholarship.
Intended use: For full-time undergraduate or graduate study at accredited postsecondary institution.
Eligibility: Applicant or parent must be member/participant of American Hellenic Educational Progressive Association. Must be of Hellenic heritage, although ancestry need not be 100 percent Greek.
Basis for selection: Applicant must demonstrate financial need, high academic achievement, depth of character, leadership, seriousness of purpose and service orientation.
Application requirements: $20 application fee. Recommendations, essay, transcript, proof of eligibility.
Additional information: Applicant must be member, or child of member, in good standing of AHEPA, Daughters of Penelope, Sons of Pericles or Maids of Athena. High school seniors eligible to apply. Visit Website for details and application.

Amount of award:	$500-$2,000
Application deadline:	March 31

Contact:
AHEPA Educational Foundation
c/o AHEPA Headquarters
1909 Q Street, NW, Suite 500
Washington, DC 20009-1007
Web: www.ahepa.org/educ_foundation

Air Force Aid Society

Air Force Aid Society Education Grant

Type of award: Scholarship.
Intended use: For full-time undergraduate study at accredited vocational, 2-year or 4-year institution in or outside United States.
Eligibility: Applicant must be dependent of active service person, veteran or deceased veteran; or spouse of active service person or deceased veteran who serves or served in the Air Force.
Basis for selection: Applicant must demonstrate financial need.
Application requirements: Proof of eligibility.
Additional information: Minimum 2.0 GPA. Veteran status alone not eligible. Veteran must either be retired Reserve with 20-plus qualifying years, or retired Air Force with at least 20 years active duty service. Air Force Reserve and Air National Guard only eligible if on active duty (all other Guard and Reserve not eligible).

Amount of award:	$1,500
Number of applicants:	9,000
Application deadline:	March 14
Notification begins:	June 9
Total amount awarded:	$6,000,000

Contact:
Air Force Aid Society
Education Assistance Department
1745 Jefferson Davis Highway, Suite 202
Arlington, VA 22202
Phone: 800-429-9475
Web: www.afas.org

Air Traffic Control Association, Inc.

Air Traffic Control Children of Specialists Scholarship

Type of award: Scholarship.
Intended use: For undergraduate or graduate study at accredited 4-year institution.
Eligibility: Parent must be air traffic control specialist. Applicant must be U.S. citizen.
Basis for selection: Major/career interest in aerospace. Applicant must demonstrate financial need, depth of character and seriousness of purpose.
Application requirements: Recommendations, transcript.
Additional information: Must be natural or adopted child of air traffic control specialist (G5-2152). Applicant's coursework must lead to a bachelor's degree or higher. Application and terms of reference can be downloaded from Website.

Amount of award:	$1,000-$1,800
Number of awards:	3
Number of applicants:	75
Application deadline:	May 1
Total amount awarded:	$4,500

Contact:
Air Traffic Control Association, Inc.
Attn: Scholarship Fund
1101 King Street, Suite 300
Arlington, VA 22314
Phone: 703-522-5717
Web: www.atca.org

Air Traffic Control Full-Time Employee Student Scholarship

Type of award: Scholarship.
Intended use: For undergraduate, graduate or non-degree study at postsecondary institution.
Eligibility: Applicant or parent must be employed by Aviation industry. Applicant must be returning adult student. Applicant must be U.S. citizen.
Basis for selection: Major/career interest in aviation; aviation repair or computer/information sciences. Applicant must demonstrate financial need, depth of character and seriousness of purpose.
Application requirements: Recommendations, transcript, proof of eligibility.
Additional information: Available only to full-time aviation career professional doing part-time study to enhance job skills. Employee applicant must work full-time in aviation-related field, and coursework must enhance aviation skills. Scholarship must be used within four years of date awarded. Application and terms of reference can be downloaded from Website.

Amount of award:	$400-$600
Number of awards:	4
Number of applicants:	45
Application deadline:	May 1
Total amount awarded:	$2,400

Contact:
Air Traffic Control Association, Inc.
Attn: Scholarship Fund
1101 King Street, Suite 300
Alexandria, VA 22314
Phone: 800-336-4583 ext. 6149
Web: www.atca.org

Air Traffic Control Half/Full-Time Student Scholarship

Type of award: Scholarship.
Intended use: For undergraduate or graduate study at accredited 4-year or graduate institution in United States.
Eligibility: Applicant must be U.S. citizen.
Basis for selection: Major/career interest in aviation or aerospace. Applicant must demonstrate financial need, depth of character and seriousness of purpose.
Application requirements: Proof of eligibility. Two recommendations, a 400-word essay on "How My Education Efforts Will Enhance My Potential Contribution to Aviation" and college transcript (high school transcript if under 30 semester hours or 45 quarter hours completed).
Additional information: Must have minimum of 30 semester hours or 45 quarter hours still to be completed before graduation and attend at least half time (six hours). Applicant's coursework must lead to bachelor's degree or higher. Application and terms of reference can be downloaded from Website.

Amount of award:	$1,500-$2,500
Number of awards:	3
Number of applicants:	300
Application deadline:	May 1
Total amount awarded:	$4,500

Contact:
Air Traffic Control Association, Inc.
Attn: Scholarship Fund
1101 King Street, Suite 300
Alexandria, VA 22314
Phone: 703-522-5717
Web: www.atca.org

Aircraft Electronics Association Educational Foundation

Bendix/King Avionics Scholarship

Type of award: Scholarship, renewable.
Intended use: For full-time undergraduate study at accredited vocational, 2-year or 4-year institution. Designated institutions: Accredited schools with avionics or aircraft repair programs.
Basis for selection: Major/career interest in aviation; aviation repair or electronics.
Application requirements: Recommendations, transcript, proof of eligibility. Applicant must submit a 300-word essay on one of the required topics.

Additional information: Available to anyone attending or planning to attend an accredited school in an avionics or aircraft repair program. Awards are announced at AEA Annual Convention and Trade Show each spring. Applicant must have a 2.5 GPA. Visit Website for additional information.

Amount of award:	$1,000
Number of awards:	1
Application deadline:	February 17
Total amount awarded:	$1,000

Contact:
Aircraft Electronics Association Educational Foundation
4217 S. Hocker Drive
Independence, MO 64055
Phone: 816-373-6565
Fax: 816-478-3100
Web: www.aea.net/educationalfoundation

BFGoodrich Component Services Scholarship

Type of award: Scholarship, renewable.
Intended use: For full-time undergraduate study at accredited vocational, 2-year or 4-year institution. Designated institutions: Accredited colleges/universities with avionics or aircraft repair programs.
Basis for selection: Major/career interest in aviation; aviation repair or electronics. Applicant must demonstrate depth of character and seriousness of purpose.
Application requirements: Recommendations, transcript, proof of eligibility.
Additional information: Available to anyone attending or planning to attend an accredited school in an avionics or aircraft repair program. Awards are announced at AEA Annual Convention and Trade Show each spring.

Amount of award:	$2,500
Number of awards:	1
Application deadline:	February 15
Total amount awarded:	$2,500

Contact:
Aircraft Electronics Association Educational Foundation
4217 S. Hocker Drive
Independence, MO 64055
Phone: 816-373-6565
Fax: 816-478-3100
Web: www.aea.net/educationalfoundation

Bud Glover Memorial Scholarship

Type of award: Scholarship, renewable.
Intended use: For full-time undergraduate study at accredited vocational, 2-year or 4-year institution. Designated institutions: Accredited schools with avionics or aircraft repair programs.
Basis for selection: Major/career interest in aviation; aviation repair or electronics. Applicant must demonstrate depth of character and seriousness of purpose.
Application requirements: Recommendations, transcript, proof of eligibility.
Additional information: Available to anyone attending or planning to attend an accredited school in an avionics or aircraft repair program. Awards are announced at AEA Annual Convention and Trade Show each spring.

Amount of award:	$1,000
Number of awards:	1
Application deadline:	February 15

Contact:
Aircraft Electronics Association Educational Foundation
4217 S. Hocker Drive
Independence, MO 64055
Phone: 816-373-6565
Fax: 816-478-3100
Web: www.aea.net/educationalfoundation

College of Aeronautics Scholarship

Type of award: Scholarship, renewable.
Intended use: For full-time undergraduate study at 2-year institution. Designated institutions: College of Aeronautics in Flushing, N.Y.
Basis for selection: Major/career interest in aviation; aviation repair or electronics. Applicant must demonstrate depth of character and seriousness of purpose.
Application requirements: Recommendations, transcript, proof of eligibility.
Additional information: Available to anyone attending or planning to attend College of Aeronautics in Flushing, N.Y. Scholarship is for duration of two-year program, at $750 per semester with maximum of $3,000 for four semesters. Awards are announced at AEA Annual Convention and Trade Show each spring.

Amount of award:	$750-$3,000
Number of awards:	1
Application deadline:	February 15

Contact:
Aircraft Electronics Association Educational Foundation
4217 S. Hocker Drive
Independence, MO 64055
Phone: 816-373-6565
Fax: 816-478-3100
Web: www.aea.net/educationalfoundation

David Arver Memorial Scholarship

Type of award: Scholarship, renewable.
Intended use: For full-time undergraduate study at accredited vocational or 2-year institution. Designated institutions: Accredited vocational/technical schools with avionics or aircraft repair programs, located in Illinois, Indiana, Iowa, Kansas, Michigan, Minnesota, Missouri, Nebraska, North Dakota, South Dakota or Wisconsin.
Basis for selection: Major/career interest in aviation; aviation repair or electronics. Applicant must demonstrate depth of character and seriousness of purpose.
Application requirements: Recommendations, transcript, proof of eligibility.
Additional information: Available to anyone attending or planning to attend an accredited school located in AEA Region Three (listed states) in an avionics or aircraft repair program. Awards are announced at AEA Annual Convention and Trade Show each spring.

Amount of award:	$1,000
Number of awards:	1
Application deadline:	February 15
Total amount awarded:	$1,000

Contact:
Aircraft Electronics Association Educational Foundation
4217 S. Hocker Drive
Independence, MO 64055
Phone: 816-373-6565
Fax: 816-478-3100
Web: www.aea.net/educationalfoundation

Dutch and Ginger Arver Scholarship

Type of award: Scholarship, renewable.
Intended use: For full-time undergraduate study at accredited vocational, 2-year or 4-year institution. Designated institutions: Accredited schools with avionics or aircraft repair programs.
Basis for selection: Major/career interest in aviation; aviation repair or electronics. Applicant must demonstrate depth of character and seriousness of purpose.
Application requirements: Recommendations, transcript, proof of eligibility.
Additional information: Available to anyone attending or planning to attend an accredited school in an avionics or aircraft repair program. Awards are announced at AEA Annual Convention and Trade Show.

Amount of award:	$1,000
Number of awards:	1
Application deadline:	February 15
Total amount awarded:	$1,000

Contact:
Aircraft Electronics Association Educational Foundation
4217 S. Hocker Drive
Independence, MO 64055
Phone: 816-373-6565
Fax: 816-478-3100
Web: www.aea.net/educationalfoundation

Field Aviation Co., Inc. Scholarship

Type of award: Scholarship, renewable.
Intended use: For full-time undergraduate study at vocational, 2-year or 4-year institution. Designated institutions: Accredited schools with avionics or aircraft repair programs, located in Canada.
Eligibility: Applicant must be high school senior.
Basis for selection: Major/career interest in aviation; aviation repair or electronics. Applicant must demonstrate depth of character and seriousness of purpose.
Application requirements: Recommendations, transcript, proof of eligibility.
Additional information: Available to anyone attending or planning to attend accredited school in avionics or aircraft repair program in Canada. Awards are announced at AEA Annual Convention and Trade Show each spring.

Amount of award:	$1,000
Number of awards:	1
Application deadline:	February 15

Contact:
Aircraft Electronics Association Educational Foundation
4217 S. Hocker Drive
Independence, MO 64055
Phone: 816-373-6565
Fax: 816-478-3100
Web: www.aea.net/educationalfoundation

Garmin Scholarship

Type of award: Scholarship, renewable.
Intended use: For full-time undergraduate study at accredited vocational, 2-year or 4-year institution. Designated institutions: Accredited schools with avionics and aircraft repair programs.
Eligibility: Applicant must be high school senior.
Basis for selection: Major/career interest in aviation; aviation repair or electronics. Applicant must demonstrate depth of character and seriousness of purpose.

Application requirements: Recommendations, transcript, proof of eligibility. Applicant must submit 300-word essay on one of the required topics.
Additional information: Available to anyone attending or planning to attend an accredited school in an avionics or aircraft repair program. Awards are announced at AEA Annual Convention and Trade Show each spring. Applicant must have 2.5 GPA. For more information, visit Website.

Amount of award:	$2,000
Number of awards:	1
Application deadline:	February 17
Total amount awarded:	$2,000

Contact:
Aircraft Electronics Association Educational Foundation
4217 S. Hocker Drive
Independence, MO 64055
Phone: 816-373-6565
Fax: 816-478-3100
Web: www.aea.net/educationalfoundation

Johnny Davis Memorial Scholarship

Type of award: Scholarship, renewable.
Intended use: For full-time undergraduate study at accredited vocational, 2-year or 4-year institution. Designated institutions: Accredited schools with avionics or aircraft repair programs.
Eligibility: Applicant must be high school senior.
Basis for selection: Major/career interest in aviation; aviation repair or electronics. Applicant must demonstrate depth of character and seriousness of purpose.
Application requirements: Recommendations, transcript, proof of eligibility. Applicant must submit 300-word essay on one of the required topics.
Additional information: Available to anyone attending or planning to attend an accredited school in an avionics or aircraft repair program. Awards are announced at AEA Annual Convention and Trade Show each spring. Applicant must have a 2.5 GPA. Visit Website for additional information.

Amount of award:	$1,000
Number of awards:	1
Application deadline:	February 17
Total amount awarded:	$1,000

Contact:
Aircraft Electronics Association Educational Foundation
4217 S. Hocker Drive
Independence, MO 64055
Phone: 816-373-6565
Fax: 816-478-3100
Web: www.aea.net/educationalfoundation

Lee Tarbox Memorial Scholarship

Type of award: Scholarship, renewable.
Intended use: For full-time undergraduate study at accredited vocational, 2-year or 4-year institution. Designated institutions: Accredited schools with avionics or aircraft repair programs.
Eligibility: Applicant must be high school senior.
Basis for selection: Major/career interest in aviation; aviation repair or electronics. Applicant must demonstrate depth of character and seriousness of purpose.
Application requirements: Recommendations, transcript, proof of eligibility. Applicant must submit a 300-word essay on one of the required topics.
Additional information: Available to anyone attending or planning to attend an accredited school in an avionics or aircraft repair program. Scholarship given by Pacific Southwest Instruments. Awards are announced at AEA Annual Convention

and Trade Show each spring. Applicant must have a minimum of 2.5 GPA. Visit Website for additional information.

Amount of award:	$2,500
Number of awards:	1
Application deadline:	February 17
Total amount awarded:	$2,500

Contact:
Aircraft Electronics Association Educational Foundation
4217 S. Hocker Drive
Independence, MO 64055
Phone: 816-373-6565
Fax: 816-478-3100
Web: www.aea.net/educationalfoundation

Leon Harris/Les Nichols Memorial to Spartan School of Aeronautics

Type of award: Scholarship, renewable.
Intended use: For full-time undergraduate study. Designated institutions: NEC Spartan School of Aeronautics in Tulsa, OK.
Basis for selection: Major/career interest in aviation; aviation repair or electronics. Applicant must demonstrate depth of character and seriousness of purpose.
Application requirements: Recommendations, transcript, proof of eligibility.
Additional information: Available to students who pursue associate's degree in applied science in aviation electronics (avionics) at NEC Spartan School of Aeronautics in Tulsa, OK. Applicant may not be currently enrolled in avionics program at Spartan. Award covers tuition for eight quarters or until associate's degree is completed, whichever comes first. All other costs (tools, living expenses, and fees) must be covered by student. Awards are announced at AEA Annual Convention and Trade Show each spring.

Amount of award:	Full tuition
Number of awards:	1
Application deadline:	February 15

Contact:
Aircraft Electronics Association Educational Foundation
4217 S. Hocker Drive
Independence, MO 64055
Phone: 816-373-6565
Fax: 816-478-3100
Web: www.aea.net/educationalfoundation

Lowell Gaylor Memorial Scholarship

Type of award: Scholarship, renewable.
Intended use: For full-time undergraduate study at accredited vocational, 2-year or 4-year institution. Designated institutions: Accredited schools with avionics or aircraft repair programs.
Basis for selection: Major/career interest in aviation; aviation repair or electronics. Applicant must demonstrate depth of character and seriousness of purpose.
Application requirements: Recommendations, transcript, proof of eligibility.
Additional information: Available to anyone attending or planning to attend an accredited school in an avionics or aircraft repair program. Awards are announced at AEA Annual Convention and Trade Show each year.

Amount of award:	$1,000
Number of awards:	1
Application deadline:	February 15

Contact:
Aircraft Electronics Association Educational Foundation
4217 S. Hocker Drive
Independence, MO 64055
Phone: 816-373-6565
Fax: 816-478-3100
Web: www.aea.net/educationalfoundation

Lowell Gaylor Memorial Scholarship

Type of award: Scholarship.
Intended use: For full-time senior study at vocational, 2-year or 4-year institution in United States. Designated institutions: Accredited vocational/technical schools with avionics or aircraft repair programs.
Eligibility: Applicant must be high school senior. Applicant must be U.S. citizen.
Basis for selection: Major/career interest in aviation; aviation repair or electronics. Applicant must demonstrate depth of character and seriousness of purpose.
Application requirements: Recommendations, essay, transcript. Applicant must submit 300-word essay on one of the required topics.
Additional information: Applicant must have a minimum of 2.5 GPA. Visit Website for additional information.

Amount of award:	$1,000
Application deadline:	February 17

Contact:
Aircraft Electronics Association Educational Foundation
4217 S. Hocker
Independence, MO 64055
Phone: 817-373-6565
Fax: 816-478-3100
Web: www.aea.net/educationalfoundation

Mid-Continent Instrument Scholarship

Type of award: Scholarship, renewable.
Intended use: For full-time undergraduate study at accredited vocational, 2-year or 4-year institution. Designated institutions: Accredited schools with avionics or aircraft repair programs.
Basis for selection: Major/career interest in aviation; aviation repair or electronics. Applicant must demonstrate depth of character and seriousness of purpose.
Application requirements: Recommendations, transcript, proof of eligibility.
Additional information: Available to anyone attending or planning to attend an accredited school in an avionics or aircraft repair program. Awards are announced at AEA Annual Convention and Trade Show each spring.

Amount of award:	$1,000
Number of awards:	1
Application deadline:	February 15
Total amount awarded:	$1,000

Contact:
Aircraft Electronics Association Educational Foundation
4217 S. Hocker Drive
Independence, MO 64055
Phone: 816-373-6565
Fax: 816-478-3100
Web: www.aea.net/educationalfoundation

Monte R. Mitchell Global Scholarship

Type of award: Scholarship, renewable.
Intended use: For full-time undergraduate study at accredited vocational or 2-year institution in or outside United States. Designated institutions: Accredited institutions with aviation maintenance technology, avionics or aircraft repair programs, located in Europe or the United States.
Eligibility: Applicant must be high school senior. Applicant must be international student or European student.
Basis for selection: Major/career interest in aviation; aviation repair or electronics. Applicant must demonstrate depth of character and seriousness of purpose.
Application requirements: Proof of eligibility.
Additional information: Available to European student pursuing degree in aviation maintenance technology, avionics or aircraft repair at accredited school in Europe or the United States. Scholarship given by Mid-Continent Instruments Co. Awards are announced at AEA Annual Convention and Trade Show each spring.

Amount of award:	$1,000
Number of awards:	1
Application deadline:	February 15
Total amount awarded:	$1,000

Contact:
Aircraft Electronics Association Educational Foundation
4217 S. Hocker Drive
Independence, MO 64055
Phone: 816-373-6565
Fax: 816-478-3100
Web: www.aea.net/educationalfoundation

Plane & Pilot Magazine/Garmin Scholarship

Type of award: Scholarship, renewable.
Intended use: For full-time undergraduate study at accredited vocational institution. Designated institutions: Accredited vocational/technical schools with avionics or aircraft repair programs.
Basis for selection: Major/career interest in aviation; aviation repair or electronics. Applicant must demonstrate depth of character and seriousness of purpose.
Application requirements: Recommendations, transcript, proof of eligibility. Applicant must submit 300-word essay on one of the required topics.
Additional information: Available to anyone attending or planning to attend an accredited vocational/technical school in an avionics or aircraft program. Awards are announced at AEA Annual Convention and Trade Show each spring. Applicant must have 2.5 GPA. Visit Website for additional information.

Amount of award:	$2,000
Number of awards:	1
Application deadline:	February 17
Total amount awarded:	$2,000

Contact:
Aircraft Electronic Association Educational Foundation
4217 S. Hocker Drive
Independence, MO 64055
Phone: 816-373-6565
Fax: 816-478-3100
Web: www.aea.net/educationalfoundation

Russell Leroy Jones Memorial Scholarship to Westwood College of Aviation Technology

Type of award: Scholarship, renewable.
Intended use: For full-time undergraduate study. Designated institutions: Westwood College of Aviation Technology in Broomfield, CO.
Basis for selection: Major/career interest in aviation; aviation repair or electronics. Applicant must demonstrate depth of character and seriousness of purpose.
Application requirements: Recommendations, transcript, proof of eligibility.
Additional information: Available to anyone planning to attend Westwood College of Aviation Technology in Broomfield, CO, for electronics/avionics program. Award covers tuition only. Tools, fees, room, and board must be paid for by student. Applicant may not be currently enrolled at Westwood College of Aviation Technology. Awards are announced at AEA Annual Convention and Trade Show each spring.

Amount of award:	$6,000
Number of awards:	3
Application deadline:	February 15

Contact:
Aircraft Electronics Association Educational Foundation
4217 S. Hocker Drive
Independence, MO 64055
Phone: 816-373-6565
Fax: 816-478-3100
Web: www.aea.net/educationalfoundation

Aircraft Owners and Pilots Association

AOPA Air Safety Foundation/ McAllister Memorial Scholarship

Type of award: Scholarship.
Intended use: For full-time junior or senior study at accredited 4-year institution in United States. Designated institutions: Institutions with aviation programs.
Eligibility: Applicant must be U.S. citizen or permanent resident.
Basis for selection: Major/career interest in aviation or aviation repair. Applicant must demonstrate financial need and high academic achievement.
Application requirements: Essay, transcript, proof of eligibility. 250-word paper on: "What should all GA pilots know about the weather?"
Additional information: Applicant must be enrolled in an aviation program at a four-year institution. Applicant must have GPA of 3.25 or better. Application available online. Five copies of entire application packet must be mailed to: Dr. David A. NewMyer, Chairperson; Aviation Management and Flight College of Applied Sciences and Arts; Southern Illinois University Carbondale; Carbondale, IL 62901-6623.

Amount of award:	$1,000
Number of awards:	1
Application deadline:	March 31
Notification begins:	July 1
Total amount awarded:	$1,000

Contact:
Aircraft Owners and Pilots Association Air Safety Foundation
McAllister Memorial Scholarship
421 Aviation Way
Frederick, MD 21701
Phone: 301-695-2177
Fax: 301-695-2343
Web: www.asf.org

Airmen Memorial Foundation

Chief Master Sergeants of the Air Force Scholarship

Type of award: Scholarship.
Intended use: For full-time undergraduate study at accredited postsecondary institution in United States.
Eligibility: Applicant must be single. Applicant must be dependent of active service person in the Air Force. Must be child of active duty or retired enlisted member of U.S. Air Force, regardless of component.
Basis for selection: Applicant must demonstrate high academic achievement, depth of character and leadership.
Application requirements: Recommendations, essay, transcript, proof of eligibility. Applicants must submit additional information they feel should be taken into consideration by selection committees. Complete "Other Considerations" form included with every scholarship application package.
Additional information: Must be single dependent, including legally adopted child or stepchild, who will not reach 23rd birthday by September 1 of award year. Applications available November 1 to March 31. For application, send SASE. Amount and number of awards vary. Visit Website for more information.

Amount of award:	$3,000
Application deadline:	April 15
Notification begins:	August 1

Contact:
Airmen Foundation Scholarships
P.O. Box 50
Temple Hills, MD 20757-0050
Phone: 800-638-0594
Web: www.amf.org

Akademos, Inc.

Akademos, Inc. TextbookX.com Scholarship

Type of award: Scholarship.
Intended use: For undergraduate or graduate study at accredited postsecondary institution in United States.
Eligibility: Applicant must be U.S. citizen, permanent resident or international student.
Basis for selection: Essay.
Application requirements: 250- to 750-word essay based on question posted on Website.
Additional information: Spring and summer scholarships offered. Awardees chosen based on essay. Visit Website for essay guidelines and deadlines, and to apply. International students with valid visas eligible. Applicant must be in good standing; cannot be relative or friend of Akademos employee.

Amount of award:	$250-$1,500
Application deadline:	June 30, December 31

Contact:
Visit Website for more information.
Web: www.textbookx.com/scholarship

Alabama Commission on Higher Education

Alabama National Guard Educational Assistance Award

Type of award: Scholarship, renewable.
Intended use: For undergraduate or graduate study at 2-year or 4-year institution. Designated institutions: Alabama public institution.
Eligibility: Applicant must be U.S. citizen residing in Alabama. Applicant must be in military service in the Reserves/National Guard. Must be active members in good standing with federally recognized unit of Alabama National Guard.
Application requirements: Proof of eligibility.
Additional information: Award covers tuition, books, fees and supplies (minus any federal veterans' benefits) at Alabama public institution.

Amount of award:	$25-$1,000
Number of awards:	775
Number of applicants:	775
Total amount awarded:	$508,916

Contact:
Alabama National Guard Unit
Phone: 334-242-2273
Fax: 334-242-0268
Web: www.studentaid.state.al.us

Alabama Student Assistance Program

Type of award: Scholarship, renewable.
Intended use: For full-time undergraduate study at vocational, 2-year or 4-year institution. Designated institutions: Eligible Alabama postsecondary institutions. Nearly 80 institutions participate in program.
Eligibility: Applicant must be residing in Alabama.
Basis for selection: Applicant must demonstrate financial need.
Application requirements: Proof of eligibility. FAFSA.
Additional information: Students urged to apply early.

Amount of award:	$300-$2,500
Number of awards:	3,849
Total amount awarded:	$1,841,270

Contact:
Applications available at high school or college financial aid office.
Phone: 334-242-2273
Fax: 334-242-0268
Web: www.studentaid.state.al.us

Alabama Student Grant

Type of award: Scholarship, renewable.

Intended use: For undergraduate study at 2-year or 4-year institution. Designated institutions: Birmingham-Southern College, Concordia College, Faulkner University, Huntingdon College, Judson College, Miles College, Oakwood College, Samford University, Southeastern Bible College, Spring Hill College, Stillman College, University of Mobile, Southern Christian University.
Eligibility: Applicant must be residing in Alabama.
Application requirements: Five proofs of Alabama residency.
Additional information: Award is not need-based. Up to $1,200 per academic year. Deadlines printed on application form.

Amount of award:	$1,200
Number of awards:	10,487
Total amount awarded:	$5,429,050

Contact:
Contact financial aid office of institution for application.
Phone: 334-242-2273
Fax: 334-242-0268
Web: www.studentaid.state.al.us

Police/Firefighters' Survivors Educational Assistance Program

Type of award: Scholarship, renewable.
Intended use: For undergraduate study at vocational, 2-year or 4-year institution. Designated institutions: Public postsecondary institutions in Alabama.
Eligibility: Applicant must be residing in Alabama. Applicant's parent must have been killed or disabled in work-related accident as fire fighter or police officer.
Application requirements: Proof of eligibility.
Additional information: Grant covers full tuition, fees, books and supplies at Alabama public institutions for dependents and eligible spouses of Alabama police officers and firefighters killed or disabled in line of duty.

Amount of award:	Full tuition
Number of awards:	19
Number of applicants:	19
Application deadline:	June 15
Total amount awarded:	$33,166

Contact:
Alabama Commission on Higher Education
P.O. Box 302000
Montgomery, AL 36130-2000
Phone: 334-242-2273
Fax: 334-242-0268
Web: www.studentaid.state.al.us

Alabama Department of Education

Alabama Robert C. Byrd Honors Scholarship

Type of award: Scholarship, renewable.
Intended use: For full-time undergraduate study at 2-year or 4-year institution in United States.
Eligibility: Applicant must be high school senior. Applicant must be U.S. citizen residing in Alabama.
Basis for selection: Applicant must demonstrate high academic achievement.

Application requirements: Nomination by high school guidance counselor. SAT/ACT scores.
Additional information: Contact high school guidance office or principal for information. Scholarship renewable for up to four years of undergraduate work. Award continues through senior year if qualifications are met. There are approximately 15 winners for each U.S. Congressional District, with seven districts in the state.

Amount of award:	$1,500
Number of awards:	105

Contact:
Robert C. Byrd Honors Scholarship Program
Alabama State Department of Education
3345 Gordon Persons Building, Box 302101
Montgomery, AL 36130-2101
Phone: 334-242-8059

Alabama Department of Postsecondary Education

Alabama Junior/Community College Athletic Scholarship

Type of award: Scholarship, renewable.
Intended use: For full-time freshman or sophomore study at 2-year institution in United States. Designated institutions: Two-year public institutions in Alabama.
Eligibility: Applicant must be U.S. citizen or permanent resident residing in Alabama.
Basis for selection: Competition/talent/interest in athletics/sports.
Application requirements: Competitive tryout will be scheduled. Must be enrolled.
Additional information: Awards not need-based. Award covers tuition and books at Alabama two-year public institutions. Eligibility based on athletic ability determined through tryouts. Renewal dependent on continued athletic participation. Award amount varies.
Contact:
Phone: 334-242-1998
Fax: 334-242-0268
Web: www.ache.state.al.us

Institutional Scholarship Waivers

Type of award: Scholarship, renewable.
Intended use: For freshman or sophomore study at accredited postsecondary institution. Designated institutions: Two-year public institutions in Alabama.
Eligibility: Applicant must be U.S. citizen or permanent resident residing in Alabama.
Basis for selection: Applicant must demonstrate high academic achievement.
Application requirements: Transcript.
Additional information: Awards not need-based. Awards based on merit. Focus of scholarship is determined by each institution. Application deadlines printed on application forms. Award may be renewed if student demonstrates academic excellence. Amount and number of awards vary.
Contact:
Phone: 334-242-1998
Fax: 334-242-0268
Web: www.ache.state.al.us

Scholarships

Alabama Department of Veterans Affairs

Alabama GI Dependents Educational Benefit

Type of award: Scholarship, renewable.
Intended use: For undergraduate or graduate study at postsecondary institution. Designated institutions: State-supported institution.
Eligibility: Applicant must be dependent of disabled veteran, deceased veteran or POW/MIA; or spouse of disabled veteran, deceased veteran or POW/MIA. Veteran must have been involved in active military duties for at least 90 days on continuous active duty. Disabled veterans must be rated at least 20% disabled due to service connected disabilities.
Application requirements: Proof of eligibility.
Additional information: Veteran parent/spouse must have been resident of Alabama at least one year prior to enlistment. Children of veterans must submit application before their 26th birthday. Spouses of veterans have no age limit.

Amount of award:	Full tuition
Number of awards:	967
Number of applicants:	1,014
Total amount awarded:	$6,585,395

Contact:
Alabama Department of Veterans Affairs
P.O. Box 1509
Montgomery, AL 36102-1509
Phone: 334-242-5077
Fax: 334-242-5102

Alcoa Foundation

Alcoa Foundation Sons and Daughters Scholarship Program

Type of award: Scholarship.
Intended use: For undergraduate study at accredited postsecondary institution.
Eligibility: Applicant or parent must be employed by Alcoa Inc. Applicant must be high school senior.
Basis for selection: Major/career interest in humanities/liberal arts. Applicant must demonstrate high academic achievement, depth of character, leadership, seriousness of purpose and service orientation.
Application requirements: Essay, transcript, proof of eligibility. Parent must be employed by Alcoa, Inc. or wholly owned subsidiaries. Applicant will choose from two given essay topics.
Additional information: Award is renewable for up to three years.

Amount of award:	$1,500
Number of awards:	150
Number of applicants:	850
Application deadline:	January 21
Notification begins:	April 22

Contact:
Alcoa Foundation, Sons and Daughters Scholarship Program
P.O. Box 4030
Iowa City, IA 52243-4030
Phone: 412-553-4786

Alexander Graham Bell Association for the Deaf and Hard of Hearing

AG Bell College Scholarship Awards

Type of award: Scholarship.
Intended use: For full-time undergraduate or graduate study at accredited 2-year, 4-year or graduate institution in or outside United States.
Eligibility: Applicant must be hearing impaired.
Basis for selection: Applicant must demonstrate financial need, high academic achievement and seriousness of purpose.
Application requirements: Recommendations, essay, transcript, proof of eligibility. Current audiogram.
Additional information: Applicant must have had hearing loss since birth or before acquiring language, with 60db or greater loss in the better ear in speech frequencies of 500, 1,000 and 2,000 Hz. Must use speech and residual hearing and/or speech-reading (lip-reading) as preferred form of communication. Must be accepted or enrolled in college/university program that primarily enrolls students with normal hearing. Application requests must be received between September 1 and January 1. Only first 500 requests will be accepted. Number of awards granted varies. Write or send e-mail (financialaid@agbell.org) to attention of Dana Hughes, financial aid coordinator.

Amount of award:	$200-$1,500
Application deadline:	March 1
Notification begins:	June 11

Contact:
Alexander Graham Bell Association for the Deaf and Hard of Hearing
Scholarship Awards Committee
3417 Volta Place, NW
Washington 20007-2778
Phone: 202-337-5220
Web: www.agbell.org

All-Ink.com

All-Ink.com College Scholarship Program

Type of award: Scholarship.
Intended use: For undergraduate or graduate study at 2-year or 4-year institution.
Eligibility: Applicant must be high school senior. Applicant must be U.S. citizen or permanent resident.
Basis for selection: Applicant must demonstrate high academic achievement.
Application requirements: 50 to 200-word essay on who has had the greated impact on your life, and a 50- to 200-word essay on what you hope to achieve in your personal and professional life after college.
Additional information: Applicant must have minimum 2.5 GPA. Applications must be completed and submitted online at www.all-ink.com/scholarship.html. Applicants will be notified of scholarship winners by posting on Website.

Number of awards: 5
Application deadline: December 31
Notification begins: January 20
Total amount awarded: $10,000
Contact:
Phone: 801-794-0123
Web: www.all-ink.com

Alliance for Young Artists and Writers

New York Times James B. Reston Writing Portfolio Award

Type of award: Scholarship.
Intended use: For freshman study at postsecondary institution.
Eligibility: Applicant must be high school senior.
Basis for selection: Competition/talent/interest in writing/journalism, based on originality, level of technical proficiency, emergence of personal voice or style. Major/career interest in journalism.
Application requirements: $10 application fee. Portfolio, essay. Completed entry form (two copies). Portfolio must contain three to eight works with table of contents listing title and category of each piece. Entry form must be signed by student's parent and teacher, counselor, or principal.
Additional information: One scholarship awarded to most outstanding nonfiction portfolio. Submission must be collection of nonfiction works intended to instruct, inform, explain, persuade, or entertain (i.e. essays, journalistic articles or editorials). Deadlines vary, contact sponsor or visit Website for details.

Amount of award: $100-$5,000
Number of awards: 1
Contact:
The Scholastic Art and Writing Awards
555 Broadway
New York, NY 10012
Phone: 212-343-6493
Web: www.artandwriting.org

Scholastic Art Portfolio Gold Award

Type of award: Scholarship.
Intended use: For freshman study at postsecondary institution.
Eligibility: Applicant must be high school senior.
Basis for selection: Competition/talent/interest in visual arts, based on originality, level of technical proficiency, and emergence of personal style or vision. Major/career interest in arts, general.
Application requirements: Portfolio, recommendations, essay, transcript. Completed portfolio entry form (available online) and signed consent form. Must submit eight works, including at least three drawings.
Additional information: Four unrestricted scholarships awarded to exemplary works. Deadlines vary. Contact sponsor or visit Website for more information.

Amount of award: $10,000
Number of awards: 4
Total amount awarded: $40,000

Contact:
The Scholastic Art and Writing Awards
555 Broadway
New York, NY 10012
Phone: 212-343-6493
Web: www.artandwriting.org

Scholastic Art Portfolio Silver Award

Type of award: Scholarship.
Intended use: For freshman study at postsecondary institution.
Eligibility: Applicant must be high school senior.
Basis for selection: Competition/talent/interest in visual arts, based on originality, level of technical proficiency, and emergence of personal style or vision. Major/career interest in arts, general.
Application requirements: Portfolio, recommendations, essay, transcript. Completed portfolio entry form (available online) and signed consent form. Must submit eight works, including at least three drawings.
Additional information: Approximately 100 students nominated for scholarships offered by participating higher education institutions. Deadlines vary. Contact sponsor or visit Website for more information.

Number of awards: 100
Contact:
The Scholastic Art and Writing Awards
555 Broadway
New York, NY 10012
Phone: 212-343-6493
Web: www.artandwriting.org

Scholastic Photography Portfolio Gold Award

Type of award: Scholarship.
Intended use: For freshman study at postsecondary institution.
Eligibility: Applicant must be high school senior.
Basis for selection: Competition/talent/interest in photography, based on originality, level of technical proficiency, and emergence of personal style or vision. Major/career interest in arts, general.
Application requirements: Portfolio, recommendations, essay, transcript. Completed portfolio entry form (available online) and signed consent form. Must submit eight works in form of prints.
Additional information: One unrestricted scholarship awarded to most outstanding photography portfolio. Deadlines vary. Contact sponsor or visit Website for more information.

Amount of award: $5,000
Number of awards: 1
Total amount awarded: $5,000
Contact:
The Scholastic Art and Writing Awards
555 Broadway
New York, NY 10012
Phone: 212-343-6493
Web: www.artandwriting.org

Scholastic Photography Portfolio Silver Award

Type of award: Scholarship.
Intended use: For freshman study at postsecondary institution.
Eligibility: Applicant must be high school senior.

Basis for selection: Competition/talent/interest in photography, based on originality, level of technical proficiency, and emergence of personal style or vision. Major/career interest in arts, general.
Application requirements: Portfolio, recommendations, essay, transcript. Completed portfolio entry form (available online) and signed consent form. Must submit eight works in form of prints.
Additional information: Approximately 50 students nominated for scholarships offered by participating higher education institutions. Deadlines vary. Contact sponsor or visit Website for more information.

　　Number of awards: 　　50
Contact:
The Scholastic Art and Writing Awards
555 Broadway
New York, NY 10012
Phone: 212-343-6493
Web: www.artandwriting.org

Scholastic Writing Portfolio Gold Award

Type of award: Scholarship.
Intended use: For freshman study at postsecondary institution.
Eligibility: Applicant must be high school senior.
Basis for selection: Competition/talent/interest in writing/journalism, based on originality, level of technical proficiency, emergence of personal voice or style. Major/career interest in English; journalism; literature or theater arts.
Application requirements: $10 application fee. Portfolio, essay. Completed entry form (two copies). Portfolio must contain three to eight works of narratives, individual poems and/or dramatic scripts demonstrating diversity and talent. Excerpts from longer works encouraged. Entry form must be signed by student's parent and teacher, counselor or principal.
Additional information: Four unrestricted scholarships awarded to exemplary works. Deadlines vary. Contact sponsor or visit Website for more information.

　　Amount of award:　　$5,000
　　Number of awards:　　4
　　Total amount awarded:　　$20,000
Contact:
The Scholastic Art and Writing Awards
555 Broadway
New York, NY 10012
Phone: 212-343-6493
Web: www.artandwriting.org

Alpha Beta Gamma International, Inc.

Alpha Beta Gamma International Scholarship

Type of award: Scholarship.
Intended use: For full-time junior or senior study at accredited 4-year institution.
Eligibility: Applicant or parent must be member/participant of Alpha Beta Gamma. Applicant must be U.S. citizen.
Basis for selection: Major/career interest in business; business, international; business/management/administration;

accounting or computer/information sciences. Applicant must demonstrate high academic achievement and leadership.
Application requirements: Recommendations. Completed institutional financial forms.
Additional information: Awarded to enrollees of two-year schools who have been accepted at four-year schools to pursue baccalaureate degrees in business or related professions, including computer and information sciences.

　　Amount of award:　　$500-$10,000
　　Number of awards:　　300
　　Number of applicants:　　400
　　Total amount awarded:　　$600,000
Contact:
Alpha Beta Gamma
Scholarship Committee
75 Grasslands Road
Valhalla, NY 10595
Web: www.abg.org

Alpha Mu Gamma National

Alpha Mu Gamma National Scholarship

Type of award: Scholarship.
Intended use: For full-time sophomore, junior, senior, master's, doctoral, first professional or postgraduate study at 2-year, 4-year or graduate institution.
Eligibility: Applicant or parent must be member/participant of Alpha Mu Gamma.
Basis for selection: Major/career interest in foreign languages. Applicant must demonstrate high academic achievement and seriousness of purpose.
Application requirements: Recommendations, transcript. Copy of Alpha Mu Gamma full membership certificate. Applicant must submit a one-page essay discussing personal, academic, and career goals and how academic and other experiences have prepared student to succeed.
Additional information: Applicant must be a full Alpha Mu Gamma member. Three $500 awards will be granted for the study of any foreign language; one $400 award for expenses toward a free, intensive one-month course of French at Laval University, Quebec, Canada; and one $200 award for the study of Esperanto or Spanish.

　　Amount of award:　　$200-$500
　　Number of awards:　　5
　　Application deadline:　　February 1
　　Notification begins:　　April 1
　　Total amount awarded:　　$2,100
Contact:
Sponsor/adviser of the local Alpha Mu Gamma chapter.
Web: www.lacitycollege.edu/activities/honor/amg/homepage.htm

Alumnae Panhellenic Association of Washington, DC

Alumnae Panhellenic Association Women's Scholarship

Type of award: Scholarship, renewable.
Intended use: For undergraduate or graduate study at 4-year institution.
Eligibility: Applicant must be female. Applicant must be residing in Washington.
Basis for selection: Major/career interest in philanthropy. Applicant must demonstrate high academic achievement, depth of character and service orientation.
Application requirements: Essay.
Additional information: Applicants must live or attend school in Washington, DC area and have a demonstrated interest in philanthropic activities. Any applications received after the deadline will not be accepted.

Amount of award:	$500
Number of awards:	3
Application deadline:	March 15
Total amount awarded:	$1,500

Contact:
Alumnae Panhellenic Association of Washington, DC
c/o Lisa Gordon
1253 Creed Drive
Annapolis, VA 21403

A.M. Castle & Co.

John M. Simpson Memorial Scholarship

Type of award: Scholarship, renewable.
Intended use: For full-time undergraduate study.
Eligibility: Applicant or parent must be employed by A. M. Castle & Co. Applicant must be high school senior.
Basis for selection: Major/career interest in humanities/liberal arts.
Application requirements: Recommendations, essay, transcript.
Additional information: For children of A.M. Castle & Co. employees only. Parent must be employed by A.M. Castle & Co. for minimum of three years. Award is $2,500 per year for four years. Student must submit SAT or ACT scores.

Amount of award:	$2,500
Number of awards:	2

Contact:
AMC & Company
3400 North Wolf Road
Franklin Park, IL 60131
Phone: 847-455-7111

AMBUCS

AMBUCS Scholars-Scholarship for Therapists

Type of award: Scholarship.
Intended use: For junior, senior or master's study at accredited 4-year or graduate institution in United States.
Eligibility: Applicant must be U.S. citizen.
Basis for selection: Major/career interest in occupational therapy; physical therapy or speech pathology/audiology. Applicant must demonstrate financial need, depth of character and service orientation.
Application requirements: Some documentation requested if named a semi-finalist.
Additional information: One additional 2-year award of $6,000 offered. Program must be accredited by appropriate health therapy association. Students must apply online. No paper applications accepted. Applicants may print enrollment certificate online. Students must send 1040 form from previous year and accompanying documents by mail if named a semi-finalist. Visit Website to apply online between January 15 and April 15 each year.

Amount of award:	$500-$1,500
Application deadline:	April 15
Notification begins:	June 20
Total amount awarded:	$225,000

Contact:
AMBUCS Resouce Center
P.O. Box 5127
High Point, NC 27262
Phone: 336-869-2166
Web: www.ambucs.com

America's Junior Miss Pageant, Inc.

Junior Miss Scholarship

Type of award: Scholarship.
Intended use: For undergraduate study at 4-year institution.
Eligibility: Applicant must be single, female, high school junior or senior. Applicant must be U.S. citizen.
Basis for selection: Competition/talent/interest in poise/talent/fitness, based on scholastic evaluation, skill in creative and performing arts, physical fitness, presence and composure, and panel interview.
Additional information: Must compete in state of legal residence. State winners expected to compete at higher levels. Must never have been married. Only seniors can compete in finals but students are encouraged to begin application process during sophomore year. Visit Website for application deadline information, as it varies from state to state.

Amount of award:	$1,000-$50,000
Number of applicants:	6,000

Contact:
America's Junior Miss Pageant
Contestant Inquiry
P.O. Box 2786
Mobile, AL 36652-2786
Phone: 800-256-5435
Fax: 334-431-0063
Web: www.ajm.org

American Alpine Club

Alpine Club A.K. Gilkey and Putnam/Bedayn Research Grant

Type of award: Research grant.
Intended use: For undergraduate or graduate study.
Eligibility: Applicant must be U.S. citizen.
Basis for selection: Major/career interest in science, general; biology; environmental science; forestry or atmospheric sciences/meteorology.
Application requirements: Recommendations, research proposal. Submit curriculum vitae, with all biographical information.
Additional information: Research proposals evaluated on scientific or technical quality and contribution to scientific endeavor germane to mountain regions. Applications available from Website.

Amount of award:	$200-$500
Application deadline:	March 1

Contact:
American Alpine Club
710 Tenth Street
Suite 100
Golden, CO 80401
Phone: 303-389-0110
Fax: 303-384-0111
Web: www.americanalpineclub.org

American Architectural Foundation

AIA/AAF Minority/Disadvantaged Scholarship

Type of award: Scholarship, renewable.
Intended use: For full-time in United States. Designated institutions: Institution must be NAAB accredited.
Eligibility: Applicant must be high school senior. Applicant must be U.S. citizen or permanent resident.
Basis for selection: Major/career interest in architecture. Applicant must demonstrate financial need.
Application requirements: Recommendations, essay, transcript, nomination by high school guidance counselor, AIA component, architect, or other individual who can speak to student's aptitude for architecture program. Statement of disadvantaged circumstances.
Additional information: Application sent to eligible students after nomination screening. Nomination form due early December. Request nomination form between Sept.15 and Dec. 1 by calling 202-626-7511. Nomination form also available

from Website. Open to high school seniors and college freshmen who plan to enter programs leading to a professional degree in architecture. Students who have completed full year of undergraduate course work not eligible. Renewable up to two years.

Amount of award:	$500-$2,000
Number of awards:	20
Application deadline:	January 15

Contact:
American Architectural Foundation
1735 New York Avenue, NW
Washington, DC 20006-5292
Web: www.archfoundation.org

American Association for Cancer Research

Science Education Awards

Type of award: Research grant.
Intended use: For full-time junior study at 4-year institution in United States or Canada.
Eligibility: Applicant must be U.S. citizen or permanent resident.
Basis for selection: Based on applicant's qualifications and interest in research, references from their mentors, and the selection committee's evaluation of the potential professional benefit of the award to the candidates. Major/career interest in biochemistry; biology; chemistry; pharmacy/pharmaceutics/pharmacology; microbiology or engineering, chemical.
Application requirements: Recommendations. Cover letter and letters of reference.
Additional information: This two-year award will consist of a waiver of registration fees for participation in the AACR annual meetings and a $1,500 stipend each year. Science students can also be enrolled in the following science programs or related disciplines: molecular biology and genetics or pathology. Applications from students who are not yet committed to cancer research are welcome. Awardees are required to attend scientific sessions at the AACR Annual Meeting for a minimum of four days and to participate in all planned activities for the awardees. They are also required to submit two comprehensive reports each year. Further information regarding the award program can be obtained by contacting AACR or visiting their Website.

Amount of award:	$1,500-$3,000
Application deadline:	December 6
Notification begins:	January 1

Contact:
American Association for Cancer Research
Public Ledger Building, Suite 826
150 S. Independence Mall West
Philadelphia, PA 19106-3483
Phone: 215-440-9300
Fax: 215-440-9412
Web: www.aacr.org

American Association of Airport Executives

AAAE Foundation Scholarship

Type of award: Scholarship.
Intended use: For full-time junior or senior study at accredited 4-year institution.
Basis for selection: Major/career interest in aviation. Applicant must demonstrate financial need and high academic achievement.
Application requirements: Recommendations, nomination by school or aviation management department. Only one recommendation per school.
Additional information: Must have 3.0 GPA. Extracurricular and community activities important. Applicant must have reached junior year in an aviation/airport management program.

Amount of award:	$1,000
Number of awards:	10
Application deadline:	May 30
Notification begins:	July 15
Total amount awarded:	$10,000

Contact:
Scholarship Coordinator
American Association of Airport Executives
601 Madison Street, Suite 400
Alexandria, VA 22314-1756
Phone: 703-824-0500
Fax: 703-820-1395
Web: www.airportnet.org

AAAE Foundation Scholarship for Native Americans

Type of award: Scholarship.
Intended use: For full-time junior or senior study at accredited 4-year institution.
Eligibility: Applicant must be American Indian.
Basis for selection: Major/career interest in aviation. Applicant must demonstrate financial need and high academic achievement.
Application requirements: Recommendations, nomination by school or aviation management department. Must apply through school scholarship or aviation management department. Only one recommendation per school.
Additional information: Must have 3.0 GPA. Extracurricular and community activities important. Applicant must have reached junior year in an aviation/airport management program.

Amount of award:	$1,000
Application deadline:	May 30

Contact:
Scholarship Coordinator, American Association of Airport Executives
601 Madison Street
Suite 400
Alexandria, VA 22314-1756
Phone: 703-824-0500
Fax: 703-820-1395
Web: www.airportnet.org

American Association of Critical Care Nurses

Critical Care Nurses Education Advancement Scholarship

Type of award: Scholarship.
Intended use: For junior, senior or graduate study.
Eligibility: Applicant or parent must be member/participant of American Association of Critical Care Nurses. At least 20% of awards will be allocated for ethnic minorities. Applicant must be U.S. citizen or permanent resident.
Basis for selection: Major/career interest in nursing or nurse practitioner. Applicant must demonstrate high academic achievement and seriousness of purpose.
Additional information: For students who do not hold RN license (applicants may hold degrees in other nursing fields). Must be currently enrolled in NLN-accredited BSN or graduate program and have cumulative GPA of 3.0 or better. Applicant must be member of National Student Nurses Association or American Association of Critical Care Nurses. Program administered by National Student Nurses Association. Application available online at www.nsna.org starting in August, through January 22. Send SASE with all inquiries.

Amount of award:	$1,500
Number of awards:	100
Application deadline:	April 1
Notification begins:	July 31

Contact:
National Student Nurses Association
45 Main Street
Suite 606
Brooklyn, NY 11201
Phone: 718-210-0705
Web: www.nsna.org

Education Advancement Scholarship

Type of award: Scholarship, renewable.
Intended use: For junior or senior study at accredited 4-year institution in United States.
Eligibility: Applicant or parent must be member/participant of American Association of Critical Care Nurses. At least 20% of awards will be allocated for ethnic minorities. Applicant must be U.S. citizen or permanent resident.
Basis for selection: Major/career interest in nursing.
Application requirements: Essay, transcript, proof of eligibility.
Additional information: Minimum 3.0 GPA required. Must be licensed nurse (RN) and American Association of Critical Care Nurses member who works in critical care unit or has had one year's experience in last three years. Current enrollment in state-accredited nursing program. Recipients announced in summer for the fall academic term.

Amount of award:	$1,500
Application deadline:	April 1

Contact:
American Association of Critical Care Nurses
101 Columbia
Aliso Viejo, CA 92656-1491
Phone: 800-394-5995
Fax: 949-362-2020
Web: www.aacn.org

American Association of School Administrators/ Discover Card, Inc.

Discover Card Tribute Award Scholarships

Type of award: Scholarship.
Intended use: For undergraduate study at accredited postsecondary institution in United States or Canada.
Eligibility: Applicant must be high school junior.
Basis for selection: Major/career interest in science, general; business; computer/information sciences or humanities/liberal arts. Applicant must demonstrate high academic achievement, leadership and service orientation.
Application requirements: Recommendations, essay, transcript. Essay must describe achievements in leadership, community service, special talents, obstacles overcome and future career plans.
Additional information: Minimum 2.75 GPA. Deadline in January. Paper and electronic applications available in October. Applicants compete first for multiple-level state scholarships; state winners compete for nine national scholarships. State and national scholarships recognize career study in the following fields: trade and technical; arts and humanities; science, business and technology. Awards may also be used for certification or licensing. Visit Website for application.

Amount of award:	$2,500-$25,000
Number of awards:	468
Number of applicants:	7,500
Total amount awarded:	$1,500,000

Contact:
American Association of School Administrators
Discover Card Tribute Award Scholarships
P.O. Box 9338
Arlington, VA 22219
Phone: 703-875-0708
Web: www.aasa.org/discover.htm

American Board of Funeral Service Education

American Board of Funeral Service Education National Scholarship

Type of award: Scholarship.
Intended use: For full-time undergraduate study at 2-year or 4-year institution in United States.
Eligibility: Applicant must be U.S. citizen or permanent resident.
Basis for selection: Major/career interest in mortuary science. Applicant must demonstrate financial need, high academic achievement, depth of character, leadership and seriousness of purpose.
Application requirements: Recommendations.
Additional information: For more information, and application visit Website. Extracurricular activites are considered for eligibility.

Amount of award:	$250-$500
Application deadline:	March 28

Contact:
American Board of Funeral Service Education
Attn: Scholarship Committee
38 Florida Avenue
Portland, ME 04103
Fax: 207-797-7686
Web: abfse.org

American Cancer Society

American Cancer Society Scholarship

Type of award: Scholarship, renewable.
Intended use: For undergraduate study at accredited postsecondary institution in United States. Designated institutions: Accredited Michigan or Indiana university, college or community college.
Eligibility: Applicant must have been diagnosed with cancer before age 21. Applicant must be no older than 20. Applicant must be U.S. citizen residing in Michigan or Indiana.
Basis for selection: Applicant must demonstrate financial need, depth of character, leadership and service orientation.
Application requirements: Recommendations, proof of eligibility.
Additional information: The American Cancer Society's college scholarships are Michigan and Indiana's first and only scholarship opportunities exclusively for students with a history of cancer.

Amount of award:	$1,000
Number of awards:	52
Number of applicants:	100
Application deadline:	April 16
Total amount awarded:	$52,000

Contact:
American Cancer Society Great Lakes Division
College Scholarship Program
1755 Abbey Road
East Lansing, MI 48823
Phone: 800-723-0360

American Center of Oriental Research

American Center of Oriental Research/Jennifer C. Groot Fellowship

Type of award: Research grant.
Intended use: For undergraduate or graduate study at 4-year or graduate institution outside United States.
Eligibility: Applicant must be U.S. citizen, international student or Canadian citizen.
Basis for selection: Competition/talent/interest in study abroad. Major/career interest in archaeology; Middle Eastern studies; ancient near eastern studies or ethnic/cultural studies.
Application requirements: Archaeological fieldwork in Jordan.

Additional information: Provides support for beginners in archaeological fieldwork who have been accepted as staff members on archaeological projects in Jordan with ASOR/CAP affiliation. Applicant must be U.S. or Canadian citizen.

Amount of award:	$1,500
Number of awards:	3
Application deadline:	February 1

Contact:
American Center of Oriental Research
Reseach Grant Coordinator
656 Beacon Street
Boston, MA 02215-2010
Phone: 617-353-6571
Fax: 617-353-6575
Web: www.bu.edu/acor

American Chemical Society

American Chemical Society Scholars Program

Type of award: Scholarship.
Intended use: For full-time freshman, sophomore, junior or senior study at accredited 2-year or 4-year institution in United States.
Eligibility: Applicant must be Alaskan native, African American, Mexican American, Hispanic American, Puerto Rican or American Indian. Applicant must be U.S. citizen or permanent resident.
Basis for selection: Major/career interest in chemistry; biochemistry; engineering, chemical; materials science; environmental science or forensics. Applicant must demonstrate financial need, high academic achievement, seriousness of purpose and service orientation.
Application requirements: Recommendations, transcript. FAFSA.
Additional information: Applicant must intend to pursue career in chemistry, biochemistry or chemical engineering. Other possible majors/career interests are chemical sciences, organic chemistry, forensics. Student must have minimum 3.0 GPA. Award up to $3,000.

Amount of award:	$3,000
Number of awards:	100
Application deadline:	February 15
Notification begins:	June 1

Contact:
American Chemical Society
Scholars Program
1155 Sixteenth Street, NW
Washington, DC 20036
Phone: 800-227-5558 ext. 6250
Web: www.chemistry.org/scholars

American Classical League/ National Junior Classical League

Latin Honor Society Scholarship

Type of award: Scholarship.

Intended use: For full-time freshman study at 2-year or 4-year institution.
Eligibility: Applicant or parent must be member/participant of National Junior Classical League. Applicant must be high school senior.
Basis for selection: Major/career interest in Classics.
Application requirements: Recommendations, essay, transcript. Application.
Additional information: Must have been member of National Junior Classics League for at least three years and must be enrolled in National Junior Classics League Latin Honor Society for current academic year and at least one preceding year. Must be planning to teach Latin or Classics. Application available online.

Amount of award:	$1,500
Number of awards:	1
Application deadline:	May 1
Total amount awarded:	$1,500

Contact:
American Classical League
Miami University
Oxford, OH 45056
Phone: 513-529-7741
Fax: 513-529-7742
Web: www.aclclassics.org

McKinlay Summer Award

Type of award: Scholarship.
Intended use: For non-degree study.
Eligibility: Applicant or parent must be member/participant of American Classical League.
Basis for selection: Major/career interest in Classics. Applicant must demonstrate financial need.
Application requirements: Recommendations.
Additional information: Must have been member of American Classical League for three years preceding application. Must be planning to teach Classics in elementary or secondary school in coming school year. May apply for independent study program funding or support to attend American Classical League Institute for first time. Total amount awarded varies each year.

Amount of award:	$1,500
Application deadline:	January 15

Contact:
American Classical League
Miami University
Oxford, OH 45056
Phone: 513-529-7741
Fax: 513-529-7742
Web: www.aclclassics.org

M.V. O'Donnell Memorial Teacher Training Award

Type of award: Scholarship.
Intended use: For junior, senior or master's study at 4-year or graduate institution.
Eligibility: Applicant or parent must be member/participant of American Classical League.
Basis for selection: Major/career interest in education, teacher or Classics. Applicant must demonstrate financial need.
Application requirements: Recommendations, transcript.
Additional information: Must be training for certification to teach Latin and have completed a substantial number of these courses.

Amount of award: $750
Application deadline: December 1, March 1
Contact:
American Classical League
Miami University
Oxford, OH 45056
Phone: 513-529-7741
Fax: 513-529-7742
Web: www.aclclassics.org

National Junior Classical League Scholarship

Type of award: Scholarship.
Intended use: For full-time freshman study at 2-year or 4-year institution.
Eligibility: Applicant or parent must be member/participant of National Junior Classical League. Applicant must be high school senior.
Basis for selection: Major/career interest in Classics or humanities/liberal arts. Applicant must demonstrate financial need, high academic achievement, depth of character, leadership, patriotism, seriousness of purpose and service orientation.
Application requirements: Recommendations, transcript, proof of eligibility.
Additional information: Preference given to applicants who intend to teach Latin, Greek or classical humanities.
Amount of award: $1,000-$1,500
Number of awards: 6
Application deadline: May 1
Total amount awarded: $4,000
Contact:
American Classical League
Miami University
Oxford, OH 45056
Phone: 513-529-7741
Fax: 513-529-7742
Web: www.aclclassics.org

American College of Musicians/National Guild of Piano Teachers

American College of Musicians $200 Scholarship

Type of award: Scholarship.
Intended use: For non-degree study.
Basis for selection: Major/career interest in music.
Application requirements: Nomination by piano teacher.
Additional information: Award to be used for piano study. Student must have been in national or international solo auditions for ten years, be Guild Paderewski winner, and be Guild High School Diploma recipient. Teacher must be member of National Guild of Piano Teachers.
Amount of award: $200
Number of awards: 150
Application deadline: September 15
Notification begins: October 1

Contact:
National Guild of Piano Teachers
International Headquarters
P.O. Box 1807
Austin, TX 78767-1807
Phone: 512-478-5775
Web: www.pianoguild.com

American College of Musicians Piano Composition Contest

Type of award: Scholarship.
Intended use: For non-degree study.
Basis for selection: Competition/talent/interest in music performance/composition, based on compositions for solo keyboard and keyboard ensemble. Compositions rated on imagination, originality and skill. Major/career interest in music.
Application requirements: Manuscript of composition.
Additional information: Teacher must be member of National Guild of Piano Teachers. Entry fees vary according to classification of students and length of composition.
Amount of award: $50-$150
Number of awards: 14
Application deadline: November 15
Contact:
National Guild of Piano Teachers
International Headquarters
P.O. Box 2215
Austin, TX 78767-2215
Phone: 512-478-5775
Web: www.pianoguild.com

Raissa Tselentis J. S. Bach Scholarship

Type of award: Scholarship.
Intended use: For non-degree study.
Basis for selection: Competition/talent/interest in music performance/composition, based on student's scores at Guild auditions. Major/career interest in music.
Application requirements: Audition, nomination by teacher.
Additional information: Competition in performance and literature of Bach. One award for early Bach, one for advanced Bach. Teacher must be member of National Guild of Piano Teachers. Entry fees vary according to classification of students.
Amount of award: $100
Number of awards: 2
Total amount awarded: $200
Contact:
National Guild of Piano Teachers
International Headquarters
P.O. Box 1807
Austin, TX 78767-1807
Phone: 512-478-5775
Web: www.pianoguild.com

American Congress on Surveying and Mapping

AAGS Joseph F. Dracup Scholarship Award

Type of award: Scholarship, renewable.
Intended use: For undergraduate study at 4-year institution.
Eligibility: Applicant or parent must be member/participant of American Congress of Surveying and Mapping.
Basis for selection: Major/career interest in surveying/mapping. Applicant must demonstrate high academic achievement and seriousness of purpose.
Application requirements: Recommendations, essay, transcript, proof of eligibility. Completed application.
Additional information: Preference will be given to applicants with significant focus on geodetic surveying. Visit Website for additional information.
    Amount of award: $2,000
    Number of awards: 1
    Application deadline: December 1
    Total amount awarded: $2,000
Contact:
American Congress on Surveying and Mapping
6 Montgomery Village Avenue
Suite 403
Gaithersburg, MD 20879
Phone: 240-632-9716 ext. 113
Fax: 240-632-1321
Web: www.acsm.net

Berntsen International Scholarship in Surveying

Type of award: Scholarship, renewable.
Intended use: For undergraduate study at 4-year institution.
Eligibility: Applicant or parent must be member/participant of American Congress of Surveying and Mapping.
Basis for selection: Major/career interest in surveying/mapping. Applicant must demonstrate high academic achievement and seriousness of purpose.
Application requirements: Recommendations, essay, transcript, proof of eligibility. Completed application.
Additional information: Open to students in four-year degree program in surveying (or in closely related degree programs such as geomatics or surveying engineering). Degree of financial need will be used, if necessary, to break ties after the primary criteria have been considered. Awarded by Berntsen International Inc. of Madison, Wisconsin. Visit Website for additional information.
    Amount of award: $1,500
    Application deadline: December 1
Contact:
American Congress on Surveying and Mapping
6 Montgomery Village Avenue
Suite 403
Gaithersburg, MD 20879
Phone: 240-632-9716 ext. 113
Fax: 240-632-1321
Web: www.acsm.net

Berntsen International Scholarship in Surveying Technology

Type of award: Scholarship, renewable.
Intended use: For undergraduate certificate study at 2-year institution.
Eligibility: Applicant or parent must be member/participant of American Congress of Surveying and Mapping.
Basis for selection: Major/career interest in surveying/mapping or cartography. Applicant must demonstrate high academic achievement and seriousness of purpose.
Application requirements: Recommendations, essay, transcript, proof of eligibility. Completed application.
Additional information: Open to students in two-year degree program in surveying technology. Awarded by Berntsen International Inc. of Madison, Wisconsin. Visit Website for additional information.
    Amount of award: $500
    Application deadline: December 1
Contact:
American Congress on Surveying and Mapping
6 Montgomery Village Avenue
Suite 403
Gaithersburg, MD 20879
Phone: 240-632-9716 ext. 112
Fax: 240-632-1321
Web: www.acsm.net

Cady McDonnell Memorial Scholarship

Type of award: Scholarship, renewable.
Intended use: For undergraduate study at 2-year or 4-year institution.
Eligibility: Applicant or parent must be member/participant of American Congress of Surveying and Mapping. Applicant must be female. Applicant must be residing in Utah, Alaska, Washington, Arizona, Nevada, California, Wyoming, Montana, Oregon, New Mexico, Idaho, Colorado or Hawaii.
Basis for selection: Major/career interest in surveying/mapping or cartography. Applicant must demonstrate high academic achievement and seriousness of purpose.
Application requirements: Recommendations, essay, transcript, proof of eligibility. Completed application and proof of legal home residence.
Additional information: Intended to recognize women students enrolled in the field of surveying who are residents of one of the listed western states. Degree of financial need will be used, if necessary, to break ties after the primary criteria have been considered. Visit Website for additional information.
    Amount of award: $1,000
    Number of awards: 1
    Application deadline: December 1
    Total amount awarded: $1,000
Contact:
American Congress on Surveying and Mapping
6 Montgomery Village Avenue
Suite 403
Gaithersburg, MD 20879
Phone: 240-632-9716 ext. 113
Fax: 240-632-1321
Web: www.acsm.net

CaGIS Scholarship Award

Type of award: Scholarship, renewable.

Intended use: For full-time undergraduate or graduate study at 4-year or graduate institution.
Eligibility: Applicant or parent must be member/participant of American Congress of Surveying and Mapping.
Basis for selection: Major/career interest in cartography or surveying/mapping. Applicant must demonstrate high academic achievement and seriousness of purpose.
Application requirements: Recommendations, essay, transcript, proof of eligibility. Completed application.
Additional information: Open to students enrolled in four-year or graduate degree program in cartography, GIS or other mapping sciences. Preference will be given to undergraduates with junior or senior standing. Awarded by the Cartography and Geographic Information Society (CaGIS). Visit Website for additional information.

    Amount of award: $1,000
    Number of awards: 1
    Application deadline: December 1
    Total amount awarded: $1,000
Contact:
American Congress on Surveying and Mapping
6 Montgomery Village Avenue
Suite 403
Gaithersburg, MD 20879
Phone: 240-632-9716 ext. 112
Fax: 240-632-1321
Web: www.acsm.net

Mary Feindt Forum for Women in Surveying Scholarship

Type of award: Scholarship, renewable.
Intended use: For undergraduate study at 4-year institution in United States.
Eligibility: Applicant or parent must be member/participant of American Congress of Surveying and Mapping. Applicant must be female.
Basis for selection: Major/career interest in surveying/mapping or cartography. Applicant must demonstrate high academic achievement and seriousness of purpose.
Application requirements: Recommendations, essay, transcript, proof of eligibility. Completed application.
Additional information: Degree of financial need will be used, if necessary, to break ties after the primary criteria have been considered. Visit Website for additional information.

    Amount of award: $1,000
    Application deadline: December 1
Contact:
American Congress on Surveying and Mapping
6 Montgomery Village Avenue
Suite 403
Gaithersburg, MD 20879
Phone: 240-632-9716 ext. 113
Fax: 240-632-1321
Web: www.acsm.net

Nettie Dracup Memorial Scholarship

Type of award: Scholarship, renewable.
Intended use: For undergraduate study at accredited 4-year institution.
Eligibility: Applicant or parent must be member/participant of American Congress of Surveying and Mapping. Applicant must be U.S. citizen.

Basis for selection: Major/career interest in surveying/mapping. Applicant must demonstrate high academic achievement and seriousness of purpose.
Application requirements: Recommendations, essay, transcript, proof of eligibility. Completed application.
Additional information: Intended to provide financial aid to U.S. citizen who is an undergraduate enrolled in geodetic surveying. Degree of financial need will be used, if necessary, to break ties after primary criteria have been considered. Visit Website for additional information.

    Amount of award: $2,000
    Application deadline: December 1
Contact:
American Congress on Surveying and Mapping
6 Montgomery Village Avenue
Suite 403
Gaithersburg, MD 20879
Phone: 240-632-9716 ext. 113
Fax: 240-632-1321
Web: www.acsm.net

NSPS Board of Governors Scholarship

Type of award: Scholarship, renewable.
Intended use: For junior study at 4-year institution.
Eligibility: Applicant or parent must be member/participant of American Congress of Surveying and Mapping.
Basis for selection: Major/career interest in surveying/mapping. Applicant must demonstrate high academic achievement and seriousness of purpose.
Application requirements: Recommendations, essay, transcript, proof of eligibility. Completed application, minimum 3.0 GPA.
Additional information: Degree of financial need will be used, if necessary, to break ties after the primary criteria have been considered. Visit Website for additional information.

    Amount of award: $1,000
    Number of awards: 1
    Application deadline: December 1
    Total amount awarded: $1,000
Contact:
American Congress on Surveying and Mapping
6 Montgomery Village Avenue
Suite 403
Gaithersburg, MD 20879
Phone: 240-632-9716 ext. 113
Fax: 240-632-1321
Web: www.acsm.net

NSPS Scholarships

Type of award: Scholarship, renewable.
Intended use: For full-time undergraduate study at 4-year institution.
Eligibility: Applicant or parent must be member/participant of American Congress of Surveying and Mapping.
Basis for selection: Major/career interest in surveying/mapping. Applicant must demonstrate high academic achievement and seriousness of purpose.
Application requirements: Recommendations, essay, transcript, proof of eligibility. Completed application.
Additional information: Intended to recognize outstanding students enrolled full-time in undergraduate surveying programs. Degree of financial need will be used, if necessary, to break ties after the primary criteria have been considered.

Awarded by National Society of Professional Surveyors. Visit Website for additional information.

Amount of award:	$1,000
Number of awards:	2
Application deadline:	December 1
Total amount awarded:	$2,000

Contact:
American Congress on Surveying and Mapping
6 Montgomery Village Avenue
Suite 403
Gaithersburg, MD 20879
Phone: 240-632-9716 ext. 113
Fax: 240-632-1321
Web: www.acsm.net

Schonstedt Scholarships in Surveying

Type of award: Scholarship, renewable.
Intended use: For undergraduate study at 4-year institution.
Eligibility: Applicant or parent must be member/participant of American Congress of Surveying and Mapping.
Basis for selection: Major/career interest in surveying/mapping. Applicant must demonstrate high academic achievement and seriousness of purpose.
Application requirements: Recommendations, essay, transcript, proof of eligibility. Completed application.
Additional information: Preference given to applicants with junior or senior standing. Degree of financial need will be used, if necessary, to break ties after primary criteria have been considered. Awarded by Schonstedt Instrument Company of Kearneysville, West Virginia. Schonstedt donates magnetic locator to surveying program at each recipient's school. Visit Website for additional information.

Amount of award:	$1,500
Number of awards:	2
Application deadline:	December 1
Total amount awarded:	$3,000

Contact:
American Congress on Surveying and Mapping
6 Montgomery Village Avenue
Suite 403
Gaithersburg, MD 20879
Phone: 240-632-9716 ext. 113
Fax: 240-632-1321
Web: www.acsm.net

American Council of the Blind

Floyd Qualls Memorial Scholarship

Type of award: Scholarship, renewable.
Intended use: For full-time undergraduate or graduate study at postsecondary institution in United States.
Eligibility: Applicant must be visually impaired.
Basis for selection: Applicant must demonstrate high academic achievement, depth of character and leadership.
Application requirements: Interview, recommendations, essay, transcript, proof of eligibility. Proof of legal blindness. Entering or transferring students must show proof of registration at accredited school.
Additional information: Applicant must be legally blind in both eyes. Must be in or currently under consideration for

postsecondary program. Two awards for entering freshmen, two for other undergraduates, two for graduates, two for vocational students. Additional scholarships available: contact ACB for more information.

Amount of award:	$2,500
Application deadline:	March 1
Notification begins:	May 15

Contact:
American Council of the Blind Scholarships
Attn: Terry Pacheco
1155 15 Street NW, Suite 1004
Washington, DC 20005
Phone: 202-467-5081 or 800-424-8666
Fax: 202-467-5085
Web: www.acb.org

American Dental Assistants Association/Oral B Laboratories

Juliette A. Southard/Oral B Laboratories Scholarship

Type of award: Scholarship.
Intended use: For undergraduate study.
Eligibility: Applicant or parent must be member/participant of American Dental Assistants Association.
Basis for selection: Major/career interest in dental assistant. Applicant must demonstrate high academic achievement, depth of character and leadership.
Application requirements: Recommendations, transcript, proof of eligibility.
Additional information: Scholarship open to high school graduates and GED certificate holders. Must be American Dental Assistants Association member or American Dental Assistants Association student member. Applicants must be enrolled in dental assisting program or be taking courses applicable to furthering career in dental assisting.

Amount of award:	$500
Number of awards:	10
Application deadline:	January 31

Contact:
American Dental Assistants Association
Dennis Marrell
35 East Wacker Drive, Suite 1730
Chicago, IL 60601
Phone: 312-541-1550
Web: www.dentalassistant.org

American Dietetic Association Foundation

Graduate, Baccalaureate or Coordinated Program Scholarships

Type of award: Scholarship, renewable.

Intended use: For full-time junior, senior or graduate study at accredited 4-year institution. Designated institutions: CADE-accredited/approved dietetics education programs.

Eligibility: Applicant must be U.S. citizen or permanent resident.

Basis for selection: Major/career interest in dietetics/nutrition. Applicant must demonstrate high academic achievement and seriousness of purpose.

Application requirements: Recommendations, proof of eligibility. GPA documentation necessary, signed by academic advisor.

Additional information: Sponsor awarded 200 scholarships to graduates and undergraduates 2002-2003. Number and amount of awards vary. All scholarships require ADA membership. To be eligible, applicant must be enrolled in the approved program a minimum of four months during the academic year. Minority status considered. Must demonstrate or show promise of being a valuable, contributing member of the profession. See Website for more information and application.

Amount of award:	$500-$5,000

Contact:
American Dietetic Association
Education Programs
216 West Jackson Blvd.
Chicago, IL 60606
Phone: 800-877-1600 ext. 5400
Web: www.eatright.org/scholelig.html

American Electroplaters and Surface Finishers Society Scholarship Committee

American Electroplaters and Surface Finishers Society Scholarship

Type of award: Scholarship, renewable.

Intended use: For full-time junior, senior or graduate study.

Basis for selection: Major/career interest in engineering, materials; engineering, chemical; engineering, environmental or chemistry.

Application requirements: Recommendations, essay, transcript. Resume.

Additional information: May apply to any field of study or research related to plating and surface finishing technologies. Award notification occurs between late July and early August. Must re-apply for renewal.

Amount of award:	$1,500
Number of applicants:	75
Application deadline:	April 15
Total amount awarded:	$10,500

Contact:
AESF Scholarship Committee
12644 Research Parkway
Orlando, FL 32826-3298
Phone: 407-281-6441

American Federation of State, County and Municipal Employees

State/County/Municipal Employees Family Scholarship

Type of award: Scholarship, renewable.

Intended use: For full-time undergraduate study at accredited 4-year institution.

Eligibility: Applicant or parent must be member/participant of American Fed. of State/County/Municipal Employees. Applicant must be high school senior.

Application requirements: Recommendations, essay, transcript, proof of eligibility. SAT or ACT scores. Essay on subject: "What AFSCME means to our family." Attach a copy of current AFSCME membership card.

Additional information: Minimum 3.0 GPA. Scholarship open to children and grandchildren of AFSCME members. Application period opens August 1.

Amount of award:	$2,000
Number of awards:	10
Number of applicants:	900
Application deadline:	December 31
Notification begins:	March 31

Contact:
American Federation of State, County and Municipal Employees
Education Department
1625 L Street NW
Washington, DC 20036
Web: www.afscme.org

State/County/Municipal Employees Jerry Clark Memorial Scholarship

Type of award: Scholarship.

Intended use: For full-time junior or senior study at accredited 4-year institution.

Eligibility: Applicant or parent must be member/participant of American Fed. of State/County/Municipal Employees.

Basis for selection: Major/career interest in political science/government. Applicant must demonstrate high academic achievement.

Application requirements: Proof of eligibility.

Additional information: Scholarship open to children and grandchildren of AFSCME members. Applicant must be a current college sophomore with a declared political science major. Winner given opportunity to intern at International Union Headquarters in Political Action department. Minimum 3.0 GPA required. Award renewable for senior year. Opens March 15th.

Amount of award:	$10,000
Number of awards:	1
Number of applicants:	30
Application deadline:	July 1
Notification begins:	August 1
Total amount awarded:	$10,000

Scholarships

Contact:
American Federation of State, County and Municipal
Employees
Education Department
1625 L Street NW
Washington, DC 20036
Web: www.afscme.org

American Floral Endowment

American Floral Endowment Harold F. Wilkins Scholarship

Type of award: Scholarship.
Intended use: For undergraduate or graduate study at postsecondary institution outside United States.
Eligibility: Applicant must be U.S. citizen.
Basis for selection: Major/career interest in horticulture.
Application requirements: Proof of eligibility. Written proof of acceptance to internship by employer or school; registration confirmation for foreign study; proof of housing accommodations and costs; confirmation for travel (visa, work permit, passport, travel reservations); and proof of insurance.
Additional information: Program designed (1) to encourage students to have internship or floricultural experience outside United States and (2) to aid floricultural students to study abroad, ro attend International Floricultural Symposium and other intellectual pursuits. Application available on Website.

  Application deadline: November 1, March 1
Contact:
American Floral Endowment
11 Glen-Ed Professional Park
Glen Carbon, IL 62034
Phone: 618-692-0045
Fax: 618-692-4045
Web: www.endowment.org

American Foundation for Aging Research

American Foundation for Aging Research Fellowship

Type of award: Research grant, renewable.
Intended use: For full-time undergraduate, master's or doctoral study in United States.
Basis for selection: AFAR areas of interest: cellular biology, immunobiology, cancer, neurobiology, biochemistry, molecular biophysics, genomics and proteomics. Those granted awards utilize modern and innovative approaches/technologies. Sociology, psychology, and health related research (eg. physical therapy/exercise physiology) not currently funded. Major/career interest in biochemistry or biomedical. Applicant must demonstrate high academic achievement.
Application requirements: $3 application fee. Recommendations, transcript, proof of eligibility, research proposal.

Additional information: Must be actively involved or planning active involvement in a specific biomedical or biochemical research project in field of aging. Also applicable toward PhD, MD, DVM and DDS degrees. Number of awards varies. Call sponsor for information regarding deadline. SASE preferred. Visit Website for additional information.

  Amount of award: $500-$1,000
  Number of applicants: 150
  Total amount awarded: $5,000
Contact:
American Foundation for Aging Research
North Carolina State University
Biochem. Dept., Campus Box 7622
Raleigh, NC 27695-7622
Phone: 919-515-5679
Fax: 919-515-2047
Web: www.agingresearchfoundation.org

American Foundation for Pharmaceutical Education

American Association of Pharmaceutical Scientists/AFPE Gateway Research Scholarship

Type of award: Research grant.
Intended use: For sophomore, junior or senior study at accredited 4-year or graduate institution.
Basis for selection: Major/career interest in pharmacy/pharmaceutics/pharmacology; biochemistry; chemistry or health sciences.
Application requirements: Recommendations, essay, transcript, research proposal. AFPE application, AFPE summary sheet, letter from faculty sponsor describing research.
Additional information: Awards intended to encourage undergraduates from any discipline to undertake mentored research experience and to consider pursuing Ph.D. in pharmaceutical science. U.S. citizenship or permanent resident status not required. $3500 is provided as a student stipend for a research project done over the full calendar year. $500 is provided to recipient to attend AAPS annual meeting. Up to $1000 may be used by sponsoring faculty member in direct support of research effort.

  Amount of award: $5,000
  Number of awards: 6
  Application deadline: January 28
  Notification begins: April 15
  Total amount awarded: $30,000
Contact:
American Foundation for Pharmaceutical Education
One Church Street, Suite 202
Rockville, MD 20850
Phone: 301-738-2160
Fax: 301-738-2161
Web: www.afpenet.org

Gateway Research Scholarship

Type of award: Research grant.
Intended use: For sophomore, junior or senior study at 4-year or graduate institution.
Basis for selection: Major/career interest in pharmacy/pharmaceutics/pharmacology.

Application requirements: Recommendations, essay, transcript, proof of eligibility, research proposal. AFPE application, AFPE summary sheet, letter from faculty sponsor describing the research.

Additional information: To encourage students in last three years of B.S. or Pharm.D. program to undertake mentored research experience and to consider pursuing the Ph.D. in pharmaceutical science. Applicant must be enrolled in degree program for one more full academic year following award of scholarship. U.S. citizenship or permanent resident status not required. $4000 is provided as student stipend for research project for full calendar year. Up to $1000 may be used by sponsoring faculty member in direct support of research effort.

Amount of award:	$5,000
Number of awards:	10
Application deadline:	January 28
Notification begins:	April 15
Total amount awarded:	$50,000

Contact:
American Foundation for Pharmaceutical Education
One Church Street
Suite 202
Rockville, MD 20850
Phone: 301-738-2160
Fax: 301-738-2161
Web: www.afpenet.org

American Foundation for the Blind

Delta Gamma Foundation Memorial Scholarship

Type of award: Scholarship.
Intended use: For undergraduate or graduate study at accredited postsecondary institution.
Eligibility: Applicant must be visually impaired. Applicant must be U.S. citizen.
Basis for selection: Major/career interest in health-related professions; rehabilitation/therapeutic services; education or education, special. Applicant must demonstrate high academic achievement, depth of character, seriousness of purpose and service orientation.
Application requirements: Recommendations, essay, transcript, proof of eligibility.
Additional information: Applicant must be legally blind and studying in the field of rehabilitation and/or the education of blind or visually impaired persons.

Amount of award:	$1,000
Number of awards:	1
Application deadline:	April 30
Total amount awarded:	$1,000

Contact:
American Foundation for the Blind
Information Center
11 Penn Plaza, Suite 300
New York, NY 10001
Phone: 212-502-7661
Fax: 212-502-7771
Web: www.afb.org

Ferdinand Torres Scholarship

Type of award: Scholarship.

Intended use: For full-time undergraduate study at postsecondary institution.
Eligibility: Applicant must be visually impaired. Applicant must be U.S. citizen or permanent resident.
Basis for selection: Applicant must demonstrate financial need, leadership, patriotism and seriousness of purpose.
Application requirements: Recommendations, essay, transcript, proof of eligibility. Send a typewritten statement of three double-spaced pages describing educational and personal goals, work experience, extracurricular activities, and how scholarship monies will be used. New immigrants should include a description of their country of origin and their reason for coming to the U.S.
Additional information: Applicant must be legally blind. Preference given to residents of New York City metropolitan area and new immigrants to the United States.

Amount of award:	$1,000
Number of awards:	1
Application deadline:	April 30
Total amount awarded:	$1,000

Contact:
American Foundation for the Blind
Information Center
11 Penn Plaza, Suite 300
New York, NY 10001
Phone: 212-506-7661
Fax: 212-502-7771
Web: www.afb.org

Freedom Scientific Technology Scholarship Award

Type of award: Scholarship.
Intended use: For undergraduate or graduate study at postsecondary institution.
Eligibility: Applicant must be visually impaired. Applicant must be high school senior. Applicant must be U.S. citizen.
Application requirements: Recommendations, essay, transcript, proof of eligibility. Send two letters of reference, proof of legal blindness and a typewritten essay of no more than three double-spaced pages.
Additional information: The Freedom Scientific Technology Scholarship Award Program will select five winners of the $1,500 award and five winners of the $2,500 award. The scholarship awards will be in the form of vouchers to be applied towards the purchase of any of Freedom Scientific's full line of products, including software, accessories, training and/or tutorials. Winners will be notified of the award amounts they will receive.

Number of awards:	10
Application deadline:	March 31

Contact:
American Foundation for the Blind
11 Penn Plaza
Suite 300
New York, NY 10001
Phone: 212-502-7661
Fax: 212-502-7771
Web: www.afb.org

R.L. Gillette Scholarship

Type of award: Scholarship, renewable.
Intended use: For full-time undergraduate study at 4-year institution.

Eligibility: Applicant must be visually impaired. Applicant must be female, high school senior. Applicant must be U.S. citizen.
Basis for selection: Major/career interest in literature or music.
Application requirements: Recommendations, essay, transcript, proof of eligibility. Evidence of admission to desired school and a performance tape not to exceed 30 minutes or a creative writing sample. A typewritten statement of no more than three double-spaced pages describing educational and personal goals, work experience, extracurricular activities, and how scholarship monies will be used.
Additional information: Applicant must be female student who is legally blind and enrolled in undergraduate degree program in literature or music.

Amount of award:	$1,000
Number of awards:	2
Application deadline:	April 30
Total amount awarded:	$2,000

Contact:
American Foundation for the Blind
11 Penn Plaza, Suite 300
New York, NY 10001
Phone: 212-502-7661
Fax: 212-502-7771
Web: www.afb.org

Rudolph Dillman Memorial Scholarship

Type of award: Scholarship.
Intended use: For undergraduate or graduate study at accredited postsecondary institution in United States.
Eligibility: Applicant must be visually impaired. Applicant must be U.S. citizen.
Basis for selection: Major/career interest in health-related professions; rehabilitation/therapeutic services or education. Applicant must demonstrate depth of character, leadership, seriousness of purpose and service orientation.
Application requirements: Recommendations, essay, transcript, proof of eligibility.
Additional information: Applicant must be legally blind and studying in the field of rehabilitation and/or education of blind or visually impaired persons.

Amount of award:	$2,500
Number of awards:	3
Application deadline:	April 30
Total amount awarded:	$7,500

Contact:
American Foundation for the Blind
Information Center
11 Penn Plaza, Suite 300
New York, NY 10001
Phone: 212-502-7600
Fax: 212-502-7771
Web: www.afb.org

Rudolph Dillman Memorial Scholarship Based on Need

Type of award: Scholarship.
Intended use: For undergraduate or graduate study at accredited postsecondary institution in United States.
Eligibility: Applicant must be visually impaired. Applicant must be U.S. citizen.
Basis for selection: Major/career interest in health-related professions; rehabilitation/therapeutic services or education.

Applicant must demonstrate financial need, depth of character, seriousness of purpose and service orientation.
Application requirements: Recommendations, essay, transcript, proof of eligibility.
Additional information: Applicant must be legally blind and studying in the field of rehabilitation and/or education of blind or visually impaired persons.

Amount of award:	$2,500
Number of awards:	4
Application deadline:	April 30
Total amount awarded:	$10,000

Contact:
American Foundation for the Blind
Information Center
11 Penn Plaza, Suite 300
New York, NY 10001
Phone: 212-502-7661
Web: www.afb.org

American Ground Water Trust

American Ground Water Trust Amtrol Scholarship

Type of award: Scholarship.
Intended use: For full-time freshman study at 2-year or 4-year institution.
Eligibility: Applicant must be high school senior. Applicant must be U.S. citizen or permanent resident.
Basis for selection: Major/career interest in geology/earth sciences; engineering, environmental; environmental science or natural resources/conservation. Applicant must demonstrate high academic achievement, leadership, seriousness of purpose and service orientation.
Application requirements: Recommendations, essay, transcript. In addition to essay, students must provide description of previously completed high school science project involving ground water resources or of non-school work experience related to environment and natural resources.
Additional information: Must be entering field related to ground water, e.g., hydrology or hydrogeology. Minimum 3.0 GPA required. Write to American Ground Water Trust for application form and details of application procedure, or visit Website for application and more information.

Amount of award:	$1,000
Number of applicants:	75
Application deadline:	June 1
Notification begins:	August 1
Total amount awarded:	$2,000

Contact:
American Ground Water Trust Scholarship
P.O. Box 1796
Concord, NH 03302
Phone: 603-228-5444
Web: www.agwt.org

American Ground Water Trust Baroid Scholarship

Type of award: Scholarship.
Intended use: For full-time freshman study at 4-year institution.

Eligibility: Applicant must be high school senior. Applicant must be U.S. citizen or permanent resident.

Basis for selection: Major/career interest in engineering, environmental; geology/earth sciences; environmental science or natural resources/conservation. Applicant must demonstrate high academic achievement, leadership, seriousness of purpose and service orientation.

Application requirements: Recommendations, essay, transcript. In addition to essay, students must provide description of previously completed high school science project involving ground water resources or of non-school work experience related to environment and natural resources.

Additional information: Must be entering field related to ground water, e.g., hydrology or hydrogeology. Minimum 3.0 GPA required. Write to American Ground Water Trust for application form and details of application procedure.

Amount of award:	$500-$2,000
Number of awards:	8
Number of applicants:	24
Application deadline:	June 1
Notification begins:	August 31
Total amount awarded:	$56,000

Contact:
American Ground Water Trust Scholarship
P.O. Box 1796
Concord, NH 03302
Phone: 603-228-5444
Web: www.agwt.org

Ben Everson Scholarship

Type of award: Scholarship.

Intended use: For full-time freshman study at 4-year institution.

Eligibility: Applicant must be high school senior. Applicant must be U.S. citizen or permanent resident.

Basis for selection: Major/career interest in ecology; engineering, environmental; geology/earth sciences; hydrology; natural resources/conservation or environmental science. Applicant must demonstrate high academic achievement and seriousness of purpose.

Application requirements: Recommendations, essay, proof of eligibility. Description of high school science/environmental project directly involving ground water, or of vacation/out-of-school work experience related to environment or natural resources. Letter establishing that one parent is employed in ground water industry.

Additional information: Applicant must intend to pursue career in ground water related field. Minimum 3.0 GPA required. Write to American Ground Water Trust or visit Website for application form.

Amount of award:	$2,500
Application deadline:	June 1
Notification begins:	August 31

Contact:
American Ground Water Trust
Ben Everson Scholarship Application
P.O. Box 1796
Concord, NH 03302
Phone: 603-228-5444
Web: www.agwt.org

American Health Information Management Association

FORE Undergraduate Scholarship

Type of award: Scholarship.

Intended use: For full-time undergraduate study. Designated institutions: Accredited institutions with health information management and technology programs.

Eligibility: Applicant or parent must be member/participant of American Health Information Management Association.

Basis for selection: Major/career interest in information systems. Applicant must demonstrate high academic achievement.

Application requirements: Recommendations, transcript, proof of eligibility.

Additional information: Applicants must be members of AHIMA and accepted into accredited health information management or health information technology program with major career interest in Health Information Management. Must have 3.0 GPA (out of 4.0). Number of awards varies.

Amount of award:	$1,000-$5,000
Application deadline:	May 30

Contact:
American Health Information Management Association
Foundation of Research and Education
233 North Michigan Avenue, Suite 2150
Chicago, IL 60601-5800
Phone: 312-233-1100
Fax: 312-233-1468
Web: www.ahima.org

American Heart Association Western States Affiliate

American Heart Association Undergraduate Student Research Program

Type of award: Research grant.

Intended use: For full-time junior or senior study at 4-year institution. Designated institutions: Cardiovascular or cerebrovascular research laboratories in California, Nevada, Utah.

Eligibility: Applicant must be U.S. citizen or permanent resident residing in California, Utah or Nevada.

Basis for selection: Major/career interest in biology; chemistry; physics or computer/information sciences. Applicant must demonstrate high academic achievement, depth of character, seriousness of purpose and service orientation.

Application requirements: Recommendations, essay, transcript, proof of eligibility.

Additional information: Applicant must be college sophomore or junior. Must have completed combined total of at least four semesters or six quarters of biological sciences, physics or chemistry. Must have completed at least one quarter of calculus, statistics, computational methods or computer science. Students are assigned to scientist-supervised laboratories to work for ten weeks during summer exploring

Scholarships

careers in heart or stroke research. Must be attending institution in or be resident of California, Utah or Nevada. Women and minorities encouraged to apply. Awardees required to participate in roundtable discussion meetings held during August to discuss research experience with supervisors and other students.

Amount of award:	$4,000
Application deadline:	February 3
Notification begins:	March 30

Contact:
American Heart Association, Western States Affiliate
Research Department
1710 Gilbreth Road
Burlingame, CA 94010-1317
Phone: 650-259-6700
Fax: 650-259-6891
Web: www.heartsource.org

American Helicopter Society, Inc.

Vertical Flight Foundation Scholarship

Type of award: Scholarship.
Intended use: For full-time junior, senior or graduate study at accredited postsecondary institution.
Basis for selection: Major/career interest in engineering; aerospace or aviation. Applicant must demonstrate high academic achievement, depth of character and seriousness of purpose.
Application requirements: Recommendations, essay, transcript. Academic endorsement by dean or professor.
Additional information: Must major in helicopter or vertical flight engineering industry. Minimum 3.0 GPA required, 3.5 recommended.

Amount of award:	$2,000-$4,000
Number of awards:	14
Number of applicants:	300
Application deadline:	February 1
Notification begins:	April 15

Contact:
Debbie Cochran, American Helicopter Society, Inc.
Vertical Flight Foundation
217 North Washington Street
Alexandria, VA 22314
Phone: 703-684-6777
Web: www.vtol.org

American Holistic Nurses' Association

Holistic Nursing Charlotte McGuire Scholarship

Type of award: Scholarship.
Intended use: For undergraduate or graduate study.
Eligibility: Applicant or parent must be member/participant of American Holistic Nurses' Association.

Basis for selection: Major/career interest in nursing. Applicant must demonstrate depth of character and seriousness of purpose.
Application requirements: Essay, transcript, proof of eligibility. Two recommendations, financial statement required. One recommendation must be from AHNA member.
Additional information: 3.0 GPA required. Experience in holistic or alternative health care practices preferred. Graduates must be member of AHNA for one year, undergraduates for six months. Amount of award varies.

Number of applicants:	6
Application deadline:	March 15
Notification begins:	May 15

Contact:
American Holistic Nurses' Association
Scholarships
P.O. Box 2130
Flagstaff, AZ 86003-2130
Phone: 800-278-2462
Fax: 928-526-2752
Web: www.ahna.org

Holistic Nursing Research Grant

Type of award: Research grant.
Intended use: For non-degree study.
Eligibility: Applicant or parent must be member/participant of American Holistic Nurses' Association.
Basis for selection: Major/career interest in nursing; health-related professions; nurse practitioner; health sciences or health education. Applicant must demonstrate seriousness of purpose and service orientation.
Application requirements: Proof of eligibility, research proposal.
Additional information: Must be member of AHNA for at least one year and be conducting research on topics related to holistic nursing. Number of awards/applicants varies.

Amount of award:	$500-$5,000
Number of awards:	2
Application deadline:	March 15
Notification begins:	May 15
Total amount awarded:	$500

Contact:
American Holistic Nurses' Association
Research Grants
P.O. Box 2130
Flagstaff, AZ 86003-2130
Phone: 800-278-2462
Fax: 928-526-2752
Web: www.ahna.org

American Hotel & Lodging Educational Foundation

American Express Scholarship Program

Type of award: Scholarship, renewable.
Intended use: For undergraduate study at 2-year or 4-year institution.
Basis for selection: Major/career interest in hotel/restaurant management or hospitality administration/management. Applicant must demonstrate financial need and high academic achievement.

Application requirements: Essay, transcript. Industry-related work experience; academic record/educational qualifications; professional, community and extracurricular activities; and personal attributes including career goals. Copy of course curriculum and copy of tax form 1040 or 1040EZ.

Additional information: Must work at hotel 20 hours a week and have 12 months' experience. Hotel must be member of American Hotel & Lodging Association. Dependents of hotel employees may also apply. Award must be used in hospitality management degree program. Amount and number of awards vary. Visit Website to download application.

Amount of award:	$500-$2,000
Number of awards:	6
Number of applicants:	24
Application deadline:	May 1
Notification begins:	June 15

Contact:
American Hotel & Lodging Educational Foundation
1201 New York Avenue, NW 600
Washington, DC 20005-3931
Phone: 202-289-3188
Fax: 202-289-3199
Web: www.ahlef.org

Ecolab Scholarship Program

Type of award: Scholarship.

Intended use: For full-time undergraduate study at 2-year or 4-year institution in United States.

Basis for selection: Major/career interest in hotel/restaurant management. Applicant must demonstrate financial need and high academic achievement.

Application requirements: Essay, transcript. Applications reviewed for industry-related experience; academic record/educational qualifications; professional, community and extracurricular activities; and personal attributes including career goals. Copy of course curriculum and copy of tax form 1040 or 1040EZ.

Additional information: Applicant must major in hotel/restaurant management and maintain minimum of 12 credit hours. Amount and number of awards vary. Visit Website to download application.

Amount of award:	$1,000-$2,000
Number of awards:	11
Number of applicants:	100
Application deadline:	June 1
Notification begins:	July 15

Contact:
American Hotel & Lodging Educational Foundation
1201 New York Avenue, NW
Suite 600
Washington, DC 20005-3931
Phone: 202-289-3188
Fax: 202-289-3199
Web: www.ahlef.org

American Indian Science & Engineering Society

A.T. Anderson Memorial Scholarship

Type of award: Scholarship.

Intended use: For full-time undergraduate or graduate study at accredited 2-year, 4-year or graduate institution in United States or Canada.

Eligibility: Applicant or parent must be member/participant of American Indian Science & Engineering Society. Applicant must be Alaskan native or American Indian. Must be member of American Indian tribe or otherwise considered to be American Indian by tribe with which affiliation is claimed, or be at least 1/4 American Indian/Alaskan Native blood.

Basis for selection: Major/career interest in science, general; engineering; medicine; natural resources/conservation; mathematics or physical sciences. Applicant must demonstrate financial need, depth of character, leadership, seriousness of purpose and service orientation.

Application requirements: Recommendations, essay, transcript, proof of eligibility. Resume.

Additional information: Minimum 2.0 GPA. Applicants must be enrolled in program leading to academic degree. Undergraduate student award $1,000 per year; graduate student award $2,000. Membership and scholarship applications available on Website. Otherwise, send SASE with information or application requests.

Amount of award:	$1,000-$2,000
Application deadline:	June 15

Contact:
AISES Scholarships
P.O. Box 9828
Albuquerque, NM 87119-9828
Phone: 505-765-1052
Web: www.aises.org

Burlington Northern Santa Fe Foundation Scholarship

Type of award: Scholarship, renewable.

Intended use: For full-time freshman, sophomore, junior or senior study at accredited postsecondary institution in United States or Canada.

Eligibility: Applicant or parent must be member/participant of American Indian Science & Engineering Society. Applicant must be Alaskan native or American Indian. Must be member of American Indian tribe or otherwise considered to be American Indian by tribe with which affiliation is claimed, or be at least 1/4 American Indian/Alaskan Native blood. Applicant must be high school senior. Applicant must be U.S. citizen residing in South Dakota, Minnesota, Washington, Kansas, Arizona, Oklahoma, California, Oregon, Montana, New Mexico, Colorado or North Dakota.

Basis for selection: Major/career interest in science, general; engineering; mathematics; physical sciences; medicine; natural resources/conservation or business. Applicant must demonstrate financial need, depth of character, leadership, seriousness of purpose and service orientation.

Application requirements: Recommendations, essay, transcript, proof of eligibility. Resume.

Additional information: Minimum 2.0 GPA. Award is renewable for four years (eight semesters) or until degree obtained, whichever comes first, assuming eligibility maintained. Membership and scholarship applications available on Website. Otherwise, include SASE with application or information requests.

Amount of award:	$2,500
Number of awards:	5
Application deadline:	April 15

Contact:
AISES Scholarships
P.O. Box 9828
Albuquerque, NM 87119-9828
Phone: 505-765-1052
Web: www.aises.org

EPA Tribal Lands Environmental Science Scholarship

Type of award: Scholarship.
Intended use: For full-time junior, senior or graduate study at accredited 4-year or graduate institution in United States.
Eligibility: Applicant or parent must be member/participant of American Indian Science & Engineering Society. Applicant must be U.S. citizen or permanent resident.
Basis for selection: Major/career interest in environmental science or engineering, environmental. Applicant must demonstrate high academic achievement, depth of character, leadership, seriousness of purpose and service orientation.
Application requirements: Recommendations, essay, transcript, proof of eligibility. Resume.
Additional information: Minimum 2.7 GPA. Those studying environmental studies, biochemistry, environmental economics or related environmental disciplines also eligible. Must show demonstrated commitment to environmental protection on tribal lands. Membership and scholarship applications available on Website. Otherwise, send SASE with information or application requests. Summer employment at EPA facility or on Indian reservation also offered contingent upon availability of resources. Non-Indians may apply.

Amount of award:	$4,000
Application deadline:	June 15

Contact:
AISES Scholarships
P.O. Box 9828
Albuquerque, NM 87119-9828
Phone: 505-765-1052
Web: www.aises.org

General Motors Engineering Scholarship

Type of award: Scholarship.
Intended use: For full-time undergraduate or graduate study at 4-year or graduate institution in United States.
Eligibility: Applicant or parent must be member/participant of American Indian Science & Engineering Society. Applicant must be Alaskan native or American Indian. Must be member of American Indian tribe or otherwise considered to be American Indian by tribe with which affiliation is claimed, or be at least 1/4 American Indian/Alaskan Native blood. Applicant must be U.S. citizen or permanent resident.
Basis for selection: Major/career interest in engineering. Applicant must demonstrate high academic achievement.
Application requirements: Recommendations, essay, transcript, proof of eligibility. Resume.
Additional information: Minimum 3.0 GPA. Must be seeking degree in engineering field. Preference given to students pursuing degree in electrical, industrial or mechanical engineering. Eligible applicants will be required to complete an online inventory of skills administered by General Motors via the Internet. Scholarship includes mandatory paid 8- to 10-week internship at Bureau of Reclamation site, which must be completed prior to graduation. Membership and scholarship applications available on Website. Otherwise, send SASE with information and application requests.

Amount of award:	$3,000
Application deadline:	June 15

Contact:
AISES Scholarships
P.O. Box 9828
Albuquerque, NM 87119-9828
Phone: 505-765-1052
Web: www.aises.org

American Institute for Foreign Study

Foreign Study/Minority Scholarship Strategic Studies Award

Type of award: Scholarship.
Intended use: For sophomore, junior or senior study in Australia, Czech Republic, Russia, South Africa, Western Europe. Designated institutions: University of Belgrano, Buenos Aires; Macquarie University, Sydney; University of Salzburg, Austria; Charles University, Prague; Richmond, The American International University in London; College International de Cannes, University of Grenoble, University of Paris IV (Sorbonne), France; Holland International Business School and Vrije Universiteit, Amsterdam; University of Limerick, Ireland; Richmond in Florence and Richmond in Rome, Italy; St. Petersburg State Polytechnic University, Russia; University of Stellenbosch, South Africa; University of Granada and University of Salamanca, Spain.
Eligibility: Applicant must be Asian American, African American, Mexican American, Hispanic American, Puerto Rican or American Indian.
Basis for selection: Competition/talent/interest in study abroad. Applicant must demonstrate financial need, high academic achievement, depth of character, leadership, seriousness of purpose and service orientation.
Application requirements: $75 application fee. Essay. Include letter of reference with application.
Additional information: Must have completed minimum 24 credits toward degree when program starts. Must be interested in multicultural/international issues and involved in multicultural/international activities. Six awards of $2,000 and two full scholarships (up to $12,000 each) including round-trip air fare, awarded each year. Award must be used for an AIFS program. Students who are unable to pay $75 application fee may submit fee waiver endorsed by their financial office or study-abroad advisor.

Amount of award:	$2,000-$12,000
Number of awards:	8
Number of applicants:	70
Application deadline:	October 15, April 15
Total amount awarded:	$32,000

Contact:
AIFS College Division
River Plaza
9 West Broad Street
Stamford, CT 06902-3788
Phone: 800-727-2437
Fax: 203-399-5597
Web: www.aifsabroad.com

International Semester Scholarship

Type of award: Scholarship.

Scholarships

Scholarships

Intended use: For freshman, sophomore, junior or senior study at postsecondary institution in Australia, Czech Republic, Russia, South Africa, Western Europe. Designated institutions: Buenos Aires; Macquarie University, Sydney; University of Salzburg, Austria; Charles University, Prague; Richmond, The American International University in London; College International de Cannes; University of Grenoble; University of Paris IV (Sorbonne), France; Holland International Business School and Vrije Universiteit, Amsterdam; University of Limerick; Richmond in Florence, Italy; Richmond in Rome, Italy; St. Petersburg State Polytechnic University, Russia; University of Stellenbosch, South Africa; University of Granada and University of Salamanca, Spain.

Basis for selection: Competition/talent/interest in study abroad. Major/career interest in international relations; social/behavioral sciences or multicultural studies. Applicant must demonstrate high academic achievement, leadership, seriousness of purpose and service orientation.

Application requirements: $75 application fee. Essay, transcript.

Additional information: Applicant must be currently enrolled college undergraduate with at least 3.0 cumulative GPA. Must be interested in multicultural/international issues and involved in multicultural/international activities. Minorities encouraged to apply. Award must be used in AIFS program. Preference given to those applying for full academic year.

Amount of award:	$1,000
Number of awards:	50
Number of applicants:	300
Application deadline:	April 15, October 15
Total amount awarded:	$50,000

Contact:
AIFS College Division
River Plaza
9 West Broad Street
Stamford, CT 06902-3788
Phone: 800-727-2437
Fax: 203-399-5597
Web: www.aifsabroad.com

International Summer Scholarship

Type of award: Scholarship.

Intended use: For freshman, sophomore, junior or senior study at postsecondary institution in Czech Republic, England, France, Italy, Poland, Russia, South Africa, Spain, traveling programs. Designated institutions: University of Salzburg, Austria; Beijing Language and Culture University, China; Charles University, Prague; Richmond, The American International University in London, England; College International de Cannes, University of Paris IV, France; Richmond in Rome and Florence, Italy; Jagiellonian University, Krakow, Poland; St. Petersburg State Polytechnic University, Russia; University of Stellenbosch, South Africa; University of Salamanca and University of Santiago de Compostela, Spain.

Basis for selection: Competition/talent/interest in study abroad. Applicant must demonstrate high academic achievement, leadership and service orientation.

Application requirements: $75 application fee. Essay. Must submit essay on benefits of study abroad.

Additional information: Applicant must be currently enrolled college undergraduate with at least 3.0 cumulative GPA. Should be interested in multicultural/international issues and involved in multicultural/international activities. Minorities strongly encouraged to apply. Award must be used on an AIFS program.

Amount of award:	$750
Number of awards:	35
Number of applicants:	200
Application deadline:	March 15
Total amount awarded:	$262,500

Contact:
AIFS College Division
River Plaza
9 West Broad Street
Stamford, CT 06902-3788
Phone: 800-727-2437
Fax: 203-399-5597
Web: www.aifsabroad.com

Moonves Scholarship

Type of award: Scholarship, renewable.

Intended use: For full-time undergraduate study at postsecondary institution. Designated institutions: Holland International Business School, The Vrije Universiteit in Amsterdam; Richmond College in Rome, Italy.

Basis for selection: Applicant must demonstrate depth of character and seriousness of purpose.

Application requirements: $50 application fee. Recommendations, essay, transcript. AIFS program application. Essay topic: benefits of study abroad.

Additional information: Awarded to students attending AIFS programs in Amsterdam and Rome (sites may change in future years). Students must meet all existing AIFS GPA requirements. Award is based on outstanding potential and innovative spirit, rather than past academic performance. Visit Website for additional information.

Amount of award:	$2,500
Number of awards:	2
Number of applicants:	50
Application deadline:	October 15, April 15
Notification begins:	November 15, May 15
Total amount awarded:	$5,000

Contact:
AIFS College Division
River Plaza
9 West Broad Street
Stamford, CT 06902-3788
Phone: 800-727-2437
Fax: 203-399-5597
Web: www.aifsabroad.com

Tcherepnine Scholarships

Type of award: Scholarship, renewable.

Intended use: For full-time undergraduate study at postsecondary institution in St. Petersburg, Russia. Designated institutions: St. Petersburg State Polytechnic University in St. Petersburg, Russia.

Basis for selection: Applicant must demonstrate high academic achievement.

Application requirements: $50 application fee. Recommendations, essay, transcript. AIFS program application. Essay topic: benefits of study abroad.

Additional information: Awarded to students attending the AIFS semester programs in St. Petersburg, Russia. Minimum 3.0 GPA. Visit Website for additional information.

Amount of award:	$2,500
Number of awards:	4
Number of applicants:	25
Application deadline:	October 15, April 15
Notification begins:	November 15, May 15
Total amount awarded:	$10,000

Contact:
AIFS College Division
River Plaza
9 West Broad Street
Stamford, CT 06902-3788
Phone: 800-727-2437
Fax: 203-399-5597
Web: www.aifsabroad.com

American Institute of Aeronautics and Astronautics

Aeronautics and Astronautics Undergraduate Scholarship

Type of award: Scholarship, renewable.
Intended use: For full-time sophomore, junior or senior study at accredited 4-year institution in United States.
Basis for selection: Major/career interest in aerospace or engineering. Applicant must demonstrate high academic achievement.
Application requirements: Recommendations, essay, transcript, proof of eligibility. Write 500- to 1,000-word essay on how academic program supports career objectives.
Additional information: Institution must be accredited by Accreditation Board for Engineering and Technology. Must have completed at least two quarters or one semester of full-time college work. Minimum 3.0 GPA. Must join American Institute of Aeronautics and Astronautics before receiving award. Not open to members of any American Institute of Aeronautics and Astronautics national committees or subcommittees. Applications must be requested by January 15 if applying by mail. Applications may be downloaded up to January 31 deadline. Applicants must reapply for renewal.

Amount of award:	$2,000
Number of awards:	30
Application deadline:	January 31
Notification begins:	June 15
Total amount awarded:	$60,000

Contact:
AIAA Foundation Undergraduate Scholarship Program
1801 Alexander Bell Drive
Suite 500
Reston, VA 20191-4344
Phone: 703-264-7536
Web: www.aiaa.org

American Institute of Architects

AIA/AAF Award for First Professional Degree Candidates

Type of award: Scholarship.
Intended use: For full-time junior, senior or master's study at accredited 4-year or graduate institution in United States.
Designated institutions: Institution must be NAAB-accredited.
Basis for selection: Major/career interest in architecture.
Application requirements: Recommendations, essay, transcript. Financial needs analysis, class ranking,
Additional information: Applicant must supply drawing along with application. Applicant must be in third year of a five-year Bachelor of Architecture program or working towards a Master's Degree in Architecture. Assists students in one of final two years of professional degree program in architecture. Applications only available from department of Architecture at NAAB- or RAIC-accredited schools.

Amount of award:	$500-$2,500
Application deadline:	February 1
Notification begins:	April 1

Contact:
American Architectural Foundation
1735 New York Avenue, NW
Washington, DC 20006-5292
Web: www.archfoundation.org

RTKL Traveling Fellowship

Type of award: Research grant
Intended use: For full-time senior or master's study at accredited 4-year or graduate institution in United States. Designated institutions: Institution must be NAAB accredited.
Basis for selection: Major/career interest in architecture.
Application requirements: Recommendations, transcript. Travel proposal budget outlining a foreign itinerary that is directly relevant to applicant's educational goals.
Additional information: Must be in or accepted in a professional degree program in architecture. Application available from NAAB-accredited institutions or the AAF. Application also available from Website.

Amount of award:	$2,500
Number of awards:	1
Application deadline:	February 15

Contact:
American Architectural Foundation
1735 New York Ave, NW
Washington, DC 20006-5292
Web: www.archfoundation.org

American Institute of Certified Public Accountants

Certified Public Accountants Minorities Scholarship

Type of award: Scholarship, renewable.
Intended use: For full-time undergraduate or graduate study at accredited 4-year or graduate institution in United States.
Eligibility: Applicant must be Alaskan native, Asian American, African American, Mexican American, Hispanic American or Puerto Rican.
Basis for selection: Major/career interest in accounting. Applicant must demonstrate high academic achievement and seriousness of purpose.
Application requirements: Recommendations, essay, transcript. Application.
Additional information: Applicant must be accounting major. For this program, AICPA defines minorities as those of black, Native American/Alaskan Native, or Pacific Island races, or of

Hispanic ethnic origin. Scholarship provides competitive awards to outstanding full-time undergraduate minority students at regionally accredited institutions to encourage their selection of accounting as a major, entry into the profession and, ultimately, achievement of CPA designation. Undergraduate students must have completed at least 30 semester hours or equivalent of college work, with at least six hours in accounting. Full-time graduate students (who are not CPAs) pursuing a master's in accounting, taxation or business administration also eligible, if they hold undergraduate degree in accounting. Notification begins the last week in August.

Amount of award:	$5,000
Number of applicants:	400
Application deadline:	July 1
Total amount awarded:	$600,000

Contact:
American Institute of Certified Public Accountants
1211 Avenue of the Americas
New York, NY 10036-8775
Phone: 212-596-6270
Web: www.aicpa.org

American Institute of Polish Culture

Harriet Irsay Grant

Type of award: Research grant.
Intended use: For full-time undergraduate study at 4-year institution.
Eligibility: Applicant must be high school senior. Applicant must be U.S. citizen.
Basis for selection: Major/career interest in journalism; communications or public relations. Applicant must demonstrate financial need and high academic achievement.
Application requirements: $25 application fee. Recommendations, transcript. Three original, signed letters of recommendation on institution letterhead, which must be sent directly to institute.
Additional information: Send SASE with application request. Application must be postmarked no later than March 17. Must be full-time student. Preference is given to American students of Polish heritage.

Amount of award:	$1,000
Number of awards:	15
Application deadline:	March 17
Notification begins:	May 5

Contact:
American Institute of Polish Culture
1440 79 Street Causeway, Suite 117
Miami, FL 33141-4135
Phone: 305-864-2349
Fax: 305-865-5150
Web: www.ampolinstitute.org

American Legion Alabama

American Legion Alabama Oratorical Contest

Type of award: Scholarship.
Intended use: For undergraduate study at postsecondary institution.
Eligibility: Applicant or parent must be member/participant of American Legion. Applicant must be enrolled in high school. Applicant must be U.S. citizen residing in Alabama.
Basis for selection: Competition/talent/interest in oratory/debate, based on breadth of knowledge, originality, application of knowledge, skill in selecting examples and analogies, logic, voice, diction, style of language, and delivery.
Application requirements: Proof of eligibility.
Additional information: Oratorical Scholarships: 1st-$5,000; 2nd-$3,000; 3rd-$2,000. For State Oratorical Contest 1st, 2nd, and 3rd place winners. State finals held in March.

Amount of award:	$2,000-$5,000
Number of awards:	3
Total amount awarded:	$10,000

Contact:
Department Adjutant
The American Legion
P.O. Box 1069
Montgomery, AL 36101-1069
Phone: 334-262-6638

American Legion Alabama Scholarship

Type of award: Scholarship, renewable.
Intended use: For undergraduate study at postsecondary institution. Designated institutions: Alabama colleges.
Eligibility: Applicant or parent must be member/participant of American Legion. Applicant must be U.S. citizen or permanent resident residing in Alabama. Applicant must be descendant of veteran; or dependent of veteran during Korean War, Persian Gulf War, WW I, WW II or Vietnam.
Application requirements: Proof of eligibility.
Additional information: Four-year scholarships at Alabama colleges. Send business-size SASE with application request.

Amount of award:	$850
Number of awards:	130
Application deadline:	May 1
Total amount awarded:	$110,500

Contact:
Department Adjutant
The American Legion
P.O. Box 1069
Montgomery, AL 36101-1069
Phone: 334-262-6638

American Legion Alabama Auxiliary

American Legion Alabama Auxiliary Scholarship

Type of award: Scholarship, renewable.

Scholarships

Intended use: For undergraduate or graduate study at postsecondary institution. Designated institutions: Alabama state-supported institutions.
Eligibility: Applicant must be U.S. citizen or permanent resident residing in Alabama. Applicant must be descendant of veteran; or dependent of veteran during Grenada conflict, Korean War, Lebanon conflict, Panama conflict, Persian Gulf War, WW I, WW II or Vietnam.
Application requirements: Proof of eligibility.
Additional information: Annual scholarships. Send SASE with request for application. Grandchildren of veterans also eligible.

Amount of award:	$850
Number of awards:	40
Application deadline:	April 1
Total amount awarded:	$34,000

Contact:
American Legion Auxiliary, Department of Alabama
Department Headquarters
120 North Jackson Street
Montgomery, AL 36104
Phone: 334-262-1176

American Legion Alaska

American Legion Alaska Oratorical Contest

Type of award: Scholarship.
Eligibility: Applicant must be enrolled in high school. Applicant must be U.S. citizen or permanent resident residing in Alaska.
Basis for selection: Competition/talent/interest in oratory/debate, based on breadth of knowledge, originality, application of knowledge on topic, skill in selecting examples and analogies, logic, voice, diction, style of language and delivery.
Application requirements: Proof of eligibility.
Additional information: High school student (grades 9-12) attending Alaska accredited institution. $1,000 for winner; $500 for 3 alternate. Must participate in local speech contests. Contest begins in January.

Amount of award:	$500-$1,000

Contact:
American Legion, Department of Alaska
Department Adjutant
1550 Charter Circle
Anchorage, AK 99508
Phone: 907-278-8598
Fax: 907-278-0041

American Legion Alaska Auxiliary

American Legion Alaska Auxiliary Scholarship

Type of award: Scholarship.
Intended use: For freshman study at postsecondary institution.
Eligibility: Applicant or parent must be member/participant of American Legion Auxiliary. Applicant must be at least 17, no

older than 24, high school senior. Applicant must be U.S. citizen or permanent resident residing in Alaska. Applicant must be dependent of veteran during Grenada conflict, Korean War, Lebanon conflict, Panama conflict, Persian Gulf War, WW I, WW II or Vietnam.
Basis for selection: Applicant must demonstrate high academic achievement.
Application requirements: Proof of eligibility.
Additional information: Scholarship to apply toward tuition, matriculation, laboratory, or similar fees (paid half first semester, half second semester). High school graduate may not have attended institution of higher education.

Amount of award:	$1,000
Application deadline:	March 15

Contact:
American Legion Auxiliary
Department of Alaska
1392 6th Avenue
Fairbanks, AK 99701

American Legion Arizona

American Legion Arizona Oratorical Contest

Type of award: Scholarship.
Eligibility: Applicant must be enrolled in high school. Applicant must be U.S. citizen or permanent resident residing in Arizona.
Basis for selection: Competition/talent/interest in Oratory/debate, based on breadth of knowledge, originality, application of knowledge on topic, skill in selecting examples and analogies, logic, voice, diction, style of language and delivery.
Additional information: Awards: 1st-$1,500, 2nd-$800, 3rd-$500. For students enrolled in accredited Arizona high school.

Application deadline:	January 15

Contact:
American Legion Arizona
4701 North 19th Avenue, Suite 200
Phoenix, AZ 85015-3779
Phone: 602-264-7706
Fax: 602-264-0029
Web: www.azlegion.org

American Legion Arizona Auxiliary

American Legion Arizona Auxiliary Health Care Occupation Scholarship

Type of award: Scholarship.
Intended use: For undergraduate study at accredited 2-year or 4-year institution. Designated institutions: Arizona accredited institution offering certificate or degree in health occupations.
Eligibility: Applicant or parent must be member/participant of American Legion Auxiliary. Applicant must be U.S. citizen residing in Arizona.
Basis for selection: Major/career interest in health-related professions or health sciences.

Additional information: Must be resident of Arizona at least one year. Preference given to immediate family members of veterans.

Amount of award:	$400
Application deadline:	May 15

Contact:
American Legion Auxiliary Department of Arizona
4701 North 19th Avenue, Suite 100
Phoenix, AZ 85015-3727
Phone: 602-241-1080
Fax: 602-274-5707

American Legion Arizona Auxiliary Nurses' Scholarship

Type of award: Scholarship.
Intended use: For sophomore study at accredited 2-year or 4-year institution. Designated institutions: Accredited Arizona institutions awarding RN degrees.
Eligibility: Applicant or parent must be member/participant of American Legion Auxiliary. Applicant must be U.S. citizen residing in Arizona.
Basis for selection: Major/career interest in nursing.
Additional information: For second-year student nurses enrolled in accredited Arizona institutions awarding RN degrees. Must be Arizona resident for at least one year. Preference given to immediate family members of veterans.

Amount of award:	$500
Application deadline:	May 15

Contact:
American Legion Auxiliary Department of Arizona
4701 North 19th Avenue, Suite 100
Phoenix, AZ 85015-3727
Phone: 602-241-1080
Fax: 602-274-5707

American Legion Arkansas

American Legion Arkansas Oratorical Contest

Type of award: Scholarship.
Intended use: For undergraduate study.
Eligibility: Applicant must be residing in Arkansas.
Basis for selection: Competition/talent/interest in oratory/debate, based on breadth of knowledge, originality, application of knowledge of topic, skill in selecting examples and analogies, logic, voice, diction, style of language and delivery.
Application requirements: Proof of eligibility.
Additional information: Oratorical Contest, State Division: 1st-$1,000, 2nd-$750, 3rd-$500, 4th-$300. Must be state oratorical winners; contestant must compete in three contests before reaching state level.

Amount of award:	$300-$1,000
Number of awards:	4
Application deadline:	March 15
Total amount awarded:	$2,550

Contact:
American Legion Arkansas
Department Adjutant
P.O. Box 3280
Little Rock, AR 72203
Phone: 501-375-1104
Fax: 501-375-4236
Web: www.arklegion.homestead.com

American Legion Arkansas Scholarship

Type of award: Scholarship.
Intended use: For undergraduate study.
Eligibility: Applicant or parent must be member/participant of American Legion. Applicant must be residing in Arkansas. Applicant must be descendant of veteran; or dependent of veteran.
Application requirements: Proof of eligibility.
Additional information: Four scholarships: amount to be determined. Must be a resident of Arkansas. Must be child, grandchild, or great-grandchild of American Legion member.

Number of awards:	4
Application deadline:	March 15

Contact:
American Legion Arkansas
Department Adjutant
P.O. Box 3280
Little Rock, AR 72203
Phone: 501-375-1104
Fax: 501-375-4236
Web: www.arklegion.homestead.com

American Legion Arkansas Auxiliary

American Legion Arkansas Auxiliary Scholarships

Type of award: Scholarship.
Intended use: For at postsecondary institution. Designated institutions: Arkansas postsecondary institutions.
Eligibility: Applicant or parent must be member/participant of American Legion Auxiliary. Applicant must be high school senior. Applicant must be U.S. citizen residing in Arkansas. Applicant must be dependent of veteran during Grenada conflict, Korean War, Lebanon conflict, Panama conflict, Persian Gulf War, WW I, WW II or Vietnam.
Application requirements: Include name of high school and SASE with application request.
Additional information: Academic Scholarship: one $1,000. Nurse Scholarship: one $500. Awards paid half first semester, half second semester. Student must be Arkansas resident attending Arkansas school.

Amount of award:	$500-$1,000
Number of awards:	2
Application deadline:	March 1
Total amount awarded:	$1,500

Scholarships

Contact:
American Legion Auxiliary Department of Arkansas
Department Secretary
1415 West 7th St.
Little Rock, AR 72201
Phone: 501-374-5836

American Legion Auxiliary, Department of Arizona

Wilma D. Hoyal/Maxine Chilton Memorial Scholarship

Type of award: Scholarship.
Intended use: For full-time sophomore, junior or senior study. Designated institutions: University of Arizona, Arizona State University, and Northern Arizona University.
Eligibility: Applicant must be U.S. citizen residing in Arizona.
Basis for selection: Major/career interest in political science/government or education, special.
Additional information: Three $600 awards payable to three designated institutions in Arizona. Applicant must be state resident at least one year. Preference given to immediate family members of veterans.

Amount of award:	$600
Number of awards:	3
Application deadline:	May 15

Contact:
American Legion Auxiliary, Department of Arizona
4701 North 19th Avenue, Suite 100
Phoenix, AZ 85015-3727
Phone: 602-241-1080
Fax: 602-274-5707

American Legion Auxiliary, Department of California

American Legion California Auxiliary Department Scholarship

Type of award: Scholarship.
Intended use: For freshman study at postsecondary institution. Designated institutions: California colleges and universities.
Eligibility: Applicant must be high school senior. Applicant must be residing in California. Applicant must be dependent of active service person or veteran during Grenada conflict, Korean War, Lebanon conflict, Panama conflict, Persian Gulf War, WW I, WW II or Vietnam.
Basis for selection: Applicant must demonstrate financial need.
Additional information: Annual scholarships: 1-$2,000; 5-$1,000; 5-$500. Must be high school senior, or graduate who has not been able to begin college due to illness or financial circumstances. See Website for application.

Amount of award:	$500-$2,000
Number of awards:	11
Application deadline:	March 15
Total amount awarded:	$9,500

Contact:
Local Auxiliary unit.
Phone: 415-861-5092
Fax: 415-861-8365
Web: www.calegionaux.org

Continuing or Re-entry Student Scholarship

Type of award: Scholarship.
Intended use: For undergraduate study at postsecondary institution. Designated institutions: California colleges and universities.
Eligibility: Applicant must be residing in California. Applicant must be dependent of active service person or veteran during Grenada conflict, Korean War, Lebanon conflict, Panama conflict, Persian Gulf War, WW I, WW II or Vietnam.
Additional information: Two $1,000 scholarships for continuing or re-entering college students. See Website for application.

Amount of award:	$1,000
Number of awards:	2
Application deadline:	March 15
Total amount awarded:	$2,000

Contact:
Local Auxiliary unit.
Phone: 415-861-5092
Fax: 415-861-8365
Web: www.calegionaux.org

Lucille Ganey Memorial Scholarship

Type of award: Scholarship.
Intended use: Designated institutions: Stephens College, Missouri.
Eligibility: Applicant must be high school senior. Applicant must be residing in California. Applicant must be dependent of active service person or veteran during Grenada conflict, Korean War, Lebanon conflict, Panama conflict, Persian Gulf War, WW I, WW II or Vietnam.
Additional information: Must be high school senior in California at time of application. Students already attending Stephens College in Missouri also eligible to apply. See Website for application.

Amount of award:	$500
Number of awards:	1
Application deadline:	March 15
Total amount awarded:	$500

Contact:
Local Auxiliary unit.
Phone: 415-861-5092
Fax: 415-861-8365
Web: www.calegionaux.org

Past Department President's Junior Scholarship

Type of award: Scholarship.
Intended use: For at postsecondary institution. Designated institutions: California colleges and universities.
Eligibility: Applicant or parent must be member/participant of American Legion Auxiliary. Applicant must be high school senior. Applicant must be residing in California. Applicant must be descendant of veteran; or dependent of veteran during Grenada conflict, Korean War, Lebanon conflict, Panama conflict, Persian Gulf War, WW I, WW II or Vietnam.

Additional information: Applicant must have consecutive membership as Junior for three years. See Website for application.

Amount of award:	$300-$1,000
Number of awards:	1
Application deadline:	April 15

Contact:
Local Auxiliary unit.
Phone: 415-861-5092
Fax: 415-861-8365
Web: www.calegionaux.org

Past President's Parley Nursing Scholarship

Type of award: Scholarship.
Intended use: For undergraduate study at postsecondary institution. Designated institutions: California postsecondary institutions.
Eligibility: Applicant must be residing in California. Applicant must be veteran; or dependent of veteran; or spouse of veteran or deceased veteran during Grenada conflict, Korean War, Lebanon conflict, Panama conflict, Persian Gulf War, WW I, WW II or Vietnam.
Basis for selection: Major/career interest in nursing.
Additional information: Applicant must be entering student or continuing student in a nursing program. Amount and number of awards vary. See Website for application.

Amount of award:	$500-$1,500
Application deadline:	April 5

Contact:
Local Auxiliary unit.
Phone: 415-861-5092
Fax: 415-861-8365
Web: www.calegionaux.org

American Legion California

American Legion California Oratorical Contest

Type of award: Scholarship.
Eligibility: Applicant must be enrolled in high school. Applicant must be residing in California.
Basis for selection: Competition/talent/interest in oratory/debate, based on breadth of knowledge, originality, application of knowledge of topic, skill in selecting examples and analogies, logic, voice, diction, style of language and delivery.
Application requirements: See local high school counselor.
Additional information: Students selected by schools to participate in district contests, followed by area and departmental finals. 1st-$1,200; 2nd-$1,000; 3rd-$800; 4th, 5th, and 6th-$700 each.

Amount of award:	$700-$1,200
Number of awards:	6

Contact:
Phone: 415-431-2400
Fax: 415-255-1571
Web: www.calegion.org

American Legion Colorado Auxiliary

American Legion Colorado Auxiliary/Past President's Parley Nurse's Scholarship

Type of award: Scholarship.
Intended use: For undergraduate study at accredited 2-year or 4-year institution. Designated institutions: Accredited nursing school in Colorado.
Eligibility: Applicant or parent must be member/participant of American Legion. Applicant must be residing in Colorado. Applicant must be veteran; or dependent of veteran; or spouse of veteran during Grenada conflict, Korean War, Lebanon conflict, Panama conflict, Persian Gulf War, WW I, WW II or Vietnam.
Basis for selection: Major/career interest in nursing.
Additional information: Number and amount of awards vary. Must live and attend nursing school in Colorado.

Application deadline:	April 15

Contact:
American Legion Colorado Auxiliary
Department Headquarters
7465 East First Avenue, Suite D
Denver, CO 80230
Phone: 303-367-5388

Department President's Scholarship

Type of award: Scholarship.
Intended use: For undergraduate study. Designated institutions: Colorado colleges and institutions.
Eligibility: Applicant or parent must be member/participant of American Legion Auxiliary. Applicant must be residing in Colorado. Applicant must be descendant of veteran; or dependent of veteran during Grenada conflict, Korean War, Lebanon conflict, Panama conflict, Persian Gulf War, WW I, WW II or Vietnam.
Additional information: Must attend school in Colorado. Two $500 awards and one $250.

Amount of award:	$250-$500
Number of awards:	3
Application deadline:	March 12
Total amount awarded:	$1,250

Contact:
American Legion Colorado Auxiliary
Department Headquarters
7465 East First Avenue, Suite D
Denver, CO 80230
Phone: 303-367-5388

Department President's Scholarship for Junior Auxiliary Members

Type of award: Scholarship.
Intended use: For undergraduate study. Designated institutions: Colorado colleges and universities.
Eligibility: Applicant or parent must be member/participant of American Legion Auxiliary. Applicant must be residing in Colorado.
Additional information: Applicant must be Colorado Junior Auxiliary member.

Amount of award: $500
Number of awards: 1
Application deadline: March 12
Contact:
American Legion Colorado Auxiliary
Department Headquarters
7465 East First Avenue, Suite D
Denver, CO 80230
Phone: 303-367-5388

American Legion Connecticut Auxiliary

Memorial Education Grant

Type of award: Scholarship.
Intended use: For undergraduate study at postsecondary institution.
Eligibility: Applicant or parent must be member/participant of American Legion. Applicant must be at least 16, no older than 23. Applicant must be residing in Connecticut.
Basis for selection: Applicant must demonstrate financial need.
Application requirements: Proof of eligibility. Apply in December.
Additional information: Half of grants awarded to child/grandchild of Connecticut AL/ALA member or to a member of Connecticut ALA/Sons of the AL. Other half awarded to child of Connecticut resident veteran. Applicant must be between the ages of 16 and 23.

Amount of award: $500
Number of awards: 4
Application deadline: March 1
Total amount awarded: $2,000
Contact:
American Legion Auxiliary
Department Headquarters
P.O. Box 266
Rocky Hill, CT 06067-0266
Phone: 860-721-5945
Fax: 860-721-5828

Past President's Parley Education Grant

Type of award: Scholarship, renewable.
Intended use: For undergraduate study at postsecondary institution.
Eligibility: Applicant or parent must be member/participant of American Legion. Applicant must be at least 16, no older than 23. Applicant must be residing in Connecticut.
Basis for selection: Applicant must demonstrate financial need.
Application requirements: Proof of eligibility. Apply in December.
Additional information: Preference given to child or grandchild of ex-servicewoman who is a CT AL/ALA member at least five years or who was a member for the five years prior to her death. Second preference to child or grandchild of CT AL/ALA member or to a member of CT ALA/Son of AL at least five years. All applicants must be between the ages of 16 and 23.

Amount of award: $500
Number of awards: 4
Application deadline: March 1
Total amount awarded: $2,000
Contact:
American Legion Auxiliary
Department Headquarters
P.O. Box 266
Rocky Hill, CT 06067-0266
Phone: 860-721-5945
Fax: 860-721-5828

American Legion Delaware Auxiliary

American Legion Delaware Auxiliary Past President's Parley Nursing Scholarship

Type of award: Scholarship.
Intended use: For undergraduate study.
Eligibility: Applicant must be residing in Delaware. Applicant must be dependent of veteran.
Basis for selection: Major/career interest in nursing.

Amount of award: $300
Number of awards: 1
Application deadline: February 28
Total amount awarded: $300
Contact:
American Legion Auxiliary
Executive Secretary
43 Blades Drive
Dover, DE 19901-5536

American Legion, Department of Connecticut

National High School Oratorical Contest

Type of award: Scholarship.
Eligibility: Applicant must be no older than 20. Applicant must be residing in Connecticut.
Basis for selection: Competition/talent/interest in Oratory/debate, based on breadth of knowledge, originality, application of knowledge of topic, skill in selecting examples and analogies, logic, voice, diction, style of language and delivery.
Additional information: Awards: 1st-$2,000; 2nd-$1,000; 3rd to 7th-$500, all in Savings Bonds. Contest open only to students attending Connecticut high school.

Amount of award: $500-$2,000
Number of awards: 7
Total amount awarded: $5,500
Contact:
American Legion, Department of Connecticut
Department Oratorical Chairman
P.O. Box 208
Rocky Hill, CT 06067
Phone: 860-721-5942

Scholarships

American Legion, Department of New Jersey

American Legion New Jersey Stutz Memorial Scholarship

Type of award: Scholarship.
Intended use: For undergraduate study at 2-year or 4-year institution.
Eligibility: Applicant must be high school senior. Applicant must be residing in New Jersey. Applicant must be dependent of veteran.
Additional information: Applicant must be natural or adopted child of The American Legion, Department of New Jersey member. Award is $1,000 per year for four years.

Amount of award:	$4,000
Number of awards:	1
Application deadline:	February 15
Total amount awarded:	$4,000

Contact:
American Legion, Department of New Jersey
Department Adjutant
135 West Hanover Street
Trenton, NJ 08618
Phone: 609-695-5418

American Legion, Department of New York

American Legion New York Dr. Hannah K. Vuolo Memorial Scholarship

Type of award: Scholarship.
Intended use: For freshman study at accredited 2-year or 4-year institution.
Eligibility: Applicant or parent must be member/participant of American Legion. Applicant must be no older than 20, high school senior. Applicant must be descendant of veteran.
Basis for selection: Major/career interest in education, teacher. Applicant must demonstrate financial need and high academic achievement.
Additional information: Applicant must be natural or adopted direct descendant of member or deceased member of American Legion, Department of New York. Must be high school senior or graduate. Preference given to New York residents.

Amount of award:	$250
Number of awards:	1
Application deadline:	May 1
Total amount awarded:	$250

Contact:
American Legion, Department of New York
Department Adjutant
112 State Street, Suite 400
Albany, NY 12207
Phone: 518-463-2215
Fax: 518-427-8443
Web: www.ny.legion.org

American Legion New York James F. Mulholland Scholarship

Type of award: Scholarship.
Intended use: For freshman study at postsecondary institution.
Eligibility: Applicant must be high school senior. Applicant must be residing in New York. Applicant must be dependent of veteran.
Basis for selection: Applicant must demonstrate financial need and high academic achievement.
Additional information: Applicant must be child of American Legion member. Must be graduating senior at New York high school.

Amount of award:	$500
Number of awards:	2
Application deadline:	May 1
Total amount awarded:	$1,000

Contact:
American Legion, Department of New York
Department Adjutant
112 State Street, Suite 400
Albany, NY 12207
Phone: 518-463-2215
Fax: 518-427-8443
Web: www.ny.legion.org

American Legion, Department of Texas

Texas Legion Oratorical Contest

Type of award: Scholarship.
Intended use: For undergraduate study at postsecondary institution.
Eligibility: Applicant must be no older than 18, enrolled in high school. Applicant must be residing in Texas.
Basis for selection: Competition/talent/interest in oratory/debate, based on breadth of knowledge, originality, application of knowledge of topic, skill in selecting examples and analogies, logic, voice, diction, style of language, and delivery. Applicant must demonstrate patriotism.
Application requirements: Proof of eligibility.
Additional information: Awards: 1st-$1,000, 2nd-$750, 3rd-$500, 4th-$250. First place winner eligible to enter national contest.

Amount of award:	$250-$1,000
Number of awards:	4
Application deadline:	August 31
Total amount awarded:	$2,500

Contact:
American Legion, Department of Texas
Oratorical Contest
3401 Ed Bluestein Blvd, Suite 200
Austin, TX 78721-2902
Phone: 512-472-4138
Fax: 512-472-0603
Web: www.txlegion.org

American Legion, Department of Wisconsin

Oratorical Contest Scholarships

Type of award: Scholarship.
Intended use: For undergraduate study.
Eligibility: Applicant must be enrolled in high school. Applicant must be residing in Wisconsin.
Basis for selection: Competition/talent/interest in oratory/debate.
Application requirements: Winners of Wisconsin high school Legion oratorical contests.
Additional information: Oratorical Contest Scholarships: Three regional contests, three regional awards $1,000 each. State winner: $2,000; regional participants $600 each.
Amount of award: $600-$2,000
Contact:
American Legion, Department of Wisconsin
Program Secretary
P.O. Box 388
Portage, WI 53901
Phone: 608-745-1090
Fax: 608-745-0179
Web: www.wilegion.org

American Legion District of Columbia

National High School Oratorical Contest

Type of award: Scholarship.
Intended use: For undergraduate study.
Eligibility: Applicant must be no older than 20. Applicant must be U.S. citizen or permanent resident residing in District of Columbia.
Basis for selection: Competition/talent/interest in oratory/debate, based on breadth of knowledge, originality, application of knowledge, skill in selecting examples and analogies, logic, voice, diction, style of language and delivery.
Application requirements: Proof of eligibility. Four Department Finalists.
Additional information: All awards in U.S. Savings Bonds: 1st-$800, 2nd-$500, 3rd-$300, 4th-$100. In addition, first place winner will receive $1,500 for participating in the next round of competition. Contest held in Washington, DC, during the third week of February.
Amount of award: $100-$800
Number of awards: 4
Application deadline: January 30
Total amount awarded: $1,600
Contact:
American Legion
Department of DC
3408 Wisconsin Avenue NW, Suite 218
Washington, DC 20016
Phone: 202-362-9151
Fax: 202-362-9152

American Legion Florida Auxiliary

American Legion Florida Auxiliary Memorial Scholarship

Type of award: Scholarship.
Intended use: For undergraduate study at vocational, 2-year or 4-year institution. Designated institutions: Florida colleges and universities.
Eligibility: Applicant or parent must be member/participant of American Legion Auxiliary. Applicant must be residing in Florida.
Application requirements: Send application requests by January 1.
Additional information: Up to $500 for junior colleges and vocational schools; $1,000 for four-year university. Members and daughters/granddaughters of members with at least three years' membership in FL unit.
Amount of award: $500-$1,000
Contact:
American Legion Auxiliary, Department of Florida
Department Secretary
P.O. Box 547917
Orlando, FL 32854-7917
Fax: 407-299-6522

American Legion Florida Auxiliary Scholarship

Type of award: Scholarship.
Intended use: For undergraduate study at vocational, 2-year or 4-year institution. Designated institutions: Florida colleges and universities.
Eligibility: Applicant or parent must be member/participant of American Legion Auxiliary. Applicant must be residing in Florida. Applicant must be dependent of veteran.
Application requirements: Proof of eligibility. Request application by January 1.
Additional information: Child of honorably discharged U.S. military veteran. Up to $500 for junior colleges and vocational schools; $1,000 for four-year university. Must be sponsored by local auxiliary unit.
Amount of award: $500-$1,000
Contact:
American Legion Auxiliary, Department of Florida
Department Secretary
P.O. Box 547917
Orlando, FL 32854-7917
Fax: 407-299-6522

American Legion Florida, Department Headquarters

American Legion Florida Scholarship

Type of award: Scholarship.
Intended use: For undergraduate study at postsecondary institution.

Scholarships

93

Eligibility: Applicant or parent must be member/participant of American Legion. Applicant must be high school senior. Applicant must be residing in Florida. Applicant must be descendant of veteran; or dependent of veteran.
Application requirements: Must be child, grandchild, great-grandchild, or legally adopted child of member in good standing of American Legion Florida.
Additional information: Scholarships: 1st-2,500; 2nd-$1,500; 3rd-$1,000; 4th-$500; 5th-$500. Applicant must be a senior attending Florida high school.

Amount of award:	$500-$2,500
Number of awards:	5
Application deadline:	March 1
Total amount awarded:	$6,000

Contact:
American Legion Florida, Department Headquarters
P.O. Box 547936
Orlando, FL 32854-7936
Phone: 407-295-2631 x37
Web: www.floridalegion.org

High School Oratorical Contest

Type of award: Scholarship.
Intended use: For at postsecondary institution.
Eligibility: Applicant must be high school senior. Applicant must be residing in Florida.
Basis for selection: Competition/talent/interest in Oratory/debate, based on breadth of knowledge, originality, application of knowledge of topic, skill in selecting examples and analogies, logic, voice, diction, style of language and delivery.
Additional information: Awards: 1st-$2,500; 2nd-$1,500; 3rd-$1,000; 4th-$500. Applicant must be enrolled in accredited Florida high school.

Amount of award:	$500-$2,500
Number of awards:	4
Application deadline:	November 1
Total amount awarded:	$5,500

Contact:
American Legion Florida, Department Headquarters
P.O. Box 547936
Orlando, FL 32854-7936
Phone: 407-295-2631 x37
Web: www.floridalegion.org

American Legion Georgia Auxiliary

American Legion Georgia Auxiliary Scholarship

Type of award: Scholarship.
Intended use: For undergraduate study at postsecondary institution.
Eligibility: Applicant must be high school senior. Applicant must be residing in Georgia. Applicant must be dependent of veteran.
Basis for selection: Applicant must demonstrate high academic achievement.
Application requirements: Essay, transcript, proof of eligibility.
Additional information: Preference given to children of deceased veterans. Must be sponsored by local Auxiliary unit.

Information and application materials available through local American Legion Auxiliary unit.

Amount of award:	$1,000
Number of awards:	2
Total amount awarded:	$2,000

Contact:
American Legion Georgia Auxiliary
Department Headquarters
3035 Mt. Zion Road
Stockbridge, GA 30281

Past President's Parley Nurses Scholarship

Type of award: Scholarship.
Intended use: For undergraduate study at 2-year or 4-year institution.
Eligibility: Applicant or parent must be member/participant of American Legion Auxiliary. Applicant must be female, high school senior. Applicant must be residing in Georgia. Applicant must be dependent of veteran.
Basis for selection: Major/career interest in nursing. Applicant must demonstrate high academic achievement.
Application requirements: Proof of eligibility.
Additional information: Amount of award and number of scholarships determined by available funds. Must be sponsored by local Auxiliary unit.
Contact:
American Legion Georgia Auxiliary
Department Headquarters
3035 Mt. Zion Road
Stockbridge, GA 30281

American Legion Hawaii, Department Headquarters

American Legion Oratorical Contest

Type of award: Scholarship.
Eligibility: Applicant must be enrolled in high school. Applicant must be residing in Hawaii.
Basis for selection: Competition/talent/interest in Oratory/debate, based on breadth of knowledge, originality, application of knowledge of topic, skill in selecting examples and analogies, logic, voice, diction, style of language and delivery.
Additional information: Awards: 1st-$500; 2nd-$300; 3rd-$100; 4th-$50. Contest normally held in February.

Amount of award:	$50-$500
Number of awards:	4
Total amount awarded:	$950

Contact:
American Legion Hawaii, Department Headquarters
612 McCully Street
Honolulu, HI 96826
Phone: 808-946-6383
Fax: 808-947-3957

American Legion Idaho Auxiliary

American Legion Idaho Auxiliary Nurse's Scholarship

Type of award: Scholarship.
Intended use: For undergraduate study at 2-year or 4-year institution.
Eligibility: Applicant must be residing in Idaho. Applicant must be veteran; or dependent of veteran.
Basis for selection: Major/career interest in nursing.
Application requirements: Application must be submitted for judging to American Legion Auxiliary Unit Presidents in local communities.
Additional information: Applicant must be Idaho resident five years prior to application.

Amount of award:	$750
Application deadline:	March 15

Contact:
American Legion Auxiliary, Department of Idaho
Department Headquarters
905 Warren Street
Boise, ID 83706
Phone: 208-342-7066
Fax: 208-342-0855

American Legion Idaho, Department Headquarters

American Legion Idaho Scholarships

Type of award: Scholarship.
Intended use: For undergraduate study at postsecondary institution. Designated institutions: Idaho postsecondary institutions.
Eligibility: Applicant or parent must be member/participant of American Legion. Applicant must be residing in Idaho.
Application requirements: Proof of eligibility.
Additional information: Scholarships determined annually. Must be child or grandchild of American Legion or Auxiliary members. See Website for more information.

Application deadline:	July 1

Contact:
American Legion Idaho, Department Headquarters
901 Warren Street
Boise, ID 83706
Phone: 208-342-7061
Fax: 208-342-1964
Web: www.idaholegion.com

Oratorical Contest

Type of award: Scholarship.
Eligibility: Applicant must be enrolled in high school. Applicant must be residing in Idaho.
Basis for selection: Competition/talent/interest in Oratory/debate, based on breadth of knowledge, originality, application of knowledge of topic, skill in selecting examples and analogies, logic, voice, diction, style of language and delivery.

Additional information: Awards: 1st-$500; 2nd-$250; 3rd-$150; 4th-$50. Visit Website for more information.

Amount of award:	$50-$500
Number of awards:	4
Total amount awarded:	$950

Contact:
American Legion Idaho, Department Headquarters
901 Warren Street
Boise, ID 83706
Phone: 208-342-7061
Fax: 208-342-1964
Web: www.idaholegion.com

American Legion Illinois

American Legion Illinois Boy Scout Scholarship

Type of award: Scholarship.
Intended use: For undergraduate study at postsecondary institution.
Eligibility: Applicant or parent must be member/participant of Boy Scouts of America. Applicant must be male, high school senior. Applicant must be residing in Illinois.
Basis for selection: Competition/talent/interest in writing/journalism.
Application requirements: Essay, proof of eligibility. 500-word essay on Legion's Americanism and Boy Scout programs.
Additional information: Boy Scout Scholarship: $1,000. Four runner-up awards: $200 each. Must be qualified Senior Boy Scout or Explorer.

Amount of award:	$200-$1,000
Number of awards:	5
Application deadline:	April 30
Total amount awarded:	$1,800

Contact:
American Legion, Department of Illinois
P.O. Box 2910
Bloomington, IL 61702
Web: www.illegion.org

American Legion Illinois Oratorical Contest

Type of award: Scholarship.
Eligibility: Applicant must be enrolled in high school. Applicant must be U.S. citizen or permanent resident residing in Illinois.
Basis for selection: Competition/talent/interest in oratory/debate, based on breadth of knowledge, originality, application of knowledge of topic, skill in selecting examples and analogies, logic, voice, diction, style of language and delivery.
Application requirements: Proof of eligibility. Applications available in the fall.
Additional information: Contest begins in January and starts at post level, to district level, to division level, to department level, then to national competition. 1st-$1,600, 2nd-$1,300, 3rd-$1,200, 4th-$1,000, 5th-$1,000; five awards for second place in each division $150 each, 3rd-$100, 4th-$75; and three awards for each district 1st-$125, 2nd-$100, 3rd-$75.

Amount of award:	$75-$1,600
Number of awards:	12
Total amount awarded:	$7,175

Contact:
American Legion, Department of Illinois
P.O. Box 2910
Bloomington, IL 61702
Web: www.illegion.org

American Legion Illinois Scholarship

Type of award: Scholarship.
Intended use: For at accredited vocational, 2-year or 4-year institution.
Eligibility: Applicant or parent must be member/participant of American Legion. Applicant must be high school senior. Applicant must be residing in Illinois.
Basis for selection: Applicant must demonstrate financial need and high academic achievement.
Application requirements: Proof of eligibility. Applications available after December 15.
Additional information: Must be a graduating high school senior and child of American Legion Post member in Illinois.

Amount of award:	$1,000
Number of awards:	20
Application deadline:	March 15
Total amount awarded:	$20,000

Contact:
American Legion
Department of Illinois
P.O. Box 2910
Bloomington, IL 61702
Phone: 309-663-0361
Web: www.illegion.org

Americanism Essay Contest Scholarship

Type of award: Scholarship.
Eligibility: Applicant must be enrolled in high school. Applicant must be residing in Illinois.
Basis for selection: Competition/talent/interest in Writing/journalism.
Application requirements: Apply at local American Legion unit.
Additional information: Applicant must write 500-word essay on selected topic. Awards: $50-$75 depending on grade level. Open to students grade 8-12 enrolled at accredited Illinois high schools.

Amount of award:	$50-$75
Application deadline:	February 2

Contact:
American Legion Illinois
P.O. Box 1426
Bloomington, IL 61702-1426
Web: www.illegion.org

American Legion Illinois Auxiliary

Ada Mucklestone Memorial Scholarship

Type of award: Scholarship.

Intended use: For undergraduate study at postsecondary institution.
Eligibility: Applicant must be high school senior. Applicant must be residing in Illinois. Applicant must be descendant of veteran; or dependent of veteran during Grenada conflict, Korean War, Lebanon conflict, Panama conflict, Persian Gulf War, WW I, WW II or Vietnam.
Application requirements: Sponsorship by local unit required. Children or grandchildren of veterans who served in eligibility dates of The American Legion.
Additional information: Prizes: First $1,200; second $1,000; several $800. Must be Illinois resident; child or grandchild of veterans. Must be senior in high school or graduate of accredited high school, but may not have attended an institution of higher learning. Applications obtained through local unit.

Amount of award:	$800-$1,200
Application deadline:	March 15

Contact:
American Legion Auxiliary Department of Illinois
P.O. Box 1426
Bloomington, IL 61702-1426
Phone: 309-663-9366

American Legion Illinois Auxiliary Special Education Teaching Scholarships

Type of award: Scholarship.
Intended use: For sophomore or junior study at 4-year institution.
Eligibility: Applicant must be U.S. citizen or permanent resident residing in Illinois.
Basis for selection: Major/career interest in education, special.
Application requirements: Proof of eligibility. Application from Local Unit. Unit sponsorship is required.
Additional information: Must be second- or third-year college student studying special education.

Amount of award:	$1,000
Application deadline:	March 15
Total amount awarded:	$1,000

Contact:
American Legion Auxiliary, Department of Illinois
P.O. Box 1426
Bloomington, IL 61702-1426
Phone: 309-663-9366

American Legion Illinois Auxiliary Student Nurse Scholarship

Type of award: Scholarship.
Intended use: For undergraduate study at 2-year or 4-year institution.
Eligibility: Applicant must be U.S. citizen or permanent resident residing in Illinois.
Basis for selection: Major/career interest in nursing.
Application requirements: Proof of eligibility. Application from Local Unit. Unit sponsorship required.

Amount of award:	$1,000
Number of awards:	1
Application deadline:	April 10
Total amount awarded:	$1,000

Contact:
American Legion Illinois Auxiliary, Department of Illinois
P.O. Box 1426
Bloomington, IL 61702-1426
Phone: 309-663-9366

Marie Sheehe Trade School Scholarship

Type of award: Scholarship.
Intended use: For undergraduate study at vocational institution. Designated institutions: Trade schools.
Eligibility: Applicant must be residing in Illinois. Applicant must be descendant of veteran; or dependent of veteran during Grenada conflict, Korean War, Lebanon conflict, Panama conflict, Persian Gulf War, WW I, WW II or Vietnam.
Application requirements: Applications from local unit. Unit sponsorship is required.
Additional information: Child or grandchild of veteran who served during the American Legion eligibility dates.

Amount of award:	$800
Number of awards:	1
Application deadline:	March 15
Total amount awarded:	$800

Contact:
American Legion Auxiliary Department of Illinois
P.O. Box 1426
Bloomington, IL 61702-1426
Phone: 309-663-9366

Mildred R. Knoles Opportunity Scholarship

Type of award: Scholarship.
Intended use: For undergraduate study at postsecondary institution.
Eligibility: Applicant must be residing in Illinois. Applicant must be veteran or descendant of veteran; or dependent of veteran during Grenada conflict, Korean War, Lebanon conflict, Panama conflict, Persian Gulf War, WW I, WW II or Vietnam.
Basis for selection: Applicant must demonstrate financial need.
Application requirements: Proof of eligibility. Applications from local unit. Unit sponsorship required.
Additional information: Awards: One $1,200; several $800. Awarded to those applicants looking to continue their education.

Amount of award:	$800-$1,200
Application deadline:	March 15

Contact:
American Legion Auxiliary, Department of Illinois
P.O. Box 1426
Bloomington, IL 61702-1426
Phone: 309-663-9366

American Legion Indiana Auxiliary

Edna M. Barcus Memorial Scholarship

Type of award: Scholarship.
Intended use: For undergraduate study at postsecondary institution. Designated institutions: Indiana postsecondary institutions.
Eligibility: Applicant must be residing in Indiana. Applicant must be dependent of veteran.
Basis for selection: Applicant must demonstrate high academic achievement.

Application requirements: Send SASE to departmental secretary.
Additional information: Applicant must attend Indiana school.

Amount of award:	$500
Application deadline:	April 1

Contact:
American Legion Auxiliary, Department of Indiana
Department Secretary
777 North Meridian Street, Room 107
Indianapolis, IN 46204
Phone: 317-630-1390
Fax: 317-630-1277

Past President's Parley Nursing Scholarship

Type of award: Scholarship.
Intended use: For undergraduate study.
Eligibility: Applicant or parent must be member/participant of American Legion Auxiliary. Applicant must be female. Applicant must be residing in Indiana.
Basis for selection: Major/career interest in nursing.
Application requirements: Send SASE to departmental secretary.
Additional information: Must be daughter of auxiliary member or deceased member; must be member of ALA, if eligible.

Amount of award:	$500
Number of awards:	1
Application deadline:	April 1
Total amount awarded:	$500

Contact:
American Legion Auxiliary, Department of Indiana
Department Secretary
777 North Meridian Street, Room 107
Indianapolis, IN 46204
Phone: 317-630-1390
Fax: 317-630-1277

American Legion Indiana, Department Headquarters

American Legion Americanism and Government Test

Type of award: Scholarship.
Eligibility: Applicant must be high school sophomore, junior or senior. Applicant must be residing in Indiana.
Additional information: Award: $500. Six state winners chosen annually (one male, one female in each grade). Test given during American Education Week in November.

Amount of award:	$500
Number of awards:	6
Total amount awarded:	$3,000

Contact:
American Legion Indiana, Department Headquarters
Americanism Office
777 North Meridian Street
Indianapolis, IN 46204
Phone: 317-630-1263

American Legion Indiana Oratorical Contest

Type of award: Scholarship.
Eligibility: Applicant must be enrolled in high school. Applicant must be residing in Indiana.
Basis for selection: Competition/talent/interest in oratory/ debate, based on breadth of knowledge, originality, application of knowledge of topic, skill in selecting examples and analogies, logic, voice, diction, style of language, and delivery.
Application requirements: Proof of eligibility. Must participate in local contests.
Additional information: Must participate in local contests and must be attending Indiana high school. State awards: 1st-$1,200, 2nd-$500, 3rd-$500, 4th-$500. Zone: four awards, $350 each.

Amount of award:	$350-$1,200
Number of awards:	8
Application deadline:	December 1
Total amount awarded:	$4,100

Contact:
American Legion Indiana, Department Headquarters
Americanism Office
777 North Meridian Street
Indianapolis, IN 46204
Phone: 317-630-1263

Frank M. McHale Memorial Scholarship

Type of award: Scholarship.
Intended use: For undergraduate study.
Eligibility: Applicant or parent must be member/participant of American Legion, Boys State. Applicant must be male, high school junior. Applicant must be residing in Indiana.
Additional information: Only Hoosier Boys Staters the year they attend are eligible. Selected by staff at Hoosier Boys State.

Number of awards:	3

Contact:
American Legion Indiana, Department Headquarters
Americanism Office
777 North Meridian Street
Indianapolis, IN 46204
Phone: 317-630-1263

American Legion Iowa

American Legion Iowa Oratorical Contest

Type of award: Scholarship.
Eligibility: Applicant must be enrolled in high school. Applicant must be U.S. citizen or permanent resident residing in Iowa.
Basis for selection: Competition/talent/interest in oratory/ debate, based on breadth of knowledge, originality, application of knowledge of topic, skill in selecting examples and analogies, logic, voice, diction, style of language, and delivery.
Application requirements: Proof of eligibility.
Additional information: Awards: 1st-$2,000; 2nd-$1,500; 3rd-$1000. Must enter Oratorical Contest at local level in September.

Amount of award:	$1,000-$2,000
Number of awards:	3
Total amount awarded:	$4,500

Contact:
American Legion Iowa
720 Lyon Street
Des Moines, IA 50309
Phone: 515-282-5068
Fax: 515-282-7583

American Legion Iowa "Boy Scout of the Year" Scholarship

Type of award: Scholarship.
Intended use: For undergraduate study at postsecondary institution.
Eligibility: Applicant or parent must be member/participant of Boy Scouts of America, Eagle Scouts. Applicant must be male. Applicant must be residing in Iowa.
Basis for selection: Applicant must demonstrate service orientation.
Application requirements: Recommendations. Eagle Scout Award.
Additional information: Tuition scholarships: first-$2,000; second-$1,500; and third-$1,000. Awarded on recommendation of Boy Scout Committee to Boy Scout who demonstrates outstanding service to religious institution, school, and community.

Amount of award:	$1,000-$2,000
Number of awards:	3
Application deadline:	February 1
Total amount awarded:	$4,500

Contact:
American Legion Iowa
720 Lyon Street
Des Moines, IA 50309
Phone: 515-282-5068
Fax: 515-282-7583

American Legion Iowa "Outstanding Citizen of Boys State" Scholarship

Type of award: Scholarship.
Intended use: For undergraduate study at postsecondary institution. Designated institutions: Eligible colleges and universities in Iowa.
Eligibility: Applicant or parent must be member/participant of American Legion, Boys State. Applicant must be male, high school senior. Applicant must be residing in Iowa.
Basis for selection: Applicant must demonstrate depth of character and patriotism.
Application requirements: Recommendations.
Additional information: Must have completed junior year in high school to attend Boys State. Awarded on recommendation of Boys State.

Amount of award:	$2,500
Number of awards:	1

Contact:
American Legion Iowa
720 Lyon Street
Des Moines, IA 50309
Phone: 515-282-5068
Fax: 515-282-7583

American Legion Iowa "Outstanding Senior Baseball Player" Scholarship

Type of award: Scholarship.
Intended use: For undergraduate study at postsecondary institution.
Eligibility: Applicant must be high school senior. Applicant must be residing in Iowa.
Basis for selection: Competition/talent/interest in athletics/sports. Applicant must demonstrate high academic achievement.
Application requirements: Recommendations.
Additional information: Must be a participant in the Iowa American Legion Senior Baseball Program. Outstanding sportsmanship, team play, and athletic ability. Awarded on recommendation of State Baseball Committee.

Amount of award:	$1,500
Number of awards:	1
Total amount awarded:	$1,500

Contact:
American Legion Iowa
720 Lyon Street
Des Moines, IA 50309
Phone: 515-282-5068
Fax: 515-282-7583

American Legion Iowa Auxiliary

American Legion Iowa Auxiliary Mary Virginia Macrea Memorial Scholarship

Type of award: Scholarship.
Intended use: For undergraduate study at 2-year or 4-year institution. Designated institutions: Eligible Iowa postsecondary institutions.
Eligibility: Applicant must be residing in Iowa. Applicant must be veteran or descendant of veteran; or dependent of veteran; or spouse of veteran or deceased veteran.
Basis for selection: Major/career interest in nursing.
Application requirements: Send SASE with application request.
Additional information: Also eligible: parents, grandchildren, great-grandchildren of veterans.

Amount of award:	$400
Number of awards:	1
Application deadline:	June 1
Total amount awarded:	$400

Contact:
American Legion Auxiliary, Department of Iowa
720 Lyon Street
Des Moines, IA 50309
Phone: 515-282-7987
Fax: 515-282-7583

Department of Iowa Scholarships

Type of award: Scholarship.
Intended use: For undergraduate study at postsecondary institution. Designated institutions: Eligible Iowa postsecondary institutions.

Eligibility: Applicant must be residing in Iowa. Applicant must be veteran or descendant of veteran; or dependent of veteran; or spouse of veteran or deceased veteran during Grenada conflict, Korean War, Lebanon conflict, Panama conflict, Persian Gulf War, WW I, WW II or Vietnam.
Application requirements: Send SASE with application request.
Additional information: For veteran.

Amount of award:	$300
Number of awards:	10
Application deadline:	June 1
Total amount awarded:	$3,000

Contact:
American Legion Auxiliary, Department of Iowa
720 Lyon Street
Des Moines, IA 50309
Phone: 515-282-7987
Fax: 515-282-7583

Harriet Hoffman Memorial Scholarship

Type of award: Scholarship.
Intended use: For undergraduate study at postsecondary institution. Designated institutions: Eligible Iowa postsecondary institutions.
Eligibility: Applicant must be residing in Iowa. Applicant must be veteran or descendant of veteran; or dependent of veteran or deceased veteran; or spouse of veteran or deceased veteran.
Basis for selection: Major/career interest in education or education, teacher.
Application requirements: Send SASE with application request.
Additional information: Teacher training scholarship. Also eligible: parent, grandchild, great-grandchild of veteran. Preference given to descendant of disabled or deceased veteran.

Amount of award:	$400
Number of awards:	1
Application deadline:	June 1
Total amount awarded:	$400

Contact:
American Legion Auxiliary, Department of Iowa
720 Lyon Street
Des Moines, IA 50309
Phone: 515-282-7987
Fax: 515-282-7583

Past President's Scholarship

Type of award: Scholarship.
Intended use: For at postsecondary institution. Designated institutions: Iowa postsecondary institutions.
Eligibility: Applicant must be residing in Iowa. Applicant must be veteran or descendant of veteran; or dependent of veteran or deceased veteran; or spouse of veteran or deceased veteran.
Application requirements: Proof of eligibility. Send SASE.
Additional information: Amount of award varies.

Application deadline:	June 1

Contact:
American Legion Iowa Auxiliary
720 Lyon Street
Des Moines, IA 50309
Phone: 515-282-7987
Fax: 515-282-7583

American Legion Kansas

Albert M. Lappin Scholarship

Type of award: Scholarship.
Intended use: For freshman or sophomore study at accredited vocational, 2-year or 4-year institution. Designated institutions: Eligible colleges, universities, and trade schools in Kansas.
Eligibility: Applicant or parent must be member/participant of American Legion. Applicant must be high school senior. Applicant must be residing in Kansas.
Additional information: Must be child of Legion or Auxiliary member.

Amount of award:	$1,000
Number of awards:	1
Application deadline:	February 15
Total amount awarded:	$1,000

Contact:
American Legion Kansas
1314 Southwest Topeka Boulevard
Topeka, KS 66612-1886
Phone: 785-232-9315

American Legion Music Scholarship

Type of award: Scholarship.
Intended use: For freshman or sophomore study at 2-year or 4-year institution. Designated institutions: Eligible Kansas colleges and universities.
Eligibility: Applicant must be high school senior. Applicant must be residing in Kansas.
Basis for selection: Major/career interest in music.
Application requirements: Proof of eligibility.

Amount of award:	$1,000
Number of awards:	1
Application deadline:	February 15
Total amount awarded:	$1,000

Contact:
American Legion Kansas
1314 Southwest Topeka Boulevard
Topeka, KS 66612-1886
Phone: 785-232-9315

Charles and Annette Hill Scholarship

Type of award: Scholarship.
Intended use: For at postsecondary institution.
Eligibility: Applicant or parent must be member/participant of American Legion. Applicant must be residing in Kansas.
Basis for selection: Major/career interest in science, general; engineering or business/management/administration.
Application requirements: Must have 3.0 GPA.
Additional information: Preference given to applicants with interest in science, engineering, or business administration.

Amount of award:	$1,000
Application deadline:	February 15

Contact:
American Legion Kansas
1314 SW Topeka Blvd.
Topeka, KS 66612-1886
Phone: 785-232-9315

Dr. Click Cowger Scholarship

Type of award: Scholarship.

Intended use: For freshman or sophomore study at vocational, 2-year or 4-year institution. Designated institutions: Eligible Kansas colleges, universities, and trade schools.
Eligibility: Applicant must be high school senior. Applicant must be residing in Kansas.
Basis for selection: Competition/talent/interest in athletics/sports.
Application requirements: Proof of eligibility.
Additional information: Must play or have played Kansas American Legion Baseball. College-level freshmen and sophomores also eligible.

Amount of award:	$500
Number of awards:	1
Application deadline:	July 15
Total amount awarded:	$500

Contact:
American Legion Kansas
1314 Southwest Topeka Boulevard
Topeka, KS 66612-1886
Phone: 785-232-9315

Hugh A. Smith Scholarship

Type of award: Scholarship.
Intended use: For freshman or sophomore study at vocational, 2-year or 4-year institution. Designated institutions: Eligible Kansas colleges, universities, and trade schools.
Eligibility: Applicant or parent must be member/participant of American Legion. Applicant must be high school senior. Applicant must be residing in Kansas.
Additional information: Applicant must be child of Kansas Legion or Auxiliary member.

Amount of award:	$500
Number of awards:	1
Application deadline:	February 15
Total amount awarded:	$500

Contact:
American Legion Kansas
1314 Southwest Topeka Boulevard
Topeka, KS 66612-1886
Phone: 785-232-9315

John and Geraldine Hobble Licensed Practical Nursing Scholarship

Type of award: Scholarship.
Intended use: For undergraduate study at accredited 2-year or 4-year institution. Designated institutions: Kansas accredited schools that award LPN diploma.
Eligibility: Applicant must be at least 18. Applicant must be residing in Kansas.
Basis for selection: Major/career interest in nursing.
Application requirements: Proof of eligibility.
Additional information: Applicant must be age 18 prior to taking Kansas State Board Examination.

Amount of award:	$300
Number of awards:	1
Application deadline:	February 15
Total amount awarded:	$300

Contact:
American Legion Kansas
1314 Southwest Topeka Boulevard
Topeka, KS 66612-1886
Phone: 785-232-9315

Legion Oratorical Contest

Type of award: Scholarship.
Intended use: For undergraduate study at postsecondary institution.
Eligibility: Applicant must be enrolled in high school. Applicant must be residing in Kansas.
Basis for selection: Competition/talent/interest in oratory/debate, based on breadth of knowledge, originality, application of knowledge of topic, skill in selecting examples and analogies, logic, voice, diction, style of language, and delivery.
Additional information: Awards: $1,500 provided by National Organization, 2nd-$500, 3rd-$250, 4th-$150. Additional awards: $1,500 provided by Emporia State University Foundation, 2nd-$500, 3rd-$250, 4th-$150 (renewable up to 4 years; must qualify for admission and attend Emporia State University). Tabor College will provide scholarship equal to 25% of previous year's tuition, runners-up at 20% (renewable up to 4 years; must qualify for admission and attend Tabor College).

Amount of award:	$150-$1,500
Number of awards:	4
Total amount awarded:	$2,400

Contact:
American Legion Kansas
1314 Southwest Topeka Boulevard
Topeka, KS 66612-1886
Phone: 785-232-9315

Rosedale Post 346 Scholarship

Type of award: Scholarship.
Intended use: For freshman or sophomore study at postsecondary institution. Designated institutions: Approved junior college, college, university, or trade school.
Eligibility: Applicant or parent must be member/participant of American Legion. Applicant must be high school senior. Applicant must be residing in Kansas.
Additional information: For children of Kansas Legion or Auxiliary members. Scholarship must be used at approved institutions.

Amount of award:	$1,500
Number of awards:	2
Application deadline:	February 15
Total amount awarded:	$3,000

Contact:
American Legion Kansas
1314 SW Topeka Blvd.
Topeka, KS 66612-1886
Phone: 785-232-9315

Ted and Nora Anderson Scholarship

Type of award: Scholarship.
Intended use: For freshman or sophomore study at vocational, 2-year or 4-year institution. Designated institutions: Eligible colleges, universities, and trade schools in Kansas.
Eligibility: Applicant or parent must be member/participant of American Legion. Applicant must be high school senior. Applicant must be residing in Kansas. Applicant must be dependent of veteran.
Application requirements: Proof of eligibility.
Additional information: Applicant must be child of Kansas Legion or Auxiliary member.

Amount of award:	$500
Number of awards:	4
Application deadline:	February 15
Total amount awarded:	$2,000

Contact:
American Legion Kansas
1314 Southwest Topeka Boulevard
Topeka, KS 66612-1886
Phone: 785-232-9315

American Legion Kansas Auxiliary

American Legion Kansas Auxiliary Department Scholarships

Type of award: Scholarship.
Intended use: For undergraduate study. Designated institutions: Kansas postsecondary institutions.
Eligibility: Applicant must be residing in Kansas. Applicant must be dependent of veteran; or spouse of veteran or deceased veteran.
Additional information: For veterans' children, spouses, or unremarried widows entering college for the first time. Eight $500 scholarships (payable in two years).

Amount of award:	$500
Number of awards:	8
Application deadline:	April 1
Total amount awarded:	$4,000

Contact:
American Legion Kansas Auxiliary
1314 SW Topeka Blvd.
Topeka, KS 66612-1886
Phone: 785-232-1396

American Legion of Kansas General Scholarship

Type of award: Scholarship.
Intended use: For freshman study at vocational, 2-year or 4-year institution. Designated institutions: Eligible Kansas institutions.
Eligibility: Applicant must be residing in Kansas. Applicant must be dependent of veteran; or spouse of veteran or deceased veteran during Grenada conflict, Korean War, Lebanon conflict, Panama conflict, Persian Gulf War, WW I, WW II or Vietnam.
Additional information: $500 total; $250 per year for two years. Applicants must be entering college for the first time. Spouses of deceased veterans must be unmarried.

Amount of award:	$500
Number of awards:	8
Application deadline:	April 1
Total amount awarded:	$4,000

Contact:
American Legion Kansas Auxiliary
Department Secretary
314 SW Topeka Boulevard
Topeka, KS 66612-1886
Phone: 785-232-1396

American Legion Kentucky

American Legion Department Oratorical Awards

Type of award: Scholarship.
Eligibility: Applicant must be enrolled in high school. Applicant must be residing in Kentucky.
Basis for selection: Competition/talent/interest in Oratory/debate, based on breadth of knowledge, originality, application of knowledge of topic, skill in selecting examples and analogies, logic, voice, diction, style of language and delivery.
Application requirements: Kentucky Department Oratorical Contest participants.
Additional information: Awards: 1st-$1,000; 2nd-$800; 3rd-$600; plus 11-$100 for district winners.

Amount of award:	$100-$1,000
Number of awards:	14
Total amount awarded:	$3,500

Contact:
American Legion Kentucky, Department Headquarters
P.O. Box 2123
Louisville, KY 40201
Phone: 502-587-1414
Fax: 502-587-6356

American Legion Kentucky Auxiliary

American Legion Kentucky Auxiliary Mary Barrett Marshall Scholarship

Type of award: Scholarship.
Intended use: For undergraduate study at vocational, 2-year or 4-year institution. Designated institutions: Eligible postsecondary institutions in Kentucky.
Eligibility: Applicant must be female. Applicant must be residing in Kentucky. Applicant must be descendant of veteran; or dependent of veteran; or spouse of veteran or deceased veteran during Grenada conflict, Korean War, Lebanon conflict, Panama conflict, Persian Gulf War, WW I, WW II or Vietnam.
Application requirements: Proof of eligibility. Wife, sister, widow, or descendant of veteran eligible for membership in American Legion.
Additional information: Include SASE with request for application.

Amount of award:	$500
Number of awards:	1
Application deadline:	April 1
Total amount awarded:	$500

Contact:
American Legion Auxiliary, Department of Kentucky
Chairman Velma Greenleaf
1448 Leafdale Road
Hodgenville, KY 42748-9379
Phone: 720-358-3341

Laura Blackburn Memorial Scholarship

Type of award: Scholarship.
Intended use: For undergraduate study.
Eligibility: Applicant must be high school senior. Applicant must be residing in Kentucky. Applicant must be descendant of veteran; or dependent of veteran during Grenada conflict, Korean War, Lebanon conflict, Panama conflict, Persian Gulf War, WW I, WW II or Vietnam.
Application requirements: Proof of eligibility. Child, grandchild, or great grandchild of veteran who served in Armed Forces during eligibility dates for membership in the American Legion.

Amount of award:	$1,000
Number of awards:	1
Application deadline:	March 31
Total amount awarded:	$1,000

Contact:
American Legion Auxiliary, Department of Kentucky
attn: Michelle Elmore
1166 Blanton Road
New Haven, KY 40051

American Legion Maine

Children and Youth Scholarship

Type of award: Scholarship.
Intended use: For undergraduate study at postsecondary institution.
Eligibility: Applicant or parent must be member/participant of American Legion. Applicant must be high school senior. Applicant must be residing in Maine.
Basis for selection: Applicant must demonstrate financial need, high academic achievement and depth of character.
Application requirements: Students must be ranked in upper half of class.
Additional information: High school seniors, college students and veterans eligible. Parent must be Maine American Legion member.

Amount of award:	$500
Number of awards:	7
Number of applicants:	300
Application deadline:	April 13
Total amount awarded:	$3,500

Contact:
American Legion Maine
Department Adjutant, State Headquarters
P.O. Box 900
Waterville, ME 04903-0900
Phone: 207-873-3229
Fax: 207-872-0501

Daniel E. Lambert Memorial Scholarship

Type of award: Scholarship.
Intended use: For undergraduate study at vocational, 2-year or 4-year institution.
Eligibility: Applicant must be high school senior. Applicant must be U.S. citizen residing in Maine. Applicant must be dependent of veteran.

Basis for selection: Applicant must demonstrate financial need and depth of character.

    Number of awards: 1
    Application deadline: May 1

Contact:
American Legion Maine
Department Adjutant, State Headquarters
P.O. Box 900
Waterville, ME 04903-0900
Phone: 207-873-3229
Fax: 207-872-0501

James V. Day Scholarship

Type of award: Scholarship.
Intended use: For freshman study at vocational, 2-year or 4-year institution.
Eligibility: Applicant or parent must be member/participant of American Legion. Applicant must be high school senior. Applicant must be residing in Maine.
Basis for selection: Applicant must demonstrate financial need, high academic achievement and depth of character.
Application requirements: Must be in top half of graduating class.
Additional information: Parent must be Maine American Legion member.

    Amount of award: $500
    Number of awards: 1
    Application deadline: May 1
    Total amount awarded: $500

Contact:
American Legion Maine
Department Adjutant, State Headquarters
P.O. Box 900
Waterville, ME 04903-0900
Phone: 207-873-3229
Fax: 207-872-0501

American Legion Maine Auxiliary

American Legion Maine Auxiliary General Scholarship

Type of award: Scholarship.
Intended use: For undergraduate study at vocational, 2-year or 4-year institution.
Eligibility: Applicant must be high school senior. Applicant must be residing in Maine. Applicant must be dependent of veteran.
Basis for selection: Applicant must demonstrate financial need.
Additional information: Only residents of Maine qualify; out-of-state applicants not considered. Send SASE with application request.

    Amount of award: $300
    Number of awards: 2
    Application deadline: April 15
    Total amount awarded: $600

Contact:
American Legion Auxiliary, Department of Maine
Department Secretary
P.O. Box 887
Bucksport, ME 04416-0887

President's Parley Nursing Scholarship

Type of award: Scholarship.
Intended use: For undergraduate study.
Eligibility: Applicant must be residing in Maine. Applicant must be descendant of veteran; or dependent of veteran during WW I or WW II.
Basis for selection: Major/career interest in nursing.
Application requirements: Proof of eligibility.
Additional information: For training in accredited nursing school. Must be graduate of accredited high school. Out-of-state applicants not considered.

    Amount of award: $300
    Number of awards: 1
    Application deadline: April 15
    Total amount awarded: $300

Contact:
American Legion Auxiliary, Department of Maine
Department Secretary
P.O. Box 887
Bucksport, ME 04416-0887

American Legion Maryland

Adler Science/Math Scholarship

Type of award: Scholarship.
Intended use: For undergraduate study at postsecondary institution.
Eligibility: Applicant must be at least 16, no older than 19. Applicant must be residing in Maryland. Applicant must be dependent of veteran.
Basis for selection: Major/career interest in science, general or mathematics.
Application requirements: Transcript.

    Amount of award: $500
    Number of awards: 1
    Application deadline: March 31
    Total amount awarded: $500

Contact:
American Legion Maryland
Department Adjutant
101 North Gay Street
Baltimore, MD 21202
Phone: 410-752-3104
Fax: 410-752-3822
Web: www.mdlegion.org

American Legion Maryland Boys State Scholarship

Type of award: Scholarship.
Intended use: For undergraduate study at postsecondary institution.
Eligibility: Applicant or parent must be member/participant of American Legion, Boys State. Applicant must be male, at least 16, no older than 19. Applicant must be residing in Maryland. Applicant must be dependent of veteran.
Application requirements: Transcript.
Additional information: Applicant must have attended Boys State program.

Amount of award: $500
Number of awards: 5
Application deadline: May 1
Total amount awarded: $2,500
Contact:
American Legion Maryland
Department Adjutant
101 North Gay Street
Baltimore, MD 21202-1405
Phone: 410-752-3104
Fax: 410-752-3822
Web: www.mdlegion.org

American Legion Maryland General Scholarship

Type of award: Scholarship.
Intended use: For undergraduate study at postsecondary institution.
Eligibility: Applicant must be at least 16, no older than 19. Applicant must be residing in Maryland. Applicant must be dependent of veteran.
Application requirements: Transcript. Applicant must not have reached 20th birthday by January 1 of calendar year application is filed.

Amount of award: $500
Number of awards: 11
Application deadline: March 31
Contact:
American Legion Maryland
Department Adjutant
101 North Gay Street
Baltimore, MD 21202-1405
Phone: 410-752-3104
Fax: 410-752-3822
Web: www.mdlegion.org

American Legion Maryland Oratorical Contest

Type of award: Scholarship.
Intended use: For undergraduate study at postsecondary institution.
Eligibility: Applicant must be at least 16, no older than 19. Applicant must be residing in Maryland.
Basis for selection: Competition/talent/interest in oratory/debate, based on breadth of knowledge, originality, application of knowledge of topic, skill in selecting examples and analogies, logic, voice, diction, style of language and delivery.
Application requirements: Proof of eligibility. Apply to nearest American Legion post.
Additional information: Awards: first-$2,500; second-$1,000; third through seventh-$500 each. Must be an American Legion Oratorical Contest department winner.

Amount of award: $500-$2,500
Number of awards: 7
Application deadline: October 1
Total amount awarded: $6,000
Contact:
Local American Legion Post
Phone: 410-752-3104
Fax: 410-752-3822
Web: www.mdlegion.org

American Legion Maryland Auxiliary

American Legion Maryland Auxiliary Nursing Scholarship

Type of award: Scholarship.
Intended use: For undergraduate study at 2-year or 4-year institution.
Eligibility: Applicant must be female, at least 16, no older than 22. Applicant must be residing in Maryland.
Basis for selection: Major/career interest in nursing. Applicant must demonstrate financial need.
Application requirements: Recommendations.
Additional information: For RN degree only. Must be daughter/step-daughter, granddaughter/step-granddaughter, great-granddaughter/step-great-granddaughter of ex-servicewoman or ex-serviceman. Submit application for Department's Past President's Parley Scholarship.

Amount of award: $2,000
Number of awards: 1
Application deadline: May 1
Total amount awarded: $2,000
Contact:
American Legion Maryland Auxiliary
Chairman, Past President's Parley Fund
1589 Sulphur Spring Road, Suite 105
Baltimore, MD 21227
Phone: 410-242-9519
Fax: 410-242-9553

American Legion Maryland Auxiliary Scholarship

Type of award: Scholarship.
Intended use: For undergraduate study at 2-year or 4-year institution. Designated institutions: Maryland college or university.
Eligibility: Applicant must be female, high school senior. Applicant must be residing in Maryland. Applicant must be dependent of veteran.
Basis for selection: Major/career interest in arts, general; science, general; business; public administration/service or education, teacher.
Additional information: Additional field of study considered: medical sciences other than nursing.

Amount of award: $2,000
Number of awards: 1
Application deadline: May 1
Total amount awarded: $2,000
Contact:
American Legion Auxiliary, Department of Maryland
Department Secretary
1589 Sulphur Spring Road, Suite 105
Baltimore, MD 21227
Phone: 410-242-9519
Fax: 410-242-9553

American Legion Massachusetts

American Legion Massachusetts General and Nursing Scholarships

Type of award: Scholarship.
Intended use: For freshman study at 2-year or 4-year institution.
Eligibility: Applicant or parent must be member/participant of American Legion. Applicant must be residing in Massachusetts. Applicant must be descendant of veteran; or dependent of veteran.
Application requirements: Parent or grandparent must be member in good standing of Department of Massachusetts American Legion.
Additional information: General Scholarships: eight-$1,000, ten-$500. Nursing Scholarship: one-$1,000.

Amount of award:	$500-$1,000
Number of awards:	19
Application deadline:	April 1
Total amount awarded:	$14,000

Contact:
American Legion Massachusetts
Department Scholarship Chair
546-2 State House
Boston, MA 02133-1044

American Legion Massachusetts Past County Commander's Scholarship

Type of award: Scholarship.
Intended use: For freshman study at 2-year or 4-year institution.
Eligibility: Applicant must be residing in Massachusetts. Applicant must be descendant of veteran; or dependent of veteran.
Application requirements: Apply at any American Legion post in Hampden County, Massachusetts.
Additional information: One $500 award; additional $250 awards contingent on availability of funds. Child or grandchild of paid-up member of Hampden County American Legion Post. May be adopted or under legal guardianship.

Amount of award:	$250-$500
Application deadline:	April 15

Contact:
American Legion Massachusetts W.J. Craven, Chairman
46 Brickett Street
Springfield, MA 01119
Phone: 413-782-0918

Department of Massachusetts Oratorical Contest

Type of award: Scholarship.
Intended use: For undergraduate study.
Eligibility: Applicant must be no older than 19. Applicant must be residing in Massachusetts.
Basis for selection: Competition/talent/interest in oratory/debate, based on breadth of knowledge, originality, application of knowledge of topic, skill selecting examples and analogies, logic, voice, diction, style of language and delivery.
Application requirements: Proof of eligibility.
Additional information: Awards: 1st-$1,000; 2nd-$800; 3rd-$700; 4th-$600.

Amount of award:	$600-$1,000
Number of awards:	4
Application deadline:	December 15
Total amount awarded:	$3,100

Contact:
American Legion Massachusetts
Department Oratorical Chair
State House, Room 546-2
Boston, MA 02133-1044

Edward & Helen DelPozzo Family Scholarship

Type of award: Scholarship.
Intended use: For freshman study.
Eligibility: Applicant must be residing in Massachusetts.
Additional information: For child or grandchild of member in good standing of AL Department of Massachusetts. Number of awards varies.

Amount of award:	$1,000
Application deadline:	April 1

Contact:
American Legion Massachusetts, Department Scholarship Chairman
546-2 State House
Boston, MA 02133-1044

American Legion Massachusetts Auxiliary

American Legion Massachusetts Auxiliary Past President's Parley Scholarship

Type of award: Scholarship.
Intended use: For undergraduate study.
Eligibility: Applicant must be residing in Massachusetts. Applicant must be dependent of veteran or deceased veteran.
Basis for selection: Major/career interest in nursing.
Additional information: Child of living or deceased veteran not eligible for Federal or Commonwealth scholarships.

Amount of award:	$200
Number of awards:	1
Application deadline:	April 1
Total amount awarded:	$200

Contact:
American Legion Massachusetts Auxiliary
Department Secretary
24 State House, Room 546-2
Boston, MA 02133-1044

American Legion Massachusetts Auxiliary Scholarship

Type of award: Scholarship.
Intended use: For undergraduate study at vocational, 2-year or 4-year institution.
Eligibility: Applicant must be at least 16, no older than 22. Applicant must be residing in Massachusetts. Applicant must be descendant of veteran; or dependent of veteran, disabled veteran

or deceased veteran during Grenada conflict, Korean War, Lebanon conflict, Panama conflict, Persian Gulf War, WW I, WW II or Vietnam.
Additional information: Awards: one-$500 and ten-$100. Must be related to living or deceased veteran as designated by American Legion eligibility.

Amount of award:	$100-$500
Number of awards:	11
Application deadline:	April 1
Total amount awarded:	$1,500

Contact:
American Legion Auxiliary, Department of Massachusetts
Department Secretary
24 State House, Room 546-2
Boston, MA 02133-1044

American Legion Michigan

American Legion Michigan Guy M. Wilson Scholarship

Type of award: Scholarship.
Intended use: For undergraduate study at 2-year or 4-year institution. Designated institutions: Michigan junior colleges, colleges and universities.
Eligibility: Applicant must be residing in Michigan.
Basis for selection: Applicant must demonstrate financial need and high academic achievement.
Application requirements: Transcript. Copy of living or deceased veteran's honorable discharge (DD-214) to be attached to application. Also include copy of most recently filed federal tax form. Application should be filed at local American Legion post.
Additional information: Son or daughter of a veteran attending Michigan high school. Must plan to attend a Michigan postsecondary institution. Minimum 2.5 GPA. Number of awards varies.

Amount of award:	$500
Application deadline:	January 1

Contact:
Deanna Clark American Legion Michigan
212 North Verlinden Avenue
Lansing, MI 48915
Phone: 517-371-4720 x25
Fax: 517-371-2401
Web: www.michiganlegion.org

American Legion Michigan Oratorical Contest

Type of award: Scholarship.
Intended use: For undergraduate study at postsecondary institution.
Eligibility: Applicant must be high school freshman, sophomore, junior or senior. Applicant must be U.S. citizen residing in Michigan.
Basis for selection: Competition/talent/interest in oratory/debate, based on ability to deliver an 8- to 10-minute speech on the United States Constitution.
Application requirements: Finalists in Zone Oratorical Contest.
Additional information: Awards: $1,000, $800, $600.

Amount of award:	$600-$1,000
Number of awards:	3
Application deadline:	January 31
Total amount awarded:	$2,400

Contact:
Deanna Clark American Legion Michigan
212 North Verlinden Avenue
Lansing, MI 48915
Phone: 517-371-4720 x25
Fax: 517-371-2401
Web: www.michiganlegion.org

William D. Brewer/Jewell W. Brewer Scholarship Trusts

Type of award: Scholarship.
Intended use: For undergraduate study at 2-year or 4-year institution. Designated institutions: Michigan colleges or universities.
Eligibility: Applicant must be residing in Michigan.
Basis for selection: Applicant must demonstrate financial need and high academic achievement.
Application requirements: Transcript. Copy of deceased or living veteran's honorable discharge (DD-214). Also include copy of most recently filed federal tax form.
Additional information: Son or daughter of a veteran attending Michigan high school. Must be planning to attend a Michigan postsecondary institution. Minimum 2.5 GPA. Applications to be filed at local American Legion post. Number of awards varies.

Amount of award:	$500
Application deadline:	January 1

Contact:
Deanna Clark American Legion Michigan
212 North Verlinden Avenue
Lansing, MI 48915
Phone: 517-371-4720 ext. 25
Fax: 517-371-2401
Web: www.michiganlegion.org

American Legion Michigan Auxiliary

American Legion Michigan Auxiliary Memorial Scholarship

Type of award: Scholarship, renewable.
Intended use: For undergraduate study at postsecondary institution. Designated institutions: Michigan educational institutions.
Eligibility: Applicant must be female, at least 16, no older than 21. Applicant must be residing in Michigan.
Basis for selection: Applicant must demonstrate financial need and high academic achievement.
Application requirements: Recommendations, transcript, proof of eligibility. Financial information.
Additional information: Applicant may be daughter, granddaughter, or great-granddaughter of honorably discharged or deceased veteran who served during eligible dates for membership in The American Legion. Can apply for renewal for second year. Visit Website for details and application.

Amount of award:	$500
Application deadline:	March 15

Contact:
Michigan American Legion Auxiliary
212 North Verlinden Avenue
Lansing, MI 48915
Phone: 517-371-4720 x21
Fax: 517-371-2401
Web: www.michalaux.org

American Legion Michigan Auxiliary National President's Scholarship

Type of award: Scholarship.
Intended use: For undergraduate study at postsecondary institution. Designated institutions: Michigan educational institutions.
Eligibility: Applicant must be high school senior. Applicant must be residing in Michigan. Applicant must be dependent of veteran during Grenada conflict, Korean War, Middle East War, Lebanon conflict, Panama conflict, Persian Gulf War, WW I, WW II or Vietnam.
Additional information: Applicant must be daughter/stepdaughter or son/stepson of veteran who served in the Armed Forces during eligibility dates for membership in American Legion.

Amount of award:	$1,000-$2,500
Number of awards:	15
Application deadline:	March 10
Total amount awarded:	$27,500

Contact:
Michigan American Legion Auxiliary
212 North Verlinden Avenue
Lansing, MI 48915
Phone: 517-371-4720 x21
Fax: 517-371-2401
Web: www.michalaux.org

American Legion Michigan Auxiliary Scholarship for Medical Careers

Type of award: Scholarship.
Intended use: For freshman study at postsecondary institution. Designated institutions: Michigan educational institutions.
Eligibility: Applicant must be residing in Michigan.
Basis for selection: Major/career interest in nursing; physical therapy or respiratory therapy. Applicant must demonstrate financial need and high academic achievement.
Application requirements: Transcript, proof of eligibility. Must be in top 25% of class. Applications available after November 15. Visit Website for details and application.
Additional information: Applicant must be daughter, granddaughter, great-granddaughter, son, wife, or widow of honorably discharged or deceased veteran who served during eligible dates for membership in The American Legion. Must be Michigan resident for one year preceding award.

Amount of award:	$500
Application deadline:	March 15

Contact:
Michigan American Legion Auxiliary
212 North Verlinden Avenue
Lansing, MI 48915
Phone: 517-371-4720 x21
Fax: 517-371-2401
Web: www.michalaux.org

American Legion Minnesota

American Legion Minnesota Legionnaire Insurance Trust Scholarship

Type of award: Scholarship.
Intended use: For undergraduate study at postsecondary institution. Designated institutions: Minnesota institution or instutitions in neighboring states with reciprocating agreements.
Eligibility: Applicant or parent must be member/participant of American Legion. Applicant must be U.S. citizen residing in Minnesota. Applicant must be descendant of veteran; or dependent of veteran. Also eligible: grandchildren, adopted children, stepchildren of American Legion member or children, adopted children, grandchildren, stepchildren of American Legion Auxiliary member.
Basis for selection: Applicant must demonstrate high academic achievement, depth of character and patriotism.
Application requirements: Proof of eligibility, nomination by Minnesota American Legion post.
Additional information: Applicant must be child/grandchild of veteran.

Amount of award:	$500
Number of awards:	3
Application deadline:	April 1
Total amount awarded:	$1,500

Contact:
American Legion Minnesota
Education Committee
20 West 12th Street, Room 300A
St. Paul, MN 55155-2000
Phone: 651-291-1800 or 866-259-9163
Web: www.mnlegion.org

American Legion Minnesota Memorial Scholarship

Type of award: Scholarship.
Intended use: For undergraduate study at postsecondary institution. Designated institutions: Minnesota institution or institution in neighboring state with reciprocating agreement.
Eligibility: Applicant or parent must be member/participant of American Legion. Applicant must be U.S. citizen residing in Minnesota.
Basis for selection: Applicant must demonstrate financial need.
Additional information: Child or grandchild of American Legion or American Legion Auxiliary member.

Amount of award:	$500
Number of awards:	6
Application deadline:	April 1
Total amount awarded:	$3,000

Contact:
American Legion Minnesota
Education Committee
20 West 12th Street, Room 300A
St. Paul, MN 55155-2000
Phone: 612-291-1800 or 866-259-9163
Web: www.mnlegion.org

American Legion Minnesota Oratorical Contest

Type of award: Scholarship.
Intended use: For at postsecondary institution.
Eligibility: Applicant must be enrolled in high school. Applicant must be U.S. citizen residing in Minnesota.
Basis for selection: Competition/talent/interest in oratory/debate, based on breadth of knowledge, originality, application of knowledge of topic, skill in selecting examples and analogies, logic, voice, diction, style of language and delivery.
Application requirements: First, second, third, and fourth place winners from Department of Minnesota Annual Oratorical Contest.
Additional information: Awards: $1,200, $900, $700, $500.

Amount of award:	$500-$1,200
Number of awards:	4
Application deadline:	December 15
Total amount awarded:	$3,300

Contact:
The American Legion
Education Committee
20 West 12th Street, Room 300A
St. Paul, MN 55155-2000
Phone: 651-291-1800 or 866-259-9163
Web: www.mnlegion.org

American Legion Minnesota Auxiliary

American Legion Minnesota Auxiliary Department Scholarship

Type of award: Scholarship.
Intended use: For undergraduate study at postsecondary institution. Designated institutions: Minnesota postsecondary institutions.
Eligibility: Applicant or parent must be member/participant of American Legion Auxiliary. Applicant must be U.S. citizen residing in Minnesota. Applicant must be descendant of veteran; or dependent of veteran.
Additional information: Child or grandchild of veteran. Must be Minnesota resident or member of AL, ALA, or SAL, Department of Minnesota.

Amount of award:	$750
Number of awards:	7
Application deadline:	March 15
Total amount awarded:	$5,250

Contact:
American Legion Auxiliary, Department of Minnesota
State Veterans Service Building
20 W 12th Street, Room 314
St. Paul, MN 55155-2069
Phone: 651-224-7634
Fax: 651-224-5243

American Legion Minnesota Auxiliary Past President's Parley Health Care Scholarship

Type of award: Scholarship.

Intended use: For undergraduate study at postsecondary institution. Designated institutions: Minnesota postsecondary institutions.
Eligibility: Applicant or parent must be member/participant of American Legion Auxiliary. Applicant must be U.S. citizen residing in Minnesota.
Basis for selection: Major/career interest in nursing; health-related professions; health sciences; medical assistant or midwifery.
Additional information: Up to three awards given. Applicable toward any educational phase of health care field.

Amount of award:	$750
Number of awards:	3
Application deadline:	March 15
Total amount awarded:	$2,250

Contact:
American Legion Auxiliary, Department of Minnesota
State Veterans Service Building
20 W. 12th Street, Room 314
St. Paul, MN 55155-2069
Phone: 651-224-7634
Fax: 651-224-5243

American Legion Mississippi Auxiliary

American Legion Mississippi Auxiliary Scholarship

Type of award: Scholarship.
Intended use: For freshman study at postsecondary institution. Designated institutions: Mississippi postsecondary institutions.
Eligibility: Applicant must be high school senior. Applicant must be residing in Mississippi. Applicant must be descendant of veteran; or dependent of veteran during Korean War, Lebanon conflict, Panama conflict, Persian Gulf War, WW I, WW II or Vietnam.
Basis for selection: Applicant must demonstrate financial need.

Amount of award:	$500
Number of awards:	1
Application deadline:	March 1
Total amount awarded:	$500

Contact:
American Legion Mississippi Auxiliary
Department Headquarters
P.O. Box 1382
Jackson, MS 39215-1382
Phone: 601-353-3681
Fax: 601-353-3682

American Legion Mississippi Auxiliary Scholarship

Type of award: Scholarship.
Intended use: For at postsecondary institution.
Eligibility: Applicant must be high school senior. Applicant must be residing in Mississippi. Applicant must be dependent of veteran during Korean War, Lebanon conflict, Panama conflict, Persian Gulf War, WW I, WW II or Vietnam.
Basis for selection: Applicant must demonstrate financial need.

Additional information: Applicant must be in senior year or graduate of accredited Mississippi high school.

Amount of award:	$500
Number of awards:	1
Application deadline:	March 1
Total amount awarded:	$500

Contact:
American Legion Mississippi Auxiliary, Department Headquarters
P.O. Box 1382
Jackson, MS 39215-1382
Phone: 601-353-3681
Fax: 601-353-3682

American Legion Missouri

American Legion Missouri Charles L. Bacon Memorial Scholarship

Type of award: Scholarship.
Intended use: For full-time undergraduate study at accredited 2-year or 4-year institution.
Eligibility: Applicant or parent must be member/participant of American Legion. Applicant must be single, no older than 21. Applicant must be U.S. citizen residing in Missouri.
Additional information: Applicants must be current member of American Legion, American Legion Auxiliary or the Sons of the American Legion, or descendent of any member.

Amount of award:	$500
Number of awards:	1
Total amount awarded:	$500

Contact:
American Legion Missouri
P.O. Box 179
Jefferson City, MO 65102
Phone: 573-893-2353
Fax: 573-893-2980
Web: www.missourilegion.org

American Legion Missouri Erman W. Taylor Memorial Scholarship

Type of award: Scholarship.
Intended use: For full-time undergraduate study at accredited 2-year or 4-year institution.
Eligibility: Applicant must be U.S. citizen residing in Missouri. Applicant must be descendant of veteran; or dependent of veteran. Must be dependent of veteran who served 90 or more days of active duty in the Armed Forces and have an honorable discharge.
Application requirements: Essay, proof of eligibility. Copy of discharge certificate for veteran parent, grandparent; essay of 500 words or less on "Which President Was the Greatest and Why." Also send evaluation form.

Amount of award:	$250
Number of awards:	1
Total amount awarded:	$250

Contact:
American Legion Missouri
P.O. Box 179
Jefferson City, MO 65102
Phone: 573-893-2353
Fax: 573-893-2980
Web: www.missourilegion.org

American Legion Missouri Oratorical Contest

Type of award: Scholarship.
Intended use: For undergraduate study at vocational, 2-year or 4-year institution.
Eligibility: Applicant must be enrolled in high school. Applicant must be residing in Missouri.
Basis for selection: Competition/talent/interest in oratory/debate, based on breadth of knowledge, originality, application of knowledge of topic, skill in selecting examples and analogies, logic, voice, diction, style of language and delivery.
Application requirements: Proof of eligibility. Must have won 1st, 2nd, 3rd, or 4th place at Department of Missouri Annual Oratorical Contest.
Additional information: Four awards offered: $2,000, $1,800, $1,600, and $1,400. Awards to be used to defray expenses of higher education.

Amount of award:	$1,400-$2,000
Number of awards:	4
Total amount awarded:	$6,800

Contact:
American Legion Missouri
Department Headquarters
P.O. Box 179
Jefferson City, MO 65102-0179
Phone: 573-893-2353
Fax: 573-893-2980
Web: www.missourilegion.org

Lillie Lois Ford Boys' Scholarship

Type of award: Scholarship.
Intended use: For undergraduate study at postsecondary institution.
Eligibility: Applicant must be male. Applicant must be U.S. citizen residing in Missouri. Applicant must be descendant of veteran; or dependent of veteran.
Basis for selection: Applicant must demonstrate financial need.
Additional information: Must have attended complete session of Boys State or Cadet Patrol Academy; not receiving any other scholarship.

Amount of award:	$1,000
Number of awards:	1
Total amount awarded:	$1,000

Contact:
Education and Scholarship Committee
1153 Greatfalls Court
Ballwin, MO 63021
Phone: 636-225-3307
Web: www.missourilegion.org

Lillie Lois Ford Girls' Scholarship

Type of award: Scholarship.
Intended use: For undergraduate study at postsecondary institution.
Eligibility: Applicant must be female. Applicant must be residing in Missouri. Applicant must be descendant of veteran; or dependent of veteran.
Basis for selection: Applicant must demonstrate financial need.
Additional information: Must have attended complete session of Girls State or Cadet Patrol Academy; not receiving any other scholarship.

Amount of award:	$1,000
Number of awards:	1
Total amount awarded:	$1,000

Contact:
Education and Scholarship Committee
1153 Greatfalls Court
Ballwin, MO 63021
Phone: 636-225-3307
Web: www.missourilegion.org

M.D. "Jack" Murphy Memorial Nurses Training Fund

Type of award: Scholarship, renewable.
Intended use: For full-time undergraduate study at 2-year or 4-year institution.
Eligibility: Applicant must be single. Applicant must be residing in Missouri.
Basis for selection: Major/career interest in nursing. Applicant must demonstrate financial need.
Additional information: Available to students training to be registered nurses. Applicant must have graduated in top 40% of high school class or have minimum "C" or equivalent standing in semester prior to applying for award. Award payment: $300 per semester. May reapply for two additional semesters.

Amount of award:	$600
Number of awards:	1
Total amount awarded:	$600

Contact:
Education and Scholarship Committee
1153 Greatfalls Court
Ballwin, MO 63021
Phone: 636-225-3307
Web: www.missourilegion.org

American Legion Missouri Auxiliary

American Legion Missouri Auxiliary Scholarship

Type of award: Scholarship.
Intended use: For freshman study at postsecondary institution.
Eligibility: Applicant must be high school senior. Applicant must be residing in Missouri. Applicant must be descendant of veteran; or dependent of veteran during Korean War, Lebanon conflict, Panama conflict, Persian Gulf War, WW I, WW II or Vietnam.
Additional information: Applicant must not have attended institution of higher learning.

Amount of award:	$500
Number of awards:	2
Application deadline:	March 15
Total amount awarded:	$1,000

Contact:
American Legion Missouri Auxiliary
Department Secretary
600 Ellis Blvd.
Jefferson City, MO 65101-2204
Phone: 573-636-9133
Fax: 573-635-3467

Past President's Parley Scholarship

Type of award: Scholarship.
Intended use: For at vocational, 2-year or 4-year institution.
Eligibility: Applicant must be high school senior. Applicant must be residing in Missouri.
Basis for selection: Major/career interest in nursing. Applicant must demonstrate depth of character.
Application requirements: Recommendations. Please include name, address, age, and photo of applicant. Four letters attesting to applicant's character: one from high school principal; one from church clergyman; one from home community representative; and one personal letter explaining "What a Nurse Profession Means to Me." Application must be submitted through an Auxiliary Unit to scholarship chairman by April 1.
Additional information: Applicant must have graduated from Missouri high school in the midterm or immediately before the Missouri Department Convention. Must be member of a veteran's family.

Amount of award:	$500
Number of awards:	1
Application deadline:	April 1

Contact:
American Legion Missouri Auxiliary
Department Secretary
600 Ellis Bvld.
Jefferson City, MO 65101-2204
Phone: 573-636-9133
Fax: 573-635-3467

American Legion Montana Auxiliary

Aloha Scholarship

Type of award: Scholarship.
Intended use: For freshman study at postsecondary institution. Designated institutions: Accredited nursing schools.
Eligibility: Applicant or parent must be member/participant of American Legion Auxiliary. Applicant must be residing in Montana.
Basis for selection: Major/career interest in nursing.
Application requirements: Recommendations. Recommendations from local Auxiliary unit, pastor, high school principal, and two local businesspeople.
Additional information: Must be child or grandchild of Auxiliary member and attending accredited school of nursing.

Amount of award:	$400
Number of awards:	1

Contact:
American Legion Montana Auxiliary
5835 Lewis & Clark Road
Wolf Creek, MT 59648
Phone: 406-235-4205

American Legion Montana Auxiliary Scholarships (1)

Type of award: Scholarship.
Intended use: For at postsecondary institution.

Eligibility: Applicant must be high school senior. Applicant must be residing in Montana. Applicant must be dependent of veteran.
Basis for selection: Based on special qualifications and 500-word essay on any topic.
Application requirements: Essay.
Additional information: Applicant must be high school senior or graduate who has not attended college. Must be state resident for at least two years.

Amount of award:	$500
Number of awards:	2
Total amount awarded:	$1,000

Contact:
American Legion Montana Auxiliary
5835 Lewis & Clark Road
Wolf Creek, MT 59648
Phone: 406-235-4205

American Legion Montana Auxiliary Scholarships (2)

Type of award: Scholarship.
Intended use: For junior study at postsecondary institution.
Eligibility: Applicant must be residing in Montana. Applicant must be dependent of veteran.
Basis for selection: Based on special qualifications and essay stating interest in children and youth.
Application requirements: Essay.
Additional information: Applicant must be child of veteran. Must have completed sophomore year in college and be going into field relating to children and youth.

Amount of award:	$500
Number of awards:	2
Total amount awarded:	$1,000

Contact:
American Legion Montana Auxiliary
5835 Lewis & Clark Road
Wolf Creek, MT 59648
Phone: 406-235-4205

American Legion National Headquarters

American Legion Auxiliary Girl Scout Achievement Award

Type of award: Scholarship.
Eligibility: Applicant must be female, enrolled in high school.
Basis for selection: Major/career interest in religion/theology.
Additional information: Applicant must be a Gold Award recipient and in 9th grade or higher. Must be an active member of religious institution and have received religious emblem. Must have demonstrated practical citizenship in church, school, scouting, and community.

Application deadline:	February 15
Total amount awarded:	$1,000

Contact:
American Legion Auxiliary
777 North Meridan Street, 3rd Floor
Indianapolis, IN 46204-1189
Phone: 317-955-3845
Web: www.legion.org

American Legion Auxiliary National President's Scholarship

Type of award: Scholarship.
Intended use: For undergraduate study at postsecondary institution.
Eligibility: Applicant must be high school senior. Applicant must be dependent of veteran during Grenada conflict, Korean War, Lebanon conflict, Panama conflict, Persian Gulf War, WW I, WW II or Vietnam.
Basis for selection: Applicant must demonstrate financial need, high academic achievement, depth of character, leadership and patriotism.
Application requirements: Applications from Unit President of Auxiliary in local community, from Department Secretary, or from Department Education Chairman. File application before March 15.
Additional information: Scholarships: Five-$2,500; five-$2,000; five-$1,500, awarded annually.

Amount of award:	$1,500-$2,500
Number of awards:	15
Application deadline:	March 15
Total amount awarded:	$30,000

Contact:
American Legion Auxiliary
Department Education Chairman
777 North Meridian Street, 3rd Floor
Indianapolis, IN 46204-1189
Phone: 317-955-3845
Web: www.legion.org

American Legion Auxiliary Spirit of Youth Scholarship for Junior Members

Type of award: Scholarship.
Intended use: For undergraduate study at postsecondary institution.
Eligibility: Applicant or parent must be member/participant of American Legion Auxiliary. Applicant must be high school senior. Applicant must be U.S. citizen.
Basis for selection: Applicant must demonstrate financial need, high academic achievement, depth of character, leadership and patriotism.
Application requirements: Proof of eligibility. Applications from Unit President of Auxiliary in local community, from Department Secretary, or from Department Education Chairman. File application before March 11.
Additional information: Junior member of three years standing, holding current membership card. One scholarship available in each of five divisions.

Amount of award:	$1,000
Number of awards:	5
Application deadline:	March 11
Total amount awarded:	$5,000

Contact:
American Legion Auxiliary
777 North Meridan, 3rd Floor
Indianapolis, IN 46204-1189
Phone: 317-955-3845
Web: www.legion.org

American Legion Eagle Scout of the Year

Type of award: Scholarship.

Intended use: For freshman, sophomore, junior or senior study at accredited postsecondary institution in United States.

Eligibility: Applicant or parent must be member/participant of Boy Scouts of America, Eagle Scouts. Applicant must be male, enrolled in high school. Applicant must be U.S. citizen.

Application requirements: Nomination. Registered, active member of Boy Scout troop, Varsity Scout team or Venturing Crew either chartered to American Legion Post/Auxiliary Unit OR applicant is son or grandson of American Legion or Auxiliary member. Request application from state or national headquarters.

Additional information: Scholarships available upon graduation from accredited high school and must be used within four years of graduation date. Awards: one-$10,000, three-$2,500.

Amount of award:	$2,500-$10,000
Number of awards:	4
Total amount awarded:	$17,500

Contact:
The American Legion
Eagle Scout of the Year
P. O. Box 1055
Indianapolis, IN 46206-1055
Phone: 317-630-1249
Web: www.legion.org

American Legion National High School Oratorical Contest

Type of award: Scholarship.

Intended use: For undergraduate study at postsecondary institution.

Eligibility: Applicant must be enrolled in high school. Applicant must be U.S. citizen or permanent resident.

Basis for selection: Competition/talent/interest in oratory/debate, based on breadth of knowledge, originality, application of knowledge of topic, skill in selecting examples and analogies, logic, voice, diction, style of language and delivery.

Application requirements: Obtain oratorical contest rules from local legion post or state department headquarters.

Additional information: Awards: State winners participating in regional level win $1,500; second-round participants not advancing to national finals receive additional $1,500. Finalists win $18,000 (first place), $16,000 (runner-up), and $14,000 (third place). Must be high school student.

Amount of award:	$1,500-$18,000
Number of awards:	54

Contact:
Local Legion Post or State American Legion Headquarters.
Web: www.legion.org

Eight and Forty Lung and Respiratory Nursing Scholarship Fund

Type of award: Scholarship.

Intended use: For undergraduate, graduate or non-degree study.

Eligibility: Applicant must be returning adult student.

Application requirements: Proof of eligibility. Contact Eight and Forty Scholarship Chairman or the American Legion Education Program.

Additional information: Applicant must be registered nurse. Program assists registered nurses with advanced preparation for positions in supervision, administration or teaching. On completion of education, must have full-time employment prospects related to lung and respiratory control in hospitals, clinics, or health departments.

Amount of award:	$3,000
Application deadline:	May 15
Notification begins:	July 1
Total amount awarded:	$3,000

Contact:
American Legion Education Program
Eight and Forty Scholarships
P.O. Box 1055
Indianapolis, IN 46206-1055

American Legion Nebraska

American Legion Nebraska Oratorical Contest

Type of award: Scholarship.

Intended use: For undergraduate study at postsecondary institution.

Eligibility: Applicant must be enrolled in high school. Applicant must be residing in Nebraska.

Basis for selection: Competition/talent/interest in oratory/debate, based on breadth of knowledge, originality, application of knowledge of topic, skill in selecting examples and analogies, logic, voice, diction, style of language and delivery.

Application requirements: Proof of eligibility. Participants of Nebraska Department Oratorical Contest.

Additional information: Awards given in U.S. Savings Bonds: 1st-$1,000, 2nd-$600, 3rd-$400, 4th-$200, plus one $100 award for 1st place in each district upon participation in area contest.

Amount of award:	$200-$1,000
Number of awards:	4

Contact:
American Legion Nebraska
Department Headquarters
P.O. Box 5205
Lincoln, NE 68505-0205
Phone: 402-464-6338
Fax: 402-464-6330
Web: www.ne.legion.org

Edgar J. Boschult Memorial Scholarship

Type of award: Scholarship.

Intended use: For undergraduate study. Designated institutions: University of Nebraska.

Eligibility: Applicant must be residing in Nebraska.

Basis for selection: Applicant must demonstrate financial need and high academic achievement.

Additional information: Must be student at University of Nebraska with high academic and ROTC standing, or military veteran attending University of Nebraska with financial need and acceptable scholastic standing.

Amount of award:	$400
Number of awards:	4
Application deadline:	March 1

Contact:
American Legion Nebraska, Department Headquarters
P.O. Box 5205
Lincoln, NE 68505-0205
Phone: 402-464-6338
Web: www.ne.legion.org

Maynard Jensen American Legion Memorial Scholarship

Type of award: Scholarship.
Intended use: For undergraduate study at vocational, 2-year or 4-year institution. Designated institutions: Nebraska postsecondary institutions.
Eligibility: Applicant must be residing in Nebraska. Applicant must be descendant of veteran; or dependent of veteran, deceased veteran or POW/MIA.
Basis for selection: Applicant must demonstrate financial need and high academic achievement.
Additional information: Must be descendant, adopted child or stepchild of American Legion member, or of POW, MIA, KIA or any deceased veteran.

Amount of award:	$500
Number of awards:	10
Application deadline:	March 1
Total amount awarded:	$5,000

Contact:
American Legion Nebraska
Department Headquarters
P.O. Box 5205
Lincoln, NE 68505-0205
Phone: 402-464-6338
Fax: 402-464-6330
Web: www.ne.legion.org

American Legion Nebraska Auxiliary

American Legion Auxiliary Junior Member Scholarship

Type of award: Scholarship.
Intended use: For undergraduate study at postsecondary institution.
Eligibility: Applicant or parent must be member/participant of American Legion Auxiliary. Applicant must be residing in Nebraska.
Additional information: Given to Nebraska's entry for Spirit of Youth Scholarship for Junior member, in event applicant does not win same.

Amount of award:	$200

Contact:
American Legion Nebraska Auxiliary
Department Education Chairman
P.O. Box 5227
Lincoln, NE 68505-0227
Phone: 402-466-1808
Web: http://www.ne.legion.org/

American Legion Nebraska Auxiliary Nurse Gift Tuition Scholarship

Type of award: Scholarship.
Intended use: For undergraduate study. Designated institutions: Hospital schools of nursing.
Eligibility: Applicant must be residing in Nebraska.
Basis for selection: Major/career interest in nursing. Applicant must demonstrate financial need.
Additional information: Awards given as funds permit. Applicant must be Nebraska resident accepted at accredited hospital school of nursing and be veteran-connected.

Amount of award:	$200-$400

Contact:
American Legion Nebraska Auxiliary
Department Headquarters
P.O. Box 5227
Lincoln, NE 68505-0227
Phone: 402-466-1808
Web: www.ne.legion.org

American Legion Nebraska Auxiliary Practical Nurse Scholarship

Type of award: Scholarship.
Intended use: For at vocational, 2-year or 4-year institution.
Eligibility: Applicant must be residing in Nebraska. Applicant must be veteran or descendant of veteran; or dependent of veteran; or spouse of veteran.
Basis for selection: Major/career interest in nursing. Applicant must demonstrate financial need.
Additional information: Must be state resident for at least three years, be accepted at school of practical nursing, and be veteran-connected.

Amount of award:	$200-$400
Application deadline:	April 1

Contact:
American Legion Nebraska Auxiliary
Department Headquarters
P.O. Box 5227
Lincoln, NE 68505-0205
Phone: 402-466-1808
Web: http://www.ne.legion.org/

American Legion Nebraska Auxiliary Roberta Marie Stretch Memorial Scholarship

Type of award: Scholarship.
Intended use: For undergraduate or master's study at 4-year or graduate institution.
Eligibility: Applicant must be residing in Nebraska. Applicant must be descendant of veteran; or dependent of veteran; or spouse of veteran.
Application requirements: Must be enrolled or accepted in undergraduate or master's program.
Additional information: Preference given to former Nebraska Girls State citizens.

Amount of award:	$400
Application deadline:	April 1

Contact:
American Legion Nebraska Auxiliary
Department Headquarters
P.O. Box 5227
Lincoln, NE 68505-0205
Phone: 402-466-1808
Web: http://www.ne.legion.org/

American Legion Nebraska Auxiliary Ruby Paul Campaign Fund Scholarship

Type of award: Scholarship.
Intended use: For freshman study at accredited 2-year or 4-year institution.
Eligibility: Applicant or parent must be member/participant of American Legion Auxiliary. Applicant must be high school senior. Applicant must be residing in Nebraska.
Basis for selection: Applicant must demonstrate high academic achievement.
Additional information: Award varies with availability of funding. Applicant must have maintained "B" or better GPA during last two semesters of senior year in high school. Must be accepted for fall term at college or university. Must be state resident for three years. Cannot be nursing student. Must be Legion member, ALA member, Sons of the American Legion member of two years' standing, or child or grandchild of Legion or ALA member of two years' standing.
  Amount of award: $100-$300
  Application deadline: April 1
Contact:
American Legion Nebraska Auxiliary
Department Headquarters
P.O. Box 5227
Lincoln, NE 68505
Phone: 402-466-1808
Web: http://www.ne.legion.org/

American Legion Nebraska President's Scholarship

Type of award: Scholarship.
Intended use: For undergraduate study at postsecondary institution.
Eligibility: Applicant must be residing in Nebraska.
Additional information: Given to Nebraska's entry for National President's Scholarship in event applicant does not win same.
  Amount of award: $200
Contact:
American Legion Nebraska Auxiliary
Department Headquarters
P.O. Box 5227
Lincoln, NE 68505-0227
Phone: 402-464-1808
Web: http://www.ne.legion.org/

Averyl Elaine Keriakedes Memorial Scholarship

Type of award: Scholarship.
Intended use: For undergraduate study. Designated institutions: University of Nebraska, Lincoln.
Eligibility: Applicant must be female. Applicant must be residing in Nebraska.

Additional information: Applicant must be veteran connected and plan to teach middle or junior high school social studies.
  Amount of award: $500
  Number of awards: 1
  Total amount awarded: $500
Contact:
American Legion Nebraska Auxiliary, Department Headquarters
P.O. Box 5227
Lincoln, NE 68505-0227
Web: http://www.ne.legion.org/

Student Aid Grant or Vocational Technical Scholarship

Type of award: Scholarship.
Intended use: For undergraduate study at vocational or 2-year institution in United States.
Eligibility: Applicant must be residing in Nebraska.
Basis for selection: Applicant must demonstrate financial need.
Additional information: Applicant must be Nebraska resident for five years and be veteran-connected.
  Amount of award: $200-$300
  Application deadline: April 1
Contact:
American Legion Nebraska Auxiliary
Department Headquarters
P.O. Box 5227
Lincoln, NE 68505-0227
Phone: 402-466-1808
Web: http://www.ne.legion.org/

American Legion Nevada Auxiliary

Past President's Parley Nurses' Scholarship

Type of award: Scholarship.
Intended use: For junior study at postsecondary institution.
Eligibility: Applicant must be residing in Nevada. Applicant must be veteran; or dependent of veteran.
Basis for selection: Major/career interest in nursing.
Additional information: $150 for each university. Applicant must have completed first two years of training.
  Amount of award: $150
Contact:
American Legion Nevada Auxiliary, Department Secretary
1718 Statz Street
North Las Vegas, NV 89030-7260

President's Scholarship and Junior Scholarship

Type of award: Scholarship.
Intended use: For at postsecondary institution.
Eligibility: Applicant must be residing in Nevada.
Additional information: President's scholarship: $300 for winner of department competition. Runner-ups: 1st-$200; 2nd-$100; 3rd-$100. Junior scholarship: $100 for winner of national competition.
  Amount of award: $100-$300

Contact:
American Legion Nevada Auxiliary, Department Secretary
1718 Statz Street
North Las Vegas, NV 89030-7260

Silver Eagle Indian Scholarship

Type of award: Scholarship.
Intended use: For undergraduate study at postsecondary institution.
Eligibility: Applicant must be American Indian. Applicant must be U.S. citizen residing in Nevada. Applicant must be descendant of veteran; or dependent of veteran.
Additional information: Applicant must be child or grandchild of American Indian veteran.

Amount of award:	$250

Contact:
American Legion Nevada Auxiliary, Department Secretary
1718 Statz Street
North Las Vegas, NV 89030-7260

American Legion Nevada, Oratorical Contest

American Legion Nevada Oratorical Contest

Type of award: Scholarship.
Intended use: For at postsecondary institution.
Eligibility: Applicant must be enrolled in high school. Applicant must be U.S. citizen or permanent resident residing in Nevada.
Basis for selection: Competition/talent/interest in Oratory/debate, based on breadth of knowledge, originality, application of knowledge of topic, skill in selecting examples and analogies, logic, voice, diction, style of language and delivery.
Additional information: Awards: 1st-$500; 2nd-$300; 3rd-$200; 4th-$150; 5th-$150, all in US Savings Bonds. Must be student enrolled in accredited Nevada high school.

Amount of award:	$150-$500
Number of awards:	5
Application deadline:	January 15
Total amount awarded:	$1,300

Contact:
Dale Salmen
P.O. Box 1799
Round Mountain, NV 89045-1799
Phone: 775-377-2529

American Legion New Hampshire

Albert T. Marcoux Memorial Scholarship

Type of award: Scholarship.
Intended use: For undergraduate study at 4-year institution.

Eligibility: Applicant or parent must be member/participant of American Legion. Applicant must be U.S. citizen residing in New Hampshire.
Application requirements: Send SASE to American Legion New Hampshire.
Additional information: Applicant must be child of living or deceased Legion or Auxiliary member; graduate of New Hampshire high school; and state resident for three years. Must be pursuing bachelor's degree.

Amount of award:	$1,000
Number of awards:	1
Application deadline:	May 1
Total amount awarded:	$1,000

Contact:
American Legion New Hampshire
Department Adjutant/State House Annex
25 Capitol Street, Room 431
Concord, NH 03301-6312
Phone: 603-271-2211

American Legion New Hampshire Boys State Scholarship

Type of award: Scholarship.
Intended use: For undergraduate study at postsecondary institution.
Eligibility: Applicant or parent must be member/participant of American Legion, Boys State. Applicant must be male. Applicant must be U.S. citizen residing in New Hampshire.
Additional information: Award given to participants of Boys State during Boys State session. Award amount varies. Recipient eligible for regional and national awards.
Contact:
American Legion New Hampshire
Department Adjutant/State House Annex
25 Capitol Street, Room 431
Concord, NH 03301-6312
Phone: 603-271-2211

American Legion New Hampshire Christa McAuliffe Memorial Scholarship

Type of award: Scholarship.
Intended use: For freshman study at 4-year institution.
Eligibility: Applicant must be U.S. citizen residing in New Hampshire.
Basis for selection: Major/career interest in education.
Application requirements: Send SASE.
Additional information: High school senior or recent graduate of New Hampshire school. Must be New Hampshire resident at least three years.

Amount of award:	$1,000
Number of awards:	1
Application deadline:	May 1
Total amount awarded:	$1,000

Contact:
American Legion New Hampshire
Department Adjutant/State House Annex
25 Capitol Street, Room 431
Concord, NH 03301-6312
Phone: 603-271-2211

American Legion New Hampshire Department Vocational Scholarship

Type of award: Scholarship.
Intended use: For freshman study at vocational institution.
Eligibility: Applicant must be enrolled in high school. Applicant must be U.S. citizen residing in New Hampshire.
Application requirements: Send SASE.
Additional information: High school student or graduate from New Hampshire school; state resident for three years.

Amount of award:	$1,000
Application deadline:	May 1
Total amount awarded:	$1,000

Contact:
American Legion New Hampshire
Department Adjutant/State House Annex
25 Capitol Street, Room 431
Concord, NH 03301-6312
Phone: 603-271-2211

American Legion New Hampshire Oratorical Contest

Type of award: Scholarship.
Intended use: For undergraduate study at postsecondary institution.
Eligibility: Applicant must be enrolled in high school. Applicant must be residing in New Hampshire.
Basis for selection: Competition/talent/interest in oratory/debate, based on breadth of knowledge, originality, application of knowledge of topic, skill in selecting examples and analogies, logic, voice, diction, style of language and delivery.
Application requirements: Proof of eligibility. Finalist in Department Oratorical Contest.
Additional information: Awards: $1,000, $750, $500, $250, and four $100.

Amount of award:	$100-$1,000
Number of awards:	8
Total amount awarded:	$2,900

Contact:
American Legion New Hampshire
Department Adjutant/State House Annex
25 Capitol Street, Room 431
Concord, NH 03301-6312
Phone: 603-271-2211

Department of New Hampshire Scholarship

Type of award: Scholarship.
Intended use: For freshman study at vocational, 2-year or 4-year institution.
Eligibility: Applicant must be enrolled in high school. Applicant must be U.S. citizen residing in New Hampshire.
Application requirements: Send SASE.
Additional information: High school student or graduate from New Hampshire school; state resident for three years.

Amount of award:	$1,000
Number of awards:	2
Application deadline:	May 1
Total amount awarded:	$2,000

Contact:
American Legion New Hampshire Scholarship Coordinator
Department Adjutant/State House Annex
25 Capitol Street, Room 431
Concord, NH 03301-6312
Phone: 603-271-2211

American Legion New Hampshire Auxiliary

Grace S. High Memorial Child Welfare Scholarship Fund

Type of award: Scholarship.
Intended use: For undergraduate study at postsecondary institution.
Eligibility: Applicant or parent must be member/participant of American Legion Auxiliary. Applicant must be female. Applicant must be U.S. citizen residing in New Hampshire.
Basis for selection: Applicant must demonstrate financial need.
Application requirements: Send SASE.
Additional information: Applicant must be high school graduate and daughter of Legion or Auxiliary member.

Amount of award:	$300
Number of awards:	2
Application deadline:	April 15
Total amount awarded:	$600

Contact:
American Legion Auxiliary, Department of New Hampshire
Department Secretary/State House Annex
25 Capitol Street, Room 432
Concord, NH 03301-6312

Marion J. Bagley Scholarship

Type of award: Scholarship.
Intended use: For undergraduate study at postsecondary institution.
Eligibility: Applicant must be U.S. citizen residing in New Hampshire.
Application requirements: Send SASE.
Additional information: Applicant must be high school graduate.

Amount of award:	$1,000
Number of awards:	1
Application deadline:	May 1
Total amount awarded:	$1,000

Contact:
American Legion Auxiliary, Department of New Hampshire
Department Secretary/State House Annex
25 Capitol St., Room 432
Concord, NH 03301-6312

Past President's Parley Nursing Scholarship

Type of award: Scholarship.
Intended use: For undergraduate study at vocational, 2-year or 4-year institution.
Eligibility: Applicant must be U.S. citizen residing in New Hampshire.

Scholarships

Basis for selection: Major/career interest in nursing. Applicant must demonstrate financial need.
Application requirements: Send SASE.
Additional information: Child of veteran given preference. One award to Registered Nurse study and one to Licensed Practical Nurse study. Award amount varies; contact sponsor for information.

Number of awards:	2
Application deadline:	May 10

Contact:
American Legion Auxiliary, Department of New Hampshire
Department Secretary/State House Annex
25 Capitol Street, Room 432
Concord, NH 03301-6312

American Legion New Jersey

American Legion New Jersey Lawrence Luterman Memorial Scholarship

Type of award: Scholarship.
Intended use: For undergraduate study at 4-year institution.
Eligibility: Applicant or parent must be member/participant of American Legion. Applicant must be high school senior. Applicant must be residing in New Jersey.
Additional information: Awards: two-$4,000 scholarships ($1,000/yr.); three-$2,000; two-$1,000. Applicant must be natural or adopted descendant of member of American Legion, Department of New Jersey.

Amount of award:	$1,000-$4,000
Number of awards:	7
Application deadline:	February 15
Total amount awarded:	$16,000

Contact:
American Legion New Jersey
Department Adjutant
135 West Hanover Street
Trenton, NJ 08618
Phone: 609-695-5418
Fax: 609-394-1532
Web: www.nj.legion.org

American Legion New Jersey Oratorical Contest

Type of award: Scholarship.
Intended use: For freshman study at postsecondary institution.
Eligibility: Applicant must be enrolled in high school. Applicant must be residing in New Jersey.
Basis for selection: Competition/talent/interest in oratory/debate, based on breadth of knowledge, originality, application of knowledge of topic, skill in selecting examples and analogies, logic, voice, diction, style of language and delivery.
Application requirements: Proof of eligibility.
Additional information: Subject: U.S. Constitution and citizenship. See high school counselor for additional information. Awards: 1st-$4,000, 2nd-$2,500, 3rd-$2,000, 4th-$1000, 5th-$1000.

Amount of award:	$1,000-$4,000
Number of awards:	5
Total amount awarded:	$10,500

Contact:
American Legion New Jersey
135 West Hanover Street
Trenton, NJ 08618
Phone: 609-695-5418
Fax: 609-394-1532
Web: www.nj.legion.org

American Legion Press Club of New Jersey Scholarship

Type of award: Scholarship.
Intended use: For freshman study at accredited 4-year institution.
Eligibility: Applicant or parent must be member/participant of American Legion. Applicant must be permanent resident residing in New Jersey.
Basis for selection: Major/career interest in communications.
Application requirements: Send SASE to Education Chairman (see contact information).
Additional information: Applicant must be child or grandchild of current member of Legion or Auxiliary, including Sons of American Legion and ALA Juniors. Graduates from either AL New Jersey Boys State or Auxiliary Girls State programs also eligible.

Amount of award:	$500
Number of awards:	1
Application deadline:	July 15
Total amount awarded:	$500

Contact:
Jack W. Keupfer, Education Chairman
American Legion Press Club of New Jersey
68 Merrill Road
Clifton, NJ 07012-1622
Phone: 973-473-5176
Web: www.nj.legion.org

David C. Goodwin Scholarship

Type of award: Scholarship.
Intended use: For at 4-year institution.
Eligibility: Applicant must be high school junior. Applicant must be residing in New Jersey.
Application requirements: Must be high school junior participating in New Jersey American Legion Baseball Program. Applications mailed to players.
Additional information: Awards: $4,000 ($1,000/year for four years); $2,000 ($500/year for four years).

Amount of award:	$2,000-$4,000
Number of awards:	2
Application deadline:	September 1
Total amount awarded:	$6,000

Contact:
American Legion New Jersey
Baseball Committee
135 West Hanover St.
Trenton, NJ 08618
Phone: 609-695-5418
Fax: 609-394-1532
Web: www.nj.legion.org

American Legion New Jersey Auxiliary

American Legion New Jersey Auxiliary Claire Oliphant Memorial Scholarship

Type of award: Scholarship.
Intended use: For freshman study at 2-year or 4-year institution.
Eligibility: Applicant must be high school senior. Applicant must be U.S. citizen residing in New Jersey. Applicant must be dependent of veteran.
Application requirements: Rules and applications distributed to all New Jersey high school guidance departments.
Additional information: Must be state resident for two years. Must be child of an honorably discharged veteran of U.S. Armed Forces.

Amount of award:	$1,800
Number of awards:	1
Application deadline:	March 15
Total amount awarded:	$1,800

Contact:
American Legion Auxiliary, Department of New Jersey
Department Secretary
1540 Kuser Road, Suite A-8
Hamilton, NJ 08619
Phone: 609-581-9580
Fax: 609-581-8429

American Legion New Jersey Auxiliary Department Scholarship

Type of award: Scholarship.
Intended use: For freshman study at 2-year or 4-year institution.
Eligibility: Applicant must be high school senior. Applicant must be U.S. citizen residing in New Jersey. Applicant must be descendant of veteran; or dependent of veteran.
Application requirements: Rules and applications distributed to all New Jersey high school guidance departments.
Additional information: Must be state resident for two years. Must be child or grandchild of honorably discharged veteran of U.S. Armed Forces. Several awards offered. Amount and number of awards vary; contact sponsor for more information.

Application deadline: March 15
Contact:
American Legion Auxiliary, Department of New Jersey
Department Secretary
1540 Kuser Road, Suite A-8
Hamilton, NJ 08619
Phone: 609-581-9580
Fax: 609-581-8429

Past President's Parley Nurses Scholarship

Type of award: Scholarship.
Intended use: For freshman study at 2-year or 4-year institution.
Eligibility: Applicant must be high school senior. Applicant must be residing in New Jersey. Applicant must be dependent of veteran.
Basis for selection: Major/career interest in nursing.

Application requirements: Rules and applications distributed to all New Jersey high school guidance departments.
Additional information: Must be state resident for two years. Must be child or grandchild of honorably discharged veteran of U.S. Armed Forces. Applicant must be enrolled in nursing program. Award amount varies. Contact sponsor for more information.

Application deadline: March 15
Contact:
American Legion Auxiliary, Department of New Jersey
Department Secretary
1540 Kuser Road, Suite A-8
Hamilton, NJ 08619
Phone: 609-581-9580
Fax: 609-581-8429

American Legion New Mexico Auxiliary

President's Parley Scholarship for Teachers of Exceptional Children

Type of award: Scholarship.
Intended use: For undergraduate, graduate or non-degree study at postsecondary institution.
Eligibility: Applicant must be residing in New Mexico.
Basis for selection: Major/career interest in education, special.
Additional information: Covers actual cost of tuition plus $50 travel; not to exceed $250. Award for additional special education training to teach exceptional children in New Mexico for one year.

Amount of award:	Full tuition
Number of awards:	1
Application deadline:	March 1

Contact:
American Legion Auxiliary, Department of New Mexico
Department Secretary
1215 Mountain Road, NE
Albuquerque, NM 87102
Phone: 505-242-9918

American Legion New York

New York State Legion Press Association Scholarship

Type of award: Scholarship.
Intended use: For full-time undergraduate study at accredited 4-year institution.
Eligibility: Applicant or parent must be member/participant of American Legion. Applicant must be residing in New York.
Basis for selection: Major/career interest in communications.
Additional information: Applicant must be child of New York Legion or Legion Auxiliary member; Sons of American Legion or ALA Juniors member; or graduate of New York American Legion Boys State or Girls State.

Amount of award:	$1,000
Number of awards:	1

Contact:
Scholarship Chairman
P.O. Box 1239
Syracuse, NY 13201-1239
Web: www.ny.legion.org

American Legion New York Auxiliary

American Legion New York Auxiliary Medical & Teaching Scholarship

Type of award: Scholarship.
Intended use: For full-time freshman study at postsecondary institution.
Eligibility: Applicant must be no older than 19. Applicant must be residing in New York. Applicant must be descendant of veteran; or dependent of veteran.
Basis for selection: Major/career interest in health-related professions or education, teacher. Applicant must demonstrate financial need.
Additional information: One scholarship in each of the ten New York Judicial Districts. Applicant must be high school senior or graduate; under age 20.

Amount of award:	$1,000
Number of awards:	10
Application deadline:	March 10
Total amount awarded:	$10,000

Contact:
Local American Legion Auxiliary Unit

American Legion New York Auxiliary Past President's Parley Student Nurses Scholarship for Girls or Boys

Type of award: Scholarship.
Intended use: For freshman study at 2-year or 4-year institution.
Eligibility: Applicant must be no older than 19, high school senior. Applicant must be residing in New York. Applicant must be descendant of veteran; or dependent of veteran during Korean War, WW I, WW II or Vietnam.
Basis for selection: Major/career interest in nursing. Applicant must demonstrate financial need.
Additional information: Applicant must be high school senior or graduate; under age 20.

Amount of award:	$1,000
Number of awards:	1
Application deadline:	March 10
Total amount awarded:	$1,000

Contact:
Local American Legion Auxiliary Unit

American Legion New York Auxiliary Scholarship

Type of award: Scholarship.
Intended use: For undergraduate study at postsecondary institution.

Eligibility: Applicant must be residing in New York. Applicant must be descendant of veteran; or dependent of veteran or deceased veteran.
Additional information: Applicant must be child/grandchild of veteran. Must be high school graduate. May use other scholarships.

Amount of award:	$1,000
Number of awards:	1
Application deadline:	March 10
Total amount awarded:	$1,000

Contact:
Local American Legion Auxiliary unit.

American Legion North Dakota

American Legion North Dakota Oratorical Contest

Type of award: Scholarship.
Intended use: For undergraduate study.
Eligibility: Applicant must be high school freshman, sophomore, junior or senior. Applicant must be residing in North Dakota.
Basis for selection: Competition/talent/interest in oratory/debate, based on breadth of knowledge, originality, application of knowledge of topic, skill in selecting examples and analogies, logic, voice, diction, style of language and delivery.
Application requirements: Proof of eligibility.
Additional information: North Dakota Oratorical Contest: 1st-$400, 2nd-$300, 3rd-$200, 4th-$100; East and West Divisional Contests: 1st-$300, 2nd-$200 each; and 10 District Contests: 1st-$300, 2nd-$200, 3rd-$100. Contact local American Legion post or department headquarters after start of school year. Local contests begin in the fall.

Amount of award:	$100-$400
Number of awards:	38
Total amount awarded:	$8,000

Contact:
American Legion North Dakota
Department Headquarters
Box 2666
Fargo, ND 58108-2666
Phone: 701-293-3120
Fax: 701-293-9951
Web: www.ndlegion.org

American Legion North Dakota Auxiliary

American Legion North Dakota Auxiliary Past President's Parley Scholarship

Type of award: Scholarship.
Intended use: For undergraduate study at 2-year or 4-year institution. Designated institutions: North Dakota hospital or nursing school.

Eligibility: Applicant or parent must be member/participant of American Legion Auxiliary. Applicant must be residing in North Dakota.
Basis for selection: Major/career interest in nursing.
Additional information: Children, grandchildren or great-grandchildren of American Legion or Auxiliary member in good standing. Must be graduate of North Dakota high school. Apply to local American Legion Auxiliary Unit.

Amount of award:	$350
Application deadline:	May 15

Contact:
American Legion Auxiliary, Department of North Dakota
Chair of Dept. Parley Scholarship Committee
P.O. Box 250
Beach, ND 58621
Phone: 701-872-3865

American Legion North Dakota Auxiliary Scholarship

Type of award: Scholarship.
Intended use: For undergraduate study at postsecondary institution. Designated institutions: North Dakota postsecondary institutions.
Eligibility: Applicant must be residing in North Dakota.
Basis for selection: Applicant must demonstrate financial need.
Additional information: Must be resident of North Dakota attending a university or college in North Dakota. Number of awards varies.

Amount of award:	$350
Application deadline:	January 15

Contact:
Local American Legion Auxiliary Unit.
Phone: 701-797-2931

American Legion of New York

American Legion New York Oratorical Contest

Type of award: Scholarship.
Intended use: For undergraduate study.
Eligibility: Applicant must be enrolled in high school. Applicant must be residing in New York.
Basis for selection: Competition/talent/interest in oratory/debate, based on breadth of knowledge, originality, application of knowledge of topic, skill in selecting examples and analogies, logic, voice, diction, style of language, and delivery.
Application requirements: Proof of eligibility. New York State Oratorical Contest finalist.
Additional information: Awards: 1st-$6,000, 2nd-$4,000, 3rd-$2,500, 4th-$2,000, 5th-$2,000. Applicant must be currently enrolled in New York high school or junior high school (public, parochial, military, private).

Amount of award:	$2,000-$6,000
Number of awards:	5
Total amount awarded:	$16,500

Contact:
American Legion, Department of New York
Department Adjutant
112 State Street, Suite 400
Albany, NY 12207
Phone: 518-463-2215
Fax: 518-427-8443
Web: www.ny.legion.org

American Legion Ohio

American Legion Ohio Scholarship

Type of award: Scholarship.
Intended use: For undergraduate study.
Eligibility: Applicant or parent must be member/participant of American Legion. Applicant must be residing in Ohio. Applicant must be dependent of deceased veteran; or spouse of deceased veteran.
Additional information: Also eligible: direct descendants of Legionnaires in good standing; direct descendants of deceased Legionnaires; spouses or children of deceased U.S. military persons who died on active duty or of injuries received on active duty. Number and amount of awards vary. Contact sponsor or visit Website for more information.

Amount of award:	$2,000
Number of awards:	18
Application deadline:	April 15

Contact:
American Legion Ohio
Department Scholarship Committee
P.O. Box 8007
Delaware, OH 43015-8007
Phone: 614-268-7072
Fax: 614-268-3048
Web: www.ohioamericanlegion.org

Department Oratorical Awards

Type of award: Scholarship.
Intended use: For undergraduate study.
Eligibility: Applicant must be enrolled in high school. Applicant must be residing in Ohio. Applicant must be dependent of veteran during Grenada conflict, Korean War, Lebanon conflict, WW I, WW II or Vietnam.
Basis for selection: Competition/talent/interest in oratory/debate, based on breadth of knowledge, originality, application of knowledge of topic, skill in selecting examples and analogies, logic, voice, diction, style of language and delivery.
Application requirements: Ohio Oratorical Contest finalist.
Additional information: Must be presently enrolled in Ohio high school (public, private, parochial or home schooled). Awards: 1st-$1,000; 2nd-$500; 3rd-$300; 4th-$200. Children or grandchildren of Gulf War veterans also considered.

Amount of award:	$200-$1,000
Number of awards:	4
Total amount awarded:	$2,000

Contact:
The American Legion
Department of Ohio
P.O. Box 8007
Delaware, OH 43015-8007
Phone: 740-362-7478
Fax: 740-362-1429
Web: www.ohioamericanlegion.org

American Legion Ohio Auxiliary

American Legion Ohio Auxiliary Scholarship

Type of award: Scholarship.
Intended use: For freshman study at postsecondary institution.
Eligibility: Applicant must be high school senior. Applicant must be residing in Ohio. Applicant must be descendant of veteran; or dependent of veteran or deceased veteran during Grenada conflict, Korean War, Lebanon conflict, Persian Gulf War, WW I, WW II or Vietnam.
Additional information: $2,000 scholarship to first-place applicant; $1,500 awarded to second-place applicant.

Amount of award:	$1,500-$2,000
Number of awards:	2
Application deadline:	March 1
Total amount awarded:	$3,500

Contact:
American Legion Ohio Auxiliary
Department Secretary
P.O. Box 2760
Zanesville, OH 43702-2760
Phone: 740-452-8245
Fax: 740-452-2620

American Legion Ohio Auxiliary Scholarship for Nurse's Training

Type of award: Scholarship.
Intended use: For undergraduate study at vocational, 2-year or 4-year institution.
Eligibility: Applicant must be residing in Ohio. Applicant must be descendant of veteran; or dependent of veteran; or spouse of veteran.
Basis for selection: Major/career interest in nursing; health-related professions; health sciences or medical assistant.
Additional information: Applicant must be spouse, child, grandchild, adopted child, or stepchild of veteran.

Amount of award:	$300-$500
Number of awards:	17
Application deadline:	May 1
Total amount awarded:	$5,500

Contact:
American Legion Auxiliary
Department Secretary
P.O. Box 2760
Zanesville, OH 43702-2760
Phone: 614-452-8245
Fax: 614-452-2620

American Legion Oregon

American Legion Oratorical Contest

Type of award: Scholarship.
Intended use: For undergraduate study.
Eligibility: Applicant must be enrolled in high school. Applicant must be U.S. citizen or permanent resident residing in Oregon.

Basis for selection: Competition/talent/interest in oratory/debate, based on breadth of knowledge, originality, application of knowledge of topic, skill in selecting examples and analogies, logic, voice, diction, style of language and delivery.
Application requirements: Proof of eligibility. Participant in Oregon Oratorical Contest.
Additional information: Awards: 1st-$500; 2nd-$400; 3rd-$300; 4th-$200. Applications available at local high schools after October 1.

Amount of award:	$200-$500
Number of awards:	4
Application deadline:	December 1
Total amount awarded:	$1,400

Contact:
American Legion Department of Oregon
P.O. Box 1730
Wilsonville, OR 97070-1730
Phone: 503-685-5006
Fax: 503-685-5008

American Legion Oregon Auxiliary

American Legion Oregon Auxiliary National President's Scholarship

Type of award: Scholarship.
Intended use: For undergraduate study at postsecondary institution.
Eligibility: Applicant must be residing in Oregon. Applicant must be dependent of veteran during Grenada conflict, Korean War, Lebanon conflict, Panama conflict, Persian Gulf War, WW I, WW II or Vietnam.
Additional information: Two awards in each Division of American Legion Auxiliary: $2,000 and $1,500.

Amount of award:	$1,500-$2,000
Number of awards:	10
Application deadline:	March 15
Total amount awarded:	$35,000

Contact:
American Legion Auxiliary, Department of Oregon
Chairman of Education
P.O. Box 1730
Wilsonville, OR 97070-1730

American Legion Oregon Auxiliary Nurses Scholarship

Type of award: Scholarship.
Intended use: For undergraduate study at accredited 2-year or 4-year institution. Designated institutions: School of nursing.
Eligibility: Applicant must be residing in Oregon. Applicant must be dependent of disabled veteran; or spouse of disabled veteran or deceased veteran.
Basis for selection: Major/career interest in nursing. Applicant must demonstrate financial need, high academic achievement, depth of character, seriousness of purpose and service orientation.
Application requirements: Proof of eligibility.

Amount of award:	$1,500
Number of awards:	1
Application deadline:	June 1
Total amount awarded:	$1,500

Contact:
American Legion Auxiliary, Department of Oregon
Chairman of Education
P.O. Box 1730
Wilsonville, OR 97070-1730

American Legion Oregon Auxiliary Scholarship

Type of award: Scholarship.
Intended use: For undergraduate study at postsecondary institution.
Eligibility: Applicant must be residing in Oregon. Applicant must be dependent of disabled veteran; or spouse of disabled veteran or deceased veteran.
Additional information: One of three grants designated for vocational or business school.

Amount of award:	$1,000
Number of awards:	3
Application deadline:	March 15
Total amount awarded:	$3,000

Contact:
American Legion Auxiliary, Department of Oregon
Chairman of Education
P.O. Box 1730
Wilsonville, OR 97070-1730

American Legion Oregon Auxiliary Spirit of Youth Scholarship

Type of award: Scholarship.
Intended use: For undergraduate study at accredited postsecondary institution.
Eligibility: Applicant or parent must be member/participant of American Legion Auxiliary. Applicant must be residing in Oregon. Applicant must be dependent of deceased veteran; or spouse of disabled veteran or deceased veteran.
Additional information: Applicant must be Junior member of American Legion Auxiliary for past three years and hold current membership. One scholarship in each division.

Amount of award:	$1,000
Application deadline:	March 15

Contact:
American Legion Auxiliary, Department of Oregon
Chairman of Education
P.O. Box 1730
Wilsonville, OR 97070-1730

American Legion Pennsylvania

American Legion Pennsylvania Joseph P. Gavenonis Scholarship

Type of award: Scholarship, renewable.
Intended use: For full-time undergraduate study at 4-year institution. Designated institutions: Pennsylvania colleges and universities.
Eligibility: Applicant or parent must be member/participant of American Legion. Applicant must be high school senior. Applicant must be residing in Pennsylvania. Applicant must be dependent of veteran or deceased veteran.
Application requirements: Proof of eligibility.

Additional information: Award is $1000 per year for four years based on grades. Applicant must be child of living member in good standing of Pennsylvania American Legion, or child of deceased Pennsylvania American Legion member.

Amount of award:	$1,000
Application deadline:	June 1

Contact:
American Legion Pennsylvania
Dept. Adjutant, Attn: Scholarship Secretary
P.O. Box 2324
Harrisburg, PA 17105-2324
Phone: 717-730-9100
Fax: 717-975-2836
Web: www.pa-legion.com

American Legion Pennsylvania Robert W. Valimont Endowment Fund Scholarship

Type of award: Scholarship, renewable.
Intended use: For full-time undergraduate study at vocational or 2-year institution. Designated institutions: Pennsylvania two-year technical or vocational schools.
Eligibility: Applicant must be residing in Pennsylvania.
Application requirements: Proof of eligibility. Membership in Pennsylvania American Legion Post not required, but must be documented if claimed.
Additional information: Award is $600 for first year; must reapply for second year. Preference given in the following order: children of Legionnaires; children of veterans; children of disabled veterans; children of deceased veterans.

Amount of award:	$600
Application deadline:	June 1
Total amount awarded:	$600

Contact:
American Legion Pennsylvania
Dept. Adjutant, Attn: Scholarship Secretary
P.O. Box 2324
Harrisburg, PA 17105-2324
Phone: 717-730-9100
Fax: 717-975-2836
Web: www.pa-legion.com

American Legion Pennsylvania Auxiliary

American Legion Pennsylvania Auxiliary Scholarship

Type of award: Scholarship.
Intended use: For undergraduate study. Designated institutions: Pennsylvania postsecondary institutions.
Eligibility: Applicant must be high school senior. Applicant must be residing in Pennsylvania. Applicant must be dependent of veteran.
Basis for selection: Applicant must demonstrate financial need.
Additional information: Award: $600 per year for four years.

Amount of award:	$2,400
Number of awards:	1
Application deadline:	March 15
Total amount awarded:	$2,400

Contact:
American Legion Auxiliary, Department of Pennsylvania
Department Education Chairman
P.O. Box 2643
Harrisburg, PA 17105
Phone: 717-763-7545
Fax: 717-763-0617

American Legion Pennsylvania Auxiliary Scholarship for Children of Deceased/Disabled Veterans

Type of award: Scholarship.
Intended use: For undergraduate study. Designated institutions: Pennsylvania postsecondary institutions.
Eligibility: Applicant must be high school senior. Applicant must be residing in Pennsylvania. Applicant must be dependent of disabled veteran or deceased veteran.
Basis for selection: Applicant must demonstrate financial need.
Additional information: Award is $600 per year for four years.

Amount of award:	$2,400
Number of awards:	1
Application deadline:	March 15
Total amount awarded:	$2,400

Contact:
American Legion Auxiliary, Department of Pennsylvania
Department Education Chairman
P.O. Box 2643
Harrisburg, PA 17105-2643
Phone: 717-763-7545
Fax: 717-763-0617

American Legion Puerto Rico Auxiliary

American Legion Puerto Rico Auxiliary Nursing Scholarship

Type of award: Scholarship.
Intended use: For undergraduate study at 2-year or 4-year institution. Designated institutions: Eligible institutions in Puerto Rico.
Eligibility: Applicant must be residing in Puerto Rico.
Basis for selection: Major/career interest in nursing.
Application requirements: Interview. Must be in nurse training program.
Additional information: $250 award for two consecutive years. Selected after filing application and attending personal interview.

Amount of award:	$250
Number of awards:	2
Application deadline:	March 15

Contact:
American Legion Auxiliary, Department of Puerto Rico
Education Chairman
P.O. Box 11424
Caparra Heights Station, PR 00922-1424

American Legion South Carolina

American Legion South Carolina Robert E. David Children's Scholarship

Type of award: Scholarship, renewable.
Intended use: For undergraduate study at 4-year institution.
Eligibility: Applicant must be residing in South Carolina. Applicant must be dependent of veteran during Grenada conflict, Korean War, Lebanon conflict, Panama conflict, Persian Gulf War, WW I, WW II or Vietnam.
Basis for selection: Applicant must demonstrate financial need and high academic achievement.
Additional information: Must have relative who is member of South Carolina American Legion. Must reapply yearly for renewal.

Amount of award:	$500
Number of awards:	10
Application deadline:	May 1
Total amount awarded:	$5,000

Contact:
American Legion South Carolina, Department Adjutant
P.O. Box 11355
132 Pickens Street
Columbia, SC 29211
Phone: 803-799-1992
Fax: 803-771-9831

American Legion South Carolina Scholarship

Type of award: Scholarship.
Intended use: For undergraduate study.
Eligibility: Applicant must be enrolled in high school. Applicant must be residing in South Carolina.
Basis for selection: Competition/talent/interest in oratory/debate.
Application requirements: Zone winners of High School Oratorical Contest. Post level contests must be completed by February 1.
Additional information: Awards: first-$1,600; second-$1,000; and third and fourth-$500. Distributed over four-year period.

Amount of award:	$500-$1,600
Number of awards:	4
Application deadline:	February 1
Total amount awarded:	$3,600

Contact:
American Legion South Carolina
P.O. Box 11355
132 Pickens St.
Columbia, SC 29211
Phone: 803-799-1992
Fax: 803-771-9831

American Legion South Carolina Auxiliary

American Legion South Carolina Auxiliary Gift Scholarship

Type of award: Scholarship.
Intended use: For undergraduate study at postsecondary institution.
Eligibility: Applicant or parent must be member/participant of American Legion Auxiliary. Applicant must be high school senior. Applicant must be residing in South Carolina.
Application requirements: Application must be completed and sent to Unit President no later than April 15.
Additional information: Must be American Legion Auxiliary member at least three consecutive years at time of application. Must have current membership card.

Amount of award:	$500
Number of awards:	2
Application deadline:	April 15
Total amount awarded:	$1,000

Contact:
American Legion Auxiliary, Department of South Carolina
Department Secretary
132 Pickens Street
Columbia, SC 29205
Phone: 803-799-6695
Fax: 803-799-7907

American Legion South Dakota

American Legion South Dakota Oratorical Contest

Type of award: Scholarship.
Intended use: For undergraduate study at postsecondary institution. Designated institutions: South Dakota postsecondary institutions.
Eligibility: Applicant must be enrolled in high school. Applicant must be residing in South Dakota.
Basis for selection: Competition/talent/interest in oratory/debate, based on breadth of knowledge, originality, application of knowledge of topic, skill in selecting examples and analogies, logic, voice, diction, style of language and delivery.
Application requirements: Proof of eligibility.
Additional information: Awards: first-$1,000; second-$500; third and fourth-$250. Redeemable within five years of date of award.

Amount of award:	$250-$1,000
Number of awards:	4
Total amount awarded:	$2,000

Contact:
American Legion South Dakota
Department Adjutant
P.O. Box 67
Watertown, SD 57201-0067
Phone: 605-886-3604

American Legion South Dakota Auxiliary

American Legion South Dakota Auxiliary College Scholarship

Type of award: Scholarship.
Intended use: For undergraduate study at vocational, 2-year or 4-year institution.
Eligibility: Applicant or parent must be member/participant of American Legion Auxiliary. Applicant must be at least 16, no older than 22. Applicant must be residing in South Dakota. Applicant must be dependent of veteran.
Additional information: Child of either veteran or Auxiliary member. College scholarships: two-$500; vocational scholarships: two-$500.

Amount of award:	$500
Number of awards:	4
Application deadline:	March 1
Total amount awarded:	$2,000

Contact:
American Legion South Dakota Auxiliary
Patricia Coyle, Department Secretary
P.O. Box 117
Huron, SD 57350-0117
Phone: 605-353-1793
Fax: 605-352-0336

American Legion South Dakota Auxiliary Nurse's Scholarship

Type of award: Scholarship.
Intended use: For undergraduate study at postsecondary institution.
Eligibility: Applicant or parent must be member/participant of American Legion Auxiliary. Applicant must be at least 16, no older than 22. Applicant must be residing in South Dakota. Applicant must be dependent of veteran.
Basis for selection: Major/career interest in nursing.
Additional information: Child of veteran or Auxiliary member.

Amount of award:	$500
Number of awards:	2
Application deadline:	March 1
Total amount awarded:	$1,000

Contact:
American Legion South Dakota Auxiliary
Patricia Coyle, Department Secretary
P.O. Box 117
Huron, SD 57350-0117
Phone: 605-353-1793
Fax: 605-352-0336

American Legion South Dakota Auxiliary Scholarship for College or Vocational

Type of award: Scholarship.
Intended use: For undergraduate or non-degree study at postsecondary institution.
Eligibility: Applicant or parent must be member/participant of American Legion Auxiliary. Applicant must be residing in South Dakota.

Additional information: Applicant must have been senior SD American Legion Auxiliary member for past three years and member for the current year.

Amount of award:	$400
Number of awards:	1
Application deadline:	March 1
Total amount awarded:	$400

Contact:
American Legion South Dakota Auxiliary
Patricia Coyle, Department Secretary
P.O. Box 117
Huron, SD 57350-0117
Phone: 605-353-1793
Fax: 605-352-0336

Thelma Foster Junior American Legion Auxiliary Members Scholarship

Type of award: Scholarship.
Intended use: For freshman study.
Eligibility: Applicant or parent must be member/participant of American Legion Auxiliary. Applicant must be high school senior. Applicant must be residing in South Dakota.
Additional information: High school senior or graduate. Junior member for past three years plus current year.

Amount of award:	$300
Number of awards:	1
Application deadline:	March 1

Contact:
American Legion South Dakota Auxiliary
Patricia Coyle, Dept. Secretary Secretary
P.O. Box 117
Huron, SD 57350-0117
Phone: 605-353-1793
Fax: 605-352-0336

Thelma Foster Senior American Legion Auxiliary Member Scholarship

Type of award: Scholarship.
Intended use: For undergraduate study.
Eligibility: Applicant or parent must be member/participant of American Legion Auxiliary. Applicant must be residing in South Dakota.
Additional information: Senior SD American Legion Auxiliary member for past three years plus current year.

Amount of award:	$300
Number of awards:	1
Application deadline:	March 1
Total amount awarded:	$300

Contact:
American Legion South Dakota Auxiliary
Patricia Coyle, Department Secretary
P.O. Box 117
Huron, SD 57350-0117
Phone: 605-353-1793
Fax: 605-352-0336

American Legion Tennessee

American Legion Tennessee Oratorical Contest

Type of award: Scholarship, renewable.
Intended use: For undergraduate study at postsecondary institution in United States.
Eligibility: Applicant must be enrolled in high school. Applicant must be residing in Tennessee.
Basis for selection: Competition/talent/interest in oratory/debate, based on breadth of knowledge, originality, application of knowledge of topic, skill in selecting examples and analogies, logic, voice, diction, style of language, and delivery.
Application requirements: Proof of eligibility. Enter high school oratorical contest through local high school.
Additional information: Scholarship awarded to top three winners. Awards: 1st-$5,000, 2nd-$2,500, 3rd-$1,500. First place winner eligible to enter national contest. National winner receives $18,000 scholarship.

Amount of award:	$1,500-$5,000
Number of awards:	3
Application deadline:	January 1
Total amount awarded:	$9,000

Contact:
American Legion Tennessee
215 8th Avenue North
Nashville, TN 37203-3583
Phone: 615-254-0568

Eagle Scout of the Year Scholarship

Type of award: Scholarship.
Intended use: For undergraduate study at postsecondary institution in United States.
Eligibility: Applicant or parent must be member/participant of Boy Scouts of America, Eagle Scouts. Applicant must be male. Applicant must be residing in Tennessee.
Application requirements: Nomination by Tennessee American Legion.
Additional information: Eagle Scout of the Year winner from Tennessee submitted to the national organization.

Amount of award:	$1,500
Number of awards:	1
Application deadline:	January 1
Total amount awarded:	$1,500

Contact:
American Legion Tennessee
215 8th Avenue North
Nashville, TN 37203-3583
Phone: 615-254-0568

American Legion Tennessee Auxiliary

American Legion Tennessee Auxiliary Vara Gray Scholarship Fund

Type of award: Scholarship.

Intended use: For freshman study at vocational, 2-year or 4-year institution.

Eligibility: Applicant must be high school senior. Applicant must be residing in Tennessee. Applicant must be dependent of veteran.

Application requirements: Recommendations, essay, nomination by local American Legion Auxiliary unit. SAT/ACT scores; 50 hours of volunteer service.

Additional information: Applicant must be child of veteran.

Amount of award:	$500
Number of awards:	3
Application deadline:	March 1
Total amount awarded:	$1,500

Contact:
American Legion Tennessee Auxiliary
Department Headquarters
4721 Trousdale Drive, Suite 131
Nashville, TN 37220
Phone: 615-781-1910
Fax: 615-781-1930

American Legion Texas Auxiliary

American Legion Texas Auxiliary General Education Scholarship

Type of award: Scholarship.

Intended use: For undergraduate study at postsecondary institution. Designated institutions: Texas postsecondary institutions.

Eligibility: Applicant must be residing in Texas. Applicant must be dependent of veteran.

Application requirements: Nomination by local unit. Unit sponsorship required.

Additional information: Obtain application from local unit.

Amount of award:	$500
Application deadline:	February 1

Contact:
American Legion Auxiliary
Department Headquarters
3401 Ed Bluestein Blvd, Suite 200
Austin, TX 78721-2902
Phone: 512-476-7278
Fax: 512-482-8391

American Legion Texas Auxiliary Medical Scholarship

Type of award: Scholarship.

Intended use: For undergraduate study at postsecondary institution.

Eligibility: Applicant must be residing in Texas. Applicant must be dependent of veteran.

Basis for selection: Major/career interest in nursing; health sciences; health-related professions or medical assistant.

Application requirements: Nomination by local unit. Unit sponsorship required.

Additional information: Obtain application from local unit.

Amount of award:	$500
Application deadline:	February 1

Contact:
American Legion Auxiliary
Department Headquarters
3401 Ed Bluestein Blvd, Suite 200
Austin, TX 78721-2902
Phone: 512-476-7278
Fax: 512-482-8391

American Legion Utah Auxiliary

American Legion Utah Auxiliary National President's Scholarship

Type of award: Scholarship.

Intended use: For undergraduate study.

Eligibility: Applicant must be high school senior. Applicant must be residing in Utah. Applicant must be dependent of veteran during Grenada conflict, Korean War, Lebanon conflict, Panama conflict, Persian Gulf War, WW I, WW II or Vietnam.

Additional information: Awards: 1-$2,000 and 1-$1,500.

Amount of award:	$1,500-$2,000
Number of awards:	2
Application deadline:	February 15
Total amount awarded:	$3,500

Contact:
American Legion Utah Auxiliary
Deanna Sargent
B-61 State Capitol Bldg.
Salt Lake City, UT 84114
Phone: 801-538-1014
Fax: 801-537-9191
Web: www.legion-aux.org

American Legion Vermont

American Legion Eagle Scout of the Year

Type of award: Scholarship.

Intended use: For undergraduate study.

Eligibility: Applicant or parent must be member/participant of Boy Scouts of America, Eagle Scouts. Applicant must be male, high school senior. Applicant must be residing in Vermont.

Additional information: Awarded to Boy Scout chosen for outstanding service to his religious institution, school and community. Applicant must have received Eagle Scout Award.

Amount of award:	$1,000
Number of awards:	1
Application deadline:	March 1
Total amount awarded:	$1,000

Contact:
American Legion of Vermont
Education and Scholarship Committee
P.O. Box 396
Montpelier, VT 05601-0396
Phone: 802-223-7131
Fax: 802-223-0318

American Legion Vermont Scholarship

Type of award: Scholarship.
Intended use: For undergraduate study at vocational, 2-year or 4-year institution.
Eligibility: Applicant must be high school senior. Applicant must be residing in Vermont.
Application requirements: Applicant must be senior at Vermont secondary school; senior from adjacent state, whose parents are legal Vermont residents; or senior from adjacent state attending Vermont school.
Additional information: Awards: Five-$1,000 paid annually for four years ($250/year); five-$500 paid annually for two years ($250/year); one-$2,000 ($1,250 first year, $250 for the following years); one-$1,500 ($750/year).

Amount of award:	$500-$2,000
Number of awards:	12
Application deadline:	April 1
Total amount awarded:	$11,000

Contact:
American Legion of Vermont
Education and Scholarship Committee
P.O. Box 396
Montpelier, VT 05601-0396
Phone: 802-223-7131
Fax: 802-223-0318

American Legion Vermont Scholarship Program

Type of award: Scholarship.
Intended use: For undergraduate study.
Eligibility: Applicant must be high school senior. Applicant must be residing in Vermont.
Basis for selection: Applicant must demonstrate financial need.
Application requirements: Parents must be Vermont residents.
Additional information: Amount and number of grants vary. Contact local American Legion post or American Legion Auxiliary unit for application.
Contact:
American Legion of Vermont
Education and Scholarship Committee
P.O. Box 396
Montpelier, VT 05601-0396
Phone: 802-223-7131
Fax: 802-223-0318

National High School Oratorical Contest

Type of award: Scholarship.
Eligibility: Applicant must be enrolled in high school. Applicant must be U.S. citizen or permanent resident residing in Vermont.
Basis for selection: Competition/talent/interest in oratory/debate, based on breadth of knowledge, originality, application of knowledge of topic, skill in selecting examples and analogies, logic, voice, diction, style of language, and delivery.
Additional information: No applications required. Selection based on prepared oration. Request rules by January 1.

Amount of award:	$2,000
Number of awards:	1
Total amount awarded:	$2,000

Contact:
American Legion of Vermont
Education and Scholarship Committee
P.O. Box 396
Montpelier, VT 05601-0396
Phone: 802-223-7131

American Legion Virginia

American Legion Virginia Oratorical Contest

Type of award: Scholarship.
Intended use: For undergraduate study at postsecondary institution.
Eligibility: Applicant must be enrolled in high school. Applicant must be residing in Virginia.
Basis for selection: Competition/talent/interest in oratory/debate, based on breadth of knowledge, originality, application of knowledge of topic, skill in selecting examples and analogies, logic, voice, diction, style of language and delivery.
Application requirements: Proof of eligibility. Speech winners of Virginia Department Oratorical Contest.
Additional information: Awards: 1st-$1,100; 2nd-$600; 3rd-$600.

Amount of award:	$600-$1,100
Number of awards:	3
Application deadline:	December 1
Total amount awarded:	$2,300

Contact:
American Legion Virginia
Department Adjutant
1708 Commonwealth Ave.
Richmond, VA 23230
Phone: 804-353-6606
Fax: 804-358-1940
Web: www.valegion.org

American Legion Virginia Auxiliary

American Legion Virginia Auxiliary Anna Gear Junior Scholarship

Type of award: Scholarship.
Intended use: For undergraduate study.
Eligibility: Applicant or parent must be member/participant of American Legion Auxiliary. Applicant must be high school senior. Applicant must be residing in Virginia.
Additional information: Junior member of American Legion Auxiliary for three years. Must be a senior attending accredited Virginia high school.

Amount of award:	$1,000
Number of awards:	1
Application deadline:	April 1
Total amount awarded:	$1,000

127

Contact:
American Legion Auxiliary, Department of Virginia
Education Chairman
1805 Chantilly Street
Richmond, VA 23230
Phone: 804-355-6410

Dr. Kate Waller Barrett Grant

Type of award: Scholarship.
Intended use: For undergraduate study at accredited vocational, 2-year or 4-year institution.
Eligibility: Applicant or parent must be member/participant of American Legion Auxiliary. Applicant must be high school senior. Applicant must be residing in Virginia. Applicant must be dependent of veteran.
Basis for selection: Applicant must demonstrate financial need.
Additional information: Applicant must be child of veteran or child of Auxiliary member. Must be senior attending accredited Virginia high school.

Amount of award:	$1,000
Number of awards:	1
Application deadline:	March 15
Total amount awarded:	$1,000

Contact:
American Legion Auxiliary, Department of Virginia
Education Chairman
1805 Chantilly Street
Richmond, VA 23230
Phone: 804-355-6410

American Legion Washington

American Legion Department Oratorical Contest

Type of award: Scholarship.
Intended use: For undergraduate study.
Eligibility: Applicant must be enrolled in high school. Applicant must be residing in Washington.
Basis for selection: Competition/talent/interest in oratory/debate, based on breadth of knowledge, originality, application of knowledge of topic, skill in selecting examples and analogies, logic, voice, diction, style of language, and delivery.
Additional information: Student participates in Post, District, Area, and Department contests.

Application deadline:	April 1
Total amount awarded:	$7,800

Contact:
American Legion Washington
Chairman, Department of Child Welfare
P.O. Box 3917
Lacey, WA 98509-3917
Phone: 360-491-4373
Fax: 360-491-7442
Web: www.walegion.org

American Legion Washington Scholarship

Type of award: Scholarship.

Intended use: For undergraduate study at accredited vocational, 2-year or 4-year institution. Designated institutions: Eligible institutions in Washington State.
Eligibility: Applicant or parent must be member/participant of American Legion. Applicant must be residing in Washington.
Basis for selection: Applicant must demonstrate financial need.
Additional information: Awards: 1-$2,500 and 1-$1,500. Must be child of living or deceased Washington Legionnaire or Auxiliary member.

Amount of award:	$1,500-$2,500
Number of awards:	2
Application deadline:	April 1
Total amount awarded:	$4,000

Contact:
American Legion Washington
Chairman, Department of Child Welfare
P.O. Box 3917
Lacey, WA 98509-3917
Phone: 360-491-4373
Fax: 360-491-7442
Web: www.walegion.org

American Legion Washington Auxiliary

American Legion Washington Auxiliary Florence Lemcke Memorial Scholarship

Type of award: Scholarship.
Intended use: For undergraduate study at 2-year or 4-year institution.
Eligibility: Applicant must be residing in Washington. Applicant must be dependent of veteran.
Basis for selection: Major/career interest in arts, general or art/art history.
Additional information: For use in field of fine arts.

Amount of award:	$500
Number of awards:	1
Application deadline:	April 1
Total amount awarded:	$500

Contact:
American Legion Washington Auxiliary
P.O. Box 5867
Lacey, WA 98509-5867

American Legion Washington Auxiliary Margarite McAlpin Nurse's Scholarship

Type of award: Scholarship.
Intended use: For undergraduate study.
Eligibility: Applicant must be residing in Washington. Applicant must be veteran or descendant of veteran; or dependent of veteran.
Basis for selection: Major/career interest in nursing.

Amount of award:	$700
Number of awards:	1
Application deadline:	April 1
Total amount awarded:	$700

Contact:
American Legion Washington Auxiliary
P.O. Box 5867
Lacey, WA 98509-5867

American Legion Washington Auxiliary Scholarships

Type of award: Scholarship.
Intended use: For undergraduate study at postsecondary institution.
Eligibility: Applicant must be residing in Washington. Applicant must be dependent of disabled veteran or deceased veteran.

Amount of award:	$500
Number of awards:	3
Application deadline:	April 1
Total amount awarded:	$1,500

Contact:
American Legion Washington Auxiliary
P.O. Box 5867
Lacey, WA 98509-5867

American Legion Washington Auxiliary Susan Burdett Scholarship

Type of award: Scholarship.
Intended use: For undergraduate study at postsecondary institution.
Eligibility: Applicant must be female. Applicant must be residing in Washington.
Additional information: Applicant must be former Evergreen Girls State Citizen (WA).

Amount of award:	$400
Number of awards:	1
Application deadline:	April 1
Total amount awarded:	$400

Contact:
American Legion Washington Auxiliary
Education Scholarships
P.O. Box 5867
Lacey, WA 98509-5867

American Legion West Virginia

American Legion West Virginia Oratorical Contest

Type of award: Scholarship.
Intended use: For freshman study.
Eligibility: Applicant must be enrolled in high school. Applicant must be residing in West Virginia.
Basis for selection: Competition/talent/interest in oratory/debate, based on breadth of knowledge, originality, application of knowledge of topic, skill in selecting examples and analogies, logic, voice, diction, style of language and delivery.
Application requirements: District Oratorical Contest winners.
Additional information: Nine district awards of $200; three section awards of $300. State winner receives $500 and four-year scholarship to West Virginia University or other state college under control of Board of Regents. Contest is held in January and February. Information may be obtained from local high school or American Legion post.

Amount of award:	$200-$500

Contact:
American Legion West Virginia
State Adjutant
2016 Kanawha Blvd. E, Box 3191
Charleston, WV 25332-3191
Phone: 304-343-7591
Fax: 304-343-7592

American Legion West Virginia Auxiliary

American Legion West Virginia Auxiliary Scholarship

Type of award: Scholarship, renewable.
Intended use: For undergraduate study at postsecondary institution. Designated institutions: West Virginia colleges and universities.
Eligibility: Applicant must be no older than 22. Applicant must be residing in West Virginia. Applicant must be dependent of veteran.
Application requirements: Proof of eligibility.
Additional information: Award: $300/year for four years. Must be high school senior or high school graduate. Award must be renewed annually, not to exceed total of four years.

Amount of award:	$300
Number of awards:	4
Application deadline:	March 1
Total amount awarded:	$1,200

Contact:
American Legion West Virginia Auxiliary
Secretary/Treasurer Mary Rose Yoho
RR 1 Box 144A
Proctor, WV 26055-9616
Phone: 304-455-3449

American Legion Wisconsin

American Legion Baseball Scholarship

Type of award: Scholarship.
Intended use: For undergraduate study.
Eligibility: Applicant must be residing in Wisconsin.
Basis for selection: Competition/talent/interest in Athletics/sports.
Application requirements: Nomination by Board of Directors.
Additional information: Applicant must be current member of Wisconsin American Legion baseball team. Must have participated in current American Legion Regional or State Championship, Junior Position Air Rifle Tournament. Award rotates yearly from region to region and is awarded at State Convention.

Amount of award:	$500
Number of awards:	1
Total amount awarded:	$500

Contact:
American Legion Wisconsin
Program Secretary
P.O. Box 388
Portage, WI 53901
Phone: 608-745-1090
Fax: 608-745-0179
Web: www.wilegion.org

American Legion Wisconsin Eagle Scout of the Year Scholarship

Type of award: Scholarship.
Intended use: For undergraduate study.
Eligibility: Applicant or parent must be member/participant of American Legion/Boys Scouts of America. Applicant must be male, high school senior. Applicant must be residing in Wisconsin.
Basis for selection: Applicant must demonstrate high academic achievement.
Additional information: Applicant must be Boy Scout, Varsity Scout or Explorer whose group is sponsored by Legion or Auxiliary post, or whose father or grandfather is Legion or Auxiliary member. $1000 award for state winner.

Amount of award:	$1,000
Number of awards:	1
Application deadline:	March 1
Total amount awarded:	$1,000

Contact:
American Legion Wisconsin
Program Secretary
P.O. Box 388
Portage, WI 53901
Phone: 608-745-1090
Fax: 608-745-0179
Web: www.wilegion.org

American Legion Wisconsin Auxiliary

American Legion Wisconsin Auxiliary Health Careers Award

Type of award: Scholarship.
Intended use: For undergraduate study at accredited postsecondary institution. Designated institutions: Hospital, university or technical school. Does not need to be four-year program.
Eligibility: Applicant or parent must be member/participant of American Legion Auxiliary. Applicant must be residing in Wisconsin. Applicant must be descendant of veteran; or dependent of veteran or deceased veteran; or spouse of veteran or deceased veteran.
Basis for selection: Major/career interest in health sciences or health-related professions. Applicant must demonstrate financial need and high academic achievement.
Additional information: Minimum 3.2 GPA. Grandchildren and great-grandchildren of veterans are eligible if Auxiliary members.

Amount of award:	$750
Number of awards:	2
Application deadline:	March 15
Total amount awarded:	$1,500

Contact:
American Legion Wisconsin Auxiliary, Department Secretary
2930 American Legion Drive
P.O. Box 140
Portage, WI 53901-0140
Phone: 608-745-0124
Fax: 608-745-1947
Web: www.amlegionauxwi.org

American Legion Wisconsin Auxiliary H.S. and Angeline Lewis Scholarship

Type of award: Scholarship.
Intended use: For undergraduate, master's or doctoral study at accredited postsecondary institution.
Eligibility: Applicant must be residing in Wisconsin. Applicant must be descendant of veteran; or dependent of veteran; or spouse of veteran or deceased veteran.
Basis for selection: Applicant must demonstrate financial need and high academic achievement.
Additional information: Minimum 3.2 GPA. Grandchildren and great-grandchildren of veterans eligible if members of Auxiliary. One award for graduate study; five awards for undergraduate study.

Amount of award:	$1,000
Number of awards:	6
Application deadline:	March 15
Total amount awarded:	$6,000

Contact:
American Legion Wisconsin Auxiliary, Department Secretary
2930 American Legion Drive
P.O. Box 140
Portage, WI 53901-0140
Phone: 608-745-0124
Fax: 608-745-1947
Web: www.amlegionauxwi.org

American Legion Wisconsin Auxiliary Merit and Memorial Scholarship

Type of award: Scholarship.
Intended use: For undergraduate study.
Eligibility: Applicant must be residing in Wisconsin. Applicant must be spouse of veteran or deceased veteran.
Basis for selection: Applicant must demonstrate financial need and high academic achievement.
Additional information: Minimum 3.2 GPA.

Amount of award:	$1,000
Number of awards:	6
Application deadline:	March 15
Total amount awarded:	$6,000

Contact:
American Legion Wisconsin Auxiliary, Department Secretary
2930 American Legion Drive
P.O. Box 140
Portage, WI 53901-0140
Phone: 608-745-0124
Fax: 608-745-1947
Web: www.amlegionauxwi.org

American Legion Wisconsin Auxiliary Registered Nurse Degree Award

Type of award: Scholarship.
Intended use: For undergraduate study at accredited postsecondary institution.
Eligibility: Applicant must be residing in Wisconsin. Applicant must be descendant of veteran; or dependent of veteran or deceased veteran; or spouse of veteran or deceased veteran.
Basis for selection: Major/career interest in nursing. Applicant must demonstrate financial need and high academic achievement.
Additional information: Must be in nursing school or accepted to accredited school of nursing, accredited hospital, or university registered nursing program. Minimum 3.2 GPA. Grandchild or great-grandchild of veteran eligible if Auxiliary member.

Amount of award:	$750
Number of awards:	2
Application deadline:	March 15
Total amount awarded:	$1,500

Contact:
American Legion Wisconsin Auxiliary, Department Secretary
2930 American Legion Drive
P.O. Box 140
Portage, WI 53901-0140
Phone: 608-745-0124
Fax: 608-745-1947
Web: www.amlegionauxwi.org

American Legion Wisconsin Auxiliary State President's Scholarship

Type of award: Scholarship.
Intended use: For undergraduate study at accredited postsecondary institution.
Eligibility: Applicant or parent must be member/participant of American Legion Auxiliary. Applicant must be residing in Wisconsin. Applicant must be descendant of veteran; or dependent of veteran; or spouse of veteran or deceased veteran.
Basis for selection: Applicant must demonstrate financial need and high academic achievement.
Additional information: Minimum 3.2 GPA. Mother of applicant or applicant must be Auxiliary member. Grandchildren and great-grandchildren of veterans eligible if Auxiliary members.

Amount of award:	$1,000
Number of awards:	3
Application deadline:	March 15
Total amount awarded:	$3,000

Contact:
American Legion Wisconsin Auxiliary, Department Secretary
2930 American Legion Drive
P.O. Box 140
Portage, WI 53901-0140
Phone: 608-745-0124
Fax: 608-745-1947
Web: www.amlegionauxwi.org

Badger Girls State Scholarship

Type of award: Scholarship.
Intended use: For undergraduate study at accredited postsecondary institution in United States.

Eligibility: Applicant must be residing in Wisconsin. Applicant must be descendant of veteran; or dependent of veteran; or spouse of veteran or deceased veteran.
Basis for selection: Applicant must demonstrate financial need and high academic achievement.
Application requirements: Must be WALA Badger Girls State Citizen of previous year.
Additional information: Number of scholarships determined annually. Applications automatically mailed yearly to eligible students.
Contact:
American Legion Auxiliary Wisconsin, Department Secretary
2930 American Legion Drive
P.O. Box 140
Portage, WI 53901
Phone: 608-745-0124
Fax: 608-745-1947
Web: www.amlegionauxwi.org

American Legion Wisconsin Auxiliary, Department Secretary

American Legion Wisconsin Auxiliary Della Van Deuren Memorial Scholarship

Type of award: Scholarship.
Intended use: For undergraduate study.
Eligibility: Applicant or parent must be member/participant of American Legion Auxiliary. Applicant must be residing in Wisconsin. Applicant must be descendant of veteran; or dependent of veteran; or spouse of veteran or deceased veteran.
Basis for selection: Applicant must demonstrate financial need and high academic achievement.
Additional information: Applicant must have minimum 3.2 GPA. Applicant's school need not be in Wisconsin. Grandchildren and great-grandchildren of veterans are eligible if they are members of American Legion Auxiliary. Applicant's mother or applicant must be member of American Legion Auxiliary.

Amount of award:	$1,000
Number of awards:	2
Application deadline:	March 15
Total amount awarded:	$2,000

Contact:
American Legion Wisconsin Auxiliary, Department Secretary
2930 American Legion Drive
P.O. Box 140
Portage, WI 53901-0140
Phone: 608-745-0214
Fax: 608-745-1947
Web: www.amlegionauxwi.org

Scholarships

131

American Legion Wyoming

American Legion Wyoming E.B. Blackmore Memorial Scholarship

Type of award: Scholarship.
Intended use: For undergraduate study at postsecondary institution.
Eligibility: Applicant or parent must be member/participant of American Legion. Applicant must be residing in Wyoming. Applicant must be veteran or descendant of veteran; or dependent of veteran.
Additional information: Wyoming students only. Applicant must be child or grandchild of Legionnaire.

Amount of award:	$1,000
Number of awards:	1
Application deadline:	May 1
Total amount awarded:	$1,000

Contact:
American Legion Wyoming
Department Adjutant
1320 Hugur Ave.
Cheyenne, WY 82001
Phone: 307-634-3035
Fax: 307-635-7093

American Legion Wyoming Oratorical Contest

Type of award: Scholarship.
Intended use: For undergraduate study at postsecondary institution.
Eligibility: Applicant must be enrolled in high school. Applicant must be residing in Wyoming.
Basis for selection: Competition/talent/interest in oratory/debate, based on breadth of knowledge, originality, application of knowledge of topic, skill in selecting examples and analogies, logic, voice, diction, style of language and delivery.
Application requirements: Proof of eligibility. Winner of state high school oratorical contest.
Additional information: Wyoming students only.

Amount of award:	$500
Number of awards:	1
Total amount awarded:	$500

Contact:
American Legion Wyoming
Department Adjutant
1320 Hugur Ave.
Cheyenne, WY 82001
Phone: 307-634-3035
Fax: 307-635-7093

American Legion Wyoming Auxiliary

American Legion Wyoming Auxiliary Past Presidents' Parley Scholarship

Type of award: Scholarship, renewable.
Intended use: For undergraduate study at 2-year or 4-year institution.
Eligibility: Applicant must be residing in Wyoming.
Basis for selection: Major/career interest in nursing or health-related professions. Applicant must demonstrate high academic achievement.
Application requirements: Must be in 3rd quarter of training and have 3.0 GPA.
Additional information: Preference given to nursing students who are children of veterans.

Amount of award:	$300
Application deadline:	May 31

Contact:
American Legion Wyoming Auxiliary
Department Secretary
P.O. Box 2198
Gillette, WY 82717
Phone: 307-686-7137

American Medical Technologists

Medical Technologists Scholarship

Type of award: Scholarship.
Intended use: For full-time undergraduate or graduate study at accredited postsecondary institution in United States.
Eligibility: Applicant must be U.S. citizen or permanent resident.
Basis for selection: Major/career interest in medical assistant; dental assistant; dental laboratory technology or medical specialties/research. Applicant must demonstrate financial need and high academic achievement.
Application requirements: Recommendations, essay, transcript, proof of eligibility. Two letters of recommendation. A typed statement stating why applicant has chosen this career must be included with application. Application must be typed. All applications and supporting documents become the property of American Medical Technologists and cannot be returned.
Additional information: Scholarship is available only to high school graduates pursuing studies in medical technology, medical laboratory technician, medical assisting, medical administrative specialist, dental assisting, phlebotomy or office laboratory technician. Students pursuing careers in other medical, health or science fields do not qualify.

Amount of award:	$500
Number of awards:	5
Application deadline:	April 1
Total amount awarded:	$2,500

Contact:
American Medical Technologists
710 Higgins Road
Park Ridge, IL 60068-5765
Phone: 847-823-5169
Fax: 847-823-0458
Web: www.amt1.com

American Meteorological Society

American Meteorological Society Undergraduate Scholarships

Type of award: Scholarship.
Intended use: For full-time senior study at accredited 4-year institution in United States.
Eligibility: Applicant must be U.S. citizen or permanent resident.
Basis for selection: Major/career interest in atmospheric sciences/meteorology; oceanography/marine studies or hydrology. Applicant must demonstrate high academic achievement and seriousness of purpose.
Application requirements: Recommendations, essay, transcript, proof of eligibility.
Additional information: Scholarships will be awarded to students entering final year of undergraduate study. Minimum 3.0 GPA. Applicants must major in atmospheric or related oceanic or hydrologic sciences, and/or must show clear intent to pursue careers in atmospheric or related sciences. Marine biology majors not eligible. Number and amount of scholarships vary. No more than two students from any one institution may enter papers in any one contest. Visit Website for more information or to download application.

> **Application deadline:** February 13

Contact:
American Meteorological Society
Fellowship/Scholarship Programs
45 Beacon Street
Boston, MA 2108-3693
Phone: 617-227-2426
Fax: 617-742-8718
Web: www.ametsoc.org/ams

American Meteorological Society/ Industry Minority Scholarship

Type of award: Scholarship.
Intended use: For full-time freshman study at accredited 4-year institution in United States.
Eligibility: Applicant must be Alaskan native, Asian American, African American, Mexican American, Hispanic American, Puerto Rican or American Indian. Applicant must be high school senior. Applicant must be U.S. citizen or permanent resident.
Basis for selection: Major/career interest in atmospheric sciences/meteorology; oceanography/marine studies or hydrology. Applicant must demonstrate high academic achievement.
Application requirements: Recommendations, essay, transcript, proof of eligibility. SAT scores.
Additional information: Award is for minority students who have traditionally been underrepresented in sciences, especially Hispanic, Native American, and black/African American students. Applicant must intend to pursue careers in atmospheric or related oceanic and hydrologic sciences. Must be entering freshman year of undergraduate study. Marine biology majors ineligible. Visit Website to download application.

> **Amount of award:** $3,000
> **Application deadline:** February 13

Contact:
American Meteorological Society
Fellowship/Scholarship Programs
45 Beacon Street
Boston, MA 2108-3693
Phone: 617-227-2426
Fax: 617-742-8718
Web: www.ametsoc.org/ams

American Meteorological Society/ Industry Undergraduate Scholarship

Type of award: Scholarship, renewable.
Intended use: For full-time junior or senior study at accredited 4-year institution in United States.
Eligibility: Applicant must be U.S. citizen or permanent resident.
Basis for selection: Major/career interest in atmospheric sciences/meteorology; hydrology; chemistry; computer/ information sciences; mathematics or physics. Applicant must demonstrate high academic achievement.
Application requirements: Recommendations, essay, transcript, proof of eligibility.
Additional information: Minimum 3.0 GPA. Applicant must major in atmospheric sciences, oceanography, hydrology, chemistry, computer sciences, math, engineering, and physics with intention to pursue career in atmospheric, oceanic and/or hydrologic sciences. Applicants must be entering junior year. Marine biology majors ineligible. Two-year scholarships are $2,000 per year. Second year funding dependent upon academic performance and faculty adviser recommendation. Visit Website to download application.

> **Amount of award:** $2,000
> **Application deadline:** February 13
> **Notification begins:** May 1

Contact:
American Meteorological Society
Fellowship/Scholarship Programs
45 Beacon Street
Boston, MA 2108-3693
Phone: 617-227-2426
Fax: 617-742-8718
Web: www.ametsoc.org/ams

Meteorological Society Father James B. MacElwane Annual Award

Type of award: Scholarship.
Intended use: For undergraduate study.
Eligibility: Applicant must be U.S. citizen or permanent resident.
Basis for selection: Competition/talent/interest in writing/ journalism. Major/career interest in atmospheric sciences/ meteorology; oceanography/marine studies or hydrology.
Application requirements: Essay, transcript, proof of eligibility. Students must submit an original paper plus four photocopies; a letter, an application including contact information.
Additional information: Award intended to stimulate interest in meteorology among college students through encouragement of original student papers concerned with some phase of atmospheric sciences. Student must be enrolled as undergraduate when paper is written. Submissions from women, minorities, and disabled students who are traditionally underrepresented in atmospheric and related oceanic and hydrologic sciences encouraged. No more than two students

from any one institution may enter papers in any one contest. Visit Website for application and information.

Amount of award:	$300
Number of awards:	1
Number of applicants:	10
Application deadline:	June 11
Total amount awarded:	$300

Contact:
American Meteorological Society
Fellowship/Scholarship Programs
45 Beacon Street
Boston, MA 02108-3693
Phone: 617-227-2426
Fax: 617-742-8718
Web: www.ametsoc.org/ams

American Morgan Horse Institute

AMHI Educational Scholarships

Type of award: Scholarship.
Intended use: For non-degree study at vocational, 2-year or 4-year institution.
Basis for selection: Major/career interest in equestrian/equine studies. Applicant must demonstrate financial need, high academic achievement, depth of character, leadership, seriousness of purpose and service orientation.
Application requirements: Recommendations, essay, transcript. Achievement with Morgan horses.
Additional information: Send SASE for application or download from Website.

Amount of award:	$1,000-$3,000
Number of awards:	5
Number of applicants:	200
Application deadline:	March 1
Notification begins:	June 1
Total amount awarded:	$15,000

Contact:
AMHI Scholarships
International Morgan Connection Scholarships
P.O. Box 837
Shelburne, VT 05482-0837
Web: www.morganhorse.com

AMHI International Morgan Connection Scholarships

Type of award: Scholarship.
Intended use: For undergraduate study at vocational, 2-year or 4-year institution.
Eligibility: Applicant must be high school senior.
Basis for selection: Major/career interest in equestrian/equine studies.
Application requirements: Recommendations, essay, transcript. Applicant must be currently showing Morgan horse in Western Seat, Hunter Seat or Saddle Seat divisions. Applicant must provide photo with application.
Additional information: One $2,000 scholarship is awarded in each of the following divisions: Western Seat, Hunter Seat and Saddle Seat.

Amount of award:	$2,000
Number of awards:	3
Application deadline:	March 1

Contact:
AMHI Scholarships
International Morgan Connection Scholarships
P.O. Box 837
Shelburne, VT 05482-0837
Web: www.morganhorse.com

AMHI van Schaik Dressage Scholarship

Type of award: Scholarship, renewable.
Intended use: For non-degree study.
Basis for selection: Major/career interest in dressage or equestrian/equine studies. Applicant must demonstrate seriousness of purpose.
Application requirements: Recommendations, essay.
Additional information: Must be dressage rider using Morgan horse. For anyone competing in and interested in advancing through levels of dressage to Fourth level and above. Download application from Website.

Amount of award:	$1,000
Number of awards:	1
Number of applicants:	50
Application deadline:	November 30
Notification begins:	January 10
Total amount awarded:	$1,000

Contact:
AMHI Scholarships
International Morgan Connection Scholarships
P.O. Box 837
Shelburne, VT 05482-0837
Web: www.morganhorse.com

American Nuclear Society

American Nuclear Society Environmental Sciences Division Scholarship

Type of award: Scholarship.
Intended use: For full-time junior or senior study at accredited 4-year institution in United States.
Eligibility: Applicant must be U.S. citizen or permanent resident.
Basis for selection: Major/career interest in environmental science; engineering, environmental; ecology; natural resources/conservation or nuclear science.
Additional information: Applicant must be an undergraduate of at least junior status pursuing a degree in a discipline related to career in environmental aspects of nuclear science or nuclear engineering. See Website for application and requirements.

Amount of award:	$2,000
Number of awards:	1
Application deadline:	February 1

Contact:
American Nuclear Society
555 North Kensington Avenue
La Grange Park, IL 60526
Phone: 708-352-6611
Fax: 708-352-0499
Web: www.ans.org

Angelo S. Bisesti Scholarship

Type of award: Scholarship.
Intended use: For full-time junior or senior study at 4-year institution in United States.
Eligibility: Applicant must be U.S. citizen or permanent resident.
Basis for selection: Major/career interest in nuclear science or engineering, nuclear.
Additional information: Applicant must be at least entering junior enrolled in program leading to degree in nuclear science, nuclear engineering, or nuclear-related field and pursuing a career in the field of commercial nuclear power. Visit Website to download application.

Amount of award:	$2,000
Number of awards:	1
Application deadline:	February 1
Total amount awarded:	$2,000

Contact:
American Nuclear Society
555 North Kensington Avenue
La Grange Park, IL 60526
Phone: 708-352-6611
Fax: 708-352-0499
Web: www.ans.org

ANS Undergraduate Scholarships

Type of award: Scholarship.
Intended use: For sophomore, junior or senior study at accredited 4-year institution in United States.
Eligibility: Applicant must be U.S. citizen or permanent resident.
Basis for selection: Major/career interest in nuclear science or engineering, nuclear.
Additional information: Maximum of four scholarships for entering sophomores in study leading to degree in nuclear science, nuclear engineering, or nuclear-related field; maximum of 21 scholarships for students who will be entering junior or senior year.

Amount of award:	$2,000
Application deadline:	February 1

Contact:
American Nuclear Society
555 North Kensington Avenue
La Grange Park, IL 60526
Phone: 708-352-6611
Fax: 708-352-0499
Web: www.ans.org

Decommissioning, Decontamination and Reutilization Scholarship

Type of award: Scholarship.
Intended use: For junior or senior study at accredited 4-year institution in United States.
Eligibility: Applicant must be U.S. citizen or permanent resident.
Basis for selection: Major/career interest in engineering, nuclear; environmental science or engineering, environmental.
Application requirements: Must join ANS.
Additional information: Applicants must be enrolled in curriculum of engineering or science associated with decommissioning/decontamination of nuclear facilities, management/characterization of nuclear waste, or restoration of environment. If awarded scholarship, student must join ANS and designate DDR Division as one professional division.

Awardee must also provide student support to DDR Division at next ANS meeting after receiving award (funding provided for travel to meeting but does not include food and lodging).

Amount of award:	$2,000
Number of awards:	1
Application deadline:	February 1

Contact:
American Nuclear Society
555 North Kensington Avenue
La Grange Park, IL 60526
Phone: 708-352-6611
Fax: 708-352-0499
Web: www.ans.org

Delayed Education Scholarship for Women

Type of award: Scholarship.
Intended use: For undergraduate study at accredited 4-year institution in United States.
Eligibility: Applicant must be female, returning adult student. Applicant must be U.S. citizen or permanent resident.
Basis for selection: Major/career interest in nuclear science or engineering, nuclear. Applicant must demonstrate financial need and high academic achievement.
Additional information: Award for mature women who have had delay in their education in field of nuclear science and engineering. One request and one application cover D.E.W.S. Award and John and Muriel Landis Award. Applicants must check appropriate box on Landis Scholarship form. Visit Website for application and requirements.

Amount of award:	$4,000
Number of awards:	1
Application deadline:	February 1

Contact:
American Nuclear Society
555 North Kensington Avenue
La Grange Park, IL 60526
Phone: 708-352-6611
Fax: 708-352-0499
Web: www.ans.org

James R. Vogt Scholarship

Type of award: Scholarship.
Intended use: For full-time undergraduate or graduate study at accredited 4-year or graduate institution.
Eligibility: Applicant must be U.S. citizen or permanent resident.
Basis for selection: Major/career interest in chemistry or nuclear science.
Additional information: Applicants must be enrolled in or proposing to enroll in radio-analytical, analytical chemistry, or analytical applications of nuclear science. Awards are $2,000 for undergraduates and $3,000 for graduate students. See Website for application and requirements.

Amount of award:	$2,000-$3,000
Number of awards:	1
Application deadline:	February 1
Notification begins:	May 9

Contact:
American Nuclear Society
555 North Kensington Avenue
La Grange Park, IL 60526
Phone: 708-352-6611
Fax: 708-352-0499
Web: www.ans.org

John and Muriel Landis Scholarship

Type of award: Scholarship.
Intended use: For undergraduate or graduate study at 4-year or graduate institution in United States.
Eligibility: Applicant must be U.S. citizen or permanent resident.
Basis for selection: Major/career interest in nuclear science or engineering, nuclear. Applicant must demonstrate financial need.
Additional information: Awarded to students with greater than average financial need. Consideration given to conditions or experiences that render student disadvantaged (poor high school/undergraduate preparation, etc.). Applicants should be planning career in nuclear science or nuclear engineering. Qualified high school seniors eligible to apply. Visit Website for application and requirements.
>   **Amount of award:** $4,000
>   **Number of awards:** 8
>   **Application deadline:** February 1

Contact:
American Nuclear Society
555 North Kensington Avenue
La Grange Park, IL 60526
Phone: 708-352-6611
Fax: 708-352-0499
Web: www.ans.org

John R. Lamarsh Scholarship

Type of award: Scholarship.
Intended use: For full-time junior or senior study at accredited 4-year institution in United States.
Eligibility: Applicant must be U.S. citizen or permanent resident.
Basis for selection: Major/career interest in nuclear science or engineering, nuclear.
Additional information: Applicant must be at least an entering junior enrolled in program leading to degree in nuclear science or nuclear engineering. See Website for application and requirements.
>   **Amount of award:** $2,000
>   **Number of awards:** 1
>   **Application deadline:** February 1

Contact:
American Nuclear Society
555 North Kensington Avenue
La Grange Park, IL 60526
Phone: 708-352-6611
Fax: 708-352-0499
Web: www.ans.org

Joseph R. Dietrich Scholarship

Type of award: Scholarship.
Intended use: For full-time junior or senior study at 4-year institution in United States.
Eligibility: Applicant must be U.S. citizen or permanent resident.
Basis for selection: Major/career interest in nuclear science; engineering, nuclear; chemistry or physics.
Additional information: Applicant must be at least an entering junior enrolled in program leading to degree in nuclear science, nuclear engineering, or nuclear-related field. See Website for application and requirements.
>   **Amount of award:** $2,000
>   **Number of awards:** 1
>   **Application deadline:** February 1

Contact:
American Nuclear Society
555 North Kensington Avenue
La Grange Park, IL 60526
Phone: 708-352-6611
Fax: 708-352-0499
Web: www.ans.org

Operations and Power Division Scholarship

Type of award: Scholarship.
Intended use: For full-time junior or senior study at 4-year institution.
Eligibility: Applicant must be U.S. citizen or permanent resident.
Basis for selection: Major/career interest in nuclear science or engineering, nuclear.
Additional information: Applicant must be at least an entering junior enrolled in a program leading to a degree in nuclear science or nuclear engineering. Application available online.
>   **Amount of award:** $2,500
>   **Number of awards:** 1
>   **Application deadline:** February 1

Contact:
American Nuclear Society
555 North Kensington Avenue
La Grange Park, IL 60526
Phone: 708-352-6611
Fax: 708-352-0499
Web: www.ans.org

Pittsburgh Local Section Scholarship

Type of award: Scholarship.
Intended use: For full-time junior, senior or graduate study at accredited 4-year or graduate institution in United States.
Eligibility: Applicant must be U.S. citizen or permanent resident residing in Pennsylvania.
Basis for selection: Major/career interest in chemistry; nuclear science or engineering, nuclear.
Application requirements: Transcript.
Additional information: Awards are $2,000 for undergraduates and $3,500 for graduate students. See Website for application and requirements.
>   **Amount of award:** $2,000-$3,500
>   **Number of awards:** 2
>   **Application deadline:** February 1

Contact:
American Nuclear Society
555 North Kensington Avenue
La Grange Park, IL 60526
Phone: 708-352-6611
Fax: 708-352-0499
Web: www.ans.org

Raymond DiSalvo Scholarship

Type of award: Scholarship.
Intended use: For full-time junior or senior study at 4-year institution in United States.
Eligibility: Applicant must be U.S. citizen or permanent resident.
Basis for selection: Major/career interest in nuclear science or engineering, nuclear.

Additional information: Applicant must be at least an entering junior enrolled in program leading to degree in nuclear science or nuclear engineering. Application available online.

Amount of award:	$2,000
Number of awards:	1
Application deadline:	February 1

Contact:
American Nuclear Society
555 North Kensington Avenue
La Grange Park, IL 60526
Phone: 708-352-6611
Fax: 708-352-0499
Web: www.ans.org

Robert G. Lacy Scholarship

Type of award: Scholarship.
Intended use: For full-time junior or senior study at 4-year institution in United States.
Eligibility: Applicant must be U.S. citizen or permanent resident.
Basis for selection: Major/career interest in nuclear science or engineering, nuclear.
Application requirements: Recommendations, transcript, proof of eligibility.
Additional information: Applicant must be at least an entering junior enrolled in a program leading to a degree in nuclear science or nuclear engineering. Application available online.

Amount of award:	$2,000
Number of awards:	1
Application deadline:	February 1
Notification begins:	May 9

Contact:
American Nuclear Society
555 North Kensington Avenue
La Grange Park, IL 60526
Phone: 708-352-6611
Fax: 708-352-0499
Web: www.ans.org

Robert T. (Bob) Liner Scholarship

Type of award: Scholarship.
Intended use: For full-time junior or senior study at 4-year institution in United States.
Eligibility: Applicant must be U.S. citizen or permanent resident.
Basis for selection: Major/career interest in nuclear science or engineering, nuclear. Applicant must demonstrate depth of character, leadership, seriousness of purpose and service orientation.
Additional information: Applicant must be at least an entering junior enrolled in a program leading to a degree in nuclear science or nuclear engineering. Application available online.

Amount of award:	$2,000
Number of awards:	1
Application deadline:	February 1

Contact:
American Nuclear Society
555 North Kensington Avenue
La Grange Park, IL 60526
Phone: 708-352-6611
Fax: 708-352-0499
Web: www.ans.org

American Physical Society

Minorities Scholarship Program

Type of award: Scholarship, renewable.
Intended use: For full-time freshman, sophomore or junior study at 2-year or 4-year institution in United States. Designated institutions: Eligible institutions must have physics department or provide for procurement of physics degree.
Eligibility: Applicant must be African American, Mexican American, Hispanic American, Puerto Rican or American Indian. Applicant must be U.S. citizen or permanent resident.
Basis for selection: Major/career interest in physics. Applicant must demonstrate high academic achievement.
Application requirements: Recommendations, essay, transcript, proof of eligibility. ACT/SAT scores. Applications available early November and due first Friday in February.
Additional information: Must be high school senior or college freshman or sophomore to apply. Additional $500 awarded to physics department at eligible institution. Visit Website for additional information.

Amount of award:	$2,000-$3,000
Number of awards:	25
Number of applicants:	100
Application deadline:	February 1
Notification begins:	May 15
Total amount awarded:	$70,000

Contact:
American Physical Society
Minorities Scholarship Program
One Physics Ellipse
College Park, MD 20740
Phone: 301-209-3232
Fax: 301-209-0865
Web: www.aps.org/educ/com/scholars

American Quarter Horse Foundation

American Quarter Horse Foundation Scholarships

Type of award: Scholarship, renewable.
Intended use: For full-time undergraduate study in United States.
Eligibility: Applicant or parent must be member/participant of American Quarter Horse Youth Association. Applicant must be at least 17, high school senior.
Basis for selection: Applicant must demonstrate financial need and high academic achievement.
Application requirements: Recommendations, essay, transcript, proof of eligibility. Essay must be one page explaining topic listed in application. Minimum 2.5 GPA. 3x5 color photograph and three reference letters.
Additional information: Applicant must have been member of American Quarter Horse Youth Association for at least three years. Notification begins May.

Amount of award:	$500-$10,000
Number of awards:	160
Number of applicants:	500
Application deadline:	February 1
Total amount awarded:	$210,000

Contact:
American Quarter Horse Foundation
Attn: Laura Owens
2601 I-40 East
Amarillo, TX 79104
Phone: 806-376-5181
Fax: 806-376-1005
Web: www.aqha.com

American Respiratory Care Foundation

J.A. Young Memorial Education Recognition Award

Type of award: Scholarship, renewable.
Intended use: For sophomore, junior or senior study at accredited vocational, 2-year or 4-year institution.
Eligibility: Applicant must be Alaskan native, Asian American, African American, Mexican American, Hispanic American, Puerto Rican or American Indian.
Basis for selection: Major/career interest in respiratory therapy. Applicant must demonstrate high academic achievement, seriousness of purpose and service orientation.
Application requirements: Recommendations, essay, transcript, proof of eligibility, nomination by school or program representative. Minimum 3.0 GPA required. Student must have six copies of an original referenced paper on some aspect of respiratory care. Two forms of letters of recommendation.
Additional information: Must have completed at least one semester in accredited respiratory care program. Preference will be given to minority applicants. If nomination cannot be obtained, student may request foundation sponsorship. Foundation prefers nominations made by representative of applicant's school or accredited respiratory training program; however, any student may initiate application.

Amount of award:	$1,000
Number of awards:	1
Number of applicants:	50
Application deadline:	May 31
Notification begins:	August 1
Total amount awarded:	$1,000

Contact:
American Respiratory Care Foundation
11030 Ables Lane
Dallas, TX 75229-4593
Phone: 972-243-2272
Web: www.aarc.org

M.B. Duggan, Jr., Memorial Education Recognition Award

Type of award: Scholarship, renewable.
Intended use: For sophomore, junior or senior study at accredited 2-year or 4-year institution in United States.
Basis for selection: Major/career interest in respiratory therapy. Applicant must demonstrate high academic achievement, depth of character, seriousness of purpose and service orientation.
Application requirements: Recommendations, essay, transcript, proof of eligibility. Minimum 3.0 GPA required. Six copies of an original referenced paper on some aspect of respiratory care. Two forms of letters of recommendation.

Additional information: Preference given to Georgia and South Carolina applicants. Must have at least one semester in Commission on Accreditation of Allied Health Education Programs-approved respiratory care program.

Amount of award:	$1,000
Number of awards:	1
Number of applicants:	50
Application deadline:	May 31
Notification begins:	August 1

Contact:
American Respiratory Care Foundation
11030 Ables Lane
Dallas, TX 75229-4593
Phone: 972-243-2272
Web: www.aarc.org

R.M. Lawrence Education Recognition Award

Type of award: Scholarship.
Intended use: For full-time junior or senior study at accredited 4-year institution in United States.
Basis for selection: Major/career interest in respiratory therapy. Applicant must demonstrate high academic achievement.
Application requirements: Recommendations, essay, transcript, proof of eligibility. Minimum 3.0 GPA required. Must provide six copies of an original referenced paper on some aspect of respiratory care. Must provide six copies of an original essay of at least 1200 words describing how this award will assist the applicant in reaching the objective of a degree, and the candidate's ultimate goals of leadership in health care.
Additional information: Must provide letter verifying enrollment in Commission on Accreditation of Allied Health Education Programs-approved respiratory care program leading to baccalaureate degree.

Amount of award:	$2,500
Number of awards:	1
Number of applicants:	50
Application deadline:	May 31
Notification begins:	August 1

Contact:
American Respiratory Care Foundation
11030 Ables Lane
Dallas, TX 75229-4593
Phone: 972-243-2272
Web: www.aarc.org

W.M. Burgin, Jr., Scholarship

Type of award: Scholarship.
Intended use: For full-time sophomore study at accredited 2-year institution in United States.
Basis for selection: Major/career interest in respiratory therapy. Applicant must demonstrate high academic achievement.
Application requirements: Recommendations, essay, transcript, proof of eligibility, nomination by school or educational program. Minimum 3.0 GPA required.
Additional information: Letter verifying enrollment in a Commission on Accreditation of Allied Health Education Programs-accredited program required. Applicants unable to obtain nomination may apply directly.

Amount of award: $2,500
Number of awards: 1
Number of applicants: 10
Application deadline: May 31
Notification begins: August 1
Contact:
American Respiratory Care Foundation
11030 Ables Lane
Dallas, TX 75229-4593
Phone: 972-243-2272
Web: www.aarc.org

American Society for Enology and Viticulture

Enology and Viticulture Scholarship

Type of award: Scholarship, renewable.
Intended use: For full-time junior, senior, master's or doctoral study at accredited 4-year or graduate institution.
Eligibility: Applicant must be U.S. citizen, permanent resident, international student, reside in North America (Canada or Mexico).
Basis for selection: Major/career interest in agriculture; food science/technology or horticulture. Applicant must demonstrate financial need and high academic achievement.
Application requirements: Recommendations, essay, transcript, proof of eligibility. Minimum 3.0 GPA for undergraduate, 3.2 GPA for graduate students. Applications will be considered complete upon receipt of following items by March 1 deadline: completed student questionnaire, written statement of intent relating to future career in wine or grape industry, interests in wine or grape industry or in related research.
Additional information: All completed forms, letters, and transcripts must be received by Scholarship Committee by March 1 for consideration for award for following scholastic year. All information (application, transcripts, and letters of recommendation) must be received together: do not have transcripts and letters sent separately. Incomplete application packets will not be considered. Applicants must be enrolled in a major or in graduate group emphasizing enology or viticulture or in curriculum emphasizing science basic to wine and grape industry. Awards may vary from year to year. Previous applicants and recipients eligible to reapply each year in open competition with new applicants.

Amount of award: $500-$3,000
Number of awards: 36
Application deadline: March 1
Notification begins: May 31
Total amount awarded: $45,000
Contact:
American Society for Enology and Viticulture
P.O. Box 1855
Davis, CA 95617-1855
Web: www.asev.org

American Society for Microbiology

ASM Minority Undergraduate Research Fellowship

Type of award: Research grant.
Intended use: For full-time undergraduate study.
Eligibility: Applicant must be Alaskan native, African American, Mexican American, Hispanic American, Puerto Rican or American Indian. Pacific Islanders also encouraged to apply. Applicant must be U.S. citizen or permanent resident.
Basis for selection: Major/career interest in microbiology. Applicant must demonstrate high academic achievement, leadership and seriousness of purpose.
Application requirements: Recommendations, transcript. Personal statement.
Additional information: Applicant must demonstrate ability to pursue graduate career (PhD) in microbiology. Program provides opportunity for minority undergraduate students to conduct summer research at selected institution for eight to 12 weeks and present research results at ASM General Meeting the following year. Fellowship offers $3,500 stipend plus housing expenses, travel, and one-year student membership to ASM. See Website for application and more details.

Amount of award: $3,500
Number of awards: 6
Application deadline: February 1
Contact:
American Society for Microbiology
Minority Undergraduate Fellowship
1752 N Street NW
Washington, DC 20036
Phone: 202-942-9283
Fax: 202-942-9329
Web: www.asm.org

ASM Undergraduate Research Fellowship

Type of award: Research grant.
Intended use: For full-time undergraduate study at 4-year institution.
Eligibility: Applicant must be U.S. citizen or permanent resident.
Basis for selection: Major/career interest in microbiology. Applicant must demonstrate high academic achievement and seriousness of purpose.
Application requirements: Recommendations, transcript. Program requires joint application from both student applicant and faculty member. Faculty member must have ongoing research project.
Additional information: Applicant must demonstrate strong interest in attending graduate school (PhD) and becoming a research scientist. Students conduct research in summer (or longer) and present results at ASM General Meeting the following year. Fellowship offers $4000 stipend, travel funding and one-year student membership to ASM. Applicant must have ASM member at institution willing to serve as mentor. Students may not receive financial support for research from any other scientific organization during the fellowship. Must have successful achievement in previous research experience. Faculty member's department head or dean must endorse project. See Website for application.

Amount of award:	$4,000
Number of awards:	20
Application deadline:	February 1

Contact:
American Society for Microbiology
Undergraduate Research Fellowship
1752 N Street NW
Washington, DC 20036
Phone: 202-942-9283
Fax: 202-942-9329
Web: www.asm.org

American Society of Civil Engineers

B. Charles Tiney Memorial ASCE Student Chapter Scholarship

Type of award: Scholarship, renewable.
Intended use: For undergraduate study at accredited postsecondary institution.
Eligibility: Applicant or parent must be member/participant of American Society of Civil Engineers.
Basis for selection: Major/career interest in engineering, civil. Applicant must demonstrate financial need, high academic achievement, depth of character and leadership.
Application requirements: Recommendations, essay, transcript, proof of eligibility. Completed application form. One-page resume. Detailed financial statement indicating how scholarship will finance applicant's education.
Additional information: Any undergraduate who is ASCE student chapter member and ASCE National Student Member may apply for this scholarship but must be in good standing at time of application. Membership applications may be submitted with scholarship application. Award is for undergraduate tuition. Visit Website for additional information and to download application.

Amount of award:	$2,000
Number of awards:	4
Application deadline:	February 10
Total amount awarded:	$8,000

Contact:
American Society of Civil Engineers
Attention: Student Services
1801 Alexander Bell Drive
Reston, VA 20191-4440
Phone: 800-548-ASCE
Web: www.asce.org/students

Freeman Fellowship

Type of award: Research grant.
Intended use: For undergraduate or graduate study in or outside United States or Canada.
Eligibility: Applicant or parent must be member/participant of American Society of Civil Engineers.
Basis for selection: Major/career interest in engineering, civil.
Application requirements: Recommendations, essay, transcript, research proposal. Resume. Detailed financial statement indicating how fellowship will finance applicant's research. Statement from institution where research will be conducted.
Additional information: Grants are made toward expenses for experiments, observations and compilations to discover new and accurate data that will be useful in engineering. Grant may be in form of prize for most useful paper relating to science/art of hydraulic construction. Travel scholarships available to ASCE members under 45, in recognition of achievement or promise. Award is to be used for expenses for research and experiments. Visit Website for additional information and to download application.

Amount of award:	$3,000-$5,000
Application deadline:	February 10

Contact:
American Society of Engineers
Attention: Student Services
1801 Alexander Bell Drive
Reston, VA 20191-4440
Phone: 800-548-ASCE ext. 6106
Web: www.asce.org/students

Samuel Fletcher Tapman ASCE Student Chapter Scholarship

Type of award: Scholarship, renewable.
Intended use: For undergraduate study at accredited postsecondary institution.
Eligibility: Applicant or parent must be member/participant of American Society of Civil Engineers.
Basis for selection: Major/career interest in engineering, civil. Applicant must demonstrate financial need, high academic achievement, depth of character and leadership.
Application requirements: Recommendations, essay, transcript, proof of eligibility. One-page resume. Detailed financial statement indicating how scholarship will finance applicant's education.
Additional information: Any undergraduate who is ASCE student chapter member and ASCE National Student Member may apply for this scholarship but must be in good standing at time of application. Membership applications may be submitted with scholarship application. Award is for undergraduate tuition. Visit Website for additional information and to download application.

Amount of award:	$2,000
Number of awards:	12
Application deadline:	February 10
Total amount awarded:	$24,000

Contact:
American Society of Civil Engineers
Attention: Student Services
1801 Alexander Bell Drive
Reston, VA 20191-4440
Phone: 800-548-ASCE
Web: www.asce.org/students

American Society of Heating/Refrigeration/Air-Conditioning Engineers, Inc.

ASHRAE Donald E. Nichols Scholarship

Type of award: Scholarship, renewable.

Intended use: For full-time undergraduate study. Designated institutions: ABET-accredited program at Tennessee Technological University.

Basis for selection: Major/career interest in air conditioning/heating/refrigeration technology or engineering. Applicant must demonstrate financial need, high academic achievement, depth of character and leadership.

Application requirements: Recommendations, transcript.

Additional information: Scholarship awarded to qualified undergraduate engineering student enrolled full-time in ABET-accredited program at Tennessee Technological University. Minimum 3.0 GPA. Must have at least one full year of undergraduate study remaining.

Amount of award:	$3,000
Number of awards:	1
Application deadline:	December 1
Total amount awarded:	$3,000

Contact:
ASHRAE - Scholarship Programs
1791 Tullie Circle, NE
Atlanta, GA 30329-2305
Phone: 404-636-8400
Fax: 404-321-5478
Web: www.ashrae.org/student/scholar.htm

ASHRAE J. Richard Mehalick Scholarship

Type of award: Research grant, renewable.

Intended use: For full-time undergraduate study in United States. Designated institutions: University of Pittsburgh.

Eligibility: Applicant must be U.S. citizen residing in Pennsylvania.

Basis for selection: Major/career interest in engineering.

Additional information: Must have at least a 3.0 GPA. Must show potential service to the HVAC Industry.

Number of awards:	1
Application deadline:	December 1
Total amount awarded:	$3,000

Contact:
ASHRAE - Scholarship Program
1791 Tullie Circle NE
Atlanta, GA 30329
Phone: 404-636-8400
Fax: 404-312-5478
Web: www.ashrae.org/student/scholar.htm

ASHRAE Region IV Benny Bootle Scholarship

Type of award: Scholarship, renewable.

Intended use: For full-time undergraduate study. Designated institutions: Schools with ABET-accredited program located within the geographic boundaries of ASHRAE's Region IV.

Basis for selection: Major/career interest in air conditioning/heating/refrigeration technology or engineering. Applicant must demonstrate financial need, high academic achievement, depth of character and leadership.

Application requirements: Recommendations, transcript.

Additional information: Scholarship awarded to qualified undergraduate engineering student enrolled full-time in ABET-accredited program at school located in ASHRAE's Region IV (currently North Carolina, South Carolina, and Georgia). Minimum 3.0 GPA. Must have at least one full year of undergraduate study remaining.

Amount of award:	$3,000
Number of awards:	1
Application deadline:	December 1
Total amount awarded:	$3,000

Contact:
ASHRAE - Scholarship Programs
1791 Tullie Circle, NE
Atlanta, GA 30329-2305
Phone: 404-636-8400
Fax: 404-321-5478
Web: www.ashrae.org/student/scholar.htm

ASHRAE Region VIII Scholarship

Type of award: Scholarship, renewable.

Intended use: For full-time undergraduate study. Designated institutions: Schools with ABET-accredited programs located within the geographic boundaries of ASHRAE's Region VIII.

Basis for selection: Major/career interest in air conditioning/heating/refrigeration technology or engineering. Applicant must demonstrate financial need, high academic achievement, depth of character and leadership.

Application requirements: Recommendations, transcript.

Additional information: Scholarship awarded to qualified undergraduate engineering student enrolled full-time in ABET-accredited program at school located in ASHRAE's Region VIII. (Region is currently Arkansas, Oklahoma, Mexico and parts of Louisiana and Texas -- parts of these states are not within the geographic boundaries of Region VIII. Contact ASHRAE for information regarding schools in this area.) Minimum 3.0 GPA. Must have at least one full year of undergraduate study remaining. Must pursue career in Heating/Ventilation/Air-Conditioning (HVAC) & Refrigeration.

Amount of award:	$3,000
Number of awards:	1
Application deadline:	December 1
Total amount awarded:	$3,000

Contact:
ASHRAE - Scholarship Program
1791 Tullie Circle, NE
Atlanta, GA 30329-2305
Phone: 404-636-8400
Fax: 404-321-5478
Web: www.ashrae.org/student/scholar.htm

ASHRAE Reuben Trane Scholarship

Type of award: Scholarship.

Intended use: For undergraduate study at accredited 4-year institution. Designated institutions: Schools with ABET-accredited program.

Basis for selection: Major/career interest in air conditioning/heating/refrigeration technology or engineering. Applicant must demonstrate financial need, high academic achievement, depth of character and leadership.

Application requirements: Recommendations, transcript.

Additional information: Minimum 3.0 GPA. Curriculum must be accredited by Accreditation Board for Engineering and Technology (ABET). Award is per year for two years, for students with two years of undergraduate study remaining.

Amount of award:	$10,000
Number of awards:	4
Application deadline:	December 1
Total amount awarded:	$40,000

Contact:
ASHRAE - Scholarship Program
1791 Tullie Circle NE
Atlanta, GA 30329-2305
Phone: 404-636-8400
Fax: 404-321-5478
Web: www.ashrae.org/student/scholar.htm

ASHRAE Undergraduate Engineering Scholarships

Type of award: Scholarship, renewable.
Intended use: For full-time undergraduate study. Designated institutions: Schools with ABET-accredited programs.
Basis for selection: Major/career interest in air conditioning/ heating/refrigeration technology or engineering. Applicant must demonstrate financial need and high academic achievement.
Additional information: Minimum 3.0 GPA. Curriculum must be accredited by Accreditation Board for Engineering and Technology (ABET). Must be currently enrolled full-time with at least one full year of undergraduate study remaining. Must pursue career in Heating/Ventilation/Air Conditioning (HVAC) and Refrigeration and demonstrate potential service to HVAC & R industry.

Amount of award:	$3,000-$5,000
Number of awards:	9
Application deadline:	December 1
Total amount awarded:	$33,000

Contact:
ASHRAE - Scholarship Program
1791 Tullie Circle NE
Atlanta, GA 30329-2305
Phone: 404-636-8400
Fax: 404-321-5478
Web: www.ashrae.org/student/scholar.htm

Heating/Refrigeration/Air-Conditioning Associate of Engineering Technology Scholarship

Type of award: Scholarship, renewable.
Intended use: For full-time undergraduate study at accredited 2-year institution.
Basis for selection: Major/career interest in air conditioning/ heating/refrigeration technology or engineering. Applicant must demonstrate financial need, high academic achievement, depth of character and leadership.
Application requirements: Recommendations, transcript.
Additional information: For students pursuing associate's degree in engineering technology. Minimum 3.0 GPA. Must intend to pursue career in Heating/Ventilation/Air Conditioning (HVAC) and/or Refrigeration.

Amount of award:	$3,000
Number of awards:	1
Application deadline:	May 1
Total amount awarded:	$3,000

Contact:
ASHRAE - Scholarship Program
1791 Tullie Circle, NE
Atlanta, GA 30329-2305
Phone: 404-636-8400
Fax: 404-321-5478
Web: www.ashrae.org/student/scholar.htm

Heating/Refrigeration/Air-Conditioning Bachelor of Engineering Technology Scholarship

Type of award: Scholarship, renewable.
Intended use: For full-time undergraduate study at accredited 4-year institution. Designated institutions: Schools with ABET-accredited programs.
Basis for selection: Major/career interest in air conditioning/ heating/refrigeration technology or engineering. Applicant must demonstrate financial need, high academic achievement, depth of character and leadership.
Application requirements: Recommendations, transcript.
Additional information: For students pursuing bachelor's degree in engineering technology. Minimum 3.0 GPA. Curriculum must be accredited by Accreditation Board for Engineering and Technology (ABET). Must intend to pursue career in Heating/Ventilation/Air-Conditioning (HVAC) and/or Refrigeration.

Amount of award:	$3,000
Number of awards:	1
Application deadline:	May 1
Total amount awarded:	$3,000

Contact:
ASHRAE - Scholarship Program
1791 Tullie Circle, NE
Atlanta, GA 30329-2305
Phone: 404-636-8400
Fax: 404-321-5478
Web: www.ashrae.org/student/scholar.htm

American Society of Interior Designers Foundation

Joel Polsky Academic Achievement Award

Type of award: Scholarship.
Intended use: For undergraduate or graduate study.
Basis for selection: Competition/talent/interest in writing/ journalism, based on graphic presentation, content, comprehensive coverage of topic, innovative subject matter, bibliography and references. Major/career interest in interior design or architecture. Applicant must demonstrate high academic achievement.
Additional information: Mainly for upperclassmen/women and graduate students. Award to recognize outstanding interior design research or thesis project. Papers should address topics such as educational research, behavioral sciences, business practices, design process, theory or other technical subjects.

Amount of award:	$1,000
Number of awards:	1
Application deadline:	April 30
Total amount awarded:	$1,000

Contact:
American Society of Interior Designers Foundation
608 Massachusetts Avenue, NE
Washington, DC 20002-6006
Phone: 202-546-3480
Fax: 202-546-3240
Web: www.asid.org

Joel Polsky Prize

Type of award: Scholarship.
Intended use: For non-degree study.
Basis for selection: Competition/talent/interest in engineering/architecture, based on graphic presentation, content, comprehensive coverage of topic, innovative subject matter, bibliography, and references. Major/career interest in interior design.
Additional information: Award to recognize outstanding contributions to the discipline of interior design through literature or visual communication. Entries should address need of public designers and students on topics such as educational research, behavioral sciences, business practice, design process, theory, or other technical subjects.

Amount of award:	$1,000
Number of awards:	1
Application deadline:	April 30
Total amount awarded:	$1,000

Contact:
American Society of Interior Designers Foundation
608 Massachusetts Avenue, NE
Washington, DC 20002-6006
Phone: 202-546-3480
Fax: 202-546-3240
Web: www.asid.org

Yale R. Burge Interior Design Competition

Type of award: Scholarship.
Intended use: For senior study.
Basis for selection: Competition/talent/interest in visual arts, based on quality of portfolio: presentation, design and planning, conceptual creativity. Major/career interest in interior design or architecture.
Application requirements: $10 application fee. Portfolio. Portfolio components submitted on slides.
Additional information: Entries must be postmarked by March 28. Contact sponsor for slide submission guidelines. Visit Website for application and more information.

Amount of award:	$750
Number of awards:	1
Application deadline:	April 1

Contact:
American Society of Interior Designers Foundation
608 Massachusetts Avenue, NE
Washington, DC 20002-6006
Phone: 202-546-3480
Web: www.asid.org

American Society of Mechanical Engineers

American Society of Mechanical Engineers Foundation Scholarship

Type of award: Scholarship.
Intended use: For full-time undergraduate study at accredited 4-year or graduate institution.
Eligibility: Applicant or parent must be member/participant of American Society of Mechanical Engineers.

Basis for selection: Major/career interest in engineering, mechanical. Applicant must demonstrate high academic achievement, depth of character and leadership.
Application requirements: Recommendations, essay, transcript. Application must be endorsed by department head.
Additional information: Applicant must be student member of ASME, enrolled in mechanical engineering or related field.

Amount of award:	$1,500
Number of awards:	16
Application deadline:	March 15
Notification begins:	June 15
Total amount awarded:	$24,000

Contact:
American Society of Mechanical Engineers
Three Park Avenue
New York, NY 10016-5990
Phone: 212-591-8131
Fax: 212-591-7143
Web: www.asme.org/education/enged/aid

ASME Petroleum Division Student Scholarship Program

Type of award: Scholarship.
Intended use: For junior or senior study at accredited 4-year institution in or outside United States. Designated institutions: ABET-accredited university or college.
Eligibility: Applicant or parent must be member/participant of American Society of Mechanical Engineers. Applicant must be U.S. citizen.
Basis for selection: Major/career interest in engineering, petroleum. Applicant must demonstrate financial need and high academic achievement.
Application requirements: Recommendations, essay, transcript. One page, typed, double-spaced essay indicating interest in some phase of petroleum industry. Completed application.
Additional information: Available to ASME student members interested in any phase of petroleum industry, including drilling, completions, facilities, pipe lines, rigs, operations, materials, equipment manufacturing, plant design and operation, maintenance, environmental protection and innovation. Submit application and checklist to: ASME Petroleum Division, Attention: Student Scholarship Program, 11757 Katy Freeway, Suite 865, Houston, TX 77079. Official transcript should be sent directly from registrar to same address. Visit Website for more information.

Amount of award:	$1,000
Number of awards:	4
Application deadline:	March 15
Notification begins:	July 1
Total amount awarded:	$4,000

Contact:
ASME Petroleum Division
Student Scholarship Program
11757 Katy Freeway, Suite 865
Houston, TX 77709
Phone: 281-493-3491
Web: www.asme-petroleumdiv.org

ASME/FIRST Robotics Competition Scholarship

Type of award: Scholarship.
Intended use: For full-time freshman study at accredited 4-year institution. Designated institutions: Schools with ABET-accredited program.

Eligibility: Applicant must be high school senior. Applicant must be U.S. citizen.

Basis for selection: Major/career interest in engineering, mechanical. Applicant must demonstrate financial need, high academic achievement and leadership.

Application requirements: Transcript, proof of eligibility, nomination by ASME member and student member active with FIRST. Completed nomination materials.

Additional information: Applications are typically due on the first Monday in March. Applicant must be active on FIRST team. Students on same team must be nominated by separate ASME members. Applicant may also enroll in mechanical engineering technology program. Applicant must have an outstanding academic record. Recipient announced at FIRST National Championship. Visit Website for more information and to download forms.

Amount of award:	$5,000
Number of awards:	7
Total amount awarded:	$35,000

Contact:
American Society of Mechanical Engineers
Three Park Avenue
New York, NY 10016-5990
Phone: 212-591-8131
Fax: 212-591-7143
Web: www.asme.org/education/enged/aid

Frank William and Dorothy Given Miller Mechanical Engineering Scholarship

Type of award: Scholarship.

Intended use: For full-time junior or senior study at accredited 4-year institution. Designated institutions: Designated institutions: schools with ABET-accredited program.

Eligibility: Applicant or parent must be member/participant of American Society of Mechanical Engineers. Applicant must be U.S. citizen.

Basis for selection: Major/career interest in engineering, mechanical. Applicant must demonstrate high academic achievement, depth of character and leadership.

Application requirements: Recommendations, essay, transcript. Application must be endorsed by department head. Applicant must be North American resident.

Additional information: Applicant must be member of ASME.

Amount of award:	$2,000
Number of awards:	2
Application deadline:	March 15
Notification begins:	June 15
Total amount awarded:	$4,000

Contact:
American Society of Mechanical Engineers
Three Park Avenue
New York, NY 10016-5990
Phone: 212-591-8131
Fax: 212-591-7143
Web: www.asme.org/education/enged/aid

F.W. "Beich" Beichley Scholarship

Type of award: Scholarship.

Intended use: For full-time junior or senior study.

Eligibility: Applicant or parent must be member/participant of American Society of Mechanical Engineers.

Basis for selection: Major/career interest in engineering, mechanical. Applicant must demonstrate financial need, high academic achievement, depth of character and leadership.

Application requirements: Recommendations, essay, transcript. Application must be endorsed by department head.

Additional information: Applicant must be member of ASME.

Amount of award:	$2,000
Number of awards:	1
Application deadline:	March 15
Notification begins:	June 15
Total amount awarded:	$2,000

Contact:
American Society of Mechanical Engineers
Three Park Avenue
New York, NY 10016-5990
Phone: 212-591-8131
Fax: 212-591-7143
Web: www.asme.org/education/enged/aid

Garland Duncan Mechanical Engineering Scholarship

Type of award: Scholarship.

Intended use: For full-time junior or senior study at accredited 4-year institution. Designated institutions: Schools with ABET-accredited program.

Eligibility: Applicant or parent must be member/participant of American Society of Mechanical Engineers.

Basis for selection: Major/career interest in engineering, mechanical. Applicant must demonstrate financial need, high academic achievement, depth of character and leadership.

Application requirements: Recommendations, essay, transcript. Application must be endorsed by department head.

Additional information: Applicant must be member of ASME.

Amount of award:	$3,500
Number of awards:	2
Application deadline:	March 15
Notification begins:	June 15
Total amount awarded:	$7,000

Contact:
American Society of Mechanical Engineers
Three Park Avenue
New York, NY 10016-5990
Phone: 212-591-8131
Fax: 212-591-7143
Web: www.asme.org/education/enged/aid

John and Elsa Gracik Mechanical Engineering Scholarship

Type of award: Scholarship.

Intended use: For full-time undergraduate study at accredited 4-year institution. Designated institutions: Schools with ABET-accredited program.

Eligibility: Applicant or parent must be member/participant of American Society of Mechanical Engineers. Applicant must be U.S. citizen.

Basis for selection: Major/career interest in engineering, mechanical. Applicant must demonstrate financial need, high academic achievement, depth of character and leadership.

Application requirements: Recommendations, essay, transcript, nomination by department head.

Additional information: Applicant must be member of ASME.

Amount of award: $1,500
Number of awards: 16
Application deadline: March 15
Notification begins: June 15
Total amount awarded: $24,000
Contact:
American Society of Mechanical Engineers
Three Park Avenue
New York, NY 10016-5990
Phone: 212-591-8131
Fax: 212-591-7143
Web: www.asme.org/education/enged/aid

Kenneth Andrew Roe Mechanical Engineering Scholarship

Type of award: Scholarship.
Intended use: For full-time junior or senior study at accredited 4-year institution. Designated institutions: Schools with ABET-accredited program or equivalent.
Eligibility: Applicant or parent must be member/participant of American Society of Mechanical Engineers. Applicant must be U.S. citizen, permanent resident, international student, North American (Canada or Mexico) resident welcome as well.
Basis for selection: Major/career interest in engineering, mechanical. Applicant must demonstrate financial need, high academic achievement, depth of character and leadership.
Application requirements: Recommendations, essay, transcript. Application must be endorsed by department head.
Additional information: Applicant must be member of ASME.
Amount of award: $10,000
Number of awards: 1
Application deadline: March 15
Notification begins: June 15
Total amount awarded: $10,000
Contact:
American Society of Mechanical Engineers
Three Park Avenue
New York, NY 10016-5990
Phone: 212-591-8131
Fax: 212-591-7143
Web: www.asme.org/education/enged/aid

Melvin R. Green Scholarship

Type of award: Scholarship.
Intended use: For full-time junior or senior study at accredited 4-year institution in United States. Designated institutions: Schools with ABET-accredited program.
Eligibility: Applicant or parent must be member/participant of American Society of Mechanical Engineers.
Basis for selection: Major/career interest in engineering, mechanical. Applicant must demonstrate high academic achievement, depth of character and leadership.
Application requirements: Recommendations, essay, transcript. Application must be endorsed by department head.
Additional information: Applicant must be student member of ASME.
Amount of award: $3,500
Number of awards: 2
Application deadline: March 15
Notification begins: June 15
Total amount awarded: $7,000

Contact:
American Society of Mechanical Engineers
Three Park Avenue
New York, NY 10016-5990
Phone: 212-591-8131
Fax: 212-591-7143
Web: www.asme.org/education/enged/aid

Robert F. Sammataro Pressure Vessels & Piping Division Scholarship

Type of award: Scholarship.
Intended use: For undergraduate study at accredited 4-year institution.
Eligibility: Applicant or parent must be member/participant of American Society of Mechanical Engineers.
Additional information: One scholarship to ASME student member, preferably with an interest in pressure vessels and piping. Interested parties may apply for ASME membership while also applying for a loan or scholarship. See website for additional requirements.
Amount of award: $1,000
Number of awards: 1
Application deadline: March 15
Notification begins: June 15, June 30
Contact:
American Society of Mechanical Engineers
Three Park Avenue
New York, NY 10016-5990
Phone: 212-591-8131
Fax: 212-591-7143
Web: www.asme.org

William J. and Marijane E. Adams, Jr., Mechanical Engineering Scholarship

Type of award: Scholarship.
Intended use: For full-time undergraduate study in United States. Designated institutions: Schools in ASME region IX: California, Nevada, Hawaii.
Eligibility: Applicant or parent must be member/participant of American Society of Mechanical Engineers.
Basis for selection: Major/career interest in engineering, mechanical. Applicant must demonstrate financial need, high academic achievement, depth of character and leadership.
Application requirements: Recommendations, essay, transcript. Minimum 2.5 GPA. Application must be endorsed by department head.
Additional information: Applicant must be member of ASME. Award designated for student with special interest in product development and design.
Amount of award: $2,000
Number of awards: 1
Application deadline: March 15
Notification begins: June 15
Total amount awarded: $2,000
Contact:
American Society of Mechanical Engineers
Three Park Avenue
New York, NY 10016-5990
Phone: 212-591-8131
Fax: 212-591-7143
Web: www.asme.org/education/enged/aid

Scholarships

American Society of Mechanical Engineers Auxiliary

Allen J. Baldwin Scholarship

Type of award: Scholarship.
Intended use: For senior study at 4-year institution in United States. Designated institutions: Must be enrolled in ABET-accredited mechanical engineering department.
Eligibility: Applicant or parent must be member/participant of American Society of Mechanical Engineers. Applicant must be U.S. citizen.
Basis for selection: Major/career interest in engineering, mechanical. Applicant must demonstrate financial need, high academic achievement and depth of character.
Additional information: For ASME student member in final year of undergraduate study in mechanical engineering. Download application from Website.

> **Amount of award:** $2,000
> **Application deadline:** March 15

Contact:
Alverta Cover
5425 Caldwell Mill Road
Birmingham, AL 35242
Phone: 205-991-6109
Web: www.asme.org/education/enged/aid

Berna Lou Cartwright Scholarship

Type of award: Scholarship.
Intended use: For senior study at 4-year institution in United States. Designated institutions: Must be enrolled in ABET-accredited mechanical engineering department.
Eligibility: Applicant or parent must be member/participant of American Society of Mechanical Engineers. Applicant must be U.S. citizen.
Basis for selection: Major/career interest in engineering, mechanical. Applicant must demonstrate financial need, high academic achievement and depth of character.
Additional information: For ASME student member in final year of undergraduate program in mechanical engineering. Download application from Website.

> **Amount of award:** $2,000
> **Application deadline:** March 15

Contact:
Alverta Cover
5425 Caldwell Mill Road
Birmingham, AL 35242
Phone: 205-991-6109
Web: www.asme.org/education/enged/aid

Sylvia W. Farny Scholarship

Type of award: Scholarship.
Intended use: For senior study at 4-year institution in United States. Designated institutions: Must be enrolled in ABET-accredited mechanical engineering department.
Eligibility: Applicant or parent must be member/participant of American Society of Mechanical Engineers. Applicant must be U.S. citizen.
Basis for selection: Major/career interest in engineering, mechanical. Applicant must demonstrate financial need, high academic achievement and depth of character.

Additional information: For ASME student members in final year of undergraduate study in mechanical engineering. Download application from Website.

> **Amount of award:** $2,000
> **Application deadline:** March 15

Contact:
Alverta Cover
5425 Caldwell Mill Road
Birmingham, AL 35242
Phone: 205-991-6109
Web: www.asme.org/education/enged/aid

American Society of Naval Engineers

Naval Engineers Scholarship

Type of award: Scholarship.
Intended use: For full-time senior or master's study at accredited 4-year or graduate institution.
Eligibility: Applicant must be U.S. citizen.
Basis for selection: Major/career interest in engineering, marine; engineering, mechanical; engineering, electrical/electronic; physical sciences or engineering, civil. Applicant must demonstrate high academic achievement.
Application requirements: Recommendations, essay, transcript.
Additional information: Award for last year of undergraduate study or one year of graduate study. Additional major/career interest: naval architecture, aeronautical engineering, ocean engineering, as well as other programs leading to careers with both military and civilian organizations requiring these educational backgrounds. Financial need may be considered.

> **Amount of award:** $2,500-$3,500
> **Number of awards:** 21
> **Number of applicants:** 90
> **Application deadline:** February 15
> **Notification begins:** May 15
> **Total amount awarded:** $55,250

Contact:
American Society of Naval Engineers
1452 Duke Street
Alexandria, VA 22314
Phone: 703-836-6727
Fax: 703-836-7491
Web: www.navalengineers.org

American Society of Travel Agents Foundation

A.J. "Andy" Spielman Travel Agents Scholarship

Type of award: Scholarship, renewable.
Intended use: For undergraduate certificate or non-degree study at accredited vocational institution in United States or Canada. Designated institutions: Recognized proprietary travel schools.
Eligibility: Applicant must be returning adult student.

Basis for selection: Major/career interest in tourism/travel. Applicant must demonstrate high academic achievement and service orientation.

Application requirements: Recommendations, transcript, proof of eligibility. 500-word essay on "Why I Have Chosen the Travel Profession for My Reentry into the Work Force." Four copies of application and required materials.

Additional information: Visit Website for application and additional requirements.

Amount of award:	$250-$3,000
Number of awards:	25
Number of applicants:	150
Total amount awarded:	$30,000

Contact:
American Society of Travel Agents Foundation
1101 King Street
Alexandria, VA 22314-2944
Phone: 703-739-2782
Fax: 703-684-8319
Web: www.astanet.com/education/edu_scholarships.asp

American Express Travel Scholarship

Type of award: Scholarship, renewable.
Intended use: For undergraduate study at accredited vocational, 2-year or 4-year institution in United States or Canada.
Eligibility: Applicant must be U.S. citizen, permanent resident, international student or Canadian citizen/resident.
Basis for selection: Major/career interest in tourism/travel.
Application requirements: Recommendations, essay, transcript, proof of eligibility. Minimum 2.5 GPA. 500-word essay detailing student's plans in travel and tourism and view of the travel industry's future. Four copies of application and required materials.
Additional information: Applicant must be enrolled in travel and tourism program. Amount of award varies. Visit Website for application and additional requirements.

Application deadline:	July 31
Notification begins:	January 1

Contact:
American Society of Travel Agents Foundation
1101 King Street
Alexandria, VA 22314-2944
Phone: 703-739-2782
Fax: 703-684-8319
Web: www.astanet.com/education/edu_scholarships.asp

American Society of Travel Agents Undergraduate Vocational Scholarship

Type of award: Scholarship.
Intended use: For undergraduate study at 2-year or 4-year institution in United States.
Eligibility: Applicant must be U.S. citizen, permanent resident, international student or or Canadian citizen.
Basis for selection: Major/career interest in tourism/travel or hospitality administration/management.
Application requirements: Recommendations, essay. Must have 2.5 GPA and submit proof of enrollment in travel or tourism courses. Must have course description and provide offical statement of tuition amount.
Additional information: Applicants attending Travel Schools also eligible. See Website for application.

Amount of award:	$250-$3,000
Number of awards:	25
Application deadline:	August 29

Contact:
American Society of Travel Agents (ASTA) Foundation
1101 King Street
Alexandria, VA 22314-2187
Phone: 703-739-2782
Fax: 703-684-8319
Web: www.astanet.com/education/edu_scholarships.asp

Arizona Chapter Dependent Scholarship Fund

Type of award: Scholarship, renewable.
Intended use: For sophomore, junior or senior study at accredited 2-year or 4-year institution. Designated institutions: Arizona postsecondary institutions.
Eligibility: Applicant or parent must be member/participant of ASTA Arizona Chapter. Applicant must be U.S. citizen or permanent resident residing in Arizona.
Basis for selection: Applicant must demonstrate high academic achievement.
Application requirements: Recommendations, transcript, proof of eligibility. Minimum 2.5 GPA. 500-word essay on applicant's career goals. Four copies of application and required materials.
Additional information: Applicant must be dependent of an ASTA Arizona Chapter Active or Active Associate member, or an employee of an Arizona ASTA member agency for a minimum of six months. Open to applicants of all majors and fields of study; major in travel and tourism not required. Applicant must be enrolled in final year at two-year college or in junior or senior year at four-year university. Visit Website for application and additional requirements.

Amount of award:	$1,500
Number of awards:	1
Application deadline:	July 31
Notification begins:	January 1
Total amount awarded:	$1,500

Contact:
American Society of Travel Agents Foundation
1101 King Street
Alexandria, VA 22314-2944
Phone: 703-739-2782
Fax: 703-684-8319
Web: www.astanet.com/education/edu_scholarships.asp

Arizona Chapter Gold Scholarship

Type of award: Scholarship, renewable.
Intended use: For sophomore, junior or senior study at accredited 4-year institution in United States. Designated institutions: Arizona colleges and universities.
Eligibility: Applicant must be U.S. citizen or permanent resident residing in Arizona.
Basis for selection: Major/career interest in tourism/travel. Applicant must demonstrate high academic achievement, seriousness of purpose and service orientation.
Application requirements: Recommendations, transcript, proof of eligibility. Minimum 2.5 GPA. 500-word essay detailing applicant's plans in travel industry and interest in business of travel and tourism. Letter of recommendation must be from educator or employer regarding applicant's credentials. Four copies of application and required materials.
Additional information: Visit Website for application and additional requirements.

Amount of award:	$3,000
Number of awards:	1
Application deadline:	July 31
Notification begins:	January 1
Total amount awarded:	$3,000

Contact:
American Society of Travel Agents Foundation
1101 King Street
Alexandria, VA 22314-2944
Phone: 703-739-2782, ext. 8721
Fax: 703-684-8319
Web: www.astanet.com/education/edu_scholarships.asp

Donald Estey Scholarship Fund-Rocky Mountain Chapter

Type of award: Scholarship.
Intended use: For undergraduate study at 2-year or 4-year institution in United States.
Eligibility: Applicant must be U.S. citizen or permanent resident residing in Wyoming, Utah or Colorado.
Basis for selection: Major/career interest in tourism/travel.
Application requirements: Recommendations, transcript.
Additional information: If professional, must be affiliated with the ASTA Rocky Mountain Chapter. Students are not required to be members of ASTA. Deadline is rolling. The maximum number of awards granted is 4.

Amount of award:	$100-$750
Number of awards:	4

Contact:
American Society of Travel Agents (ASTA) Foundation
1101 King Street, Suite 200
Alexandria, VA 22314-2187
Phone: 703-739-2782
Fax: 703-684-8319
Web: www.astanet.com/education/edu_scholarship@asp

George Reinke Scholarships

Type of award: Scholarship.
Intended use: For freshman or sophomore study.
Eligibility: Applicant must be U.S. citizen.
Basis for selection: Major/career interest in tourism/travel.
Application requirements: Recommendations, essay, transcript. 500-word essay on career goals in travel and tourism industry.
Additional information: See Website for more information. The maximum number of awards granted is 6.

Amount of award:	$2,000
Number of awards:	6
Application deadline:	July 28, December 22

Contact:
American Society of Travel Agents (ASTA) Foundation
1101 King Street, Suite 200
Alexander, Va 22314-2187
Phone: 703-739-2782
Fax: 703-684-8319
Web: www.astanet.com/education/edu_scholarships.asp

Healy Scholarship

Type of award: Scholarship, renewable.
Intended use: For freshman, sophomore, junior or senior study at accredited 4-year institution in United States or Canada.
Eligibility: Applicant must be U.S. citizen, permanent resident, international student or Canadian citizen/resident.

Basis for selection: Major/career interest in tourism/travel. Applicant must demonstrate high academic achievement and service orientation.
Application requirements: Recommendations, transcript, proof of eligibility. Minimum 2.5 GPA. 500-word essay suggesting improvements in travel industry. Four copies of application and required materials.
Additional information: Visit Website for application and additional requirements.

Amount of award:	$2,000
Number of awards:	1
Application deadline:	July 31
Notification begins:	January 1

Contact:
American Society of Travel Agents Foundation
1101 King Street
Alexandria, VA 22314-2944
Phone: 703-739-2782
Fax: 703-684-8319
Web: www.astanet.com/education/edu_scholarships.asp

Holland America Line-Westours, Inc., Scholarship

Type of award: Scholarship, renewable.
Intended use: For undergraduate study at accredited vocational, 2-year or 4-year institution in United States.
Eligibility: Applicant must be U.S. citizen, permanent resident, international student or Canadian citizen/resident.
Basis for selection: Major/career interest in tourism/travel. Applicant must demonstrate high academic achievement, seriousness of purpose and service orientation.
Application requirements: Recommendations, transcript, proof of eligibility. 500-word essay on future of cruise industry. Minimum 2.5 GPA. Four copies of application and required materials.
Additional information: Visit Website for application and additional requirements.

Amount of award:	$3,000
Number of awards:	2
Application deadline:	July 31
Notification begins:	January 1
Total amount awarded:	$6,000

Contact:
American Society of Travel Agents Foundation
1101 King Street
Alexandria, VA 22314-2944
Phone: 703-739-2782
Fax: 703-684-8319
Web: www.astanet.com/education/edu_scholarships.asp

Joseph R. Stone Scholarship

Type of award: Scholarship, renewable.
Intended use: For freshman, sophomore, junior or senior study at accredited 2-year or 4-year institution in United States or Canada.
Eligibility: Applicant must be U.S. citizen, permanent resident, international student or Canadian citizen/resident.
Basis for selection: Major/career interest in tourism/travel. Applicant must demonstrate high academic achievement.
Application requirements: Recommendations, transcript, proof of eligibility. 500-word essay on applicant's goals in travel industry. Minimum 2.5 GPA. Four copies of application and required materials.

Additional information: One parent must be employed by travel industry. Visit Website for application and additional requirements.

Amount of award:	$2,400
Number of awards:	3
Application deadline:	July 31
Notification begins:	January 1
Total amount awarded:	$7,200

Contact:
American Society of Travel Agents Foundation
1101 King Street
Alexandria, VA 22314-2944
Phone: 703-739-2782
Fax: 703-684-8319
Web: www.astanet.com/education/edu_scholarships.asp

Northern California Chapter/ Richard Epping Scholarship

Type of award: Scholarship, renewable.
Intended use: For undergraduate study at accredited vocational, 2-year or 4-year institution in United States. Designated institutions: Colleges, universities and recognized proprietary travel and tourism schools in California and Northern Nevada.
Eligibility: Applicant must be U.S. citizen or permanent resident residing in California or Nevada.
Basis for selection: Major/career interest in tourism/travel. Applicant must demonstrate high academic achievement, depth of character, seriousness of purpose and service orientation.
Application requirements: Recommendations, transcript, proof of eligibility. Minimum 2.5 GPA. 500-word essay on why applicant desires profession in travel and tourism industry. Four copies of application and required materials.
Additional information: Applicant must be resident of Northern California or Northern Nevada. Must attend school in California or Northern Nevada. Recipient must make presentation at NorCal ASTA chapter meeting within six months of receiving scholarship. Application deadlines and notification dates vary. Visit Website for application and additional information.

Amount of award:	$2,000
Number of awards:	1
Application deadline:	July 31
Notification begins:	January 1
Total amount awarded:	$2,000

Contact:
American Society of Travel Agents Foundation
1101 King Street
Alexandria, VA 22314-2944
Phone: 703-739-2782
Fax: 703-684-8319
Web: www.astanet.com/education/edu_scholarships.asp

Princess Cruises and Princess Tours Scholarship

Type of award: Scholarship, renewable.
Intended use: For undergraduate study at accredited vocational, 2-year or 4-year institution in United States or Canada.
Eligibility: Applicant must be U.S. citizen, permanent resident, international student or Canadian citizen/resident.
Basis for selection: Major/career interest in tourism/travel. Applicant must demonstrate high academic achievement, seriousness of purpose and service orientation.

Application requirements: Recommendations, transcript, proof of eligibility. Minimum 2.5 GPA. 300-word essay on two features cruise ships will need to offer passengers in next ten years. Four copies of application and required materials.
Additional information: Visit Website for application and additional requirements.

Amount of award:	$2,000
Number of awards:	2
Application deadline:	July 31
Notification begins:	January 1
Total amount awarded:	$4,000

Contact:
American Society of Travel Agents Foundation
1101 King Street
Alexandria, VA 22314-2944
Phone: 703-739-2782
Fax: 703-684-8319
Web: www.astanet.com/education/edu_scholarships.asp

Southern California Chapter/ Pleasant Hawaiian Holidays Scholarship

Type of award: Scholarship, renewable.
Intended use: For undergraduate study at accredited 4-year institution in United States.
Eligibility: Applicant must be U.S. citizen.
Basis for selection: Major/career interest in tourism/travel. Applicant must demonstrate high academic achievement, seriousness of purpose and service orientation.
Application requirements: Recommendations, transcript, proof of eligibility. Minimum 2.5 GPA. 500-word essay on applicant's goals in travel industry and statement explaining why applicant should receive award. Four copies of application and required materials.
Additional information: One award for student from Southern California region; one award for student from anywhere in the United States. Visit Website for application and more details.

Amount of award:	$2,500
Number of awards:	2
Application deadline:	July 31
Notification begins:	January 1
Total amount awarded:	$5,000

Contact:
American Society of Travel Agents Foundation
1101 King Street
Alexandria, VA 22314-2944
Phone: 703-739-2782
Fax: 703-684-8319
Web: www.astanet.com/education/edu_scholarships.asp

American Water Ski Educational Foundation

American Water Ski Educational Foundation Scholarship

Type of award: Scholarship.
Intended use: For full-time sophomore, junior or senior study at 2-year or 4-year institution.

Scholarships

Eligibility: Applicant or parent must be member/participant of American Water Ski Association. Applicant must be U.S. citizen.

Basis for selection: Applicant must demonstrate financial need, high academic achievement, depth of character, leadership and seriousness of purpose.

Application requirements: Recommendations, essay, transcript.

Additional information: Must be a member of American Water Ski Association.

Amount of award:	$1,500
Number of awards:	6
Application deadline:	March 1

Contact:
American Water Ski Educational Foundation
799 Overlook Drive
Winter Haven, FL 33884
Phone: 863-324-4341
Fax: 863-324-3996
Web: usawaterski.org

American Welding Society Foundation, Inc.

Airgas-Terry Jarvis Memorial Scholarship

Type of award: Scholarship.

Intended use: For full-time sophomore, junior or senior study at 4-year institution in United States.

Eligibility: Applicant must be at least 18. Applicant must be U.S. citizen.

Basis for selection: Major/career interest in welding.

Application requirements: Recommendations, transcript, proof of eligibility. Applicant must have interest in pursuing career with industrial gas or welding equipment distributor.

Additional information: Must have interest in pursuing a minimum four-year degree in welding engineering or welding engineering technology. Minimum 2.8 GPA overall, with 3.0 GPA in engineering courses. Priority given to residents of Florida, Alabama, and Georgia. Applicant does not have to be a member of the American Welding Society.

Amount of award:	$2,500
Number of awards:	1
Number of applicants:	8
Application deadline:	January 15

Contact:
American Welding Society Foundation, Inc.
Attn: Scholarships
550 Northwest LeJeune Road
Miami, FL 33126
Phone: 800-443-9353
Web: www.aws.org

American Welding Society District Scholarship

Type of award: Scholarship.

Intended use: For undergraduate study at accredited vocational, 2-year or 4-year institution in United States.

Eligibility: Applicant must be U.S. citizen.

Basis for selection: Major/career interest in welding. Applicant must demonstrate financial need, high academic achievement, depth of character, leadership and seriousness of purpose.

Application requirements: Recommendations, transcript, proof of eligibility.

Amount of award:	$500-$1,000
Number of awards:	150
Application deadline:	March 1
Notification begins:	July 1
Total amount awarded:	$110,000

Contact:
American Welding Society Foundation, Inc.
Attn: Scholarships
550 Northwest LeJeune Road
Miami, FL 33126
Phone: 800-443-9353

Donald F. Hastings Scholarship

Type of award: Scholarship, renewable.

Intended use: For sophomore, junior or senior study at 4-year institution in United States.

Eligibility: Applicant must be U.S. citizen.

Basis for selection: Major/career interest in welding. Applicant must demonstrate financial need and seriousness of purpose.

Application requirements: Recommendations, transcript, proof of eligibility. Minimum of 2.5 GPA. Interest in pursuing minimum four-year degree in welding engineering or welding engineering technology.

Additional information: Priority given to residents of Ohio and California.

Amount of award:	$2,500
Number of awards:	1
Number of applicants:	23
Application deadline:	January 15
Notification begins:	March 15

Contact:
American Welding Society Foundation, Inc.
Attn: Scholarships
550 Northwest LeJeune Road
Miami, FL 33126
Phone: 800-443-9353

Edward J. Brady Memorial Scholarship

Type of award: Scholarship, renewable.

Intended use: For sophomore, junior or senior study at 4-year institution.

Eligibility: Applicant must be U.S. citizen.

Basis for selection: Major/career interest in welding or engineering. Applicant must demonstrate financial need and seriousness of purpose.

Application requirements: Recommendations, essay, transcript, proof of eligibility. Proposed curriculum, brief biography, proof of hands-on welding experience. Minimum 2.5 GPA.

Additional information: Interest in pursuing minimum four-year degree in welding engineering or welding engineering technology.

Amount of award:	$2,500
Number of awards:	1
Number of applicants:	12
Application deadline:	January 15
Notification begins:	March 15

Contact:
American Welding Society Foundation, Inc.
Attn: Scholarships
550 Northwest LeJeune Road
Miami, FL 33126
Phone: 800-443-9353

Howard E. Adkins Memorial Scholarship

Type of award: Scholarship, renewable.
Intended use: For full-time junior or senior study at 4-year institution.
Eligibility: Applicant must be U.S. citizen.
Basis for selection: Major/career interest in welding. Applicant must demonstrate high academic achievement and seriousness of purpose.
Application requirements: Recommendations, transcript, proof of eligibility. Minimum GPA of 3.2 in engineering, scientific and technical subjects; minimum overall GPA of 2.8. Interest in pursuing minimum four-year degree in welding engineering or welding engineering technology.
Additional information: Priority given to residents of Kentucky and Wisconsin.

Amount of award:	$2,500
Number of awards:	1
Number of applicants:	19
Application deadline:	January 15
Notification begins:	March 15

Contact:
American Welding Society Foundation Inc.
Attn: Scholarships
550 Northwest LeJeune Road
Miami, FL 33126
Phone: 800-443-9353

James A. Turner, Jr., Memorial Scholarship

Type of award: Scholarship, renewable.
Intended use: For full-time sophomore, junior or senior study at accredited 4-year institution.
Eligibility: Applicant must be U.S. citizen.
Basis for selection: Major/career interest in welding or business/management/administration. Applicant must demonstrate financial need and seriousness of purpose.
Application requirements: Recommendations, transcript, proof of eligibility. Minimum GPA of 2.5. Verification of employment, brief biography, financial aid report, proposed curriculum. Interest in pursuing management career in welding.
Additional information: Must work minimum of 10 hours per week at welding store.

Amount of award:	$3,000
Number of awards:	1
Number of applicants:	3
Application deadline:	January 15
Notification begins:	March 15

Contact:
American Welding Society Foundation, Inc.
Attn: Scholarships
550 Northwest LeJeune Road
Miami, FL 33126
Phone: 800-443-9353

John C. Lincoln Memorial Scholarship

Type of award: Scholarship, renewable.
Intended use: For sophomore, junior or senior study at 4-year institution.
Eligibility: Applicant must be U.S. citizen.
Basis for selection: Major/career interest in welding. Applicant must demonstrate financial need and seriousness of purpose.
Application requirements: Recommendations, transcript, proof of eligibility. Minimum GPA of 2.5. Interest in pursuing minimum four-year degree in welding engineering or welding engineering technology.

Amount of award:	$2,500
Number of awards:	1
Number of applicants:	21
Application deadline:	January 15
Notification begins:	March 15

Contact:
American Welding Society Foundation, Inc.
Attn: Scholarships
550 Northwest LeJeune Road
Miami, FL 33126
Phone: 800-443-9553

Matsuo Bridge Company Ltd of Japan Scholarship

Type of award: Scholarship.
Intended use: For junior, senior or graduate study at accredited 4-year or graduate institution in United States.
Eligibility: Applicant must be at least 18.
Basis for selection: Major/career interest in welding or engineering, civil.
Application requirements: Recommendations, transcript, proof of eligibility. Minimum 3.0 GPA required. Valid passport.
Additional information: Scholarship provides a two- to three-week training opportunity at Matsuo Bridge Company's facilities and job sites in Japan to individuals interested in pursuing a career in civil engineering, welding engineering, or welding engineering technology. Priority given to applicants residing in California, Texas, Oregon, or Washington. Applicant does not have to be a member of the American Welding Society but must agree to participate in AWS Foundation or Matsuo Bridge Company sponsored publicity.

Amount of award:	$2,500
Number of awards:	1
Application deadline:	January 15

Contact:
American Welding Society Foundation, Inc.
Attn: Scholarships
550 Northwest LeJeune Road
Miami, FL 33126
Phone: 800-443-9353
Web: www.aws.org

Miller Electric Manufacturing Company Ivic Scholarship

Type of award: Scholarship.
Intended use: For undergraduate study at accredited vocational, 2-year or 4-year institution in United States.
Eligibility: Applicant must be U.S. citizen.

Basis for selection: Major/career interest in welding. Applicant must demonstrate depth of character, leadership and seriousness of purpose.

Additional information: Competition based on AWS National Welding Trials.

Amount of award:	$40,000
Number of awards:	1

Contact:
American Welding Society Foundation, Inc.
Attn: Scholarships
550 Northwest LeJeune Road
Miami, FL 33126
Phone: 800-443-9353

Praxair International Scholarship

Type of award: Scholarship, renewable.

Intended use: For full-time sophomore, junior or senior study at 4-year institution.

Eligibility: Applicant must be U.S. citizen, international student or Canadian citizen/resident.

Basis for selection: Major/career interest in welding. Applicant must demonstrate financial need, leadership and service orientation.

Application requirements: Recommendations, transcript, proof of eligibility. Minimum GPA of 2.5. Interest in pursuing minimum four-year degree in welding engineering or welding engineering technology.

Amount of award:	$2,500
Number of awards:	1
Number of applicants:	17
Application deadline:	January 15
Notification begins:	March 15

Contact:
American Welding Society Foundation, Inc.
Praxair Scholarship
550 Northwest LeJeune Road
Miami, FL 33126
Phone: 800-443-9353

William B. Howell Memorial Scholarship

Type of award: Scholarship, renewable.

Intended use: For undergraduate study at accredited 4-year institution in United States.

Eligibility: Applicant must be at least 18. Applicant must be U.S. citizen.

Basis for selection: Major/career interest in welding. Applicant must demonstrate financial need.

Application requirements: Recommendations, transcript, proof of eligibility. Interest in pursuing a four-year degree in welding program at accredited four-year university.

Additional information: Minimum 2.5 GPA required. Priority given to residents of Florida, Michigan, and Ohio. Applicant does not have to be a member of the American Welding Society.

Amount of award:	$2,500
Number of awards:	1
Application deadline:	January 15

Contact:
American Welding Society Foundation, Inc.
Attn: Scholarships
550 Northwest LeJeune Road
Miami, FL 33126
Phone: 800-443-9353
Web: www.aws.org

An Uncommon Legacy Foundation, Inc.

Lesbian Leadership Scholarship

Type of award: Scholarship.

Intended use: For full-time undergraduate or graduate study in United States.

Eligibility: Applicant should be lesbian. Applicant must be female.

Basis for selection: Applicant must demonstrate financial need, high academic achievement, depth of character, leadership, seriousness of purpose and service orientation.

Application requirements: Recommendations, essay, transcript, proof of eligibility. Minimum 3.0 GPA.

Additional information: Applicants must be lesbian college students who show potential for leadership and demonstrate commitment or contribution to lesbian community. Applicant pool and number of awards granted varies. Write to foundation or visit Website for application.

Amount of award:	$2,500
Application deadline:	July 1
Notification begins:	December 15

Contact:
An Uncommon Legacy Foundation, Inc.
Legacy Scholarship Committee
P.O. Box 33727
Washington, DC 20033
Phone: 202-265-1926
Fax: 202-265-1927
Web: www.uncommonlegacy.org

Annie's Homegrown, Inc.

Annie's Environmental Studies Scholarships

Type of award: Scholarship.

Intended use: For full-time undergraduate or graduate study at accredited 4-year or graduate institution in United States. Designated institutions: Accredited U.S. colleges and universities.

Basis for selection: Major/career interest in environmental science or ecology. Applicant must demonstrate high academic achievement, depth of character and seriousness of purpose.

Application requirements: Recommendations, essay, transcript.

Additional information: Applicants must be focused on environmental studies. Criteria in selection place more emphasis on commitment to preserving and protecting the environment than on grades/GPA. Application and more information available on Website.

Amount of award:	$1,000
Number of awards:	25
Application deadline:	January 1, June 30
Total amount awarded:	$25,000

Contact:
Annie's Scholarship Program
P.O. Box 554
Wakefield, MA 01880
Phone: 781-224-1172
Web: www.annies.com

Scholarships

AOPA Air Safety Foundation

Donald Burnside Memorial Scholarship

Type of award: Scholarship.
Intended use: For junior or senior study at 4-year institution.
Eligibility: Applicant must be U.S. citizen.
Basis for selection: Major/career interest in aviation.
Application requirements: Essay with a maximum of 250 words on: "What is the biggest safety issue associated with new avionics technology?"
Additional information: Applicant must have a GPA of at least 3.25. Application available on Website. Five copies of entire application packet must be mailed to: Dr. David A. NewMyer, Chairperson; Aviation Management and Flight College of Applied Sciences and Arts; Southern Illinois University Carbondale; Carbondale, IL 62901-6623.

Amount of award:	$1,000
Number of awards:	1
Application deadline:	March 31
Notification begins:	July 1
Total amount awarded:	$1,000

Contact:
AOPA Air Safety Foundation
Donald Burnside Memorial Scholarship
421 Aviation Way
Frederick, MD 21701
Phone: 301-695-2177
Fax: 301-695-2343
Web: www.asf.org

Appaloosa Youth Foundation

Appaloosa Youth Foundation Educational Scholarships

Type of award: Scholarship, renewable.
Intended use: For full-time undergraduate or graduate study at accredited postsecondary institution in United States.
Eligibility: Applicant or parent must be member/participant of Appaloosa Horse Club. Applicant must be U.S. citizen or permanent resident.
Basis for selection: Based on scholastic aptitude, involvement in the Appaloosa industry, leadership potential, sportsmanship, community and civic responsibility, and general knowledge and accomplishments in horsemanship.
Application requirements: Recommendations, essay, transcript, proof of eligibility. Photo, SAT or ACT scores. GPA of 3.5 for one scholarship, GPA of 2.5 for other scholarships.
Additional information: Applicant must be member of Appaloosa Horse Club or Appaloosa Youth Association. One scholarship requires intent to pursue equine-related studies.

Amount of award:	$1,000-$2,000
Application deadline:	June 10
Notification begins:	July 15
Total amount awarded:	$10,000

Contact:
Appaloosa Youth Foundation Scholarship Committee
2720 Pullman Road
Moscow, ID 83843
Phone: 208-882-5578
Fax: 208-882-8150
Web: www.appaloosa.com

Arizona Board of Regents

Arizona Tuition Waiver for Non-Residents

Type of award: Scholarship, renewable.
Intended use: For full-time undergraduate or graduate study. Designated institutions: Arizona State University, Northern Arizona University, and University of Arizona.
Eligibility: Applicant must be residing in Arizona.
Basis for selection: Applicant must demonstrate financial need and high academic achievement.
Application requirements: Students seeking need-based waiver must file FAFSA. Merit waiver requirements vary. Graduate students seeking merit waivers apply to graduate academic department. Must contact designated institution for application process.
Additional information: Waivers generally used to recruit nonresident students with strong academic backgrounds or special talents, but applicant can be resident. Financial need and academic achievement/talent considered separately. Must maintain academic progress and complete community service requirement to renew. Additional Websites: NAU: www.nau.edu; UA: www.arizona.edu. Selection process and application requirements vary by institution.
Contact:
Contact school's financial aid office.
Web: www.asu.edu

Arizona Tuition Waivers for Children/Spouses of Slain Public Servants

Type of award: Scholarship, renewable.
Intended use: For undergraduate study at accredited postsecondary institution. Designated institutions: Arizona State University, Northern Arizona University, and University of Arizona.
Eligibility: Applicant must be U.S. citizen or permanent resident residing in Arizona. Applicant's parent must have been killed or disabled in work-related accident as fire fighter, police officer or public safety officer.
Application requirements: Proof of eligibility. Documentation of eligibility by Arizona Peace Officers, Arizona Fire Fighters, or Arizona Emergency Paramedics.
Additional information: Eligible public safety categories include emergency medical service. Students must meet university admissions criteria and maintain satisfactory academic progress to renew. Parent must have been Arizona state firefighter or police officer. Waiver may also cover summer courses.

153

Contact:
Arizona Board of Regents
2020 North Central Avenue
Suite 230
Phoenix, AZ 85004-4593
Phone: 602-229-2500
Fax: 602-229-2555

Arizona Tuition Waivers for Residents

Type of award: Scholarship, renewable.
Intended use: For undergraduate or graduate study at postsecondary institution. Designated institutions: Arizona State University, Northern Arizona University, and University of Arizona.
Eligibility: Applicant must be residing in Arizona.
Application requirements: Nomination by Arizona high schools or Arizona home-schooling families. Students seeking need-based waiver must file FAFSA. Graduate students seeking merit waivers apply to graduate academic department. Evidence for merit awards includes test scores, grades, and special talent.
Additional information: Awarded to students who demonstrate financial need, merit, or both. Eligibility for waivers generally established one year prior to enrollment. Must meet university admissions criteria and maintain satisfactory academic progress to renew. Additional Websites: NAU: www.nau.edu; UA: www.arizona.edu. Selection process and requirements may vary by institution.

   Amount of award: Full tuition
Contact:
Arizona high school counselor or institution's admissions office.
Web: www.asu.edu

Arkansas Department of Higher Education

Academic Challenge Scholarship

Type of award: Scholarship, renewable.
Intended use: For full-time undergraduate study at postsecondary institution. Designated institutions: Approved Arkansas college or university.
Eligibility: Applicant must be high school senior. Applicant must be U.S. citizen or permanent resident residing in Arkansas.
Basis for selection: Applicant must demonstrate financial need and high academic achievement.
Application requirements: Transcript. Completed application, ACT, and family federal income tax forms for two years preceding high school graduation.
Additional information: Applications available online and at high school counselor's office. Award is renewable annually up to four years, provided student maintains minimum cumulative GPA of 2.75 and at least 30 semester credit hours per academic year. Visit Website for more information.

   Amount of award: $3,000
   Application deadline: June 1
Contact:
Arkansas Department of Higher Education
114 E. Capitol Street
Little Rock, AR 72201-3818
Phone: 800-547-8839
Web: www.arkansaschallenge.com

Arkansas Department of Higher Education Arkansas Student Assistance Grant

Type of award: Scholarship.
Intended use: For undergraduate study at postsecondary institution. Designated institutions: Approved postsecondary institutions.
Eligibility: Applicant must be high school senior. Applicant must be U.S. citizen or permanent resident residing in Arkansas.
Basis for selection: Applicant must demonstrate financial need.
Application requirements: FAFSA.
Additional information: Awards made on first-come, first-served basis to Arkansas residents, based on information provided on FAFSA. Submit FAFSA early for best chance.

   Amount of award: $600
   Number of awards: 6,000
   Application deadline: April 15
   Total amount awarded: $3,200,000
Contact:
Arkansas Dept. of Higher Education
144 E. Capitol Street
Little Rock, AR 72201
Phone: 501-371-2050 or 800-54-STUDY
Fax: 501-371-2001
Web: www.arscholarships.com

Arkansas Department of Higher Education Teacher Assistance Resource (STAR) Program

Type of award: Scholarship, renewable.
Intended use: For undergraduate study.
Eligibility: Applicant must be U.S. citizen or permanent resident residing in Arkansas.
Basis for selection: Major/career interest in education, teacher; education, special or education. Applicant must demonstrate financial need.
Additional information: Loan-forgiveness program for students entering field of teaching. Awards subject to applicant's agreement to teach in subject shortage area of math, science, foreign language, special education or ESL. Awards also made to applicants who agree to teach in Arkansas public school experiencing critical shortage of teachers. Recipients required to teach one year for every year loan received in order to have loan forgiven.

   Amount of award: $3,000-$6,000
   Application deadline: June 1
   Total amount awarded: $1,500,000
Contact:
Arkansas Department of Higher Education
114 E. Capitol Street
Little Rock, AR 72201
Phone: 501-371-2050 or 800-54-STUDY
Fax: 501-371-2001
Web: www.arscholarships.com

Arkansas Law Enforcement Officers' Dependents Scholarship

Type of award: Scholarship, renewable.

Intended use: For undergraduate study at accredited vocational, 2-year or 4-year institution. Designated institutions: Arkansas public institutions.

Eligibility: Applicant must be U.S. citizen or permanent resident residing in Arkansas. Applicant's parent must have been killed or disabled in work-related accident as fire fighter, police officer or public safety officer.

Application requirements: Proof of eligibility. Documentation of eligibility.

Additional information: All eligible applicants will receive tuition waver. Children/spouses of Highway and Transportation Department employees disabled or killed in work-related accident also eligible. Applicant must be Arkansas resident for at least six months. Dependent child applicant may be no older than 23; no age restriction for spouse. Application deadlines are as follows: August 1 for the fall term; December 1 for the spring/winter Terms; May 1 for summer I term; and July 1 for summer II term. Visit Website or call 501-371-2050 or 800-54-STUDY for more information or to obtain application.

    Amount of award: Full tuition
Contact:
Arkansas Department of Higher Education
114 E. Capitol Street
Little Rock, AR 72201-3818
Phone: 800-54-STUDY
Web: www.arkansashighered.com

Arkansas Missing/Killed in Action Dependents Scholarship

Type of award: Scholarship, renewable.
Intended use: For full-time undergraduate, master's or non-degree study at accredited vocational, 2-year, 4-year or graduate institution.
Eligibility: Applicant must be U.S. citizen or permanent resident residing in Arkansas. Applicant must be dependent of deceased veteran or POW/MIA; or spouse of deceased veteran or POW/MIA who served in the Army, Air Force, Marines, Navy, Coast Guard or Reserves/National Guard during Persian Gulf War or Vietnam. Parent/spouse must have been Arkansas resident prior to enlistment.
Application requirements: Proof of eligibility.
Additional information: Child/spouse of person killed in action or missing in action. Applicant must be Arkansas resident for at least six months. Application deadlines for summer May 1 and July 1. Visit Website or call 501-371-2050 or 800-54-STUDY for an application.

    Application deadline: August 1, December 1
Contact:
Arkansas Department of Higher Education
114 E. Capitol Street
Little Rock, AR 72201-3818
Phone: 800-547-8839
Web: www.arkansashighered.com

Governor's Scholars Program

Type of award: Scholarship, renewable.
Intended use: For full-time undergraduate study at postsecondary institution. Designated institutions: Approved Arkansas college or university.
Eligibility: Applicant must be high school senior. Applicant must be U.S. citizen or permanent resident residing in Arkansas.
Basis for selection: Applicant must demonstrate high academic achievement and leadership.

Application requirements: Completed application. Applicants must have at least 3.50 grade point average or score at least 27 on ACT or at least combined score of 1220 on SAT to qualify. Governor's Distinguished Scholars must have at least a 32 composite ACT or a 1410 combined SAT score or have been selected as a National Merit Finalist or National Achievement Scholar.

Additional information: Governor's Distinguished Scholars automatically receive an award equal to tuition, mandatory fees, room and board, up to $10,000 per year at any Arkansas institution. Other chosen applicants receive award of $4,000 per year. Award is renewable annually up to four years, provided student maintains minimum cumulative GPA of 3.0 and at least 30 semester credit hours or equivalent per academic year. Governor's Distinguished Scholars must maintain a minimum 3.25 GPA. Applications available from high school counselor's office. Visit Website for more information.

    Amount of award: $4,000
    Number of awards: 75
    Application deadline: February 1
    Total amount awarded: $400,000
Contact:
Arkansas Department of Higher Education
114 E. Capitol Street
Little Rock, AR 72201-3818
Phone: 800-547-8839
Web: www.arkansashighered.com

Second Effort Scholarship

Type of award: Scholarship, renewable.
Intended use: For undergraduate study at postsecondary institution. Designated institutions: Arkansas college or university.
Eligibility: Applicant must be returning adult student. Applicant must be U.S. citizen or permanent resident residing in Arkansas.
Basis for selection: Applicant must demonstrate high academic achievement.
Application requirements: Applicant must not have graduated from high school. Students do not apply for this award. Those scholars who achieved one of ten best scores on Arkansas High School Diploma test during previous calendar year are contacted directly by Arkansas Department of Higher Education.
Additional information: This scholarship was established to recognize importance of Arkansas High School Diploma (GED) Program and to encourage those students who successfully pass the Arkansas High School test to enroll in Arkansas postsecondary institutions. Award is renewable annually up to four years (or equivalent if student enrolled part-time), provided student maintains minimum cumulative GPA of 2.5. Eligible students are notified by Arkansas Dept. of Higher Education.

    Amount of award: $1,000
Contact:
Arkansas Department of Higher Education
114 E. Capitol Street
Little Rock, AR 72201-3818
Phone: 800-547-8839
Web: www.arkansashighered.com

Scholarships

Armed Forces Communications and Electronics Association

AFCEA Copernicus Foundation Scholarship For Computer Graphic Design

Type of award: Scholarship.
Intended use: For full-time sophomore or junior study at accredited 4-year institution in United States.
Eligibility: Applicant must be U.S. citizen.
Basis for selection: Major/career interest in computer graphics.
Application requirements: Recommendations, essay, transcript. Must send single sample of original, digital artwork along with 200-word essay describing image and how it was created. Digital artwork must be created solely by applicant, not group effort or improvement on existing site.
Additional information: Graphic can be submitted in .JPEG or .GIF format on CD, zip disk or diskette, or, if URL is provided, it can be viewed at Website. Applicants judged on artistic creativity as well as mastery of Web technology. If Websites are submitted, one graphic from site must be identified for consideration; entire sites not eligible.

Amount of award:	$2,000
Number of awards:	1
Application deadline:	October 15
Total amount awarded:	$2,000

Contact:
Armed Forces Communications and Electronics Association
Educational Foundation
4400 Fair Lakes Court
Fairfax, VA 22033-3899
Phone: 800-336-4583, ext. 6149
Fax: 703-631-4693
Web: www.afcea.org

AFCEA General Emmett Paige Scholarship

Type of award: Scholarship.
Intended use: For full-time sophomore or junior study at accredited 4-year institution in United States.
Eligibility: Applicant must be U.S. citizen. Applicant must be in military service or veteran; or dependent of active service person, veteran or POW/MIA; or spouse of active service person, veteran or POW/MIA.
Basis for selection: Major/career interest in aerospace; computer/information sciences; engineering, computer; physics; mathematics or engineering, electrical/electronic. Applicant must demonstrate high academic achievement, depth of character, leadership, patriotism, seriousness of purpose and service orientation.
Application requirements: Recommendations, transcript, proof of eligibility. Freshman veteran students must have letters from employer or supervisor or copy of performance evaluation, fitness report or similar document. Proof of eligibility can be copy of discharge form DD214, certificate of service, facsimile of applicant's current DOD or Coast Guard identification card.
Additional information: Send SASE or visit Website for application (available after November 1). Must have minimum

3.4 GPA. Graduating high school seniors not eligible, but veterans enrolled as freshmen are eligible to apply; spouses or dependents must be enrolled as sophomores or juniors at time of application.

Amount of award:	$2,000
Number of awards:	10
Application deadline:	March 1
Notification begins:	June 1
Total amount awarded:	$20,000

Contact:
Armed Forces Communications and Electronics Association
Educational Foundation
4400 Fair Lakes Court
Fairfax, VA 22033-3899
Phone: 703-631-6149
Fax: 703-631-4693
Web: www.afcea.org

AFCEA General John A. Wickham Scholarship

Type of award: Scholarship.
Intended use: For full-time sophomore or junior study at accredited 4-year institution in United States.
Eligibility: Applicant must be U.S. citizen.
Basis for selection: Major/career interest in aerospace; electronics; computer/information sciences; physics; mathematics or engineering, electrical/electronic. Applicant must demonstrate high academic achievement, depth of character, leadership, patriotism, seriousness of purpose and service orientation.
Application requirements: Transcript. Minimum 3.5 GPA. Two letters of recommendation from faculty members having personal knowledge of candidate's program, achievements and potential.
Additional information: Send SASE or visit Website for application. Student must be sophomore or junior enrolled full time at time of application.

Amount of award:	$2,000
Number of awards:	15
Application deadline:	May 1
Notification begins:	June 1
Total amount awarded:	$30,000

Contact:
Armed Forces Communications and Electronics Association
Educational Foundation
4400 Fair Lakes Court
Fairfax, VA 22033-3899
Phone: 800-336-4583 ext. 6149
Fax: 703-631-4693
Web: www.afcea.org

AFCEA Professional Part-Time Scholarship

Type of award: Scholarship.
Intended use: For half-time sophomore, junior or senior study at accredited 2-year or 4-year institution in United States.
Eligibility: Applicant must be U.S. citizen.
Basis for selection: Major/career interest in engineering, electrical/electronic; aerospace; engineering, computer; information systems; physics or mathematics. Applicant must demonstrate high academic achievement.
Application requirements: Transcript, proof of eligibility. Completed applications must be received by September 15, but not before August 15.

Scholarships

Additional information: Scholarship awarded to part-time students pursuing eligible undergraduate program while currently employed in government or industry. Distance learning programs not eligible. Student must be enrolled in at least two classes per semester with major in science or technology degree program. Minimum 3.5 GPA required.

> **Amount of award:** $1,500
> **Application deadline:** September 15

Contact:
Armed Forces Communications and Electronics Association
Educational Foundation
4400 Fair Lakes Court
Fairfax, VA 22033-3899
Phone: 703-631-6149
Fax: 703-631-4693
Web: www.afcea.org

AFCEA ROTC Scholarships

Type of award: Scholarship.
Intended use: For full-time sophomore or junior study at accredited 4-year institution in United States.
Eligibility: Applicant or parent must be member/participant of Reserve Officers Training Corps (ROTC). Applicant must be U.S. citizen.
Basis for selection: Major/career interest in aerospace; engineering, electrical/electronic; computer/information sciences; engineering, computer; physics; mathematics; science, general or electronics. Applicant must demonstrate high academic achievement, depth of character, leadership, patriotism, seriousness of purpose and service orientation.
Application requirements: Transcript, nomination by professor of military science, naval science or aerospace studies. Recommendations from ROTC commander and professor in stated major.
Additional information: Applicant must be in ROTC. For application information, contact commander of ROTC unit. Candidates must be enrolled as sophomores or juniors at time of application.

> **Amount of award:** $2,000
> **Number of awards:** 60
> **Application deadline:** April 1
> **Notification begins:** June 1
> **Total amount awarded:** $120,000

Contact:
Armed Forces Communications and Electronics Association
Educational Foundation
4400 Fair Lakes Court
Fairfax, VA 22033-3899
Phone: 703-631-6149
Fax: 703-631-4693
Web: www.afcea.org

AFCEA Sgt. Jeannette L. Winters, USMC Memorial Scholarship

Type of award: Scholarship.
Intended use: For sophomore, junior or senior study at accredited 4-year institution in United States.
Eligibility: Applicant must be U.S. citizen.
Basis for selection: Major/career interest in aerospace; computer/information sciences; mathematics; engineering or physics. Applicant must demonstrate high academic achievement, depth of character, leadership, patriotism, seriousness of purpose and service orientation.
Application requirements: Recommendations, transcript, proof of eligibility. Send as proof either a Certificate of Service,

Discharge Form DD214, or facsimile of a current Department of Defense Identification Card.
Additional information: For Marines on active duty, or those honorably discharged. Must have minimum 3.4 GPA. Qualified sophomore, junior or senior undergraduate students enrolled either part-time or full-time in an eligible degree program. Send SASE or visit Website for application (available after July 1).

> **Amount of award:** $2,000
> **Number of awards:** 1
> **Application deadline:** September 15
> **Notification begins:** October 15
> **Total amount awarded:** $2,000

Contact:
Armed Forces Communications and Electronics Association
4400 Fair Lakes Court
Fairfax, VA 22033-3899
Phone: 800-336-4583 ext. 6149
Fax: 703-631-4693
Web: www.afcea.org

AFCEA/Orincon IT Scholarship

Type of award: Scholarship.
Intended use: For full-time sophomore or junior study at accredited 4-year institution in United States. Designated institutions: Postsecondary institutions in greater San Diego, California, area.
Eligibility: Applicant must be U.S. citizen residing in California.
Basis for selection: Major/career interest in aerospace; electronics; computer/information sciences; physics; mathematics or engineering, electrical/electronic. Applicant must demonstrate high academic achievement, depth of character, leadership, patriotism, seriousness of purpose and service orientation.
Application requirements: Transcript. Two letters of recommendation required.
Additional information: Minimum 3.5 GPA required.

> **Amount of award:** $3,000
> **Number of awards:** 1
> **Application deadline:** May 1
> **Notification begins:** June 1

Contact:
Armed Forces Communications and Electronics Association
Educational Foundation
4400 Fair Lakes Court
Fairfax, VA 22033-3899
Phone: 800-336-4583 ext. 6149
Fax: 703-631-4693
Web: www.afcea.org

Vice Admiral Jerry O. Tuttle, USN (Ret.), and Mrs. Barbara A. Tuttle Science and Technology Scholarship

Type of award: Scholarship.
Intended use: For full-time sophomore, junior or senior study at accredited 4-year institution in United States. Designated institutions: Accredited technological institute or technology program at accredited four-year college/university.
Eligibility: Applicant must be U.S. citizen.
Basis for selection: Major/career interest in computer/information sciences; engineering, computer or electronics. Applicant must demonstrate high academic achievement.
Application requirements: Recommendations, transcript.
Additional information: Student must be sophomore or junior enrolled full time in technology related field at time of

157

application. Priority consideration will be given to military enlisted candidate.

Amount of award:	$2,000
Number of awards:	1
Application deadline:	November 1

Contact:
Armed Forces Communications and Electronics Association
Educational Foundation
4400 Fair Lakes Court
Fairfax, VA 22033-3899
Phone: 703-631-6149
Fax: 703-631-4693
Web: www.afcea.org

Armenian General Benevolent Union

Armenian General Benevolent Union International Scholarship Program

Type of award: Scholarship, renewable.
Intended use: For full-time undergraduate or graduate study in countries outside of U.S.
Eligibility: Applicant must be Armenian. Applicant must be U.S. citizen or permanent resident.
Basis for selection: Competition/talent/interest in Study abroad. Applicant must demonstrate financial need, high academic achievement, depth of character, leadership, seriousness of purpose and service orientation.
Application requirements: Recommendations, transcript, proof of eligibility.
Additional information: Students must provide verification of enrollment. Must be of Armenian descent.

Amount of award:	$300-$1,200
Number of awards:	400
Number of applicants:	450
Application deadline:	May 15
Notification begins:	September 15
Total amount awarded:	$475,000

Contact:
Armenian General Benevolent Union
Mrs. Maral Achian
55 E. 59th Street
New York, NY 10022-1112
Phone: 212-319-6383
Fax: 212-319-6507
Web: www.agbu.org

ARMY Emergency Relief

MG James Ursano Scholarship Fund

Type of award: Scholarship, renewable.
Intended use: For full-time freshman, sophomore, junior or senior study at accredited vocational, 2-year or 4-year institution.
Eligibility: Applicant must be single, at least 16, no older than 22. Applicant must be U.S. citizen or permanent resident.

Applicant must be dependent of active service person, veteran or deceased veteran who serves or served in the Army.
Basis for selection: Applicant must demonstrate financial need, high academic achievement and leadership.
Application requirements: Transcript, proof of eligibility.
Additional information: Applicants must be enrolled, accepted or pending acceptance as full-time dependent students for entire academic year in postsecondary institutions approved by Department of Education for Title IV funds. Applicants must maintain at least 2.0 GPA. Application may be downloaded from Website.

Amount of award:	$700-$1,800
Number of awards:	2,114
Number of applicants:	3,295
Application deadline:	March 1
Notification begins:	June 1
Total amount awarded:	$2,539,200

Contact:
ARMY Emergency Relief/MG James Ursano Scholarship Fund
7200 Stovall Street
Alexandria, VA 22332-0600
Web: www.aerhq.org

ARRL Foundation, Inc.

ARRL Albuquerque Amateur Radio Club Scholarship/Toby Cross Scholarship

Type of award: Scholarship.
Intended use: For undergraduate study at accredited postsecondary institution in United States.
Eligibility: Applicant must be residing in New Mexico.
Basis for selection: Competition/talent/interest in amateur radio. Applicant must demonstrate financial need.
Application requirements: Recommendations, essay, transcript, proof of eligibility. One-page essay on role amateur radio has played in their life.
Additional information: Must be amateur radio operator holding any class license. Number of awards varies, but is usually one per year. Application may be obtained on Website.

Amount of award:	$500
Number of awards:	1
Application deadline:	February 1

Contact:
ARRL Foundation Inc./Scholarship Program
225 Main Street
Newington, CT 06111
Phone: 860-594-0200
Fax: 860-594-0259
Web: www.arrl.org/arrlf/scholgen.html

ARRL Donald Riebhoff Memorial Scholarship

Type of award: Scholarship.
Intended use: For undergraduate or graduate study at accredited postsecondary institution in United States.
Eligibility: Applicant or parent must be member/participant of American Radio Relay League.
Basis for selection: Competition/talent/interest in amateur radio. Major/career interest in international relations. Applicant must demonstrate financial need.

Application requirements: Recommendations, transcript, proof of eligibility.
Additional information: Must be amateur radio operator with technician class license. Application may be obtained on Website.

Amount of award:	$1,000
Number of awards:	1
Application deadline:	February 1

Contact:
ARRL Foundation Inc./Scholarship Program
225 Main Street
Newington, CT 06111
Phone: 860-594-0200
Fax: 860-594-0259
Web: www.arrl.org/arrlf/scholgen.html

ARRL Earl I. Anderson Scholarship

Type of award: Scholarship.
Intended use: For undergraduate or graduate study at accredited postsecondary institution. Designated institutions: Postsecondary institutions in Illinois, Indiana, Florida or Michigan.
Eligibility: Applicant or parent must be member/participant of American Radio Relay League. Applicant must be residing in Michigan, Indiana, Illinois or Florida.
Basis for selection: Competition/talent/interest in amateur radio. Major/career interest in engineering, electrical/electronic. Applicant must demonstrate financial need.
Application requirements: Recommendations, transcript, proof of eligibility.
Additional information: Must be amateur radio operator holding any class license. Application may be obtained on Website.

Amount of award:	$1,250
Number of awards:	3
Application deadline:	February 1

Contact:
ARRL Foundation, Inc./Scholarship Program
225 Main Street
Newington, CT 06111
Phone: 860-594-0200
Fax: 860-594-0259
Web: www.arrl.org/arrlf/scholgen.html

ARRL Eugene "Gene" Sallee, W4YFR Memorial Scholarship

Type of award: Scholarship.
Intended use: For undergraduate or graduate study at accredited postsecondary institution in United States.
Eligibility: Applicant must be residing in Georgia.
Basis for selection: Competition/talent/interest in amateur radio. Applicant must demonstrate financial need and high academic achievement.
Application requirements: Recommendations, transcript, proof of eligibility.
Additional information: Must be amateur radio operator with technician plus class license. Minimum 3.0 GPA. Application may be obtained on Website.

Amount of award:	$500
Number of awards:	1
Application deadline:	February 1
Total amount awarded:	$500

Contact:
ARRL Foundation Inc./Scholarship Program
225 Main Street
Newington, CT 06111
Phone: 860-594-0200
Fax: 860-594-0259
Web: www.arrl.org/arrlf/scholgen.html

ARRL Henry Broughton, K2AE Memorial Scholarship

Type of award: Scholarship.
Intended use: For undergraduate study at accredited 4-year institution in United States.
Eligibility: Applicant must be residing in New York.
Basis for selection: Competition/talent/interest in amateur radio. Major/career interest in engineering or science, general. Applicant must demonstrate financial need.
Application requirements: Recommendations, transcript, proof of eligibility.
Additional information: Applicant must live within 70-mile radius of Schenectady, New York. Must be amateur radio operator with general class license. May offer additional awards if funding permits. Application may be obtained on Website.

Amount of award:	$1,000
Number of awards:	1
Application deadline:	February 1

Contact:
ARRL Foundation, Inc./Scholarship Program
225 Main Street
Newington, CT 06111
Phone: 860-594-0200
Fax: 860-594-0259
Web: www.arrl.org/arrlf/scholgen.html

ARRL Scholarship Honoring Senator Barry Goldwater, K7UGA

Type of award: Scholarship.
Intended use: For undergraduate or graduate study at accredited postsecondary institution in United States.
Basis for selection: Competition/talent/interest in amateur radio. Major/career interest in radio/television/film or communications. Applicant must demonstrate financial need.
Application requirements: Recommendations, transcript.
Additional information: Must be amateur radio operator with novice license. Application may be obtained on Website.

Amount of award:	$5,000
Number of awards:	1
Application deadline:	February 1
Total amount awarded:	$5,000

Contact:
ARRL Foundation Inc./Scholarship Program
225 Main Street
Newington, CT 06111
Phone: 860-594-0200
Fax: 860-594-0259
Web: www.arrl.org/arrlf/scholgen.html

Charles Clarke Cordle Memorial Scholarship

Type of award: Scholarship.
Intended use: For undergraduate or graduate study at accredited postsecondary institution. Designated institutions: Georgia or Alabama postsecondary institutions.
Eligibility: Applicant must be residing in Alabama or Georgia.

Basis for selection: Competition/talent/interest in amateur radio. Applicant must demonstrate financial need.
Application requirements: Recommendations, transcript.
Additional information: Must have at least 2.5 GPA. Must be amateur radio operator holding any class license. Application may be obtained from Website.

Amount of award:	$1,000
Number of awards:	1
Application deadline:	February 1
Total amount awarded:	$1,000

Contact:
ARRL Foundation Inc./Scholarship Program
225 Main Street
Newington, CT 06111
Phone: 860-594-0200
Fax: 860-594-0259
Web: www.arrl.org/aarlf/scholgen.html

Charles N. Fisher Memorial Scholarship

Type of award: Scholarship.
Intended use: For undergraduate or graduate study at accredited postsecondary institution in United States.
Eligibility: Applicant must be residing in California or Arizona.
Basis for selection: Competition/talent/interest in amateur radio. Major/career interest in communications; electronics or engineering, electrical/electronic. Applicant must demonstrate financial need.
Application requirements: Recommendations, transcript.
Additional information: Must be amateur radio operator holding any class license. California candidates must reside in Los Angeles, Orange, San Diego and Santa Barbara areas. Application may be obtained on Website.

Amount of award:	$1,000
Number of awards:	1
Application deadline:	February 1
Total amount awarded:	$1,000

Contact:
ARRL Foundation Inc./Scholarship Program
225 Main Street
Newington, CT 06111
Phone: 860-594-0200
Fax: 860-594-0259
Web: www.arrl.org/arrlf/scholgen.html

Chicago FM Club Scholarships

Type of award: Scholarship.
Intended use: For undergraduate study at accredited vocational, 2-year or 4-year institution in United States.
Eligibility: Applicant must be U.S. citizen residing in Wisconsin, Indiana or Illinois.
Basis for selection: Competition/talent/interest in amateur radio. Applicant must demonstrate financial need.
Application requirements: Recommendations, transcript.
Additional information: Student must be U.S. citizen or within three months of becoming U.S. citizen. Must be amateur radio operator with technician license. Number of awards varies. Application may be obtained on Website.

Amount of award:	$500
Application deadline:	February 1

Contact:
ARRL Foundation Inc./Scholarship Program
225 Main Street
Newington, CT 06111
Phone: 860-594-0200
Fax: 860-594-0259
Web: www.arrl.org/arrlf/scholgen.html

Dr. James L. Lawson Memorial Scholarship

Type of award: Scholarship.
Intended use: For undergraduate or graduate study at accredited postsecondary institution. Designated institutions: New England and New York postsecondary institutions.
Eligibility: Applicant must be residing in Vermont, New York, New Hampshire, Connecticut, Maine, Massachusetts or Rhode Island.
Basis for selection: Competition/talent/interest in amateur radio. Major/career interest in communications or electronics. Applicant must demonstrate financial need.
Application requirements: Recommendations, transcript.
Additional information: Must be amateur radio operator holding general license. Application may be obtained on Website.

Amount of award:	$500
Number of awards:	1
Application deadline:	February 1
Total amount awarded:	$500

Contact:
ARRL Foundation Inc./Scholarship Program
225 Main Street
Newington, CT 06111
Phone: 860-594-0200
Fax: 860-594-0259
Web: www.arrl.org/arrlf/scholgen.html

Edmond A. Metzger Scholarship

Type of award: Scholarship.
Intended use: For undergraduate, graduate or non-degree study at accredited postsecondary institution. Designated institutions: Illinois, Indiana, Wisconsin postsecondary institutions.
Eligibility: Applicant or parent must be member/participant of American Radio Relay League. Applicant must be residing in Wisconsin, Indiana or Illinois.
Basis for selection: Competition/talent/interest in amateur radio. Major/career interest in engineering, electrical/electronic. Applicant must demonstrate financial need.
Application requirements: Recommendations, transcript, proof of eligibility.
Additional information: Must be amateur radio operator with novice license. Application may be obtained on Website.

Amount of award:	$500
Number of awards:	1
Application deadline:	February 1
Total amount awarded:	$500

Contact:
ARRL Foundation Inc./Scholarship Program
225 Main Street
Newington, CT 06111
Phone: 860-594-0200
Fax: 860-594-0259
Web: www.arrl.org/arrlf/scholgen.html

The General Fund Scholarships

Type of award: Scholarship.
Intended use: For undergraduate or graduate study at accredited postsecondary institution in United States.
Eligibility: Applicant or parent must be member/participant of American Radio Relay League.
Basis for selection: Competition/talent/interest in amateur radio. Major/career interest in radio/television/film or communications. Applicant must demonstrate financial need.
Application requirements: Recommendations, transcript.
Additional information: Must be amateur radio operator holding any class license. Number of awards varies. Application may be obtained on Website.

   Amount of award: $1,000
   Application deadline: February 1
Contact:
ARRL Foundation Inc./Scholarship Program
225 Main Street
Newington, CT 06111
Phone: 860-594-0200
Fax: 860-594-0259
Web: www.arrl.org/arrlf/scholgen.html

Irving W. Cook WAOCGS Scholarship

Type of award: Scholarship.
Intended use: For undergraduate or graduate study at accredited postsecondary institution in United States.
Eligibility: Applicant must be residing in Kansas.
Basis for selection: Competition/talent/interest in amateur radio. Major/career interest in communications; electronics or engineering, electrical/electronic. Applicant must demonstrate financial need.
Application requirements: Recommendations, transcript.
Additional information: Must be amateur radio operator holding any class license. Application may be obtained on Website.

   Amount of award: $1,000
   Number of awards: 1
   Application deadline: February 1
   Total amount awarded: $1,000
Contact:
ARRL Foundation Inc./Scholarship Program
225 Main Street
Newington, CT 06111
Phone: 860-594-0200
Fax: 860-594-0259
Web: www.arrl.org/arrlf/scholgen.html

K2TEO Martin J. Green, Sr., Memorial Scholarship

Type of award: Scholarship.
Intended use: For undergraduate or graduate study at accredited postsecondary institution in United States.
Basis for selection: Competition/talent/interest in amateur radio. Major/career interest in radio/television/film; communications or engineering, electrical/electronic. Applicant must demonstrate financial need.
Application requirements: Recommendations, transcript.
Additional information: Must be amateur radio operator with general license. Preference given to student ham from family of ham operators. Application may be obtained on Website.

   Amount of award: $1,000
   Number of awards: 1
   Application deadline: February 1
   Total amount awarded: $1,000
Contact:
ARRL Foundation, Inc./Scholarship Program
225 Main Street
Newington, CT 06111
Phone: 860-594-0200
Fax: 860-594-0259
Web: www.arrl.org/arrlf/scholgen.html

L. Phil Wicker Scholarship

Type of award: Scholarship.
Intended use: For undergraduate, graduate or non-degree study at accredited postsecondary institution. Designated institutions: Institutions in North Carolina, South Carolina, Virginia, West Virginia.
Eligibility: Applicant must be residing in Virginia, West Virginia, North Carolina or South Carolina.
Basis for selection: Competition/talent/interest in amateur radio. Major/career interest in communications; electronics or engineering, electrical/electronic. Applicant must demonstrate financial need.
Application requirements: Recommendations, transcript.
Additional information: Must be amateur radio operator holding general license. Preference to bachelor's or higher degree. Application may be obtained on Website.

   Amount of award: $1,000
   Number of awards: 1
   Application deadline: February 1
   Total amount awarded: $1,000
Contact:
ARRL Foundation Inc./Scholarship Program
225 Main Street
Newington, CT 06111
Phone: 860-594-0200
Fax: 860-594-0259
Web: www.arrl.org/arrlf/schlogen.html

Mary Lou Brown Scholarship

Type of award: Scholarship.
Intended use: For undergraduate or graduate study at accredited postsecondary institution in United States.
Eligibility: Applicant must be residing in Oregon, Montana, Alaska, Idaho or Washington.
Basis for selection: Competition/talent/interest in amateur radio. Applicant must demonstrate financial need.
Application requirements: Recommendations, transcript.
Additional information: Minimum 3.0 GPA with demonstrated interest in promoting Amateur Radio Service. Must be amateur radio operator with general license. Application may be obtained on Website.

   Amount of award: $2,500
   Application deadline: February 1
Contact:
ARRL Foundation Inc./Scholarship Program
225 Main Street
Newington, CT 06111
Phone: 860-594-0200
Fax: 860-594-0259
Web: www.arrl.org/arrlf/scholgen.html

The Mississippi Scholarship

Type of award: Scholarship.

Intended use: For undergraduate or graduate study at accredited 4-year or graduate institution. Designated institutions: Postsecondary institutions in Mississippi.
Eligibility: Applicant must be no older than 30. Applicant must be residing in Mississippi.
Basis for selection: Competition/talent/interest in amateur radio. Major/career interest in communications; electronics or engineering, electrical/electronic. Applicant must demonstrate financial need.
Application requirements: Recommendations, transcript, proof of eligibility.
Additional information: Must be amateur radio operator with any class license. Application may be obtained on Website.

Amount of award:	$500
Number of awards:	1
Application deadline:	February 1
Total amount awarded:	$500

Contact:
ARRL Foundation Inc./Scholarship Program
225 Main Street
Newington, CT 06111
Phone: 860-594-0200
Fax: 860-594-0259
Web: www.arrl.org/arrlf/scholgen.html

New England FEMARA Scholarship

Type of award: Scholarship.
Intended use: For undergraduate, graduate or non-degree study at accredited postsecondary institution in United States.
Eligibility: Applicant must be residing in Vermont, Connecticut, New Hampshire, Maine, Massachusetts or Rhode Island.
Basis for selection: Competition/talent/interest in amateur radio. Applicant must demonstrate financial need.
Application requirements: Recommendations, transcript.
Additional information: Must be amateur radio operator holding technician license. Number of awards varies. Application may be obtained on Website.

Amount of award:	$600
Number of awards:	8
Application deadline:	February 1

Contact:
ARRL Foundation Inc./Scholarship Program
225 Main Street
Newington, CT 06111
Phone: 860-594-0200
Fax: 860-594-0259
Web: www.arrl.org/arrlf/scholgen.html

Paul and Helen L. Grauer Scholarship

Type of award: Scholarship.
Intended use: For undergraduate or graduate study at accredited postsecondary institution in United States. Designated institutions: Postsecondary institutions in Iowa, Kansas, Missouri and Nebraska.
Eligibility: Applicant must be residing in Iowa, Nebraska, Kansas or Missouri.
Basis for selection: Competition/talent/interest in amateur radio. Major/career interest in communications or electronics. Applicant must demonstrate financial need.
Application requirements: Recommendations, transcript.
Additional information: Must be amateur radio operator with novice license. Application may be obtained on Website.

Amount of award:	$1,000
Number of awards:	1
Application deadline:	February 1
Total amount awarded:	$1,000

Contact:
ARRL Foundation Inc./Scholarship Program
225 Main Street
Newington, CT 06111
Phone: 860-594-0200
Fax: 860-594-0259
Web: www.arrl.org/arrlf/scholgen.html

The PHD ARA Scholarship

Type of award: Scholarship.
Intended use: For undergraduate, graduate or non-degree study at accredited postsecondary institution in United States.
Eligibility: Applicant must be residing in Iowa, Nebraska, Kansas or Missouri.
Basis for selection: Competition/talent/interest in amateur radio. Major/career interest in journalism; computer/information sciences or engineering, electrical/electronic. Applicant must demonstrate financial need.
Application requirements: Recommendations, transcript.
Additional information: Must be amateur radio operator holding any class license. May be child of deceased radio amateur. Application may be obtained on Website.

Amount of award:	$1,000
Number of awards:	1
Application deadline:	February 1
Total amount awarded:	$1,000

Contact:
ARRL Foundation Inc./Scholarship Program
225 Main Street
Newington, CT 06111
Phone: 860-594-0200
Fax: 860-594-0259
Web: www.arrl.org/arrlf/scholgen.html

Six Meter Club of Chicago Scholarship

Type of award: Scholarship.
Intended use: For undergraduate study at accredited vocational, 2-year or 4-year institution in United States. Designated institutions: Postsecondary institutions in Illinois.
Eligibility: Applicant must be residing in Illinois.
Basis for selection: Competition/talent/interest in amateur radio. Applicant must demonstrate financial need.
Application requirements: Recommendations, transcript.
Additional information: Must be amateur radio operator holding any class license. Award open to remaining ARRL Central Division (Indiana, Wisconsin) if no qualified Illinois student identified. Application may be obtained on Website.

Amount of award:	$500
Number of awards:	1
Application deadline:	February 1
Total amount awarded:	$500

Contact:
ARRL Foundation Inc./Scholarship Program
225 Main Street
Newington, CT 06111
Phone: 860-594-0200
Fax: 860-594-0259
Web: www.arrl.org/arrlf/scholgen.html

Tom and Judith Comstock Scholarship

Type of award: Scholarship.
Intended use: For undergraduate study at accredited 2-year or 4-year institution in United States.
Eligibility: Applicant must be high school senior. Applicant must be residing in Oklahoma or Texas.
Basis for selection: Competition/talent/interest in amateur radio. Applicant must demonstrate financial need.
Application requirements: Recommendations, transcript.
Additional information: AARL member with any class license eligible to apply. Application may be obtained on Website.

Amount of award:	$1,000
Number of awards:	1
Application deadline:	February 1
Total amount awarded:	$1,000

Contact:
ARRL Foundation Inc./Scholarship Program
225 Main Street
Newington, CT 06111
Phone: 860-594-0200
Fax: 860-594-0259
Web: www.arrl.org/arrlf/scholgen.html

"You've Got a Friend in Pennsylvania" Scholarship

Type of award: Scholarship.
Intended use: For undergraduate, graduate or non-degree study at accredited postsecondary institution. Designated institutions: Pennsylvania postsecondary institutions.
Eligibility: Applicant or parent must be member/participant of American Radio Relay League. Applicant must be residing in Pennsylvania.
Basis for selection: Competition/talent/interest in amateur radio. Applicant must demonstrate financial need.
Application requirements: Recommendations, transcript, proof of eligibility.
Additional information: Must be amateur radio operator with general license. Application may be obtained from Website.

Amount of award:	$1,000
Number of awards:	1
Application deadline:	February 1
Total amount awarded:	$1,000

Contact:
ARRL Foundation Inc./Scholarship Program
225 Main Street
Newington, CT 06111
Phone: 860-594-0200
Fax: 860-594-0259
Web: www.arrl.org/arrlf/scholgen.html

The Art Institutes

Best Teen Chef Culinary Scholarship Competition

Type of award: Scholarship.
Intended use: For undergraduate study at 2-year or 2-year institution in United States. Designated institutions: Art Institute schools that offer culinary arts programs.

Eligibility: Applicant must be enrolled in high school.
Basis for selection: Competition/talent/interest in culinary arts, based on ability and originality in meal preparation. Major/career interest in culinary arts or hotel/restaurant management.
Application requirements: Essay, transcript. Resume. Plan for two-course menu, including original recipes.
Additional information: In addition to three full-tuition scholarships the total of which exceeds $30, 000, financial awards are given. Regional semifinalists notified by April 1, with first-place winner competing in the national event slated for May. For more information and deadline details, visit Website or contact nearest Art Institute.

Amount of award:	Full tuition
Number of awards:	3
Application deadline:	February 5

Contact:
The Art Institutes
210 Sixth Ave, 33rd Floor
Pittsburgh, PA 15222
Phone: 888-328-7900
Fax: 412-562-1732
Web: www.artinstitutes.edu/nc

Arthur and Doreen Parrett Scholarship Trust Fund

Arthur and Doreen Parrett Scholarship

Type of award: Scholarship, renewable.
Intended use: For full-time sophomore, junior, senior, master's, doctoral or first professional study.
Eligibility: Applicant must be residing in Washington.
Basis for selection: Major/career interest in science, general; engineering; dentistry or medicine. Applicant must demonstrate financial need and high academic achievement.
Application requirements: Recommendations, transcript.
Additional information: Applicants must have completed first year of college. Include SASE with inquiries and information will be forwarded.

Amount of award:	$500-$1,400
Number of awards:	8
Number of applicants:	200
Application deadline:	July 31
Notification begins:	September 1
Total amount awarded:	$14,500

Contact:
Arthur and Doreen Parrett Scholarship Trust Fund
1420 5th Avenue, Suite 2100
Seattle, WA 98111-7206

ASCAP Foundation

ASCAP Morton Gould Young Composers Award

Type of award: Scholarship, renewable.
Intended use: For non-degree study.

Eligibility: Applicant must be at least 30. Applicant must be U.S. citizen, permanent resident, international student or Foreign student must have student visa.

Basis for selection: Competition/talent/interest in music performance/composition. Major/career interest in music.

Application requirements: Must submit score or manuscript of one original concert music work, biographical information, list of compositions to date, and, if available, tape of submitted composition along with application.

Additional information: Amount and number of awards vary.

   Application deadline: March 1

Contact:
ASCAP Foundation Morton Gould Young Composers Awards
c/o Fran Richard, Concert Music
One Lincoln Plaza
New York, NY 10023
Phone: 212-621-6219
Web: www.ASCAPFoundation.org

Rudolf Nissim Composers Competition

Type of award: Scholarship.
Intended use: For non-degree study.
Eligibility: Applicant or parent must be member/participant of American Society of Composers/Authors/Publishers.
Basis for selection: Competition/talent/interest in music performance/composition. Major/career interest in music.
Application requirements: Proof of eligibility. Application form. Must submit original music composition, which has not been professionally performed, for a large ensemble that requires a conductor.
Additional information: Applicant must be an ASCAP member. Number and amount of award varies.

Amount of award:	$5,000
Number of awards:	1
Number of applicants:	260
Application deadline:	November 15
Notification begins:	January 15
Total amount awarded:	$5,000

Contact:
Fran Richard, Concert Music
The ASCAP Foundation
One Lincoln Plaza
New York, NY 10023

Asian American Journalists Association

Asian-American Journalists Association Scholarship

Type of award: Scholarship.
Intended use: For undergraduate or graduate study at 2-year or 4-year institution in United States.
Eligibility: Applicant must be high school senior.
Basis for selection: Based on commitment to the field of journalism, sensitivity to Asian-American issues as demonstrated by community involvement, journalistic ability, scholastic ability and financial need. Major/career interest in journalism or film/video. Applicant must demonstrate financial need, high academic achievement, depth of character, seriousness of purpose and service orientation.

Application requirements: Portfolio, recommendations, essay, transcript. Resume. Applicant must show a strong commitment to the Asian-American community.
Additional information: Asian heritage not required. Visit Website for application and more information.

Amount of award:	$1,000-$5,000
Number of awards:	15
Application deadline:	April 9

Contact:
Asian American Journalists Association
Scholarship Committee
1182 Market Street, Suite 320
San Francisco, CA 94102
Phone: 415-346-2051
Fax: 415-346-6343
Web: www.aaja.org

Internship Grant for Broadcast Intern

Type of award: Scholarship.
Intended use: For full-time undergraduate study at 4-year institution.
Eligibility: Applicant must be at least 18.
Basis for selection: Major/career interest in journalism.
Application requirements: Recommendations, essay, proof of eligibility. Three copies of essay, resume, proof of age, statement of financial need and internship verification.
Additional information: Applicant must have already secured summer internship at a broadcasting company before applying for internship.

Amount of award:	$1,500
Number of awards:	1
Application deadline:	April 23

Contact:
Asian American Journalists Association
1182 Market Street
Suite 320
San Francisco, CA 94102
Phone: 415-346-2051
Web: www.aaja.org

Internship Grants for Print/New Media

Type of award: Scholarship.
Intended use: For at postsecondary institution.
Eligibility: Applicant must be at least 18.
Basis for selection: Major/career interest in journalism. Applicant must demonstrate financial need.
Application requirements: Recommendations, essay, proof of eligibility. Three copies of essay, resume, proof of age, statement of financial need and internship verification.
Additional information: Applicants must have already secured a summer internship at a print or online company before applying for internship grant. Number of awards varies yearly.

Amount of award:	$1,500
Number of awards:	5
Application deadline:	April 23

Contact:
Asian American Journalists Association
1182 Market Street
San Francisco, CA 94102
Phone: 415-346-2051
Fax: 416-346-6343
Web: www.aaja.org

A.S.J. Media, LLC./ BlackNews.com Scholarship Fund

BlackNews.com Scholarship

Type of award: Scholarship.
Intended use: For undergraduate or graduate study at 2-year or 4-year institution in United States.
Eligibility: Applicant must be African American. Applicant must be U.S. citizen.
Basis for selection: Competition/talent/interest in Writing/journalism, essay based on why applicant thinks black news mediums are important to the black community. Applicant must demonstrate depth of character, leadership and seriousness of purpose.
Application requirements: Applicant must submit a 2-page essay and register with BlackNews.com's Website.
Additional information: For additional information, visit the Website.

Amount of award:	$1,000
Application deadline:	July 15

Contact:
A.S.J. Media, LLC./BlackNews.com Scholarship Fund
7740 W. Manchester Ave., Suite 210
Playa Del Rey, CA 90293
Web: www.BlackNews.com

ASM International Foundation

ASM International Foundation Scholarship Awards

Type of award: Scholarship, renewable.
Intended use: For full-time sophomore, junior or senior study at accredited 4-year institution in or outside United States.
Eligibility: Applicant or parent must be member/participant of ASM International.
Basis for selection: Major/career interest in materials science or engineering. Applicant must demonstrate high academic achievement, depth of character, leadership, seriousness of purpose and service orientation.
Application requirements: Recommendations, essay, transcript. Personal statement (maximum two pages). Two letters of recommendation. Photograph for publication.
Additional information: These scholarships are open to international student members. Also open to those in related science or engineering disciplines. Visit Website for application and full details.

Amount of award:	$1,000
Number of awards:	12
Application deadline:	May 1
Notification begins:	July 15
Total amount awarded:	$12,000

Contact:
ASM International Foundation
Scholarship Program
9639 Kinsman Road
Materials Park, OH 44073-0002
Phone: 440-338-5151
Fax: 440-338-4634
Web: www.asminternational.org

ASM Outstanding Scholars Awards

Type of award: Scholarship, renewable.
Intended use: For full-time sophomore study at accredited 4-year institution in or outside United States.
Eligibility: Applicant or parent must be member/participant of ASM International.
Basis for selection: Major/career interest in engineering or materials science. Applicant must demonstrate high academic achievement, depth of character and seriousness of purpose.
Application requirements: Recommendations, essay, transcript. Personal statement (two page maximum). Two letters of recommendation. Photograph for publication.
Additional information: Also open to those in related science or engineering disciplines. These scholarships are open to international student members. Visit Website for application and full details.

Amount of award:	$2,000
Number of awards:	3
Application deadline:	May 1
Notification begins:	July 15
Total amount awarded:	$6,000

Contact:
ASM International Foundation
Scholarship Programs
9639 Kinsman Road
Materials Park, OH 44073-0002
Phone: 440-338-5151
Fax: 440-338-4634
Web: www.asminternational.org

ASM Technical and Community College Scholarship

Type of award: Scholarship, renewable.
Intended use: For full-time sophomore study at accredited vocational, 2-year or 4-year institution in or outside United States.
Eligibility: Applicant or parent must be member/participant of ASM International.
Basis for selection: Major/career interest in engineering or engineering, electrical/electronic. Applicant must demonstrate high academic achievement, depth of character and seriousness of purpose.
Application requirements: Recommendations, essay, transcript. Personal statement (two page maximum). Two letters of recommendation. Photograph for publication.
Additional information: This award is open to student members attending technical or community colleges and training to be technicians in various engineering fields. These scholarship awards are also open to international student members. Visit Website for application and full details.

Amount of award:	$500
Number of awards:	10
Application deadline:	May 1
Notification begins:	July 15
Total amount awarded:	$5,000

Contact:
ASM International Foundation
9639 Kinsman Road
Materials Park, OH 44073-0002
Phone: 440-338-5151
Fax: 440-338-4634
Web: www.asminternational.org

George A. Roberts Scholarships

Type of award: Scholarship, renewable.
Intended use: For full-time sophomore, junior or senior study at accredited 4-year institution in United States.
Eligibility: Applicant or parent must be member/participant of ASM International.
Basis for selection: Major/career interest in engineering or materials science. Applicant must demonstrate financial need, high academic achievement, depth of character and seriousness of purpose.
Application requirements: Recommendations, essay, transcript. Personal statement (two page maximum). Two letters of recommendation. Photograph for publication.
Additional information: Also open to those in related science or engineering disciplines. Visit Website for application and full details.

Amount of award:	$6,000
Number of awards:	7
Application deadline:	May 1
Notification begins:	July 15
Total amount awarded:	$42,000

Contact:
ASM International Foundation
Scholarship Programs
9639 Kinsman Road
Materials Park, OH 44073-0002
Phone: 440-388-5151
Fax: 440-388-4634
Web: asminternational.org

Nicholas J. Grant Scholarship

Type of award: Scholarship, renewable.
Intended use: For full-time sophomore, junior or senior study at accredited 4-year institution in United States.
Eligibility: Applicant or parent must be member/participant of ASM International.
Basis for selection: Major/career interest in engineering or materials science. Applicant must demonstrate financial need, high academic achievement, depth of character and seriousness of purpose.
Application requirements: Recommendations, essay, transcript. Personal statement (two page maximum). Two letters of recommendation. Photograph for publication.
Additional information: Scholarship award is one year full tuition. Also open to those in related science or engineering disciplines. Visit Website for application and full details.

Number of awards:	1
Application deadline:	May 1
Notification begins:	July 15

Contact:
ASM International Foundation
Scholarship Programs
9639 Kinsman Road
Materials Park, OH 44073-0002
Phone: 440-338-5151
Fax: 440-338-4634
Web: www.asminternational.org

William Park Woodside Founder's Scholarship

Type of award: Scholarship, renewable.
Intended use: For full-time sophomore, junior or senior study at accredited 4-year institution in United States.
Eligibility: Applicant or parent must be member/participant of ASM International.
Basis for selection: Major/career interest in engineering or materials science. Applicant must demonstrate financial need, high academic achievement, depth of character and seriousness of purpose.
Application requirements: Recommendations, essay, transcript. Personal statement (two page maximum). Two letters of recommendation. Also send photograph for publication.
Additional information: This scholarship provides recipient with one year full tuition up to $10,000. Also open to those in related science or engineering disciplines. Visit Website for application and full details.

Amount of award:	$10,000
Number of awards:	1
Application deadline:	May 1
Notification begins:	July 15
Total amount awarded:	$10,000

Contact:
ASM International Foundation
Scholarship Programs
9639 Kinsman Road
Materials Park, OH 44073-002
Phone: 440-338-5151
Fax: 440-338-4634
Web: www.asminternational.org

Associated Builders and Contractors, CEF

Trimmer Education Foundation Scholarship

Type of award: Scholarship, renewable.
Intended use: For sophomore, junior or senior study at 2-year or 4-year institution.
Eligibility: Applicant or parent must be member/participant of Associated Builders and Contractors. Architecture and most engineering programs excluded. Minimum GPA 2.85 overall with 3.0 in major, or GPA of 3.0 overall if no courses in major have been completed.
Basis for selection: Major/career interest in construction management or construction. Applicant must demonstrate financial need and high academic achievement.
Application requirements: Recommendations, transcript. Academic evaluation, completed by student's academic advisor. Copy of Student Aid Report (first page of FAFSA). Application may not be faxed.
Additional information: Minimum 3.0 GPA required. Must be active member of Associated Builders and Contractors (ABC) Student Chapter or work for an ABC member. Must have completed at least one year of associate or baccalaureate degree program and have one full year remaining. Construction-related employment history considered.

Amount of award:	$1,000-$2,500
Application deadline:	May 30

Contact:
Scholarship Coordinator
Associated Builders and Contractors, CEF
4250 North Fairfax Drive, 9th Floor
Arlington, VA 22203
Phone: 703-812-2008
Fax: 703-812-8234
Web: www.abc.org/studentchapters

Associated General Contractors Education and Research Foundation

AGC Education and Research Undergraduate Scholarship

Type of award: Scholarship, renewable.
Intended use: For full-time freshman, sophomore or junior study at accredited 4-year institution. Designated institutions: Must be enrolled in an ABET or ACCE accredited program to be eligible.
Eligibility: Applicant must be U.S. citizen or permanent resident.
Basis for selection: Major/career interest in engineering, civil; engineering, construction or construction.
Application requirements: Recommendations, transcript. Application form.
Additional information: Must be enrolled in or planning to enroll in a full-time, four- or five-year university program of construction or civil engineering. Applications are available September 1 from AGC office or Website. Seniors with one full academic year of course work remaining are eligible.

Amount of award:	$2,000-$8,000
Application deadline:	November 1

Contact:
Association of General Contractors Education and Research Foundation
Attn: Floretta Slade, Director of Programs
333 John Carlyle Street, Suite 200
Alexandria, VA 22314
Phone: 703-837-5342
Fax: 703-837-5402
Web: www.agcfoundation.org

Associated General Contractors James L. Allhands Essay Competition

Type of award: Scholarship.
Intended use: For full-time senior study at accredited 4-year institution. Designated institutions: ABET- or ACCE-accredited universities.
Basis for selection: Competition/talent/interest in writing/journalism, based on essay concerning construction/contracting, which must have a management orientation and demonstrate clarity of thought, completeness, specific examples supporting opinions, grammar, neatness, adherence to contest rules. Major/career interest in engineering, civil; engineering, construction or construction.
Application requirements: Essay.
Additional information: First prize is $1,000 and all expenses-paid trip to AGC convention; First prize sponsor/ advisor receives $500 plus all expenses-paid trip to convention. Second prize is $500. Third prize is $300. Competition is management oriented, not technical.

Amount of award:	$300-$1,000
Number of awards:	3
Number of applicants:	50
Application deadline:	November 1

Contact:
Association of General Contractors Education and Research Foundation
Attn: Floretta Slade, Director of Programs
333 John Carlyle Street, Suite 200
Alexandria, VA 22314
Phone: 703-837-5342
Fax: 703-837-5402
Web: www.agcfoundation.org

Associated Press

Associated Press/APTRA-CLETE Roberts Memorial Journalism Scholarship

Type of award: Scholarship.
Intended use: For undergraduate or graduate study at 4-year or graduate institution in United States. Designated institutions: Students must be enrolled in California or Nevada college or university.
Eligibility: Applicant must be residing in California or Nevada.
Basis for selection: Major/career interest in journalism or radio/television/film.
Application requirements: Recommendations, essay. May submit examples of broadcast-related work.
Additional information: For study in broadcast journalism. Applications due mid-December. Application forms are available online. Visit Website for more information and application.

Amount of award:	$1,500
Number of awards:	4
Notification begins:	September 10
Total amount awarded:	$6,000

Contact:
APTRA
100 Milmar Way
Los Gatos, CA 95032
Web: www.aptra.org

Association for Library and Information Science Foundation

ALISE Bodhan S. Wynar Research Paper Competition

Type of award: Scholarship.
Intended use: For non-degree study.
Eligibility: Applicant or parent must be member/participant of Association for Library/Information Science Education.

Basis for selection: Competition/talent/interest in research paper, based on any aspect of librarianship or information studies. Major/career interest in library science.
Application requirements: Proof of eligibility. Paper must not exceed 75 double-spaced pages. Send seven copies of research paper.
Additional information: Up to two awards given. Visit Website for detailed explanation of requirements. Research papers prepared by joint investigators eligible; at least one author must be member of ALISE by deadline date. Winners expected to present papers at ALISE annual meeting.

Amount of award:	$2,500
Number of awards:	2
Application deadline:	September 13
Total amount awarded:	$5,000

Contact:
ALISE National Office
Attn: ALISE Awards
1009 Commerce Park Drive, Suite 150
Oak Ridge, TN 37839
Phone: 865-425-0155
Fax: 865-481-0390
Web: www.alise.org

ALISE Methodology Paper Competition

Type of award: Scholarship.
Intended use: For non-degree study.
Eligibility: Applicant or parent must be member/participant of Association for Library/Information Science Education.
Basis for selection: Competition/talent/interest in research paper, based on description of methodology or technique, relevance of methodology or technique to library and information science, practical applications of technique toward library and information science research, and clarity and organization of presentation. Major/career interest in library science.
Application requirements: Paper must not exceed 25 double-spaced pages. Send seven copies of paper, with 200-word abstract.
Additional information: Papers completed in pursuit of master's or doctoral degrees are eligible, as are papers generated as result of research grant or other source of funding. Papers prepared by joint authors eligible; at least one author must be member of ALISE. Winners expected to present papers at ALISE annual meeting.

Amount of award:	$500
Number of awards:	1
Application deadline:	September 13
Total amount awarded:	$500

Contact:
ALISE National Office
Attn: ALISE Awards
1009 Commerce Park Drive, Suite 150
Oak Ridge, TN 37839
Phone: 865-425-0155
Fax: 865-481-0390
Web: www.alise.org

ALISE Research Grant Award

Type of award: Research grant.
Intended use: For non-degree study.
Eligibility: Applicant or parent must be member/participant of Association for Library/Information Science Education.

Basis for selection: Major/career interest in library science. Applicant must demonstrate high academic achievement.
Application requirements: Proof of eligibility, research proposal. Proposal must not exceed 20 double-spaced pages. Send seven copies of proposal.
Additional information: Visit Website for detailed explanation of requirements. Must be member of ALISE as of deadline date. More than one grant may be awarded; however, total amount of funding for all grants not to exceed $5,000. Research grant award cannot be used to support doctoral dissertation.

Amount of award:	$5,000
Number of awards:	1
Application deadline:	October 15
Total amount awarded:	$5,000

Contact:
ALISE National Office
Attn: ALISE Awards
1009 Commerce Park Drive, Suite 150
Oak Ridge, TN 37839
Phone: 865-425-0155
Fax: 865-481-0390
Web: www.alise.org

Association for Women in Architecture Foundation

Women in Architecture Scholarship

Type of award: Scholarship, renewable.
Intended use: For full-time junior, senior, master's, doctoral or first professional study at 4-year or graduate institution.
Eligibility: Applicant must be female. Applicant must be residing in California.
Basis for selection: Major/career interest in architecture; interior design; engineering; landscape architecture or urban planning. Applicant must demonstrate financial need, high academic achievement and seriousness of purpose.
Application requirements: Interview, portfolio, recommendations, essay, transcript.
Additional information: Must be California resident or attend California school to qualify. Student must have completed at least one year in architecture or related program leading to degree. Applications may be downloaded from Website.

Amount of award:	$1,000-$2,500
Number of awards:	3
Number of applicants:	60
Application deadline:	April 25
Notification begins:	February 1
Total amount awarded:	$5,000

Contact:
Association for Women in Architecture Foundation
386 Beech Ave.
Unit B4
Torrence, CA 90501-6202
Phone: 310-533-4042
Web: www.awa-la.org

Association for Women in Communications

Association for Women in Communications Scholarship

Type of award: Scholarship.
Intended use: For full-time junior, senior or graduate study at accredited 4-year or graduate institution. Designated institutions: Must attend schools in Washington state.
Eligibility: Applicant must be residing in Washington.
Basis for selection: Major/career interest in communications; journalism; radio/television/film; film/video or graphic arts/design. Applicant must demonstrate financial need, high academic achievement, depth of character and service orientation.
Application requirements: Recommendations, essay, transcript. Writing sample.
Additional information: Must attend or plan to attend an accredited four-year college.

Amount of award:	$1,000-$1,500
Number of awards:	2
Application deadline:	February 15

Contact:
Association for Women in Communications
1412 SW 102 Street
#224
Seattle, WA 98146
Phone: 206-654-2929
Web: www.womcom.org

Association of American Geographers

Anne U. White Fund

Type of award: Research grant, renewable.
Intended use: For undergraduate, graduate or non-degree study at postsecondary institution.
Eligibility: Applicant or parent must be member/participant of Association of American Geographers. Applicant must be U.S. citizen.
Basis for selection: Major/career interest in geography.
Application requirements: Research proposal. Both spouses must complete background information forms. Applicant must send six (6) copies of completed application.
Additional information: Fund enables member of AAG to engage in useful field studies jointly with his/her spouse. Must have been member for at least two years at time of application. Report summarizing results and documenting expenses underwritten by grant must be submitted within 12 months after receiving award.

Amount of award:	$1,000-$1,500
Number of awards:	6
Number of applicants:	9
Application deadline:	December 31
Notification begins:	March 1
Total amount awarded:	$7,300

Contact:
Association of American Geographers
1710 16 Street, NW
Washington, DC 20009-3198
Phone: 202-234-1450
Web: www.aag.org

Association of Certified Fraud Examiners

Ritchie-Jennings Memorial Scholarship

Type of award: Scholarship.
Intended use: For full-time undergraduate or graduate study.
Basis for selection: Major/career interest in criminal justice/law enforcement or accounting.
Application requirements: Recommendations, essay, transcript. Applicant must provide three letters of recommendation, including at least one from a Certified Fraud Examiner or a local CFE chapter, plus additional recommendations from employer, faculty members or academic advisors. Essay must be no more than 500 words and must explain why the applicant deserves the scholarship and how the awareness of fraud will affect his or her professional career development.

Amount of award:	$1,000
Number of awards:	15
Number of applicants:	200
Application deadline:	April 30
Total amount awarded:	$15,000

Contact:
Association of Certified Fraud Examiners
The Gregor Building
716 West Avenue
Austin, TX 78701
Phone: 800-245-3321 or 512-478-9070
Fax: 512-478-9297
Web: www.cfenet.com/services/scholarships.asp

Association of Energy Service Companies

Energy Service Scholarship

Type of award: Scholarship, renewable.
Intended use: For full-time undergraduate or non-degree study at accredited vocational, 2-year or 4-year institution.
Eligibility: Applicant or parent must be employed by Association of Energy Service Companies.
Basis for selection: Applicant must demonstrate financial need, high academic achievement, depth of character, leadership and service orientation.
Application requirements: Essay, transcript. ACT or SAT scores.
Additional information: Student or parent must be employed by a member company of the Association of Energy Service Companies.

Amount of award:	$1,000
Number of awards:	40
Number of applicants:	150
Application deadline:	March 15
Notification begins:	May 15
Total amount awarded:	$40,000

Contact:
Association of Energy Service Companies
Jim Yancy
10200 Richmond Avenue
Houston, TX 77642
Phone: 800-692-0771
Fax: 713-781-7542
Web: www.aesc.net

Association of State Dam Safety Officials

Dam Safety Officials Scholarship

Type of award: Scholarship.
Intended use: For senior study in United States.
Eligibility: Applicant must be U.S. citizen.
Basis for selection: Major/career interest in engineering, civil. Applicant must demonstrate financial need, high academic achievement, depth of character, leadership, seriousness of purpose and service orientation.
Application requirements: Recommendations, essay, transcript.
Additional information: Decisions based on grades, career goals, and extracurricular activities.

Amount of award:	$2,500
Number of awards:	2
Number of applicants:	50
Application deadline:	February 15
Notification begins:	May 11
Total amount awarded:	$5,000

Contact:
Association of State Dam Safety Officials
450 Old Vine Street, 2nd Floor
Lexington, KY 40507
Phone: 859-257-5140
Fax: 859-323-1958
Web: www.damsafety.org

Astraea National Lesbian Action Foundation

Margot Karle Scholarship

Type of award: Scholarship.
Intended use: For full-time undergraduate study at 4-year institution in United States. Designated institutions: City University of New York (CUNY) schools.
Eligibility: Applicant must be female. Applicant must be U.S. citizen.
Basis for selection: Applicant must demonstrate depth of character, leadership and seriousness of purpose.
Application requirements: Recommendations, essay, transcript.

Additional information: Visit Website for more information.

Number of awards:	2
Application deadline:	June 1

Contact:
Astraea National Lesbian Action Foundation
116 East 16th Street, 7th floor
New York, NY 10003
Phone: 212-529-8021
Fax: 212-982-3321
Web: www.astraea.org

Atlanta Association of Black Journalists

Xernona Clayton Scholarship

Type of award: Scholarship.
Intended use: For undergraduate study at accredited 4-year institution. Designated institutions: Georgia colleges and universities.
Eligibility: Applicant must be African American. Applicant must be U.S. citizen residing in Georgia.
Basis for selection: Major/career interest in communications; journalism; English; public relations or radio/television/film. Applicant must demonstrate depth of character and leadership.
Application requirements: Essay, transcript. Application form and samples of published work. Minimum 3.0 GPA required.
Additional information: Scholarships of $5,000, $3,000 and $2,000 awarded. Visit Website for details and application.

Amount of award:	$2,000-$5,000
Number of awards:	3
Total amount awarded:	$10,000

Contact:
Atlanta Association of Black Journalists
P.O. Box 54128
Atlanta, GA 30308
Phone: 404-508-4612
Web: www.aabj.org

Automotive Hall of Fame

Automotive Educational Fund Scholarship

Type of award: Scholarship, renewable.
Intended use: For full-time undergraduate study at accredited 2-year, 4-year or graduate institution in United States.
Basis for selection: Major/career interest in automotive technology; engineering, mechanical; engineering, chemical or engineering, electrical/electronic.
Application requirements: Recommendations, transcript, proof of eligibility. High school seniors must have proof of acceptance to postsecondary institution.
Additional information: Applicant must have interest in pursuing automotive career. SASE must be received in order to get scholarship application. All required materials must be submitted with application to be considered. Only award recipients will be notified.

Amount of award:	$250-$2,000
Number of awards:	13
Application deadline:	May 30

Contact:
Automotive Hall of Fame
21400 Oakwood Blvd.
Dearborn, MI 48124-4078
Phone: 313-240-4000
Fax: 313-240-8641
Web: www.automotivehalloffame.org

AXA Achievement Scholarship

AXA Achievement Scholarship in Association with U.S. News & World Report

Type of award: Scholarship.
Intended use: For full-time undergraduate study at accredited 2-year or 4-year institution in United States.
Eligibility: Applicant must be high school senior. Applicant must be U.S. citizen.
Basis for selection: Based on a non-academic outstanding achievement. Major/career interest in humanities/liberal arts. Applicant must demonstrate depth of character, leadership and service orientation.
Application requirements: Recommendations. Must demonstrate achievement in a non-academic activity or project. Consideration will also be given to other extra curricular activities in school and community, work experience, and the applicants academic record over the past four years.
Additional information: Fifty-two students, to be known as AXA Achievers, will be selected to receive $10, 000. scholarships, one from each state, the Distric of Columbia and Puerto Rico. From among the state recipients, ten students will be named national AXA Achievers. They will be selected to receive national awards at $15,000 each for a total of $25,000 per national recipient. Visit Website for more information or to download an application. Questions about the application process may be directed to Scholarship America's toll free number or by email to axaachievement@scholarshipamerica.org.

Amount of award:	$10,000-$25,000
Number of awards:	10
Application deadline:	December 15
Notification begins:	March 15

Contact:
AXA Achievement Scholarship
Scholarship Management Services, Scholarship
One Scholarship Way, P.O. Box 297
Saint Peter, MN 56082
Phone: 800-537-4180
Web: www.axa-achievement.com

Ayn Rand Institute

Atlas Shrugged Essay Contest

Type of award: Scholarship.
Intended use: For undergraduate or graduate study at 2-year or 4-year institution.
Basis for selection: Competition/talent/interest in Writing/journalism, Essay on the Ayn Rand novel Atlas Shrugged.
Application requirements: Essay no fewer than 1000 and not more than 1200 words. Typewritten and double-spaced.
Additional information: Applicant must be enrolled in full-time college degree program at time of entry. Stapled cover sheet must include name and address of entrant, entrant's email address (if available), name and address of entrant's university, topic selected and declared major. Applicant chooses from three topic questions on Atlas Shrugged.

Amount of award:	$400-$5,000
Application deadline:	September 16
Notification begins:	October 21
Total amount awarded:	$10,000

Contact:
The Ayn Rand Institute
Atlas Shurgged Essay Contest, Dept.
2121 Alton Parway, Suite 250
Irvine, CA 92606
Phone: 949-222-6550
Fax: 949-222-6558
Web: www.aynrand.org

Barry M. Goldwater Scholarship and Excellence In Education Foundation

Barry M. Goldwater Scholarship

Type of award: Scholarship, renewable.
Intended use: For full-time sophomore or junior study at accredited 4-year institution in United States. Designated institutions: Those listed in Directory of Postsecondary Institutions published by US Department of Education.
Eligibility: Applicant must be U.S. citizen or permanent resident.
Basis for selection: Major/career interest in engineering; mathematics; natural sciences; science, general; computer/information sciences; medical specialties/research; astronomy or geology/earth sciences. Applicant must demonstrate high academic achievement, depth of character, leadership and seriousness of purpose.
Application requirements: Recommendations, transcript, proof of eligibility, nomination by college faculty representative. Minimum 3.0 GPA required. Essay (600 words or less) relating to student's chosen career. Nominations of resident aliens must include letter of nominee's intent to obtain U.S. citizenship and photocopy of Alien Registration Card.
Additional information: Bulletin of information, nomination materials, application and list of faculty representatives available on Website. Students must be nominated by university's Goldwater Scholarship faculty representative. Applicants must be legal resident of state from which they are candidates. Residents of District of Columbia, Puerto Rico, Guam, American Samoa, Virgin Islands, and Commonwealth of North Mariana Islands also eligible.

Amount of award:	$7,500
Number of awards:	309
Number of applicants:	1,155
Application deadline:	February 1
Notification begins:	April 1

Scholarships

Contact:
Barry M. Goldwater/Excellence In Education Foundation
6225 Brandon Avenue, Suite 315
Springfield, VA 22150-2519
Phone: 703-756-6012
Fax: 703-756-6015
Web: www.act.org/goldwater

Contact:
Best Book Buys
2400 Lincoln Avenue
Altadena, CA 91001
Phone: 626-296-6263
Fax: 626-296-6261
Web: www.bestwebbuys.com/books/scholarship.html

Bemis Company Foundation

Bemis Company Foundation Scholarship

Type of award: Scholarship, renewable.
Intended use: For undergraduate study at accredited vocational, 2-year or 4-year institution.
Eligibility: Applicant or parent must be employed by Bemis Company.
Basis for selection: Applicant must demonstrate financial need, high academic achievement, depth of character, leadership, seriousness of purpose and service orientation.
Application requirements: Transcript, proof of eligibility.
Additional information: Award may be renewed up to three times if applicant is attending four-year school.

Amount of award:	$1,000-$5,000
Number of awards:	60
Number of applicants:	249
Total amount awarded:	$600,000

Contact:
Bemis Company Foundation
222 South Ninth Street
Suite 2300
Minneapolis, MN 55402-4099
Phone: 612-376-3000
Web: www.bemis.com

Best Book Buys

Best Book Buys Scholarship

Type of award: Scholarship.
Intended use: For undergraduate or graduate study at vocational, 2-year, 4-year or graduate institution in United States.
Eligibility: Applicant must be U.S. citizen or permanent resident.
Basis for selection: Major/career interest in journalism; literature; publishing or political science/government.
Application requirements: Essay.
Additional information: Applicant must be currently enrolled in school during contest period and in good academic standing. Must use online application at Best Book Buys Website. Eligibility proof required from winners. Visit Website for more information and for essay topic, which changes each year.

Amount of award:	$300-$1,500
Number of awards:	6
Number of applicants:	11,388
Application deadline:	December 15
Total amount awarded:	$3,000

Best Buy Children's Foundation

Best Buy Scholarships

Type of award: Scholarship.
Intended use: For full-time at vocational, 2-year or 4-year institution in United States.
Eligibility: Applicant must be high school senior.
Basis for selection: Major/career interest in advertising. Applicant must demonstrate high academic achievement, leadership and service orientation.
Additional information: Award amount varies; up to three scholarships granted in each U.S. Congressional District and the District of Columbia. Only online applications will be accepted. See Website for more information.

Amount of award:	$1,000-$2,000
Number of awards:	1,308
Application deadline:	February 15
Total amount awarded:	$2,180,000

Contact:
Web: www.bestbuy.com

Bethesda Lutheran Homes and Services, Inc.

Developmental Disabilities Nursing Scholastic Achievement Scholarship

Type of award: Scholarship.
Intended use: For full-time junior, senior, master's or doctoral study at accredited 2-year, 4-year or graduate institution.
Eligibility: Applicant must be Lutheran.
Basis for selection: Major/career interest in nursing. Applicant must demonstrate high academic achievement, seriousness of purpose and service orientation.
Application requirements: Recommendations, essay, transcript, proof of eligibility.
Additional information: Minimum 3.0 GPA required. Must be working toward registered nurse (R.N.) degree. Preference given to those interested in working with developmentally disabled persons.

Amount of award:	$1,500
Number of awards:	2
Application deadline:	March 15
Notification begins:	May 1
Total amount awarded:	$3,000

Contact:
Bethesda Lutheran Homes and Services, Inc.
Coordinator, Outreach Programs
600 Hoffmann Drive
Watertown, WI 53094
Phone: 800-369-4636 ext. 416
Fax: 920-262-6513
Web: www.blhs.org

Developmental Disability Scholastic Achievement Scholarship

Type of award: Scholarship.
Intended use: For full-time junior, senior or graduate study at accredited 4-year or graduate institution in United States.
Eligibility: Applicant must be Lutheran.
Basis for selection: Major/career interest in social work; education; psychology; mental health/therapy; education, special; education, early childhood; education, teacher; speech pathology/audiology; occupational therapy or health-related professions. Applicant must demonstrate financial need, high academic achievement, seriousness of purpose and service orientation.
Application requirements: Recommendations, essay, transcript, proof of eligibility.
Additional information: Preference given to those interested in working with persons with mental retardation. Minimum 3.0 GPA. Also available for students of Lutheran theology.

Amount of award:	$1,500
Number of awards:	3
Application deadline:	March 15
Notification begins:	May 1
Total amount awarded:	$4,500

Contact:
Bethesda Lutheran Homes and Services, Inc.
Coordinator, Outreach Programs
600 Hoffmann Drive
Watertown, WI 53094
Phone: 800-369-4636 ext. 416
Fax: 920-262-6513
Web: www.blhs.org

Birthright Israel

Birthright Israel Gift

Type of award: Scholarship.
Intended use: For undergraduate study.
Eligibility: Applicant must be at least 18, no older than 26. Applicant must be Jewish.
Application requirements: Proof of eligibility.
Additional information: All eligible applicants receive free trip to Israel under the auspices of Aish HaTorah, Hillel and other organizations. Round-trip airfare and 10 days of program activity funded. Must not have visited Israel previously on an educational peer-group trip. International program seeks to "make Israel accessible to every Jewish youth regardless of his or her affiliation, nationality or economic status." Visit Website or contact sponsor for current offerings.
Contact:
Email: information@birthrightisrael.com
Phone: 888-99-ISRAEL
Web: www.birthrightisrael.com

Blinded Veteran's Association

Katherine F. Gruber Scholarship Program

Type of award: Scholarship, renewable.
Intended use: For full-time freshman, sophomore, junior, senior or graduate study at accredited postsecondary institution in United States.
Eligibility: Parent must be visually impaired. Applicant must be U.S. citizen. Applicant must be dependent of disabled veteran; or spouse of disabled veteran who served in the Army, Air Force, Marines, Navy or Coast Guard.
Application requirements: Recommendations, essay, transcript.
Additional information: Dependent children and spouses of blinded veterans of U.S. Armed Forces are eligible. Veteran must meet definition of blindness used by Blinded Veteran's Association; blindness may be service-connected or non-service-connected.

Amount of award:	$1,000-$2,000
Number of awards:	12
Number of applicants:	25
Application deadline:	April 12
Notification begins:	January 1
Total amount awarded:	$24,000

Contact:
Katherine F. Gruber Scholarship Program
Blinded Veteran's Association
477 H Street NW
Washington, DC 20001-2694
Phone: 202-371-8880
Fax: 202-371-8258

BMI Foundation, Inc.

BMI Student Composer Awards

Type of award: Scholarship.
Intended use: For undergraduate or graduate study at accredited 4-year institution.
Eligibility: Applicant must be no older than 25.
Basis for selection: Competition/talent/interest in Music performance/composition, based on composition of classical concert music. Major/career interest in music. Applicant must demonstrate seriousness of purpose.
Application requirements: Student must be a citizen of a Western Hemisphere country (North, South, or Central America).
Additional information: Applicant must be under age of 26 on December 31 of year prior to deadline. Applicant must be enrolled in accredited public, private, or parochial secondary schools; in accredited colleges or conservatories of music; or engaged in private study of music with recognized and established teachers. Visit Website for applications, which usually become available in November.

Amount of award:	$500-$5,000
Application deadline:	February 6

Contact:
Ralph N. Jackson
BMI Student Composer Awards
320 W. 57th Street
New York, NY 10019
Web: www.bmi.com/bmifoundation

John Lennon Scholarship

Type of award: Scholarship.
Intended use: For undergraduate or graduate study.
Eligibility: Applicant must be at least 15, no older than 24.
Basis for selection: Competition/talent/interest in Music performance/composition, based on best song of any genre with original music and lyrics. Major/career interest in music or performing arts.
Application requirements: Nomination by participating school, college, community music organization or youth orchestra, or Music Educators National Conference (MENC).
Additional information: Each participating organization may submit one entry from a current student or an alumnus/alumna who meets eligibility requirements. Students interested in applying should check with school or group to see if it is a participant or whether it wishes to apply for inclusion.

Amount of award:	$5,000-$10,000
Number of awards:	3
Application deadline:	January 26
Total amount awarded:	$20,000

Contact:
BMI Foundation, Inc.
Attn: David Sanjek, Dir. J. Lennon Schol.
320 W. 57th Street
New York, NY 10019
Web: www.bmi.com/bmifoundation

The Boeing Company

The Boeing Company Undergraduate Scholarships

Type of award: Scholarship.
Intended use: For undergraduate study at 4-year institution in United States. Designated institutions: Boeing's partner colleges and universities.
Additional information: Scholarships are based upon merit and are made by the college with cooperation from Boeing. Available to students who attend one of Boeing's partner colleges and universities. Contact school adviser for more information.

Number of awards:	1

Contact:
Contact school adviser.
Web: www.boeing.com

Historically Black Colleges and Minority Institutions Scholarships

Type of award: Scholarship.
Intended use: For undergraduate study at 4-year institution in United States.
Eligibility: Applicant must be African American.
Additional information: Scholarships awarded to students attending the following schools: Atlanta Consortium (Morehouse, Spelman, and Morris Brown colleges, and Clark Atlanta University), North Carolina A&T State University, Alabama A&M University, Florida A&M University, Howard University, Tuskegee University, University of Texas-El Paso, Prairie View A&M University, Southern University, University of Hawaii. Contact college adviser for application and more information.
Contact:
Contact college adviser.
Web: www.boeing.com

Boy Scouts of America

Boy Scouts of America/Eastern Orthodox Committee on Scouting Scholarship

Type of award: Scholarship.
Intended use: For full-time freshman study at accredited 4-year institution in United States.
Eligibility: Applicant or parent must be member/participant of Boy Scouts of America. Applicant must be male, high school senior. Applicant must be Eastern Orthodox. Applicant must be U.S. citizen.
Basis for selection: Applicant must demonstrate depth of character and service orientation.
Application requirements: Applicant must submit four letters of recommendation with application, one from each of following groups: religious institution, school, community leader, and head of Scouting unit.
Additional information: Offers one $1,000 scholarship and one $500 scholarship upon acceptance to four-year accredited college or university. Eligible applicant must be registered member of Boy Scouts unit; Eagle Scout; active member of Eastern Orthodox Church; have received Alpha Omega Religious Award; have demonstrated practical citizenship in his church, school, Scouting unit, and community.

Amount of award:	$500-$1,000
Number of awards:	2
Application deadline:	April 15
Total amount awarded:	$1,500

Contact:
EOCS Scholarship Committee
862 Guy Lombardo Avenue
Freeport, NY 11520
Phone: 516-868-4050
Fax: 516-868-4052
Web: www.eocs.org

E. Urner Goodman Scholarship

Type of award: Scholarship.
Intended use: For full-time undergraduate or graduate study.
Eligibility: Applicant or parent must be member/participant of Boy Scouts of America. Applicant must be male. Applicant must be U.S. citizen or permanent resident.
Additional information: Open to Arrowmen planning career in professional service of Boy Scouts. Amounts of individual scholarships vary each year. Send SASE with notation on lower left corner, "Order of the Arrow Scholarship Application."

Application deadline:	January 15
Notification begins:	March 1

Contact:
Boy Scouts of America National Order of the Arrow S214
1325 West Walnut Hill Lane
P.O. Box 152079
Irving, TX 75015-2079
Phone: 972-580-2032
Fax: 972-580-2502

National Eagle Scout Scholarship

Type of award: Scholarship.
Intended use: For undergraduate study at accredited 2-year or 4-year institution.
Eligibility: Applicant or parent must be member/participant of Boy Scouts of America, Eagle Scouts. Applicant must be male, high school senior. Applicant must be U.S. citizen or permanent resident.
Basis for selection: Applicant must demonstrate financial need, high academic achievement and leadership.
Application requirements: Recommendations, transcript. Must have SAT of at least 1090 or ACT of 26.
Additional information: Applicant must be Eagle Scout. First contact should be at local council office for form 58-702. Must be endorsed by professional or volunteer scout leader. Applicants considered for five kinds of awards: one non-renewable $3,000 award, four awards of $1,000 per year for four years, four awards of $2,000 per year for four years, one Mabel and Lawrence S. Cooke scholarship of up to $12,000 per year for four years, and four $20,000 scholarships ($5,000 a year for four years) given annually. Award may not be used at military institution.

Amount of award:	$3,000-$48,000
Number of applicants:	2,500
Application deadline:	February 28
Notification begins:	June 1
Total amount awarded:	$212,000

Contact:
Boy Scouts of America
1325 West Walnut Hill Lane
Irving, TX 75015-2079
Phone: 972-580-2032
Web: www.scouting.org

Boys and Girls Clubs of Greater San Diego

Spence Reese Scholarship

Type of award: Scholarship, renewable.
Intended use: For full-time freshman, sophomore, junior or senior study at accredited 4-year institution in United States.
Eligibility: Applicant must be male, high school senior. Applicant must be U.S. citizen or permanent resident.
Basis for selection: Major/career interest in law; political science/government; engineering or medicine. Applicant must demonstrate financial need and high academic achievement.
Application requirements: $10 application fee. Recommendations, essay, transcript. SAT.
Additional information: Award is renewable for four years of study. Send SASE with application request after January 1 of graduating year. Application also availible on Website. Finalists interview in San Diego. Travel expenses will be reimbursed.

Amount of award:	$2,000
Number of awards:	4
Number of applicants:	200
Application deadline:	May 15
Notification begins:	June 1
Total amount awarded:	$32,000

Contact:
Boys and Girls Clubs of Greater San Diego
Support Services
4635 Clairemont Mesa Blvd.
San Diego, CA 92117
Phone: (619) 298-3250
Fax: (619) 298-3615
Web: www.bgcsd.com

British Government

Marshall Scholarships

Type of award: Scholarship.
Intended use: For full-time undergraduate or master's study at graduate institution in United Kingdom.
Eligibility: Applicant must be U.S. citizen.
Basis for selection: Competition/talent/interest in study abroad. Major/career interest in political science/government. Applicant must demonstrate high academic achievement, depth of character, leadership, seriousness of purpose and service orientation.
Application requirements: Interview, recommendations, essay, transcript. Endorsement by President or Dean of educational institution, or employer if no longer in school; description of proposed plan of study.
Additional information: Must pursue British first (bachelor's) or higher degree. Must have bachelor's from accredited U.S. institution by start of award year; may not have graduated more than two years previous. Must have minimum 3.7 GPA in academic courses. Award distributed in two yearly installments. Award period is two academic years, but in exceptional case may be extended a year. Americans already studying for or holding British degree or degree-equivalent qualification not eligible. Applications available after June 1. Applications submitted regionally; visit British Council Website for addresses. Application available on Website.

Amount of award:	$50,000
Number of awards:	40
Number of applicants:	1,000

Contact:
The British Council Marshall Scholarships
3100 Massachusetts Avenue NW
Washington, DC 20008-3600
Phone: 202-588-7854
Web: www.marshallscholarship.org

Broadcast Education Association

Abe Voron Scholarship

Type of award: Scholarship.

Intended use: For full-time junior, senior or graduate study at 4-year or graduate institution. Designated institutions: BEA member institution.

Basis for selection: Major/career interest in radio/television/film. Applicant must demonstrate high academic achievement, depth of character and seriousness of purpose.

Application requirements: Recommendations, essay, transcript. Application, waiver form. Should be able to show evidence of potential.

Additional information: All scholarships must be applied to study at campus where at least one department is BEA institutional member. Obtain application forms from campus faculty or visit Website to download forms and get additional information. Deadline for requesting mailed application is September 1. Awards for tuition and fees. Current scholarship holders are not eligible for reappointment in year following award.

Amount of award:	$5,000
Number of awards:	1
Application deadline:	September 15

Contact:
Broadcast Education Association
1771 N Street, N.W.
Washington, DC 20036-2891
Phone: 888-380-7222
Web: www.beaweb.org/scholarships.html

Alexander M. Tanger Scholarship

Type of award: Scholarship.
Intended use: For full-time junior, senior or graduate study at 4-year or graduate institution in United States. Designated institutions: BEA member institution.
Basis for selection: Major/career interest in radio/television/film; communications or film/video. Applicant must demonstrate high academic achievement, depth of character and seriousness of purpose.
Application requirements: Recommendations, essay, transcript. Completed application, waiver form. Should be able to show evidence of potential in electronic media.
Additional information: All scholarships must be applied to study at campus where at least one department is BEA institutional member. Obtain official application forms from campus faculty or visit Website to download forms and for additional information. Deadline for requesting mailed application is September 1. Awards for tuition and fees. Current scholarship holders are not eligible for reappointment in year following award.

Amount of award:	$5,000
Number of awards:	1
Application deadline:	September 15

Contact:
Broadcast Education Association
1771 N Street, N.W.
Washington, DC 20036-2891
Phone: 888-380-7222
Web: www.beaweb.org/scholarships.html

Andrew M. Economos Scholarship

Type of award: Scholarship.
Intended use: For full-time junior, senior or graduate study at 4-year or graduate institution. Designated institutions: BEA member institution.
Basis for selection: Major/career interest in radio/television/film. Applicant must demonstrate high academic achievement, depth of character and seriousness of purpose.

Application requirements: Recommendations, essay, transcript. Application. Waiver sheet. Should be able to show evidence of potential in radio career.

Additional information: Scholarships must be applied to study at campus where at least one department is BEA institutional member. Obtain application from campus faculty or visit Website. Deadline for requesting mailed application is September 1. Awards for tuition and fees. Current scholarship holders are not eligible for reappointment in year following award.

Amount of award:	$5,000
Number of awards:	1
Application deadline:	September 15
Total amount awarded:	$5,000

Contact:
Broadcast Education Association
1771 N Street, N.W.
Washington, DC 20036-2891
Phone: 888-380-7222
Web: www.beaweb.org/scholarships.html

The Broadcasters' Foundation Helen J. Sioussat

Type of award: Scholarship.
Intended use: For full-time junior, senior or graduate study at 4-year or graduate institution. Designated institutions: BEA member universities.
Basis for selection: Major/career interest in radio/television/film. Applicant must demonstrate high academic achievement, depth of character and seriousness of purpose.
Application requirements: Recommendations, essay, transcript. Application. Waiver sheet. Should be able to show evidence of potential in electronic media.
Additional information: Scholarships must be applied to study at campus where at least one department is BEA institutional member. Obtain application from campus faculty or visit Website to download forms and for additional information. Deadline for requesting mailed application is September 1. Awards for tuition and fees. Current scholarship holders are not eligible for reappointment in year following award.

Amount of award:	$1,250
Number of awards:	2
Application deadline:	September 15
Total amount awarded:	$2,500

Contact:
Broadcast Education Association
1771 N Street, N.W.
Washington, DC 20036-2891
Phone: 888-380-7222
Web: www.beaweb.org/scholarships.html

Country Radio Broadcasters, Inc Scholarships

Type of award: Scholarship.
Intended use: For full-time junior, senior or graduate study at 4-year or graduate institution. Designated institutions: BEA member institutions.
Basis for selection: Major/career interest in radio/television/film.
Application requirements: Recommendations, essay, transcript. Application. Waiver form. Should be able to show evidence of potential in media.
Additional information: Scholarships must be applied to study at campus where at least one department is BEA institutional member. Obtain application from campus faculty or

visit Website. Deadline for requesting mailed application is September 1. Awards for tuition and fees. Current scholarship holders are not eligible for reappointment in year following award.

Amount of award:	$3,000
Number of awards:	10
Application deadline:	September 15
Total amount awarded:	$30,000

Contact:
Broadcast Education Association
1771 N Street, N.W.
Washington, DC 20036-2891
Phone: 888-380-7222
Web: www.beaweb.org/scholarships.html

Harold E. Fellows Scholarship

Type of award: Scholarship.
Intended use: For full-time junior, senior or graduate study at 4-year or graduate institution. Designated institutions: BEA member institutions.
Basis for selection: Major/career interest in radio/television/film. Applicant must demonstrate high academic achievement, depth of character and seriousness of purpose.
Application requirements: Recommendations, essay, transcript. Application. Waiver sheet. NAB station employment/internship affidavit. Should be able to show evidence of potential in electronic media.
Additional information: Scholarships must be applied to study at campus where at least one department is BEA institutional member. Obtain application from campus faculty or visit Website to download. Deadline for requesting mailed application is September 1. Awards for tuition and fees. Current scholarship holders are not eligible for reappointment in year following award.

Amount of award:	$1,250
Number of awards:	4
Application deadline:	September 15
Total amount awarded:	$5,000

Contact:
Broadcast Education Association
1771 N Street, N.W.
Washington, DC 20036-2891
Phone: 888-380-7222
Web: www.beaweb.org/scholarships.html

Philo T. Farnsworth Scholarship

Type of award: Scholarship.
Intended use: For full-time junior, senior or graduate study at 4-year or graduate institution. Designated institutions: BEA member institutions.
Basis for selection: Major/career interest in radio/television/film or film/video. Applicant must demonstrate high academic achievement, depth of character and seriousness of purpose.
Application requirements: Recommendations, essay, transcript. Application. Waiver sheet. Should be able to show evidence of potential in electronic media.
Additional information: Scholarships must be applied to study at campus where at least one department is BEA institutional member. Obtain application from campus faculty or visit Website. Deadline for requesting mailed application is September 1. Awards for tuition and fees. Current scholarship holders are not eligible for reappointment in year following award.

Amount of award:	$1,250
Number of awards:	1
Application deadline:	September 15

Contact:
Broadcast Education Association
1771 N Street, N.W.
Washington, DC 20036-2891
Phone: 888-380-7222
Web: www.beaweb.org/scholarships.html

Two Year Community College BEA Award

Type of award: Scholarship.
Intended use: For full-time freshman or sophomore study at 2-year institution. Designated institutions: BEA 2-year/community college.
Basis for selection: Major/career interest in radio/television/film. Applicant must demonstrate high academic achievement, depth of character and seriousness of purpose.
Application requirements: Recommendations, essay, transcript. Application. Waiver form. Should be able to show evidence of potential in electronic media.
Additional information: Scholarships must be applied to study at campus where at least one department is BEA institutional member. Obtain application from campus faculty or visit Website. Deadline for requesting mailed application is September 1. Awards for tuition and fees. Current scholarship holders are not eligible for reappointment in year following award.

Amount of award:	$1,500
Number of awards:	2
Application deadline:	September 15
Total amount awarded:	$3,000

Contact:
Broadcast Education Association
1771 N Street, N.W.
Washington, DC 20036-2891
Phone: 888-380-7222
Web: www.beaweb.org/scholarships.html

Walter S. Patterson Scholarship

Type of award: Scholarship.
Intended use: For full-time junior, senior or graduate study at 4-year or graduate institution. Designated institutions: BEA member institution.
Basis for selection: Major/career interest in radio/television/film. Applicant must demonstrate high academic achievement, depth of character and seriousness of purpose.
Application requirements: Recommendations, essay, transcript. Completed application, waiver sheet. Should be able to show evidence of potential.
Additional information: All scholarships must be applied to study at campus where at least one department is BEA institutional member. Obtain official application forms from campus faculty or visit Website to download forms and for additional information. Deadline for requesting mailed application is September 1. Awards for tuition and fees. Current scholarship holders are not eligible for reappointment in year following award.

Amount of award:	$1,250
Number of awards:	2
Application deadline:	September 15
Total amount awarded:	$2,500

Scholarships

177

Contact:
Broadcast Education Association
1771 N Street, N.W.
Washington, DC 20036-2891
Phone: 888-380-7222
Web: www.beaweb.org/scholarships.html

Brown and Caldwell

Dr. W. Wes Eckenfelder Jr. Scholarship

Type of award: Scholarship.
Intended use: For full-time undergraduate or graduate study at 2-year or 4-year institution in United States.
Eligibility: Applicant must be U.S. citizen or permanent resident.
Basis for selection: Major/career interest in engineering, civil; engineering, chemical; engineering, environmental; geology/earth sciences; biology; public health; ecology or hydrology. Applicant must demonstrate depth of character, leadership and seriousness of purpose.
Application requirements: Transcript. Student must also provide a 250-word essay on the topic "Why I chose to major in one of the environmental disciplines." Applicant must also submit two written recommendations; at least one from a university or college official; completed application form; academic advisor's contact information.
Additional information: Student must have a minimum of 3.0 GPA. Please visit Website for additional information.

    Amount of award: $3,000
    Application deadline: January 31
Contact:
Brown and Caldwell
Attn: HR/Scholarship Programs
201 N. Civic Drive, Suite 115
Walnut Creek, CA 94598
Phone: 800-727-2224
Web: www.BrownAndCaldwell.com

Building Industry Association

BIA North County Division Scholarship

Type of award: Scholarship.
Intended use: For undergraduate study.
Eligibility: Applicant must be high school senior. Applicant must be residing in California.
Basis for selection: Major/career interest in engineering, civil; real estate; construction; finance/banking; landscape architecture; engineering, construction; law; accounting; architecture or electronics. Applicant must demonstrate high academic achievement.
Application requirements: Interview, essay, proof of eligibility. Application form. Applicant must be senior at eligible North County high school in California.
Additional information: For high school seniors in California's North County interested in careers in the building

industry. Open to students considering career as developer, contractor, civil/structural/soils engineer, designer, banker, accountant, planner, landscape architect, framer, plumber, electrician or other related professions. See Website for application and list of eligible high schools.

    Amount of award: $1,000-$6,000
    Number of awards: 22
    Application deadline: April 5
    Total amount awarded: $47,750
Contact:
North County Building Industry Association
Tom Blessent, Chairman
10179 Huennekens Street
San Diego, CA 92121
Phone: 858-558-4500
Web: www.biasandiego.org

Building Industry Association Scholarship

Type of award: Scholarship, renewable.
Intended use: For undergraduate study at 2-year or 4-year institution.
Basis for selection: Major/career interest in architecture; construction; engineering, civil; finance/banking; business; real estate; urban planning; interior design; advertising or law. Applicant must demonstrate financial need and high academic achievement.
Application requirements: Essay, transcript. Application form. Student must have completed one course in their field prior to application.
Additional information: For students with interest and potential in the building industry. Open to students with majors in related areas, such as advertising, finance, construction, management, architecture, carpentry, city planning, business, real estate, law and interior design. Applicants must have completed one course in field prior to application. Notification in December.

    Amount of award: $750-$1,500
    Application deadline: November 15
Contact:
Building Industry Association
HBC Scholarship Committee
6226 Greenwich Drive, Suite A
San Diego, CA 92122
Phone: 858-450-1221
Web: www.biasandiego.org

Bureau of Indian Affairs

Higher Education Grant Program

Type of award: Scholarship, renewable.
Intended use: For full-time undergraduate study at accredited 2-year or 4-year institution in United States.
Eligibility: Applicant must be American Indian. Member of or at least one-quarter degree descendant of member of federally recognized tribe.
Basis for selection: Applicant must demonstrate financial need.
Application requirements: Proof of eligibility. Proof of Native American Tribal Affiliation.
Additional information: Student must be accepted at/enrolled in nationally accredited higher education institution for study

toward associate or bachelor's degree. Student should contact tribe of which he or she is member, nearest Bureau of Indian Affairs, or address below.

Amount of award:	$500-$2,500
Number of awards:	12,000
Number of applicants:	16,000

Contact:
Office of Indian Education Programs
1849 C. ST. NW
MS 3512-MIB
Washington 20240

Bureau of Indian Affairs-Oklahoma Area Education Office

Bureau of Indian Affairs-Oklahoma Area Quapaw Tribe and Ottawa Tribe Scholarship Grant

Type of award: Scholarship.
Intended use: For undergraduate study.
Eligibility: Applicant must be American Indian. Must be enrolled member of the Quapaw Tribe and Ottawa Tribe.
Application requirements: Recommendations, essay, transcript, proof of eligibility.
Additional information: Must maintain 2.0 GPA. Contact Bureau of Indian Affairs-Oklahoma Area Education Office for application and additional information.

Application deadline:	July 15, October 15
Notification begins:	July 30, October 30

Contact:
Bureau of Indian Affairs-Oklahoma Area Education Office
4149 Highline Blvd., Suite 380
Oklahoma City, OK 73108
Phone: 405-605-6051 ext. 303

Bureau of Indian Affairs-Osage Tribal Education Committee Award

Type of award: Scholarship.
Intended use: For undergraduate or graduate study at postsecondary institution in United States.
Eligibility: Applicant must be American Indian. Must be member of Osage Tribe.
Application requirements: Recommendations, transcript, proof of eligibility.
Additional information: Minimum 2.0 GPA. Contact Bureau of Indian Affairs-Oklahoma Area Education Office for application and additional information. Deadline for summer study applications is May 1; notification begins May 15.

Application deadline:	July 1, December 31
Notification begins:	July 15, January 15

Contact:
Burea of Indian Affairs-Oklahoma Area Education Office
4149 Highline Blvd., Suite 380
Oklahoma City, OK 73108
Phone: 405-605-6051 ext.303

Business and Professional Women's Foundation

Business and Professional Women's Career Advancement Scholarship

Type of award: Scholarship.
Intended use: For junior, senior, master's or first professional study at accredited 4-year or graduate institution in United States.
Eligibility: Applicant must be female, at least 25. Applicant must be U.S. citizen.
Basis for selection: Major/career interest in science, general; education, teacher; engineering; law; computer/information sciences; humanities/liberal arts; social/behavioral sciences or business/management/administration. Applicant must demonstrate financial need.
Application requirements: Recommendations, essay, transcript, proof of eligibility. Tax forms.
Additional information: Also for applicants in the fields of paralegal studies and science or professional degrees (J.D., D.D.S., M.D.) Must be within 24 months of receiving degree, demonstrate critical financial need and have definite career plan. Must be accepted into an accredited program. Application available January 1 through April 1. Send business-size, double-stamped SASE.

Amount of award:	$500-$2,500
Number of awards:	43
Number of applicants:	1,519
Application deadline:	January 1, April 15
Notification begins:	July 31
Total amount awarded:	$40,000

Contact:
Business and Professional Women's Foundation
Scholarship and Loan Programs
2012 Massachusetts Avenue NW
Washington, DC 20036
Phone: 202-293-1200 ext. 169
Fax: 202-861-0298
Web: www.bpwusa.org

Butler Manufacturing Company Foundation

Butler Manufacturing Company Foundation Scholarship

Type of award: Scholarship, renewable.
Intended use: For full-time freshman, sophomore, junior or senior study at accredited 4-year institution.
Eligibility: Applicant or parent must be employed by Butler Manufacturing Co. & subsidiaries. Applicant must be high school senior.
Basis for selection: Applicant must demonstrate financial need, high academic achievement, depth of character, leadership and service orientation.
Application requirements: Recommendations, essay, transcript. SAT 1 or ACT required.
Additional information: Applicant's parent must be employed by Butler Mfg. Co. or wholly-owned subsidiary. Contact human resources office at workplace for information

Scholarships

and application. Application deadline is mid-February.
Subsidiaries are: Bucon, Lester Building Systems, Vistawall.

Amount of award:	$2,500
Number of awards:	8
Number of applicants:	50
Notification begins:	April 15
Total amount awarded:	$80,000

Contact:
Butler Manufacturing Company Foundation
P.O. Box 419917
Kansas City, MO 64141-6917
Phone: 816-968-3208

Centennial Scholarship

Type of award: Scholarship, renewable.
Intended use: For full-time undergraduate study at accredited vocational or 2-year institution. Designated institutions: Two Year Junior or Community College or Vocational/Technical Associate Degree or Certification.
Eligibility: Applicant or parent must be employed by Butler Manufacturing Co. & subsidiaries. Applicant must be no older than 21.
Basis for selection: Applicant must demonstrate high academic achievement, depth of character, leadership and seriousness of purpose.
Application requirements: Essay, transcript. Applicant must be financially dependent upon parent.
Additional information: Applicant must be a dependent child with high school diploma or GED.

Amount of award:	$1,000
Number of awards:	4
Number of applicants:	14

Contact:
Butler Manufacturing Company Foundation
P.O. Box 419917
Kansas City, MO 64141-6917
Phone: 816-968-3208

Calgon

Take Me Away to College Scholarship

Type of award: Scholarship.
Intended use: For full-time undergraduate study at accredited 4-year institution in United States.
Eligibility: Applicant must be female, at least 18. Applicant must be U.S. citizen or permanent resident.
Basis for selection: Major/career interest in humanities/liberal arts. Applicant must demonstrate high academic achievement.
Application requirements: Only online submissions accepted. Apply between March 15 and July 31.
Additional information: Award based on academic performance, extracurricular activities and essay response. Minimum 3.0 GPA. Applicant must enter online. $7000 first prize, $3500 second prize, $2000 third prize and five $1000 runner-up prizes.

Amount of award:	$1,000-$7,000
Number of awards:	8
Application deadline:	February 14
Total amount awarded:	$17,500

Contact:
Web: www.takemeaway.com

California Alliance for Arts Education

Emerging Young Artist Award

Type of award: Scholarship, renewable.
Eligibility: Applicant must be high school senior. Applicant must be residing in California.
Basis for selection: Competition/talent/interest in Performing arts, based on artistic achievement. Major/career interest in music; theater arts or theater/production/technical.
Application requirements: $10 application fee. Portfolio. Applicant must submit a work sample and written application.
Additional information: Applicant must be high school senior looking to pursue a career in the arts. Applications are available for download at Website.

Amount of award:	$1,000-$20,000
Number of awards:	12
Number of applicants:	500
Application deadline:	February 1
Total amount awarded:	$28,000

Contact:
California Alliance for Arts Education
495 E. Colorado Blvd.
Pasadena, CA 91101
Phone: 626-578-9315
Fax: 626-578-9894
Web: www.artsed411.org

California Association of Realtors Scholarship Foundation

California Association of Realtors Scholarship

Type of award: Scholarship.
Intended use: For undergraduate or graduate study at 2-year or 4-year institution. Designated institutions: California colleges or universities.
Eligibility: Applicant must be U.S. citizen residing in California.
Basis for selection: Major/career interest in real estate. Applicant must demonstrate financial need.
Application requirements: Interview, recommendations, essay, transcript, proof of eligibility. Minimum 2.6 GPA. Must have completed minimum of 12 college level course units within last four years. At least two courses must be in real estate or real estate related. Must submit an essay of at least 300 words explaining why real estate is career goal.
Additional information: Students attending two-year colleges eligible for $1,000 award; four-year college/university students eligible for $2,000 award. Renewable one time only. Deadlines are rolling. Application and information available at Website.

Amount of award:	$1,000-$2,000
Number of awards:	2
Application deadline:	January 2

Scholarships

Contact:
California Association of Realtors Scholarship Foundation
525 South Virgil Avenue
Los Angeles, CA 90020
Phone: 213-739-8200
Fax: 213-739-7724
Web: www.car.org

California Chicano News Media Association

Joel Garcia Memorial Scholarship

Type of award: Scholarship, renewable.
Intended use: For full-time undergraduate or graduate study at accredited postsecondary institution. Designated institutions: Out-of-state residents restricted to California schools.
Eligibility: Applicant must be Mexican American, Hispanic American or Puerto Rican. Applicant must be U.S. citizen or permanent resident.
Basis for selection: Competition/talent/interest in Writing/journalism. Major/career interest in journalism. Applicant must demonstrate financial need, high academic achievement, seriousness of purpose and service orientation.
Application requirements: Interview, recommendations, essay, transcript, proof of eligibility. Applicant must include samples of work: newspaper clips, photographs, audio or television tapes.
Additional information: Applicant must be Latino. Can be resident of California attending school in or out of state, or non-resident attending school in California. Must provide proof of full-time enrollment.

Amount of award:	$500-$2,000
Number of awards:	34
Number of applicants:	200
Application deadline:	April 5
Notification begins:	January 3
Total amount awarded:	$26,000

Contact:
California Chicano News Media Association
3800 S. Figueroa Street
Los Angeles, CA 90037-1206
Phone: 213-743-4960
Fax: 213-743-4989
Web: www.ccnma.org

California Farm Bureau

California Farm Bureau Scholarship

Type of award: Scholarship, renewable.
Intended use: For full-time freshman, sophomore, junior or senior study at accredited 4-year institution. Designated institutions: Four-year schools in California.
Eligibility: Applicant must be U.S. citizen.
Basis for selection: Major/career interest in agriculture; agribusiness; veterinary medicine or engineering, agricultural.
Application requirements: Recommendations, essay, transcript.
Additional information: Applications may be obtained from local County Farm Bureau office. Applicant must be preparing for career in agricultural industry. Award must be used at California four-year school.

Amount of award:	$2,000-$2,750
Application deadline:	March 1
Notification begins:	May 30

Contact:
California Farm Bureau Scholarship Foundation
2300 River Plaza Drive
Sacramento, CA 95833
Phone: 916-561-5520
Web: www.cfbf.com

California Grange Foundation

Deaf Activities Scholarship

Type of award: Scholarship.
Intended use: For undergraduate or graduate study at accredited vocational, 2-year or 4-year institution in United States.
Basis for selection: Major/career interest in deafness studies. Applicant must demonstrate depth of character, seriousness of purpose and service orientation.
Additional information: For students who are entering, continuing or returning to college to pursue studies that will benefit deaf communities. Award amounts vary. Applications and additional information available after February 1.

Application deadline:	April 1

Contact:
California Grange Foundation
Scholarship Committee
2101 Stockton Blvd.
Sacramento, CA 95817
Phone: 916-454-5805
Fax: 916-739-8189
Web: www.grangeonline.org

Doris Deaver Memorial Scholarship

Type of award: Scholarship.
Intended use: For freshman study at accredited vocational, 2-year or 4-year institution in United States.
Eligibility: Applicant or parent must be member/participant of Fraternal Grange. Applicant must be high school senior. Applicant must be residing in California.
Basis for selection: Applicant must demonstrate service orientation.
Additional information: Award amounts vary. Applicant must be member of California Fraternal Grange and must demonstrate Grange service orientation. Applications and additional information available after February 1.

Application deadline:	April 1

Contact:
California Grange Foundation
Scholarship Committee
2101 Stockton Blvd.
Sacramento, CA 95817
Phone: 916-454-5805
Fax: 916-739-8189
Web: www.grangeonline.com

Peter Marinoff Memorial Scholarship

Type of award: Scholarship.
Intended use: For undergraduate study at accredited vocational, 2-year or 4-year institution in United States.
Eligibility: Applicant or parent must be member/participant of Fraternal Grange. Applicant must be residing in California.
Basis for selection: Applicant must demonstrate service orientation.
Additional information: Award amounts vary. Applicant must be member of California Fraternal Grange and must demonstrate Grange service orientation. Available to high school seniors and undergraduate students. Applications and additional information available after February 1.

    Application deadline: April 1
Contact:
California Grange Foundation
Scholarship Committee
2101 Stockton Blvd.
Sacramento, CA 95817
Phone: 916-454-5805
Fax: 916-739-8189
Web: www.grangeonline.org

Sehlmeyer Scholarship

Type of award: Scholarship.
Intended use: For full-time sophomore, junior or senior study at accredited vocational, 2-year or 4-year institution in United States.
Eligibility: Applicant or parent must be member/participant of Fraternal Grange. Applicant must be residing in California.
Basis for selection: Applicant must demonstrate service orientation.
Additional information: Applicant must be member of California Fraternal Grange. Award amounts vary. Applications and additional information available after February 1.

    Amount of award: $250-$2,000
    Number of awards: 10
    Number of applicants: 17
    Application deadline: April 1
Contact:
California Grange Foundation
Scholarship Committee
2101 Stockton Blvd.
Sacramento, CA 95817
Phone: 916-454-5805
Fax: 916-739-8189
Web: www.grangeonline.org

California Masonic Foundation

California Masonic Foundation Scholarship

Type of award: Scholarship, renewable.
Intended use: For full-time undergraduate study at accredited 2-year or 4-year institution.
Eligibility: Applicant must be high school senior. Applicant must be U.S. citizen residing in California.

Basis for selection: Applicant must demonstrate financial need and high academic achievement.
Application requirements: Recommendations, essay, transcript, proof of eligibility. 1040 tax return, FAFSA.
Additional information: Minimum 3.0 GPA. Most awards are renewable. While not required, some preference is given to applicants with Masonic relationships and/or Masonic Youth Group membership. Number of awards granted is based on availability of funds. Visit Website for information and application.

    Amount of award: $1,000-$12,000
    Number of applicants: 1,400
    Application deadline: February 15
    Total amount awarded: $918,316
Contact:
California Masonic Foundation
1111 California Street
San Francisco, CA 94108-2284
Web: www.californiamasons.org

California's Junior Miss Program

California's Junior Miss Competition

Type of award: Scholarship.
Intended use: For undergraduate study at accredited 2-year or 4-year institution in United States.
Eligibility: Applicant must be single, female, high school junior. Applicant must be U.S. citizen residing in California.
Basis for selection: Based on interview, scholastics, poise, talent and fitness. Applicant must demonstrate high academic achievement.
Application requirements: Interview. Minimum 3.0 GPA required.
Additional information: Initial inquiry should be made by December 31 of junior year in high school. Awards not limited to state Junior Miss finalists; winners of various judged categories also receive awards. Winner of Junior Miss pageant will receive $10,000 on the state level, other prizes of varying amounts may be awarded on the local level.

    Number of awards: 20
    Number of applicants: 60
    Application deadline: January 1
    Notification begins: August 17
    Total amount awarded: $30,000
Contact:
California's Junior Miss Program
3523 Glenbrook Lane
Napa, CA 94558
Phone: 707-224-5112
Web: www.ajm.org/california

California Student Aid Commission

Cal Grant A & B Entitlement Award Program

Type of award: Scholarship, renewable.
Intended use: For undergraduate study at postsecondary institution. Designated institutions: Qualifying California postsecondary schools.
Eligibility: Applicant must be high school senior. Applicant must be U.S. citizen or permanent resident residing in California.
Basis for selection: Applicant must demonstrate financial need and high academic achievement.
Application requirements: Continuing college students (freshmen, sophomores and juniors) must submit FAFSA to federal processor and GPA Verification Form to California Student Aid Commission.
Additional information: Awards given to all eligible applicants. Applicants must have income and assets below established levels. Minimum 3.0 GPA for Cal Grant A; minimum 2.0 GPA for Cal Grant B. Cal Grant A provides tuition and fees. Cal Grant B provides access grant for first year and then both access grant and tuition and fees for second year. If attending a California community college, award can be reserved for up to two years until transfer to tuition/fee charging college, provided qualifications are still met. Students with no available GPA can submit SAT, ACT or GED scores. Visit Website or contact CSAC for more details.

Amount of award:	$700-$11,259
Number of applicants:	150,000
Application deadline:	March 2
Total amount awarded:	$175,900,000

Contact:
California Student Aid Commission
Grant Services Division
P.O. Box 419027
Rancho Cordova, CA 95741-9027
Phone: 888-224-7268
Web: www.csac.ca.gov

Cal Grant C Award Program

Type of award: Scholarship, renewable.
Intended use: For undergraduate study at postsecondary institution. Designated institutions: Qualifying California postsecondary and vocational institutions.
Eligibility: Applicant must be U.S. citizen or permanent resident residing in California.
Basis for selection: Applicant must demonstrate financial need.
Application requirements: Students must submit FAFSA to federal processor and GPA Verification Form to CSAC.
Additional information: Applicants must have income and assets below certain established levels. Applicants must plan to enroll in a vocational/occupational program of at least four months. Students with no available GPA can submit SAT, ACT or GED scores. Visit Website or contact CSAC for more details.

Amount of award:	$576-$3,168
Number of awards:	7,761
Number of applicants:	23,000
Application deadline:	January 1
Notification begins:	May 15
Total amount awarded:	$14,000,000

Contact:
California Student Aid Commission
Grant Services Division
P.O. Box 419027
Rancho Cordova, CA 95741-9027
Phone: 888-224-7268
Web: www.csac.ca.gov

California Child Development Teacher and Supervisor Grant Program

Type of award: Scholarship.
Intended use: For undergraduate study at accredited 2-year or 4-year institution. Designated institutions: California public or private postsecondary institutions with approved child development classes.
Eligibility: Applicant must be U.S. citizen or permanent resident residing in California.
Basis for selection: Major/career interest in education, early childhood or education, teacher. Applicant must demonstrate financial need and seriousness of purpose.
Application requirements: Proof of eligibility by college or employer. Application. Recommendations from institution faculty. Points based on GPA, income and EFC. Applicant must be pursuing permit to teach/supervise in field of child care and development.
Additional information: Recipients attending two-year postsecondary institutions will receive up to $1,000 annually for up to two years. Recipients attending four-year institutions will receive up to $2,000 annually for up to two years. Applicants continuing beyond two years may reapply but cannot cumulatively receive more than $6,000 through the program. Recipients must maintain at least half-time enrollment in approved course of study leading to Child Development Permit; maintain satisfactory academic progress; meet federal Selective Service registration requirements; and commit to one year of full-time employment in a licensed child care center for every year they receive the grant. The commission can award up to 100 new recipients each year. Application deadlines and notification dates vary. Visit Website for information and application.

Amount of award:	$1,000-$2,000

Contact:
California Student Aid Commission
Specialized Programs
P.O. Box 41029
Rancho Cordova, CA 95741-9029
Phone: 888-224-7268
Fax: 916-526-7977
Web: www.csac.ca.gov

California Law Enforcement Personnel Dependents Grant

Type of award: Scholarship, renewable.
Intended use: For undergraduate study at accredited 2-year or 4-year institution. Designated institutions: California postsecondary institutions accredited by Western Association of Schools and Colleges (WASC).
Eligibility: Applicant must be U.S. citizen residing in California. Applicant's parent must have been killed or disabled in work-related accident as fire fighter, police officer or public safety officer.
Basis for selection: Applicants are dependants or spouses of law enforcement officials (fire fighter, police officer or public

safety officer) who were killed or 100% disabled as a result of an accident or injury in the performance of duty. Applicant must demonstrate financial need.

Application requirements: Proof of eligibility. Application, copy of current Student Aid Report, birth certificate (not required for spouse). Applicant must be natural/adopted child or spouse, at time of death/injury, of CA peace/law enforcement officer, officer/employee of Dept. Corrections/Youth Authority, or firefighter.

Additional information: Additional application requirements: dependent/spouse of A) peace/law enforcement officers: death certificate of parent/spouse and coroner's report (if appropriate), police report and any other necessary documentation; B) officers/employees of Dept. of Corrections/Youth Authority: death certificate of parent/spouse, coroner's report (if appropriate) and documentation showing death/total disability was caused by the direct action of inmate; C) firefighters: death certificate of parent/spouse, coroner's report (if appropriate) and any other necessary documentation. All must include findings of Worker's Compensation Appeals Board or other evidence that fatality/disabling accident/injury is compensable under Division 4.0 and 4.5 of the Labor Code.

Amount of award:	$100-$11,259
Number of awards:	16
Total amount awarded:	$93,571

Contact:
California Student Aid Commision
Specialized Programs
P.O. Box 419029
Rancho Cordova, CA 95741-9027
Phone: 888-224-7268
Fax: 916-526-7977
Web: www.csac.ca.gov

California Robert C. Byrd Honors Scholarship

Type of award: Scholarship, renewable.
Intended use: For full-time undergraduate study at accredited 2-year or 4-year institution in United States.
Eligibility: Applicant must be high school senior. Applicant must be U.S. citizen residing in California.
Basis for selection: Applicant must demonstrate high academic achievement.
Application requirements: Nomination by high school.
Additional information: Students are awarded individually by their school based on merit. Contact guidance office for information. GED students may apply directly. Renewable up to four years.

Amount of award:	$1,500
Number of awards:	862
Number of applicants:	1,621
Notification begins:	May 15
Total amount awarded:	$5,200,000

Contact:
California Student Aid Commission
Robert C. Byrd Honors Scholarship Program
P.O. Box 419027
Rancho Cordova, CA 95741-9027
Phone: 888-224-7268
Fax: 916-526-7977
Web: www.csac.ca.gov

Competitive Cal Grant A and B Award Programs

Type of award: Scholarship, renewable.

Intended use: For undergraduate study at postsecondary institution. Designated institutions: Qualifying California postsecondary schools.
Eligibility: Applicant must be U.S. citizen or permanent resident residing in California.
Basis for selection: Applicant must demonstrate financial need and high academic achievement.
Application requirements: Continuing college students (current freshmen, sophomores and juniors) must submit FAFSA to federal processor and GPA Verification Form to California Student Aid Commission. Both forms must be postmarked by March 2.
Additional information: Applicants must have income and assets below established levels. Must have minimum 2.0 GPA. Competitive grant program awards used for same purpose as entitlement grants but not guaranteed to all applicants. Cal Grant A awards intended to help low- and middle-income families pay tuition and fees. Cal Grant B awards up to $1,551 to disadvantaged and low-income families toward living expenses and costs for transportation, supplies and books. Students with no available GPA can submit SAT, ACT or GED scores. Deadlines: March 2 for continuing college students; September 2 for California Community College students. Visit Website or contact CSAC for more details.

Amount of award:	$700-$11,259
Number of awards:	22,500
Number of applicants:	350,000
Application deadline:	March 2, September 2
Notification begins:	May 1, October 1
Total amount awarded:	$48,000,000

Contact:
California Student Aid Commission
Grant Services Division
P.O. Box 419027
Rancho Cordova, CA 95741-9027
Phone: 888-224-7268
Web: www.csac.ca.gov

California Teachers Association

California Teachers Association Martin Luther King, Jr., Memorial Scholarship

Type of award: Scholarship.
Intended use: For undergraduate or graduate study at accredited postsecondary institution.
Eligibility: Applicant or parent must be member/participant of California Teachers Association. Applicant must be Alaskan native, Asian American, African American, Mexican American, Hispanic American, Puerto Rican or American Indian.
Basis for selection: Major/career interest in education; education, teacher or education, special. Applicant must demonstrate financial need.
Application requirements: Proof of eligibility.
Additional information: Must be active CTA or student CTA member, or dependent child of active, deceased or retired CTA member. Must be ethnic minority. High school seniors may also apply. Amount of award varies. In order to receive funds, scholarship recipients must show proof of registration in approved credential or degree program. Visit Website for more information.

Number of applicants: 150
Application deadline: March 15
Notification begins: May 1
Contact:
California Teachers Association Human Rights Department
P.O. Box 921
Burlingame, CA 94011-0921
Phone: 650-697-1400
Fax: 650-552-5002
Web: www.cta.org

CTA Scholarship for Dependent Children

Type of award: Scholarship, renewable.
Intended use: For full-time undergraduate or graduate study at accredited postsecondary institution.
Eligibility: Applicant or parent must be member/participant of California Teachers Association.
Basis for selection: Major/career interest in education. Applicant must demonstrate high academic achievement, depth of character, leadership, seriousness of purpose and service orientation.
Application requirements: Transcript, proof of eligibility. Application. Scholarships awarded based on overall achievement in four categories: 1) involvement in and sensitivity to human, social and civic issues; 2) characteristics such as responsibility, reliability and integrity; 3) academic and vocational potential; and 4) special and personal achievements.
Additional information: Eligible graduating high school seniors, undergraduates, and graduates. Applicant must be dependent child of active, retired or deceased member of CTA. Applicant must be claimed as a dependent on current year's IRS tax forms. In order to receive funds, scholarship recipients must show proof of registration in approved credential or degree program. Visit Website for more information.

Amount of award: $2,000
Number of awards: 25
Number of applicants: 1,000
Application deadline: February 15
Notification begins: May 1
Contact:
California Teachers Association Human Rights Department
P.O. Box 921
Burlingame, CA 94011-0921
Phone: 650-697-1400
Fax: 650-552-5002
Web: www.cta.org

CTA Scholarships for Members

Type of award: Scholarship, renewable.
Intended use: For undergraduate or graduate study at accredited postsecondary institution.
Eligibility: Applicant or parent must be member/participant of California Teachers Association.
Basis for selection: Major/career interest in education, teacher. Applicant must demonstrate high academic achievement, depth of character, leadership, seriousness of purpose and service orientation.
Application requirements: Transcript. Application. Scholarships awarded based on overall achievement in four categories: 1) involvement in and sensitivity to human, social and civic issues; 2) characteristics such as responsibility, reliability and integrity; 3) academic and vocational potential; and 4) special and personal achievements.

Additional information: Applicant must be active member of CTA (including members working on emergency credential). In order to receive funds, scholarship recipients must show proof of registration in approved credential or degree program. Visit Website for more information.

Amount of award: $2,000
Number of awards: 5
Number of applicants: 150
Application deadline: February 15
Notification begins: May 1
Total amount awarded: $10,000
Contact:
California Teachers Association Human Rights Department
P.O. Box 921
Burlingame, CA 94011-0921
Phone: 650-697-1400
Fax: 650-552-5002
Web: www.cta.org

L. Gordon Bittle Memorial Scholarship for Student CTA

Type of award: Scholarship, renewable.
Intended use: For full-time undergraduate or graduate study at accredited postsecondary institution. Designated institutions: Can be teacher credential program at accredited postsecondary institution.
Eligibility: Applicant or parent must be member/participant of California Teachers Association. Applicant must be residing in California.
Basis for selection: Major/career interest in education; education, teacher or education, special. Applicant must demonstrate high academic achievement, depth of character and service orientation.
Application requirements: Transcript. Application. Scholarships are awarded based on overall achievement in four categories: 1) involvement in and sensitivity to human, social and civic issues; 2) characteristics such as responsibility, reliability and integrity; 3) academic and vocational potential; and 4) special and personal achievements.
Additional information: Not available to CTA members currently working in public schools. Applicant must be active member of Student CTA. In order to receive funds, scholarship recipients must show proof of registration in approved credential or degree program. Visit Website for more information.

Amount of award: $2,000
Number of awards: 3
Number of applicants: 20
Application deadline: February 15
Notification begins: May 1
Total amount awarded: $6,000
Contact:
California Teachers Association Human Rights Department
P.O. Box 921
Burlingame, CA 94011-0921
Phone: 650-697-1400
Fax: 650-552-5002
Web: www.cta.org

Scholarships

CAP Charitable Foundation

The Ron Brown Scholar Program

Type of award: Scholarship, renewable.
Intended use: For full-time undergraduate study at 4-year institution in United States.
Eligibility: Applicant must be African American. Applicant must be high school senior. Applicant must be U.S. citizen.
Basis for selection: Applicant must demonstrate financial need, high academic achievement, depth of character, leadership, seriousness of purpose and service orientation.
Application requirements: Recommendations, essay, transcript.
Additional information: In addition to financial assistance, scholars get other benefits: summer internships, career guidance, placement opportunities, mentors, and leadership training. The scholarships are not limited to specific fields or career objectives and may be used to pursue any academic discipline. Funding is available for four years; a total of $40,000.

Amount of award:	$10,000
Number of awards:	10
Application deadline:	January 9

Contact:
Ron Brown Scholar Program
Attention: Ms. Fran Hardey
1160 Pepsi Place, Suite 206
Charlottesville, VA 22901
Phone: 434-964-1588
Web: www.ronbrown.org

Case Western Reserve University

Marc A. Klein Playwriting Award

Type of award: Scholarship.
Intended use: For undergraduate or graduate study at 2-year or 4-year institution in United States.
Basis for selection: Competition/talent/interest in performing arts, based on creativity, originality. Major/career interest in theater arts.
Application requirements: Send a stage manuscript.
Additional information: Manuscripts must be endorsed by faculty member of university theater or drama department. Only plays that have not been professionally produced can be entered. Musicals and children's plays will not be accepted. May submit only one script accompanied by endorsed Klein application form.

Amount of award:	$1,000
Number of awards:	1
Number of applicants:	40
Application deadline:	December 1
Notification begins:	August 1

Contact:
Marc A. Klein Playwriting Award
CWRU Department of Theater and Dance
10900 Euclid Ave.
Cleveland, OH 44106-7077
Phone: 216-368-4868
Fax: 216-368-5184

Catching the Dream

MESBEC Scholarships

Type of award: Scholarship, renewable.
Intended use: For full-time undergraduate or graduate study at accredited postsecondary institution in United States.
Eligibility: Applicant must be Alaskan native or American Indian. Must be an enrolled member of a tribe. Must be one-quarter Native American. Applicant must be U.S. citizen or permanent resident.
Basis for selection: Major/career interest in mathematics; engineering; computer/information sciences; business; education or science, general. Applicant must demonstrate high academic achievement, depth of character, leadership, seriousness of purpose and service orientation.
Application requirements: Recommendations, essay, transcript, proof of eligibility.
Additional information: Deadlines: March 15 for summer funding; April 15 for fall; September 15 for spring.

Amount of award:	$500-$5,000
Number of awards:	200
Number of applicants:	200
Total amount awarded:	$300,000

Contact:
Catching the Dream
8200 Mountain Road NE
Suite 203
Albuquerque, NM 87110
Phone: 505-262-2351
Fax: 505-262-0534

Native American Leadership in Education Scholarship

Type of award: Scholarship, renewable.
Intended use: For full-time undergraduate or graduate study at accredited postsecondary institution in United States.
Eligibility: Applicant must be Alaskan native or American Indian. Must be an enrolled member of a tribe. Must be one-quarter Native American. Applicant must be U.S. citizen or permanent resident.
Basis for selection: Major/career interest in education. Applicant must demonstrate high academic achievement, depth of character, leadership, seriousness of purpose and service orientation.
Application requirements: Recommendations, essay, transcript, proof of eligibility.
Additional information: Deadlines: March 15 for summer funding; April 15 for fall; September 15 for spring.

Amount of award:	$500-$5,000
Number of awards:	30
Number of applicants:	40
Total amount awarded:	$100,000

Contact:
Catching the Dream
8200 Mountain Road NE
Suite 203
Albuquerque, NM 87110
Phone: 505-262-2351
Fax: 505-262-0534

Tribal Business Management Scholarship

Type of award: Scholarship, renewable.

Intended use: For full-time undergraduate, graduate or postgraduate study at accredited postsecondary institution in United States.
Eligibility: Applicant must be Alaskan native or American Indian. Must be enrolled member of a tribe. Must be at least one-quarter Native American. Applicant must be U.S. citizen or permanent resident.
Basis for selection: Major/career interest in business; economics; finance/banking; hotel/restaurant management or accounting. Applicant must demonstrate high academic achievement, depth of character, leadership, seriousness of purpose and service orientation.
Application requirements: Recommendations, essay, transcript, proof of eligibility.
Additional information: Scholarships are for fields of study directly related to tribal business development and management. Application deadlines: March 15 for summer semester; April 15 for fall semester; September 15 for spring semester.

Amount of award:	$500-$5,000
Number of awards:	15
Number of applicants:	30
Application deadline:	April 15, September 15
Total amount awarded:	$30,000

Contact:
Catching the Dream
8200 Mountain Road NE
Suite 203
Albuquerque, NM 87110
Phone: 505-262-2351
Fax: 505-262-0534

Catholic Aid Association

Catholic Aid Association Scholarship

Type of award: Scholarship.
Intended use: For full-time freshman study at vocational, 2-year or 4-year institution in United States.
Eligibility: Applicant or parent must be member/participant of Catholic Aid Association.
Basis for selection: Applicant must demonstrate financial need, high academic achievement, depth of character, leadership, seriousness of purpose and service orientation.
Application requirements: Essay, transcript, proof of eligibility. Application form required. Essay must outline interests and vocational goals.
Additional information: Open to college freshmen and high school seniors. Must have been member of Catholic Aid Association for two years. Application forms change every year. $300 awards go to those who are or will be attending state schools, while $500 awards go to those who are or will be attending Catholic universities. Applications can be downloaded from Website, but hard copy must be mailed in. Essays are graded by outside vendor before being judged by Catholic Aid Association.

Amount of award:	$300-$500
Application deadline:	February 15

Contact:
Catholic Aid Association
3499 North Lexington Avenue
St. Paul, MN 55126
Phone: 651-490-0170
Fax: 651-490-0170
Web: www.catholicaid.com

Catholic Workman Fraternal Benefit Society

National Catholic Workman Scholarship

Type of award: Scholarship, renewable.
Intended use: For full-time undergraduate or non-degree study at accredited postsecondary institution in United States.
Eligibility: Applicant or parent must be member/participant of Catholic Workman Fraternal Life Association.
Basis for selection: Applicant must demonstrate high academic achievement, leadership and service orientation.
Application requirements: Recommendations, essay, transcript, proof of eligibility. SAT/ACT scores. Minimum 2.5 GPA. Must have volunteer background.
Additional information: Applicant must be member of Catholic Workman Fraternal Life Association. Visit Website for more informaton.

Amount of award:	$500-$1,000
Number of awards:	20
Number of applicants:	50
Application deadline:	July 1
Notification begins:	August 25
Total amount awarded:	$16,000

Contact:
Catholic Workman Fraternal Life Association
Scholarship Program
1201 1st St. NE
New Prague, MN 56071
Phone: 800-346-6231
Web: www.catholicworkman.org

Center for Education Solutions

A. Patrick Charnon Memorial Scholarship

Type of award: Scholarship.
Intended use: For full-time undergraduate study at accredited 4-year institution in United States.
Eligibility: Applicant must be U.S. citizen or permanent resident.
Basis for selection: Major/career interest in governmental public relations; humanities/liberal arts; social/behavioral sciences or sociology. Applicant must demonstrate seriousness of purpose and service orientation.
Application requirements: Essay, transcript. Include three letters of recommendation with completed application form.

Additional information: One annual scholarship awarded to an undergraduate student who has demonstrated commitment to building communities. Selection committee looks for candidates who have shown tolerance, compassion and respect for all people and a commitment to these values by their actions. Non-traditional students may apply. See Website for application. Application may also be obtained by mailing SASE to address below. Relatives of selection committee ineligible for award. Recipients may re-apply for up to four years as long as award requirements are met.

Amount of award:	$1,500
Number of awards:	1
Number of applicants:	549
Application deadline:	April 1
Notification begins:	August 1

Contact:
A. Patrick Charnon Memorial Scholarship
The Center for Education Solutions
P.O. Box 208
San Francisco, CA 94104
Web: www.cesresources.org

Central Intelligence Agency

CIA Undergraduate Scholarship

Type of award: Scholarship, renewable.
Intended use: For full-time freshman, sophomore, junior or senior study at accredited 4-year institution in United States.
Eligibility: Applicant must be at least 18, high school senior. Applicant must be U.S. citizen.
Basis for selection: Major/career interest in engineering; computer/information sciences or economics. Applicant must demonstrate financial need, high academic achievement, depth of character, leadership, patriotism, seriousness of purpose and service orientation.
Application requirements: Transcript. SAT/ACT scores. Resume.
Additional information: Award offers applicant chance to work at the CIA over college summers. Salary paid, as well as $15,000 award. Minority or disabled applicants preferred. Service commitment to CIA must be fulfilled or recipient must repay award. Minimum 3.0 GPA; 1000 SAT/21 ACT required. Applicants with family income over $70,000 not eligible. Applicants with family income between $60,000 and $70,000 accepted only if family has four or more dependents. Applicants must be 18 by April of senior year in high school; if not, they can apply for the scholarship in their freshman year of college.

Amount of award:	$15,000
Number of applicants:	300
Application deadline:	November 1
Notification begins:	June 30
Total amount awarded:	$15,000

Contact:
Central Intelligence Agency
Recruitment Center
P.O. Box 4090
Reston, VA 20195
Fax: 703-613-7875

C.G. Fuller Foundation

C.G. Fuller Foundation Scholarship

Type of award: Scholarship, renewable.
Intended use: For full-time undergraduate study at 4-year institution. Designated institutions: South Carolina colleges and universities.
Eligibility: Applicant must be high school senior. Applicant must be residing in South Carolina.
Basis for selection: Applicant must demonstrate financial need and high academic achievement.
Application requirements: Interview, recommendations, transcript.
Additional information: Apply through financial aid office of university. Applications distributed between end of October and end of November. Applicant must have minimum 3.0 GPA and SAT score of 1100 or higher. Recipient must be South Carolina resident attending college in South Carolina. Total amount awarded and number of awards vary with changes in funding.

Amount of award:	$2,000
Number of awards:	15
Number of applicants:	200
Application deadline:	April 15
Notification begins:	August 1

Contact:
C.G. Fuller Foundation, c/o Bank of America
P.O. Box 448
SC3-240-04-17
Columbia, SC 29202-0448

Chairscholars Foundation, Inc.

Chairscholars Scholarship

Type of award: Scholarship, renewable.
Intended use: For full-time freshman study at postsecondary institution.
Eligibility: Applicant must be physically challenged. Applicant must be single, no older than 21, high school senior. Applicant must be U.S. citizen.
Basis for selection: Applicant must demonstrate financial need, depth of character, leadership, seriousness of purpose and service orientation.
Application requirements: Recommendations, essay, transcript, proof of eligibility. Photograph and 300-500 word essay outlining how you became physically challenged, how your situation has affected your family, and what your goals are for the future. Applicant must list any contributions to the community.
Additional information: Eight of the awardees for this scholarship receive four $5,000 awards, given yearly. Applicant must have a "major" physical challenge but does not have to be confined to a wheelchair. Applicant must be unable to attend college without financial aid. Applicant must have at least a B+ GPA and must submit ACT or SAT scores.

Amount of award:	$3,000-$20,000
Number of awards:	12
Number of applicants:	250
Application deadline:	February 28
Total amount awarded:	$300,000

Contact:
Chairscholars Foundation, Inc.
16101 Carencia Ln.
Odessa, FL 33556
Web: chairscholars.org

Charles & Lucille King Family Foundation, Inc.

Charles & Lucille King Family Foundation Scholarships

Type of award: Scholarship, renewable.
Intended use: For full-time junior or senior study at 4-year institution in United States.
Basis for selection: Major/career interest in communications or radio/television/film.
Application requirements: Recommendations. Personal statement. Application form with financial information.
Additional information: Award is renewable for college undergraduates pursuing television, film or communication studies.
    Amount of award: $1,250-$2,500
    Number of awards: 20
    Application deadline: April 1
Contact:
Charles & Lucille King Family Foundation, Inc.
366 Madison Avenue, 10th Floor
New York, NY 10017
Phone: 212-682-2913
Fax: 212-949-0728
Web: www.kingfoundation.org

Charles A. and Anne Morrow Lindbergh Foundation

Lindbergh Foundation Grant

Type of award: Research grant.
Intended use: For non-degree study.
Basis for selection: Major/career interest in environmental science; aviation; natural resources/conservation; education or health sciences.
Application requirements: Research proposal. Project must address a balance between technology and nature.
Additional information: Applicant research or educational project should address balance between technological advancement and environmental preservation.
    Amount of award: $1,000-$10,580
    Number of awards: 10
    Number of applicants: 200
    Application deadline: June 15
    Notification begins: April 15

Contact:
The Charles A. and Anne Morrow Lindbergh Foundation
2150 Third Avenue North
Suite 310
Anoka, MN 55303-2200
Phone: 763-576-1596
Fax: 763-576-1664
Web: www.lindberghfoundation.org

Charter Fund

Charter Fund Scholarship

Type of award: Scholarship.
Intended use: For full-time freshman study.
Eligibility: Applicant must be high school senior. Applicant must be U.S. citizen residing in Colorado.
Basis for selection: Applicant must demonstrate financial need.
Application requirements: Interview. Personal letter. ACT/SAT scores.
    Amount of award: $100-$2,500
    Number of awards: 90
    Application deadline: May 7
    Notification begins: July 15
    Total amount awarded: $100,000
Contact:
Charter Fund- Jeanette Montoya
370 17th Street, Suite 5300
Denver, CO 80202
Phone: 303-572-1727
Fax: 303-628-3839
Web: www.piton.org

Chesapeake Corporation Foundation

Chesapeake Corporation Scholarship

Type of award: Scholarship, renewable.
Intended use: For full-time freshman, sophomore, junior or senior study.
Eligibility: Applicant or parent must be employed by Chesapeake Corporation. Applicant must be high school senior.
Basis for selection: Applicant must demonstrate high academic achievement.
Application requirements: SAT/ACT scores.
Additional information: Applicant or parent must be employed by Chesapeake Corporation.
    Amount of award: $3,500
    Number of applicants: 8
    Application deadline: November 15
    Total amount awarded: $7,000
Contact:
Chesapeake Corporation Foundation
James Center II
1021 East Cary Street, Box 2350
Richmond, VA 23218-2350
Web: www.cskcorp.com

Chesterfield Film Company

Chesterfield Writer's Film Project

Type of award: Scholarship.
Intended use: For non-degree study.
Basis for selection: Competition/talent/interest in writing/journalism, based on writing samples in any genre (film, fiction, theater); no specific format required. Major/career interest in film/video.
Application requirements: $40 application fee. Writing samples.
Additional information: Selection based on demonstrated writing ability. Fellowships last one year and fellows receive a $20,000 stipend. Up to five awards each year, but sponsor reserves the right to grant fewer awards in any given year. Successful submissions also considered for professional production, with additional remuneration if produced. No specific eligibility criteria; fiction, theater and film writers may apply. Several thousand applications received each year. Visit Website for more information.

Amount of award:	$20,000
Number of awards:	5
Application deadline:	June 21

Contact:
Chesterfield Film Company
1158 26th Street
Box 544
Santa Monica, CA 90403
Phone: 213-683-3977
Web: www.chesterfield-co.com

Cheyenne-Arapaho Tribes of Oklahoma-Concho Agency

Cheyenne-Arapaho Federal Aid Grants

Type of award: Scholarship, renewable.
Intended use: For undergraduate or graduate study at accredited 2-year, 4-year or graduate institution in United States.
Eligibility: Applicant must be American Indian. Must be enrolled member of Cheyenne-Arapaho Tribe of OK, certified by Concho Agency to be one-quarter Cheyenne-Arapaho or more.
Basis for selection: Applicant must demonstrate financial need and high academic achievement.
Application requirements: Transcript, proof of eligibility. FAFSA, Cheyenne-Arapaho FNA. GED certificate accepted. Complete application including letter explaining educational plans.
Additional information: Applicant must be entering degree-granting program. Student receives $1,000 per semester for full-time enrollment. Part-time enrollment: three credit hours $250; six credit hours $500; nine credit hours $750. Summer and part-time applicants considered. Summer application deadline is April 1.

Amount of award:	$1,000
Number of awards:	130
Number of applicants:	150
Application deadline:	June 1, November 1

Contact:
Cheyenne-Arapaho Tribe of Oklahoma-Concho Agency
Department of Education
P.O. Box 38
Concho, OK 73022
Phone: 405-262-0345 or 800-247-4612
Fax: 405-262-0745

Child Nutrition Foundation

CNF Lincoln Food Service Research Grants

Type of award: Research grant.
Intended use: For non-degree study at postsecondary institution.
Eligibility: Applicant or parent must be member/participant of American School Food Service Foundation.
Basis for selection: Major/career interest in dietetics/nutrition or food production/management/services. Applicant must demonstrate high academic achievement and seriousness of purpose.
Application requirements: Proof of eligibility, research proposal. Letter of support.
Additional information: Must be active member of ASFSA or be supervised on grant by active ASFSA member. Level of study is nonacademic research (no need to be enrolled in master's program). Research must be applicable to child nutrition and must support ASFSA grant program mission.

Amount of award:	$2,500
Number of awards:	2
Application deadline:	April 30
Notification begins:	June 1
Total amount awarded:	$5,000

Contact:
CNF Financial Aid Manager
700 S. Washington St.
Suite 300
Alexandria, VA 22314
Phone: 800-877-8822 ext. 150
Web: www.asfsa.org/continuinged/assistance/scholarships

Schwan's Food Service Scholarship

Type of award: Scholarship, renewable.
Intended use: For undergraduate or graduate study at accredited postsecondary institution.
Eligibility: Applicant or parent must be member/participant of American School Food Service Foundation.
Basis for selection: Major/career interest in food production/management/services; dietetics/nutrition; food science/technology or culinary arts. Applicant must demonstrate high academic achievement, leadership, seriousness of purpose and service orientation.
Application requirements: Essay, transcript, proof of eligibility. Course description, two recommendations.
Additional information: Distance learning accepted for correspondence courses. Must major or intend to pursue career in school food service or child nutrition. Applicant or parent must be current ASFSA member for at least one year.

Scholarships are primarily for undergraduates; occasionally awarded to graduate students. Vocational and junior colleges accepted.

Amount of award:	$150-$1,000
Number of awards:	55
Application deadline:	April 15
Notification begins:	June 1
Total amount awarded:	$40,000

Contact:
CNF Financial Aid Manager
700 S. Washington St.
Suite 300
Alexandria, VA 22314
Phone: 800-877-8822 ext.150
Web: www.asfsa.org/continuinged/assistance/scholarships

Choctaw Nation of Oklahoma

Choctaw Nation Higher Eduation Program

Type of award: Scholarship, renewable.
Intended use: For undergraduate or graduate study at accredited 2-year, 4-year or graduate institution in United States.
Eligibility: Applicant must be American Indian. Must be enrolled member of Choctaw Tribe and have Certificate Documenting Indian Blood (CDIB) and tribal membership card.
Basis for selection: Financial need for grant and minimum 2.5 GPA for scholarship. Applicant must demonstrate financial need.
Application requirements: Transcript, proof of eligibility. Proof of Choctaw descent. FAFSA.
Additional information: Must first apply for federal financial assistance. Grant will assist with any unmet need up to award amount. Must reapply for renewal. Also, $2,000 scholarship program now in effect for those with minimum 2.5 GPA; financial need is not required, but FAFSA must be completed.

Amount of award:	$2,000
Number of awards:	2,500
Number of applicants:	4,300
Application deadline:	March 15
Notification begins:	July 15

Contact:
Choctaw Nation of Oklahoma
Higher Education Department
P.O. Drawer 1210
Durant, OK 74702-1210
Phone: 800-522-6170

Christian Record Services

Christian Record Services Scholarship

Type of award: Scholarship, renewable.
Intended use: For full-time undergraduate study in United States.

Eligibility: Applicant must be visually impaired. Applicants must be legally blind or blind.
Basis for selection: Applicant must demonstrate financial need and high academic achievement.
Application requirements: Recommendations. Also include photo and bio.
Additional information: Applicants must be legally blind or blind. Awardees must reapply yearly. Applications accepted beginning November 1.

Amount of award:	$500
Number of awards:	10
Number of applicants:	67
Application deadline:	April 1
Notification begins:	May 15
Total amount awarded:	$5,000

Contact:
Christian Record Services
4444 South 52 Street
Lincoln, NE 68516
Phone: 402-488-0981
Fax: 402-488-7582

The Christophers

The Christophers Video Contest for College Students

Type of award: Scholarship.
Intended use: For undergraduate study at postsecondary institution.
Basis for selection: Video or film that captures theme, artistic and technical proficiency. Major/career interest in film/video.
Application requirements: Entries must be submitted in NTSC format on standard, full-sized VHS tape. Entries over five minutes will not be considered.
Additional information: Video contest for college students. Visit Website for contest's annual theme and additional information. Winning entries aired nationwide via Christopher Closeup television series.

Amount of award:	$100-$3,000
Application deadline:	June 11

Contact:
The Christophers
12. E. 48th Street
New York, NY 10017
Phone: 212-759-4050
Fax: 212-838-5073
Web: www.christophers.org/contests.html

The Coca-Cola Foundation

First Generation Scholarship Program

Type of award: Scholarship, renewable.
Intended use: For full-time undergraduate study at accredited 2-year or 4-year institution in United States. Designated institutions: 430 eligible institutions throughout U.S. and China.
Eligibility: Applicant must be high school senior. Applicant must be U.S. citizen, permanent resident, international student or Chinese citizens.

Basis for selection: Applicant must demonstrate financial need.
Application requirements: Proof of eligibility.
Additional information: Applicant must be first in immediate family to seek college education if U.S. resident; or first in village to seek higher education if in China. Must maintain 3.0 GPA and full-time status to renew. Contact individual institution to see if scholarship is currently available. Visit Website for list of eligible institutions.

Amount of award:	$5,000

Contact:
The Coca-Cola Foundation
P.O. Drawer 1734
Atlanta, GA 30301
Phone: 404-676-2568
Web: www.thecocacolacompany.com

Coca-Cola Scholars Foundation, Inc.

Coca-Cola Scholars Program

Type of award: Scholarship, renewable.
Intended use: For full-time undergraduate study at accredited 4-year institution in United States.
Eligibility: Applicant must be high school senior. Applicant must be U.S. citizen or permanent resident.
Basis for selection: Applicant must demonstrate high academic achievement, depth of character, leadership, seriousness of purpose and service orientation.
Additional information: Must be attending high school in United States or territories. Minimum 3.0 GPA required at the end of junior year high school. Award is for four years, $1000 or $5000 per year. Notification begins December 31 for semifinalists; end of February for finalists. Children of Coca-Cola employees not eligible.

Amount of award:	$4,000-$20,000
Number of awards:	250
Number of applicants:	100,000
Application deadline:	October 31
Notification begins:	December 31
Total amount awarded:	$1,800,000

Contact:
Coca-Cola Scholars Foundation
P.O. Box 442
Atlanta, GA 30301-0442
Phone: 800-306-2653
Web: www.coca-colascholars.org

Coca-Cola Two-Year Colleges Scholarship

Type of award: Scholarship.
Intended use: For undergraduate study at 2-year institution in United States. Designated institutions: Two-year degree granting institution.
Eligibility: Applicant must be U.S. citizen or permanent resident.
Basis for selection: Major/career interest in humanities/liberal arts. Applicant must demonstrate high academic achievement, depth of character and service orientation.
Application requirements: Nomination by college in which student is enrolled or planning to enroll. College will submit nomination/application.

Additional information: Applicant/nominee must have completed 100 hours community service within past 12 months. Minimum 2.5 GPA at time of nomination. Must be planning to enroll in at least two courses during next term. Children of Coca-Cola employees not eligible. Up to two nominations from each campus.

Amount of award:	$1,000
Number of awards:	400
Application deadline:	May 31
Notification begins:	July 15
Total amount awarded:	$400,000

Contact:
Coca-Cola Two-Year Colleges Scholarship Program
P.O. Box 1615
Atlanta, GA 30301-1615
Phone: 800-306-2653
Web: www.coca-colascholars.org

COLAGE (Children of Lesbians and Gays Everywhere) and the Family Pride Coalition

Lee Dubin Scholarship

Type of award: Scholarship, renewable.
Intended use: For undergraduate study at accredited postsecondary institution.
Eligibility: Applicant must have at least one lesbian, gay, bisexual, or transgender parent.
Basis for selection: Applicant must demonstrate financial need, depth of character, leadership and service orientation.
Application requirements: Application, essay, proof of enrollment, grade verification, financial aid information.
Additional information: Students working to combat homophobia and increase positive awareness of LGBT families encouraged to apply. Applicants must maintain a minimum 2.0 GPA. Previous applicants or awardees encouraged to re-apply. Applicants encouraged to be willing to be named publicly in association with Family Pride Coalition, COLAGE and the Lee Dubin Scholarship. Application deadline is the third Friday in April.

Amount of award:	$1,000
Number of awards:	5
Application deadline:	April 16
Total amount awarded:	$5,000

Contact:
COLAGE Scholarship Committee
3543 18th Street, #1
San Francisco, CA 94110
Phone: 415-861-KIDS (5437)
Web: www.colage.org

The College Board/The Robert Wood Johnson Foundation

Young Epidemiology Scholars Student Competition

Type of award: Scholarship.
Intended use: For undergraduate study at 4-year institution in United States.
Eligibility: Applicant must be high school junior or senior. Applicant must be U.S. citizen or permanent resident.
Basis for selection: Major/career interest in epidemiology; sociology; science, general or mathematics.
Application requirements: Essay, proof of eligibility. An individual research project that applies epidemiological principles to health-related area is also required.
Additional information: YES research project should shed light on a health problem, using methods employed by epidemiologists. Deadline in January. See Website for more information.

    Amount of award: $1,000-$50,000
    Number of awards: 120
Contact:
The College Board/Robert Wood Johnson Foundation
YES Program
11911 Freedom Drive, Suite 300
Reston, VA 20190-5602
Phone: 703-707-8999
Fax: 703-707-5599
Web: www.collegeboard.com/yes

College Foundation of North Carolina

North Carolina Jagannathan Scholarships

Type of award: Scholarship, renewable.
Intended use: For full-time undergraduate study at 4-year institution in United States. Designated institutions: Constituent institutions of the University of North Carolina.
Eligibility: Applicant must be high school senior. Applicant must be U.S. citizen or permanent resident residing in North Carolina.
Basis for selection: Applicant must demonstrate financial need, high academic achievement and leadership.
Application requirements: Proof of eligibility, nomination by high school guidance counselor; financial office of UNC institution; Tolaram Polymers, Cookson Fibers or related company. Also send SAT scores, College Scholarship Service's PROFILE (register by January 26; file by February 7), and documented proof of financial need.
Additional information: Special consideration given to students whose parents are employees of Tolaram Polymers, Cookson Fibers and related companies. Application availible at all North Carolina public high schools.

    Amount of award: $3,500
    Number of awards: 4
    Number of applicants: 150
    Application deadline: February 14
    Total amount awarded: $42,000
Contact:
College Foundation of North Carolina
P.O. Box 12100
Raleigh, NC 27605-2100
Phone: 888-234-6400
Web: www.cfnc.org

North Carolina Student Incentive Grant

Type of award: Scholarship, renewable.
Intended use: For full-time undergraduate study at vocational, 2-year or 4-year institution. Designated institutions: Approved institutions in North Carolina.
Eligibility: Applicant must be residing in North Carolina.
Basis for selection: Applicant must demonstrate financial need.

    Amount of award: $700
    Number of awards: 4,820
    Number of applicants: 60,500
    Application deadline: March 15
    Total amount awarded: $2,839,046
Contact:
College Foundation of North Carolina
P.O. Box 12100
Raleigh, NC 27605-2100
Phone: 888-234-6400
Web: www.cfnc.org

Colorado Commission on Higher Education

Colorado Leveraging Education Assistance Program/Supplemental Leaveraging Education Assistance Program

Type of award: Scholarship.
Intended use: For undergraduate study at accredited postsecondary institution. Designated institutions: Eligible postsecondary institutions in Colorado.
Eligibility: Applicant must be residing in Colorado.
Basis for selection: Applicant must demonstrate financial need.
Application requirements: FAFSA.
Additional information: Must demonstrate substantial financial need. Contact college financial aid office for information and application. Maximum award is $5,000. Award is not renewable; student must apply each year.
Contact:
Colorado Commission on Higher Education
1380 Lawrence Street
Suite 1200
Denver, CO 80204
Phone: 303-866-2723
Web: www.state.co.us/cche

Scholarships

193

Colorado Nursing Scholarship

Type of award: Scholarship.
Intended use: For undergraduate or post-bachelor's certificate study at vocational, 2-year or 4-year institution. Designated institutions: Eligible postsecondary institution in Colorado participating in state programs that offer nursing degrees or certificates.
Eligibility: Applicant must be U.S. citizen residing in Colorado.
Basis for selection: Major/career interest in nursing; nurse practitioner or midwifery. Applicant must demonstrate financial need.
Application requirements: FAFSA.
Additional information: Minimum of six credit hours. Must reapply each year. Visit Website for additional information. Student may download application on Website, but applicant's school must approve form and provide information before submission.

Amount of award:	Full tuition
Application deadline:	April 1

Contact:
Colorado Commission on Higher Education
1380 Lawrence Street
Suite 1200
Denver, CO 80204
Phone: 303-866-2723
Web: www.state.co.us/cche

Colorado Student Grant

Type of award: Scholarship.
Intended use: For full-time undergraduate study at postsecondary institution. Designated institutions: Eligible postsecondary institutions in Colorado.
Eligibility: Applicant must be residing in Colorado.
Basis for selection: Applicant must demonstrate financial need.
Application requirements: FAFSA.
Additional information: Contact college financial aid office or visit Website for additional information, deadline and application.

Amount of award:	$5,000

Contact:
Colorado Commission on Higher Education
1380 Lawrence Street
Suite 1200
Denver, CO 80204
Phone: 303-866-2723
Web: www.state.co.us/cche

Colorado Undergraduate Merit Award

Type of award: Scholarship, renewable.
Intended use: For undergraduate study at accredited postsecondary institution. Designated institutions: Eligible postsecondary institutions in Colorado.
Eligibility: Applicant must be residing in Colorado.
Basis for selection: Applicant must demonstrate high academic achievement.
Application requirements: Student must maintain 3.0 GPA to be considered for renewal.
Additional information: Amount of award varies but cannot exceed tuition. Institutions may make awards for academic excellence or special talents, including music and athletics.

Contact college financial aid office for details and application or visit Website for additional information.
Contact:
Colorado Commission on Higher Education
1380 Lawrence Street
Suite 1200
Denver, CO 80204
Phone: 303-866-2723
Web: www.state.co.us/cche

Colorado Work-Study Program

Type of award: Scholarship.
Intended use: For undergraduate study at postsecondary institution. Designated institutions: Designated postsecondary institutions in Colorado.
Eligibility: Applicant must be residing in Colorado.
Basis for selection: Applicant must demonstrate financial need.
Application requirements: Applicant must demonstrate financial need and/or need to work.
Additional information: This is a part-time employment program designed to assist students with financial need or work experience. Amount of award cannot exceed need. Contact college financial aid office or visit Website for additional information. Award is not renewable.
Contact:
Colorado Commission on Higher Education
1380 Lawrence Street
Suite 1200
Denver, CO 80204
Phone: 303-866-2723
Web: www.state.co.us/cche

Colorado Masons Benevolent Fund Association

Colorado Masons Scholarship

Type of award: Scholarship, renewable.
Intended use: For full-time undergraduate study at accredited vocational, 2-year or 4-year institution in United States. Designated institutions: Can only be used at Colorado institutions.
Eligibility: Applicant must be high school senior. Applicant must be residing in Colorado.
Basis for selection: Applicant must demonstrate financial need, high academic achievement and depth of character.
Additional information: Applicant must be a graduating senior at a public high school. Contact high school college counselor for application details. Do not contact the association directly.

Amount of award:	$7,000
Number of awards:	53
Number of applicants:	53
Application deadline:	March 7
Total amount awarded:	$265,000

Contact:
Scholarship Administrator
1130 Panorama Drive
Colorado Springs, CO 80904
Phone: 800-482-4441, ext 29
Fax: 800-440-3520
Web: www.coloradomasons.org

Colorado Society of CPAs Educational Foundation

Colorado CPAs Ethnic-College and University Scholarship

Type of award: Scholarship, renewable.
Intended use: For undergraduate or graduate study at accredited 2-year or 4-year institution in United States. Designated institutions: Colorado colleges and universities with accredited accounting programs.
Eligibility: Applicant must be Asian American, African American, Mexican American, Hispanic American, Puerto Rican or American Indian. Applicant must be U.S. citizen residing in Colorado.
Basis for selection: Major/career interest in accounting. Applicant must demonstrate financial need and high academic achievement.
Application requirements: Transcript, proof of eligibility.
Additional information: Must have completed eight semester hours of accounting courses to be eligible to apply. Minimum 3.0 GPA required. Visit Website to download application.

Amount of award:	$1,000
Number of awards:	2
Application deadline:	June 30, November 30
Total amount awarded:	$2,000

Contact:
Colorado Society of CPAs Educational Foundation
7979 East Tufts Avenue, Suite 500
Denver, CO 80237-2845
Phone: 800-523-9082
Web: www.cocpa.org

Colorado CPAs Gordon Scheer Scholarship

Type of award: Scholarship, renewable.
Intended use: For junior, senior or graduate study at accredited 4-year or graduate institution in United States. Designated institutions: Colorado colleges and universities with accredited accounting programs.
Eligibility: Applicant must be U.S. citizen residing in Colorado.
Basis for selection: Major/career interest in accounting. Applicant must demonstrate high academic achievement.
Application requirements: Interview, recommendations, transcript, proof of eligibility. Letter of reference from accounting faculty member.
Additional information: Minimum 3.5 GPA necessary to qualify. No financial information required. Visit Website to download application.

Amount of award:	$1,250
Number of awards:	1
Application deadline:	June 30
Total amount awarded:	$1,250

Contact:
Colorado Society of CPAs Educational Foundation
7979 East Tufts Avenue, Suite 500
Denver, CO 80237-2843
Phone: 800-523-9082
Web: www.cocpa.org

Colorado Society of CPAs General Scholarship

Type of award: Scholarship, renewable.
Intended use: For junior, senior or graduate study at accredited 4-year or graduate institution in United States. Designated institutions: Colorado colleges and universities with an accredited accounting program.
Eligibility: Applicant must be U.S. citizen residing in Colorado.
Basis for selection: Major/career interest in accounting. Applicant must demonstrate financial need and high academic achievement.
Application requirements: Transcript, proof of eligibility.
Additional information: Must have completed eight semester hours in accounting to be eligible to apply. Minimum 3.0 GPA required. Visit Website to download application.

Amount of award:	$1,000
Number of awards:	12
Application deadline:	June 30, November 30
Total amount awarded:	$12,000

Contact:
Colorado Society of CPAs Educational Foundation
7979 East Tufts Avenue, Suite 500
Denver, CO 80237-2843
Phone: 800-523-9082
Web: www.cocpa.org

Columbus Citizens Foundation, Inc.

Columbus Citizens Foundation College Scholarship Program

Type of award: Scholarship, renewable.
Intended use: For undergraduate study.
Eligibility: Applicant must be high school senior. Applicant must be Italian.
Basis for selection: Applicant's per-capita income must not exceed $20,000. Must exhibit service to community and school, academic excellence, financial need and pride in Italian-American heritage. Applicant must demonstrate financial need, high academic achievement and service orientation.
Application requirements: Interview, recommendations, essay, transcript. 3 letters of recommendation, two from academic source and one from non-academic source. Two essays: one outlining applicant's pride in Italian-American heritage and one about a famous Italian-American.
Additional information: Applicant must be graduating high school seniors and have an average of 80 or higher (on a scale of 100). Award is renewable for up to 4 years of study. Applicants who reach semi-finalist round after review of initial materials must travel to New York City for an interview. Applications availible on the Website beginning in January.

Number of awards:	25
Application deadline:	February 28

Contact:
Columbus Citizens Foundation College Scholarship Program
8 East 69th Street
New York, NY 10021-4906
Phone: 212-249-9923
Fax: 212-737-4413
Web: www.columbuscitizensfd.org

Columbus Citizens Foundation High School Scholarship Program

Type of award: Scholarship, renewable.
Intended use: For undergraduate study.
Eligibility: Applicant must be high school freshman. Applicant must be Italian.
Basis for selection: Applicant must demonstrate financial need, high academic achievement and service orientation.
Application requirements: Interview, recommendations, essay, transcript. 2 letters of recommendation, one from academic source and one from non-academic source. Personal essay outlining applicant's pride in Italian-American heritage.
Additional information: Applicant must be entering high school and have an average of 80 or higher (on a scale of 100). Applicant's income must not exceed $20,000. Must exhibit service to community and school, academic excellence, financial need and pride in Italian-American heritage. Applicants who reach semi-finalist round after review of initial materials must travel to New York City for an interview. Applications availible on the Website beginning in January.

    Number of awards: 25
    Application deadline: March 1
Contact:
Columbus Citizens Foundation High School Scholarship Program
8 East 69th Street
New York, NY 10021-4906
Phone: 212-249-9923
Fax: 212-737-4413
Web: www.columbuscitizensfd.org

Cone Mills Corporation

Cone Mills Scholarship Program

Type of award: Scholarship, renewable.
Intended use: For full-time undergraduate study at accredited vocational, 2-year or 4-year institution in United States.
Eligibility: Applicant or parent must be employed by Cone Mills Corporation. Applicant must be high school senior. Applicant must be U.S. citizen.
Basis for selection: Applicant must demonstrate high academic achievement.
Application requirements: Essay, transcript, proof of eligibility. CSS PROFILE application required.

    Amount of award: $500-$2,500
    Number of awards: 8
    Number of applicants: 24
    Application deadline: February 28
    Notification begins: April 30
    Total amount awarded: $56,000
Contact:
Cone Mills Corporation
Scholarship Program
804 Green Valley Road
Greensboro, NC 27408
Phone: 910-379-6252
Fax: 910-379-6930

Congressional Black Caucus Foundation, Inc.

Congressional Black Caucus Foundation Spouses Scholarship

Type of award: Scholarship, renewable.
Intended use: For full-time undergraduate or graduate study at accredited 4-year institution.
Eligibility: Applicant must be U.S. citizen or permanent resident residing in Ohio, New York, Louisiana, Virginia, California, Mississippi, Illinois, Missouri, Michigan, Texas, Maryland, Pennsylvania, Georgia, Florida, South Carolina, District of Columbia, Virgin Islands, Indiana, New Jersey or North Carolina.
Basis for selection: Applicant must demonstrate financial need.
Application requirements: Transcript. Minimum 2.5 GPA. Applicant must reside or attend school in Congressional Black Caucus member's district.
Additional information: Must reside or attend school in congressional district represented by Black Caucus member. Selection made at district level. List of eligible districts and members' addresses provided by national office. Award amounts vary. Employees or relatives of CBC members, CBC Spouses, CBCF and/or General Mills are not eligible for this program. To obtain local contact information, see Website or e-mail spouses@cbcfonline.org. Contact the Congressional Black Caucus member representing the district of the school that the applicant attends or his/her place of residence.

    Application deadline: May 15, September 15
Contact:
Phone: 202-263-2800
Fax: 202-775-0773
Web: www.cbcfonline.org

Congressional Hispanic Caucus Institute

CHCI Scholarship Award

Type of award: Scholarship.
Intended use: For full-time undergraduate or graduate study at accredited 2-year, 4-year or graduate institution in United States.
Eligibility: Applicant must be Mexican American, Hispanic American or Puerto Rican. Applicant must be U.S. citizen or permanent resident.
Basis for selection: Applicant must demonstrate financial need, depth of character, leadership and service orientation.
Application requirements: Recommendations, essay, transcript, proof of eligibility. Applicant must submit completed

application, resume, responses to three essays, current tax return, SAR, current official transcript and three letters of recommendation.
Additional information: Student must be of Latin American descent.

Amount of award:	$2,000-$5,000
Number of awards:	40
Number of applicants:	40
Application deadline:	April 15
Total amount awarded:	$155,000

Contact:
Congressional Hispanic Caucus Institute
504 C Street, NE
Washington, DC 20002
Phone: 202-543-1771
Fax: 202-546-2143
Web: www.chciyouth.org

Congressional Hispanic Caucus Institute Scholarship Awards

Type of award: Scholarship.
Intended use: For undergraduate or graduate study at postsecondary institution.
Eligibility: Applicant must be Mexican American or Hispanic American.
Basis for selection: Demonstrated history of service to community. Applicant must demonstrate leadership and service orientation.
Additional information: No GPA requirement. Students attending community college receive $1,000; those attending four-year or graduate/professional schools receive $2,500.

Amount of award:	$1,000-$2,500
Application deadline:	April 15

Contact:
Congressional Hispanic Caucus Institute
911 2nd Street NE
Washington, DC 20002
Phone: 202-543-1771
Fax: 202-546-2143
Web: www.chciyouth.org

Connecticut Building Congress Scholarship Fund

Connecticut Building Congress Scholarship

Type of award: Scholarship, renewable.
Intended use: For undergraduate or graduate study at 2-year or 4-year institution in United States.
Eligibility: Applicant must be residing in Connecticut.
Basis for selection: Major/career interest in engineering, construction; architecture or construction management. Applicant must demonstrate financial need and high academic achievement.
Application requirements: Interview, recommendations, essay, transcript. Application. Student Aid Report.
Additional information: Applicant must be Connecticut resident but may attend school outside of state. Finalists notified in June; they will meet with a panel of judges for interviews in July.

Amount of award:	$500-$2,000
Number of awards:	5
Number of applicants:	85
Application deadline:	March 15, June 1
Total amount awarded:	$10,000

Contact:
Connecticut Building Congress Scholarship Fund
2600 Dixwell Avenue, Suite 7
Hamden, CT 06514
Phone: 203-281-3183
Fax: 203-248-8932
Web: www.cbc-ct.org

Connecticut Department of Higher Education

Connecticut Aid for Public College Students

Type of award: Scholarship, renewable.
Intended use: For undergraduate study. Designated institutions: Public institutions in Connecticut.
Eligibility: Applicant must be U.S. citizen residing in Connecticut.
Basis for selection: Applicant must demonstrate financial need.
Additional information: Awards up to amount of unmet financial need. Apply at financial aid office at Connecticut public college.

Amount of award:	$400-$6,000
Number of awards:	11,000
Total amount awarded:	$19,759,261

Contact:
Contact school's financial aid office.

Connecticut Aid to Dependents of Deceased/Disabled/MIA Veterans

Type of award: Scholarship.
Intended use: For undergraduate or graduate study.
Eligibility: Applicant must be U.S. citizen residing in Connecticut. Applicant must be dependent of disabled veteran, deceased veteran or POW/MIA; or spouse of disabled veteran, deceased veteran or POW/MIA. Death or disability must be service related.
Basis for selection: Applicant must demonstrate financial need.
Application requirements: Proof of eligibility.
Additional information: Parent/spouse must have been Connecticut resident prior to enlistment.

Amount of award:	$400
Number of awards:	6
Number of applicants:	6
Total amount awarded:	$2,400

Contact:
Connecticut Department of Higher Education
61 Woodland Street
Hartford, CT 06105-2391
Phone: 860-947-1855
Fax: 860-947-1311

Connecticut Capitol Scholarship Program

Type of award: Scholarship, renewable.
Intended use: For undergraduate study.
Eligibility: Applicant must be high school senior. Applicant must be U.S. citizen or permanent resident residing in Connecticut.
Basis for selection: Applicant must demonstrate financial need and high academic achievement.
Additional information: Must rank in top fifth of class or have SAT score of at least 1200. May be used at institutions in Connecticut or at institutions that have reciprocity agreements with Connecticut.

Amount of award:	$2,000
Number of awards:	4,500
Number of applicants:	7,500
Application deadline:	February 15
Notification begins:	June 30
Total amount awarded:	$5,500,000

Contact:
High school guidance office for application
Phone: 860-947-1855
Fax: 860-947-1311
Web: www.ctdhe.commnet.edu

Connecticut Independent College Student Grant

Type of award: Scholarship, renewable.
Intended use: For undergraduate study at 4-year institution in United States. Designated institutions: Private institutions in Connecticut.
Eligibility: Applicant must be U.S. citizen residing in Connecticut.
Basis for selection: Applicant must demonstrate financial need.
Additional information: Applications can be obtained at college financial aid office.

Amount of award:	$8,000
Number of awards:	4,500
Total amount awarded:	$18,776,929

Contact:
Contact school's financial office.

Connecticut Minority Incentive Grant

Type of award: Scholarship.
Intended use: For junior or senior study. Designated institutions: Connecticut college or university teacher preparation program.
Eligibility: Applicant must be residing in Connecticut.
Basis for selection: Based on nomination. Major/career interest in education.
Application requirements: Nomination.
Additional information: Award for minority juniors or seniors enrolled in Connecticut college or university teacher preparation program. Grants up to $5000/year for two years; loan reimbursement of $2500/year for up to four years of teaching in Connecticut public school. Visit Website for more information or contact education dean at Connecticut colleges and universities that offer teacher preparation programs by October 23.

Amount of award:	$2,500-$5,000
Application deadline:	October 23

Contact:
Education Dean at CT colleges with teacher preparation programs
Phone: 800-842-0229
Fax: 860-947-1810
Web: www.ctdhe.org

Connecticut Robert C. Byrd Honors Scholarship

Type of award: Scholarship, renewable.
Intended use: For freshman, sophomore, junior or senior study.
Eligibility: Applicant must be high school senior. Applicant must be U.S. citizen residing in Connecticut.
Basis for selection: Applicant must demonstrate high academic achievement.
Additional information: Must rank in top two percent of high school graduating class.

Amount of award:	$1,500
Number of awards:	206
Number of applicants:	700
Total amount awarded:	$478,000

Contact:
Connecticut Department of Higher Education
61 Woodland Street
Hartford, CT 06105-2391
Phone: 860-947-1855
Fax: 860-947-1311
Web: www.ctdhe.commnet.edu

Connecticut Tuition Set Aside Aid

Type of award: Scholarship, renewable.
Intended use: For undergraduate study at 2-year or 4-year institution in United States. Designated institutions: Public institutions in Connecticut.
Eligibility: Applicant must be U.S. citizen residing in Connecticut.
Basis for selection: Applicant must demonstrate financial need.
Additional information: Awards up to unmet financial need. Apply at financial aid office of institution. Scholarship awarded through Connecticut public colleges.
Contact:
Financial aid office of Connecticut public colleges

Connecticut Tuition Waiver for Senior Citizens

Type of award: Scholarship.
Intended use: For undergraduate study at 2-year institution. Designated institutions: Public two-year intitutions in Connecticut.
Eligibility: Applicant must be returning adult student. Applicant must be U.S. citizen residing in Connecticut.
Application requirements: Proof of eligibility.
Additional information: Waivers approved on space available basis. Apply through financial aid office of institution.

Amount of award:	Full tuition

Contact:
Financial aid office of Connecticut public colleges.

Connecticut Tuition Waiver for Veterans

Type of award: Scholarship, renewable.

Intended use: For undergraduate study. Designated institutions: Connecticut public institution.
Eligibility: Applicant must be U.S. citizen residing in Connecticut. Applicant must be veteran. Must have served during time of conflict.
Application requirements: Proof of eligibility.
Additional information: Must have been Connecticut resident at time of enlistment.

Amount of award:	Full tuition

Contact:
Financial aid office of Connecticut public colleges.

Connecticut Tuition Waiver for Vietnam MIA/POW Dependents

Type of award: Scholarship.
Intended use: For undergraduate study. Designated institutions: Connecticut public institutions.
Eligibility: Applicant must be U.S. citizen residing in Connecticut. Applicant must be dependent of POW/MIA; or spouse of POW/MIA during Vietnam.
Application requirements: Proof of eligibility.
Additional information: Apply at financial aid office of institution. Awarded through Connecticut public colleges.
Contact:
Connecticut public colleges.

Connecticut League for Nursing

Connecticut Nursing Scholarship

Type of award: Scholarship.
Intended use: For senior or graduate study at accredited postsecondary institution. Designated institutions: Connecticut nursing school accredited by National League of Nursing.
Eligibility: Applicant must be U.S. citizen residing in Connecticut.
Basis for selection: Major/career interest in nursing. Applicant must demonstrate financial need, high academic achievement, leadership and seriousness of purpose.
Application requirements: Recommendations, essay, transcript, proof of eligibility.
Additional information: One undergraduate and one graduate award given. Applicants must have 20 credit hours in nursing courses to be eligible for graduate scholarship; undergraduates must have completed one year of two-year program or three years of four-year program; RN students must be entering senior year in upper-division BSN program. Awardees notified in late November.

Amount of award:	$1,000
Number of awards:	2
Number of applicants:	15
Application deadline:	October 15
Total amount awarded:	$2,000

Contact:
Connecticut League for Nursing
P.O. Box 365
Wallingford, CT 06492
Phone: 203-265-4248

Consortium of Information and Telecommunication Executives, Inc.

CITE-NY Association Scholarship

Type of award: Scholarship.
Intended use: For undergraduate study in United States.
Eligibility: Applicant must be African American. Applicant must be high school senior. Applicant must be U.S. citizen or permanent resident residing in New York.
Basis for selection: Major/career interest in business; computer/information sciences; engineering or communications. Applicant must demonstrate financial need, high academic achievement, depth of character, leadership and service orientation.
Application requirements: Recommendations, essay, transcript, proof of eligibility.
Additional information: Recipient must be a New York State resident and must attend local CITE Scholarship awards dinner to accept award.

Amount of award:	$1,500
Number of awards:	2
Application deadline:	April 30
Notification begins:	July 7
Total amount awarded:	$3,000

Contact:
Verizon
230 West 36th Street
New York, NY 10018
Phone: 212-643-2522
Web: citeny.org

Four-Year Scholarship

Type of award: Scholarship.
Intended use: For undergraduate study.
Eligibility: Applicant must be African American. Applicant must be high school senior. Applicant must be U.S. citizen.
Basis for selection: Applicant must demonstrate financial need and high academic achievement.
Application requirements: Recommendations, essay, transcript, proof of eligibility. 3.0 GPA.
Additional information: Applicant's total family income must not exceed $60,000. An immediate family member or anyone who has legal/permanent residence in the household of any employee of the Verizon Corporation or an affiliated subsidary is ineligible for this scholarship. In order to receive the award, recipient must agree to attend CITE's annual conference in its entirety. (CITE will pay conference, travel, lodging, and most board expenses for recipient.)

Amount of award:	$2,000
Application deadline:	April 12
Notification begins:	May 20

Contact:
Verizon
230 West 36th Street
New York, NY 10018
Phone: 212-643-2522
Web: citeny.org

Scholarships

Corporate Express

Corporate Express Scholarship

Type of award: Scholarship.
Intended use: For full-time undergraduate study at accredited vocational, 2-year or 4-year institution.
Eligibility: Applicant or parent must be employed by Corporate Express. Applicant must be no older than 24.
Basis for selection: Applicant must be a child of a full-time Express employee. Applicant must demonstrate high academic achievement and leadership.
Application requirements: Recommendations, essay, transcript, proof of eligibility. Must be 24 years old or younger at time of deadline. Statement of educational and career goals, work experience and community activities.
Additional information: Must be child or ward of full-time employee of Corporate Express who has worked for company for over one year at time of application. For further information or an application, contact Corporate Express Scholarship Program directly.

Amount of award:	$3,000
Number of awards:	45
Number of applicants:	50
Application deadline:	March 15
Total amount awarded:	$135,000

Contact:
Corporate Express Scholarship Program
Scholarship Management Services, CSFA
1505 Riverview Road, P.O. Box 297
St. Peter, MN 56082
Phone: 507-931-1682

Corporation for National and Community Service

Presidential Freedom Scholarship

Type of award: Scholarship.
Intended use: For freshman study at accredited 2-year or 4-year institution in United States.
Eligibility: Applicant must be high school junior or senior. Applicant must be U.S. citizen or permanent resident.
Basis for selection: Based on record of community service. Must have 100 hours of community service for 12 months prior to applying. Applicant must demonstrate service orientation.
Application requirements: Nomination by high school. Student should have performed outstanding service in his/her community.
Additional information: Each high school in United States may select two students who have performed outstanding service to their community. High school must secure $500 from the community to match the $500 the corporation provides.

Amount of award:	$1,000
Number of awards:	10,000
Application deadline:	July 2, June 30
Notification begins:	June 1, August 1
Total amount awarded:	$10,000,000

Contact:
Presidential Freedom Scholarship
1150 Connecticut Avenue, N.W.
Suite 1100
Washington, DC 20036
Phone: 866-291-7700 (toll-free)
Fax: 202-742-5393
Web: www.nationalservice.org/scholarships/

Costume Society of America

Adele Filene Travel Award

Type of award: Scholarship.
Intended use: For undergraduate study at 2-year or 4-year institution in United States.
Basis for selection: Major/career interest in ethnic/cultural studies; art/art history; arts, general or history.
Application requirements: Recommendations, essay. References and abstract of paper or poster presentation.
Additional information: Open to international students and US citizens. Must be a member of Costume Society of America. Award assists students' travel expenses to Costume Society of America National symposium to present juried paper or poster.

Amount of award:	$500
Number of awards:	3
Application deadline:	March 1

Contact:
Costume Society of America
PO Box 73
Earlesville, MD 21919-0073
Phone: 410-275-1619
Fax: 410-275-8936
Web: www.costumesocietyamerica.com

Stella Blum Research Grant

Type of award: Research grant.
Intended use: For undergraduate study at vocational, 2-year or 4-year institution in United States.
Basis for selection: Major/career interest in art/art history; arts, general; history; museum studies or performing arts.
Application requirements: Recommendations, transcript. Must submit application, references and written proposal researching North American costumes.
Additional information: Open to international students as well as U.S. Citizens. Must be a member of Costume Society of America researching a North American costume topic as part of a degree requirement.

Amount of award:	$3,000
Number of awards:	1
Application deadline:	May 1
Total amount awarded:	$3,000

Contact:
Costume Society of America
PO Box 73
Earleville, MD 21919
Phone: 410-275-1619
Fax: 410-275-8936
Web: www.costumesocietyamerica.com

Council on International Educational Exchange

Bowman Travel Grants

Type of award: Scholarship.
Intended use: For full-time undergraduate study at accredited 4-year institution in Africa, Asia, Latin America, the Middle East, and select European countries.
Eligibility: Applicant must be enrolled in high school. Applicant must be U.S. citizen or permanent resident.
Basis for selection: Applicant must demonstrate financial need, depth of character, seriousness of purpose and service orientation.
Application requirements: Recommendations, essay, transcript, proof of eligibility. Financial aid information.
Additional information: Grant provides voucher for round trip tickets to non-traditional study destinations. Applicant must be an undergraduate participating in study, work, or volunteer program in Council ISP Centers or institutions that are Official International Student Identity Card (ISIC), issuing offices in approved countries, or must be enrolled at a Council Member Institution or Official ISIC issuing office in U.S. Students with limited education abroad experience encouraged to apply. High school students also eligible. Award amounts vary. Application available on Website.

Number of awards:	18
Application deadline:	March 15, October 15
Notification begins:	April 15, November 15

Contact:
Council-International Educational Exchange
Bowman Travel Grant Committee
633 Third Ave., 20th Floor
New York, NY 10017
Phone: 800-40-STUDY ext. 2756
Web: www.ciee.org/STEP

Department of Education Scholarship for Programs in China

Type of award: Scholarship.
Intended use: For junior, senior, master's, doctoral or postgraduate study at 4-year or graduate institution in China. Designated institutions: Council on International Educational Exchange Study Centers at Peking University or Nanjing University.
Eligibility: Applicant must be U.S. citizen or permanent resident.
Basis for selection: Competition/talent/interest in study abroad. Major/career interest in foreign languages; education or asian studies. Applicant must demonstrate financial need and seriousness of purpose.
Application requirements: Transcript, proof of eligibility. Applicant must submit essay outlining his or her interest in Chinese studies. Minimum of 100 words.
Additional information: Must have two years college-level mandarin Chinese and intend to teach language or area studies. Additional fields of study include ethnic and cultural studies, asian studies, Chinese language and literature. Upon return from China, program participants should submit an essay of 250-500 words reflecting on their experiences. Application available on Website.

Amount of award:	$500-$4,000
Application deadline:	April 15, November 15

Contact:
Council-International Study Progams
Attn: Daniel Olds, Program Officer - Asia
205 E. 42nd Street
New York, NY 10017
Phone: 800-40-STUDY ext 2756
Web: www.ciee.org/isp

International Study Programs (ISP) Scholarship

Type of award: Scholarship.
Intended use: For full-time undergraduate or graduate study at accredited 4-year or graduate institution. Designated institutions: Applicants must be from Academic Consortium member institutions (a complete list of member institutions is on Website).
Basis for selection: Applicant must demonstrate financial need, high academic achievement, depth of character and seriousness of purpose.
Application requirements: Recommendations, essay, transcript, proof of eligibility. Copy of FAFSA Student Aid Report or CSS/Financial Aid Profile and all other required financial aid information, additional photocopy of all materials.
Additional information: Available to Council Study Center applicants only. Applicants must be from Academic Consortium member institutions. Visit Website for list of member institutions. Applicants should demonstrate preparation for program through course work, volunteer work, or internships. The same application package may be used for the Bailey and ISP scholarship. Application available on Website.

Amount of award:	$500-$1,000
Number of awards:	42
Application deadline:	March 15, November 1
Notification begins:	April 15, December 15

Contact:
Council-International Study Programs
Scholarship Committee
633 Third Ave., 20th Floor
New York, NY 10017
Phone: 800-40-STUDY ext. 2756
Web: www.ciee.org/isp

Robert B. Bailey III Minority Scholarship

Type of award: Scholarship.
Intended use: For full-time undergraduate or graduate study at 2-year or 4-year institution. Designated institutions: Council-ISP Africa, Asia, Australia/New Zealand, Europe, Latin America, and Middle East study centers.
Eligibility: Applicant must be U.S. citizen.
Basis for selection: Major/career interest in international studies. Applicant must demonstrate financial need.
Application requirements: Recommendations, essay. Copy of FAFSA Student Aid Report or CSS/Financial Aid Profile and all other required financial aid. Must be self-identified member of under-represented group in study abroad.
Additional information: Open to Council Study Center (CSC) applicants only. Applicants should demonstrate preparation for program through course work, volunteer work or internships. Same application package may be used for Bailey and ISP scholarships. Visit Website for details and application.

Amount of award:	$500
Application deadline:	March 15, October 15

Contact:
Council-International Study Progams
Attn: Scholarship Coordinator
633 Third Avenue, 20th Floor
New York, NY 10017
Phone: 800-40-STUDY ext. 2756
Web: www.ciee.org/isp

Courage Center Vocational Services-United Way Organization

Scholarship for People with Disabilities

Type of award: Scholarship.
Intended use: For undergraduate study at accredited vocational, 2-year or 4-year institution.
Eligibility: Applicant must be visually impaired, hearing impaired or physically challenged. Applicant must be U.S. citizen residing in Minnesota.
Basis for selection: Applicant must demonstrate financial need, depth of character, leadership and seriousness of purpose.
Application requirements: Interview, essay, proof of eligibility.
Additional information: If not a Minnesota resident, student must be U.S. citizen who participated in Courage Center services. Student must have a sensory impairment or physical disability. Selection emphasis is placed on the applicant's intentions and achievements.

Amount of award:	$500-$1,000
Number of awards:	14
Number of applicants:	16
Application deadline:	May 31
Total amount awarded:	$12,500

Contact:
Courage Center (United Way Organization) Vocational Services Dept.
Leanne Jackson-Butala
3915 Golden Valley Rd.
Golden Valley, MN 55422-4298
Phone: 763-520-0507
Fax: 763-520-0577
Web: www.courage.org

Course Technology

Help Desk Scholarship

Type of award: Scholarship.
Intended use: For undergraduate study at vocational, 2-year or 4-year institution in United States. Designated institutions: Public or private colleges, universities, or career schools.
Eligibility: Applicant must be U.S. citizen.
Basis for selection: Major/career interest in information systems or computer/information sciences. Applicant must demonstrate seriousness of purpose.
Application requirements: Essay. Application. Essay should be one to two pages in length and address one of the following topics: (1) Describe a Help Desk internship that you've recently

held and how it will help you land a job in the Help Desk industry; (2) Identify the ways in which you can contribute to the Help Desk field.
Additional information: Applicant must be enrolled in a Help Desk course of study at the time of entry and intend to persue a career in the Help Desk industry. Winner will be selected based on thoughtfulness of essay. Application available on Website.

Amount of award:	$1,000
Number of awards:	1
Application deadline:	May 17
Notification begins:	May 30
Total amount awarded:	$1,000

Contact:
Course Technology
c/o A Angie Laughlin
25 Thomson Place
Boston, MA 02210
Phone: 800-648-7450 ext. 8299
Web: www.course.com/helpdesk/scholarship.cfm

Cymdeithas Gymreig/ Philadelphia

Cymdeithas Gymreig (Welsh Society) Philadelphia Scholarship

Type of award: Scholarship.
Intended use: For full-time freshman, sophomore or junior study at accredited 2-year or 4-year institution in United States. Designated institutions: Must attend institutions in Delaware, Maryland, New Jersey or Pennsylvania.
Eligibility: Applicant must be Welsh. Applicant must be residing in Delaware, New Jersey, Maryland or Pennsylvania.
Basis for selection: Applicant must demonstrate high academic achievement, leadership, seriousness of purpose and service orientation.
Application requirements: Recommendations, essay, transcript, proof of eligibility. Proof of Welsh descent. Proof of participation in Welsh activities. SASE is required or sponsor will not respond.
Additional information: Applicant or parent must be member of or be active in Welsh organization, church, or activities. If inquiry does not have proof of Welsh descent and evidence of participation in Welsh activities, sponsor will not reply. Applicant may study in Wales if primary residence is within 150 miles of Philadelphia. Must rank in top third of class. Five to seven awards totalling $5,000 to $7,000 are given anually.

Amount of award:	$500-$1,000
Number of awards:	5
Number of applicants:	300
Application deadline:	March 1
Notification begins:	June 1
Total amount awarded:	$5,000

Contact:
Cymdeithas Gymreig/Philadelphia
Hen Dy Hapus 367 South River Street
Wilkes-Barre, PA 18702
Phone: 570-822-4871

Cystic Fibrosis Foundation

Cystic Fibrosis Student Traineeship

Type of award: Research grant, renewable.
Intended use: For full-time senior, master's or doctoral study at accredited 4-year or graduate institution in United States.
Basis for selection: Major/career interest in medical specialties/research.
Application requirements: Recommendations, research proposal.
Additional information: Trainees must work with faculty sponsor on research project related to cystic fibrosis. Applications accepted throughout the year, but should be submitted at least two months prior to projected start date of project.

Amount of award:	$1,500

Contact:
Cystic Fibrosis Foundation
Office of Grants Management
6931 Arlington Road
Bethesda, MD 20814
Phone: 301-951-4422
Fax: 301-907-2563

Dairy Management, Inc.

Dairy Product Marketing Scholarship

Type of award: Scholarship, renewable.
Intended use: For full-time sophomore, junior or senior study at accredited 4-year institution.
Eligibility: Applicant must be U.S. citizen.
Basis for selection: Major/career interest in advertising; marketing; food production/management/services or food science/technology. Applicant must demonstrate high academic achievement, leadership and seriousness of purpose.
Application requirements: Recommendations, transcript. Student must have commitment to career in dairy.
Additional information: Applications available through Food Science Department Chairperson or financial aid officer of applicant's institution as well as online at Website listed below. Nineteen recipients receive $1500 and one recipient receives $2500.

Amount of award:	$1,500-$2,500
Number of awards:	20
Number of applicants:	30
Application deadline:	May 30
Notification begins:	July 30
Total amount awarded:	$7,500

Contact:
Dairy Management Inc.
10255 West Higgins Road
Suite 900
Rosemont, IL 60018
Web: www.dairyshrine.org

Dairy Management, Inc., and the National Dairy Shrine

NDS/DMI Milk Marketing Scholarship

Type of award: Scholarship, renewable.
Intended use: For full-time sophomore, junior or senior study at 4-year institution.
Basis for selection: Major/career interest in dairy; marketing; food production/management/services; food science/technology; agricultural education; agricultural economics or animal sciences. Applicant must demonstrate high academic achievement.
Application requirements: Proof of eligibility. Two letters of recommendation required: one must be from faculty member in applicant's major department.
Additional information: Applications available through Food Science Department Chairperson or financial aid officer of applicant's institution as well as online at Website. Must have commitment to career in dairy-food related disciplines. Top-rated applicant will receive $1,500 and six other winners receive $1,000 each.

Amount of award:	$1,000-$1,500
Number of applicants:	25
Application deadline:	March 15
Total amount awarded:	$7,500

Contact:
National Dairy Shrine
1224 Alton Darby Creek Road
Columbus, OH 43228-9792
Web: www.dairyshrine.org

The Dallas Foundation

The Dallas Foundation Scholarship Funds

Type of award: Scholarship.
Intended use: For full-time undergraduate study at accredited 2-year or 4-year institution in United States. Designated institutions: Accredited colleges or universities in Dallas, Texas.
Eligibility: Applicant must be U.S. citizen or permanent resident residing in Texas.
Basis for selection: Major/career interest in athletic training; architecture; engineering or religion/theology. Applicant must demonstrate seriousness of purpose.
Application requirements: Recommendations, transcript, proof of eligibility. In some cases, applicant must be nominated by dean.
Additional information: Foundation offers a number of scholarship funds, each with a different purpose and eligibility requirements. Deadlines vary. Visit Website for program profiles and application.

Amount of award:	$250-$8,000
Application deadline:	March 28, April 15

Contact:
The Dallas Foundation Attn: Cathy Barker
900 Jackson Street
Suite 150
Dallas, TX 75202
Phone: 214-741-9898
Web: www.dallasfoundation.org

Harrell & Hamilton Architectural Scholarship Fund

Type of award: Scholarship.
Intended use: For undergraduate study at 4-year institution in United States. Designated institutions: Participating schools.
Eligibility: Applicant must be U.S. citizen residing in Texas.
Basis for selection: Major/career interest in architecture.
Additional information: Scholarship award rotates annually among the eight accredited Texas architecture schools.
   Amount of award: $2,500
   Application deadline: March 28
Contact:
Dallas Architectural Foundation
1444 Oak Lawn Avenue
Suite 600
Dallas, TX 75207
Phone: 214-741-9898
Web: www.dallasfoundation.org

HKS/John Humphries Minority Scholarship

Type of award: Scholarship.
Intended use: For undergraduate study at 4-year institution in or outside United States.
Eligibility: Applicant must be Alaskan native, Asian American, African American, Mexican American, Hispanic American, Puerto Rican or American Indian. Applicant must be U.S. citizen or permanent resident residing in Texas.
Basis for selection: Major/career interest in architecture.
Additional information: Applicant must be between 17 and 25, and a resident of Dallas County for at least one year at time of application.
   Amount of award: Full tuition
   Application deadline: March 28
Contact:
The Dallas Architectural Foundation
1444 Oak Lawn Avenue
Suite 600
Dallas, TX 75207
Phone: 214-742-3242
Web: www.dallasfoundation.org

Wendy Ella Guiford Scholarship Fund

Type of award: Scholarship, renewable.
Intended use: For undergraduate study at 4-year institution.
Eligibility: Applicant must be high school senior. Applicant must be U.S. citizen or permanent resident residing in Texas.
Basis for selection: Major/career interest in architecture.
Application requirements: Interview. Applicants must be available for personal interviews with scholarship committee if requested.
Additional information: Must be a resident of Dallas-Fort Worth area.
   Amount of award: $2,000
   Application deadline: April 3

Contact:
Wendy Ella Guilford Scholarship Foundation
8300 Horseshoe Bend
Fort Worth, TX 76131
Phone: 214-741-9898
Web: www.dallasfoundation.org

Datatel Scholars Foundation

Angelfire Scholarship

Type of award: Scholarship.
Intended use: For undergraduate, graduate or non-degree study at accredited postsecondary institution. Designated institutions: Datatel client college/university.
Eligibility: Applicant must be Vietnam veteran, spouse or child of Vietnam veteran, or refugee from Cambodia, Laos, or Vietnam during 1964-1975 time frame.
Basis for selection: Applicant evaluated on following scale: 40% Personal Essay; 30% Academic Merit; 20% Achievements; 10% Letter of Recommendation. Applicant must demonstrate high academic achievement, depth of character and seriousness of purpose.
Application requirements: Recommendations, essay, transcript, proof of eligibility, nomination by Datatel client institution.
Additional information: Deadline to request application is January 31. Visit Website to apply and for list of eligible institutions.
   Amount of award: $700-$2,000
   Application deadline: January 31
   Notification begins: May 1
Contact:
Datatel Scholars Foundation
4375 Fair Lakes Court
Fairfax, VA 22033
Phone: 800-486-4332
Fax: 703-968-4625
Web: www.datatel.com

Datatel Scholars Foundation Scholarship

Type of award: Scholarship.
Intended use: For undergraduate, graduate or non-degree study at accredited postsecondary institution. Designated institutions: Datatel client college/university.
Basis for selection: Applicants evaluated on following scale: 40% Quality of Essay Statement; 30% Academic Merit; 20% Achievements; 10% Letters of Recommendation. Major/career interest in humanities/liberal arts. Applicant must demonstrate high academic achievement, depth of character and seriousness of purpose.
Application requirements: Recommendations, essay, transcript, proof of eligibility, nomination by Datatel client institution.
Additional information: When requesting application, include institution name for determination of qualification. Visit Website to apply. Application request deadline is January 31.
   Amount of award: $700-$2,000
   Application deadline: January 31
   Notification begins: May 1

Contact:
Datatel Scholars Foundation
4375 Fair Lakes Court
Fairfax, VA 22033
Phone: 800-486-4332
Fax: 703-968-4625
Web: www.datatel.com

Nancy Goodhue Lynch Scholarship

Type of award: Scholarship.
Intended use: For undergraduate, graduate or non-degree study at accredited postsecondary institution. Designated institutions: Datatel client college/university.
Basis for selection: Applicants evaluated on following scale: 40% Personal Essay; 30% Academic Merit; 20% Achievements; 10% Letters of Recommendation. Major/career interest in computer/information sciences; engineering, computer; engineering, electrical/electronic; information systems; electronics; computer graphics or robotics. Applicant must demonstrate high academic achievement, depth of character and seriousness of purpose.
Application requirements: Recommendations, essay, transcript, proof of eligibility, nomination by Datatel client institution.
Additional information: Scholarship for student enrolled in technology-related degree program. Apply on Website. Deadline to request application is January 31. Visit sponsor website for list of eligible institutions.

Amount of award:	$5,000
Number of awards:	1
Application deadline:	January 31
Notification begins:	May 1
Total amount awarded:	$5,000

Contact:
Datatel Scholars Foundation
4375 Fair Lakes Court
Fairfax, VA 22033
Phone: 800-486-4322
Fax: 703-968-4625
Web: www.datatel.com

Returning Student Scholarship

Type of award: Scholarship.
Intended use: For undergraduate, graduate or non-degree study at accredited postsecondary institution. Designated institutions: Datatel client college/university.
Eligibility: Applicant must be returning adult student.
Basis for selection: Applicants evaluated on following scale: 40% Personal Essay; 30% Academic Merit; 20% Achievements; 10% Letters of Recommendation.
Application requirements: Recommendations, essay, transcript, proof of eligibility, nomination by Datatel client institution.
Additional information: Intended for any student returning to school after a five-year absence or more. Deadline to request application is January 31. Visit Website to apply and for a list of eligible institutions.

Amount of award:	$1,000
Number of awards:	50
Application deadline:	January 31
Notification begins:	May 1
Total amount awarded:	$50,000

Contact:
Datatel Scholars Foundation
4375 Fair Lakes Court
Fairfax, VA 22033
Phone: 800-486-4322
Fax: 703-968-4625
Web: www.datatel.com

Daughters of Penelope

Alexandra A. Sonenfeld Award

Type of award: Scholarship.
Intended use: For undergraduate study at accredited vocational, 2-year or 4-year institution in United States.
Eligibility: Applicant or parent must be member/participant of Daughters of Penelope. Applicant must be female. Applicant must be Greek. Applicant must be U.S. citizen, permanent resident, international student or Canadian citizen.
Basis for selection: Applicant must demonstrate financial need and high academic achievement.
Application requirements: Recommendations, essay, transcript, proof of eligibility. Also include parents' IRS forms, federal aid forms, and SAT or ACT scores.
Additional information: Applicant must be a high school senior or recent graduate and have member of immediate family or legal guardian (court appointed) in the Daughters of Penelope, Order of AHEPA, or Maids of Athena and in good standing for at least two years. Applicant must not be a past recipient of any undergraduate award from the Daughters of Penelope National Scholarship program.

Amount of award:	$1,500
Number of awards:	1
Application deadline:	June 1
Total amount awarded:	$1,500

Contact:
Daughters of Penelope
1909 Q Street, NW
Suite 500
Washington, DC 20009
Phone: 202-234-9741
Fax: 202-483-6983

Daughters of Penelope Past Grand Presidents' Award

Type of award: Scholarship.
Intended use: For freshman study at vocational, 2-year or 4-year institution.
Eligibility: Applicant or parent must be member/participant of Daughters of Penelope. Applicant must be female. Applicant must be Greek. Applicant must be U.S. citizen, permanent resident, international student or Canadian citizen.
Basis for selection: Applicant must demonstrate financial need and high academic achievement.
Application requirements: Recommendations, essay, transcript, proof of eligibility. Include SAT/ACT scores, copy of parents' IRS forms, federal aid forms.
Additional information: Applicant must be high school senior or recent graduate and have member of immediate family or legal guardian (court appointed) in the Daughters of Penelope, Order of AHEPA, or Maids of Athena in good standing for minimum of two years. Applicant must not be a

past recipient of any undergraduate award from the Daughters of Penelope National Scholarship program.

- **Amount of award:** $1,500
- **Number of awards:** 1
- **Application deadline:** June 1

Contact:
Daughters of Penelope
1909 Q Street NW
Suite 500
Washington, DC 20009
Phone: 202-234-9741
Fax: 202-483-6983

Emily Tamaras Memorial Award

Type of award: Scholarship.

Intended use: For undergraduate study at accredited vocational, 2-year or 4-year institution.

Eligibility: Applicant or parent must be member/participant of Daughters of Penelope. Applicant must be female. Applicant must be Greek. Applicant must be U.S. citizen, permanent resident, international student or Canadian citizen.

Basis for selection: Applicant must demonstrate high academic achievement.

Application requirements: Recommendations, essay, transcript, proof of eligibility. Include SAT or ACT scores.

Additional information: Applicant must be high school senior or recent graduate, and have member of immediate family or legal guardian (court appointed) in the Daughters of Penelope, Order of AHEPA, or Maids of Athena and in good standing for minimum of two years. Applicant must not be a past recipient of any undergraduate award from the Daughters of Penelope National Scholarship program.

- **Amount of award:** $1,000
- **Number of awards:** 1
- **Application deadline:** June 1

Contact:
Daughters of Penelope
1909 Q Street, NW
Suite 500
Washington, DC 20009
Phone: 202-234-9741
Fax: 202-483-6983

Eos #1 Mother Lodge Chapter Award

Type of award: Scholarship.

Intended use: For undergraduate study at accredited vocational, 2-year or 4-year institution in United States.

Eligibility: Applicant or parent must be member/participant of Daughters of Penelope. Applicant must be female. Applicant must be Greek. Applicant must be U.S. citizen, permanent resident, international student or Canadian citizen.

Basis for selection: Applicant must demonstrate high academic achievement.

Application requirements: Recommendations, essay, transcript, proof of eligibility. Include SAT or ACT scores.

Additional information: Applicant must be a high school senior or recent graduate, and have member of immediate family or legal guardian (court appointed) in the Daughters of Penelope, Order of AHEPA, or Maids of Athena and in good standing for at least two years. Applicant must not be a past recipient of any undergraduate award from the Daughters of Penelope National Scholarship program.

- **Amount of award:** $1,000
- **Number of awards:** 1
- **Application deadline:** June 1

Contact:
Daughters of Penelope
1909 Q Street, NW
Suite 500
Washington, DC 20009
Phone: 202-234-9741
Fax: 202-483-6983

Kottis Family Award

Type of award: Scholarship.

Intended use: For freshman study at vocational, 2-year or 4-year institution.

Eligibility: Applicant or parent must be member/participant of Daughters of Penelope. Applicant must be female. Applicant must be Greek. Applicant must be U.S. citizen, permanent resident, international student or Canadian citizen.

Basis for selection: Applicant must demonstrate high academic achievement.

Application requirements: Recommendations, essay, transcript, proof of eligibility. Include SAT or ACT scores.

Additional information: Applicant must be high school senior or recent graduate, and have member of immediate family or legal guardian (court appointed) in the Daughters of Penelope, Order of AHEPA or Maids of Athena in good standing for minimum of two years. Applicant must not be a past recipient of any undergraduate award from the Daughters of Penelope National Scholarship program.

- **Amount of award:** $1,000
- **Number of awards:** 1
- **Application deadline:** June 1

Contact:
Daughters of Penelope
1909 Q Street, NW
Suite 500
Washington, DC 20009
Phone: 202-234-9741
Fax: 202-483-6983

Mary M. Verges Award

Type of award: Scholarship.

Intended use: For freshman study at vocational, 2-year or 4-year institution.

Eligibility: Applicant or parent must be member/participant of Daughters of Penelope. Applicant must be female. Applicant must be Greek. Applicant must be U.S. citizen, permanent resident, international student or Canadian citizen.

Basis for selection: Applicant must demonstrate high academic achievement.

Application requirements: Recommendations, essay, transcript, proof of eligibility. Include SAT or ACT scores.

Additional information: Applicant must be high school senior or recent graduate and have member of immediate family in the Daughters of Penelope, Order of AHEPA, or Maids of Athena in good standing for minimum of two years. Applicant must not be a past recipient of any undergraduate award from the Daughters of Penelope National Scholarship program.

- **Amount of award:** $1,000
- **Number of awards:** 1
- **Application deadline:** June 1

Scholarships

Contact:
Daughters of Penelope
1909 Q Street, NW
Suite 500
Washington, DC 20009
Phone: 202-234-9741
Fax: 202-483-6983

Past Grand Presidents' Memorial Award

Type of award: Scholarship.
Intended use: For freshman study at vocational, 2-year or 4-year institution.
Eligibility: Applicant or parent must be member/participant of Daughters of Penelope. Applicant must be female. Applicant must be Greek. Applicant must be U.S. citizen, permanent resident, international student or Canadian citizen.
Basis for selection: Applicant must demonstrate high academic achievement.
Application requirements: Recommendations, essay, transcript, proof of eligibility. Include SAT/ACT scores.
Additional information: Applicant must be high school senior or recent graduate and have member of immediate family or legal guardian (court appointed) in the Daughters of Penelope, Order of AHEPA, or Maids of Athena and in good standing for minimum of two years. Applicant must not be a past recipient of any undergraduate award from the Daughters of Penelope National Scholarship program.

Amount of award:	$1,000
Number of awards:	1
Application deadline:	June 1

Contact:
Daughters of Penelope
1909 Q Street NW
Suite 500
Washington, DC 20009
Phone: 202-234-9741
Fax: 202-483-6983

Daughters of Union Veterans of the Civil War 1861-1865, Inc.

Grand Army of the Republic Living Memorial Scholarship

Type of award: Scholarship.
Intended use: For full-time junior, senior or graduate study at accredited 4-year institution in United States.
Eligibility: Applicant must be U.S. citizen. Applicant must be during Civil War. Applicant must be descendant of Union Civil War soldier.
Basis for selection: Applicant must demonstrate high academic achievement, depth of character, leadership, patriotism, seriousness of purpose and service orientation.
Application requirements: Recommendations, transcript. Ancestor's military record required. Must send self-addressed, stamped envelope (SASE) when requesting information.
Additional information: Must be lineal descendant of Union Veteran of Civil War. Minimum 3.75 GPA required. Applicant must have completed freshman year in a 4-year college/

university. Request for information and application honored only with SASE. Number of awards granted may vary.

Amount of award:	$200
Number of awards:	3
Application deadline:	April 30
Notification begins:	August 30

Contact:
Daughters of Union Veterans of the Civil War 1861-1865, Inc.
503 South Walnut Street
Springfield, IL 62704-1932

Davidson Institute

Davidson Fellows Scholarship

Type of award: Scholarship.
Intended use: For undergraduate study.
Eligibility: Applicant must be no older than 18, enrolled in high school. Applicant must be U.S. citizen or permanent resident.
Basis for selection: Major/career interest in science, general; literature or music.
Additional information: Applicant awarded for accomplishment that is recognized as significant by experts in that field and has the potential to make positive contribution to society. Applications accepted in the following categories: science, technology, mathematics, music, literature, philosophy and "outside the box"; not competitive, but to recognize the extraordinary. Work may be exceptionally creative application of existing knowledge, new idea with high impact, innovative solution with broad-range implications, important advancement that can be replicated and built upon, interdisciplinary discovery, prodigious performance and another demonstration of extraordinary accomplishment.

Amount of award:	$10,000-$50,000
Number of awards:	15
Application deadline:	March 25
Total amount awarded:	$400,000

Contact:
Davidson Institute
9665 Gateway Drive
Suite B
Reno, NV 89521
Phone: 775-852-DIDT
Fax: 775-852-2184
Web: www.davidsonfellows.org

Davis-Roberts Scholarship Fund

Davis-Roberts Scholarship

Type of award: Scholarship, renewable.
Intended use: For full-time undergraduate study at 2-year or 4-year institution.
Eligibility: Applicant or parent must be member/participant of Wyoming Job's Daughters/DeMolay. Applicant must be U.S. citizen residing in Wyoming.
Basis for selection: Applicant must demonstrate financial need.

Application requirements: Recommendations, essay, transcript. Applicant's photograph.
Additional information: Applicant must be member of Wyoming Job's Daughters/DeMolay.

Amount of award:	$500
Number of awards:	5
Number of applicants:	15
Application deadline:	June 15
Notification begins:	July 1
Total amount awarded:	$2,500

Contact:
Davis-Roberts Scholarship Fund
c/o Gary D. Skillern
P.O. Box 20645
Cheyenne, WY 82003

DEED

Demonstration of Energy-Efficient Developments Program Scholarship

Type of award: Scholarship.
Intended use: For undergraduate or graduate study at 2-year or 4-year institution in United States or Canada.
Eligibility: Applicant must be U.S. citizen.
Basis for selection: Major/career interest in electronics; engineering, electrical/electronic or engineering, mechanical.
Application requirements: Applicants must complete a research project and must be members of the Demonstration of Energy-Efficient Developments Program.

Amount of award:	$4,000
Number of awards:	10
Application deadline:	January 15, July 15
Total amount awarded:	$40,000

Contact:
DEED
2301 M Street NW
Washington, DC 20037
Phone: 202-467-2960
Fax: 202-467-2992
Web: www.appanet.org

Delaware Higher Education Commission

Charles L. Hebner Memorial Scholarship

Type of award: Scholarship, renewable.
Intended use: For full-time undergraduate study. Designated institutions: University of Delaware or Delaware State University.
Eligibility: Applicant must be high school senior. Applicant must be residing in Delaware.
Basis for selection: Applicant must demonstrate high academic achievement.
Additional information: Applicant must rank in top half of graduating class. Minimum SAT score of 900. Major in humanities or social sciences; preference given to political

science majors. Award covers tuition, fees, room, board, and books at University of Delaware or Delaware State University.

Number of awards:	6
Number of applicants:	93
Application deadline:	March 14
Total amount awarded:	$615,000

Contact:
Delaware Higher Education Commission
820 North French Street
Wilmington, DE 19801
Phone: 302-577-3240
Fax: 302-577-6765
Web: www.doe.state.de.us/high-ed

Delaware B. Bradford Barnes Scholarship

Type of award: Scholarship, renewable.
Intended use: For full-time freshman study. Designated institutions: University of Delaware.
Eligibility: Applicant must be high school senior. Applicant must be permanent resident residing in Delaware.
Basis for selection: Applicant must demonstrate high academic achievement.
Application requirements: Essay, transcript, proof of eligibility. Applicant must be Delaware resident.
Additional information: Must rank in top 25 percent of high school class. Minimum SAT score of 1200 (27 on ACT) required. Awards full tuition, fees, room, board and books at the University of Delaware.

Amount of award:	Full tuition
Number of awards:	4
Number of applicants:	65
Application deadline:	February 7
Notification begins:	March 1

Contact:
Delaware Higher Education Commission
820 North French Street
Wilmington, DE 19801
Phone: 302-577-3240
Fax: 302-577-6765
Web: www.doe.state.de.us/high-ed

Delaware Diamond State Scholarship

Type of award: Scholarship, renewable.
Intended use: For full-time freshman study at accredited vocational, 2-year or 4-year institution in United States.
Eligibility: Applicant must be high school senior. Applicant must be permanent resident residing in Delaware.
Basis for selection: Applicant must demonstrate high academic achievement.
Application requirements: Essay, transcript, proof of eligibility. Proof of residency.
Additional information: Must rank in top 25 percent of high school class. Minimum SAT score of 1200 (27 on ACT) required.

Amount of award:	$1,250
Number of awards:	50
Number of applicants:	275
Application deadline:	March 31
Notification begins:	May 1
Total amount awarded:	$250,000

Contact:
Delaware Higher Education Commission
820 North French Street
Wilmington, DE 19801
Phone: 302-577-3240
Fax: 302-577-6765
Web: www.doe.state.de.us/high-ed

Delaware Education Fund for Children of Deceased Military Personnel/State Police

Type of award: Scholarship, renewable.
Intended use: For undergraduate study. Designated institutions: Public institutions in Delaware.
Eligibility: Applicant must be at least 16, no older than 24. Applicant must be permanent resident residing in Delaware. Applicant must be dependent of deceased veteran. Applicant's parent must have been killed or disabled in work-related accident as police officer.
Application requirements: Proof of eligibility. Must be Delaware resident.
Additional information: Parent must have been Delaware State Police officer killed in line of duty, or veteran residing in Delaware at time of death. Awards full tuition and fees for four years at a Delaware public institution or reduced award for Delaware private institution or out-of-state school.

| Amount of award: | Full tuition |

Contact:
Delaware Higher Education Commission
820 North French Street
Wilmington, DE 19801
Phone: 302-577-3240
Fax: 302-577-6765
Web: www.doe.state.de.us/high-ed

Delaware Herman M. Holloway, Sr., Memorial Scholarship

Type of award: Scholarship, renewable.
Intended use: For full-time freshman study. Designated institutions: Delaware State University.
Eligibility: Applicant must be high school senior. Applicant must be U.S. citizen residing in Delaware.
Basis for selection: Applicant must demonstrate high academic achievement.
Application requirements: Essay, transcript, proof of eligibility. Must complete application.
Additional information: Minimum 3.25 GPA and minimum SAT score of 850 required. Awards full tuition, fees, room, board and books at Delaware State University.

Amount of award:	Full tuition
Number of awards:	2
Number of applicants:	26
Application deadline:	March 14
Notification begins:	May 1
Total amount awarded:	$17,750

Contact:
Delaware Higher Education Commission
820 North French Street
Wilmington, DE 19801
Phone: 302-577-3240
Fax: 302-577-6765
Web: www.doe.state.de.us/high-ed

Delaware Legislative Essay Scholarship

Type of award: Scholarship.
Intended use: For undergraduate study.
Eligibility: Applicant must be high school senior. Applicant must be residing in Delaware.
Application requirements: Essay, 500 to 2000 words, on historical topic. (Topic changes annually.)
Additional information: Applicant must be Delaware resident.

Amount of award:	$500-$5,500
Number of awards:	62
Number of applicants:	90
Application deadline:	December 5
Total amount awarded:	$40,000

Contact:
Delaware Higher Education Commission
820 North French St
Wilmington, DE 19801
Phone: 302-577-3240
Fax: 302-577-6765
Web: www.doe.state.de.us/high-ed

Delaware Robert C. Byrd Honors Scholarship

Type of award: Scholarship, renewable.
Intended use: For full-time undergraduate study.
Eligibility: Applicant must be high school senior. Applicant must be residing in Delaware.
Basis for selection: Applicant must demonstrate high academic achievement.
Additional information: Applicant must be high school senior in top 25 percent of graduating class. Minimum SAT score of 1200.

Amount of award:	$1,500
Number of awards:	20
Number of applicants:	275
Application deadline:	March 31
Total amount awarded:	$108,000

Contact:
Delaware Higher Education Commission
820 North French St
Wilmington, DE 19801
Phone: 302-577-3240
Fax: 302-577-6765
Web: www.doe.state.de.us/high-ed

Delaware Scholarship Incentive Program (SCIP)

Type of award: Scholarship.
Intended use: For full-time freshman, sophomore, junior, senior, master's, doctoral or first professional study at accredited 2-year, 4-year or graduate institution. Designated institutions: Delaware or Pennsylvania postsecondary institutions; other state postsecondary institutions with restrictions.
Eligibility: Applicant must be residing in Delaware.
Basis for selection: Applicant must demonstrate financial need.
Application requirements: Transcript. FAFSA.
Additional information: Must be Delaware resident. May be used outside of Delaware and Pennsylvania if program of study is not offered at tax-supported institution in Delaware.

Amount of award:	$700-$2,200
Number of awards:	1,040
Number of applicants:	11,000
Application deadline:	April 15
Notification begins:	July 1
Total amount awarded:	$1,455,000

Contact:
Delaware Higher Education Commission
820 North French Street
Wilmington, DE 19801
Phone: 302-577-3240
Fax: 302-577-6765
Web: www.doe.state.de.us/high-ed

Optometry Scholarhip Program

Type of award: Scholarship.
Intended use: For full-time undergraduate study.
Eligibility: Applicant must be residing in Delaware.
Basis for selection: Major/career interest in optometry/ophthalmology. Applicant must demonstrate financial need.
Application requirements: Transcript. FAFSA.

Amount of award:	$4,000
Number of awards:	4
Number of applicants:	2
Application deadline:	March 31

Contact:
Delaware Higher Education Commission
820 North French Street
Wilmington, DE 19801
Phone: 302-577-3240
Fax: 302-577-6765
Web: www.doe.state.de.us/high-ed

Delta Delta Delta Foundation

Delta Delta Delta Undergraduate Scholarship

Type of award: Scholarship.
Intended use: For sophomore, junior or senior study at 4-year institution.
Eligibility: Applicant or parent must be member/participant of Delta Delta Delta Fraternity.
Basis for selection: Applicant must demonstrate financial need, high academic achievement and service orientation.
Additional information: Campus, chapter and community involvement important. Applicants must be initiated members of Delta Delta Delta in good standing with chapter. Number of awards varies.

Amount of award:	$500-$2,500
Number of applicants:	120
Application deadline:	February 1
Total amount awarded:	$60,000

Contact:
Delta Delta Delta Foundation
P.O. Box 5987
Arlington, TX 76005
Phone: 817-633-8001, 213
Web: www.trideltafoundation.org

Delta Gamma Foundation

Delta Gamma Scholarship

Type of award: Scholarship.
Intended use: For sophomore, junior or senior study at accredited 4-year institution in or outside United States.
Eligibility: Applicant or parent must be member/participant of Delta Gamma. Applicant must be female.
Basis for selection: Applicant must demonstrate high academic achievement.
Application requirements: Recommendations, essay, transcript.
Additional information: Student must be a member of Delta Gamma. Minimum 3.0 GPA. Notifications given in June.

Amount of award:	$1,000
Number of awards:	182
Application deadline:	February 1
Total amount awarded:	$182,000

Contact:
Delta Gamma Foundation
3250 Riverside Drive
P.O. Box 21397
Columbus, OH 43221-0397
Phone: 614-481-8169

Department For The Blind & Vision Impaired

Virginia Assistance for the Visually Handicapped

Type of award: Scholarship.
Intended use: For full-time undergraduate study at postsecondary institution.
Eligibility: Applicant must be a Virginia citizen who has been determined eligible for Vocational Rehabilitation Services. Applicant must be residing in Virginia.
Basis for selection: Sponsorship must be directly related to a specific vocational objective as developed through an individualized plan for employment.
Application requirements: Vocational Rehab Application.
Additional information: Award is an education sponsorship as part of a Vocational Rehabilitation Program. Available only when need exists after federal, state and private funding have been used.
Contact:
Virginia Department for the Blind and Vision Impaired
Phone: 800-622-2155
Web: www.vdbvi.org

Department of Rehabilitative Services

Virginia Rehabilitative Services College Program

Type of award: Scholarship.

Intended use: For undergraduate study at postsecondary institution.

Eligibility: Applicant must be visually impaired, hearing impaired, physically challenged or learning disabled. Applicant must be residing in Virginia.

Basis for selection: Applicant must demonstrate financial need.

Application requirements: Proof of eligibility. Proof must be furnished at least 60 days before start of school or educational program.

Additional information: Applicant must have a disability and an employment goal. Funding is available to eligible individuals only if need remains after other federal, state and private sources are used. Program provides vocational rehabilitation and related services to Virginians with disabilities in order to foster the skills necessary to achieve greater self-sufficiency, independence and employment. Contact nearest Department of Rehabilitative Services office or visit Website for numbers.

Contact:
Web: www.vadrs.org

Descendents of the Signers of the Declaration of Independence, Inc.

Descendents of the Signers of the Declaration of Independence Scholarship

Type of award: Scholarship, renewable.

Intended use: For full-time freshman, sophomore, junior or senior study at accredited 4-year or graduate institution in United States.

Eligibility: Applicant or parent must be member/participant of Descendants of the Signers of the Declaration of Independence.

Basis for selection: Applicant must demonstrate high academic achievement, depth of character, leadership, patriotism, seriousness of purpose and service orientation.

Application requirements: Recommendations, transcript, proof of eligibility. Submit membership number and ancestor's name with request for application and information with SASE.

Additional information: Applicant must be a direct lineal descendant of a signer of the Declaration of Independence. The first-year winner gets an allowance of $500 to attend a ceremony and receive award at Independence Hall on July 4th. Preference given to persons involved in community, school activities and volunteer work. Applicant must reapply for renewal.

Amount of award:	$3,100
Number of awards:	3
Number of applicants:	30
Application deadline:	March 15
Notification begins:	May 1
Total amount awarded:	$9,300

Contact:
Descendents of the Signers of the Declaration of Independence, Inc.
Attn: Susan Peterson, Chairman
43 Brickmill Road
Bedford, NH 03110
Phone: 603-472-2913

Discover Financial Services, Inc. & American Assoc. of School Administrators

Discover Card Tribute Award Scholarship Program

Type of award: Scholarship.

Intended use: For undergraduate study at accredited vocational, 2-year or 4-year institution.

Eligibility: Applicant must be high school junior. Applicant must be U.S. citizen or permanent resident.

Basis for selection: Applicant must demonstrate depth of character, leadership, seriousness of purpose and service orientation.

Application requirements: Statement of future goals.

Additional information: Applicant must be high school junior enrolled in public or accredited private school in U.S. and have a minimum cumulative GPA of 2.75 for the 9th and 10th grades only. Applicants must demonstrate achievement in three of the four following areas: special talents, leadership, community service, and obstacles overcome, as they will be judged on how well they address their chosen criteria areas. Application materials are distributed each fall to high schools and national community-based, youth-serving organizations. Beginning October 1 each year, application materials are available online at both AASA's and Discover Card's Websites. Application materials cannot be faxed or e-mailed. Please note that it takes 4-6 weeks to receive applications by mail. Check Website for deadlines.

Amount of award:	$2,500-$25,000
Number of awards:	459
Number of applicants:	9,515
Total amount awarded:	$1,372,500

Contact:
Discover Card Tribute Awards
AASA
P.O. Box 9338
Arlington, VA 22219
Web: www.aasa.org/discover.htm

District of Columbia Office of Postsecondary Education

District of Columbia Leveraging Educational Assistance Partnership Program

Type of award: Scholarship, renewable.

Intended use: For undergraduate study at 2-year or 4-year institution in United States.

Eligibility: Applicant must be U.S. citizen or permanent resident residing in District of Columbia.

Basis for selection: Applicant must demonstrate financial need and high academic achievement.

Application requirements: Proof of eligibility. Student Aid Report generated by FAFSA.

Additional information: Must be enrolled or accepted for enrollment in an undergraduate program (AAS, BA, BS) in a college or university certified as eligible by U.S. Department of Education. Must be resident of D.C. for 18 months prior to application. Must be eligible for Title IV aid. Considered on "first come, first served" basis for as long as funds are available.

Amount of award:	$1,500
Application deadline:	June 28

Contact:
LEAP Program State Education Office
One Judiciary Square
350 North
Washington, DC 20001
Phone: 202-727-6436

Dolphin Scholarship Foundation

Dolphin Scholarship

Type of award: Scholarship, renewable.
Intended use: For full-time undergraduate study.
Eligibility: Applicant must be single, no older than 24. Applicant must be U.S. citizen. Must be child or stepchild of: (1) member/former member of Submarine Force who has qualified in submarines and has served at least eight years or died while on active duty; or (2) Navy member who served minimum of ten years active duty in submarine support activities.
Basis for selection: Applicant must demonstrate financial need, high academic achievement, depth of character, leadership and seriousness of purpose.
Application requirements: Recommendations, essay, transcript, proof of eligibility.
Additional information: Scholarship open only to high school or undergraduate college children/stepchildren of naval personnel. Must be under the age of 24 at time of deadline.

Amount of award:	$3,000
Number of awards:	131
Number of applicants:	215
Application deadline:	March 15
Notification begins:	April 25
Total amount awarded:	$393,000

Contact:
Dolphin Scholarship Foundation
5040 Virginia Beach Blvd., Suite 104A
Virginia Beach, VA 23462
Phone: 757-671-3200
Fax: 757-671-3330
Web: www.dolphinscholarship.org

U.S. Submarine Veterans of World War II Scholarship

Type of award: Scholarship, renewable.
Intended use: For full-time undergraduate study at accredited vocational, 2-year or 4-year institution outside United States.
Eligibility: Applicant must be single, no older than 24, high school senior. Applicant must be U.S. citizen. Applicant must be dependent of veteran who served in the Navy during WW II.
Basis for selection: Applicant must demonstrate financial need, high academic achievement, depth of character, leadership and seriousness of purpose.
Application requirements: Recommendations, essay, transcript, proof of eligibility.

Additional information: Must be child/stepchild of paid-up, regular member of U.S. Submarine Veterans of World War II. Grandchildren are not eligible. Send application requests to organization. Applicant must be high school senior or have graduated from high school not more than four years prior to application, and must be under age 24 at application deadline. Requests for applications should include sponsor's U.S. Submarine Veterans of World War II membership number.

Amount of award:	$3,000
Number of awards:	5
Number of applicants:	5
Application deadline:	April 15
Notification begins:	May 31
Total amount awarded:	$15,000

Contact:
US Submarine Veterans of World War II
Scholarship Program
5040 Virginia Beach Blvd., Suite 104-A
Virginia Beach, VA 23462
Phone: 757-671-3200
Fax: 757-671-3330

e-CollegeDegree.com

e-CollegeDegree.com Online Education Scholarship

Type of award: Scholarship.
Intended use: For undergraduate study at postsecondary institution. Designated institutions: Online colleges or universities.
Eligibility: Applicant must be at least 18, high school senior. Applicant must be U.S. citizen or permanent resident.
Additional information: Program designed to help pay online education. Only online applications accepted.

Amount of award:	$1,000
Number of awards:	2
Application deadline:	December 15

Contact:
Visit Website for additional information.
Web: www.e-collegedegree.com

EAA Aviation Foundation, Inc.

David Alan Quick Scholarship

Type of award: Scholarship, renewable.
Intended use: For junior or senior study at accredited postsecondary institution.
Basis for selection: Major/career interest in aerospace or aviation. Applicant must demonstrate financial need, depth of character, leadership and service orientation.
Application requirements: $5 application fee. Recommendations, essay, transcript. Submit completed application, application fee and supporting materials by March 30.
Additional information: Applicant must be a junior or senior in good standing. Must be pursuing degree in aerospace or

aeronautical engineering at accredited college/university. Visit Website for details and application.

Amount of award:	$1,000
Number of awards:	1
Application deadline:	March 30
Total amount awarded:	$1,000

Contact:
Scholarship Office
EAA Aviation Foundation, Inc.
P.O. Box 3065
Oshkosh, WI 54903-3065
Phone: 920-426-6884
Fax: 920-426-6865
Web: www.eaa.org/education/scholarships

EAA Aviation Achievement Scholarship

Type of award: Scholarship.
Intended use: For undergraduate study at postsecondary institution.
Basis for selection: Major/career interest in aviation. Applicant must demonstrate financial need, depth of character, leadership and service orientation.
Application requirements: $5 application fee. Recommendations, essay, transcript. Submit completed application, application fee and supporting materials by March 30.
Additional information: Applicants should be active in recreational aviation endeavors. Award is to encourage, recognize and support excellence in aviation students. Visit Website for details and application.

Amount of award:	$500
Number of awards:	2
Application deadline:	March 30
Total amount awarded:	$1,000

Contact:
Scholarship Office
EAA Aviation Foundation, Inc.
P.O. Box 3065
Oshkosh, WI 54903-3065
Phone: 920-426-6884
Fax: 920-426-6865
Web: www.eaa.org/education/scholarships

Friendship One Flight Training Scholarships

Type of award: Scholarship.
Intended use: For non-degree study.
Basis for selection: Major/career interest in aviation. Applicant must demonstrate financial need, depth of character, leadership and service orientation.
Application requirements: $5 application fee. Recommendations, essay, transcript, proof of eligibility. Submit completed application, application fee and supporting materials by March 30. Include copy of FAA medical, airmen's certificate and flight instructor progress report.
Additional information: Award is for flight training. Applicant must have attended the resident youth EAA Air Academy in Oshkosh, Wisconsin. Scholarships may be awarded as two $5,000 grants for commercial flight training, or as one $5,000 grant for commercial flight training and two $2,500 grants for private pilot training. Visit Website for details and application.

Amount of award:	$5,000
Number of awards:	2
Application deadline:	March 30
Total amount awarded:	$10,000

Contact:
Scholarship Office
EAA Aviation Foundation, Inc.
P.O. Box 3065
Oshkosh, WI 54903-3065
Phone: 920-426-6884
Fax: 920-426-6865
Web: www.eaa.org/education/scholarships

Hansen Scholarship

Type of award: Scholarship, renewable.
Intended use: For undergraduate study at accredited 2-year or 4-year institution.
Basis for selection: Major/career interest in aerospace or aviation. Applicant must demonstrate high academic achievement, depth of character, leadership and service orientation.
Application requirements: $5 application fee. Recommendations, essay, transcript. Submit completed application, application fee and supporting materials by March 30.
Additional information: Renewable scholarship for student in good academic standing enrolled in accredited college/ university or technical college pursuing degree in aerospace engineering or aeronautical engineering. Financial need not required. Visit Website for details and application.

Amount of award:	$1,000
Number of awards:	1
Application deadline:	March 30
Total amount awarded:	$1,000

Contact:
Scholarship Office
EAA Aviation Foundation, Inc.
P.O. Box 3065
Oshkosh, WI 54903-3065
Phone: 920-426-6884
Fax: 920-426-6865
Web: www.eaa.org/education/scholarships

Herbert L. Cox Memorial Scholarship

Type of award: Scholarship.
Intended use: For undergraduate study at accredited 4-year institution.
Basis for selection: Major/career interest in aviation. Applicant must demonstrate financial need, depth of character, leadership and service orientation.
Application requirements: $5 application fee. Recommendations, essay, transcript. Submit completed application, application fee, and supporting materials by March 30.
Additional information: Award for student accepted or attending four-year accredited college/university in pursuit of degree leading to career in aviation. Visit Website for details and application.

Amount of award:	$500
Number of awards:	1
Application deadline:	March 30
Total amount awarded:	$500

Contact:
Scholarship Office
EAA Aviation Foundation, Inc.
P.O. Box 3065
Oshkosh, WI 54903-3065
Phone: 920-426-6884
Fax: 920-426-6865
Web: www.eaa.org/education/scholarships/index.html

H.P. "Bud" Milligan Aviation Scholarship

Type of award: Scholarship, renewable.
Intended use: For undergraduate study at accredited postsecondary institution. Designated institutions: College/ university, technical school or aviation academy with accredited aviation program.
Basis for selection: Major/career interest in aviation. Applicant must demonstrate depth of character, leadership and service orientation.
Application requirements: $5 application fee. Recommendations, essay, transcript. Submit completed application, application fee and supporting materials by March 30.
Additional information: Renewable scholarship for students enrolled in accredited aviation program at college, technical school or aviation academy. Financial need not required. Visit Website for details and application.

Amount of award:	$1,000
Number of awards:	1
Application deadline:	March 30
Total amount awarded:	$1,000

Contact:
Scholarship Office
EAA Aviation Foundation, Inc.
P.O. Box 3065
Oshkosh, WI 54903-3065
Phone: 920-426-6884
Fax: 920-426-6865
Web: www.eaa.org/education/scholarships

Payzer Scholarship

Type of award: Scholarship.
Intended use: For undergraduate study at accredited postsecondary institution.
Basis for selection: Major/career interest in engineering; mathematics; physical sciences or biology. Applicant must demonstrate financial need, depth of character, leadership and service orientation.
Application requirements: $5 application fee. Recommendations, essay, transcript. Submit completed application, application fee and supporting materials by March 30.
Additional information: Applicant must be accepted/enrolled in postsecondary school with emphasis on technical information. Visit Website for details and application.

Amount of award:	$5,000
Number of awards:	1
Application deadline:	March 30
Total amount awarded:	$5,000

Contact:
Scholarship Office
EAA Aviation Foundation, Inc.
P.O. Box 3065
Oshkosh, WI 54903-3065
Phone: 920-426-6884
Fax: 920-426-6865
Web: www.eaa.org/education/scholarships

Richard Lee Vernon Aviation Scholarship

Type of award: Scholarship.
Intended use: For undergraduate or graduate study at postsecondary institution. Designated institutions: Aviation technical school or postsecondary institution with recognized professional aviation training program.
Basis for selection: Major/career interest in aviation. Applicant must demonstrate financial need.
Application requirements: $5 application fee. Recommendations, essay, transcript, proof of eligibility. Submit completed application, application fee and supporting materials by March 30. Include copy of FAA medical, airmen's certificate and flight instructor progress report.
Additional information: Award for student accepted to a course of study in a recognized aviation training program in postsecondary institution or aviation technical school. Applicant must be pursuing training leading to professional aviation occupation. Visit Website for details and application.

Amount of award:	$500
Number of awards:	1
Application deadline:	March 30
Total amount awarded:	$500

Contact:
Scholarship Office
EAA Aviation Foundation, Inc.
P.O. Box 3065
Oshkosh, WI 54903-3065
Phone: 920-426-6884
Fax: 920-426-6865
Web: www.eaa.org/education/scholarships

Eaton Corporation

Eaton Multicultural Scholars Program

Type of award: Scholarship, renewable.
Intended use: For full-time sophomore, junior or senior study at accredited 4-year institution in United States. Designated institutions: Targeted institutions across the United States.
Eligibility: Applicant must be Alaskan native, Asian American, African American, Mexican American, Hispanic American, Puerto Rican or American Indian. Applicant must be U.S. citizen or permanent resident.
Basis for selection: Major/career interest in engineering; engineering, computer; engineering, mechanical; engineering, electrical/electronic; computer/information sciences; manufacturing; electronics; engineering, materials or accounting. Applicant must demonstrate high academic achievement.
Application requirements: Recommendations, essay, transcript. Application, ACT/SAT scores, SAR and school's financial aid letter.

Additional information: Provides renewable annual scholarship in addition to paid summer internships, mentoring and other benefits. Visit Website for application and list of target schools. Must be engineering major. Must have completed one year in accredited engineering program, have acceptable GPA, and have three remaining years of coursework to complete before earning B.A. All applications reviewed by Inroads.

Contact:
EMSP c/o Inroads
1360 West. Ninth St., Suite 330
Cleveland, OH 44113
Phone: 800-533-2192
Web: www.eaton.com/careers

Edmund F. Maxwell Foundation

Edmund F. Maxwell Foundation Scholarship

Type of award: Scholarship, renewable.
Intended use: For full-time freshman study.
Eligibility: Applicant must be U.S. citizen or permanent resident residing in Washington.
Basis for selection: Applicant must demonstrate financial need, high academic achievement, depth of character, leadership, seriousness of purpose and service orientation.
Application requirements: Essay, transcript.
Additional information: Combined SAT I must be greater than 1200. College or university must be independent. Must submit financial need assessment with application. Only residents of western Washington are eligible. Applicants are encouraged to apply early in the year. Visit Website for more information.

Amount of award:	$3,500
Application deadline:	April 30
Notification begins:	June 1

Contact:
Edmund F. Maxwell Foundation
P.O. Box 22537
Seattle, WA 98122-0537
Web: www.maxwell.org

Education and Research Foundation, Society of Nuclear Medicine

Nuclear Medicine Student Fellowship Award

Type of award: Research grant.
Intended use: For undergraduate, master's, doctoral or first professional study at postsecondary institution.
Basis for selection: Major/career interest in nuclear medicine.
Application requirements: Recommendations, research proposal. Resume. Letter addressed to the Education and Research Foundation requesting fellowship support. Preceptor

for project: either nuclear medicine physician or nuclear medicine scientist.
Additional information: For summer research internship. Minimum of two months. Competence in physical and/or biological aspects of radioactivity essential. Will assist in clinical and basic research activities in nuclear medicine. Total amount awarded varies. Recipients of awards are required to provide the foundation with a 1,000-word resume of their activities prior to receipt of final monthly allocation.

Amount of award:	$1,000-$3,000
Application deadline:	November 15

Contact:
Susan C. Weiss
CNMT
1060 Arbor Lane
Northfield, IL 60093
Phone: 847-446-4176
Web: www.snmerf.org

Paul Cole Scholarship

Type of award: Scholarship.
Intended use: For full-time undergraduate study at accredited 2-year or 4-year institution.
Basis for selection: Major/career interest in nuclear medicine. Applicant must demonstrate financial need and high academic achievement.
Application requirements: Recommendations, essay, transcript. 2.5 GPA or better. Proof of acceptance or enrollment in nuclear medicine technology program.
Additional information: Application must be submitted and signed by director of nuclear medicine technology program on behalf of student. Special consideration will be given to applicants who are not only academically capable but whose financial situation is such that, without the scholarship, they might not be able to attend the training program. Visit Website for more information.

Amount of award:	$1,000
Number of awards:	24
Number of applicants:	125
Application deadline:	October 15
Total amount awarded:	$24,000

Contact:
Susan C. Weiss, Executive
1060 Arbor Lane
Northfield, IL 60093
Phone: 847-446-4176
Web: www.snmerf.org

Educational Communications Scholarship Foundation

Educational Communications Scholarship

Type of award: Scholarship.
Intended use: For undergraduate study at accredited postsecondary institution.
Eligibility: Applicant must be enrolled in high school. Applicant must be U.S. citizen or permanent resident.
Basis for selection: Based on grade point average, achievement test scores, leadership qualifications, work

experience, evaluation of an essay and with some consideration for financial need. Awards are to be applied toward educational costs at an accredited college or university. Payments will be issued directly to the institution's financial aid office and applied to the student's account. Major/career interest in education or communications. Applicant must demonstrate high academic achievement and leadership.

Application requirements: Must have taken the ACT or SAT.

Additional information: Recipients selected by independent committee of professional educators on basis of GPA, achievement, test scores, work experience and financial need. Request application from local high school. ECSF distributes to 24,000 high schools by January each year.

Amount of award:	$1,000
Number of awards:	200
Application deadline:	May 15
Notification begins:	June 15, August 5
Total amount awarded:	$200,000

Contact:
Educational Communications Scholarship Foundation
721 N. McKinley Road
Lake Forest, IL 60045
Phone: 847-295-6650
Fax: 847-295-3972
Web: www.honoring.com

Elie Wiesel Foundation for Humanity

Elie Wiesel Prize in Ethics

Type of award: Scholarship.
Intended use: For full-time junior or senior study at 4-year institution in United States.
Basis for selection: Competition/talent/interest in writing/journalism, based on essay on ethical dilemma, issue or question related to the contest's annual topic. Major/career interest in ethnic/cultural studies; social/behavioral sciences or governmental public relations.
Application requirements: Proof of eligibility. Letter from college/university verifying full-time junior or senior status. Sponsorship by faculty member. Students must request updated guidelines and application form.
Additional information: Application deadline is first Friday in December. Send SASE after August 1 for application materials. Application and all information available on Website.

Amount of award:	$500-$5,000
Number of awards:	5
Notification begins:	May 31
Total amount awarded:	$10,000

Contact:
Elie Wiesel Prize in Ethics
The Elie Wiesel Foundation for Humanity
529 Fifth Avenue, Suite 1802
New York, NY 10017
Phone: 212-490-7777
Fax: 212-490-6006
Web: www.eliewieselfoundation.org

Elizabeth Glaser Pediatric AIDS Foundation

Elizabeth Glaser Pediatric AIDS Foundation Short-Term Scientific Awards

Type of award: Research grant.
Intended use: For non-degree study in United States.
Basis for selection: Major/career interest in medical specialties/research or medicine. Applicant must demonstrate seriousness of purpose.
Application requirements: Research proposal.
Additional information: Major/career interest in pediatric research. Program provides funding for travel and short-term study to initiate critical research project, obtain preliminary data, learn new techniques or sponsor workshop.

Amount of award:	$10,000

Contact:
Program Manager Short-term Scientific Awards
2950 31st Street
Suite 125
Santa Monica, CA 90405
Phone: 310-314-1459
Fax: 310-314-1469
Web: www.pedaids.org

Elizabeth Greenshields Foundation

The Elizabeth Greenshields Grant

Type of award: Scholarship, renewable.
Intended use: For undergraduate, graduate or non-degree study.
Basis for selection: Major/career interest in arts, general.
Application requirements: Slides.
Additional information: For artists (fine arts) in the early stages of careers creating representational or figurative works through painting, drawing, printmaking or sculpture. Must make a commitment to making art a lifetime career. Applications are welcome throughout the year. All amounts are in Canadian dollars. Funds may be used for any art-related purpose.

Amount of award:	$10,000
Number of awards:	60
Number of applicants:	500

Contact:
Elizabeth Greenshields Foundation
1814 Sherbrooke Street West, Suite 1
Montreal
Quebec, Canada, H3H 1E4
Phone: 514-937-9225
Fax: 514-937-0141

Elks National Foundation

Elks Most Valuable Student Scholarship

Type of award: Scholarship.
Intended use: For full-time freshman, sophomore, junior or senior study in United States.
Eligibility: Applicant or parent must be member/participant of Elks. Applicant must be high school senior. Applicant must be U.S. citizen.
Basis for selection: Applicant must demonstrate financial need, high academic achievement and leadership.
Application requirements: Recommendations, essay, transcript. SAT 1, ACT.
Additional information: Applications available starting September 15 from local Benevolent and Protective Order of Elks Lodge; also available on Website or by sending SASE to foundation. Award is distributed over four years. Membership in Elks not required. Applications submitted to local Elks Lodge for entry into competition. Judging occurs at lodge, district and state level before reaching national competition.

Amount of award:	$4,000-$60,000
Number of awards:	500
Application deadline:	January 9
Notification begins:	May 15
Total amount awarded:	$2,216,000

Contact:
Elks National Foundation
2750 North Lakeview Avenue
Chicago, IL 60614-1889
Web: www.elks.org/enf

Elks National Foundation Legacy Awards

Type of award: Scholarship.
Intended use: For full-time freshman study at accredited postsecondary institution in United States. Designated institutions: Institutions in Guam, Panama, Puerto Rico and the Philippines for eligible applicants who are residents of those countries.
Eligibility: Applicant or parent must be member/participant of Elks. Applicant must be high school senior. Applicant must be U.S. citizen.
Basis for selection: Based on leadership and scholarship.
Application requirements: Recommendations, transcript. SAT/ACT scores, biographical questionnaire, Legacy Award application.
Additional information: Applicant must be child or grandchild of Elk who is a paid-up member in good standing for two years. Application available after August 1 from local lodge's scholarship chairman, from Website or by sending SASE to foundation. Visit Website for additional information.

Amount of award:	$1,000
Number of awards:	500
Total amount awarded:	$500,000

Contact:
Elks National Foundation
2750 North Lakeview Avenue
Chicago, IL 60614-1889
Web: www.elks.org/enf

Enesco Group, Inc.

Enesco Scholarship

Type of award: Scholarship.
Intended use: For full-time undergraduate or graduate study at accredited 2-year, 4-year or graduate institution.
Eligibility: Applicant or parent must be employed by Enesco Corporation.
Basis for selection: Test scores, grades, class standing, and school and community involvement. Applicant must demonstrate high academic achievement, leadership, seriousness of purpose and service orientation.
Application requirements: Recommendations, essay, transcript. SAT, PSAT or ACT scores. Minimum B average.
Additional information: For children of regular full-time or regular part-time associates of Enesco Group, Inc. only. Pre-application must be submitted in early September. Entry form must then be submitted to high school counselor by November 1 and returned to ENESCO by December 1. Number and amount of awards vary.

Application deadline:	December 1

Contact:
Scholarship Coordinator
Enesco Group, Inc.
225 Windsor Drive
Itasca, IL 60143
Phone: 800-4-ENESCO
Web: www.enesco.com

Engineers Foundation of Ohio

Engineers Foundation of Ohio Scholarship

Type of award: Scholarship.
Intended use: For freshman study at accredited 4-year institution in United States. Designated institutions: Must be used at ABET-accredited school in Ohio or at Notre Dame University.
Eligibility: Applicant must be high school senior. Applicant must be U.S. citizen residing in Ohio.
Basis for selection: Major/career interest in engineering or engineering, civil. Applicant must demonstrate high academic achievement, leadership, seriousness of purpose and service orientation.
Application requirements: Transcript. SAT/ACT scores. Minimum 3.0 GPA.
Additional information: Award may be renewable in some circumstances.

Amount of award:	$500-$2,500
Number of awards:	25
Number of applicants:	324
Application deadline:	December 16

Contact:
Engineers Foundation of Ohio
4795 Evanswood Drive
Suite 201
Columbus, OH 43229-7216
Phone: 614-846-1177
Fax: 614-846-1131

The Entomological Foundation

The Entomological Foundation Undergraduate Scholarship

Type of award: Scholarship.
Intended use: For full-time sophomore, junior or senior study at 4-year institution in United States or Canada.
Basis for selection: Competition/talent/interest in study abroad. Major/career interest in entomology; zoology; biology or science, general.
Application requirements: Essay, transcript. Application packet, including biographical information; statement of interest, financial need, and qualifications; recommendations; application form. Submit as e-mail to melodie@entfdn.org. All files must be in Adobe pdf format or Microsoft Word-compatible.
Additional information: Applicants must have completed at least one course or project in entomology. Must have accumulated 30 semester hours by time award is given. Preference given to students with financial need. Transcript may be sent separately. One $2,000 award sponsored by BioQuip Products. Visit Website for more information. Applications must be submitted electronically; paper applications not accepted.

Amount of award:	$1,500-$2,000
Number of awards:	4
Number of applicants:	72
Application deadline:	May 31
Notification begins:	September 30
Total amount awarded:	$6,500

Contact:
The Entomological Foundation
Undergraduate Scholarship
9332 Annapolis Road, Suite 210
Lanham, MD 20706-3115
Phone: 301-459-9082
Fax: 301-459-9084
Web: www.entfdn.org

Stan Beck Fellowship

Type of award: Scholarship.
Intended use: For undergraduate study at 4-year or graduate institution.
Eligibility: Applicant must be Alaskan native, Asian American, African American, Mexican American, Hispanic American, Puerto Rican or American Indian.
Basis for selection: Applicant must demonstrate financial need.
Application requirements: Recommendations, essay, transcript, proof of eligibility, nomination.
Additional information: Award amount varies. Need is based on physical limitations or economic, minority, or environmental conditions. Award amount is based on the earnings from the investment. Applications must be submitted electonically. See Website for additional information.

Amount of award:	$2,000
Number of awards:	1
Number of applicants:	10
Application deadline:	July 1

Contact:
The Entomological Foundation
9332 Annapolis Road #210
Lanham, MD 20706
Phone: 301-459-9082
Fax: 301-459-9084
Web: www.entfdn.org

Epilepsy Foundation of America

Behavioral Sciences Student Fellowship

Type of award: Research grant.
Intended use: For undergraduate or graduate study in United States.
Basis for selection: Major/career interest in social/behavioral sciences; sociology; social work; psychology; anthropology; nursing; economics; rehabilitation/therapeutic services or political science/government.
Application requirements: Research proposal. Completed application and fifteen copies.
Additional information: Three-month fellowship for work on an epilepsy study project. A professor or advisor must accept responsibility for supervision of student and project. Other appropriate fields include vocational rehabilitation, counseling, political science and subjects relevant to epilepsy research or practice. Women and minorities are especially encouraged to apply. Visit Website for more information.

Amount of award:	$3,000
Application deadline:	March 1

Contact:
Epilepsy Foundation of America - Programs and Research
Cathy Morris, Administrative Coordinator
4351 Garden City Drive
Landover, MD 20785-2267
Phone: 301-459-3700
Fax: 301-577-2684
Web: www.epilepsyfoundation.org/grants

Equality Maine

Joel Abromson Scholarship

Type of award: Scholarship.
Intended use: For undergraduate study at postsecondary institution.
Eligibility: Applicant must be high school senior. Applicant must be U.S. citizen or permanent resident residing in Maine.
Basis for selection: Essay. Applicant must demonstrate depth of character and service orientation.
Application requirements: Recommendations, essay, proof of eligibility.
Additional information: Open to any high school senior regardless of sexual orientation. Applicant must have proof of college acceptance. Visit Website for essay question, deadline, and additional information.

Scholarships

Amount of award: $500-$1,000
Number of awards: 2
Number of applicants: 50
Notification begins: May 1
Contact:
Equality Maine
P.O. Box 1951
Portland, ME 04104
Web: www.mlgpa.org

Equibal/The Perfect Body

Blemfree Online Scholarship Essay Contest

Type of award: Scholarship, renewable.
Intended use: For undergraduate study.
Eligibility: Applicant must be at least 18. Applicant must be U.S. citizen or permanent resident.
Basis for selection: Competition/talent/interest in Writing/journalism, baed on 500-word essay with bibliography. Essay must be based on following statement: "Describe why you believe an education is essential to professional success in the beauty industry and what role you believe continuing education will play in your future success." Major/career interest in cosmetology/hairdressing.
Application requirements: Essay. Must be enrolled in or be accepted to accredited beauty college, cosmetology school or esthetics program. Also open to already licensed professionals taking business-related courses as part of their continuing education. Candidates must also complete Nufree training program.
Additional information: Scholarships available to owners and employees of Nufree Registered salons, and their dependent children. Visit Website for application and more information.
  Amount of award: $2,500
  Notification begins: May 1
Contact:
Equibal/The Perfect Body
Essay Contest Coordinator
P.O. Box 180
Unionville, NY 10988
Web: thebodyperfect.com

Executive Women International

Executive Women International Scholarship

Type of award: Scholarship, renewable.
Intended use: For full-time undergraduate study at accredited 4-year institution in United States.
Eligibility: Applicant must be female, high school junior.
Basis for selection: Applicant must demonstrate high academic achievement, depth of character, leadership, seriousness of purpose and service orientation.
Application requirements: Interview, recommendations, essay. Applicants must have sponsoring teacher at their school. Must have a major/career interest in a professional field.

Additional information: Applicant must reside within boundaries of participating EWI chapter. Scholarship awarded each academic year, for up to five consecutive years, until student completes degree.
  Amount of award: $1,000-$10,000
  Application deadline: March 1
  Notification begins: April 15
Contact:
Executive Women International
515 South 700 East
Suite 2A
Salt Lake City, UT 84102
Phone: 801-355-2800
Fax: 801-355-2852
Web: www.executivewomen.org

Explorers Club

Explorers Club Youth Activity Fund

Type of award: Research grant.
Intended use: For undergraduate or graduate study.
Eligibility: Applicant must be U.S. citizen.
Basis for selection: Based on scientific and practical merit of proposal, competence of the investigator, and appropriateness of budget. Major/career interest in natural sciences. Applicant must demonstrate financial need and seriousness of purpose.
Application requirements: Recommendations, essay, research proposal. Request application form from club. Two letters of recommendation must be submitted with application. Physical release must accompany completed application.
Additional information: Applications will not be considered if they do not include two letters of recommendation. Recipients of grants must provide a one to two-page report on their exploration or research within the year of receiving the grant. Photographs are encouraged. Grants are made primarily to graduate students, but undergraduates are eligible. Send SASE when requesting application.
  Amount of award: $300-$1,200
  Number of awards: 20
  Number of applicants: 200
  Application deadline: January 15, April 1
Contact:
Explorers Club
The Exploration Fund Committee
46 East 70 Street
New York, NY 10021
Phone: 212-628-8383
Fax: 212-288-4449

Federal Employee Education and Assistance Fund

Federal Employee Education and Assistance Fund Scholarship

Type of award: Scholarship.
Intended use: For undergraduate, master's or doctoral study at accredited 2-year, 4-year or graduate institution.

Eligibility: Applicant or parent must be employed by Federal/U.S. Government.

Basis for selection: Applicant must demonstrate high academic achievement.

Application requirements: Recommendations, essay, transcript.

Additional information: Current civilian federal and postal employees with minimum three years service and their dependents are eligible. Applicant must have completed community service activities. Must have 3.0 GPA. Employee applicants eligible for part-time study; dependents must enroll full-time. Send SASE for application materials or download from Website beginning mid-January.

Amount of award:	$300-$1,500
Number of awards:	401
Number of applicants:	4,788
Application deadline:	March 30
Notification begins:	August 31

Contact:
Federal Employee Education and Assistance Fund
8441 West Bowles Avenue
Suite 200
Littleton, CO 80123-9501
Phone: 800-323-4140
Web: www.feea.org

Finance Authority of Maine

Maine Robert C. Byrd Honors Scholarship

Type of award: Scholarship, renewable.

Intended use: For full-time undergraduate study at 2-year or 4-year institution.

Eligibility: Applicant must be high school senior. Applicant must be U.S. citizen residing in Maine.

Basis for selection: Applicant must demonstrate high academic achievement.

Application requirements: Essay, transcript. High school profile from guidance office; SAT scores, class rank, list of scholastic achievements, awards and honors.

Additional information: Information available through Maine high school guidance offices and Finance Authority of Maine. Applicants do not need to complete FAFSA. See Website for further details.

Amount of award:	$1,500
Application deadline:	April 15

Contact:
Finance Authority of Maine
5 Community Drive
P.O. Box 949
Augusta, ME 04332-0949
Phone: 207-623-3263 or 800-228-3734
Fax: 207-623-0095
Web: www.famemaine.com

FIRST - Floriculture Industry Research and Scholarship Trust

Barbara Carlson Scholarship

Type of award: Scholarship.

Intended use: For sophomore, junior, senior or graduate study at accredited vocational, 2-year, 4-year or graduate institution in United States or Canada.

Eligibility: Applicant must be U.S. citizen, permanent resident, international student or Canadian citizen.

Basis for selection: Major/career interest in horticulture. Applicant must demonstrate financial need and high academic achievement.

Application requirements: Recommendations, transcript. Application. Statement of academic and professional intentions. Minimum 3.0 GPA.

Additional information: Applicant must intern or work for public gardens. Number and amount of scholarships vary. Applications are available from January to May. Send SASE with completed application for acknowledgment of receipt. Visit Website for application and more information.

Amount of award:	$500-$2,000
Number of awards:	1
Application deadline:	May 1

Contact:
Floriculture Industry Research and Scholarship Trust
Scholarship Applications
P.O. Box 280
East Lansing, MI 48826-0280
Phone: 517-333-4617
Fax: 517-333-4494
Web: www.firstinfloriculture.org

Carl F. Dietz Memorial Scholarship

Type of award: Scholarship.

Intended use: For full-time sophomore, junior or senior study at accredited 2-year or 4-year institution in United States or Canada.

Eligibility: Applicant must be U.S. citizen, permanent resident, international student or Canadian citizen.

Basis for selection: Major/career interest in horticulture. Applicant must demonstrate financial need and high academic achievement.

Application requirements: Recommendations, transcript. Statement of academic and professional intent. Minimum 3.0 GPA.

Additional information: Study of horticulture or career interest in horticulture required. Applicant must have interest in horticultural allied trades (i.e., supply sales, trade press, greenhouse equipment, etc.). Number and amount of awards vary each year; students should contact FIRST directly to obtain the latest application form, which lists all current scholarships and requirements. Applications available from January 1 to May 1. Download application from Website, or send SASE or printed self-addressed mailing label to FIRST.

Amount of award:	$500-$2,000
Number of awards:	1
Application deadline:	May 1

Contact:
Floriculture Industry Research and Scholarship Trust
Scholarship Applications
P.O. Box 280
East Lansing, MI 48826-0280
Phone: 517-333-4617
Fax: 517-333-4494
Web: www.firstinfloriculture.org

Dosatron International Scholarship

Type of award: Scholarship.
Intended use: For junior, senior or graduate study at accredited 4-year or graduate institution in United States or Canada.
Eligibility: Applicant must be U.S. citizen, permanent resident, international student or Canadian citizen.
Basis for selection: Major/career interest in horticulture. Applicant must demonstrate financial need and high academic achievement.
Application requirements: Recommendations, transcript. Application. Statement of academic and professional intent. Minimum 3.0 GPA.
Additional information: Applicant must have interest in floriculture production, with a career goal of working in a greenhouse. Number and amount of scholarships vary. Applications are available from January to May. Send SASE with completed application for acknowledgment of receipt. Visit Website for applications and more information.

Amount of award:	$500-$2,000
Application deadline:	May 1

Contact:
Floriculture Industry Research and Scholarship Trust
Scholarship Applications
P.O. Box 280
East Lansing, MI 48826-0280
Phone: 517-333-4617
Fax: 517-333-4494
Web: www.firstinfloriculture.org

Earl J. Small Growers Scholarship

Type of award: Scholarship.
Intended use: For full-time sophomore, junior or senior study at accredited 4-year institution in United States or Canada.
Eligibility: Applicant must be U.S. citizen, permanent resident, international student or Canadian citizen.
Basis for selection: Major/career interest in horticulture.
Application requirements: Recommendations, transcript. Statement of academic and professional intent. Minimum 3.0 GPA.
Additional information: Study of horticulture or career interest in horticulture required. To apply for this scholarship, applicant must have interest in greenhouse production and potted plants. Number and amount of scholarships changes each year; students should contact FIRST directly to obtain the latest application form, which lists all current scholarships and requirements. Applications available from January 1 to May 1. Download application from Website, or send SASE or printed self-addressed mailing label to FIRST.

Amount of award:	$500-$2,000
Number of awards:	1
Application deadline:	May 1

Contact:
Floriculture Industry Research and Scholarship Trust
Scholarship Applications
P.O. Box 280
East Lansing, MI 48826-0280
Phone: 517-333-4617
Fax: 517-333-4494
Web: www.firstinfloriculture.org

Ed Markham International Scholarship

Type of award: Scholarship.
Intended use: For sophomore, junior, senior or graduate study at accredited 2-year, 4-year or graduate institution in United States or Canada.
Eligibility: Applicant must be U.S. citizen, permanent resident, international student or Canadian citizen.
Basis for selection: Major/career interest in horticulture or marketing. Applicant must demonstrate financial need and high academic achievement.
Application requirements: Recommendations, transcript. Application. Statement of academic and professional intent. Minimum 3.0 GPA.
Additional information: Must have interest in studying horticulture marketing through international travel. Number and amount of scholarships vary. Applications are available from January 1 to May 1. Send SASE with completed application for acknowledgment of receipt. Visit Website for applications and more information.

Amount of award:	$500-$2,000
Application deadline:	May 1

Contact:
Floriculture Industry Research and Scholarship Trust
Scholarship Applications
P.O. Box 280
East Lansing, MI 48826-0280
Phone: 517-333-4617
Fax: 517-333-4494
Web: www.firstinfloriculture.org

Fran Johnson Non-Traditional Scholarship

Type of award: Scholarship.
Intended use: For full-time undergraduate study at accredited 4-year or graduate institution in United States or Canada.
Eligibility: Applicant must be returning adult student. Applicant must be U.S. citizen, permanent resident, international student or Canadian citizen.
Basis for selection: Major/career interest in horticulture. Applicant must demonstrate financial need and high academic achievement.
Application requirements: Recommendations, transcript. Statement of academic and professional intent.
Additional information: Study of horticulture or career interest in horticulture required. Specific interest in bedding plants or floral crops required. Must have been out of academic setting for at least five years and re-entering school. Number and amount of awards vary each year; students should contact FIRST directly to obtain the latest application form, which lists all current scholarships and requirements. Applications available from January 1 to May 1; download from Website, or send SASE or printed self-addressed mailing label to FIRST.

Amount of award:	$500-$2,000
Number of awards:	1
Application deadline:	May 1

Contact:
Floriculture Industry Research and Scholarship Trust
Scholarship Applications
P.O. Box 280
East Lansing, MI 48826-0280
Phone: 517-333-4617
Fax: 517-333-4494
Web: www.firstinfloriculture.org

Harold Bettinger Memorial Scholarship

Type of award: Scholarship.
Intended use: For full-time sophomore, junior or senior study at accredited 4-year or graduate institution in United States or Canada.
Eligibility: Applicant must be U.S. citizen, permanent resident, international student or Canadian citizen.
Basis for selection: Major/career interest in horticulture; business or marketing. Applicant must demonstrate financial need and high academic achievement.
Application requirements: Recommendations, transcript. Statement of academic and professional intent. Minimum 3.0 GPA.
Additional information: Study of horticulture or career interest in horticulture required. To apply for this scholarship, applicant's major or minor must be in business and/or marketing with intent to apply it to a horticulture-related business. Number and amount of awards vary each year; students should contact FIRST directly to obtain the latest application form, which lists all of the current scholarships and requirements. Applications available from January 1 to May 1; download application from Website, or send SASE or printed self-addressed mailing label to FIRST.

Amount of award:	$500-$2,000
Number of awards:	1
Application deadline:	May 1

Contact:
Floriculture Industry Research and Scholarship Trust
Scholarship Applications
P.O. Box 280
East Lansing, MI 48826-0280
Phone: 517-333-4617
Fax: 517-333-4494
Web: www.firstinfloriculture.org

Jacob Van Namen Marketing Scholarship

Type of award: Scholarship.
Intended use: For sophomore, junior or senior study at accredited 2-year or 4-year institution in United States or Canada.
Eligibility: Applicant must be U.S. citizen, permanent resident, international student or Canadian citizen/resident.
Basis for selection: Major/career interest in horticulture; agribusiness; marketing; botany or agriculture. Applicant must demonstrate financial need and high academic achievement.
Application requirements: Recommendations, transcript. Application. Statement of academic and professional intent. Minimum 3.0 GPA.
Additional information: Applicant must have interest in agribusiness marketing and distribution of floral products. Number and amount of scholarships vary. Applications are available from January 1 to May 1. Send SASE with completed application for acknowledgment of receipt. Visit Website for application and more information.

Amount of award:	$500-$2,000
Number of awards:	1
Application deadline:	May 1

Contact:
Floriculture Industry Research and Scholarship Trust
Scholarship Applications
P.O. Box 280
East Lansing, MI 48826-0280
Phone: 517-333-4617
Fax: 517-333-4494
Web: www.firstinfloriculture.org

Jerry Baker Scholarship

Type of award: Scholarship.
Intended use: For full-time freshman study at accredited 4-year institution in United States or Canada.
Eligibility: Applicant must be high school senior. Applicant must be U.S. citizen, permanent resident, international student or Canadian citizen/resident.
Basis for selection: Major/career interest in horticulture or landscape architecture. Applicant must demonstrate financial need and high academic achievement.
Application requirements: Recommendations, transcript. Statement of academic and professional intent.
Additional information: Study of horticulture or career interest in horticulture, landscaping or gardening required. Number and amount of awards vary; students should contact FIRST directly to obtain the latest application form, which lists all current scholarships and requirements. Scholarship applications available from January 1 to May 1; download from Website, or send SASE or printed self-addressed mailing label to FIRST.

Amount of award:	$500-$2,000
Application deadline:	May 1

Contact:
Floriculture Industry Research and Scholarship Trust
Scholarship Applications
P.O. Box 280
East Lansing, MI 48826-0280
Phone: 517-333-4617
Fax: 517-333-4494
Web: www.firstinfloriculture.org

Jerry Wilmot Scholarship

Type of award: Scholarship.
Intended use: For full-time sophomore, junior or senior study at accredited 2-year or 4-year institution in United States or Canada.
Eligibility: Applicant must be U.S. citizen, permanent resident, international student or Canadian citizen/resident.
Basis for selection: Major/career interest in horticulture; business; finance/banking or business/management/administration. Applicant must demonstrate financial need and high academic achievement.
Application requirements: Recommendations, transcript. Essay stating academic and professional intent. Minimum 3.0 GPA.
Additional information: Study of horticulture or career interest in horticulture required. Applicant must major or minor in business or finance with intent to apply it to garden center management. Number and amount of award varies; students should contact FIRST directly to obtain the latest application form, which lists all current scholarships and requirements. Application available from January 1 to May 1; download from Website, send SASE or printed self-addressed mailing label to FIRST.

Amount of award: $500-$2,000
Number of awards: 1
Application deadline: May 1
Contact:
Floriculture Industry Research and Scholarship Trust
Scholarship Applications
P.O. Box 280
East Lansing, MI 48826-0280
Phone: 517-333-4617
Fax: 517-333-4494
Web: www.firstinfloriculture.org

J.K. Rathmell, Jr., Memorial for Work/Study Abroad

Type of award: Scholarship.
Intended use: For full-time junior, senior or graduate study at accredited 4-year or graduate institution in or outside United States or Canada.
Eligibility: Applicant must be U.S. citizen, permanent resident, international student or Canadian citizen.
Basis for selection: Competition/talent/interest in Study abroad. Major/career interest in horticulture or landscape architecture. Applicant must demonstrate financial need, high academic achievement, depth of character and seriousness of purpose.
Application requirements: Recommendations, transcript. Statement of academic and professional intent. Minimum 3.0 GPA.
Additional information: Study of horticulture or career interest in horticulture required. Applicants must plan work/study abroad and submit specific plan for such. Preference given to those planning to work or study for six months or longer. Must have interest in floriculture, ornamental horticulture or landscape architecture. Must include letter of invitation from host institution abroad. Number and amount of awards vary; students should contact FIRST directly to obtain the latest application form, which lists all current scholarships and requirements. Applications available from January 1 to May 1; download from Website, or send SASE or printed self-addressed mailing label to FIRST.
Amount of award: $500-$2,000
Number of awards: 1
Application deadline: May 1
Contact:
Floriculture Industry Research snd Scholarship Trust
Scholarship Applications
P.O. Box 280
East Lansing, MI 48826-0280
Phone: 517-333-4617
Fax: 517-333-4494
Web: www.firstinfloriculture.org

Paris Fracasso Production Floriculture Scholarship

Type of award: Scholarship.
Intended use: For junior or senior study at accredited 4-year institution in United States or Canada.
Eligibility: Applicant must be U.S. citizen, permanent resident, international student or Canadian citizen/resident.
Basis for selection: Major/career interest in horticulture. Applicant must demonstrate financial need and high academic achievement.
Application requirements: Recommendations, transcript. Application. Statement of academic and professional intent. Minimum 3.0 GPA.

Additional information: Applicant must have interest in career in floriculture production. Number and amount of scholarships vary. Applications are available from January to May. Send SASE with completed application for acknowledgment of receipt. Visit Website for applications and more information.
Amount of award: $500-$2,000
Number of awards: 1
Application deadline: May 1
Contact:
Floriculture Industry Research and Scholarship Trust
Scholarship Applications
P.O. Box 280
East Lansing, MI 48826-0280
Phone: 517-333-4617
Fax: 517-333-4494
Web: www.firstinfloriculture.org

Vocational Horticulture Scholarship

Type of award: Scholarship.
Intended use: For full-time undergraduate certificate, freshman, sophomore or non-degree study at accredited vocational or 2-year institution in United States or Canada.
Eligibility: Applicant must be U.S. citizen, permanent resident, international student or Canadian citizen.
Basis for selection: Major/career interest in horticulture. Applicant must demonstrate financial need and high academic achievement.
Application requirements: Recommendations, transcript. Essay stating academic and professional intent. Minimum 3.0 GPA.
Additional information: Must intend to become floriculture plant producer or operations manager. Number and amount of awards vary each year; students should contact FIRST directly to obtain the latest application form, which lists all current scholarships and requirements. Applications available from January 1 to May 1. Download application from Website, or send SASE or printed self-addressed mailing label to FIRST.
Amount of award: $500-$2,000
Number of awards: 1
Application deadline: May 1
Contact:
Floriculture Industry Research and Scholarship Trust
Scholarship Applications
P.O. Box 280
East Lansing, MI 48826-0280
Phone: 517-333-4617
Fax: 517-333-4494
Web: www.firstinfloriculture.org

First Marine Division Association, Inc.

First Marine Division Association Scholarship

Type of award: Scholarship, renewable.
Intended use: For full-time undergraduate study at accredited 2-year or 4-year institution in United States.
Eligibility: Applicant must be high school senior. Applicant must be U.S. citizen. Applicant must be dependent of disabled veteran or deceased veteran who served in the Marines.

Basis for selection: Applicant must demonstrate depth of character and seriousness of purpose.
Application requirements: Essay, proof of eligibility.
Additional information: This program is to assist dependents of deceased or 100 percent permanently disabled veterans of service with the First Marine Division in furthering education toward a bachelor's degree. Contact office by phone, fax or mail for additional information and application deadlines.

Amount of award:	$1,500
Number of awards:	58
Number of applicants:	250
Total amount awarded:	$74,750

Contact:
First Marine Division Association, Inc.
14325 Willard Road
Suite 107
Chantilly, VA 20151-2110
Phone: 703-803-3195
Fax: 703-803-7114
Web: www.1stmarinedivisionassociation.org

Fisher Communications, Inc.

Fisher Broadcasting Scholarship for Minorities

Type of award: Scholarship.
Intended use: For full-time sophomore, junior or senior study at accredited vocational, 2-year or 4-year institution in United States.
Eligibility: Applicant must be Alaskan native, Asian American, African American, Mexican American, Hispanic American, Puerto Rican or American Indian. Applicant must be U.S. citizen.
Basis for selection: Major/career interest in radio/television/film; journalism; communications or marketing. Applicant must demonstrate financial need, depth of character, seriousness of purpose and service orientation.
Application requirements: Interview, recommendations, essay, transcript, proof of eligibility.
Additional information: Amount of award varies each year. Minimum 2.5 GPA. Must have career interest in broadcast communications or broadcast journalism. Washington, Oregon, Idaho and Montana state residents may attend school in any state. Also open to applicants from other states attending school in Washington, Oregon, Idaho and Montana. Successful applicants may also be offered summer employment with Fisher Broadcasting at appropriate pay for position being filled. Only finalists will be interviewed.

Number of awards:	4
Number of applicants:	18
Application deadline:	April 30
Notification begins:	July 1
Total amount awarded:	$12,323

Contact:
Fisher Communications Inc.
100 Fourth Ave. N Ste 440
Seattle, WA 98109
Web: www.fsci.com/broadcasting/scholarship.htm

Florida Department of Education

Children of Deceased or Disabled Veterans or Children of Servicemen Classified as Prisoners of War or Missing in Action Scholarship Program

Type of award: Scholarship, renewable.
Intended use: For full-time undergraduate study at postsecondary institution. Designated institutions: Eligible Florida postsecondary institutions.
Eligibility: Applicant must be U.S. citizen or permanent resident residing in Florida. Applicant must be dependent of disabled veteran, deceased veteran or POW/MIA during Grenada conflict, Korean War, Middle East War, Lebanon conflict, Panama conflict, Persian Gulf War, WW I, WW II or Vietnam.
Basis for selection: Applicant must demonstrate financial need.
Application requirements: Proof of eligibility. Completed Florida Financial Aid Aplication by April 1; Military and residency status of parent must be verified by Florida Department of Veterans' Affairs. Must meet eligibility requirements for receipt of state aid. Consult Bureau of Student Financial Assistance for additional details regarding specific conflicts and additional residency requirements.
Additional information: Award amount covers tuition/fees for one academic year at eligible Florida public postsecondary institution; renewable up to four years (eight semesters). Award for eligible private schools based on Florida public tuition/fees costs. Renewal applicant must maintain minimum 2.0 GPA. Visit Website for additional information and qualification specifications.

Amount of award:	Full tuition
Application deadline:	April 1

Contact:
Florida Department of Veterans Affairs
Executive Director
P.O. Box 31003
St. Petersburg, FL 33731-8903
Phone: 888-827-2004
Web: www.FloridaStudentFinancialAid.org

Critical Occupational Therapist or Physical Therapist Shortage Tuition Reimbursement Program

Type of award: Scholarship, renewable.
Intended use: For non-degree study.
Eligibility: Applicant must be U.S. citizen or permanent resident residing in Florida.
Basis for selection: Major/career interest in occupational therapy or physical therapy.
Application requirements: Proof of eligibility. Minimum of 3.0 GPA on all approved courses. Must be licensed or have valid temporary permit as therapist from Florida Department of Business and Professional Regulation and provide proof of same. Must be currently employed as full-time therapist in Florida public school or developmental research minimum of three years. Postsecondary Certification Form (PDF).

Additional information: Provides assistance to licensed therapists who take courses to improve their skills and knowledge and who have been employed as full-time therapists in Florida public schools for at least three years. Recipients receive up to $78 per credit hour for maximum of nine semester hours per academic year (or equivalent).
Contact:
Florida Department of Education
Office of Student Financial Assistance
1940 North Monroe Street, Suite 70
Tallahassee, FL 32303-4759
Phone: 888-827-2004
Web: www.FloridaStudentFinancialAid.org

Ethics in Business Scholarship

Type of award: Scholarship.
Intended use: For undergraduate study at 2-year or 4-year institution. Designated institutions: Florida community colleges and eligible private colleges and universities.
Basis for selection: Major/career interest in business.
Additional information: Scholarships funded by private and state contributions. Awards dependent on private matching funds. Contact financial aid office at participating institutions for more information.
Contact:
Florida Department of Education
1940 North Monroe Street
Tallahassee, FL 32303-4759
Phone: 888-827-2004
Web: www.FloridaStudentFinancialAid.org

Florida Academic Scholars Award

Type of award: Scholarship, renewable.
Intended use: For undergraduate study at postsecondary institution. Designated institutions: Eligible Florida postsecondary institutions.
Eligibility: Applicant must be high school senior. Applicant must be U.S. citizen or permanent resident residing in Florida.
Basis for selection: Applicant must demonstrate high academic achievement and service orientation.
Application requirements: Send ACT or SAT scores. Applicant should have 75 hours of community service experience. Must 1) be National Merit Scholarship finalist/Achievement Scholar/Finalist or National Hispanic Scholar; 2) be International Baccalaureate (IB) Diploma recipient or have completed IB curriculum with at least 1270/SAT or 28/ACT; or 3) have earned 3.5 GPA. GED Diplomas are also accepted. Two years of foreign language study necessary. Application must be completed before high school graduation.
Additional information: Bright Futures Scholarship Program breaks down as follows: public institution: scholarship covers full tuition and fees with up to $600 stipend; private institution: covers equivalent amount. In addition, high school senior with highest academic ranking in each county, based on GPA and SAT/ACT score, will receive annual Top Scholars Award of $1,500. Applications available from high school guidance office, Office of Financial Assistance or online. Check Website for additional information and requirements.
Amount of award: Full tuition
Contact:
Florida Department of Education
Bright Futures Scholarship Program
124 Collins, 325 West Gaines Street
Tallahassee, FL 32399-0400
Phone: 888-827-2004
Web: www.FloridaStudentFinancialAid.org

Florida Gold Seal Vocational Scholars Award

Type of award: Scholarship, renewable.
Intended use: For undergraduate study at vocational, 2-year or 4-year institution. Designated institutions: Eligible Florida postsecondary institutions.
Eligibility: Applicant must be high school senior. Applicant must be U.S. citizen or permanent resident residing in Florida.
Basis for selection: Applicant must demonstrate high academic achievement.
Application requirements: CPT, SAT or ACT. Application must be completed before high school graduation.
Additional information: At public institution, scholarship covers 75 percent of tuition and fees; at private institution, it covers equivalent amount. Applications available from high school guidance office, Office of Financial Assistance or online. Check Website for additional information and requirements.
Contact:
Florida Department of Education
Bright Futures Scholarship Program
124 Collins, 325 West Gaines Street
Tallahassee, FL 32303-4759
Phone: 888-827-2004
Web: www.FloridaStudentFinancialAid.org

Florida Merit Scholars Award

Type of award: Scholarship.
Intended use: For undergraduate study at 2-year or 4-year institution. Designated institutions: Eligible Florida postsecondary institutions.
Eligibility: Applicant must be high school senior. Applicant must be U.S. citizen or permanent resident residing in Florida.
Basis for selection: Applicant must demonstrate high academic achievement.
Application requirements: Send ACT/SAT scores. Applicant must 1) be National Merit Scholarship finalist, Achievement Scholar/Finalist or National Hispanic Scholar; 2) have completed International Baccalaureate IB curriculum/home education program/GED/Early Admissions with at least 970/SAT or 20/ACT; or 3) have earned 3.0 GPA with SAT/ACT scores as stated. Two years of foreign language study necessary. Application must be completed before high school graduation.
Additional information: At public institution, scholarship covers 75 percent of tuition and fees; at private institution, it covers equivalent amount. Applications available from high school guidance office, Office of Financial Assistance or online. Check Website for additional information and requirements.
Contact:
Florida Department of Education
Bright Futures Scholarship Program
124 Collins, 325 West Gaines Street
Tallahassee, FL 32399-0400
Phone: 888-827-2004
Web: www.FloridaStudentFinancialAid.org

Florida Robert C. Byrd Honors Scholarship

Type of award: Scholarship, renewable.
Intended use: For full-time undergraduate study at 2-year, 4-year or graduate institution in United States. Designated institutions: Eligible Florida or non-Florida public or private non-profit postsecondary institution.

Eligibility: Applicant must be high school senior. Applicant must be U.S. citizen or permanent resident residing in Florida.
Basis for selection: Applicant must demonstrate high academic achievement.
Application requirements: Proof of eligibility, nomination by high school principal or Adult Education Director. Send ACT or SAT scores. Applicant must meet registration requirements of Selective Service System. Completed Florida Financial Aid Application and ED 80-0016 (PDF) the same year in which student graduates from H.S. or received GED.
Additional information: Application requires unweighted cumulative GPA and SAT or ACT scores. Applicants are ranked with members of designated geographical region. Total amounts awarded determined annually.

   Application deadline: April 15
Contact:
Florida Department of Education
Office of Student Financial Assistance
1940 North Monroe Street, Suite 70
Tallahassee, FL 32303-4759
Phone: 888-827-2004
Web: www.FloridaStudentFinancialAid.org

Florida Seminole and Miccosukee Indian Scholarship

Type of award: Scholarship, renewable.
Intended use: For undergraduate or graduate study at vocational, 2-year, 4-year or graduate institution in United States. Designated institutions: Eligible Florida postsecondary institutions.
Eligibility: Applicant must be American Indian. Must be member of or eligible for membership in Seminole or Miccosukee Tribes in Florida. Applicant must be U.S. citizen or permanent resident residing in Florida.
Basis for selection: Applicant must demonstrate financial need.
Application requirements: Proof of eligibility. Florida Financial Aid Application, FAFSA.
Additional information: Award amount and deadline determined by tribe. Application not required for scholarship renewal. Applications can be obtained from the following addresses: Miccosukee Tribe of Florida, c/o Higher Education Committee, P.O. Box 440021 Tamiami Station, Miami, FL 33144, ph: 305-223-8380; or Seminole Tribe of Florida, c/o Higher Education Committee, 6300 Stirling Road, Hollywood, FL 33024, ph: 954-966-6300. For further information, contact Florida Department of Education Office of Student Financial Assistance or visit Website.
Contact:
Florida Department of Education
Office of Student Financial Assistance
1940 North Monroe Street, Suite 70
Tallahassee, FL 32303-4759
Phone: 888-827-2004
Web: www.FloridaStudentFinancialAid.org

Florida Student Assistance Grant Program

Type of award: Scholarship, renewable.
Intended use: For full-time undergraduate study at 2-year or 4-year institution. Designated institutions: Eligible Florida public and private postsecondary institutions.
Eligibility: Applicant must be U.S. citizen or permanent resident residing in Florida.

Basis for selection: Applicant must demonstrate financial need.
Application requirements: Proof of eligibility. FAFSA. Minimum 2.0 cumulative GPA for renewal applicants.
Additional information: Each participating institution determines application deadlines, student eligibility and award amounts. Applicant must not have previously received a bachelor's degree. Applications available from high school guidance offices and participating schools' financial aid offices. FAFSA deadline determined by participating institution.
   Amount of award: $200-$1,300
Contact:
Florida Department of Education
Office of Student Financial Assistance
1940 North Monroe Street, Suite 70
Tallahassee, FL 32303-4759
Phone: 888-827-2004
Web: www.FloridaStudentFinancialAid.org

Jose Marti Scholarship Challenge Grant

Type of award: Scholarship, renewable.
Intended use: For full-time undergraduate or graduate study at 2-year, 4-year or graduate institution in United States. Designated institutions: Eligible Florida postsecondary institutions.
Eligibility: Applicant must be Mexican American, Hispanic American or Puerto Rican. Applicant must be high school senior. Applicant must be U.S. citizen or permanent resident residing in Florida.
Basis for selection: Applicant must demonstrate financial need and high academic achievement.
Application requirements: 3.0 GPA and FAFSA.
Additional information: Must be of Spanish culture and born in Mexico or Spain or a Hispanic country of the Caribbean, Central America or South America, or child of same. Must meet Florida eligibility criteria for state student aid. Award number is limited to the amount of available funds; renewals take priority over new awards. A renewal application is not required with a 3.0 GPA and 12 undergraduate or nine graduate credit hours. Applications available from high school guidance office or college office of financial aid. Visit Website for more information.
   Amount of award: $2,000
   Application deadline: April 1
Contact:
Florida Department of Education
Office of Student Financial Assistance
1940 North Monroe Street, Suite 70
Tallahassee, FL 32303-4759
Phone: 888-827-2004
Web: www.FloridaStudentFinancialAid.org

Mary McLeod Bethune Scholarship

Type of award: Scholarship, renewable.
Intended use: For full-time undergraduate study at 4-year institution in United States. Designated institutions: Bethune-Cookman College, Edward Waters College, Florida A&M University or Florida Memorial College.
Eligibility: Applicant must be high school senior. Applicant must be residing in Florida.
Basis for selection: Applicant must demonstrate financial need and high academic achievement.
Application requirements: Minimum 3.0 cumulative GPA for renewal applicants.

Additional information: Minimum 3.0 high school GPA required. Applicant must maintain residency in Florida for purposes other than education for a minimum of 12 consecutive months prior to the first day of class of the academic term for which funds are requested. Deadlines established by participating institutions. Award is $3,000 per academic year, renewable for up to eight semesters or 12 quarters. Applicant must submit a renewal application. General award availability contingent on matching funds raised by the eligible institutions. Applications can be obtained from any of four designated institutions' financial aid offices or by contacting the Office of Student Financial Assistance.

Amount of award: $3,000

Contact:
Florida Department of Education
Office of Student Financial Assistance
1940 North Monroe Street, Suite 70
Tallahassee, FL 32303-4759
Phone: 888-827-2004
Web: www.FloridaStudentFinancialAid.org

Rosewood Family Scholarship Program

Type of award: Scholarship, renewable.
Intended use: For full-time undergraduate study at vocational, 2-year or 4-year institution in United States. Designated institutions: State university, public community college or public postsecondary vocational-technical school in Florida. Certificate programs must be minimum 900 clock hours.
Eligibility: Applicant must be Alaskan native, Asian American, African American, Mexican American, Hispanic American, Puerto Rican or American Indian. Applicant must be U.S. citizen or permanent resident residing in Florida.
Basis for selection: Applicant must demonstrate financial need.
Application requirements: FAFSA. If not Florida resident, copy of Student Aid Report (SAR) must be postmarked to Florida Bureau of Student Financial Assistance by May 15th (along with FAFSA).
Additional information: Descendants of African-American Rosewood families affected by the incidents of January 1923 given priority over other applicants. Award covers annual cost of tuition and fees up to $4,000 per semester for up to eight semesters. Visit Website for more information.

Amount of award: $4,000
Number of awards: 25
Total amount awarded: $100,000

Contact:
Florida Department of Education
Office of Student Financial Assistance
1940 North Monroe Street, 70
Tallahassee, FL 32303-4759
Phone: 888-827-2004
Web: www.FloridaStudentFinancialAid.org

William L. Boyd, IV, Florida Resident Access Grant

Type of award: Scholarship, renewable.
Intended use: For full-time undergraduate study at accredited 4-year institution. Designated institutions: Eligible private, non-profit Florida colleges and universities.
Eligibility: Applicant must be U.S. citizen or permanent resident residing in Florida.
Application requirements: Proof of eligibility. Renewal applicant must have minimum 2.0 cumulative GPA.

Additional information: Applicant must not have previously received a bachelor's degree and may not use award for study of divinity or theology. Applications available from eligible institutions financial aid offices. Award amount determined by Florida Legislature on yearly basis.

Amount of award: Full tuition

Contact:
Florida Department of Education
Office of Student Financial Assistance
1940 North Monroe Street, Suite 70
Tallahassee, FL 32303-4759
Phone: 888-827-2004
Web: www.FloridaStudentFinancialAid.org

Florida Division of Blind Services

Florida Educational Assistance for the Blind

Type of award: Scholarship, renewable.
Intended use: For full-time undergraduate, graduate or non-degree study at vocational, 2-year, 4-year or graduate institution in United States.
Eligibility: Applicant must be visually impaired. Applicant must be U.S. citizen or permanent resident residing in Florida.
Basis for selection: Must be determined eligible for vocational rehabilitation services based on a bilateral visual impairment and require educational assistance for an employment outcome. Applicant must demonstrate financial need and seriousness of purpose.
Application requirements: Transcript, proof of eligibility. Must be a client of State of Florida Division of Blind Services and eligible for vocational rehabilitation. Applicant must first secure federal or state scholarships/grants/loans.
Additional information: Tuition, books, reader's service fees and maintenance awarded for out-of-state institutions. Only tuition paid for in-state institutions. Deadline dates vary.

Amount of award: Full tuition

Contact:
Florida State Division of Blind Services
1350 Executive Center Drive
Tallahassee, FL 32399
Phone: 850-488-1330
Fax: 850-487-1804

Ford Motor Company

Ford/American Indian College Fund Corporate Scholars Program

Type of award: Scholarship, renewable.
Intended use: For sophomore, junior or senior study at 4-year institution. Designated institutions: Participating colleges and universities.
Eligibility: Applicant must be Alaskan native or American Indian. Applicant must be U.S. citizen.
Basis for selection: Major/career interest in computer/information sciences; engineering, electrical/electronic;

accounting; finance/banking; information systems or marketing. Applicant must demonstrate depth of character and leadership.
Application requirements: Essay, transcript, proof of eligibility. Must be American Indian or Alaska Native with proof of enrollment or descendancy. Must include small color photo.
Additional information: Student must demonstrate leadership and commitment to the American Indian community and be attending one of the participating colleges or universities. Award is up to $5,000 for those attending tribal universities and up to $10,000 for those attending universities outside the tribal system. Applicant must have minimum 3.0 GPA.

Amount of award:	$5,000-$10,000
Number of applicants:	40
Application deadline:	March 15

Contact:
Ford Motor Company
8333 Greenwood Blvd
Denver, CO 80221
Phone: 303-426-8900
Fax: 303-426-1200
Web: www.collegefund.org

Foundation for Surgical Technology

Foundation for Surgical Technology Scholarship Fund

Type of award: Scholarship.
Intended use: For undergraduate study at accredited vocational or 2-year institution in United States.
Basis for selection: Major/career interest in surgical technology. Applicant must demonstrate financial need or high academic achievement. Major/career interest in surgical technology. Applicant must demonstrate financial need and high academic achievement.
Application requirements: Recommendations, transcript, proof of eligibility. Must be recommended by CAAHEP instructor.
Additional information: Applicant must be currently enrolled in surgical technology program approved by CAAHEP. Interested students may visit Website to download scholarship application, or call and request document #1015.

Amount of award:	$500-$2,500
Number of awards:	10
Number of applicants:	108
Application deadline:	April 1
Notification begins:	May 15
Total amount awarded:	$10,500

Contact:
Foundation for Surgical Technology
Scholarship Administrator
7108-C South Alton Way, Suite 200
Centennial, CO 80112-2106
Phone: 303-694-9130
Fax: 303-694-9169
Web: www.ffst.org

Foundation of Research & Education (FORE)

Fore Undergraduate Merit Scholarship

Type of award: Scholarship.
Intended use: For undergraduate study.
Basis for selection: Major/career interest in health-related professions. Applicant must demonstrate high academic achievement.
Application requirements: Recommendations, transcript, proof of eligibility. Three references from educators and/or employers.
Additional information: Applicant must be member of AHIMA. Applicant must be enrolled in a health information administration or health information technology program accredited by the Commission on Accreditation of Allied Health Education Programs and cannot be completing studies before December 2004. Applicant must have minimum GPA of 3.0 out of 4.0 or 4.0 out of 5.0. Applicant must be taking a minumim of eight quarter hours/six semester hours and be pursuing a degree. Applicants are asked not to call regarding receipt of applications. Verification of receipt will be sent via mail. Visit Website for more information.

Amount of award:	$1,000-$5,000
Application deadline:	May 30
Notification begins:	August 31

Contact:
AHIMA/FORE Attn. Undergraduate Scholarships
233 N. Michigan Ave.
Suite 2150
Chicago, IL 60601-5800
Phone: 312-233-1100
Fax: 312-233-1090
Web: www.ahima.org

Foundation of the National Student Nurses Association, Inc.

National Student Nurses Association Scholarship

Type of award: Scholarship.
Intended use: For full-time undergraduate study at accredited 2-year or 4-year institution. Designated institutions: State-approved schools of nursing or pre-nursing.
Eligibility: Applicant must be U.S. citizen or permanent resident.
Basis for selection: Major/career interest in nursing or nurse practitioner. Applicant must demonstrate financial need, high academic achievement and service orientation.
Application requirements: $10 application fee. Recommendations, essay, transcript, proof of eligibility. Must be enrolled in nursing or pre-nursing program. National Student Nurses Association members must submit proof of membership.
Additional information: All applicants considered for the following scholarships: General Scholarships, Career Mobility Scholarships, Breakthrough to Nursing Scholarships for Ethnic

People of Color, Specialty Scholarships, and Promise of Nursing Scholarships. Awards granted in spring for use in summer and following academic year. Include business-sized SASE with $.60 postage when requesting application. Applications available from August through January 15. Visit Website to download application.

Amount of award:	$1,000–$2,500
Application deadline:	January 22
Notification begins:	March 1
Total amount awarded:	$120,000

Contact:
Foundation of the National Student Nurses Association, Inc.
45 Main Street
Suite 606
Brooklyn, NY 11201
Phone: 718-210-0705
Web: www.nsna.org

Francis Ouimet Scholarship Fund

Francis Ouimet Scholarship

Type of award: Scholarship, renewable.
Intended use: For full-time undergraduate study.
Eligibility: Applicant must be residing in Massachusetts.
Basis for selection: Competition/talent/interest in athletics/sports. Applicant must demonstrate financial need, high academic achievement and service orientation.
Application requirements: Interview, recommendations, essay, transcript, proof of eligibility. Applicants must have completed two years' service to golf as caddies or helpers in the pro shop, or course superintendent operations. Service must have been done in Massachusetts. Applicants must submit recommendations from guidance counselor and three club officials, and submit official (FAFSA & CSS/Profile) financial data.
Additional information: High school seniors may apply if they meet golf course criterion. Contact Donna Palen at The Ouimet Fund Office in midsummer to be put on an application mailing list for awards following school year. Application packages are mailed in early September. Awards announced following August.

Amount of award:	$1,000–$6,000
Application deadline:	December 1

Contact:
Francis Ouimet Scholarship Fund
Donna Palen, Scholarship Administrator
300 Arnold Palmer Blvd.
Norton, MA 02766
Phone: 774-430-9090
Fax: 774-430-9091
Web: www.ouimet.org

Fred G. Zahn Foundation

Fred G. Zahn Foundation Scholarship

Type of award: Scholarship, renewable.

Intended use: For undergraduate study at accredited 2-year, 4-year or graduate institution in United States. Designated institutions: Washington state colleges and universities.
Eligibility: Applicant must be residing in Washington.
Basis for selection: Applicant must demonstrate financial need and high academic achievement.
Application requirements: Transcript. Letter detailing the cost of student's course of study and extracurricular activities, other financial resources available including part-time employment, career plans and work experience. Student Aid Report. Transcripts from all schools student has attended including high school.
Additional information: Must have graduated from Washington state high school. Minimum 3.75 GPA. May obtain additional information and application at eligible Washington state institution. Do not contact foundation.

Amount of award:	$1,500
Number of awards:	4
Number of applicants:	400
Application deadline:	April 15
Notification begins:	June 1

Contact:
Financial aid department of eligible Washington college or university.

Freedom from Religion Foundation

Blanche Fearn Memorial Award

Type of award: Scholarship.
Intended use: For undergraduate study.
Eligibility: Applicant must be high school senior.
Basis for selection: Competition/talent/interest in writing/journalism, based on essay on why student is freethinker; essay most suitable for atheistic and agnostic student. Major/career interest in social/behavioral sciences; political science/government or humanities/liberal arts.
Application requirements: Essay, proof of eligibility. Submit 3-4 typed, double-spaced pages with standard margins. Include autobiographical paragraph giving permanent address, phone numbers and e-mail. Identify high school and college/university to be attended. Include intended major and other interests.
Additional information: Applicant must be college-bound high school senior. Essay topics and requirements change annually and are announced in February. Students are requested not to inquire before then. Awards are $1,000 first place, $500 second place, $250 third place. Send SASE or visit Website for additional information.

Amount of award:	$250–$1,000
Number of applicants:	121
Application deadline:	July 1
Notification begins:	September 1
Total amount awarded:	$1,750

Contact:
Freedom From Religion Foundation
High School Essay Competition
P.O. Box 750
Madison, WI 53701
Phone: 608-250-8900
Web: www.ffrf.org/essay.html

FFRF Student Activist Award

Type of award: Scholarship.
Intended use: For undergraduate study at postsecondary institution.
Basis for selection: Major/career interest in social/behavioral sciences; political science/government or humanities/liberal arts.
Additional information: Given to students who have done something specific to separate church and state (e.g., stopped religious programs in public schools, been a plaintiff in a chuch-state lawsuit, etc.).

Amount of award:	$1,000
Number of awards:	2
Application deadline:	June 30
Total amount awarded:	$2,000

Contact:
Freedom From Religion Foundation
P.O. Box 750
Madison, WI 53701
Phone: 608-250-8900
Web: www.ffrf.org

Phyllis Stevenson Grams Memorial Award

Type of award: Scholarship.
Intended use: For full-time undergraduate or graduate study at postsecondary institution.
Eligibility: Applicant must be U.S. citizen.
Basis for selection: Competition/talent/interest in writing/journalism, based on essay on free thought concerning religion; essay most suitable for atheistic and agnostic student. Major/career interest in social/behavioral sciences; political science/government or humanities/liberal arts.
Application requirements: Essay. Submit 5-6 typed, double-spaced pages with standard margins, Include autobiographical paragraph giving both campus and permanent addresses, phone numbers and email. Identify college/university, major and interests.
Additional information: Applicant must be a currently enrolled college student. Essay topics and requirements change annually and are announced in February. Students are requested not to inquire before then. Awards are $1,000 first place, $500 second place, $250 third place. Send SASE or visit Website for additional information.

Amount of award:	$250-$1,000
Number of applicants:	116
Application deadline:	July 1
Notification begins:	September 1
Total amount awarded:	$1,750

Contact:
Freedom from Religion Foundation
College Essay Competition
P.O. Box 750
Madison, WI 53701
Phone: 608-256-8900
Web: www.ffrf.org/essay.html

Garden Club of America

F.M. Peacock Native Bird Habitat Scholarship

Type of award: Scholarship.

Intended use: For senior or graduate study at graduate institution.
Basis for selection: Major/career interest in ornithology.
Additional information: Grant for advanced study of U.S. winter/summer habitat of threatened or endangered native birds. Awarded in cooperation with the Cornell Lab of ornithology. No phone calls. For further information, send SASE.

Amount of award:	$4,000
Number of awards:	1
Application deadline:	January 15
Total amount awarded:	$4,000

Contact:
Cornell Lab of Ornithology
Scott Sutcliffe
159 Sapsucker Woods Road
Ithaca, NY 14850
Fax: 607-254-2415
Web: www.gcamerica.org

Garden Club of America Summer Environmental Awards

Type of award: Scholarship.
Intended use: For freshman, sophomore or junior study at 4-year institution.
Basis for selection: Major/career interest in environmental science or ecology.
Application requirements: Must send business-size SASE.
Additional information: Two or more awards for summer study in field of ecology and environmental studies.

Amount of award:	$1,500
Number of awards:	2
Application deadline:	February 10

Contact:
Garden Club of America
Attn: Scholarship Committee Summer Studies
14 East 60th Street
New York, NY 10022
Phone: 212-753-8287
Fax: 212-753-0134
Web: www.gcamerica.org

Katharine M. Grosscup Scholarship

Type of award: Scholarship.
Intended use: For junior, senior or graduate study at accredited 4-year or graduate institution in United States.
Eligibility: Applicant must be residing in Michigan, Ohio, West Virginia, Indiana, Kentucky or Pennsylvania.
Basis for selection: Major/career interest in horticulture. Applicant must demonstrate financial need and high academic achievement.
Application requirements: Interview, recommendations, transcript.
Additional information: Several scholarships available. Preference given to residents of Pennsylvania, Ohio, West Virginia, Michigan, Indiana and Kentucky. Please do not contact by phone. Application available on Website.

Amount of award:	$3,000
Application deadline:	February 1

Contact:
Grosscup Scholarship Committee/Cleveland Botanical Garden
11030 East Blvd, Attn: Mrs. Nancy Stevenson
Cleveland, OH 44106
Web: www.gcamerica.org

The Loy McCandless Marks Scholarship

Type of award: Scholarship.
Intended use: For junior, senior or graduate study at accredited 4-year or graduate institution in or outside United States.
Eligibility: Applicant must be U.S. citizen.
Basis for selection: Major/career interest in horticulture or botany.
Additional information: Complementary funding for science student to assist with tropical ornamental horticulture project. For graduate or advanced undergraduate students to study and do research at appropriate foreign institution specializing in study of tropical plants. Visit Website for application.

Amount of award:	$2,000
Number of awards:	1
Application deadline:	January 15

Contact:
Garden Club of America
Attn: Scholarship Committee Summer Studies
14 East 60th Street
New York, NY 10022
Phone: 212-753-8287
Fax: 212-753-0134
Web: www.gcamerica.org

Georgia Student Finance Commission

Georgia Governor's Scholarship

Type of award: Scholarship, renewable.
Intended use: For full-time undergraduate study at accredited 2-year or 4-year institution. Designated institutions: Public or private colleges and universities in Georgia.
Eligibility: Applicant must be high school senior. Applicant must be U.S. citizen or permanent resident residing in Georgia.
Basis for selection: Applicant must demonstrate high academic achievement, depth of character, leadership, patriotism, seriousness of purpose and service orientation.
Application requirements: Completed Governor's Scholarship application.
Additional information: Must be valedictorian, salutatorian, STAR Student or designated Georgia Scholar. Must enroll at eligible Georgia school within seven months of high school graduation. Must maintain 3.0 GPA with 30 semester hours earned each year to renew.

Amount of award:	$1,000
Number of awards:	2,758
Total amount awarded:	$4,114,504

Contact:
Georgia Student Finance Commission
2082 East Exchange Place
Suite 100
Tucker, GA 30084
Phone: 800-546-4673
Fax: 770-724-9031

Georgia Hope Scholarship - GED Recipient

Type of award: Scholarship.

Intended use: For undergraduate study at accredited vocational, 2-year or 4-year institution. Designated institutions: Any branch of University System of Georgia, Georgia Department of Technical and Adult Education, or HOPE-eligible private college/university in Georgia.
Eligibility: Applicant must be U.S. citizen or permanent resident residing in Georgia.
Application requirements: Proof of eligibility.
Additional information: Must have received GED from Georgia Department of Technical and Adult Education after June 30, 1993. Submit HOPE voucher upon enrollment. Students receiving GED from DTAE receive voucher automatically.

Amount of award:	$500
Number of awards:	4,947
Total amount awarded:	$2,467,836

Contact:
Georgia Student Finance Commission
2082 East Exchange Place, Suite 100
Tucker, GA 30084
Phone: 800-546-HOPE
Fax: 770-724-9031
Web: www.gsfc.org

Georgia Hope Scholarship - Private Institution

Type of award: Scholarship, renewable.
Intended use: For full-time undergraduate study at accredited 2-year or 4-year institution. Designated institutions: Georgia private colleges or universities.
Eligibility: Applicant must be U.S. citizen or permanent resident residing in Georgia.
Basis for selection: Applicant must demonstrate high academic achievement.
Application requirements: Must complete Georgia Tuition Equalization Grant (TEG) Application.
Additional information: Award designed to help academically outstanding pupils. Must be attending eligible college or university in Georgia. Minimum 3.0 GPA required.

Amount of award:	$1,500-$3,000
Number of awards:	14,861
Total amount awarded:	$39,490,821

Contact:
Georgia Student Finance Commission
2082 East Exchange Place, Suite 100
Tucker, GA 30084
Phone: 800-546-HOPE
Fax: 770-724-9031

Georgia Hope Scholarship - Public College or University

Type of award: Scholarship, renewable.
Intended use: For undergraduate study at accredited 2-year or 4-year institution. Designated institutions: Eligible Georgia public colleges or universities.
Eligibility: Applicant must be U.S. citizen or permanent resident residing in Georgia.
Basis for selection: Applicant must demonstrate high academic achievement.
Application requirements: Proof of eligibility. Submit FAFSA or HOPE application.
Additional information: Minimum 3.0 GPA. HOPE assistance includes any tuition, mandatory fees. Also includes book allowance for up to $150 per semester. Applicant must

Scholarships

have graduated high school after 1993. Must be designated HOPE scholar.

Amount of award:	Full tuition
Number of awards:	76,692
Total amount awarded:	$189,979,288

Contact:
Georgia Student Finance Commission
2082 East Exchange Place
Suite 100
Tucker, GA 30084
Phone: 800-546-HOPE
Fax: 770-724-9031

Georgia Hope Scholarship - Public Technical Institution

Type of award: Scholarship, renewable.
Intended use: For undergraduate certificate study at accredited vocational, 2-year or 4-year institution. Designated institutions: Branch or affiliate of the Georgia Department of Technical and Adult Education or branch of the University System of Georgia.
Eligibility: Applicant must be U.S. citizen or permanent resident residing in Georgia.
Application requirements: FAFSA or HOPE appplication.
Additional information: Scholarship covers tuition, mandatory fees plus book allowance up to $150 per semester for full-time students. Must be enrolled, matriculated technical certificate or diploma student.

Amount of award:	Full tuition
Number of awards:	104,707
Total amount awarded:	$86,910,529

Contact:
Georgia Student Finance Commission
2082 East Exchange Place
Suite 100
Tucker, GA 30084
Phone: 800-546-HOPE
Fax: 770-724-9052

Georgia Law Enforcement Personnel Dependents Grant

Type of award: Scholarship, renewable.
Intended use: For full-time undergraduate study at accredited vocational, 2-year or 4-year institution. Designated institutions: Georgia's private or public colleges or public technical institutes.
Eligibility: Applicant must be U.S. citizen or permanent resident residing in Georgia. Applicant's parent must have been killed or disabled in work-related accident as fire fighter, police officer or public safety officer.
Application requirements: Proof of eligibility. LEPD Grant application.
Additional information: Must complete preliminary document that verifies claim with parent's former employer and doctors. Application deadline is last day of registration for school term. Parent must have been permanently disabled or killed in the line of duty as Georgia police officer, firefighter or corrections officer.

Amount of award:	$2,000
Total amount awarded:	$64,270

Contact:
Georgia Student Finance Commission
2082 East Exchange Place
Suite 100
Tucker, GA 30084
Phone: 800-546-4673
Fax: 770-724-9031

Georgia LEAP Grant

Type of award: Scholarship, renewable.
Intended use: For undergraduate study.
Eligibility: Applicant must be residing in Georgia.
Basis for selection: Applicant must demonstrate financial need.
Application requirements: FAFSA.

Amount of award:	$300-$2,000
Number of awards:	3,135
Total amount awarded:	$1,475,500

Contact:
Georgia Student Finance Commission
2082 East Exchange Place
Suite 100
Tucker, GA 30084
Phone: 800-546-4673
Fax: 770-724-9031

Georgia Robert C. Byrd Scholarship

Type of award: Scholarship, renewable.
Intended use: For full-time undergraduate study at accredited 2-year or 4-year institution in United States.
Eligibility: Applicant must be high school senior. Applicant must be U.S. citizen or permanent resident residing in Georgia.
Basis for selection: Applicant must demonstrate high academic achievement, depth of character, leadership, seriousness of purpose and service orientation.
Application requirements: Recommendations, essay, transcript, proof of eligibility. Obtain application from high school guidance office.
Additional information: Application submitted to the Georgia Department of Education.

Amount of award:	$1,500
Number of awards:	703
Total amount awarded:	$1,023,545

Contact:
Georgia Student Finance Commission
Grants and Scholarships Section
2082 East Exchange Place, Suite 100
Tucker, GA 30084
Phone: 800-546-4673
Fax: 770-724-9031

Georgia Tuition Equalization Grant

Type of award: Scholarship, renewable.
Intended use: For full-time undergraduate study at accredited 4-year institution. Designated institutions: Agnes Scott College, American Intercontinental University, Andrew College, Atlanta Christian College, Atlanta College of Art, Art Institute of Atlanta, Berry College, Brenau College, Brewton-Parker College, Clark Atlanta University, Covenant College, DeVry Institute, Emmanuel College, Emory University, Georgia Military College, Ga. Baptist College of Nursing, LaGrange College, Life College, Mercer University, Morehouse College, Morris Brown College, Oglethorpe University, Oxford College, Paine College, Piedmont College, Reinhardt College, Savannah College of Art, Shorter College, Spelman College, South

College, Thomas College, Toccoa Falls College, Truett-McConnell College, Wesleyan College, Young Harris College. Also Clemson University, Florida A&M University, Florida State University, Troy State University at Dothan, University of Tennessee/Chattanooga.

Eligibility: Applicant must be U.S. citizen or permanent resident residing in Georgia.

Application requirements: Proof of eligibility. Mileage affidavit (for out-of-state schools only).

Additional information: Must be enrolled full-time at eligible private college or university in Georgia, or be a junior or senior with no Georgia public college within 50 miles of home and enrolled at eligible public college outside Georgia. Application deadlines set by schools.

Amount of award:	$800
Number of awards:	34,477
Total amount awarded:	$33,123,310

Contact:
Georgia Student Finance Commission
2082 East Exchange Place
Suite 100
Tucker, GA 30084
Phone: 800-546-4673
Fax: 770-724-9031

Glamour Magazine

Top Ten College Women Competition

Type of award: Scholarship.
Intended use: For full-time junior study at accredited 4-year institution.
Eligibility: Applicant must be female.
Basis for selection: Applicant must demonstrate high academic achievement, depth of character, leadership, seriousness of purpose and service orientation.
Application requirements: Recommendations, essay, transcript. List of activities and organizations; black-and-white or color photograph.
Additional information: Must be goal-oriented female and full-time junior. Selection based on meritorious attributes. Applications available October 1. Award includes trip to New York City.

Amount of award:	$1,500
Number of awards:	10
Number of applicants:	800
Application deadline:	February 10
Notification begins:	June 15
Total amount awarded:	$15,000

Contact:
Glamour Magazine
4 Times Square
16th floor
New York, NY 10036-6593
Phone: 800-244-4526 or 212-286-6667
Fax: 212-286-6922
Web: www.glamour.com

Golden Key International Honor Society

Art International

Type of award: Scholarship.
Intended use: For undergraduate or graduate study at accredited postsecondary institution.
Eligibility: Applicant or parent must be member/participant of Golden Key National Honor Society.
Basis for selection: Competition/talent/interest in Visual arts, based on artistic merit.
Application requirements: Entries accepted in the following eight categories: painting, drawing, mixed media, sculpture, photography, applied art, printmaking, and computer-generated art/illustration/graphic design/set design. Submit application form with slides.
Additional information: Open to Golden Key members only. $1,000 awarded to winners in each of eight categories; $100 awarded to up to 10 finalists in each category. Winning entries published in CONCEPTS and displayed at annual convention. One entry per member per category. Visit Website for details and application.

Amount of award:	$100-$1,000
Number of awards:	88
Number of applicants:	600
Application deadline:	April 1
Total amount awarded:	$16,000

Contact:
Art International
Golden Key International Honor Society
P.O. Box 23737
Nashville, TN 37202-3737
Phone: 800-377-2401 or 404-373-2400
Fax: 404-373-7033
Web: www.goldenkey.org

Business Achievement Awards

Type of award: Scholarship.
Intended use: For undergraduate or graduate study at accredited postsecondary institution.
Eligibility: Applicant or parent must be member/participant of Golden Key National Honor Society.
Basis for selection: Based on creativity and viability of business plan created in response to problem posed by an honorary member in business field. Major/career interest in business.
Application requirements: Recommendations, transcript. Application form and business plan. Business plan must not exceed three typed pages.
Additional information: Open to Golden Key members only. Must submit creative, viable business plan based on fundamental knowledge of business and marketing. First-place winner receives $1,000; second place, $750; third place, $500. Visit Website for details and application.

Amount of award:	$500-$1,000
Number of awards:	3
Application deadline:	March 1
Total amount awarded:	$2,250

Contact:
Business Achievement Awards
Golden Key International Honor Society
P.O. Box 23737
Nashville, TN 37202-3737
Phone: 800-377-2401 or 404-377-2400
Fax: 404-373-7033
Web: www.goldenkey.org

Claes Nobel Earth Ethics Award

Type of award: Scholarship.
Intended use: For undergraduate or graduate study at accredited postsecondary institution.
Eligibility: Applicant or parent must be member/participant of Golden Key National Honor Society.
Application requirements: Essay. Essay must respond to question: "How do you define earth ethics and how do you apply that definition in your everyday life?"
Additional information: Open to Golden Key members only. $1,000 awarded to student who exhibits dedication to environmental awareness and responsibility. Winning essay will be published in CONCEPTS magazine. Visit Website for details and application.

Amount of award:	$1,000
Number of awards:	1
Application deadline:	February 15
Total amount awarded:	$1,000

Contact:
Claes Nobel Earth Ethics Award
Attn: Scholarships
P.O. Box 23737
Nashville, TN 37202-3737
Phone: 800-377-2401 or 404-377-2400
Fax: 404-373-7033
Web: www.goldenkey.org

Education Achievement Awards

Type of award: Scholarship.
Intended use: For undergraduate or graduate study at accredited postsecondary institution.
Eligibility: Applicant or parent must be member/participant of Golden Key National Honor Society.
Basis for selection: Based on creativity of originality of lesson plan created in response to problem posed by an honorary member in education field. Major/career interest in education.
Application requirements: Recommendations, transcript. Application form and response to problem. Response should be in the form of an original thematic unit comprised of individual lesson plans.
Additional information: Open to Golden Key members only. Must submit creative, dynamic and inclusive original lesson plan based on fundamental knowledge of education. First-place winner receives $1,000; second place, $750; third place, $500. Visit Website for details and application.

Amount of award:	$500-$1,000
Number of awards:	3
Application deadline:	March 1
Total amount awarded:	$2,250

Contact:
Education Achievement Awards
Golden Key International Honor Society
1189 Ponce de Leon Avenue
Atlanta, GA 30306-4624
Phone: 800-377-2401 or 404-377-2400
Fax: 404-373-7033
Web: www.goldenkey.org

Engineering Achievement Awards

Type of award: Scholarship.
Intended use: For undergraduate or graduate study at accredited postsecondary institution.
Eligibility: Applicant or parent must be member/participant of Golden Key National Honor Society.
Basis for selection: Based on creativity and viability of response to problem posed by an honorary member in engineering field. Major/career interest in engineering.
Application requirements: Application form and response to problem. Must use sound mechanical/electrical/computer engineering techniques to develop solution.
Additional information: Open to Golden Key members only. First-place winner receives $1,000; second place, $750; third place, $500. Visit Website for details and application.

Amount of award:	$500-$1,000
Number of awards:	3
Application deadline:	March 1
Total amount awarded:	$2,250

Contact:
Engineering Achievement Awards
Golden Key International Society
P.O. Box 23737
Nashville, TN 37202-3737
Phone: 800-377-2401 or 404-377-2400
Fax: 404-373-7033
Web: www.goldenkey.org

Excellence in Speech and Debate Awards

Type of award: Scholarship.
Intended use: For undergraduate or graduate study.
Eligibility: Applicant or parent must be member/participant of Golden Key National Honor Society.
Basis for selection: Competition/talent/interest in Oratory/debate, based on viability of argument and verbal/nonverbal communication skills as displayed in videotaped monologue.
Application requirements: Application form. Videotaped monologue no more than five minutes in length.
Additional information: Only Golden Key members eligible to apply. Selected finalists will be asked to attend annual convention for public debate; winner will be selected based on live presentation. Visit Website for details and application.

Application deadline:	April 1

Contact:
Excellence in Speech and Debate Awards
Golden Key International Society
Attn: Scholarships
Nashville, TN 30306-4624
Phone: 800-377-2401 or 404-377-2400
Fax: 404-373-7033
Web: www.goldenkey.org

Ford Motor Company/Golden Key Undergraduate Scholarships

Type of award: Scholarship.
Intended use: For junior or senior study at accredited postsecondary institution.
Eligibility: Applicant or parent must be member/participant of Golden Key National Honor Society.
Basis for selection: Applicant must demonstrate high academic achievement, leadership and service orientation.
Application requirements: New member profile.
Additional information: Must be new member of Golden Key Honor Society. Every new member joining prior to invitation deadline automatically considered for award. Award amount: $500 minimum. Application deadline same as chapter's membership deadline and varies with school chapters. Two applicants (one junior, one senior) per chapter per school.

Number of awards:	600
Total amount awarded:	$300,000

Contact:
Golden Key International Honor Society
P.O. Box 23737
Nashville, TN 37202-3737
Phone: 800-377-2401 or 404-377-2400
Fax: 404-373-7033
Web: www.goldenkey.org

GEICO/Golden Key Adult Scholar Awards

Type of award: Scholarship.
Intended use: For undergraduate study at accredited postsecondary institution.
Eligibility: Applicant or parent must be member/participant of Golden Key National Honor Society. Applicant must be at least 25, returning adult student.
Basis for selection: Applicant must demonstrate high academic achievement.
Application requirements: Recommendations, essay, transcript. Send official application form along with all requested materials no later than April 1.
Additional information: Only undergraduate Golden Key members 25 years of age or older are eligible to apply. Visit Website for details and application.

Amount of award:	$1,000
Number of awards:	10
Number of applicants:	100
Application deadline:	April 1
Total amount awarded:	$10,000

Contact:
Golden Key International Honor Society
Attn: Scholarships
P.O. Box 23737
Nashville, TN 37202-3737
Phone: 800-377-2401 or 404-377-2400
Fax: 404-373-7033
Web: www.gknhs.gsu.edu

Golden Key Research Travel Grants

Type of award: Research grant.
Intended use: For undergraduate study.
Eligibility: Applicant or parent must be member/participant of Golden Key National Honor Society.
Basis for selection: Applicant must demonstrate high academic achievement.

Application requirements: Application form, statement of purpose, details of Golden Key activities, evidence of invitation to present at professional conference/research symposia, and recent transcript.
Additional information: Only undergraduate Golden Key members eligible to apply. Grant for members to travel to professional conferences and research symposia where they have been invited to present. Grants may also assist students who need funding to pursue field research related to honors thesis. Visit Website for details and application.

Amount of award:	$500
Number of awards:	10
Number of applicants:	75
Application deadline:	April 15, October 15
Total amount awarded:	$5,000

Contact:
Golden Key International Honor Society
Attn: Scholarships
P.O. Box 23737
Nashville, TN 37202-3737
Phone: 800-377-2401 or 404-377-2400
Fax: 404-373-7033
Web: www.gknhs.gsu.edu

Golden Key Service Award

Type of award: Scholarship.
Intended use: For undergraduate or graduate study at accredited postsecondary institution.
Eligibility: Applicant or parent must be member/participant of Golden Key National Honor Society.
Basis for selection: Applicant must demonstrate service orientation.
Application requirements: Recommendations, essay. Application form and requested materials must be postmarked no later than February 15.
Additional information: Only Golden Key members enrolled as students during previous academic year eligible to apply. Winner will receive $500; winner's chapter will receive $250; and charity of winner's choice will receive $250. Visit Website for details and application.

Amount of award:	$1,000
Number of awards:	1
Application deadline:	February 15
Total amount awarded:	$1,000

Contact:
Golden Key International Honor Society
Attn: Scholarships
P.O. Box 23737
Nashville, TN 37202-3737
Phone: 800-377-2401 or 404-377-2400
Fax: 404-373-7033
Web: www.goldenkey.org

Golden Key Study Abroad Scholarships

Type of award: Scholarship.
Intended use: For undergraduate study.
Eligibility: Applicant or parent must be member/participant of Golden Key National Honor Society.
Basis for selection: Competition/talent/interest in Study abroad, based on academic record and active participation in Golden Key activities. Applicant must demonstrate high academic achievement.
Application requirements: Transcript. Application form. Details of Golden Key activities. Description of planned study

program at host university. Statement of relevance of program to degree.

Additional information: Only undergraduate Golden Key members eligible to apply. Up to five scholarships awarded per deadline. Visit Website for details and application.

Amount of award:	$2,000
Number of awards:	10
Number of applicants:	200
Application deadline:	April 15, October 15
Total amount awarded:	$20,000

Contact:
Golden Key Study Abroad Scholarships
Golden Key National Honor Society
P.O. Box 23737
Nashville, TN 37202-3737
Phone: 800-377-2401 or 404-377-2400
Fax: 404-373-7033
Web: www.goldenkey.org

Information Systems Achievement Awards

Type of award: Scholarship.
Intended use: For undergraduate or graduate study at accredited postsecondary institution.
Eligibility: Applicant or parent must be member/participant of Golden Key National Honor Society.
Basis for selection: Based on creativity and viability of response to problem posed by an honorary member within information systems field. Major/career interest in information systems.
Application requirements: Recommendations, transcript. Application form and response to problem. Response may be in the form of essay or design.
Additional information: Open to Golden Key members only. Must submit creative, viable response based on fundamental knowledge of information systems. First-place winner receives $1,000; second place, $750; third place, $500. Visit Website for details and application.

Amount of award:	$500-$1,000
Number of awards:	3
Application deadline:	March 1
Total amount awarded:	$2,250

Contact:
Golden Key International Honor Society
Attn: Scholarships
P.O. Box 23737
Nashville, TN 37202-3737
Phone: 800-377-2401 or 404-377-2400
Fax: 404-373-7033
Web: www.goldenkey.org

International Student Leader Award

Type of award: Scholarship.
Intended use: For undergraduate or graduate study at accredited postsecondary institution.
Eligibility: Applicant or parent must be member/participant of Golden Key National Honor Society.
Basis for selection: Based on leadership and involvement in Golden Key activities, campus and community leadership, and academic merit. Applicant must demonstrate high academic achievement, leadership and service orientation.
Application requirements: Recommendations, essay, transcript. Include list of personal Golden Key involvement and extracurricular activities.

Additional information: Open to Golden Key members only. Applicant must be active member in good standing. Must be currently enrolled in an undergraduate or graduate program in accredited college/university. Visit Website for details and application.

Amount of award:	$1,000
Number of awards:	1
Application deadline:	May 1
Total amount awarded:	$1,000

Contact:
International Student Leader Award
Golden Key International Honor Society
P.O. Box 23737
Nashville, TN 37202-3737
Phone: 800-377-2401 or 404-377-2400
Fax: 404-373-7033
Web: www.goldenkey.org

Literary Achievement Awards

Type of award: Scholarship.
Intended use: For undergraduate or graduate study at accredited postsecondary institution.
Eligibility: Applicant or parent must be member/participant of Golden Key National Honor Society.
Basis for selection: Competition/talent/interest in writing/journalism.
Application requirements: Entries accepted in the following four categories: fiction, non-fiction, poetry, and feature writing. Entry must be original composition; previously published works not accepted. Submit application form with entry.
Additional information: Open to Golden Key members only. $1,000 awarded to winners in each of four categories. Winning entries also published in CONCEPTS. Only one entry per member per category. Visit Website for details and application.

Amount of award:	$1,000
Number of awards:	4
Application deadline:	April 1
Total amount awarded:	$4,000

Contact:
Golden Key International Honor Society
Attn: Scholarships
P.O. Box 23737
Nashville, TN 30202-3737
Phone: 800-377-2401 or 404-377-2400
Fax: 404-373-7033
Web: www.goldenkey.org

Performing Arts Showcase

Type of award: Scholarship.
Intended use: For undergraduate or graduate study at accredited postsecondary institution.
Eligibility: Applicant or parent must be member/participant of Golden Key National Honor Society.
Basis for selection: Competition/talent/interest in Performing arts, based on submitted video cassette entry (not to exceed ten minutes in length).
Application requirements: Entries accepted in the following six categories: dance, drama, film, vocal performance, instrumental performance and original musical composition. Entry must be submitted on VHS videotape (compact discs and audio cassettes accepted for original musical composition only). Must include application form with entry.
Additional information: Only Golden Key members eligible to apply. Winners receive $1,000 and opportunity to perform at annual convention. Only one entry per member per category. Visit Website for details and application.

Amount of award: $1,000
Number of awards: 6
Number of applicants: 300
Application deadline: March 1
Total amount awarded: $6,000
Contact:
Golden Key International Honor Society
Attn: Scholarships
P.O. Box 23737
Nashville, TN 37202-3737
Phone: 800-377-2401 or 404-377-2400
Fax: 404-373-7033
Web: www.gknhs.gsu.edu

Student Scholastic Showcase

Type of award: Scholarship.
Intended use: For undergraduate study at accredited postsecondary institution.
Eligibility: Applicant or parent must be member/participant of Golden Key National Honor Society.
Basis for selection: Based on quality of undergraduate research.
Application requirements: Research paper with abstract and faculty letter of support. Include Student Scholastic Showcase application form with entry.
Additional information: Only undergraduate Golden Key members eligible to apply. Alumni also eligible, but entry must have been undergraduate research. Only one submission per member. Every applicant will receive one-year subscription to Scientific American. Visit Website for details and application.
Amount of award: $1,000
Number of awards: 4
Number of applicants: 100
Application deadline: March 1
Total amount awarded: $4,000
Contact:
Student Scholastic Showcase
Golden Key International Honor Society
P.O. Box 23737
Nashville, TN 37202-3737
Phone: 800-377-2401 or 404-377-2400
Fax: 404-373-7033
Web: www.goldenkey.org

Golden State Minority Foundation

Golden State Minority Foundation Scholarship

Type of award: Scholarship.
Intended use: For full-time undergraduate or graduate study at 4-year institution in United States.
Eligibility: Applicant must be Asian American, African American, Mexican American or American Indian. Applicant must be U.S. citizen residing in California.
Basis for selection: Major/career interest in economics; insurance/actuarial science; business; health services administration or engineering.
Additional information: Student must not be employed more than 28 hours per week. Applicant must have minimum 3.0 GPA.

Amount of award: $2,000
Number of awards: 75
Application deadline: April 1
Contact:
Golden State Minority Foundation
1055 Wilshire Blvd. #1115
Los Angeles, CA 90017-2431
Phone: 213-482-6300
Fax: 213-482-6305
Web: www.gsmf.org

Golf Course Superintendents Association of America

GCSAA Legacy Awards

Type of award: Scholarship.
Intended use: For full-time undergraduate study at accredited 2-year, 4-year or graduate institution.
Eligibility: Applicant or parent must be member/participant of Golf Course Superintendents Association of America.
Application requirements: Recommendations, essay, transcript. Applicant must be child or grandchild of GCSAA member.
Additional information: Applicants must be child or grandchild of GCSAA members who have been active for at least five years. Must be enrolled full-time at accredited postsecondary institution or, if high school senior, must be accepted for following academic year. Must be studying field unrelated to golf course management. Award is funded by Syngenta Professional Products. Visit Website or contact via e-mail (psmith@gcsaa.org) for additional information.
Amount of award: $1,500
Number of awards: 20
Application deadline: April 15
Total amount awarded: $30,000
Contact:
Scholarships/Student Programs Manager, Pam Smith
1421 Research Park Drive
Lawrence, KS 66049
Phone: 800-472-7878 ext. 678
Fax: 785-832-4449
Web: www.gcsaa.org

GCSAA Scholars Competition

Type of award: Scholarship.
Intended use: For sophomore, junior or senior study at accredited 2-year or 4-year institution.
Eligibility: Applicant or parent must be member/participant of Golf Course Superintendents Association of America.
Basis for selection: Major/career interest in turf management. Applicant must demonstrate high academic achievement.
Application requirements: Recommendations, transcript.
Additional information: Applicant must be a Golf Course Superintendents Association of America (GCSAA) member. Must be planning career as a golf course superintendent and have successfully completed at least 24 credit hours or equivalent of one year of full-time study. Visit Website or contact via e-mail address (psmith@gcsaa.org) for additional information.

Amount of award:	$500-$6,000
Number of awards:	24
Application deadline:	June 1

Contact:
Scholarship/Student Programs Manager, Pam Smith
1421 Research Park Drive
Lawrence, KS 66049-3859
Phone: 800-472-7878 ext. 678
Fax: 785-832-4449
Web: www.gcsaa.org

GCSAA Student Essay Contest

Type of award: Scholarship.
Intended use: For undergraduate or graduate study at accredited 2-year, 4-year or graduate institution.
Eligibility: Applicant or parent must be member/participant of Golf Course Superintendents Association of America.
Basis for selection: Based on seven- to twelve-page essay focusing on golf course management. Major/career interest in turf management.
Additional information: Applicant must be member of Golf Course Superintendents Association of America (GCSAA). Applicant must be pursuing degree in turfgrass science, agronomy or any field related to golf course management. First, $2,000; 2nd, $1,500; 3rd, $1,000. Visit Website or contact via e-mail (psmith@gcsaa.org) for additional information.

Amount of award:	$1,000-$2,000
Number of awards:	3
Number of applicants:	12
Application deadline:	March 31
Total amount awarded:	$4,500

Contact:
Scholarship/Student Programs Manager, Pam Smith
1421 Research Park Drive
Lawrence, KS 66049
Phone: 800-472-7878 ext. 678
Fax: 785-832-4449
Web: www.gcsaa.org

Scotts Company Scholars Program

Type of award: Scholarship.
Intended use: For freshman, sophomore or junior study at accredited 2-year or 4-year institution.
Basis for selection: Major/career interest in turf management.
Application requirements: Recommendations, transcript.
Additional information: Five finalists are selected for summer internships, receive a $500 award and an opportunity to compete for two $2,500 scholarships. Applicants must be pursuing a career in the green industry. Women, minorities, and persons with disabilities encouraged to apply. Visit Website or contact via e-mail (psmith@gcsaa.org) for additional information.

Amount of award:	$500-$2,500
Number of awards:	7
Application deadline:	March 1
Total amount awarded:	$7,500

Contact:
Scholarship/Student Programs Manager, Pam Smith
1421 Research Park Drive
Lawrence, KS 66049
Phone: 800-472-7878 ext. 678
Fax: 785-832-4449
Web: www.gcsaa.org

Grange Insurance Association

Grange Insurance Scholarship

Type of award: Scholarship.
Intended use: For full-time undergraduate or graduate study at accredited vocational, 2-year, 4-year or graduate institution.
Eligibility: Applicant or parent must be member/participant of Fraternal Grange. Applicant must be U.S. citizen or permanent resident residing in Wyoming, California, Oregon, Montana, Idaho, Washington or Colorado.
Basis for selection: Applicant must demonstrate financial need, high academic achievement, depth of character, leadership, patriotism, seriousness of purpose and service orientation.
Application requirements: Recommendations, essay, transcript. Financial need, scholastic ability.
Additional information: Applicant or parent must be permanent resident of the designated state and member of The Grange in that state. Applicant or parent need not have insurance with The Grange. Applicants must be GIG policyholders or children and grandchildren of GIG policyholders within the 7 states in which GIG operates: CA, CO, ID, MT, OR, WA and WY, or children and grandchildren of Grange members or the children and grandchildren of GIG company employees. Previous recipients also eligible to apply.

Amount of award:	$750-$1,000
Number of awards:	25
Number of applicants:	117
Application deadline:	April 15
Notification begins:	May 15
Total amount awarded:	$19,500

Contact:
Grange Insurance Association
Scholarship Coordinator
P.O. Box 21089
Seattle, WA 98111-3089
Phone: 800-247-2643 ext. 2200

Greater Kanawha Valley Foundation

Greater Kanawha Valley Scholarship Program

Type of award: Scholarship, renewable.
Intended use: For full-time undergraduate or graduate study at postsecondary institution. Designated institutions: West Virginia institutions.
Eligibility: Applicant must be residing in West Virginia.
Basis for selection: Applicant must demonstrate financial need, high academic achievement, depth of character and leadership.
Application requirements: Recommendations, essay, transcript.
Additional information: Greater Kanawha Valley Foundation offers several scholarships. Visit Website for complete listing. Student must have a minimum of 20 ACT.

Amount of award: $1,000
Number of applicants: 1,300
Application deadline: February 14
Notification begins: May 1
Contact:
Greater Kanawha Valley Foundation
P.O. Box 3041
Charleston, WV 25331
Phone: 304-346-3620
Web: www.tgkvf.org

Guideposts

Young Writers Contest

Type of award: Scholarship.
Intended use: For undergraduate study at accredited 2-year or 4-year institution.
Eligibility: Applicant must be high school junior or senior.
Basis for selection: Competition/talent/interest in writing/ journalism, based on nonfiction article (maximum 1,200 words), must be in first-person, written in style of Guideposts magazine, and demonstrating writer's faith in God. Major/career interest in publishing; communications or journalism.
Application requirements: Essay.
Additional information: Prizes must be used within five years after high school. Only high school juniors and seniors may compete. Submission of a true, first-person story in which the applicant writes of a significant experience required. Guideposts employees and their children not eligible.
Amount of award: $250-$10,000
Number of awards: 20
Number of applicants: 4,000
Application deadline: November 25
Notification begins: January 4
Total amount awarded: $38,500
Contact:
Youth Writing Contest/ Guideposts
Christine Pisani
16 East 34 Street, 21st Floor
New York, NY 10016
Web: www.guideposts.org

Hall/McElwain Merit Scholarships

National Eagle Scout Merit Scholarships

Type of award: Scholarship.
Intended use: For freshman, sophomore or junior study.
Eligibility: Applicant or parent must be member/participant of Boy Scouts of America, Eagle Scouts. Applicant must be male, high school senior.
Basis for selection: Applicant must demonstrate leadership.
Application requirements: Recommendations, proof of eligibility. Applicant must have been granted the Eagle Scout rank. Must have strong record of participation in activities outside of scouting. Recommendation must be from volunteer or professional Scout leader.

Additional information: Only those applications postmarked after November 1 but no later than February 28 and received by March 5 will be considered. Do not fax applications. Visit Website for more information and to download application.
Amount of award: $1,500
Number of awards: 80
Application deadline: February 28
Notification begins: June 15
Contact:
Eagle Scout Service S220
Boy Scouts of America
1325 W. Walnut Hill Lane, P.O. Box 152079
Irving, TX 75015-2079
Phone: 972-580-2032
Web: www.scouting.org/nesa/scholar

Harness Tracks of America

Harness Tracks of America Scholarship

Type of award: Scholarship.
Intended use: For full-time undergraduate or graduate study at accredited postsecondary institution.
Eligibility: Applicant or parent must be member/participant of Harness Racing Industry.
Basis for selection: Applicant must demonstrate financial need and high academic achievement.
Application requirements: Essay, transcript, proof of eligibility. Submit FAFSA; U.S. or Canadian tax return.
Additional information: Must be child of licensed driver, trainer, breeder, owner or caretaker of harness horses or be personally active in harness racing industry. Children of deceased industry members also eligible. Recommendations not required but considered if included with application. Awards based on financial need, academic excellence and active harness racing involvement. Visit Website for more information.
Amount of award: $7,500
Number of awards: 6
Number of applicants: 121
Application deadline: June 15
Notification begins: September 15
Total amount awarded: $45,000
Contact:
Harness Tracks of America
4640 East Sunrise Road
Suite 200
Tucson, AZ 85718
Phone: 520-529-2525
Fax: 520-529-3235
Web: www.harnesstracks.com

Harry S. Truman Scholarship Foundation

Harry S. Truman Scholarship

Type of award: Scholarship.
Intended use: For full-time senior or graduate study at 4-year or graduate institution.

Eligibility: Applicant must be U.S. citizen.
Basis for selection: Major/career interest in public administration/service; governmental public relations; political science/government or education. Applicant must demonstrate high academic achievement, leadership and service orientation.
Application requirements: Recommendations, essay, transcript, nomination by participating institutions. Must have a signed Institution Nomination Form, a signed Nominee Information Form, and an analysis of public policy issue.
Additional information: Applicants must participate in Truman Scholars Leadership Week, Awards Ceremony at Harry S. Truman Library, and Truman Scholars Washington Summer Institute. Each scholarship provides $26,000: awardees receive up to $2,000 for senior year and up to $24,000 for graduate study. Open to all fields of study as long as candidate plans to use degree in public service. Must be in top 25 percent of class. Visit Website for application and important dates.

> **Number of awards:** 78

Contact:
Harry Truman Scholarship Foundation
712 Jackson Place NW
Washington, DC 20006
Web: www.truman.gov

The Hartt School Community Division

Young Composers Award

Type of award: Scholarship.
Intended use: For freshman study.
Eligibility: Applicant must be at least 13, no older than 18, enrolled in high school. Applicant must be U.S. citizen.
Basis for selection: Competition/talent/interest in music performance/composition, based on original musical composition. Major/career interest in music.
Application requirements: $15 application fee. Proof of eligibility. Original musical composition. Certification of composition by music teacher. Four copies of the score.
Additional information: Each applicant may submit only one work. Composer's name may not appear on submission. Pseudonyms required. Students must not be enrolled in any undergraduate program at the time of application. There are two age categories, 13-15 and 16-18. Prizes vary. All submissions reviewed by independent jury. $15 application fee. Visit Website for additional information.

> **Amount of award:** $250-$1,000
> **Number of awards:** 5
> **Notification begins:** June 15

Contact:
The Hartt School Community Division
University of Hartford
200 Bloomfield Avenue
West Hartford, CT 06117
Phone: 860-768-7768
Web: www.nationalguild.org

Havana National Bank

McFarland Charitable Foundation Scholarship

Type of award: Scholarship, renewable.
Intended use: For full-time undergraduate study at accredited vocational, 2-year or 4-year institution in United States.
Eligibility: Applicant must be residing in Illinois.
Basis for selection: Major/career interest in nursing. Applicant must demonstrate seriousness of purpose.
Application requirements: $5 application fee. Interview, recommendations, transcript, proof of eligibility. Letter of acceptance to RN program.
Additional information: Award recipients must contractually obligate themselves to return to Havana, Illinois, and work as registered nurses for two years for each year of funding. Cosigner is required. To fund RN programs only.

> **Amount of award:** $1,000-$14,000
> **Number of awards:** 7
> **Number of applicants:** 30
> **Application deadline:** May 1
> **Notification begins:** June 15
> **Total amount awarded:** $75,000

Contact:
Havana National Bank
112 South Orange
P.O. Box 200
Havana, IL 62644-0200
Phone: 309-543-3361

Hawaii Community Foundation

Aiea General Hospital Association Scholarship

Type of award: Scholarship, renewable.
Intended use: For full-time undergraduate or graduate study at accredited 2-year, 4-year or graduate institution in United States.
Eligibility: Applicant must be U.S. citizen or permanent resident residing in Hawaii.
Basis for selection: Major/career interest in health-related professions. Applicant must demonstrate financial need, high academic achievement and depth of character.
Application requirements: Recommendations, essay, transcript. Application form and two letters of recommendation.
Additional information: Minimum 2.7 GPA. New applicants must be undergraduates. Applicant must be resident of Leeward Oahu zip codes: 96701, 96706, 96707, 96782, 96792 or 98797. Amount and number of awards vary and may change yearly. Notifications mailed between April and June.

> **Amount of award:** $1,000
> **Number of awards:** 25
> **Application deadline:** March 1

Contact:
Hawaii Community Foundation Scholarships
1164 Bishop Street
Suite 800
Honolulu, HI 96813
Phone: 808-537-6333 or 888-731-3863
Fax: 808-521-6286
Web: www.hawaiicommunityfoundation.org

Alma White-Delta Kappa Gamma Scholarship

Type of award: Scholarship.
Intended use: For full-time junior, senior or graduate study at accredited postsecondary institution in United States.
Eligibility: Applicant must be U.S. citizen or permanent resident residing in Hawaii.
Basis for selection: Major/career interest in education. Applicant must demonstrate financial need, high academic achievement and depth of character.
Application requirements: Recommendations, essay, transcript. Two letters of recommendation required.
Additional information: Applicants must have permanent address in Hawaii. Notifications mailed between April and June. Amount and number of awards vary and may change yearly. Visit Website for details and application.

Amount of award:	$1,250
Number of awards:	14
Application deadline:	March 1

Contact:
Hawaii Community Foundation Scholarships
1164 Bishop Street
Suite 800
Honolulu, HI 96813
Phone: 808-537-6333 or 888-731-3863
Fax: 808-521-6286
Web: www.hawaiicommunityfoundation.org

Ambassador Minerva Jean Falcon Hawaii Scholarship

Type of award: Scholarship.
Intended use: For full-time undergraduate or graduate study at accredited 2-year or 4-year institution. Designated institutions: Hawaii schools.
Eligibility: Applicant must be of Filipino ancestry. Applicant must be U.S. citizen or permanent resident residing in Hawaii.
Basis for selection: Applicant must demonstrate financial need, high academic achievement, depth of character and service orientation.
Application requirements: Recommendations, essay, transcript. Submit essay (maximum two pages, double-spaced) on how you plan to be involved in the community as a Filipino-American student.
Additional information: Amount of scholarship varies yearly. Applicants must have permanent address in Hawaii. Notifications mailed between April and June. Visit Website for details and application.

Amount of award:	$1,000
Number of awards:	1
Application deadline:	March 1

Bal Dasa Scholarship Fund

Type of award: Scholarship.
Intended use: For full-time undergraduate study at accredited 2-year or 4-year institution in United States.
Eligibility: Applicant must be a graduate of Waipahu High School. Applicant must be U.S. citizen or permanent resident residing in Hawaii.
Basis for selection: Applicant must demonstrate financial need, high academic achievement and depth of character.
Application requirements: Recommendations, essay, transcript.
Additional information: Amount of scholarship varies yearly. Applicants must have permanent address in Hawaii. Notifications mailed between April and June. Visit Website for details and application.

Amount of award:	$1,500
Number of awards:	1
Application deadline:	March 1

Contact:
Hawaii Community Foundation Scholarships
1164 Bishop Street
Suite 800
Honolulu, HI 96813
Phone: 808-537-6333 or 888-731-3863
Fax: 808-521-6286
Web: www.hawaiicommunityfoundation.org

Bick Bickson Scholarship Fund

Type of award: Scholarship.
Intended use: For full-time undergraduate or graduate study at accredited 2-year or 4-year institution in United States.
Eligibility: Applicant must be U.S. citizen or permanent resident residing in Hawaii.
Basis for selection: Major/career interest in marketing; law or tourism/travel. Applicant must demonstrate financial need, high academic achievement and depth of character.
Additional information: Student need not apply for this scholarship. Foundation will pull eligible students from overall pool of applicants and contact awardee. Notifications mailed between April and June. Amount of award may change yearly. Visit the Website for further information.

Contact:
Hawaii Community Foundation Scholarships
1164 Bishop Street
Suite 800
Honolulu, HI 96813
Phone: 808-537-6333 or 888-731-3863
Fax: 808-521-6286
Web: www.hawaiicommunityfoundation.org

Blossom Kalama Evans Memorial Scholarship

Type of award: Scholarship, renewable.
Intended use: For full-time junior, senior or graduate study at accredited 4-year or graduate institution in United States.

Eligibility: Applicant must be U.S. citizen or permanent resident residing in Hawaii.
Basis for selection: Major/career interest in hawaiian studies. Applicant must demonstrate financial need, high academic achievement and depth of character.
Application requirements: Recommendations, essay, transcript.
Additional information: Minumum 2.7 GPA. Hawaiian language students also eligible. Preference given to students of Hawaiian ancestry. Amount and number of awards vary. Applicants must have permanent address in Hawaii. Applicants who take up mainland residency must have relatives living in Hawaii. Other former Hawaii residents considered on case-by-case basis. Notifications mailed between April and June. Hawaiian Girls Golf Association members not eligible.

Amount of award:	$1,444
Number of awards:	9
Application deadline:	March 1

Contact:
Hawaii Community Foundation Scholarships
1164 Bishop Street
Suite 800
Honolulu, HI 96813
Phone: 808-537-6333 or 888-731-3863
Fax: 808-521-6286
Web: www.hcf-hawaii.org

Camille C. Chidiac Fund

Type of award: Scholarship.
Intended use: For full-time undergraduate study at accredited 2-year or 4-year institution in United States.
Eligibility: Applicant must be a senior at Ka'u High School. Applicant must be high school senior. Applicant must be U.S. citizen or permanent resident residing in Hawaii.
Basis for selection: Applicant must demonstrate financial need, high academic achievement and depth of character.
Application requirements: Recommendations, essay, transcript. Submit short essay on why it is important for Hawaii students to be internationally aware.
Additional information: Amount of scholarship varies yearly. Notifications mailed between April and June. Visit Website for details and application.

Amount of award:	$1,000
Number of awards:	1
Application deadline:	March 1

Contact:
Hawaii Community Foundation Scholarships
1164 Bishop Street
Suite 800
Honolulu, HI 96813
Phone: 808-537-6333 or 888-731-3863
Fax: 808-521-6286
Web: www.hawaiicommunityfoundation.org

Castle & Cooke Mililani Technology Park Scholarship Fund

Type of award: Scholarship.
Intended use: For full-time freshman study at accredited 2-year or 4-year institution in United States.
Eligibility: Applicant must be high school senior. Applicant must be U.S. citizen or permanent resident residing in Hawaii.
Basis for selection: Major/career interest in science, general; engineering or computer/information sciences. Applicant must demonstrate financial need, high academic achievement and depth of character.

Application requirements: Recommendations, essay, transcript.
Additional information: Applicants must be graduating senior from Leilehua, Mililani, or Waialua high schools. Preference given to majors in technology fields. Applicants must have permanent address in Hawaii. Notifications mailed between April and June. Amount and number of awards vary and may change yearly. Visit Website for details and application.

Amount of award:	$1,000
Number of awards:	5
Application deadline:	March 1

Contact:
Hawaii Community Foundation Scholarships
1164 Bishop Street
Suite 800
Honolulu, HI 96813
Phone: 808-537-6333 or 888-731-3863
Fax: 808-521-6286
Web: www.hawaiicommunityfoundation.org

Community Scholarship Fund

Type of award: Scholarship, renewable.
Intended use: For full-time undergraduate or graduate study at accredited 2-year or 4-year institution in United States.
Eligibility: Applicant must be U.S. citizen or permanent resident residing in Hawaii.
Basis for selection: Major/career interest in arts, general; architecture; education; humanities/liberal arts or social/behavioral sciences. Applicant must demonstrate financial need, high academic achievement, depth of character and service orientation.
Application requirements: Recommendations, essay, transcript.
Additional information: Minimum 3.0 GPA. Applicant must demonstrate accomplishment, motivation, initiative, and vision, and intention of returning to or staying in Hawaii to work. Applicants must have permanent address in Hawaii. Notifications mailed between April and June. Amount and number of awards vary and may change yearly. Visit Website for details and application.

Amount of award:	$1,000
Number of awards:	97
Application deadline:	March 1

Contact:
Hawaii Community Foundation Scholarships
1164 Bishop Street
Suite Street
Honolulu, HI 96813
Phone: 808-537-6333 or 888-731-3863
Fax: 808-521-6286
Web: www.hawaiicommunityfoundation.org

Cora Aguda Manayan Fund

Type of award: Scholarship, renewable.
Intended use: For full-time undergraduate or graduate study at accredited postsecondary institution in United States.
Eligibility: Applicant must be of Filipino ancestry. Preference given to students studying in Hawaii. Applicant must be U.S. citizen or permanent resident residing in Hawaii.
Basis for selection: Major/career interest in health-related professions. Applicant must demonstrate financial need, high academic achievement and depth of character.
Application requirements: Recommendations, essay, transcript.

Additional information: Minumum 2.7 GPA. Amount and number of awards vary and may change yearly. Applicants must have permanent address in Hawaii. (Applicants who take up mainland residency must have relatives living in Hawaii. Other former Hawaii residents considered on a case-by-case basis.) Notifications mailed between April and June.

Amount of award:	$520
Number of awards:	25
Application deadline:	March 1

Contact:
Hawaii Community Foundation Scholarships
1164 Bishop Street
Suite 800
Honolulu, HI 96813
Phone: 808-537-6333 or 888-731-3863
Fax: 808-521-6286
Web: www.hawaiicommunityfoundation.org

Dan & Pauline Lutkenhouse & Tropical Garden Scholarship

Type of award: Scholarship.
Intended use: For full-time undergraduate or graduate study at accredited 2-year or 4-year institution in United States.
Eligibility: Applicant must be resident of Hilo Coast and Hamakua Coast, north of Wailuku River. Applicant must be U.S. citizen or permanent resident residing in Hawaii.
Basis for selection: Major/career interest in agriculture; science, general; medicine or nursing. Applicant must demonstrate financial need, high academic achievement and depth of character.
Additional information: Student need not apply for this scholarship. Foundation will pull eligible students from overall pool of applicants and notify awardee. Amount of award may change yearly. Notifications mailed between April and June.

Contact:
Hawaii Community Foundation Scholarships
1164 Bishop Street
Suite 800
Honolulu, HI 96813
Phone: 808-537-6333 or 888-731-3863
Fax: 808-521-6286
Web: www.hawaiicommunityfoundation.org

David L. Irons Memorial Scholarship Fund

Type of award: Scholarship.
Intended use: For full-time undergraduate study at accredited 2-year or 4-year institution in United States.
Eligibility: Applicant must be a senior at Punahou School. Applicant must be high school senior. Applicant must be U.S. citizen or permanent resident residing in Hawaii.
Basis for selection: Applicant must demonstrate financial need, high academic achievement and depth of character.
Application requirements: Recommendations, essay, transcript. Include answers to the following questions in personal statement: 1) What are your educational and career goals; 2) Why did you choose these goals; 3) How would you spend a free day; 4) Who is a hero of yours and what is an overriding quality that makes this person your hero?
Additional information: Notifications mailed between April and June. Amount of award may change yearly. Visit Website for details and application.

Amount of award:	$1,000
Number of awards:	2
Application deadline:	March 1

Contact:
Hawaii Community Foundation Scholarships
1164 Bishop Street
Suite 800
Honolulu, HI 96813
Phone: 808-537-6333 or 888-731-3863
Fax: 808-521-6286
Web: www.hawaiicommunityfoundation.org

Dolly Ching Scholarship Fund

Type of award: Scholarship.
Intended use: For full-time undergraduate study at accredited postsecondary institution in United States. Designated institutions: Any institution in University of Hawaii system.
Eligibility: Must be high school senior from island of Kauai. Applicant must be high school senior. Applicant must be U.S. citizen or permanent resident residing in Hawaii.
Basis for selection: Applicant must demonstrate financial need, high academic achievement, depth of character and service orientation.
Application requirements: Recommendations, essay, transcript. Two letters of recommendation.
Additional information: Notifications mailed between April and June. Amount and number of awards vary and may change yearly.

Amount of award:	$1,250
Number of awards:	2
Application deadline:	March 1

Contact:
Hawaii Community Foundation Scholarships
1164 Bishop Street
Suite 800
Honolulu, HI 96813
Phone: 808-537-6333 or 888-731-3863
Fax: 808-521-6286
Web: www.hawaiicommunityfoundation.org

Dorice & Clarence Glick Classical Music Scholarship

Type of award: Scholarship.
Intended use: For full-time undergraduate or graduate study at accredited 2-year or 4-year institution in United States.
Eligibility: Applicant must be residing in Hawaii.
Basis for selection: Major/career interest in music. Applicant must demonstrate financial need, high academic achievement and depth of character.
Application requirements: Recommendations, essay, transcript. Describe in personal statement how program of study relates to classical music.
Additional information: Must major in music, with emphasis on classical music. Applicants must have permanent address in Hawaii. Notifications mailed between April and June. Amount and number of awards vary and may change yearly. Visit Website for details and application.

Amount of award:	$1,000
Number of awards:	8
Application deadline:	March 1

Contact:
Hawaii Community Foundation Scholarships
1164 Bishop Street
Suite 800
Honolulu, HI 96813
Phone: 808-537-6333 or 888-731-3863
Fax: 808-521-6286
Web: www.hawaiicommunityfoundation.org

Dr. Hans & Clara Zimmerman Foundation Education Scholarship

Type of award: Scholarship.
Intended use: For full-time undergraduate or graduate study at accredited 2-year or 4-year institution in United States.
Eligibility: Applicant must be U.S. citizen or permanent resident residing in Hawaii.
Basis for selection: Major/career interest in health sciences; health services administration; health-related professions; public health or social work. Applicant must demonstrate financial need, high academic achievement, depth of character and leadership.
Application requirements: Recommendations, essay, transcript. Personal statement describing participation in community service projects or activities.
Additional information: Applicant must be a non-traditional student who has worked for at least 2 years and is returning to school in the United States. Minimum 2.7 GPA. Applicants must have permanent address in Hawaii. Notifications mailed between April and June. Amount and number of awards vary and may change yearly. Visit Website for details and application.

Amount of award:	$2,000
Number of awards:	42
Application deadline:	March 1

Contact:
Hawaii Community Foundation Scholarships
1164 Bishop Street
Suite 800
Honolulu, HI 96813
Phone: 808-537-6333 or 888-731-3863
Fax: 808-521-6286
Web: www.hawaiicommunityfoundation.org

Dr. Hans and Clara Zimmerman Foundation Health Scholarship

Type of award: Scholarship, renewable.
Intended use: For full-time junior, senior or graduate study at accredited postsecondary institution in United States.
Eligibility: Applicant must be U.S. citizen or permanent resident residing in Hawaii.
Basis for selection: Major/career interest in education, teacher. Applicant must demonstrate financial need, high academic achievement and depth of character.
Application requirements: Recommendations, essay, transcript. Personal statement should include description of participation in community service projects or activities.
Additional information: For nontraditional students who worked at least two years and will return to United States. Minimum 2.7 GPA. Must demonstrate leadership potential. Amount and number of awards vary and may change yearly. Applicants must have permanent address in Hawaii. Notifications mailed between April and June.

Amount of award:	$3,458
Number of awards:	220
Application deadline:	March 1

Contact:
Hawaii Community Foundation Scholarships
1164 Bishop Street
Suite 800
Honolulu, HI 96813
Phone: 808-537-6333 or 888-731-3863
Fax: 808-521-6286
Web: www.hawaiicommunityfoundation.org

Earl Bakken Engineering Scholarship

Type of award: Scholarship.
Intended use: For full-time undergraduate or graduate study at accredited 2-year or 4-year institution in United States.
Eligibility: Applicant must be U.S. citizen or permanent resident residing in Hawaii.
Basis for selection: Major/career interest in engineering. Applicant must demonstrate financial need, high academic achievement and depth of character.
Application requirements: Recommendations, essay, transcript.
Additional information: Applicants must have permanent address in Hawaii. Preference given to students of Hawaiian ethnicity. Amount of award may change yearly. Visit Website for details and application.

Application deadline:	March 1

Contact:
Hawaii Community Foundation Scholarships
1164 Bishop Street
Suite 800
Honolulu, HI 96813
Phone: 808-537-6333 or 888-731-3863
Fax: 808-521-6286
Web: www.hawaiicommunityfoundation.org

Edward J. Doty Scholarship

Type of award: Scholarship.
Intended use: For full-time junior, senior or graduate study at accredited 2-year or 4-year institution in United States.
Eligibility: Applicant must be U.S. citizen or permanent resident residing in Hawaii.
Basis for selection: Major/career interest in gerontology. Applicant must demonstrate financial need, high academic achievement and depth of character.
Additional information: Student need not apply for this scholarship. Foundation will pull eligible students from overall pool of applicants, and contact awardee. Amount of award may change yearly. Notifications mailed between April and June.

Amount of award:	$2,000
Number of awards:	1

Contact:
Hawaii Community Foundation Scholarships
1164 Bishop Street
Suite 800
Honolulu, HI 96813
Phone: 808-537-6333 or 888-731-3863
Fax: 808-521-6286
Web: www.hawaiicommunityfoundation.org

Edward Payson and Bernice Pi'ilani Irwin Scholarship Trust Fund

Type of award: Scholarship.
Intended use: For full-time junior, senior or graduate study at accredited 4-year institution in United States.
Eligibility: Applicant must be U.S. citizen or permanent resident residing in Hawaii.
Basis for selection: Major/career interest in journalism or communications. Applicant must demonstrate financial need, high academic achievement and depth of character.
Application requirements: Recommendations, essay, transcript.
Additional information: Applicants must have permanent address in Hawaii. (Applicants who take up mainland residency

must have relatives living in Hawaii. Other former Hawaii residents considered on a case-by-case basis.) Notifications mailed between April and June. Amount and number of awards vary and may change yearly. Visit Website for details and application.

Amount of award:	$1,832
Number of awards:	19
Application deadline:	March 1

Contact:
Hawaii Community Foundation Scholarships
1164 Bishop Street
Suite 800
Honolulu, HI 96813
Phone: 808-537-6333 or 888-731-3863
Fax: 808-521-6286
Web: www.hawaiicommunityfoundation.org

E.E. Black Scholarship

Type of award: Scholarship, renewable.
Intended use: For full-time undergraduate study at accredited postsecondary institution in United States.
Eligibility: Applicant or parent must be employed by Tesoro Petroleum Companies, Inc. Applicant must be U.S. citizen or permanent resident residing in Hawaii.
Basis for selection: Applicant must demonstrate financial need, high academic achievement and depth of character.
Application requirements: Recommendations, essay, transcript. Name of Tesoro employee and relationship.
Additional information: Minimum 3.0 GPA. Amount and number of awards vary and may change yearly. Applicants must have permanent address in Hawaii. (Applicants who take up mainland residency must have relatives living in Hawaii. Other former Hawaii residents considered on a case-by-case basis.) Notifications mailed between April and June.

Amount of award:	$1,111
Number of awards:	9
Application deadline:	March 1

Contact:
Hawaii Community Foundation Scholarships
1164 Bishop Street
Suite 800
Honolulu, HI 96813
Phone: 808-537-6333 or 888-731-3863
Fax: 808-521-6286
Web: www.hawaiicommunityfoundation.org

Eiro Yamada Memorial Scholarship

Type of award: Scholarship.
Intended use: For full-time undergraduate or graduate study at accredited 2-year or 4-year institution in United States.
Eligibility: Applicant must be U.S. citizen residing in Hawaii. Applicant must be descendant of veteran during WW II. Applicant must be direct descendant of World War II veteran of 100th, 442nd, MIS or 1399th units.
Basis for selection: Applicant must demonstrate financial need, high academic achievement and depth of character.
Application requirements: Recommendations, essay, transcript, proof of eligibility. Name of veteran and relationship to applicant required.
Additional information: Applicants who take up mainland residency must have relatives living in Hawaii. Other former Hawaii residents considered on a case-by-case basis. Amount and number of awards vary. Notifications mailed between April and June. Visit Website for details and application.

Application deadline:	March 1

Contact:
Hawaii Community Foundation Scholarships
1164 Bishop Street
Suite 800
Honolulu, HI 96813
Phone: 808-537-6333 or 888-731-3863
Fax: 808-521-6286
Web: www.hawaiicommunityfoundation.org

Ellison Onizuka Memorial Scholarship

Type of award: Scholarship.
Intended use: For full-time undergraduate study at accredited 2-year or 4-year institution in United States.
Eligibility: Applicant must be high school senior. Applicant must be U.S. citizen or permanent resident residing in Hawaii.
Basis for selection: Major/career interest in aerospace. Applicant must demonstrate financial need and depth of character.
Application requirements: Recommendations, transcript, nomination by high school principal.
Additional information: Amount and number of awards vary and may change yearly. Applicants must have permanent address in Hawaii. (Applicants who take up mainland residency must have relatives living in Hawaii. Other former Hawaii residents considered on case-by-case basis.) Contact high school principal to apply.

Contact:
Hawaii Community Foundation Scholarships
1164 Bishop Street
Suite 800
Honolulu, HI 96813
Phone: 808-537-6333 or 888-731-3863
Fax: 808-521-6286
Web: www.hawaiicommunityfoundation.org

Esther Kanagawa Memorial Art Scholarship

Type of award: Scholarship.
Intended use: For full-time undergraduate or graduate study at accredited 2-year or 4-year institution in United States.
Eligibility: Applicant must be U.S. citizen or permanent resident residing in Hawaii.
Basis for selection: Major/career interest in art/art history. Applicant must demonstrate financial need, high academic achievement and depth of character.
Application requirements: Recommendations, essay, transcript.
Additional information: Must major in Fine Art. Scholarship not for students studying video, film, or the performing arts. Applicants must have permanent address in Hawaii. Notifications mailed between April and June. Amount of award varies yearly. Visit Website for details and application.

Application deadline:	March 1

Contact:
Hawaii Community Foundation Scholarships
1164 Bishop Street
Suite 800
Honolulu, HI 96813
Phone: 808-537-6333 or 888-731-3863
Fax: 808-521-6286
Web: www.hawaiicommunityfoundation.org

Scholarships

The Filipino Nurses' Organization of Hawaii Scholarship

Type of award: Scholarship.
Intended use: For full-time undergraduate study at accredited 2-year or 4-year institution in United States.
Eligibility: Applicant must be of Filipino ancestry. Applicant must be U.S. citizen or permanent resident residing in Hawaii.
Basis for selection: Major/career interest in nursing. Applicant must demonstrate financial need, high academic achievement, depth of character and service orientation.
Application requirements: Recommendations, essay, transcript.
Additional information: Applicants must have permanent address in Hawaii. Notifications mailed between April and June. Visit Website for details and application. Amount of award may vary yearly.

   Application deadline: March 1
Contact:
Hawaii Community Foundation Scholarships
1164 Bishop Street
Suite 800
Honolulu, HI 96813
Phone: 808-537-6333 or 888-731-3863
Fax: 808-521-6286
Web: www.hcf-hawaii.org

Financial Women International Scholarship

Type of award: Scholarship.
Intended use: For full-time junior, senior or graduate study at accredited 2-year or 4-year institution in United States.
Eligibility: Applicant must be female. Applicant must be U.S. citizen or permanent resident residing in Hawaii.
Basis for selection: Major/career interest in business. Applicant must demonstrate financial need, high academic achievement and depth of character.
Application requirements: Applicant must demonstrate strong academic potential (generally a 3.5 GPA), accomplishment and motivation.
Additional information: Student need not apply for this scholarship. Foundation will pull eligible students from overall pool of applicants and contact awardee. Amount of award may change yearly. Notifications mailed between April and June.

   Amount of award: $600
   Number of awards: 2
Contact:
Hawaii Community Foundation Scholarships
1164 Bishop Street
Suite 800
Honolulu, HI 96813
Phone: 808-537-6333 or 888-731-3863
Fax: 808-521-6286
Web: www.hawaiicommunityfoundation.org

Fletcher & Fritzi Hoffmann Education Fund

Type of award: Scholarship.
Intended use: For full-time undergraduate study at accredited vocational, 2-year or 4-year institution. Designated institutions: Hawaii colleges and vocational schools.
Eligibility: Must be long time resident of the Hamakua Coast in Hawaii. Applicant must be U.S. citizen or permanent resident residing in Hawaii.

Basis for selection: Applicant must demonstrate financial need, high academic achievement and depth of character.
Application requirements: Recommendations, essay, transcript. Submit essay on family's history and roots in the Hamakua area.
Additional information: Preference given to students from families who worked in the sugar plantation industry. Notifications mailed between April and June. Amount of award may change yearly. Visit Website for details and application.

   Application deadline: March 1
Contact:
Hawaii Community Foundation Scholarships
1164 Bishop Street
Suite 800
Honolulu, HI 96813
Phone: 808-537-6333 or 888-731-3863
Fax: 808-521-6286
Web: www.hawaiicommunityfoundation.org

Frances S. Watanabe Memorial Scholarship

Type of award: Scholarship, renewable.
Intended use: For undergraduate or graduate study at accredited postsecondary institution in United States.
Eligibility: Applicant or parent must be member/participant of Hawaii Construction Industry Federal Credit Union. Applicant must be U.S. citizen or permanent resident residing in Hawaii.
Basis for selection: Applicant must demonstrate financial need, high academic achievement and depth of character.
Application requirements: Recommendations, essay, transcript. Name of member of Hawaii Construction Industry Federal Credit Union.
Additional information: Amount and number of awards vary and may change yearly. Applicants must have permanent address in Hawaii. (Applicants who take up mainland residency must have relatives living in Hawaii. Other former Hawaii residents considered on case-by-case basis.) Credit union members must belong to Amana Street location. Notifications mailed between April and June.

   Amount of award: $650
   Number of awards: 5
   Application deadline: March 1
Contact:
Hawaii Community Foundation Scholarships
1164 Bishop Street
Sutie 800
Honolulu, HI 96813
Phone: 808-537-6333 or 888-731-3863
Fax: 808-521-6286
Web: www.hawaiicommunityfoundation.org

Friends of Hawaii Public Housing Scholarship

Type of award: Scholarship.
Intended use: For full-time undergraduate or graduate study at accredited 2-year or 4-year institution in United States.
Eligibility: Applicant must be U.S. citizen or permanent resident residing in Hawaii.
Basis for selection: Applicant must demonstrate financial need, high academic achievement and depth of character.
Application requirements: Recommendations, essay, transcript, proof of eligibility. Indicate name of public housing complex in personal statement. Applicant must have permanent address in Hawaii.

Additional information: Applicant must be resident of a public housing unit in Hawaii. Visit Website for details and application. Amount and number of awards may change yearly.

Amount of award:	$750
Number of awards:	4
Application deadline:	March 1

Contact:
Hawaii Community Foundation Scholarships
1164 Bishop Street
Suite 800
Honolulu, HI 96813
Phone: 808-537-6333 or 888-731-3863
Fax: 808-521-6286
Web: www.hawaiicommunityfoundation.org

Henry and Dorothy Castle Memorial Scholarship

Type of award: Scholarship, renewable.
Intended use: For full-time undergraduate or graduate study at accredited postsecondary institution in United States.
Eligibility: Applicant must be U.S. citizen or permanent resident residing in Hawaii.
Basis for selection: Major/career interest in education, early childhood. Applicant must demonstrate financial need, high academic achievement, depth of character, seriousness of purpose and service orientation.
Application requirements: Recommendations, essay, transcript. Essay stating interests and goals in early childhood education, and plans to contribute to field.
Additional information: Amount and number of awards vary and may change yearly. Applicants must have permanent address in Hawaii. (Applicants who take up mainland residency must have relatives living in Hawaii. Other former Hawaii residents considered on case-by-case basis.) Notifications mailed between April and June. Scholarship is funded by Samuel N. & Mary Castle Foundation.

Amount of award:	$1,300
Number of awards:	15
Application deadline:	March 1

Contact:
Hawaii Community Foundation Scholarships
1164 Bishop Street
Suite 800
Honolulu, HI 96813
Phone: 808-537-6333 or 888-731-3863
Fax: 808-521-6286
Web: www.hawaiicommunityfoundation.org

Jean Fitzgerald Scholarship Fund

Type of award: Scholarship, renewable.
Intended use: For full-time freshman or graduate study at accredited 2-year or 4-year institution in United States.
Eligibility: Applicant or parent must be member/participant of Hawaii Pacific Tennis Association. Applicant must be female. Applicant must be U.S. citizen or permanent resident residing in Hawaii.
Basis for selection: Applicant must demonstrate financial need, high academic achievement and depth of character.
Application requirements: Recommendations, essay, transcript.
Additional information: Minimum 2.7 GPA. Must be incoming freshman. Applicant must be active member of Hawaii Pacific Tennis Association for last four years. Applicants must have permanent address in Hawaii. Amount and number of awards vary and may change yearly.

Amount of award:	$3,000
Number of awards:	3
Application deadline:	March 1

Contact:
Hawaii Community Foundation Scholarships
1164 Bishop Street
Suite 800
Honolulu, HI 96813
Phone: 808-537-6333 or 888-731-3863
Fax: 808-521-6286
Web: www.hawaiicommunityfoundation.org

John Dawe Dental Education Fund

Type of award: Scholarship, renewable.
Intended use: For full-time undergraduate or graduate study at accredited postsecondary institution in United States.
Eligibility: Applicant must be U.S. citizen or permanent resident residing in Hawaii.
Basis for selection: Major/career interest in dentistry; dental hygiene or dental assistant. Applicant must demonstrate financial need, high academic achievement and depth of character.
Application requirements: Recommendations, essay, transcript, proof of eligibility. Must submit Dawe Supplemental Financial Form (obtain from Hawaii Community Foundation). Two letters of recommendation required.
Additional information: Dental hygiene applicants must submit a letter from their school confirming enrollment in the dental hygiene program. Applicants must have permanent address in Hawaii. Amount and number of awards vary and may change yearly.

Amount of award:	$1,050
Number of awards:	10
Application deadline:	March 1

Contact:
Hawaii Community Foundation Scholarships
1164 Bishop Street
Suite 800
Honolulu, HI 96813
Phone: 808-537-6333 or 888-731-3863
Fax: 808-521-6286
Web: www.hawaiicommunityfoundation.org

John Ross Foundation

Type of award: Scholarship, renewable.
Intended use: For full-time undergraduate or graduate study at accredited postsecondary institution in United States.
Eligibility: Applicant must be U.S. citizen or permanent resident residing in Hawaii.
Basis for selection: Applicant must demonstrate financial need, high academic achievement and depth of character.
Application requirements: Recommendations, essay, transcript. Personal statement should discuss applicant's plan to remain on or return to the Big Island.
Additional information: Students do not need to apply; foundation will pull eligible students from overall pool. Foundation will contact student if scholarship if awarded. Minimum 2.7 GPA. Preference given to undergraduates born on, having ancestors from, and planning to reside on the Big Island. Preference given to undergraduates. Notifications mailed between April and June. Amount of award varies yearly.

Amount of award:	$1,000
Number of awards:	19

Contact:
Hawaii Community Foundation Scholarships
1164 Bishop Street
Suite 800
Honolulu, HI 96813
Phone: 808-537-6333 or 888-731-3863
Fax: 808-521-6286
Web: www.hawaiicommunityfoundation.org

Juliette M. Atherton Scholarship

Type of award: Scholarship, renewable.
Intended use: For full-time undergraduate, graduate or non-degree study at accredited postsecondary institution in United States.
Eligibility: Applicant must be Protestant. Applicant must be U.S. citizen or permanent resident residing in Hawaii.
Basis for selection: Major/career interest in religion/theology. Applicant must demonstrate financial need, high academic achievement, depth of character, leadership, seriousness of purpose and service orientation.
Application requirements: Recommendations, essay, transcript, proof of eligibility. Children of ministers must provide in their personal statement: parent's current position, church/parish name, denomination, place and date of ordination, and name of seminary attended.
Additional information: Applicant must meet one of the following criteria: (1) be a dependant child of an active, ordained Protestant minister in an established denomination in Hawaii; (2) be planning to attend an accredited graduate school of theology with goal of ordination as Protestant minister; (3) be an ordained Protestant minister planning to pursue an advanced degree related to profession or education in a field related to ministry through coursework, workshops, or seminars. Applicant must have permanent address in Hawaii. Amount and number of awards vary and may change yearly.
  Amount of award: $2,100
  Number of awards: 62
  Application deadline: March 1
Contact:
Hawaii Community Foundation Scholarships
1164 Bishop Street
Suite 800
Honolulu, HI 96813
Phone: 808-537-6333 or 888-731-3863
Fax: 808-521-6286
Web: www.hawaiicommunityfoundation.org

Ka'iulani Home for Girls Trust Scholarship

Type of award: Scholarship, renewable.
Intended use: For full-time undergraduate or graduate study at accredited postsecondary institution in United States.
Eligibility: Applicant must be female. Applicant must be U.S. citizen or permanent resident residing in Hawaii.
Basis for selection: Applicant must demonstrate financial need, high academic achievement and depth of character.
Application requirements: Recommendations, essay, transcript, proof of eligibility. First-time applicants include birth certificate to verify ancestry.
Additional information: Minimum 2.7 GPA, Hawaiian ancestry. Applicants must have permanent address in Hawaii. Notifications mailed between April and June. Amount and number of awards vary and may change yearly.

  Amount of award: $650
  Number of awards: 280
  Application deadline: March 1
Contact:
Hawaii Community Foundation Scholarships
1164 Bishop Street
Suite 800
Honolulu, HI 96813
Phone: 808-537-6333 or 888-731-3863
Fax: 808-521-6286
Web: www.hawaiicommunityfoundation.org

Ka'a'awa Community Fund

Type of award: Scholarship.
Intended use: For full-time undergraduate or graduate study at accredited 2-year or 4-year institution in United States.
Eligibility: Applicant must be resident of the Ka'a'awa area on Windward O'ahu. Applicant must be U.S. citizen or permanent resident residing in Hawaii.
Basis for selection: Applicant must demonstrate financial need, high academic achievement and depth of character.
Application requirements: Recommendations, essay, transcript.
Additional information: Preference given to long time residents of Ka'a'awa area. Notifications mailed between April and June. Amount and number of awards vary and may change yearly. Visit Website for details and application.
  Amount of award: $650
  Number of awards: 6
  Application deadline: March 1
Contact:
Hawaii Community Foundation Scholarships
1164 Bishop Street
Suite 800
Honolulu, HI 96813
Phone: 808-537-6333 or 888-731-3863
Fax: 808-521-6286
Web: www.hawaiicommunityfoundation.org

Kapolei Community & Business Scholarship

Type of award: Scholarship.
Intended use: For full-time undergraduate study at accredited 2-year or 4-year institution in United States.
Eligibility: Applicant must be a senior from Campbell, Nanakuli or Waianae high schools. Applicant must be high school senior. Applicant must be U.S. citizen or permanent resident residing in Hawaii.
Basis for selection: Applicant must demonstrate financial need, high academic achievement and depth of character.
Additional information: Student need not apply for this scholarship. Foundation will pull eligible students from overall pool of applicants, and contact awardee. Notifications mailed between April and June. Amount of award may vary yearly.
  Amount of award: $500
  Number of awards: 3
Contact:
Hawaii Community Foundation Scholarships
1164 Bishop Street
Suite 800
Honolulu, HI 96813
Phone: 808-537-6333 or 888-731-3863
Fax: 808-521-6286
Web: www.hawaiicommunityfoundation.org

Kawasaki-McGaha Scholarship Fund

Type of award: Scholarship.
Intended use: For full-time undergraduate study. Designated institutions: Hawaii Pacific University.
Eligibility: Applicant must be permanent resident residing in Hawaii.
Basis for selection: Major/career interest in computer/information sciences or international studies. Applicant must demonstrate financial need, high academic achievement and depth of character.
Application requirements: Recommendations, essay, transcript.
Additional information: Applicants must have permanent address in Hawaii. Notifications mailed between April and June. Amount and number of awards vary and may change yearly. Visit Website for details and application.

Amount of award:	$857
Number of awards:	7
Application deadline:	March 1

Contact:
Hawaii Community Foundation Scholarships
1164 Bishop Street
Suite 800
Honolulu, HI 96813
Phone: 808-537-6333 or 888-731-3863
Fax: 808-521-6286
Web: www.hawaiicommunityfoundaiton.org

Kellie Ann Andrade Scholarship Fund

Type of award: Scholarship.
Intended use: For full-time undergraduate study. Designated institutions: Pacific Rim Bible Institute.
Eligibility: Applicant must be U.S. citizen or permanent resident residing in Hawaii.
Basis for selection: Applicant must demonstrate financial need, high academic achievement and depth of character.
Application requirements: Recommendations, essay, transcript.
Additional information: Applicant must have permanent address in Hawaii. Applicants who take up mainland residency must have relatives living in Hawaii. Other former Hawaii residents considered on a case-by-case basis. Notifications mailed between April and June. Amount of award may change yearly. Visit Website for details and application.

Amount of award:	$1,000
Number of awards:	1
Application deadline:	March 1

Contact:
Hawaii Community Foundation Scholarships
1164 Bishop Street
Suite 800
Honolulu, HI 96813
Phone: 808-537-6333 or 888-731-3863
Fax: 808-521-6286
Web: www.hawaiicommunityfoundation.org

King Kekaulike High School Scholarship

Type of award: Scholarship.
Intended use: For full-time undergraduate study at accredited 2-year or 4-year institution in United States.
Eligibility: Applicant must be a senior at King Kekaulike High School. Applicant must be high school senior. Applicant must be U.S. citizen or permanent resident residing in Hawaii.
Basis for selection: Applicant must demonstrate financial need, high academic achievement, depth of character and service orientation.
Application requirements: Recommendations, essay, transcript. Submit 500-word essay on how well Na Alii 3 R's (Respect, Relevance, and Rigor) relate to your future goals.
Additional information: Minimum 2.8 GPA and three or more hours of community service. Children of KKHS staff members not eligible. Amount of award may change yearly. Notifications mailed between April and June. Visit Website for details and application.

Amount of award:	$1,200
Number of awards:	1
Application deadline:	March 1

Contact:
Hawaii Community Foundation Scholarships
1164 Bishop Street
Suite 800
Honolulu, HI 96813
Phone: 808-537-6333 or 888-731-3863
Fax: 808-521-6286
Web: www.hawaiicommunityfoundation.org

K.M. Hatano Scholarship

Type of award: Scholarship, renewable.
Intended use: For full-time undergraduate study at accredited 4-year institution in United States. Designated institutions: Four-year college or university in Hawaii.
Eligibility: Applicant must be high school senior. Applicant must be U.S. citizen or permanent resident residing in Hawaii.
Basis for selection: Applicant must demonstrate financial need, high academic achievement and depth of character.
Application requirements: Recommendations, essay, transcript.
Additional information: Amount and number of awards vary and may change yearly. Applicant must be resident of Maui, including Lanai and Molokai. Contact Hyatt Regency Maui for more information.

Amount of award:	$1,000
Number of awards:	5
Application deadline:	March 1

Contact:
Hawaii Community Foundation Scholarships
1164 Bishop Street
Suite 800
Honolulu, HI 96813
Phone: 808-537-6333 or 888-731-3863
Fax: 808-521-6286
Web: www.hawaiicommunityfoundation.org

Kohala Ditch Education Fund

Type of award: Scholarship.
Intended use: For full-time undergraduate study at accredited 2-year or 4-year institution in United States.
Eligibility: Applicant must be a senior at Kohala High School. Applicant must be high school senior. Applicant must be U.S. citizen or permanent resident residing in Hawaii.
Basis for selection: Applicant must demonstrate financial need, high academic achievement and depth of character.
Application requirements: Recommendations, essay, transcript.

Additional information: Amount of award may change yearly. Notifications mailed between April and June. Visit Website for details and application.

Amount of award:	$1,000
Number of awards:	2
Application deadline:	March 1

Contact:
Hawaii Community Foundation Scholarships
1164 Bishop Street
Suite 800
Honolulu, HI 96813
Phone: 808-537-6333 or 888-731-3863
Fax: 808-521-6286
Web: www.hawaiicommunityfoundation.org

Koloa Scholarship

Type of award: Scholarship, renewable.
Intended use: For full-time undergraduate or graduate study at accredited vocational, 2-year or 4-year institution in United States.
Eligibility: Applicant must be U.S. citizen or permanent resident residing in Hawaii.
Basis for selection: Applicant must demonstrate financial need, high academic achievement and depth of character.
Application requirements: Recommendations, essay, transcript. Essay must explain personal understanding of meaning of "aloha," list of books or other publications read on Hawaii's history, and list of relatives born in Koloa District, including relationship to you, place of and approximate year of birth. Two recommendation letters required.
Additional information: Applicant must be resident of one of the following Kauai areas in Hawaii: Koloa, including Omao and Poipu (96756), Lawai (96765) or Kalaheo (96741). Amount of award varies and may change yearly. Minimum 2.0 GPA.

Amount of award:	$1,000
Number of awards:	5
Application deadline:	March 1

Contact:
Hawaii Community Foundation Scholarships
1164 Bishop Street
Suite 800
Honolulu, HI 96813
Phone: 808-537-6333 or 888-731-3863
Fax: 808-521-6286
Web: www.hawaiicommunityfoundation.org

Kurt W. Schneider Memorial Scholarship Fund

Type of award: Scholarship.
Intended use: For full-time undergraduate study at accredited 2-year or 4-year institution in United States.
Eligibility: Applicant must be a senior at Lanai High School. Applicant must be high school senior. Applicant must be U.S. citizen or permanent resident residing in Hawaii.
Basis for selection: Major/career interest in tourism/travel. Applicant must demonstrate financial need, high academic achievement and depth of character.
Application requirements: Recommendations, essay, transcript.
Additional information: Preference given to travel industry management majors. Notifications mailed between April and June. Amount of award may change yearly. Visit Website for details and application.

Amount of award:	$1,500
Number of awards:	2
Application deadline:	March 1

Contact:
Hawaii Community Foundation Scholarships
1164 Bishop Street
Suite 800
Honolulu, HI 96813
Phone: 808-537-6333 or 888-731-3863
Fax: 808-521-6286
Web: www.hawaiicommunityfoundation.org

Laura N. Dowsett Fund

Type of award: Scholarship.
Intended use: For full-time junior, senior or graduate study at accredited 2-year or 4-year institution in United States.
Eligibility: Applicant must be U.S. citizen or permanent resident residing in Hawaii.
Basis for selection: Major/career interest in occupational therapy. Applicant must demonstrate financial need, high academic achievement and depth of character.
Application requirements: Recommendations, essay, transcript. At least one letter of recommendation should be from someone in the occupational therapy field.
Additional information: Applicants must have permanent address in Hawaii. Applicants who take up mainland residency must have relatives living in Hawaii. Other former Hawaii residents considered on a case-by-case basis. Notifications mailed between April and June. Amount and number of awards vary and may change yearly.

Amount of award:	$1,833
Number of awards:	6
Application deadline:	March 1

Contact:
Hawaii Community Foundation Scholarships
1164 Bishop Street
Suite 800
Honolulu, HI 96813
Phone: 808-537-6333 or 888-731-3863
Fax: 808-521-6286
Web: www.hcf-hawaii.org

Margaret Jones Memorial Nursing Scholarship

Type of award: Scholarship, renewable.
Intended use: For full-time junior, senior or graduate study at accredited 4-year or graduate institution in United States.
Eligibility: Applicant must be U.S. citizen or permanent resident residing in Hawaii.
Basis for selection: Major/career interest in nursing. Applicant must demonstrate financial need, high academic achievement and depth of character.
Application requirements: Recommendations, essay, transcript.
Additional information: Applicants must be enrolled in BSN, MSN or doctoral nursing program in Hawaii. Preference may be given to members of Hawaii Nurses Association. Minimum 3.0 GPA. Applicants must have permanent address in Hawaii. Notifications mailed between April and June. Amount and number of awards vary and change yearly.

Amount of award:	$940
Number of awards:	16
Application deadline:	March 1

Contact:
Hawaii Community Foundation Scholarships
1164 Bishop Street
Suite 800
Honolulu, HI 96813
Phone: 808-537-6333 or 888-731-3863
Fax: 808-521-6286
Web: www.hawaiicommunityfoundation.org

Marion MacCarrell Scott Scholarship

Type of award: Scholarship, renewable.
Intended use: For full-time undergraduate or graduate study at accredited postsecondary institution in United States. Designated institutions: Institutions on U.S. mainland.
Eligibility: Applicant must be U.S. citizen or permanent resident residing in Hawaii.
Basis for selection: Major/career interest in political science/ government; history; economics; anthropology; international relations; sociology; geography; law; psychology or philosophy. Applicant must demonstrate financial need, high academic achievement and depth of character.
Application requirements: Recommendations, essay, transcript. Essay (2-3 typed pages, double-spaced) must demonstrate commitment to international understanding and world peace. Must describe how learning experiences relate to international understanding and world peace and enhance knowledge to achieve such goals.
Additional information: Must be graduate of Hawaii public high school and attend accredited mainland U.S. college or university. Minimum 2.8 GPA. Applicant must have permanent address in Hawaii. Notifications mailed between April and June. Amount and number of awards vary and may change yearly.

Amount of award:	$2,460
Number of awards:	203
Application deadline:	March 1

Contact:
Hawaii Community Foundation Scholarships
1164 Bishop Street
Suite 800
Honolulu, HI 96813
Phone: 808-537-6333 or 888-731-3863
Fax: 808-521-6286
Web: www.hawaiicommunityfoundation.org

Mary Josephine Bloder Scholarship

Type of award: Scholarship.
Intended use: For full-time undergraduate study at accredited 2-year or 4-year institution in United States.
Eligibility: Applicant must be senior at Lahainaluna High School. Applicant must be high school senior. Applicant must be U.S. citizen or permanent resident residing in Hawaii.
Basis for selection: Applicant must demonstrate financial need, high academic achievement and depth of character.
Application requirements: Recommendations, essay, transcript. Must have high GPA in sciences, two letters of recommendation.
Additional information: Preference given to boarding students. Amount and number of awards vary and may change yearly. Notifications mailed between April and June. Visit Website for details and application.

Amount of award:	$1,550
Number of awards:	8
Application deadline:	March 1

Contact:
Hawaii Community Foundation Scholarships
1164 Bishop Street
Suite 800
Honolulu, HI 96813
Phone: 808-537-6333 or 888-731-3863
Fax: 808-521-6286
Web: www.hawaiicommunityfoundation.org

Mildred Towle Trust Fund Scholarship

Type of award: Scholarship, renewable.
Intended use: For full-time undergraduate or graduate study at accredited postsecondary institution in or outside United States.
Eligibility: Applicant must be residing in Hawaii.
Basis for selection: Applicant must demonstrate financial need, high academic achievement and depth of character.
Application requirements: Recommendations, essay, transcript.
Additional information: Award for Hawaii residents studying as undergraduate or graduate at Boston University or as a junior or higher in foreign country. African-Americans studying in Hawaii also eligible. Minimum GPA 3.0. Notifications mailed between April and June. Amount and number of awards vary and may change yearly.

Amount of award:	$800
Number of awards:	46
Application deadline:	March 1

Contact:
Hawaii Community Foundation Scholarships
1164 Bishop Street
Suite 800
Honolulu, HI 96813
Phone: 808-537-6333 or 888-731-3863
Fax: 808-521-6286
Web: www.hawaiicommunityfoundation.org

Nick Van Pernis Scholarship

Type of award: Scholarship.
Intended use: For full-time undergraduate study at accredited 2-year or 4-year institution in United States.
Eligibility: Applicant must be graduate of public or private school in the North Kona, South Kona, North Kohala or Ka'u districts. Applicant must be U.S. citizen or permanent resident residing in Hawaii.
Basis for selection: Major/career interest in oceanography/ marine studies; bioengineering; health sciences or education, early childhood. Applicant must demonstrate financial need, high academic achievement, depth of character and service orientation.
Application requirements: Recommendations, essay, transcript. Submit essay explaining how your career may benefit the lives of Hawaii residents upon completing your education. Record of community service required.
Additional information: Amount and number of awards may vary yearly. Notifications mailed between April and June. Visit Website for details and application.

Amount of award:	$750
Number of awards:	2
Application deadline:	March 1

Contact:
Hawaii Community Foundation Scholarships
1164 Bishop Street
Suite 800
Honolulu, HI 96813
Phone: 808-537-6333 or 888-731-3863
Fax: 808-521-6286
Web: www.hawaiicommunityfoundation.org

Oscar and Rosetta Fish Fund

Type of award: Scholarship.
Intended use: For full-time undergraduate or graduate study. Designated institutions: Any University of Hawaii campus, excluding Manoa.
Eligibility: Applicant must be U.S. citizen or permanent resident residing in Hawaii.
Basis for selection: Major/career interest in business. Applicant must demonstrate financial need, high academic achievement and depth of character.
Application requirements: Recommendations, essay, transcript.
Additional information: Must attend school at any University of Hawaii campus, excluding Manoa. Applicants must have permanent address in Hawaii. Notifications mailed between April and June. Amount and number of awards vary and may change yearly. Visit Website for details and application.

Amount of award:	$1,500
Number of awards:	25
Application deadline:	March 1

Contact:
Hawaii Community Foundation Scholarships
1164 Bishop Street
Suite 800
Honolulu, HI 96813
Phone: 808-537-6333 or 888-731-3863
Fax: 808-521-6286
Web: www.hawaiicommunityfoundation.org

PHG Foundation Scholarship

Type of award: Scholarship.
Intended use: For undergraduate study at accredited 2-year or 4-year institution in United States.
Eligibility: Applicant must be U.S. citizen or permanent resident residing in Hawaii.
Basis for selection: Major/career interest in art/art history. Applicant must demonstrate financial need, high academic achievement and depth of character.
Application requirements: Recommendations, essay, transcript. Minimum 2.7 GPA.
Additional information: Minimum GPA 2.7. Scholarship not for students studying video, film, performing arts or culinary arts. Applicants must have permanent address in Hawaii. Notifications mailed between April and June. Amount and number of awards vary and may change yearly. Visit Website for details and application.

Amount of award:	$1,000
Number of awards:	5
Application deadline:	March 1

Contact:
Hawaii Community Foundation Scholarships
1164 Bishop Street
Suite 800
Honolulu, HI 96813
Phone: 808-537-6333 or 888-731-3863
Fax: 808-521-6286
Web: www.hawaiicommunityfoundation.org

Ron Bright Scholarship

Type of award: Scholarship.
Intended use: For full-time undergraduate study at accredited 2-year or 4-year institution in United States.
Eligibility: Applicant must be high school senior. Applicant must be U.S. citizen or permanent resident residing in Hawaii.
Basis for selection: Major/career interest in education. Applicant must demonstrate financial need, high academic achievement and depth of character.
Application requirements: Recommendations, essay, transcript. Submit grades from first semester of 12th grade.
Additional information: Applicant must be senior from one of these public Windward Oahu high schools: Castle, Kahuku, Kailua, Kalaheo, or Olomana. Preference given to students with extracurricular activities in the performing arts. Applicants must have permanent address in Hawaii. Notifications mailed between April and June. Amount and number of awards vary and may change yearly. Visit Website for details and application.

Application deadline:	March 1

Contact:
Hawaii Community Foundation Scholarships
1164 Bishop Street
Suite 800
Honolulu, HI 96813
Phone: 808-537-6333 or 888-731-3863
Fax: 808-521-6286
Web: www.hawaiicommunityfoundation.org

Rosemary & Nellie Ebrie Fund

Type of award: Scholarship.
Intended use: For full-time undergraduate or graduate study at accredited 2-year or 4-year institution in United States.
Eligibility: Applicant must be of Hawaiian ancestry. Must be long-term resident born on the island of Hawaii. Applicant must be U.S. citizen or permanent resident residing in Hawaii.
Basis for selection: Applicant must demonstrate financial need, high academic achievement and depth of character.
Additional information: Student need not apply for this scholarship. Foundation will pull eligible students from overall pool of applicants, and contact awardee. Amount of award may change yearly. Notifications mailed between April and June.

Amount of award:	$676
Number of awards:	37

Contact:
Hawaii Community Foundation Scholarships
1164 Bishop Street
Suite 800
Honolulu, HI 96813
Phone: 808-537-6333 or 888-731-3863
Fax: 808-521-6286
Web: www.hawaiicommunityfoundation.org

Shuichi, Katsu and Itsuyo Suga Scholarship

Type of award: Scholarship.
Intended use: For full-time undergraduate or graduate study at accredited 2-year or 4-year institution in United States.
Eligibility: Applicant must be U.S. citizen or permanent resident residing in Hawaii.
Basis for selection: Major/career interest in mathematics; physics; science, general or computer/information sciences. Applicant must demonstrate financial need, high academic achievement and depth of character.

Application requirements: Minimum 3.0 GPA.
Additional information: Student need not apply for this scholarship. Foundation will pull eligible students from overall pool of applicants, and contact awardee. Amount of award may change yearly. Notifications mailed between April and June.

Amount of award:	$1,000
Number of awards:	6

Contact:
Hawaii Community Foundation Scholarships
1164 Bishop Street
Suite 800
Honolulu, HI 96813
Phone: 808-537-6333 or 888-731-3863
Fax: 808-521-6286
Web: www.hawaiicommunityfoundation.org

Thz Fo Farm Fund

Type of award: Scholarship.
Intended use: For full-time undergraduate or graduate study at accredited postsecondary institution in United States.
Eligibility: Chinese ancestry. Applicant must be Chinese. Applicant must be U.S. citizen or permanent resident residing in Hawaii.
Basis for selection: Major/career interest in gerontology. Applicant must demonstrate financial need, high academic achievement and depth of character.
Application requirements: Minimum 2.7 GPA.
Additional information: Student need not apply for this scholarship. Foundation will pull eligible students from overall pool of applicants, and contact awardee. Amount of award may change yearly. Notifications mailed between April and June.

Amount of award:	$1,000
Number of awards:	4

Contact:
Hawaii Community Foundation Scholarships
1164 Bishop Street
Suite 800
Honolulu, HI 96813
Phone: 808-537-6333 or 888-731-3863
Fax: 808-521-6286
Web: www.hawaiicommunityfoundation.org

Tommy Lee Memorial Scholarship Fund

Type of award: Scholarship.
Intended use: For full-time undergraduate study at accredited 2-year or 4-year institution in United States.
Eligibility: Applicant must be residing in the Waialua or Hale'iwa areas. Applicant must be high school senior. Applicant must be U.S. citizen or permanent resident residing in Hawaii.
Basis for selection: Applicant must demonstrate financial need, high academic achievement and depth of character.
Application requirements: Recommendations, essay, transcript. Two letters of recommendation required.
Additional information: Must be a high school senior residing in the Waialua or Hale'iwa areas. Notifications mailed between April and June. Amount of award may change yearly. Visit Website for details and application.

Amount of award:	$1,000
Number of awards:	2
Application deadline:	March 1

Contact:
Hawaii Community Foundation Scholarships
1164 Bishop Street
Suite 800
Honolulu, HI 96813
Phone: 808-537-6333 or 888-731-3863
Fax: 808-521-6286
Web: www.hawaiicommunityfoundation.org

Toraji & Toki Yoshinaga Scholarship

Type of award: Scholarship.
Intended use: For full-time sophomore study at accredited 2-year or 4-year institution. Designated institutions: Hawaii college/university that is not part of the University of Hawaii system.
Eligibility: Applicant must be U.S. citizen or permanent resident residing in Hawaii.
Basis for selection: Applicant must demonstrate financial need, high academic achievement and depth of character.
Additional information: Student need not apply for this scholarship. Foundation will pull eligible students from overall pool of applicants, and contact awardee. Amount of award may change yearly. Notifications mailed between April and June.

Amount of award:	$1,000
Number of awards:	2

Contact:
Hawaii Community Foundation Scholarships
1164 Bishop Street
Suite 800
Honolulu, HI 96813
Phone: 808-537-6333 or 888-731-3863
Fax: 808-521-6286
Web: www.hawaiicommunityfoundation.org

University of Redlands Hawaii Scholarship

Type of award: Scholarship, renewable.
Intended use: For full-time freshman study. Designated institutions: University of Redlands.
Eligibility: Applicant must be U.S. citizen or permanent resident residing in Hawaii.
Basis for selection: Applicant must demonstrate financial need, high academic achievement, depth of character, leadership and service orientation.
Application requirements: Recommendations, essay, transcript. Must submit FAFSA by February 15. Include University of Redlands federal code (001322). Two letters of recommendation required. All application materials due by March 1. No exceptions.
Additional information: Scholarship renewable for three years by maintaining 3.0 GPA. Prior acceptance for admission to University of Redlands not needed to apply. Notifications mailed between April and June. Visit Website for details and application. Amount of award varies yearly.

Amount of award:	$5,000
Number of awards:	4
Application deadline:	March 1

Contact:
Hawaii Community Foundation Scholarships
164 Bishop Street
Suite 800
Honolulu, HI 96813
Phone: 808-537-6333 or 888-731-3863
Fax: 808-521-6286
Web: www.hawaiicommunityfoundation.org

Vicki Willder Scholarship Fund

Type of award: Scholarship.
Intended use: For full-time undergraduate study at accredited 2-year or 4-year institution in United States.
Eligibility: Applicant must be employee or dependent of employee of Kamehameha Schools food services department or a graduate of Kamehameha Schools. Applicant must be U.S. citizen or permanent resident residing in Hawaii.
Basis for selection: Major/career interest in culinary arts or tourism/travel. Applicant must demonstrate financial need, high academic achievement and depth of character.
Application requirements: Recommendations, essay, transcript.
Additional information: Preference given to students majoring in culinary arts or travel industry management. Amount and number of awards vary and may change yearly. Notifications mailed between April and June. Visit Website for details and application.

Amount of award:	$1,042
Number of awards:	36
Application deadline:	March 1

Contact:
Hawaii Community Foundation Scholarships
1164 Bishop Street
Suite 800
Honolulu, HI 96813
Phone: 808-537-6333 or 888-731-3863
Fax: 808-521-6286
Web: www.hawaiicommunityfoundation.org

Walter H. Kupau Memorial Fund

Type of award: Scholarship.
Intended use: For full-time undergraduate study at accredited 2-year or 4-year institution in United States.
Eligibility: Applicant or parent must be member/participant of Hawaii Carpenter's Union Local 745. Applicant must be U.S. citizen or permanent resident residing in Hawaii.
Basis for selection: Applicant must demonstrate financial need, high academic achievement and depth of character.
Application requirements: Recommendations, essay, transcript. Name and social security number of Local 745 member, along with relationship to applicant.
Additional information: Applicant must be descendant of Hawaii Carpenter's Union Local 745 members in good standing, with preference given to descendants of retired members. Amount and number of awards vary. Visit the Website for further information.

Application deadline:	March 1

Contact:
Hawaii Community Foundation Scholarships
1164 Bishop Street
Suite 800
Honolulu, HI 96813
Phone: 808-537-6333 or 888-731-3863
Fax: 808-521-6286
Web: www.hawaiicommunityfoundation.org

William James & Dorothy Bading Lanquist Fund

Type of award: Scholarship.
Intended use: For full-time undergraduate or graduate study at accredited 2-year or 4-year institution in United States.
Eligibility: Applicant must be U.S. citizen or permanent resident residing in Hawaii.
Basis for selection: Major/career interest in physical sciences. Applicant must demonstrate financial need, high academic achievement and depth of character.
Application requirements: Recommendations, essay, transcript.
Additional information: Must major in the physical sciences or related fields, excluding biological and social sciences. Applicants must have permanent address in Hawaii. Notifications mailed between April and June. Amount and number of awards vary and may change yearly. Visit Website for details and application.

Amount of award:	$1,000
Number of awards:	16
Application deadline:	March 1

Contact:
Hawaii Community Foundation Scholarships
1164 Bishop Street
Suite 800
Honolulu, HI 96813
Phone: 808-537-6333 or 888-731-3863
Fax: 808-521-6286
Web: www.hawaiicommunityfoundation.org

Hawaii Postsecondary Education Commission

Hawaii Student Incentive Grant

Type of award: Scholarship, renewable.
Intended use: For undergraduate or graduate study at accredited postsecondary institution. Designated institutions: Participating public and private institutions in Hawaii system.
Eligibility: Applicant must be U.S. citizen residing in Hawaii.
Basis for selection: Applicant must demonstrate financial need.
Application requirements: Applicant must be eligible for Pell grant.
Additional information: Deadlines vary by campus. Contact school's financial aid office.

Amount of award:	Full tuition
Number of awards:	480
Total amount awarded:	$375,000

Contact:
Financial aid office of University of Hawaii campus
Web: www.hawaii.edu

Hawaii Tuition Waiver

Type of award: Scholarship, renewable.
Intended use: For undergraduate or graduate study at accredited postsecondary institution. Designated institutions: University of Hawaii campuses.
Eligibility: Applicant must be U.S. citizen or permanent resident residing in Hawaii.

Scholarships

Basis for selection: Applicant must demonstrate financial need and high academic achievement.
Additional information: Applicant may demonstrate either financial need or high academic achievement. Deadline varies by campus.

Amount of award:	Full tuition
Number of awards:	7,500
Total amount awarded:	$10,000,000

Contact:
Contact financial aid office of University of Hawaii campus.
Web: www.hawaii.edu

Helicopter Association International

Aviation Maintenance Technician Scholarship Award

Type of award: Scholarship.
Intended use: For non-degree study. Designated institutions: U.S. helicopter airframe and engine manufacturers or Southern Illinois University.
Basis for selection: Major/career interest in aviation repair.
Application requirements: Recommendations, nomination by FAA-approved Airframe and Powerplant (A&P) school.
Additional information: For students who wish to study helicopter maintenance. Applicant must be about to graduate from FAA-approved Aviation Maintenance Technician School, or a recent recipient of Airframe and Powerplant (A&P) certificate. Applications available on Website.

Amount of award:	$500-$1,500
Number of awards:	5
Number of applicants:	50
Application deadline:	October 1
Total amount awarded:	$4,300

Contact:
Aviation Maintenance Technician Scholarship
Helicopter Association International
1635 Prince Street
Alexandria, VA 22314-2818
Phone: 703-683-4646
Fax: 703-683-4745
Web: www.rotor.com

HEPC

PROMISE Scholarship Program

Type of award: Scholarship, renewable.
Intended use: For full-time undergraduate study at 2-year or 4-year institution in United States. Designated institutions: Alderson-Broaddus, Appalacian Bible College, Bethany College, Bluefield State College, Concord College, Davis & Elkins College, Eastern WV Community & Technical College, Fairmont State College, Glenville State College, Marshall University, Ohio Valley College, Potomac State College of WVU, Salem International University, Shepherd College, Southern WV Community & Technical College, University of Charleston, West Liberty State College, WV Northern Community College, WV State College, West Virginia University, WVU Intstitute of Technology, WVU at Parkersburg, West Virginia Wesleyan College, Wheeling Jesuit University.
Eligibility: Applicant must be high school senior. Applicant must be U.S. citizen residing in West Virginia.
Basis for selection: Applicant must demonstrate high academic achievement.
Additional information: Provides recipients full tuition scholarship to state college or university in West Virginia or equivalent to in-state private college. Student must have minimum 3.0 GPA, obtain composite score of 21 with minimum subscore of 20 in each area on any single ACT test or combined SAT score of 1000 with mimimum 490 verbal, 480 math scores. Visit Website for application.

Amount of award:	Full tuition
Number of awards:	3,483
Number of applicants:	4,063
Application deadline:	January 31
Total amount awarded:	$10,200,000

Contact:
HEPC
PROMISE Scholarship Program
1018 Kanawha Boulevard, East, Suite 700
Charleston, WV 25301
Phone: 304-558-4417; 877-WVPROMISE
Web: www.promisescholarships.org

Herschel C. Price Educational Foundation

Herschel C. Price Educational Scholarship

Type of award: Scholarship, renewable.
Intended use: For undergraduate or graduate study at accredited 2-year, 4-year or graduate institution in United States. Designated institutions: West Virginia colleges and universities.
Eligibility: Applicant must be U.S. citizen residing in West Virginia.
Basis for selection: Applicant must demonstrate financial need and high academic achievement.
Application requirements: Interview, transcript. Application.
Additional information: Applicant must reside in West Virginia or attend West Virginia college/university. Achievement in community activities also considered. Preference shown to undergraduates. A limited number of applications are released and must be requested in January or August.

Amount of award:	$250-$5,000
Number of awards:	225
Number of applicants:	400
Application deadline:	April 1, October 1
Notification begins:	May 15, November 15
Total amount awarded:	$245,000

Contact:
Herschel C. Price Educational Foundation
PO Box 412
Huntington, WV 25708-0412
Phone: 304-529-3852

Scholarships

Hilgenfeld Foundation for Mortuary Education c/o ABFSE

Mortuary Education Grant

Type of award: Scholarship.
Intended use: For undergraduate, graduate or non-degree study at postsecondary institution.
Eligibility: Applicant must be U.S. citizen.
Basis for selection: Major/career interest in mortuary science. Applicant must demonstrate financial need, high academic achievement, depth of character, leadership and seriousness of purpose.
Application requirements: Transcript.
Additional information: For individuals pursuing careers in funeral service industry, including licensure and higher degrees. Applicants must be enrolled in funeral service program. Contact American Board of Funeral Education for required application.

Amount of award:	$250-$500
Number of awards:	60
Number of applicants:	120
Total amount awarded:	$25,000

Contact:
American Board of Funeral Service Education
38 Florida Avenue
Portland, ME 04103

Hispanic Heritage Awards Foundation

Hispanic Heritage Youth Awards

Type of award: Scholarship.
Intended use: For undergraduate study at postsecondary institution.
Eligibility: Applicant must be Mexican American, Hispanic American or Puerto Rican. At least one parent of Hispanic ancestry. Applicant must be high school senior. Applicant must be U.S. citizen or permanent resident.
Basis for selection: Meritorious achievements in applicant's chosed discipline, compelling essay responses, contribution to community, overall character as role model, strong letter of recommendation. Applicant must demonstrate high academic achievement, depth of character, leadership and service orientation.
Application requirements: Recommendations, transcript, proof of eligibility.
Additional information: Visit Website for updates regarding Youth Awards Program. Foundation offers regional and national awards in number of categories. Amount of award and application deadlines vary by year; application available online.

Amount of award:	$2,000-$7,000
Number of awards:	78
Total amount awarded:	$250,000

Contact:
Hispanic Heritage Awards Foundation
Hispanic Heritage Youth Awards
2600 Virginia Avenue, Suite #406
Washington, DC 20037
Phone: 202-861-9797
Fax: 202-861-9799
Web: www.hispanicheritageawards.org

Hispanic Scholarship Fund

College Scholarship Fund

Type of award: Scholarship.
Intended use: For full-time sophomore, junior, senior or graduate study at postsecondary institution in or outside United States. Designated institutions: Colleges in United States, Puerto Rico or U.S. Virgin Islands.
Eligibility: Applicant must be Mexican American, Hispanic American or Puerto Rican. One parent must be fully Hispanic, or both parents half Hispanic. Applicant must be U.S. citizen or permanent resident.
Basis for selection: Applicant must demonstrate financial need, high academic achievement, seriousness of purpose and service orientation.
Application requirements: Recommendations, essay, transcript, proof of eligibility. Financial aid award letter, SAR, copy of permanent resident card or passport stamped I-551 (if applicable).
Additional information: Applicant must have earned minimum of 12 undergraduate college credits in United States, Puerto Rico or U.S. Virgin Islands. Minimum 2.7 GPA. Visit Website or contact via e-mail for more information and tips on how to apply.

Amount of award:	$1,000-$2,500
Application deadline:	October 15
Total amount awarded:	$9,000,000

Contact:
General Selection Committee
Hispanic Scholarship Fund
55 Second St, Suite 1500
San Francisco, CA 94105
Phone: 877-HSF-INFO
Fax: 415-808-2302
Web: www.hsf.net

Community College Transfer Scholarship

Type of award: Scholarship.
Intended use: For undergraduate study at accredited postsecondary institution in United States. Designated institutions: Accredited four-year postsecondary institutions in the United States, Puerto Rico, or U.S. Virgin Islands.
Eligibility: Applicant must be Mexican American, Hispanic American or Puerto Rican. One parent must be fully Hispanic, or both parents half Hispanic. Applicant must be U.S. citizen or permanent resident.
Basis for selection: Applicant must demonstrate financial need and high academic achievement.
Application requirements: Recommendations, essay, transcript, proof of eligibility. Completed and signed application, letter of recommendation from school administrator

or teacher, Student Aid Report (if available) and copy of Permanent Resident card (if applicable).

Additional information: Award designed to assist Latinos making transition from community college to four-year accredited postsecondary institution. Applicant must plan to transfer to four-year institution in fall or spring of next academic year. Minimum 3.0 GPA. Send business-size SASE with application request or download from Website at beginning of application period.

    Amount of award: $1,000-$2,500
    Application deadline: February 15

Contact:
Community College Transfer Program
Hispanic Scholarship Fund
55 Second Street, Suite 1500
San Francisco, CA 94104
Phone: 877-HSF-INFO
Fax: 415-808-2302
Web: www.hsf.net

National High School Program

Type of award: Scholarship.
Intended use: For full-time freshman study at accredited postsecondary institution in or outside United States. Designated institutions: Accredited postsecondary institutions in United States, Puerto Rico, or U.S. Virgin Islands.
Eligibility: Applicant must be Mexican American, Hispanic American or Puerto Rican. Must be of at least half Hispanic background with one parent fully Hispanic, or both parents half Hispanic. Applicant must be high school senior. Applicant must be U.S. citizen or permanent resident.
Basis for selection: Applicant must demonstrate financial need, high academic achievement and seriousness of purpose.
Application requirements: Recommendations, essay, transcript, proof of eligibility. Application, ACT/SAT scores, Student Aid Report (if available), copy of permanent resident card (if applicable).
Additional information: Award designed to assist Latinos making transition from high school to two-year and four-year accredited postsecondary institutions. Applicant must have definite plans to attend college/university in fall semester following graduation. Minimum 3.0 GPA. If applicant is planning to attend community college, he or she must be planning to transfer and pursue BA degree. Number of awards granted varies. Send business-size SASE with application request or download from Website at beginning of application period.

    Amount of award: $1,000-$2,500
    Application deadline: February 15

Contact:
Hispanic Scholarship Fund High School Program
55 Second Street
Suite 1500
San Francisco, CA 94105
Phone: 877-HSF-INFO
Fax: 415-808-2302
Web: www.hsf.net

The Hoover Carden Scholarship Fund

The Hoover Carden Scholarship

Type of award: Scholarship, renewable.
Intended use: For senior study.
Eligibility: Applicant must be U.S. citizen or permanent resident residing in Texas.
Basis for selection: Major/career interest in animal sciences or agriculture. Applicant must demonstrate leadership and service orientation.
Additional information: Applicant must have high school diploma with a minimum 2.75 GPA, and SAT score of 800 or ACT of 18 to receive scholarship funds. Open to high school seniors or students enrolled in institute of higher learning. Priority given to students of Prairie View A&M University and applicants with former 4-H membership experience.

    Amount of award: $1,500
    Application deadline: February 28

Contact:
The Hoover Carden Scholarship Fund
P.O. Box 2425
Prairie View, TX 77446

Hopi Tribe Grants and Scholarship Program

Hopi BIA Higher Education Grant

Type of award: Scholarship, renewable.
Intended use: For undergraduate or graduate study at accredited 2-year, 4-year or graduate institution.
Eligibility: Applicant must be American Indian. Must be enrolled member of the Hopi Tribe.
Basis for selection: Applicant must demonstrate financial need.
Application requirements: Must apply each academic year or semester.
Additional information: Entering freshmen must have 2.0 GPA for high school coursework or minimum composite score of 45% on GED Exam. Continuing students must have 2.0 GPA for all graduate coursework.

    Amount of award: $2,500
    Application deadline: July 31, November 30

Contact:
Hopi Tribe Grants and Scholarship Program
P.O. Box 123
Kykotsmovi, AZ 86039
Phone: 800-762-9630
Fax: 928-734-9575

Hopi Scholarship

Type of award: Scholarship, renewable.
Intended use: For full-time undergraduate or graduate study at accredited 4-year or graduate institution.
Eligibility: Applicant must be American Indian. Must be enrolled member of the Hopi Tribe.
Basis for selection: Applicant must demonstrate high academic achievement.
Application requirements: Must apply each academic year.

Additional information: Entering freshmen must be in top 10 percent of graduating class or have minimum of 21 on ACT or 930 on SAT. Undergraduate students must have and maintain 3.0 GPA; graduate, postgraduate and professional students must have 3.25 GPA for all graduate coursework. $1,000 award given each semester. Number of awards varies.

Amount of award:	$1,000
Application deadline:	July 31, November 30

Contact:
Hopi Tribe Grants and Scholarship Program
P.O. Box 123
Kykotsmovi, AZ 86039
Phone: 800-762-9630
Fax: 928-734-9575

Hopi Supplemental Grant

Type of award: Scholarship, renewable.
Intended use: For undergraduate or graduate study at accredited 2-year, 4-year or graduate institution.
Eligibility: Applicant must be American Indian. Must be enrolled member of the Hopi Tribe.
Basis for selection: Applicant must demonstrate financial need.
Application requirements: Must apply each academic year or semester.
Additional information: Entering freshmen must have 2.0 GPA for high school coursework or minimum composite score of 45 percent on the GED Exam. Continuing students must have 2.0 GPA for all college work. $1,500 may be awarded each semester.

Amount of award:	$1,500
Application deadline:	July 31, November 30

Contact:
Hopi Tribe Grants and Scholarship Program
P.O. Box 123
Kykotsmovi, AZ 86039
Phone: 800-762-9630
Fax: 928-734-9575

Hopi Tribal Priority Scholarship

Type of award: Scholarship, renewable.
Intended use: For full-time junior, senior or graduate study at accredited 4-year or graduate institution.
Eligibility: Applicant must be American Indian. Must be enrolled member of the Hopi Tribe.
Basis for selection: Major/career interest in law; natural resources/conservation; education; business; engineering; health-related professions or medical specialties/research. Applicant must demonstrate financial need, high academic achievement, depth of character, leadership and seriousness of purpose.
Application requirements: Recommendations, transcript.
Additional information: Applicant must show certification of Indian blood. Award is based on amount of college cost. Applicant must have college submit financial needs analysis to determine amount of award. Tuition, books, room and board covered until graduation.

Amount of award:	Full tuition
Number of awards:	3
Application deadline:	July 31

Contact:
Hopi Tribe Grants and Scholarship Program
P.O. Box 123
Kykotsmovi, AZ 86039
Phone: 800-762-9630
Fax: 928-734-9575

Horace Mann Companies

Horace Mann Scholarship Program

Type of award: Scholarship, renewable.
Intended use: For full-time undergraduate study at accredited 2-year or 4-year institution.
Eligibility: Applicant or parent must be employed by U.S. public school district or public college/university. Applicant must be high school senior.
Basis for selection: Applicant must demonstrate high academic achievement, depth of character, leadership and service orientation.
Application requirements: Recommendations, essay, transcript, proof of eligibility. List of activities and honors.
Additional information: Student must have B average and minimum 23 on ACT or 1100 on SAT. Parent must be employed by U.S. public or private school district or by public or private college/university. Awards are given as follows: one $10,000 award, five $4,000 awards, and twenty $1,000 awards. Application available online only.

Amount of award:	$1,000-$10,000
Number of awards:	26
Number of applicants:	10,000
Application deadline:	February 12
Notification begins:	March 31
Total amount awarded:	$50,000

Contact:
Horace Mann Scholarship Program
1 Horace Mann Plaza
Springfield, IL 62715-0001
Web: www.horacemann.com

Horatio Alger Association

Horatio Alger Association Florida Scholarship Program

Type of award: Scholarship.
Intended use: For undergraduate study.
Eligibility: Must be resident of Broward, Martin or St. Lucie county. Applicant must be high school senior. Applicant must be U.S. citizen residing in Florida.
Basis for selection: Applicant must demonstrate financial need.
Application requirements: Application. Minimum 2.0 GPA. Student must have overcome great obstacles in his/her life.
Additional information: Program assists Florida high school seniors who have faced and overcome great obstacles. Applicant should have strong commitment to use college degree in service to others. Must plan to pursue bachelor's degree. See Website for application.

Amount of award:	$2,500-$10,000
Number of awards:	100
Application deadline:	October 15

Contact:
Horatio Alger Association
99 Canal Center Plaza
Alexandria, VA 22314
Phone: 703-684-9444
Fax: 703-684-9445
Web: www.horatioalger.org/scholarships

Horatio Alger Association Indiana Scholarship Program

Type of award: Scholarship.
Intended use: For undergraduate study.
Eligibility: Applicant must be high school senior. Applicant must be U.S. citizen residing in Indiana.
Basis for selection: Applicant must demonstrate high academic achievement.
Application requirements: Application. Minimum 2.0 GPA. Student must have overcome great obstacles in his/her life.
Additional information: Program assists Indiana high school seniors who have faced and overcome great obstacles. Applicant should have strong commitment to us college degree in service to others. Must plan to pursue bachelor's degree. See Website for application.

Amount of award:	$2,500-$10,000
Number of awards:	16
Application deadline:	October 15

Contact:
Horatio Alger Association
99 Canal Center Plaza
Alexandria, VA 22314
Phone: 703-684-9444
Fax: 703-684-9445
Web: www.horatioalger.org/scholarships

Horatio Alger Association Minnesota Scholarship Program

Type of award: Scholarship.
Intended use: For undergraduate study.
Eligibility: Must be resident of Anoka, Carver, Dakota, Hennepin, Ramsey, Scott or Washington county. Applicant must be high school senior. Applicant must be U.S. citizen residing in Minnesota.
Basis for selection: Applicant must demonstrate financial need.
Application requirements: Application. Minimum 2.0 GPA. Student must have overcome great obstacles in his/her life.
Additional information: Program assists Minnesota high school seniors who have faced and overcome great obstacles. Applicant should have strong commitment to use college degree in service to others. Must plan to pursue bachelor's degree. See Website for application.

Amount of award:	$2,500-$10,000
Number of awards:	42
Application deadline:	October 15

Contact:
Horatio Alger Association
99 Canal Center Plaza
Alexandria, VA
Phone: 703-684-9444
Fax: 703-684-9445
Web: www.horatioalger.org/scholarships

Horatio Alger Association Missouri Scholarship Program

Type of award: Scholarship.
Intended use: For undergraduate study.
Eligibility: Applicant must be high school senior. Applicant must be U.S. citizen residing in Missouri.
Application requirements: Application. Minimum 2.0 GPA. Student must have overcome great obstacles in his/her life.

Additional information: Program assists Missouri high school seniors who have faced and overcome great obstacles. Applicant should have strong commitment to use college degree in service to others. Must plan to pursue bachelor's degree. See Website for application.

Amount of award:	$2,500-$10,000
Number of awards:	100
Application deadline:	October 15

Contact:
Horatio Alger Association
99 Canal Center Plaza
Alexandria, VA 22314
Phone: 703-684-9444
Fax: 703-684-9445
Web: www.horatioalger.org/scholarships

Horatio Alger Association Montana Scholarship Program

Type of award: Scholarship.
Intended use: For undergraduate study. Designated institutions: University of Montana institutions.
Eligibility: Applicant must be high school senior. Applicant must be U.S. citizen residing in Montana.
Basis for selection: Applicant must demonstrate financial need.
Application requirements: Application. Minimum 2.0 GPA. Student must have overcome great obstacles in his/her life.
Additional information: Program assists Montana high school seniors who have faced and overcome great obstacles. Applicant should have strong commitment to us college degree in service to others. Must plan to pursue bachelor's degree. See Website for application.

Amount of award:	$2,500-$10,000
Number of awards:	100
Application deadline:	October 15

Contact:
Horatio Alger Association
99 Canal Center Plaza
Alexandria, VA 22314
Phone: 703-684-9444
Fax: 703-684-9445
Web: www.horatioalger.org/scholarships

Horatio Alger Association Pennsylvania Scholarship Program

Type of award: Scholarship.
Intended use: For undergraduate study.
Eligibility: Applicant must be high school senior. Applicant must be U.S. citizen residing in Pennsylvania.
Basis for selection: Applicant must demonstrate financial need.
Application requirements: Application. Minimum 2.0 GPA. Student must have overcome great obstacles in his/her life.
Additional information: Program assists Pennsylvania high school seniors who have faced and overcome great obstacles. Applicant should have strong commitment to use college degree in service to others. Must plan to pursue bachelor's degree. See Website for application.

Amount of award:	$2,500-$10,000
Number of awards:	100
Application deadline:	October 15

Scholarships

Contact:
Horatio Alger Association
99 Canal Center Drive
Alexandria, VA 22314
Phone: 703-684-9444
Fax: 703-684-9445
Web: www.horatioalger.org/scholarships

Horatio Alger Association/Delaware Scholarship Program

Type of award: Scholarship.
Eligibility: Applicant must be high school senior. Applicant must be U.S. citizen residing in Delaware.
Basis for selection: Applicant must demonstrate financial need.
Application requirements: Application. Minimum 2.0 GPA. Student must have overcome great obstacles in his/her life.
Additional information: Program assists Delaware high school seniors who have faced and overcome great obstacles. Applicants should have strong commitment to use college degree in service to others. Must plan to pursue bachelor's degree. See Website for application.

Amount of award:	$10,000
Number of awards:	1,000
Application deadline:	October 15
Total amount awarded:	$2,500

Contact:
Horatio Alger Association
99 Canal Center Drive
Alexandria, VA 22314
Phone: 703-684-9444
Fax: 703-684-9445
Web: www.horatioalger.org/scholarships

Horatio Alger Association/Iowa Scholarship Program

Type of award: Scholarship.
Intended use: For undergraduate study. Designated institutions: University of Iowa.
Eligibility: Applicant must be high school senior. Applicant must be residing in Iowa.
Basis for selection: Applicant must demonstrate financial need.
Application requirements: Application. Minimum 2.0 GPA. Student must have overcome great obstacles in his/her life.
Additional information: Program assists Iowa high school seniors who have faced and overcome great obstacles. Applicant should have strong commitment to use college degree in service to others. Must plan to pursue bachelor's degree. See Website for application.

Amount of award:	$3,000-$10,000
Number of awards:	100
Application deadline:	October 15

Contact:
Horatio Alger Association
99 Canal Center Plaza
Alexandria, VA 22314
Phone: 703-684-9444
Fax: 703-684-9445
Web: www.horatioalger.org/scholarships

Horatio Alger California Scholarship Program

Type of award: Scholarship.

Intended use: For undergraduate study at accredited 2-year or 4-year institution.
Eligibility: Applicant must be high school senior. Applicant must be U.S. citizen residing in California.
Basis for selection: Applicant must demonstrate financial need, seriousness of purpose and service orientation.
Application requirements: Essay. Application. Minimum 2.0 GPA. Student must have overcome great obstacles in his/her life.
Additional information: Program assists California high school seniors who have faced and overcome great obstacles. Applicant should have strong commitment to use college degree in service to others. Must plan to pursue bachelor's degree. See Website for application.

Amount of award:	$1,000-$10,000
Number of awards:	1,300
Application deadline:	October 15

Contact:
Horatio Alger Association
99 Canal Center Plaza
Alexandria, VA 22314
Phone: 703-684-9444
Fax: 703-684-9445
Web: www.horatioalger.org/scholarships

Horatio Alger Louisiana Scholarship Program

Type of award: Scholarship.
Intended use: For undergraduate study at accredited 2-year or 4-year institution. Designated institutions: Accredited Louisiana colleges.
Eligibility: Applicant must be high school senior. Applicant must be U.S. citizen residing in Louisiana.
Basis for selection: Applicant must demonstrate financial need, seriousness of purpose and service orientation.
Application requirements: Essay. Application. Minimum 2.0 GPA. Student must have overcome great obstacles in his/her life.
Additional information: Program assists Louisiana high school seniors who have faced and overcome great obstacles. Applicant should have strong commitment to use college degree in service to others. Must plan to pursue bachelor's degree. See Website for application.

Amount of award:	$1,000-$10,000
Number of awards:	1,300
Application deadline:	October 15

Contact:
Horatio Alger Association
99 Canal Center Plaza
Alexandria, VA 22314
Phone: 703-684-9444
Fax: 703-684-9445
Web: www.horatioalger.org/scholarships

Horatio Alger National Scholarship

Type of award: Scholarship.
Intended use: For undergraduate study at accredited 2-year or 4-year institution.
Eligibility: Applicant must be high school senior. Applicant must be U.S. citizen.
Basis for selection: Major/career interest in humanities/liberal arts. Applicant must demonstrate financial need, seriousness of purpose and service orientation.

Application requirements: Essay. Send application form. Minimum 2.0 GPA. Student must have overcome great obstacles in his/her life.

Additional information: Program assists high school seniors who have faced and overcome great obstacles. Applicant should have strong commitment to use college degree in service to others. Must plan to pursue bachelor's degree. Visit Website for application.

Amount of award:	$1,000-$10,000
Number of awards:	1,300
Application deadline:	October 15

Contact:
Horatio Alger Association
99 Canal Center Plaza
Alexandria, VA 22314
Phone: 703-684-9444
Fax: 703-684-9445
Web: www.horatioalger.org/scholarships

Horatio Alger Nebraska Scholarship Program

Type of award: Scholarship.
Intended use: For undergraduate study at accredited 2-year or 4-year institution.
Eligibility: Applicant must be high school senior. Applicant must be U.S. citizen residing in Nebraska.
Basis for selection: Applicant must demonstrate financial need, seriousness of purpose and service orientation.
Application requirements: Essay. Application. Minimum 2.0 GPA. Student must have overcome great obstacles in his/her life.
Additional information: Program assists Nebraska high school seniors who have faced and overcome great obstacles. Applicant should have strong commitment to use college degree in service to others. Must plan to pursue bachelor's degree. Must show critical financial need. See Website for application.

Amount of award:	$1,000-$10,000
Number of awards:	1,300
Application deadline:	October 15

Contact:
Horatio Alger Association
99 Canal Center Plaza
Alexandria, VA 22314
Phone: 703-684-9444
Fax: 703-684-9445
Web: www.horatioalger.org/scholarships

Horation Alger Association Kentucky Scholarship Program

Type of award: Scholarship.
Intended use: For undergraduate study.
Eligibility: Applicant must be high school senior. Applicant must be U.S. citizen residing in Kentucky.
Basis for selection: Applicant must demonstrate financial need.
Application requirements: Application. Minimum 2.0 GPA. Student must have overcome great obstacles in his/her life.
Additional information: Program assists Kentucky high school seniors who have faced and overcome great obstacles. Applicant should have strong commitment to use college degree in service to others. Must plan to pursue bachelor's degree. See Website for application.

Amount of award:	$2,500-$10,000
Number of awards:	16
Application deadline:	October 15

Contact:
Horation Alger Association
99 Canal Center Plaza
Alexandria, VA 22314
Phone: 703-684-9444
Fax: 703-684-9445
Web: www.horatioalger.org/scholarships

Horizons Foundation

Horizons Foundation Scholarship

Type of award: Scholarship.
Intended use: For junior, senior or graduate study at accredited 4-year institution in United States.
Eligibility: Applicant must be U.S. citizen.
Basis for selection: Major/career interest in military science; computer/information sciences; physics; mathematics; business; law; international relations; political science/government; economics or engineering. Applicant must demonstrate financial need and high academic achievement.
Application requirements: Recommendations, essay, transcript. Application.
Additional information: Scholarship intended to provide financial assistance to individuals either employed or planning careers in defense or national security areas. Minimum 3.25 GPA. Studies must be aimed at national defense/national security. Visit Website for details and application (no phone calls).

Amount of award:	$500-$2,000
Application deadline:	July 1, November 1

Contact:
Horizons Foundation
c/o National Defense Industrial Association
2111 Wilson Blvd., Suite 400
Arlington, VA 22201-3061
Phone: 703-247-2552
Fax: 703-522-1885
Web: wid.ndia.org

Horticultural Research Institute

Carville M. Akehurst Memorial Scholarship

Type of award: Scholarship.
Intended use: For full-time junior or senior study at accredited postsecondary institution.
Eligibility: Applicant must be residing in Virginia, West Virginia or Maryland.
Basis for selection: Major/career interest in horticulture or landscape architecture. Applicant must demonstrate high academic achievement.
Application requirements: Recommendations, transcript. Faculty Referral Form.
Additional information: Applicant must be resident of Maryland, Virginia or West Virginia. Minimum 2.7 overall GPA and minimum 3.0 in major. Must have junior standing in four-year curriculum or senior standing in two-year curriculum.

Preference given to applicants who plan to work within industry following graduation. Previous winners eligible for additional funding. Visit Website for application and more information. Applications accepted in June.

Amount of award:	$1,000-$2,500
Application deadline:	April 1

Contact:
Horticultural Research Institute
1000 Vermont Avenue NW
Suite 300
Washington, DC 20005-4914
Phone: 202-789-2900
Fax: 202-789-1893
Web: www.anla.org/research/scholarships

Horticultural Research Institute Spring Meadow Scholarship

Type of award: Scholarship.
Intended use: For full-time at accredited postsecondary institution.
Eligibility: Applicant must be residing in Virginia, West Virginia or Maryland.
Application requirements: Recommendations, transcript. Faculty Referral Form.
Additional information: Applicant must be resident of Maryland, Virginia, or West Virginia. Minimum 2.25 overall GPA, and minimum 2.7 in major. Must have junior standing in four-year curriculum or senior standing in two-year curriculum. Preference given to applicants who plan to work within industry following graduation. Previous winners eligible for additional funding. Visit Website for application and more information. Applications accepted in June.

Amount of award:	$1,000-$2,500
Application deadline:	April 1

Contact:
Horticultural Research Institute
1000 Vermont Avenue NW
Washington, DC 20005-4914
Phone: 202-789-2900
Fax: 202-789-1893
Web: www.anla.org/research/scholarships

Timothy Bigelow Scholarship

Type of award: Scholarship.
Intended use: For full-time undergraduate or graduate study at accredited 2-year, 4-year or graduate institution.
Eligibility: Applicant must be residing in Vermont, New Hampshire, Connecticut, Maine, Massachusetts or Rhode Island.
Basis for selection: Major/career interest in landscape architecture or horticulture. Applicant must demonstrate financial need, high academic achievement, depth of character and seriousness of purpose.
Application requirements: Recommendations, essay, transcript. Applicant must submit one-page resume of background, employment history, and education and two-page cover letter.
Additional information: Must have at least 2.25 GPA for undergraduates and 3.0 GPA for graduate students. Must be enrolled in accredited landscape/horticulture program. Applicant must have senior standing in two-year program, junior standing in four-year program, or graduate standing.

Amount of award:	$2,500
Number of awards:	3
Application deadline:	April 1
Notification begins:	July 1

Contact:
Endowment Program Administrator
Horticultural Research Institute
1000 Vermont Ave. NW, Suite 300
Washington, DC 20005-4914
Phone: 202-789-2900 ext. 3014
Fax: 202-789-1893
Web: www.anla.org/research/scholarships

Usrey Family Scholarship

Type of award: Scholarship, renewable.
Intended use: For full-time undergraduate or graduate study at vocational, 2-year, 4-year or graduate institution in United States. Designated institutions: California state college or university.
Eligibility: Non-resident applicants who attend California school are also eligible. Applicant must be residing in California.
Basis for selection: Major/career interest in landscape architecture or horticulture.
Application requirements: Recommendations, essay, transcript. Cover letter and resume. Minimum 2.5 GPA (overall); minimum 2.7 GPA in major.
Additional information: Applicant must be student enrolled in California state college or university in undergraduate or graduate landscape horticulture program. Visit Website for application.

Amount of award:	$1,000
Number of awards:	1
Application deadline:	April 1
Total amount awarded:	$1,000

Contact:
Endowment Program Administrator, Horticultural Research Institute
1000 Vermont Ave. NW
Suite 300
Washington, DC 20005-4914
Phone: 202-789-5980 ext.3014
Fax: 202-789-1893
Web: www.anla.org/research/scholarships

Household International (HFC)

Household Scholar Award and Financial Aid Grant program

Type of award: Scholarship.
Intended use: For full-time undergraduate study at accredited 2-year or 4-year institution.
Eligibility: Applicant or parent must be employed by Household International (HFC).
Basis for selection: Applicant must demonstrate financial need.
Application requirements: Proof of eligibility. Must be dependent child of benefit-eligible Household employee.
Additional information: To apply for Scholar Award, applicant must be dependent child of benefit-eligible employee of Household International and high school senior. Scholar Award is one-time award of $1500. To apply for Financial Aid Grant, applicant must be dependent child of benefit-eligible employee of Household International and either high school senior or currently enrolled undergraduate at accredited

university. Financial Aid Grants awarded in amounts up to $2,000 per year. Contact employer for details.

Amount of award:	$1,500-$2,000
Number of awards:	42
Number of applicants:	153
Application deadline:	April 1
Total amount awarded:	$228,000

Contact:
Scholar Award and Financial Aid Coordinator Household International
2700 Sanders Road
Prospect Heights, IL 60070
Fax: 847-564-7094
Web: www.household.com

Houston Livestock Show and Rodeo

Go Texan Scholarships

Type of award: Scholarship.
Intended use: For undergraduate study. Designated institutions: Texas postsecondary institutions.
Eligibility: Applicant must be high school senior. Applicant must be U.S. citizen residing in Texas.
Basis for selection: Applicant must demonstrate financial need, high academic achievement, depth of character, leadership and service orientation.
Application requirements: Recommendations, essay, transcript, proof of eligibility. SAT/ACT scores.
Additional information: Must be two-year or four-semester member in good standing of Texas 4-H or Texas FFA. One-year $2,500 scholarship awarded to eligible student from each of 60 Area Go Texan counties. Award may be upgraded to two-year $5,000 scholarship. Scholarship increased to four-year $10,000 awards for top performing counties in each of 10 Area Go Texan districts. Contact sponsor or visit Website for details and application. SAT scores must be at least 910 combined, and ACT scores at least 19. Deadline for submitting application in April.

Amount of award:	$2,500-$10,000
Number of awards:	60

Contact:
Houston Livestock Show and Rodeo
Office of Education Programs
P.O. Box 20070
Houston, TX 77225
Phone: 832-667-1000
Web: www.rodeohouston.com/education

Opportunity Scholarship

Type of award: Scholarship.
Intended use: For full-time undergraduate study. Designated institutions: Texas postsecondary institutions.
Eligibility: Applicant must be high school senior. Applicant must be U.S. citizen residing in Texas.
Basis for selection: Applicant must demonstrate financial need, high academic achievement, depth of character, leadership and service orientation.
Application requirements: Recommendations, essay, transcript, proof of eligibility. Must pass TAAS Mastery/Exit Level exam. Must submit up to three references; two-page, double-spaced narrative describing college importance and

career goals; SAT/ACT scores (minimum 830 SAT, 17 ACT); class standing; photograph.
Additional information: Criteria for selection based on 50% financial need, 35% academics, and 15% leadership and community involvement. Must be graduating in top half of class from specified school districts in Brazoria, Chambers, Fort Bend, Galveston, Harris, Liberty, Montgomery and Waller counties. Visit Website for listing of eligible school districts and additional information. For applications, contact guidance counselor or call Mike Nathanson. Deadline for submitting application in April.

Amount of award:	$10,000
Number of awards:	100
Total amount awarded:	$1,000,000

Contact:
Houston Livestock Show and Rodeo
Office of Education Programs
P.O. Box 20070
Houston, TX 77225
Phone: 832-667-1000
Web: www.rodeohouston.com/education

ICMA Retirement Corporation

ICMA Retirement Corporation Vantagepoint Public Employee Memorial Scholarship Fund

Type of award: Scholarship.
Intended use: For full-time undergraduate or graduate study at accredited postsecondary institution.
Eligibility: Applicant must be high school senior.
Basis for selection: Academics, involvement in school/community, work experience, outside appraisal, goals and aspirations, unusual personal or family circumstances. Applicant must demonstrate financial need, high academic achievement, leadership and service orientation.
Application requirements: Recommendations, essay, transcript, proof of eligibility. Application, statement of goals and aspirations, official letter from deceased employee's place of work certifying employee died in line of duty.
Additional information: Program established to assist children and/or spouses of deceased public employees. Amount of awards vary. Ten or more awards available in following categories: fire and rescue, law enforcement, and general public employees. Applications must be postmarked no later than March 31 each year.

Amount of award:	$10,000
Number of awards:	7
Application deadline:	March 31
Total amount awarded:	$40,000

Contact:
Vantagepoint Public Memorial Scholarship Program
c/o Scholarship America
1505 Riverview Road, PO Box 297
St. Peter, MN 56082
Phone: 507-931-1682
Web: www.icmarc.org/vantagescholar/

Idaho State Board of Education

Atwell J. Parry Work Study Program

Type of award: Scholarship.
Intended use: For undergraduate study at postsecondary institution in United States. Designated institutions: Participating Idaho institutions.
Eligibility: Applicant must be U.S. citizen or permanent resident residing in Idaho.
Basis for selection: Applicant must demonstrate financial need.
Additional information: Students may be employed on campus or in approved off-campus jobs. Educational need is considered.
Contact:
Contact financial aid office of Idaho college or university
Phone: 208-334-2270
Web: www.idahoboardofed.org/scholarships/work.asp

Idaho Governor's Challenge Scholarship

Type of award: Scholarship, renewable.
Intended use: For full-time undergraduate study at postsecondary institution. Designated institutions: Idaho colleges and universities.
Eligibility: Applicant must be high school senior. Applicant must be residing in Idaho.
Basis for selection: Applicant must demonstrate high academic achievement, leadership and service orientation.
Application requirements: SAT/ACT scores.
Additional information: Number of awards depends on availability of funds. Applicant must be high school senior at Idaho high school. Minimum 2.8 GPA. Must have demonstrated commitment to public service. For more information contact high school guidance counselor or Idaho State Board of Education.
  Amount of award: $3,000
  Application deadline: December 15
Contact:
Idaho State Board of Education
P.O. Box 83720
Boise, ID 83720-0037
Phone: 208-334-2270
Web: www.idahoboardofed.org/scholarships/challenge.asp

Idaho Minority and "At-Risk" Student Scholarship

Type of award: Scholarship.
Intended use: For full-time undergraduate study. Designated institutions: Boise State University, Idaho State University, North Idaho College, Eastern Idaho Technical College, Lewis-Clark State College, University of Idaho, College of Southern Idaho, Albertson College.
Eligibility: Applicant must be physically challenged. Applicant must be African American, Mexican American, Hispanic American, Puerto Rican or American Indian. Applicant must be U.S. citizen residing in Idaho.
Application requirements: Must be graduate of Idaho high school.
Additional information: Must be talented student at risk of failing to realize ambitions due to cultural, economic or physical circumstances. Migrant farm workers, migrant farm worker dependents and first-generation college students given special consideration. Contact high school counselor or financial aid office of participating postsecondary institutions for specific eligibility requirements and application.
  Amount of award: $3,000
  Number of awards: 45
  Total amount awarded: $120,000
Contact:
High school counselor or financial aid office
Web: www.idahoboardofed.org/scholarships/minority.asp

Idaho Promise Category B Scholarship

Type of award: Scholarship.
Intended use: For full-time freshman study at postsecondary institution. Designated institutions: Idaho colleges and universities.
Eligibility: Applicant must be no older than 21. Applicant must be residing in Idaho.
Application requirements: Must have completed high school, or equivalent, in Idaho.
Additional information: Minimum 3.0 GPA. Minimum ACT score of 20. Must be younger than 22 on July 1 of academic term of the award. For more information, contact college or university.
  Amount of award: $500
Contact:
Idaho State Board of Education
P.O. Box 83720
Boise, ID 83720-0027
Phone: 208-334-2270
Web: www.idahoboardofed.org/scholarships/promiseb.asp

Idaho Robert C. Byrd Scholarship

Type of award: Scholarship, renewable.
Intended use: For full-time freshman study at 2-year or 4-year institution.
Eligibility: Applicant must be high school senior. Applicant must be U.S. citizen or permanent resident residing in Idaho.
Basis for selection: Applicant must demonstrate high academic achievement.
Application requirements: Recommendations, transcript, proof of eligibility.
Additional information: Application and information available through high school guidance office after February 15.
  Amount of award: $1,500
  Application deadline: April 9
Contact:
Idaho State Board of Education
P.O. Box 83720
Boise, ID 83720-0037
Phone: 208-332-1574
Web: www.idahoboardofed.org/scholarships/byrd.asp

Idaho State Board of Education Robert R. Lee Promise A Category Scholarship

Type of award: Scholarship, renewable.
Intended use: For freshman study at postsecondary institution.
Eligibility: Applicant must be high school senior. Applicant must be residing in Idaho.
Additional information: Applicant must have minimum 28 ACT and 3.5 GPA and be in top ten percent of graduating class.

Applicants for professional-technical programs must have minimum 2.8 GPA and take COMPASS exam.

Amount of award:	$3,000
Number of awards:	125
Number of applicants:	3,000
Application deadline:	December 15
Total amount awarded:	$327,000

Contact:
Idaho State Board of Education
P.O. Box 83720
Boise, ID 83720-0027
Phone: 208-334-2270
Web: www.idahoboardofed.org

Leveraging Educational Assistance State Partnership Program (LEAP)

Type of award: Scholarship, renewable.
Intended use: For undergraduate or graduate study at vocational, 2-year, 4-year or graduate institution. Designated institutions: Eligible Idaho public or private colleges and universities.
Eligibility: Applicant must be U.S. citizen or permanent resident.
Basis for selection: Applicant must demonstrate financial need.
Application requirements: FAFSA.
Additional information: Formerly Idaho State Student Incentive Grant. Institution makes recommendations to Idaho State Board of Education. Awards of up to $5,000 for full-time students. Contact financial aid office of Idaho public colleges and universities for materials or additional information.

Amount of award:	$5,000
Number of awards:	1,578
Total amount awarded:	$644,543

Contact:
Financial aid offices at Idaho colleges
Web: www.idahoboardofed.org/scholarships/leap.asp

IEEE Computer Society

Lance Stafford Larson Student Scholarship

Type of award: Scholarship.
Intended use: For full-time undergraduate study at postsecondary institution.
Eligibility: Applicant or parent must be member/participant of IEEE Computer Society.
Basis for selection: Competition/talent/interest in research paper, based on technical content, writing skills and overall presentation. Major/career interest in computer/information sciences.
Application requirements: Essay, proof of eligibility.
Additional information: Applicant must be a student member of IEEE Computer Society.

Application deadline:	October 31
Total amount awarded:	$500

Contact:
IEEE Computer Society
1730 Massachusetts Ave., NW
Washington, DC 20036-1992
Web: www.computer.org

Richard E. Merwin Award

Type of award: Scholarship.
Intended use: For full-time junior, senior or graduate study at accredited 4-year or graduate institution.
Eligibility: Applicant or parent must be member/participant of IEEE Computer Society.
Basis for selection: Major/career interest in computer/ information sciences; engineering, computer or science, general. Applicant must demonstrate seriousness of purpose.
Application requirements: Recommendations, proof of eligibility.
Additional information: Minimum 2.5 GPA required. Applicant must participate in IEEE Computer Society's student branch chapter. Student winners for previous year are not eligible.

Amount of award:	$3,000
Application deadline:	September 15

Contact:
IEEE Computer Society
1730 Massachusetts Ave., NW
Washington, DC 20036-1992
Web: www.computer.org

Upsilon Pi Epsilon Award

Type of award: Scholarship.
Intended use: For full-time undergraduate or graduate study.
Eligibility: Applicant or parent must be member/participant of IEEE Computer Society.
Basis for selection: Major/career interest in computer/ information sciences. Applicant must demonstrate high academic achievement and seriousness of purpose.
Application requirements: Transcript, proof of eligibility. Three letters of recommendation.
Additional information: Applicant must be member of IEEE Computer Society. Past student winners of computer society's Richard Merwin Award or UPE/CS Award not eligible.

Amount of award:	$500
Application deadline:	October 31

Contact:
IEEE Computer Society
1730 Massachusetts Ave., NW
Washington, DC 20036-1992
Web: www.computer.org

Illinois Student Assistance Commission

Bonus Incentive Grant (BIG)

Type of award: Scholarship.
Intended use: For undergraduate study at 2-year or 4-year institution in United States. Designated institutions: Approved Illinois public and private colleges, universities and hospital schools.
Eligibility: Applicant must be U.S. citizen or permanent resident residing in Illinois.
Additional information: Bonus Incentive Grants are non-need based grants available to beneficiaries of Illinois College Savings Bonds, if at least 70% of bond proceeds are used for costs at eligible institution. Grant amounts range from $15 to $440 per bond, depending on its maturity. Grants can be used

for educational purposes only. Contact sponsor for more information.

Number of awards:	1,175
Application deadline:	May 30
Total amount awarded:	$573,720

Contact:
Illinois Student Assistance Commission
ISAC College Zone Counselor
1755 Lake Cook Road
Deerfield, IL 60015
Phone: 800-899-ISAC
Web: www.collegezone.com

Grant Program for Dependents of Police/Fire/Correctional Officers

Type of award: Scholarship, renewable.
Intended use: For undergraduate or graduate study at 2-year, 4-year or graduate institution. Designated institutions: ISAC-approved institutions in Illinois.
Eligibility: Applicant must be U.S. citizen or permanent resident residing in Illinois. Applicant's parent must have been killed or disabled in work-related accident as fire fighter, police officer or public safety officer.
Application requirements: Proof of eligibility.
Additional information: Grant for tuition and fees for spouse and children of Illinois policemen, firemen or corrections officers killed or at least 90 percent disabled in line of duty. Award amount adjusted annually. Applicant need not be Illinois resident at time of enrollment. Beneficiaries may receive the equivalent of eight semesters or 12 quarters of assistance. Contact ISAC or visit Website for additional information.

Amount of award:	Full tuition
Number of awards:	55
Total amount awarded:	$202,661

Contact:
Illinois Student Assistance Commission
ISAC College Zone Counselor
1755 Lake Cook Road
Deerfield, IL 60015
Phone: 800-899-ISAC
Web: www.collegezone.com

Illinois Future Teacher Corps

Type of award: Scholarship, renewable.
Intended use: For senior or graduate study at accredited 2-year or 4-year institution. Designated institutions: Approved Illinois public and private four-year colleges and universities offering teacher program, and certain other degree-granting institutions.
Eligibility: Applicant must be U.S. citizen or permanent resident residing in Illinois.
Basis for selection: Major/career interest in education; education, teacher or education, early childhood. Applicant must demonstrate financial need and high academic achievement.
Application requirements: Submit FAFSA and Teacher Education Program Application.
Additional information: Scholarships for students planning to pursue careers as preschool, elementary, and secondary school teachers in Illinois. Priority given to students with financial need, minority students, and those planning to teach in teacher shortage discipline and/or hard-to-staff school. Based on teaching commitment made, awards may be up to $5,000 or $10,000 (and, in some cases, may be increased additional $5,000) per year for payment of tuition, fees, room, and board.

Must fullfill teaching commitment or repay funds received plus interest.

Amount of award:	$5,000-$15,000
Number of awards:	552
Application deadline:	March 1
Total amount awarded:	$2,613,336

Contact:
Illinois Student Assistance Commission
ISAC College Zone Counselor
1755 Lake Cook Road
Deerfield, IL 60015
Phone: 800-899-ISAC
Web: www.collegezone.com

Illinois National Guard Grant

Type of award: Scholarship, renewable.
Intended use: For undergraduate or graduate study at 2-year or 4-year institution. Designated institutions: Illinois public institutions.
Eligibility: Applicant must be residing in Illinois. Applicant must be in military service in the Reserves/National Guard. Must have served at least one year of active duty in Illinois National Guard or Naval Militia.
Application requirements: Proof of eligibility.
Additional information: Available to enlisted and company grade officers up to rank of captain who have served one year active duty or are currently on active duty status. Award covers tuition and certain fees. Recipients may use award for eight semesters or 12 quarters (or the equivalent). Award amount varies. Deadlines are: 10/1 for full year, 3/1 for second/third term, and 6/15 for summer term. Applications available from ISAC or National Guard units. Contact ISAC or National Guard units or visit Website for additional information.

Amount of award:	Full tuition
Number of awards:	2,075
Application deadline:	October 1, March 1
Total amount awarded:	$4,159,591

Contact:
Illinois Student Assistance Commission
ISAC College Zone Counselor
1755 Lake Cook Road
Deerfield, IL 60015
Phone: 800-899-ISAC
Web: www.collegezone.com

Illinois Veteran Grant (IVG) Program

Type of award: Scholarship, renewable.
Intended use: For undergraduate or graduate study at postsecondary institution. Designated institutions: Public institutions in Illinois.
Eligibility: Applicant must be U.S. citizen or permanent resident residing in Illinois. Applicant must be veteran.
Application requirements: Proof of eligibility. Must have been Illinois resident six months prior to entering service and must have returned to Illinois to reside within six months of leaving service.
Additional information: Provides payment of tuition and certain fees to qualified Illinois veterans or military service members with at least one year of active duty in U.S. Armed Forces and who served honorably. Grant is available for equivalent of four academic years of full-time enrollment for undergraduate and graduate study. Not required to enroll for minimum number of credit hours each term. One-time

application only; college must be notified of intent to use grant within two months after end of each term.

Amount of award:	Full tuition
Number of awards:	11,622
Total amount awarded:	$19,245,547

Contact:
Illinois Student Assistance Commission
ISAC College Zone Counselor
1755 Lake Cook Road
Deerfield, IL 60015
Phone: 800-899-ISAC
Web: www.collegezone.com

Merit Recognition Scholarship

Type of award: Scholarship.
Intended use: For freshman study at postsecondary institution. Designated institutions: ISAC-approved institutions in Illinois or approved United States Service academies.
Eligibility: Applicant must be high school senior. Applicant must be U.S. citizen or permanent resident residing in Illinois.
Basis for selection: Applicant must demonstrate high academic achievement.
Application requirements: Proof of eligibility.
Additional information: Financial need not factor in determining MRS recipients. Must rank in top five percent of Illinois high school class at end of third semester prior to graduation or score in top 5% of Illinois students taking college entrance tests during designated time frame. Recipients must use award within one year of high school graduation and must be enrolled for undergraduate study at least half-time. High school counselors designate eligible students. Non-U.S. citizen resident of Illinois may be eligible. Contact ISAC or high school counselor or visit Website for additional information.

Amount of award:	$1,000
Number of awards:	5,327
Total amount awarded:	$5,240,500

Contact:
Illinois Student Assistance Commission
ISAC College Zone Counselor
1755 Lake Cook Road
Deerfield, IL 60015
Phone: 800-899-ISAC
Web: www.collegezone.com

Minority Teachers of Illinois Scholarship

Type of award: Scholarship, renewable.
Intended use: For undergraduate or graduate study at postsecondary institution. Designated institutions: ISAC-approved institutions in Illinois.
Eligibility: Applicant must be Alaskan native, Asian American, African American, Mexican American, Hispanic American, Puerto Rican or American Indian. Applicant must be U.S. citizen or permanent resident residing in Illinois.
Basis for selection: Major/career interest in education, teacher or education.
Application requirements: Teacher Education Program application. Applicant should be in a course of study leading to a teacher certification.
Additional information: Recipient must sign teaching commitment to teach one year for each year assistance is received. Must teach at nonprofit Illinois preschool, elementary or secondary school with at least 30% minority enrollment. If teaching commitment is not fulfilled, scholarship converts to

loan and entire amount, plus interest, must be paid. Contact ISAC or visit Website for additional information.

Amount of award:	$5,000
Number of awards:	549
Application deadline:	March 1
Total amount awarded:	$2,578,871

Contact:
Illinois Student Assistance Commission
ISAC College Zone Counselor
1755 Lake Cook Road
Deerfield, IL 60015
Phone: 800-899-ISAC
Web: www.collegezone.com

Monetary Award Program (MAP)

Type of award: Scholarship, renewable.
Intended use: For undergraduate study at 2-year or 4-year institution. Designated institutions: ISAC/MAP-approved institutions in Illinois.
Eligibility: Applicant must be U.S. citizen or permanent resident residing in Illinois.
Basis for selection: Applicant must demonstrate financial need.
Application requirements: FAFSA.
Additional information: Non-U.S. citizens who are residents of Illinois may be eligible. Must reapply every year for renewal. Contact ISAC or visit Website for application, deadline, and additional information. Amount of award dependent on legislative action and available funding in any given year.

Amount of award:	$300-$4,968
Number of awards:	140,744
Number of applicants:	450,000
Total amount awarded:	$372,360,503

Contact:
Illinois Student Assistance Commission
ISAC College Zone Counselor
1755 Lake Cook Road
Deerfield, IL 60015
Phone: 800-899-ISAC
Web: www.collegezone.com

Robert C. Byrd Honors Scholarship Program

Type of award: Scholarship, renewable.
Intended use: For full-time undergraduate study at accredited postsecondary institution in United States.
Eligibility: Applicant must be high school senior. Applicant must be U.S. citizen or permanent resident residing in Illinois.
Basis for selection: Applicant must demonstrate high academic achievement.
Additional information: Provides scholarships of up to $1,500 (subject to federal funding) for maximum of four academic years. Applicant must be high school senior and be enrolled, or accepted for enrollment, as full-time undergraduate. Eligibility based on standardized test scores, high school rank, and GPA.

Amount of award:	$1,500
Number of awards:	1,146
Application deadline:	January 15
Total amount awarded:	$1,675,438

Contact:
Illinois Student Assistance Commission
ISAC College Zone Counselor
1755 Lake Cook Road
Deerfiled, IL 60015
Phone: 800-899-ISAC
Web: www.collegezone.com

Silas Purnell Illinois Incentive for Access

Type of award: Scholarship.
Intended use: For freshman study at postsecondary institution. Designated institutions: ISAC-approved institutions.
Eligibility: Applicant must be U.S. citizen or permanent resident residing in Illinois.
Basis for selection: Applicant must demonstrate financial need.
Application requirements: FAFSA.
Additional information: Applicant must have been determined by federal needs calculation to have an expected family contribution (EFC) of $500 or less. Applicants with EFC of zero awarded $1000; EFC of $500 awarded $500. Must meet Monetary Award Program eligibility requirements. Non-U.S. citizen who is Illinois resident may be eligible. Contact ISAC or visit Website for additional information.

Amount of award:	$500-$1,000
Number of applicants:	45,000

Contact:
Illinois Student Assistance Commission
ISAC College Zone Counselor
1755 Lake Cook Road
Deerfield, IL 60015
Phone: 800-899-ISAC
Web: www.collegezone.com

Silas Purnell Illinois Incentive for Access Grant (IIA)

Type of award: Scholarship.
Intended use: For freshman study at 2-year or 4-year institution in United States. Designated institutions: Approved Illinois public and private institutions, hospital schools, and certain other degree-granting institutions.
Eligibility: Applicant must be U.S. citizen or permanent resident residing in Illinois.
Basis for selection: Applicant must demonstrate financial need.
Application requirements: Proof of eligibility. FAFSA.
Additional information: Grant for freshman students who, based on federal need calculation, have been determined to have no or extremely limited family resources. Qualified freshman enrolled at least half time may receive up to $500 or $1000 (depending on funding) for college expenses. Apply using FAFSA after January 1 preceeding academic year. Funding for IIA Grant limited; apply early.

Number of awards:	21,426
Total amount awarded:	$7,960,250

Contact:
Illinois Student Assistance Commission
ISAC College Zone Counselor
1755 Lake Cook Road
Deerfield, IL 60015
Phone: 800-899-ISAC
Web: www.collegezone.com

Student-to-Student Grant

Type of award: Scholarship, renewable.
Intended use: For undergraduate study at postsecondary institution. Designated institutions: Participating institutions in Illinois.
Eligibility: Applicant must be U.S. citizen or permanent resident residing in Illinois.
Basis for selection: Applicant must demonstrate financial need.
Additional information: Voluntary student contributions are matched, dollar for dollar, by ISAC, and paid to participating institutions. Need-based grants are then made available to needy students through procedures established by the campus financial aid administrator and the local student government. Deadline for application set by individual schools. Recipient must attend on at least half-time basis. Must reapply for renewal. Contact ISAC or visit Website for additional information.

Number of awards:	3,453
Number of applicants:	4,500
Total amount awarded:	$949,153

Contact:
Illinois Student Assistance Commission
ISAC College Zone Counselor
1755 Lake Cook Road
Deerfield, IL 60015
Phone: 800-899-ISAC
Web: www.collegezone.com

Immune Deficiency Foundation

Immune Deficiency Foundation Scholarship

Type of award: Scholarship, renewable.
Intended use: For undergraduate study at accredited vocational, 2-year or 4-year institution.
Eligibility: Applicant must be U.S. citizen or permanent resident.
Basis for selection: Applicant must demonstrate financial need, depth of character and leadership.
Application requirements: Documentation of diagnosis.
Additional information: Applicants must have documented diagnosis of primary immune deficiency disease. Immune Deficiency Foundation program is supported through an educational grant from the American Red Cross, Aventis Behring, Baxter Healthcare Corp, Bayer Corp, 777 Enterprises and ZLB Bioplasma, Inc.

Amount of award:	$750-$2,000
Application deadline:	March 31
Total amount awarded:	$25,000

Contact:
Immune Deficieny Foundation Scholarship
40 West Chesapeake Ave.
Suite 308
Towson, MD 21204
Phone: 410-321-6647 or 800-296-4433
Fax: 410-321-9165

Independent Colleges of Southern California

Macerich Scholarship

Type of award: Scholarship, renewable.
Intended use: For full-time undergraduate study at accredited 4-year institution in United States. Designated institutions: California Lutheran University, Claremont McKenna College, Loyola Marymount University, Mount St. Mary's College, Occidental College, Scripps College, University of Redlands, Whittier College, Chapman University, Harvey Mudd College, Pepperdine University, Pitzer College, Pomona College, Univerity of La Verne, University of San Diego, Westmont College.
Eligibility: Applicant must be high school senior. Applicant must be residing in California.
Basis for selection: Applicant must demonstrate high academic achievement and service orientation.
Application requirements: Recommendations, essay, transcript, proof of eligibility. List of extracurricular activities along with FA release and application.
Additional information: Applicant must attend designated high schools near one of three Macerich shopping centers: Lakewood, Cerritos, and Stonewood. Deadline and additional information available on Website.

Amount of award:	$10,000
Number of awards:	3
Total amount awarded:	$30,000

Contact:
Independent Colleges of Southern California
555 S. Flower Street
Los Angeles, CA 90071
Phone: 213-553-9380
Fax: 213-553-9346
Web: www.cal-colleges.org

Ralph M. Parsons Memorial Scholarship

Type of award: Scholarship.
Intended use: For full-time undergraduate study at accredited 4-year institution in United States. Designated institutions: California Lutheran University, Claremont McKenna College, Loyola Marymount University, Mount St. Mary's College, Occidental College, Scripps College, University of Redlands, Whittier College, Chapman University, Harvey Mudd College, Pepperdine University, Pitzer College, Pomona College, Univerity of La Verne, University of San Diego, Westmont College, Claremont Graduate University.
Eligibility: Applicant or parent must be employed by The Parsons Corporation. Applicant must be high school senior. Applicant must be residing in California.
Application requirements: Recommendations, essay, transcript, proof of eligibility. SAT/ACT scores.
Additional information: Open to high school seniors or current undergraduates who are relatives of employees of The Parsons Corporation or its subsidiaries. To obtain application, visit Website or write to sponsor. Deadline and additional information available on Website.

Contact:
Independent Colleges of Southern California
555 S. Flower Street
Los Angeles, CA 90071
Phone: 213-553-9380
Fax: 213-553-9346
Web: www.cal-colleges.org

Indiana Student Assistance Commission

Frank O'Bannon Grant

Type of award: Scholarship, renewable.
Intended use: For full-time undergraduate study at 2-year or 4-year institution. Designated institutions: Eligible Indiana schools.
Eligibility: Applicant must be U.S. citizen or permanent resident residing in Indiana.
Basis for selection: Applicant must demonstrate financial need.
Application requirements: FAFSA.
Additional information: Renewal recipients must maintain satisfactory academic progress. Summer work-study program available to recipients.

Amount of award:	$200-$9,100
Number of awards:	38,000
Number of applicants:	150,000
Application deadline:	March 1
Notification begins:	July 1
Total amount awarded:	$98,499,549

Contact:
Indiana Student Assistance Commission
150 West Market Street, Suite 500
Indianapolis, IN 46204
Web: www.in.gov/ssaci

Indiana Hoosier Scholar Program

Type of award: Scholarship.
Intended use: For full-time freshman study at accredited vocational, 2-year or 4-year institution. Designated institutions: Eligible Indiana postsecondary schools (list provided to applicants).
Eligibility: Applicant must be high school senior. Applicant must be U.S. citizen or permanent resident residing in Indiana.
Basis for selection: Applicant must demonstrate high academic achievement.
Application requirements: Proof of eligibility, nomination by high school guidance counselor. Nomination forms must be submitted by March 1.
Additional information: List of eligible Indiana colleges provided with application. Applicant must be in top 20 percent of high school class.

Amount of award:	$500
Number of awards:	840
Number of applicants:	840
Application deadline:	March 1
Notification begins:	April 15
Total amount awarded:	$420,000

Contact:
Contact high school guidance counselor for further information.
Web: www.in.gov/ssaci

Scholarships

Indiana Minority Teacher Scholarship

Type of award: Scholarship, renewable.
Intended use: For full-time undergraduate or graduate study at accredited 4-year or graduate institution. Designated institutions: Indiana schools.
Eligibility: Applicant must be African American, Mexican American, Hispanic American or Puerto Rican. Applicant must be U.S. citizen or permanent resident residing in Indiana.
Basis for selection: Major/career interest in education; education, special; occupational therapy or physical therapy. Applicant must demonstrate high academic achievement.
Application requirements: Proof of eligibility. Applicant must be black or Hispanic except if applicant is entering field of special education, occupational or physical therapy.
Additional information: 2.0 GPA required.

Amount of award:	$1,000-$4,000
Number of awards:	317
Number of applicants:	317
Total amount awarded:	$378,410

Contact:
Contact financial aid office of applicant's chosen college.
Phone: 317-232-2350
Fax: 317-232-3260
Web: www.in.gov/ssaci

Indiana Nursing Scholarship

Type of award: Scholarship, renewable.
Intended use: For undergraduate study at accredited vocational, 2-year or 4-year institution. Designated institutions: Eligible Indiana schools (list provided to applicants).
Eligibility: Applicant must be U.S. citizen residing in Indiana.
Basis for selection: Major/career interest in nursing. Applicant must demonstrate financial need and high academic achievement.
Application requirements: Proof of eligibility. FASFA.
Additional information: 2.0 GPA required. Must be admitted to eligible Indiana school. Commitment to work two years as nurse in any Indiana health care setting required. Contact financial aid office of institution for application or e-mail Indiana Student Assistance Commission. Deadline varies by institution.

Amount of award:	$50-$5,000
Number of awards:	540
Number of applicants:	540
Total amount awarded:	$416,915

Contact:
Contact financial aid office of chosen institution
Web: www.in.gov/ssaci

Indiana Robert C. Byrd Honors Scholarship

Type of award: Scholarship, renewable.
Intended use: For full-time freshman, sophomore, junior or senior study at accredited 2-year or 4-year institution in United States.
Eligibility: Applicant must be high school senior. Applicant must be U.S. citizen residing in Indiana.
Basis for selection: Applicant must demonstrate high academic achievement.
Application requirements: Transcript, proof of eligibility.
Additional information: Must have minimum 1300 SAT, 29 ACT, or 65 GED. Cannot be in debt to federal Ggvernment or

been sentenced for drug offense. Award total cannot exceed $6,000 over four years.

Amount of award:	$1,500
Number of awards:	556
Number of applicants:	556
Application deadline:	April 24
Notification begins:	June 1
Total amount awarded:	$817,401

Contact:
Contact high school guidance counselor for information
Web: www.in.gov/ssaci

Indiana Special Education Services Scholarship

Type of award: Scholarship, renewable.
Intended use: For full-time undergraduate study at accredited 4-year institution in United States. Designated institutions: Eligible Indiana schools (list provided to applicants).
Eligibility: Applicant must be U.S. citizen residing in Indiana.
Basis for selection: Major/career interest in education, special. Applicant must demonstrate high academic achievement.
Application requirements: Proof of eligibility.
Additional information: Scholarship selection made by individual schools. Minimum 2.0 GPA required to renew scholarship. Applicants must pursue or intend to pursue course of study that would enable student upon graduation to teach in accredited elementary or secondary school in Indiana. Must fulfill teaching requirements following graduation or reimburse.

Amount of award:	$1,000
Number of awards:	96
Number of applicants:	96
Total amount awarded:	$89,200

Contact:
Financial aid office of chosen institution
Web: www.in.gov/ssaci

Indiana Twenty-First Century Scholars Program

Type of award: Scholarship.
Intended use: For full-time undergraduate study at accredited 2-year or 4-year institution. Designated institutions: Participating two- or four-year schools in Indiana.
Eligibility: Applicant must be high school senior. Applicant must be U.S. citizen or permanent resident residing in Indiana.
Basis for selection: Applicant must demonstrate financial need.
Application requirements: Proof of eligibility. FAFSA.
Additional information: Must have minimum 2.0 high school GPA. Must enroll in 7th or 8th grade by taking pledge to remain drug, alcohol and crime free. Must file affirmation that pledge was fulfilled in high school senior year. Full tuition waiver up to $6,516 after other financial aid applied.

Amount of award:	Full tuition
Application deadline:	March 10
Notification begins:	July 1
Total amount awarded:	$7,627,156

Contact:
Indiana Student Assistance Commission
150 West Market Street, Suite 500
Indianapolis, IN 46204
Phone: 317-232-2350
Fax: 317-232-3260

National Guard Supplemental Grant

Type of award: Scholarship, renewable.
Intended use: For undergraduate study at 2-year or 4-year institution. Designated institutions: Indiana public colleges.
Eligibility: Applicant must be residing in Indiana. Member of Indiana Air and Army National Guard.
Basis for selection: Applicant must apply for the Indiana Higher Education Grant and meet Indiana National Guard criteria.
Application requirements: FAFSA and ING application.
Additional information: Applicant must meet requirements for the Indiana Higher Education Grant, be in active drilling status, and be certified by Indiana National Guard (ING). Applicant must maintain satisfactory academic progress.

Amount of award:	$200-$6,516
Number of awards:	945
Number of applicants:	945
Application deadline:	March 1
Notification begins:	September 1
Total amount awarded:	$2,456,005

Contact:
Indiana Student Assistance Commission
150 West Market Street
Suite 500
Indianapolis, IN 46201
Web: www.in.gov/ssaci

Institute for Humane Studies

A World Connected Essay Contest

Type of award: Scholarship.
Intended use: For full-time undergraduate or graduate study at postsecondary institution.
Eligibility: Applicant must be no older than 25, enrolled in high school.
Basis for selection: Clarity, rigor and eloquence of essay.
Application requirements: Application.
Additional information: Topic of essay contest, guidelines, entry form and additional information available on Website. Essay must be 600 to 2,500 words, excluding footnotes. See Website for submission guidelines.

Amount of award:	$250-$5,000
Application deadline:	June 1

Contact:
Institute for Humane Studies
A World Connected Essay Contest
3301 N. Fairfax Drive, Suite 440
Arlington, VA 22201
Web: www.aworldconnected.org

Humane Studies Fellowship

Type of award: Scholarship.
Intended use: For full-time junior, senior or graduate study.
Basis for selection: Applicant must demonstrate high academic achievement.
Application requirements: $25 application fee. Recommendations, essay, transcript. Applicants must submit test scores (GRE, LSAT, GMAT, SAT, ACT, etc.), two recommendations, two essays, and writing sample. Sample is typically draft dissertation or academic paper; 30 word maximum.
Additional information: Applicants must demonstrate interest in classical liberal/libertarian tradition. Amounts awarded take into account the cost of tuition at the recipient's institution and any other funds received. Number of fellowships awarded each year varies. IHS begins accepting applications in mid-late September.

Amount of award:	$2,000-$12,000
Application deadline:	December 31

Contact:
Institute for Humane Studies at George Mason University
3301 N. Fairfax Drive
Suite 440
Arlington, VA 22201
Phone: 703-993-4880 or 800-697-8799
Fax: 703-993-4890
Web: www.theihs.org

Institute of Food Technologists

Institute of Food Technologists Freshman Scholarship

Type of award: Scholarship, renewable.
Intended use: For full-time freshman study at 4-year institution in United States or Canada. Designated institutions: Educational institutions with approved program in food science/technology.
Eligibility: Applicant must be high school senior.
Basis for selection: Major/career interest in food science/technology. Applicant must demonstrate high academic achievement.
Application requirements: Minimum 2.5 GPA required. Previous scholarship recipients must be IFT members to reapply. Applicant must have a well-rounded personality.
Additional information: Applicant must be high school senior or high school graduate entering college for first time. Must enroll in IFT-approved program. Program descriptions and application available through Website or via fax. All other inquiries and completed applications should be directed to the department head of the approved school.

Amount of award:	$1,000-$1,500
Number of awards:	25
Application deadline:	February 15
Notification begins:	April 15
Total amount awarded:	$25,500

Contact:
Institute of Food Technologists
Scholarship Department
525 West Van Buren, Suite 1000
Chicago, IL 60607
Phone: 312-782-8424
Fax: 312-782-8348
Web: www.ift.org

Institute of Food Technologists Junior/Senior Scholarship

Type of award: Scholarship, renewable.

Intended use: For full-time sophomore, junior or senior study at 4-year institution in United States or Canada. Designated institutions: Educational institutions with approved program in food science/technology.
Basis for selection: Major/career interest in food science/technology. Applicant must demonstrate high academic achievement.
Application requirements: Minimum 2.5 GPA required. Previous scholarship recipients must be IFT members to reapply.
Additional information: Must be enrolled in IFT-approved program. Program description and application available through Website or via fax. All other inquiries and completed applications should be directed to the department head of the approved school.

Amount of award:	$1,000-$2,250
Number of awards:	61
Application deadline:	February 1
Total amount awarded:	$72,250

Contact:
Scholarship Department
Institute of Food Technologists
525 W. Van Buren, Suite 1000
Chicago, IL 60601
Phone: 312-782-8424
Fax: 312-782-8348
Web: www.ift.org

Institute of Food Technologists Sophomore Scholarship

Type of award: Scholarship, renewable.
Intended use: For full-time freshman study at 4-year institution in United States or Canada. Designated institutions: Educational institutions with approved program in food science/technology.
Basis for selection: Major/career interest in food science/technology. Applicant must demonstrate high academic achievement.
Application requirements: Recommendations, essay, transcript, proof of eligibility. Minimum 2.5 GPA required. Previous scholarship recipients must be IFT members to reapply.
Additional information: Applicant must be college freshman. Must be enrolled in or plan to enroll in IFT-approved program. Program descriptions and application available through Website or via fax. All other inquiries and completed applications should be directed to the department head of approved school.

Amount of award:	$1,000
Number of awards:	23
Application deadline:	March 1
Total amount awarded:	$23,000

Contact:
Institute of Food Technologists
Scholarship Department
525 West Van Buren, Suite 1000
Chicago, IL 60607
Phone: 312-782-8424
Fax: 312-782-8348
Web: www.ift.org

Quality Assurance Division Junior/ Senior Scholarship

Type of award: Scholarship, renewable.
Intended use: For full-time sophomore, junior or senior study at 4-year institution in United States or Canada. Designated

institutions: Educational institutions with approved program in food science/technology.
Basis for selection: Major/career interest in food science/technology. Applicant must demonstrate high academic achievement.
Application requirements: Recommendations, essay, transcript, proof of eligibility. Minimum 2.5 GPA required. Previous scholarship recipients must be IFT members to reapply.
Additional information: Must be enrolled in IFT-approved program. Preference given to applicants who are taking or have taken at least one course in quality assurance and demonstrate definite interest. Program descriptions and application available through Website or via fax. All other inquiries and completed applications should be directed to department head of approved school.

Amount of award:	$2,000
Number of awards:	2
Application deadline:	February 1
Notification begins:	April 15
Total amount awarded:	$4,000

Contact:
Institute of Food Technologists
Scholarship Department
525 West Van Buren, Suite 1000
Chicago, IL 60607
Phone: 312-782-8424
Fax: 312-782-8348
Web: www.ift.org

Institute of International Education

Anna K. Meredith Fund Scholarship

Type of award: Scholarship.
Intended use: For undergraduate study in Florence, Italy. Designated institutions: Studio Art Centers International (SACI).
Basis for selection: Competition/talent/interest in study abroad. Major/career interest in arts, general or art/art history. Applicant must demonstrate financial need.
Application requirements: Portfolio. Submit portfolio of 20 labeled slides of own work. Student aid report from home school or recent tax return if not currently enrolled.
Additional information: Number of awards offered varies according to budget.

Amount of award:	$500-$2,000
Application deadline:	March 31, October 1

Contact:
Institute of International Education
809 United Nations Plaza
U.S. Student Programs, SACI Coordinator
New York, NY 10017-3580
Phone: 212-984-5548
Fax: 212-984-5325
Web: www.saci-florence.org

Clare Brett Smith Scholarship

Type of award: Scholarship.
Intended use: For undergraduate or graduate study in Florence, Italy. Designated institutions: Studio Art Centers International (SACI).

Basis for selection: Competition/talent/interest in study abroad. Major/career interest in arts, general.
Application requirements: Portfolio. Must submit portfolio of 20 labeled slides of own work or two short papers. Student aid report from home school, or recent tax return if not currently enrolled.
Additional information: Applicant must be studying photography. Number of awards varies yearly according to budget.

Amount of award:	$1,000
Application deadline:	March 31, October 1

Contact:
Institute of International Education
809 United Nations Plaza
U.S. Student Programs, SACI Coordinator
New York, NY 10017-3580
Phone: 212-984-5548
Fax: 212-984-5325
Web: www.saci-florence.org

Freeman-ASIA Award Program

Type of award: Scholarship.
Intended use: For full-time undergraduate study at 2-year or 4-year institution in Cambodia, China, Hong Kong, Indonesia, Japan, Korea, Laos, Macao, Malaysia, Mongolia, Philippines, Singapore, Taiwan, Thailand, Vietnam.
Eligibility: Applicant must be U.S. citizen or permanent resident.
Basis for selection: Major/career interest in asian studies. Applicant must demonstrate financial need, high academic achievement, depth of character and service orientation.
Application requirements: Proof of eligibility. Personal statement, service proposal. Applicant must currently receive Need-Based Financial Aid or demonstrate through FAFSA verifiable need for financial assistance for study abroad in Asia. Applicant must have at least one term of enrollment remaining at home institution following return from study in Asia.
Additional information: Priority given to students with no experience in Asia. Applicants must have applied or been accepted to study abroad program in approved Asian country or region. Program must be sponsored by U.S. accredited institution and award college credit. Applicants must design projects to educate about and encourage study abroad in Asia upon returning to United States. Award amounts: $5,000 for fall or spring semester, $7,000 for academic year, $3,000 for summer term. Deadlines: April 2 for fall/academic year (application start date February 9), October 15 for spring (application start date September 1), March 5 for summer (application start date January 23). Must file electronic application; hard copies of application received through mail not accepted.

Amount of award:	$3,000-$7,000

Contact:
Institute of International Education
Freeman-Asia Award Program
809 UN Plaza
New York, NY 10017-3580
Phone: 212-984-5542
Fax: 212-984-5325
Web: www.iie.org/Freeman-ASIA

IIE/Cora Faye Williamson Scholarship

Type of award: Scholarship.

Intended use: For undergraduate or graduate study in Florence, Italy. Designated institutions: Studio Art Centers International (SACI).
Basis for selection: Competition/talent/interest in Study abroad. Major/career interest in arts, general or art/art history.
Application requirements: Portfolio.
Additional information: Offered to assist undergraduate or graduate student meet academic objectives. May be used to offset any costs associated with significant study-abroad experience. Preferences given to students from East Texas, especially from Beaumont area, or from Lamar University in particular.

Application deadline:	March 31, October 1

Contact:
Institute of International Education
809 United Nations Plaza
U.S. Student Programs, SACI Coordinator
New York, NY 10017-3580
Phone: 212-984-5548
Fax: 212-984-5235
Web: www.saci-florence.org

International Incentive Awards

Type of award: Scholarship.
Intended use: For sophomore, junior or senior study in Florence, Italy. Designated institutions: Studio Art Centers International (SACI).
Basis for selection: Competition/talent/interest in study abroad. Major/career interest in arts, general or art/art history. Applicant must demonstrate financial need and high academic achievement.
Application requirements: Portfolio. Must submit portfolio of 20 labeled slides of own work or 2 short papers. Must submit student aid report from home school. Must fill out FAFSA online and forward student aid information to foundation.
Additional information: Must be at least sophomore with minimum 3.0 GPA. Studio arts accepted fields of study. Special efforts are made to encourage applications from minorities and underrepresented groups. Up to two awards offered each semester.

Amount of award:	$1,500
Number of awards:	2
Application deadline:	March 31, October 1

Contact:
Institute of International Education
809 United Nations Plaza
U.S. Student Programs, SACI Coordinator
New York, NY 10017-3580
Phone: 212-984-5548
Fax: 212-984-5325

Jules Maidoff Scholarship

Type of award: Scholarship.
Intended use: For undergraduate or graduate study in Florence, Italy. Designated institutions: Studio Art Centers International (SACI).
Basis for selection: Competition/talent/interest in Study abroad. Major/career interest in arts, general or art/art history. Applicant must demonstrate financial need.
Application requirements: Portfolio.
Additional information: Awarded to students exhibiting both exceptional artistic talent and financial need.

Amount of award:	Full tuition
Application deadline:	March 31, October 1

Contact:
Institute of International Education
809 United Nations Plaza
U.S. Student Programs, SACI Coordinator
New York, NY 10017-3580
Phone: 212-984-5548
Fax: 212-984-5325
Web: www.saci-florence.org

Lele Cassin Scholarship

Type of award: Scholarship.
Intended use: For undergraduate or graduate study in Florence, Italy. Designated institutions: Studio Art Centers International (SACI).
Basis for selection: Competition/talent/interest in Study abroad. Major/career interest in film/video.
Application requirements: Submit video (no longer than 15 minutes) of own work.
Additional information: For video-filmmaking student. Number of awards offered varies yearly according to budget.

  Amount of award: $1,000
  Application deadline: March 31, October 1
Contact:
Institute of International Education
809 United Nations Plaza
U.S. Students Programs, SACI Coordinator
New York, NY 10017-3580
Phone: 212-984-5548
Fax: 212-984-5325
Web: www.saci-florence.org

Institute of Materials, Minerals and Mining

Centenary Scholarship

Type of award: Scholarship.
Intended use: For freshman or sophomore study in or outside United States.
Eligibility: Applicant or parent must be member/participant of Institution of Mining and Metallurgy.
Basis for selection: Major/career interest in geology/earth sciences. Applicant must demonstrate high academic achievement.
Application requirements: Application.
Additional information: Award is for projects, visits, etc., furthering applicant's career development. Applicant must be student-member of Institute of Materials, Minerals and Mining. Application forms available from Institute. Recipients expected to produce reports on their use of the award for publication.

  Number of awards: 1
  Application deadline: March 15
Contact:
Institute of Materials, Minerals and Mining
Danum House
South Parade
Doncaster, EN DNI-2DY
Phone: 44-1302-320486
Fax: 44-1302-380900
Web: www.iom3.org

Institute of Real Estate Management Foundation

George M. Brooker Collegiate Scholarship for Minorities

Type of award: Scholarship.
Intended use: For full-time junior, senior, master's or doctoral study at accredited 4-year or graduate institution.
Eligibility: Applicant must be Alaskan native, Asian American, African American, Mexican American, Hispanic American, Puerto Rican or American Indian. Applicant must be U.S. citizen.
Basis for selection: Major/career interest in real estate; business or business/management/administration. Applicant must demonstrate high academic achievement, depth of character, leadership and seriousness of purpose.
Application requirements: Interview, recommendations, essay, transcript.
Additional information: Must have 3.0 GPA in major. Must intend to enter the field of real estate management. Undergraduate scholarships $1,000; graduate $2,500. Award notification is made on an ongoing basis.

  Amount of award: $1,000-$2,500
  Number of awards: 3
  Application deadline: March 31
  Total amount awarded: $4,500
Contact:
Institute of Real Estate Management Foundation
Foundation Administrator
430 North Michigan Avenue
Chicago, IL 60611
Phone: 312-329-6008
Web: www.irem.org

Int'l Union of Electr., Salaried, Machine, and Furn. Wrkrs Dept. of Education

James B. Carey Scholarship

Type of award: Scholarship.
Intended use: For full-time undergraduate study in United States.
Eligibility: Applicant or parent must be member/participant of International Union of EESMF Workers, AFL-CIO. Applicant must be enrolled in high school.
Basis for selection: Applicant must demonstrate depth of character and service orientation.
Application requirements: Recommendations, essay, transcript, proof of eligibility. Local Union Seal.
Additional information: Available to children and grandchildren of all IUE-CWA members and employees (including retired or deceased members and employees). For application and more information, visit Website.

Amount of award:	$1,000
Number of awards:	9
Number of applicants:	300
Application deadline:	March 31
Total amount awarded:	$9,000

Contact:
Trudy Humphrey, IUE Department of Education
Int'l Union of EESMF Workers, AFL-CIO
1275 K Street, N.W.
Washington, DC 20005-4064
Web: www.iue-cwa.org

Paul Jennings Scholarship

Type of award: Scholarship.
Intended use: For full-time undergraduate study in United States.
Eligibility: Applicant or parent must be member/participant of International Union of EESMF Workers, AFL-CIO. Applicant must be high school senior.
Basis for selection: Major/career interest in nursing or engineering. Applicant must demonstrate depth of character, leadership and service orientation.
Application requirements: Recommendations, essay, transcript, proof of eligibility.
Additional information: Award available to children and grandchildren of IUE-CWA members who are now or have been local union elected officials. Families of full-time International union officers or employees not eligible.

Amount of award:	$3,000
Number of awards:	1
Number of applicants:	100
Application deadline:	March 31
Total amount awarded:	$3,000

Contact:
Trudy Humphrey
IEU-CWA
1275 K Street, N.W.
Washington, DC 20005-4064
Web: www.iue-cwa.org

Intel Corporation

Intel International Science and Engineering Fair

Type of award: Scholarship.
Intended use: For freshman study.
Eligibility: Applicant must be enrolled in high school. Applicant must be U.S. citizen.
Basis for selection: Merit at Intel ISEF-affiliated regional or state fair. Major/career interest in science, general or engineering.
Additional information: World's largest precollege science competition. Students compete at Intel ISEF-affiliated regional or state fair; winners advance to Intel ISEF. Individual and team projects eligible if entry requirements met. All paper work must be received by Science Service within 10 days after regional or state fair is held. Please consult Website for full details.

Amount of award:	$100-$50,000
Number of awards:	700
Number of applicants:	1,200
Total amount awarded:	$3,000,000

Contact:
Intel ISEF
Science Service
1719 N Street NW
Washington, DC 20036
Web: www.intel.com/education or www.sciserv.org/sts

Intel Science Talent Search

Type of award: Scholarship.
Intended use: For undergraduate study.
Eligibility: Applicant must be high school senior. Applicant must be U.S. citizen.
Basis for selection: Competition/talent/interest in science project, based on individual research reports in science, math or engineering; scientific originality and creative thinking. Major/career interest in biology; science, general; physics or mathematics.
Application requirements: Interview, recommendations, essay, transcript, proof of eligibility. 20-page research report on independent research in science, math or engineering; standardized test scores; and entry form.
Additional information: Highly competitive program for college-bound students. Open only to high school seniors meeting all entry requirements. Consult Website for full details and deadline dates. Semifinalist awards: $1000 to 300 high school seniors and their high schools annually. Finalist awards: 40 entrants selected for all-expense-paid trip to Washington, DC, in March, where they compete for $530,000 in scholarships.

Amount of award:	$1,000-$100,000
Number of awards:	40
Number of applicants:	1,600
Total amount awarded:	$1,100,000

Contact:
Intel STS, Science Service
1719 N Street NW
Washington, DC 20036
Web: www.intel.com/education or www.sciserve.org/sts

International Association of Fire Fighters

W.H. McClennan Scholarship

Type of award: Scholarship, renewable.
Intended use: For full-time undergraduate or graduate study.
Eligibility: Applicant or parent must be member/participant of International Association of Fire Fighters. Applicant's parent must have been killed or disabled in work-related accident as fire fighter.
Basis for selection: Applicant must demonstrate financial need, high academic achievement, depth of character, seriousness of purpose and service orientation.
Application requirements: Recommendations, essay, transcript, proof of eligibility. Two letters of recommendations.
Additional information: Applicants must be children of firefighters who were killed in the line of duty and were members in good standing of the IAFF at the time of their deaths.

Amount of award:	$2,500
Number of awards:	26
Number of applicants:	26
Application deadline:	February 1
Notification begins:	June 1
Total amount awarded:	$65,000

Contact:
International Association of Fire Fighters
1750 New York Avenue, NW
Washington, DC 20006
Phone: 202-737-8484

International Buckskin Horse Association, Inc.

Buckskin Horse Association Scholarship

Type of award: Scholarship, renewable.
Intended use: For full-time undergraduate study at accredited postsecondary institution in United States.
Eligibility: Applicant or parent must be member/participant of International Buckskin Horse Association. Applicant must be high school senior. Applicant must be U.S. citizen.
Basis for selection: Applicant must demonstrate financial need, high academic achievement, depth of character, leadership and seriousness of purpose.
Application requirements: Portfolio, recommendations, proof of eligibility.
Additional information: Applicant must be association member for at least two years.

Amount of award:	$500-$1,500
Number of awards:	13
Number of applicants:	15
Application deadline:	February 1
Notification begins:	September 15
Total amount awarded:	$10,750

Contact:
International Buckskin Horse Association, Inc.
P.O. Box 268
Shelby, IN 46377
Web: www.ibha.net

International Executive Housekeepers Association

IEHA Educational Foundation Scholarship

Type of award: Scholarship.
Intended use: For undergraduate or non-degree study at accredited postsecondary institution.
Eligibility: Applicant or parent must be member/participant of International Executive Housekeepers Association.
Basis for selection: Major/career interest in hospitality administration/management.
Application requirements: Essay, transcript. Letter from school official verifying enrollment. Original and three copies of

prepared manuscript must be double-spaced, maximum 2,000 words. Photographs must be black and white glossy prints.
Additional information: Applicant must be member of IEHA. This scholarship will be awarded to student(s) submitting best original manuscript on housekeeping within any industry segment, (eg, hospitality, healthcare, education, rehabilitation centers, government buildings, etc.). Other major/career interest: facilities management. Can be used for IEHA Certification program. No set limit on number of awards granted.

| Amount of award: | $800 |
| Application deadline: | January 10 |

Contact:
International Executive Housekeepers Association
Educational Foundation Scholarships
1001 Eastwind Drive, Suite 301
Westerville, OH 43081-3361
Phone: 800-200-6342 or 614-895-7166
Fax: 614-895-1248
Web: www.ieha.org

International Foodservice Editorial Council

Foodservice Communicators Scholarship

Type of award: Scholarship.
Intended use: For full-time undergraduate or master's study at accredited postsecondary institution in United States.
Basis for selection: Major/career interest in food science/technology; food production/management/services; culinary arts or communications. Applicant must demonstrate financial need, high academic achievement, depth of character, leadership, seriousness of purpose and service orientation.
Application requirements: Recommendations, transcript, proof of eligibility.
Additional information: Applicant must work or pursue academic study in both culinary arts and communications. Applications may be requested by e-mail or downloaded from Website. Four to six awards granted each year for total of $8,000 to $15,000.

Amount of award:	$1,000-$3,750
Number of awards:	4
Number of applicants:	675
Application deadline:	March 15
Notification begins:	July 1
Total amount awarded:	$15,000

Contact:
International Foodservice Editorial Council (IFEC)
P.O. Box 491
Hyde Park, NY 12538
Phone: 845-229-6973
Fax: 845-229-6993
Web: www.ifec-is-us.com

Foodservice Editorial Communicators Scholarship

Type of award: Scholarship.
Intended use: For full-time undergraduate study at 2-year or 4-year institution in United States.

Eligibility: Applicant must be U.S. citizen or permanent resident.

Basis for selection: Must demonstrate skills and interest in combined fields of foodservice and communication arts. Major/career interest in food production/management/services; food science/technology; communications; English; journalism; marketing; graphic arts/design; culinary arts; hotel/restaurant management or dietetics/nutrition. Applicant must demonstrate depth of character, leadership, seriousness of purpose and service orientation.

Application requirements: Recommendations, transcript. Application. Two letters of recommendation. Essay questions.

Additional information: For students pursuing career in foodservices communication.

Amount of award:	$1,000-$3,750
Application deadline:	March 15

Contact:
International Foodservice Editorial Council
IFEC Scholarship Program
P.O. Box 491
Hyde Park, NY 12538
Phone: 845-229-6973
Fax: 845-229-6993
Web: www.ifec-is-us.com

International Furnishings and Design Association Educational Foundation

International Furnishings and Design Association Student Scholarships

Type of award: Scholarship.

Intended use: For full-time undergraduate or graduate study at accredited postsecondary institution in or outside United States. Designated institutions: Full-time, post-secondary institutions outside U.S., U.S. institutions, accredited schools.

Basis for selection: Major/career interest in design; marketing; arts, general; graphic arts/design or education. Applicant must demonstrate high academic achievement, depth of character, seriousness of purpose and service orientation.

Application requirements: Recommendations, essay, transcript.

Additional information: Some scholarships require IFDA membership. Student membership fee is $45. Applicants must have completed at least one semester of postsecondary school. Number and award amounts vary. See Website for further requirements and applications for Charles E. Mayo Student Scholarship, IFDA Student Scholarships, Vercille Voss Scholarship, and Ruth Clark Scholarship.

Amount of award:	$1,000-$1,500
Application deadline:	March 31

Contact:
IFDA Educational Foundation
c/o Audra Whitelock
9591 Donnan Castle Court
Laurel, MD 20723
Web: www.ifdaef.org

International Order of the King's Daughters and Sons

Health Career Scholarship

Type of award: Scholarship, renewable.

Intended use: For full-time junior, senior, master's or first professional study at accredited 4-year or graduate institution in United States or Canada.

Eligibility: Applicant must be U.S. citizen, international student or Canadian.

Basis for selection: Major/career interest in medicine; dentistry; pharmacy/pharmaceutics/pharmacology; nursing; health sciences or health-related professions. Applicant must demonstrate financial need, high academic achievement, depth of character, leadership, seriousness of purpose and service orientation.

Application requirements: Recommendations, essay, transcript, proof of eligibility.

Additional information: Physical therapy, occupational therapy, and other health-related majors also eligible, except pre-med. To request application, student must write to director, stating field and present level of study, and include business-size SASE. Canadian students must send self-addressed envelope; no postage required. Nursing students must have completed first year of schooling; others must be at least college juniors. Awards made in early June and distributed in August.

Amount of award:	$500-$1,000
Number of awards:	50
Number of applicants:	350
Total amount awarded:	$58,000

Contact:
International Order of the King's Daughters and Sons
Director, Health Careers Department
P.O. Box 1040
Chautauqua, NY 14722-1040
Web: www.iokds.org

North American Indian Scholarship

Type of award: Scholarship, renewable.

Intended use: For full-time undergraduate study at accredited 2-year or 4-year institution in United States.

Eligibility: Applicant must be American Indian. Proof of Native American heritage. Applicant must be U.S. citizen.

Basis for selection: Applicant must demonstrate financial need, depth of character, leadership, seriousness of purpose and service orientation.

Application requirements: Recommendations, essay, transcript, proof of eligibility. Written documentation of Reservation Registration and other requirements.

Additional information: Offers scholarships with no restrictions as to tribal affiliations or Indian blood quantum. For more information, send SASE to director of North American Indian Dept.

Number of awards:	50
Notification begins:	July 1

Contact:
International Order of the King's Daughters and Sons
Director, North American Indian Dept.
P.O. Box 1040
Chautauqua, NY 14722-1040
Web: www.iokds.org

Scholarships

Intertribal Timber Council

Truman D. Picard Scholarship

Type of award: Scholarship, renewable.
Intended use: For full-time undergraduate or graduate study at accredited 2-year, 4-year or graduate institution in United States.
Eligibility: Applicant must be Alaskan native or American Indian. Must be enrolled member of a federally recognized tribe. Applicant must be U.S. citizen.
Basis for selection: Major/career interest in natural resources/conservation; forestry; wildlife/fisheries or agriculture. Applicant must demonstrate financial need, high academic achievement, depth of character, leadership, seriousness of purpose and service orientation.
Application requirements: Recommendations, transcript. Resume, and two-page (maximum) letter of application.
Additional information: Check Website for application acceptance dates.

Amount of award:	$1,200-$1,800
Number of awards:	10
Number of applicants:	70
Notification begins:	November 1
Total amount awarded:	$18,000

Contact:
Intertribal Timber Council
Education Committee
1112 NE 21st Avenue
Portland, OR 97232-2114
Phone: 503-282-4296
Fax: 503-282-1274
Web: www.itcnet.org

Iowa College Student Aid Commission

Iowa Grant

Type of award: Scholarship, renewable.
Intended use: For freshman, sophomore, junior or senior study at vocational, 2-year or 4-year institution. Designated institutions: Iowa colleges.
Eligibility: Applicant must be U.S. citizen or permanent resident residing in Iowa.
Basis for selection: Applicant must demonstrate financial need.
Application requirements: Proof of eligibility. FAFSA.
Additional information: Award amount may be adjusted downward for part-time study.

Amount of award:	$1,000
Number of awards:	1,202
Number of applicants:	4,685
Application deadline:	January 1
Notification begins:	March 20
Total amount awarded:	$467,799

Contact:
Iowa College Student Aid Commission
200 Tenth Street, Fourth Floor
Des Moines, IA 50309-3609
Web: www.iowacollegeaid.org

Iowa National Guard Educational Assistance Program

Type of award: Scholarship, renewable.
Intended use: For undergraduate study.
Eligibility: Applicant must be U.S. citizen residing in Iowa. Applicant must be in military service in the Reserves/National Guard.
Application requirements: National Guard application.
Additional information: Applicant must be in military service in the Iowa Reserves/National Guard. Selection is based on National Guard designation.

Amount of award:	$2,490
Number of awards:	1,144
Total amount awarded:	$1,223,064

Contact:
National Guard Education Officer
7700 NW Beaver Drive
Johnston, IA 50131
Web: www.iowacollegeaid.org

Iowa Robert C. Byrd Honor Scholarship

Type of award: Scholarship.
Intended use: For full-time undergraduate study at accredited 2-year or 4-year institution in United States.
Eligibility: Applicant must be high school senior. Applicant must be U.S. citizen or permanent resident residing in Iowa.
Basis for selection: Applicant must demonstrate high academic achievement.
Application requirements: Recommendations, essay, transcript, proof of eligibility. 28 ACT or 1240 SAT and 3.5 GPA.
Additional information: Eligible applicants must have completed 3 years of science beyond general science including 2 years of lab science, 2 years of the same foreign language, 4 years of English, 3 years of social studies, and 3 years of math beyond general math and pre-algebra.

Amount of award:	$1,500
Number of awards:	70
Number of applicants:	450
Application deadline:	February 1
Notification begins:	July 15

Contact:
Iowa College Student Aid Commission
200 Tenth Street, Fourth Floor
Des Moines, IA 50309-3609
Phone: 515-242-3380
Fax: 515-242-3388
Web: www.iowacollegeaid.org

Iowa Tuition Grant

Type of award: Scholarship, renewable.
Intended use: For undergraduate study at accredited 2-year or 4-year institution. Designated institutions: Private colleges in Iowa.
Eligibility: Applicant must be U.S. citizen or permanent resident residing in Iowa.
Basis for selection: Applicant must demonstrate financial need.
Application requirements: Proof of eligibility. FAFSA.

Amount of award:	$4,000
Number of awards:	14,667
Number of applicants:	23,961
Application deadline:	July 1

Contact:
Iowa College Student Aid Commission
200 Tenth Street, Fourth Floor
Des Moines, IA 50309-3609
Phone: 515-242-3344
Fax: 515-242-3388
Web: www.iowacollegeaid.org

Iowa Vocational-Technical Tuition Grant

Type of award: Scholarship, renewable.
Intended use: For undergraduate study at vocational institution. Designated institutions: Iowa community colleges.
Eligibility: Applicant must be U.S. citizen or permanent resident residing in Iowa.
Basis for selection: Applicant must demonstrate financial need.
Application requirements: Proof of eligibility. Financial aid forms.
Additional information: Only vocational-technical career majors considered.

Amount of award:	$600-$1,200
Number of awards:	5,129
Number of applicants:	20,261
Application deadline:	July 1
Total amount awarded:	$2,337,786

Contact:
Iowa College Student Aid Commission
200 Tenth Street, Fourth Floor
Des Moines, IA 50309-3609
Web: www.iowacollegeaid.org

State of Iowa Scholarship

Type of award: Scholarship.
Intended use: For full-time freshman study at accredited vocational, 2-year or 4-year institution. Designated institutions: Iowa schools.
Eligibility: Applicant must be high school senior. Applicant must be U.S. citizen or permanent resident residing in Iowa.
Basis for selection: Applicant must demonstrate high academic achievement.
Application requirements: Proof of eligibility.
Additional information: Must rank in top 15 percent of class and have taken ACT or SAT test. For class ranking and other criteria for selection, consult with high school guidance counselor.

Amount of award:	$400
Number of awards:	1,700
Number of applicants:	4,306
Application deadline:	November 1
Notification begins:	February 1
Total amount awarded:	$477,000

Contact:
Iowa College Student Aid Commission
200 Tenth Street, Fourth Floor
Des Moines, IA 50309-3609
Phone: 515-242-3373
Fax: 515-242-3388
Web: www.iowacollegeaid.org

Ispat Inland Inc.

Ispat Inland Foundation Scholarship Program

Type of award: Scholarship, renewable.
Intended use: For full-time undergraduate study at accredited 4-year institution.
Eligibility: Applicant must be high school senior.
Basis for selection: Academic performance, extracurricular activities, character and essay. Applicant must demonstrate high academic achievement, depth of character and leadership.
Application requirements: Recommendations, essay, transcript.
Additional information: Student should be child or legal ward of active, retired or deceased full-time employee of Ispat Inland Inc. Foundation scholarship may be used only for tuition, fees, books, supplies and required equipment. Program will include one-time $1,000 honorary award or maximum $2,500 renewable award per year based on financial need.

Amount of award:	$1,000-$2,500
Number of awards:	102
Number of applicants:	139
Application deadline:	February 13
Total amount awarded:	$198,000

Contact:
Legacy Foundation Inc.
Attn: Jan Smyth, Program Officer
1000 E. 80th Place, North Tower 420
Merrillville, IN 46410
Phone: 219-736-1880
Fax: 219) 736-1940

Italian Catholic Federation

Italian Catholic Federation Scholarship

Type of award: Scholarship, renewable.
Intended use: For full-time freshman study at accredited 2-year or 4-year institution.
Eligibility: Applicant must be high school senior. Applicant must be Italian. Applicant must be Roman Catholic. Applicant must be U.S. citizen residing in California, Illinois, Arizona or Nevada.
Basis for selection: Applicant must demonstrate financial need and high academic achievement.
Application requirements: Recommendations, essay, transcript. Include copy of first two pages of parents' recent federal tax return.
Additional information: Applicants must live in Arizona, California, Illinois or Nevada, where branches of Federation are established. Minimum 3.2 GPA. Also open to non-Italian students whose parents or grandparents are members of Federation. First year's scholarship award is $400. Larger amounts available for advanced scholarships.

Amount of award:	$400-$1,000
Number of awards:	200
Number of applicants:	600
Application deadline:	March 15
Notification begins:	May 1
Total amount awarded:	$70,000

Scholarships

Contact:
Italian Catholic Federation
675 Hegenberger Road, #230
Oakland, CA 94621
Phone: 510-633-9058

Jackie Robinson Foundation

Education and Leadership Development Program

Type of award: Scholarship, renewable.
Intended use: For full-time undergraduate study at accredited 4-year institution in United States.
Eligibility: Applicant must be Alaskan native, Asian American, African American, Mexican American, Hispanic American, Puerto Rican or American Indian. Applicant must be high school senior. Applicant must be U.S. citizen.
Basis for selection: Applicant must demonstrate financial need, high academic achievement and leadership.
Application requirements: Interview, recommendations, essay, transcript. Applicant must have been accepted to accredited 4-year college or university.
Additional information: Applications sent October through March upon receipt of written request. Award amount varies up to $6,000. Applications may be reproduced.

Amount of award:	$3,000-$6,000
Number of awards:	241
Application deadline:	April 1
Notification begins:	September 1
Total amount awarded:	$13,000,000

Contact:
Jackie Robinson Foundation
Attn: Scholarship Programs
3 West 35 Street, 11th Floor
New York, NY 10001-2204
Phone: 212-290-8600
Web: www.jackierobinson.org

James Beard Foundation

Friends of James Beard Scholarships

Type of award: Scholarship.
Intended use: For undergraduate, graduate or non-degree study in or outside United States or Canada. Designated institutions: Institution with approved program in culinary arts.
Basis for selection: Major/career interest in culinary arts.
Application requirements: Recommendations, transcript. Essay, income tax returns and proof of residency may be required as well.
Additional information: Applications available online in December and accepted in January. Visit Website for criteria and additional information.

Application deadline:	May 15

Contact:
Director of Scholarship Program, Caroline Stuart
54 Constock Road
New Canaan, CT 06840
Web: www.jamesbeard.org

James F. Byrnes Foundation

James F. Byrnes Scholarship

Type of award: Scholarship, renewable.
Intended use: For full-time freshman study at accredited 4-year institution.
Eligibility: Applicant must be high school senior. Applicant must be U.S. citizen residing in South Carolina.
Basis for selection: Applicant must demonstrate financial need, high academic achievement, depth of character, leadership, patriotism, seriousness of purpose and service orientation.
Application requirements: Interview, recommendations, essay, transcript. SAT/ACT scores, photograph, autobiography (three typed pages maximum) describing home situation, death of parent/s, desire for college education, college ambitions, reasons financial assistance is needed, how college will be financed, etc. Two nonrelative references (one from current guidance counselor or teacher) required.
Additional information: Applicant must be high school senior or college freshman. Applicant must have 2.5 GPA. One or both parents of applicant must be deceased. Visit Website for additional information.

Amount of award:	$2,750
Number of applicants:	200
Application deadline:	February 15
Notification begins:	April 20
Total amount awarded:	$177,000

Contact:
James F. Byrnes Foundation
P.O. Box 6781
Columbia, SC 29260-6781
Phone: 803-254-9325
Fax: 803-254-9354
Web: www.byrnesscholars.org

Japanese American Association of New York

Japanese American General Scholarship

Type of award: Scholarship.
Intended use: For full-time freshman study at accredited 2-year or 4-year institution in United States.
Eligibility: Applicant must be Asian American. Applicant must be high school senior. Applicant must be Japanese. Applicant must be U.S. citizen or permanent resident residing in Connecticut, New York or New Jersey.
Basis for selection: Applicant must demonstrate financial need, high academic achievement and service orientation.
Application requirements: Recommendations, essay, transcript. SAT scores, photograph. Letter of recommendation from a JAA member if no one in family is a member.
Additional information: Two awards given are need-based.

Application deadline:	May 7

Contact:
Japanese American Association of New York
15 West 44 Street
New York, NY 10036
Phone: 212-840-6942
Fax: 212-840-0616
Web: www.jaany.org

Japanese American Music Scholarship Competition

Type of award: Scholarship.
Intended use: For undergraduate or graduate study at postsecondary institution.
Eligibility: Applicant must be Asian American. Applicant must be Japanese. Applicant must be U.S. citizen, permanent resident, international student or Japanese citizen.
Basis for selection: Competition/talent/interest in music performance/composition, based on string performance. Major/career interest in music.
Application requirements: Photograph.
Additional information: Open to Japanese students and students of Japanese descent. Please contact sponsor and/or visit Website for future competitions.

Amount of award:	$1,500
Number of awards:	4
Number of applicants:	30
Total amount awarded:	$6,000

Contact:
Japanese American Association of New York
15 West 44 Street
New York, NY 10036
Phone: 212-840-6942
Fax: 212-840-0616
Web: www.jaany.org

Jaycee War Memorial Fund

Charles R. Ford Scholarship

Type of award: Scholarship.
Intended use: For undergraduate study at postsecondary institution.
Eligibility: Applicant or parent must be member/participant of Jaycees. Applicant must be returning adult student. Applicant must be U.S. citizen.
Basis for selection: Applicant must demonstrate financial need, high academic achievement and leadership.
Application requirements: $5 application fee. Nomination by Applicant's state Junior Chamber organization. Send SASE and application fee between July 1 and February 1 to obtain application. Check or money order payable to The War Memorial Fund.
Additional information: Intended for active member who wishes to return to college or university to complete his or her education. Applicants must send request for applications and completed applications to Karen Fitzgerald. State President selects semi-finalist and forwards application to U.S. Junior Chamber of Commerce by March 15. Visit Website for additional information.

Amount of award:	$2,500
Number of awards:	1
Application deadline:	March 1
Notification begins:	May 15

Contact:
Jaycee War Memorial Fund
Ford Scholarship, c/o Karen Fitzgerald
P.O. Box 7
Tulsa, OK 74102-0007
Phone: 918-584-2481 ext. 434
Web: www.usjaycees.org

Jaycee War Memorial Scholarship

Type of award: Scholarship.
Intended use: For full-time undergraduate study at accredited 2-year or 4-year institution.
Eligibility: Applicant or parent must be member/participant of Jaycees. Applicant must be enrolled in high school. Applicant must be U.S. citizen.
Basis for selection: Applicant must demonstrate financial need, high academic achievement and leadership.
Application requirements: $5 application fee.
Additional information: To receive an application, send a business-size SASE with application fee between July 1 and February 1. Make check or money order payable to the Jaycee War Memorial Fund. Visit Website for additional information.

Amount of award:	$1,000
Number of awards:	25
Application deadline:	March 1
Notification begins:	May 15
Total amount awarded:	$25,000

Contact:
Jaycee War Memorial Fund
Jaycee War Memorial Scholarship
Dept. 94922
Tulsa, OK 74194-0001
Phone: 918-584-2481
Web: www.usjaycees.org

Thomas Wood Baldridge Scholarship

Type of award: Scholarship.
Intended use: For full-time undergraduate study at accredited 2-year or 4-year institution.
Eligibility: Applicant or parent must be member/participant of Jaycees. Applicant must be U.S. citizen.
Basis for selection: Applicant must demonstrate financial need, high academic achievement and leadership.
Application requirements: $5 application fee.
Additional information: Any Jaycee descendent is eligible. To receive an application, send a business-size SASE along with application fee between July 1 and February 1. Make check or money order payable to the Jaycee War Memorial Fund. Visit Website for additional information.

Amount of award:	$3,000
Number of awards:	1
Application deadline:	March 1
Total amount awarded:	$3,000

Contact:
Jaycee War Memorial Fund
Baldridge Scholarship
P.O. Box 7
Tulsa, OK 74102-0007
Phone: 918-584-2481
Web: www.usjaycees.org

Scholarships

281

Jeannette Rankin Foundation

Women's Education Fund

Type of award: Scholarship.
Intended use: For undergraduate study at accredited vocational, 2-year or 4-year institution in United States.
Eligibility: Applicant must be female, at least 35, returning adult student. Applicant must be U.S. citizen.
Basis for selection: Must display courage and attainable goals. Applicant must demonstrate financial need, depth of character and service orientation.
Application requirements: Recommendations, essay. Applicant must be 35+ as of April 1, and meet low-income guidelines.
Additional information: Download application from Website from November through mid-February, or send SASE with application request. E-mail address: info@rankinfoundation.org.

Amount of award:	$2,000
Number of awards:	30
Number of applicants:	1,900
Application deadline:	March 1
Notification begins:	June 30
Total amount awarded:	$60,000

Contact:
Jeannette Rankin Foundation
P.O. Box 6653
Athens, GA 30604
Phone: 706-208-1211
Web: www.rankinfoundation.org

Jewish Vocational Service

JVS Jewish Community Scholarship Fund

Type of award: Scholarship, renewable.
Intended use: For full-time undergraduate or graduate study at accredited postsecondary institution in United States.
Designated institutions: Accredited postsecondary institutions in U.S., including trade schools.
Eligibility: Applicant must be Jewish. Applicant must be U.S. citizen or permanent resident residing in California.
Basis for selection: Applicant must demonstrate financial need, seriousness of purpose and service orientation.
Application requirements: Recommendations, essay, transcript. FAFSA and tax returns.
Additional information: Minimum 2.5 GPA required. Must be Jewish, legal permanent resident of Los Angeles County with verifiable financial need. Visit Website for electronic application.

Amount of award:	$500-$6,000
Number of awards:	107
Number of applicants:	250
Application deadline:	April 15
Total amount awarded:	$216,250

Contact:
JVS Jewish Community Scholarship Fund
6505 Wilshire Blvd., Suite 200
Los Angeles, CA 90048
Phone: 323-761-8888 ext. 8868
Fax: 323-761-8575
Web: www.jvsla.org

Jewish War Veterans of the United States of America

Jewish War Veterans of the United States of America Bernard Rotberg Memorial Scholarship

Type of award: Scholarship.
Intended use: For freshman study at accredited 4-year institution. Designated institutions: Accredited four-year college/university, or three-year hospital school of nursing.
Eligibility: Applicant must be high school senior. Applicant must be Jewish.
Basis for selection: Merit. Applicant must demonstrate financial need and high academic achievement.
Application requirements: Application.
Additional information: Applicant must be direct descendant of JWV member. Must be in upper 25% of high school class; must have participated in extracurricular activities in school as well as in Jewish community. Number of awards given each year varies.

Amount of award:	$1,000
Application deadline:	May 3

Contact:
Jewish War Veterans of the United States of America
National Scholarship Committee
1811 R Street NW
Washington, DC 20009
Phone: 202-265-6280
Fax: 202-234-5662
Web: www.jwv.org

Jewish War Veterans of the United States of America JWV Grant

Type of award: Research grant.
Intended use: For freshman study at accredited vocational or 4-year institution. Designated institutions: Accredited four-year college/university, or three-year hospital school of nursing.
Eligibility: Applicant must be high school senior. Applicant must be Jewish.
Basis for selection: Applicant must demonstrate financial need and high academic achievement.
Application requirements: Application.
Additional information: Applicant must be direct descendant of JWV member. Must be in upper 25% of high school class; must have participated in extracurricular activities in school as well as in Jewish community. Number of awards given each year varies.

Amount of award:	$500
Application deadline:	May 3

Contact:
Jewish War Veterans of the United States of America
National Scholarship Committee
1811 R Street NW
Washington, DC 20009
Phone: 202-265-6280
Fax: 202-234-5662
Web: www.jwv.org

Jewish War Veterans of the United States of America XX Olympiad Memorial Award

Type of award: Scholarship.
Intended use: For undergraduate study at accredited 4-year institution.
Eligibility: Applicant must be enrolled in high school. Applicant must be Jewish.
Basis for selection: Applicant must demonstrate high academic achievement, leadership and service orientation.
Additional information: Selection based on merit with focus on athletic achievement.

Amount of award:	$100-$500
Number of awards:	3
Application deadline:	June 30

Contact:
Jewish War Veterans of the United States of America
National Scholarship Committee
1811 R Street NW
Washington, DC 20009
Phone: 202-265-6280
Fax: 202-234-5662
Web: www.jwv.org

Louis S. Silver Grant

Type of award: Research grant.
Intended use: For freshman study at accredited 4-year institution. Designated institutions: Accredited four-year college/university, or three-year hospital school of nursing.
Eligibility: Applicant must be high school senior. Applicant must be Jewish.
Basis for selection: Applicant must demonstrate financial need and high academic achievement.
Application requirements: Application.
Additional information: Applicant must be direct descendant of JWV member. Must be in upper 25% of high school class; must have participated in extracurricular activities in school as well as in Jewish community. Number of awards given each year varies.

Amount of award:	$750
Application deadline:	May 3

Contact:
Jewish War Veterans of the United States of America
National Scholarship Committee
1811 R St. NW
Washington, DC 20009
Phone: 202-265-6280
Fax: 202-234-5662
Web: www.jwv.org

Kansas Board of Regents

Kansas Comprehensive Grant

Type of award: Scholarship, renewable.
Intended use: For full-time undergraduate study at accredited 4-year institution in United States. Designated institutions: Kansas postsecondary institutions.
Eligibility: Applicant must be U.S. citizen or permanent resident residing in Kansas.
Basis for selection: Applicant must demonstrate financial need.
Application requirements: Proof of eligibility. FAFSA.
Additional information: Up to $1,100 for those attending public institutions; up to $3,000 for those attending private institutions.

Number of awards:	1
Application deadline:	April 1
Notification begins:	May 1

Contact:
Kansas Board of Regents
1000 SW Jackson St.
Suite 520
Topeka, KS 66612-1368
Phone: 785-296-3517
Fax: 785-296-0983
Web: www.kansasregents.com

Kansas Ethnic Minority Scholarship

Type of award: Scholarship, renewable.
Intended use: For full-time undergraduate study at 2-year or 4-year institution. Designated institutions: Kansas postsecondary institutions.
Eligibility: Applicant must be Alaskan native, Asian American, African American, Mexican American, Hispanic American, Puerto Rican or American Indian. Applicant must be U.S. citizen or permanent resident residing in Kansas.
Basis for selection: Applicant must demonstrate financial need and high academic achievement.
Application requirements: $10 application fee. Proof of eligibility, research proposal, nomination. 3.0 GPA. State of Kansas Student Aid Application. FAFSA.

Amount of award:	$1,850
Number of awards:	204
Application deadline:	May 1
Total amount awarded:	$348,746

Contact:
Kansas Board of Regents
1000 SW Jackson St.
Suite 520
Topeka, KS 66612-1368
Phone: 785-296-3517
Fax: 785-296-0983
Web: www.kansasregents.com

Kansas Nursing Service Scholarship

Type of award: Scholarship, renewable.
Intended use: For full-time undergraduate, master's or non-degree study at postsecondary institution. Designated institutions: Kansas postsecondary schools with approved nursing programs.
Eligibility: Applicant must be U.S. citizen or permanent resident residing in Kansas.

283

Basis for selection: Major/career interest in nursing. Applicant must demonstrate financial need and high academic achievement.

Application requirements: $10 application fee. Application. State of Kansas Student Aid Application. FAFSA.

Additional information: Must obtain sponsorship from adult-care home licensed under the Adult Care Home Licensure Act; state agency that employs LPNs or RNs; or state-licensed medical care facility, psychiatric hospital, home health agency or local health department. Must agree to work in Kansas one year for each year that scholarship is received. If recipient does not meet obligation, award becomes loan.

Amount of award:	$2,500-$3,500
Number of awards:	152
Application deadline:	May 1
Total amount awarded:	$443,489

Contact:
Kansas Board of Regents
1000 SW Jackson St.
Suite 520
Topeka, KS 66612-1368
Phone: 785-296-3518
Fax: 785-296-0983
Web: www.kansasregents.com

Kansas ROTC Service Scholarship

Type of award: Scholarship.

Intended use: For full-time undergraduate study. Designated institutions: Kansas postsecondary institutions.

Eligibility: Applicant or parent must be member/participant of Reserve Officers Training Corps (ROTC). Applicant must be residing in Kansas.

Application requirements: Application.

Additional information: Applicant must be Kansas resident enrolled in Kansas ROTC program. Must be full-time undergraduate with at least 12 credit hours. Scholarship limited to eight semesters. Award amount may be up to tuition and costs of average four-year regents institution; average award is $1,650.

Amount of award:	$2,528
Number of awards:	76
Application deadline:	November 1, March 1
Notification begins:	June 1
Total amount awarded:	$191,836

Contact:
Kansas Board of Regents
Director of Student Financial Assistance
1000 SW Jackson St., Suite 520
Topeka, KS 66612-1368
Phone: 785-296-3518
Fax: 785-296-0983
Web: www.kansasregents.com

Kansas State Scholarship

Type of award: Scholarship, renewable.

Intended use: For full-time undergraduate study at postsecondary institution in United States. Designated institutions: Kansas postsecondary institutions.

Eligibility: Applicant must be enrolled in high school. Applicant must be residing in Kansas.

Basis for selection: Applicant must demonstrate financial need and high academic achievement.

Application requirements: $10 application fee. Proof of eligibility. Complete State of Kansas Student Aid Application, FAFSA.

Additional information: Applicant must be Kansas resident and must be designated State Scholar in senior year of high school. Must have high GPA (average: 3.9) and ACT scores (average: 29).

Amount of award:	$1,000
Number of awards:	1,226
Application deadline:	May 1
Total amount awarded:	$1,201,275

Contact:
Kansas Board of Regents
1000 SW Jackson St.
Suite 520
Topeka, KS 66612-1368
Phone: 785-296-3517
Fax: 785-296-0983
Web: www.kansasregents.com

Kansas Teacher Service Scholarship

Type of award: Scholarship, renewable.

Intended use: For full-time freshman, sophomore, junior, senior, post-bachelor's certificate or first professional study at 4-year or graduate institution. Designated institutions: Kansas postsecondary institutions.

Eligibility: Applicant must be residing in Kansas.

Basis for selection: Major/career interest in education, teacher or education, special. Applicant must demonstrate high academic achievement.

Application requirements: $10 application fee. Recommendations, transcript, proof of eligibility. Complete State of Kansas Student Aid Application, FAFSA.

Additional information: Applicant must be Kansas resident enrolled in Kansas school that offers education degree. Must identify a "hard-to-fill" or "underserved" area. Must not have teaching license. Scholarships are competitive; selection based on ACT score, GPA, high school rank, transcript and recommendation.

Amount of award:	$5,000
Number of awards:	7,357
Application deadline:	May 1
Total amount awarded:	$11,000,000

Contact:
Kansas Board of Regents
1000 SW Jackson St.
Suite 520
Topeka, KS 66612-1368
Phone: 785-296-3517
Fax: 785-296-0983
Web: www.kansasregents.com

Kansas Vocational Education Scholarship

Type of award: Scholarship, renewable.

Intended use: For full-time undergraduate study at vocational, 2-year or 4-year institution. Designated institutions: Kansas postsecondary institutions.

Eligibility: Applicant must be U.S. citizen or permanent resident residing in Kansas.

Basis for selection: Based on vocational examination.

Application requirements: $10 application fee. Proof of eligibility. Must take Kansas vocational examination, offered in November and March.

Additional information: Applicant must be Kansas resident and graduate of Kansas high school. Must take vocational test given on first Saturday of November or March and complete Vocational Education application. Renewals awarded first;

remaining scholarships offered to those with highest exam scores.

Amount of award:	$500
Number of awards:	88
Application deadline:	May 1, February 1
Notification begins:	May 15
Total amount awarded:	$411,911

Contact:
Kansas Board of Regents
1000 SW Jackson St.
Suite 520
Topeka, KS 66612-0983
Phone: 785-296-3518
Fax: 785-296-0983
Web: www.kansasregents.com

Kaplan, Inc.

Kaplan/Newsweek "My Turn" Essay Contest

Type of award: Scholarship.
Intended use: For full-time freshman or sophomore study at 2-year or 4-year institution.
Eligibility: Applicant must be enrolled in high school.
Basis for selection: Competition/talent/interest in writing/journalism. Based on personal opinion or experience essay on topic chosen by student. Major/career interest in publishing.
Application requirements: Essay.
Additional information: Winning essays may be published by Newsweek. Call Kaplan for entry form including official rules. Completed entries may be sent to address listed. Essays must be original and factually accurate. They are judged on effectiveness; creativity; insight; organization and development; consistent use of language; variety in sentence structure and vocabulary; and use of proper grammar, spelling and punctuation. Visit Website for more information.

Amount of award:	$1,000-$5,000
Number of awards:	10
Application deadline:	March 1
Notification begins:	April 17
Total amount awarded:	$15,000

Contact:
Kaplan, Inc.
Community Outreach Director
888 Seventh Avenue
New York, NY 10106
Phone: 800-KAP-TEST
Web: www.kaptest.com/essay

Kappa Kappa Gamma Foundation

Kappa Kappa Gamma Scholarship

Type of award: Scholarship.
Intended use: For full-time undergraduate or graduate study at 4-year or graduate institution in United States.
Eligibility: Applicant or parent must be member/participant of Kappa Kappa Gamma.

Basis for selection: Applicant must demonstrate high academic achievement.
Additional information: Applicant must be an active member of Kappa Kappa Gamma fraternity. Applicant must be U.S. citizen or permanent resident from Canada. Minimum 3.0 GPA.

Amount of award:	$3,000
Application deadline:	February 1

Contact:
Kappa Kappa Gamma Foundation
P.O. Box 38
Columbus, OH 43216-0038
Phone: 614-228-6515
Fax: 614-228-7809
Web: www.kappakappagamma.org

KarMel Scholarship Committee

KarMel Scholarship

Type of award: Scholarship.
Intended use: For undergraduate study at vocational, 2-year or 4-year institution in United States.
Eligibility: Applicant must be high school senior. Applicant must be U.S. citizen.
Basis for selection: Applicant must demonstrate depth of character, leadership and seriousness of purpose.
Application requirements: Application consists of artistic work and application (available on Website).
Additional information: Applicant does not have to be gay/lesbian/bi to apply for scholarship. However, applicant must submit works to include gay/lesbian/bi content. Scholarship is divided into two categories: Best "Written" Gay/Lesbian/Bi Themed Work and Best "Artistic" Gay/Lesbian/Bi Themed Work. Applicant may submit up to three works in both categories. Written work of any length will be accepted. All applicants may submit work via e-mail or postal mail. Please visit Website for complete additional information.

Amount of award:	$200-$400
Number of awards:	2
Application deadline:	March 31
Total amount awarded:	$700

Contact:
KarMel Scholarship Committee
P.O. Box 70382
Sunnyvale, CA 94086
Web: www.karenandmelody.com/karmelscholarship.html

Kentucky Higher Education Assistance Authority (KHEAA)

Kentucky College Access Program Grant (CAP)

Type of award: Scholarship, renewable.
Intended use: For undergraduate study at 2-year or 4-year institution. Designated institutions: Postsecondary institutions in Kentucky.

Eligibility: Applicant must be U.S. citizen or permanent resident residing in Kentucky.
Basis for selection: Applicant must demonstrate financial need.
Application requirements: Proof of eligibility. FAFSA; applicant ineligible if family contribution exceeds $3,550.
Additional information: May be used at eligible schools. Visit Website for additional information.

Amount of award:	$50-$1,400
Number of awards:	34,536
Number of applicants:	132,491
Notification begins:	April 15
Total amount awarded:	$34,590,124

Contact:
Kentucky Higher Education Assistance Authority (KHEAA)
Grant Programs
1050 U.S. 127 South
Frankfort, KY 40601-4323
Phone: 800-928-8926
Fax: 502-695-7373
Web: www.kheaa.com

Kentucky Educational Excellence Scholarship (KEES)

Type of award: Scholarship, renewable.
Intended use: For undergraduate study at accredited vocational, 2-year or 4-year institution in United States or Canada. Designated institutions: Participating public and private postsecondary institutions in Kentucky and selected out-of-state institutions if program of study not offered in Kentucky.
Eligibility: Applicant must be enrolled in high school. Applicant must be U.S. citizen or permanent resident residing in Kentucky.
Basis for selection: Applicant must demonstrate high academic achievement.
Application requirements: Minimum annual high school GPA of 2.5. Supplemental award is given for highest ACT or equivalent SAT score achieved by HS graduation, based on minimum ACT score of 15. High School districts routinely report annual year-end grades to Kentucky Department of Education.
Additional information: Recipient must be enrolled in postsecondary program at least half-time. Scholarship is earned each year of high school. Visit Website or contact via e-mail (tphelps@kheaa.com) for additional information.

Amount of award:	$125-$2,500
Number of awards:	43,676
Total amount awarded:	$37,985,700

Contact:
Kentucky Higher Education Assistance Authority (KHEAA)
1050 U.S. 127 South
Frankfort, KY 40601-4323
Phone: 800-928-8926
Fax: 502-696-7373
Web: www.kheaa.com

Kentucky Tuition Grant

Type of award: Scholarship, renewable.
Intended use: For full-time undergraduate study at 2-year or 4-year institution. Designated institutions: Eligible private institutions in Kentucky.
Eligibility: Applicant must be U.S. citizen residing in Kentucky.
Basis for selection: Applicant must demonstrate financial need.

Application requirements: Proof of eligibility. FAFSA.
Additional information: Visit Website for additional information.

Amount of award:	$200-$2,600
Number of awards:	8,846
Number of applicants:	15,372
Notification begins:	April 15
Total amount awarded:	$13,380,950

Contact:
Kentucky Higher Education Assistance Authority
Grant Programs
1050 U.S. 127 South
Frankfort, KY 40601-4323
Phone: 800-928-8926
Fax: 502-695-7373
Web: www.kheaa.com

Knights of Columbus

Matthews/Swift Educational Trust - Military Dependants

Type of award: Scholarship, renewable.
Intended use: For full-time undergraduate study at 4-year institution in United States. Designated institutions: Catholic colleges and universities.
Eligibility: Applicant or parent must be member/participant of Knights of Columbus. Applicant must be Roman Catholic. Applicant must be dependent of disabled veteran, deceased veteran or POW/MIA who served in the Army, Air Force, Marines, Navy, Coast Guard or Reserves/National Guard during Korean War, Persian Gulf War, WW II or Vietnam. Parent must have been Knights of Columbus member when killed in action during a period of conflict or died as result of service-connected disability. Parent permanently and totally disabled as result of criminal violence while performing duties must have kept Knights of Columbus membership active.
Application requirements: Proof of eligibility.
Additional information: Award pays tuition, room, board, books and incidental fees at a Catholic college. No application deadline.

Amount of award:	Full tuition
Number of awards:	10
Number of applicants:	10

Contact:
Knights of Columbus
Director of Scholarship Aid
P.O. Box 1670
New Haven, CT 06507-0901
Phone: 203-752-4332

Matthews/Swift Educational Trust - Police/Firefighters

Type of award: Scholarship, renewable.
Intended use: For full-time undergraduate study at 4-year institution in United States. Designated institutions: Catholic colleges and universities.
Eligibility: Applicant or parent must be member/participant of Knights of Columbus. Applicant must be Roman Catholic. Applicant's parent must have been killed or disabled in work-related accident as fire fighter or police officer.
Application requirements: Proof of eligibility. Applicant's father must have been killed or permanently and totally

disabled as the result of criminal violence while performing his duties as a full-time fire fighter or law enforcement officer.

Additional information: Award pays tuition, room, board, books and incidental fees at a Catholic college. No application deadline.

Amount of award:	Full tuition
Number of awards:	10
Number of applicants:	10

Contact:
Knights of Columbus
Director of Scholarship Aid
P.O. Box 1670
New Haven, CT 06507-0901
Phone: 203-752-4332

Pro Deo/Pro Patria Scholarship

Type of award: Scholarship, renewable.

Intended use: For full-time undergraduate study at 4-year institution in United States. Designated institutions: Catholic colleges and universities.

Eligibility: Applicant or parent must be member/participant of Knights of Columbus. Applicant must be high school senior. Applicant must be Roman Catholic. Applicant must be U.S. citizen.

Basis for selection: Applicant must demonstrate high academic achievement.

Application requirements: Recommendations, essay, transcript, proof of eligibility.

Additional information: Must be Knights of Columbus member in good standing; child of such a member or deceased member; or member in good standing of Columbian Squires. There are 12 scholarships designated for students at the Catholic University of America in Washington, DC; 50 scholarships available to students entering other Catholic colleges in the United States. Scholarships are renewable for up to four years, pending satisfactory academic performance. Scholarship applications must be filed by March 1. Obtain application from Director of Scholarship Aid, Knights of Columbus, in New Haven, CT.

Amount of award:	$1,500
Number of awards:	62
Number of applicants:	600
Application deadline:	March 1
Notification begins:	May 1
Total amount awarded:	$93,000

Contact:
Knights of Columbus
Director of Scholarship Aid
P.O. Box 1670
New Haven, CT 06510-0901
Phone: 203-752-4332

Kosciuszko Foundation

Kosciuszko Foundation Tuition Scholarships

Type of award: Scholarship, renewable.

Intended use: For full-time senior or graduate study at 4-year or graduate institution in United States.

Eligibility: Applicant must be Polish. Applicant must be U.S. citizen or permanent resident.

Basis for selection: Major/career interest in polish language/studies. Applicant must demonstrate financial need, high academic achievement, seriousness of purpose and service orientation.

Application requirements: $25 application fee. Essay, transcript, proof of eligibility. Proof of Polish descent, two letters of recommendation from professors, two passport photos 1.5"x1.5" with full name on reverse side of each. Graduates must submit copies of degee diplomas.

Additional information: Minimum 3.0 GPA. $25 nonrefundable application fee. Applicant must be entering upper-level postsecondary or graduate program. Limit of two tuition scholarships per individual. Only one member per immediate family awarded at once. Eligible applicants must be either U.S. citizens of Polish descent, Polish citizens with permanent residentcy status in U.S., or U.S. citizens pursuing Polish studies as major. Students of other nationalities doing work in Polish studies considered. Student must reapply for renewal of award. Visit Website or call for application. Applications available from October 1 to December 30.

Amount of award:	$1,000-$7,000
Application deadline:	January 15
Notification begins:	May 15

Contact:
Kosciuszko Foundation
15 East 65 Street
New York, NY 10021-6595
Phone: 212-734-2130
Fax: 212-628-4552
Web: www.kosciuszkofoundation.org

Kosciuszko Foundation Year Abroad Program

Type of award: Scholarship, renewable.

Intended use: For sophomore, junior, senior or graduate study at 4-year or graduate institution in United States in Poland. Designated institutions: A year of studies at the Jagiellonian University, Institute of Polish Diaspora and Ethnic Studies, formerly the Polonia Institute, Krakow.

Eligibility: Applicant must be U.S. citizen or permanent resident.

Basis for selection: Competition/talent/interest in study abroad. Major/career interest in polish language/studies. Applicant must demonstrate high academic achievement.

Application requirements: $50 application fee. Essay, transcript. Three letters of reference (two academic), certificate of proficiency in Polish, physician's certificate and printout of HIV test results, two passport-sized photos 1.5"x1.5" with full name on reverse side of each. Graduates must submit copies of degree diplomas.

Additional information: Must have interest in Polish subjects and/or involvement in Polish-American community. Scholarship covers tuition and stipend for housing and living expenses for one academic year or semester. Airfare not included. Minimum 3.0 GPA. $50 nonrefundable application fee. Interview may be required. Previous recipients and candidates may reapply. Visit Website for more information and application. Applications available from October 1 to December 30.

Amount of award:	Full tuition
Application deadline:	January 15

Contact:
Kosciuszko Foundation
Year Abroad Program
15 East 65th Street
New York, NY 10021
Phone: 212-734-2130
Fax: 212-628-4552
Web: www.kosciuszkofoundation.org

The Lagrant Foundation

Lagrant Scholarships

Type of award: Scholarship.
Intended use: For full-time freshman, sophomore or junior study at accredited 4-year institution.
Eligibility: Applicant must be Alaskan native, Asian American, African American, Mexican American, Hispanic American, Puerto Rican or American Indian. Applicant must be high school senior. Applicant must be U.S. citizen.
Basis for selection: Major/career interest in advertising; marketing or public relations.
Application requirements: Essay, transcript. Minimum 2.5 GPA. Resume. Two-page typed essay outlining career goals, accomplishments, reasons why he/she should be selected, and steps he/she will take to increase ethnic representation in this field. Include paragraph indicating how education is currently financed and why financing in coming year is needed, explaining college and/or community activities, describing any honors or awards received, and (if employed) indicating hours worked and responsibilites.
Additional information: Chosen applicant must attend the Lagrant Foundation's career development workshop and awards reception to receive scholarship. In addition, recipient must make a one-year commitment to maintain contact with TLF to receive professional guidance and academic support.

Amount of award:	$5,000
Number of awards:	10
Application deadline:	March 31
Total amount awarded:	$50,000

Contact:
The Lagrant Foundation
555 S. Flowers Street, Suite 700
Los Angeles, CA 90071-2300
Phone: 323-469-8680
Fax: 323-469-8683
Web: www.lagrantfoundation.org

Lambda Alpha

National Dean's List Scholarship

Type of award: Scholarship.
Intended use: For senior study at accredited 4-year institution in United States in U.S. territories.
Eligibility: Applicant or parent must be member/participant of Lambda Alpha. Applicant must be U.S. citizen or permanent resident.
Basis for selection: Major/career interest in anthropology. Applicant must demonstrate high academic achievement and seriousness of purpose.

Application requirements: Recommendations, transcript, nomination by faculty sponsor from department of anthropology. Resume.
Additional information: Institution must have chartered Lambda Alpha chapter. Apply in junior year.

Amount of award:	$1,000
Number of awards:	1
Number of applicants:	15
Application deadline:	March 1
Notification begins:	April 1
Total amount awarded:	$1,000

Contact:
Lambda Alpha
Department of Anthropology
Ball State University
Muncie, IN 47306-0435
Phone: 765-285-1575
Web: www.lambdaalpha.com

Landscape Architecture Foundation

David T. Woolsey Scholarship

Type of award: Scholarship.
Intended use: For full-time junior, senior or graduate study at accredited 4-year or graduate institution.
Eligibility: Applicant must be permanent resident residing in Hawaii.
Basis for selection: Major/career interest in landscape architecture. Applicant must demonstrate service orientation.
Application requirements: Portfolio, recommendations, essay, proof of eligibility. Also include (1) typed, double-spaced autobiography and statement of personal and professional goals (minimum 500 words); (2) sample of design work (three 8x10 photos); (3) two letters of recommendation including one from design instructor; and (4) proof of Hawaii residency.
Additional information: Applicant must be enrolled in landscape architecture program at accredited college/university.

Amount of award:	$1,000
Number of awards:	1
Application deadline:	April 6
Total amount awarded:	$1,000

Contact:
Landscape Architecture Foundation
818 18th Street
Suite 810
Washington, DC 20006
Phone: 202-331-7070
Web: www.laprofession.org

LAF/CLASS Fund (California Landscape Architectural Student Scholarship) University Program

Type of award: Scholarship.
Intended use: For junior or senior study at accredited postsecondary institution in United States. Designated institutions: University of California Davis, California Polytechnic at Pomona and at San Luis Obispo.
Eligibility: Applicant must be residing in California.
Basis for selection: Major/career interest in landscape architecture. Applicant must demonstrate financial need.

Application requirements: Recommendations. Academic, community and professional involvement. 300-word statement on the profession; 100-word statement on intended use of funds. Two faculty recommendation letters. One confidential department head recommendation. Faxed applications will not be accepted.

Additional information: Open to students at University of California at Davis, and at California Polytechnic Pomona and San Luis Obispo. Two scholarships per institution.

Amount of award:	$1,500
Number of awards:	6
Application deadline:	April 1

Contact:
Landscape Architecture Foundation
818 18th Street
Suite 810
Washington, DC 20006
Phone: (202) 331-7070
Web: www.laprofession.org/financial/scholarships.htm

LAF/CLASS Fund Landscape Architecture Program

Type of award: Scholarship.
Intended use: For full-time undergraduate study. Designated institutions: University of California, Berkeley; University of California, Los Angeles; University of California, Davis; Cal Poly Pomona; Cal Poly San Luis Obispo.
Eligibility: Applicant must be residing in California.
Basis for selection: Major/career interest in landscape architecture. Applicant must demonstrate financial need and service orientation.
Application requirements: Recommendations, essay, transcript. Academic, community and professional involvement background. 300-word statement on the profession. 100-word statement on intended use of funds. Two faculty recommendation letters. One confidential department head recommendation, cover sheet and personal profile (details on Website). Faxed applications will not be accepted.
Additional information: For use at designated institutions only. Two awards per institution.

Amount of award:	$500
Number of awards:	10
Application deadline:	April 6

Contact:
Landscape Architecture Foundation
818 18th Street
Suite 810
Washington, DC 20006
Phone: 202-331-7070
Web: www.laprofession.org/financial/scholarships.htm

LAF/CLASS Fund Scholarship Ornamental Horticulture Program

Type of award: Scholarship.
Intended use: For junior or senior study at accredited postsecondary institution in United States. Designated institutions: California Polytechnic at Pomona or San Luis Obispo, or University of California at Davis.
Eligibility: Applicant must be residing in California.
Basis for selection: Major/career interest in horticulture.
Application requirements: Recommendations. Academic, community and professional involvement background. 300-word statement on profession. 100-word statement on intended use of funds. Two faculty recommendation letters. One confidential department head recommendation, cover sheet and personal

profile (details on Website). Faxed applications will not be accepted.
Additional information: For juniors or seniors enrolled in ornamental horticulture curriculum at California Polytechnic at Pomona or San Luis Obispo, or University of California at Davis. One award per institution.

Amount of award:	$1,000
Number of awards:	3
Application deadline:	April 6
Total amount awarded:	$3,000

Contact:
Landscape Architecture Foundation
818 18th Street
Suite 810
Washington, DC 20006
Phone: 202-331-7070
Web: www.laprofession.org/financial/scholarships.htm

Rain Bird Company Scholarship

Type of award: Scholarship.
Intended use: For full-time junior, senior or post-bachelor's certificate study at accredited 4-year institution.
Basis for selection: Major/career interest in landscape architecture; horticulture; construction or urban planning. Applicant must demonstrate financial need and high academic achievement.
Application requirements: 300-word essay stating career goals and expected contribution to landscape architecture. Financial aid forms.
Additional information: Third-, fourth-, and fifth-year undergraduates eligible. Visit Website for more information.

Amount of award:	$1,000
Number of awards:	1
Number of applicants:	30
Application deadline:	April 6
Total amount awarded:	$1,000

Contact:
Landscape Architecture Foundation
818 18th Street
Suite 810
Washington, DC 20006
Phone: 202-331-7070
Web: www.laprofession.org/financial/scholarships.htm

Raymond E. Page Scholarship

Type of award: Scholarship.
Intended use: For full-time sophomore, junior or senior study at accredited 4-year institution.
Basis for selection: Major/career interest in landscape architecture; horticulture; urban planning or construction. Applicant must demonstrate financial need and seriousness of purpose.
Application requirements: Recommendations, essay. A two-page essay detailing financial need and how award will be used; recommendation from current professor who is familiar with that applicant's character and intent to pursue education in landscape architecture.
Additional information: Award is for students committed to directing the profession of landscape architecture by answering the challenges of tomorrow. Visit Website for more information.

Amount of award:	$1,000
Number of awards:	1
Application deadline:	April 6
Total amount awarded:	$1,000

Contact:
Landscape Architecture Foundation
818 18th Street
Suite 810
Washington, DC 20006
Phone: 202-331-7070
Web: www.laprofession.org/financial/scholarships.htm

Latin American Educational Foundation

Latin American Educational Scholarship

Type of award: Scholarship, renewable.
Intended use: For full-time undergraduate or non-degree study at accredited postsecondary institution in United States.
Eligibility: Applicant must be Mexican American, Hispanic American or Puerto Rican. Must have Hispanic heritage or be actively involved in Hispanic community. Applicant must be residing in Colorado.
Basis for selection: Applicant must demonstrate financial need and high academic achievement.
Application requirements: Recommendations, essay, transcript, proof of eligibility.
Additional information: Minimum 3.0 GPA required. SAT or ACT scores required for high school seniors. Recipients must fulfill ten hours of community service during the award year.

Amount of award:	$250-$2,000
Number of awards:	302
Number of applicants:	500
Application deadline:	February 15
Notification begins:	May 31

Contact:
Executive Director
924 West Colfax Avenue
Suite 103
Denver, CO 80204
Phone: 303-446-0541
Fax: 303-446-0526
Web: www.laef.org

League of United Latin American Citizens

LULAC National Scholarship Fund Honors Awards

Type of award: Scholarship.
Intended use: For full-time undergraduate or graduate study at accredited 2-year, 4-year or graduate institution in United States.
Eligibility: Applicant must be Mexican American, Hispanic American or Puerto Rican. Applicant must be U.S. citizen or permanent resident.
Basis for selection: Applicant must demonstrate high academic achievement.
Application requirements: Essay, transcript, proof of eligibility. Application. Verification of admittance to institution student will attend (letter of acceptance, transcript, or letter from registrar). Personal essay of no more than 300 words, typed or neatly printed. ACT or SAT scores. ACT can be sent directly with code #9891. Minimum 3.25 GPA.
Additional information: Applicant must have applied to or be enrolled in a college, university, or graduate school, including 2-year colleges, excluding vocational schools. Students are ineligible for a scholarship if related to a scholarship committee member, the Council President, or an individual contributor to the local funds of the Council. Entering freshmen must have scored at least 20 on ACT or 840 on SAT. See Website for list of participating LULAC Councils. Local LULAC Council may require additional information and/or personal interview.

Amount of award:	$250-$1,000
Application deadline:	March 31
Notification begins:	May 15

Contact:
Contact local LULAC Council for more information and application.
Phone: 202-833-6130
Web: www.lulac.org/Programs/Scholar.html

LULAC National Scholarship Fund National Scholastic Achievement Awards

Type of award: Scholarship.
Intended use: For full-time undergraduate or graduate study at accredited 2-year, 4-year or graduate institution in United States.
Eligibility: Applicant must be Mexican American, Hispanic American or Puerto Rican. Applicant must be U.S. citizen or permanent resident.
Basis for selection: Applicant must demonstrate high academic achievement.
Application requirements: Essay, transcript, proof of eligibility. Application. Verification of admittance to institution student will attend (letter of acceptance, transcript, or letter from registrar). Personal essay of no more than 300 words, typed or neatly printed. ACT or SAT scores. ACT can be sent directly with code #9891. Minimum 3.5 GPA.
Additional information: Applicant must have applied to or be enrolled in a college, university, or graduate school, including 2-year colleges, excluding vocational schools. Students are ineligible for a scholarship if related to a scholarship committee member, the Council President, or an individual contributor to the local funds of the Council. Entering freshmen must have scored at least 23 on ACT or 970 on SAT. Minimum amount of award is $1000. See Website for list of participating LULAC Councils. Local LULAC Council may require additional information and/or personal interview.

Application deadline:	March 31
Notification begins:	May 15

Contact:
Contact Local LULAC Council for more information.
Phone: 202-833-6130
Web: www.lulac.org/Programs/Scholar.html

LULAC National Scholarshp Fund General Awards

Type of award: Scholarship.
Intended use: For undergraduate or graduate study at accredited 2-year, 4-year or graduate institution in United States.

Eligibility: Applicant must be Mexican American, Hispanic American or Puerto Rican. Applicant must be U.S. citizen or permanent resident.
Basis for selection: Applicant must demonstrate financial need, high academic achievement, depth of character, leadership and service orientation.
Application requirements: Essay, transcript, proof of eligibility. Completed and signed application. Verification of admittance or enrollment (transcript, letter of acceptance, letter from registrar). Personal essay of not more than 300 words, typed or neatly printed.
Additional information: Applicant must have applied to or be enrolled in a college, university, or graduate school, including 2-year colleges, excluding vocational schools. Students are ineligible for a scholarship if related to a scholarship committee member, the Council President, or an individual contributor to the local funds of the Council. See Website for list of participating LULAC Councils. Local LULAC Council may require additional information and/or personal interview.

Amount of award:	$250-$1,000
Application deadline:	March 31
Notification begins:	May 15

Contact:
Contact Local LULAC Council for more information.
Phone: 202-833-6130
Web: www.lulac.org/Programs/Scholar.html

League of United Latin American Citizens and General Electric Fund

GE Business/Engineering Scholarship for Minority Students

Type of award: Scholarship, renewable.
Intended use: For full-time sophomore study at accredited 4-year institution in United States.
Eligibility: Applicant must be U.S. citizen or permanent resident.
Basis for selection: Major/career interest in business or engineering. Applicant must demonstrate high academic achievement, seriousness of purpose and service orientation.
Application requirements: Recommendations, essay, transcript, proof of eligibility. Minimum 3.25 GPA. Application. Personal statement of no more than 300 words describing professional and career goals.
Additional information: Applicant must be a minority student entering their sophomore year in the fall. Applicant must submit letters of reference from three adults (at least one being a college professor) addressed to the GE/LULAC Scholarship Selection Committee. Include a complete telephone number and mailing address for each reference. GE/LULAC Scholarship recipients may be offered temporary summer or internship positions with GE businesses; however the students are under no obligation to accept GE employment. Application available on Website.

Amount of award:	$5,000
Number of awards:	2
Application deadline:	June 15
Notification begins:	August 15
Total amount awarded:	$10,000

Contact:
GE Fund/LULAC Scholarship Program
2000 "L" Street NW, Ste. #610
Washington, DC 20036
Phone: (202) 833-6130
Web: www.lulac.org/Programs/Scholar.html

League of United Latin American Citizens and General Motors Corporation

GM Engineering Scholarship For Minority Students

Type of award: Scholarship, renewable.
Intended use: For full-time undergraduate study at 4-year institution. Designated institutions: Colleges or Universities approved by LULAC and GM.
Eligibility: Applicant must be Alaskan native, African American, Mexican American, Hispanic American, Puerto Rican or American Indian.
Basis for selection: Major/career interest in engineering. Applicant must demonstrate high academic achievement, seriousness of purpose and service orientation.
Application requirements: Recommendations, essay, transcript. Minimum 3.2 college GPA, or 3.5 high school GPA for entering freshmen. Entering freshmen must have minimum 23 ACT score or 970 SAT score. Application. Personal statement of no more than 300 words describing professional and career goals.
Additional information: Applicant must be a minority student persuing a bachelor's degree in engineering. Applicant must submit letters of reference from three adults (at least one being a teacher or professor) addressed to the GM/LULAC Scholarship Selection Committee. Include a complete telephone number and mailing address for each reference. Must maintain satisfactory academic progress to be eligible for renewal. See Website for application. Scholarship recipients may be offered temporary summer or internship positions with GM businesses; however students are not obligated to accept such offers.

Amount of award:	$2,000
Number of awards:	20
Application deadline:	July 15
Notification begins:	August 15
Total amount awarded:	$40,000

Contact:
Leage of United Latin American Citizens (LULAC)
GM/LULAC Scholarship Selection Committee
2000 L Street, NW, Suite 610
Washington, DC 20036
Phone: 202-833-6130
Web: www.lulac.org/Programs/Scholar.html

Learning For Life

Floyd Boring Award

Type of award: Scholarship.
Intended use: For undergraduate study at accredited 2-year or 4-year institution.

Eligibility: Applicant or parent must be member/participant of Learning for Life. Applicant must be U.S. citizen or permanent resident.
Basis for selection: Major/career interest in criminal justice/law enforcement. Applicant must demonstrate depth of character, leadership, seriousness of purpose and service orientation.
Application requirements: Recommendations, essay, proof of eligibility, nomination. 1,000 word essay describing act for which applicant is being nominated, Three letters of recommendation from school officials, post or organizational leaders, and community or church leaders attesting to candidacy. Statement from post advisor describing nominee's act. Black-and-white photo (preferably in uniform). Must submit original and one copy of all materials.
Additional information: Applicant's achievements should reflect high degree of motivation, commitment, and community concern that epitomizes law enforcement profession. Visit Website for more information and to download application.

Amount of award:	$2,000
Number of awards:	2
Application deadline:	March 15
Total amount awarded:	$4,000

Contact:
National Law Enforcement Scholarships and Awards
1325 West Walnut Hill Lane
P.O. Box 152079
Irving, TX 75015-2079
Phone: 972-580-2433
Fax: 972-580-2502
Web: www.learning-for-life.org/exploring

Frank D. Visceglia Memorial Scholarship

Type of award: Scholarship, renewable.
Intended use: For full-time freshman study at accredited 4-year institution.
Eligibility: Applicant or parent must be member/participant of Boy Scouts of America, Eagle Scouts. Applicant must be male, high school senior. Applicant must be U.S. citizen or permanent resident residing in New Jersey.
Additional information: Must be New Jersey Eagle Scout. Preference given to applicants whose service projects relate to environment and/or economy.

Amount of award:	$1,000
Number of awards:	1
Number of applicants:	12
Application deadline:	June 30
Total amount awarded:	$1,000

Contact:
Frank D. Visceglia Memorial Scholarship Program
Dennis Kohl, Scout Executive
222 Columbia Turnpike
Florham Park, NJ 07932

National Technical Investigators' Captain James J. Regan Memorial Scholarship

Type of award: Scholarship.
Intended use: For full-time undergraduate study.
Eligibility: Applicant or parent must be member/participant of Learning for Life. Applicant must be high school senior. Applicant must be U.S. citizen or permanent resident.

Basis for selection: Major/career interest in criminal justice/law enforcement. Applicant must demonstrate high academic achievement, leadership and seriousness of purpose.
Application requirements: Recommendations, essay, transcript, proof of eligibility. Secure certification from post advisor, head of participating organization, Learning for Life representative. Three letters of recommendation (two from outside of law enforcement), personal statement on "What Significance I Place on a Technological Background in Law Enforcement," 250-word minimum essay on "How Will Technology Affect Law Enforcement in the 21st Century" and black-and-white photo (preferably in uniform). Must submit original and four copies of all materials.
Additional information: Program open to Learning for Life's Law Enforcement Explorers. Visit Website for more information and to download application.

Amount of award:	$500
Number of awards:	2
Total amount awarded:	$1,000

Contact:
National Law Enforcement Scholarships and Awards
1325 West Walnut Hill Lane
P.O. Box 152079
Irving, TX 75015-2079
Phone: 972-580-2433
Fax: 972-580-2502
Web: www.learning-for-life.org/exploring

Sheryl A. Horak Law Enforcement Explorer Scholarship

Type of award: Scholarship.
Intended use: For full-time undergraduate study at accredited 2-year or 4-year institution.
Eligibility: Applicant or parent must be member/participant of Learning for Life. Applicant must be high school senior. Applicant must be U.S. citizen or permanent resident.
Basis for selection: Major/career interest in criminal justice/law enforcement. Applicant must demonstrate high academic achievement, leadership and service orientation.
Application requirements: Recommendations, essay. Secure certification from post advisor, head of participating organization, Learning for Life representative. Three letters of recommendation (two from outside of law enforcement), 500-word minimum essay on "Why I Want to Pursue a Career in Law Enforcement" and black-and-white photo (preferably in uniform). Must submit original and two copies of all materials.
Additional information: Program open to Learning for Life's Law Enforcement Explorers. Visit Website for more information and to download application.

Amount of award:	$1,000
Number of awards:	1

Contact:
National Law Enforcement Scholarships and Awards
1325 West Walnut Hill Lane
P.O. Box 152079
Irving, TX 75015-2418
Phone: 972-580-2433
Fax: 972-580-2502
Web: www.learning-for-life.org/exploring

Lighthouse International

Lighthouse College-Bound Award

Type of award: Scholarship.
Intended use: For full-time freshman study at accredited 2-year or 4-year institution in United States. Designated institutions: Schools in New York, New Jersey, Pennsylvania, Connecticut, Massachusetts, Maine, Vermont, New Hampshire, Rhode Island, Delaware, Maryland, Washington, D.C.
Eligibility: Applicant must be visually impaired. Applicant must be high school senior. Applicant must be U.S. citizen residing in Vermont, New York, Maine, Delaware, Maryland, Pennsylvania, Massachusetts, District of Columbia, Connecticut, New Hampshire, New Jersey or Rhode Island.
Basis for selection: Applicant must demonstrate high academic achievement.
Application requirements: Recommendations, essay, transcript, proof of eligibility. Documentation of legal blindness from State Commission for the Blind. Recommendations required: one personal, one academic. Personal essay should be at least 500 words. Transcript must be official. Letter of acceptance to college.
Additional information: College-bound high school seniors or recent high school graduates now planning to begin college may apply. Student must be blind or partially sighted.

Amount of award:	$5,000
Number of awards:	1
Application deadline:	March 31
Total amount awarded:	$5,000

Contact:
Lighthouse International
Scholarship Awards Program
111 East 59 Street
New York, NY 10022
Phone: 212-821-9428
Fax: 212-821-9703
Web: www.lighthouse.org/scholarship_awards.htm

Lighthouse Undergraduate Award I

Type of award: Scholarship.
Intended use: For full-time undergraduate study at postsecondary institution. Designated institutions: Schools in New Jersey, New York, Pennsylvania, Connecticut, Massachusetts, Maine, New Hampshire, Rhode Island, Vermont, Delaware, Maryland, Washington D.C.
Eligibility: Applicant must be visually impaired. Applicant must be U.S. citizen residing in Vermont, New York, Maine, Delaware, Maryland, Pennsylvania, Massachusetts, District of Columbia, Connecticut, New Hampshire, New Jersey or Rhode Island.
Basis for selection: Applicant must demonstrate high academic achievement.
Application requirements: Recommendations, essay, transcript, proof of eligibility. Documentation of legal blindness from State Commission for the Blind. Recommendations required: one personal, one academic. Personal essay should be at least 500 words. Transcript must be official.

Amount of award:	$5,000
Number of awards:	1
Application deadline:	March 31
Total amount awarded:	$5,000

Contact:
Lighthouse International
Scholarship Awards Program
111 East 59 Street
New York, NY 10022
Phone: 212-821-9428
Fax: 212-821-9703
Web: www.lighthouse.org/scholarship_awards.htm

Lighthouse Undergraduate Incentive Award II

Type of award: Scholarship.
Intended use: For full-time undergraduate study. Designated institutions: Schools in New York, New Jersey, Pennsylvania, Connecticut, Massachusetts, Rhode Island, Vermont, New Hampshire, Maine, Deleware, Maryland and Washington, D.C.
Eligibility: Applicant must be visually impaired. Applicant must be returning adult student. Applicant must be U.S. citizen residing in Vermont, New York, Maine, Delaware, Maryland, Pennsylvania, Massachusetts, District of Columbia, Connecticut, New Hampshire, New Jersey or Rhode Island.
Basis for selection: Applicant must demonstrate high academic achievement.
Application requirements: Recommendations, essay, transcript, proof of eligibility. Documentation of legal blindness from State Commission for the Blind. Recommendations required: one personal, one academic. Personal essay should be at least 500 words. Transcript must be official.
Additional information: This award is for adult students pursuing an undergraduate degree after an absence of ten years or more from high school or an accredited program. Students may apply at any time immediately prior to, or during, their course of study. Visit Website for more information and to be placed on the mailing list for an application.

Amount of award:	$5,000
Number of awards:	1
Application deadline:	March 31
Total amount awarded:	$5,000

Contact:
Lighthouse International
Scholarship Awards Program
111 East 59 Street
New York, NY 10022
Phone: 212-821-9428
Fax: 212-821-9703
Web: www.lighthouse.org/scholarship_awards.htm

Long and Foster Scholarship Program

Long and Foster Scholarship Program

Type of award: Scholarship.
Intended use: For freshman study at 4-year institution in United States.
Eligibility: Applicant must be high school senior. Applicant must be U.S. citizen residing in District of Columbia, Virginia, Delaware, Maryland or Pennsylvania.
Basis for selection: Applicant must demonstrate financial need, depth of character, leadership, seriousness of purpose and service orientation.

Scholarships

Additional information: Applicant must submit SAT scores and have minimum of 3.0 GPA. Application deadline in early March.

Amount of award:	$1,000
Number of awards:	125
Total amount awarded:	$125,000

Contact:
Long and Foster Scholarship Program
11351 Random Hills Road
Fairfax, VA 22030-6082
Phone: 703-359-1500
Web: www.longandfoster.com/scholarships

Los Padres Foundation

Los Padres Foundation Scholarships

Type of award: Scholarship.
Intended use: For undergraduate study at 2-year or 4-year institution in United States.
Eligibility: Applicant must be Mexican American, Hispanic American or Puerto Rican. Applicant must be high school senior. Applicant must be U.S. citizen.
Basis for selection: Applicant must demonstrate seriousness of purpose and service orientation.
Application requirements: Application.
Additional information: Applicant must have minimum 2.75 GPA. Application available at financial aid office.

Amount of award:	$2,000
Application deadline:	January 17

Contact:
Los Padres Foundation
289 Grant Avenue
Jersey City, NJ 07305
Phone: 201-451-6229
Fax: 201-451-5893
Web: www.lospadresfoundation.org

Louisiana Department of Veterans Affairs

Louisiana Veterans Affairs Educational Assistance for Dependent Children

Type of award: Scholarship, renewable.
Intended use: For full-time undergraduate, graduate or non-degree study at vocational, 2-year, 4-year or graduate institution. Designated institutions: Louisiana public institutions.
Eligibility: Applicant must be at least 16, no older than 25. Applicant must be residing in Louisiana. Applicant must be dependent of disabled veteran or deceased veteran. Deceased veteran must have died of service-related disability.
Application requirements: Proof of eligibility. Must obtain certification of eligibility and application from parish veterans assistance counselor.
Additional information: Award is a tuition waiver at all Louisiana state-supported schools. Disability must be at least 90 percent as rated by U.S. Department of Veterans Affairs to qualify. Applicant also eligible if disability rating is 60 percent or more but employability rating is 100 percent unemployable. Award amounts vary and may be applied only toward state public schools.

Amount of award:	Full tuition

Contact:
Louisiana Department of Veterans Affairs
P.O. Box 94095, Capitol Station
Baton Rouge, LA 70804-9095
Web: www.ldva.org

Louisiana Veterans Affairs Educational Assistance for Surviving Spouse

Type of award: Scholarship, renewable.
Intended use: For full-time undergraduate, graduate or non-degree study at postsecondary institution. Designated institutions: Louisiana public institutions.
Eligibility: Applicant must be single. Applicant must be residing in Louisiana. Applicant must be spouse of deceased veteran.
Application requirements: Proof of eligibility. Must obtain certification of eligibility and application from parish veterans assistance counselor.
Additional information: Award is tuition waiver at all Louisiana state-supported schools. Veteran must have been a Lousiana resident at least 12 months prior to disability or death.

Amount of award:	Full tuition

Contact:
Louisiana Department of Veterans Affairs
P.O. Box 94095, Capitol Station
Baton Rouge, LA 70804-9095
Web: www.ldva.org

Louisiana Office of Student Financial Assistance

Louisiana Leveraging Educational Assistance Partnership

Type of award: Scholarship, renewable.
Intended use: For full-time undergraduate study at vocational, 2-year or 4-year institution. Designated institutions: Louisiana postsecondary institutions.
Eligibility: Applicant must be U.S. citizen, international student or eligible non-U.S. citizen. Applicant must be residing in Louisiana.
Basis for selection: Applicant must demonstrate financial need.
Application requirements: FAFSA.
Additional information: Applicant must have lived in Louisiana a year before applying. Must have minimum of 45 on GED, 20 on ACT, or high school or postsecondary GPA minimum of 2.0. May not be in default on any student loan or grant. Must be registered with Selective Service if required. Award may be used at state technical institutions or proprietary schools. Must reapply for renewal annually. Contact financial aid office of institution.

Amount of award:	$200-$2,000
Number of awards:	3,000
Application deadline:	July 1
Total amount awarded:	$2,000,000

Contact:
Louisiana Office of Student Financial Assistance
P.O. Box 91202
Baton Rouge, LA 70821-9202
Phone: 800-259-5626 ext. 1012
Fax: 225-922-0790
Web: www.osfa.state.la.us

Louisiana Rockefeller Wildlife Scholarship

Type of award: Scholarship, renewable.
Intended use: For full-time undergraduate or graduate study at 4-year or graduate institution. Designated institutions: Louisiana public institutions.
Eligibility: Applicant must be U.S. citizen, international student or eligible non-U.S. citizen. Applicant must be residing in Louisiana.
Basis for selection: Major/career interest in wildlife/fisheries; forestry or oceanography/marine studies. Applicant must demonstrate high academic achievement.
Application requirements: FAFSA. Application.
Additional information: Minimum 2.5 GPA required. May not be in default on any educational loan or grant. Must attain degree in eligible field at Louisiana public college or university or repay funds received, plus interest. Must achieve cumulative GPA of at least 2.5 at end of each spring semester and have earned at least 24 hours total credit by end of academic year (fall and spring). Recipients receive $500 for each semester. Cumulative amount of $7,000 will be awarded for up to five years of undergraduate and two years of graduate study.

Amount of award:	$1,000
Number of awards:	60
Number of applicants:	150
Application deadline:	July 1
Total amount awarded:	$60,000

Contact:
Louisiana Office of Student Financial Assistance
P.O. Box 91202
Baton Rouge, LA 70821-9202
Phone: 800-259-5626 ext. 1012
Fax: 225-925-4969
Web: www.osfa.state.la.us

Louisiana Tuition Opportunity Program for Students Award

Type of award: Scholarship, renewable.
Intended use: For full-time undergraduate study at postsecondary institution. Designated institutions: Eligible Louisiana postsecondary institutions.
Eligibility: Applicant must be U.S. citizen residing in Louisiana.
Basis for selection: Applicant must demonstrate high academic achievement.
Application requirements: Must submit FAFSA by May 1 for priority consideration, or by July 1 for full award consideration.
Additional information: All eligible students funded. Applicant must be Louisiana resident for at least two years prior to high school graduation. Must have minimum high school cumulative GPA of 2.5 in core curriculum courses. Minimum ACT score equal to or greater than state average for prior year. Must enroll as first-time, full-time undergraduate by semester following first anniversary of high school graduation. Awards are for amount equal to tuition at public institution attended or the weighted average tuition amount for attendance

at institution that is a member of Louisiana Association of Independent Colleges and Universities. Amount of award varies.

Amount of award:	Full tuition
Application deadline:	July 1

Contact:
Louisiana Office of Student Financial Assistance
P.O. Box 91202
Baton Rouge, LA 70821-9202
Phone: 800-259-5626 ext. 1012
Fax: 225-922-0790
Web: www.osfa.state.la.us

Louisiana Tuition Opportunity Program for Students Honors Award

Type of award: Scholarship, renewable.
Intended use: For full-time undergraduate study. Designated institutions: Eligible Louisiana postsecondary institutions.
Eligibility: Applicant must be U.S. citizen residing in Louisiana.
Basis for selection: Applicant must demonstrate high academic achievement.
Application requirements: Must submit FAFSA by May 1 for priority consideration, or by July 1 for full award consideration.
Additional information: All eligible students funded. Must be Louisiana resident for at least two years prior to graduation. Minimum ACT score of 27 required. Must complete 16.5 core unit curriculum and have minimum high school GPA of 3.5 in core curriculum classes. Must enroll as first-time, full-time undergraduate by semester following the first anniversary of high school graduation. Awards are for amount equal to tuition at public institution or weighted average tuition amount for attendance at institution that is member of Louisiana Association of Independent Colleges and Universities. Additional stipend of $800 per academic year. Amount of award varies.

Application deadline:	July 1

Contact:
Louisiana Office of Student Financial Assistance
P.O. Box 91202
Baton Rouge, LA 70821-9202
Phone: 800-259-5626 ext. 1012
Fax: 225-922-0790
Web: www.osfa.state.la.us

Louisiana Tuition Opportunity Program for Students Performance Award

Type of award: Scholarship, renewable.
Intended use: For full-time undergraduate study. Designated institutions: Eligible Louisiana postsecondary institutions.
Eligibility: Applicant must be U.S. citizen residing in Louisiana.
Basis for selection: Applicant must demonstrate high academic achievement.
Application requirements: Must submit FAFSA by May 1 for priority consideration; no later than July 1 for for full award consideration.
Additional information: All eligible students funded. Must be Louisiana resident. Minimum ACT score of 23 required. Must complete 16.5 core unit curriculum and have minimum high school GPA of 3.5 in core curriculum classes. Alternate

GPA information for Performance Award only: minimum cumulative GPA of 3.0, with ten or more honors, advanced placement or gifted courses completed within the core. Recipient must enroll as first-time, full-time undergraduate by semester following first anniversary of high school graduation. Awards are for amount equal to tuition at public institution attended or the weighted average tuition for attendance at institution that is a member of Louisiana Association of Independent Colleges and Universities. Additional stipend of $400 per academic year. Amount of award varies.

  Amount of award: Full tuition
  Application deadline: July 1
Contact:
Louisiana Office of Student Financial Assistance
P.O. Box 91202
Baton Rouge, LA 70821-9202
Phone: 800-259-5626 ext. 1012
Fax: 225-922-0790
Web: www.osfa.state.la.us

Louisiana Tuition Opportunity Program for Students Tech Award

Type of award: Scholarship, renewable.
Intended use: For full-time undergraduate study at vocational institution in United States. Designated institutions: Louisiana public postsecondary vocational or technical institutions.
Eligibility: Applicant must be U.S. citizen or permanent resident residing in Louisiana.
Basis for selection: Applicant must demonstrate high academic achievement.
Application requirements: Must submit FAFSA by May 1 for priority consideration, or by July 1 for full award consideration.
Additional information: All eligible students funded. Applicant must be Louisiana resident for at least two years prior to high school graduation. Minors who apply for citizenship within 60 days of their 18th birthday are also eligible. Minimum ACT score of 17 required. Must complete core curriculum and have minimum 2.5 high school GPA. Must enroll as first-time, full-time undergraduate by semester following first anniversary of high school graduation. Awards are for amount equal to tuition at public institutions that offer a vocational or technical education certificate or diploma program or a nonacademic undergraduate degree.

  Amount of award: Full tuition
  Application deadline: July 1
Contact:
Louisiana Office of Student Financial Assistance
P.O. Box 91202
Baton Rouge, LA 70821-9202
Phone: 800-259-5626 ext. 1012
Fax: 255-922-0790
Web: www.osfa.state.la.us

Lucent Technologies Foundation

Lucent Global Science Scholars Program

Type of award: Scholarship.

Intended use: For full-time undergraduate study at accredited 4-year institution in United States.
Eligibility: Applicant must be high school senior. Applicant must be U.S. citizen.
Basis for selection: Major/career interest in physical sciences; computer/information sciences; engineering; information systems; mathematics; aerospace or astronomy. Applicant must demonstrate high academic achievement.
Application requirements: Recommendations, essay, transcript, proof of eligibility. Two letters of recommendation required. Describe interest and achievements in math and science in 500-word essay. Include one passport-size photo, as well as photocopies of SAT/ACT scores.
Additional information: Applicant must demonstrate competency in spoken and written English. Visit Website for further details and to download application. Notification begins in April.

  Amount of award: $5,000
  Number of awards: 23
  Application deadline: February 25
Contact:
The Lucent Global Science Scholars Program
Institute of International Education
809 United Nations Plaza
New York, NY 10017
Phone: 212-984-5419
Web: www.iie.org/programs/lucent

Luso-American Education Foundation

Luso-American Education Foundation Scholarship

Type of award: Scholarship.
Intended use: For undergraduate study at accredited 2-year or 4-year institution.
Eligibility: Applicant or parent must be member/participant of Portuguese Continental Union.
Basis for selection: Applicant must demonstrate financial need, high academic achievement, depth of character, leadership and seriousness of purpose.
Application requirements: Recommendations, essay, transcript, proof of eligibility, nomination. SAT scores, report from secondary school or college attended by student.
Additional information: Applicant must have been LAEF member with at least one year in good standing. If not currently enrolled in college or university, must plan to enroll in the current academic year. Award amount based on individual financial need. Contact sponsor for more information.

  Application deadline: February 15
  Notification begins: April 30
Contact:
Luso-American Education Foundation
Scholarship Committee
7 Hartwell Ave.
Lexington, MA 02421
Phone: 781-676-2002
Fax: 781-376-2033
Web: www.luso-american.org

Maine Department of Agriculture, Food and Rural Resources

Maine Rural Rehabilitation Fund

Type of award: Scholarship.
Intended use: For full-time undergraduate study at postsecondary institution. Designated institutions: Institution offering agricultural degree.
Eligibility: Applicant must be high school senior. Applicant must be residing in Maine.
Basis for selection: Major/career interest in agribusiness; agricultural economics; agricultural education; agriculture; animal sciences or engineering, agricultural. Applicant must demonstrate financial need and high academic achievement.
Additional information: Applicant must be Maine resident studying agriculture. Cumulative 2.7 GPA or 3.0 GPA most recent semester. Amount of awards vary. Contact sponsor or visit Website for application.

Amount of award:	$500-$2,000
Number of awards:	4
Application deadline:	June 15
Total amount awarded:	$4,000

Contact:
Maine Department of Agriculture, Food and Rural Resources
28 State House Station
Augusta, ME 04333-4470
Phone: 207-287-3871
Fax: 207-287-7548
Web: www.state.me.us/agriculture

Maine Division of Veterans Services

Maine Veterans Services Dependents Educational Benefits

Type of award: Scholarship.
Intended use: For undergraduate or graduate study at vocational, 2-year or 4-year institution. Designated institutions: State of Maine-supported institutions.
Eligibility: Applicant must be at least 16, no older than 21. Applicant must be residing in Maine. Applicant must be dependent of disabled veteran, deceased veteran or POW/MIA; or spouse of disabled veteran or deceased veteran. Must apply for program prior to 22nd birthday or before 26th birthday if applicant was enrolled in the U.S. Armed Forces. Age limits apply to child applicants only, not spouses.
Application requirements: Proof of eligibility. All applicants: proof of veteran's disability; child of veteran: birth certificate; stepchild of veteran: birth certificate and parent's marriage certificate to veteran; adopted child: birth certificate, adoption certificate; adopted child with natural parent as veteran: birth certificate, proof of paternity to natural parent; spouse: marriage certificate.
Additional information: Parent or spouse must have been resident of Maine prior to enlistment or resident of Maine for five years preceding application for aid. Applicant must be dependent of 100% permanently and totally disabled veteran or deceased veteran. Provides tuition at all branches of University of Maine system, all State of Maine vocational-technical colleges, and Maine Maritime Academy for eight semesters to be used within six years.

Amount of award:	Full tuition

Contact:
Maine Division of Veterans Services
117 State House Station
Augusta, ME 04333-0117
Phone: 207-626-4464
Fax: 207-626-4471

Maine Innkeepers Association

Maine Innkeepers Association Scholarship

Type of award: Scholarship.
Intended use: For full-time undergraduate study at accredited vocational or 4-year institution in United States. Designated institutions: Institutions with fully accredited programs in hotel administration or culinary arts.
Eligibility: Applicant must be U.S. citizen or permanent resident residing in Maine.
Basis for selection: Major/career interest in culinary arts; hotel/restaurant management or hospitality administration/management. Applicant must demonstrate financial need and high academic achievement.
Application requirements: Recommendations, essay, transcript.
Additional information: Applicant must be Maine resident who is high school senior or college undergraduate. Application deadline is last Friday in March.

Amount of award:	$250-$1,000
Number of applicants:	35

Contact:
Maine Innkeepers Association
Scholarship Chairperson
304 US Route 1
Freeport, ME 04032
Phone: 207-865-6100
Fax: 207-865-6120
Web: www.maineinns.com

Maine Metal Products Association

Maine Metal Products Association Scholarship

Type of award: Scholarship.
Intended use: For undergraduate study at postsecondary institution.
Eligibility: Applicant must be permanent resident residing in Maine.
Basis for selection: Major/career interest in engineering. Applicant must demonstrate financial need, high academic

achievement, depth of character, leadership, seriousness of purpose and service orientation.
Application requirements: Recommendations, essay, transcript, proof of eligibility, nomination.
Additional information: Applicant must have career interest in Maine metals industry or related academic majors. Amount of award varies based on need and fund account. Visit Website for more information.

Number of awards:	12
Number of applicants:	30
Application deadline:	June 1
Total amount awarded:	$12,000

Contact:
Laurie Cook, Office Manager
Maine Metal Products Association
28 Stroudwater St. Suite #4
Westbrook, ME 04092
Phone: 207-854-2153
Fax: 207-854-3865
Web: www.maine-metals.org

Maine Recreation and Parks Association

Maine Recreation and Parks Association Scholarship

Type of award: Scholarship.
Intended use: For full-time undergraduate study. Designated institutions: Institutions with parks & recreation or leisure studies programs.
Eligibility: Applicant must be U.S. citizen.
Basis for selection: Major/career interest in parks/recreation. Applicant must demonstrate high academic achievement.
Application requirements: Recommendations, transcript. Send three copies of requested materials. Must send SASE to receive application form.
Additional information: For parks and recreation or leisure studies majors only. Students who intend to study physical education, wildlife management, natural resources or law enforcement are not eligible. Out-of-state applicant must attend college in Maine; Maine residents may attend out-of-state college. One $500 award reserved for high school seniors; remaining awards are for enrolled undergraduates.

Amount of award:	$500-$750
Number of awards:	3
Application deadline:	April 1
Total amount awarded:	$2,000

Contact:
Maine Recreation and Parks Association
c/o Gorham Recreation Department
270 Main St.
Gorham, ME 04038

Maine Restaurant Association

Russ Casey Scholarship

Type of award: Scholarship.

Intended use: For undergraduate or graduate study at accredited 2-year, 4-year or graduate institution. Designated institutions: New England colleges and universities.
Eligibility: Applicant must be U.S. citizen residing in Maine.
Basis for selection: Major/career interest in culinary arts. Applicant must demonstrate high academic achievement.
Application requirements: Transcript. Two recommendations from high school or college teachers, one from restaurant owner/manager or allied member of Maine Restaurant Association. Cover letter detailing applicant's interest in and connection to food service industry in 300 words or less.
Additional information: Open to Maine students pursuing career in food service industry.

Amount of award:	$1,000
Number of awards:	3
Number of applicants:	20
Application deadline:	May 1
Total amount awarded:	$3,000

Contact:
Maine Restaurant Association
P.O. Box 5060
5 Wade St.
Augusta, ME 04332

Maine Society of Professional Engineers

Maine Society of Professional Engineers Scholarship Program

Type of award: Scholarship.
Intended use: For freshman study at 2-year or 4-year institution in United States.
Eligibility: Applicant must be high school senior. Applicant must be permanent resident residing in Maine.
Basis for selection: Major/career interest in engineering or engineering, civil.
Application requirements: Recommendations, essay, transcript. Must submit SAT/ACT scores.
Additional information: Applicant must intend to earn a degree in engineering and to enter the practice of engineering after graduation. One or more scholarships awarded each year.

Amount of award:	$1,500
Number of awards:	1
Application deadline:	March 1
Notification begins:	May 30

Contact:
Robert G. Martin, P.E. NSPE
Maine Society of Professional Engineers
1387 Augusta Road
Belgrade, ME 04917-3732
Phone: 207-495-2244

Maine State Society of Washington, DC

Maine State Society of Washington, DC, Foundation Scholarship Program

Type of award: Scholarship.
Intended use: For full-time sophomore, junior or senior study at accredited 4-year institution. Designated institutions: Public or private colleges or universities in Maine.
Eligibility: Applicant must be no older than 25. Applicant must be U.S. citizen residing in Maine.
Basis for selection: Applicant must demonstrate high academic achievement and seriousness of purpose.
Application requirements: Portfolio, essay, transcript, proof of eligibility. Must have completed one academic year with 3.0 GPA.
Additional information: Must have been born in Maine or have been legal resident of Maine for at least four years or have at least one parent who was born in Maine or who has been legal resident of Maine for at least four years. Applicant must currently attend college in Maine, with a minimum GPA of 3.0 for latest academic year. Requests for applications must include SASE. Applications may be downloaded at Website.

Amount of award:	$1,000-$2,000
Number of awards:	8
Application deadline:	April 1
Total amount awarded:	$8,000

Contact:
Maine State Society Scholarship Foundation
3508 Wilson Street
Fairfax, VA 22030
Web: www.mainestatesociety.org

Manomet Center for Conservation Sciences

Kathleen S. Anderson Award

Type of award: Research grant.
Intended use: For junior, senior or graduate study in or outside United States. Designated institutions: Institutions in Western Hemisphere.
Basis for selection: Major/career interest in ornithology. Applicant must demonstrate leadership and seriousness of purpose.
Application requirements: Recommendations, research proposal.
Additional information: Research grant: Either one $1,000 award or two $500 awards. Kathleen Anderson is asked to choose winner from five finalists submitted by Manomet staff.

Amount of award:	$500-$1,000
Number of awards:	2
Number of applicants:	25
Application deadline:	December 1
Notification begins:	March 1
Total amount awarded:	$1,000

Contact:
Manomet Center for Conservation Sciences
Kathleen Anderson Award
81 Stage Point Road, P.O. Box 1770
Manomet, MA 02345
Phone: 508-224-6521
Fax: 508-224-9220
Web: www.manomet.org

Marin Community Foundation

Goldman Family Fund: New Leader Scholarship

Type of award: Scholarship, renewable.
Intended use: For full-time junior or senior study. Designated institutions: University of California, Berkeley; California State University, Hayward; San Francisco State University; San Jose State University; Sonoma State University.
Eligibility: Applicant must be U.S. citizen or permanent resident residing in California.
Basis for selection: Major/career interest in psychology; medicine; political science/government; economics; Latin american studies; sociology or social work. Applicant must demonstrate financial need, high academic achievement, leadership and service orientation.
Application requirements: Interview, recommendations, essay, transcript. Minimum 3.2 GPA, financial statement.
Additional information: Preference given to recent immigrants and students of color. Applicants should demonstrate commitment to giving back to their communities and plan to pursue career in public, legal, psychological, health or social services.

Amount of award:	$6,000
Number of awards:	8
Number of applicants:	52
Application deadline:	March 15
Total amount awarded:	$25,000

Contact:
Marin Education Fund
New Leader Scholarship of Goldman Family Fund
781 Lincoln Ave., Suite 140
San Rafael, CA 94901
Phone: 415-459-4240
Fax: 415-459-0527
Web: www.goldmanfamilyfund.org, www.marineducationfund.org

Marine Corps Scholarship Foundation

Marine Corps Scholarship

Type of award: Scholarship, renewable.
Intended use: For undergraduate study at accredited vocational, 2-year or 4-year institution in United States.
Eligibility: Applicant must be high school senior. Applicant must be U.S. citizen. Applicant must be dependent of active service person or veteran in the Marines. Must be child of

active Marine, Marine reservist, or Marine who has received honorable discharge.
Basis for selection: Applicant must demonstrate financial need.
Application requirements: Recommendations, essay, transcript, proof of eligibility. FAFSA. Photo of applicant is also required.
Additional information: Gross family income must not exceed 58K. Must be dependent of Marine or of former Marine with honorable record. Undergraduates attending post-high school vocational/technical institutions are also eligible.

Amount of award:	$500-$2,500
Number of awards:	848
Number of applicants:	1,100
Application deadline:	April 1
Total amount awarded:	$1,500,000

Contact:
Marine Corps Scholarship Foundation
P.O. Box 3008
Princeton, NJ 08543-3008
Phone: 800-292-7777
Fax: 609-452-2259
Web: www.marine-scholars.org

Maryland Higher Education Commission Office of Student Financial Assistance

Guaranteed Access Grant

Type of award: Scholarship, renewable.
Intended use: For full-time undergraduate study at accredited postsecondary institution. Designated institutions: Degree-granting institutions in Maryland.
Eligibility: Applicant must be U.S. citizen or permanent resident residing in Maryland.
Basis for selection: Applicant must demonstrate financial need.
Application requirements: Proof of eligibility. File FAFSA and G. A. Grant application by March 1 each award year.
Additional information: Applicant must have completed college preparatory program or vocational/technical program and begin college within one year of completing high school. GPA 2.5. Must meet Guaranteed Access Family Grant income requirements; award equals 100% of student's financial need.

Amount of award:	$400-$11,600
Number of awards:	733
Application deadline:	March 1
Total amount awarded:	$3,961,794

Contact:
Maryland Higher Ed. Commission Office of Student Financial Assistance
Guaranteed Access Grant
839 Bestgate Road, Suite 400
Annapolis, MD 21401-3103
Phone: 410-260-4565 or 800-974-1024
Fax: 410-260-3200
Web: www.mhec.state.md.us

Maryland Child Care Provider Scholarship

Type of award: Scholarship, renewable.
Intended use: For undergraduate study at accredited 2-year or 4-year institution in United States. Designated institutions: Maryland schools.
Eligibility: Applicant must be U.S. citizen or permanent resident residing in Maryland.
Basis for selection: Major/career interest in education or education, early childhood.
Application requirements: Must complete CCP application.
Additional information: Applicants and parents (if applicant is dependent) must be Maryland residents. Minimum 2.0 GPA. Must be enrolled in program leading to degree in child development or early childhood education. Awardees agree to work as child care provider in Maryland. Must work one year for each year, or portion thereof, award held, beginning within twelve months of graduation. Award may be renewed if eligibility is maintained. Funds may not be available to award all eligible students.

Amount of award:	$500-$2,000
Number of awards:	60
Application deadline:	June 15
Notification begins:	August 15
Total amount awarded:	$71,500

Contact:
Maryland Higher Ed. Commission Office of Student Financial Assistance
Child Care Provider Scholarship Program
839 Bestgate Road, Suite 400
Annapolis, MD 21401-1781
Phone: 410-260-4565 or 800-974-1024
Fax: 410-260-3200
Web: www.mhec.state.md.us

Maryland Delegate Scholarship

Type of award: Scholarship, renewable.
Intended use: For undergraduate or graduate study at vocational, 2-year, 4-year or graduate institution. Designated institutions: Maryland institutions.
Eligibility: Applicant must be high school senior. Applicant must be U.S. citizen, international student or or eligible non-U.S. citizen. Applicant must be residing in Maryland.
Application requirements: Proof of eligibility, nomination by local state delegate. FAFSA.
Additional information: Applicant's parents (if applicant is dependent) must be Maryland residents. Rolling application deadline. Certain vocational programs eligible. Out-of-state institutions eligible only if major not offered in Maryland. Each State Delegate makes awards to students. Non-U.S. citizens living in Maryland may be eligible. Applicants must reapply yearly for renewal and maintain satisfactory academic progress.

Amount of award:	$200-$15,700
Number of awards:	2,599
Application deadline:	March 1
Notification begins:	July 1
Total amount awarded:	$2,300,306

Contact:
Maryland Higher Ed. Commission Office of Student Financial
Assistance
Delegate Scholarship
839 Bestgate Road, Suite 400
Annapolis, MD 21401-3013
Phone: 410-260-4558 or 800-974-1024
Fax: 410-260-3200
Web: www.mhec.state.md.us

Maryland Developmental Disabilities Mental Health, Child Welfare, and Juvenile Justice Workforce Tuition Assistance Program

Type of award: Scholarship, renewable.
Intended use: For undergraduate or graduate study at 2-year
or 4-year institution. Designated institutions: Maryland schools.
Eligibility: Applicant must be U.S. citizen or permanent
resident residing in Maryland.
Basis for selection: Major/career interest in nursing;
rehabilitation/therapeutic services; occupational therapy; social
work; physical therapy; education, special or psychology.
Application requirements: Transcript, proof of eligibility.
Additional information: Applicants must major in human
services degree program or any other concentration in the
healing arts or programs providing support services to
individuals with special needs including child welfare and
juvenile justice. Awardees must agree to provide direct support
or care to individuals with developmental disabilities or to work
as a first-line supervisor of employees providing direct support
or care in a community-based program or repay the scholarship
with interest. Must begin service obligation within six months
of graduation. Priority given to applicants currently employed at
eligible institutions. Late applicants will be considered as long
as funds are available.

Amount of award:	$2,000-$3,000
Number of awards:	297
Application deadline:	July 1
Total amount awarded:	$564,250

Contact:
Maryland Higher Ed. Commission Office of Student Financial
Assistance
839 Bestgate Road, Suite 400
Annapolis, MD 24101-3013
Phone: 410-260-4565 or 800-974-1024
Web: www.mhec.state.md.us

Maryland Distinguished Scholar: Achievement

Type of award: Scholarship, renewable.
Intended use: For full-time undergraduate study at 2-year or
4-year institution. Designated institutions: Eligible Maryland
institutions.
Eligibility: Applicant must be high school junior. Applicant
must be U.S. citizen or permanent resident residing in
Maryland.
Basis for selection: Applicant must demonstrate high
academic achievement.
Application requirements: Transcript, nomination by High
school guidance counselor at end of first semester of junior
year. Applicant's highest SAT 1 scores from tests taken in
January of junior year or earlier used with GPA to determine

final eligibility. PSAT or ACT scores may be submitted if
student has not taken SAT 1.
Additional information: Applicant's parents (if applicant is
dependent) must be Maryland residents. Minimum 3.7 GPA.
Students not funded initially will be placed on waiting list;
funds may not be available to award all eligible students.
Award is automatically renewed up to three additional years if
annual minimum GPA is 3.0 and other eligibility requirements
are maintained.

Amount of award:	$3,000
Number of awards:	1,014
Notification begins:	June 30
Total amount awarded:	$2,986,500

Contact:
Maryland Higher Ed. Commission Office of Student Financial
Assistance
Distinguished Scholar Program
839 Bestgate Road, Suite 400
Annapolis, MD 21401-3013
Phone: 410-260-4565 or 800-974-1024
Fax: 410-260-3200
Web: www.mhec.state.md.us

Maryland Distinguished Scholar: National Merit and National Achievement Finalists

Type of award: Scholarship, renewable.
Intended use: For full-time undergraduate study at 2-year or
4-year institution in United States. Designated institutions:
Eligible Maryland institutions.
Eligibility: Applicant must be high school junior. Applicant
must be U.S. citizen or permanent resident residing in
Maryland.
Application requirements: Applicant must be National Merit
Finalist or National Achievement Finalist.
Additional information: Applicant's parents (if applicant is
dependent) must be Maryland residents. Minimum 3.7 GPA.
Students not funded initially will be placed on waiting list;
funds may not be available to award all eligible students.
Award is automatically renewed up to three additional years, if
annual minimum GPA is 3.0 and other eligibility requirements
are maintained.

Amount of award:	$3,000
Number of awards:	216
Total amount awarded:	$634,500

Contact:
Maryland Higher Ed. Commission Office of Student Financial
Assistance
Distinguished Scholar Program
839 Bestgate Road, Suite 400
Annapolis, MD 21401-3013
Phone: 410-260-4565 or 800-735-2258
Fax: 410-260-3200
Web: www.mhec.state.md.us

Maryland Distinguished Scholar: Talent

Type of award: Scholarship, renewable.
Intended use: For full-time undergraduate study at 2-year or
4-year institution. Designated institutions: Eligible Maryland
schools.
Eligibility: Applicant must be high school junior. Applicant
must be U.S. citizen or permanent resident residing in
Maryland.

Basis for selection: Competition/talent/interest in performing arts. Major/career interest in performing arts; theater arts or music.

Application requirements: Audition, nomination by High school in spring of junior year. In early June, nominated students must appear in person for audition or portfolio review before panel of professional judges.

Additional information: Awards for dance, drama, visual arts, and vocal and instrumental music. Winners determined by panel of judges. Applicant's parents (if applicant is dependent) must be Maryland residents. Students not funded initially will be placed on waiting list; funds may not be available to award all eligible students. Award is automatically renewed if annual minimum GPA is 3.0 and other eligibility requirements are maintained.

Amount of award:	$3,000
Number of awards:	210
Total amount awarded:	$622,500

Contact:
Maryland Higher Ed. Commission Office of Student Financial Assistance
Distinguished Scholar Program
839 Bestgate Road, Suite 400
Annapolis, MD 21401-3013
Phone: 410-260-4565 or 800-974-1024
Fax: 410-260-3200
Web: www.mhec.state.md.us

Maryland Distinguished Scholar: Teacher Education Program

Type of award: Scholarship, renewable.
Intended use: For full-time freshman, sophomore, junior or senior study at accredited 2-year or 4-year institution. Designated institutions: Eligible Maryland institutions.
Eligibility: Applicant must be residing in Maryland.
Basis for selection: Major/career interest in education, teacher; education, early childhood or education, special.
Application requirements: Eligible applicants will be contacted by the Maryland Office of Student Financial Assistance. Applicants planning to teach in critical shortage area receive priority; others are ranked on basis of GPA by class standing.
Additional information: Applicant's parents (if applicant is dependent) must be Maryland residents. Applicant must be recipient of Distinguished Scholar Award and enroll in approved course of study leading to teacher certification. Awardees agree to work as teacher in Maryland or pay back scholarship with interest. Must work one year for each year, or portion thereof, award held and begin service obligation within 12 months of graduation. Award automatically renewed if 3.0 GPA maintained. Students not funded initially will be placed on waiting list; funds may not be available to award all eligible students.

Amount of award:	$3,000
Number of awards:	64
Application deadline:	July 1
Notification begins:	August 31
Total amount awarded:	$192,000

Contact:
Maryland Higher Ed. Commission Office of Student Financial Assistance
Distinguished Scholar Teacher Ed. Program
839 Bestgate Road, Suite 400
Annapolis, MD 21401-3013
Phone: 410-260-4565 or 800-974-1024
Fax: 410-260-3200
Web: www.mhec.state.md.us

Maryland Educational Assistance Grant

Type of award: Scholarship, renewable.
Intended use: For full-time undergraduate study at 2-year or 4-year institution. Designated institutions: Maryland postsecondary schools.
Eligibility: Applicant must be U.S. citizen or permanent resident residing in Maryland.
Basis for selection: Applicant must demonstrate financial need.
Application requirements: Proof of eligibility. Must file FAFSA before March 1.
Additional information: Applicant's parents (if applicant is dependent) must be Maryland resident. Grant equals 35% of financial need. Applicants are ranked by Expected Family Contribution (EFC); those with lowest EFC are awarded first. Award may be renewed if eligibility is maintained and FAFSA is submitted by March 1 each year. Funds may not be available to award all eligible students each year.

Amount of award:	$400-$2,700
Number of awards:	18,819
Application deadline:	March 1
Notification begins:	April 15
Total amount awarded:	$34,012,606

Contact:
Maryland Higher Ed. Commission Office of Student Financial Assistance
Educational Assistance Grant
839 Bestgate Road, Suite 400
Annapolis, MD 21401-3013
Phone: 410-260-4565 or 800-974-1024
Fax: 410-260-3200
Web: www.mhec.state.md.us

Maryland Edward T. Conroy Memorial Scholarship Program

Type of award: Scholarship, renewable.
Intended use: For undergraduate or graduate study. Designated institutions: Eligible Maryland institutions.
Eligibility: Applicant must be U.S. citizen. Applicant must be veteran or disabled while on active duty; or dependent of veteran, disabled veteran or deceased veteran; or spouse of disabled veteran, deceased veteran or POW/MIA who served in the Army during Vietnam. If applicant is dependent of disabled US Armed Forces veteran, the veteran must be declared 100% disabled as direct result of military service. If applicant is disabled veteran, applicant must have declared disability of 25% or greater and have exhausted/become no longer eligible for federal veteran's educational benefits. Applicant may also be the dependent or surviving spouse of a victim of the September 11, 2001 attack who died as a result of the World Trade Center, Pentagon, or United Airlines Flight 93 tragedies. Also open to dependent or surviving spouse (not remarried) of a state or local public safety employee or volunteer who died in the line of duty. State or local public safety employees or

Scholarships

volunteers who were 100% disabled in the line of duty may also apply.

Application requirements: Must file Conroy application.
Additional information: The parent, veteran, POW, public safety employee or volunteer specified above must have been a resident of Maryland at the time of death or when declared disabled or have a disability of 25% or greater and have exhausted/become no longer eligible for federal veteran's educational benefits. Amount of award may be equal to tuition and fees, but may not exceed $7,200.

Amount of award:	$7,200
Number of awards:	72
Application deadline:	July 30
Total amount awarded:	$255,944

Contact:
Maryland Higher Ed. Commission Office of Student Financial Assistance
Edward T. Conroy Memorial Grant Program
839 Bestgate Road, Suite 400
Annapolis, MD 21401-3013
Phone: 410-260-4565 or 800-974-1024
Fax: 410-260-3200
Web: www.mhec.state.md.us

Maryland Firefighter, Ambulance and Rescue Squad Member Tuition Reimbursement Program

Type of award: Scholarship, renewable.
Intended use: For undergraduate study. Designated institutions: Degree-granting Maryland institutions.
Eligibility: Applicant must be U.S. citizen or permanent resident residing in Maryland.
Basis for selection: Major/career interest in fire science/technology or medical emergency.
Application requirements: Transcript, proof of eligibility.
Additional information: Applicant must be active career/volunteer firefighter or ambulance/rescue squad member serving the Maryland community while taking courses. Funds may not be available to award all eligible students. To renew award, student must maintain satisfactory academic progress and remain enrolled in eligible program. Payment is made one year after completion of study if recipient continues as firefighter or ambulance/resque squad member during the intervening year. Career interest in emergency medical technology eligible.

Amount of award:	$4,550
Number of awards:	153
Application deadline:	July 1
Total amount awarded:	$311,912

Contact:
Maryland Higher Ed. Commission Office of Student Financial Assistance
Reimbursement of Firefighters
839 Bestgate Road, Suite 400
Annapolis, MD 21401-3013
Phone: 410-260-4565 or 800-974-1024
Fax: 410-260-3200
Web: www.mhec.state.md.us

Maryland Jack F. Tolbert Memorial Grant

Type of award: Scholarship, renewable.
Intended use: For full-time undergraduate study at vocational institution. Designated institutions: Private career schools in Maryland.

Eligibility: Applicant must be U.S. citizen or permanent resident residing in Maryland.
Basis for selection: Applicant must demonstrate financial need.
Application requirements: Nomination by financial aid counselor at private career school. Must submit FAFSA by 3/1.
Additional information: Applicant's parents (if applicant is dependent) must be Maryland residents. Award can only be held for one semester per academic year, for two years (two awards in all).

Amount of award:	$200
Number of awards:	1,000
Total amount awarded:	$200,000

Contact:
Maryland Higher Ed. Commission Office of Student Financial Assistance
Jack F. Tolbert Memorial Grant
839 Bestgate Road, Suite 400
Annapolis, MD 21401-3013
Phone: 410-260-4565 or 800-974-1024
Fax: 410-260-3200
Web: www.mhec.state.md.us

Maryland Part-Time Grant Program

Type of award: Scholarship, renewable.
Intended use: For half-time freshman, sophomore, junior or senior study. Designated institutions: Maryland institutions.
Eligibility: Applicant must be residing in Maryland.
Basis for selection: Applicant must demonstrate financial need.
Additional information: Applicant's parents (if applicant is dependent) must be Maryland residents. Applicant must be taking 6 to 11 semester credit hours. Apply through financial aid office of Maryland institution. Funds may not be available to award all eligible students. To renew award, student must maintain satisfactory academic progress and submit FAFSA by March 1 each year; may receive award up to eight years.

Amount of award:	$200-$1,000
Number of awards:	3,173
Total amount awarded:	$1,800,000

Contact:
Maryland Higher Ed. Commission Office of Student Financial Assitance
Part-Time Grant Program
839 Bestgate Road, Suite 400
Annapolis, MD 21401-3013
Phone: 410-260-4565 or 800-974-1024
Fax: 410-260-3200
Web: www.mhec.state.md.us

Maryland Physical/Occupational Therapists and Assistants Grant

Type of award: Scholarship, renewable.
Intended use: For full-time undergraduate study at 2-year or 4-year institution. Designated institutions: Maryland institutions with professional program leading to licensure in physical/occupational therapy.
Eligibility: Applicant must be U.S. citizen or permanent resident residing in Maryland.
Basis for selection: Major/career interest in physical therapy or occupational therapy. Applicant must demonstrate high academic achievement.
Application requirements: Transcript. File FAFSA application.

Scholarships

Additional information: Applicant's parents (if applicant is dependent) must be Maryland residents. Awardees agree to work in facility that provides service to handicapped children. Must work one year for each year, or portion thereof, award held, or repay scholarship with interest. Service obligation must begin within six months of graduation. Award may be renewed up to three years if student maintains satisfactory academic progress and remains enrolled in eligible program.

Amount of award:	$2,000
Number of awards:	7
Application deadline:	July 1
Notification begins:	August 1
Total amount awarded:	$12,000

Contact:
Maryland Higher Ed. Commission Office of Student Financial Assistance
Physical and Occupational Therapy Program
839 Bestgate Road, Suite 400
Annapolis, MD 21401-3013
Phone: 410-260-4565 or 800-974-1024
Fax: 410-260-3200
Web: www.mhec.state.md.us

Maryland Senatorial Scholarship

Type of award: Scholarship, renewable.
Intended use: For freshman, sophomore, junior, senior, master's or doctoral study at postsecondary institution. Designated institutions: Maryland schools.
Eligibility: Applicant must be residing in Maryland.
Basis for selection: Applicant must demonstrate financial need.
Application requirements: Nomination by local state senator. File FAFSA by March 1.
Additional information: Applicants and parents (if applicant is dependent) must be Maryland residents. SAT or ACT required for freshmen at four-year institutions unless applicant graduated from high school five years prior to aid application or has earned 24 college credit hours. Only certain vocational programs and institutions eligible. Out-of-state institutions eligible with approved unique major status only if major not offered in Maryland. Most State Senators make awards to students in election district. Contact State Senator's office for further information and requirements. Award will be automatically renewed if satisfactory academic progress is maintained. Full-time students may be awarded four years total, part-time students eight years total.

Amount of award:	$200-$2,000
Number of awards:	5,411
Application deadline:	March 1
Total amount awarded:	$6,122,547

Contact:
Maryland Higher Ed. Commission Office of Student Financial Assitance
Senatorial Scholarship Program
839 Bestgate Road, Suite 400
Annapolis, MD 21401-3013
Phone: 410-260-4565 or 800-974-1024
Fax: 410-260-3200
Web: www.mhec.state.mc.us

Maryland Sharon Christa McAuliffe Memorial Teacher Education Award

Type of award: Scholarship, renewable.

Intended use: For undergraduate or graduate study at 2-year, 4-year or graduate institution. Designated institutions: Eligible Maryland institutions.
Eligibility: Applicant must be U.S. citizen or permanent resident residing in Maryland.
Basis for selection: Major/career interest in education, teacher or education, special. Applicant must demonstrate high academic achievement.
Application requirements: Essay, transcript. Submit McAuliffe Award application, and resume.
Additional information: Applicants must be certified teacher changing to critical shortage area, or undergraduate with at least 60 credits or college graduate wishing to be certified and teach in critical shortage area. Applicant's parents (if applicant is dependent) must be Maryland residents. Must have 3.0 GPA. Must have major/career interest in critical shortage field identified by Maryland State Department of Education. Awardees agree to work in Maryland public school teaching in critical shortage field for which student became certified for one year for each year of the award, or repay scholarship with interest. Service obligation must begin within 12 months of graduation. Funds may not be available to award all eligible students; they will initially be placed on waiting list. Award may be renewed for one additional year if student maintains eligibility.

Amount of award:	$14,775
Number of awards:	87
Application deadline:	December 31
Total amount awarded:	$528,268

Contact:
Maryland Higher Ed. Commission Office of Student Financial Assistance
S.C. McAuliffe Mem. Teacher Education Award
839 Bestgate Road, Suite 400
Annapolis, MD 21401-3013
Phone: 410-260-4565 or 800-974-1024
Fax: 410-260-3200
Web: www.mhec.state.md.us

Maryland State Nursing Scholarship and Living Expenses Grant

Type of award: Scholarship, renewable.
Intended use: For undergraduate or graduate study at accredited 2-year, 4-year or graduate institution. Designated institutions: Maryland schools.
Eligibility: Applicant must be U.S. citizen or permanent resident residing in Maryland.
Basis for selection: Major/career interest in nursing. Applicant must demonstrate financial need.
Application requirements: FAFSA filed by March 1, State Nursing Scholarship by June 30.
Additional information: Must have 3.0 GPA. Grant may provide up to $3,000 for living expenses; applicants must demonstrate financial need to receive grant. Award renewed automatically if minimum 3.0 annual GPA in college course work is maintained; student remains enrolled in eligible program and maintains satisfactory academic progress standards of institution; and, if receiving Living Expenses Grant, continues to demonstrate financial need. Applicants must agree to work as full-time nurse at eligible organization in Maryland (licensed hospital, public health agency, nursing home, home health agency, or adult day care center), one year for each year of award, or repay scholarship with interest. Service obligation must begin within six months of graduation.

Amount of award: $200-$3,000
Number of awards: 416
Application deadline: June 30
Notification begins: July 31
Total amount awarded: $891,000
Contact:
Maryland Higher Ed. Commission Office of Student Financial
Assitance
State Nursing Scholarship
839 Bestgate Road, Suite 400
Annapolis, MD 21401-3013
Phone: 410-260-4565 or 800-974-1024
Fax: 410-260-3200
Web: www.mhec.state.md.us

Maryland Tuition Reduction for Non-Resident Nursing Students

Type of award: Scholarship, renewable.
Intended use: For half-time undergraduate study at
postsecondary institution. Designated institutions: Maryland
public institutions with degree-granting nursing program.
Eligibility: Applicant must be U.S. citizen.
Basis for selection: Major/career interest in nursing.
Additional information: Must be resident of state other than
Maryland and accepted into Maryland degree-granting nursing
program at two- or four-year public institution. Must enroll as
full-time (12+ credits per semester) or part-time (6-11 credits
per semester). Awardees agree to work as nurse in state of
Maryland following graduation; two-years service required if
attending community college, four years if attending four-year
public institution. Service must begin within six months of
graduation. Award amount varies; college may reduce tuition so
that non-residents pay tuition charged to Maryland resident.
Contact:
Maryland Higher Ed. Commission Office of Student Financial
Assistance
Out-of-State Nursing Program
839 Bestgate Road, Suite 400
Annapolis, MD 21401-3013
Phone: 410-260-4565 or 800-974-1024
Fax: 410-260-3200
Web: www.mhec.state.md.us

Tuition Waiver for Foster Care Recipients

Type of award: Scholarship, renewable.
Intended use: For undergraduate study at 2-year or 4-year
institution. Designated institutions: Eligible programs at public
Maryland institutions.
Eligibility: Applicant must be no older than 21. Applicant
must be residing in Maryland.
Application requirements: Complete and file FAFSA.
Contact the financial aid office of the institution you will attend
to have the waiver activated.
Additional information: Applicant must have resided in a
foster care home in Maryland at the time of high school
graduation or completion of GED examination. Also open to
applicants who resided in a Maryland foster care home on 14th
birthday and were subsequently adopted. The Department of
Human Resources must confirm applicant's eligibility.
Applicant must be enrolled as a degree-seeking student before
age of 21. Award renewal possible if satisfactory academic
progress and enrollment in eligible program maintained.
Amount of award: Full tuition
Application deadline: March 1

Contact:
Maryland Higher Ed. Commission Office of Student Financial
Assistance
839 Bestgate Road, Suite 400
Annapolis, MD 21401-3013
Phone: 410-260-4565 or 800-974-1024
Fax: 410-260-3200
Web: www.mhec.state.md.us

Massachusetts Board of Higher Education

Massachusetts Christian A. Herter Memorial Scholarship Program

Type of award: Scholarship, renewable.
Intended use: For full-time undergraduate study at accredited
vocational, 2-year or 4-year institution.
Eligibility: Applicant must be high school sophomore or
junior. Applicant must be U.S. citizen or permanent resident
residing in Massachusetts.
Basis for selection: Applicant must demonstrate financial
need, depth of character and seriousness of purpose.
Application requirements: Interview, recommendations,
essay, transcript, nomination by high school principal,
counselor, teacher, or social service agency. Minimum 2.5 GPA.
Additional information: Program provides grant assistance
for students from low income or disadvantaged backgrounds
who have had to overcome adverse circumstances. Selection
made during sophomore and junior years in high school. Award
amount is up to half of student's demonstrated financial need.
Number of awards: 25
Number of applicants: 200
Application deadline: April 15
Total amount awarded: $900,000
Contact:
Office of Student Financial Assistance
Massachusetts Board of Higher Education
454 Broadway, Suite 200
Revere, MA 02151
Phone: 617-727-9420
Fax: 617-727-0667
Web: www.osfa.mass.edu

Massachusetts Gilbert Grant

Type of award: Scholarship, renewable.
Intended use: For full-time undergraduate study at accredited
2-year or 4-year institution. Designated institutions: Independent
colleges or hospital schools of nursing.
Eligibility: Applicant must be residing in Massachusetts.
Basis for selection: Applicant must demonstrate financial
need.
Additional information: Deadline depends on institution.
Amount of award: $250-$2,500
Number of awards: 9,200
Total amount awarded: $23,000,000
Contact:
Apply to college financial aid office.
Phone: 617-727-9420
Fax: 617-727-0667
Web: www.osfa.mass.edu

Massachusetts MASSgrant Program

Type of award: Scholarship, renewable.
Intended use: For full-time undergraduate study at accredited vocational, 2-year or 4-year institution. Designated institutions: Schools in Massachusetts, Connecticut, Maine, New Hampshire, Vermont, Rhode Island, Pennsylvania, Maryland, or Washington, DC.
Eligibility: Applicant must be U.S. citizen or permanent resident residing in Massachusetts.
Basis for selection: Applicant must demonstrate financial need.
Additional information: Applicant must have expected family contribution of less than $3,850 and be eligible for Title IV financial aid. Applicant must maintain satisfactory academic progress.

Amount of award:	$300-$2,300
Number of awards:	32,000
Number of applicants:	250,000
Application deadline:	May 1
Notification begins:	June 15
Total amount awarded:	$33,000,000

Contact:
Office of Student Financial Assistance
Massachusetts Board of Higher Education
454 Broadway, Suite 200
Revere, MA 02151
Phone: 617-727-9420
Fax: 617-727-0667
Web: www.osfa.mass.edu

Massachusetts Public Service Program

Type of award: Scholarship, renewable.
Intended use: For full-time undergraduate study at accredited 2-year or 4-year institution. Designated institutions: Massachusetts institutions.
Eligibility: Applicant must be U.S. citizen or permanent resident residing in Massachusetts. Applicant must be dependent of deceased veteran or POW/MIA. Applicant's parent must have been killed or disabled in work-related accident as fire fighter, police officer or public safety officer.
Application requirements: Proof of eligibility.
Additional information: Award in form of entitlement grant. Death of veteran, POW/MIA, police officer or firefighter parent must have been service related or in line of duty for applicant to be eligible for program. Applicant must be resident of Massachusetts at least one year prior to start of school. For recipients attending Massachusetts public college or university, award shall equal cost of tuition. Recipients attending Massachusetts independent college or university, award will be up to $2,500.

Amount of award:	$800-$2,500
Number of awards:	30
Number of applicants:	30
Application deadline:	May 1
Notification begins:	June 1
Total amount awarded:	$3,400

Contact:
Office of Student Financial Assistance
Massachusetts Board of Higher Education
454 Broadway, Suite 200
Revere, MA 02151
Phone: 617-727-9420
Fax: 617-727-0667
Web: www.osfa.mass.edu

Massachusetts Tuition Waiver

Type of award: Scholarship.
Intended use: For undergraduate study at 2-year or 4-year institution. Designated institutions: Massachusetts public institutions.
Eligibility: Applicant must be residing in Massachusetts.
Basis for selection: Applicant must demonstrate financial need.
Additional information: Amount of award varies depending on tuition; up to 100% of billed tuition may be waived (not including fees). Deadline depends on institution.

Number of awards:	25,755
Total amount awarded:	$18,095,495

Contact:
Apply to financial aid office at public college.
Phone: 617-727-9420
Fax: 617-727-0667
Web: www.osfa.mass.edu

Massachusetts Department of Education

Massachusetts Robert C. Byrd Honors Scholarship

Type of award: Scholarship, renewable.
Intended use: For full-time undergraduate study at postsecondary institution.
Eligibility: Applicant must be high school senior. Applicant must be residing in Massachusetts.
Basis for selection: Applicant must demonstrate high academic achievement, leadership and service orientation.
Application requirements: Nomination.
Additional information: Minimum 3.5 GPA required. Students are nominated by high school. See guidance officer for additional information and application procedure.

Amount of award:	$1,500
Number of awards:	132
Number of applicants:	235
Application deadline:	June 1
Total amount awarded:	$832,500

Contact:
Massachusetts Department of Education
Sally Teixeira
350 Main Street
Malden, MA 02148-5023
Phone: 781-338-6304

Massachusetts Federation of Polish Women's Clubs c/o Kosciuszko Foundation

Massachusetts Federation of Polish Women's Clubs Scholarships

Type of award: Scholarship.

Intended use: For full-time sophomore, junior or senior study at postsecondary institution in United States.

Eligibility: Applicant must be Polish. Applicant must be U.S. citizen or permanent resident.

Basis for selection: Selection based on academic excellence, motivation, and interest in Polish subjects or involvement in Polish-American community. Applicant must demonstrate financial need and high academic achievement.

Application requirements: $25 application fee. Recommendations, essay, transcript, proof of eligibility. Complete Kosciuszko Foundation tuition scholarship application form, available from October through December. Discuss background and academic and career goals in personal statement. Two letters of recommendation required. Provide proof of Polish ancestry. Include two passport photos 1.5" x 1.5" with full name printed on reverse side of each. Send SASE to confirm receipt of materials.

Additional information: Applicant must be member of Massachusetts Federation of Polish Women's Clubs. Children and grandchildren of federation members also eligible. Minimum 3.0 GPA. Only one member per immediate family may receive Massachusetts Federation of Polish Women's Scholarship during any given academic year. $25 nonrefundable application fee. Notifications made in writing in May.

> **Amount of award:** $1,250
> **Application deadline:**   January 15

Contact:
Kosciuszko Foundation
15 East 65th Street
New York, NY 10021
Phone: 212-734-2130
Fax: 212-628-4552
Web: www.kosciuszkofoundation.org

MBNA Foundation

MBNA Cleveland Scholars Program

Type of award: Scholarship, renewable.

Intended use: For full-time senior study at accredited 4-year institution in United States. Designated institutions: Ohio colleges and universities.

Eligibility: Applicant must be high school senior. Applicant must be U.S. citizen or permanent resident residing in Ohio.

Basis for selection: Applicant must demonstrate financial need, high academic achievement, depth of character, leadership, seriousness of purpose and service orientation.

Application requirements: Interview, recommendations, essay, transcript, proof of eligibility. Applicants must provide SAT or ACT scores, MBNA Financial Aid Summary, high school academic records, Candidate Recommendation Forms with application.

Additional information: Applicant must live with parents or legal guardians in city of Cleveland and graduate from a Cleveland high school. SAT I or ACT must be taken no later than December of senior year. Minimum 2.5 GPA required. Request application packets through school guidance counselors or via phone. Number of scholarships awarded varies. Award includes assigned advisors and paid summer job eligibility. Renewable for a maximum of four years. Children of MBNA employees are not eligible for this program. Visit Website for more information and application deadline.

> **Amount of award:** $7,500

Contact:
MBNA Scholars Programs Educational Testing Service
Scholarship and Recognition Programs
P.O. Box 6730
Princeton, NJ 08541-6730
Phone: 888-763-0472
Web: www.mbna.com

MBNA Delaware Scholars Program

Type of award: Scholarship, renewable.

Intended use: For full-time undergraduate study at accredited 4-year institution. Designated institutions: Delaware colleges and universities.

Eligibility: Applicant must be high school senior. Applicant must be U.S. citizen or permanent resident residing in Delaware.

Basis for selection: Applicant must demonstrate financial need, high academic achievement, depth of character, leadership, seriousness of purpose and service orientation.

Application requirements: Interview, recommendations, essay, transcript, proof of eligibility. Applicants must provide SAT or ACT scores, MBNA Financial Aid Summary, high school academic records, Candidate Recommendation Forms with application.

Additional information: Open to Delaware residents enrolling in Delaware institutions or in the University of Delaware's Parallel Program. SAT I or ACT must be taken no later than December of senior year. Minimum 2.5 GPA required. Request MBNA Scholarship Program information/packets through school guidance counselors or via phone. Number of scholarships awarded varies. Award includes assigned advisors and paid summer job eligibility. Renewable for a maximum of four years (eight consecutive semesters). Children of MNBA employees not eligible for this program. Visit Website for more information and application deadline.

> **Amount of award:** $7,500

Contact:
MBNA Scholars Programs Educational Testing Service
Scholarship and Recognition Programs
P.O. Box 6730
Princeton, NJ 08541-6730
Phone: 800-441-7048
Web: www.mbna.com

MBNA Historically Black Colleges and Universities Scholars Program

Type of award: Scholarship, renewable.

Intended use: For full-time undergraduate study at accredited 4-year institution. Designated institutions: Historically Black Colleges and Universities.

Eligibility: Applicant must be African American. Applicant must be high school senior. Applicant must be U.S. citizen or permanent resident residing in Delaware.

Basis for selection: Applicant must demonstrate financial need, high academic achievement, depth of character, leadership, seriousness of purpose and service orientation.

Application requirements: Interview, recommendations, essay, transcript, proof of eligibility. SAT or ACT scores. MBNA Financial Aid Summary. Candidate Recommendation Forms. Completed Application.

Additional information: Open to Delaware residents enrolling in Historically Black Colleges and Universities. SAT I or ACT must be taken no later than December of senior year. Minimum 2.5 GPA required. Request MBNA Scholarship Program information/packets through school guidance

Scholarships

counselors or via phone. Number of scholarships awarded varies. Award includes assigned advisors and paid summer internship eligibility. Award is renewable for a maximum of four years/eight consecutive semesters. Children of MNBA employees not eligible for this program. Visit Website for more information and application deadline.

Amount of award: $7,500

Contact:
MBNA Foundation
P.O. Box 6730
Princeton, NJ 08541-6730
Phone: 800-441-7048 ext. 25155
Web: www.mbna.com

MBNA Maine Scholars Program

Type of award: Scholarship, renewable.
Intended use: For full-time undergraduate study at 4-year institution in United States or Canada.
Eligibility: Applicant must be high school senior. Applicant must be U.S. citizen or permanent resident residing in Maine.
Basis for selection: Applicant must demonstrate financial need, high academic achievement, depth of character, leadership, seriousness of purpose and service orientation.
Application requirements: Interview, recommendations, essay, transcript, proof of eligibility. SAT/ACT scores. MBNA Financial Aid Summary. High school academic records. Candidate Recommendation Forms (in application packet).
Additional information: Open to graduating high school seniors who live in Knox or Waldo counties or following Maine school districts: 1, 9, 27, and Chebeague, Cliff Island, Long Island, Peaks Island, Frenchboro, Islesford, Cranberry Isle, Swans Island, and Monhegan. Applicant must be enrolling full-time in four-year accredited college and live with parents or legal guardians in their home state. SAT/ACT must be taken no later than December of senior year. Minimum 2.5 GPA. Request application through school guidance counselors or sponsor contact. Number of scholarships awarded varies. Award includes assigned advisors and paid summer internship eligibility, but attendance not mandatory. Renewable each year for maximum of four years (eight consecutive semesters). Children of MNBA employees not eligible. Visit Website for more information and application deadline.

Amount of award: $1,000-$7,500

Contact:
MBNA Scholars Programs Educational Testing Service
Scholarship and Recognition Programs
P.O. Box 6730
Princeton, NJ 08541-6730
Phone: 800-386-6262 ext. 65878
Web: www.mbna.com

Menominee Indian Tribe of Wisconsin

Menominee Adult Vocational Training Grant

Type of award: Scholarship, renewable.
Intended use: For undergraduate or non-degree study at accredited vocational or 2-year institution in United States.
Eligibility: Applicant must be American Indian. Applicant must be enrolled member of Menominee Indian tribe of Wisconsin.

Basis for selection: Applicant must demonstrate financial need.
Application requirements: Submit completed FAFSA and Menominee Tribal Grant Application.
Additional information: Award also applicable toward associate's degree. Must apply through college financial aid office.

Amount of award: $100-$2,200
Number of awards: 35
Number of applicants: 35
Application deadline: October 30, March 1

Contact:
Menominee Indian Tribe of Wisconsin
P.O. Box 910
Keshena, WI 54135
Phone: 715-799-5118/5110
Fax: 715-799-5102

Menominee Higher Education Scholarship

Type of award: Scholarship, renewable.
Intended use: For full-time undergraduate study at accredited 2-year or 4-year institution in United States.
Eligibility: Applicant must be American Indian. Applicant must be enrolled member of Menominee Indian tribe.
Basis for selection: Applicant must demonstrate financial need.
Application requirements: Submit completed FAFSA and Menominee Tribal Grant Application.
Additional information: Applications and deadline dates available through Tribal Education office.

Amount of award: $100-$2,200
Number of awards: 97
Number of applicants: 97

Contact:
Menominee Indian Tribe of Wisconsin
P.O. Box 910
Keshena, WI 54135
Phone: 715-799-5118/5110
Fax: 715-799-5102

Mexican American Grocers Association Foundation

Mexican American Grocers Association Scholarship

Type of award: Scholarship.
Intended use: For full-time sophomore, junior or senior study at accredited 4-year institution in United States.
Eligibility: Applicant must be Mexican American, Hispanic American or Puerto Rican.
Basis for selection: Major/career interest in business or business/management/administration. Applicant must demonstrate financial need and high academic achievement.
Application requirements: Essay, transcript.
Additional information: Minimum 2.5 GPA. Applications may be obtained beginning in April by sending a SASE. Completed application must be postmarked between June 1 and July 31. Awards presented in October or November.

Amount of award:	$500-$1,500
Number of awards:	25
Number of applicants:	1,000
Application deadline:	July 31
Notification begins:	August 15

Contact:
Mexican-American Grocers Association Foundation
Attn: Jackie Solis/Scholarship Coordinator
405 North San Fernando Road
Los Angeles, CA 90031
Phone: 323-227-1565

Michigan Higher Education Assistance Authority

Michigan Adult Part-Time Grant

Type of award: Scholarship, renewable.
Intended use: For half-time undergraduate study at 2-year or 4-year institution. Designated institutions: Michigan public or private nonprofit institutions.
Eligibility: Applicant must be U.S. citizen or permanent resident residing in Michigan.
Basis for selection: Applicant must demonstrate financial need.
Application requirements: Proof of eligibility. FAFSA.
Additional information: Number of awards varies. Apply to college financial aid office. Applications may be made at any time.

Amount of award:	$600
Number of applicants:	7,648

Contact:
College financial aid office
Web: www.michigan.gov/mistudentaid

Michigan Competitive Scholarship

Type of award: Scholarship, renewable.
Intended use: For freshman, sophomore, junior or senior study at 2-year or 4-year institution. Designated institutions: Michigan public or private nonprofit educational institutions.
Eligibility: Applicant must be U.S. citizen or permanent resident residing in Michigan.
Basis for selection: Applicant must demonstrate financial need.
Application requirements: FAFSA and qualifying ACT score.

Amount of award:	$100-$1,300
Number of awards:	29,612
Application deadline:	March 1
Total amount awarded:	$42,863,186

Contact:
Michigan Higher Education Assistance Authority
Office of Scholarships and Grants
P.O. Box 30462
Lansing, MI 48909-7962
Web: www.michigan.gov/mistudentaid

Michigan Educational Opportunity Grant

Type of award: Scholarship, renewable.

Intended use: For undergraduate study at postsecondary institution. Designated institutions: Michigan public and private nonprofit institutions.
Eligibility: Applicant must be U.S. citizen or permanent resident residing in Michigan.
Basis for selection: Applicant must demonstrate financial need.
Application requirements: Proof of eligibility. FAFSA.
Additional information: Applicant must be enrolled at least part time.

Amount of award:	$1,000
Number of awards:	5,424
Total amount awarded:	$2,225,357

Contact:
College financial aid office
Web: www.michigan.gov/mistudentaid

Michigan Robert C. Byrd Honors Scholarship

Type of award: Scholarship, renewable.
Intended use: For full-time undergraduate study at accredited postsecondary institution in United States.
Eligibility: Applicant must be high school senior. Applicant must be U.S. citizen or permanent resident residing in Michigan.
Basis for selection: Applicant must demonstrate high academic achievement.
Application requirements: Nomination by high school guidance counselor.

Amount of award:	$1,500
Total amount awarded:	$1,409,995

Contact:
Michigan Higher Education Assistance Authority
Office of Scholarships and Grants
P.O. Box 30462
Lansing, MI 48909-7966
Web: www.michigan.gov/mistudentaid

Michigan Tuition Grant

Type of award: Scholarship, renewable.
Intended use: For undergraduate, master's or doctoral study at 2-year, 4-year or graduate institution. Designated institutions: Michigan private nonprofit institutions.
Eligibility: Applicant must be U.S. citizen or permanent resident residing in Michigan.
Basis for selection: Applicant must demonstrate financial need.
Application requirements: FAFSA.

Amount of award:	$100-$2,000
Number of awards:	30,544
Application deadline:	March 1
Total amount awarded:	$57,401,294

Contact:
Michigan Higher Education Assistance Authority
Office of Scholarships and Grants
P.O. Box 30462
Lansing, MI 48909-7962
Web: www.michigan.gov/mistudentaid

Scholarships

Michigan Society of Professional Engineers

Michigan Society of Professional Engineers Scholarships

Type of award: Scholarship.
Intended use: For undergraduate study at accredited 4-year institution. Designated institutions: Must be an ABET accredited school in Michigan.
Eligibility: Applicant must be high school senior. Applicant must be U.S. citizen residing in Michigan.
Basis for selection: Major/career interest in engineering. Applicant must demonstrate high academic achievement, depth of character and leadership.
Application requirements: Recommendations, essay, transcript. 3.0 GPA, 26 ACT score for high school seniors, evidence of involvement in extracurricular activities, 500-word essay describing interest in engineering for undergraduates.
Additional information: State applicant must attend college in Michigan. Some scholarships for graduating high school seniors and some for undergraduates; majority of awards are for high school seniors. January deadline for high school seniors; April deadline for undergraduates. Undergraduates must be members of MSPE. Contact guidance counselor or local MSPE chapter for application and specific eligibility requirements.

Amount of award:	$1,500-$3,000
Number of awards:	42
Application deadline:	January 1, April 2
Notification begins:	April 1

Contact:
Scholarship Coordinator Michigan Society of Professional Engineers
P.O. Box 15276
Lansing, MI 48901-5276
Phone: 517-487-9388
Fax: 517-487-0635
Web: www.michiganspe.org

Microscopy Society of America

Microscopy Presidential Student Award

Type of award: Scholarship.
Intended use: For undergraduate or graduate study.
Basis for selection: Competition/talent/interest in research paper, based on the quality of the paper submitted for presentation at the Annual Microscopy and Microanalysis meeting. Applicant must be the first author of the submitted paper. Successful applicants must present papers at meeting to receive award. Major/career interest in science, general; biology; chemistry; physics or natural sciences.
Application requirements: Research paper (original and four copies). Supporting letter from MSA member, preferably a research advisor.
Additional information: Award consists of free registration for Annual Microscopy and Microanalysis meeting, copy of proceedings and invitation to special events. MSA also reimburses awardees for round-trip travel and student housing.

Awards are based on the quality of the paper submitted for presentation at the meeting. For more details, see Website's "Call for Abstracts" section under Microscopy and Microanalysis.

Number of awards:	10
Application deadline:	February 15
Notification begins:	March 20

Contact:
Microscopy Society of America
230 East Ohio Street
Suite 400
Chicago, IL 60611
Phone: 800-538-3672
Web: www.msa.microscopy.com

Microscopy Society of America Undergraduate Research Scholarship

Type of award: Research grant.
Intended use: For full-time junior or senior study.
Basis for selection: Major/career interest in science, general; biology; physics; chemistry or natural sciences. Applicant must demonstrate seriousness of purpose.
Application requirements: Recommendations, research proposal. Original and four copies of application form, resume including career goals and microscopy training, budget for proposed funds, and research proposal not more than three pages long. Four copies of letter from supervisor of laboratory where work will be done confirming that applicant and research project are acceptable. Two letters of reference from scientists or university faculty familiar with applicant's capabilities (four copies of each, if possible).
Additional information: Award for students interested in pursuing microscopy as career or major research tool. Applicant should be sponsored by MSA member. Must supply abstract of research project. Must have junior or senior standing by the time the work is initiated. Funds must be spent within year of award date, but in special cases may be extended to cover additional research during summer semester following graduation.

Amount of award:	$3,000
Number of awards:	6
Number of applicants:	20
Application deadline:	December 31
Notification begins:	April 1
Total amount awarded:	$16,000

Contact:
Microscopy Society of America
Undergraduate Research Scholarship
230 East Ohio Street, Suite 400
Chicago, IL 60611
Phone: 800-538-3672
Fax: 312-644-8557
Web: www.msa.microscopy.com

Microsoft Corporation

Microsoft General Scholarship

Type of award: Scholarship.
Intended use: For full-time undergraduate study. Designated institutions: College or university in the United States, Canada, or Mexico.

Basis for selection: Major/career interest in computer/ information sciences; engineering, computer; mathematics or physics. Applicant must demonstrate financial need and high academic achievement.
Application requirements: Recommendations, essay, transcript. Resume. Minimum 3.0 GPA.
Additional information: Scholarship will cover 100 percent of tuition for one academic year. All recipients required to complete salaried summer internship of 12 weeks or more at Microsoft in Redmond, Washington. Applicant must be enrolled in degree-granting program in computer science, computer engineering or related technical discipline, with demonstrated interest in computer science. See Website for important dates, more information and application.
> **Total amount awarded:** $540,000

Contact:
Microsoft Scholarship Program
Microsoft Corporation
One Microsoft Way
Redmond, WA 98052-8303
Web: www.microsoft.com/college/scholarships

Microsoft Minority Technical Scholarship

Type of award: Scholarship.
Intended use: For full-time undergraduate study. Designated institutions: College or university in the United States, Canada or Mexico.
Eligibility: Applicant must be African American, Mexican American, Hispanic American, Puerto Rican or American Indian.
Basis for selection: Major/career interest in computer/ information sciences; engineering, computer; mathematics or physics. Applicant must demonstrate financial need and high academic achievement.
Application requirements: Recommendations, essay, transcript. Resume. Minimum 3.0 GPA.
Additional information: Scholarship will cover 100 percent of tuition for one academic year. All recipients required to complete salaried summer internship of 12 weeks or more at Microsoft in Redmond, Washington. Applicant must be enrolled in degree-granting program in computer science, computer engineering or related technical discipline, with demonstrated interest in computer science. See Website for important dates, more information and application.
> **Total amount awarded:** $540,000

Contact:
Microsoft Scholarship Program
Microsoft Corporation
One Microsoft Way
Redmond, WA 98052-8303
Web: www.microsoft.com/college/scholarships

Microsoft Women's Technical Scholarship

Type of award: Scholarship.
Intended use: For full-time undergraduate study. Designated institutions: College or university in United States, Canada, or Mexico.
Eligibility: Applicant must be female.
Basis for selection: Major/career interest in computer/ information sciences; engineering, computer; mathematics or physics. Applicant must demonstrate financial need and high academic achievement.

Application requirements: Recommendations, essay, transcript. Resume. Minimum 3.0 GPA.
Additional information: Scholarship will cover 100 percent of tuition for one academic year. All recipients required to complete salaried summer internship of 12 weeks or more at Microsoft in Redmond, Washington. Applicant must be enrolled in degree-granting program in computer science, computer engineering or related technical discipline, with demonstrated interest in computer science. See Website for important dates, more information and application.
> **Total amount awarded:** $540,000

Contact:
Microsoft Scholarship Program
Microsoft Corporation
One Microsoft Way
Redmond, WA 98052-8303
Web: www.microsoft.com/college/scholarships

Midwestern Higher Education Compact

Midwest Student Exchange Program

Type of award: Scholarship, renewable.
Intended use: For full-time undergraduate, master's, doctoral or first professional study at accredited 2-year, 4-year or graduate institution in United States. Designated institutions: Participating institutions in Kansas, Michigan, Minnesota, Missouri, Nebraska, and North Dakota.
Eligibility: Applicant must be residing in Michigan, Minnesota, Nebraska, Kansas, Missouri or North Dakota.
Application requirements: Proof of eligibility.
Additional information: Reduced tuition rate for Kansas, Michigan, Minnesota, Missouri, Nebraska, and North Dakota residents attending participating out-of-state institutions in one of five other states in designated institutions or programs of study. For information, contact high school counselor or college admissions officer. For a list of participating institutions and programs, and for individual state contact information, visit MHEC Website.
> **Amount of award:** Full tuition
> **Number of awards:** 2,533
> **Total amount awarded:** $9,340,000

Contact:
Midwestern Higher Education Compact - MSEP Program Officer
1300 South 2nd Street
Suite 130
Minneapolis, MN 55454-1079
Phone: 612-626-1602
Fax: 612-626-8290
Web: www.mhec.org

Military Order of the Purple Heart

Military Order of the Purple Heart Scholarship

Type of award: Scholarship, renewable.

Intended use: For full-time undergraduate study at vocational, 2-year, 4-year or graduate institution.

Eligibility: Applicant must be U.S. citizen. Applicant must be descendant of veteran; or dependent of veteran.

Basis for selection: Applicant must demonstrate high academic achievement.

Application requirements: $5 application fee. Recommendations, essay, transcript, proof of eligibility. Two letters of recommendation, SAT/ACT scores, copy of birth certificate, 200-300 words or more essay explaining "Why I Wish to Attend College," proof of Purple Heart Award or copy of Life Membership Card.

Additional information: Must have 3.5 GPA or higher. Contact the Military Order of the Purple Heart or for applications, deadline information, award amounts and other details. Applications available October 1. Applicant must be a direct descendent (child, grandchild--natural or adopted) or the spouse of an MOPH member in good standing.

    Amount of award: $1,750
    Application deadline: March 31
Contact:
Military Order of the Purple Heart
Scholarship Coordinator
5413-B Backlick Road
Springfield, VA 22151
Phone: 703-642-5360
Fax: 703-642-2054
Web: www.PurpleHeart.org

Minnesota Department of Veterans Affairs

Minnesota Educational Assistance for Veterans

Type of award: Research grant.

Intended use: For undergraduate or graduate study at postsecondary institution. Designated institutions: All Minnesota institutions except the University of Minnesota.

Eligibility: Applicant must be residing in Minnesota. Applicant must be veteran.

Application requirements: Proof of eligibility.

Additional information: Applicant must have exhausted eligible federal educational benefits. Grant is one-time award. Information also available from institution or county veterans service officer.

    Amount of award: $750
Contact:
Minnesota Department of Veterans Affairs
Veterans Service Building, 2nd Floor
20 West 12 Street
St. Paul, MN 55155

Minnesota Educational Assistance for War Orphans

Type of award: Scholarship, renewable.

Intended use: For full-time undergraduate study at accredited vocational, 2-year or 4-year institution. Designated institutions: Approved Minnesota schools.

Eligibility: Applicant must be residing in Minnesota. Applicant must be dependent of deceased veteran. Veteran's death must have been on active duty or service connected.

Application requirements: Proof of eligibility.

Additional information: All recipients receive stipend and tuition waiver. Program not accepted at University of Minnesota. Information also available from institution or county veterans service officer. Applicant must be resident of Minnesota for two years prior to application and parent must have been in Minnesota at time of active duty. Available until recipient obtains bachelor's degree or equivalent.

    Amount of award: $750
Contact:
Minnesota Department of Veterans Affairs
Veterans Service Building, 2nd Floor
20 West 12 Street
St. Paul, MN 55155-2079

Minnesota Higher Education Services Office

Minnesota Post-Secondary Child Care Grant

Type of award: Scholarship, renewable.

Intended use: For freshman, sophomore, junior or senior study at accredited vocational, 2-year or 4-year institution. Designated institutions: Eligible Minnesota schools.

Eligibility: Applicant must be U.S. citizen or permanent resident residing in Minnesota.

Basis for selection: Applicant must demonstrate financial need.

Additional information: Apply at college's financial aid office. Eligibility limited to applicants with children 12 years or younger. Award amount prorated upon enrollment. Maximum of $2,200 per eligible child per academic year. Applicant cannot receive Aid to Families with Dependent Children, Minnesota Family Investment Program, tuition reciprocity, or be in default of loan. Those with bachelor's degree or eight semesters or 12 quarters of credit, or equivalent, are not eligible. Applicant must be enrolled at least half-time in nonsectarian program and must be in good academic standing. Award based on family income and size. Deadlines established by individual institution.

    Amount of award: $2,200
    Number of awards: 2,429
    Total amount awarded: $4,750,526
Contact:
MHESO
1450 Energy Park Drive, Suite 350
St. Paul, MN 55108-5227
Phone: 651-642-0567 or 800-657-3866
Web: www.mheso.state.mn.us

Minnesota Safety Officers Survivors Program

Type of award: Scholarship.

Intended use: For undergraduate or non-degree study at accredited postsecondary institution.

Eligibility: Applicant must be residing in Minnesota. Applicant's parent must have been killed or disabled in work-related accident as fire fighter, police officer or public safety officer.

Application requirements: Proof of eligibility. Eligibility certificate.

Additional information: Must be enrolled in degree or certificate program at institution participating in State Grant Program. Also eligible if parent or spouse, not officially employed in public safety, was killed while assisting public safety officer or offering emergency medical assistance. Obtain eligibility certificate from Department of Public Safety, 211 Transportation Building, St. Paul, MN 55155. Apply through financial aid office.

Number of awards:	12
Number of applicants:	12
Total amount awarded:	$38,191

Contact:
MHESO
1450 Energy Park Drive, Suite 350
St. Paul, MN 55108-5227
Phone: 651-642-0567 or 800-657-3866
Web: www.mheso.state.mn.us

Minnesota State Grant Program

Type of award: Scholarship, renewable.
Intended use: For undergraduate study at accredited vocational, 2-year or 4-year institution. Designated institutions: Minnesota institutions.
Eligibility: Applicant must be U.S. citizen or permanent resident residing in Minnesota.
Basis for selection: Applicant must demonstrate financial need.
Application requirements: Proof of eligibility.
Additional information: Must not have completed four years of college. If not Minnesota high school graduate and parents not residents of Minnesota, applicant must be resident of Minnesota for at least one year. Cannot be in default on loans or delinquent on child-support payments. FAFSA used as application for Minnesota State Grant. Application deadline is 14 days from term start date.

Amount of award:	$100-$7,662
Number of awards:	6,500
Number of applicants:	133,000
Application deadline:	June 30
Total amount awarded:	$115,700,000

Contact:
MHESO
1450 Energy Park Drive, Suite 350
St. Paul, MN 55108-5227
Phone: 651-642-0567 or 800-657-3866
Web: www.mheso.state.mn.us

Miss America Organization

Albert A. Marks, Jr., Scholarship for Teacher Education

Type of award: Scholarship, renewable.
Intended use: For undergraduate or graduate study at postsecondary institution.
Eligibility: Applicant must be female.
Basis for selection: Major/career interest in education. Applicant must demonstrate financial need and high academic achievement.
Application requirements: Recommendations, essay, transcript, proof of eligibility.
Additional information: Must be pursuing a degree (undergraduate, masters or higher) in education. Must have

competed in Miss America system in local, state or national level after 1993. Notification begins in September.

Application deadline:	June 30

Contact:
Miss America Organization
Two Miss America Way
Atlantic City, NJ 08401
Phone: 609-345-7571 ext. 27
Fax: 609-347-6079
Web: www.missamerica.org

Dr. & Mrs. David B. Allman Medical Scholarship

Type of award: Scholarship, renewable.
Intended use: For undergraduate or graduate study at postsecondary institution.
Eligibility: Applicant must be female.
Basis for selection: Major/career interest in medicine. Applicant must demonstrate financial need and high academic achievement.
Application requirements: Recommendations, essay, transcript, proof of eligibility. MCAT scores.
Additional information: Must be pursuing a degree (undergraduate, graduate or higher) in medicine. Must have competed in Miss America system at local, state or national level after 1993. Notification begins in August.

Application deadline:	June 30

Contact:
Miss America Organization
Two Miss America Way
Suite 1000
Atlantic City, NJ 08401
Phone: 609-345-7571 ext. 27
Fax: 609-347-6079
Web: www.missamerica.org

Eugenia Vellner Fischer Award for the Performing Arts

Type of award: Scholarship, renewable.
Intended use: For undergraduate or graduate study at postsecondary institution.
Eligibility: Applicant must be female.
Basis for selection: Major/career interest in performing arts. Applicant must demonstrate financial need and high academic achievement.
Application requirements: Recommendations, essay, transcript, proof of eligibility.
Additional information: Must be pursuing degree (undergraduate, master or higher) in the performing arts, such as dance or music. Must have competed in Miss America system in local, state or national level after 1993. Notification begins in September.

Application deadline:	June 30

Contact:
Miss America Organization
Two Miss America Way
Atlantic City, NJ 08401
Phone: 609-345-7571 ext. 27
Fax: 609-347-6079
Web: www.missamerica.org

Leonard C. Horn Award for Legal Studies

Type of award: Scholarship, renewable.

Intended use: For undergraduate or graduate study at postsecondary institution.
Eligibility: Applicant must be female.
Basis for selection: Major/career interest in law.
Application requirements: Recommendations, essay, transcript, proof of eligibility. LSAT score.
Additional information: Must be pursuing degree (undergraduate, masters or higher) in field of law. Must have competed within Miss America system at local, state or national level after 1993. Notification begins in September.

   Application deadline: June 30
Contact:
Miss America Organization
Two Atlantic Way
Suite 1000
Atlantic City, NJ 08401
Phone: 609-345-7571 ext. 27
Fax: 609-347-6079
Web: www.missamerica.org

Miss America Competition Awards

Type of award: Scholarship.
Intended use: For undergraduate, graduate or non-degree study at accredited postsecondary institution.
Eligibility: Applicant must be single, female, at least 17, no older than 24. Applicant must be U.S. citizen.
Basis for selection: Competition/talent/interest in poise/talent/fitness. Applicant must demonstrate depth of character, leadership, patriotism, seriousness of purpose and service orientation.
Application requirements: Proof of eligibility.
Additional information: Local winners go on to compete at state level, and state winners compete for Miss America. Contestants will apply their talent, intelligence, and speaking ability, and exercise their commitment to community service. Cash and tuition-based scholarships available at every level of competition. Some scholarships awarded at the National Level are as follows: first runner-up receives $40,000; second runner-up receives $30,000; third runner-up receives $25,000; fourth runner-up receives $20,000; and Miss America receives $50,000 in scholarship monies. Deadlines for local competitions vary. Contact the Miss America Organization for more information or visit Website.

   Amount of award: $2,000-$50,000
   Total amount awarded: $40,000,000
Contact:
Miss America Organization
Two Miss America Way
Suite 1000
Atlantic City, NJ 08401
Phone: 609-345-7571 ext. 27
Fax: 609-347-6079
Web: www.missamerica.org

Mississippi Office of State Student Financial Aid

Gulf Coast Research Laboratory Minority Summer Grant

Type of award: Research grant.
Intended use: For undergraduate or graduate study. Designated institutions: Gulf Coast Research Laboratory.

Eligibility: Applicant must be Alaskan native, Asian American, African American, Mexican American, Hispanic American, Puerto Rican or American Indian. Applicant must be U.S. citizen or permanent resident residing in Mississippi.
Basis for selection: Major/career interest in oceanography/marine studies or environmental science.
Additional information: Must be undergraduate or graduate student at Mississippi college or university. Program provides summer grants for minority students to attend classes or conduct independent study at Gulf Coast Research Laboratory in Gulf Coast Research Laboratory Summer Academic Institute. Four- to ten-week program. Stipend for four week program is $100, for five week program $125 and for ten week program $250. College credit possible, depending on grant holder's educational institution. Number of awards depends upon availability of funds. Call 228-872-4200 or 800-327-2980 for application. Apply early for best results.

   Application deadline: March 31
Contact:
Mississippi Office of Student Financial Aid
3825 Ridgewood Road
Jackson, MS 39211-6453
Phone: 601-432-6997
Fax: 601-432-6527
Web: www.ihl.state.ms.us

Mississippi Office of Student Financial Aid

Leveraging Educational Assistance Partnership Program (LEAP)

Type of award: Scholarship, renewable.
Intended use: For full-time undergraduate study at accredited 2-year or 4-year institution. Designated institutions: Mississippi colleges and universities.
Eligibility: Applicant must be enrolled in high school. Applicant must be U.S. citizen or permanent resident residing in Mississippi.
Basis for selection: Applicant must demonstrate financial need and high academic achievement.
Application requirements: Recommendations, proof of eligibility. FAFSA.
Additional information: Must meet general requirements for participation in federal student aid program. Award amount varies. Apply to college financial aid office.
Contact:
Mississippi Student Financial Aid
3825 Ridgewood Road
Jackson, MS 39211-6453
Phone: 601-432-6997
Web: www.ihl.state.ms.us

Mississippi Eminent Scholars Grant

Type of award: Scholarship, renewable.
Intended use: For full-time undergraduate study at accredited vocational, 2-year or 4-year institution. Designated institutions: Eligible Mississippi institutions.
Eligibility: Applicant must be high school senior. Applicant must be residing in Mississippi.
Basis for selection: Applicant must demonstrate high academic achievement.

Additional information: Applicant must be high school senior and resident of Mississippi for at least one year. Must have minimum 3.5 GPA. Must have ACT of 29 or SAT of 1280, or be recognized as a semifinalist or finalist by the National Merit Scholarship Program or the National Achievement Scholarship Program.

    Amount of award: $2,500
    Application deadline: September 15
Contact:
Mississippi Student Financial Aid
3825 Ridgewood Road
Jackson, MS 39211-6453
Phone: 601-432-6997
Web: www.ihl.state.ms.us

Mississippi Higher Education Legislative Plan for Needy Students

Type of award: Scholarship, renewable.
Intended use: For full-time freshman or sophomore study at accredited 2-year or 4-year institution. Designated institutions: Eligible Mississippi institutions.
Eligibility: Applicant must be U.S. citizen residing in Mississippi.
Basis for selection: Applicant must demonstrate financial need.
Application requirements: Application. FAFSA.
Additional information: Minimum 2.5 GPA and 20 on ACT. Must be legal resident of Mississippi for at least two years. Student's family must have adjusted gross income of $36,500 or less over the prior two years. Amount and number of awards depend upon availability of funds. Apply early for best results.

    Application deadline: March 31
Contact:
Mississippi Office of Student Financial Aid
3825 Ridgewood Road
Jackson, MS 39211-6453
Phone: 601-432-6997
Web: www.ihl.state.ms.us

Mississippi Law Enforcement Officers & Firemen Scholarship

Type of award: Scholarship, renewable.
Intended use: For full-time undergraduate study at 2-year or 4-year institution. Designated institutions: Mississippi public colleges and universities.
Eligibility: Applicant must be residing in Mississippi. Applicant's parent must have been killed or disabled in work-related accident as fire fighter, police officer or public safety officer.
Application requirements: Proof of eligibility.
Additional information: Award covers tuition, housing, and fees at Mississippi public institutions. Spouses also eligible.

    Amount of award: Full tuition
Contact:
Mississippi Office of Student Financial Aid
3825 Ridgewood Road
Jackson, MS 39211-6453
Phone: 601-432-6997
Fax: 601-432-6527
Web: www.ihl.state.ms.us

Mississippi Resident Tuition Assistance Grant

Type of award: Scholarship, renewable.

Intended use: For full-time undergraduate study at accredited vocational, 2-year or 4-year institution. Designated institutions: Eligible Mississippi institutions.
Eligibility: Applicant must be U.S. citizen residing in Mississippi.
Application requirements: Submit FAFSA and Student Aid Report.
Additional information: Applicant must be resident of Mississippi for no less than one year. Must be receiving less than full Federal Pell Grant. First-time freshman applicants (high school seniors) must have minimum 2.5 GPA and ACT score of 15. Other first-time applicants must have 2.5 GPA. Award is up to $500 per year for freshmen and sophomores; up to $1,000 per year for juniors and seniors. Recipients must maintain 2.5 GPA to reapply. Applicants must not be in default on an educational loan.

    Amount of award: $500-$1,000
    Application deadline: September 15
Contact:
Mississippi Student Financial Aid
3825 Ridgewood Road
Jackson, MS 39211-6453
Phone: 601-432-6997
Web: www.ihl.state.ms.us

Mississippi Southeast Asia POW/MIA Scholarship

Type of award: Scholarship, renewable.
Intended use: For full-time undergraduate study at 2-year or 4-year institution. Designated institutions: Mississippi public institutions.
Eligibility: Applicant must be U.S. citizen or permanent resident residing in Mississippi. Applicant must be dependent of POW/MIA who served in the Army, Air Force, Marines or Navy during Vietnam.
Application requirements: Proof of eligibility.
Additional information: Award covers cost of tuition, housing and fees at a Mississippi public institution. Notification upon receipt of required documents.

    Amount of award: Full tuition
Contact:
Mississippi Office of Student Financial Aid
3825 Ridgewood Road
Jackson, MS 39211-6453
Phone: 601-432-6997
Fax: 601-432-6527
Web: www.ihl.state.ms.us

Missouri Department of Elementary and Secondary Education

Missouri Minority Teaching Scholarship

Type of award: Scholarship, renewable.
Intended use: For full-time undergraduate or master's study at accredited 2-year or 4-year institution in United States. Designated institutions: Missouri institutions.
Eligibility: Applicant must be Alaskan native, Asian American, African American, Mexican American, Hispanic American,

Puerto Rican or American Indian. Applicant must be returning adult student, high school senior. Applicant must be residing in Missouri.
Basis for selection: Major/career interest in education. Applicant must demonstrate high academic achievement.
Application requirements: Recommendations, essay, transcript, proof of eligibility.
Additional information: Must rank in top 25 percent of class. Must score in top 25 percent on ACT or SAT. If in college, may have 3.0 GPA at 30 hours to qualify. If college graduate, may receive award if returning to a master's level math or science education program. Upon graduation, recipient must teach for five years in Missouri public schools or scholarship becomes loan.

Amount of award:	$3,000
Number of awards:	100
Application deadline:	February 15
Notification begins:	April 15

Contact:
Missouri Department of Elementary and Secondary Education
Educator Recruitment and Retention
P.O. Box 480
Jefferson City, MO 65102
Phone: 573-751-1668
Fax: 573-526-3580
Web: www.dese.mo.gov

Missouri Robert C. Byrd Honors Scholarship

Type of award: Scholarship, renewable.
Intended use: For undergraduate study at accredited 4-year institution in United States. Designated institutions: Eligible Missouri institutions.
Eligibility: Applicant must be high school senior. Applicant must be U.S. citizen or permanent resident residing in Missouri.
Basis for selection: Applicant must demonstrate high academic achievement.
Application requirements: Transcript.
Additional information: Applicant must be completing high school or GED in year of application. Must be in top 10 percent of class or have GED score at or above national 90th percentile. Final selection at each congressional district level based on SAT/ACT scores and GPA. Award amount varies; contact sponsor for more information. Applicant's high school guidance counselor must sign and verify application form. After graduating from a Missouri postsecondary institution, student must teach in Missouri for five years.

Amount of award:	$1,500
Application deadline:	April 15
Notification begins:	October 1

Contact:
Missouri Department of Elementary and Secondary Education
Robert C. Byrd Honors Scholarship
P.O. Box 480
Jefferson City, MO 65102
Phone: 573-751-1668
Fax: 573-526-3580
Web: www.dese.mo.gov

Missouri Teacher Education Scholarship

Type of award: Scholarship.
Intended use: For full-time freshman or sophomore study.
Designated institutions: Accredited Missouri schools.

Eligibility: Fifteen percent of awards set aside for minorities. Applicant must be high school senior. Applicant must be U.S. citizen residing in Missouri.
Basis for selection: Major/career interest in education. Applicant must demonstrate high academic achievement.
Application requirements: Recommendations, essay, transcript, proof of eligibility. ACT/SAT and class rank.
Additional information: Must rank in top 15 percent of graduating class or score in top 15 percent on ACT, SAT I, or other standardized tests. Must teach in Missouri public school for five years after graduation or scholarship becomes a loan.

Amount of award:	$2,000
Number of awards:	240
Number of applicants:	500
Application deadline:	February 15
Notification begins:	April 15
Total amount awarded:	$240,000

Contact:
Missouri Department of Elementary and Secondary Education
Educator Recruitment and Retention
P.O. Box 480
Jefferson City, MO 65102
Phone: 573-751-1668
Fax: 573-526-3580
Web: www.dese.mo.gov

Missouri Department of Higher Education

Charles Gallagher Student Financial Assistance Program

Type of award: Scholarship, renewable.
Intended use: For full-time undergraduate study at accredited vocational, 2-year or 4-year institution in United States. Designated institutions: Approved Missouri public or private schools.
Eligibility: Applicant must be U.S. citizen or permanent resident residing in Missouri.
Basis for selection: Applicant must demonstrate financial need.
Application requirements: Proof of eligibility. FAFSA must be received by central processor by April 1.
Additional information: May be used only toward first postsecondary degree. May not be used for theology or divinity studies. Awards vary, depending on cost of school.

Amount of award:	$100-$1,500
Number of awards:	13,797
Number of applicants:	108,000
Application deadline:	April 1
Notification begins:	July 1
Total amount awarded:	$17,323,495

Contact:
Missouri Department of Higher Education
3515 Amazonas Drive
Jefferson City, MO 65109
Phone: 800-473-6757
Fax: 573-751-6635
Web: www.dhe.mo.gov

Marguerite Ross Barnett Memorial Scholarship

Type of award: Scholarship, renewable.
Intended use: For half-time undergraduate study at postsecondary institution in United States. Designated institutions: Participating Missouri schools.
Eligibility: Applicant must be at least 18. Applicant must be U.S. citizen or permanent resident residing in Missouri.
Basis for selection: Applicant must demonstrate financial need.
Application requirements: Proof of eligibility. Applicant must complete FAFSA and be employed and compensated for at least 20 hours per week.
Additional information: For students employed while attending school part-time. Apply early; scholarship awarded on first-come, first-served basis for nonrenewal students. Maximum award is tuition charged at school of part-time enrollment; amount of tuition charged to Missouri undergraduate resident enrolled part-time in same class level at University of Missouri-Columbia; or demonstrated financial need. Employer must verify applicant's employment. Recipient may not be pursuing degree in theology or divinity. Application available on Website.

    Application deadline: April 1
Contact:
Missouri Department of Higher Education
3515 Amazonas Drive
Jefferson City, MO 65109
Phone: 800-473-6757
Fax: 573-751-6635
Web: www.dhe.mo.gov

Missouri College Guarantee Program

Type of award: Scholarship.
Intended use: For full-time undergraduate study at postsecondary institution in United States. Designated institutions: Participating Missouri schools.
Eligibility: Applicant must be U.S. citizen or permanent resident residing in Missouri.
Basis for selection: Applicant must demonstrate financial need and high academic achievement.
Application requirements: Proof of eligibility. FAFSA. Must have participated in high school extracurricular activities.
Additional information: Maximum award is based on fees charged at University of Missouri campus with the largest enrollment and standard book allowance determined by board. Minimum 20 on ACT/950 on SAT. Minimum 2.5 GPA. Recipient may not be pursuing degree in theology or divinity.
    Application deadline: April 1
Contact:
Missouri Department of Higher Education
3515 Amazonas Drive
Jefferson City, MO 65109
Phone: 800-473-6757
Fax: 573-751-6635
Web: www.dhe.mo.gov

Missouri Department of Higher Education Vietnam Veteran's Survivor Grant Program

Type of award: Scholarship.

Intended use: For full-time undergraduate study at postsecondary institution. Designated institutions: Missouri postsecondary institutions.
Eligibility: Applicant must be residing in Missouri. Applicant must be dependent of deceased veteran; or spouse of deceased veteran.
Additional information: For children and spouses of Vietnam veterans whose death was attributed to or caused by exposure to toxic chemicals during Vietnam conflict. Applicant cannot pursue degree in theology or divinity. Applications accepted in January; end date based on fund availability. Amount of award varies. Maximum amount is the least of actual tuition charged at school where applicant is enrolled, or the average amount of tuition charged to an undergraduate Missouri resident enrolled full-time in same class level and academic major at regional four-year public Missouri institutions.
    Number of awards: 11
    Total amount awarded: $30,790
Contact:
Missouri Department of Higher Education
3515 Amazonas Drive
Jefferson City, MO 65109
Phone: 800-473-6757
Fax: 573-751-6635
Web: www.dhe.mo.gov

Missouri Higher Education Academic Scholarship

Type of award: Scholarship, renewable.
Intended use: For full-time undergraduate study at accredited vocational, 2-year or 4-year institution in United States. Designated institutions: Approved Missouri public or private schools.
Eligibility: Applicant must be U.S. citizen or permanent resident residing in Missouri.
Basis for selection: Applicant must demonstrate high academic achievement.
Application requirements: Proof of eligibility. Academic progress required.
Additional information: Program also known as "Bright Flight." May not be used for theology or divinity studies. SAT/ACT scores required for determining academic achievement; composite scores must be in top three percent of state students. Must achieve qualifying scores by June assessment date of senior year. Application deadline is June assessment date of senior year. No paper application needed. Check with high school counselor or financial aid administrator for additional information. Also see Website.
    Amount of award: $2,000
    Number of awards: 7,538
    Total amount awarded: $14,308,835
Contact:
Missouri Department of Higher Education
3515 Amazonas Drive
Jefferson City, MO 65109
Phone: 800-473-6757
Fax: 573-751-6635
Web: www.dhe.mo.gov

Missouri Public Service Survivor Grant

Type of award: Scholarship, renewable.
Intended use: For full-time undergraduate study at accredited vocational, 2-year or 4-year institution in United States.

Designated institutions: Approved Missouri public or private schools.

Eligibility: Applicant must be U.S. citizen or permanent resident residing in Missouri. Applicant's parent must have been killed or disabled in work-related accident as fire fighter, police officer or public safety officer.

Application requirements: Proof of eligibility.

Additional information: For spouses or children of Missouri public safety officers, including law enforcement, firefighters, corrections, water safety and conservation officers, killed or totally and permanently disabled in the line of duty. Children or spouses of Missouri Department of Highway and Transportation employees also eligible if parent died during performance of job. May not be used for theology or divinity studies. Award amounts vary; contact sponsor for information. Estimated amount is based on 12 credit hours at chosen institution or no more than 12 hours at University of Missouri. Application date is based on fund availability.

Number of awards:	15
Total amount awarded:	$37,354

Contact:
Missouri Department of Higher Education
3515 Amazonas Drive
Jefferson City, MO 65109
Phone: 800-473-6757
Fax: 573-751-6635
Web: www.dhe.mo.gov

Missouri League for Nursing

Missouri League for Nursing Scholarship

Type of award: Scholarship, renewable.

Intended use: For full-time sophomore, junior, senior or master's study.

Eligibility: Applicant must be U.S. citizen residing in Missouri.

Basis for selection: Major/career interest in nursing. Applicant must demonstrate financial need and high academic achievement.

Application requirements: 3.0 GPA, second year or more in nursing school.

Additional information: Scholarship must be used for study in Missouri. Amount of award varies. Applications can be obtained from dean of nationally recognized accredited schools of nursing in Missouri.

Number of awards:	3
Number of applicants:	60
Application deadline:	October 20
Notification begins:	September 1

Contact:
Contact dean of school of nursing programs in Missouri.

Montana Board of Regents of Higher Education

Leveraging Educational Assistance Partnership Program

Type of award: Scholarship.

Intended use: For undergraduate study. Designated institutions: Montana postsecondary institutions.

Eligibility: Applicant must be residing in Montana.

Basis for selection: Applicant must demonstrate financial need.

Amount of award:	$200-$600
Number of awards:	800
Total amount awarded:	$370,000

Contact:
Contact college financial aid office for application information.

Montana Tuition Fee Waiver for Dependents of POW/MIA

Type of award: Scholarship.

Intended use: For undergraduate or graduate study at accredited postsecondary institution. Designated institutions: Montana University system institutions.

Eligibility: Applicant must be residing in Montana. Applicant must be dependent of POW/MIA; or spouse of POW/MIA.

Application requirements: The following information must be provided: 1) Proof that your parent or spouse was declared by the Secretary of Defense to be a prisoner of war or missing or captured in connection with the conflict in Southeast Asia after January 1, 1961; 2) Proof that you are the spouse or child and dependent of the prisoner of war; 3) Proof that the prisoner of war was a Montana resident at the time he or she became a prisoner of war. Eligibility for waiver continues until completion of B.A. or certification of completion, as long as eligibility requirements continue to be met.

Additional information: Contact college financial aid office for application information.

Amount of award:	Full tuition

Contact:
Montana Board of Regents of Higher Eduaction
PO Box 203101
Helena, MT 59620-3101

Montana Tuition Fee Waiver for Veterans

Type of award: Scholarship.

Intended use: For undergraduate or graduate study. Designated institutions: Montana University system institutions.

Eligibility: Applicant must be permanent resident residing in Montana. Applicant must be veteran. Must have been honorably discharged person who served with the United States forces during wartime.

Application requirements: Proof of eligibility. Veterans who have served in the armed forces subsequent to the conflict in Vietnam are eligible for a fee waiver if the following conditions are met: 1) The veteran has been awarded an Armed Forces Expeditionary Medal for service in Lebanon, Grenada, or Panama or the veteran served in a combat theater in the Persian Gulf between August 2, 1990 and April 11, 1991 and received the Southwest Asia Service Medal; 2) The veteran is pursuing his or her initial undergraduate degree.

Additional information: Must have used up all federal veterans educational assistance benefits. Contact college financial aid office.

Amount of award:	Full tuition

Contact:
Montana University System
PO Box 203101
Helena, MT 59620-3101
Web: www.mgslp.state.mt.us

Montana University System Community College Honor Scholarship

Type of award: Scholarship.
Intended use: For junior study at 4-year institution.
Designated institutions: Montana University system institutions.
Eligibility: Applicant must be residing in Montana.
Basis for selection: Applicant must demonstrate high academic achievement.
Application requirements: Recommendations, proof of eligibility. Must be graduate with associate degree from and be recommended by president/faculty of accredited Montana community college.
Additional information: Holder of scholarship must enter Montana University System within nine months after receiving associate degree. Award provides for tuition/fee waiver in any unit of Montana University System. The waiver will be valid through the completion of the first academic year (two semesters) of enrollment, exclusive of any credits earned prior to high school or community college graduation.

Amount of award:	Full tuition

Contact:
Financial aid office of community college.
Web: www.mgslp.state.mt.us

Montana University System High School Honor Scholarship

Type of award: Scholarship.
Intended use: For freshman study at 4-year institution.
Designated institutions: Montana University system campus and Dawson, Flathead Valley, or Miles community colleges.
Eligibility: Applicant must be high school senior. Applicant must be U.S. citizen, international student or foreign student who has been exchange student. Applicant must be residing in Montana.
Basis for selection: Applicant must demonstrate high academic achievement.
Application requirements: Recommendations, transcript, proof of eligibility.
Additional information: Obtain information from high school guidance counselor who completes application for recommended students. Must have 3.0 GPA. Terms of award and which fees are covered specified at time scholarship is awarded. The scholarship must be utilized within nine months after high school graduation. The waiver will be valid through the completion of the first academic year, exclusive of any credit earned prior to high school graduation. Eligibility will continue for no more than three years after the date of issuance, provided satisfactory academic progress is maintained.

Amount of award:	Full tuition
Application deadline:	March 31

Contact:
Montana Board of Regents of Higher Education
PO Box 203101
Helena, MT 59620-3101
Web: www.mgslp.state.mt.us

Montana Trappers Association

MTA Doug Slifka Memorial Scholarship

Type of award: Scholarship.
Intended use: For undergraduate study. Designated institutions: Any college or university.
Eligibility: Applicant must be at least 15, no older than 25. Applicant must be residing in Montana.
Basis for selection: Major/career interest in environmental science; life sciences; natural resources/conservation or wildlife/fisheries. Applicant must demonstrate depth of character and seriousness of purpose.
Application requirements: Interview, recommendations, essay, transcript. Essay or story on trapping or conservation. Recommendations by MTA members, teachers, or other important individuals. Endorsement of MTA District Director (or subdirector) where applicant resides. Student involvement in activities that include MTA programs, trapping, school programs, and community service.
Additional information: Applicant may be member of MTA, member's sibling, or minor dependent of member. MTA member in question must have been member of Association for one year prior to application. MTA members out of state and their families also eligible to apply. Furbearer, wild life management, natural resources and other life science are preferred but others will be considered. For application, complete request form on Website or contact local director, officer or committee member for application.

Amount of award:	$500
Number of awards:	2
Application deadline:	June 1
Total amount awarded:	$1,000

Contact:
Montana Trappers Association MTA Scholarship Committee
C/O Eugene Couch, Committee Chair
39474 Highway 81
Lewistown, MT 59457
Phone: 406-538-9734
Web: www.montanatrappers.org/scholarship.htm

Myasthenia Gravis Foundation

Viets Medical Student/Graduate Student Fellowship

Type of award: Research grant.
Intended use: For full-time junior, senior or first professional study at accredited 4-year or graduate institution in United States.

Eligibility: Applicant must be U.S. citizen or permanent resident.
Basis for selection: Major/career interest in medicine.
Application requirements: Recommendations, proof of eligibility, research proposal. Eight copies of recommendation from sponsoring preceptor, letter of interest, curriculum vitae of applicant and sponsoring preceptor.
Additional information: Focus of research must be myasthenia gravis or related field.

Amount of award:	$3,000
Number of awards:	4
Number of applicants:	10
Application deadline:	March 15
Total amount awarded:	$12,000

Contact:
Research Grant Committee
Myasthenia Gravis Foundation
1821 University Avenue W, Suite S256
St. Paul, MN 55104
Phone: 800-541-5454
Fax: 651-917-1835
Web: www.myasthenia.org

Myasthenia Gravis Foundation of America

Myasthenia Gravis Foundation Nursing Research Fellowship

Type of award: Research grant.
Intended use: For full-time undergraduate or graduate study at accredited 4-year or graduate institution in United States.
Eligibility: Applicant must be U.S. citizen or permanent resident.
Basis for selection: Major/career interest in nursing.
Application requirements: Recommendations, research proposal. Four copies: cover letter, proposed budget, curriculum vitae of applicant and sponsoring preceptor, proposed work plan.
Additional information: For nursing students or professionals interested in studying problems encountered by patients with Myasthenia Gravis or related neuromuscular conditions.

Amount of award:	$3,000

Contact:
Research Grant Committee
Myasthenia Gravis Foundation of America
1821 University Ave W, Suite S256
St. Paul, MN 55104
Phone: 800-541-5454
Fax: 651-917-1835
Web: www.myasthenia.org

NAACP

Lillian and Samuel Sutton Scholarship

Type of award: Scholarship.
Intended use: For undergraduate or graduate study.

Eligibility: Applicant must be African American. Applicant must be U.S. citizen.
Basis for selection: Major/career interest in education. Applicant must demonstrate financial need, high academic achievement and depth of character.
Application requirements: Recommendations, transcript, proof of eligibility.
Additional information: High school and undergraduate applicants must have minimum 2.5 GPA. Graduate students must have minimum 3.0 GPA. Undergraduate awards are $1,000; graduate awards are $2,000. Undergraduates must be full-time students; graduate students may be full or part time. NAACP membership is highly desirable. Request application in writing. For more information, see Website.

Amount of award:	$1,000-$2,000
Application deadline:	March 28

Contact:
NAACP: Education Department
ATTN: Scholarship Request
4805 Mt. Hope Drive
Baltimore, MD 21215
Phone: 410-580-5760
Web: www.naacp.org

NAACP Legal Defense and Education Fund, Inc.

Herbert Lehman Scholarship for African American Students

Type of award: Scholarship, renewable.
Intended use: For full-time freshman study at accredited 4-year institution in United States.
Eligibility: Applicant must be African American. Applicant must be high school senior. Applicant must be U.S. citizen.
Basis for selection: Applicant must demonstrate financial need, high academic achievement, depth of character, leadership, seriousness of purpose and service orientation.
Application requirements: Recommendations, essay, transcript. Send completed application.
Additional information: For initial application, must be entering first year of college where African Americans are substantially underrepresented. Application request should be made in writing between November 15 and March 15 with statement of career and educational goals, reason why assistance is needed, and name of college to be attended.

Amount of award:	$2,000
Application deadline:	April 15
Notification begins:	July 1

Contact:
The Herbert Lehman Fund
NAACP Legal Defense and Educational Fund, Inc
99 Hudson Street Suite 1600
New York, NY 10013
Phone: 212-965-2200 or 212-965-2225
Fax: 212-219-1595
Web: www.naacpldf.org

NAACP Special Contribution Fund

Agnes Jones Jackson Scholarship

Type of award: Scholarship, renewable.
Intended use: For full-time undergraduate or graduate study at 2-year, 4-year or graduate institution.
Eligibility: Applicant or parent must be member/participant of National Association for Advancement of Colored People. Applicant must be no older than 25.
Application requirements: Recommendations, transcript, proof of eligibility. Include financial aid forms or copies of parents latest income tax forms. Send one personal reference, one academic reference and one NAACP reference (from an officer).
Additional information: Must be current regular member of NAACP for at least one year or fully paid life member. Minimum 2.5 GPA for undergraduates, 3.0 for graduate students. Award amounts: $1,500 undergraduate, $2,500 graduate. Graduate students can be full-time or part-time. Applications may be requested after January 1; include business-sized SASE.

Amount of award:	$1,500-$2,500
Application deadline:	March 28
Notification begins:	July 31

Contact:
NAACP Special Contribution Fund
Education Department
4805 Mount Hope Drive
Baltimore, MD 21215-3297
Phone: 410-580-5760
Web: www.naacp.org

Earl G. Graves/NAACP Scholarship Award

Type of award: Scholarship.
Intended use: For full-time junior, senior, master's or doctoral study at accredited 4-year or graduate institution in United States.
Basis for selection: Major/career interest in business. Applicant must demonstrate high academic achievement.
Application requirements: Recommendations, transcript, proof of eligibility.
Additional information: Applicants must be in top 20% of their class. May apply during sophomore year.

Amount of award:	$5,000
Application deadline:	March 28
Notification begins:	July 31

Contact:
NAACP Special Contribution Fund
4805 Mount Hope Drive
Baltimore, MD 21215
Web: www.naacp.org

NAACP/NASA Louis Stokes Science & Technology Award

Type of award: Scholarship.
Intended use: For full-time freshman study at accredited 4-year institution in United States. Designated institutions: Historically Black college or university.
Eligibility: Applicant must be U.S. citizen.

Basis for selection: Major/career interest in engineering; chemistry; biology or physics. Applicant must demonstrate financial need and high academic achievement.
Application requirements: Recommendations, transcript. Letter of recommendation from NAACP officer and two from teachers or professors in field of study.
Additional information: Minimum 2.5 GPA required. NAACP membership and participation is highly desirable.

Amount of award:	$2,000
Application deadline:	March 28
Notification begins:	July 31

Contact:
NAACP Special Contribution Fund
405 Mount Hope Drive
Baltimore, MD 21215
Web: www.naacp.org

Roy Wilkins Scholarship

Type of award: Scholarship.
Intended use: For full-time freshman study at accredited 2-year or 4-year institution in United States.
Eligibility: Applicant or parent must be member/participant of National Association for Advancement of Colored People. Applicant must be high school senior. Applicant must be U.S. citizen.
Application requirements: Recommendations, transcript, proof of eligibility. One recommendation should be from NAACP officer. Send financial aid forms along with copy of letter of acceptance from college or university.
Additional information: Minimum 2.5 GPA. Applications may be requested after January 1. Include business-sized SASE.

Amount of award:	$1,000
Application deadline:	March 28
Notification begins:	July 31

Contact:
NAACP Special Contribution Fund
Education Department
4805 Mount Hope Drive
Baltimore, MD 21215-3297
Web: www.naacp.org

Sutton Education Scholarship

Type of award: Scholarship, renewable.
Intended use: For full-time undergraduate or graduate study at accredited 2-year, 4-year or graduate institution in United States.
Eligibility: Applicant or parent must be member/participant of National Association for Advancement of Colored People. Applicant must be U.S. citizen.
Basis for selection: Major/career interest in education. Applicant must demonstrate high academic achievement and leadership.
Application requirements: Recommendations, transcript, proof of eligibility. One recommendation should be from NAACP officer. Financial aid forms. Also include recent transcript of grades, acceptance letter from college or university and two letters of recommendation from teachers or professors in the major field of study.
Additional information: For students majoring in field with teacher certification. Undergraduates must have minimum 2.5 GPA, graduate students must have minimum 3.0 GPA. Applications available in January. Include business-sized SASE. Graduate students may be enrolled part-time.

Amount of award:	$1,000-$2,000
Application deadline:	April 30
Notification begins:	July 31

Contact:
NAACP Special Contribution Fund
Education Department
4805 Mount Hope Drive
Baltimore, MD 21215-3297
Web: www.naacp.org

Willems Scholarship

Type of award: Scholarship, renewable.
Intended use: For full-time undergraduate or graduate study at accredited 2-year, 4-year or graduate institution in United States.
Eligibility: Applicant or parent must be member/participant of National Association for Advancement of Colored People. Applicant must be male. Applicant must be U.S. citizen.
Basis for selection: Major/career interest in engineering; chemistry; physics or mathematics. Applicant must demonstrate financial need and high academic achievement.
Application requirements: Recommendations, transcript, proof of eligibility. One recommendation should be from NAACP officer and two from teachers or professors in the field of study. Financial aid forms.
Additional information: Applications may be requested after January 1. Send 9- by 12-inch SASE. Minimum 2.0 GPA for undergraduates and 3.0 GPA for graduate students. Award is $2,000 for undergraduates, $3,000 for graduate students. Graduate students may be enrolled part-time.

Amount of award:	$2,000-$3,000
Application deadline:	April 30
Notification begins:	July 31

Contact:
NAACP Special Contribution Fund
Education Department
4805 Mount Hope Drive
Baltimore, MD 21215-3297
Web: www.naacp.org

NASA Alabama Space Grant Consortium

NASA Space Grant Undergraduate Scholarship

Type of award: Scholarship, renewable.
Intended use: For full-time junior or senior study at accredited 4-year institution. Designated institutions: Alabama Space Grant member universities: University of Alabama Huntsville, Alabama A&M, University of Alabama, University of Alabama Birmingham, University of South Alabama, Auburn University, Tuskegee University.
Eligibility: Applicant must be U.S. citizen residing in Alabama.
Basis for selection: Major/career interest in aerospace; engineering or science, general. Applicant must demonstrate high academic achievement.
Application requirements: Recommendations, essay, transcript, nomination by faculty advisor at Alabama consortium member institution. Include resume.
Additional information: Applicants must have 3.0 or greater GPA and attend Alabama University. Must be in final term of sophomore year or later when applying. The Consortium actively encourages women, minority, and physically challenged students to apply, but others not excluded.

Amount of award:	$1,000
Number of awards:	35
Application deadline:	March 1

Contact:
NASA Alabama Space Grant Consortium
University of Alabama in Huntsville
Materials Science Building, 205
Huntsville, AL 35899
Phone: 256-824-6800
Fax: 256-824-6061
Web: www.uah.edu/ASGC/

NASA Alaska Space Grant Program

Alaska Student Rocket Project Scholarship

Type of award: Research grant, renewable.
Intended use: For undergraduate or graduate study in United States. Designated institutions: University of Alaska.
Eligibility: Applicant must be U.S. citizen.
Basis for selection: Major/career interest in aerospace; engineering or science, general.
Application requirements: Recommendations, transcript, nomination by University of Alaska faculty member willing to supervise proposed aerospace research project. Resume, research proposal, cover letter describing career goals and space-related interests. Applicant must be current student at University of Alaska.
Additional information: Provides students with hands-on experience in all aspects of rocket and payload testing and launching. Internships awarded to students who assume leadership positions in interdisciplinary student team. Size of award commensurate with scope of proposed project, usually less than $5,000. More details and research proposal forms available on Website.

Notification begins:	June 1

Contact:
Alaska Space Grant Program Office
Univ. of Alaska Fairbanks
P.O. Box 755919
Fairbanks, AK 99775-5919
Phone: 907-474-6833
Fax: 907-474-2696
Web: www.uaf.edu/asgp

Student Research Scholarship

Type of award: Research grant, renewable.
Intended use: For full-time undergraduate or graduate study at accredited 4-year institution in United States. Designated institutions: University of Alaska at Fairbanks and Anchorage, University of Alaska Southeast, Alaska Pacific University.
Eligibility: Applicant must be U.S. citizen.
Basis for selection: Major/career interest in aerospace; astronomy; engineering or physics.
Application requirements: Recommendations, essay, transcript, research proposal, nomination by University of Alaska faculty member willing to supervise proposed aerospace research project. Resume, research proposal, cover letter describing career goals and space-related interests. Applicant must be current student at University of Alaska.

Additional information: Awardee receives support for working on a specific aerospace-related research project. Must be used at an Alaska Space Grant Consortium member institution. Number of scholarships and amount of funding vary; most awards $5,000 or less. Deadline usually in April or May. Contact sponsor for information.

    Application deadline: March 3
    Notification begins: June 1
Contact:
Alaska Space Grant Program Office
Univ. of Alaska Fairbanks
P.O. Box 755919
Fairbanks, AK 99775-5919
Phone: 907-474-6833
Fax: 907-474-2696
Web: www.uaf.edu/asgp

NASA Arkansas Space Grant Consortium

NASA Space Grant Arkansas Undergraduate Scholarship

Type of award: Scholarship.
Intended use: For full-time undergraduate study in United States. Designated institutions: Arkansas Space Grant Consortium members: University of Arkansas at Little Rock, Arkansas State University, Arkansas Tech University, Harding University, Henderson State University, Hendrix College, Lyon College, Ouachita Baptist University, University of Arkansas at Fayetteville, University of Arkansas at Pine Bluff, University of Arkansas for Medical Sciences, University of Central Arkansas, University of the Ozarks, and University of Arkansas at Monticello.
Eligibility: Applicant must be U.S. citizen residing in Arkansas.
Basis for selection: Major/career interest in aerospace; astronomy; chemistry; engineering; physics or medicine. Applicant must demonstrate high academic achievement.
Application requirements: Research proposal. Sponsoring faculty member or mentor.
Additional information: Awards must be used at Consortium Member institutions in Arkansas. For any space-related research. Applications usually accepted September through November; contact campus program office. Application deadlines vary by campus. Minimum 3.0 GPA preferred.
    Amount of award: $250-$5,000
Contact:
Contact local campus Space Grant representative.
Phone: 501-569-8212 501-569-8212
Fax: 501-569-8039
Web: asgc.ualr.edu

NASA Connecticut Space Grant Consortium

NASA Space Grant Connecticut Undergraduate Fellowship

Type of award: Research grant, renewable.
Intended use: For full-time undergraduate study at accredited 4-year institution in United States. Designated institutions: Connecticut Space Grant Consortium member institutions including University of Connecticut, University of Hartford, University of New Haven, Trinity College.
Eligibility: Applicant must be U.S. citizen.
Basis for selection: Major/career interest in aerospace; engineering or science, general.
Application requirements: Recommendations, transcript, proof of eligibility. Resume.
Additional information: Must be used at a Connecticut Consortium member institution. Consortium actively encourages women, minority, and disabled students to apply.
    Amount of award: $2,500
    Number of awards: 10
    Application deadline: April 1
    Total amount awarded: $25,000
Contact:
NASA Space Grant Connecticut Space Grant Consortium
University of Hartford
200 Bloomfield Ave.
West Hartford, CT 06117
Phone: (860) 768-4813
Fax: (860) 768-5073
Web: uhaweb.hartford.edu/ctspgrant/pdf_files.html

NASA Delaware Space Grant Consortium

Delaware Space Grant Undergraduate Summer Scholarship

Type of award: Scholarship, renewable.
Intended use: For full-time undergraduate study. Designated institutions: University of Delaware, Delaware Technical and Community College, Franklin and Marshall College, Gettysburg College, Lehigh University, Swarthmore College, Delaware State University at Dover, Villanova University, Wilmington College.
Eligibility: Applicant must be U.S. citizen.
Basis for selection: Major/career interest in aerospace; astronomy; engineering; physics; engineering, materials; oceanography/marine studies; geography or geology/earth sciences.
Application requirements: Recommendations, transcript. Applicant statement.
Additional information: Applicants must have proven interest in space science-related studies. Recipient must attend a Delaware Space Grant Consortium member institution.
    Amount of award: $1,400-$3,000
    Application deadline: March 1
    Notification begins: March 15
    Total amount awarded: $25,350

Scholarships

Contact:
Delaware Space Grant Consortium Program Office
University of Delaware
217 Sharp Lab
Newark, DE 19716
Phone: 302-831-1094
Fax: 302-831-1843
Web: www.delspace.org

NASA District of Columbia Space Grant Consortium

NASA District of Columbia Undergraduate Scholarship

Type of award: Scholarship, renewable.
Intended use: For undergraduate or graduate study. Designated institutions: The American University, Gallaudet University, George Washington University, Howard University, University of District of Columbia.
Eligibility: Applicant must be U.S. citizen.
Basis for selection: Major/career interest in science, general; mathematics; engineering; aerospace; physical education; political science/government or engineering. Applicant must demonstrate high academic achievement.
Application requirements: Recommendations, transcript, proof of eligibility.
Additional information: Number of grants, amounts of funding, deadlines, and application requirements vary by year and by institutions. Contact sponsor for more information.
Contact:
District of Columbia Space Grant Consortium,
American University Department of Physics
McKinley Building Room 102
Washington, DC 20016-8058
Phone: 202-885-2755
Fax: 202-885-2723
Web: www.dcspacegrant.org

NASA Georgia Space Grant Consortium

NASA Space Grant Georgia Fellowship Program

Type of award: Scholarship, renewable.
Intended use: For full-time junior, senior, master's or doctoral study at accredited postsecondary institution in United States. Designated institutions: Clark Atlanta University, Columbus State University, Georgia Institute of Technology, Kennesaw State University, Mercer University, Morehouse College, Spelman College, State University of West Georgia, University of Georgia.
Eligibility: Applicant must be U.S. citizen residing in Georgia.
Basis for selection: Major/career interest in engineering; science, general; aerospace; physics; atmospheric sciences/meteorology; computer/information sciences; education or chemistry. Applicant must demonstrate seriousness of purpose and service orientation.

Application requirements: Interview, portfolio, recommendations, essay, transcript.
Additional information: Funding available for students in all areas of engineering and science, and many areas of social science.

Amount of award:	$550-$1,100

Contact:
Georgia Space Grant Consortium
Georgia Tech-Aerospace and Engineering
Space Science and Technology Bldg., Room 210
Atlanta, GA 30332-0150
Phone: 404-894-0521
Fax: 404-894-9313
Web: www.ae.gatech.edu/research/gsgc

NASA Hawaii Space Grant Consortium

NASA Space Grant Hawaii Undergraduate Fellowship

Type of award: Scholarship.
Intended use: For full-time junior or senior study in United States. Designated institutions: Consortium member schools. Consortium members are: University of Hawaii at Manoa and Hilo, Honolulu, Kapiolani, Leeward, Maui, and Windward Community Colleges.
Eligibility: Applicant must be U.S. citizen residing in Hawaii.
Basis for selection: Major/career interest in astronomy; geology/earth sciences; oceanography/marine studies; physics; zoology; law or geography.
Application requirements: Applicants must be sponsored by a faculty member willing to act as the student's mentor during the award period.
Additional information: Additional fields include math, physics, engineering, computer sciences and life sciences that are concerned with understanding, utilization or exploration of space with investigation of Earth from space. Full-time undergraduates at Manoa, Hilo with major declared can apply for two-semester fellowships. Stipend of $3,000 per semester. Also up to $500 for supplies or travel. Recipients expected to work 10-15 hours per week on space-related projects. Women, under-represented minorities (specifically Native Hawaiians, Filipinos, other Pacific Islanders, Native Americans, Blacks, Hispanics), physically challenged students who have interest in space-related fields are particularly encouraged to apply. Freshmen and sophomores may also apply.

Amount of award:	$3,000
Number of awards:	20
Application deadline:	June 15, December 1

Contact:
Hawaii Space Grant College
University of Hawaii
1680 East West Road
Honolulu, HI 96822
Phone: 808-956-3138
Web: www.spacegrant.hawaii.edu

NASA Idaho Space Grant Consortium

NASA Idaho Space Grant Undergraduate Scholarship

Type of award: Scholarship, renewable.
Intended use: For full-time undergraduate study at accredited 4-year institution. Designated institutions: Albertson College of Idaho, Boise State University, College of Southern Idaho, Idaho State University, Lewis Clark State College, North Idaho College, Northwest Nazarene University, BYU-Idaho, and the University of Idaho.
Eligibility: Applicant must be U.S. citizen residing in Idaho.
Basis for selection: Major/career interest in engineering; mathematics; science, general or education.
Application requirements: Recommendations, essay, transcript. Include high school and college transcripts.
Additional information: Applicants must attend Idaho Space Grant Consortium member institution in Idaho and maintain a 3.0 GPA. Application should include ACT/SAT scores, if available. Consortium actively encourages women, minority students, and disabled students to apply. Application essay should not exceed 500 words. Applications may be downloaded from Website.

Amount of award:	$500-$1,000
Application deadline:	March 1
Notification begins:	May 1
Total amount awarded:	$22,000

Contact:
NASA Space Grant Idaho Space Grant Consortium
University of Idaho
P.O. Box 441011
Moscow, ID 83844-1011
Web: www.uidaho.edu/nasa_isgc

NASA Illinois Space Grant Consortium

NASA Space Grant Illinois Undergraduate Scholarship

Type of award: Scholarship, renewable.
Intended use: For full-time undergraduate study. Designated institutions: University of Illinois.
Eligibility: Applicant must be U.S. citizen residing in Illinois.
Basis for selection: Major/career interest in engineering or aerospace. Applicant must demonstrate high academic achievement.
Application requirements: Transcript.
Additional information: Must be enrolled in aerospace engineering at University of Illinois. Contact sponsor for deadline information. Recipient required to work on research or design project.

Amount of award:	$500-$1,000

Contact:
Associate Director/ Illinois Space Grant Consortium
U of Illinois-Urbana, 306 Talbot Lab
104 S. Wright St.
Urbana, IL 61801-2935
Phone: 217-244-8048
Fax: 217-244-0720
Web: www.ae.uiuc.edu/ISGC

NASA Indiana Space Grant Consortium

NASA Space Grant Indiana Undergraduate Scholarship

Type of award: Scholarship, renewable.
Intended use: For undergraduate study. Designated institutions: Indiana Space Grant Consortium member institutions: Purdue University at West Lafayette, Purdue University at Hammond, University of Notre Dame in South Bend, Indiana University in Bloomington, Ball State University, Taylor University, Valparaiso University, IUPUI, University of Evansville.
Eligibility: Applicant must be U.S. citizen residing in Indiana.
Basis for selection: Major/career interest in science, general; mathematics; engineering or aerospace. Applicant must demonstrate high academic achievement.
Additional information: Number of grants, amount of funding, deadlines and application requirements vary by institution; contact sponsor for more information. Must be used at Indiana Space Grant Consortium member institution. Applicant must be studying to work in a NASA-related field. Application can be obtained on Website.

Amount of award:	$1,000
Application deadline:	December 1

Contact:
NASA: Indiana Space Grant Consortium
500 Stadium Mall Drive
West Lafayette, IN 47907-1282
Phone: 765-494-5873
Web: www.insgc.org

NASA Kentucky Space Grant Consortium

NASA Space Grant Kentucky Undergraduate Scholarship

Type of award: Scholarship, renewable.
Intended use: For full-time undergraduate study at accredited 4-year institution in United States. Designated institutions: Consortium member institution: Centre College, Eastern Kentucky University, Kentucky Center for Space Enterprise, Kentucky State University, Morehead State University, Murray State University, Northern Kentucky University, Thomas More College, Transylvania University, University of Kentucky, University of Louisville, Western Kentucky University.
Eligibility: Applicant must be U.S. citizen residing in Kentucky.

Basis for selection: Major/career interest in aerospace; astronomy; education; engineering or physics.

Application requirements: Interview, recommendations, essay, transcript, research proposal, nomination by professor/mentor at participating institution. Research proposal, written with mentor.

Additional information: Preference given to schools that waive tuition for recipient. Consortium actively encourages women, minority, and physically challenged students to apply. Deadline is in early April. Check Website for exact date. Applicants doing work related to space exploration may qualify for funding, whatever their field of study may be. An additional $500 is offered for use in support of student's mentored research project.

    Amount of award: $3,000
    Number of awards: 2
    Number of applicants: 4

Contact:
NASA Space Grant Kentucky Space Grant Consortium
Western Kentucky University
Dept. of Phys., TCCW 246, One Big Red Way
Bowling Green, KY 42101-3576
Phone: 270-745-4156
Web: www.wku.edu/KSGC

NASA Maine Space Grant Consortium

NASA Space Grant Maine Consortium Annual Scholarship and Fellowship Program

Type of award: Research grant, renewable.

Intended use: For full-time undergraduate or graduate study at accredited 4-year or graduate institution. Designated institutions: University of Maine (Orono), University of Southern Maine, University of New England, Maine Maritime Academy.

Eligibility: Applicant must be U.S. citizen residing in Maine.

Basis for selection: Major/career interest in astronomy; geology/earth sciences; geophysics; engineering; aerospace; biology or medicine.

Additional information: Application requirements vary by institution. Visit Website for additional details.

Contact:
Maine Space Grant Consortium
87 Winthrop Street
Suite 200
Augusta, ME 04330
Phone: 877-397-7223
Web: www.msgc.org

NASA Michigan Space Grant Consortium

NASA Space Grant Michigan Undergraduate Fellowship

Type of award: Research grant, renewable.

Intended use: For undergraduate study at accredited 4-year or graduate institution. Designated institutions: Michigan Space Grant Consortium member institutions.

Eligibility: Applicant must be U.S. citizen residing in Michigan.

Basis for selection: Major/career interest in aerospace; engineering; science, general or mathematics. Applicant must demonstrate high academic achievement.

Application requirements: Recommendations, essay, transcript. Two letters of recommendation.

Additional information: Offers support in form of graduate and undergraduate research and public service fellowships to students in aerospace, space science, Earth system science and other related science, engineering or math fields. Students working on educational research topics in math, science or technology also eligible to apply. Preference given to projects directly related to aerospace, space science, Earth system science and directly related educational efforts. Announcements for next funding interval can be found on Website.

    Amount of award: $2,500-$5,000

Contact:
NASA Space Grant Michigan Space Grant Consortium
U of Michigan
2455 Hayward Street - 2106 SRB
Ann Arbor, MI 98109-2143
Phone: 734-764-9508
Fax: 734-763-0437
Web: www.umich.edu/~msgc

NASA Mississippi Space Grant Consortium

NASA Space Grant Mississippi Undergraduate Scholarship

Type of award: Scholarship, renewable.

Intended use: For full-time undergraduate or graduate study in United States. Designated institutions: University of Mississippi, Jackson State University, University of Southern Mississippi, Mississippi State University, Alcorn State University, Delta State University, Mississippi University for Women, Mississippi Valley State University, Coahoma Community College, Hinds Community College-Utica Campus, Itawamba Community College, Meridian Community College, Mississippi Delta Community College, Mississippi Gulf Coast Community College, Northeast Mississippi Community College, and Pearl River Community College.

Eligibility: Applicant must be U.S. citizen residing in Mississippi.

Basis for selection: Major/career interest in engineering; mathematics; science, general or aerospace. Applicant must demonstrate high academic achievement, leadership and seriousness of purpose.

Application requirements: Nomination by faculty mentor at participating Mississippi Space Grant Consortium member institution.

Additional information: Award amounts per term vary; contact sponsor. Awardees must attend Mississippi Space Grant Consortium member institution. Selection criteria vary by institution; most consider GPA, field of study and written essay. Most awards require research or public service activity. List of campus contacts available online. Applicants from groups traditionally underrepresented in space-related fields encouraged.

Number of awards: 66
Contact:
NASA Space Grant Mississippi Space Grant Consortium
217 Vardaman Hall
P.O. Box 1848
University, MS 38677-1848
Phone: 662-915-1187
Fax: 662-915-3927
Web: www.olemiss.edu/programs/nasa/spacegrant.html

NASA Missouri Space Grant Consortium

NASA Missouri State Space Grant Undergraduate Scholarship

Type of award: Scholarship, renewable.
Intended use: For full-time undergraduate study at accredited 4-year institution in United States. Designated institutions: Southwest Missouri State University, University of Missouri - Columbia, University of Missouri - Rolla, University of Missouri - St. Louis, and Washington University in St. Louis.
Eligibility: Applicant must be residing in Missouri.
Basis for selection: Major/career interest in aerospace; astronomy; engineering; geology/earth sciences or physics.
Application requirements: Recommendations, essay, transcript.
Additional information: Program encourages applications from eligible space science students. Awardees must attend Missouri Space Grant Consortium member institution. Women, minority students, and physically challenged students are actively encouraged to apply. Deadline varies but is usually the first week in March. Check sponsor for exact date. Awards normally granted sometime in May.

Amount of award: $2,000-$3,000
Number of awards: 30
Total amount awarded: $75,000
Contact:
NASA Missouri Space Grant Consortium
University of Missouri - Rolla
226 Mechanical. Eng. Bldg.
Rolla, MO 65401-0249
Phone: 573-341-4887
Fax: 573-341-4607
Web: www.umr.edu/~spaceg

NASA Montana Space Grant Consortium

NASA Space Grant Montana Undergraduate Scholarship Program

Type of award: Scholarship, renewable.
Intended use: For full-time undergraduate study at accredited 2-year or 4-year institution in United States. Designated institutions: Montana Space Grant Consortium member institutions.

Eligibility: Applicant must be U.S. citizen residing in Montana.
Basis for selection: Major/career interest in aerospace; biology; chemistry; geology/earth sciences; physics; astronomy; computer/information sciences; engineering, chemical; engineering, civil or engineering, electrical/electronic. Applicant must demonstrate depth of character and leadership.
Additional information: Awards for one year, renewable on a competitive basis. Visit Website for more information.

Amount of award: $1,000
Application deadline: April 1
Contact:
NASA Space Grant Montana Space Grant Consortium
Montana State University
P.O. Box 173835
Bozeman, MT 59717-3835
Phone: 406-994-4223
Fax: 406-994-4452
Web: www.spacegrant.montana.edu

NASA Nebraska Space Grant Consortium

NASA Space Grant Nebraska Undergraduate Scholarships

Type of award: Scholarship, renewable.
Intended use: For undergraduate or graduate study in United States. Designated institutions: Nebraska Space Grant Consortium member institution. Member institutions include: Chadron State College, College of St. Mary, Creighton University, Grace University, Metro Community College, Nebraska Indian Community College, University of Nebraska - Lincoln, University of Nebraska at Kearney, University of Nebraska at Omaha, University of Nebraska Medical Center, Western Nebraska Community College, Hastings College and Little Priest Tribal College.
Eligibility: Non-residents are eligible if attending institution in Nebraska. Applicant must be U.S. citizen residing in Nebraska.
Basis for selection: Major/career interest in aerospace; aviation; energy research; engineering; science, general or mathematics.
Application requirements: Transcript, proof of eligibility. Proof of US Citizenship reqired.
Additional information: Award amounts vary. View Website to access application.

Application deadline: April 30
Contact:
NASA Nebraska Space Grant Consortium
Aviation Institute, Engineering #116
6001 Dodge St.
Omaha, NE 68182
Web: http://nasa.unomaha.edu

NASA Nevada Space Grant Consortium

NASA Space Grant Nevada Undergraduate Scholarship

Type of award: Scholarship.
Intended use: For full-time undergraduate study at accredited postsecondary institution in United States. Designated institutions: Nevada (UCCSN) institution.
Eligibility: Applicant must be U.S. citizen residing in Nevada.
Basis for selection: Major/career interest in science, general; engineering; education; economics; business; mathematics or computer/information sciences.
Application requirements: Essay. GPA. Career goal statement, including applicant's motivation toward aerospace career.
Additional information: Math, science, engineering, or majors in relevant fields eligible to apply. Applications available on Website. Contact institution of interest for more detailed information, deadlines, award amounts and application requirements.

Amount of award:	$2,500
Application deadline:	December 15, March 15

Contact:
NASA Space Grant Nevada Space Grant Consortium
James V. Taranik, PhD; or Lori M. Rountree
University of Nevada, Reno
Reno, NV 89557-0138
Phone: 775-784-6261
Fax: 775-327-2235
Web: www.unr.edu/spacegrant

NASA New Mexico Space Grant Consortium

NASA Space Grant New Mexico Undergraduate Scholarship

Type of award: Research grant, renewable.
Intended use: For full-time sophomore, junior or senior study at accredited 4-year institution in United States. Designated institutions: New Mexico State University.
Eligibility: Applicant must be U.S. citizen residing in New Mexico.
Basis for selection: Major/career interest in astronomy; biology; chemistry; computer/information sciences; engineering, chemical; engineering, civil; engineering, electrical/electronic; engineering, mechanical; physics or mathematics.
Application requirements: Research proposal, nomination by Faculty-mentor. Transcript with declared undergraduate major.
Additional information: Applicant must attend New Mexico State University and have minimum 3.0 GPA. Preference given to applicants who can show nonfederal matching funds. Women, minority students, and physically challenged students encouraged to apply. Applications and deadline details on Website.

Amount of award:	$2,000
Number of awards:	5
Total amount awarded:	$100,000

Contact:
NASA Space Grant New Mexico Space Grant Consortium
Program Office, New Mexico State University
Wells Hall, Bay 4, at Wells & Locust St.
Las Cruces, NM 88003-0001
Phone: 505-646-6414
Fax: 505-646-7791
Web: spacegrant.nmsu.edu

NASA North Carolina Space Grant Consortium

NASA Space Grant North Carolina Consortium Undergraduate Scholarship

Type of award: Scholarship.
Intended use: For full-time sophomore, junior or senior study. Designated institutions: North Carolina Space Grant Consortium member institution. Consortium members include: North Carolina State University, North Carolina Central University, Duke University, North Carolina A&T State University, Winston-Salem State University, University of North Carolina at Charlotte, University of North Carolina at Chapel Hill, University of North Carolina at Pembroke.
Eligibility: Applicant must be returning adult student. Applicant must be U.S. citizen residing in North Carolina.
Basis for selection: Major/career interest in science, general; engineering or aerospace. Applicant must demonstrate high academic achievement.
Application requirements: Recommendations, transcript, research proposal, nomination by faculty member.

Amount of award:	$4,000
Number of awards:	5
Number of applicants:	12
Application deadline:	January 31
Total amount awarded:	$20,000

Contact:
NASA Space Grant North Carolina Space Grant Consortium
Box 7515
Raleigh, NC 27511
Phone: 919-515-5937 or 919-515-4240
Fax: 919-515-5934
Web: www.mae.ncsu.edu/spacegrant

NASA North Dakota Space Grant Consortium

NASA Space Grant North Dakota Consortium Lillian Goettler Scholarship

Type of award: Scholarship.
Intended use: For full-time undergraduate study in United States. Designated institutions: North Dakota State University.
Eligibility: Applicant must be female. Applicant must be U.S. citizen residing in North Dakota.

Additional information: Awarded to female undergraduate science or mathematics student, ideally involved in research project of interest to NASA. Minimum 3.5 GPA. Contact coordinator for deadline information.

> **Amount of award:** $2,500

Contact:
North Dakota Space Grant Consortium
U of North Dakota, Space Studies Dept.
PO Box 9008
Grand Forks, ND 58202-9008
Phone: 701-777-4856
Web: www.space.edu/spacegrant

NASA Space Grant North Dakota Undergraduate Scholarship

Type of award: Scholarship, renewable.
Intended use: For full-time undergraduate study. Designated institutions: North Dakota community colleges, public colleges and universities, and tribal colleges.
Eligibility: Applicant must be U.S. citizen residing in North Dakota.
Basis for selection: Major/career interest in biology; chemistry; engineering; geology/earth sciences; computer/information sciences or mathematics.
Application requirements: Recommendations, transcript, nomination by sponsoring North Dakota Space Grant Consortium member institution.
Additional information: Three awards of $500 are available at each of the two-year public and tribal colleges; three $750 scholarships are provided to four-year public state universities. Awardees must attend North Dakota Space Grant Consortium member institution. Consortium actively encourages women, minority students, and physically challenged students to apply. Deadlines vary. Contact institutions directly.

> **Amount of award:** $500-$750

Contact:
NASA Space Grant North Dakota Space Grant Consortium
U of North Dakota, Space Studies Dept.
P.O. Box 9008
Grand Forks, ND 58202-9008
Phone: 701-777-4856
Web: www.space.edu/spacegrant

Pearl I. Young Scholarship

Type of award: Scholarship.
Intended use: For full-time undergraduate study in United States. Designated institutions: University of North Dakota.
Eligibility: Applicant must be female. Applicant must be U.S. citizen or permanent resident residing in North Dakota.
Basis for selection: Major/career interest in biology; chemistry; engineering; geology/earth sciences; computer/information sciences or mathematics.
Additional information: Awarded to female undergraduate science or mathematics student. Applicants must have minimum 3.5 GPA and ideally be involved in research project of interest to NASA. Contact coordinator for deadline information.

> **Amount of award:** $2,500
> **Number of awards:** 1

Contact:
NASA Space Grant North Dakota Space Grant Consortium
U of North Dakota, Space Studies Dept.
P.O. Box 9008
Grand Forks, ND 58202-9008
Phone: 701-777-4856
Web: www.space.edu/spacegrant

NASA Ohio Space Grant Consortium

NASA Ohio Space Grant Junior/ Senior Scholarship Program

Type of award: Scholarship, renewable.
Intended use: For full-time junior or senior study at accredited 4-year institution. Designated institutions: Ohio Space Grant Consortium members include: Case Western Reserve University, Cedarville College, Central State University, Cleveland State University, Marietta College, Ohio Northern University, Ohio University, Ohio State University, University of Akron, University of Cincinnati, University of Dayton, University of Toledo, Wilberforce University, Wright State University, Miami University, and Youngstown State University.
Eligibility: Applicant must be U.S. citizen residing in Ohio.
Basis for selection: Major/career interest in aerospace or engineering.
Application requirements: Recommendations, essay, transcript.
Additional information: Awards are $2,000 for juniors, $3,000 for seniors. Must attend a Consortium member institution.

> **Amount of award:** $2,000-$3,000
> **Number of awards:** 50
> **Number of applicants:** 150
> **Application deadline:** January 31
> **Notification begins:** April 30
> **Total amount awarded:** $130,000

Contact:
NASA Ohio Space Grant Consortium
OAI
22800 Cedar Point Road
Cleveland, OH 44142
Web: www.osgc.org

NASA Oregon Space Grant Consortium

NASA Space Grant Oregon Community College Scholarship

Type of award: Scholarship.
Intended use: For full-time freshman or sophomore study at accredited 2-year institution in United States. Designated institutions: Lane Community College, Central Oregon Community College, Portland Community College.
Eligibility: Applicant must be U.S. citizen residing in Oregon.
Basis for selection: Major/career interest in aerospace; science, general or engineering.
Application requirements: Recommendations, essay, transcript.
Additional information: Please see Website for additional information and deadlines.

> **Amount of award:** $1,000
> **Number of awards:** 10
> **Total amount awarded:** $10,000

Contact:
Oregon NASA Space Grant Consortium
Oregon State University
94 Kerr Administration Building
Corvalis, OR 97331-2103
Phone: 541-737-2414
Web: www.oregonspacegrant.orst.edu

NASA Space Grant Oregon Undergraduate Scholarship

Type of award: Scholarship.
Intended use: For full-time undergraduate study at accredited 2-year or 4-year institution in United States. Designated institutions: Oregon State University, University of Oregon, Portland State University, Eastern Oregon University, Southern Oregon University, Oregon Institute of Technology, Linfield College, Hatfield Marine Science Center, Pine Mountain Observatory.
Eligibility: Applicant must be U.S. citizen residing in Oregon.
Basis for selection: Major/career interest in science, general; engineering or aerospace. Applicant must demonstrate high academic achievement.
Application requirements: Recommendations, essay, transcript.
Additional information: Must attend one of the designated institutions. Contact Space Grant Consortium representative on campus for additional information. Please see Website for additional information and application deadlines.

Amount of award:	$1,000
Number of awards:	10
Total amount awarded:	$10,000

Contact:
Oregon NASA Space Grant Consortium
Oregon State University
94 Kerr Administration Building
Corvalis, OR 97331-2103
Phone: 541-737-2414
Web: www.oregonspacegrant.orst.edu

NASA Pennsylvania Space Grant Consortium

NASA Space Grant Pennsylvania Undergraduate Scholarship

Type of award: Scholarship.
Intended use: For full-time junior or senior study at accredited 4-year institution in United States. Designated institutions: Pennsylvania State University, Carnegie Mellon University, Lincoln University, Abington College, Susquehanna University, Temple University, West Chester University, University of Pittsburgh.
Eligibility: Applicant must be U.S. citizen residing in Pennsylvania.
Basis for selection: Major/career interest in science, general; mathematics; engineering; education; aerospace or astronomy.
Application requirements: Recommendations, essay, transcript.
Additional information: Competitive scholarships provided for undergraduates at Pennsylvania Space Grant Consortium member institutions. Sylvia Stein Memorial Space Grant Scholarship at Penn State University (two one-year scholarships

for $4,000 per year) awarded to outstanding undergraduate with extensive community service. Other awards and eligibility requirements vary with institution. Contact campus Space Grant Consortium representative for details. Consortium actively encourages women, minority, and physically challenged students to apply.
Contact:
NASA Pennsylvania Space Grant Consortium
Penn State, University Park
2217 Earth-Engineering Sciences Building
University Park, PA 16802
Web: www.psu.edu/spacegrant

NASA Rhode Island Space Grant Consortium

NASA Space Grant Rhode Island Summer Undergraduate Scholarship

Type of award: Scholarship.
Intended use: For sophomore, junior or senior study at postsecondary institution. Designated institutions: Rhode Island Space Grant Consortium member institutions: Brown University, Bryant College, Community College of Rhode Island, Roger Williams University, Rhode Island College, Rhode Island School of Design, Salve Regina University, University of Rhode Island, Wheaton College.
Eligibility: Applicant must be U.S. citizen residing in Rhode Island.
Basis for selection: Major/career interest in physics; engineering; biology; geology/earth sciences or aerospace. Applicant must demonstrate high academic achievement.
Application requirements: Interview, recommendations, essay, transcript. Research proposal, resume.
Additional information: Applicants must be students at Rhode Island Space Grant affiliated college or university. Applications accepted in late February, deadline in early March; call sponsor for exact dates. Number of awards may vary. Topics of study in space sciences also funded. Students should contact campus representative or the Rhode Island Space Grant office.

Amount of award:	$4,000
Number of awards:	2

Contact:
NASA Rhode Island Space Grant Consortium
Brown University
Box 1846
Providence, RI 02912
Phone: 401-863-2889
Fax: 401-863-1292
Web: www.spacegrant.brown.edu/RI_Space_Grant

NASA Space Grant Rhode Island Undergraduate Academic Year Scholarship

Type of award: Scholarship, renewable.
Intended use: For sophomore, junior or senior study at postsecondary institution. Designated institutions: Rhode Island Space Grant Consortium member institutions: Brown University, Bryant College, Community College of Rhode Island, Roger Williams University, Rhode Island College,

Rhode Island School of Design, Salve Regina University, University of Rhode Island, Wheaton College.
Eligibility: Applicant must be U.S. citizen residing in Rhode Island.
Basis for selection: Major/career interest in physics; engineering; biology; geology/earth sciences or aerospace. Applicant must demonstrate high academic achievement.
Application requirements: Interview, recommendations, essay, transcript. Resume.
Additional information: Applicants must be students at Rhode Island Space Grant affiliated college or university. Applications accepted in late February, deadline in early March; call sponsor for exact dates. Number of awards may vary. Topics of study in space sciences also funded. Students should contact their campus representative or the Rhode Island Space Grant office.

Amount of award:	$4,000
Number of awards:	3

Contact:
NASA Rhode Island Space Grant Consortium
Brown University
Box 1846
Providence, RI 02912
Phone: 401-863-2889
Fax: 401-863-1292
Web: www.spacegrant.brown.edu/RI_Space_Grant

NASA Rocky Mountain Space Grant Consortium

Rocky Mountain Space Grant Consortium Undergraduate Scholarship

Type of award: Scholarship, renewable.
Intended use: For full-time undergraduate study in United States. Designated institutions: Utah State University, University of Utah, Brigham Young University, University of Denver, Weber State University and Southern Utah University.
Eligibility: Applicant must be U.S. citizen.
Basis for selection: Major/career interest in science, general; aerospace or engineering. Applicant must demonstrate high academic achievement.
Application requirements: Recommendations, transcript, research proposal. Resume.
Additional information: Award varies from year to year. Contact sponsor for deadline information. Must be used at a Rocky Mountain Space Grant Consortium member institution.

Amount of award:	$200-$1,000

Contact:
Rocky Mountain NASA Space Grant Consortium
Utah State University
EL Building, Room 302
Logan, UT 84332-4140
Phone: 435-797-3666
Fax: 435-797-3382
Web: www.rmc.sdl.usu.edu

NASA South Carolina Space Grant Consortium

Kathryn D. Sullivan Science and Engineering Undergraduate Fellowship

Type of award: Scholarship, renewable.
Intended use: For full-time senior study at 4-year institution. Designated institutions: SCSGC member institutions.
Eligibility: Applicant must be high school senior. Applicant must be U.S. citizen residing in South Carolina.
Basis for selection: Major/career interest in science, general; engineering or mathematics.
Application requirements: Recommendations, essay, transcript, nomination by faculty advisor.
Additional information: Applicants must attend South Carolina member institution. Applicants must have sponsorship from faculty advisor. Awards are $3,500 per semester. The Consortium actively encourages women, minority, and disabled students to apply. Application deadline usually in January.

Amount of award:	$7,000
Number of awards:	1
Application deadline:	January 27

Contact:
NASA South Carolina Space Grant Consortium
Tara B. Scozzaro, MPA
College of Charleston Department of Geology
Charleston, SC 29424
Phone: 843-953-5463
Fax: 843-953-5446
Web: www.cofc.edu/~scsgrant/

NASA Space Grant South Carolina Research Program

Type of award: Research grant, renewable.
Intended use: For full-time junior or senior study at accredited 4-year institution in United States. Designated institutions: Benedict College, The Citadel, Clemson University, Coastal Carolina University, Furman University, South Carolina State University, University of Charleston, University of South Carolina, Medical University of South Carolina, University of the Virgin Islands, and Wofford College.
Eligibility: Applicant must be U.S. citizen residing in South Carolina.
Basis for selection: Major/career interest in science, general or mathematics.
Application requirements: Recommendations, essay, transcript, research proposal, nomination by and sponsorship from faculty advisor.
Additional information: Applicants must attend a South Carolina Space Grant Consortium member institution and be studying to work in a NASA-related field. Research awards available for academic year or summer research. The Consortium actively encourages women, minority, and disabled students to apply. Application deadline is usually January of every year. Check with sponsor to find out exact date. Applications can be downloaded from Website.

Amount of award:	$3,000
Number of applicants:	25

Contact:
NASA Space Grant South Carolina Space Grant Consortium
College of Charleston
Department of Geology
Charleston, SC 29424
Phone: 843-953-5463
Fax: 843-953-5446
Web: www.cofc.edu/~scsgrant/

NASA Space Grant South Carolina Undergraduate Academic Year Research Program

Type of award: Research grant, renewable.
Intended use: For full-time undergraduate study at accredited 4-year institution in United States. Designated institutions: Benedict College, The Citadel, Clemson University, Coastal Carolina University, Furman University, South Carolina State University, University of Charleston, University of South Carolina, Medical University of South Carolina, University of the Virgin Islands, and Wofford College.
Eligibility: Applicant must be U.S. citizen residing in South Carolina.
Basis for selection: Academic record, research related to NASA. Major/career interest in mathematics; science, general; astronomy; aerospace; engineering, mechanical; geophysics; geology/earth sciences or atmospheric sciences/meteorology. Applicant must demonstrate high academic achievement.
Application requirements: Recommendations, essay, transcript, research proposal, nomination by faculty advisor. Applicant must study at accredited 4-year space grant institution.
Additional information: Applicants must attend a South Carolina Space Grant Consortium member institution. Applicants must have sponsorship from a faculty advisor. Applicants may have a field of study or interest related to any NASA enterprise. The Consortium actively encourages women, minority, and disabled students to apply.

Amount of award:	$3,000
Application deadline:	January 4

Contact:
NASA South Carolina Space Grant Consortium
Tara B. Scozzaro MPA
College of Charleston Department of Geology
Charleston, SC 29424
Phone: 843-953-5463
Fax: 843-953-5446
Web: www.cofc.edu/~scsgrant/

NASA Space Grant Minnesota Space Grant Consortium

NASA Space Grant Minnesota Undergraduate Scholarship

Type of award: Scholarship, renewable.
Intended use: For full-time undergraduate study at accredited 4-year institution in United States. Designated institutions: Augsburg College, Bethel College, Bemidji State University, Carleton College, College of St. Catherine, Fond du Lac Community College, Leech Lake Tribal College, Macalaster College, Normandale Community College, University of Minnesota - Duluth, University of Minnesota - Twin Cities, University of St. Thomas, Concordia College, Southwest State U.
Eligibility: Applicant must be U.S. citizen.
Basis for selection: Major/career interest in aerospace; astronomy; atmospheric sciences/meteorology; biology; botany; chemistry; engineering, biomedical; engineering, chemical; engineering, civil or engineering, computer.
Application requirements: Recommendations, transcript.
Additional information: Applicants must include letter of intent and show 3.2 or greater GPA. Awardees must attend a Minnesota Space Grant Consortium member institution. The Consortium actively encourages women, minority, and physically challenged students to apply. Applicant must be attending a Minnesota State school but does not have to be a resident of the state.

Amount of award:	$1,000-$3,000
Number of awards:	15
Number of applicants:	40
Application deadline:	March 1
Notification begins:	May 15

Contact:
NASA Space Grant Minnesota Space Grant Consortium
University of Minnesota
Dept. of Aerospace Engineering & Mechanics
Minneapolis, MN 55455
Web: www.aem.umn.edu/msgc

NASA Texas Space Grant Consortium

NASA Space Grant Texas Undergraduate Scholarship Program

Type of award: Scholarship.
Intended use: For full-time senior study at accredited 4-year institution in United States. Designated institutions: Texas Space Grant member institutions.
Eligibility: Applicant must be U.S. citizen residing in Texas.
Basis for selection: Major/career interest in aerospace. Applicant must demonstrate high academic achievement.
Application requirements: Recommendations, essay, transcript, proof of eligibility.
Additional information: Awardees must be sophomores or juniors at time of application and must attend Texas Space Grant Consortium member institution. Deadline in mid-March.

Amount of award:	$1,000
Number of awards:	15
Number of applicants:	40
Application deadline:	April 16
Total amount awarded:	$15,000

Contact:
Texas Space Grant Consortium
3925 W. Braker Lane
Suite 200
Austin, TX 78749-5321
Web: www.tsgc.utexas.edu

Scholarships

NASA Vermont Space Grant Consortium

NASA Space Grant Vermont Consortium Undergraduate Scholarships

Type of award: Scholarship, renewable.
Intended use: For full-time undergraduate study in United States. Designated institutions: Vermont colleges and universities.
Eligibility: Applicant must be high school senior. Applicant must be U.S. citizen residing in Vermont.
Basis for selection: Major/career interest in science, general; engineering; mathematics; aerospace or physics.
Application requirements: Recommendations, essay, transcript.
Additional information: Open to high school seniors who intend to be enrolled full time in the following year. Applicant must be enrolled in program relevant to NASA's goals at a Vermont institution. Minimum 3.0 GPA. Out-of-state recipients qualify for in-state tuition. Three awards designated for Native American applicants; three scholarships designated for Burlington Technical Center Aviation & Technical Center, Aerospace Work Force Development and Aviation Technical School. Can be used at any accredited Vermont institution of higher education.

Amount of award:	$1,500
Number of awards:	10
Number of applicants:	30
Application deadline:	March 1
Notification begins:	March 15

Contact:
Vermont Space Grant Consortium
Votey Bldg, College of Engineering and Math
University of Vermont
Burlington, VT 05405-0156
Phone: 802-656-1429
Web: www.emba.uvm.edu/VSGC

NASA Virginia Space Grant Consortium

Aerospace Undergraduate Research Scholarship Program

Type of award: Scholarship.
Intended use: For full-time junior or senior study at accredited 4-year institution in United States. Designated institutions: College of William and Mary, Hampton University, Old Dominion University, University of Virginia, Virginia Tech.
Eligibility: Applicant must be U.S. citizen residing in Virginia.
Basis for selection: Major/career interest in aerospace; astronomy; biology; chemistry; computer/information sciences; education; engineering; geology/earth sciences; mathematics or physics. Applicant must demonstrate high academic achievement.
Application requirements: Recommendations, essay, transcript, research proposal. Resume.

Additional information: Any undergraduate major that includes coursework related to an understanding of aerospace is eligible. Minimum 3.0 GPA. Awards can include $3,000 stipend plus $1,000 travel/research during the academic year, and $3,500 stipend plus $1,000 travel/research during the summer (ten weeks). Awardees must attend a Virginia Space Grant Consortium member institution. The consortium actively encourages women, minorities and students with disabilities to apply. Application deadline is early February.

Amount of award:	$3,000-$8,500
Number of awards:	12
Number of applicants:	30
Notification begins:	April 15

Contact:
Virginia Space Grant Consortium
Old Dominion University Peninsula Center
600 Butler Farm Road
Hampton, VA 23666
Phone: 757-766-5210
Fax: 757-766-5205
Web: www.vsgc.odu.edu

NASA Space Grant Teacher Education Scholarship

Type of award: Scholarship.
Intended use: For full-time undergraduate study in United States. Designated institutions: College of William and Mary, Hampton University, Old Dominion University, University of Virginia, Virginia Tech.
Eligibility: Applicant must be high school senior. Applicant must be U.S. citizen.
Basis for selection: Major/career interest in education; computer/information sciences; mathematics or science, general.
Application requirements: Recommendations, essay, transcript.
Additional information: Applicants must be enrolled in course of study leading to pre-college teacher certification. Priority given to technology, education, mathematics, and earth/space/environmental science majors. Women, minorities and students with disabilities are encouraged to apply. Application deadline is early February.

Amount of award:	$1,000
Number of awards:	10
Number of applicants:	20
Notification begins:	April 1
Total amount awarded:	$10,000

Contact:
Virginia Space Grant Consortium
Old Dominion University Peninsula Center
2713-D Magruder Blvd.
Hampton, VA 23666
Phone: 757-766-5210
Fax: 757-766-5205
Web: www.vsgc.odu.edu

NASA Space Grant Virginia Community College Scholarship

Type of award: Scholarship.
Intended use: For sophomore study in United States. Designated institutions: Virginia community colleges.
Eligibility: Applicant must be U.S. citizen residing in Virginia.
Basis for selection: Major/career interest in aerospace; computer/information sciences; electronics; engineering; mathematics or science, general.

Application requirements: Recommendations, essay, transcript. Resume, photograph and biographical information.

Additional information: Awards are generally to full-time students (12 semester hours), but part-time students (six to nine hours) demonstrating academic achievements are also eligible. Minimum 3.0 GPA. Scholarship is open to students at all community colleges in Virginia. Application deadline may vary. Women, minorities and students with disabilities are encouraged to apply. Application deadline is early February.

Amount of award:	$1,500
Number of awards:	10
Number of applicants:	20
Notification begins:	April 1

Contact:
Virginia Space Grant Consortium
600 Butler Farm Road
Hampton, VA 23666
Phone: 757-766-5210
Fax: 757-766-5205
Web: www.vsgc.odu.edu

NASA West Virginia Space Grant Consortium

NASA Space Grant West Virginia Consortium Undergraduate Scholarship

Type of award: Scholarship, renewable.

Intended use: For full-time undergraduate study at accredited 4-year institution in United States. Designated institutions: West Virginia University, Bethany College, Fairmont State College, Marshall University, Salem International University, Shepherd College, West Virginia University Institute of Technology, West Virginia State College, Wheeling-Jesuit University, West Liberty State College, and West Virginia Wesleyan College.

Eligibility: Applicant must be U.S. citizen residing in West Virginia.

Basis for selection: Major/career interest in aerospace; science, general or engineering. Applicant must demonstrate high academic achievement and seriousness of purpose.

Application requirements: Research proposal.

Additional information: Consortium makes it possible for undergraduate scholars to work with faculty members in their major department on research project to supplement classwork. Alternatively, some undergraduate scholars participate in the Consortium Challenge Program, working with elementary students on their science projects. Application deadline usually falls in mid- to late-September.

Amount of award:	$1,000-$2,000
Number of applicants:	16

Contact:
West Virginia Space Grant Consortium
College of Engineering and Mineral Resources
P.O. Box 6070, G60 ESB
Morgantown, WV 26506-6070
Phone: 304-293-4099
Fax: 304-293-4970
Web: www.nasa.wvu.edu

NASA Space Grant West Virginia Undergraduate Fellowship Scholarship

Type of award: Scholarship, renewable.

Intended use: For full-time undergraduate study at accredited 4-year institution in United States. Designated institutions: West Virginia University, Bethany College, Fairmont State College, Marshall University, Salem International University, Shepherd College, West Virginia University Institute of Technology, West Virginia State College, Wheeling-Jesuit University, West Liberty State College and West Virginia Wesleyan College.

Eligibility: Applicant must be U.S. citizen residing in West Virginia.

Basis for selection: Major/career interest in aerospace; science, general or engineering. Applicant must demonstrate high academic achievement and seriousness of purpose.

Application requirements: Research proposal.

Additional information: Space Grant Fellowships provide full tuition, fees, and room and board for four years to selected students. During their four-year tenure as Fellows, some students work with Consortium professors and NASA advisors on aerospace project, and spend three summers working at NASA Center on project. Other students work with researchers at their respective colleges and gain valuable experience during those three summers. Visit Website for more information and to download application.

Amount of award:	Full tuition

Contact:
NASA Space Grant West Virginia Space Grant Consortium
West Virginia U, NASA Space Grant Prog.
P.O. Box 6070
Morgantown, WV 26506-6070
Phone: 304-293-4099 ext.3737
Fax: 304-293-4970
Web: www.nasa.wvu.edu

NASA Wisconsin Space Grant Consortium

NASA Academy Wisconsin Awards

Type of award: Scholarship.

Intended use: For full-time junior, senior or graduate study at accredited 4-year or graduate institution in United States. Designated institutions: NASA Field Centers.

Eligibility: Applicant must be U.S. citizen residing in Wisconsin.

Basis for selection: Major/career interest in aerospace; engineering; science, general; robotics or geology/earth sciences. Applicant must demonstrate high academic achievement, depth of character, leadership and seriousness of purpose.

Application requirements: Recommendations, transcript. SAT/ACT scores. Minimum 3.0 GPA. Two-page statement of intent, interest, and experience in space, aerospace, or space-related studies.

Additional information: Awards include competitive scholarships and fellowships for research programs at NASA Field Centers such as Goddard Space Flight Center and Ames Research Center. Amount of awards varies. Deadline varies based on Field Center. Applications sent directly to Academy not accepted. See Website for requirements and details or contact Sharon Brandt at address below.

Application deadline: January 31

Contact:
Program Manager, Wisconsin Space Grant Consortium
Dept. of Natural and Applied Sciences, UW-GB
2420 Nicolet Drive
Green Bay, WI 54311-7001
Phone: 920-465-2941
Fax: 920-465-2376
Web: www.uwgb.edu/WSGC

NASA Space Grant Wisconsin Consortium Undergraduate Scholarship

Type of award: Scholarship, renewable.
Intended use: For full-time undergraduate study at accredited 4-year institution in United States. Designated institutions: Alverno College; Carroll College; College of the Menominee Nation: Lawrence University: Marquette University: Medical College of Wisconsin; Milwaukee School of Engineering; Ripon College; University of Wisconsin at Green Bay, La Crosse, Madison, Milwaukee, Oshkosh, Parkside and Whitewater.
Eligibility: Applicant must be U.S. citizen residing in Wisconsin.
Basis for selection: Major/career interest in aerospace; astronomy; engineering; physics; science, general; architecture; law; business or medicine. Applicant must demonstrate high academic achievement.
Application requirements: Recommendations, essay, transcript. SAT/ACT scores.
Additional information: Applicant must attend Wisconsin Space Grant Consortium member institution and reside in Wisconsin during school year. Minimum 3.0 GPA. Qualified students may also apply for summer session's Undergraduate Research Award. Consortium actively encourages women, minorities and students with disabilities to apply. See Website for application and details.

  Amount of award: $3,500
  Application deadline: February 14
Contact:
Thomas Achtor, Wisconsin Space Grant Consortium
University of Wisconsin - Green Bay
2420 Nicolet Drive
Green Bay, WI 54311-7001
Phone: 920-465-2941
Fax: 920-465-2376
Web: www.uwgb.edu/WSGC

NASA Space Grant Wisconsin Undergraduate Research Awards

Type of award: Research grant, renewable.
Intended use: For full-time undergraduate study at accredited 4-year institution in United States. Designated institutions: Alverno College, Carroll College, College of the Menominee Nation, Lawrence University, Marquette University, Medical College of Wisconsin, Milwaukee School of Engineering, Ripon College, St. Norbert College, and University of Wisconsin Green Bay, La Crosse, Madison, Milwaukee, Oshkosh, Parkside, and Whitewater.
Eligibility: Applicant must be U.S. citizen residing in Wisconsin.

Basis for selection: Major/career interest in aerospace; astronomy; engineering; physics; science, general or aviation. Applicant must demonstrate high academic achievement.
Application requirements: Recommendations, transcript, research proposal. Proposal and budget for project related to aerospace, space science or other space-related studies. SAT/ACT scores.
Additional information: Applicants must attend WSGC member college and universities. Awards are for one year. Minimum 3.0 GPA. WSGC actively encourages women, minority students, and disabled students to apply. See Website to download application and complete list of eligible institutions.

  Amount of award: $4,000
  Application deadline: February 14
Contact:
NASA Space Grant Wisconsin Space Grant Consortium c/o Thomas Achtor
Space Science and Engineering Center
1225 W. Dayton Street, Room 251
Madison, WI 53706-1280
Phone: 608-263-4206
Fax: 608-262-5974
Web: www.uwgb.edu/wsgc

Space Grant Wisconsin Consortium Undergraduate Research Award

Type of award: Research grant.
Intended use: For full-time undergraduate study at 2-year or 4-year institution. Designated institutions: Alverno College; Carroll College; College of the Menominee Nation: Lawrence University: Marquette University: Medical College of Wisconsin; Milwaukee School of Engineering; Ripon College; the University of Wisconsin at Green Bay, La Crosse, Madison, Milwaukee, Oshkosh, Parkside and Whitewater.
Eligibility: Applicant must be U.S. citizen.
Basis for selection: Major/career interest in aerospace; astronomy; engineering; science, general; architecture; law; business or medicine. Applicant must demonstrate high academic achievement and seriousness of purpose.
Application requirements: Recommendations, transcript, research proposal. Completed appplication packet. Agreement by faculty or research staff member on campus to act as adviser for project. Project proposal with budget. SAT/ACT scores. Two letters of recommendation.
Additional information: Funding for qualified students to create and implement a small research study related to aerospace, space science or other interdisciplinary space-related studies. For academic year or summer term use. Award up to $3,500; additional $500 may be awarded for exceptional expenses. Minimum 3.0 GPA required. Consortium encourages applications from women, minorities and students with disabilities. For more information, contact Wisconsin Space Grant Consortium.

  Amount of award: $3,500
  Application deadline: March 1
Contact:
Wisconsin Space Grant Consortium
Space Science and Engineering Center
1225 W. Dayton Street, Room 251
Madison, WI 53706-1280
Phone: 608-263-4206
Fax: 608-262-5974
Web: www.uwgb.edu/wsgc

NASA Wyoming Space Grant Consortium

NASA Space Grant Wyoming Undergraduate Research Fellowships

Type of award: Research grant.
Intended use: For undergraduate study at accredited postsecondary institution in United States. Designated institutions: Eligible Wyoming institutions.
Eligibility: Applicant must be U.S. citizen.
Basis for selection: Major/career interest in aerospace; engineering; science, general or energy research. Applicant must demonstrate high academic achievement.
Application requirements: Transcript, proof of eligibility, research proposal.
Additional information: Funding for research projects available through Wyoming Space Grant program. Contact project coordinator at the University of Wyoming. Proposals that cannot be funded from other sources given priority. Research expected to result in refereed publication. Underrepresented groups encouraged to apply. Visit Website for more details. Contact sponsor for complete list of eligible Wyoming institutions.

Amount of award:	$5,000
Number of awards:	10
Number of applicants:	20
Application deadline:	February 16
Total amount awarded:	$45,000

Contact:
NASA Space Grant Wyoming Space Grant Consortium
P.O. Box 3905
University of Wyoming
Laramie, WY 82071-3905
Phone: 307-766-2862
Web: wyomingspacegrant.uwyo.edu

NASA/Delaware Space Grant Consortium

Delaware Space Grant Undergraduate Tuition Scholarship

Type of award: Scholarship, renewable.
Intended use: For full-time undergraduate study. Designated institutions: University of Delaware, Delaware Technical and Community College, Franklin and Marshall College, Gettysburg College, Lehigh University, Swarthmore College, Delaware State University at Dover, Villanova University, Wilmington College.
Eligibility: Applicant must be U.S. citizen.
Basis for selection: Major/career interest in aerospace; astronomy; communications; engineering; geography; geology/earth sciences; geophysics; physics or oceanography/marine studies.
Application requirements: Recommendations, transcript. Applicant statement.

Additional information: Applicants must have proven interest in space-related studies. Recipient must attend Delaware Space Grant Consortium member institution.

Amount of award:	$4,000
Application deadline:	March 1
Notification begins:	March 15
Total amount awarded:	$21,145

Contact:
Delaware Space Grant Consortium Program Office
University of Delaware
217 Sharp Lab
Newark, DE 19716
Phone: 302-831-1094
Fax: 302-831-1843
Web: www.delspace.org

National Academy for Nuclear Training

Scholarship Educational Assistance Program

Type of award: Scholarship, renewable.
Intended use: For full-time sophomore, junior or senior study at accredited 4-year institution in United States. Designated institutions: Institutions with accredited programs in relevant fields of study.
Eligibility: Applicant must be U.S. citizen.
Basis for selection: Major/career interest in engineering, chemical; engineering, mechanical; engineering, electrical/electronic or engineering, nuclear. Applicant must demonstrate high academic achievement, depth of character, leadership, seriousness of purpose and service orientation.
Application requirements: Recommendations, essay, transcript, proof of eligibility, nomination by department head. Minimum 3.0 GPA.
Additional information: Renewal up to three years for eligible students. Additional field of study: power generation health physics. Study of chemical engineering must include nuclear or power option. Applicant should be considering career in nuclear utility industry. For additional information and important dates, contact by e-mail or visit Website.

Amount of award:	$2,500
Number of awards:	150
Total amount awarded:	$375,000

Contact:
National Academy for Nuclear Training Scholarship Program
301 ACT Drive, P.O. Box 4030
Iowa City, IA 52243-4030
Phone: 800-294-7492
Web: www.nei.org/nantscholarships

National Alliance for Excellence, Inc.

National Alliance for Excellence Honored Scholars and Artists Program

Type of award: Scholarship.
Intended use: For full-time undergraduate or graduate study at accredited 2-year, 4-year or graduate institution in or outside United States.
Eligibility: Applicant must be U.S. citizen.
Basis for selection: Major/career interest in humanities/liberal arts; accounting; arts, general or education.
Application requirements: $5 application fee. Recommendations.
Additional information: These highly competitive awards go to the country's best and brightest and are presented by govenors, senators and congressional representatives. There is no application deadline as this is a year-round competition. Application can be received by sendiing a SASE with request or by visiting Website.

Amount of award:	$1,000-$5,000
Number of awards:	50
Number of applicants:	9,000

Contact:
National Alliance for Excellence, Inc.
1070-H Hwy34, #205
Matawan, NJ 07747
Phone: 732-765-1730
Fax: 732-765-1732
Web: www.excellence.org

National Amateur Baseball Federation, Inc.

National Amateur Baseball Federation Scholarship

Type of award: Scholarship, renewable.
Intended use: For undergraduate study in United States or Canada.
Eligibility: Applicant or parent must be member/participant of National Amateur Baseball Federation.
Basis for selection: Competition/talent/interest in athletics/sports. Major/career interest in athletic training. Applicant must demonstrate financial need and high academic achievement.
Application requirements: Recommendations, transcript, proof of eligibility. Written statement. Previous awards to candidates from sponsoring association.
Additional information: Amount of award determined annually. Applicant must have participated in National Amateur Baseball Federation event and be sponsored by National Amateur Baseball Federation member association. Send SASE for application packet.

Amount of award:	$500-$1,000
Number of awards:	10
Number of applicants:	12
Application deadline:	September 1
Total amount awarded:	$9,000

Contact:
National Amateur Baseball Federation
Attn: Chairman Awards Committee
P.O. Box 705
Bowie, MD 20718
Phone: 301-262-5005
Web: www.nabf.com

National Art Materials Trade Association

National Art Materials Scholarship

Type of award: Scholarship.
Intended use: For undergraduate or graduate study at accredited postsecondary institution in or outside United States.
Eligibility: Applicant or parent must be member/participant of National Art Materials Trade Association.
Basis for selection: Applicant must demonstrate financial need, high academic achievement, depth of character, seriousness of purpose and service orientation.
Application requirements: Essay, transcript. Proof of acceptance.
Additional information: NAMTA will award two $1,500 academic scholarships to employees or family members of NAMTA member firms. Two $2,500 art scholarships will be awarded to any student majoring in, or planning to major in, any art-related field.

Amount of award:	$1,500-$2,500
Number of awards:	4
Number of applicants:	83
Application deadline:	April 1
Notification begins:	June 1
Total amount awarded:	$8,000

Contact:
Katharine D. Coffey, National Art Materials Trade Association
15806 Brookway Drive
Suite 300
Huntersville, NC 28078
Phone: 704-892-6244
Fax: 704-892-6247
Web: www.namta.org

National Association of Black Accountants Inc.

NABA National Scholarship Program

Type of award: Scholarship.
Intended use: For full-time undergraduate or master's study at 4-year or graduate institution.
Eligibility: Applicant or parent must be member/participant of National Association of Black Accountants. Applicant must be Alaskan native, Asian American, African American, Mexican American, Hispanic American, Puerto Rican or American Indian.
Basis for selection: Major/career interest in accounting or business. Applicant must demonstrate depth of character, leadership and service orientation.

Application requirements: Essay, transcript, proof of eligibility. Application. Personal biography discussing career objectives, leadership abilities, community activities, and involvement with NABA (500 words or less). Student Aid Report. Financial aid transcript from financial aid office (if applicant is U.S. citizen). Resume.

Additional information: Applicants must have 2.5 GPA or better. Applicants may join association upon submission of scholarship application.

Amount of award:	$500-$6,000
Number of awards:	45
Number of applicants:	120
Application deadline:	December 31
Notification begins:	April 15
Total amount awarded:	$100,000

Contact:
National Association of Black Accountants Inc.
National Scholarship Program
7249-A Hanover Parkway
Greenbelt, MD 20770
Phone: 301-474-6222
Fax: 301-474-3114
Web: www.nabainc.org

National Association of Black Journalists

NABJ Non-Sustaining Scholarship

Type of award: Scholarship.
Intended use: For undergraduate, master's, doctoral, first professional or postgraduate study at accredited 4-year or graduate institution.
Eligibility: Applicant must be African American. Applicant must be U.S. citizen.
Basis for selection: Major/career interest in journalism or radio/television/film.
Application requirements: Recommendations, essay, transcript, nomination. Applicant must maintain minimum 2.5 GPA, and attend NABJ convention to work on the convention student project. Essay must demonstrate why applicant wants to become a journalist. Resume required.
Additional information: Must become member of National Association of Black Journalists before award is given and participate in the NABJ Mentor Program. Applicants of African descent from countries outside the United States are also eligible. Several $2500 scholarships are given, while only one $5000 scholarship is awarded. Applicant must either be going into a journalism degree program, have a position on their school newspaper or have a position on their campus TV station, radio station or Website.

Amount of award:	$2,500-$5,000
Application deadline:	April 15

Contact:
NABJ--Scholarship Programs
8701 Adelphi Road
Adelphi, MD 20783-1716
Phone: 301-445-7100
Fax: 301-445-7101
Web: www.nabj.org

National Association of Insurance Women Education Foundation

NAIW Education Foundation College Scholarship

Type of award: Scholarship.
Intended use: For junior, senior or graduate study at accredited 4-year or graduate institution.
Basis for selection: Major/career interest in insurance/actuarial science.
Application requirements: Essay, transcript. Three letters of recommendation. Application (must be signed by candidate and representative of college/university).
Additional information: Applicant must be major or minor in insurance, risk management or actuarial science with a minimum 3.0 GPA. Must have completed or be currently enrolled in two insurance, actuarial science or risk-management-related courses, a minimum of three credit hours each. Application must be received by NAIW by March 1. Postmark dates have no bearing on the deadline. See Website to download form.

Amount of award:	$1,000-$4,000
Application deadline:	March 1

Contact:
NAIW Education Foundation
5310 31st Street
Suite 302
Tulsa, OK 74135
Phone: 918-622-1816
Fax: 918-622-1821
Web: www.naiwfoundation.org

National Association of Insurance Women- Portland Maine Chapter

Junior Achievement of Maine Scholarship

Type of award: Scholarship.
Intended use: For undergraduate study at accredited postsecondary institution in United States.
Eligibility: Applicant must be high school senior. Applicant must be residing in Maine.
Basis for selection: Major/career interest in business. Applicant must demonstrate high academic achievement.
Application requirements: Recommendations, essay, proof of eligibility.
Additional information: Must have participated in Junior Achievement programs during high school or volunteered to teach a junior achievement class during current year as high school or college student.

Amount of award:	$1,000
Number of awards:	1
Number of applicants:	10
Application deadline:	February 1
Notification begins:	May 1
Total amount awarded:	$1,000

Contact:
Scholarship Coordinator Junior Achievement of Maine
Dana Warp Mill
90 Bridge Street, Suite 120
Westbrook, ME 04092
Web: maine.ja.org

National Association of Letter Carriers

Costas G. Lemonopoulos Scholarship

Type of award: Scholarship, renewable.
Intended use: For full-time freshman, sophomore, junior or senior study at 4-year institution. Designated institutions: St. Petersburg Junior College or four-year public Florida university.
Eligibility: Applicant or parent must be member/participant of National Association of Letter Carriers.
Basis for selection: Applicant must demonstrate high academic achievement.
Application requirements: Transcript. SAT/ACT scores (copy must be sent by student) and NALC form.
Additional information: Open to children of NALC members. High school seniors and college students may apply. Limit two awards. Must apply through NALC. Winners notified in late September. Awards paid in December by the Pinellas County Community Foundation of Clearwater, Florida. Complete information published each April, with coupon, in the NALC Postal Record.

Amount of award:	$400-$1,000
Number of awards:	20
Number of applicants:	75
Application deadline:	June 1

Contact:
National Association of Letter Carriers
100 Indiana Avenue NW
Washington, DC 20001-2144
Web: www.nalc.org

William C. Doherty Scholarship

Type of award: Scholarship, renewable.
Intended use: For full-time freshman, sophomore, junior or senior study at accredited 4-year institution.
Eligibility: Applicant or parent must be member/participant of National Association of Letter Carriers. Applicant must be high school senior.
Basis for selection: Applicant must demonstrate financial need and high academic achievement.
Application requirements: Recommendations, essay, transcript, proof of eligibility. SAT/ACT scores (copy must be sent by student).
Additional information: Applicant must be child of letter carrier NALC member in good standing (active, retired or deceased). Applications are printed in July through November issues of NALC newsletter. Students will be notified through newsletter.

Amount of award:	$1,000-$4,000
Number of awards:	6
Application deadline:	December 31
Total amount awarded:	$21,000

Contact:
National Association of Letter Carriers
100 Indiana Avenue NW
Washington, DC 20001
Web: www.nalc.org

National Association of Water Companies (NJ Chapter)

Water Companies (NJ Chapter) Scholarship

Type of award: Scholarship.
Intended use: For freshman, sophomore, junior, senior or graduate study at accredited 2-year, 4-year or graduate institution in United States. Designated institutions: Institutions in New Jersey.
Eligibility: Applicant must be U.S. citizen residing in New Jersey.
Basis for selection: Major/career interest in hydrology; natural resources/conservation; science, general; engineering, environmental; finance/banking; communications; accounting; business; computer/information sciences or law. Applicant must demonstrate financial need, high academic achievement, depth of character, leadership, seriousness of purpose and service orientation.
Application requirements: Recommendations, essay, transcript. Essay must illustrate interest in investor-owned water utility field.
Additional information: Applicant must have interest in relating fields of study to water industry. Acceptable fields of study also include consumer affairs and human resources. At least five years residence in New Jersey required. Minimum 3.0 GPA.

Amount of award:	$2,500
Number of awards:	2
Number of applicants:	25
Application deadline:	April 1
Notification begins:	June 1
Total amount awarded:	$5,000

Contact:
Nat'l Assn. of Water Companies (NJ Chapter) Attn: A. Bruce O'Connor
c/o Middlesex Water Company
1500 Ronson Road
Iselin, NJ 08830
Phone: 732-634-1502 ext. 211

National Association of Women in Construction

Women in Construction: Founders' Scholarship

Type of award: Scholarship.
Intended use: For full-time undergraduate study at accredited postsecondary institution in United States.
Eligibility: Applicant must be U.S. citizen.
Basis for selection: Major/career interest in construction; construction management; engineering, construction or architecture. Applicant must demonstrate financial need and high academic achievement.
Application requirements: Interview, recommendations, transcript.
Additional information: Number and amount of awards vary. Interest in construction, extracurricular activities and employment experience also taken into consideration. Applicants must have completed one term of study in construction-related field. Must have current GPA of 3.0 or higher. Only semifinalists will be interviewed. Visit Website for additional information and to download application.

Amount of award:	$1,500-$2,000
Application deadline:	April 1
Notification begins:	April 1

Contact:
National Association of Women in Construction
327 South Adams Street
Fort Worth, TX 76104
Phone: 800-552-3506
Web: www.nawic.org

National Athletic Trainers' Association

Athletic Trainers' Curriculum Scholarship

Type of award: Scholarship.
Intended use: For full-time undergraduate or master's study at accredited 4-year or graduate institution. Designated institutions: Contact Association for list of institutions.
Eligibility: Applicant or parent must be member/participant of National Athletic Trainers Association.
Basis for selection: Major/career interest in athletic training. Applicant must demonstrate high academic achievement.
Application requirements: Recommendations, essay, transcript, proof of eligibility.
Additional information: Minimum 3.2 GPA required. Must be planning a career in athletic training.

Amount of award:	$2,000
Application deadline:	February 1
Notification begins:	April 15

Contact:
National Athletic Trainers' Association
2952 Stemmons Freeway
Dallas, TX 75247
Web: www.nata.org

Athletic Trainers' Student Writing Contest

Type of award: Scholarship.
Intended use: For undergraduate or graduate study at 2-year, 4-year or graduate institution.
Eligibility: Applicant or parent must be member/participant of National Athletic Trainers Association.
Basis for selection: Competition/talent/interest in writing/journalism, based on paper related to the athletic training profession. Major/career interest in athletic training. Applicant must demonstrate high academic achievement.
Application requirements: Essay, proof of eligibility.
Additional information: Applicants must submit one original and two copies of essay. Topic may be case report, literature review, experimental report, analysis of training room techniques, etc. Must not have been published or be under consideration for publication. Award varies depending on availability of funds. See NATA News bulletin for more information.

Number of awards:	1
Application deadline:	March 1
Notification begins:	April 15

Contact:
National Athletic Trainers' Association Student Writing Contest
Life University, 1269 Barclay Circle
Marietta, GA 30060
Web: www.nata.org

Athletic Trainers' Undergraduate Scholarship

Type of award: Scholarship.
Intended use: For full-time junior or senior study at 4-year institution.
Eligibility: Applicant or parent must be member/participant of National Athletic Trainers Association.
Basis for selection: Applicant must demonstrate high academic achievement.
Application requirements: Recommendations, essay, transcript, proof of eligibility.
Additional information: Minimum 3.2 GPA required. Intention to pursue the profession of athletic training as career required. Must be sponsored by a certified athletic trainer.

Amount of award:	$2,000
Number of awards:	59
Application deadline:	February 1
Notification begins:	April 15
Total amount awarded:	$118,000

Contact:
National Athletic Trainers' Association
Research and Education Foundation
2952 Stemmons Freeway
Dallas, TX 75247
Web: www.nata.org

National Black Nurses Association

Black Nurses Scholarship

Type of award: Scholarship.
Intended use: For undergraduate or graduate study.

Eligibility: Applicant or parent must be member/participant of National Black Nurses' Association. Applicant must be African American.

Basis for selection: Major/career interest in nursing or nurse practitioner. Applicant must demonstrate seriousness of purpose and service orientation.

Application requirements: Recommendations, essay, transcript. Evidence of participation in both student nursing activities and the African-American community. Five-page double-spaced essay describing extracurricular activities, community involvement, how role as nurse can improve the health and/or social conditions of African Americans and statement about future goals in nursing. Two letters of recommendation from school of nursing and local chapter or nurse from local area.

Additional information: Applicants must be currently enrolled in a nursing program and have at least one full year of school left. Must be in good academic standing. Call association for current information on program.

Amount of award:	$500-$2,000
Number of awards:	10
Number of applicants:	50
Application deadline:	April 15
Notification begins:	July 1

Contact:
National Black Nurses Association
8630 Fenton Street
Silver Spring, MD 20910
Phone: 301-589-3200
Fax: 301-589-3223
Web: www.nbna.org

National Black Police Association

Alphonso Deal Scholarship

Type of award: Scholarship.
Intended use: For freshman study at 2-year or 4-year institution in United States.
Eligibility: Applicant must be enrolled in high school. Applicant must be U.S. citizen.
Basis for selection: Major/career interest in law or criminal justice/law enforcement. Applicant must demonstrate high academic achievement, depth of character, seriousness of purpose and service orientation.
Application requirements: Recommendations, essay, transcript. Applicant must be accepted by a college or university prior to date of award.
Additional information: Award provides higher education training for the betterment of the criminal justice system.

Amount of award:	$500
Number of awards:	5
Number of applicants:	2,500
Application deadline:	June 1
Total amount awarded:	$2,500

Contact:
National Black Police Association Scholarship Award
3251 Mount Pleasant Street, NW
Washington, DC 20010-2103
Phone: 202-986-2070
Fax: 202-986-0410
Web: www.blackpolice.org

National Dairy Council

Scholar Athlete Milk Mustache of the Year Awards

Type of award: Scholarship.
Intended use: For undergraduate study.
Eligibility: Applicant must be high school senior.
Basis for selection: Competition/talent/interest in Athletics/sports, selection based on academic performance, athletic excellence, leadership skills and community service. Major/career interest in sports/sports administration. Applicant must demonstrate high academic achievement, leadership and service orientation.
Application requirements: Essay. A description, in 75 words or less, of how drinking milk is part of applicant's life and training regimen.
Additional information: In addition to scholarship, winners receive spot in SAMMY Hall of Fame located in Milk House at Disney's Wide World of Sports and trip to Disney World to be honored in special ceremony. SAMMY award winners will be selected based on four criteria: academic performance, athletic excellence, leadership skills and community service. Visit Website for application, important dates, and more information.

Amount of award:	$7,500
Number of awards:	25
Total amount awarded:	$187,500

Contact:
Visit Website for more information.
Web: www.whymilk.com

National Dairy Shrine

Dairy Student Recognition Program

Type of award: Scholarship.
Intended use: For senior study.
Basis for selection: Major/career interest in dairy; food production/management/services or food science/technology. Applicant must demonstrate leadership.
Application requirements: Recommendations, essay, nomination by college or university dairy science departments.
Additional information: Cash awards for graduating seniors planning career in dairy cattle. Two candidates eligible per institution. First-place winner receives $1,500, second place $1,000, third through seventh, $500. National Dairy Shrine chooses final winners. Students who placed in top five in previous years not eligible for further competition.

Amount of award:	$500-$1,500
Number of awards:	10
Number of applicants:	20
Application deadline:	March 15
Notification begins:	June 10
Total amount awarded:	$6,000

Contact:
National Dairy Shrine
1224 Alton Darby Creek Road
Columbus, OH 43228-9792
Web: www.dairyshrine.org

Marshall E. McCullough Undergraduate Scholarship

Type of award: Scholarship.
Intended use: For full-time senior study at accredited 4-year institution in United States.
Eligibility: Applicant must be high school senior. Applicant must be U.S. citizen.
Basis for selection: Major/career interest in animal sciences; dairy; communications or journalism.
Application requirements: Recommendations, essay.
Additional information: Two awards: one for $2,500; one for $1,000. Must major in dairy/animal science with communications emphasis or agricultural journalism with dairy/animal science emphasis.

Amount of award:	$1,000-$2,500
Number of awards:	2
Application deadline:	March 15
Notification begins:	July 1

Contact:
National Dairy Shrine
1224 Alton Darby Creek Road
Columbus, OH 43228-9792
Phone: 614-878-5333
Fax: 614-870-9792
Web: www.dairyshrine.org

National Dairy Shrine Kildee Scholarship

Type of award: Scholarship.
Intended use: For undergraduate study.
Basis for selection: Major/career interest in food production/management/services; food science/technology or dairy.
Additional information: May request application from Website or National Dairy Shrine.

Number of awards:	1
Number of applicants:	18
Application deadline:	March 15
Total amount awarded:	$2,000

Contact:
National Dairy Shrine
1224 Alton Darby Creek
Columbus, OH 43228
Web: www.dairyshrine.org

National Dairy Shrine Klussendorf Scholarship

Type of award: Scholarship.
Intended use: For undergraduate study.
Basis for selection: Major/career interest in food production/management/services; food science/technology or dairy.
Additional information: May request application from Website or National Dairy Shrine.

Amount of award:	$1,000
Number of awards:	1
Number of applicants:	9
Application deadline:	March 15
Total amount awarded:	$1,000

Contact:
National Dairy Shrine
1224 Alton Darby Creek
Columbus, OH 43228
Web: www.dairyshrine.org

National Dairy Shrine/Iager Dairy Scholarship

Type of award: Scholarship.
Intended use: For undergraduate study.
Basis for selection: Major/career interest in food production/management/services; food science/technology or dairy.
Additional information: May request application from Website or National Dairy Shrine.

Amount of award:	$1,000
Application deadline:	March 15

Contact:
National Dairy Shrine
1224 Alton Darby Creek
Columbus, OH 43228
Web: www.dairyshrine.org

National Environmental Health Association

American Academy of Sanitarians Scholarship

Type of award: Scholarship.
Intended use: For full-time junior, senior or graduate study at accredited 4-year or graduate institution.
Basis for selection: Major/career interest in environmental science or public health. Applicant must demonstrate financial need, high academic achievement and seriousness of purpose.
Application requirements: Recommendations, transcript, proof of eligibility. Three letters of recommendation (one from active NEHA member, two from faculty members at applicant's school).
Additional information: Undergraduates must be enrolled in an Environmental Health Accreditation Council accredited school or National Environmental Health Association Institutional/Educational or sustaining member school (list available at sponsor Website). Graduates must be enrolled in environmental health science and/or public health program.

Application deadline:	February 1

Contact:
National Environmental Health Association
NEHA/AAS Scholarship
720 South Colorado Blvd South Tower, 970
Denver, CO 80246-1925
Phone: 303-756-9090
Web: www.neha.org

National Federation of the Blind

Computer Science Scholarship

Type of award: Scholarship, renewable.
Intended use: For full-time undergraduate or graduate study at postsecondary institution.
Eligibility: Applicant must be visually impaired.
Basis for selection: Major/career interest in computer/information sciences; engineering, computer or computer

graphics. Applicant must demonstrate financial need, high academic achievement and service orientation.

Application requirements: Recommendations, transcript. Personal letter from applicant, letter from state officer of Federation, two letters of recommendation, score reports for all standardized tests taken for college admission (high school seniors only).

Additional information: Applicant must be legally blind. Recipients of federation scholarships need not be members of National Federation of the Blind. Visit Website to download application. All applications must be filed in hard copy by mail.

Amount of award:	$3,000
Number of awards:	1
Application deadline:	March 31
Notification begins:	June 1
Total amount awarded:	$3,000

Contact:
National Federation of the Blind Scholarship Committee
Mrs. Peggy Elliott, Chairman
805 Fifth Avenue
Grinnell, IA 50112
Phone: 641-236-3366
Web: www.nfb.org

E.U. Parker Memorial Scholarship

Type of award: Scholarship, renewable.

Intended use: For full-time undergraduate or graduate study at postsecondary institution.

Eligibility: Applicant must be visually impaired.

Basis for selection: Applicant must demonstrate financial need, high academic achievement and service orientation.

Application requirements: Recommendations, transcript. Personal letter from applicant, letter from state officer of Federation, two letters of recommendation, score reports for all standardized tests taken for college admission (high school seniors only).

Additional information: Applicant must be legally blind. Recipients of federation scholarships need not be members of National Federation of the Blind. Visit Website to download application. All applications must be filed in hardcopy by mail.

Amount of award:	$3,000
Number of awards:	1
Application deadline:	March 31
Notification begins:	June 1
Total amount awarded:	$3,000

Contact:
National Federation of the Blind Scholarship Committee
Mrs. Peggy Elliott, Chairman
805 Fifth Avenue
Grinnell, IA 50112
Phone: 641-236-3366
Web: www.nfb.org

Hank LeBonne Scholarship

Type of award: Scholarship.

Intended use: For full-time undergraduate or graduate study at postsecondary institution in United States.

Eligibility: Applicant must be visually impaired.

Application requirements: Recommendations, transcript. Personal letter from applicant, letter from state officer of Federation, two letters of recommendation, score reports for all standardized tests taken for college admission (high school seniors only).

Additional information: Visit Website to download application. All applications must be filed in hard copy by mail.

Amount of award:	$5,000
Application deadline:	March 31

Contact:
National Federation for the Blind
Mrs. Peggy Elliot, Chairman
805 Fifth Avenue
Grinnell, IA 50112
Phone: 641-236-3366
Web: www.nfb.org

Hermione Grant Calhoun Scholarship

Type of award: Scholarship, renewable.

Intended use: For full-time undergraduate or graduate study at postsecondary institution.

Eligibility: Applicant must be visually impaired. Applicant must be female.

Basis for selection: Applicant must demonstrate financial need, high academic achievement and service orientation.

Application requirements: Recommendations, transcript. Personal letter from applicant, letter from state officer of Federation, two letters of recommendation, score reports for all standardized tests taken for college admission (high school seniors only).

Additional information: Applicant must be a legally blind woman. Recipients of federation scholarships need not be members of National Federation of the Blind. Visit Website to download application. All applications must be filed in hard copy by mail.

Amount of award:	$3,000
Number of awards:	1
Application deadline:	March 31
Notification begins:	June 1
Total amount awarded:	$3,000

Contact:
National Federation of the Blind Scholarship Committee
Mrs. Peggy Elliott, Chairman
805 Fifth Avenue
Grinnell, IA 50112
Phone: 641-236-3366
Web: www.nfb.org

Howard Brown Rickard Scholarship

Type of award: Scholarship, renewable.

Intended use: For full-time undergraduate or graduate study at postsecondary institution.

Eligibility: Applicant must be visually impaired.

Basis for selection: Major/career interest in law; medicine; engineering; architecture or natural sciences. Applicant must demonstrate financial need, high academic achievement and service orientation.

Application requirements: Recommendations, transcript. Personal letter from applicant, letter from state officer of Federation, two letters of recommendation, score reports for all standardized tests taken for college admission (high school seniors only).

Additional information: Applicant must be legally blind. Recipients of federation scholarships need not be members of National Federation of the Blind. Visit Website to download application. All applications must be filed in hard copy by mail.

Amount of award:	$3,000
Number of awards:	1
Application deadline:	March 31
Notification begins:	June 1
Total amount awarded:	$3,000

Contact:
National Federation of the Blind Scholarship Committee
Mrs. Peggy Elliott, Chairman
805 Fifth Avenue
Grinnell, IA 50112
Phone: 621-236-3366
Web: www.nfb.org

Jennica Ferguson Memorial Scholarship

Type of award: Scholarship, renewable.
Intended use: For full-time undergraduate or graduate study at postsecondary institution.
Eligibility: Applicant must be visually impaired.
Basis for selection: Applicant must demonstrate financial need, high academic achievement and service orientation.
Application requirements: Recommendations, transcript. Personal letter from applicant, letter from state officer of Federation, two letters of recommendation, score reports for all standardized tests taken for college admission (high school seniors only).
Additional information: Applicant must be legally blind. Recipients of federation scholarships need not be members of National Federation of the Blind. Visit Website to download application. Applications should be filed in hard copy and by mail.

Amount of award:	$5,000
Number of awards:	1
Application deadline:	March 31
Notification begins:	June 1
Total amount awarded:	$5,000

Contact:
National Federation of the Blind Scholarship Committee
Mrs. Peggy Elliott, Chairman
805 Fifth Avenue
Grinnell, IA 50112
Phone: 641-236-3366
Web: www.nfb.org

Kenneth Jernigan Memorial Scholarship

Type of award: Scholarship, renewable.
Intended use: For full-time undergraduate or graduate study.
Eligibility: Applicant must be visually impaired.
Basis for selection: Applicant must demonstrate financial need, high academic achievement and service orientation.
Application requirements: Recommendations, transcript. Personal letter from applicant, letter from state officer of Federation, two letters of recommendation, score reports for all standardized tests taken for college admission (high school seniors only).
Additional information: Applicant must be legally blind. Recipients of federation scholarships need not be members of Federation. Visit Website to download application. All applications must be filed in hard copy by mail.

Amount of award:	$12,000
Number of awards:	1
Application deadline:	March 31
Notification begins:	June 1
Total amount awarded:	$12,000

Contact:
National Federation of the Blind Scholarship Committee
Mrs. Peggy Elliott, Chairman
805 Fifth Avenue
Grinnell, IA 50112
Phone: 641-236-3366
Web: www.nfb.org

Kucher-Killian Memorial Scholarship

Type of award: Scholarship, renewable.
Intended use: For full-time undergraduate or graduate study at postsecondary institution.
Eligibility: Applicant must be visually impaired.
Basis for selection: Applicant must demonstrate financial need, high academic achievement and service orientation.
Application requirements: Recommendations, transcript. Personal letter from applicant, letter from state officer of Federation, two letters of recommendation, score reports for all standardized tests taken for college admission (high school seniors only).
Additional information: Applicant must be legally blind. Recipients of federation scholarships need not be members of National Federation of the Blind. Visit Website to download application. All applications must be filed in hard copy by mail.

Amount of award:	$3,000
Number of awards:	1
Application deadline:	March 31
Notification begins:	June 1
Total amount awarded:	$3,000

Contact:
National Federation of the Blind Scholarship Committee
Mrs. Peggy Elliott, Chairman
805 Fifth Avenue
Grinnell, IA 50112
Phone: 641-236-3366
Web: www.nfb.org

Melva T. Owen Memorial Scholarship

Type of award: Scholarship, renewable.
Intended use: For full-time undergraduate or graduate study at postsecondary institution.
Eligibility: Applicant must be visually impaired.
Basis for selection: Applicant must demonstrate financial need, high academic achievement and service orientation.
Application requirements: Recommendations, transcript. Personal letter from applicant, letter from state officer of Federation, two letters of recommendation, score reports for all standardized tests taken for college admission (high school seniors only).
Additional information: Applicant must be legally blind. Field of study should be directed toward attaining financial independence. Excludes study of religion and those seeking only to further general or cultural education. Recipients of federation scholarships need not be members of National Federation of the Blind. Visit Website to download application. All applications must be filed in hard copy by mail.

Amount of award:	$10,000
Number of awards:	1
Application deadline:	March 31
Notification begins:	June 1

Contact:
National Federation of the Blind Scholarship Committee
Mrs. Peggy Elliott, Chairman
805 Fifth Avenue
Grinnell, IA 50112
Phone: 641-236-3366
Web: www.nfb.org

Michael and Marie Marucci Scholarship

Type of award: Scholarship, renewable.
Intended use: For full-time undergraduate or graduate study at postsecondary institution.
Eligibility: Applicant must be visually impaired.
Basis for selection: Major/career interest in foreign languages; literature; history; geography; political science/government; international studies or international relations. Applicant must demonstrate financial need, high academic achievement and service orientation.
Application requirements: Recommendations, transcript. Personal letter from applicant, letter from state officer of Federation, two letters of recommendation, score reports for all standardized tests taken for college admission (high school seniors only).
Additional information: Applicant must be legally blind. Applicant must be studying foreign language or comparative literature; pursuing degree in history, geography or political science with concentration in international studies; or majoring in any discipline that involves study abroad. Must also show evidence of competence in foreign language. Recipients of federation scholarships need not be members of National Federation of the Blind. Visit Website to download application. All applications must be filed in hard copy by mail.

Amount of award:	$5,000
Number of awards:	22
Application deadline:	March 31
Notification begins:	June 1

Contact:
National Federation of the Blind Scholarship Committee
Mrs. Peggy Elliott, Chairman
805 Fifth Avenue
Grinnell, IA 50112
Phone: 641-236-3366
Web: www.nfb.org

National Federation of the Blind Educator of Tomorrow Award

Type of award: Scholarship, renewable.
Intended use: For full-time undergraduate or graduate study at postsecondary institution.
Eligibility: Applicant must be visually impaired.
Basis for selection: Major/career interest in education, teacher or education. Applicant must demonstrate financial need, high academic achievement and service orientation.
Application requirements: Recommendations, transcript. Personal letter from applicant, letter from state officer of Federation, two letters of recommendation, score reports for all standardized tests taken for college admission (high school seniors only).
Additional information: Applicant must be legally blind. Must be planning career in elementary, secondary, or postsecondary teaching. Recipients of federation scholarships need not be memebers of National Federation of the Blind. Visit Website to download application. All applications must be filed in hard copy by mail.

Amount of award:	$3,000
Number of awards:	1
Application deadline:	March 31
Notification begins:	June 1
Total amount awarded:	$3,000

Contact:
National Federation of the Blind Scholarship Committee
Mrs. Peggy Elliott, Chairman
805 Fifth Avenue
Grinnell, IA 50112
Phone: 641-236-3366
Web: www.nfb.org

National Federation of the Blind Scholarships

Type of award: Scholarship, renewable.
Intended use: For full-time undergraduate or graduate study at postsecondary institution.
Eligibility: Applicant must be visually impaired.
Basis for selection: Major/career interest in humanities/liberal arts. Applicant must demonstrate financial need, high academic achievement and service orientation.
Application requirements: Recommendations, transcript. Personal letter from applicant, letter from state officer of Federation, two letters of recommendation, score reports for all standardized tests taken for college admission (high school seniors only).
Additional information: Applicant must be legally blind. Recipients of federation scholarships need not be members of National Federation of the Blind. Award amounts are $3,000 and $7,000. Visit Website to download application. All applications should be filed in hard copy by mail.

Amount of award:	$3,000-$7,000
Number of awards:	18
Application deadline:	March 31
Notification begins:	June 1

Contact:
National Federation of the Blind Scholarship Committee
Mrs. Peggy Elliott, Chairman
805 Fifth Avenue
Grinnell, IA 50112
Phone: 641-236-3366
Web: www.nfb.org

Sally Jacobsen Memorial Scholarship

Type of award: Scholarship.
Intended use: For full-time undergraduate or graduate study at postsecondary institution.
Eligibility: Applicant must be visually impaired.
Application requirements: Recommendations, transcript. Personal letter from applicant, letter from state officer of Federation, two letters of recommendation, score reports for all standardized tests taken for college admission (high school seniors only).
Additional information: Applicant must be legally blind. Applicant must be studying education or have an interest in working with multi-handicapped people.

Amount of award:	$5,000
Number of awards:	1
Application deadline:	March 31
Notification begins:	June 1

Contact:
National Federation of the Blind Scholarship Committee
805 Fifth Avenue
Grinnell, IA 50112
Phone: 641-236-3366
Web: www.nfb.org

National Foster Parent Association

Benjamin Eaton Scholarship

Type of award: Scholarship.
Intended use: For undergraduate or non-degree study at postsecondary institution.
Eligibility: Applicant or parent must be member/participant of National Foster Parent Association. Applicant must be high school senior.
Basis for selection: Applicant must demonstrate financial need.
Application requirements: Recommendations, essay, transcript. Photograph, extracurricular activities.
Additional information: For postsecondary education in both degree- and non-degree-granting institutions. Consideration to applicants with physical disability, handicap or other special needs. Foster children, adoptive children and birth children of licensed, approved foster parents who are members of NFPA are eligible. Applications accepted year-round.

Amount of award:	$1,000
Number of awards:	5
Number of applicants:	50
Application deadline:	March 31
Notification begins:	May 31
Total amount awarded:	$5,000

Contact:
NFPA Scholarship
7512 Stanich Ave. #6
Gig Harbor, WA 98335
Phone: 800-557-5238
Fax: 253-853-4001
Web: www.nfpainc.org

The National Future Farmers of America

National FFA Organization Scholarship Program

Type of award: Scholarship.
Intended use: For undergraduate study.
Eligibility: Applicant must be high school senior.
Basis for selection: Major/career interest in agribusiness; agriculture; agricultural economics or agricultural education.
Additional information: Each year the National FFA Organization awards more than $2 million in scholarships to FFA members as well as a number to high schoolers who are not members. Contact National FFA for further information. To request an application, email scholarships@ffa.org. Visit www.ffa.org/programs/scholarships for more information.

Amount of award:	$1,000-$10,000
Application deadline:	February 15
Notification begins:	June 15

Contact:
The National FFA
Attn. Scholarship Office
P.O. Box 68960
Indianapolis, IN 46268-0960
Phone: 317-802-4321
Fax: 317-802-5321
Web: www.ffa.org

National Ground Water Association

NGWREF Len Assante Scholarship Fund

Type of award: Scholarship.
Intended use: For full-time undergraduate study at accredited 2-year or 4-year institution.
Eligibility: Applicant or parent must be member/participant of National Ground Water Association. Applicant must be high school senior.
Basis for selection: Applicant must demonstrate financial need, high academic achievement, depth of character, leadership, patriotism, seriousness of purpose and service orientation.
Application requirements: Essay, transcript, proof of eligibility. Essay should be one-page biography. Applicant or relative must be member/participant of National Ground Water Association.
Additional information: Application also open to extended relatives of National Ground Water Association members. Minimum 2.5 GPA. Amount and number of awards vary annually. Application available at Website.

Amount of award:	$500-$2,000
Number of applicants:	14
Application deadline:	April 1

Contact:
National Ground Water Assocation: Len Assante Scholarship Fund
c/o Michelle Islam
601 Dempsey Road
Westerville, OH 43081
Phone: 800-551-7379
Web: www.ngwa.org

National Institute for Labor Relations Research

Future Teacher Scholarship

Type of award: Scholarship.
Intended use: For undergraduate or graduate study at accredited postsecondary institution in United States.
Basis for selection: Based entirely on essay written by applicant about desire to teach. Major/career interest in education.

Application requirements: Essay, transcript, proof of eligibility.

Additional information: Must major in education. Applicants must demonstrate potential for completion of degree program and obtainment of teaching license. Must also demonstrate understanding of principles of voluntary unionism and problems of compulsory unionism in relation to education.

Amount of award:	$1,000
Number of awards:	1
Application deadline:	December 31
Notification begins:	April 30

Contact:
National Institute for Labor Relations Research
Attn: Scholarship Coordinator
5211 Port Royal Road, Suite 510
Springfield, VA 22151
Phone: 703-321-9606
Fax: 703-321-7342
Web: www.nilrr.org

William B. Ruggles Right to Work Scholarship

Type of award: Scholarship.

Intended use: For undergraduate or graduate study at accredited 2-year or 4-year institution.

Basis for selection: Major/career interest in journalism. Applicant must demonstrate high academic achievement, depth of character and seriousness of purpose.

Application requirements: Essay, transcript. Essay must be 500 words and demonstrate understanding of principles of voluntary unionism.

Additional information: Applicants must demonstrate potential for completion of degree program. Must also demonstrate understanding of principles of voluntary unionism and economic and social problems of compulsory unionism.

Amount of award:	$2,000
Number of awards:	1
Number of applicants:	150
Application deadline:	December 31
Total amount awarded:	$2,000

Contact:
National Institute for Labor Relations Research
Attn: Scholarship Coordinator
5211 Port Royal Road, Suite 510
Springfield, VA 22151
Phone: 703-321-9606
Fax: 703-321-7342
Web: www.nilrr.org

National Institutes of Health

National Institutes of Health Undergraduate Scholarship Program

Type of award: Scholarship.

Intended use: For full-time undergraduate study at accredited 4-year institution in United States.

Eligibility: Applicant must be U.S. citizen or permanent resident.

Basis for selection: Career interest in biomedical research or behavorial or social science research related to health. Major/ career interest in biology; medical specialties/research; bioengineering; engineering, biomedical; health sciences or social/behavioral sciences. Applicant must demonstrate financial need and high academic achievement.

Application requirements: Recommendations, transcript, proof of eligibility. Must show commitment to pursuing career in biomedical research. Applicant must be from disadvantaged background and demonstrate high academic achievement.

Additional information: Up to 15 awards given. Minimum 3.5 GPA or rank in top 5 percent of class. Student must work 10 consecutive weeks (in summer) during scholarship year, and 12 months as full-time employee at NIH labs after graduation for each year that scholarship is awarded. Award covers tuition, fees and qualified educational and living expenses up to $20,000.

Amount of award:	$20,000
Application deadline:	February 28

Contact:
NIH Office of Loan Repayment and Scholarship
2 Center Drive, Room 2E30
MSC 0230
Bethesda, MD 20892-0230
Phone: (800) 528-7689
Web: ugsp.info.nih.gov

National Inventors Hall of Fame

Collegiate Inventors Competition

Type of award: Scholarship.

Intended use: For full-time undergraduate study.

Basis for selection: Competition/talent/interest in Science project, 1500-word essay describing invention. Include title page and one-paragraph overview of invention. Entries judged on potential to society and scope of use.

Application requirements: Essay. Applicant must provide advisor letter, 500 words maximum; four copies of application and three copies of any supplementary material; diagrams, illustrations, photos, slides or videos of invention.

Additional information: Amount of awards vary. Entry must include summary of current literature and patent search, test data and invention's benefit. Competition accepts individual and team entries. Students must be (or have been) enrolled full-time at least part of 12-month period prior to date entry submitted. For teams, at least one member must meet full-time eligibility criteria. Other team members must have been enrolled on part-time basis (at minimum) sometime during 24-month period prior to date entry submitted.

Amount of award:	$5,000-$50,000
Number of awards:	6
Application deadline:	June 1

Contact:
The Collegiate Inventors Competition
The National Inventors Hall of Fame
221 South Broadway St.
Akron, OH 44308-1505
Phone: 330-849-6887
Web: www.invent.org

National Italian American Foundation

Emanuele and Emilia Inglese Memorial Scholarship

Type of award: Scholarship.
Intended use: For undergraduate study at accredited postsecondary institution.
Eligibility: Italian Americans who can trace lineage to Lombardy region in Italy. Applicant must be Italian. Applicant must be U.S. citizen or permanent resident.
Basis for selection: Applicant must demonstrate financial need and high academic achievement.
Application requirements: Transcript. Application, Teacher Evaluation Form, Student Aid Report from FAFSA.
Additional information: Applicant must be first-generation of family to attend college. Minimum 3.0 GPA. Applications must be submitted online.

   Application deadline: April 30
Contact:
The Inglese Memorial Scholarship c/o NIAF
1860 19th Street NW
Washington, DC 20009
Phone: 202-387-0600
Fax: 202-387-0800
Web: www.niaf.org

National Italian American Foundation Scholarship Program

Type of award: Scholarship.
Intended use: For full-time undergraduate or graduate study at accredited 4-year or graduate institution in United States or Canada.
Eligibility: "Italian-American" defined as having at least one ancestor who immigrated from Italy. Also open to those who are not of Italian descent but intend to persue Italian-related majors or minors academically. Applicant must be Italian. Applicant must be U.S. citizen or permanent resident.
Basis for selection: Major/career interest in Italian-american studies or Italian. Applicant must demonstrate financial need, high academic achievement, depth of character, leadership, patriotism, seriousness of purpose and service orientation.
Application requirements: Recommendations, transcript. Minimum 3.25 GPA. FAFSA. Completed application submitted online. Teacher evaluation may be filed online using student's file number established when application was submitted. Changes to online applicatoin may be made up until date of deadline.
Additional information: Awards in two categories. General Category I Awards: Open to Italian American students who demonstrate outstanding potential and high academic achievement who wish to persue any area of study. General Category II Awards: Open to those students from any ethnic background majoring or minoring in Italian Language, Italian studies, Italian American Studies or related fields. Awards are given based on academic performance, field of study, career objectives, and the potential, commitment, and demonstrated ability to make significant contributions to chosen field of study. Financial need will be considered for some scholarships. Recipients are awarded money in one year only, but are encouraged to reapply in subsequent years.

Amount of award: $2,000-$5,000
Number of awards: 100
Number of applicants: 3,000
Application deadline: April 30
Notification begins: June 30
Contact:
The National Italian American Foundation
1860 19th Street NW
Washington, DC 20009
Phone: 202-387-0600
Fax: 202-387-0800
Web: www.niaf.org

National Italian American Foundation Scholarship Program

Type of award: Scholarship.
Intended use: For undergraduate study in United States.
Eligibility: Italian Americans must have at least one ancestor that immigrated from Italy. Applicant must be Italian. Applicant must be U.S. citizen or permanent resident.
Basis for selection: Applicant must demonstrate high academic achievement.
Application requirements: Transcript. Application. FAFSA. Teacher Evaluation Form must be submitted online.
Additional information: Two categories of applicants eligible: General Category I includes Italian Americans; General Category II includes students of any ethnic background majoring or minoring in Itallian language, Italian American Studies, or related field. Minimum 3.25 GPA.

   Amount of award: $2,000-$5,000
   Application deadline: April 30
   Notification begins: June 30
Contact:
National Italian American Foundation
1860 19th Street NW
Washington, DC 20009
Web: www.niaf.org

National Jewish Committee on Scouting, Boy Scouts of America

Chester M. Vernon Memorial Eagle Scout Scholarship

Type of award: Scholarship, renewable.
Intended use: For full-time undergraduate study at accredited 2-year or 4-year institution.
Eligibility: Applicant or parent must be member/participant of Boy Scouts of America, Eagle Scouts. Applicant must be male, high school senior. Applicant must be Jewish. Applicant must be U.S. citizen or permanent resident.
Basis for selection: Applicant must demonstrate financial need, depth of character, leadership and service orientation.
Application requirements: Applicants must submit at least four letters of recommendation with nomination application. One letter required from leaders of each of the following groups: religious institution, school, community, and Scouting unit.
Additional information: Recipient of scholarship receives $1,000 per year for four years. Applicant must be registered,

active member of a Boy Scout troop, Varsity Scout team, or Venturing crew. Must have received Eagle Scout Award. Must be active member of synagogue and received Ner Tamid or Etz Chaim emblem. Contact National Jewish Committee on Scouting to request application form. Visit Website for more information.

Amount of award:	$1,000
Number of awards:	1
Application deadline:	December 31
Notification begins:	March 1
Total amount awarded:	$4,000

Contact:
National Jewish Committee on Scouting, BSA
1325 W. Walnut Hill Lane
P.O. Box 152079
Irving, TX 75015
Phone: 972-580-2171
Fax: 972-580-2535
Web: www.jewishscouting.org

Frank L. Weil Memorial Eagle Scout Scholarship

Type of award: Scholarship.
Intended use: For full-time undergraduate study at accredited 2-year or 4-year institution.
Eligibility: Applicant or parent must be member/participant of Boy Scouts of America, Eagle Scouts. Applicant must be male, high school senior. Applicant must be Jewish. Applicant must be U.S. citizen or permanent resident.
Basis for selection: Applicant must demonstrate depth of character, leadership and service orientation.
Application requirements: Recommendations. Applicants must submit at least four letters of recommendation with nomination application. One letter required from leaders of each of the following groups: religious institution, school, community, and Scouting unit.
Additional information: Recipient of scholarship receives $1,000. Two $500 second-place scholarship awards also given. Applicant must be registered, active member of a Boy Scout troop, Varsity Scout team, or Venturing crew. Must have received Eagle Scout Award. Must be active member of synagogue and received Ner Tamid emblem. Contact National Jewish Committee on Scouting to request application form. Visit Website for more information.

Amount of award:	$500-$1,000
Number of awards:	3
Application deadline:	December 31
Notification begins:	March 1
Total amount awarded:	$2,000

Contact:
National Jewish Committee on Scouting, BSA
1325 West Walnut Hill Lane
P.O. Box 152079
Irving, TX 75015-2079
Phone: 972-580-2171
Fax: 972-580-2535
Web: www.jewishscouting.org

National League of American Pen Women

American Pen Women Award: Arts

Type of award: Scholarship.
Intended use: For non-degree study.
Eligibility: Applicant must be female, at least 35. Applicant must be U.S. citizen.
Basis for selection: Competition/talent/interest in visual arts, Quality, originality, workmanship, creativity, and/or performance. Major/career interest in arts, general.
Application requirements: $8 application fee. Portfolio, proof of eligibility. Proof of age and U.S. citizenship: birth certificate, copy of passport page, or voter's registration with driver's license. Send packages no larger than 8x10 via regular mail only.
Additional information: Awards offered in even-numbered years. Portfolio must include three four-by-six color prints (no slides) in any media. Photographic entries should submit three four-by-six color or black-and-white photographs. Submission may not have previously won an award. Awards to be used to further artistic purpose. Include business-size SASE with all information requests. In order to have pictures returned and receive list of winners, applicant should include SASE. Must send SASE or no reply will be sent. In addition to grant, recipients receive two-year paid Honorary Associate membership in NLAPW.
Contact:
National League of American Pen Women
1300 Seventeenth Street, N.W.
Washington, DC 20036-1973

American Pen Women Award: Letters

Type of award: Scholarship.
Intended use: For non-degree study.
Eligibility: Applicant must be female, at least 35. Applicant must be U.S. citizen.
Basis for selection: Competition/talent/interest in writing/ journalism, based on quality, originality, workmanship, creativity, and/or performance. Major/career interest in journalism; publishing or communications.
Application requirements: $8 application fee. Portfolio, proof of eligibility. Proof of age and U.S. citizenship: birth certificate, copy of passport page, or voter's registration and driver's license. Packages should be no larger than 8x10 and should not be sent via regular mail.
Additional information: Awards offered in even-numbered years. Applicant may submit essay or short story not exceeding 4,000 words, three poems, television script or play, first chapter of a novel with outline, or an editorial. Submission may not have previously won an award. Awards to be used to further artistic purpose. Include business-size SASE with all information requests. Will return manuscripts if sufficient postage and mailer are sent. Will send list of winners if SASE is sent. In addition to the grant, recipients receive two-year paid Honorary Associate membership in the NLAPW.

Number of awards:	1
Total amount awarded:	$1,000

Contact:
National League of American Pen Women
1300 Seventeenth Street, N.W.
Washington, DC 20036-1973

Scholarships

American Pen Women Award: Music

Type of award: Scholarship.
Intended use: For non-degree study.
Eligibility: Applicant must be female, at least 35. Applicant must be U.S. citizen.
Basis for selection: Competition/talent/interest in music performance/composition, Quality, originality, workmanship, creativity, and/or performance. Major/career interest in music.
Application requirements: $8 application fee. Portfolio, proof of eligibility. Proof of U.S. citizenship and age: birth certificate, copy of passport page, or voter's registration with driver's license. Packages should be no larger than 8x10 and should not be sent via regular mail.
Additional information: Awards offered in even-numbered years. Applicants must submit two scores of at least 10 minutes and at most 25 minutes. Must not have received previous award for work. One score must have been written within past five years. Awards to be used to further creative purpose. Include business-size SASE with information requests. To have score returned and receive list of winners, include appropriate SASE. In addition to grant, recipient will receive two-year paid Honorary Associate membership in NLAPW.

Number of awards:	1
Total amount awarded:	$1,000

Contact:
National League of American Pen Women
National League of American Pen Women
1300 Seventeenth Avenue, N.W.
Washington, DC 20036-1973

National Merit Scholarship Corporation

Achievement Scholarship Awards

Type of award: Scholarship.
Intended use: For full-time undergraduate study in United States.
Eligibility: Applicant must be African American. Applicant must be enrolled in high school. Applicant must be U.S. citizen or permanent resident.
Basis for selection: Abilities, skills, accomplishments. Applicant must demonstrate high academic achievement and leadership.
Application requirements: Recommendations, essay.
Additional information: A privately financed academic competition for black American high school students. To enter, students must meet published participation requirements and request consideration in program when they take PSAT/NMSQT and enter National Merit Program. Entry requirements published each year in PSAT/NMSQT Student Bulletin, sent to schools for distribution to students before October test administration, and on NMSC's Website. Some 1,500 of highest scoring participants named Semifinalists on regional representation basis. Semifinalists must meet additional requirements and advance to Finalist standing to compete for about 800 Achievement Scholarship awards offered annually. There are 700 National Achievement $2,500 Scholarships for which all Finalists compete and about 100 corporate-sponsored scholarships for Finalists who meet specified criteria of sponsoring organization.

Number of awards:	775
Number of applicants:	115,000
Total amount awarded:	$2,700,000

Contact:
National Achievement Scholarship Program
1560 Sherman Avenue
Suite 200
Evanston, IL 60201-4897
Web: www.nationalmerit.org

Merit Scholarship Program Awards

Type of award: Scholarship.
Intended use: For full-time undergraduate study in United States.
Eligibility: Applicant must be enrolled in high school. Applicant must be U.S. citizen or permanent resident.
Basis for selection: Abilities, skills, accomplishments. Applicant must demonstrate high academic achievement and leadership.
Application requirements: Recommendations, essay.
Additional information: Open to U.S. high school students who take PSAT/NMQST in specified year in high school and meet other entry requirements. Entry requirements published each year in PSAT/NMQST Student Bulletin, sent to schools for distribution to students before October test administration, and on NMSC's Website. Some 16,000 high scoring participants designated. Semifinalists on state representational basis. Applications sent to students through their schools. Semifinalists must meet additional requirements and advance to Finalist standing to be considered for Merit Scholar awards. About 8,000 awards of three types offered annually: 2,500 National Merit $2,500 Scholarships for which all Finalists compete; about 1,100 corporate-sponsored Merit Scholarship awards for Finalists who meet criteria of sponsoring corporate organization; and 4,400 college-sponsored Merit Scholarship awards for Finalists who will attend sponsor college/university. Corporate organizations also provide about 1,600 Special Scholarships for other high performers in competition who are not Finalists. Permanent residents eligible if in process of becoming U.S. citizen.

Number of awards:	9,600
Notification begins:	March 7
Total amount awarded:	$43,500,000

Contact:
National Merit Scholarship Program
1560 Sherman Avenue
Suite 200
Evanston, IL 60201-4897
Web: www.nationalmerit.org

National Poultry & Food Distributors Association

NPFDA Scholarship

Type of award: Scholarship, renewable.
Intended use: For full-time junior or senior study at 4-year institution in United States.
Basis for selection: Major/career interest in dietetics/nutrition; agriculture; agricultural economics; agribusiness; food science/technology or business, international. Applicant must demonstrate high academic achievement.

Application requirements: Essay, transcript, proof of eligibility. Application, recommendation by dean or department head. 1-2 page statement about applicant's goals and aspirations.

Additional information: Poultry science, animal science or related agricultural business majors also eligible.

Amount of award:	$1,500-$2,000
Number of awards:	4
Number of applicants:	115
Application deadline:	May 31
Total amount awarded:	$6,500

Contact:
National Poultry & Food Distributors Association
958 McEver Road Ext., Unit B-8
Gainesville, GA 30504
Phone: 770-535-9901
Fax: 770-535-7385
Web: www.npfda.org

National Press Photographers Foundation

Bob East Scholarship Fund

Type of award: Scholarship.

Intended use: For undergraduate or graduate study in United States.

Eligibility: Applicant must be U.S. citizen or permanent resident residing in Florida.

Basis for selection: Portfolio, which must include at least five single images in addition to picture story. Major/career interest in journalism. Applicant must demonstrate financial need.

Application requirements: Portfolio, recommendations. #10 SASE. Must be undergraduate in first three and one half years of college, or be planning to pursue postgraduate work and offer indication of acceptance in such program.

Additional information: Open to students studying photojournalism for newspapers.

Application deadline:	March 1
Total amount awarded:	$2,000

Contact:
The Miami Herald
Attn: Chuck Fadely
One Herald Plaza
Miami, FL 33132
Phone: 305-376-2015
Web: www.nppa.org

College Photographer of the Year Competition

Type of award: Scholarship.

Intended use: For undergraduate study at 4-year institution in United States or Canada.

Basis for selection: Major/career interest in journalism. Applicant must demonstrate financial need and high academic achievement.

Application requirements: Portfolio, recommendations, proof of eligibility. #10 SASE.

Additional information: Contest recognizes outstanding work of student photojournalists. NPPF Booster club provides $1,000 Col. William Lookadoo Award and $500 Milton Frier Award.

Amount of award:	$500-$1,000
Number of awards:	2
Application deadline:	October 1
Total amount awarded:	$1,500

Contact:
University of Missouri School of Journalism
David Rees, CPOY Dir.
106 Lee Hills Hall
Columbia, MO 65211
Phone: 573-882-4442
Web: www.nppa.org

National Press Photographers Foundation Still Scholarship

Type of award: Scholarship.

Intended use: For sophomore, junior or senior study at 4-year institution in United States or Canada.

Basis for selection: Major/career interest in journalism. Applicant must demonstrate financial need and high academic achievement.

Application requirements: Portfolio, recommendations, proof of eligibility. #10 SASE. Must have at least one half year of undergraduate schooling remaining at time of award.

Additional information: Awards aimed at those with journalism potential, but with little opportunity and great need. Must have completed one year at recognized four-year college or university having courses in photojournalism. Must be continuing in program leading to bachelor's degree.

Amount of award:	$2,000
Number of awards:	1
Application deadline:	March 1
Total amount awarded:	$2,000

Contact:
Bill Sanders
640 NW 100 Way
Coral Springs, FL 33071
Phone: 954-341-9718
Web: www.nppa.org

National Press Photographers Foundation Television News Scholarship

Type of award: Scholarship.

Intended use: For junior or senior study at 4-year institution in United States or Canada.

Basis for selection: Major/career interest in theater/production/ technical or journalism. Applicant must demonstrate financial need and high academic achievement.

Application requirements: Portfolio, recommendations, essay, proof of eligibility. #10 SASE. Videotape containing no more than three complete stories no longer than six minutes total with voice narration and natural sound. One-page biographical sketch including personal statement addressing professional goals.

Additional information: Must be enrolled in recognized four-year college or university having courses in TV news photojournalism. Must be continuing program leading to bachelor's degree.

Amount of award:	$1,000
Number of awards:	1
Application deadline:	March 1
Total amount awarded:	$1,000

Contact:
Dave Hamer
3702 N. 53rd Street
Omaha, NE 68104
Web: www.nppa.org

Reid Blackburn Scholarship

Type of award: Scholarship.
Intended use: For sophomore study at 4-year institution in United States or Canada.
Basis for selection: Major/career interest in journalism. Applicant must demonstrate financial need, high academic achievement and seriousness of purpose.
Application requirements: Portfolio, recommendations, essay, proof of eligibility. #10 SASE, philosophy and goals statement. Must have at least half year of undergraduate schooling remaining at time of award.
Additional information: Must have completed at least one year at recognized four-year college or university having courses in photojournalism. Must be continuing program leading to bachelor's degree.

Number of awards:	1
Application deadline:	March 1
Total amount awarded:	$2,000

Contact:
The Columbian
Attn: Jeremiah Coughlan
701 W. 8th Street
Vancouver, WA 98660
Phone: 360-694-3391
Web: www.nppa.org

National Restaurant Association Educational Foundation

Academic Scholarship for High School Seniors

Type of award: Scholarship.
Intended use: For undergraduate study at vocational, 2-year or 4-year institution. Designated institutions: Food service-related postsecondary programs.
Eligibility: Applicant must be high school senior. Applicant must be U.S. citizen or permanent resident.
Basis for selection: Major/career interest in food science/ technology; hotel/restaurant management; food science/ technology; culinary arts or marketing.
Application requirements: Recommendations, transcript. One to three letters of recommendation, must be accepted into accredited restaurant/food service related postsecondary program and plan to enroll in minimum of two terms for following school year.
Additional information: Minimum 2.75 high school GPA required. Must have minimum 250 hours of foodservice-related work experience. To apply, visit Website.

Amount of award:	$2,000
Application deadline:	April 16
Notification begins:	May 19

Contact:
National Restaurant Association Educational Foundation
Scholarships and Mentoring Initiative
175 W. Jackson Blvd., Suite 1500
Chicago, IL 60604-5834
Phone: 800-765-2122 ext. 733
Fax: 312-566-9726
Web: www.nraef.org

Academic Scholarship for Undergraduate Students

Type of award: Scholarship.
Intended use: For sophomore, junior, senior or post-bachelor's certificate study at accredited vocational, 2-year or 4-year institution in United States.
Eligibility: Applicant must be U.S. citizen or permanent resident.
Basis for selection: Major/career interest in food production/ management/services; culinary arts; hotel/restaurant management; hospitality administration/management; food science/technology or food science/technology.
Application requirements: Recommendations, transcript. One to three letters of recommendation; must be on business letterhead from a current or previous employer in the restaurant or food service industry.
Additional information: Applicant must have completed at least one term of two- or four-year degree program. Must have performed minimum 750 hours foodservice-related work. Minimum 2.75 GPA. For application and more information, visit Website.

Amount of award:	$2,000
Application deadline:	April 30
Notification begins:	January 6, June 16

Contact:
National Restaurant Assn. Educational Foundation
Scholarships and Mentoring Initiative
175 West Jackson Boulevard, Suite 1500
Chicago, IL 60606-5834
Phone: 800-765-2122 ext. 733
Fax: 312-566-9726
Web: www.nraef.org

ProStart National Certificate of Achievement Scholarship

Type of award: Scholarship.
Intended use: For undergraduate study at 2-year or 4-year institution in United States. Designated institutions: Accredited Hospitality Management Program.
Eligibility: Applicant must be high school senior. Applicant must be U.S. citizen or permanent resident.
Basis for selection: Major/career interest in food production/ management/services; food science/technology; culinary arts or hotel/restaurant management.
Application requirements: Transcript. If student applies via Internet, application must be printed out and returned with required accompanying materials. Documentation received separately will be automatically disqualified. Must earn ProStart National Certificate of Achievement by August 16, 2004.

Amount of award:	$2,000
Application deadline:	August 16

Contact:
National Restaurant Association Educational Foundation
Scholarships and Mentoring Initiative
175 W. Jackson Blvd., Suite 1500
Chicago, IL 60604-2702
Phone: 800-765-2122 x733
Fax: 312-566-9726
Web: www.nraef.org

National Rifle Association

Jeanne E. Bray Law Enforcement Dependents Scholarship

Type of award: Scholarship.
Intended use: For undergraduate or graduate study at accredited 2-year, 4-year or graduate institution in United States.
Eligibility: Applicant or parent must be member/participant of National Rifle Association. Applicant must be U.S. citizen. Applicant's parent must have been killed or disabled in work-related accident as police officer.
Basis for selection: GPA, SAT and ACT scores.
Application requirements: Recommendations, essay, transcript, proof of eligibility. SAT score of 950 or ACT score of 25.
Additional information: Number of awards varies. Parent must be active, disabled, deceased, discharged, or retired law enforcement officer and member of National Rifle Association. Applicant must also be NRA member. Minimum 2.5 GPA. Award given for up to four years or until applicable monetary cap is reached, as long as student maintains eligibility. Applications accepted on continuous basis.

Amount of award:	$500-$2,000
Application deadline:	November 15
Notification begins:	February 15

Contact:
National Rifle Association, Attn: Sandy S. Elkin
Jeanne E. Bray Memorial Scholarship
11250 Waples Mill Road
Fairfax, VA 22030
Phone: 703-267-1131
Fax: 703-267-1083
Web: www.nra.org

National Science Teachers Association

Toshiba ExploraVision Award

Type of award: Scholarship.
Intended use: For undergraduate or non-degree study in United States or Canada.
Eligibility: Applicant must be enrolled in high school.
Basis for selection: Competition/talent/interest in science project, based on scientific accuracy, creativity, communication and feasibility of vision. Major/career interest in science, general.
Application requirements: Essay. Written description of research and design project, five graphics simulating Web pages. Applicant must attend public, private or home school in United States or Canada. Must be full-time student, no older than 21.
Additional information: Technology study project. Open to grades K-12. Each student member of first-place team receives $10,000 savings bond, each student member of second-place team receives $5,000 savings bond, and regional winners receive digital camera. Contact sponsor for entry kit, and visit Website to download application.

Amount of award:	$5,000-$10,000
Application deadline:	February 1
Notification begins:	March 1
Total amount awarded:	$340,000

Contact:
Toshiba/NSTA ExploraVision Awards
1840 Wilson Boulevard
Arlington, VA 22201-3000
Phone: 800-EXPLOR9
Web: www.exploravision.org

National Sculpture Society

The Alex J. Ettl Grant

Type of award: Scholarship.
Intended use: For non-degree study.
Eligibility: Applicant must be U.S. citizen or permanent resident.
Basis for selection: Competition/talent/interest in Visual arts, based on exceptional ability as demonstrated in work. Major/career interest in art/art history; arts, general or arts management. Applicant must demonstrate seriousness of purpose.
Application requirements: Portfolio. Applicant must submit at least ten 8x10 photographs or slides of at least eight different works, and brief biography. Photographs should be labeled on back with applicant's name, title of work, size, medium and date of execution. Include SASE for return of photographs.
Additional information: Award for figurative or realist sculptor with demonstrated commitment to sculpting and outstanding ability in life's work. National Sculpture Society members not eligible. Notifications given in February. Award presented in formal Honors and Awards Dinner in May.

Amount of award:	$4,000
Number of awards:	1
Application deadline:	January 8

Contact:
The Alex J. Ettl Grant
National Sculpture Society
237 Park Avenue
New York, NY 10017
Phone: 212-764-5645
Web: www.nationalsculpture.org

National Sculpture Competition

Type of award: Scholarship.
Intended use: For non-degree study.
Basis for selection: Competition/talent/interest in Visual arts, Proven talent in figurative sculpting. Major/career interest in art/art history; arts management or arts, general.
Additional information: Event is two-part competition; second part is on-site. Entrants may participate in either or both parts, and should indicate preference on application. Part one: Young Sculptor Awards for sculptor with best work in bas-relief

($1000); sculptor who reaches for excellence in representational sculpture ($750); sculpture who strives to uplift the human spirit through medium of his/her art ($350); meritorious body of work (medal). Entrants need not be present to be considered for awards; notifications given by mail if entrants do not participate in part two of competition. Part two: The Figure Modeling Contest is on-site and awards three winners $300, $500, and $1000. Visit Website for more information and to download application and schedule information.

Amount of award:	$300-$1,000
Number of awards:	7
Application deadline:	April 5
Total amount awarded:	$3,900

Contact:
National Sculpture Competition
National Sculpture Society
237 Park Avenue
New York, NY 10017
Phone: 212-764-5645
Web: www.nationalsculpture.org

Sculpture Society Scholarship

Type of award: Scholarship, renewable.
Intended use: For undergraduate, master's or doctoral study at postsecondary institution in United States.
Eligibility: Applicant must be U.S. citizen or permanent resident.
Basis for selection: Competition/talent/interest in Visual arts, based on slides or photos of figurative or representational sculpture created by the applicant. Major/career interest in arts, general. Applicant must demonstrate financial need.
Application requirements: Portfolio, recommendations, essay, proof of eligibility. 1) Brief letter of application or biography explaining background in sculpture; 2) 8-10 photographs of at least three works; 3) proof of financial need; 4) two recommendation letters.
Additional information: Must be studying figurative sculpture. Number of awards varies. Please include SASE.

Amount of award:	$1,000
Number of awards:	6
Number of applicants:	40
Application deadline:	April 30
Notification begins:	June 15
Total amount awarded:	$6,000

Contact:
National Sculpture Society
237 Park Avenue, Ground Floor
New York, NY 10017
Phone: 212-764-5645
Web: www.nationalsculpture.org

National Security Agency

National Security Agency Stokes Scholars Program

Type of award: Scholarship, renewable.
Intended use: For full-time undergraduate study at accredited 4-year institution in United States.
Eligibility: Applicant must be high school senior. Applicant must be U.S. citizen.
Basis for selection: Interest in majors leading to a career in Intelligence Analysis. Major/career interest in computer/

information sciences; mathematics; engineering, computer; engineering, electrical/electronic; engineering or foreign languages. Applicant must demonstrate high academic achievement, depth of character, leadership, patriotism, seriousness of purpose and service orientation.
Application requirements: Interview, recommendations, transcript, proof of eligibility. Must have minimum 3.0 GPA, SAT score of 1100 and/or ACT score of 25. Must undergo polygraph and security screening.
Additional information: Current applications available after September 1 of each year.

Amount of award:	Full tuition
Number of awards:	20
Number of applicants:	800
Application deadline:	November 30
Notification begins:	April 1

Contact:
National Security Agency Stokes Scholars Program
P.O. Box 1661
MB3, Suite 6779, Stokes Scholars Program
Fort Meade, MD 20755-6779
Phone: 410-854-4725 or 866-672-4473, opt. 3
Fax: 410-854-3002
Web: www.nsa.gov

National Society of Accountants Scholarship Foundation

National Society of Accountants Scholarship

Type of award: Scholarship.
Intended use: For undergraduate study at accredited vocational, 2-year or 4-year institution in United States.
Eligibility: Applicant must be U.S. citizen, international student or Canadian citizen.
Basis for selection: Major/career interest in accounting. Applicant must demonstrate financial need, high academic achievement and leadership.
Application requirements: Transcript. Application and appraisal form. Students applying in college freshman year must submit high school transcript.
Additional information: Minimum 3.0 GPA. Competition's most outstanding student receives additional stipend. Applications available on Website in October, or call or write sponsor.

Amount of award:	$500-$1,000
Number of awards:	40
Number of applicants:	1,200
Application deadline:	March 10
Total amount awarded:	$40,000

Contact:
National Society of Accountants
Scholarship Foundation
1010 North Fairfax Street
Alexandria, VA 22314-1574
Phone: 800-966-6679
Fax: 703-549-2512
Web: www.nsacct.org

National Society of Black Engineers

Fulfilling the Legacy Scholarship

Type of award: Scholarship.
Intended use: For undergraduate or graduate study at accredited postsecondary institution.
Eligibility: Applicant or parent must be member/participant of National Society of Black Engineers. Applicant must be U.S. citizen.
Basis for selection: Major/career interest in engineering. Applicant must demonstrate high academic achievement, depth of character, leadership, seriousness of purpose and service orientation.
Application requirements: Essay, transcript, proof of eligibility.
Additional information: Number of awards and amount depend on total contributions made by members and others. NSBE membership required. General information available on Website in September. All inquiries should be sent to scholarships@nsbe.org. Society does not provide paper application. All eligible applicants must apply online through their membership account.
    Application deadline: January 7
Contact:
National Society of Black Engineers
1425 Duke Street
Alexandria, VA 22314
Phone: 703-549-2207
Fax: 703-683-5312
Web: www.nsbe.org

National Society of Black Engineers Corporate Scholarships Program

Type of award: Scholarship.
Intended use: For undergraduate study at 4-year institution.
Eligibility: Applicant or parent must be member/participant of National Society of Black Engineers.
Basis for selection: Major/career interest in engineering, computer; engineering, electrical/electronic or engineering, mechanical.
Additional information: Various corporate scholarships available. NSBE membership required and general information available on Website in September. All inquiries should be sent to scholarships@nsbe.org. Society does not provide paper application. All eligible applicants must apply online through their membership account.
    Application deadline: January 7
Contact:
National Society of Black Engineers
1454 Duke Street
Alexandria, VA 22314
Phone: 703-549-2207
Fax: 703-683-5312
Web: www.nsbe.org

National Society of Black Engineers Golden Torch Awards

Type of award: Scholarship.
Intended use: For undergraduate study at 4-year institution.

Eligibility: Applicant or parent must be member/participant of National Society of Black Engineers. Applicant must be enrolled in high school.
Basis for selection: Applicant must demonstrate depth of character, leadership and service orientation.
Application requirements: Recommendations, essay, transcript.
Additional information: NSBE Jr. membership required and general information available on Website in September. All inquiries should be sent to scholarships@nsbe.org. Society does not provide paper application. All eligible applicants must apply online through their membership account.
    Application deadline: January 7
Contact:
National Society of Black Engineers
1454 Duke Street
Alexandria, VA 22314
Phone: 703-549-2207
Fax: 703-683-5312
Web: www.nsbe.org

National Society of Black Engineers Leroy Callendar Award Program

Type of award: Scholarship.
Intended use: For undergraduate study at 4-year institution.
Eligibility: Applicant or parent must be member/participant of National Society of Black Engineers. Applicant must be enrolled in high school. Applicant must be residing in Iowa, South Dakota, Texas, Arkansas, Kansas, Louisiana, Oklahoma, Nebraska, Missouri or North Dakota.
Basis for selection: Applicant must demonstrate high academic achievement and service orientation.
Application requirements: Recommendations.
Additional information: Applicants must reside in Region V of NSBE National Convention. NSBE Jr. membership required. General information available on Website in September. All inquiries should be sent to scholarships@nsbe.org. Society does not provide paper application. All eligible applicants must apply online through their membership account.
    Amount of award: $500
    Number of awards: 2
    Application deadline: January 7
Contact:
National Society of Black Engineers
1454 Duke Street
Alexandria, VA 22314
Phone: 703-549-2207
Fax: 703-683-5312
Web: www.nsbe.org

National Society of Black Engineers/GE African American Forum Scholarship

Type of award: Scholarship.
Intended use: For junior or senior study at postsecondary institution in United States. Designated institutions: Universities geographically located East of the Mississippi River (Regions I - IV).
Eligibility: Applicant or parent must be member/participant of National Society of Black Engineers. Applicant must be African American. Applicant must be U.S. citizen.
Basis for selection: Major/career interest in engineering, mechanical; engineering, electrical/electronic or engineering. Applicant must demonstrate high academic achievement.

Application requirements: Essay, transcript, proof of eligibility. Resume.
Additional information: Minimum 3.0 GPA required. Service to NSBE and/or other professional, campus and community activities considered when selecting awardees. NSBE membership required. General information available on Website in September. All inquiries should be sent to scholarships@nsbe.org. Society does not provide paper application. All eligible applicants must apply online through their membership account. Mail transcript and resume.

Application deadline:	January 7
Total amount awarded:	$2,500

Contact:
National Society of Black Engineers
1454 Duke Street
Alexandria, VA 22314
Phone: 703-549-2207 ext. 305
Fax: 703-683-5312
Web: www.nsbe.org

NSBE Fellows Scholarship

Type of award: Scholarship.
Intended use: For full-time undergraduate or graduate study at accredited 4-year or graduate institution in United States.
Eligibility: Applicant or parent must be member/participant of National Society of Black Engineers. Applicant must be U.S. citizen.
Basis for selection: Major/career interest in engineering. Applicant must demonstrate high academic achievement, depth of character, leadership, seriousness of purpose and service orientation.
Application requirements: Essay, transcript, proof of eligibility.
Additional information: Intended for applicants dedicated to Society's cause and other community organizations, and show promise in their studies and professional pursuits. NSBE membership required. General information available on Website in September. All inquiries should be sent to scholarships@nsbe.org. Society does not provide paper application. All eligible applicants must apply online through their membership account.

Amount of award:	$1,000-$5,000
Application deadline:	January 7

Contact:
National Society of Black Engineers
1454 Duke St.
Alexandria, VA 22314
Phone: 703-549-2207
Fax: 703-683-5312
Web: www.nsbe.org

National Society of the Sons of the American Revolution

Sons of the American Revolution Eagle Scout Scholarship

Type of award: Scholarship.
Intended use: For undergraduate study.
Eligibility: Applicant or parent must be member/participant of Eagle Scouts. Applicant must be male, no older than 18.

Basis for selection: Applicant must demonstrate depth of character, leadership and patriotism.
Application requirements: Essay, proof of eligibility. Essay should be 500 words on Revoluntionary War, subject of applicant's choice. Application form and four generations ancestor chart.
Additional information: Open to all Eagle Scouts currently registered in active unit who have not reached 19th birthday during year of application. Competition conducted in three phases: Chapter (local), Society (state), and National. Applicants need only apply at Chapter level. Winners at local level entered into state competition; state winners used in National contest. Number of awards varies. State awards may also be available. For more information, contact State Eagle Scout Chairman. On homepage, look for "Youth Programs" and "Eagle Scout." Detailed criteria and application forms can be downloaded from Website as well as names and addresses of state chairman to whom inquiries can be made and applications submitted.

Amount of award:	$2,000-$8,000
Number of awards:	3
Application deadline:	December 31
Total amount awarded:	$14,000

Contact:
National Eagle Scout Committee Chair, Robert Eugene Burt, Chairman
219 Allen Avenue
Key Largo, FL 33037
Web: www.sar.org

National Speakers Association

National Speakers Association Scholarship

Type of award: Scholarship.
Intended use: For full-time junior, senior or graduate study.
Basis for selection: Major/career interest in communications; public relations or radio/television/film. Applicant must demonstrate high academic achievement, leadership and seriousness of purpose.
Application requirements: Recommendations, essay, transcript.
Additional information: Applicant must have an above-average academic record and major or minor in speech or communication-related studies. Application available on Website.

Amount of award:	$4,000
Number of awards:	4
Application deadline:	June 1
Notification begins:	September 1
Total amount awarded:	$16,000

Contact:
National Speakers Association
1500 South Priest Drive
Tempe, AZ 85281
Phone: 480-968-2552
Fax: 480-968-0911
Web: www.nsaspeaker.org/about/foundation.shtml

National Stone, Sand & Gravel Association

Jennifer Curtis Byler Scholarship Fund for the Study of Public Affairs

Type of award: Scholarship.
Intended use: For full-time undergraduate study in United States.
Eligibility: Applicant must be high school senior.
Basis for selection: Major/career interest in public administration/service. Applicant must demonstrate high academic achievement, seriousness of purpose and service orientation.
Application requirements: Recommendations, essay. Completed application. Recommendation must come from faculty advisor. Essay should be 300-500 words on applicant's plans for career in public affairs. Recommendation from employer if applicant has work experience in public affairs though summer job, internship or co-op program.
Additional information: Applicant must be graduating high school senior or student already enrolled in public affairs program in college. Must be child of aggregate company employee. Must demonstrate commitment to career in public affairs. Visit Website for details and application.

  Number of awards: 1
  Application deadline: December 31
Contact:
Jennifer Curtis Byler Scholarship
c/o NSSGA
2101 Wilson Blvd., Suite 100
Arlington, VA 22201
Phone: 703-525-8788 or 800-342-1415
Fax: 703-525-7782
Web: www.nssga.org/careers/scholarships.htm

National Tourism Foundation

National Tourism Foundation Academy of Travel and Tourism Foundation Scholarship

Type of award: Scholarship.
Intended use: For undergraduate study at accredited postsecondary institution.
Eligibility: Applicant must be high school senior.
Basis for selection: Major/career interest in tourism/travel.
Application requirements: Recommendations, essay. NTF scholarship application, list of work and/or internship experience in tourism industry, two letters of recommendation (one from director of Academy and other from teacher, internship supervisor or mentor). Must also submit typewritten one page essay on importance of entering tourism-related career. Essay is signed to verify that it is original.
Additional information: Program open to students at National Academy Foundation's Academy of Travel and Tourism. Minimum 3.0 GPA.

  Amount of award: $500
  Application deadline: May 10

Contact:
National Tourism Foundation
546 East Main Street
Lexington, KY 40508
Phone: 800-682-8886
Fax: 859-226-4437
Web: www.nftonline.org

National Tourism Foundation New Horizons Kathy LeTarte Scholarship

Type of award: Scholarship.
Intended use: For full-time junior study at accredited 4-year institution in United States or Canada.
Eligibility: Applicant must be residing in Michigan.
Basis for selection: Major/career interest in tourism/travel. Applicant must demonstrate high academic achievement.
Application requirements: Recommendations, essay, transcript. Application, two letters of recommendation (one from tourism-related faculty member and other from tourism industry professional), resume. Must also submit typewritten, double-spaced, referenced and signed essay not exceeding two pages (excluding reference page) on one of following topics: International Inbound Tourism, Intergenerational Travel, Effects of Technological Advancements on Tourism, Cultural Diversity, Impact of Group Tourism, Career Opportunities in the Industry, Niche Marketing or Heritage Tourism. Essay is signed to verify that it is original.
Additional information: Minimum 3.0 GPA. Scholarship open to students from Michigan studying travel and tourism anywhere in North America.

  Amount of award: $1,000
  Application deadline: May 10
Contact:
National Tourism Foundation
546 East Main Street
Lexington, KY 40508
Phone: 800-682-8886
Fax: 859-226-4437
Web: www.ntfonline.org

National Tourism Foundation Tauck Scholars Award

Type of award: Scholarship.
Intended use: For full-time sophomore or junior study at 4-year institution.
Basis for selection: Major/career interest in tourism/travel.
Application requirements: Recommendations, essay, transcript. Application, two letters of recommendation (one from tourism-related faculty member and other from tourism industry professional), resume. Must also submit typewritten, double-spaced, referenced and signed essay not exceeding two pages (excluding reference page) on one of following topics: International Inbound Tourism, Intergenerational Travel, Effects of Technological Advancements on Tourism, Cultural Diversity, Impact of Group Tourism, Career Opportunities in the Industry, Niche Marketing or Heritage Tourism. Essay is signed to verify that it is original.
Additional information: Minimum 3.0 GPA. Two-year award at $1,500 per year.

  Amount of award: $3,000
  Number of awards: 4
  Application deadline: May 10

357

Contact:
National Tourism Foundation
546 East Main Street
Lexington, KY 40508
Phone: 800-682-8886
Fax: 859-226-4437
Web: www.ntfonline.org

Pat & Jim Host Scholarship

Type of award: Scholarship.
Intended use: For full-time undergraduate study at 4-year institution. Designated institutions: Kentucky colleges/universities.
Eligibility: Applicant must be residing in Kentucky.
Basis for selection: Major/career interest in tourism/travel or hotel/restaurant management. Applicant must demonstrate financial need and high academic achievement.
Application requirements: Recommendations, essay, transcript. Application, two letters of recommendation (one from tourism-related faculty member and other from tourism industry professional), student aid report. Must also submit typewritten, double-spaced, referenced and signed essay not exceeding two pages (excluding reference page) on one of following topics: Economic Impart of Tourism, Tour Planning for Seniors, Adventure Touring, Importance of the Group Tourism Industry, Environmental Impact of Tourism, Promoting Destinations to Groups, Rural Area Tourism Planning and The Effects of Crime on Tourism. Essay is signed to verify that it is original.
Additional information: Minimum 3.0 GPA. Four-year award; upon yearly renewal, awardee must provide original copy of transcript showing satisfactory academic progress and no change in major course of study.

Amount of award:	$2,000
Application deadline:	May 10

Contact:
National Tourism Foundation
546 East Main Street
Lexington, KY 40508
Phone: 800-682-8886
Fax: 859-226-4437
Web: www.ntfonline.org

Societe Des Casinso Du Quebec Scholarship

Type of award: Scholarship.
Intended use: For full-time junior or senior study at 2-year or 4-year institution in United States or Canada.
Eligibility: Must be Quebec resident.
Basis for selection: Major/career interest in hotel/restaurant management or tourism/travel. Applicant must demonstrate high academic achievement.
Application requirements: Recommendations, essay, transcript, proof of eligibility. NTF scholarship application, two letters of recommendation (one from tourism-related faculty member and the other from tourism industry professional), resume. Must also submit typewritten, double-spaced, referenced and signed essay not exceeding two pages (excluding reference page) on one of the following topics: International Inbound Tourism, Intergenerational Travel, Effects of Technological Advancements on Tourism, Cultural Diversity, Impact of Group Tourism, Career Opportunities in Industry, Niche Marketing or Heritage Tourism. Essay is signed to verify that it is original.

Additional information: Minimum 3.0 GPA. Visit Website for updates and additional information.

Amount of award:	$1,000
Number of awards:	1
Application deadline:	May 10
Total amount awarded:	$1,000

Contact:
National Tourism Foundation
546 East Main Street
Lexington, KY 40508
Phone: 800-682-8886
Web: www.ntfonline.org

Tampa/Hillsborough Legacy Scholarship

Type of award: Scholarship.
Intended use: For full-time junior or senior study at 2-year or 4-year institution in United States. Designated institutions: Florida institutions.
Eligibility: Applicant must be residing in Florida.
Basis for selection: Major/career interest in hotel/restaurant management or tourism/travel. Applicant must demonstrate high academic achievement.
Application requirements: Recommendations, essay, transcript, proof of eligibility. NTF scholarship application, two letters of recommendation (one from tourism-related faculty member and the other from tourism industry professional), resume. Must also submit typewritten, double-spaced, referenced and signed essay not exceeding two pages (excluding reference page) on one of the following topics: International Inbound Tourism, Intergenerational Travel, Effects of Technological Advancements on Tourism, Cultural Diversity, Impact of Group Tourism, Career Opportunities in Industry, Niche Marketing or Heritage Tourism. Essay is signed to verify that it is original.
Additional information: Minimum 3.0 GPA. Visit Website for updates and additional information.

Amount of award:	$1,000
Number of awards:	1
Application deadline:	May 10
Total amount awarded:	$1,000

Contact:
National Tourism Foundation
546 East Main Street
Lexington, KY 40508
Phone: 800-682-8886
Web: www.ntfonline.org

Tourism Foundation Cleveland Legacy 1 Scholarship

Type of award: Scholarship.
Intended use: For full-time junior or senior study at 2-year or 4-year institution in United States.
Eligibility: Applicant must be residing in Ohio.
Basis for selection: Major/career interest in tourism/travel or hotel/restaurant management. Applicant must demonstrate high academic achievement.
Application requirements: Recommendations, essay, transcript. NTF scholarship application, two letters of recommendation (one from tourism-related faculty member and other from tourism industry professional), resume. Must also submit typewritten, double-spaced, referenced and signed essay not exceeding two pages (excluding reference page) on one of following topics: International Inbound Tourism, Intergenerational Travel, Effects of Technological Advancements

Scholarships

on Tourism, Cultural Diversity, Impact of Group Tourism, Career Opportunities in the Industry, Niche Marketing or Heritage Tourism. Essay is signed to verify that it is original.
Additional information: Minimum 3.0 GPA. Visit Website for updates and additional information.

Amount of award:	$1,000
Number of awards:	1
Application deadline:	May 10

Contact:
National Tourism Foundation
546 East Main Street
Lexington, KY 40508
Phone: 800-682-8886
Web: www.ntfonline.org

Tourism Foundation Cleveland Legacy 2 Scholarship

Type of award: Scholarship.
Intended use: For full-time junior or senior study at 2-year or 4-year institution in United States.
Eligibility: Applicant must be residing in Ohio.
Basis for selection: Major/career interest in tourism/travel or hotel/restaurant management. Applicant must demonstrate high academic achievement.
Application requirements: Recommendations, essay, transcript. NTF scholarship application, two letters of recommendation (one from tourism-related faculty member and other from tourism industry professional), resume. Must also submit typewritten, double-spaced, referenced and signed essay not exceeding two pages (excluding reference page) on one of following topics: International Inbound Tourism, Intergenerational Travel, Effects of Technological Advancements on Tourism, Cultural Diversity, Impact of Group Tourism, Career Opportunities in the Industry, Niche Marketing or Heritage Tourism. Essay is signed to verify that it is original.
Additional information: Minimun 3.0 GPA. Visit Website for updates and additional information.

Amount of award:	$1,000
Number of awards:	1
Application deadline:	May 10
Total amount awarded:	$1,000

Contact:
National Tourism Foundation
546 East Main Street
Lexington, KY 40508
Phone: 800-682-8886
Web: www.ntfonline.org

Tourism Foundation Tulsa Scholarship

Type of award: Scholarship.
Intended use: For full-time undergraduate study at 4-year institution in United States. Designated institutions: Institutions in Oklahoma only.
Eligibility: Applicant must be U.S. citizen or permanent resident residing in Oklahoma.
Basis for selection: Major/career interest in tourism/travel or hotel/restaurant management. Applicant must demonstrate high academic achievement.
Application requirements: Recommendations, essay, transcript. NTF scholarship application, two letters of recommendation (one from tourism-related faculty member and other from professional in tourism industry), resume. Must also submit typewritten, double-spaced, referenced and signed essay not exceeding two pages (excluding reference page) on one of

following topics: International Inbound Tourism, Intergenerational Travel, Effects of Technological Advancements on Tourism, Cultural Diversity, Impact of Group Tourism, Career Opportunities in the Industry, Niche Marketing or Heritage Tourism. Essay is signed to verify that it is original.
Additional information: Visit Website for updates and additional information.

Amount of award:	$500
Number of awards:	1
Application deadline:	May 10
Total amount awarded:	$500

Contact:
National Tourism Foundation
546 East Main Street
Lexington, KY 40508
Phone: 800-682-8886
Web: www.ntfonline.org

Tourism Foundation Yellow Ribbon Scholarship

Type of award: Scholarship.
Intended use: For undergraduate study at postsecondary institution. Designated institutions: Schools in North America.
Eligibility: Applicant must be visually impaired, hearing impaired or physically challenged.
Basis for selection: Major/career interest in tourism/travel or hotel/restaurant management. Applicant must demonstrate high academic achievement.
Application requirements: Recommendations, essay, transcript, proof of eligibility. Application. Two recommendation letters (one from tourism-related faculty member; one from tourism industry professional). Resume. Typed, signed, and referenced essay (minimum 500 words) explaining how education will be used in making career in travel/tourism.
Additional information: Available to students with physical or sensory disability. Minimum 3.0 GPA for students entering postsecondary institution; minimum 2.5 GPA at college level. Visit Website for updates and more information.

Amount of award:	$2,500
Number of awards:	1
Application deadline:	May 10
Total amount awarded:	$2,500

Contact:
National Tourism Foundation
546 East Main Street
Lexington, KY 40508
Phone: 800-682-8886
Fax: 859-226-4437
Web: www.ntfonline.org

Travel and Tourism Research Association

Type of award: Scholarship.
Intended use: For undergraduate study at postsecondary institution.
Basis for selection: Projects judged based on ability to improve measurements, decrease costs and improve information for better application and understanding by management. Major/career interest in tourism/travel.
Application requirements: Application, resume.
Additional information: Program available to individual or organization responsible for development of travel research technique or methodology. Project must show significant benefits to travel and tourism industry. In addition to

scholarship, $300 is awarded to attend TTRA's convention. Applications accepted in March.

Amount of award:	$2,000
Number of awards:	1
Application deadline:	May 10

Contact:
National Tourism Foundation
546 East Main Street
Lexington, KY 40508
Phone: 800-682-8886
Fax: 859-226-4437
Web: www.ntfonline.org

National Urban League

American Chemical Society Minority Scholars Program

Type of award: Scholarship.
Intended use: For full-time undergraduate or graduate study at accredited 2-year or 4-year institution in United States.
Eligibility: Applicant must be minority student who is either high school senior, college senior, community college graduate, transfer student or community college freshman. Applicant must be high school senior. Applicant must be U.S. citizen or permanent resident.
Basis for selection: Major/career interest in chemistry; biochemistry or engineering, chemical. Applicant must demonstrate financial need, high academic achievement and seriousness of purpose.
Application requirements: Recommendations, transcript.
Additional information: Approximately 75 new awards valued at up to $2,500 each will be made to students who pursue bachelor's degree in chemistry, biochemistry, chemical engineering or chemically related field; and up to $2,500 will be awarded to students who pursue two-year technology program certificate. Visit Website for more information.

Amount of award:	$2,500
Number of awards:	75
Application deadline:	February 15

Contact:
National Urban League Scholarship Programs
120 Wall Street
New York, NY 10005
Phone: 888-839-0467 or 212-558-5300
Web: www.nul.org

Freddie Mac Scholarships

Type of award: Scholarship, renewable.
Intended use: For freshman or sophomore study at accredited 2-year or 4-year institution in United States.
Eligibility: Applicant must be African American. Applicant must be high school senior. Applicant must be U.S. citizen or permanent resident.
Basis for selection: Applicant must demonstrate financial need, high academic achievement and seriousness of purpose.
Additional information: Scholarships awarded to students from low- and moderate-income families in urban communities. Students must demonstrate potential for success in competitive academic environment. Initial funding $5,000 per year for first two years of college study. Visit Website for more information.

Amount of award:	$5,000
Number of awards:	15
Application deadline:	January 15

Contact:
National Urban League Scholarship Programs
120 Wall Street
New York, NY 10005
Phone: 888-839-0467
Web: www.nul.org

Jerry Bartow Scholarship Fund

Type of award: Scholarship.
Intended use: For full-time sophomore, junior or senior study at 4-year institution. Designated institutions: Historically Black Colleges/Universities (HBCUs) participating in Black Executive Exchange Program (BEEP).
Eligibility: Applicant must be African American. Applicant must be U.S. citizen or permanent resident.
Basis for selection: Major/career interest in business/management/administration; computer/information sciences or education.
Additional information: Awardees notified by BEEP office and should be available to receive award at BEEP's Annual Conference; travel and hotel arrangements provided. Visit Website for details.

Amount of award:	$1,500
Number of awards:	2
Application deadline:	January 15
Total amount awarded:	$3,000

Contact:
National Urban League Scholarship Programs
120 Wall Street
New York, NY 10005
Phone: 888-839-0467
Web: www.nul.org

National Urban League National Achievers Society Scholars Award

Type of award: Scholarship.
Intended use: For full-time undergraduate study at accredited 4-year institution in United States.
Eligibility: Applicant must be African American. Applicant must be high school senior. Applicant must be U.S. citizen or permanent resident.
Basis for selection: Applicant must demonstrate high academic achievement.
Application requirements: Transcript, proof of eligibility. Application, questionnaire, test scores, two statements of personal recommendation (from school official and nonrelative/community representative).
Additional information: Minimum 2.7 GPA. Student must be inducted member of Urban League/Congress of National Black Churches (CNBC) Achievers Society or McKnight Achievers. Award up to $10,000 for up to four years. Visit Website for details and application.

Amount of award:	$10,000
Number of awards:	100
Application deadline:	January 15

Contact:
National Urban League Scholarship Programs
120 Wall Street
New York, NY 10005
Phone: 888-839-0467
Web: www.nul.org

National Urban League/Congress of National Black Churches Scholars Award

Type of award: Scholarship.
Intended use: For full-time undergraduate study at accredited 4-year institution in United States.
Eligibility: Applicant must be African American. Applicant must be high school senior. Applicant must be U.S. citizen or permanent resident.
Basis for selection: Applicant must demonstrate high academic achievement, leadership and service orientation.
Application requirements: Recommendations, transcript. Application, questionnaire, test scores, two statements of personal recommendation (from school official and nonrelative/community representative).
Additional information: Minimum 2.7 GPA. Award up to $10,000 for up to four years. Special consideration given to candidates affiliated with one of CAAA partner organizations and with Urban League. Visit Website for details and application.

Amount of award:	$10,000
Number of awards:	100
Application deadline:	January 15

Contact:
National Urban League Scholarship Programs
120 Wall Street
New York, NY 10005
Phone: 888-839-0467
Web: www.nul.org

Reginald K. Brack, Jr., NULITES Scholarship

Type of award: Scholarship.
Intended use: For undergraduate study in United States.
Eligibility: Applicant must be African American. Applicant must be high school senior. Applicant must be U.S. citizen or permanent resident.
Basis for selection: Major/career interest in communications; journalism; public relations; publishing or journalism. Applicant must demonstrate financial need, high academic achievement and service orientation.
Application requirements: Letter of recommendation from an Urban League affiliate CEO or a NULITES Advisor/Youth Development Director/Education Director.
Additional information: Awarded to current or former National Urban League Incentives To Excel & Succeed (NULITES) program participants. Minimum "B" average or 3.0 GPA. Award given annually for four years. Visit Website for more information.

Amount of award:	$2,500
Application deadline:	January 15

Contact:
National Urban League Scholarship Programs
120 Wall Street
New York, NY 10005
Phone: 888-839-0467
Web: www.nul.org

University of Rochester Urban League Scholarship

Type of award: Scholarship.
Intended use: For full-time undergraduate study. Designated institutions: University of Rochester.

Eligibility: Applicant must be African American.
Basis for selection: Applicant must demonstrate financial need.
Application requirements: Submit admissions application no later than January 31 to University of Rochester. Include letter of intent to proceed with scholarship nomination process.
Additional information: Award is $6,000/year for four years. Candidates who apply for scholarship will not be required to submit $50 admissions application fee. Visit Urban League Website or contact University of Rochester admissions office for details and application. Also visit www.rochester.edu for information.

Amount of award:	$24,000
Application deadline:	January 15

Contact:
National Urban League Scholarship Programs
120 Wall Street
New York, NY 10005
Phone: 888-839-0467 or 212-558-5300
Web: www.nul.org

Native Daughters of the Golden West

Native Daughters of the Golden West Scholarship

Type of award: Scholarship, renewable.
Intended use: For full-time undergraduate or graduate study at accredited postsecondary institution in United States. Designated institutions: California.
Eligibility: Applicant or parent must be member/participant of Native Daughters of the Golden West. Applicant must be U.S. citizen residing in California. Applicant must be veteran; or dependent of active service person or veteran.
Basis for selection: Applicant must be born in California. Major/career interest in business; education; social work or nursing. Applicant must demonstrate financial need, high academic achievement, depth of character, leadership, patriotism, seriousness of purpose and service orientation.
Application requirements: Recommendations, essay, transcript, nomination by local club or parlor.
Additional information: High school seniors and college freshmen may apply.

Amount of award:	$850-$1,500
Application deadline:	April 15
Notification begins:	May 15

Contact:
Native Daughters of the Golden West
543 Baker Street
San Francisco, CA 94117-1405

Navy Supply Corps Foundation

Navy Supply Corps Foundation Scholarship

Type of award: Scholarship, renewable.

361

Intended use: For full-time undergraduate study at accredited 2-year or 4-year institution.

Eligibility: Applicant must be U.S. citizen. Applicant must be dependent of veteran who served in the Navy. Applicant must be dependent child or spouse of Navy Supply Corps/Warrant Officer or associated supply enlisted ratings (MS, DK, SK, AK, LI, PC, and SH) on active duty, reserve status, retired-with-pay, or deceased.

Basis for selection: Applicant must demonstrate financial need, high academic achievement, depth of character, leadership and service orientation.

Application requirements: Transcript, proof of eligibility.

Additional information: Minimum 3.0 GPA required. Any family member of Foundation member or enlisted member (active duty, reservist, or retired) is eligible for consideration. Only applications downloaded from Website accepted.

Amount of award:	$1,000-$10,000
Application deadline:	April 10
Notification begins:	April 30

Contact:
Navy Supply Corps Foundation
Navy Supply Corps School
1425 Prince Avenue
Athens, GA 30606-2205
Phone: 706-354-4111
Web: www.usnscf.com

Navy-Marine Corps Relief Society

Vice Admiral E.P. Travers Scholarship

Type of award: Scholarship, renewable.

Intended use: For full-time undergraduate study.

Eligibility: Applicant must be U.S. citizen. Applicant must be in military service; or dependent of active service person; or spouse of active service person in the Marines or Navy.

Basis for selection: Applicant must demonstrate financial need.

Application requirements: Proof of eligibility. Current military ID required for dependent and service member.

Additional information: Minimum 2.0 GPA. Applicant must be the dependent child of an active duty or retired Navy or Marine Corps service member.

Amount of award:	$2,000
Application deadline:	March 1

Contact:
Navy-Marine Corps Relief Society NMCRS Education Division
801 North Randolph Street
Suite 1228
Arlington, VA 22203-1978
Phone: 703-696-4960
Fax: 703-696-0144
Web: www.nmcrs.org

NCAA

The Freedom Forum/NCAA Sports Journalism Scholarship

Type of award: Scholarship.

Intended use: For senior study. Designated institutions: NCAA member institutions.

Basis for selection: Based on quality of three examples of sports journalism work such as newspaper articles, program copy, published photographs, editorials, television and/or radio scripts. VHS tapes and cassettes accepted. Major/career interest in journalism.

Application requirements: Portfolio, recommendations, transcript. Request application and information from Chief Executive Officer of Faculty Athletics Representatives or Chairperson of Journalism School/Department of NCAA member institutions. Application also printable from Website. All materials, including transcripts, essay question statement, writing samples and recommendation letters, should be mailed with completed application.

Additional information: Students must apply during junior year of college. Eight scholarships awarded at NCAA member institutions. Applications available in September.

Amount of award:	$3,000
Number of awards:	8
Application deadline:	December 13

Contact:
NCAA Leadership Advisory Board
P.O. Box 6222
Indianapolis, IN 46207-6222
Phone: (317) 917-6816
Web: www.ncaa.org/leadership_advisory_board

NCAA Division I Degree-Completion Program

NCAA Division I Degree-Completion Award Program

Type of award: Scholarship.

Intended use: For senior study at 4-year institution. Designated institutions: Colleges in Division I of the NCAA.

Basis for selection: Competition/talent/interest in athletics/sports. Major/career interest in athletic training. Applicant must demonstrate financial need, depth of character, leadership and service orientation.

Application requirements: Recommendations, transcript. Endorsement and signature from dean of college or head of department and director of athletics; statement and signature from financial aid office.

Additional information: Applicants must have received athletics-related grant-in-aid at NCAA Division I institution. Must have less than 30 semester hours or 45 quarter hours remaining to complete degree and be attainable within two semesters or three-quarters. Must be entering at least sixth year of postsecondary education. Application materials available at office of Director of Athletics on member school campuses. Must also submit IRS forms. Awards will not exceed full athletics-related grant-in-aid as defined by institution and is renewable for second term, given completion of 12 hours with 2.0 GPA or better.

Number of applicants: 313
Total amount awarded: $950,000
Contact:
NCAA Division I Degree-Completion Program
Karen Cooper
P.O. Box 6222
Indianapolis, IN 46206-6222
Phone: 317-917-6307
Fax: 317-917-6364
Web: www.ncaa.org

Nebraska State Department of Education

Nebraska Robert C. Byrd Honors Scholarship

Type of award: Scholarship, renewable.
Intended use: For full-time freshman study at accredited postsecondary institution in United States. Designated institutions: Excludes U.S. military academies.
Eligibility: Applicant must be high school senior. Applicant must be U.S. citizen or permanent resident residing in Nebraska.
Basis for selection: Applicant must demonstrate high academic achievement.
Application requirements: Transcript. ACT scores.
Additional information: Renewable up to four years with good academic standing. Minimum ACT score of 30. Applications mailed to counselors at all Nebraska high schools in January.

Amount of award: $1,500
Application deadline: March 15
Total amount awarded: $252,000
Contact:
Nebraska State Department of Education
Robert C. Byrd Scholarship
P.O. Box 94987
Lincoln, NE 68509-4987
Phone: 402-471-3962
Web: www.nde.state.ne.us/byrd

Nevada Department of Education

Nevada Robert C. Byrd Honors Scholarship

Type of award: Scholarship, renewable.
Intended use: For undergraduate study at postsecondary institution.
Eligibility: Applicant must be high school senior. Applicant must be U.S. citizen or permanent resident residing in Nevada.
Basis for selection: Applicant must demonstrate high academic achievement, depth of character and seriousness of purpose.
Additional information: Applicant must be Nevada High School Scholar. Minimum 3.5 GPA and SAT score of 1100 or ACT score of 25 required.

Amount of award: $1,500
Number of awards: 40
Number of applicants: 975
Contact:
Contact high school guidance counselor.

Nevada Student Incentive Grant

Type of award: Scholarship.
Intended use: For undergraduate or graduate study at vocational, 2-year, 4-year or graduate institution. Designated institutions: Nevada institutions.
Eligibility: Applicant must be U.S. citizen or permanent resident residing in Nevada.
Basis for selection: Applicant must demonstrate financial need.

Amount of award: $5,000
Number of awards: 988
Total amount awarded: $494,774
Contact:
Contact financial aid office of institution.
Phone: 775 687 9228

New England Board of Higher Education

New England Board of Higher Education's Regional Student Program

Type of award: Scholarship.
Intended use: For undergraduate or graduate study in United States. Designated institutions: 78 New England public colleges and universities.
Eligibility: Applicant must be permanent resident residing in Vermont, New Hampshire, Connecticut, Maine, Massachusetts or Rhode Island.
Application requirements: Applicant must pursue approved major listed in annual program catalog.
Additional information: Regional Student Program provides New England residents with a tuition discount when they study approved majors not offered at public institutions in their own state at out-of-state public colleges in New England. Approved majors listed in annual catalog.
Contact:
New England Board of Higher Education
45 Temple Place
Boston, MA 2111
Phone: 617-357-9620
Web: www.nebhe.org

New Hampshire Postsecondary Education Commission

New Hampshire Incentive Program

Type of award: Scholarship, renewable.

Intended use: For undergraduate study at accredited vocational, 2-year or 4-year institution. Designated institutions: Eligible institutions in New England.
Eligibility: Applicant must be U.S. citizen or permanent resident residing in New Hampshire.
Basis for selection: Applicant must demonstrate financial need.
Application requirements: Proof of eligibility. FAFSA.

Amount of award:	$125-$1,000
Number of awards:	2,858
Application deadline:	May 1
Total amount awarded:	$1,496,894

Contact:
New Hampshire Postsecondary Education Commission
3 Barrell Court, Suite 300
Concord, NH 03301-8543
Phone: 603-271-2555
Fax: 603-271-2696
Web: www.nh.us/postsecondary

New Hampshire Scholarship for Orphans of Veterans

Type of award: Scholarship, renewable.
Intended use: For full-time undergraduate or graduate study at vocational, 2-year or 4-year institution.
Eligibility: Applicant must be at least 16, no older than 25. Applicant must be U.S. citizen residing in New Hampshire. Applicant must be dependent of disabled veteran or deceased veteran during Korean War, WW I, WW II or Vietnam.
Application requirements: Proof of eligibility.
Additional information: Parent must have been legal resident of New Hampshire at time of service-related death.

Amount of award:	$1,000
Number of awards:	9
Number of applicants:	10
Total amount awarded:	$9,000

Contact:
New Hampshire Postsecondary Education Commission
3 Barrell Court, Suite 300
Concord, NH 03301-8543
Phone: 603-271-2555
Fax: 603-271-2696
Web: www.nh.gov/postsecondary

Workforce Incentive Program

Type of award: Scholarship, renewable.
Intended use: For full-time undergraduate or graduate study at accredited 2-year, 4-year or graduate institution. Designated institutions: New Hampshire institutions.
Eligibility: Applicant must be U.S. citizen or permanent resident residing in New Hampshire.
Basis for selection: Major/career interest in education, special; foreign languages or nursing. Applicant must demonstrate financial need.
Additional information: Award offered is $500 per semester. Contact financial aid office at New Hampshire institution or Melanie Deshaies at New Hampshire Postsecondary Education Commission.

Amount of award:	$1,000
Number of awards:	50
Number of applicants:	60
Application deadline:	June 1, December 15
Total amount awarded:	$28,000

Contact:
New Hampshire Postsecondary Education Commission
3 Barrell Court
Suite 300
Concord, NH 03301-8543
Phone: 603-271-2555
Fax: 603-271-2696
Web: www.nh.gov/postsecondary

New Jersey Commission on Higher Education

New Jersey Educational Opportunity Fund Grant

Type of award: Scholarship, renewable.
Intended use: For full-time freshman, sophomore, junior, senior or graduate study at accredited 2-year or 4-year institution. Designated institutions: 41 participating New Jersey community colleges and four-year colleges and universities.
Eligibility: Applicant must be U.S. citizen or permanent resident residing in New Jersey.
Basis for selection: Applicant must demonstrate financial need.
Application requirements: File or renew FAFSA by October 1.
Additional information: For students from educationally disadvantaged backgrounds with demonstrated financial need. Must be New Jersey resident for at least 12 consecutive months prior to receiving grant. Students are admitted into EOF program by college. Program includes summer sessions, tutoring and counseling. Graduate award up to $4,150. Contact financial aid office at institution.

Amount of award:	$200-$2,100
Application deadline:	October 1

Contact:
New Jersey Commission on Higher Education
P.O. Box 542
Trenton, NJ 08625-0542
Phone: 800-792-8670
Web: www.hesaa.org

New Jersey Department of Military and Veterans Affairs

New Jersey POW/MIA Program

Type of award: Scholarship, renewable.
Intended use: For full-time freshman, sophomore, junior or senior study at accredited 4-year institution in United States. Designated institutions: New Jersey schools.
Eligibility: Applicant must be residing in New Jersey. Applicant must be dependent of active service person or POW/MIA. Parent must have been officially declared Prisoner of War or Missing in Action after January 1, 1960.
Application requirements: Proof of eligibility.
Additional information: Award is full-tuition waiver (no room, board or expenses) at eligible institution.

Amount of award: Full tuition
Number of awards: 2
Application deadline: October 1, March 1
Total amount awarded: $10,552
Contact:
New Jersey Department of Military and Veterans Affairs
DVP
P.O. Box 340
Trenton, NJ 08625-7005
Phone: 609-530-6854
Fax: 609-530-7075
Web: www.state.nj.us/military

New Jersey Veteran Tuition Credit Program

Type of award: Scholarship, renewable.
Intended use: For undergraduate or graduate study at postsecondary institution in United States.
Eligibility: Applicant must be residing in New Jersey. Applicant must be veteran who served in the Army, Air Force, Marines, Navy, Coast Guard or Reserves/National Guard during Vietnam. Must have served in Armed Forces between December 31, 1960, and May 7, 1975. Must have been New Jersey resident at time of induction or discharge, or for at least a year prior to application, excluding active duty time.
Application requirements: Proof of eligibility.
Additional information: Must be New Jersey resident for at least one year prior to application.
Amount of award: $200-$400
Number of awards: 43
Application deadline: October 1, March 1
Total amount awarded: $12,700
Contact:
New Jersey Department of Military and Veterans Affairs
DVP
P.O. Box 340
Trenton, NJ 08625-7005
Phone: 609-530-6854
Fax: 609-530-7075
Web: www.state.nj.us/military

New Jersey Higher Education Student Assistance Authority

New Jersey Edward J. Bloustein Distinguished Scholars

Type of award: Scholarship, renewable.
Intended use: For full-time undergraduate study at accredited 2-year or 4-year institution. Designated institutions: Approved NJ colleges, universities, and degree-granting proprietary institutions.
Eligibility: Applicant must be high school senior. Applicant must be U.S. citizen or permanent resident residing in New Jersey.
Basis for selection: Applicant must demonstrate high academic achievement.
Application requirements: Transcript, nomination by high school. SAT/ACT scores.

Additional information: Open to students with high SAT scores ranking in top 10% of their junior class. Must be a New Jersey resident for at least 12 consecutive months prior to receiving the award. Candidates nominated for consideration by high schools at the end of junior year will be notified in the fall of senior year. Students may not apply directly to this program. Candidates will be selected for consideration by their secondary schools based upon standard of academic criteria. See guidance counselor for more information.
Amount of award: $950
Contact:
New Jersey Higher Education Student Assistance Authority
4 Quakerbridge Plaza, P.O. Box 540
Trenton, NJ 08625-0540
Phone: 800-792-8670
Web: www.hesaa.org

New Jersey Survivor Tuition Benefits Program

Type of award: Scholarship, renewable.
Intended use: For undergraduate study at accredited 2-year or 4-year institution. Designated institutions: Approved NJ colleges, universities and degree-granting institutions.
Eligibility: Applicant must be U.S. citizen residing in New Jersey. Applicant's parent must have been killed or disabled in work-related accident as fire fighter, police officer or public safety officer.
Application requirements: Proof of eligibility.
Additional information: Parent or spouse must have been New Jersey firefighter, law enforcement or emergency service personnel killed in line of duty. Applications available by calling State of New Jersey Office of Student Assistance toll-free financial aid hotline. Grants pay cost of tuition up to highest tuition charged at a New Jersey public postsecondary school.
Amount of award: Full tuition
Application deadline: October 1, March 1
Contact:
New Jersey Higher Education Student Assistance Authority
4 Quakerbridge Plaza, P.O. Box 540
Trenton, NJ 08625-0540
Phone: 800-792-8670
Web: www.hesaa.org

New Jersey Tuition Aid Grants (TAG)

Type of award: Scholarship, renewable.
Intended use: For full-time freshman, sophomore, junior or senior study at accredited 2-year or 4-year institution in United States. Designated institutions: Approved New Jersey colleges, universities and degree-granting proprietary institutions.
Eligibility: Applicant must be U.S. citizen or permanent resident residing in New Jersey.
Basis for selection: Applicant must demonstrate financial need.
Application requirements: Proof of eligibility. FAFSA.
Additional information: Renewal students must maintain satisfactory academic progress. Deadline for fall and spring awards: June 1 for renewal students; October 1 for new applicants who did not receive Tuition Aid Grant in the prior academic year. Visit Website for more information.
Amount of award: $868-$7,272
Application deadline: June 1, October 1

Contact:
New Jersey Higher Education Student Assistance Authority
4 Quakerbridge Plaza, P.O. Box 540
Trenton, NJ 08625-0540
Phone: 800-792-8670
Web: www.hesaa.org

New Jersey Urban Scholars

Type of award: Scholarship, renewable.
Intended use: For undergraduate study at accredited 2-year or 4-year institution in United States. Designated institutions: Approved New Jersey colleges, universities, and degree-granting institutions.
Eligibility: Applicant must be high school senior. Applicant must be U.S. citizen or permanent resident residing in New Jersey.
Basis for selection: Applicant must demonstrate high academic achievement.
Application requirements: Nomination by high school. Applicant must attend public secondary schools in state's urban and economically distressed areas.
Additional information: Open to students in top 10 percent of their high school class, with minimum 3.0 GPA or equivalent, attending high schools in New Jersey's urban and economically distressed areas. Candidates nominated for consideration by high schools at end of junior year will receive notification by fall of senior year. Students may not apply directly for award. See guidance counselors for more information.

 Amount of award: $950
Contact:
New Jersey Higher Education Student Assistance Authority
4 Quakerbridge Plaza
P.O. Box 540
Trenton, NJ 08625-0540
Phone: 800-792-8670
Fax: 609-588-2228
Web: www.hesaa.org

New Jersey Scholarship Foundation

AIA New Jersey Scholarship Foundation

Type of award: Scholarship, renewable.
Intended use: For full-time sophomore, junior, senior, master's or first professional study at accredited postsecondary institution. Designated institutions: Accredited architectural schools.
Eligibility: Applicant must be permanent resident residing in New Jersey.
Basis for selection: Major/career interest in architecture. Applicant must demonstrate financial need, high academic achievement and seriousness of purpose.
Application requirements: $5 application fee. Portfolio, recommendations, essay, transcript, proof of eligibility. FAFSA.
Additional information: Applicant must be New Jersey resident and have completed one year at accredited institution.

 Amount of award: $1,500-$2,500
 Number of applicants: 12
 Application deadline: April 30
 Notification begins: July 15

Contact:
New Jersey Scholarship Foundation Inc.
c/o Robert Zaccone
212 White Avenue
Old Tappan, NJ 07675

New Jersey Society of Architects

New Jersey Society of Architects Scholarship

Type of award: Scholarship.
Intended use: For full-time sophomore, junior, senior or master's study at accredited 4-year or graduate institution in United States.
Eligibility: Applicant must be residing in New Jersey.
Basis for selection: Major/career interest in architecture. Applicant must demonstrate financial need and high academic achievement.
Application requirements: $5 application fee. Portfolio, recommendations, essay, transcript. Photos of projects and FAFSA.
Additional information: Number of awards varies. Total amount awarded $5,000-$10,000.

 Amount of award: $1,000-$2,000
 Application deadline: April 30
 Notification begins: June 30

Contact:
New Jersey Society of Architects
AIA New Jersey Schol. Fndn c/o. R. Zaccone
212 White Avenue
Old Tappan, NJ 07675
Phone: 201-767-9575
Fax: 201-767-5541

New Jersey State Golf Association

Caddie Scholarship

Type of award: Scholarship, renewable.
Intended use: For full-time undergraduate study at accredited 2-year or 4-year institution in United States. Designated institutions: Accredited members of Association of American Colleges and Universities.
Basis for selection: Competition/talent/interest in Athletics/sports. Applicant must demonstrate financial need and high academic achievement.
Application requirements: Recommendations, proof of eligibility. Applicants must caddie at least one year at a member New Jersey State Golf Association golf club. Recommendation from golf club.
Additional information: Minimum 2.5 GPA. Must be in top 50% of class and have minimum combined SAT I score of 800. Foundation also offers one full scholarship award, which covers tuition, fees, room and board at Rutgers University.

Amount of award: $1,500-$3,000
Number of awards: 200
Application deadline: May 1
Notification begins: June 30
Total amount awarded: $320,000
Contact:
New Jersey State Golf Association
Caddie Scholarship Foundation
P.O. Box 6947
Freehold, NJ 07728
Phone: 732-780-4822
Web: www.njsga.org

New Mexico Commission on Higher Education

New Mexico Athlete Scholarship

Type of award: Scholarship, renewable.
Intended use: For undergraduate study at accredited 2-year or 4-year institution. Designated institutions: Selected New Mexico public institutions.
Eligibility: Applicant must be U.S. citizen or permanent resident residing in New Mexico.
Additional information: Awards vary, but are applied toward tuititon and fees. For more information, application, and deadlines, contact athletic department or financial aid office of any New Mexico public postsecondary institution. Non-resident eligible if attending eligible New Mexico institution.
Contact:
New Mexico Commission on Higher Education
Financial Aid and Student Services
1068 Cerrillos Road
Santa Fe, NM 87501
Phone: 800-279-9777
Web: www.nmche.org

New Mexico Legislative Endowment Program

Type of award: Scholarship, renewable.
Intended use: For undergraduate study at accredited postsecondary institution. Designated institutions: Public postsecondary New Mexico institutions.
Eligibility: Applicant must be U.S. citizen or permanent resident residing in New Mexico.
Basis for selection: Applicant must demonstrate financial need.
Application requirements: FAFSA.
Additional information: Contact financial aid office of any public postsecondary institution in New Mexico. Four-year public institutions may award up to $2,500 per student per academic year. Two-year public institutions may award up to $1,000 per student per year. Part-time students eligible for prorated awards. Deadlines set by institution.
Amount of award: $1,000-$2,500
Contact:
New Mexico Commission on Higher Education
Financial Aid and Student Services
1068 Cerrillos Road
Santa Fe, NM 87501
Phone: 800-279-9777
Web: www.nmche.org

New Mexico Scholars Program

Type of award: Scholarship, renewable.
Intended use: For undergraduate study at accredited 2-year or 4-year institution. Designated institutions: Public or private nonprofit institutions in New Mexico.
Eligibility: Applicant must be at least 16, no older than 21. Applicant must be U.S. citizen or permanent resident residing in New Mexico.
Basis for selection: Applicant must demonstrate financial need and high academic achievement.
Application requirements: SAT/ACT score, FAFSA.
Additional information: Tuition waiver (tuition, books and required fees). Number of awards based on availability of funds. Must be graduate of New Mexico high school. Must score at least 1020 on SAT, 25 on ACT or rank in top five percent of high school graduating class and have family income no greater than $30,000 per year. Contact financial aid office of New Mexico postsecondary institution of choice for information and application. Application deadlines set by institution.
Amount of award: Full tuition
Contact:
New Mexico Commission on Higher Education
Financial Aid and Student Services
1068 Cerrillos Road
Santa Fe, NM 87501
Phone: 800-279-9777
Web: www.nmche.org

New Mexico Student Choice Program

Type of award: Scholarship, renewable.
Intended use: For undergraduate study at postsecondary institution. Designated institutions: St. John's College, College of Southwest, College of Santa Fe.
Eligibility: Applicant must be U.S. citizen or permanent resident residing in New Mexico.
Basis for selection: Applicant must demonstrate financial need.
Application requirements: FAFSA.
Additional information: Award varies, with maximum based on highest tuition at New Mexico public university. Apply to financial aid office at one of three private non-profit colleges where award may be used. Must be enrolled in eligible institution as undergraduate. Part-time students eligible for prorated awards.
Contact:
New Mexico Commission on Higher Education
Financial Aid and Student Services
1068 Cerrillos Road
Santa Fe, NM 87501
Phone: 800-279-9777
Web: www.nmche.org

New Mexico Student Incentive Grant

Type of award: Scholarship, renewable.
Intended use: For undergraduate study at accredited postsecondary institution. Designated institutions: Public and selected private nonprofit New Mexico postsecondary institutions.
Eligibility: Applicant must be U.S. citizen or permanent resident residing in New Mexico.
Basis for selection: Applicant must demonstrate financial need.

Application requirements: FAFSA.
Additional information: Must demonstrate exceptional financial need. Contact financial aid office of New Mexico public postsecondary institutions or eligible private nonprofits for information, application and deadline. Part-time students eligible for prorated awards.

Amount of award: $200-$2,500
Contact:
New Mexico Commission on Higher Education
Financial Aid and Student Services
1068 Cerrillos Road
Santa Fe, NM 87501
Phone: 800-279-9777
Web: www.nmche.org

New Mexico Three Percent Scholarship

Type of award: Scholarship, renewable.
Intended use: For undergraduate or graduate study at accredited postsecondary institution. Designated institutions: Public New Mexico postsecondary institutions.
Eligibility: Applicant must be U.S. citizen or permanent resident residing in New Mexico.
Basis for selection: Applicant must demonstrate depth of character and leadership.
Application requirements: Transcript.
Additional information: Maximum award covers tuition and required fees. One-third of scholarships awarded on basis of financial need. Contact school's financial aid office for details. Each postsecondary institution establishes its own eligibility requirements and application deadlines.

Amount of award: Full tuition
Contact:
New Mexico Commission on Higher Education
1068 Cerrillos Road
Santa Fe, NM 85701
Phone: 800-279-9777
Web: www.nmche.org

New Mexico Vietnam Veteran's Scholarship

Type of award: Scholarship, renewable.
Intended use: For undergraduate or master's study at postsecondary institution. Designated institutions: Public and selected private non-profit postsecondary institutions in New Mexico.
Eligibility: Applicant must be U.S. citizen residing in New Mexico. Applicant must be veteran during Vietnam.
Application requirements: Proof of eligibility. Coursework must be certified by New Mexico Veterans' Service Commission (call 505-827-6300).
Additional information: Maximum award provides tuition/fees and book allowance on first come, first served basis. Eligibility must be certified by New Mexico Veterans Service Commission. Contact financial aid office of any New Mexico public postsecondary institution for information, deadline and application.

Amount of award: Full tuition
Contact:
New Mexico Veteran's Service Commission
P.O. Box 2324
Santa Fe, NM 87503
Phone: 505-827-6300
Web: www.nmche.org

New York Association of Black Journalists

Stephen H. Gayle Essay Contest

Type of award: Scholarship.
Intended use: For undergraduate study in United States. Designated institutions: Applicant must attend school in New York City, Westchester County or Long Island.
Eligibility: Applicant must be enrolled in high school. Applicant must be U.S. citizen residing in New York.
Basis for selection: Competition/talent/interest in writing/journalism, based on essay on a current affairs topic. Major/career interest in journalism. Applicant must demonstrate seriousness of purpose.
Application requirements: Essay, transcript. Proof of enrollment, writing samples, cover letter and resume.
Additional information: High school students eligible. Recipients will be honored at the NYABJ Awards dinner in December. Graduate scholarships also available. Contact NYABJ or see Website for essay topic and additional details. Essay judged on originality, creativity, style, accuracy and thoroughness of reporting.

Amount of award: $500-$2,500
Application deadline: November 17
Contact:
New York Association of Black Journalists
P.O. Box 230243
Ansonia Station
New York, NY 10023
Phone: 212-522-6969
Web: www.nyabj.org

New York Lottery

Leaders of Tomorrow Scholarship

Type of award: Scholarship.
Intended use: For full-time undergraduate study at accredited vocational, 2-year or 4-year institution in United States. Designated institutions: Eligible New York State postsecondary institutions.
Eligibility: Applicant must be high school senior. Applicant must be permanent resident residing in New York.
Basis for selection: Applicant must demonstrate high academic achievement, leadership and service orientation.
Application requirements: Transcript, proof of eligibility. Applicant should have at least B-average based on seven semesters of high school.
Additional information: $4,000 scholarship paid over four years, at $1,000 per year. One student from every public and private high school in New York State is awarded scholarship. Student must plan to attend New York State-accredited college, university, trade school or community college. Deadline in March; check Website for exact date. Awardees cannot accept full-cost-of-attendance scholarship from another source. Students with parents/guardians employed by New York State Lottery, its contractors, or CASDA are not eligible.

Amount of award: $1,000
Number of awards: 1,200
Number of applicants: 2,010
Notification begins: May 31
Total amount awarded: $1,033,000

Contact:
CASDA (Capital Area School Development Association)
One University Place - A 409
East Campus
Rensselaer, NY 12144-3456
Phone: 518-525-2788
Fax: 518-525-2797
Web: www.nylottery.org

New York State Education Department

New York State Readers Aid Program

Type of award: Scholarship, renewable.
Intended use: For undergraduate, master's or doctoral study at 2-year, 4-year or graduate institution.
Eligibility: Applicant must be visually impaired or hearing impaired. Applicant must be residing in New York.
Application requirements: Proof of eligibility.
Additional information: Number of awards varies. Applications available at degree-granting institutions. For deaf or blind students, award provides funds for notetakers, readers, or interpreters.

Amount of award:	$1,000
Total amount awarded:	$300,000

Contact:
Office of Vocational and Ed. Services for People with Disabilities
Readers Aid Program
Education Building, Room 1601
Albany, NY 12234
Phone: 518-474-5652
Fax: 518-473-6073
Web: www.vesid.nysed.gov

New York State Robert C. Byrd Federal Honors Scholarship

Type of award: Scholarship, renewable.
Intended use: For full-time undergraduate study at accredited 2-year or 4-year institution in United States.
Eligibility: Applicant must be high school senior. Applicant must be U.S. citizen or permanent resident residing in New York.
Basis for selection: Applicants will be ranked within county of legal residence based on final ranking score composed of 75% GPA and 25% SAT score. Applicant must demonstrate high academic achievement.
Application requirements: Applications available in early fall at student's high school.
Additional information: Must have 1250 SAT score, minimum unweighted 95.00 GPA in selected academic courses or 310 GED score.

Amount of award:	$1,500
Number of awards:	400
Application deadline:	March 1

Contact:
New York State Education Department
Scholarship Processing Unit
Room 1078 EBA
Albany, NY 12234
Phone: 518-486-1319
Fax: 518-486-5346
Web: www.highered.nysed.gov/kiap/scholarships/home.htm

New York State Education Department, the University of the State of New York

New York State Higher Education Opportunity Program

Type of award: Scholarship.
Intended use: For undergraduate study at 2-year or 4-year institution. Designated institutions: Independent New York State colleges and universities.
Eligibility: Applicant must be residing in New York.
Basis for selection: Applicant must demonstrate financial need.
Additional information: Applicant must be resident of New York State for one year preceding entry into HEOP and be academically and economically disadvantaged. Contact college or university of interest for application and additional information, and apply at time of admission. Support services include presession summer program and tutoring, counseling, and special coursework during academic year. Award amounts vary; contact sponsor for information.
Contact:
New York State Education Department, University of the State of NY
Collegiate & Prof'l. Development Prgms. Unit
Room 1071 EBA
Albany, NY 12234
Phone: 518-474-5313

New York State Grange

Grange Denise Scholarship

Type of award: Scholarship, renewable.
Intended use: For full-time undergraduate study at 2-year or 4-year institution.
Eligibility: Applicant must be residing in New York.
Basis for selection: Major/career interest in agriculture; agribusiness; agricultural education; agricultural economics or natural resources/conservation. Applicant must demonstrate financial need.
Application requirements: Recommendations, transcript. Three recommendations.
Additional information: Send SASE for application.

Amount of award:	$1,000
Number of awards:	6
Number of applicants:	20
Application deadline:	April 15
Notification begins:	June 15
Total amount awarded:	$6,000

Scholarships

Contact:
New York State Grange
100 Grange Place
Cortland, NY 13045
Phone: 607-756-7553

Grange Susan W. Freestone Education Award

Type of award: Scholarship, renewable.
Intended use: For full-time undergraduate or graduate study at 2-year or 4-year institution in United States.
Eligibility: Applicant or parent must be member/participant of New York State Grange. Applicant must be residing in New York.
Basis for selection: Applicant must demonstrate financial need, depth of character and service orientation.
Additional information: Applicant must be current Grange member in New York state to qualify for grant. Send SASE for application. Award granted by scholarship committee, based on many factors.

Amount of award:	$1,000
Number of awards:	2
Number of applicants:	5
Application deadline:	April 15
Notification begins:	June 15
Total amount awarded:	$2,000

Contact:
New York State Grange
100 Grange Place
Cortland, NY 13045
Phone: 607-756-7553

New York State Higher Education Services Corporation

Awards for Children of Veterans

Type of award: Scholarship.
Intended use: For full-time undergraduate or non-degree study at 2-year or 4-year institution. Designated institutions: Postsecondary institutions in New York.
Eligibility: Applicant must be residing in New York. Applicant must be dependent of veteran, disabled veteran or deceased veteran during Grenada conflict, Korean War, Lebanon conflict, Panama conflict, Persian Gulf War, WW I, WW II or Vietnam.
Application requirements: Proof of eligibility. FAFSA and Express TAP Application.
Additional information: Student's parents must have been disabled or deceased veteran, prisoner of war or classified as Missing In Action. Students whose parent(s) have been recipient of Armed Forces, Navy or Marine Corps expeditionary medal for participation in operations in Lebanon, Grenada and Panama also eligible. Visit Website for additional information.

Amount of award:	$450
Application deadline:	May 1

Contact:
New York State Higher Education Services Corporation
Grants and Scholarships
99 Washington Avenue
Albany, NY 12255
Phone: 888-NYS-HESC
Web: www.hesc.com

City University Seek/College Discovery Program

Type of award: Scholarship.
Intended use: For undergraduate study at 2-year or 4-year institution. Designated institutions: City University of New York campuses only.
Eligibility: Applicant must be U.S. citizen or permanent resident residing in New York.
Basis for selection: Applicant must demonstrate financial need.
Application requirements: Proof of eligibility. FAFSA.
Additional information: Applicant must be both academically and economically disadvantaged. Apply to financial aid office of CUNY. Available at City University of New York and community college campuses. For SEEK, student must have resided in New York state for at least one year; for College Discovery, student must have resided in New York City for at least one year.
Contact:
City University of New York
Office of Admission Services
101 West 31 Street
New York, NY 10001-3503
Phone: 212-947-4800
Web: www.cuny.edu

New York State Aid for Part-time Study Program

Type of award: Scholarship, renewable.
Intended use: For half-time undergraduate study at accredited postsecondary institution. Designated institutions: Postsecondary institutions in New York.
Eligibility: Applicant must be U.S. citizen or permanent resident residing in New York.
Basis for selection: Applicant must demonstrate financial need.
Application requirements: Proof of eligibility.
Additional information: Must fall within income limits. Campus-based program; recipients selected and award amount determined by school. Apply to financial aid office of institution. Maximum award is $2,000. Must not have used up TAP eligibility or be in default on Federal Family Education Loan. Student must maintain minimum 2.0 GPA. Visit Website for additional information.

Amount of award:	$2,000

Contact:
New York State Higher Education Services Corporation
Grants and Scholarships
99 Washington Avenue
Albany, NY 12255
Phone: 888-NYS-HESC
Web: www.hesc.com

Scholarships

New York State Memorial Scholarship for Families of Deceased Police/Volunteer Firefighters/Peace Officers and Emergency Medical Service Workers

Type of award: Scholarship, renewable.
Intended use: For full-time undergraduate study at 2-year or 4-year institution. Designated institutions: New York institutions.
Eligibility: Applicant must be U.S. citizen residing in New York. Applicant's parent must have been killed or disabled in work-related accident as fire fighter, police officer or public safety officer.
Application requirements: Proof of eligibility. Must submit Memorial Scholarship Supplement, FAFSA and Express TAP Application.
Additional information: Spouse and/or children of police officer/firefighter/peace officer/ EMS worker who died as result of injuries sustained in line of duty in service to NYS are eligible. Award will equal applicant's actual tuition cost or SUNY undergraduate tuition cost, whichever is less. Also provides funds to meet non-tuition costs, such as room and board, books, supplies and transportation. Visit Website for additional information.

    Application deadline: May 1
Contact:
New York State Higher Education Services Corporation
Grants and Scholarships
99 Washington Avenue
Albany, NY 12255
Phone: 888-NYS-HESC
Web: www.hesc.com

New York State Tuition Assistance Program

Type of award: Scholarship, renewable.
Intended use: For full-time undergraduate or graduate study at accredited postsecondary institution in United States. Designated institutions: TAP-eligible postsecondary schools in New York.
Eligibility: Applicant must be U.S. citizen or permanent resident residing in New York.
Basis for selection: Applicant must demonstrate financial need.
Application requirements: Proof of eligibility.
Additional information: Must fall within income limits. Submit FAFSA and receive prefilled Express TAP Application (ETA) to review, sign and return. Institution must be approved by New York State Education Department to offer TAP eligible programs of study. Award subject to budget appropriations. Visit Website for additional information and current dollar range.

    Amount of award: $75-$5,000
    Application deadline: May 1
Contact:
New York State Higher Education Services Corporation
Grants and Scholarships
99 Washington Avenue
Albany, NY 12255
Phone: 888-NYS-HESC
Web: www.hesc.com

New York State Vietnam Veteran Tuition Award/Persian Gulf Veteran Tuition Award

Type of award: Scholarship, renewable.
Intended use: For undergraduate or graduate study at accredited vocational, 2-year, 4-year or graduate institution in United States. Designated institutions: Approved postsecondary schools in New York.
Eligibility: Applicant must be returning adult student. Applicant must be U.S. citizen or permanent resident residing in New York. Applicant must be veteran during Persian Gulf War or Vietnam. Must have served in armed forces in Indochina between December 1961 and May 1975 for Vietnam Veteran Tuition Award. Must have served in hostilities beginning August 2, 1990 for Persian Gulf Veteran Tuition Award. Must have other than dishonorable charge for either.
Application requirements: Proof of eligibility. FAFSA. Express Tap Application (ETA). Documentation of Indochina service or Persian Gulf service.
Additional information: Maximum award is $2,000 annually for full-time students; $1,000 annually for part-time students. Students must have also applied for TAP and Federal Pell Grant awards. Visit Website for additional information.

    Amount of award: $1,000-$2,000
    Application deadline: May 1
Contact:
New York State Higher Education Services Corporation
Grants and Scholarships
99 Washington Avenue
Albany, NY 12255
Phone: 888-NYS-HESC
Web: www.hesc.com

New York State Native American Education Unit

New York State Native American Student Aid Program

Type of award: Scholarship, renewable.
Intended use: For undergraduate study at accredited vocational, 2-year or 4-year institution. Designated institutions: New York institutions.
Eligibility: Applicant must be American Indian. Must be on official tribal roll of New York State tribe, or be a child of enrolled member. Applicant must be U.S. citizen residing in New York.
Application requirements: Proof of eligibility. Tribal certification form, documentation of high school graduation and college acceptance letter.
Additional information: Must reapply to renew award each semester. Minimum 2.0 semester GPA required. Summer application deadline May 20. Students taking 12 or more credits receive $1,000; under 12 credits $85 per credit hour.

    Amount of award: $1,000
    Application deadline: July 15, December 31

Contact:
New York State Native American Education Unit
New York State Education Department
Room 465, Education Building Annex
Albany, NY 12234
Phone: 518-474-0537
Fax: 518-474-3666

Nisei Student Relocation Commemorative Fund

Nisei Student Relocation Commemorative Fund

Type of award: Scholarship.
Intended use: For freshman study at vocational, 2-year or 4-year institution in United States.
Eligibility: Applicant must be Southeast Asian (Vietnamese, Cambodian, Hmong, Laotian, Amerasian) refugee or immigrant. Applicant must be high school senior.
Basis for selection: Applicant must demonstrate financial need and high academic achievement.
Application requirements: Recommendations, essay, transcript.
Additional information: Applicant must be high school senior living in city/area/region of the United States where scholarships awarded as determined annually by organization's board of directors. Location changes yearly; contact group for information. Number of awards varies.

Amount of award:	$500-$2,000
Number of applicants:	80
Application deadline:	March 31
Total amount awarded:	$37,500

Contact:
Nisei Student Relocation Commemorative Fund
c/o Y. Kobayashi or J. Hibino
19 Scenic Drive
Portland, CT 06480
Phone: 860-342-1731

NJ Higher Education Student Assistance

New Jersey Higher Education Student Assistance Authority Pilot Part-Time Tuition Aid Grant

Type of award: Scholarship, renewable.
Intended use: For half-time undergraduate study at postsecondary institution. Designated institutions: Participating New Jersey county colleges.
Eligibility: Applicant must be residing in New Jersey.
Basis for selection: Applicant must demonstrate financial need.
Application requirements: FAFSA.
Additional information: Renewals accepted June 1. Application and additional information can be obtained on Website.

Amount of award:	$116-$375
Application deadline:	October 1, March 1

Contact:
NJ Higher Education Student Assistance Authority
P.O. Box 540
Trenton, NJ 08625
Phone: 888-792-8670
Web: www.hesaa.org

NJ Higher Education Student Assistance Authority

New Jersey Higher Education Student Assistance Authority Dana Christmas Scholarship for Heroism

Type of award: Scholarship.
Intended use: For undergraduate or graduate study at 4-year or graduate institution.
Eligibility: Applicant must be enrolled in high school. Applicant must be residing in New Jersey.
Additional information: Honors young New Jersey residents for acts of heroism. Application can be obtained by calling HESAA or by visiting Website.

Amount of award:	$10,000
Application deadline:	October 15

Contact:
NJ Higher Education Student Assistance Authority
P.O. Box 540
Trenton, NJ 08625
Phone: 800-792-8670
Web: www.hesaa.org

Noncommissioned Officers Association

Noncommissioned Officers Association Scholarship for Children of Members

Type of award: Scholarship, renewable.
Intended use: For full-time undergraduate study at accredited 4-year institution in United States.
Eligibility: Applicant or parent must be member/participant of Non-Commissioned Officers Association.
Application requirements: Recommendations, essay, transcript. Include two letters of recommendation from school, one personal letter of recommendation from an adult who is not a relative, autobiography, ACT or SAT scores, and minumum 200-word essay on Americanism.
Additional information: Applicant must be dependent of member of Noncommissioned Officers Association. Applicant can apply for academic grant only.

Amount of award:	$900-$1,000
Number of awards:	12
Number of applicants:	150
Application deadline:	March 31

Contact:
Noncommissioned Officers Association
P.O. Box 33610
San Antonio, TX 78265
Phone: 210-653-6161
Fax: 210-637-3337
Web: www.ncoausa.org

Noncommissioned Officers Association Scholarship for Spouses

Type of award: Scholarship, renewable.
Intended use: For full-time undergraduate study at 4-year institution in United States.
Eligibility: Applicant or parent must be member/participant of Non-Commissioned Officers Association. Applicant must be U.S. citizen. Must be spouse of non-commissioned officer or petty officer.
Application requirements: Transcript. Send copy of high school diploma or GED, brief biographical background, certificates of completion for any other courses of training, letter of intent describing degree course of study, plans for completion of a degree program, and a closing paragraph on "What a College Degree Means to Me."
Additional information: Must be spouse of member of Noncommissioned Officers Association. Recipient must apply for auxiliary membership in Noncommissioned Officers Association.

Amount of award:	$900
Number of awards:	4
Number of applicants:	30
Application deadline:	March 31

Contact:
Noncommissioned Officers Association
P.O. Box 33610
San Antonio, TX 78265
Phone: 210-653-6161
Fax: 210-637-3337
Web: www.ncoausa.org

North American Limousin Junior Association

Limousin Award of Excellence

Type of award: Scholarship.
Intended use: For undergraduate study at 2-year or 4-year institution.
Eligibility: Applicant or parent must be member/participant of North American Limousin Junior Association. Applicant must be at least 19, no older than 21.
Basis for selection: Major/career interest in agriculture. Applicant must demonstrate high academic achievement, depth of character, leadership, patriotism, seriousness of purpose and service orientation.
Application requirements: Interview, recommendations, proof of eligibility.
Additional information: Up to three awards given. Experience with Limousin cattle preferred. Proven excellence in

Limousin activities as well as leadership skills demonstrated in NALJA, 4-H and FFA.

Amount of award:	$750
Application deadline:	May 15
Notification begins:	July 25

Contact:
North American Limousin Junior Association
7383 South Alton Way
Englewood, CO 80112
Phone: 303-220-1693
Web: www.nalf.org

North American Limousin Limouselle Foundation

Limouselle Scholarship

Type of award: Scholarship.
Intended use: For undergraduate or graduate study at 2-year or 4-year institution.
Eligibility: Applicant or parent must be member/participant of North American Limousin Junior Association.
Basis for selection: Major/career interest in agriculture; agribusiness; agricultural economics or agricultural education. Applicant must demonstrate financial need, high academic achievement, depth of character, leadership, patriotism, seriousness of purpose and service orientation.
Application requirements: Transcript, proof of eligibility.
Additional information: Must rank in top third of class.

Amount of award:	$500
Number of awards:	3
Application deadline:	May 15
Notification begins:	July 25

Contact:
North American Limousin Foundation
7383 South Alton Way
Englewood, CO 80112
Phone: 303-220-1693
Web: www.nalf.org

North Carolina Association of Educators

Mary Morrow-Edna Richards Scholarship

Type of award: Scholarship.
Intended use: For full-time junior study in United States.
Eligibility: Applicant must be residing in North Carolina.
Basis for selection: Major/career interest in education or education, teacher. Applicant must demonstrate financial need, high academic achievement, depth of character, leadership and service orientation.
Application requirements: Recommendations, essay, transcript. Must be enrolled in a teacher education program.
Additional information: Must agree to teach in North Carolina for two years after graduation. Application should be made through college or university with department of education head during junior year. Other eligible students may request application forms from NCAE office. Preference may be

given to Student NCAE members or children of NCAE members. Number of awards varies annually according to funding, minimum four per year. Application is due on the second Monday in January.

Amount of award:	$1,000
Number of awards:	10
Number of applicants:	50
Notification begins:	February 15
Total amount awarded:	$10,000

Contact:
North Carolina Association of Educators
P.O. Box 27347
Raleigh, NC 27611
Phone: 800-662-7924 ext. 216
Web: www.ncae.org

North Carolina Bar Association

North Carolina Law Enforcement Dependents Scholarship

Type of award: Scholarship, renewable.
Intended use: For full-time undergraduate, master's, doctoral or first professional study at accredited postsecondary institution.
Eligibility: Applicant must be no older than 27. Applicant must be residing in North Carolina. Applicant's parent must have been killed or disabled in work-related accident as police officer or public safety officer.
Basis for selection: Applicant must demonstrate financial need.
Application requirements: Essay, transcript, proof of eligibility. Photo (optional).
Additional information: Applicant's parent must have been working as North Carolina law enforcement officer at time of death or disablement. Amount awarded depends on available funding, number of applicants and cost of institution.

Number of applicants:	17
Application deadline:	April 1
Notification begins:	May 31

Contact:
North Carolina Bar Association
Young Lawyers Division Scholarship Committee
P. O. Box 3688
Cary, NC 27519
Phone: 919-677-0561
Web: www.ncbar.org

North Carolina Department of Community Colleges

Allen Ryan Todd Scholarship

Type of award: Scholarship.
Intended use: For undergraduate study at 2-year institution.
Designated institutions: North Carolina community college.
Eligibility: Applicant must be residing in North Carolina.

Basis for selection: Major/career interest in education. Applicant must demonstrate financial need and high academic achievement.
Application requirements: Essay, proof of eligibility.
Additional information: Applicant must be resident of "low wealth" county, as designated by Department of Public Instruction. Must be enrolled in, or intend to enroll in, associate's degree program in education at North Carolina community college.

Amount of award:	$1,661
Number of awards:	2
Total amount awarded:	$3,322

Contact:
North Carolina Department of Community Colleges
200 West Jones Street
Raleigh, NC 27603-1379
Phone: 919-733-7051 ext. 440
Fax: 919-733-0680

George W. Ballard Memorial Scholarship

Type of award: Scholarship.
Intended use: For undergraduate study at 2-year institution. Designated institutions: North Carolina community colleges: Alamance Community College, Cape Fear Community College, Central Piedmont Community College, Gaston Community College and Guilford Community College.
Eligibility: Applicant must be residing in North Carolina.
Basis for selection: Major/career interest in air conditioning/heating/refrigeration technology. Applicant must demonstrate financial need.
Application requirements: Essay.
Additional information: One scholarship, which grants a maximum of 90 percent of full-time tuition to recipient, rotates among designated colleges. Funds distributed in two equal payments. Number of awards granted are rotated annually among designated North Carolina community colleges.

Number of awards:	1

Contact:
North Carolina Department of Community Colleges
200 West Jones St.
Raleigh, NC 27603-1379
Phone: 919-733-7051 ext. 440
Fax: 919-733-0680

North Carolina Community Colleges Bell South Telephone/Telegraph Scholarship

Type of award: Scholarship, renewable.
Intended use: For freshman, sophomore or non-degree study. Designated institutions: North Carolina schools.
Eligibility: Applicant must be returning adult student. Applicant must be residing in North Carolina.
Basis for selection: Applicant must demonstrate financial need.
Additional information: Must enroll in degree or diploma program at one of eight eligible community colleges located in Bell South service area. Must apply through financial aid office at institution. Employees displaced because of obsolete job skills also eligible. Criteria subject to change.

Amount of award:	$1,335
Number of awards:	2
Total amount awarded:	$2,670

Contact:
Must apply through financial aid office at institution.

North Carolina Community Colleges Sprint College Transfer Scholarship

Type of award: Scholarship.
Intended use: For full-time freshman or sophomore study at 2-year institution.
Eligibility: Applicant must be residing in North Carolina.
Additional information: Must be enrolled in transfer program at community college in service area of Sprint Telecommunication Company. Apply through financial aid office of institution where enrolled. Priority given to African-American students.

Amount of award:	$500
Number of awards:	20
Total amount awarded:	$10,000

Contact:
North Carolina Department of Community Colleges
200 West Jones Street
Raleigh, NC 27603-1379

North Carolina Community Colleges Sprint Scholarship

Type of award: Scholarship.
Intended use: For full-time freshman, sophomore or non-degree study at 2-year institution. Designated institutions: North Carolina community colleges in Sprint service area.
Eligibility: Applicant must be residing in North Carolina.
Basis for selection: Applicant must demonstrate financial need.
Additional information: Priority given to minorities and displaced workers.

Amount of award:	$550
Number of awards:	70
Total amount awarded:	$38,500

Contact:
North Carolina Department of Community Colleges
200 West Jones Street
Raleigh, NC 27603-1379
Phone: 919-807-7106
Fax: 919-715-1999
Web: www.ncccs.cc.nc.us

North Carolina Community Colleges Wachovia Technical Scholarship

Type of award: Scholarship.
Intended use: For full-time sophomore study at 2-year institution.
Eligibility: Applicant must be residing in North Carolina.
Basis for selection: Applicant must demonstrate financial need and high academic achievement.
Additional information: Must be enrolled in second year of two-year education/technical program. Apply through financial aid office of institution where enrolled.

Amount of award:	$500
Number of awards:	113
Total amount awarded:	$56,500

Contact:
North Carolina Department of Community Colleges
200 West Jones Street
Raleigh, NC 27603-1379

Progress Energy Inc. Community College Scholarship Program

Type of award: Scholarship.
Intended use: For full-time undergraduate study at 2-year institution. Designated institutions: North Carolina community colleges: Cape Fear Community College, Fayetteville Technical Community College and Wake Technical Community College.
Eligibility: Applicant must be residing in North Carolina.
Basis for selection: Major/career interest in business; electronics or engineering, electrical/electronic. Applicant must demonstrate financial need and high academic achievement.
Application requirements: Must be North Carolina resident.
Additional information: Scholarship provides financial support to students residing in Progress Energy Inc.'s service area who are seeking two-year degrees that enhance the economic development of the service area. Applicant must be enrolled full-time or must intend to enroll as a new student in approved course of study at designated institution. Partial scholarships may be offered to continuing students who have completed half of the required course of study at one of the three colleges.

Amount of award:	$15,000
Number of awards:	3
Total amount awarded:	$45,000

Contact:
North Carolina Department of Community Colleges
200 West Jones St
Raleigh, NC 27603-1379
Phone: 919-733-7051 ext. 440
Fax: 919-733-0680

North Carolina Division of Veterans Affairs

North Carolina Scholarships for Children of War Veterans

Type of award: Scholarship.
Intended use: For undergraduate or graduate study at accredited postsecondary institution. Designated institutions: North Carolina schools.
Eligibility: Applicant must be dependent of disabled veteran, deceased veteran or POW/MIA who served in the Army, Air Force, Marines, Navy or Coast Guard. Parent must have served during a period of war.
Basis for selection: Applicant must demonstrate financial need and high academic achievement.
Application requirements: Interview, transcript, proof of eligibility. Birth certificate.
Additional information: Award is tuition waiver plus minimum room and board expenses for up to four years. Parent must have been North Carolina resident at time of enlistment or child must have been born in and resided permanently in North Carolina. Parent must have served during period of war.

Amount of award: Full tuition
Number of applicants: 555
Application deadline: March 31
Notification begins: July 15
Contact:
North Carolina Division of Veterans Affairs
1315 Mail Service Center
Albemarle Building, Suite 1065
Raleigh, NC 27699-1315

North Carolina Division of Vocational Rehabilitation Services

North Carolina Vocational Rehabilitation Award

Type of award: Scholarship, renewable.
Intended use: For full-time undergraduate study at vocational, 2-year or 4-year institution. Designated institutions: North Carolina institutions.
Eligibility: Applicant must be physically challenged or learning disabled. Applicant must be residing in North Carolina.
Application requirements: Interview, proof of eligibility. Applicant must have a mental or physical disability that is an impediment to employment.
Additional information: This program provides educational assistance for individuals who meet the eligibility requirements and require training to reach their vocational goals.
Amount of award: $2,428
Contact:
North Carolina Division of Vocational Rehabilitation Services
2801 Mail Service Center
Raleigh, NC 27699-2801
Phone: 919-855-3500
Fax: 919-715-0616

North Carolina State Education Assistance Authority

Atkinson Scholarship

Type of award: Scholarship.
Intended use: For freshman study.
Eligibility: Applicant must be high school senior. Applicant must be residing in North Carolina.
Additional information: Apply through the financial aid office of your UNC system school.
Number of awards: 16
Number of applicants: 50
Total amount awarded: $25,600

Contact:
North Carolina State Education Assistance Authority
P.O. Box 14223
Research Triangle Park, NC 27709
Phone: 800-700-1775 x624
Fax: 919-549-8481
Web: www.ncseaa.edu

Dickson Scholarship

Type of award: Scholarship.
Intended use: For undergraduate study.
Eligibility: Applicant must be residing in North Carolina.
Additional information: Apply through financial aid office of UNC system schools. Amount of award subject to available income.
Contact:
North Carolina State Education Assistance Authority
P.O. Box 14223
Research Triangle Park, NC 27709
Phone: 800-700-1775, X313
Fax: 919-549-8481
Web: www.ncseaa.edu

James Lee Love Scholarship

Type of award: Scholarship.
Intended use: For full-time undergraduate study in United States. Designated institutions: University of North Carolina System Schools.
Eligibility: Applicant must be residing in North Carolina.
Basis for selection: Applicant must demonstrate financial need and high academic achievement.
Application requirements: 3.0 GPA.
Additional information: Apply at financial aid office of University of North Carolina system school. Amount of award subject to available income.
Contact:
North Carolina State Education Assistance Authority
P.O. Box 13663
RTP, NC 27709-3663

NC Sherrif's Association Criminal Justice Scholarship

Type of award: Scholarship.
Intended use: For undergraduate study.
Eligibility: Applicant must be residing in North Carolina.
Additional information: Application available at the financial aid office of UNC Charlotte, UNC Pembroke, UNC Wilmington, Western Carolina University, NC State University, NC Central Universtiy, Fayetteville State University, Elizabeth City State University, East Carolina University and Appalachian State University. Amount awarded $1000 per semester.
Amount of award: $2,000
Number of awards: 10
Number of applicants: 50
Total amount awarded: $20,000
Contact:
North Carolina State Education Assistance Authority
P.O. Box 13663
Research Triangle Park, NC 27709-3663
Phone: 800-700-1775 x673
Web: www.ncseaa.edu

North Carolina Aubrey Lee Brooks Scholarship

Type of award: Scholarship, renewable.
Intended use: For full-time undergraduate study at 4-year institution in United States. Designated institutions: North Carolina State University, University of North Carolina at Chapel Hill, and University of North Carolina at Greensboro.
Eligibility: Applicant must be high school senior. Applicant must be U.S. citizen residing in North Carolina.
Basis for selection: Applicant must demonstrate financial need, depth of character, leadership and seriousness of purpose.
Application requirements: Proof of eligibility. College Scholarship Service's Financial Aid PROFILE by January 22; mail completed profile to CSS by January 31.
Additional information: Scholarship awards are $6300 per year, plus a one-time computer award of $3000. The scholarship pays additional amounts for approved summer study or internships. Applications available through high school. Applicants must reside in one of the following counties: Alamance, Bertie, Caswell, Durham, Forsyth, Granville, Guilford, Orange, Person, Rockingham, Stokes, Surry, Swain and Warren.

Number of awards:	16
Application deadline:	February 3
Total amount awarded:	$6,300

Contact:
North Carolina State Education Assistance Authority
P.O. Box 13663
RTP, NC 27709-3663
Phone: 800-700-1775, ext 650
Web: www.cfnc.org

North Carolina Legislative Tuition Grant

Type of award: Scholarship, renewable.
Intended use: For full-time undergraduate study at accredited 2-year or 4-year institution. Designated institutions: North Carolina private institutions.
Eligibility: Applicant must be U.S. citizen or permanent resident residing in North Carolina.
Application requirements: Complete application at North Carolina private institution.
Additional information: Award is not applicable for theology, divinity or religious education programs. Applicants should contact North Carolina private institution they attend or North Carolina State Education Assistance Authority. Student must maintain full-time status.

Amount of award:	$1,800
Number of awards:	24,078
Application deadline:	October 1
Total amount awarded:	$43,911,790

Contact:
North Carolina State Education Assistance Authority
P.O. Box 13663
Research Triangle Park, NC 27709-3663
Phone: 1-800-700-1775 ext. 650
Web: www.cfnc.org

State Contractual Scholarship Fund

Type of award: Scholarship, renewable.
Intended use: For undergraduate study at accredited 2-year or 4-year institution. Designated institutions: Degree seeking programs at private institutions in North Carolina.

Eligibility: Applicant must be U.S. citizen or permanent resident residing in North Carolina.
Basis for selection: Applicant must demonstrate financial need.
Application requirements: Proof of eligibility.
Additional information: Theology/divinity students not eligible. Contact school's financial aid office or NCSEAA for more information. Students must be enrolled in a degree seeking program.
Contact:
North Carolina State Education Assistance Authority
P.O. Box 13663
Research Triangle Park, NC 27709-3663
Phone: 1-800-700-1775 x650
Web: www.cfnc.org

North Dakota University System

North Dakota Indian Scholarship Program

Type of award: Scholarship, renewable.
Intended use: For full-time undergraduate or graduate study.
Eligibility: Applicant must be American Indian. Must be enrolled member of Indian tribe. Applicant must be U.S. citizen residing in North Dakota.
Basis for selection: Applicant must demonstrate financial need.
Application requirements: Proof of eligibility. Applicant must have 2.0 GPA.

Amount of award:	$700-$2,000
Number of awards:	150
Number of applicants:	600
Application deadline:	July 15

Contact:
North Dakota University System
Indian Scholarship Program
600 East Boulevard - Dept. 215
Bismarck, ND 58505-0230
Phone: 701-328-9661
Web: www.ndus.nodak.edu

North Dakota Scholars Program

Type of award: Scholarship, renewable.
Intended use: For full-time undergraduate study at 2-year or 4-year institution. Designated institutions: Postsecondary institutions in North Dakota.
Eligibility: Applicant must be high school senior. Applicant must be residing in North Dakota.
Basis for selection: Applicant must demonstrate high academic achievement.
Application requirements: Proof of eligibility.
Additional information: Applicant must take ACT between October and June of junior year and score in the upper five percentile of all North Dakota ACT test takers. Must maintain 3.5 GPA for renewal. Class rank at the end of junior year may also be considered. Contact sponsor for more information and deadline.

Amount of award:	$1,700-$2,800
Number of awards:	50
Number of applicants:	400

Contact:
North Dakota University System
600 East Boulevard
Dept. 215
Bismarck, ND 58505-0230
Phone: 701-328-4114
Web: www.ndus.nodak.edu

North Dakota State Grant

Type of award: Scholarship, renewable.
Intended use: For full-time undergraduate study at vocational, 2-year or 4-year institution. Designated institutions: North Dakota schools.
Eligibility: Applicant must be U.S. citizen or permanent resident residing in North Dakota.
Basis for selection: Applicant must demonstrate financial need.
Application requirements: Proof of eligibility. FAFSA.
Additional information: Application automatic with FAFSA.

Amount of award:	$600
Number of awards:	2,600
Number of applicants:	28,000
Application deadline:	March 15
Total amount awarded:	$2,220,000

Contact:
North Dakota University System
Student Financial Assistance Program
600 East Boulevard - Dept. 215
Bismarck, ND 58505-0230
Phone: 701-328-4114
Web: www.ndus.nodak.edu

Northern Cheyenne Tribal Education Department

Northern Cheyenne Higher Education Program

Type of award: Scholarship, renewable.
Intended use: For undergraduate study at postsecondary institution.
Eligibility: Applicant must be American Indian. Must be enrolled with the Northern Cheyenne Tribe. Applicant must be U.S. citizen.
Basis for selection: Applicant must demonstrate financial need.
Application requirements: Recommendations, essay, transcript, proof of eligibility. Northern Cheyenne Tribal Application. FAFSA.
Additional information: Award amount varies, depends on unmet need. Deadlines: October 1 for spring, April 1 for summer, and March 1 for fall.

Amount of award:	$175-$6,000
Number of awards:	64
Number of applicants:	175
Notification begins:	August 1, November 1
Total amount awarded:	$257,455

Contact:
Northern Cheyenne Tribal Education Department
Attn: Norma Bixby
Box 307
Lame Deer, MT 59043
Phone: 406-477-6602

Northwest Danish Foundation

Danish Foundation Scholarship

Type of award: Scholarship, renewable.
Intended use: For undergraduate or graduate study at postsecondary institution in or outside United States. Designated institutions: May be used at institutions in Denmark.
Eligibility: Applicant or parent must be member/participant of Northwest Danish Foundation. Applicant must be Danish. Applicant must be U.S. citizen or permanent resident residing in Oregon or Washington.
Basis for selection: Applicant must demonstrate depth of character and service orientation.
Application requirements: Recommendations, essay, transcript. Two recommendations, personal essay on educational goals, and Danish heritage or commitment to the Danish community required.
Additional information: Spouses of persons of Danish descent eligible as well as applicants of non-Danish descent. Must demonstrate interest/involvement in Danish culture and community. One recommendation must be from non-family member of Danish community, explaining applicant's involvement in Danish activities/community. Application deadline is April 1 by 4:30 pm.

Amount of award:	$250-$1,000
Number of awards:	20
Number of applicants:	40
Application deadline:	April 1
Notification begins:	May 1
Total amount awarded:	$15,000

Contact:
Northwest Danish Foundation
1833 North 105th Street
Suite 203
Seattle, WA 98133-8973
Phone: 206-523-2363 or 800-564-7736
Fax: 206-523-3263
Web: www.northwestdanishfoundation.org

Oak Ridge Institute for Science and Education

National Oceanic and Atmospheric Administration Educational Partnership Program with Minority Serving Institutions Undergraduate Scholarship

Type of award: Scholarship.
Intended use: For junior or senior study at 4-year institution. Designated institutions: Minority serving institutions, including Hispanic serving institutions, historically black colleges and universities, and tribal colleges and universities. Internship assignments at NOAA sites.
Basis for selection: Must be pursuing degrees in areas related to NOAA. Major/career interest in science, general; biology; cartography; chemistry; computer/information sciences;

engineering; environmental science; geography; mathematics or physics.

Additional information: Provides scholarships and internships for juniors and seniors attending minority serving institutions and pursuing degrees in fields related to the National Oceanic and Atmospheric Administration. Application deadline in January. Award is tuition and fees up to $4,000. Internship pays weekly stipend of $650. Weekly housing allowance of $100 during internship. See Website for application and more information.

Amount of award:	$4,000
Number of awards:	10

Contact:
Oak Ridge Institute for Science and Education
P.O. Box 117
Oak Ridge, TN 37831-0117
Phone: 865-576-9279
Web: www.orau.gov/orise/educ.htm

Office of Civilian Radioactive Waste Management Historically Black Colleges and Universities Scholarship

Type of award: Scholarship.
Intended use: For junior or senior study at accredited 4-year institution in United States. Designated institutions: Historically Black Colleges and Universities.
Eligibility: Applicant must be U.S. citizen.
Basis for selection: Major/career interest in science, general; mathematics; social/behavioral sciences or engineering.
Application requirements: Applicant must be in junior or senior year during program participation.
Additional information: Provides scholarships and practical experience for students from Historically Black Colleges and Universities pursuing degrees in areas related to the Office of Civilian Radioactive Waste Management. Tuition and fees paid to maximum $8,000 per year. Monthly stipend of $600. January deadline.

Amount of award:	Full tuition
Number of awards:	10
Application deadline:	January 27

Contact:
Web: www.orau.gov/orise/educ.htm

Ohio Board of Regents

Ohio Academic Scholarship

Type of award: Scholarship, renewable.
Intended use: For full-time freshman, sophomore, junior or senior study at accredited 2-year or 4-year institution. Designated institutions: Ohio schools.
Eligibility: Applicant must be high school senior. Applicant must be U.S. citizen or permanent resident residing in Ohio.
Basis for selection: Applicant must demonstrate high academic achievement.
Application requirements: ACT scores.
Additional information: Contact high school guidance counselors.

Amount of award:	$2,000
Number of awards:	1,000
Number of applicants:	4,500
Application deadline:	March 1
Notification begins:	May 1
Total amount awarded:	$7,000,000

Contact:
Ohio Board of Regents
P.O. Box 182452
Columbus, OH 43218-2452
Phone: 614-752-9528 or 888-833-1133 ext. 29528

Ohio Instructional Grant

Type of award: Scholarship.
Intended use: For full-time undergraduate study at accredited 2-year or 4-year institution. Designated institutions: Ohio schools and some select Pennsylvania schools.
Eligibility: Applicant must be U.S. citizen or permanent resident residing in Ohio.
Basis for selection: Applicant must demonstrate financial need.
Additional information: By completing the FAFSA form, you automatically apply for this grant. Number of awards given varies.

Amount of award:	$174-$5,466
Application deadline:	October 1
Notification begins:	March 1
Total amount awarded:	$93,600,000

Contact:
Ohio Board of Regents
P.O. Box 182452
Columbus, OH 43218-2452
Phone: 614-466-7420 or 888-833-1133

Ohio Safety Officers College Memorial Fund

Type of award: Scholarship, renewable.
Intended use: For freshman, sophomore, junior or senior study at vocational, 2-year or 4-year institution. Designated institutions: Ohio schools.
Eligibility: Applicant must be U.S. citizen or permanent resident residing in Ohio.
Application requirements: Proof of eligibility.
Additional information: Parent or spouse must have been firefighter or police officer killed in line of duty. Apply at college financial aid office.

Amount of award:	Full tuition
Number of awards:	46
Number of applicants:	46
Total amount awarded:	$121,068

Contact:
Barbara Metheney, Program Administrator
Ohio Board of Regents
P.O. Box 182452
Columbus, OH 43218-2452
Phone: 614-752-9535 or 888-833-1133 ext. 29535
Web: www.regents.state.oh.us

Ohio Student Choice Grant

Type of award: Scholarship, renewable.
Intended use: For full-time freshman, sophomore, junior or senior study at 4-year institution. Designated institutions: Award must be used at private nonprofit Ohio colleges or universities.
Eligibility: Applicant must be U.S. citizen or permanent resident residing in Ohio.

Additional information: Apply at college financial aid office.

Amount of award:	$1,002
Number of awards:	45,000
Total amount awarded:	$24,200,000

Contact:
Barbara Metheney, Program Administrator
Ohio Board of Regents
P.O. Box 182452
Columbus, OH 43218-2452
Phone: 614-752-9535 or 888-833-1133 ext. 29535
Web: www.regents.state.oh.us

Ohio War Orphans Scholarship

Type of award: Scholarship, renewable.
Intended use: For full-time freshman, sophomore, junior or senior study at accredited 2-year or 4-year institution. Designated institutions: Ohio schools.
Eligibility: Applicant must be at least 16, no older than 21. Applicant must be U.S. citizen or permanent resident residing in Ohio. Applicant must be dependent of veteran, disabled veteran, deceased veteran or POW/MIA. Child of wartime veteran or POW/MIA in Asian war eligible.
Application requirements: Proof of eligibility.

Amount of award:	Full tuition
Number of applicants:	341
Application deadline:	July 1
Notification begins:	August 1
Total amount awarded:	$3,600,000

Contact:
Sarina Wilks, Program Administrator
Ohio Board of Regents
P.O. Box 182452
Columbus, OH 43218-2452
Phone: 614-752-9528 or 1-888-833-1133 x29528

Part-time Student Instructional Grant Program

Type of award: Scholarship, renewable.
Intended use: For half-time freshman, sophomore, junior or senior study at accredited 2-year or 4-year institution.
Eligibility: Applicant must be U.S. citizen residing in Ohio.
Basis for selection: Applicant must demonstrate financial need.
Additional information: For application, contact college financial aid office.

Number of awards:	30,000
Total amount awarded:	$10,000,000

Contact:
Barbara Metheney, Program Administrator
Ohio Board of Regents
P.O. Box 182452
Columbus, OH 43218-2452
Phone: 614-752-9535 or 1-888-833-1133 x29535

Ohio National Guard

Ohio National Guard Scholarship Program

Type of award: Scholarship, renewable.
Intended use: For freshman, sophomore, junior or senior study at accredited postsecondary institution. Designated institutions: Degree-granting institutions in Ohio, approved by Ohio Board of Regents.
Eligibility: Applicant or parent must be member/participant of Ohio National Guard. Applicant must be in military service. Must enlist, reenlist, or extend current enlistment to equal six years with Ohio National Guard. Must remain in good standing.
Application requirements: Proof of eligibility. Must be member of Ohio National Guard. Must not already possess baccalaureate degree.
Additional information: Minimum of six credit hours. Award covers 100 percent instructional and general fee for state-assisted institutions; average of state-assisted universities for proprietary institutions. Application deadlines: fall-July 1, winter-November 1, spring-February 1, summer-April 1.

Amount of award:	Full tuition
Number of awards:	5,000

Contact:
Adjutant General's Department
Ohio National Guard Scholars
2825 West Dublin Granville Road
Columbus, OH 43235
Phone: 888-400-6484

Ohio Newspapers Foundation

Harold K. Douthit Scholarship

Type of award: Scholarship.
Intended use: For freshman study at 4-year institution. Designated institutions: In Ohio counties; Cuyahoga, Loraine, Huron, Erie, Wood, Sandusky, Ottawa, Geauga, or Lucas.
Eligibility: Applicant must be high school senior. Applicant must be U.S. citizen residing in Ohio.
Basis for selection: Major/career interest in journalism. Applicant must demonstrate financial need and high academic achievement.
Application requirements: Recommendations, essay, transcript. Samples of published work.
Additional information: 3.0 GPA required.

Amount of award:	$1,000
Number of awards:	1
Number of applicants:	14
Application deadline:	March 31
Total amount awarded:	$1,000

Contact:
Ohio Newspapers Foundation
1335 Dublin Road
Suite 216-B
Columbus, OH 43215
Phone: 614-486-6677
Fax: 614-486-4940
Web: www.ohionews.org

Ohio Newspapers Minority Scholarship

Type of award: Scholarship.
Intended use: For full-time freshman study. Designated institutions: Ohio colleges and universities.
Eligibility: Applicant must be Alaskan native, Asian American, African American, Mexican American, Hispanic American, Puerto Rican or American Indian. Applicant must be residing in Ohio.

Basis for selection: Major/career interest in journalism. Applicant must demonstrate high academic achievement.
Application requirements: Recommendations, essay, transcript, proof of eligibility. Students may include writing samples or published articles.
Additional information: Minimum 2.5 GPA.

Amount of award:	$1,500
Number of awards:	3
Number of applicants:	8
Application deadline:	March 31
Notification begins:	May 15
Total amount awarded:	$4,500

Contact:
Ohio Newspapers Foundation
1335 Dublin Road
Suite 216-B
Columbus, OH 43215
Phone: 614-486-6677
Fax: 614-486-4940
Web: www.ohionews.org

University Journalism Scholarship

Type of award: Scholarship.
Intended use: For sophomore, junior or senior study. Designated institutions: Ohio college or university.
Eligibility: Applicant must be enrolled in high school. Applicant must be residing in Ohio.
Basis for selection: Major/career interest in journalism.
Additional information: Student must have 2.5 GPA, two letters of recommendation.

Amount of award:	$1,500
Number of awards:	1
Number of applicants:	6
Application deadline:	March 31

Contact:
Ohio Newspaper Foundation
1335 Dublin Road
Suite 216-B
Columbus, OH 43215
Phone: (614) 486-6677
Fax: (614) 486-4940
Web: www.ohionews.org

Oklahoma Engineering Foundation

Oklahoma Engineering Foundation Scholarship

Type of award: Scholarship, renewable.
Intended use: For undergraduate study at accredited 4-year institution in United States. Designated institutions: Oklahoma Christian University of Science & Arts, Oklahoma State University, University of Oklahoma, Oral Roberts University, University of Tulsa.
Eligibility: Applicant must be high school senior. Applicant must be U.S. citizen residing in Oklahoma.
Basis for selection: Major/career interest in engineering. Applicant must demonstrate depth of character, leadership and service orientation.
Application requirements: Interview, essay, transcript. Minimum 3.0 GPA. ACT composite of 23-32.

Additional information: Must be used at specific institutions in Oklahoma. Contact office for more information.

Amount of award:	$500-$1,000
Number of awards:	12
Number of applicants:	52
Application deadline:	November 15
Notification begins:	August 30
Total amount awarded:	$12,000

Contact:
Executive Director
201 Northeast 27th St.
Room 125
Oklahoma City, OK 73105
Phone: 405-528-1435
Web: www.ospe.org

Oklahoma National Guard

National Guard Tuition Waiver

Type of award: Scholarship.
Intended use: For undergraduate study at 2-year or 4-year institution.
Eligibility: Applicant must be residing in Oklahoma. Applicant must be bona fide member in good standing of Oklahoma National Guard. Applicant must not currently hold a bachelor's or graduate degree.
Application requirements: Proof of eligibility. Submit Statement of Understanding and Certificate of Basic Eligibility.
Additional information: Award covers cost of tuition. Applicant must be enrolled in degree-granting program. Waivers not awarded for certificate-granting courses, continuing education courses or career technology courses.

Amount of award:	Full tuition

Contact:
Oklahoma National Guard
Phone: 800-858-1840
Fax: 405-225-9230
Web: www.okhighered.org

Oklahoma State Department of Education Professional Services Division

Robert C. Byrd Honors Scholarship Program

Type of award: Scholarship, renewable.
Intended use: For full-time undergraduate study at postsecondary institution.
Eligibility: Applicant must be high school senior. Applicant must be U.S. citizen or permanent resident residing in Oklahoma.
Basis for selection: Applicant must demonstrate high academic achievement.
Application requirements: Recommendations, essay, transcript.

Additional information: Students receive $1,500 for first year of study at eligible postsecondary institution. Scholarships are renewable for up to three additional years of study provided students continue to meet eligibility requirements as defined by the institution they are attending.

    Amount of award: $1,500
Contact:
Oklahoma State Department of Education
Oliver Hodge Building
2500 N. Lincoln Boulevard
Oklahoma City, OK 73105-4599
Phone: 405-521-2808
Web: www.sde.state.ok.us

Oklahoma State Regents for Higher Education

Academic Scholars Program

Type of award: Scholarship.
Intended use: For full-time undergraduate study at 2-year or 4-year institution in United States. Designated institutions: Oklahoma postsecondary institutions.
Basis for selection: Major/career interest in humanities/liberal arts. Applicant must demonstrate high academic achievement.
Application requirements: Transcript, proof of eligibility. Application.
Additional information: Scholarships are awarded to students with high academic performance who plan to attend Oklahoma public or private university. Application deadline varies.

    Amount of award: $1,800-$5,500
Contact:
Oklahoma State Regents for Higher Education
P.O. Box 108850
Oklahoma City, OK 73101-8850
Phone: 800-858-1840 or 405-225-9239
Fax: 405-225-9230
Web: www.okhighered.org

Future Teachers Scholarship

Type of award: Scholarship, renewable.
Intended use: For undergraduate or graduate study at accredited 2-year or 4-year institution.
Eligibility: Applicant must be U.S. citizen or permanent resident residing in Oklahoma.
Basis for selection: Major/career interest in education; education, special; mathematics; foreign languages; science, general; art/art history or speech pathology/audiology. Applicant must demonstrate high academic achievement.
Application requirements: Essay, transcript, proof of eligibility, nomination by by college based on academic record. Completed application. SAT/ACT scores.
Additional information: Application deadline varies. Visit Website for more information.

    Amount of award: $500-$1,500
Contact:
Oklahoma State Regents For Higher Education
P.O. Box 108850
Oklahoma City, OK 73101-8850
Phone: 800-858-1840 or 405-225-9239
Fax: 405-225-9230
Web: www.okhighered.org

Heartland Scholarship Fund

Type of award: Scholarship.
Intended use: For full-time undergraduate study at accredited 2-year or 4-year institution.
Eligibility: Applicant must be residing in Oklahoma.
Application requirements: Proof of eligibility. For details, contact Oklahoma State Regents for Higher Education.
Additional information: Applicant must be dependent child of individual killed as a result of the April 19, 1995, bombing of Alfred P. Murrah Federal Building in Oaklahoma City. Awards covers cost of tuition, fees, books, and room and board.

    Amount of award: $3,500-$5,500
Contact:
Oklahoma State Regents for Higher Education
P.O. Box 108850
Oklahoma City, OK 73101-8500
Phone: 800-858-1840 or 405-225-9239
Fax: 405-225-9230
Web: www.okhighered.org

Independent Living Act (Department of Human Services Tuition Waiver)

Type of award: Scholarship.
Intended use: For undergraduate study at postsecondary institution.
Eligibility: Applicant must be no older than 21. Applicant must be residing in Oklahoma.
Application requirements: Proof of eligibility.
Additional information: Awards tuition waivers to eligible individuals who have been or are in the Oklahoma Department of Human Services foster care program.

    Amount of award: Full tuition
Contact:
Oklahoma State Regents for Higher Education
P.O. Box 108850
Oklahoma City, OK 73101
Phone: 800-858-1840 or 405-225-9100
Fax: 405-225-9230
Web: www.okhighered.org

Oklahoma Higher Learning Access Program (OHLAP)

Type of award: Scholarship.
Intended use: For undergraduate study at 2-year or 4-year institution.
Eligibility: Applicant must be high school freshman or sophomore. Applicant must be residing in Oklahoma.
Basis for selection: Applicant must demonstrate financial need, high academic achievement and seriousness of purpose.
Additional information: Scholarship for students in families earning less than $50,000 per year. Student must enroll in the program in the eighth, ninth or tenth grade and demonstrate commitment to academic success in high school. Award amount varies; tuition at public institutions or portion of tuition at private institutions in Oklahoma. See counselor or visit Website for details.

    Application deadline: June 30

Contact:
Oklahoma State Regents for Higher Education
655 Research Parkway
Suite 200
Oklahoma City, OK 73104
Phone: 800-858-1840 or 405-225-9239
Fax: 405-225-9230
Web: www.okhighered.org/ohlap

Oklahoma Tuition Aid Grant

Type of award: Scholarship, renewable.
Intended use: For undergraduate or graduate study at vocational, 2-year or 4-year institution. Designated institutions: Approved Oklahoma postsecondary and vocational-technical institutions.
Eligibility: Applicant must be U.S. citizen or permanent resident residing in Oklahoma.
Basis for selection: Applicant must demonstrate financial need.
Application requirements: Proof of eligibility. Completed FAFSA.
Additional information: Applications accepted through June 30. For best consideration, apply by April 30.

Amount of award:	$1,000
Application deadline:	June 30

Contact:
Oklahoma Tuition Aid Grant Program
P.O. Box 108850
Oklahoma City, OK 73101-8850
Phone: 877-662-6231
Web: www.otag.org

Regional University Baccalaureate Scholarship

Type of award: Scholarship, renewable.
Intended use: For full-time undergraduate study at postsecondary institution.
Eligibility: Applicant must be residing in Oklahoma.
Basis for selection: Applicant must demonstrate high academic achievement.
Application requirements: Applicant must have ACT score of at least 30 or be National Merit Semifinalist or Commended Student.
Additional information: These scholarships are awarded based on the academic merit of Oklahoma residents who plan to attend an Oklahoma regional university. Application deadlines vary by institution.

Amount of award:	$3,000

Contact:
Oklahoma State Regents for Higher Education
PO Box 108850
Oklahoma City, OK 73104-9131
Phone: 800-858-1840 or 405-225-9131
Fax: 405-225-9230
Web: www.okhighered.org

OMNE/Nursing Leaders of Maine

OMNE/Nursing Leaders of Maine Scholarship

Type of award: Scholarship.
Intended use: For undergraduate study at accredited 4-year or graduate institution. Designated institutions: Accredited Maine nursing schools.
Eligibility: Applicant must be U.S. citizen residing in Maine.
Basis for selection: Major/career interest in nursing. Applicant must demonstrate seriousness of purpose and service orientation.
Application requirements: Recommendations, transcript, proof of eligibility. Enrollment in baccalaureate program.
Additional information: Applicant must be Maine resident.

Amount of award:	$500
Number of awards:	2
Number of applicants:	12
Application deadline:	May 1
Total amount awarded:	$1,000

Contact:
Sherry Rogers, RN, MS
Redington Fairview General Hospital
P.O. Box 468
Skowhegan, ME 04976
Phone: 207-474-5121
Fax: 207-474-2670
Web: www.omne.org

ONS Foundation

Ethnic Minority Bachelors Scholarships

Type of award: Scholarship.
Intended use: For undergraduate study in United States. Designated institutions: Schools accredited by the National League for Nursing.
Eligibility: Applicant must be Asian American, African American, Mexican American, Hispanic American, Puerto Rican or American Indian.
Basis for selection: Major/career interest in nursing or oncology. Applicant must demonstrate high academic achievement, depth of character, leadership and service orientation.
Application requirements: $5 application fee. Essay, transcript, proof of eligibility.
Additional information: Must have current license to practice as a registered nurse or practical (vocational) nurse and must be currently enrolled in a bachelor's degree nursing program at school accredited by National League for Nursing.

Amount of award:	$2,000
Number of awards:	3
Application deadline:	February 1
Notification begins:	March 15
Total amount awarded:	$6,000

Contact:
ONS Foundation
125 Enterprise Drive
Pittsburgh, PA 15275-1214
Phone: 412-859-6100
Fax: 412-859-6160
Web: www.onsfoundation.org

Oncology Nursing Certification Corporation Bachelor's Scholarships

Type of award: Scholarship.
Intended use: For undergraduate study in United States. Designated institutions: Schools accredited by National League for Nursing.
Basis for selection: Major/career interest in nursing or oncology. Applicant must demonstrate high academic achievement, depth of character, leadership and service orientation.
Application requirements: $5 application fee. Essay, transcript, proof of eligibility.
Additional information: Must have current license to practice as a registered nurse or practical (vocational) nurse and currently enrolled in a bachelors nursing degree program at school accredited by National League for Nursing.

Amount of award:	$2,000
Number of awards:	10
Application deadline:	February 1
Notification begins:	March 15
Total amount awarded:	$20,000

Contact:
ONS Foundation
125 Enterprise Drive
Pittsburgh, PA 15275-1214
Phone: 412-859-6100
Fax: 412-859-6160
Web: www.onsfoundation.org

Roberta Pierce Scofield Bachelors Scholarships

Type of award: Scholarship.
Intended use: For undergraduate study. Designated institutions: Schools accredited by the National League for Nursing.
Basis for selection: Major/career interest in nursing or oncology. Applicant must demonstrate high academic achievement, depth of character, leadership and service orientation.
Application requirements: $5 application fee. Essay, transcript, proof of eligibility.
Additional information: Must have current license to practice as registered nurse or practical (vocational) nurse and must be currently enrolled in a bachelor's degree nursing program at school accredited by National League for Nursing.

Amount of award:	$2,000
Number of awards:	3
Application deadline:	February 1
Notification begins:	March 15
Total amount awarded:	$6,000

Contact:
ONS Foundation
125 Enterprise Drive
Pittsburgh, PA 15275-1214
Phone: 412-859-6100
Fax: 412-859-6160
Web: www.onsfoundation.org

OP Loftbed

OP Loftbed $500 Scholarship Award

Type of award: Scholarship.
Intended use: For full-time undergraduate study at accredited postsecondary institution in United States. Designated institutions: Accredited U.S. colleges and universities.
Eligibility: Applicant must be U.S. citizen.
Basis for selection: Creativity of answers to given set of questions.
Application requirements: Send transcript only when requested.
Additional information: Applications must be submitted on Website, which includes set of questions that must be answered and judged. Faxed or mailed entries will not be accepted. Guidelines and additional information available online.

Amount of award:	$500
Application deadline:	July 31

Contact:
Visit Website for entry form and additional information.
Web: www.oploftbed.com

Oregon Student Assistance Commission

Agricultural Women-in-Network Scholarship

Type of award: Scholarship, renewable.
Intended use: For full-time junior or senior study at accredited 4-year institution. Designated institutions: Four-year colleges in Idaho, Oregon, or Washington.
Eligibility: Applicant must be U.S. citizen or permanent resident residing in Oregon.
Basis for selection: Major/career interest in agriculture. Applicant must demonstrate high academic achievement.
Application requirements: Transcript. FAFSA and two essays required.
Additional information: Preference given to female students. Visit Website for details and application. For those with disabilities: TYY 541-687-7395 (voice), 800-452-8807 ext. 7395.

Amount of award:	$500
Application deadline:	March 1

Contact:
Oregon Student Assistance Commission
Grants and Scholarship Division
1500 Valley River Drive, Suite 100
Eugene, OR 97401
Phone: 541-687-7400 or 800-452-8807
Web: www.osac.state.or.us

Alpha Delta Kappa/Harriet Simmons Scholarship

Type of award: Scholarship, renewable.
Intended use: For full-time senior or graduate study at accredited postsecondary institution in United States.
Eligibility: Applicant must be U.S. citizen or permanent resident residing in Oregon.

Scholarships

Basis for selection: Major/career interest in education or education, teacher. Applicant must demonstrate financial need and high academic achievement.
Application requirements: Essay, transcript. FAFSA. Two essays required.
Additional information: Applicants must be elementary or secondary education majors. Visit Website for details and application. For those with disabilities: TYY 541-687-7395 (voice), 800-452-8807 ext. 7395.

Amount of award:	$500
Application deadline:	March 1

Contact:
Oregon Student Assistance Commission
Grants and Scholarship Division
1500 Valley River Drive, Suite 100
Eugene, OR 97401-2146
Phone: 541-687-7400 or 800-452-8807
Web: www.osac.state.or.us

American Ex-Prisoner of War, Peter Connacher Memorial Scholarship

Type of award: Scholarship, renewable.
Intended use: For full-time undergraduate or graduate study at postsecondary institution in United States.
Eligibility: Applicant must be U.S. citizen or permanent resident residing in Oregon. Must be American former prisoner of war or descendant.
Basis for selection: Applicant must demonstrate financial need and high academic achievement.
Application requirements: Essay, transcript, proof of eligibility. Include FAFSA. Two essays required. Submit copy of POW's military discharge papers and proof of POW status. State relationship to POW on supporting documents.
Additional information: Visit Website for details and application. For those with disabilities: TYY 542-687-7395 (voice), 800-452-8807 ext. 7395.

Amount of award:	$500
Application deadline:	March 1

Contact:
Oregon Student Assistance Commission
Grants and Scholarship Division
1500 Valley River Drive, Suite 100
Eugene, OR 97401-2146
Phone: 541-687-7400 or 800-452-8807
Web: www.osac.state.or.us

Ben Selling Scholarship

Type of award: Scholarship, renewable.
Intended use: For full-time sophomore, junior or senior study at postsecondary institution in United States.
Eligibility: Applicant must be U.S. citizen or permanent resident residing in Oregon.
Basis for selection: Applicant must demonstrate financial need and high academic achievement.
Application requirements: Transcript. FAFSA and two essays required. Minimum 3.5 GPA.
Additional information: Wells Fargo employees, children, or near relatives must provide complete disclosure of employment status. Visit Website for details and application. For those with disabilities: TYY 541-687-7395 (voice), 800-452-8807 ext. 7395.

Amount of award:	$500
Application deadline:	March 1

Contact:
Oregon Student Assistance Commission
Grants and Scholarship Division
1500 Valley River Drive, Suite 100
Eugene, OR 97401-2146
Phone: 541-687-7400 or 800-452-8807
Web: www.osac.state.or.us

Benjamin Franklin/Edith Green Scholarship

Type of award: Scholarship.
Intended use: For full-time undergraduate study at accredited 4-year institution. Designated institutions: Oregon four-year public colleges.
Eligibility: Applicant must be high school senior. Applicant must be U.S. citizen or permanent resident residing in Oregon.
Basis for selection: Applicant must demonstrate financial need and high academic achievement.
Application requirements: Transcript. FAFSA and two essays required. Must have a 2.5+ GPA and show improvements in grades from freshman year.
Additional information: Applicant must be graduating senior from Oregon high school and planning to attend a college or university in Oregon. Visit Website for details and application. For those with disabilities: TYY 542-687-7395 (voice), 800-452-8807 ext. 7395.

Amount of award:	$500
Application deadline:	March 1

Contact:
Oregon Student Assistance Commission
Grants and Scholarship Division
1500 Valley River Drive, Suite 100
Eugene, OR 97401-2146
Phone: 541-687-7400 or 800-452-8807
Web: www.osac.state.or.us

Bertha P. Singer Scholarship

Type of award: Scholarship, renewable.
Intended use: For full-time undergraduate or graduate study at accredited postsecondary institution. Designated institutions: Oregon colleges.
Eligibility: Applicant must be U.S. citizen or permanent resident residing in Oregon.
Basis for selection: Major/career interest in nursing.
Application requirements: Transcript, proof of eligibility. FAFSA and two essays required. Minimum 3.0 GPA. Must provide documentation of enrollment in third year of four-year nursing degree program or second year of two-year associate degree nursing program.
Additional information: Employees of U.S. Bancorp., their children or near relatives are not eligible. Visit Website for details and application. For those with disabilities: TYY 541-687-7395 (voice), 800-452-8807 ext. 7395.

Amount of award:	$500
Application deadline:	March 1

Contact:
Oregon Student Assistance Commission
Grants and Scholarship Division
1500 Valley River Drive, Suite 100
Eugene, OR 97401-2146
Phone: 541-687-7400 or 800-452-8807
Web: www.osac.state.or.us

Crowley Family Scholarship

Type of award: Scholarship, renewable.

Intended use: For undergraduate or graduate study at postsecondary institution in United States.
Eligibility: Applicant must be U.S. citizen or permanent resident residing in Oregon.
Basis for selection: Major/career interest in education.
Application requirements: Essay, transcript. FAFSA and two essays required.
Additional information: For graduates of Medford, Oregon, high schools. Preference given to female students demonstrating strong work ethic and interest in community service. Applicants returning to school to pursue education as a career are encouraged to apply. Visit Website for details and application. For those with disabilities: TYY 541-687-7395 (voice), 800-452-8807 ext. 7395.

  Application deadline: March 1
Contact:
Oregon Student Assistance Commission
Grants and Scholarship Division
1500 Valley River Drive, Suite 100
Eugene, OR 97401-2146
Phone: 541-687-7400 or 800-452-8807
Web: www.osac.state.or.us

David Family Scholarship

Type of award: Scholarship, renewable.
Intended use: For sophomore, junior, senior or graduate study at postsecondary institution in United States.
Eligibility: Applicant must be U.S. citizen or permanent resident residing in Oregon.
Basis for selection: Applicant must demonstrate financial need and high academic achievement.
Application requirements: Essay, transcript. Include FAFSA. Two essays required. Minimum 2.5 GPA.
Additional information: Intended for residents of Clackamas, Lane, Multnomah and Washington counties. Preference given to applicants enrolling at least half-time in upper-division or graduate programs at four-year colleges. Visit Website for details and application. For those with disabilities: TYY 542-687-7395 (voice), 800-452-8807 ext. 7395.
  Amount of award: $500
  Application deadline: March 1
Contact:
Oregon Student Assistance Commission
Grants and Scholarship Division
1500 Valley River Drive, Suite 100
Eugene, OR 97401-2146
Phone: 541-687-7400 or 800-452-8807
Web: www.osac.state.or.us

Dorothy Campbell Memorial Scholarship

Type of award: Scholarship, renewable.
Intended use: For full-time undergraduate study at accredited 4-year institution. Designated institutions: Four-year colleges in Oregon.
Eligibility: Applicant must be female. Applicant must be U.S. citizen or permanent resident residing in Oregon.
Basis for selection: Applicant must demonstrate financial need and high academic achievement.
Application requirements: Essay, transcript. Include FAFSA. Two essays required. Minimum 2.75 GPA. Additional essay: one page describing strong and continuing interest in golf and contribution the sport has made to applicant's development.
Additional information: Must be female graduate of any Oregon high school. Visit Website for details and application.

For those with disabilities: TYY 541-687-7395 (voice), 800-452-8807 ext. 7395.
  Amount of award: $500
  Application deadline: March 1
Contact:
Oregon Student Assistance Commission
Grants and Scholarship Division
1500 Valley River Drive, Suite 100
Eugene, OR 97401-2146
Phone: 541-687-7400 or 800-452-8807
Web: www.osac.state.or.us

Fashion Group International of Portland Scholarship

Type of award: Scholarship.
Intended use: For sophomore, junior or senior study at postsecondary institution in United States. Designated institutions: Postsecondary institutions in Oregon, Washington, Idaho and California.
Eligibility: Applicant must be U.S. citizen or permanent resident residing in Oregon.
Basis for selection: Major/career interest in fashion/fashion design/modeling.
Application requirements: Transcript. FAFSA and two essays required.
Additional information: Minimum 3.0 GPA. Semifinalists will be interviewed by donor group in Portland. See Website for details and application. For those with disabilities: TYY 541-687-7395 (voice), 800-452-8807 ext. 7395.
  Application deadline: March 1
Contact:
Oregon Student Assistance Commission
Grants and Scholarship Division
1500 Valley River Drive, Suite 100
Eugene, OR 97401-2146
Phone: 541-687-7400 or 800-452-8807
Web: www.osac.state.or.us

Ford Opportunity Program

Type of award: Scholarship, renewable.
Intended use: For full-time undergraduate study at accredited 4-year institution. Designated institutions: Oregon colleges or community colleges.
Eligibility: Applicant must be U.S. citizen or permanent resident residing in Oregon.
Basis for selection: Applicant must demonstrate financial need and high academic achievement.
Application requirements: Transcript. FAFSA and two essays required. Minimum 3.0 GPA or 2650 GED score, unless application is accompanied by Special Recommendation Form from counselor or OSAC. Interviews will be required of all semifinalists.
Additional information: Must be single head of household with custody of dependent child/children. Visit Website for details and application. For those with disabilities: TYY 541-687-7395 (voice), 800-452-8807 ext. 7395. Counselors who wish to intervene on behalf of applicant who does not meet minimum requirements should check Financial Aid Handbook for recommendation form or call 800-452-8807 ext. 7388.
  Number of awards: 30
  Application deadline: March 1

Contact:
Oregon Student Assistance Commission
Grants and Scholarship Division
1500 Valley River Drive, Suite 100
Eugene, OR 97401-2146
Phone: 541-687-7400 or 800-452-8807
Web: www.osac.state.or.us

Ford Scholars Program

Type of award: Scholarship, renewable.
Intended use: For full-time undergraduate study at accredited 4-year institution. Designated institutions: Oregon colleges or community colleges.
Eligibility: Applicant must be U.S. citizen or permanent resident residing in Oregon.
Basis for selection: Applicant must demonstrate financial need and high academic achievement.
Application requirements: Transcript. FAFSA and two essays required. Minimum 3.0 GPA or 2650 GED score, unless application is accompanied by Special Recommendation Form from counselor or OSAC.
Additional information: Intended for high school seniors/graduates who have not yet been full-time undergraduates, or for individuals who have completed two years at Oregon community college and are entering junior year at Oregon four-year college. Visit Website for details and application. For those with disabilities: TYY 541-687-7395 (voice), 800-452-8807 ext. 7395. Counselors who wish to intervene on behalf of applicant who does not meet minimum requirements should check Financial Aid Handbook for recommendation form or call 800-452-8807 ext. 7388.

Amount of award:	$500
Application deadline:	March 1

Contact:
Oregon Student Assistance Commission
Grants and Scholarship Division
1500 Valley River Drive, Suite 100
Eugene, OR 97401-2146
Phone: 541-687-7400 or 800-452-8807
Web: www.osac.state.or.us

Friends of Oregon Students Scholarship

Type of award: Scholarship.
Intended use: For undergraduate or graduate study at 4-year or graduate institution in United States.
Eligibility: Applicant must be returning adult student. Applicant must be U.S. citizen or permanent resident residing in Oregon.
Basis for selection: Major/career interest in health education; social work; public health; education; nursing; physical therapy; environmental science; mental health/therapy; education, teacher or education, special. Applicant must demonstrate service orientation.
Application requirements: Transcript. FAFSA and two essays required. Preferences: 1) volunteer or work experience relevant to chosen profession; 2) graduate of public alternative Oregon high school or GED recipient or transferring from Oregon community college to 4-year college; 3) GPA of 2.5 over last three quarters of solid course work. Applicant must go to donor's Website for information on additional essays and reference letters: www.hffund.org.
Additional information: For non-traditional students (e.g., older, returning, single parent) who are working and will continue to work at least 20 hours weekly while attending

college at least 3/4 time. Must be pursuing career in the helping professions. Visit Website for details and application. For those with disabilities: TYY 541-687-7395 (voice), 800-452-8807 ext. 7395.

Amount of award:	$500
Application deadline:	March 1

Contact:
Oregon Student Assistance Commission
Grant Division/Friends of Oregon Students
1500 Valley River Drive, Suite 100
Eugene, OR 97401-2146
Phone: 541-687-7400 or 800-452-8807
Web: www.osac.state.or.us

Glenn Jackson Scholars

Type of award: Scholarship, renewable.
Intended use: For full-time undergraduate study at postsecondary institution in United States.
Eligibility: Applicant or parent must be employed by Oregon Department of Transportation/Parks and Recreation Dept. Applicant must be high school senior. Applicant must be U.S. citizen or permanent resident residing in Oregon.
Application requirements: Transcript. FAFSA and two essays required by OSAC. Two additional essays: two one-page essays: (1) "How do you plan to finance your college education?" and (2) "If you could have a personal meeting with the Governor of Oregon, what would you talk about and why?"
Additional information: Must be dependent of employee or retiree of Oregon Department of Transportation or Parks and Recreation Department. Employees must have been employed by their department at least three years. Visit Website for details and application. For those with disabilities: TYY 541-687-7395 (voice), 800-452-8807 ext. 7395.

Amount of award:	$500
Application deadline:	March 1

Contact:
Oregon Student Assistance Commission
Grants and Scholarship Division
1500 Valley River Drive, Suite 100
Eugene, OR 97401-2146
Phone: 541-687-7400 or 800-452-8807
Web: www.osac.state.or.us

Howard Vollum American Indian Scholarship

Type of award: Scholarship, renewable.
Intended use: For undergraduate study at postsecondary institution in United States.
Eligibility: Applicant must be American Indian. For American Indian residents of Clackamas, Multnomah, or Washington County in Oregon, or Clark County, Washington. Applicant must be high school senior. Applicant must be U.S. citizen or permanent resident residing in Oregon or Washington.
Basis for selection: Major/career interest in science, general; computer/information sciences; mathematics; engineering or engineering, computer. Applicant must demonstrate high academic achievement and service orientation.
Application requirements: Transcript, proof of eligibility. FAFSA and two essays. Additional essay topic: "How do you view your cultural heritage and its importance to you?" Submit certification of tribal enrollment or American Indian ancestry: photocopy of (1) tribal enrollment card that includes enrollment number and/or blood quantum, (2) Johnson O'Malley student eligibility form or (3) letter from tribe stating blood quantum and/or enrollment number of parent or grandparent.

387

Additional information: Preference given to applicants with demonstrated commitment to the American Indian community. Visit Website for details and application. For those with disabilities: TYY 541-687-7395 (voice), 800-452-8807 ext. 7395.

  Application deadline: March 1
Contact:
Oregon Student Assistance Commission
Grants and Scholarship Division
1500 Valley River Drive, Suite 100
Eugene, OR 97401-2146
Phone: 541-687-7400 or 800-452-8807
Web: www.osac.state.or.us

Ida M. Crawford Scholarship

Type of award: Scholarship, renewable.
Intended use: For full-time undergraduate study at accredited postsecondary institution in United States.
Eligibility: Applicant must be U.S. citizen residing in Oregon.
Basis for selection: Applicant must demonstrate financial need and high academic achievement.
Application requirements: Transcript, proof of eligibility. FAFSA and two essays required. Minimum 3.5 GPA. Student must submit proof of birth in US.
Additional information: Must be graduate of accredited Oregon high school. Not available to students majoring in law, medicine, music, theology, or teaching. U.S. Bancorp employees, their children and near relatives not eligible. Visit Website for details and application. For those with disabilities: TYY 541-687-7395 (voice), 800-452-8807 ext. 7395.

  Amount of award: $500
  Application deadline: March 1
Contact:
Oregon Student Assistance Commission
Grants and Scholarship Division
1500 Valley River Drive, Suite l00
Eugene, OR 97401-2146
Phone: 541-687-7400 or 800-452-8807
Web: www.osac.state.or.us

Jackson Foundation Journalism Scholarship

Type of award: Scholarship, renewable.
Intended use: For full-time undergraduate study. Designated institutions: Oregon postsecondary institutions.
Eligibility: Applicant must be U.S. citizen or permanent resident residing in Oregon.
Basis for selection: Major/career interest in journalism. Applicant must demonstrate financial need and high academic achievement.
Application requirements: Transcript. FAFSA and two essays required.
Additional information: Must be graduate of Oregon high school. Visit Website for details and application. For those with disabilities: TYY 541-687-7395 (voice), 800-452-8807 ext. 7395.

  Amount of award: $500
  Application deadline: March 1
Contact:
Oregon Student Assistance Commission
Grants and Scholarship Division
1500 Valley River Drive, Suite 100
Eugene, OR 97401-2146
Phone: 541-687-7400 or 800-452-8807
Web: www.ossc.state.or.us

James Carlson Memorial Scholarship

Type of award: Scholarship.
Intended use: For full-time senior or graduate study at accredited 4-year institution in United States.
Eligibility: Applicant must be Asian American, African American, Mexican American, Hispanic American, Puerto Rican or American Indian. Applicant must be U.S. citizen or permanent resident residing in Oregon.
Basis for selection: Major/career interest in education; education, teacher; education, special or education, early childhood. Applicant must demonstrate financial need and high academic achievement.
Application requirements: Transcript. FAFSA and two essays required.
Additional information: Available to elementary, secondary education majors entering senior or fifth-year or graduate students in fifth-year for elementary or secondary certificate. Preference given to African-American, Asian, Hispanic, and Native American ethnic groups; dependents of Oregon Education Association members; and others committed to teach autistic children. Visit Website for details and application. For those with disabilities: TYY 541-687-7395 (voice), 800-452-8807 ext. 7395.

  Amount of award: $500
  Application deadline: March 1
Contact:
Oregon Student Assistance Commission
Grants and Scholarship Division
1500 Valley River Drive, Suite 100
Eugene, OR 97401-2146
Phone: 541-687-7400 or 800-452-8807
Web: www.osac.state.or.us

Jerome B. Steinbach Scholarship

Type of award: Scholarship.
Intended use: For full-time sophomore, junior or senior study at accredited postsecondary institution in United States.
Eligibility: Applicant must be U.S. citizen residing in Oregon.
Basis for selection: Applicant must demonstrate financial need and high academic achievement.
Application requirements: Transcript. FAFSA and two essays required. Minimum 3.5 GPA required. Must submit proof of U.S. birth.
Additional information: U.S. Bancorp employees, their children and near relatives not eligible. Visit Website for details and application. For those with disabilities: TYY 542-687-7395 (voice), 800-452-8807 ext. 7395.

  Amount of award: $500
  Application deadline: March 1
Contact:
Oregon Student Assistance Commission
Grants and Scholarship Division
1500 Valley River Drive, Suite l00
Eugene, OR 97401-2146
Phone: 541-687-7400 or 800-452-8807
Web: www.osac.state.or.us

Jose D. Garcia Migrant Education Scholarship

Type of award: Scholarship.
Intended use: For freshman study at postsecondary institution in United States.

Eligibility: Applicant must be U.S. citizen or permanent resident residing in Oregon.
Application requirements: Transcript. FAFSA and two essays required. Must be high school graduate or GED recipient. Must enter parents' names in Item 16 of Application.
Additional information: Applicant must be participant in Oregon Migrant Education Program who are high school graduates or GED recipients. Visit Website for details and application. For those with disabilities: TYY 541-687-7395 (voice), 800-452-8807 ext. 7395.

  Amount of award: $500
  Application deadline: March 1
Contact:
Oregon Student Assistance Commission
Grants and Scholarship Division
1500 Valley River Drive, Suite 100
Eugene, OR 97401-2146
Phone: 541-687-7400 or 800-452-8807
Web: www.osac.state.or.us

Kaiser-Permanente Dental Assistant Scholarship

Type of award: Scholarship.
Intended use: For full-time undergraduate certificate study. Designated institutions: Accredited dental assistant programs at Blue Mountain Community College, Chemeketa Community College, Concorde Career Institute, Lane Community College, Linn-Benton Community College, Portland Community Colleges and Concorde Career Institute.
Eligibility: Applicant must be U.S. citizen or permanent resident residing in Oregon.
Basis for selection: Major/career interest in dental assistant. Applicant must demonstrate financial need.
Application requirements: Transcript. FAFSA and two essays required.
Additional information: Visit Website for details and application. For those with disabilities: TYY 541-687-7395 (voice), 800-452-8807 ext. 7395.

  Amount of award: $500
  Application deadline: March 1
Contact:
Oregon Student Assistance Commission
Grants and Scholarship Division
1500 Valley River Drive, Suite 100
Eugene, OR 97401-2146
Phone: 541-687-7400 or 800-452-8807
Web: www.osac.state.or.us

Laurence R. Foster Memorial Scholarship

Type of award: Scholarship, renewable.
Intended use: For junior, senior or graduate study at accredited 4-year institution in United States. Designated institutions: 4-year institutions.
Eligibility: Applicant must be U.S. citizen or permanent resident residing in Oregon.
Basis for selection: Major/career interest in nursing; medical specialties/research; physician assistant; public health; medical assistant; health-related professions; bioengineering; engineering, biomedical or nurse practitioner. Applicant must demonstrate service orientation.
Application requirements: Transcript. FAFSA and two essays required. Provide three names/phone numbers of references and additional one-page essay describing interest,

experience (if any) in public health career, migrant clinics, or community primary care clinics.
Additional information: Applicant must be seeking career in public health, not private practice. General preference given to applicants of diverse cultures. Preference also given to graduate students majoring in public health, and to undergraduates entering junior/senior-year health programs. Visit Website for details and application. For those with disabilities: TYY 541-687-7395 (voice), 800-452-8807 ext. 7395.

  Amount of award: $500
  Application deadline: March 1
Contact:
Oregon Student Assistance Commission
Grants and Scholarship Division
1500 Valley River Drive, Suite 100
Eugene, OR 97401-2146
Phone: 541-687-7400 or 800-452-8807
Web: www.osac.state.or.us

Maria C. Jackson-General George A. White Scholarship

Type of award: Scholarship, renewable.
Intended use: For full-time undergraduate or graduate study. Designated institutions: Oregon postsecondary institutions.
Eligibility: Applicant must be U.S. citizen or permanent resident residing in Oregon. Applicant must have served, or applicant's parent must serve or have served, in U.S. Armed Forces and resided in Oregon at time of enlistment.
Basis for selection: Applicant must demonstrate financial need and high academic achievement.
Application requirements: Transcript, proof of eligibility. FAFSA and two essays required. Minimum 3.75 GPA. Provide documentation (DD93, DD214, discharge papers).
Additional information: U.S. Bancorp employees, children, and near relatives not eligible. Visit Website for details and application. For those with disabilities: TYY 541-687-7395 (voice), 800-452-8807 ext. 7395.

  Application deadline: March 1
Contact:
Oregon Student Assistance Commission
Grants and Scholarship Division
1500 Valley River Drive, Suite 100
Eugene, OR 97401-2146
Phone: 541-687-7400 or 800-452-8807
Web: www.osac.state.or.us

Mark Hass Journalism Scholarship

Type of award: Scholarship.
Intended use: For full-time undergraduate study at accredited postsecondary institution in United States.
Eligibility: Applicant must be high school senior. Applicant must be U.S. citizen or permanent resident residing in Oregon.
Basis for selection: Major/career interest in journalism. Applicant must demonstrate financial need and high academic achievement.
Application requirements: Transcript. FAFSA and two essays required.
Additional information: Visit Website for details and application. For those with disabilities: TYY 541-687-7395 (voice), 800-452-8807 ext. 7395.

  Application deadline: March 1

Contact:
Oregon Student Assistance Commission
Grants and Scholarship Division
1500 Valley River Drive, Suite 100
Eugene, OR 97401-2146
Phone: 541-687-7400 or 800-452-8807
Web: www.osac.state.or.us

Mentor Graphics Scholarship

Type of award: Scholarship, renewable.
Intended use: For full-time junior or senior study at accredited 4-year institution in United States.
Eligibility: Applicant must be U.S. citizen or permanent resident residing in Oregon.
Basis for selection: Major/career interest in computer/information sciences; engineering, electrical/electronic or engineering, computer. Applicant must demonstrate financial need.
Application requirements: Transcript. FAFSA and two essays required.
Additional information: Available to graduates of an Oregon high school who are entering junior or senior year in college. One award reserved for female, African-American, Native American, or Hispanic applicant. Visit Website for details and application. For those with disabilities: TYY 541-687-7395 (voice), 800-452-8807 ext. 7395.

    Amount of award: $500
    Application deadline: March 1
Contact:
Oregon Student Assistance Commission
Grants and Scholarship Division
1500 Valley River Drive, Suite 100
Eugene, OR 97401-2146
Phone: 541-687-7400 or 800-452-8807
Web: www.osac.state.or.us

Oregon AFL-CIO Scholarship

Type of award: Scholarship.
Intended use: For full-time undergraduate study at postsecondary institution in United States.
Eligibility: Applicant must be high school senior. Applicant must be U.S. citizen or permanent resident residing in Oregon.
Basis for selection: Applicant must demonstrate financial need and high academic achievement.
Application requirements: Transcript. FAFSA and two essays required by OSAC. An additional essay required by AFL-CIO either [1] describe your own experience as an employee and why it leads you to believe that workers do (or do not) need a union on the job, or [2] explain why it is that many people who work full-time can not provide a decent standard of living for their families and what you believe should be done about it.
Additional information: Preference may be given to applicants from union families. Visit Website for details and application. For those with disabilities: TYY 541-687-7395 (voice), 800-452-8807 ext. 7395.

    Amount of award: $500
    Application deadline: March 1
Contact:
Oregon Student Assistance Commission
Grants and Scholarship Division
1500 Valley River Drive, Suite 100
Eugene, OR 97401-2146
Phone: 541-687-7400 or 800-452-8807
Web: www.osac.state.or.us

Oregon Collectors Association Bob Hasson Memorial Scholarship Fund Essay

Type of award: Scholarship.
Intended use: For full-time freshman study at postsecondary institution. Designated institutions: Oregon colleges and vocational schools.
Eligibility: Applicant must be high school senior. Applicant must be U.S. citizen or permanent resident residing in Oregon.
Basis for selection: Based on three- to four-page essay: "The Proper Use of Credit in the 21st Century." Applicant must demonstrate financial need.
Application requirements: Essay, transcript. Include FAFSA. Applicant's name/address/social security number, parent name/telephone number, high school name/telephone number, and name of intended college must appear on first page of essay.
Additional information: Applicant must be enrolling in Oregon college within 12 months of high school graduation. Children and grandchildren of owners and officers of collection agencies in Oregon not eligible. Finalists must read their essays at Association's annual spring meeting. Essays may be printed/published at discretion of Oregon Collectors Association. Apply only by mailing essays to ORCA Scholarship Fund, PO Box 42409, Portland OR 97242 or online at www.orcascholarshipfund.com. Visit Website for details and application. For those with disabilities: TYY 541-687-7395 (voice), 800-452-8807 ext. 7395.

    Amount of award: $1,500-$3,000
    Application deadline: March 1
Contact:
ORCA Scholarship Fund
PO Box 42409
Portland, OR 97242
Phone: 541-687-7400 or 800-452-8807
Web: www.orcascholarshipfund.com

Oregon Dungeness Crab Commission

Type of award: Scholarship.
Intended use: For full-time undergraduate study at postsecondary institution in United States.
Eligibility: Applicant or parent must be employed by Oregon Dungeness Crab Fishermen. Applicant must be high school senior. Applicant must be U.S. citizen or permanent resident residing in Oregon.
Basis for selection: Applicant must demonstrate financial need and high academic achievement.
Application requirements: Transcript. FAFSA and two essays required. Identify name of vessel in place of "worksite" on item 16 of application.
Additional information: For dependents of licensed Oregon Dungeness Crab fishermen or crew. Visit Website for details and application. For those with disabilities: TYY 541-687-7395 (voice), 800-452-8807 ext. 7395.

    Amount of award: $500
    Application deadline: March 1
Contact:
Oregon Student Assistance Comm ission
Grants and Scholarship Division
1500 Valley River Drive, Suite 100
Eugene, OR 97401-2146
Phone: 541-687-7400 or 800-452-8807
Web: www.osac.state.or.us

Scholarships

Oregon Education Association Scholarship

Type of award: Scholarship, renewable.
Intended use: For full-time undergraduate study at accredited postsecondary institution.
Eligibility: Applicant must be high school senior. Applicant must be U.S. citizen or permanent resident residing in Oregon.
Basis for selection: Major/career interest in education, teacher. Applicant must demonstrate high academic achievement.
Application requirements: Transcript. FAFSA and two essays required.
Additional information: For graduating seniors of any Oregon public high school who plan to become teachers. Applicant must attend a college or university in Oregon. Student must also be planning to complete baccalaureate degree and teaching certificate requirements. Visit Website for details and application. For those with disabilities: TYY 541-687-7395 (voice), 800-452-8807 ext. 7395.

   Amount of award: $500
   Application deadline: March 1
Contact:
Oregon Student Assistance Commission
Grants and Scholarship Division
1500 Valley River Drive, Suite 100
Eugene, OR 97401
Phone: 541-687-7400 or 800-452-8807
Web: www.osac.state.or.us

Oregon Metro Federal Credit Union Scholarship

Type of award: Scholarship, renewable.
Intended use: For full-time freshman study at postsecondary institution in United States.
Eligibility: Applicant or parent must be member/participant of Oregon Metro Federal Credit Union. Applicant must be U.S. citizen or permanent resident residing in Oregon.
Basis for selection: Applicant must demonstrate financial need and high academic achievement.
Application requirements: Transcript. FAFSA and two essays required.
Additional information: Must be graduate of Oregon high school and member of Oregon Metro Federal Credit Union. Preference given to graduating high school seniors attending Oregon colleges. Visit Website for details and application. For those with disabilities: TYY 541-687-7395 (voice), 800-452-8807 ext. 7395.

   Amount of award: $500
   Application deadline: March 1
Contact:
Oregon Student Assistance Commission
Grants and Scholarship Division
1500 Valley River Drive, Suite 100
Eugene, OR 97401-2146
Phone: 541-687-7400 or 800-452-8807
Web: www.osac.state.or.us

Oregon Occupational Safety and Health Division Workers Memorial Scholarship

Type of award: Scholarship, renewable.
Intended use: For full-time undergraduate or graduate study at postsecondary institution in United States.

Eligibility: Applicant must be U.S. citizen or permanent resident residing in Oregon. Applicant's parent must have been killed or disabled in work-related accident as public safety officer.
Basis for selection: Applicant must demonstrate financial need and high academic achievement.
Application requirements: Transcript, proof of eligibility. FAFSA and two essays required by OSAC. Additional 500-word essay: "How has the injury or death of your parent or spouse affected or influenced your decision to further your education?" Must provide name, social security number or workers compensation claim number of worker permanently disabled or fatally injured; date of death or injury; location of incident; exact relationship to disabled or fatally injured worker.
Additional information: Must be high school graduate or GED recipient. Must be dependent or spouse of Oregon worker permanently disabled on job or the recipient of fatality benefits as dependent or spouse of worker fatally injured in Oregon. Visit Website for details and application. For those with disabilities: TYY 541-687-7395 (voice), 800-452-8807 ext. 7395.

   Amount of award: $500
   Application deadline: March 1
Contact:
Oregon Student Assistance Commission
Grants and Scholarship Division
1500 Valley River Drive, Suite 100
Eugene, OR 97401-2146
Phone: 541-687-7400 or 800-452-8807
Web: www.osac.state.or.us

Oregon Robert C. Byrd Honors Scholarship

Type of award: Scholarship, renewable.
Intended use: For full-time undergraduate study at accredited postsecondary institution in United States.
Eligibility: Applicant must be high school senior. Applicant must be U.S. citizen or permanent resident residing in Oregon.
Basis for selection: Applicant must demonstrate high academic achievement.
Application requirements: Transcript. FAFSA and two essays required. Minimum 3.85 GPA or Oregon GED of 3300. Minimum 1300 on SAT or 29 on ACT.
Additional information: Must be graduating senior of Oregon high school. Fifteen recipients per federal congressional district. Visit Website for details and application. For those with disabilities: TYY 542-687-7395 (voice), 800-452-8807 ext. 7395.

   Amount of award: $500
   Application deadline: March 1
Contact:
Oregon Student Assistance Commission
Grants and Scholarship Division
1500 Valley River Drive, Suite 100
Eugene, OR 97401-2146
Phone: 541-687-7400 or 800-452-8807
Web: www.osac.state.or.us

Oregon Scholarship Fund Community College Student Award

Type of award: Scholarship, renewable.
Intended use: For full-time undergraduate study. Designated institutions: Oregon colleges.
Eligibility: Applicant must be U.S. citizen or permanent resident residing in Oregon.

Application requirements: Transcript. FAFSA and two essays required.

Additional information: Must be Oregon resident enrolled or planning to enroll in community college programs. Visit Website for details and application. For those with disabilities: TYY 541-687-7395 (voice), 800-452-8807 ext. 7395.

> **Amount of award:** $500
> **Application deadline:** March 1

Contact:
Oregon Student Assistance Commission
Grants and Scholarship Division
1500 Valley River Drive, Suite 100
Eugene, OR 97401-2146
Phone: 541-687-7400 or 800-452-8807
Web: www.osac.state.or.us

Oregon Trucking Association

Type of award: Scholarship.
Intended use: For full-time undergraduate study at postsecondary institution in United States.
Eligibility: Applicant or parent must be member/participant of Oregon Trucking Association (OTA). Applicant must be high school senior. Applicant must be U.S. citizen or permanent resident residing in Oregon.
Basis for selection: Applicant must demonstrate financial need and high academic achievement.
Application requirements: Transcript. FAFSA and two essays required.
Additional information: Intended for graduating seniors of any Oregon high school who are children of Oregon Trucking Association (OTA) members or children of employees (for at least one year) of OTA members. Visit Website for details and application. For those with disabilities: TYY 541-687-7395 (voice), 800-452-8807 ext. 7395.

> **Amount of award:** $500
> **Application deadline:** March 1

Contact:
Oregon Student Assistance Commission
Grants and Scholarship Division
1500 Valley River Drive, Suite 100
Eugene, OR 97401-2146
Phone: 541-687-7400 or 800-452-8807
Web: www.osac.state.or.us

Pendleton Postal Workers (APWU Local 110) Scholarship

Type of award: Scholarship.
Intended use: For full-time freshman study at postsecondary institution in United States.
Eligibility: Applicant or parent must be member/participant of Pendleton Postal Workers (APWU Local 110). Applicant must be high school senior. Applicant must be U.S. citizen or permanent resident residing in Oregon.
Basis for selection: Applicant must demonstrate high academic achievement.
Application requirements: Transcript. FAFSA and two essays required by OSAC. An additional essay topic: "What has the labor movement accomplished historically for working people?"
Additional information: Applicants must be dependents/descendants of active, retired or deceased members of Pendleton APWU #110 at least one year preceding application deadline. Visit Website for details and application. For those with disabilities: TYY 541-687-7395 (voice), 800-452-8807 ext. 7395.

Amount of award: $500
Application deadline: March 1
Contact:
Oregon Student Assistance Commission
Grants and Scholarship Division
1500 Valley River Drive, Suite 100
Eugene, OR 97401-2146
Phone: 541-687-7400 or 800-452-8807
Web: www.osac.state.or.us

Professional Land Surveyors of Oregon Scholarship

Type of award: Scholarship, renewable.
Intended use: For full-time sophomore, junior or senior study at postsecondary institution. Designated institutions: Oregon postsecondary institutions.
Eligibility: Applicant must be U.S. citizen or permanent resident residing in Oregon.
Basis for selection: Major/career interest in surveying/mapping.
Application requirements: Transcript. FAFSA and two essays required. One additional essay: brief statement of education-career goals relating to land surveying. Two references including names, addresses, and phone numbers.
Additional information: Students must be enrolled in curricula leading to land-surveying career. Community college applicants must intend to transfer to eligible four-year schools. Four-year applicants must intend to take Fundamentals of Land Surveying (FLS) exam. Visit Website for details and application. For those with disabilities: TYY 541-687-7395 (voice), 800-452-8807 ext. 7395.

> **Amount of award:** $500
> **Application deadline:** March 1

Contact:
Oregon Student Assistance Commission
Grants and Scholarship Division
1500 Valley River Drive, Suite 100
Eugene, OR 97401-2146
Phone: 541-687-7400 or 800-452-8807
Web: www.osac.state.or.us

Richard F. Brentano Memorial Scholarship

Type of award: Scholarship, renewable.
Intended use: For full-time undergraduate study at postsecondary institution in United States.
Eligibility: Applicant or parent must be employed by Waste Control Systems, Inc. Applicant must be no older than 24. Applicant must be U.S. citizen or permanent resident residing in Oregon.
Basis for selection: Applicant must demonstrate high academic achievement.
Application requirements: Transcript. FAFSA and two essays required.
Additional information: Intended for children or IRS-legal dependents (24 years of age and under) of employees of Waste Control Systems, Inc., and subsidiaries. Exception: age extended to maximum 26 for children or IRS-legal dependents entering U.S. Armed Forces directly from high school. Employees must have been employed by Waste Control Systems one year as of application deadline. Visit Website for details and application. For those with disabilities: TYY 541-687-7395 (voice), 800-452-8807 ext. 7395.

> **Amount of award:** $500
> **Application deadline:** March 1

Contact:
Oregon Student Assistance Commission
Grants and Scholarship Division
1500 Valley Drive, Suite 100
Eugene, OR 97401-2146
Phone: 541-687-7400 or 800-452-8807
Web: www.osac.state.or.us

Roger W. Emmons Memorial Scholarship

Type of award: Scholarship, renewable.
Intended use: For full-time undergraduate study at accredited postsecondary institution in United States.
Eligibility: Applicant or parent must be employed by Oregon Refuse & Recycling Association. Applicant must be high school senior. Applicant must be U.S. citizen or permanent resident residing in Oregon.
Basis for selection: Applicant must demonstrate high academic achievement.
Application requirements: Transcript, proof of eligibility. FAFSA and two essays required.
Additional information: Must be graduating senior of any Oregon high school. Parent(s) or grandparent(s) must have been solid waste company member(s) or employees (for at least three years) of members of Oregon Refuse & Recycling Association. Visit Website for details and application. For those with disabilities: TYY 542-687-7395 (voice), 800-452-8807 ext. 7395.

Amount of award:	$500
Application deadline:	March 1

Contact:
Oregon Student Assistance Commission
Grants and Scholarship Division
1500 Valley River Drive, Suite l00
Eugene, OR 97401-2146
Phone: 541-687-7400 or 800-452-8807
Web: www.osac.state.or.us

Teamsters Clyde C. Crosby/Joseph M. Edgar Memorial Scholarship

Type of award: Scholarship, renewable.
Intended use: For full-time undergraduate study at postsecondary institution in United States.
Eligibility: Applicant must be high school senior. Applicant must be U.S. citizen or permanent resident residing in Oregon.
Basis for selection: Applicant must demonstrate financial need and high academic achievement.
Application requirements: Transcript. FAFSA and two essays required. Minimum 3.0 cumulative GPA.
Additional information: Must be child or dependent stepchild of active, retired, disabled or deceased member of local unions affiliated with Joint Council of Teamsters #37. Qualifying members must have been active at least one year. Visit Website for details and application. For those with disabilities: TYY 541-687-7395 (voice), 800-452-8807 ext. 7395.

Amount of award:	$500
Application deadline:	March 1

Contact:
Oregon Student Assistance Commission
Grants and Scholarship Division
1500 Valley River Drive, Suite 100
Eugene, OR 97401-2146
Phone: 541-687-7400 or 800-452-8807
Web: www.osac.state.or.us

Teamsters Council #37 Federal Credit Union Scholarship

Type of award: Scholarship.
Intended use: For undergraduate or graduate study at postsecondary institution in United States.
Eligibility: Applicant must be high school senior. Applicant must be U.S. citizen or permanent resident residing in Oregon.
Basis for selection: Applicant must demonstrate financial need and high academic achievement.
Application requirements: Transcript. FAFSA and two essays required by OSAC. Additional essay topic: "The Importance of Preserving the Right to Strike in a Free Enterprise System." Applicant must have cumulative GPA between 2.0 and 3.0 and be enrolled at least half-time in college.
Additional information: For members (or dependents) of Council #37 credit union. Members must have been active in local affiliated with the Joint Council of Teamsters #37 at least one year. Visit Website for details and application. For those with disabilities: TYY 541-687-7395 (voice), 800-452-8807 ext. 7395.

Amount of award:	$500
Application deadline:	March 1

Contact:
Oregon Student Assistance Commission
Grants and Scholarship Division
1500 Valley River Drive, Suite 100
Eugene, OR 97401-2146
Phone: 541-687-7400 or 800-452-8807
Web: www.osac.state.or.us

Teamsters Local 305 Scholarship

Type of award: Scholarship, renewable.
Intended use: For full-time undergraduate study at postsecondary institution in United States.
Eligibility: Applicant must be high school senior. Applicant must be U.S. citizen or permanent resident residing in Oregon.
Basis for selection: Applicant must demonstrate financial need and high academic achievement.
Application requirements: Transcript. FAFSA and two essays required.
Additional information: Must be child or dependent stepchild of active, retired, disabled, or deceased members of Local 305 of the Joint Council of Teamsters #37. Members must have been active at least one year. Visit Website for details and application. For those with disabilities: TYY 541-687-7395 (voice), 800-452-8807 ext. 7395.

Amount of award:	$500
Application deadline:	March 1

Contact:
Oregon Student Assistance Commission
Grants and Scholarship Division
1500 Valley River Drive, Suite 100
Eugene, OR 97401-2146
Phone: 541-687-7400 or 800-452-8807
Web: www.osac.state.or.us

Walter and Marie Schmidt Scholarship

Type of award: Scholarship, renewable.
Intended use: For undergraduate study at accredited postsecondary institution in United States.
Eligibility: Applicant must be U.S. citizen or permanent resident residing in Oregon.

Scholarships

393

Basis for selection: Major/career interest in nursing or gerontology. Applicant must demonstrate financial need and high academic achievement.

Application requirements: Transcript. FAFSA and two essays required by OSAC. Additional essay describing desire to pursue nursing career in geriatric health care.

Additional information: Available to students enrolling in programs to become registered nurses and intending to pursue careers in geriatric healthcare. Priority given to students from Lane County students. U.S. Bancorp employees, children and near relatives not eligible. Visit Website for details and application. For those with disabilities: TYY 542-687-7395 (voice), 800-452-8807 ext. 7395.

Amount of award:	$500
Application deadline:	March 1

Contact:
Oregon Student Assistance Commission
Grants and Scholarship Division
1500 Valley River Drive, Suite 100
Eugene, OR 97401-2146
Phone: 541-687-7400 or 800-452-8807
Web: www.osac.state.or.us

Organization of Chinese Americans

OCA/Avon Foundation College Scholarship

Type of award: Scholarship.
Intended use: For full-time undergraduate study in United States.
Eligibility: Applicant must be Asian American. Applicant must be female. Applicant must be U.S. citizen or permanent resident.
Basis for selection: Applicant must demonstrate financial need and high academic achievement.
Application requirements: Recommendations, essay, transcript. FAFSA.
Additional information: Applicant must be entering college freshman in fall. Applicant must have GPA of at least 3.0. Deadlines vary. Check with Website or sponsor for exact deadline.

Amount of award:	$2,000
Number of awards:	10
Number of applicants:	300
Application deadline:	May 15
Total amount awarded:	$20,000

Contact:
Organization of Chinese Americans
1001 Connecticut Avenue NW, #601
Washington, DC 20036
Phone: 202-223-5500
Fax: 202-296-0540
Web: www.ocanatl.org

OCA/LIPS Foundation Gold Mountain College Scholarship

Type of award: Scholarship.
Intended use: For full-time undergraduate study.
Eligibility: Applicant must be Asian American. Applicant must be U.S. citizen or permanent resident.

Basis for selection: Applicant must demonstrate financial need and high academic achievement.
Application requirements: Recommendations, essay.
Additional information: Applicant must be entering college freshman and the first person in family to go to college. Must submit FAFSA.

Amount of award:	$2,000
Number of awards:	10
Number of applicants:	250
Application deadline:	May 15
Total amount awarded:	$20,000

Contact:
Organization of Chinese Americans
1001 Connecticut Avenue NW, #601
Washington, DC 20036
Phone: 202-223-5500
Fax: 202-296-0540
Web: www.ocanatl.org

OCA/Verizon Foundation College Scholarship

Type of award: Scholarship.
Intended use: For full-time freshman study.
Eligibility: Applicant must be Asian American. Applicant must be U.S. citizen or permanent resident.
Basis for selection: Applicant must demonstrate financial need and high academic achievement.
Application requirements: Recommendations, essay. FAFSA.
Additional information: Contact sponsor for more information.

Amount of award:	$2,000
Number of awards:	25
Application deadline:	May 15
Total amount awarded:	$50,000

Contact:
Organization of Chinese Americans
1001 Connecticut Ave., NW
#601
Washington, DC 20036
Phone: 202-223-5500
Fax: 202-296-0540
Web: www.ocanatl.org

The Orthotic and Prosthetic Education and Development Fund

Chester Haddan Scholarship Program

Type of award: Scholarship.
Intended use: For senior study at accredited 2-year or 4-year institution in United States. Designated institutions: Accredited orthotic and prosthetic programs.
Eligibility: Applicant must be U.S. citizen.
Basis for selection: Major/career interest in orthotics/ prosthetics; medical specialties/research or mental health/ therapy. Applicant must demonstrate financial need, depth of character, seriousness of purpose and service orientation.
Application requirements: Recommendations, transcript by Students may apply directly, or a professor may nominate them.

Application. Letter of reference. 200-word essay on why student wants to work in orthotics or prosthetics.
Additional information: Applicants must be willing to contribute to their own education financially.

Amount of award:	$1,000
Application deadline:	January 20
Notification begins:	March 21
Total amount awarded:	$1,000

Contact:
The Academy, Orthotic and Prosthetic Education and Development Fund
526 King Street
Suite 201
Alexandria, VA 22314
Phone: 703-836-0788, ext. 206
Web: www.oandp.org/education

Dan McKeever Scholarship Program

Type of award: Scholarship.
Intended use: For undergraduate study at 2-year or 4-year institution in United States. Designated institutions: Accredited orthotic and prosthetic program.
Eligibility: Applicant must be U.S. citizen.
Basis for selection: Major/career interest in orthotics/prosthetics; medical specialties/research or mental health/therapy. Applicant must demonstrate financial need, leadership, seriousness of purpose and service orientation.
Application requirements: Recommendations, transcript by Students may apply directly, or a professor may nominate them. Application. Letter of reference. 200-word essay on why student wants to work in orthotics or prosthetics.
Additional information: Applicant must maintain minimum 3.0 GPA. Applicants must be willing to contribute to their own education financially.

Amount of award:	$1,000
Number of awards:	3
Application deadline:	May 31
Total amount awarded:	$3,000

Contact:
The Academy, Orthotic and Prosthetic Education and Development Fund
526 King Street
Suite 201
Alexandria, VA 22314
Phone: 703-836-0788, ext. 206
Web: www.oandp.org/education

Ken Chagnon Scholarship

Type of award: Scholarship.
Intended use: For senior study at 2-year or 4-year institution in United States. Designated institutions: Accredited orthotic and prosthetic program.
Eligibility: Applicant must be U.S. citizen.
Basis for selection: Major/career interest in orthotics/prosthetics; medical specialties/research or mental health/therapy. Applicant must demonstrate financial need, leadership and seriousness of purpose.
Application requirements: Recommendations, transcript by Students may apply directly for the scholarship, or a professor may nominate them. Application. Letter of reference. 200-word essay on why student wants to work in orthotics or prosthetics.
Additional information: Applicants must be willing to contribute financially to their education. Must show exceptional technical aptitude.

Amount of award:	$500
Number of awards:	1
Application deadline:	January 20
Notification begins:	March 21
Total amount awarded:	$500

Contact:
The Academy, Orthotic and Prosthetic Education and Development Fund
526 King Street
Suite 201
Alexandria, VA 22314
Phone: 703-836-0788, ext. 206
Web: www.oandp.org/education

Osage Tribal Education Committee

Osage Tribal Education Scholarship

Type of award: Scholarship, renewable.
Intended use: For undergraduate or graduate study at accredited postsecondary institution in United States.
Eligibility: Applicant must be American Indian. Must be a member of the Osage Nation of Oklahoma. Applicant must be U.S. citizen.
Application requirements: Must provide proof of Osage Indian blood.
Additional information: Must maintain 2.0 GPA. Deadline for summer funding is May 1. July 1 deadline is for fall semester; December 31 is for spring deadline. Application must be received by Committee by deadline.

Number of awards:	220
Number of applicants:	250
Application deadline:	July 1, December 31

Contact:
Osage Tribal Education Committee
Oklahoma Area Education Office
4149 Highline Boulevard, Suite 380
Oklahoma City, OK 73108
Phone: 405-605-6051 ext. 304
Fax: 405-605-6057

Outdoor Writers Association of America, Inc.

Bodie McDowell Scholarship

Type of award: Scholarship.
Intended use: For full-time junior, senior or graduate study at 2-year or 4-year institution in United States. Designated institutions: Any OWAA-accredited school of journalism and mass communication.
Eligibility: Applicant must be U.S. citizen.
Basis for selection: Major/career interest in journalism; communications; film/video; arts, general or public relations.
Application requirements: Recommendations, essay, transcript.
Additional information: Candidate should have career goal in outdoor communications, demonstrated by submission to OWAA of printed, film or taped material, job history, course

...idence of good faith. Outdoor
Outdo...ly included. For a listing of schools
...AA's scholarship program, visit Website.
...rd: $2,500-$3,500
...ards: 3
...eadline: January 1, March 1

...s Association of America, Inc.
...t.

...T 59801
...728-7434
...owaa.org

PACE International Union

PACE International Union Scholarship

Type of award: Scholarship.
Intended use: For full-time freshman study at 4-year institution in United States.
Eligibility: Applicant or parent must be employed by PACE International Union. Applicant must be high school senior. Applicant must be U.S. citizen or permanent resident.
Basis for selection: Applicant must demonstrate financial need, high academic achievement, depth of character, leadership, patriotism, seriousness of purpose and service orientation.
Application requirements: Essay, transcript.
Additional information: Scholarship recipients required to take one course in labor relations. Applicant or parent must be a member of PACE International Union.

Amount of award:	$1,000
Number of awards:	20
Number of applicants:	1,500
Application deadline:	March 15
Notification begins:	June 15

Contact:
Scholarship Coordinator
PACE International Union
P.O. Box 1475
Nashville, TN 37202
Phone: 615-834-8590
Web: www.paceunion.org

Papercheck.com

Papercheck.com Charles Shafae' Scholarship Fund

Type of award: Scholarship.
Intended use: For undergraduate study at accredited postsecondary institution in United States.
Eligibility: Applicant must be U.S. citizen or permanent resident.
Basis for selection: Essay. Applicant must demonstrate high academic achievement.
Application requirements: Transcript. Essay must have minimum 1,000 words and be in MLA format. Include works cited page with minimum of two sources.

Additional information: Two awards for essay contest. Minimum 3.2 GPA. Applicant must be in good standing at institution. Visit Website for essay questions, guidelines, and deadlines. Complete entry form online. Contact via e-mail.

Amount of award:	$500
Number of awards:	2

Contact:
Visit Website for application and more information.
Phone: 866-693-EDIT
Web: www.papercheck.com

Par Aide

Par Aide's Joseph S. Garske Collegiate Grant Program

Type of award: Scholarship, renewable.
Intended use: For undergraduate study at postsecondary institution.
Eligibility: Applicant must be high school senior.
Basis for selection: Applicant must demonstrate leadership.
Application requirements: Essay, transcript. 500-word essay explaining reason for wanting to pursue higher education.
Additional information: Minimum 2.0 GPA. Applicant's parent or stepparent must be GCSAA member for five or more consecutive years and must be a currently active GCSAA member in one of the following classifications: A, Superintendent Member, C, Retired-A, Retired-B or AA life. Children or stepchildren of deceased members eligible if member was active for five years at time of death. Children of those employed by Par Aide, the Environmental Institute for Golf's Board of Trustees, the GCSAA Board of Directors, and GCSAA staff are not eligible for this program.

Amount of award:	$2,500
Application deadline:	March 15
Notification begins:	May 15

Contact:
Golf Course Superintendents Association of America
Garske Grant Program
1421 Research Park Drive
Lawrence, KS 66049-3859
Phone: 785-841-2240
Web: www.gcsaa.org

Patient Advocate Foundation

Scholarships for Survivors

Type of award: Scholarship.
Intended use: For full-time undergraduate or graduate study at accredited 2-year, 4-year or graduate institution.
Eligibility: Applicant must be U.S. citizen.
Basis for selection: Applicant must demonstrate depth of character and leadership.
Application requirements: Recommendations, essay, transcript, proof of eligibility. Previous year's tax returns.
Additional information: Applicants must pursue course of study that renders them immediately employable after graduation. Student must be a survivor of a life-threatening,

chronic or debilitating disease. Must maintain an overall 3.0 GPA. Must complete 20 hours of community service for the year the scholarship will be dispensed.

Amount of award:	$5,000
Number of awards:	8
Application deadline:	May 1
Total amount awarded:	$40,000

Contact:
Patient Advocate Foundation
753 Thimble Shoals Blvd., Suite B
Newport News, VA 23606
Web: www.patientadvocate.org

Peacock Productions, Inc.

The Audria M. Edwards Scholarship Fund

Type of award: Scholarship, renewable.
Intended use: For full-time undergraduate study at 2-year or 4-year institution in United States.
Eligibility: Applicant must be U.S. citizen residing in Oregon or Washington.
Basis for selection: Major/career interest in arts, general. Applicant must demonstrate depth of character and leadership.
Application requirements: Proof of eligibility.
Additional information: Applicant must be pursuing a degree in academic, trade, vocational or the arts. Please visit Website for application information.

Amount of award:	$500-$3,500
Number of awards:	10
Number of applicants:	27
Application deadline:	May 1
Total amount awarded:	$18,000

Contact:
Peacock Productions, Inc.
Audria M. Edwards Scholarship Fund
P.O. Box 8854
Portland, OR 97207-8854
Web: www.peacockinthepark.com/scholarship.shtm

Penguin Putnam Inc.

Signet Classic Student Scholarship Essay Contest

Type of award: Scholarship.
Intended use: For undergraduate study.
Eligibility: Applicant must be high school junior or senior. Applicant must be U.S. citizen or permanent resident.
Basis for selection: Competition/talent/interest in writing/journalism, based on style, content, grammar and originality; judges look for clear, concise writing that is articulate, logically organized and well-supported. Major/career interest in English or literature.
Application requirements: Essay, proof of eligibility, nomination by high school English teacher. Essay must be submitted by high school English teacher on behalf of student, along with cover letter on school letterhead.
Additional information: Entrant must read designated book and answer one of several book-related questions in two- to

three-page essay. Visit Website for details and applic... contact high school English department. Winner also ... Signet Classic library for school.

Amount of award:	$1,000
Number of awards:	5
Application deadline:	April 15
Notification begins:	June 15
Total amount awarded:	$5,000

Contact:
Penguin Putnam Inc. Signet Classic Student Scholarship Essay Contest
375 Hudson Street
New York, NY 10014
Phone: 212-366-2377
Web: www.penguinputnam.com/scessay

Peninsula Community Foundation

Bobette Bibo Gugliotta Memorial Scholarship for Creative Writing

Type of award: Scholarship, renewable.
Intended use: For full-time undergraduate or graduate study at 2-year, 4-year or graduate institution.
Eligibility: Applicant must be high school senior.
Basis for selection: Major/career interest in journalism.
Application requirements: Applicants must submit samples of creative writing.
Additional information: Award is $2000 for an undergraduate or graduate student, $500 for a graduating high school senior. Applicants must have graduated from high school located on the San Francisco Peninsula, from Daly City through Mountain View. Recipients may not re-apply.

Amount of award:	$500-$2,000
Number of awards:	2
Application deadline:	March 1

Contact:
Peninsula Community Foundation
1700 South
El Camino Real, Suite 300
San Mateo, CA 94402-3049
Phone: 650-358-9369
Fax: 650-358-9817
Web: www.pcf.org

Mervin G. Morris Educational Scholarship Program

Type of award: Scholarship.
Intended use: For undergraduate study at 2-year or 4-year institution.
Eligibility: Applicant must be high school senior. Applicant must be residing in California.
Additional information: Applicant must be the child or grandchild of any Mervyn's team member. Applicant should contact the human resources department at Mervyn's for more information and an application.

Amount of award:	$1,000-$5,000
Number of awards:	16
Application deadline:	March 14

Penin₅ Foundation
no Real

₄02-3049
₀369
₁7
org

Mrs. Sze Lee Memorial
rship

award: Scholarship.
ded use: For undergraduate study at vocational, 2-year or
4-year institution.
Eligibility: Applicant must be high school senior. Applicant
must be U.S. citizen residing in California.
Basis for selection: Applicant must demonstrate leadership
and service orientation.
Additional information: Applicant must be an employee or
dependent of employee of the San Francisco Airport or
companies/airlines based at the airport. Employees must have
minimum of three years service.

Amount of award:	$2,000
Number of awards:	12
Application deadline:	March 5
Total amount awarded:	$24,000

Contact:
Peninsula Community Foundation
1700 South El Camino Real
Ste. 300
San Mateo, CA 94402-3049
Phone: 650-358-9369
Fax: 650-358-9817
Web: www.pcf.org

Pennsylvania Higher Education Assistance Agency

Pennsylvania Grant Program

Type of award: Scholarship, renewable.
Intended use: For undergraduate study at accredited
vocational, 2-year or 4-year institution in United States.
Designated institutions: Pennsylvania postsecondary institutions.
Eligibility: Applicant must be residing in Pennsylvania.
Basis for selection: Applicant must demonstrate financial
need.
Application requirements: Proof of eligibility. FAFSA.
Additional information: Grants are portable to approved
institutions in other states. Number and amount of awards vary.

Amount of award:	$300-$3,300
Application deadline:	May 1

Contact:
Pennsylvania Higher Education Assistance Agency
State Grant and Special Programs Divisions
1200 North Seventh Street
Harrisburg, PA 17102-1444
Phone: 800-692-7392
Web: www.pheaa.org

Pennsylvania Robert C. Byrd Honors Scholarship

Type of award: Scholarship, renewable.
Intended use: For full-time freshman study at accredited
2-year or 4-year institution in United States.
Eligibility: Applicant must be high school senior. Applicant
must be U.S. citizen or permanent resident residing in
Pennsylvania.
Basis for selection: Applicant must demonstrate high
academic achievement.
Application requirements: Transcript. SAT/ACT or GED
scores.
Additional information: Applicant must rank in top five
percent of class, have 3.5 GPA, 1150 on SAT (25 on ACT), or
355 on GED, and must enroll following graduation. Information
available from high school guidance office.

Amount of award:	$1,500
Application deadline:	May 1

Contact:
Pennsylvania Higher Education Assistance Agency
Robert C. Byrd Scholarship
P.O. Box 8114
Harrisburg, PA 17105-8114
Phone: 800-692-7392
Web: www.pheaa.org

Phi Delta Kappa International

Phi Delta Kappa Scholarship for Prospective Educators

Type of award: Scholarship.
Intended use: For full-time freshman study at accredited
postsecondary institution outside United States.
Eligibility: Applicant must be high school senior.
Basis for selection: Major/career interest in education.
Applicant must demonstrate high academic achievement,
leadership, seriousness of purpose and service orientation.
Application requirements: Recommendations, essay,
transcript.
Additional information: Minimum four awards to racial
minorities and two to dependents of PDK members. Minimum
3.5 GPA required, 3.7 recommended. Two of the scholarships
are renewable. Make application to local chapter.

Amount of award:	$1,000-$5,000
Number of awards:	30
Number of applicants:	800
Application deadline:	January 15
Notification begins:	June 1
Total amount awarded:	$30,000

Contact:
Phi Delta Kappa Headquarters
Scholarship Program
Box 789, 408 N. Union Street
Bloomington, IN 47402-0789
Phone: 812-766-1156 or 800-766-1156
Web: www.pdkintl.org

The Phillips Foundation

Ronald Reagan Future Leaders Scholarship Program

Type of award: Scholarship, renewable.
Intended use: For sophomore, junior or senior study at 2-year or 4-year institution in United States.
Eligibility: Applicant must be U.S. citizen.
Basis for selection: Major/career interest in political science/government. Applicant must demonstrate financial need, high academic achievement, depth of character, leadership, seriousness of purpose and service orientation.
Application requirements: Recommendations, essay, transcript. Applicants must submit a 500 to 750 word essay describing their backgrounds, career objectives, and scope of participation in leadership activities promoting freedom, American values, and constitutional principles. Two letters of recommendation. Supporting documentation or materials which provide evidence of the applicant's active involvement in campus or community leadership.
Additional information: Award amounts are $2,500, $5,000, $7,500 and $10,000. Check Website for additional information.

Amount of award:	$10,000
Number of awards:	2
Application deadline:	January 15
Total amount awarded:	$20,000

Contact:
The Phillips Foundation
Attn: Jeff Hollingsworth
7811 Montrose Road, Suite 100
Potomac, MD 20854
Phone: 301-340-7788, ext. 6028
Web: www.thephillipsfoundation.org

Physician Assistant Foundation

Physician Assistant Scholarship

Type of award: Scholarship.
Intended use: For undergraduate study. Designated institutions: Any physician assistant program accredited by Committee on Allied Health Education and Accreditation/Commission on Accreditation of Allied Health Education Programs.
Eligibility: Applicant or parent must be member/participant of American Academy of Physician Assistants.
Basis for selection: Applicant must demonstrate financial need, high academic achievement, seriousness of purpose and service orientation.
Application requirements: Transcript, proof of eligibility. Letter from financial aid office verifying aid if any. Passport-size photo.
Additional information: Applicant must have completed first semester of P.A. program. Must be student member of American Academy of Physician Assistants at time of application. Number of awards varies.

Amount of award:	$2,000
Number of awards:	48
Number of applicants:	250
Application deadline:	February 1
Notification begins:	May 15

Contact:
Francesca M. Rusk, Foundation Manager
Physician Assistant Foundation
950 North Washington Street
Alexandria, VA 22314
Phone: 703-519-5686
Fax: 703-684-1924
Web: www.aapa.org/paf/app-scholarship.html

Playtex Products, Inc.

Playtex Scholarship

Type of award: Scholarship, renewable.
Intended use: For full-time freshman study at accredited 4-year institution in United States or Canada.
Eligibility: Applicant or parent must be employed by Playtex Products, Inc. and subsidiaries. Applicant must be high school senior.
Basis for selection: Applicant must demonstrate high academic achievement, depth of character, leadership, seriousness of purpose and service orientation.
Application requirements: Recommendations, essay, transcript, proof of eligibility. SAT/ACT scores.
Additional information: Parent or guardian must have completed one year of continuous service with Playtex by time of application. Canadian and Puerto Rican citizens also qualify. Two scholarships were given in most recent year, six were renewed.

Amount of award:	$2,000
Number of awards:	8
Application deadline:	November 19
Notification begins:	May 1
Total amount awarded:	$16,000

Contact:
Playtex Products Scholarship Program
300 Nyala Farms Road
Westport, CT 06880
Web: www.playtexproducts.com

Plumbing-Heating-Cooling Contractors - National Assoc. Educational Foundation

Delta Faucet Company Scholarship

Type of award: Scholarship.
Intended use: For full-time undergraduate study at accredited 2-year or 4-year institution in United States.
Basis for selection: Major/career interest in air conditioning/heating/refrigeration technology; architecture; business; engineering, construction or construction management.

Application requirements: Recommendations, essay, transcript. Submit SAT/ACT scores.

Additional information: High school seniors and college students are eligible to apply. Applicants must pursue studies in a major related to the plumbing-heating-cooling industry and must be sponsored by an active member of PHCC--National Association. Funds provided by Delta Faucet Company and administered by PHCC Educational Foundation.

Amount of award:	$2,500
Number of awards:	6
Number of applicants:	45
Application deadline:	June 1
Total amount awarded:	$15,000

Contact:
Delta Faucet Company Scholarship Program
P.O. Box 6808
180 S. Washington Street
Falls Church, VA 22046
Phone: 800-533-7694
Fax: 703-237-7442
Web: www.phccweb.org

Plumbing-Heating-Cooling Contractors - National Association Educational Foundation Scholarship

Type of award: Scholarship, renewable.

Intended use: For full-time undergraduate study at accredited postsecondary institution in United States.

Eligibility: Applicant must be high school senior.

Basis for selection: Major/career interest in air conditioning/heating/refrigeration technology; architecture; business; engineering, construction or construction management. Applicant must demonstrate high academic achievement.

Application requirements: Interview, recommendations, transcript. Application.

Additional information: High school seniors and college students are eligible to apply. Applicants must pursue studies in a major related to the plumbing-heating-cooling industry and must be sponsored by an active member of PHCC-National Association. The award for four-year students is $12,000 ($3,000 per year for up to four years), while the award for two-year students is $3,000 ($1,500 per year for up to two years). Recipients must continue study in a p-h-c-related major and maintain 2.0 GPA or better throughout period for which scholarship is awarded.

Amount of award:	$3,000-$12,000
Number of awards:	5
Application deadline:	May 1
Notification begins:	August 1
Total amount awarded:	$48,000

Contact:
PHCC Educational Foundation
180 S. Washington St.
P.O. Box 6808
Falls Church, VA 22046
Phone: 800-533-7694
Fax: 703-237-7442
Web: www.phccweb.org

Polish American Club of North Jersey c/o Kosciuszko Foundation

The Polish American Club of North Jersey Scholarships

Type of award: Scholarship, renewable.

Intended use: For full-time undergraduate or graduate study at accredited postsecondary institution in United States.

Eligibility: Applicant must be Polish. Applicant must be U.S. citizen or permanent resident.

Basis for selection: Selection based on academic excellence, motivation, and interest in Polish subjects or involvement in the Polish-American community. Applicant must demonstrate financial need and high academic achievement.

Application requirements: $25 application fee. Recommendations, essay, transcript, proof of eligibility. Complete Kosciuszko Foundation tuition scholarship application form, available from October through December. Discuss background and academic and career goals in personal statement. Two letters of recommendation required. Provide proof of Polish ancestry. Include two passport-sized photos with full name printed on reverse side of each. Send SASE to confirm receipt of materials.

Additional information: Applicant must be an active member of Polish American Club of North Jersey. Children and grandchildren of Polish American Club of North Jersey members also eligible. Minimum 3.0 GPA. Only one member per immediate family may receive a Polish American Club of North Jersey Scholarship during any given academic year. Submit application, $25 non-refundable application fee and supporting materials to Kosciuszko Foundation. E-mailed and faxed materials wll not be considered. Notifications made in writing in May.

Amount of award:	$1,000-$2,000
Number of awards:	5
Application deadline:	January 15
Total amount awarded:	$8,000

Contact:
Kosciuszko Foundation
15 East 65th Street
New York, NY 10021
Phone: 212-734-2130
Web: www.kosciuszkofoundation.org

Polish National Alliance of Brooklyn, USA, Inc. c/o Kosciuszko Foundation

The Polish National Alliance of Brooklyn, USA, Inc. Scholarships

Type of award: Scholarship, renewable.

Intended use: For full-time undergraduate study at accredited postsecondary institution in United States.

Eligibility: Applicant or parent must be member/participant of Polish National Alliance of Brooklyn. Applicant must be Polish. Applicant must be U.S. citizen or permanent resident.

Basis for selection: Selection based on academic excellence, motivation, and interest in Polish subjects or involvement in the Polish-American community. Applicant must demonstrate financial need and high academic achievement.

Application requirements: $25 application fee. Recommendations, essay, transcript, proof of eligibility. Complete Kosciuszko Foundation tuition scholarship application form, available from October through December. Discuss background and academic and career goals in personal statement. Two letters of recommendation required. Provide proof of Polish ancestry. Include two passport-sized photos with full name printed on reverse side of each. Send SASE to confirm receipt of materials.

Additional information: Applicant must be member in good standing of Polish National Alliance of Brooklyn, USA, Inc. Minimum 3.0 GPA. Only one member per immediate family may receive scholarship during any given academic year. Submit application, $25 non-refundable application fee and supporting materials to Kosciuszko Foundation. E-mailed and faxed materials wll not be considered. Notifications made in writing in May.

Amount of award:	$2,000
Number of awards:	4
Application deadline:	January 15
Total amount awarded:	$8,000

Contact:
Kosciuszko Foundation
15 East 65th Street
New York, NY 10021
Phone: 212-734-2130
Web: www.kosciuszkofoundation.org

Presbyterian Church (USA)

Ira Page Wallace Bible Scholarship

Type of award: Scholarship.
Intended use: For undergraduate study in United States. Designated institutions: Barber-Scotia College, Johnson C. Smith University, Knoxville College, Mary Holmes College, Stillman College.
Eligibility: Applicant must be African American. Applicant must be Presbyterian. Applicant must be U.S. citizen.
Basis for selection: Major/career interest in religion/theology. Applicant must demonstrate financial need and high academic achievement.
Additional information: Must demonstrate superior academic progress in Bible studies. Contact chairperson of Department of Religion at school for application information.

Amount of award:	$3,938
Number of awards:	5
Total amount awarded:	$19,687

Contact:
Presbyterian Church (USA)
Office of Racial Ethnic Schools and Colleges
100 Witherspoon Street, 3012
Louisville, KY 40202-1396
Phone: 888-728-7228 ext. 5646
Web: www.pcusa.org/highereducation

National Presbyterian Scholarship

Type of award: Scholarship, renewable.
Intended use: For full-time undergraduate study in United States. Designated institutions: Presbyterian-related institutions.

Eligibility: Applicant must be high school senior. Applicant must be Presbyterian. Applicant must be U.S. citizen or permanent resident.
Basis for selection: Applicant must demonstrate financial need and high academic achievement.
Application requirements: Recommendations, transcript. Applicant must send a recommendation from church pastor; biographical questionaire and record from high school guidance counselor.
Additional information: SAT/ACT must be taken no later than December 15 of senior year of high school. Must be preparing to enter one of the participating colleges related to the Presbyterian Church (USA). Applications and additional requirements available after December 1.

Amount of award:	$500-$1,400
Number of awards:	440
Application deadline:	January 31
Notification begins:	March 1

Contact:
Presbyterian Church (USA)
Financial Aid for Studies
100 Witherspoon Street, M067A
Louisville, KY 40202-1396
Phone: 888-728-7228 ext.8235
Fax: 502-569-8766
Web: www.pcusa.org/financialaid

Presbyterian Appalachian Scholarship

Type of award: Scholarship, renewable.
Intended use: For full-time undergraduate study at postsecondary institution in United States.
Eligibility: Applicant must be Presbyterian. Applicant must be U.S. citizen or permanent resident.
Basis for selection: Applicant must demonstrate financial need and high academic achievement.
Application requirements: Transcript, proof of eligibility.
Additional information: Must be member of Presbyterian Church (USA) and reside in Appalachian region. Nontraditional-age students with no previous college experience encouraged to apply. Must be high school graduate or GED recipient. Previous recipients must reapply for renewal.

Amount of award:	$100-$1,000
Number of awards:	148
Application deadline:	July 1
Notification begins:	August 7

Contact:
Presbyterian Church (USA)
Financial Aid for Studies
100 Witherspoon Street, M067
Louisville, KY 40202-1396
Phone: 888-728-7228 x5745
Fax: 502-569-8766
Web: www.pcusa.org/financialaid

Presbyterian Student Opportunity Scholarship

Type of award: Scholarship.
Intended use: For full-time undergraduate study at accredited 2-year or 4-year institution in United States.
Eligibility: Applicant must be Asian American, African American, Mexican American, Hispanic American, Puerto Rican or American Indian. Applicant must be high school senior. Applicant must be Presbyterian. Applicant must be U.S. citizen or permanent resident.

401

Basis for selection: Applicant must demonstrate financial need.
Application requirements: Recommendations, proof of eligibility.
Additional information: Applications available after February 1. Possibility of renewal, however award recipients must reapply annually.

Amount of award:	$100-$1,000
Number of awards:	156
Number of applicants:	365
Application deadline:	May 1
Notification begins:	June 1
Total amount awarded:	$175,000

Contact:
Presbyterian Church (USA)
Financial Aid for Studies
100 Witherspoon Street, M067
Louisville, KY 40202-1396
Phone: 888-728-7228 ext. 5745
Fax: 502-569-8766
Web: www.pcusa.org/financialaid

Samuel Robinson Award

Type of award: Scholarship.
Intended use: For full-time junior or senior study at 4-year institution. Designated institutions: One of 69 colleges related to Presbyterian Church (USA).
Eligibility: Applicant must be Presbyterian. Applicant must be U.S. citizen or permanent resident.
Application requirements: Essay.
Additional information: One time award. Applicant must successfully recite answers of the Westminster Shorter Catechism and write a 2,000-word essay on assigned topic related to the Catechism. Amount of award based on annual funds.

Application deadline:	April 1
Notification begins:	May 15

Contact:
Presbyterian Church (USA)
Financial Aid for Studies
100 Witherspoon Street, M067
Louisville, KY 40202-1396
Phone: 888-728-7228 ext.5745
Fax: 502-569-8766
Web: www.pcusa.org/financialaid

Press Club of Houston Educational Foundation

Press Club of Houston Scholarship

Type of award: Scholarship.
Intended use: For full-time junior or senior study at accredited 4-year institution in United States.
Eligibility: Applicant must be U.S. citizen.
Basis for selection: Major/career interest in journalism or radio/television/film. Applicant must demonstrate financial need and high academic achievement.
Application requirements: Interview, recommendations, transcript. Writing samples, statement from college financial aid office of current financial aid package, statement of parents' annual income.

Additional information: Applicant must be student at college in Greater Houston Area (Harris, Brazoria, Chambers, Fort Bend, Galveston, Liberty, Montgomery, and Waller Counties) or resident of Greater Houston Area attending college anywhere. Applications available after January 1; write to sponsor to request application materials. Total amount available for awards depends on proceeds from annual Gridiron Show.

Amount of award:	$500-$3,000
Application deadline:	April 1

Contact:
Press Club of Houston Educational Foundation
Scholarship Chairman
P.O. Box 541038
Houston, TX 77254-1038
Phone: 713-349-0204
Web: www.houstonpressclub.com

Prevent Blindness America

Prevent Blindness America Investigator Award

Type of award: Scholarship.
Intended use: For undergraduate, master's, doctoral or first professional study. Designated institutions: Colleges and universities in U.S. and Canada.
Basis for selection: Major/career interest in medicine or optometry/ophthalmology.
Application requirements: Research proposal.
Additional information: Clinical research based on the prevention of blindness and the socioeconomic impact of vision-related disease and safety.

Amount of award:	$25,000-$50,000
Application deadline:	March 1
Notification begins:	May 15

Contact:
Prevent Blindness America Investigator Award
500 East Remington Road
Director, Program Services
Schaumburg, IL 60173
Phone: 847-843-2020
Fax: 847-843-8458
Web: www.preventblindness.org

The Princess Grace Foundation USA

Princess Grace Award for Dance

Type of award: Scholarship.
Intended use: For undergraduate or graduate study at accredited 4-year or graduate institution.
Eligibility: Applicant must be U.S. citizen or permanent resident.
Application requirements: Nomination by dean or department head.
Additional information: Dance scholarships are available for dance students who have completed at least one year of professional training, undergraduate, or graduate work at a non-

profit institution. Dance students must be nominated by a dean or department chair. Award amount varies.

Number of awards:	6
Number of applicants:	43
Application deadline:	April 30
Total amount awarded:	$75,000

Contact:
Princess Grace Foundation-USA
150 E. 58th Street
25th Floor
New York, NY 10155
Phone: 212-317-1470
Fax: 212-317-1473
Web: www.pgfusa.com

Princess Grace Award For Film

Type of award: Scholarship.
Intended use: For senior or graduate study at accredited 4-year institution.
Eligibility: Applicant must be U.S. citizen or permanent resident.
Basis for selection: Major/career interest in film/video.
Application requirements: Nomination.
Additional information: Award amount varies. Film scholarships are available to help undergraduate seniors or graduate students produce their thesis projects.

Number of awards:	6
Number of applicants:	36
Application deadline:	June 1
Total amount awarded:	$55,557

Contact:
The Princess Grace Foundation - USA
150 E. 58th Street
25th Floor
New York, NY 10155
Phone: 212-317-1470
Fax: 212-317-1473
Web: www.pgfusa.com

Princess Grace Award For Playwriting

Type of award: Scholarship.
Intended use: For undergraduate study in United States.
Eligibility: Applicant must be U.S. citizen or permanent resident.
Basis for selection: Major/career interest in playwriting/screen writing.
Additional information: The Playwright grant is available directly to an individual through a residency at New Dramatists, Inc. in New York. Playwrights may submit applications independently; they do not have to be nominated. See Website for application.

Amount of award:	$7,500
Number of awards:	1
Number of applicants:	276
Application deadline:	March 31

Contact:
The Princess Grace Foundation- USA
150 E. 58th Street
25th Floor
New York, NY 10155
Phone: 212-317-1470
Fax: 212-317-1473
Web: www.pgfusa.com

Princess Grace Award For Theatre

Type of award: Scholarship.
Intended use: For senior or master's study at accredited 4-year or graduate institution.
Eligibility: Applicant must be U.S. citizen or permanent resident.
Basis for selection: Major/career interest in arts, general.
Application requirements: Nomination.
Additional information: Theater scholarships are awarded to students for their last year (undergraduate or graduate) of professional training in acting, directing, scenic, lighting, sound, and costume design. Award amount varies. Students must be nominated by dean or department chair.

Number of awards:	6
Number of applicants:	52
Application deadline:	March 31
Total amount awarded:	$73,068

Contact:
The Princess Grace Foundation - USA
150 E. 58th Street
25th Floor
New York, NY 10155
Phone: 212-317-1470
Fax: 212-317-1473
Web: www.pgfusa.com

Print and Graphics Scholarship Foundation

PGSF Annual Scholarship Competition

Type of award: Scholarship, renewable.
Intended use: For full-time undergraduate study at 2-year or 4-year institution.
Eligibility: Applicant must be high school senior. Applicant must be U.S. citizen.
Basis for selection: Major/career interest in graphic arts/design; printing or publishing. Applicant must demonstrate high academic achievement.
Application requirements: Recommendations, transcript. Biographical information including extracurricular activities and academic honors. SAT, for high school students. Photocopy of intended course of study.
Additional information: To renew, recipients must maintain 3.0 GPA and continue as a graphic arts or printing technology major. Application deadlines are March 1 for high school seniors and high school graduates not currently attending college, and April 1 for current undergraduate students. Application requirements and criteria may vary by trust fund member institution. Contact sponsor for application or download from Website.

Amount of award:	$1,000-$1,500
Number of awards:	300
Number of applicants:	2,000
Application deadline:	March 1, April 1
Notification begins:	June 30

Contact:
Print and Graphics Scholarship Foundation
200 Deer Run Road
Sewickley, PA 15154
Web: www.pgsf.org

Procter and Gamble Fund

Procter and Gamble Fund Scholarship Competition

Type of award: Scholarship.
Intended use: For full-time undergraduate study at 2-year or 4-year institution in United States.
Eligibility: Applicant or parent must be employed by Procter and Gamble.
Basis for selection: Applicant must demonstrate high academic achievement, depth of character and leadership.
Application requirements: Recommendations, transcript, proof of eligibility. Submit SRP profile.
Additional information: Applicant's parent must be Procter & Gamble employee. Parents may obtain application for their child(ren) from their office. 25% of applicants are awarded scholarships.

Amount of award:	$2,500
Number of awards:	141
Number of applicants:	565
Application deadline:	January 15
Notification begins:	April 15
Total amount awarded:	$352,500

Contact:
Procter and Gamble Fund Scholarship Competition
P.O. Box 599
Cincinnati, OH 45201-0599
Phone: 513-983-2139
Fax: 513-983-2173

Professional Association of Georgia Educators Foundation, Inc.

PAGE Foundation Scholarships

Type of award: Scholarship.
Intended use: For junior, senior or post-bachelor's certificate study at accredited postsecondary institution in United States.
Eligibility: Applicant or parent must be member/participant of Professional Association of GA Educators /Student Professional Association of GA Educators. Applicant must be U.S. citizen or permanent resident residing in Georgia.
Basis for selection: Major/career interest in education. Applicant must demonstrate high academic achievement and service orientation.
Application requirements: Recommendations, essay, transcript. Application. Minimum 3.0 GPA.
Additional information: Must be PAGE, SPAGE member. Intended for future teachers and certified teachers seeking advanced degrees. Must agree to teach in Georgia for three years. Applications available from September to April, and due in April. Scholarships awarded in July. Visit Website for additional information, deadlines, and application procedures.

Amount of award:	$1,000
Number of awards:	15
Number of applicants:	100
Application deadline:	April 30
Total amount awarded:	$15,000

Contact:
PAGE Foundation
P.O. Box 942270
Atlanta, GA 31141-2270
Phone: 800-334-6861
Fax: 770-216-9672
Web: www.pagefoundation.org

Professional Grounds Management Society

Anne Seaman Memorial Scholarship

Type of award: Scholarship.
Intended use: For undergraduate or graduate study at postsecondary institution.
Basis for selection: Major/career interest in horticulture.
Application requirements: Recommendations, transcript, proof of eligibility. Cover letter, resume, and application.
Additional information: Additional fields of study: Plant nursery, arboriculture, turf care and grounds management. Applications accepted April through June. Applicants must be sponsored by PGMS members or not eligible to apply.

Amount of award:	$500-$1,500
Number of awards:	3
Number of applicants:	100
Application deadline:	July 2
Notification begins:	October 1
Total amount awarded:	$3,000

Contact:
Professional Grounds Management Society
720 Light Street
Baltimore, MD 21230
Phone: 410-223-2861
Fax: 410-752-8295
Web: www.pgms.org

Puerto Rico Department of Education

Puerto Rico Robert C. Byrd Honors Scholarship

Type of award: Scholarship, renewable.
Intended use: For full-time undergraduate study in United States.
Eligibility: Applicant must be high school senior. Applicant must be U.S. citizen residing in Puerto Rico.
Basis for selection: Applicant must demonstrate high academic achievement and leadership.
Application requirements: Interview, recommendations, essay, transcript, proof of eligibility. Show college acceptance.
Additional information: Minimum 3.5 GPA, evidence of leadership, and 3,000 points of PEAU. Candidates selected by local committee from local Puerto Rican school region; interview required. Scholarship offered to students studying in schools in Puerto Rico. Contact high school guidance office for information and application materials.

Amount of award:	$1,500
Number of awards:	401
Total amount awarded:	$601,500

Contact:
Eligio Hernandez- Department of Education
Educational Development Office
P.O. Box 190759, Suite 1106
San Juan, PR 00919-0759
Phone: 787-759-2000 ext. 2657, 2655

Quill and Scroll Foundation

Edward J. Nell Memorial Scholarship

Type of award: Scholarship.
Intended use: For full-time freshman study at accredited 2-year or 4-year institution in United States.
Eligibility: Applicant must be high school senior. Applicant must be U.S. citizen.
Basis for selection: Major/career interest in journalism. Applicant must demonstrate seriousness of purpose.
Application requirements: Essay. Statement of intent to major in journalism.
Additional information: Open only to winners of Quill and Scroll Annual National Yearbook Excellence or International Writing/Photo Contests at any time during high school career. Yearbook Excellence deadline is November 1. Writing/Photo deadline is February 5.

Amount of award:	$500-$1,500
Number of applicants:	43

Contact:
Quill and Scroll Foundation
School of Journalism and Mass Communication
312 West Seashore Hall
Iowa City, IA 52242-1401
Web: www.uiowa.edu/~quill-sc

Radio and Television News Directors Foundation

Carole Simpson Scholarship

Type of award: Scholarship.
Intended use: For full-time sophomore, junior or senior study at 4-year or graduate institution.
Eligibility: Preference given to undergraduate minority students.
Basis for selection: Major/career interest in journalism; radio/ television/film or communications. Applicant must demonstrate depth of character and seriousness of purpose.
Application requirements: Recommendations, essay, proof of eligibility. Audio or video tape of one to three work samples, maximum 15 minutes, with accompanying scripts. Statement explaining reasons for seeking career in broadcast or cable journalism, and specific career preferences of radio or television, reporting, producing, or news management. Dean or faculty sponsor letter of reference certifying eligibilty.
Additional information: Must have at least one full year of school remaining. Application must be postmarked by May 10.

Previous Radio and Television News Directors Foundation scholarship or internship winners not eligible.

Amount of award:	$2,000
Number of awards:	1
Number of applicants:	20
Application deadline:	May 10
Notification begins:	July 1

Contact:
Radio and Television News Directors Foundation
1600 K Street NW
Suite 700
Washington, DC 20036
Phone: 202-467-5218
Web: www.rtndf.org

Ed Bradley Scholarship

Type of award: Scholarship.
Intended use: For full-time sophomore, junior, senior or graduate study at 4-year or graduate institution.
Eligibility: Priority given to minority undergraduate students.
Basis for selection: Major/career interest in journalism; radio/ television/film or communications. Applicant must demonstrate seriousness of purpose.
Application requirements: Recommendations, essay, proof of eligibility. Audio or video tape of one to three work samples, maximum length 15 minutes total, with accompanying scripts. Essay explaining reasons for seeking a career in broadcast or cable journalism, and specific career preferences of radio or television, reporting, producing, or news management. Dean or faculty sponsor endorsement letter certifying eligibility.
Additional information: Must have at least one full year of school remaining. Application must be postmarked by May 10th. Previous Radio and Television News Directors Foundation scholarship or internship winners not eligible. Preference given to minority undergraduates.

Amount of award:	$10,000
Number of awards:	1
Application deadline:	May 10
Notification begins:	July 1
Total amount awarded:	$10,000

Contact:
Radio and Television News Directors Foundation
1600 K Street NW
Suite 700
Washington, DC 20006
Phone: 202-467-5218
Web: www.rtndf.org

The George Foreman Tribute to Lyndon B. Johnson Scholarship

Type of award: Scholarship.
Intended use: For full-time sophomore, junior or senior study at 4-year institution in United States. Designated institutions: University of Texas at Austin.
Eligibility: Applicant must be U.S. citizen or permanent resident residing in Texas.
Basis for selection: Major/career interest in journalism.
Additional information: This award was developed by George Foreman, television commentator and former heavyweight champion, for a broadcast journalism student at the University of Texas-Austin. Application must be postmarked by May 10th. For more information and application requirements, visit Website.

Amount of award: $6,000
Number of awards: 1
Application deadline: May 10
Notification begins: June 8
Contact:
Radio and Television News Directors Foundation
1600 K St., NW Suite 700
Washington, DC 20006
Phone: 202-659-6510
Fax: 202-223-4007
Web: www.rtnda.org

Ken Kashiwahara Scholarship

Type of award: Scholarship.
Intended use: For full-time sophomore, junior or senior study at postsecondary institution in United States.
Eligibility: Applicant must be Alaskan native, Asian American, African American, Mexican American, Hispanic American, Puerto Rican or American Indian. Applicant must be U.S. citizen or permanent resident.
Basis for selection: Major/career interest in journalism.
Application requirements: Recommendations, essay. Resume, taped examples of work.
Additional information: Applicant must be in good standing to be eligible for this award. Preference is given to an undergraduate student of color. Award is for students majoring in broadcast and electronic journalism. Application must be postmarked by May 10.
Amount of award: $2,500
Number of awards: 1
Number of applicants: 150
Application deadline: May 10
Notification begins: July 1
Total amount awarded: $2,500
Contact:
Radio and Television News Directors Foundation
1600 K Street NW
Suite 700
Washington, DC 20006
Phone: 202-659-6510
Fax: 202-223-4007
Web: www.rtnda.org

Lou and Carole Prato Sports Reporting Scholarship

Type of award: Scholarship.
Intended use: For full-time sophomore, junior or senior study.
Basis for selection: Major/career interest in radio/television/ film.
Application requirements: Portfolio, recommendations, essay, proof of eligibility. Resume. One to three examples (audio or video cassettes) showing journalistic skills, accompanied by script.
Additional information: Award is for student planning a career as a sports reporter in television or radio. Applicant must have one or more years of school remaining and can be enrolled in any major as long as career intent is radio or television news. Applications must be postmarked by May 10. Visit Website for more information.
Number of awards: 1
Application deadline: May 10
Total amount awarded: $1,000

Contact:
RTNDF Scholarships
1600 K Street
Suite 700
Washington, DC 20006
Phone: 202-467-5218
Web: www.rtndf.org

Mike Reynolds Scholarship

Type of award: Scholarship.
Intended use: For full-time sophomore, junior or senior study in United States.
Basis for selection: Major/career interest in communications; film/video or journalism. Applicant must demonstrate financial need.
Application requirements: Portfolio, recommendations, essay, proof of eligibility. Resume. One to three examples (audio or video cassettes) showing journalistic skills, accompanied by script.
Additional information: Preference given to undergraduate student demonstrating need for financial assistance. Applicant should indicate media-related jobs held and contribution made to funding of education. Applicant must have one or more years of school remaining. Visit Website for more information. Applications must be postmarked by May 10th.
Application deadline: May 10
Total amount awarded: $1,000
Contact:
RTNDF Scholarships
1600 K Street NW
Suite 700
Washington, DC 20006
Phone: 202-467-5218
Web: www.rtndf.org

Presidents' $2,500 Scholarships

Type of award: Scholarship.
Intended use: For full-time sophomore, junior or senior study at 2-year or 4-year institution.
Basis for selection: Major/career interest in journalism; communications or radio/television/film. Applicant must demonstrate high academic achievement and seriousness of purpose.
Application requirements: Recommendations, essay. One to three samples showing reporting or producing skills on audio or video tape, accompanied by scripts. Letter of endorsement from dean or faculty adviser certifying proof of eligibility.
Additional information: Previous winners not eligible. Must have at least one full year of school remaining. Application must be postmarked by May 3rd. Applicant may be enrolled in any major so long as career intent is television or radio news.
Amount of award: $2,500
Number of awards: 2
Number of applicants: 100
Application deadline: May 10
Notification begins: June 8
Total amount awarded: $9,000
Contact:
Radio and Television News Directors Foundation
RTNDF Scholarships
1000 Connecticut Avenue, NW Suite 615
Washington, DC 20036
Phone: 202-467-5218
Web: www.rtndf.org

Rainbow Unity Foundation

Rainbow Unity Memorial Scholarship

Type of award: Scholarship, renewable.
Intended use: For undergraduate study at postsecondary institution.
Eligibility: Applicant must be U.S. citizen residing in Iowa.
Basis for selection: Applicant must demonstrate financial need and high academic achievement.
Application requirements: Recommendations, essay, transcript, proof of eligibility. Three sealed letters of recommendation that contain applicant's full name. Copy of current driver's license or ID.
Additional information: Aplicant must self-identify as gay, lesbian, bisexual or transgendered. Must maintain 3.0 GPA. Visit Website to download application form.

Amount of award:	$1,000
Application deadline:	August 1

Contact:
Rainbow Unity Foundation
Rainbow Unity Memorial Scholarship
P.O. Box 241733
Omaha, NE 68124-1733
Web: www.rainbowunity.org

Real Estate Educators Association

Harwood Memorial Scholarship

Type of award: Scholarship, renewable.
Intended use: For full-time undergraduate study in United States.
Eligibility: Applicant must be U.S. citizen.
Basis for selection: Major/career interest in real estate.
Application requirements: Recommendations, transcript. Recommendations must come from REEA member.
Additional information: Must have Real Estate Educators Association member on campus. Must have completed two semesters of college work and be currently enrolled in undergraduate program specializing in real estate. Minimum 3.2 GPA. Number of awards vary.

Amount of award:	$250-$500
Application deadline:	January 31

Contact:
Real Estate Educators Association
407 Wekiva Springs Road
Suite 241
Longwood, FL 32779

Recording for the Blind and Dyslexic

Marion Huber Learning Through Listening Award

Type of award: Scholarship.
Intended use: For undergraduate study.
Eligibility: Applicant or parent must be member/participant of Recording for the Blind & Dyslexic. Applicant must be learning disabled. Applicant must be high school senior.
Basis for selection: Applicant must demonstrate high academic achievement, leadership and service orientation.
Application requirements: Essay, transcript. Must obtain two teacher/school administrator referrals. Applicant must be enterprising.
Additional information: Must be a registered member of Recording for the Blind and Dyslexic for at least one year prior to the application deadline. Must have 3.0 GPA or better in grades 10-12.

Amount of award:	$2,000-$6,000
Number of awards:	6
Number of applicants:	200
Application deadline:	February 21
Total amount awarded:	$24,000

Contact:
Recording for the Blind & Dyslexic
c/o Public Affairs Office
20 Roszel Road
Princeton, NJ 08540
Phone: 609-520-8044
Web: www.rfbd.org

Mary P. Oenslager Scholastic Achievement Award

Type of award: Scholarship.
Intended use: For undergraduate study.
Eligibility: Applicant or parent must be member/participant of Recording for the Blind & Dyslexic. Applicant must be visually impaired.
Basis for selection: Applicant must demonstrate high academic achievement, leadership, or service orientation. Applicant must demonstrate high academic achievement, leadership and service orientation.
Application requirements: Essay, transcript. Two professors/college administrators report forms must be completed.
Additional information: Applicant must be legally blind and must receive a bachelor's degree from an accredited four-year college or university in the U.S. or its territories during the current year. Must have minimum 3.0 GPA on 4.0 scale (or equivalent if based on a different grading system). Must be a registered member of Recording for the Blind and Dyslexic for at least one year prior to application deadline. Continuing education beyond a bachelor's degree is not required.

Amount of award:	$1,000-$6,000
Number of awards:	9
Number of applicants:	50
Application deadline:	February 21
Notification begins:	May 31
Total amount awarded:	$30,000

Contact:
Recording for the Blind & Dyslexic
c/o Public Affairs Office
20 Roszel Road
Princeton, NJ 08540
Phone: 609-520-8095
Web: www.rfbd.org

Red River Valley Association

Red River Valley Fighter Pilots Association (RRVA) Scholarship Program

Type of award: Scholarship, renewable.
Intended use: For undergraduate or graduate study at accredited 2-year, 4-year or graduate institution in United States.
Eligibility: Applicant must be U.S. citizen. Applicant must be dependent of deceased veteran or POW/MIA; or spouse of deceased veteran or POW/MIA. Must be spouse or child of member of any branch of the U.S. Armed Forces listed as KIA or MIA since August 1964. Immediate dependents of military aircrew members killed in non-combat missions and dependents of current or deceased RRVA members in good standing also eligible.
Basis for selection: Applicant must demonstrate financial need.
Application requirements: Transcript, proof of eligibility.
Additional information: Award funds sent directly to school to be used for tuition, books and other academic expenditures, including room and board for full-time students. See Website for application and more information.

Amount of award:	$500-$3,500
Number of awards:	32
Number of applicants:	42
Application deadline:	May 15
Total amount awarded:	$57,000

Contact:
Red River Valley Association
P.O. Box 1916
Harrisonburg, VA 22801
Phone: 540-442-7782
Fax: 540-433-3105
Web: www.river-rats.org

Reserve Officers Association

Henry J. Reilly Memorial College Scholarship

Type of award: Scholarship, renewable.
Intended use: For full-time undergraduate study at accredited 4-year institution in United States.
Eligibility: Applicant or parent must be member/participant of Reserve Officers Association or ROAL. Applicant must be U.S. citizen.

Basis for selection: Applicant must demonstrate high academic achievement, depth of character, leadership and seriousness of purpose.
Application requirements: Essay, transcript, proof of eligibility. Must have registered for the draft, if eligible.
Additional information: Applicant, parent, or grandparent must be member of either Reserve Officers Association or ROAL. Designated for study at regionally accredited institution. Must meet minimum SAT/ACT score requirements. Minimum 3.0 GPA. Application deadline end of April. Visit Website for more information.

Amount of award:	$500
Notification begins:	June 15

Contact:
Reserve Officers Association
Ms. Mickey Hagen
One Constitution Avenue, NE
Washington, DC 20002-5655
Phone: 800-809-9448; 202-479-2200
Fax: 202-646-7762
Web: www.roa.org

Rhode Island Higher Education Assistance Authority

College Bound Fund Academic Promise Scholarship

Type of award: Scholarship, renewable.
Intended use: For full-time undergraduate study at 2-year or 4-year institution. Designated institutions: Rhode Island institutions.
Eligibility: Applicant must be U.S. citizen or permanent resident residing in Rhode Island.
Basis for selection: Applicant must demonstrate financial need and high academic achievement.
Application requirements: FAFSA. SAT or ACT.
Additional information: Applicant must be a Rhode Island resident. Initial eligibility based on SAT/ACT scores and expected family contribution; renewal subject to maintenance of specified GPA yearly. Award must be used at Title IV eligible institutions.

Amount of award:	$2,500
Number of awards:	100
Number of applicants:	1,080
Application deadline:	March 1
Total amount awarded:	$250,000

Contact:
Rhode Island Higher Education Assistance Authority
560 Jefferson Blvd.
Warwick, RI 02886
Phone: 401-736-1100
Fax: 401-732-3541
Web: www.riheaa.org

Rhode Island State Grant

Type of award: Scholarship, renewable.
Intended use: For undergraduate study at accredited vocational, 2-year or 4-year institution in or outside United States or Canada. Designated institutions: Accredited schools in U.S., Canada or Mexico.

Eligibility: Applicant must be U.S. citizen or permanent resident residing in Rhode Island.
Basis for selection: Applicant must demonstrate financial need.
Application requirements: FAFSA. Must meet all Title IV eligibility requirements.

Amount of award:	$300-$1,400
Number of awards:	11,500
Number of applicants:	38,000
Application deadline:	March 1
Total amount awarded:	$13,309,302

Contact:
Rhode Island Higher Education Assistance Authority
560 Jefferson Boulevard
Warwick, RI 02886
Phone: 401-736-1100
Fax: 401-736-1178
Web: grants@riheaa.org

Richard F. Walsh/Alfred W. Di Tolla/Harold P. Spivak Foundation

Richard F. Walsh/Alfred W. Di Tolla/Harold P. Spivak Scholarship

Type of award: Scholarship, renewable.
Intended use: For full-time undergraduate study at accredited 4-year institution.
Eligibility: Applicant or parent must be employed by International Alliance of Theatrical Stage Employees. Applicant must be high school senior.
Basis for selection: Applicant must demonstrate high academic achievement.
Application requirements: Recommendations, transcript. SAT, College Entrance Examination, or results of equivalent examination.
Additional information: Must be son or daughter of member in good standing of the International Alliance of Theatrical Stage Employees. Renewable throughout undergraduate studies.

Amount of award:	$1,750
Number of awards:	2
Application deadline:	December 31
Notification begins:	May 1
Total amount awarded:	$3,500

Contact:
Richard F. Walsh/Alfred W. Di Tolla /Harold P. Spivak
Foundation
1430 Broadway
20th Floor
New York, NY 10018
Phone: 212-730-1770

Rocky Mountain Coal Mining Institute

Rocky Mountain Coal Mining Scholarship

Type of award: Scholarship, renewable.
Intended use: For full-time junior or senior study in United States. Designated institutions: Mining schools approved by Rocky Mountain Coal Mining Institute.
Eligibility: Applicant must be U.S. citizen residing in Utah, Texas, Arizona, Wyoming, Montana, New Mexico, Colorado or North Dakota.
Basis for selection: Major/career interest in engineering; engineering, mining or geology/earth sciences. Applicant must demonstrate high academic achievement.
Application requirements: Interview, recommendations.
Additional information: Applicant must be a full-time college sophomore or junior to apply. Must have interest in western coal mining as possible career. Recommended GPA of 3.0 or above. One new award made per Rocky Mountain Coal Mining Institute member state per year. Can be renewed as senior or post-grad. Money paid directly to school as tuition reimbursement. Applications available after September 1.

Amount of award:	$2,000
Number of awards:	16
Number of applicants:	30
Application deadline:	February 1
Notification begins:	March 1
Total amount awarded:	$32,000

Contact:
Rocky Mountain Coal Mining Institute
8057 S. Yukon Way
Littletown, CO 80128-5510
Phone: 303-948-3300
Fax: 303-948-1132
Web: www.rmcmi.org

Roger Von Amelunxen Foundation

Roger Von Amelunxen Scholarship

Type of award: Scholarship, renewable.
Intended use: For full-time undergraduate study.
Eligibility: Applicant or parent must be employed by U.S. Customs.
Basis for selection: Applicant must demonstrate high academic achievement, depth of character, leadership, seriousness of purpose and service orientation.
Application requirements: Recommendations, transcript.
Additional information: Number and amount of awards vary. Scholarship available only to children of U.S. Customs employees.

Amount of award:	$1,000-$4,000
Application deadline:	August 1
Notification begins:	August 31

Contact:
Roger Von Amelunxen Foundation
8321 Edgerton Boulevard
Jamaica, NY 11432
Phone: 718-641-4800

Ronald McDonald House Charities

African American Future Achievers Scholarship Program

Type of award: Scholarship.
Intended use: For full-time undergraduate study at accredited 2-year or 4-year institution.
Eligibility: Applicant must be African American. Applicant must have at least one parent of African American heritage. Applicant must be high school senior.
Basis for selection: Applicant must demonstrate leadership and service orientation.
Application requirements: Recommendations, essay, transcript, proof of eligibility. Application. High school transcript must contain class rank and SAT/ACT test scores. Personal statement, not to exceed two pages, must provide information about applicant's African American background, community involvement, career goals, and desire to contribute to community. Unique personal or financial circumstances may be added. One-page letter of recommendation from teacher or school official should detail applicant's background, achievements, leadership abilities and community involvement. Should be personalized, not a form letter.
Additional information: Applicant must reside within geographic boundaries of participating program. Geographic areas are listed on Website. Most local chapters of RMHC award students a minimum of $1,000; amounts may vary in some program areas. Students should contact their local RMHC chapter for further details. See Website for contact information and application.

Amount of award:	$1,000
Application deadline:	February 1

Contact:
RMHC/Future Achievers Scholarship Program
Scholarship Program Administrators
P.O. Box 22376
Nashville, TN 37202
Phone: 630-623-7048
Web: www.rmhc.org

ASIA (Asian-Pacific Students Increasing Achievement) Scholarship Program

Type of award: Scholarship.
Intended use: For full-time undergraduate study at accredited 2-year or 4-year institution.
Eligibility: Applicant must be Alaskan native or Asian American. Applicant must have at least one parent of Asian-Pacific heritage.
Basis for selection: Applicant must demonstrate leadership and service orientation.
Application requirements: Recommendations, essay, transcript, proof of eligibility. Application. High school transcript must contain class rank and SAT/ACT scores.

Personal statement, not to exceed two pages, must provide information about applicant's Asian-Pacific background, community involvement, career goals, and desire to contribute to community. Unique personal or financial circumstances may be added. One-page letter of recommendation from teacher or school official should detail applicant's background, achievements, leadership abilities and community involvement. Should be personalized, not a form letter.
Additional information: Applicant must reside within geographic boundaries of participating program. Geographic areas are listed on Website. Most local chapters of RMHC award students a minimum of $1,000; amounts may vary in some program areas. Students should contact their local RMHC chapter for further details. See Website for contact information and application.

Amount of award:	$1,000
Application deadline:	February 1

Contact:
RMHC/ASIA Scholarship Program Scholarship Program Administrators
P.O. Box 22376
Nashville, TN 37202
Phone: 630-623-7048
Web: www.rmhc.org

HACER (Hispanic American Commitment to Educational Resources) Scholarship Program

Type of award: Scholarship.
Intended use: For full-time undergraduate study at accredited 2-year or 4-year institution.
Eligibility: Applicant must be Mexican American, Hispanic American or Puerto Rican. Applicant must have at least one parent of Hispanic heritage. Applicant must be high school senior.
Basis for selection: Applicant must demonstrate leadership and service orientation.
Application requirements: Recommendations, essay, transcript, proof of eligibility. Application. High school transcript must contain class rank and SAT/ACT scores. Personal statement, not to exceed two pages, must provide information about applicant's Hispanic background, community involvement, career goals, and desire to contribute to community. Unique personal or financial circumstances may be added. One-page letter of recommendation from teacher or school official should detail applicant's background, achievements, leadership abilities and community involvement. Should be personalized, not a form letter.
Additional information: Applicant must reside within geographic boundaries of participating program. Geographic areas are listed on Website. Most local chapters of RMHC award students a minimum of $1,000; amounts may vary in some program areas. Students should contact their local RMHC chapter for further details. See Website for contact information and application.

Amount of award:	$1,000
Application deadline:	February 1

Contact:
RMHC/HACER Scholarship Program Scholarship Program Administrators
P.O. Box 22376
Nashville, TN 37202
Phone: 630-623-7048
Web: www.rmhc.org

The R.O.S.E. Fund

The R.O.S.E. (Regaining One's Self Esteem) Scholarship

Type of award: Scholarship, renewable.
Intended use: For undergraduate study at accredited 2-year or 4-year institution in United States. Designated institutions: Accredited New England instituitons.
Eligibility: Applicant must be female. Applicant must be U.S. citizen or permanent resident residing in Vermont, New Hampshire, Maine, Massachusetts or Rhode Island.
Basis for selection: Applicant must demonstrate financial need.
Application requirements: Recommendations, essay, transcript, proof of eligibility, nomination by someone other than applicant. One- to two-page typed statement written by nominator. Three letters of recommendation required (two from applicant's teachers and one personal reference, not including applicant's nominator). Copy of high school diploma/GED or transcript. Description of applicant's accomplishments. Copy of FAFSA and tax return.
Additional information: The R.O.S.E. Scholarship acknowledges women who are survivors of violence or abuse. Up to $10,000 for tuition and expenses at any college/university in New England. Preference will be given to students that have completed one year of college. Applicant must show evidence of self-help in financing one's education. Visit Website for details and application.
  Application deadline: June 8
  Total amount awarded: $10,000
Contact:
The R.O.S.E. Fund Scholarship
175 Federal Street
Suite 455
Boston, MA 02110
Phone: 617-482-5400
Fax: 617-482-3443
Web: www.rosefund.org

The Rotary Foundation

Academic-Year Ambassadorial Scholarship

Type of award: Scholarship.
Intended use: For junior, senior or graduate study at postsecondary institution in proposed host country.
Eligibility: Applicant must be international student or citizen of country that has Rotary clubs.
Basis for selection: Competition/talent/interest in Study abroad. Major/career interest in political science/government or foreign languages. Applicant must demonstrate high academic achievement, leadership, seriousness of purpose and service orientation.
Application requirements: Interview, recommendations, essay, transcript, proof of eligibility. Language certification.
Additional information: Deadlines will be set by the local Rotary clubs. Applicant must have interest in international understanding and peace. Scholarship provides funding for one academic year of study in another country. Covers tuition, room and board, round-trip transportation, and one month of language training (if necessary). Must have completed two years of postsecondary work or have appropriate professional experience, and be proficient in the language of the proposed host country. Number of awards varies from year to year. Spouses or dependents of Rotarians ineligible. Visit Website or check with local Rotary Club for more information and scholarship availability.
  Amount of award: $25,000
Contact:
The Rotary Foundation
One Rotary Center
1560 Sherman Avenue
Evanston, IL 60201-3698
Phone: 847-866-3000
Web: www.rotary.org

Cultural Ambassadorial Scholarship

Type of award: Scholarship.
Intended use: For junior, senior, graduate or non-degree study in at designated language institute.
Eligibility: Applicant must be U.S. citizen, international student or citizen of country that has Rotary clubs.
Basis for selection: Competition/talent/interest in study abroad. Major/career interest in foreign languages. Applicant must demonstrate leadership, seriousness of purpose and service orientation.
Application requirements: Interview, recommendations, essay, transcript, proof of eligibility. Language certification.
Additional information: Deadlines will be set by the local Rotary clubs. Scholarship for three or six months of intensive language study in foreign country at designated language institute. Must have completed at least one year of college-level course work of proposed language. Spouses or dependents of Rotarians ineligible. Funding covers tuition, round-trip transportation, and homestay expenses (not to exceed $12,000 for three-month study; $19,000 for six-month study). Applications will be considered for those interested in studying English, French, German, Hebrew, Japanese, Italian, Mandarin Chinese, Polish, Russian, Portuguese, Spanish, Swahili and Swedish. Number of awards varies from year to year. Check with local Rotary Club for more information and scholarship availability.
  Amount of award: $12,000-$19,000
  Number of awards: 150
Contact:
The Rotary Foundation
One Rotary Center
1560 Sherman Avenue
Evanston, IL 60201-3698
Phone: 847-866-3000
Web: www.rotary.org

Multi-Year Ambassadorial Scholarship

Type of award: Scholarship.
Intended use: For junior, senior, master's or doctoral study at postsecondary institution in in proposed host country.
Eligibility: Applicant must be U.S. citizen, international student or citizen of country that has Rotary clubs.
Basis for selection: Competition/talent/interest in study abroad. Applicant must demonstrate leadership, seriousness of purpose and service orientation.
Application requirements: Interview, recommendations, essay, transcript, proof of eligibility. Language certification.

Additional information: Deadlines set by local Rotary Clubs. Provides partial funding for two years of degree-oriented study abroad. Must have completed two years of postsecondary work or have appropriate professional experience and be proficient in the language of the proposed host country. Spouse or dependents of Rotarians ineligible. Check with local Rotary Club for more information and scholarship availability.

Amount of award: $25,000
Contact:
The Rotary Foundation
One Rotary Center
1560 Sherman Avenue
Evanston, IL 60201-3698
Phone: 847-866-3000
Web: www.rotary.org

ROTC/Air Force

ROTC/Air Force Four-Year Scholarship (Types 1, 2 and 7)

Type of award: Scholarship.
Intended use: For freshman study at accredited 4-year institution in United States.
Eligibility: Applicant must be at least 17, no older than 25, high school senior. Applicant must be U.S. citizen.
Basis for selection: Major/career interest in engineering; mathematics; physics; computer/information sciences; meteorology or architecture. Applicant must demonstrate high academic achievement.
Application requirements: Interview, recommendations, transcript.
Additional information: Minimum 3.0 GPA. Minimum test scores: 24 ACT or 1100 SAT. Opportunities available in any major. Applicants must not have been enrolled in college full-time prior to application. Type One provides full tuition, fees and textbook allowance, without restriction. $150 per month stipend during academic year. Type Two provides tuition, fees up to $15,000 per year. $150 per month stipend during academic year. Type Seven scholarships provide tuition and fees at institutions with a tuition of $9,000 or less. $150 per month stipend during academic year. Scholarship board decides which type of scholarship is offered. Scholarship recipients agree to serve four years active duty.

Amount of award: Full tuition
Application deadline: December 1
Contact:
Contact local ROTC recruiter.
Phone: 800-USA-ROTC

ROTC/Air Force Three-Year Scholarship (Types 2 and Targeted)

Type of award: Scholarship.
Intended use: For sophomore study at accredited 4-year institution in United States.
Eligibility: Applicant must be at least 17, no older than 30. Applicant must be U.S. citizen.
Basis for selection: Major/career interest in engineering; mathematics; physics; computer/information sciences or architecture. Applicant must demonstrate high academic achievement.
Application requirements: Interview, recommendations, transcript.

Additional information: Minimum 3.0 GPA. Minimum test scores: 24 ACT or 1100 SAT. Opportunities available in any major. Type two provides tuition, fees allowance up to $15,000 per year. $150-400 per month stipend during academic year. Targeted scholarships provide full tuition and fees at "low cost" school (mostly state institutions). $150-450 per month stipend during academic year. ROTC scholarship board decides which type of scholarship is offered. Tuition cap of $9,000 per year. Recipients agree to serve four years active duty.

Amount of award: Full tuition
Application deadline: December 1
Contact:
HQ/Air Force ROTC/RROO
551 East Maxwell Boulevard
Maxwell AFB, AL 36112
Phone: 866-423-7682

ROTC/United States Army

ROTC/United States Army Four-Year Historically Black College/University Scholarship

Type of award: Scholarship.
Intended use: For freshman study at accredited 4-year institution in United States. Designated institutions: AL A&M, Tuskegee, U of AK-Pine Bluff, Howard, FL A&M, Fort Valley St., Grambling St., Southern U, A&M Coll, Bowie St., Morgan St., Alcorn St., Jackson St., Lincoln U, Elizabeth City St., NC A&T St., St. Augustine's, Central St. (OH), SC St., Prairie View A&M U, Hampton U, Norfolk St., WV St.
Eligibility: Applicant must be at least 17, no older than 25, high school senior. Applicant must be U.S. citizen.
Basis for selection: Applicant must demonstrate high academic achievement and depth of character.
Application requirements: Interview, transcript. Class rank. SAT or ACT score.
Additional information: Minimum SAT score of 920 or ACT score of 19. Minimum college GPA of 2.5 on 4.0 scale. Scholarships are offered at different levels up to $17,000 annually, providing college tuition and educational fees. Same requirements as Army ROTC four-year Scholarship. Limited number of scholarships for attendance at Historically Black College or University. Tax-free substinence allowance ($250/month first year, increasing each year) for up to ten months each year the scholarship is in effect, plus an allowance for books and other educational items. Scholarships do not pay flight fees. To apply, complete item 11 on the first page of the application. You will still be considered for the national four-year scholarship program. First school choice must be one of the schools identified in the list of HBCUs. If first school choice is not one of these schools, application will not be considered for these dedicated HBCU scholarships. Contact local ROTC recruiter for further information.

Total amount awarded: $17,000
Contact:
Army ROTC Scholarship
Fort Monroe
VA 23651-5238
Phone: 800-USA-ROTC

United States Army Four-Year Nursing Scholarship

Type of award: Scholarship.
Intended use: For freshman study at accredited 4-year institution in United States.
Eligibility: Applicant must be at least 17, no older than 25. Applicant must be U.S. citizen.
Basis for selection: Major/career interest in military science or nursing. Applicant must demonstrate high academic achievement and depth of character.
Application requirements: Interview, transcript.
Additional information: Minimum SAT score of 920 or ACT score of 19. Minimum college GPA of 2.5 on 4.0 scale. Scholarships are offered at different levels up to $16,000 annually, providing college tuition and educational fees. All applicants are considered for each level. Designated book allowance. Tax-free subsistence allowance ($250/month first year, increasing each year) for up to ten months each year the scholarship is in effect, plus an allowance for books and other educational items. Scholarships do not pay flight fees. Limited numbers of three- and two-year scholarships are available once a student is on campus. Applicants should check with the Professor of Military Science once they are attending classes. Contact local Army ROTC recruiter. Individuals applying for nurse program scholarships must indicate "JXX" as choice of major in item four of page eight of the four-year scholarship application; item three should include approved institution applicant wishes to attend.
Contact:
Army ROTC Scholarship
Fort Monroe
VA 23651-5238
Phone: 800-USA-ROTC

United States Army Four-Year Scholarship

Type of award: Scholarship.
Intended use: For freshman study at accredited 4-year institution in United States.
Eligibility: Applicant must be at least 17, no older than 26. Applicant must be U.S. citizen.
Basis for selection: Major/career interest in military science. Applicant must demonstrate high academic achievement and depth of character.
Application requirements: Interview, recommendations, transcript. SAT/ACT scores. High school class rank.
Additional information: Tuition waiver up to $17,000 per year, plus tax-free subsistence allowance ($250/month first year, increasing each year) for up to ten months each year the scholarship is in effect, plus an allowance for books and other educational items. Minimum SAT score of 1100 or ACT score of 24. Must have minimum 2.5 GPA on 4.0 scale. Limited numbers of three- and two-year scholarships are available once student is on campus; students should check with professor of Military Science once they are attending classes. Contact local Army ROTC recruiter. Must enlist in Army Reserve or Army National Guard for minimum eight years.
Contact:
Army ROTC Scholarship
Fort Monroe
VA 23651-5238
Phone: 800-USA-ROTC

Royce Builders

RoyceBuilders.com Foundation for Youth Scholarship

Type of award: Scholarship, renewable.
Intended use: For undergraduate study at postsecondary institution.
Eligibility: Applicant must be high school senior. Applicant must be residing in Texas.
Basis for selection: Applicant must demonstrate financial need, high academic achievement and service orientation.
Application requirements: Recommendations, essay, transcript.
Additional information: For students graduating from school districts within the Houston Gulf Coast area.

Amount of award:	$2,500
Number of awards:	56
Application deadline:	April 15
Total amount awarded:	$140,000

Contact:
Royce Builders
Foundation for Youth
7850 North Sam Houston Parkway West
Houston, TX 77064
Phone: 281-569-1109
Web: www.rbffy.com

Sachs Foundation

Sachs Scholarship

Type of award: Scholarship, renewable.
Intended use: For full-time undergraduate study at accredited 2-year or 4-year institution.
Eligibility: Applicant must be African American. Applicant must be high school senior. Applicant must be U.S. citizen or permanent resident residing in Colorado.
Basis for selection: Applicant must demonstrate financial need, high academic achievement, depth of character and leadership.
Application requirements: Interview, recommendations, transcript, proof of eligibility. Financial statement.
Additional information: Must be resident of Colorado for more than five years. Must maintain high academic achievement throughout college for renewal consideration.

Amount of award:	$4,000
Number of applicants:	300
Application deadline:	March 1
Notification begins:	March 15
Total amount awarded:	$1,000,000

Contact:
Sachs Foundation
90 South Cascade Avenue
Suite 1410
Colorado Springs, CO 80903
Phone: 719-633-2353

Screen Actors Guild Foundation

John L. Dales Standard Scholarship

Type of award: Scholarship.
Intended use: For full-time undergraduate or graduate study at accredited 2-year, 4-year or graduate institution in United States.
Eligibility: Applicant or parent must be member/participant of Screen Actor's Guild.
Basis for selection: Applicant must demonstrate financial need.
Application requirements: Recommendations, essay, transcript, proof of eligibility. Most recent federal income tax return and additional financial information. SAT/ACT scores.
Additional information: Must be member of Guild for five years with lifetime earnings of $30,000 or child of ten-year Guild member with lifetime earnings of $60,000. Guild employees, scholarship committee members, Foundation trustees and their relatives are not eligible. Consult office or visit Website for more information.

Amount of award:	$3,000-$5,000
Application deadline:	March 15
Notification begins:	November 1

Contact:
Screen Actors Guild Foundation
John L. Dales Scholarship Fund
5757 Wilshire Boulevard
Los Angeles, CA 90036
Phone: 323-549-6649
Fax: 323-549-6710
Web: www.sagfoundation.org

John L. Dales Transitional Scholarship

Type of award: Scholarship.
Intended use: For full-time undergraduate or graduate study at accredited postsecondary institution in United States.
Eligibility: Applicant or parent must be member/participant of Screen Actor's Guild.
Basis for selection: Applicant must demonstrate financial need.
Application requirements: Recommendations, essay, transcript, proof of eligibility. Most recent federal income tax return and additional financial information. SAT/ACT scores.
Additional information: Must be Guild member for at least ten years and have lifetime earnings of $60,000. Guild employees, scholarship committee members, Foundation board members, their families, relatives or employees not eligible. Not to be used for a theater or related study degree. For those reentering school to make a transition to another field of study. Award based on financial need; amount varies from year to year.

Amount of award:	$3,000-$5,000
Application deadline:	March 15
Notification begins:	November 1

Contact:
Screen Actors Guild Foundation
John L. Dales Scholarship Fund
5757 Wilshire Boulevard
Los Angeles, CA 90036
Phone: 323-549-6649
Fax: 323-549-6710
Web: www.sagfoundation.org

Seabee Memorial Scholarship Association, Inc.

Seabee Memorial Scholarship

Type of award: Scholarship, renewable.
Intended use: For full-time undergraduate study at accredited 4-year institution in United States.
Eligibility: Applicant must be U.S. citizen. Applicant must be descendant of veteran who served in the Navy. Applicant must be a child or grandchild of a Seabee or member of Naval Civil Engineer Corps - deceased, retired, reserve, active or honorably discharged.
Basis for selection: Applicant must demonstrate financial need, depth of character, leadership, patriotism, seriousness of purpose and service orientation.
Application requirements: Essay, transcript, proof of eligibility. Submit completed application form.
Additional information: Download application from Website.

Amount of award:	$1,000-$5,000
Number of applicants:	350
Application deadline:	April 15
Notification begins:	June 15

Contact:
Scholarship Committee
P.O. Box 6574
Silver Spring, MD 20916
Phone: 301-570-2850
Fax: 301-570-2873
Web: www.seabee.org

Seattle Jaycees

Seattle Jaycees Scholarship

Type of award: Scholarship, renewable.
Intended use: For undergraduate or graduate study at accredited postsecondary institution. Designated institutions: Postsecondary institutions in state of Washington.
Basis for selection: Major/career interest in urban planning or social/behavioral sciences. Applicant must demonstrate depth of character and service orientation.
Application requirements: $5 application fee. Transcript. Include resume and proof of community service.
Additional information: Send SASE to receive application; send application fee with completed application. Scholarships granted for exemplary civic involvement, volunteerism and community service.

Amount of award:	$1,000
Number of awards:	20
Number of applicants:	480
Application deadline:	April 1

Contact:
Seattle Jaycees
Scholarship Committee
109 West Mercer Street
Seattle, WA 98119
Phone: 206-286-2014
Fax: 206-286-4459
Web: www.seattlejaycees.org

Second Marine Division Association Memorial Scholarship Fund

Second Marine Division Scholarship

Type of award: Scholarship, renewable.
Intended use: For full-time undergraduate study at accredited vocational, 2-year or 4-year institution.
Eligibility: Applicant must be single. Applicant must be descendant of veteran who served in the Marines. Must be child or grandchild of person who serves or served in the Second Marine Division, U.S. Marine Corps, or a unit attached to the Division.
Basis for selection: Applicant must demonstrate financial need, high academic achievement, depth of character, leadership, patriotism, seriousness of purpose and service orientation.
Application requirements: Recommendations, essay, transcript, proof of eligibility. Must include SASE when requesting application.
Additional information: Annual family income $42,000 or less. Minimum 2.5 GPA. Must reapply for renewal.

Amount of award:	$1,000
Number of awards:	32
Number of applicants:	32
Application deadline:	April 1
Notification begins:	September 30
Total amount awarded:	$32,000

Contact:
Second Marine Division Association Memorial Scholarship Fund
P.O. Box 8180
Camp Lejeune, NC 28547

SEG Foundation

SEG Foundation Scholarship

Type of award: Scholarship, renewable.
Intended use: For undergraduate or graduate study in or outside United States.
Eligibility: Applicant must be high school senior.
Basis for selection: Major/career interest in physics; mathematics or geology/earth sciences. Applicant must demonstrate financial need, high academic achievement and seriousness of purpose.
Application requirements: Recommendations, essay, transcript, proof of eligibility. An applicant in need of financial assistance will also be considered. However, the competence of the student as indicated by the application is given first consideration. Results of aptitude tests, college entrance exams, National Merit Scholarship competition, etc., are not required but should be furnished if taken.
Additional information: Applicant must intend to pursue college course directed toward a career in geophysics. Amount and number of awards vary. Visit Website for more information and to download application.

Amount of award:	$500-$12,000
Number of awards:	115
Application deadline:	March 1
Total amount awarded:	$200,500

Contact:
SEG Foundation
P.O. Box 702740
Tulsa, OK 74170-2740
Phone: 918-497-5538
Fax: 918-497-5560
Web: www.seg.org

Senator George J. Mitchell Scholarship Research Institute

Senator George J. Mitchell Scholarship Fund

Type of award: Scholarship, renewable.
Intended use: For full-time freshman study at accredited 2-year or 4-year institution in United States. Designated institutions: Four-year or two-year accredited Maine college or university.
Eligibility: Applicant must be U.S. citizen residing in Maine.
Basis for selection: Applicant must demonstrate financial need, high academic achievement and service orientation.
Application requirements: Essay, transcript, proof of eligibility. Application form, letter from guidance counselor, SAR, copy of financial aid award from college student plans to attend.
Additional information: One award made to graduating senior from every public high school in Maine. Total scholarship award is $4,000 with students receiving $1,000 in each of their four years of college. Maine residents entering their first year at a college or university are eligible. Those entering two-year degree programs are eligible to apply (award up to $2000).

Amount of award:	$2,000-$4,000
Number of awards:	130
Number of applicants:	1,000
Application deadline:	April 1, May 1
Notification begins:	June 1

Contact:
Senator George J. Mitchell Scholarship Research Institute
22 Monument Square
Suite 200
Portland, ME 04101
Phone: 207-773-7700
Web: www.mitchellinstitute.org

Seneca Nation and BIA

Seneca Nation Higher Education Program

Type of award: Scholarship, renewable.
Intended use: For undergraduate or graduate study at accredited 2-year, 4-year or graduate institution.
Eligibility: Applicant must be American Indian. Must be an enrolled member of Seneca Nation of Indians. Applicant must be U.S. citizen.
Basis for selection: Applicant must demonstrate financial need.
Application requirements: Essay, transcript, proof of eligibility. Tribal enrollment proof, letter of reference from person not a relative.
Additional information: Amount and number of awards vary. Residency requirements: Level 1- New York state residents living on the reservation; Level 2- New York state residents living in New York; Level 3- enrolled members living outside New York. Applicants of any age can apply. Application deadlines: Fall - July 1; Spring - December 1; Summer - May 1. Contact sponsor or see Website for more information.
Contact:
Seneca Nation of Indians
Higher Education Program
P.O. Box 231
Salamanca, NY 14779
Phone: 716-945-1790 ext.3013
Fax: 716-945-7170
Web: www.sni.org

Sertoma International

Sertoma Communicative Disorders Scholarship Program

Type of award: Scholarship.
Intended use: For full-time graduate study. Designated institutions: Must be accredited by ASHA's Council on Academic Accreditation.
Eligibility: Applicant must be U.S. citizen or permanent resident.
Basis for selection: Major/career interest in speech pathology/audiology.
Application requirements: Recommendations, essay, transcript. Verified 3.2 cumulative GPA on all undergraduate and graduate level course work.

Application deadline: March 30

Contact:
Sertoma International
Attn: $2,500 Scholarships
1912 East Meyer Boulevard
Kansas City, MO 64132-1174
Web: www.sertoma.org

Sertoma Scholarships for Hearing-Impaired Students

Type of award: Scholarship, renewable.
Intended use: For full-time undergraduate study at 4-year institution in United States.
Eligibility: Applicant must be hearing impaired. Applicant must be U.S. citizen or permanent resident.
Basis for selection: Applicant must demonstrate high academic achievement, depth of character and seriousness of purpose.
Application requirements: Recommendations, transcript, proof of eligibility. Minimum 3.2 GPA. Application form, statement of purpose, letter of acceptance from college or university, documentation of hearing impairment in form of recent audiogram or signed statement by hearing health professional.
Additional information: Applicant must be deaf or hearing impaired. May reapply for up to four years. Winners notified in June. Visit Website for application and more information.

Amount of award:	$1,000
Number of awards:	25
Application deadline:	May 1
Total amount awarded:	$25,000

Contact:
Sertoma International
Scholarships for Hearing-Impaired Students
1912 East Meyer Boulevard
Kansas City, MO 64132-1174
Web: www.sertoma.org

Sertoma Scholarships for Students Who Are Hearing Impaired

Type of award: Scholarship.
Intended use: For full-time undergraduate study at 4-year institution.
Eligibility: Applicant must be U.S. citizen or permanent resident.
Basis for selection: Applicant must demonstrate high academic achievement.
Application requirements: Recommendations, essay, transcript. Appplicant must have a clinically significant bilateral hearing loss. Recent audiogram or statement from hearing health professional. GPA of 3.2.
Additional information: Associate degrees and degrees from commmunity colleges or vocational programs do not qualify.

Amount of award:	$1,000
Application deadline:	May 1

Contact:
Sertoma International
Attn: $1,000 Scholarships
1912 East Meyer Boulevard
Kansas City, MO 64132-1174
Web: www.sertoma.org

Service Employees International Union, California State Council

Charles Hardy Memorial Scholarship

Type of award: Scholarship, renewable.
Intended use: For full-time freshman study at accredited 4-year institution in United States.
Eligibility: Applicant or parent must be member/participant of Service Employees International Union. Applicant must be high school senior. Applicant must be residing in California.
Application requirements: Recommendations, essay, transcript.
Additional information: Parent must be a member of the Service Employees International Union. Visit Website for application and online test.

Amount of award:	$1,000
Number of awards:	4
Number of applicants:	4
Application deadline:	March 15
Total amount awarded:	$4,000

Contact:
Service Employees International Union, California State Council
1007 7th Street
4th Floor
Sacramento, CA 95814-3407
Phone: 916-442-3838
Fax: 916-442-0976
Web: www.seiu.org

Shoshone Tribe

Shoshone Tribal Scholarship

Type of award: Scholarship, renewable.
Intended use: For undergraduate study at accredited vocational, 2-year or 4-year institution in United States.
Eligibility: Applicant must be American Indian. Must be enrolled member of Eastern Shoshone Tribe.
Basis for selection: Applicant must demonstrate financial need.
Application requirements: Transcript, proof of eligibility.
Additional information: Must first apply for Pell Grant and appropriate campus-based aid. Minimum 2.5 GPA required. Award renewable for maximum ten semesters. Application deadline for summer is April 15.

Amount of award:	$50-$5,000
Number of awards:	90
Number of applicants:	100
Application deadline:	June 1, November 15
Total amount awarded:	$300,000

Contact:
Shoshone Education Program
P.O. Box 628
Fort Washakie, WY 82514
Phone: 307-332-3538, ext. 15

Sid Richardson Memorial Fund

Sid Richardson Scholarship

Type of award: Scholarship, renewable.
Intended use: For full-time undergraduate or graduate study at accredited postsecondary institution.
Basis for selection: Major/career interest in humanities/liberal arts. Applicant must demonstrate financial need and high academic achievement.
Application requirements: Essay, transcript, proof of eligibility. Submit SAT or ACT scores.
Additional information: Those eligible to apply for a Sid Richardson Memorial Fund are direct descendants (children or grandchildren) of persons presently employed (or retired) with a minimum of three years' full-time service for one or more of the following companies: Barbnet Investment Company, Perry R. Bass Inc., Bass Brothers Enterprises Inc., Bass Enterprises Production Company, City Center Development Company, Leapartners, L.P. (dba Sid Richardson Gasoline Company, - Jal), Richardson and Bass Oil Company, Richardson Aviation, Richardson Oils, Inc., Richardson Products II Company, Sid Richardson Carbon Company, Sid Richardson Gasoline Co., Sid Richardson Refining Company, Sid W. Richardson Foundation SRCG Aviation, Inc., or San Jose Cattle Company. Direct requests for applications to Peggy Laskoski, Sid Richardson Memorial Fund, and include name, social security number, place and approximate dates of employment of qualifying employee. Requests by fax welcome.

Amount of award:	$500-$6,000
Number of awards:	52
Number of applicants:	105
Application deadline:	March 31
Total amount awarded:	$181,500

Contact:
Sid Richardson Memorial Fund
309 Main Street
Fort Worth, TX 76102
Phone: 817-336-0494
Fax: 817-332-2176

Siemens Foundation

Siemens Awards for Advanced Placement

Type of award: Scholarship.
Intended use: For full-time freshman study at accredited 4-year institution.
Eligibility: Applicant must be high school freshman, sophomore or junior. Applicant must be U.S. citizen or permanent resident.
Basis for selection: Competition/talent/interest in Academics, based on the highest AP grades of five across seven subjects: Caculus BC, Computer Science AB, Statistics, Chemistry, Biology, Environmental Science and Physics C (Physics C: Mechanics and Physics C: Electricity and Magnetism each count as 1/2). Major/career interest in science, general; engineering; computer/information sciences; mathematics; physics; chemistry or biology. Applicant must demonstrate high academic achievement.

Application requirements: Must take AP exams.
Additional information: Each Fall, the two highest-ranking male and two highest-ranking female students are chosen from each of the six College Board Regions. Thus, four students are chosen from each of the six regions for a total of twenty-four awards of $3,000 each. A top male and top female student will receive an additional award of $5,000. Applicant must be in high school when award is given.

Amount of award:	$3,000-$8,000
Number of awards:	24
Number of applicants:	85,909
Notification begins:	October 19
Total amount awarded:	$82,000

Contact:
Siemens Foundation, Program Associate
11911 Freedom Drive, Suite 300
Reston, VA 20190
Phone: 800-626-9795
Fax: 571-262-5970
Web: www.siemens-foundation.org

Siemens Westinghouse Competition in Math, Science and Technology

Type of award: Scholarship.
Intended use: For full-time undergraduate or graduate study at accredited 4-year or graduate institution.
Eligibility: Applicant must be U.S. citizen or permanent resident.
Basis for selection: Competition/talent/interest in science project, based on competition of science research project displaying originality, creativity, academic rigor, and clarity of expression; comprehensiveness; creativity; experimental work; field knowledge; future work; interpretation; literature review; scientific importance and validity. Major/career interest in biology; chemistry; engineering; environmental science; materials science; mathematics or physics.
Application requirements: Proof of eligibility, research proposal. A 20-page (maximum) research report followed by a poster presentation and oral presentation for regional finalists. Candidate Data Sheet signed by school Principal. Completed Project Advisor or Mentor Comments Form. Applicant must be a high school senior or high school student as part of a two or three member team.
Additional information: The competition is to encourage students to do research. It gives young scientists the opportunity to present their research to leading scientists in their field. If the student is selected as a Regional Finalist, he/she will be awarded an expense paid trip to compete at one of six regional competitions. At a regional event, after presenting a poster, giving an oral presentation, and participating in a question and answer session, the student or team of students will qualify for either a $1,000 or $3,000 scholarship. If the student advances to National Finalist, then the student or team of students will qualify for a $10,000 to $100,000 scholarship. Download application from Website.

Amount of award:	$1,000-$100,000
Number of awards:	60
Number of applicants:	1,142
Application deadline:	October 1
Notification begins:	October 24
Total amount awarded:	$450,000

Contact:
Siemens Westinghouse Competition Program Manager
c/o The College Board
11911 Freedom Drive, Suite 300
Reston, VA 20190
Phone: 800-626-9795
Fax: 703-707-5599
Web: www.collegeboard.com/siemens

Slovak Gymnastic Union Sokol, USA

Milan Getting Scholarship

Type of award: Scholarship, renewable.
Intended use: For full-time undergraduate study at accredited 4-year institution.
Eligibility: Applicant or parent must be member/participant of Slovak Gymnastic Union Sokol, USA. Applicant must be high school junior or senior. Applicant must be U.S. citizen.
Basis for selection: Applicant must demonstrate high academic achievement, depth of character, leadership, patriotism and seriousness of purpose.
Application requirements: Recommendations, transcript. Write sponsor for application form.
Additional information: Applicant must be member of Slovak Gymnastic Union Sokol, USA, in good standing for at least three years. Recipient must attend four-year college or university. Minimum scholastic average of C+ or equivalent required. Recipients chosen on the basis of scholastic merit, leadership and character. Award renewable for four years. Number of awards varies.

Amount of award:	$500
Number of awards:	4
Application deadline:	April 1

Contact:
Slovak Gymnastic Union Sokol, USA
P.O. Box 189
East Orange, NJ 07019
Phone: 973-676-0280

Slovenian Women's Union of America

Slovenian Women's Union Scholarship

Type of award: Scholarship.
Intended use: For full-time freshman study at accredited 2-year or 4-year institution in United States.
Eligibility: Applicant or parent must be member/participant of Slovenian Women's Union of America. Applicant must be high school senior.
Basis for selection: Applicant must demonstrate financial need, high academic achievement, depth of character, leadership and service orientation.
Application requirements: Recommendations, transcript. Include resume and/or personal statement/autobiography.
Additional information: Applicant must be member of Slovenian Women's Union or active participant of

organization's activities for three years. Open to women and men with interest in promoting Slovene culture. Contact Mary Turvey for more information.

Amount of award:	$1,000
Number of awards:	5
Number of applicants:	7
Application deadline:	March 1
Total amount awarded:	$5,000

Contact:
Slovenian Women's Union of America
Scholarship Director
52 Oakridge Drive
Marguette, MI 49855
Phone: 906-249-4288
Web: http://members.aol.com/sherryew/swu/swuscholarship.html

Slovenian Women's Union Scholarship For Returning Adults

Type of award: Scholarship.
Intended use: For undergraduate certificate or non-degree study at 2-year or 4-year institution in United States.
Eligibility: Applicant or parent must be member/participant of Slovenian Women's Union of America. Applicant must be returning adult student.
Basis for selection: Applicant must demonstrate financial need, high academic achievement, depth of character, leadership and service orientation.
Application requirements: Resume and/or personal statement/autobiography.
Additional information: Applicant must be member of Slovenian Women's Union or active participant of organization's activities for the three years. Open to men and women with interest in promoting Slovene culture. Contact Mary Turvey for more information.

Amount of award:	$500
Number of awards:	2
Application deadline:	March 1
Total amount awarded:	$1,000

Contact:
Slovenian Women's Union of America
Scholarship Director
52 Oakridge Dr.
Marquette, MI 49855
Phone: 906-249-4288
Web: http://members.aol.com/sherryew/swu/swuscholarship.html

Sociedad Honoraria Hispanica

Joseph S. Adams Scholarship

Type of award: Scholarship.
Intended use: For full-time freshman study in United States.
Eligibility: Applicant or parent must be member/participant of Sociedad Honoraria Hispanica. Applicant must be high school senior.
Basis for selection: Major/career interest in Latin american studies or foreign languages. Applicant must demonstrate high academic achievement, depth of character, leadership, patriotism, seriousness of purpose and service orientation.
Application requirements: Recommendations, essay, transcript, proof of eligibility, nomination by local high school chapter sponsor. Must be presently enrolled in high school

Spanish or Portuguese class. SHH members should contact their sponsor not the national director regarding application.
Additional information: Applicant must be active senior member of the honor society. All majors eligible; strong interest in Latin American Studies, Spanish, Portuguese preferred. Contact high school sponsor of Sociedad Honoraria Hispanica for official application before December 31. One member per chapter may apply; scholarship is not renewable.

Amount of award:	$1,000-$2,000
Number of awards:	44
Number of applicants:	200
Application deadline:	February 15
Notification begins:	April 15
Total amount awarded:	$52,000

Contact:
Contact high school sponsor of Sociedad Honoraria Hispanica
Phone: 847-550-0455
Fax: 847-550-0460
Web: www.sociedadhonorariahispanica.org

Society For Range Management

Masonic Range Science Scholarship

Type of award: Scholarship.
Intended use: For full-time freshman or sophomore study.
Eligibility: Applicant must be high school senior.
Basis for selection: Major/career interest in range science. Applicant must demonstrate high academic achievement and leadership.
Application requirements: Recommendations, essay, transcript, nomination by SRM, NACD or SWCS member. Application, SAT/ACT scores, two reference letters.
Additional information: Award amount may vary. Given to high school senior or college freshman or sophomore who is planning to major in or is majoring in range science at a college or university with range science program. Maximum of eight semesters. Student must maintain 2.5 GPA first two semesters; 3.0 GPA any subsequent semester. Visit Website for more information and to download application. Applications should be mailed to: Paul Loeffler, Texas General Land Office, 710 E. Holland, Suite 3, Alpine, TX 79830.

Amount of award:	$1,000-$8,000
Number of awards:	1
Number of applicants:	145

Contact:
Society for Range Management
445 Union Boulevard, Suite 230
Lakewood, CO 80228-1259
Phone: 303-986-3309
Web: www.rangelands.org

Society for Technical Communication

Society for Technical Communication Scholarship Program

Type of award: Scholarship.
Intended use: For full-time undergraduate or graduate study at accredited 2-year, 4-year or graduate institution.
Basis for selection: Major/career interest in graphic arts/design; communications or computer/information sciences. Applicant must demonstrate high academic achievement.
Application requirements: Recommendations, essay, transcript. Application. Must have at least one year of postsecondary education to be eligible.
Additional information: Two awards for undergraduates, two for graduate students. Applicants must be full-time students, have completed at least one year of postsecondary education, have major/career interest in technical communication and have a potential contribution to the profession. Additional contact: Society for Technical Communication, 901 North Stuart Street, Suite 904, Arlington, VA, 22203-1822. Phone: 703-522-4114. Application deadline mid-February.

Amount of award:	$1,000
Number of awards:	4
Notification begins:	April 15
Total amount awarded:	$4,000

Contact:
Ms. Lenore S. Ridgway
19 Johnston Avenue
Kingston, NY 12401-5211
Phone: 845-339-4927
Web: www.stc.org

Society of Actuaries/ Casualty Actuarial Society

Joint CAS/SOA Minority Scholarships for Actuarial Students

Type of award: Scholarship.
Intended use: For full-time undergraduate or graduate study at accredited 4-year or graduate institution.
Eligibility: Applicant must be Alaskan native, African American, Mexican American, Hispanic American, Puerto Rican or American Indian. Applicant must be U.S. citizen or permanent resident.
Basis for selection: Major/career interest in insurance/actuarial science or mathematics. Applicant must demonstrate financial need and high academic achievement.
Application requirements: Recommendations, transcript, proof of eligibility, nomination by faculty members or actuarial supervisors. SAT/ACT scores. CSS PROFILE application required. Financial statement and student aid report.
Additional information: Applicant must be admitted to institution offering actuarial science program or courses that will prepare student for actuarial career. Award amount varies. Also awards advanced calculators to recipients. Open to

minority groups that are underrepresented in the actuarial profession.

Application deadline:	April 15
Notification begins:	July 15

Contact:
Society of Actuaries/Casualty Actuarial Society
Minority Scholarship Coordinator
475 North Martingale Road, Suite 600
Schaumburg, IL 60173-2226
Phone: 847-706-3509
Web: www.beanactuary.org

Society of Automotive Engineers

Society of Automotive Engineers (SAE) Engineering Scholarships

Type of award: Scholarship.
Intended use: For full-time freshman study at accredited 4-year institution in United States.
Eligibility: Applicant must be high school senior. Applicant must be U.S. citizen.
Basis for selection: Major/career interest in engineering. Applicant must demonstrate high academic achievement, depth of character and leadership.
Application requirements: $5 application fee. Essay, transcript.
Additional information: Awards vary from $400 to full tuition. Some awards may have additional criteria. Must have 3.0 GPA and rank in 90th percentile on ACT composite or SAT I.

Amount of award:	Full tuition
Number of awards:	53
Application deadline:	December 1
Notification begins:	June 1
Total amount awarded:	$278,000

Contact:
Society of Automotive Engineers
Customer Service
400 Commonwealth Drive
Warrendale, PA 15096-0001
Phone: 724-776-4970 or 877-606-7323
Web: www.sae.org/students/scholarships

Society of Automotive Engineers (SAE) Longterm Member Sponsored Scholarship

Type of award: Scholarship.
Intended use: For full-time senior study at 4-year institution.
Eligibility: Applicant or parent must be member/participant of Society of Automotive Engineers.
Basis for selection: Must demonstrate support for SAE activities and programs. Applicant must demonstrate leadership.
Application requirements: Proof of eligibility.
Additional information: Applicant must be an active SAE student member. Must be junior in college at time of application.

Amount of award:	$1,000
Number of awards:	4
Application deadline:	April 1
Notification begins:	June 1
Total amount awarded:	$4,000

Contact:
Society of Automotive Engineers
Customer Service
400 Commonwealth Drive
Warrendale, PA 15096-0001
Phone: 724-776-4970
Web: www.sae.org/students/scholarships

Society of Automotive Engineers (SAE) Yanmar Scholarship

Type of award: Scholarship, renewable.
Intended use: For full-time senior study at 4-year institution.
Eligibility: Applicant must be U.S. citizen, international student or Canadian citizen or Mexican citizen.
Basis for selection: Major/career interest in engineering. Applicant must demonstrate leadership.
Application requirements: Essay, transcript, proof of eligibility.
Additional information: Must pursue course of study or research related to conservation of energy in transportation, agriculture, construction or power generation. Emphasis is placed on research or study related to internal combustion engine. Must be junior in college at time of application. Citizen of North America.

Amount of award:	$2,000
Number of awards:	1
Application deadline:	April 1
Notification begins:	June 1
Total amount awarded:	$2,000

Contact:
Society of Automotive Engineers
Customer Service
400 Commonwealth Drive
Warrendale, PA 15096-0001
Phone: 724-776-4970
Web: www.sae.org/students/scholarships

Society of Daughters of the United States Army

Society of Daughters of United States Army Scholarship Program

Type of award: Scholarship, renewable.
Intended use: For full-time undergraduate study at accredited postsecondary institution.
Eligibility: Applicant must be female. Applicant must be dependent of veteran or deceased veteran who served in the Army. Applicant must be a daughter or granddaughter only (including step or adopted) of a career warrant (WO 1-5) or commissioned (2nd & 1st LT, CPT, MAJ, LTC, COL, or General) officer of the U.S. Army who: (1) is currently on active duty, or (2) retired from active duty after at least 20 years of service, or (3) was medically retired before 20 years of active service, or (4) died while on active duty, or (5) died after retiring from active duty with 20 or more years of service. U.S. Army must have been the officer's primary occupation.

Basis for selection: Applicant must demonstrate high academic achievement, depth of character, leadership, patriotism and seriousness of purpose.
Additional information: Minimum 3.0 GPA. Scholarhips are awarded for undergraduate study only. Applicant must include name, rank, component (Active, Regular, Reserve) and inclusive dates of active service of parent or grandparent. Number of awards varies annually. Send business-sized SASE and one letter of request only. Do not send birth certificate or original documents. Do not use registered/certified mail. All application submissions become the property of DUSA.

Amount of award:	$1,000
Number of applicants:	600
Application deadline:	March 1
Notification begins:	June 15

Contact:
Society of Daughters of the United States Army
Mary P. Maroney, Chairman
11804 Grey Birch Place
Reston, VA 20191-4223

Society of Exploration Geophysicists

Society of Exploration Geophysicists Scholarship

Type of award: Scholarship, renewable.
Intended use: For full-time undergraduate or graduate study at accredited 4-year or graduate institution in United States.
Eligibility: Applicant must be high school senior.
Basis for selection: Major/career interest in geophysics; geology/earth sciences or physics. Applicant must demonstrate financial need and high academic achievement.
Application requirements: Recommendations, transcript, proof of eligibility.
Additional information: Number of scholarships available yearly depends on the number of sponsors and the amount they contribute. Applicants must intend to pursue career in exploration geophysics (graduate students in operations, teaching, or research). Visit Website for more information.

Number of awards:	118
Application deadline:	March 1
Total amount awarded:	$211,750

Contact:
SEG Foundation
P.O. Box 702740
Tulsa, OK 74137-2740
Web: www.seg.org

Society of Hispanic Professional Engineers Foundation

Hispanic Professional Engineers Educational Grant

Type of award: Scholarship, renewable.

Intended use: For full-time undergraduate or graduate study at 2-year, 4-year or graduate institution.

Basis for selection: Major/career interest in engineering or science, general. Applicant must demonstrate financial need and high academic achievement.

Application requirements: Recommendations, essay. Application.

Additional information: All sciences except medicine eligible. Include SASE with application request, or download application from Website. Amount of award varies. Applications available beginning of September.

Number of awards:	313
Number of applicants:	990
Application deadline:	May 15
Notification begins:	June 15
Total amount awarded:	$250,000

Contact:
Society of Hispanic Professional Engineers Foundation
3900 Whiteside Street
Los Angeles, CA 90063
Web: www.shpefoundation.org

Society of Manufacturing Engineers Education Foundation

Albert E. Wischmeyer Memorial Scholarship Award

Type of award: Scholarship, renewable.

Intended use: For undergraduate study at accredited 4-year institution in United States or Canada. Designated institutions: New York schools with manufacturing engineering, manufacturing engineering technology, or mechanical technology degree program.

Eligibility: Applicant must be high school senior. Applicant must be U.S. citizen or permanent resident residing in New York.

Basis for selection: Major/career interest in manufacturing or engineering. Applicant must demonstrate high academic achievement.

Application requirements: Recommendations, essay, transcript. Student statement. Resume. One copy and five originals of application materials.

Additional information: Applicants must reside in Western New York State (West of Interstate 81). Applicant must be graduating high school seniors or current undergraduate students. Minimum GPA 3.0. Applicants must reapply for renewal. Financial need a consideration only between two otherwise equal applicants. Award amount may increase depending on endowment funds. Application available on Website.

Amount of award:	$1,900
Number of awards:	2
Application deadline:	February 1
Total amount awarded:	$3,800

Contact:
Society of Manufacturing Engineers
Scholarship Review Committee
One SME Drive, P.O. Box 930
Dearborn, MI 48121-0930
Phone: 313-271-1500
Web: www.sme.org/foundation

Arthur and Gladys Cervenka Scholarship

Type of award: Scholarship, renewable.

Intended use: For full-time sophomore, junior or senior study at accredited 4-year institution in United States or Canada. Designated institutions: Schools with manufacturing engineering degree program.

Basis for selection: Major/career interest in manufacturing or engineering. Applicant must demonstrate high academic achievement.

Application requirements: Recommendations, essay, transcript. Student statement. Resume. One original and five copies of application materials. Supply foundation with name of intended college or university.

Additional information: Preference given but not limited to students attending colleges or universities in state of Florida. Applicants must be enrolled in manufacturing engineering or technology degree program and must have completed a minimum of 30 college credit hours. Minimum 3.0 GPA. Applicants must reapply for renewal. Financial need a consideration only between two otherwise equal applicants. Application available on Website.

Amount of award:	$1,250
Number of awards:	1
Application deadline:	February 1
Total amount awarded:	$1,250

Contact:
Society of Manufacturing Engineers
Scholarship Review Committee
One SME Drive, P.O. Box 930
Dearborn, MI 48121-0930
Phone: 313-271-1500
Web: www.sme.org/foundation

Caterpillar Scholars Award

Type of award: Scholarship, renewable.

Intended use: For full-time freshman, sophomore, junior or senior study at 4-year institution in United States or Canada. Designated institutions: Schools with manufacturing engineering degree program.

Basis for selection: Major/career interest in manufacturing or engineering. Applicant must demonstrate high academic achievement.

Application requirements: Recommendations, essay, transcript. Statement letter. Resume. One original and five copies of application materials. Supply foundation with name of intended college or university; freshmen must supply SAT scores.

Additional information: Applicants must be enrolled in manufacturing engineering degree program and must have completed a minimum of 30 college credit hours. Minority applicants may apply as incoming freshmen. Minimum 3.0 GPA. Applicants must reapply for renewal. Summer internships may be offered to select Caterpillar scholars. Financial need a consideration only between two otherwise equal applicants. Application available on Website.

Amount of award:	$2,000
Number of awards:	5
Application deadline:	February 1
Total amount awarded:	$10,000

Contact:
Society of Manufacturing Engineers
Scholarship Review Committee
One SME Drive, P.O. Box 930
Dearborn, MI 48121-0930
Phone: 313-271-1500
Web: www.sme.org/foundation

Chapter 4 Lawrence A. Wacker Memorial Scholarship

Type of award: Scholarship, renewable.
Intended use: For undergraduate study at accredited 4-year institution in United States or Canada. Designated institutions: Wisconsin schools with manufacturing engineering, mechanical engineering, or industrial engineering degree program.
Eligibility: Applicant must be high school senior. Applicant must be U.S. citizen or permanent resident residing in Wisconsin.
Basis for selection: Major/career interest in manufacturing; engineering or engineering, mechanical. Applicant must demonstrate high academic achievement.
Application requirements: Recommendations, essay, transcript. Student statement. Resume. One original and five copies of application materials.
Additional information: Applicants must be seeking a bachelor's degree in manufacturing, mechanical or industrial engineering. Minimum 3.0 GPA. One scholarship granted to graduating high school senior, the other granted to current undergraduate. First preference given to SME Chapter 4 members or spouses, children, or grandchildren of members. Second preference given to residents of Milwaukee, Ozaukee, Washington and Waukesha counties. Third preference given to Wisconsin residents. Applicants must reapply for renewal. Financial need a consideration only between two otherwise equal applicants. Application available on Website.

Amount of award:	$1,500
Number of awards:	2
Application deadline:	February 1
Total amount awarded:	$3,000

Contact:
Society of Manufacturing Engineers
Scholarship Review Committee
One SME Drive, P.O. Box 930
Dearborn, MI 48121-0930
Phone: 313-271-1500
Web: www.sme.org/foundation

Clinton J. Helton Manufacturing Scholarship Award

Type of award: Scholarship.
Intended use: For full-time sophomore, junior or senior study at accredited 4-year institution in United States. Designated institutions: Colorado State University, all University of Colorado campuses.
Eligibility: Applicant must be residing in Colorado.
Basis for selection: Major/career interest in manufacturing or engineering. Applicant must demonstrate high academic achievement and depth of character.
Application requirements: Recommendations, essay, transcript. Student statement. Resume. One original and five

copies of application materials. Supply foundation with name of intended college or university.
Additional information: Applicants must be enrolled in manufacturing engineering or technology degree program and must have completed at least 30 credit hours. Minimum 3.3 GPA. Applicants must reapply for renewal. Financial need a consideration only between two otherwise equal applicants. Application available on Website.

Amount of award:	$3,500
Number of awards:	1
Application deadline:	February 1
Total amount awarded:	$3,500

Contact:
Society of Manufacturing Engineers Education Foundation
Scholarship Review Committee
One SME Drive, P.O. Box 930
Dearborn, MI 48121-0930
Phone: 313-271-1500
Web: www.sme.org/foundation

Community College Scholarship

Type of award: Scholarship, renewable.
Intended use: For full-time freshman or sophomore study at accredited vocational or 2-year institution in United States or Canada. Designated institutions: Community colleges, trade schools, or other two-year-degree-granting institutions with manufacturing or related degree program.
Basis for selection: Major/career interest in manufacturing. Applicant must demonstrate high academic achievement.
Application requirements: Recommendations, essay, transcript. Student statement. Resume. One original and five copies of application materials. Supply foundation with name of intended college or university.
Additional information: Applicants must be enrolled in manufacturing engineering or closely related degree program and must have completed less than 60 college credit hours. Minimum 3.0 GPA. Applicants must reapply for renewal. Financial need a consideration only between two otherwise equal applicants. Application available on Website.

Amount of award:	$1,000
Number of awards:	3
Application deadline:	February 1
Total amount awarded:	$3,000

Contact:
Society of Manufacturing Engineers
Scholarship Review Committee
One SME Drive, P.O. Box 930
Dearborn, MI 48121-0930
Phone: 313-271-1500
Web: www.sme.org/foundation

Connie and Robert T. Gunter Scholarship

Type of award: Scholarship.
Intended use: For full-time sophomore, junior or senior study at accredited 4-year institution in United States. Designated institutions: Georgia Institute of Technology, Georgia Southern College, Southern College of Technology.
Basis for selection: Major/career interest in manufacturing or engineering. Applicant must demonstrate high academic achievement, depth of character and seriousness of purpose.
Application requirements: Recommendations, essay, transcript. Student statement. Resume. One original and five copies of application materials. Supply foundation with name of intended college or university.

Additional information: Applicants must be enrolled in manufacturing engineering degree program and must have completed at least 30 credit hours. Minimum 3.5 GPA. Applicants must reapply for renewal. Financial need a consideration only between two otherwise equal applicants. Application available on Website.

Amount of award:	$1,000
Number of awards:	1
Application deadline:	February 1
Total amount awarded:	$1,000

Contact:
Society of Manufacturing Engineers Education Foundation
Scholarship Review Committee
One SME Drive, P.O. Box 930
Dearborn, MI 48121-0930
Phone: 313-271-1500
Web: www.sme.org/foundation

Detroit Chapter One - Founding Chapter Scholarship Award

Type of award: Scholarship, renewable.
Intended use: For undergraduate or graduate study at accredited 4-year or graduate institution in United States or Canada. Designated institutions: Wayne State University, Lawrence Technological University, University of Detroit Mercy, Focus: HOPE Center for Advanced Technologies, Henry Ford Community College.
Eligibility: Applicant or parent must be member/participant of Society of Manufacturing Engineers.
Basis for selection: Major/career interest in manufacturing or engineering. Applicant must demonstrate high academic achievement, depth of character and leadership.
Application requirements: Recommendations, essay, transcript. Student statement. Resume. Must demonstrate good character and leadership. One original and five copies of application materials. Supply foundation with name of intended college or university.
Additional information: Awarded to one student each at associate, baccalaureate, and graduate levels. Applicants must be enrolled in manufacturing engineering, manufacturing engineering technology or closely related degree or certificate program. Applicants must plan to attend one of the select schools listed, be involved in one of the SME Student Chapters at the select schools listed, and have an overall minimum GPA of 3.0. Applicants must reapply for renewal. Financial need a consideration only between two otherwise equal applicants. Application available on Website.

Amount of award:	$1,000
Number of awards:	3
Application deadline:	February 1
Total amount awarded:	$3,000

Contact:
Society of Manufacturing Engineers Education Foundation
Scholarship Review Committee
One SME Drive, P.O. Box 930
Dearborn, MI 48121-0930
Phone: 313-271-1500
Web: www.sme.org/foundation

Directors Scholarship

Type of award: Scholarship, renewable.
Intended use: For full-time sophomore, junior or senior study at accredited 4-year institution in United States or Canada.

Basis for selection: Major/career interest in manufacturing. Applicant must demonstrate high academic achievement and leadership.
Application requirements: Recommendations, essay, transcript. Student statement. Resume. One original and five copies of application materials. Supply foundation with name of intended college or university.
Additional information: Applicants must have completed a minimum of 30 college credit hours. Minimum 3.5 GPA. Applicants must reapply for renewal. Preference given to students who demonstrate leadership skills in community, academic, or professional environment. Financial need a consideration only between two otherwise equal applicants. Application available on Website.

Amount of award:	$5,000
Number of awards:	1
Application deadline:	February 1
Total amount awarded:	$5,000

Contact:
Society of Manufacturing Engineers
Scholarship Review Committee
One SME Drive, P.O. Box 930
Dearborn, MI 48121-0930
Phone: 313-271-1500
Web: www.sme.org/foundation

Edward S. Roth Manufacturing Engineering

Type of award: Scholarship, renewable.
Intended use: For full-time undergraduate study at accredited 4-year institution in United States. Designated institutions: California Polytechnic State University, California State Polytechnic University, University of Miami, Bradley University, Central State University, Miami University, Boston University, Worcester Polytechnic Institute, University of Massachusetts, St. Cloud State University, The University of Texas - Pan American, Brigham Young University, Utah State University.
Eligibility: Applicant must be Alaskan native, Asian American, African American, Mexican American, Hispanic American, Puerto Rican or American Indian. Applicant must be U.S. citizen.
Basis for selection: Major/career interest in manufacturing or engineering. Applicant must demonstrate financial need, high academic achievement, depth of character and seriousness of purpose.
Application requirements: Recommendations, essay, transcript. Student statement. Resume. One original and five copies of application materials. Supply foundation with name of intended college or university.
Additional information: Applicants must be enrolled in manufacturing engineering degree program. Minimum 3.0 GPA. Preference given to students demonstrating financial need, minority students and students participating in co-op program. Applicants must reapply for renewal. Application available on Website.

Amount of award:	$2,500
Number of awards:	1
Application deadline:	February 1
Total amount awarded:	$2,500

Contact:
Society of Manufacturing Engineers Education Foundation
Scholarship Review Committee
One SME Drive, P.O. Box 930
Dearborn, MI 48121-0930
Phone: 313-271-1500
Web: www.sme.org/foundation

Guiliano Mazzetti Scholarship

Type of award: Scholarship, renewable.
Intended use: For full-time sophomore, junior or senior study at accredited 4-year institution in United States or Canada. Designated institutions: Schools with manufacturing engineering degree program.
Basis for selection: Major/career interest in manufacturing or engineering. Applicant must demonstrate high academic achievement.
Application requirements: Recommendations, essay, transcript. Student statement. Resume. One original and five copics of application materials. Supply foundation with name of intended college or university.
Additional information: Applicants must be enrolled in manufacturing engineering, technology, or closely related field degree program, and must have completed a minimum of 30 college credit hours. Minimum GPA 3.0. Applicants must reapply for renewal. Financial need a consideration only between two otherwise equal applicants. Application available on Website.

Amount of award:	$1,500
Number of awards:	2
Application deadline:	February 1
Total amount awarded:	$3,000

Contact:
Society of Manufacturing Engineers
Scholarship Review Committee
One SME Drive, P.O. Box 930
Dearborn, MI 48121-0930
Phone: 313-271-1500
Web: www.sme.org/foundation

Kalamazoo Chapter 116 - Roscoe Douglas Scholarship Award

Type of award: Scholarship, renewable.
Intended use: For full-time sophomore, junior or senior study at accredited 2-year or 4-year institution in United States. Designated institutions: Glen Oaks Community College, Jackson Community College, Kalamazoo Valley Community College, Kellogg Community College, Southwestern Michigan College, Western Michigan University.
Basis for selection: Major/career interest in manufacturing or engineering. Applicant must demonstrate high academic achievement, depth of character and seriousness of purpose.
Application requirements: Recommendations, essay, transcript. Student statement. Resume. One original and five copies of application materials. Supply foundation with name of intended college or university.
Additional information: Applicants must be enrolled in manufacturing engineering or manufacturing engineering technology degree program and must have completed at least 30 credit hours. Minimum 3.0 GPA. Applicants must reapply for renewal. Financial need a consideration only between two otherwise equal applicants. Application available on Website.

Amount of award:	$1,500
Number of awards:	1
Application deadline:	February 1
Total amount awarded:	$1,500

Contact:
Society of Manufacturing Engineers
Scholarship Review Committee
One SME Drive, P.O. Box 930
Dearborn, MI 48121-0930
Phone: 313-271-1500
Web: www.sme.org/foundation

Lucile B. Kaufman Women's Scholarship

Type of award: Scholarship, renewable.
Intended use: For full-time sophomore, junior or senior study at 4-year institution in United States or Canada. Designated institutions: Schools with manufacturing engineering degree program.
Eligibility: Applicant must be female.
Basis for selection: Major/career interest in manufacturing or engineering. Applicant must demonstrate high academic achievement.
Application requirements: Recommendations, essay, transcript. Statement letter. Resume. One original and five sets of application materials. Supply foundation with name of intended college or university.
Additional information: Applicants must be enrolled in manufacturing engineering or manufacturing engineering technology degree program and must have completed minimum of 30 credits. Minimum 3.5 GPA. Applicants must reapply for renewal. Financial need a consideration only between two otherwise equal applicants. Application available on Website. For additional award opportunities, visit Society of Women Engineers Website at www.swe.org.

Amount of award:	$1,000
Number of awards:	1
Application deadline:	February 1
Total amount awarded:	$1,000

Contact:
Society of Manufacturing Engineers
Scholarship Review Committee
One SME Drive, P.O. Box 930
Dearborn, MI 48121-0930
Phone: 313-271-1500
Web: www.sme.org/foundation

Myrtle and Earl Walker Scholarship

Type of award: Scholarship, renewable.
Intended use: For full-time freshman, sophomore, junior or senior study at accredited 4-year institution in United States or Canada. Designated institutions: Schools with manufacturing engineering degree program.
Basis for selection: Major/career interest in manufacturing or engineering. Applicant must demonstrate high academic achievement.
Application requirements: Recommendations, essay, transcript. Student statement. Resume. One original and five copies of application materials. Supply foundation with name of intended college or university.
Additional information: Applicants must be enrolled in manufacturing engineering degree or technology program and must have completed minimum 15 credits. Minimum 3.5 GPA. Applicants must reapply for renewal. Financial need a

consideration only between two otherwise equal applicants. Application available on Website.

Amount of award:	$1,000
Number of awards:	25
Application deadline:	February 1
Total amount awarded:	$25,000

Contact:
Society of Manufacturing Engineers
Scholarship Review Committee
One SME Drive, P.O. Box 930
Dearborn, MI 48121-0930
Phone: 313-271-1500
Web: www.sme.org/foundation

S-B Power Tool Scholarship Award

Type of award: Scholarship, renewable.
Intended use: For full-time sophomore, junior or senior study at accredited 4-year institution in United States or Canada. Designated institutions: Arkansas, Illinois, and North Carolina schools with manufacturing engineering degree program.
Eligibility: Applicant must be U.S. citizen or permanent resident.
Basis for selection: Major/career interest in manufacturing or engineering. Applicant must demonstrate high academic achievement.
Application requirements: Recommendations, essay, transcript. Student statement. Resume. One original and five copies of application materials. Supply foundation with name of intended college or university.
Additional information: Applicants must be enrolled in manufacturing engineering degree program and must have completed a minimum of 30 college credit hours. Minimum 3.5 GPA. Applicants must reapply for renewal. Financial need a consideration only between two otherwise equal applicants. Application available on Website. Sponsored by S-B Power Tool Company through the SME Education Foundation.

Amount of award:	$1,500
Number of awards:	1
Application deadline:	February 1
Total amount awarded:	$1,500

Contact:
Society of Manufacturing Engineers
Scholarship Review Committee
One SME Drive, P.O. Box 930
Dearborn, MI 48121
Phone: 313-271-1500 ext. 1707 or ext. 1709
Web: www.sme.org/foundation

St. Louis Chapter 17 Scholarship

Type of award: Scholarship.
Intended use: For full-time freshman, sophomore or junior study at accredited 2-year or 4-year institution in United States. Designated institutions: Jefferson College, Mineral Area College, St. Louis Community College at Florissant Valley, University of Missouri, Southeast Missouri State University, Southern Illinois University.
Eligibility: Applicant or parent must be member/participant of Society of Manufacturing Engineers.
Basis for selection: Major/career interest in manufacturing; engineering or engineering, mechanical. Applicant must demonstrate high academic achievement, depth of character and seriousness of purpose.
Application requirements: Recommendations, essay, transcript. Student statement. Resume. One original and five copies of application materials. Supply foundation with name of intended college or university.

Additional information: Applicants must be enrolled in manufacturing engineering or related degree program and be member of SME Chapter 17 student chapter. Sophomores at two-year institutions must be accepted to eligible four-year institution to receive award. Minimum 3.5 GPA at application; 3.0 GPA must be maintained. Applicants must reapply for renewal. Financial need a consideration only between two otherwise equal applicants. Application available on Website.

Amount of award:	$1,000
Number of awards:	4
Application deadline:	February 1
Total amount awarded:	$2,000

Contact:
Society of Manufacturing Engineers
Scholarship Review Committee
One SME Drive, P.O. Box 930
Dearborn, MI 48121-0930
Phone: 313-271-1500
Web: www.sme.org/foundation

Walt Bartram Memorial Education Award (Region 12)

Type of award: Scholarship, renewable.
Intended use: For full-time undergraduate study at accredited 2-year or 4-year institution in United States or Canada. Designated institutions: Schools with manufacturing engineering program within Desert Pacific Region 12 (Arizona, New Mexico, Southern California).
Eligibility: Applicant or parent must be member/participant of Society of Manufacturing Engineers. Applicant must be high school senior. Applicant must be residing in California, New Mexico or Arizona.
Basis for selection: Major/career interest in manufacturing or engineering. Applicant must demonstrate high academic achievement, depth of character and seriousness of purpose.
Application requirements: Recommendations, essay, transcript. Student statement. Resume. One original and five copies of application materials. Supply foundation with name of intended college or university.
Additional information: Applicants must reside within Desert Pacific Region 12, and, unless high school senior, must be member of SME. Applicants must be enrolled in manufacturing engineering or closely related degree program. Minimum 3.5 GPA. Financial need a consideration only between two otherwise equal applicants. Application available on Website.

Amount of award:	$500-$1,200
Number of awards:	1
Application deadline:	February 1
Total amount awarded:	$1,200

Contact:
Society of Manufacturing Engineers
Scholarship Review Committee
One SME Drive, P.O. Box 930
Dearborn, MI 48121-0930
Phone: 313-271-1500
Web: www.sme.org/foundation

Wayne Kay Co-op Scholarship

Type of award: Scholarship, renewable.
Intended use: For full-time sophomore, junior or senior study in United States or Canada.
Basis for selection: Major/career interest in manufacturing or engineering. Applicant must demonstrate high academic achievement.

Application requirements: Recommendations, essay, transcript, proof of eligibility. Supply foundation with name of intended college or university. Two letters of recommendation from employer(s) and letter of support from faculty member at college or university. Must provide evidence of demonstrated excellence that may include a project completed for their employer and must be related to manufacturing engineering or technology.

Additional information: Applicants must be enrolled in manufacturing engineering or technology degree program and working through co-op program in a manufacturing-related environment. Applicants must have completed a minimum of 30 college credit hours. Minimum GPA 3.0. Applicants must reapply for renewal. Financial need a consideration only between two otherwise equal applicants. Application available on Website.

Amount of award:	$2,500
Number of awards:	2
Application deadline:	February 1
Total amount awarded:	$5,000

Contact:
Society of Manufacturing Engineers
Scholarship Review Committee
One SME Drive, P.O. Box 930
Dearborn, MI 48121-0930
Phone: 313-271-1500
Web: www.sme.org/foundation

Wayne Kay High School Scholarship

Type of award: Scholarship, renewable.
Intended use: For full-time freshman study at accredited 4-year institution in United States or Canada. Designated institutions: Schools with manufacturing engineering degree program.
Eligibility: Applicant must be high school senior.
Basis for selection: Major/career interest in manufacturing or engineering. Applicant must demonstrate high academic achievement.
Application requirements: Recommendations, essay, transcript. Student statement. Resume. One original and five copies of application materials. Supply foundation with name of intended college or university.
Additional information: Applicants must be a high school senior committed to enrolling in manufacturing engineering degree or technology program. Minimum 3.0 GPA. Award is $1,000 for first year, renewable for $1,500 for second year based on recipient's academic excellence and career path. Financial need a consideration only between two otherwise equal applicants. Application available on Website.

Amount of award:	$1,000-$2,500
Number of awards:	2
Application deadline:	February 1
Total amount awarded:	$5,000

Contact:
Society of Manufacturing Engineers
Scholarship Review Committee
One SME Drive, P.O. Box 930
Dearborn, MI 48121-0930
Phone: 313-271-1500
Web: www.sme.org/foundation

Wayne Kay Scholarship

Type of award: Scholarship, renewable.

Intended use: For full-time sophomore, junior or senior study at accredited 4-year institution in United States or Canada. Designated institutions: Schools with manufacturing engineering degree program.
Basis for selection: Major/career interest in manufacturing or engineering. Applicant must demonstrate high academic achievement.
Application requirements: Recommendations, essay, transcript. Student statement. Resume. One original and five copies of application materials. Supply foundation with name of intended college or university.
Additional information: Applicants must be enrolled in manufacturing engineering or technology degree program and must have completed 30 credit hours. Minimum 3.0 GPA. Applicants must reapply for renewal. Financial need a consideration only between two otherwise equal applicants. Application available on Website.

Amount of award:	$2,500
Number of awards:	10
Application deadline:	February 1
Total amount awarded:	$25,000

Contact:
Society of Manufacturing Engineers
Scholarship Review Committee
One SME Drive, P.O. Box 930
Dearborn, MI 48121-0930
Phone: 313-271-1500
Web: www.sme.org/foundation

William E. Weisel Scholarship

Type of award: Scholarship, renewable.
Intended use: For full-time sophomore, junior or senior study at 4-year institution in United States or Canada. Designated institutions: Schools with manufacturing engineering degree programs.
Basis for selection: Major/career interest in manufacturing; engineering or robotics. Applicant must demonstrate high academic achievement.
Application requirements: Recommendations, essay, transcript. Student statement. Resume. One original and six copies of application materials. Supply foundation with name of intended college or university.
Additional information: Applicant must be U.S. or Canadian citizen. Applicants must be enrolled in manufacturing engineering degree program and must have completed minimum of 30 credits. Must be seeking a career in robotics or automated systems used in manufacturing, or robotics used in medical field. Minimum 3.5 GPA. Applicants must reapply for renewal. Financial need a consideration only between two otherwise equal applicants. Application available on Website.

Amount of award:	$1,000
Number of awards:	1
Application deadline:	February 1
Total amount awarded:	$1,000

Contact:
Society of Manufacturing Engineers
Scholarship Review Committee
One SME Drive, P.O. Box 930
Dearborn, MI 48121-0930
Phone: 313-271-1500
Web: www.sme.org/foundation

Society of Physics Students

Society of Physics Students Leadership Scholarship

Type of award: Scholarship.
Intended use: For full-time senior study at 4-year institution.
Eligibility: Applicant or parent must be member/participant of Society of Physics Students.
Basis for selection: Major/career interest in physics. Applicant must demonstrate high academic achievement and seriousness of purpose.
Application requirements: Recommendations, transcript. Application. Letters from at least two full-time faculty members must be filed in support of application.
Additional information: Awards payable in equal installments at the beginning of each semester or quarter of full-time study in the final year of study leading to a baccalaureate degree. Applicants must have junior or higher standing. Must be active participant in Society of Physics Students. Must show intention for continued scholastic development in physics. Number of awards varies. Obtain application from Website or SPS Chapter Advisers.

Amount of award:	$1,000-$4,000
Application deadline:	February 15
Notification begins:	April 1

Contact:
SPS Scholarships Committee
One Physics Ellipse
College Park, MD 20740
Phone: 301-209-3007
Web: www.spsnational.org

Society of Plastics Engineers

Composites Division/Harold Giles Scholarship

Type of award: Scholarship, renewable.
Intended use: For full-time undergraduate or graduate study at vocational, 2-year, 4-year or graduate institution.
Basis for selection: Major/career interest in chemistry; engineering; engineering, chemical; engineering, materials; engineering, mechanical or physics. Applicant must demonstrate financial need.
Application requirements: Recommendations, transcript. A one-to-two page typed statement telling why the applicant is applying for the scholarship, the applicants qualifications, and the applicant's educational and career goals. Three recommendation letters: two from teachers or school officials and one from an employer or non-relative.
Additional information: All applicants must be in good standing with their colleges and have a demonstrated or expressed interest in the plastics industry. Visit Website for more information.

Number of awards:	1
Application deadline:	January 15
Total amount awarded:	$1,000

Contact:
Society of Plastics Engineers
14 Fairfield Drive
P.O. Box 403
Brookfield, CT 06804
Phone: 203-740-5447
Fax: 203-775-1157
Web: www.4spe.org

Extrusion Division/Lew Erwin Memorial Scholarship

Type of award: Scholarship.
Intended use: For full-time senior or graduate study at vocational, 2-year, 4-year or graduate institution.
Basis for selection: Major/career interest in chemistry; engineering; engineering, chemical; engineering, materials; engineering, mechanical or physics. Applicant must demonstrate financial need.
Application requirements: Recommendations, research proposal. A one- to two-page typed statement explaining why applicant is applying for scholarship, plus his/her qualifications and educational and career goals in the plastics industry. Recommendation letter from faculty adviser associated with project.
Additional information: All applicants must be in good academic standing with their colleges and have a demonstrated or expressed interest in the plastics industry. Applicants must be working on a Senior or MS research project in the field of polymer extrusion which the scholarship will help support. The project must be described in writing, including background, objective, and proposed experiments. Recipient will be expected to furnish a final research summary report. Visit Website for more information.

Amount of award:	$2,500
Number of awards:	1
Application deadline:	March 1
Total amount awarded:	$2,500

Contact:
Society of Plastics Engineers
14 Fairfield Drive
P.O. Box 403
Brookfield, CT 06804-0403
Phone: 203-740-5447
Fax: 203-775-1157
Web: www.4spe.org

Fleming/Blaszcak Scholarship

Type of award: Scholarship.
Intended use: For full-time undergraduate or graduate study at 4-year or graduate institution.
Eligibility: Applicant must be Mexican American. Applicants must be of Mexican descent. Applicant must be permanent resident.
Basis for selection: Major/career interest in chemistry; engineering; engineering, chemical; engineering, materials; engineering, mechanical or physics. Applicant must demonstrate financial need.
Application requirements: Recommendations, transcript. A one- to two-page typed statement telling why the applicant is applying for the scholarship, the applicant's qualifications, and the applicant's educational and career goals in the plastics industry. Three recommendation letters: two from teachers or school officials and one from an employer or non-relative.
Additional information: Applicant must be of Mexican heritage, a Mexican citizen, or a legal resident of the United

States. All applicants must be in good standing with their colleges and have a demonstrated or expressed interest in the plastics industry. Visit Website for more information.

Amount of award:	$2,000
Number of awards:	1
Application deadline:	January 15
Total amount awarded:	$2,000

Contact:
Society of Plastics Engineers
14 Fairfield Drrive
P.O. Box 403
Brookfield, CT 06804-0403
Phone: 203-740-5447
Fax: 203-775-1157
Web: www.4spe.org

Polymer Modifiers and Additives Division Scholarships

Type of award: Scholarship.

Intended use: For full-time undergraduate study at vocational, 2-year or 4-year institution.

Basis for selection: Major/career interest in chemistry; engineering; engineering, chemical; engineering, materials; engineering, mechanical or physics. Applicant must demonstrate financial need.

Application requirements: Recommendations, transcript. A one- to two-page typed statement telling why the applicant is applying for the scholarship, the applicant's qualifications, and the applicant's educational and career goals in the plastics industry. Three recommendation letters: two from teachers or school officials and one from an employer or non-relative.

Additional information: All applicants must be in good standing with their colleges and have a demonstrated or expressed interest in the plastics industry. Visit Website for more information.

Amount of award:	$4,000
Number of awards:	2
Application deadline:	January 15
Total amount awarded:	$8,000

Contact:
Society of Plastics Engineers
14 Fairfield Drive
P.O. Box 403
Brookfield, CT 06804-0471
Phone: 203-740-5447
Fax: 203-775-1157
Web: www.4spe.org

Robert E. Cramer/Product Design and Development Division/Middle-Michigan Section Scholarship

Type of award: Scholarship.

Intended use: For full-time undergraduate study at vocational, 2-year or 4-year institution.

Eligibility: Applicant must be residing in Michigan.

Basis for selection: Major/career interest in chemistry; engineering; engineering, chemical; engineering, materials; engineering, mechanical or physics. Applicant must demonstrate financial need.

Application requirements: Recommendations, transcript. A one- to two-page typed statement telling why the applicant is applying for the scholarship, the applicant's qualifications, and the applicant's career and educational goals in the plastics

industry. Three recommendation letters: two from teachers or school officials and one from an employer or non-relative.

Additional information: All applicants must be in good standing with their colleges and have a demonstrated or expressed interest in the plastics industry. Visit Website for more information.

Amount of award:	$1,000
Number of awards:	1
Application deadline:	January 15
Total amount awarded:	$1,000

Contact:
Society of Plastics Engineers
14 Fairfield Drive
P.O. Box 403
Brookfield, CT 06804-0403
Phone: 203-740-5447
Fax: 203-775-1157
Web: www.4spe.org

Robert E. Daily/Detroit Section Scholarship

Type of award: Scholarship.

Intended use: For full-time undergraduate study at vocational, 2-year or 4-year institution.

Basis for selection: Major/career interest in chemistry; engineering; engineering, materials; engineering, chemical; engineering, mechanical or physics. Applicant must demonstrate financial need.

Application requirements: Recommendations, transcript. A one- to two-page typed statement telling why the applicant is applying for the scholarship, the applicant's qualifications, and the applicant's educational and career goals in the plastics industry. Three recommendation letters: two from teachers or school officials and one from an employer or non-relative.

Additional information: All applicants must be in good standing with their colleges and have a demonstrated or expressed interest in the plastics industry. Visit Website for more information.

Amount of award:	$4,000
Number of awards:	1
Application deadline:	January 15
Total amount awarded:	$4,000

Contact:
Society of Plastics Engineers
14 Fairfield Drive
P.O. Box 403
Brookfield, CT 06804-0471
Phone: 203-740-0487
Fax: 203-775-1157
Web: www.4spe.org

Society of Plastics Engineers General Scholarships

Type of award: Scholarship, renewable.

Intended use: For full-time undergraduate study at vocational, 2-year or 4-year institution.

Basis for selection: Major/career interest in chemistry; engineering; engineering, chemical; engineering, mechanical; engineering, materials or physics. Applicant must demonstrate financial need and seriousness of purpose.

Application requirements: Recommendations, transcript. A one- to two-page typed statement telling why the applicant is applying for the scholarship, the applicant's qualifications, and the applicant's educational and career goals in the plastics industry. Three recommendation letters: two from teachers or school officials and one from and employer or non-relative.

Additional information: Scholarships are awarded for one year only, but applicants may apply to be re-awarded for up to three additional years. All applicants must be in good standing with their colleges and must have a demonstrated or expressed interest in the plastics industry. Visit Website for more information.

Amount of award:	$4,000
Number of awards:	12
Application deadline:	January 15
Total amount awarded:	$48,000

Contact:
Society of Plastics Engineers
14 Fairfield Drive
P.O. Box 403
Brookfield, CT 06804-0403
Phone: 203-740-5447
Fax: 203-775-1157
Web: www.4spe.org

Ted Neward Scholarship

Type of award: Scholarship.
Intended use: For full-time undergraduate or graduate study at vocational, 2-year or 4-year institution.
Eligibility: Applicant must be U.S. citizen.
Basis for selection: Major/career interest in chemistry; engineering; engineering, chemical; engineering, materials; engineering, mechanical or physics. Applicant must demonstrate financial need.
Application requirements: Recommendations, transcript. A one- to two-page typed statement telling why the applicant is applying for the scholarship, the applicant's qualifications, and the applicant's educational and career goals in the plastics industry. Three letters of recommendation: two from teachers or school officials and one from an employer or non-relative.
Additional information: All applicants must be in good standing with their colleges and have a demonstrated or expressed interest in the plastics industry. Visit Website for more information.

Amount of award:	$3,000
Number of awards:	1
Application deadline:	January 15
Total amount awarded:	$3,000

Contact:
Society of Plastics Engineers
14 Fairfield Drive
P.O. Box 403
Brookfield, CT 06804-0403
Phone: 203-740-5447
Fax: 203-775-1157
Web: 4spe.org

Thermoforming Division Memorial Scholarships

Type of award: Scholarship.
Intended use: For full-time undergraduate or graduate study at vocational, 2-year, 4-year or graduate institution.
Basis for selection: Major/career interest in chemistry; engineering; engineering, chemical; engineering, materials; engineering, mechanical or physics. Applicant must demonstrate financial need.
Application requirements: Recommendations, transcript. One- to two-page typed statement explaining why applicant is applying for scholarship, plus his/her qualifications and

educational and career goals. Applicants must also include statement detailing their exposure to the thermostat industry, including courses, research conducted or jobs held. Three recommendation letters: two from teachers or school officials, and one from an employer or other non-relative.
Additional information: All applicants must be in good standing with their colleges and have a demonstrated or expressed interest in the plastics industry. Visit Website for more information.

Amount of award:	$5,000
Number of awards:	2
Application deadline:	January 15
Total amount awarded:	$10,000

Contact:
Society of Plastics Engineers
14 Fairfield Drive
P.O. Box 403
Brookfield, CT 06084-0403
Phone: 203-740-5447
Fax: 203-775-1157
Web: www.4spe.org

Thermoset Division/ James MacKenzie Memorial Scholarship

Type of award: Scholarship.
Intended use: For full-time undergraduate study at vocational, 2-year or 4-year institution.
Basis for selection: Major/career interest in chemistry; engineering; engineering, chemical; engineering, materials; engineering, mechanical or physics. Applicant must demonstrate financial need.
Application requirements: Recommendations, transcript. A one- to two-page typed statement telling why the applicant is applying for the scholarship, the applicant's qualifications, and the applicant's educational and career goals in the plastics industry. Applicants must also include a statement detailing their exposure to the thermoset industry. Three recommendation letters: two from teachers or school officials and one from an employer or non-relative.
Additional information: All applicants must be in good academic standing with their colleges and have a demonstrated or expressed interest in the plastics industry. Applicants for this award must have experience in the thermoset industry, such as courses taken, research conducted, or jobs held. Visit Website for more information.

Amount of award:	$2,000
Number of awards:	1
Application deadline:	January 15
Total amount awarded:	$2,000

Contact:
Society of Plastics Engineers
14 Fairfield Drive
P.O. Box 403
Brookfield, CT 06084-0403
Phone: 203-740-5447
Fax: 203-775-1157
Web: www.4spe.org

Society of Professional Journalists, Greater Los Angeles Professional Chapter

Bill Farr Scholarship

Type of award: Scholarship, renewable.
Intended use: For full-time junior, senior or graduate study at accredited 4-year institution in United States.
Eligibility: Applicant must be U.S. citizen.
Basis for selection: Based on applicant's accomplishments and potential. Major/career interest in journalism.
Application requirements: Essay, proof of eligibility. Proof of enrollment in journalism program. Resume, clips, samples of work, and 500- to 700-word essay. References.
Additional information: Applicant must be resident of Los Angeles, Ventura or Orange counties, or attending university in one of those counties. Scholarship awarded based on accomplishments and potential. Financial need considered in making selection between equally qualified applicants. Must reapply for renewal. Visit Website for details and application.
  Amount of award: $500-$1,000
Contact:
SPJ/LA Scholarships Department of Journalism
California State University, Long Beach
1250 Bellflower
Long Beach, CA 90840
Web: www.spj.org/losangeles

Carl Greenberg Scholarship

Type of award: Scholarship, renewable.
Intended use: For full-time junior, senior or graduate study at accredited 4-year institution in United States.
Basis for selection: Major/career interest in journalism.
Application requirements: Essay, proof of eligibility. Proof of enrollment in journalism program. Resume, clips, samples of work, and 500- to 700-word essay. References.
Additional information: Award for investigative or political reporting. Applicant must be resident of Los Angeles, Ventura or Orange counties, or attending university in one of those counties. Scholarship awarded based on applicant's accomplishments and potential. Must reapply for renewal. Visit Website for details and application.
  Amount of award: $1,000
Contact:
SPJ/LA Scholarships Department of Journalism
California State University, Long Beach
1250 Bellflower
Long Beach, CA 90840
Web: www.spj.org/losangeles

Helen Johnson Scholarship

Type of award: Scholarship, renewable.
Intended use: For full-time junior, senior or graduate study at accredited 4-year institution in United States.
Basis for selection: Major/career interest in journalism.
Application requirements: Essay, proof of eligibility. Proof of enrollment in journalism program. Include resume, samples of work, and 500- to 700-word essay. References.
Additional information: Award for broadcast journalism students. Applicant must be resident of Los Angeles, Ventura or Orange counties, or attending university in one of those counties. Scholarship awarded based on applicant's accomplishments; financial need considered in making selections between equally qualified applicants. Must reapply for renewal. Visit Website for details and application.
  Amount of award: $500-$1,000
Contact:
SPJ/LA Scholarships Department of Journalism
California State University, Long Beach
1250 Bellflower
Long Beach, CA 90840
Web: www.spj.org/losangeles

Ken Inouye Scholarship

Type of award: Scholarship, renewable.
Intended use: For full-time junior, senior or graduate study at accredited 4-year institution in United States.
Eligibility: Must be member of ethnic minority. Applicant must be U.S. citizen.
Basis for selection: Major/career interest in journalism.
Application requirements: Essay, proof of eligibility. Proof of enrollment in journalism program. Resume, clips, samples of work, and 500- to 700-word essay. References.
Additional information: Applicant must be resident of Los Angeles, Ventura or Orange counties, or attending university in one of those counties. Scholarship awarded based on applicant's accomplishments and potential. Financial need considered in making selections between equally qualified applicants. Must reapply for renewal. Visit Website for details and application.
  Amount of award: $500-$1,000
  Application deadline: March 15
Contact:
SPJ/LA Scholarships Department of Journalism
California State University, Long Beach
1250 Bellflower
Long Beach, CA 90840
Web: www.spj.org/losangeles

Society of Women Engineers

Admiral Grace Murray Hopper Scholarship

Type of award: Scholarship.
Intended use: For full-time freshman study at accredited 4-year institution in United States.
Eligibility: Applicant must be female, high school senior. Applicant must be U.S. citizen or permanent resident.
Basis for selection: Major/career interest in engineering. Applicant must demonstrate high academic achievement.
Application requirements: Recommendations, essay, transcript, proof of eligibility.
Additional information: Applicants must be enrolled or plan to be enrolled in an ABET- or CSAB-accredited program or SWE approved school. Minimum 3.5 GPA. Preference given to computer-related engineering majors. Application forms available through the Deans of Engineering at eligible schools, through SWE sections, SWE student sections and from SWE Headquarters. Include SASE with requests for hard copy from SWE Headquarters. Application form also available on Website. Applicants considered for all scholarships for which they are eligible and need submit only one application package.

Scholarships

Amount of award: $1,000
Number of awards: 5
Application deadline: May 15
Notification begins: September 15
Total amount awarded: $5,000
Contact:
Society of Women Engineers
World Headquarters
230 E. Ohio Street, Suite 400
Chicago, IL 60611-3265
Phone: 312-596-5223
Fax: 312-644-8557
Web: www.swe.org

Adobe Systems Computer Science Scholarships

Type of award: Scholarship.
Intended use: For full-time junior or senior study at accredited 4-year institution in United States.
Eligibility: Applicant must be female. Applicant must be U.S. citizen or permanent resident.
Basis for selection: Major/career interest in computer/information sciences. Applicant must demonstrate high academic achievement.
Application requirements: Recommendations, essay, transcript, proof of eligibility.
Additional information: Preference given to students attending selected San Francisco Bay area schools and computer science majors. Applicants must be enrolled or plan to be enrolled in an ABET- or CSAB-accredited program or SWE approved school. Minimum 3.0 GPA. Application forms available through the Deans of Engineering at eligible schools, through SWE sections, SWE student sections and from SWE Headquarters. Include SASE with requests for hard copy from SWE Headquarters. Application form also available on Website.
Amount of award: $1,500-$2,000
Number of awards: 2
Application deadline: February 1
Notification begins: May 15
Total amount awarded: $3,500
Contact:
Society of Women Engineers
World Headquarters
230 E. Ohio Street, Suite 400
Chicago, IL 60611-3265
Phone: 312-596-5223
Fax: 312-644-8557
Web: www.swe.org

Agilient Mentoring Scholarship

Type of award: Scholarship.
Intended use: For full-time sophomore or junior study at accredited 4-year institution in United States.
Eligibility: Applicant must be female.
Basis for selection: Major/career interest in engineering, biomedical; engineering, computer; engineering, electrical/electronic; computer/information sciences or engineering, mechanical.
Application requirements: Recommendations, essay, transcript, proof of eligibility.
Additional information: Minimum 3.0 GPA. Applicants must be enrolled or plan to be enrolled in an ABET- or CSAB-accredited program. Application forms available through the deans of engineering at eligible schools and from SWE sections, SWE student sections and SWE Headquarters. Include

SASE with requests for hard copy from SWE Headquarters. Application form also available on Website. Applicants considered for all scholarships for which they are eligible and need submit only one application package.
Amount of award: $1,000
Number of awards: 1
Application deadline: February 1
Contact:
Society of Women Engineers
230 E. Ohio Street
Suite 400
Chicago, IL 60611-3265
Phone: 316-596-5223
Fax: 312-596-5252
Web: www.swe.org

Anne Maureen Whitney Barrow Memorial

Type of award: Scholarship.
Intended use: For full-time undergraduate study at accredited 4-year institution in United States.
Eligibility: Applicant must be female, high school senior. Applicant must be U.S. citizen or permanent resident.
Basis for selection: Major/career interest in engineering.
Application requirements: Recommendations, essay, transcript, proof of eligibility.
Additional information: Minimum 3.5 GPA. Applicants must be enrolled or plan to be enrolled in an ABET- or CSAB-accredited program. Application forms available through the deans of engineering at eligible schools and from SWE sections, SWE student sections and SWE Headquarters. Include SASE with requests for hard copy from SWE Headquarters. Application form also available on Website. Applicants considered for all scholarships for which they are eligible and need submit only one application package.
Amount of award: $5,000
Number of awards: 1
Application deadline: May 15
Contact:
Society of Women Engineers
230 E. Ohio Street
Suite 400
Chicago, IL 60611-3265
Phone: 312-596-5223
Fax: 312-596-5252
Web: hq@swe.org

Arizona Section Scholarship

Type of award: Scholarship.
Intended use: For full-time freshman study at accredited 4-year institution in United States.
Eligibility: Applicant must be high school senior. Applicant must be U.S. citizen or permanent resident residing in Arizona.
Basis for selection: Major/career interest in engineering. Applicant must demonstrate high academic achievement.
Application requirements: Recommendations, essay, transcript, proof of eligibility.
Additional information: Must be Arizona resident or attending school in Arizona. Minimum 3.5 GPA. Applicants must be enrolled or plan to be enrolled in an ABET- or CSAB-accredited program. Application forms available through the deans of engineering at eligible schools and from SWE sections, SWE student sections and SWE Headquarters. Include SASE with requests for hard copy from SWE Headquarters. Application form also available on Website. Applicants

considered for all scholarships for which they are eligible and need submit only one application package.

Amount of award:	$1,000
Number of awards:	2
Application deadline:	May 15

Contact:
Society of Women Engineers
230 E. Ohio Street
Suite 400
Chicago, IL 60611-3265
Phone: 312-596-5223
Fax: 312-596-5252
Web: www.swe.org

B. J. Harrod Scholarships

Type of award: Scholarship.
Intended use: For full-time freshman study at accredited 4-year institution in United States.
Eligibility: Applicant must be female, high school senior. Applicant must be U.S. citizen or permanent resident.
Basis for selection: Major/career interest in engineering. Applicant must demonstrate high academic achievement.
Application requirements: Recommendations, essay, transcript, proof of eligibility. Two letters of reference: one from a high school teacher, one from a person who knows the applicant, but not a family member.
Additional information: Applicants must be enrolled or plan to be enrolled in an ABET- or CSAB-accredited program or SWE approved school. Minimum 3.5 GPA. Application forms available through the Deans of Engineering at eligible schools, through SWE sections, SWE student sections and from SWE Headquarters. Include SASE with requests for hard copy from SWE Headquarters. Application form also available on Website. Applicants considered for all scholarships for which they are eligible and need submit only one application package.

Amount of award:	$1,500
Number of awards:	2
Application deadline:	May 15
Notification begins:	September 15
Total amount awarded:	$3,000

Contact:
Society of Women Engineers
World Headquarters
230 E. Ohio Street, Suite 400
Chicago, IL 60611-3265
Phone: 312-596-5223
Fax: 312-644-8557
Web: www.swe.org

B. K. Krenzer Reentry Scholarship

Type of award: Scholarship.
Intended use: For undergraduate or graduate study at accredited 4-year or graduate institution in United States.
Eligibility: Applicant must be female, returning adult student. Applicant must be U.S. citizen or permanent resident.
Basis for selection: Major/career interest in engineering; engineering, electrical/electronic; engineering, structural or engineering, mechanical. Applicant must demonstrate high academic achievement.
Application requirements: Recommendations, essay, transcript, proof of eligibility.
Additional information: Application deadline: 05/15 for freshman, 02/01 for upper classmen. Eligibility restricted to women who have been out of school for at least two years prior to reentry. Also open to women who have been out of engineering workforce and school at least two years. Preference

given to degreed engineers. Applicants must be enrolled or plan to be enrolled in an ABET- or CSAB-accredited program. Minimum 3.0 GPA after first year of reentry. Application forms available through the Deans of Engineering at eligible schools, through SWE sections, SWE student sections and from SWE Headquarters. Include SASE with requests for hard copy from SWE Headquarters. Application form also available on Website. Applicants considered for all scholarships for which they are eligible and need submit only one application package.

Amount of award:	$2,000
Number of awards:	1
Notification begins:	September 15
Total amount awarded:	$2,000

Contact:
Society of Women Engineers
World Headquarters
230 E. Ohio Street, Suite 400
Chicago, IL 60611-3265
Phone: 312-596-5223
Fax: 312-596-5252
Web: www.swe.org

Bechtel Corporation Scholarship

Type of award: Scholarship.
Intended use: For full-time sophomore, junior or senior study at accredited 4-year institution in United States.
Eligibility: Applicant or parent must be member/participant of Society of Women Engineers. Applicant must be female. Applicant must be U.S. citizen or permanent resident.
Basis for selection: Major/career interest in engineering, chemical; engineering, electrical/electronic; engineering, environmental; engineering, mechanical; engineering or architecture. Applicant must demonstrate high academic achievement.
Application requirements: Recommendations, essay, transcript, proof of eligibility.
Additional information: Architectural engineering majors also eligible to apply. Applicants must be enrolled or plan to be enrolled in an ABET- or CSAB-accredited program. Minimum 3.0 GPA. Application forms available through the deans of engineering at eligible schools, and from SWE sections, SWE student sections and SWE Headquarters. Include SASE with requests for hard copy from SWE Headquarters. Application form also available on Website. Applicants considered for all scholarships for which they are eligible and need submit only one application package.

Amount of award:	$1,400
Number of awards:	2
Application deadline:	February 1
Notification begins:	May 1
Total amount awarded:	$2,800

Contact:
Society of Women Engineers
World Headquarters
230 E. Ohio Street, Suite 400
Chicago, IL 60611-3265
Phone: 312-596-5223
Fax: 312-596-5252
Web: www.swe.org

Bertha Lamme Memorial Scholarhsip

Type of award: Scholarship.
Intended use: For full-time freshman study at 4-year institution in United States.

Eligibility: Applicant must be female. Applicant must be U.S. citizen.
Basis for selection: Major/career interest in engineering, electrical/electronic.
Additional information: Minimum 3.5 GPA. Applicants must be enrolled or plan to be enrolled in an ABET- or CSAB-accredited program. Application forms available through the deans of engineering at eligible schools and from SWE sections, SWE student sections and SWE Headquarters. Include SASE with requests for hard copy from SWE Headquarters. Application form also available on Website. Applicants considered for all scholarships for which they are eligible and need submit only one application package.

Amount of award:	$1,200
Number of awards:	1
Application deadline:	May 15

Contact:
Society of Women Engineers
230 E. Ohio Street
Suite 400
Chicago, IL 60611-3265
Phone: 312-596-5223
Fax: 312-596-5252
Web: www.swe.org

Caterpillar Inc. Scholarship

Type of award: Scholarship.
Intended use: For full-time undergraduate or graduate study at 4-year or graduate institution in United States.
Eligibility: Applicant must be female. Applicant must be U.S. citizen or permanent resident.
Basis for selection: Major/career interest in engineering.
Application requirements: Recommendations, essay, transcript, proof of eligibility.
Additional information: Minimum 2.8 GPA. Applicants must be enrolled or plan to be enrolled in an ABET- or CSAB-accredited program. Application forms available through the deans of engineering at eligible schools and from SWE sections, SWE student sections and SWE Headquarters. Include SASE with requests for hard copy from SWE Headquarters. Application form also available on Website. Applicants considered for all scholarships for which they are eligible and need submit only one application package.

Amount of award:	$2,400
Number of awards:	3
Application deadline:	February 1

Contact:
Society of Women Engineers
230 E. Ohio Street
Suite 400
Chicago, IL 60611-3265
Phone: 312-596-5223
Fax: 312-596-5252
Web: www.swe.org

Chevron Texaco Corporation Scholarships

Type of award: Scholarship.
Intended use: For full-time sophomore or junior study at accredited 4-year institution in United States.
Eligibility: Applicant or parent must be member/participant of Society of Women Engineers. Applicant must be female.
Basis for selection: Major/career interest in engineering, civil; engineering, chemical; engineering, petroleum; engineering,

mechanical or engineering, electrical/electronic. Applicant must demonstrate high academic achievement.
Application requirements: Recommendations, essay, transcript, proof of eligibility. Must be an active SWE Student Member.
Additional information: One award each for sophomore and junior engineering student. Applicants must be enrolled or plan to be enrolled in an ABET- or CSAB-accredited program. Minimum 3.5 GPA. Application forms available through the Deans of Engineering at eligible schools, through SWE sections, SWE student sections and from SWE Headquarters. Include SASE with requests for hard copy from SWE Headquarters. Application form also available on Website. Applicants considered for all scholarships for which they are eligible and need submit only one application package.

Amount of award:	$2,000
Number of awards:	7
Application deadline:	February 1
Notification begins:	May 1
Total amount awarded:	$14,000

Contact:
Society of Women Engineers
World Headquarters
230 E. Ohio Street, Suite 400
Chicago, IL 60611-3265
Phone: 312-596-5223
Fax: 312-596-5252
Web: www.swe.org

DaimlerChrysler Corporation Fund Scholarships

Type of award: Scholarship, renewable.
Intended use: For full-time sophomore study at accredited 4-year institution in United States.
Eligibility: Applicant or parent must be member/participant of Society of Women Engineers. Applicant must be female. Applicant must be U.S. citizen or permanent resident.
Basis for selection: Major/career interest in engineering, electrical/electronic or engineering, mechanical. Applicant must demonstrate high academic achievement.
Application requirements: Recommendations, essay, transcript, proof of eligibility.
Additional information: Applicants must be enrolled or plan to be enrolled in an ABET- or CSAB-accredited program. Minimum 3.0 GPA. Application forms available through the deans of engineering at eligible schools and from SWE sections, SWE student sections and SWE Headquarters. Include SASE with requests for hard copy from SWE Headquarters. Application form also available on Website. Applicants considered for all scholarships for which they are eligible and need submit only one application package.

Amount of award:	$2,000
Number of awards:	1
Application deadline:	February 1
Notification begins:	May 15

Contact:
Society of Women Engineers
World Headquarters
230 E. Ohio Street, Suite 400
Chicago, IL 60611-3265
Phone: 312-596-5223
Fax: 312-596-5252
Web: www.swe.org

David Sarnoff Research Center Scholarship

Type of award: Scholarship.
Intended use: For full-time junior study at accredited 4-year institution.
Eligibility: Applicant must be female. Applicant must be U.S. citizen or permanent resident.
Basis for selection: Major/career interest in engineering or computer/information sciences. Applicant must demonstrate high academic achievement.
Application requirements: Recommendations, essay, transcript, proof of eligibility.
Additional information: Applicants must be enrolled or plan to be enrolled in an ABET- or CSAB-accredited program. Minimum 3.5 GPA. Application forms available through the Deans of Engineering at eligible schools, through SWE sections, SWE student sections and from SWE Headquarters. Include SASE with requests for hard copy from SWE Headquarters. Application form also available on Website. Applicants considered for all scholarships for which they are eligible and need submit only one application package.

Amount of award:	$1,500
Number of awards:	1
Application deadline:	February 1
Notification begins:	May 15
Total amount awarded:	$1,500

Contact:
Society of Women Engineers
World Headquarters
230 E. Ohio Street, Suite 400
Chicago, IL 60611-3265
Phone: 312-596-5223
Fax: 312-596-5252
Web: www.swe.org

Dell Computer Corporation Scholarship

Type of award: Scholarship.
Intended use: For full-time sophomore or junior study at 4-year institution in United States or Canada.
Eligibility: Applicant must be female. Applicant must be U.S. citizen or permanent resident.
Basis for selection: Major/career interest in engineering, electrical/electronic; engineering, computer; engineering, mechanical or computer/information sciences. Applicant must demonstrate financial need.
Application requirements: Recommendations, essay, transcript, proof of eligibility.
Additional information: Minimum 3.0 GPA. Applicants must be enrolled or plan to be enrolled in an ABET- or CSAB-accredited program. Application forms available through the deans of engineering at eligible schools and from SWE sections, SWE student sections and SWE Headquarters. Include SASE with requests for hard copy from SWE Headquarters. Application form also available on Website. Applicants considered for all scholarships for which they are eligible and need submit only one application package.

Amount of award:	$2,250
Number of awards:	2
Application deadline:	February 1

Contact:
Society of Women Engineers
230 E. Ohio Street
Suite 400
Chicago, IL 60611-3265
Phone: 312-596-5223
Fax: 312-596-5252
Web: www.swe.org

Dorothy Lemke Howarth Scholarships

Type of award: Scholarship.
Intended use: For full-time sophomore study at accredited 4-year institution.
Eligibility: Applicant must be female. Applicant must be U.S. citizen.
Basis for selection: Major/career interest in engineering. Applicant must demonstrate high academic achievement.
Application requirements: Recommendations, essay, transcript, proof of eligibility.
Additional information: Applicants must be enrolled or plan to be enrolled in an ABET- or CSAB-accredited program. Minimum 3.0 GPA. Application forms available through the Deans of Engineering at eligible schools, through SWE sections, SWE student sections and from SWE Headquarters. Include SASE with requests for hard copy from SWE Headquarters. Application form also available on Website. Applicants considered for all scholarships for which they are eligible and need submit only one application package.

Amount of award:	$2,000
Number of awards:	5
Application deadline:	February 1
Notification begins:	May 15
Total amount awarded:	$10,000

Contact:
Society of Women Engineers
World Headquarters
230 E. Ohio Street, Suite 400
Chicago, IL 60611-3265
Phone: 312-596-5223
Fax: 312-596-5252
Web: www.swe.org

Dorothy M. & Earl S. Hoffman Scholarships

Type of award: Scholarship, renewable.
Intended use: For full-time freshman study at accredited 4-year institution in United States.
Eligibility: Applicant must be female, high school senior. Applicant must be U.S. citizen or permanent resident.
Basis for selection: Major/career interest in engineering. Applicant must demonstrate high academic achievement.
Application requirements: Recommendations, essay, transcript, proof of eligibility.
Additional information: Applicants must be enrolled or plan to be enrolled in an ABET- or CSAB-accredited program. Preference given to students attending Bucknell University and Rensselaer Polytechnic University. Minimum 3.5 GPA. Application forms available through the deans of engineering at eligible schools and from SWE sections, SWE student sections and SWE Headquarters. Include SASE with requests for hard copy from SWE Headquarters. Application form also available on Website. Applicants considered for all scholarships for which they are eligible, therefore need only submit one application package.

Amount of award: $3,000
Number of awards: 5
Application deadline: May 15
Notification begins: September 15
Contact:
Society of Women Engineers
World Headquarters
230 E. Ohio Street, Suite 400
Chicago, IL 60611-3265
Phone: 312-596-5223
Fax: 312-644-8557
Web: www.swe.org

Dorothy Morris Scholarship

Type of award: Scholarship.
Intended use: For full-time sophomore, junior or senior study at 4-year institution in United States.
Eligibility: Applicant must be female. Applicant must be U.S. citizen.
Basis for selection: Major/career interest in engineering.
Application requirements: Recommendations, essay, transcript, proof of eligibility.
Additional information: Minimum 3.0 GPA. Limited to graduates of New Jersey high schools. Applicants must be enrolled or plan to be enrolled in an ABET- or CSAB-accredited program. Application forms available through the deans of engineering at eligible schools and from SWE sections, SWE student sections and SWE Headquarters. Include SASE with requests for hard copy from SWE Headquarters. Application forms also available on Website. Applicants considered for all scholarships for which they are eligible and need submit only one application package.
Amount of award: $1,000
Number of awards: 1
Application deadline: February 1
Contact:
Society of Women Engineers
230 E. Ohio Street
Suite 400
Chicago, IL 60611-3265
Phone: 312-596-5223
Fax: 312-596-5252
Web: www.swe.org

DuPont Company Scholarship

Type of award: Scholarship.
Intended use: For full-time freshman study at 4-year institution in United States or Canada. Designated institutions: Institutions in eastern U.S.
Eligibility: Applicant must be female, high school senior. Applicant must be U.S. citizen or permanent resident.
Basis for selection: Major/career interest in engineering, chemical or engineering, mechanical.
Additional information: Limited to schools in eastern U.S. Minimum 3.0 GPA. Applicants must be enrolled or plan to be enrolled in an ABET- or CSAB-accredited program. Application forms available through the deans of engineering at eligible schools and from SWE sections, SWE student sections and SWE Headquarters. Include SASE with requests for hard copy from SWE Headquarters. Application form also available on Website. Applicants considered for all scholarships for which they are eligible and need submit only one application package.
Amount of award: $2,000
Number of awards: 2

Contact:
Society of Women Engineers
230 E. Ohio Street
Suite 400
Chicago, IL 60611-3265
Phone: 312-596-5223
Fax: 312-596-5252
Web: www.swe.org

DuPont Scholarships

Type of award: Scholarship.
Intended use: For full-time freshman, sophomore, junior or senior study at accredited 4-year institution in United States.
Eligibility: Applicant must be female. Applicant must be U.S. citizen or permanent resident.
Basis for selection: Major/career interest in engineering, chemical or engineering, mechanical. Applicant must demonstrate high academic achievement.
Application requirements: Recommendations, essay, transcript, proof of eligibility.
Additional information: Two awards for incoming freshmen; two for sophomores, juniors, seniors. Limited to schools in the eastern United States. Applicants must be enrolled or plan to be enrolled in an ABET- or CSAB-accredited program. Minimum 3.0 GPA. Application forms available through the Deans of Engineering at eligible schools, through SWE sections, SWE student sections and from SWE Headquarters. Include SASE with requests for hard copy from SWE Headquarters. Application form also available on Website. Applicants considered for all scholarships for which they are eligible and need submit only one application package. Early deadline is for sophomores, juniors, seniors.
Amount of award: $2,000
Number of awards: 4
Application deadline: February 1, May 15
Notification begins: May 1, September 15
Total amount awarded: $8,000
Contact:
Society of Women Engineers
World Headquarters
230 E. Ohio Street, Suite 400
Chicago, IL 60611-3265
Phone: 312-596-5223
Fax: 312-596-5252
Web: www.swe.org

Exelon Scholarship

Type of award: Scholarship.
Intended use: For full-time freshman study at 4-year institution in United States or Canada.
Eligibility: Applicant must be female, high school senior. Applicant must be U.S. citizen or permanent resident.
Basis for selection: Major/career interest in engineering.
Additional information: Minimum 3.5 GPA. Applicants must be enrolled or plan to be enrolled in an ABET- or CSAB-accredited program. Application forms available through the deans of engineering at eligible schools and from SWE sections, SWE student sections and SWE Headquarters. Include SASE with requests for hard copy from SWE Headquarters. Application form also available on Website. Applicants considered for all scholarships for which they are eligible and need submit only one application package.
Amount of award: $1,000
Number of awards: 4
Application deadline: May 15

Contact:
Society of Women Engineers
230 E. Ohio Street
Suite 400
Chicago, IL 60611-3265
Phone: 312-596-5223
Fax: 312-596-5252
Web: www.swe.org

Ford Motor Company Scholarship

Type of award: Scholarship.
Intended use: For sophomore, junior, senior or graduate study at accredited 4-year or graduate institution.
Eligibility: Applicant must be female.
Basis for selection: Major/career interest in engineering, electrical/electronic or engineering, mechanical. Applicant must demonstrate leadership.
Additional information: Minimum 3.0 GPA. Applicants must be enrolled or plan to be enrolled in an ABET- or CSAB-accredited program. Application forms available through the deans of engineering at eligible schools and from SWE sections, SWE student sections and SWE Headquarters. Include SASE with requests for hard copy from SWE Headquarters. Application form also available on Website. Applicants considered for all scholarships for which they are eligible and need submit only one application package.

Amount of award:	$2,000
Number of awards:	7
Application deadline:	February 1

Contact:
Society of Women Engineers
230 E. Ohio Street
Suite 400
Chicago, IL 60611
Phone: 312-596-5223
Fax: 312-644-8557
Web: www.swe.org

General Electric Fund Scholarships

Type of award: Scholarship, renewable.
Intended use: For full-time freshman study at accredited 4-year institution.
Eligibility: Applicant must be female, high school senior. Applicant must be U.S. citizen.
Basis for selection: Major/career interest in engineering. Applicant must demonstrate high academic achievement.
Application requirements: Recommendations, essay, transcript, proof of eligibility.
Additional information: Fund includes travel grant to attend the SWE National Conference. Award is renewable for three years. Applicants must be enrolled or plan to be enrolled in an ABET- or CSAB-accredited program. Minimum 3.5 GPA. Application forms available through the Deans of Engineering at eligible schools, through SWE sections, SWE student sections and from SWE Headquarters. Include SASE with requests for hard copy from SWE Headquarters. Application form also available on Website. Applicants considered for all scholarships for which they are eligible and need submit only one application package.

Amount of award:	$1,000
Number of awards:	3
Application deadline:	May 15
Notification begins:	September 15
Total amount awarded:	$3,000

Contact:
Society of Women Engineers
World Headquarters
230 E. Ohio Street, Suite 400
Chicago, IL 60611-3265
Phone: 312-596-5223
Fax: 312-596-5252
Web: www.swe.org

General Motors Foundation Scholarships

Type of award: Scholarship, renewable.
Intended use: For full-time junior study at accredited 4-year institution in United States.
Eligibility: Applicant must be female. Applicant must be U.S. citizen or permanent resident.
Basis for selection: Major/career interest in engineering; automotive technology; engineering, electrical/electronic; engineering, mechanical; engineering, chemical or engineering, materials. Applicant must demonstrate financial need, high academic achievement and leadership.
Application requirements: Recommendations, essay, transcript, proof of eligibility.
Additional information: Industrial engineering and manufacturing engineering majors also eligible to apply. Applicants must be enrolled or plan to be enrolled in an ABET- or CSAB-accredited program or SWE approved school. Applicants should have career interest in automotive industry or manufacturing. Foundation provides travel grant to attend the SWE National Convention and Student Conference. Minimum 3.5 GPA. Application forms available through the Deans of Engineering at eligible schools, through SWE sections, SWE student sections and from SWE Headquarters. Include SASE with requests for hard copy from SWE Headquarters. Application form also available on Website. Applicants considered for all scholarships for which they are eligible and need submit only one application package.

Amount of award:	$1,225
Number of awards:	2
Application deadline:	February 1
Notification begins:	May 15

Contact:
Society of Women Engineers
World Headquarters
230 E. Ohio Street, Suite 400
Chicago, IL 60611-3265
Phone: 312-596-5223
Fax: 312-644-8557
Web: www.swe.org

Guidant Corporation Scholarship

Type of award: Scholarship.
Intended use: For full-time senior study at 4-year institution in United States.
Eligibility: Applicant must be female. Applicant must be U.S. citizen or permanent resident.
Basis for selection: Major/career interest in engineering, chemical; computer/information sciences; engineering, electrical/electronic; engineering, mechanical or engineering, materials. Applicant must demonstrate high academic achievement.
Application requirements: Recommendations, essay, transcript, proof of eligibility.
Additional information: Minimum 3.0 GPA. Applicants must be enrolled or plan to be enrolled in an ABET- or CSAB-

accredited program. Application forms available through the deans of engineering at eligible schools and from SWE sections, SWE student sections and SWE Headquarters. Include SASE with requests for hard copy from SWE Headquarters. Application form also available on Website. Applicants considered for all scholarships for which they are eligible and need submit only one application package.

Amount of award:	$5,000
Number of awards:	2
Application deadline:	February 1

Contact:
Society of Women Engineers
230 E. Ohio Street
Suite 400
Chicago, IL 60611-3265
Phone: 312-596-5223
Fax: 312-596-5252
Web: www.swe.org

Ivy Parker Memorial Scholarship

Type of award: Scholarship.
Intended use: For full-time junior or senior study at accredited 4-year institution in United States.
Eligibility: Applicant must be female. Applicant must be U.S. citizen or permanent resident.
Basis for selection: Major/career interest in engineering. Applicant must demonstrate financial need and high academic achievement.
Application requirements: Recommendations, essay, transcript, proof of eligibility.
Additional information: Applicants must be enrolled or plan to be enrolled in an ABET- or CSAB-accredited program. Minimum 3.0 GPA. Application forms available through the Deans of Engineering at eligible schools, through SWE sections, SWE student sections and from SWE Headquarters. Include SASE with requests for hard copy from SWE Headquarters. Application form also available on Website. Applicants considered for all scholarships for which they are eligible and need submit only one application package.

Amount of award:	$2,500
Number of awards:	1
Application deadline:	February 1
Notification begins:	May 15
Total amount awarded:	$2,500

Contact:
Society of Women Engineers
World Headquarters
230 E. Ohio Street, Suite 400
Chicago, IL 60611-3265
Phone: 312-596-5223
Fax: 312-596-5252
Web: www.swe.org

Judith Resnik Memorial Scholarship

Type of award: Scholarship.
Intended use: For full-time sophomore, junior or senior study at accredited 4-year institution.
Eligibility: Applicant or parent must be member/participant of Society of Women Engineers. Applicant must be female. Applicant must be U.S. citizen or permanent resident.
Basis for selection: Major/career interest in engineering or aerospace. Applicant must demonstrate high academic achievement.

Application requirements: Recommendations, essay, transcript, proof of eligibility.
Additional information: Must be aeronautical/aerospace engineering or astronautical engineering major. Applicants must be enrolled or plan to be enrolled in an ABET- or CSAB-accredited program. Minimum 3.0 GPA. Application forms available through the Deans of Engineering at eligible schools, through SWE sections, SWE student sections and from SWE Headquarters. Include SASE with requests for hard copy from SWE Headquarters. Application form also available on Website. Applicants considered for all scholarships for which they are eligible and need submit only one application package.

Amount of award:	$2,500
Number of awards:	1
Application deadline:	February 1
Notification begins:	May 15
Total amount awarded:	$2,500

Contact:
Society of Women Engineers
World Headquarters
230 E. Ohio Street, Suite 400
Chicago, IL 60611-3265
Phone: 312-596-5223
Fax: 312-596-5252
Web: www.swe.org

Lillian Moller Gilbreth Scholarship

Type of award: Scholarship.
Intended use: For full-time junior or senior study at accredited 4-year institution in United States.
Eligibility: Applicant must be female. Applicant must be U.S. citizen or permanent resident.
Basis for selection: Major/career interest in engineering. Applicant must demonstrate high academic achievement.
Application requirements: Recommendations, essay, transcript, proof of eligibility.
Additional information: Applicants must be enrolled or plan to be enrolled in an ABET- or CSAB-accredited program. Minimum 3.0 GPA. Application forms available through the Deans of Engineering at eligible schools, through SWE sections, SWE student sections and from SWE Headquarters. Include SASE with requests for hard copy from SWE Headquarters. Application form also available on Website. Applicants considered for all scholarships for which they are eligible and need submit only one application package.

Amount of award:	$6,000
Number of awards:	1
Application deadline:	February 1
Notification begins:	May 15
Total amount awarded:	$6,000

Contact:
Society of Women Engineers
World Headquarters
230 E. Ohio Street, Suite 400
Chicago, IL 60611-3265
Phone: 312-596-5223
Fax: 312-596-5252
Web: www.swe.org

Lockheed Aeronautics Company Scholarships

Type of award: Scholarship.
Intended use: For full-time junior study at accredited 4-year institution in United States.

Eligibility: Applicant must be female. Applicant must be U.S. citizen or permanent resident.

Basis for selection: Major/career interest in engineering, electrical/electronic or engineering, mechanical. Applicant must demonstrate high academic achievement.

Application requirements: Recommendations, essay, transcript, proof of eligibility.

Additional information: Awards given to one student in each of above majors. Applicants must be enrolled or plan to be enrolled in an ABET- or CSAB-accredited program. Minimum 3.5 GPA. Application forms available through the Deans of Engineering at eligible schools, through SWE sections, SWE student sections and from SWE Headquarters. Include SASE with requests for hard copy from SWE Headquarters. Application form also available on Website. Applicants considered for all scholarships for which they are eligible and need submit only one application package.

Amount of award:	$1,000
Number of awards:	2
Application deadline:	February 1
Notification begins:	May 15
Total amount awarded:	$2,000

Contact:
Society of Women Engineers
World Headquarters
230 E. Ohio Street, Suite 400
Chicago, IL 60611-3265
Phone: 312-596-5223
Fax: 312-596-5252
Web: www.swe.org

Lockheed Martin Corporation Scholarships

Type of award: Scholarship.

Intended use: For full-time freshman study at accredited 4-year institution in United States.

Eligibility: Applicant must be female, high school senior. Applicant must be U.S. citizen or permanent resident.

Basis for selection: Major/career interest in engineering. Applicant must demonstrate high academic achievement.

Application requirements: Recommendations, essay, transcript, proof of eligibility.

Additional information: Includes travel grant for the SWE National Conference. Applicants must be enrolled or plan to be enrolled in an ABET- or CSAB-accredited program or SWE-approved school. Minimum 3.5 GPA. Application forms available through the deans of engineering at eligible schools and from SWE sections, SWE student sections and SWE Headquarters. Include SASE with requests for hard copy from SWE Headquarters. Application form also available on Website. Applicants considered for all scholarships for which they are eligible therefore need only submit one application package.

Amount of award:	$3,000
Number of awards:	2
Application deadline:	May 15
Notification begins:	September 15
Total amount awarded:	$6,000

Contact:
Society of Women Engineers
World Headquarters
230 E. Ohio Street, Suite 400
Chicago, IL 60611-3265
Phone: 312-596-5223
Fax: 312-596-5252
Web: www.swe.org

MASWE Scholarships

Type of award: Scholarship.

Intended use: For full-time sophomore, junior or senior study at accredited 4-year institution in United States.

Eligibility: Applicant must be female. Applicant must be U.S. citizen or permanent resident.

Basis for selection: Major/career interest in engineering. Applicant must demonstrate financial need and high academic achievement.

Application requirements: Recommendations, essay, transcript, proof of eligibility.

Additional information: Applicants must be enrolled or plan to be enrolled in an ABET- or CSAB-accredited program. Minimum 3.0 GPA. Application forms available through the Deans of Engineering at eligible schools, through SWE sections, SWE student sections and from SWE Headquarters. Include SASE with requests for hard copy from SWE Headquarters. Application form also available on Website. Applicants considered for all scholarships for which they are eligible and need submit only one application package.

Amount of award:	$2,000
Number of awards:	4
Application deadline:	February 1
Notification begins:	May 15
Total amount awarded:	$8,000

Contact:
Society of Women Engineers
World Headquarters
230 E. Ohio Street, Suite 400
Chicago, IL 60611-3265
Phone: 312-596-5223
Fax: 312-596-5252
Web: www.swe.org

Meridith Thoms Memorial Scholarships

Type of award: Scholarship.

Intended use: For full-time sophomore, junior or senior study at accredited 4-year institution in United States.

Eligibility: Applicant must be female. Applicant must be U.S. citizen or permanent resident.

Basis for selection: Major/career interest in engineering. Applicant must demonstrate high academic achievement.

Application requirements: Recommendations, essay, transcript, proof of eligibility.

Additional information: Minimum GPA 3.0. Applicants must be enrolled or plan to be enrolled in an ABET- or CSAB-accredited program. Application forms available through the deans of engineering at eligible schools and from SWE sections, SWE student sections and SWE Headquarters. Include SASE with requests for hard copy from SWE Headquarters. Application form also available on Website. Applicants considered for all scholarships for which they are eligible and need submit only one application package.

Amount of award:	$2,000
Number of awards:	6
Application deadline:	February 1
Notification begins:	May 15
Total amount awarded:	$12,000

Contact:
Society of Women Engineers
World Headquarters
230 E. Ohio Street, Suite 400
Chicago, IL 60611-3265
Phone: 312-596-5223
Fax: 312-596-5252
Web: www.swe.org

Microsoft Corporation Scholarships

Type of award: Scholarship.
Intended use: For full-time sophomore, junior, senior or master's study at accredited 4-year institution in United States.
Eligibility: Applicant must be female. Applicant must be U.S. citizen or permanent resident.
Basis for selection: Major/career interest in engineering, computer or computer/information sciences. Applicant must demonstrate high academic achievement.
Application requirements: Recommendations, essay, transcript, proof of eligibility.
Additional information: Graduate students eligible only in first year of master's study. Applicants must be enrolled or plan to be enrolled in an ABET- or CSAB-accredited program or SWE-approved school. Minimum 3.5 GPA. Application forms available through the deans of engineering at eligible schools and from SWE sections, SWE student sections and SWE Headquarters. Include SASE with requests for hard copy from SWE Headquarters. Application form also available on Website. Applicants considered for all scholarships for which they are eligible and need submit only one application package.

Amount of award:	$2,500
Number of awards:	2
Application deadline:	February 1
Notification begins:	May 15
Total amount awarded:	$5,000

Contact:
Society of Women Engineers
World Headquarters
230 E. Ohio Street, Suite 400
Chicago, IL 60611-3265
Phone: 312-596-5223
Fax: 312-644-8557
Web: www.swe.org

New Jersey Scholarship

Type of award: Scholarship.
Intended use: For full-time freshman study at accredited 4-year institution in United States.
Eligibility: Applicant must be female, high school senior. Applicant must be U.S. citizen or permanent resident residing in New Jersey.
Basis for selection: Major/career interest in engineering. Applicant must demonstrate high academic achievement.
Application requirements: Recommendations, essay, transcript, proof of eligibility.
Additional information: Applicants must be enrolled or plan to be enrolled in an ABET- or CSAB-accredited program or SWE approved school. Minimum 3.5 GPA. Application forms available through the Deans of Engineering at eligible schools, through SWE sections, SWE student sections and from SWE Headquarters. Include SASE with requests for hard copy from SWE Headquarters. Application form also available on Website. Applicants considered for all scholarships for which they are eligible and need submit only one application package.

Amount of award:	$1,500
Number of awards:	1
Application deadline:	May 15
Notification begins:	September 15
Total amount awarded:	$1,500

Contact:
Society of Women Engineers
World Headquarters
230 E. Ohio Street, Suite 400
Chicago, IL 60611-3265
Phone: 312-596-5223
Fax: 312-644-8557
Web: www.swe.org

Northrop Grumman Corporation Scholarship

Type of award: Scholarship.
Intended use: For full-time sophomore, junior or senior study at accredited 4-year institution in United States.
Eligibility: Applicant must be female. Applicant must be U.S. citizen or permanent resident.
Basis for selection: Major/career interest in aerospace; engineering, chemical; engineering, computer; computer/information sciences; engineering, electrical/electronic or engineering, materials. Applicant must demonstrate high academic achievement.
Application requirements: Recommendations, essay, transcript, proof of eligibility.
Additional information: Minimum 3.0 GPA. Applicants must be enrolled or plan to be enrolled in ABET- or CSAB-accredited program. Application forms available through the deans of engineering at eligible schools and from SWE sections, SWE student sections and SWE Headquarters. Include SASE with requests for hard copy from SWE Headquarters. Application form also available on Website. Applicants considered for all scholarships for which they are eligible and need submit only one application package.

Amount of award:	$5,000
Number of awards:	2
Application deadline:	February 1

Contact:
Society of Women Engineers
230 E. Ohio Street
Suite 400
Chicago, IL 60611-3265
Phone: 312-596-5223
Fax: 312-596-5252
Web: www.swe.org

Olive Lynn Salembier Reentry Scholarship

Type of award: Scholarship.
Intended use: For undergraduate or graduate study at accredited 4-year or graduate institution in United States.
Eligibility: Applicant must be female. Applicant must be U.S. citizen or permanent resident.
Basis for selection: Major/career interest in engineering.
Application requirements: Recommendations, essay, transcript, proof of eligibility.
Additional information: Eligibility restricted to women who have been out of school for at least two years prior to reentry. Also open to women who have been out of engineering workforce and school at least two years. Applicants must be enrolled or plan to be enrolled in an ABET- or CSAB-accredited program or SWE approved school. Minimum 3.0

Scholarships

GPA after first year of reentry. Application forms available through the Deans of Engineering at eligible schools, through SWE sections, SWE student sections and from SWE Headquarters. Include SASE with requests for hard copy from SWE Headquarters. Application form also available on Website. Applicants considered for all scholarships for which they are eligible and need submit only one application package.

Amount of award:	$2,000
Number of awards:	1
Application deadline:	May 15
Notification begins:	September 15
Total amount awarded:	$2,000

Contact:
Society of Women Engineers
World Headquarters
230 E. Ohio Street, Suite 400
Chicago, IL 60611-3265
Phone: 312-596-5223
Fax: 312-644-8557
Web: www.swe.org

Past Presidents Scholarships

Type of award: Scholarship.

Intended use: For full-time sophomore, junior, senior or graduate study at accredited 4-year or graduate institution in United States.

Eligibility: Applicant must be female. Applicant must be U.S. citizen.

Basis for selection: Major/career interest in engineering. Applicant must demonstrate high academic achievement.

Application requirements: Recommendations, essay, transcript, proof of eligibility. 3.0/4.0 Minimum GPA.

Additional information: Applicants must be enrolled or plan to be enrolled in an ABET- or CSAB-accredited program or SWE approved school. Application forms available through the Deans of Engineering at eligible schools, through SWE sections, SWE student sections and from SWE Headquarters. Include SASE with requests for hard copy from SWE Headquarters. Application form also available on Website. Applicants considered for all scholarships for which they are eligible therefore need only submit one application package.

Amount of award:	$1,500
Number of awards:	2
Application deadline:	February 1
Notification begins:	May 15
Total amount awarded:	$3,000

Contact:
Society of Women Engineers
World Headquarters
230 E. Ohio Street, Suite 400
Chicago, IL 60611-3265
Phone: 312-596-5223
Fax: 312-644-8557
Web: www.swe.org

Rockwell Corporation Scholarships

Type of award: Scholarship.

Intended use: For full-time junior study at accredited 4-year institution in United States.

Eligibility: Applicant must be Alaskan native, Asian American, African American, Mexican American, Hispanic American, Puerto Rican or American Indian. Applicant must be female. Applicant must be U.S. citizen or permanent resident.

Basis for selection: Major/career interest in engineering. Applicant must demonstrate leadership.

Application requirements: Recommendations, essay, transcript, proof of eligibility.

Additional information: Preference given to members of groups underrepresented in engineering. Must demonstrate leadership potential. Applicants must be enrolled or plan to be enrolled in an ABET- or CSAB-accredited program. Minimum 3.5 GPA. Application forms available through the deans of engineering at eligible schools and from SWE sections, SWE student sections and SWE Headquarters. Include SASE with requests for hard copy from SWE Headquarters. Application form also available on Website. Applicants considered for all scholarships for which they are eligible and need submit only one application package.

Amount of award:	$3,000
Number of awards:	2
Application deadline:	February 1
Notification begins:	May 15
Total amount awarded:	$6,000

Contact:
Society of Women Engineers
World Headquarters
230 E. Ohio Street, Suite 400
Chicago, IL 60611-3265
Phone: 312-596-5223
Fax: 312-596-5252
Web: www.swe.org

Susan Miszkowitz Memorial Scholarship

Type of award: Scholarship.

Intended use: For full-time sophomore, junior or senior study at accredited 4-year institution in United States.

Eligibility: Applicant must be female. Applicant must be U.S. citizen or permanent resident.

Basis for selection: Major/career interest in engineering. Applicant must demonstrate high academic achievement.

Additional information: Minimum 3.0 GPA. Applicants must be enrolled or plan to be enrolled in an ABET- or CSAB-accredited program. Application forms available through the deans of engineering at eligible schools and from SWE sections, SWE student sections and SWE Headquarters. Include SASE with requests for hard copy from SWE Headquarters. Application form also available on Website. Applicants considered for all scholarships for which they are eligible and need submit only one application package.

Amount of award:	$1,000
Number of awards:	1
Application deadline:	February 1

Contact:
Society of Women Engineers
230 E. Ohio Street
Suite 400
Chicago, IL 60611-3265
Phone: 312-596-5223
Fax: 312-596-5252
Web: www.swe.org

Soicety of Women Engineers

General Electric Foundation Scholarship

Type of award: Scholarship.
Intended use: For full-time freshman study at 4-year institution in United States or Canada.
Eligibility: Applicant must be female, high school senior. Applicant must be U.S. citizen.
Basis for selection: Major/career interest in engineering.
Additional information: Minimum 3.5 GPA. Applicants must be enrolled or plan to be enrolled in an ABET- or CSAB-accredited program. Scholarship includes a travel grant for the SWE National Conference. Application forms available through the deans of engineering at eligible schools and from SWE sections, SWE student sections and SWE Headquarters. Include SASE with requests for hard copy from SWE Headquarters. Application form also available on Website. Applicants considered for all scholarships for which they are eligible and need submit only one application package.

Amount of award:	$1,250
Number of awards:	3
Application deadline:	May 15

Contact:
Society of Women Engineers
230 E. Ohio Street
Suite 400
Chicago, IL 60611-3265
Phone: 312-596-5223
Fax: 312-596-5252
Web: www.swe.org

Soil and Water Conservation Society

Donald A. Williams Soil Conservation Scholarship

Type of award: Scholarship.
Intended use: For undergraduate study.
Eligibility: Applicant or parent must be member/participant of Soil and Water Conservation Society.
Basis for selection: Major/career interest in natural resources/conservation. Applicant must demonstrate financial need, depth of character and seriousness of purpose.
Additional information: Must have been member of SWCS for more than one year. Must demonstrate integrity, ability, and competence in line of work. Must have completed at least one year of full-time employment and be currently employed in a natural resource conservation endeavor. Send SASE or visit Website for application.

Amount of award:	$1,500
Number of awards:	3
Application deadline:	February 12
Total amount awarded:	$4,500

Contact:
Soil and Water Conservation Society
945 SW Ankeny Road
Ankeny, IA 50021
Phone: 515-289-2331
Fax: 515-289-1227
Web: www.swcs.org

Melville H. Cohee Student Leader Conservation Scholarship

Type of award: Scholarship.
Intended use: For full-time junior, senior or master's study at accredited 4-year or graduate institution.
Eligibility: Applicant or parent must be member/participant of Soil and Water Conservation Society.
Basis for selection: Major/career interest in natural resources/conservation; agricultural economics; forestry; engineering, agricultural; hydrology or wildlife/fisheries. Applicant must demonstrate high academic achievement and leadership.
Additional information: Must have been member of SWCS for more than one year; chapter must have had at least 15 members. Applicant must have minimum 3.0 GPA. Applicant may not be employee or immediate family member of scholarship selection committee. Those studying soils, planned land use management, wildlife biology, rural sociology, agronomy or water management also eligible. May not be combined with other SWCS scholarships. Visit Website for application and additional information.

Amount of award:	$1,000
Number of awards:	2
Application deadline:	February 12
Total amount awarded:	$2,000

Contact:
Soil and Water Conservation Society
945 SW Ankeny Road
Ankeny, IA 50021
Phone: 515-289-2331
Fax: 515-289-1227
Web: www.swcs.org

Sons of Italy Foundation

Henry Salvatori Scholarship

Type of award: Scholarship.
Intended use: For full-time undergraduate study.
Eligibility: Applicant must be high school senior. Applicant must be Italian. Applicant must be U.S. citizen.
Basis for selection: Applicant must demonstrate high academic achievement, depth of character, leadership, patriotism, seriousness of purpose and service orientation.
Application requirements: $25 application fee. Recommendations, essay, transcript, proof of eligibility. SAT/ACT scores. Two letters of recommendation from public figures who have demonstrated the ideals of liberty, freedom and equality in their work.
Additional information: Applicant must be of some Italian descent. Application deadline in late January. Contact sponsor for exact date and application materials after beginning of October.

Amount of award:	$5,000
Number of awards:	1
Total amount awarded:	$5,000

Contact:
Soil and Water Conservation Society
945 SW Ankeny Road
Ankeny, IA 50021
Phone: 515-289-2331
Fax: 515-289-1227
Web: www.swcs.org

Scholarships

Contact:
Order of Sons of Italy in America
219 E Street NE
Washington, DC 20002
Phone: 202-547-5106
Web: www.osia.org

Sons of Italy National Leadership Grant

Type of award: Scholarship.
Intended use: For full-time undergraduate, master's, doctoral or first professional study at accredited 4-year or graduate institution in United States.
Eligibility: Applicant must be Italian. Applicant must be U.S. citizen.
Basis for selection: Applicant must demonstrate high academic achievement, depth of character, leadership, seriousness of purpose and service orientation.
Application requirements: $25 application fee. Essay, transcript, proof of eligibility. SAT/ACT scores; activities list or resume; two recommendations; application fee.
Additional information: Applicant must be of some Italian descent. Amount and number of awards vary. Call for information on deadlines, availability of awards and application fees beginning October.

Amount of award:	$4,000-$25,000
Number of awards:	12
Application deadline:	February 28

Contact:
Order of Sons of Italy in America
219 E Street NE
Washington, DC 20002
Phone: 202-547-5106
Web: www.osia.org

Sons of Norway Foundation

Astrid G. Cates Scholarship Fund and Myrtle Beinhauer Scholarship

Type of award: Scholarship.
Intended use: For undergraduate study at postsecondary institution.
Eligibility: Applicant or parent must be member/participant of Sons of Norway. Applicant must be U.S. citizen.
Basis for selection: Applicant must demonstrate financial need, high academic achievement, depth of character and service orientation.
Application requirements: Recommendations, transcript, proof of eligibility.
Additional information: Applicant, parent or grandparent must be a current member of Sons of Norway. Student must include the following information with application: GPA, what type of study is intended and at which institution, and when. Related fees must be specified as well as long-term career goals, involvement in the Sons of Norway, and extracurricular activities, and financial need. The Astrid G. Cates Scholarship ranges from $500 to $750; the Myrtle Beinhauer Scholarship is $3,000 and is awarded to the most qualified of all candidates. A student can be awarded a maximum of two scholarships within a five-year period.

Amount of award:	$500-$3,000
Number of awards:	6
Number of applicants:	99
Application deadline:	March 1
Notification begins:	May 1

Contact:
Sons of Norway Foundation
c/o Sons of Norway
1455 West Lake Street
Minneapolis, MN 55408
Web: www.sonsofnorway.com

King Olav V Norwegian-American Heritage Fund

Type of award: Scholarship.
Intended use: For full-time undergraduate or graduate study at accredited postsecondary institution.
Eligibility: Applicant must be at least 18. Applicant must be international student or Norwegian or American.
Basis for selection: Major/career interest in Scandinavian studies/research. Applicant must demonstrate financial need, high academic achievement, depth of character, leadership and service orientation.
Application requirements: Recommendations, essay, transcript, proof of eligibility. Three letters of recommendation. Essay of 500 words or less with the reasons for applying gor a scholarship, the course of study to be pursued, the length of the course, the name of the instituiton which applicant will attend and its tuitions and costs, and the amount of financial assitance required. Also applicants need to state how their course of study will benefit their community and be in accord with the goals and objectives of the Sons of Norway Foundation. Grade Point Average, participation in school and community activities, work experience, education and carrer goals are also factors.
Additional information: Open to Americans who have demonstrated keen and sincere interest in Norwegian heritage or Norwegians who have demonstrated interest in American heritage and now desire to further study their heritage (arts, crafts, literature, history, music, folklore, etc.) at recognized educational institution.

Amount of award:	$250-$3,000
Number of awards:	9
Number of applicants:	100
Application deadline:	March 1
Notification begins:	May 1
Total amount awarded:	$10,000

Contact:
Sons of Norway Foundation
1455 West Lake Street
Minneapolis, MN 55408
Web: www.sonsofnorway.com

Nancy Lorraine Jensen Memorial Scholarship

Type of award: Scholarship, renewable.
Intended use: For full-time freshman, sophomore, junior or senior study.
Eligibility: Applicant or parent must be member/participant of Sons of Norway. Applicant must be female, at least 17, no older than 35. Applicant must be U.S. citizen.
Basis for selection: Major/career interest in chemistry; physics; engineering, electrical/electronic or engineering, mechanical. Applicant must demonstrate high academic achievement, depth of character and seriousness of purpose.

Application requirements: Recommendations, essay, transcript, proof of eligibility. Statement of SAT or ACT scores, an essay, grade transcript from school and three letters of recommendation.

Additional information: Employees of NASA Goddard Space Flight Center, Greenbelt, Maryland, for at least three years also eligible. Minimum SAT score of 1200 or ACT score of 26. Must apply each year.

Amount of award:	Full tuition
Number of awards:	1
Application deadline:	March 1

Contact:
Sons of Norway Foundation
1455 West Lake Street
Minneapolis, MN 55408
Web: www.sonsofnorway.com

South Carolina Commission on Higher Education

LIFE Scholarship Program

Type of award: Scholarship, renewable.
Intended use: For full-time undergraduate study at 2-year or 4-year institution. Designated institutions: Eligible public and private institutions in South Carolina.
Eligibility: Applicant must be high school senior. Applicant must be U.S. citizen or permanent resident residing in South Carolina.
Basis for selection: Applicant must demonstrate high academic achievement.
Application requirements: Transcript, proof of eligibility.
Additional information: Applicant must be a full-time enrolled degree-seeking undergradute. First-time entering freshman must meet two of three criteria: 3.0 high school GPA on the uniform grading scale; score at least 1100 on SAT or 24 on ACT; rank in top 30 percent of graduating class. Students should contact institution's financial aid office.

Amount of award:	$3,000-$5,000
Number of awards:	20,340
Total amount awarded:	$54,300,000

Contact:
South Carolina Commission on Higher Education
1333 Main Street, Suite 200
Columbia, SC 29201
Phone: 803-737-2260
Fax: 803-737-2297
Web: www.che.sc.gov

Lottery Tuition Assistance Program

Type of award: Scholarship, renewable.
Intended use: For undergraduate study at 2-year institution in United States. Designated institutions: Eligible South Carolina institutions.
Eligibility: Applicant must be residing in South Carolina.
Basis for selection: Applicant must demonstrate financial need.
Application requirements: Proof of eligibility. FAFSA.
Additional information: Award may be as high as cost of tuition; up to $876/semester for full-time students and up to $73/credit hour if part time. All federal grants and need-based grants must be awarded first before determining amount for which student is eligible. Student must be degree-seeking and enrolled in minimum of six credit hours. See Website for further information.

Amount of award:	$73-$876

Contact:
South Carolina Commission on Higher Education
1333 Main Street, Suite 200
Columbia, SC 29201
Phone: 803-737-2260
Fax: 803-737-2297
Web: www.che.sc.gov

Palmetto Fellows Scholarship Program

Type of award: Scholarship, renewable.
Intended use: For full-time undergraduate study at 4-year institution. Designated institutions: Eligible South Carolina public and private institutions.
Eligibility: Applicant must be high school senior. Applicant must be U.S. citizen or permanent resident residing in South Carolina.
Basis for selection: Applicant must demonstrate high academic achievement.
Application requirements: Transcript. Online application, test scores.
Additional information: Must score 1200 on SAT or 27 on ACT, earn a cumulative 3.5 GPA, and rank in top five percent of sophomore or junior class. High school graduates or students who have completed a home-school program as prescribed by law may be eligible. Scholarship must be used toward the cost of attendance at a four-year degree-granting institution. For more information, contact guidance counselor or the commission.

Amount of award:	$6,700
Number of awards:	4,000
Total amount awarded:	$17,000,000

Contact:
South Carolina Commission on Higher Education
1333 Main Street, Suite 200
Columbia, SC 29201
Phone: 803-737-2260 or 877-349-7183
Fax: 803-737-2297
Web: www.che.sc.gov

South Carolina HOPE Scholarships

Type of award: Scholarship.
Intended use: For freshman study at 4-year institution in United States. Designated institutions: Eligible South Carolina public or private college/university.
Eligibility: Applicant must be high school senior. Applicant must be U.S. citizen or permanent resident residing in South Carolina.
Basis for selection: Applicant must demonstrate high academic achievement.
Application requirements: Transcript, proof of eligibility.
Additional information: There is no application. College or university will determine eligibility based upon official high school transcript and will notify students directly. Student must earn at least a cumulative 3.0 GPA. Student must certify that he/she has not been convicted of any felonies or drug/alcohol misdemeanors within the past academic year. May also contact institution's financial aid office for more information.

Amount of award:	$2,650

Contact:
South Carolina Commission on Higher Education
1333 Main St., Suite 200
Columbia, SC 29201
Phone: 803-737-2260
Fax: 803-737-2297
Web: www.che.sc.gov

South Carolina Need-Based Grants Program

Type of award: Scholarship.
Intended use: For undergraduate study at 2-year or 4-year institution outside United States. Designated institutions: South Carolina public and independent institutions.
Eligibility: Applicant must be U.S. citizen or permanent resident residing in South Carolina.
Basis for selection: Applicant must demonstrate financial need.
Application requirements: FAFSA.
Additional information: Students eligible to receive award for maximum of eight full-time equivalent terms or until degree is earned, whichever is less. Must enroll in at least 12 credit hours per semester if full-time or six credit hours per semester if part-time.

Amount of award:	$1,250-$2,500
Number of awards:	20,000
Total amount awarded:	$12,000,000

Contact:
Financial aid office at public college or university or
S.C. Higher Ed. Tuition Grants Commission
1333 Main Street, Suite 200
Columbia, SC 29201
Phone: 803-737-2260 or 877-349-7183
Fax: 803-737-2297
Web: www.che.sc.gov

South Carolina Higher Education Tuition Grants Commission

South Carolina Tuition Grants

Type of award: Scholarship, renewable.
Intended use: For full-time undergraduate study at accredited 2-year or 4-year institution in United States. Designated institutions: SACS-accredited South Carolina private, nonprofit institutions.
Eligibility: Applicant must be U.S. citizen residing in South Carolina.
Basis for selection: Applicant must demonstrate financial need.
Application requirements: FAFSA.
Additional information: Award amount varies. Recipient may reapply for up to four years of grant assistance. Incoming freshmen must score 900 on SAT or 19 on the ACT, or graduate in upper 3/4 of high school class. Upperclassmen must complete 24 semester hours and meet college's satisfactory progress requirements. Application is automatic with FAFSA; submit to federal processor and list eligible college in college choice section. All eligible applicants funded if deadline is met. Contact campus financial aid office for details.

Application deadline:	June 30

Contact:
South Carolina Higher Education Tuition Grants Commission
101 Business Park Blvd., Suite 2100
Columbia, SC 29203-9498
Phone: 803-896-1120
Fax: 803-896-1126
Web: www.sctuitiongrants.com

South Dakota Board of Regents

South Dakota Annis I. Fowler/Kaden Scholarship

Type of award: Scholarship.
Intended use: For freshman study. Designated institutions: University of South Dakota, Black Hills State University, Dakota State University or Northern State University.
Eligibility: Applicant must be U.S. citizen residing in South Dakota.
Basis for selection: Major/career interest in education. Applicant must demonstrate financial need, high academic achievement, depth of character, leadership, seriousness of purpose and service orientation.
Application requirements: Recommendations, essay, transcript, proof of eligibility. Transcript must include class rank, cumulative GPA, and list of courses to be taken during senior year. Complete Fowler/Kaden application form. Two letters of recommendation. Copy of applicant's ACT scores.
Additional information: Open to high school seniors who have a cumulative GPA of 3.0 after three years. Applicants must select elementary education as major field. Special consideration given to applicants with demonstrated motivation, a disability, or who are self-supporting.

Amount of award:	$1,200
Number of awards:	2
Application deadline:	February 9

Contact:
South Dakota Board of Regents
Scholarship Committee
306 E. Capitol Avenue, Suite 200
Pierre, SD 57501-3159
Phone: 605-773-3455

South Dakota Ardell Bjugstad Scholarship

Type of award: Scholarship.
Intended use: For freshman study at postsecondary institution in United States.
Eligibility: Applicant must be American Indian. Member of federally recognized Indian tribe whose reservation is in North Dakota or South Dakota. Applicant must be high school senior. Applicant must be U.S. citizen residing in South Dakota or North Dakota.
Basis for selection: Major/career interest in agribusiness; agriculture; natural resources/conservation or environmental science. Applicant must demonstrate high academic achievement, depth of character, leadership and seriousness of purpose.
Application requirements: Recommendations, transcript, proof of eligibility. Transcript must include class rank and

cumulative GPA. Completed Bjugstad Scholarship application form. Two letters of recommendation.
Additional information: Verification of tribal enrollment required.

Amount of award:	$500
Number of awards:	1
Application deadline:	February 9

Contact:
South Dakota Board of Regents
Scholarship Committee
306 E. Capitol Avenue, Suite 200
Pierre, SD 57502-3159
Phone: 605-773-3455

South Dakota Haines Memorial Scholarship

Type of award: Scholarship.
Intended use: For full-time sophomore, junior or senior study at accredited 4-year institution in United States. Designated institutions: South Dakota public universities including: BHSU, DSU, NSU, SDSU, USD.
Eligibility: Applicant must be residing in South Dakota.
Basis for selection: Major/career interest in education. Applicant must demonstrate depth of character, leadership, seriousness of purpose and service orientation.
Application requirements: Essay, transcript, proof of eligibility. Include resume with completed Haines Scholarship application form. Must submit two two-page essays: one essay describing personal philosophy and another describing philosophy of education.
Additional information: Minimum 2.5 GPA.

Amount of award:	$2,150
Number of awards:	1
Application deadline:	February 9
Notification begins:	March 27

Contact:
South Dakota Board of Regents Scholarship Committee
306 E. Capitol, Suite 200
Pierre, SD 57501-3159
Phone: 605-773-3455

South Dakota Marlin R. Scarborough Memorial Scholarship

Type of award: Scholarship.
Intended use: For full-time junior study at accredited 4-year institution in United States. Designated institutions: South Dakota public universities.
Eligibility: Applicant must be residing in South Dakota.
Basis for selection: Major/career interest in humanities/liberal arts. Applicant must demonstrate high academic achievement, depth of character, leadership, seriousness of purpose and service orientation.
Application requirements: Essay, transcript, proof of eligibility, nomination by a participating South Dakota public university. Completed Scarborough Scholarship application form. Must submit essay explaining leadership and academic qualities, career plans, and educational interests.
Additional information: For junior year study only. Must be sophomore at time of application. Minimum 3.5 GPA. Must have completed three full semesters at same university. Call or e-mail sponsor for deadlines and application.

Amount of award:	$1,000
Number of awards:	1

Contact:
South Dakota Board of Regents Scholarship Committee
306 East Capitol, Suite 200
Pierre, SD 57501-3159
Phone: 605-773-3455

South Dakota Department of Education

South Dakota Robert C. Byrd Honors Scholarship

Type of award: Scholarship, renewable.
Intended use: For full-time undergraduate study in United States.
Eligibility: Applicant must be high school senior. Applicant must be U.S. citizen or permanent resident residing in South Dakota.
Basis for selection: Applicant must demonstrate high academic achievement.
Application requirements: Transcript. Must have ACT score of 30 or above.
Additional information: Applicant must be a high school senior with a minimum 3.5 GPA.

Amount of award:	$1,500
Number of awards:	80
Number of applicants:	200
Application deadline:	May 1
Notification begins:	March 1
Total amount awarded:	$115,000

Contact:
South Dakota Department of Education
700 Governors Drive
Pierre, SD 57501-2291
Phone: 605-773-5669
Fax: 605-773-6139
Web: www.state.sd.us/deca

South Dakota Military and Veterans Affairs

South Dakota National Guard Tuition Assistance

Type of award: Scholarship, renewable.
Intended use: For undergraduate study at vocational or 4-year institution.
Eligibility: Applicant or parent must be member/participant of South Dakota National Guard. Applicant must be residing in South Dakota. Applicant or parent must be currently serving in South Dakota National Guard.
Application requirements: Proof of eligibility.
Additional information: Provides tuition/fee waiver of 50 percent.

Amount of award:	Full tuition
Number of awards:	500
Number of applicants:	500
Total amount awarded:	$125,000

Contact:
SDNG Unit or South Dakota Department of Military and
Veterans Affairs
Soldiers and Sailors Building
500 East Capitol Avenue
Pierre, SD 57501-5070
Phone: 605-773-3269

Southern Nursery Organization

Southern Nursery Organization Sidney B. Meadows Scholarship

Type of award: Scholarship.
Intended use: For junior, senior, master's or doctoral study at 4-year or graduate institution.
Eligibility: Applicant must be U.S. citizen.
Basis for selection: Major/career interest in horticulture.
Additional information: Must be enrolled in ornamental horticulture or related discipline in good standing. Minimum 2.25 GPA for undergraduates, 3.0 for graduates. Must be resident of one of 16 states in Southern Nursery Organization. For list of states, application, and additional information, visit Website.

Amount of award:	$2,500
Application deadline:	May 31

Contact:
Southern Nursery Organization
1827 Power Ferry Road
Building 4, Suite 100
Atlanta, GA 30339
Web: www.sna.org/education

Southwest Student Services Corporation

Anne Lindeman Memorial Scholarship

Type of award: Scholarship.
Intended use: For junior or senior study at 4-year institution in United States. Designated institutions: Arizona universities.
Eligibility: Applicant must be U.S. citizen residing in Arizona.
Basis for selection: Major/career interest in education; health sciences or social/behavioral sciences. Applicant must demonstrate high academic achievement.
Application requirements: Recommendations, essay, transcript. Resume, application. Minimum 2.5 GPA.

Amount of award:	$1,000
Number of awards:	3
Application deadline:	April 1
Total amount awarded:	$3,000

Contact:
Southwest Student Services Corporation
Attn: Anne Lindeman Scholarship Committee
P.O. Box 41595
Mesa, AZ 85274
Fax: 480-461-6595
Web: www.sssc.com

Arizona Community College Scholarship

Type of award: Scholarship, renewable.
Intended use: For full-time undergraduate study at 2-year institution. Designated institutions: Arizona community colleges.
Eligibility: Applicant must be high school senior. Applicant must be residing in Arizona.
Basis for selection: Applicant must demonstrate high academic achievement.
Application requirements: Essay, transcript. Must demonstrate community service achievement.
Additional information: Notification in mid-May. Scholarship is renewable for one additional year if recipient maintains 2.5 GPA.

Amount of award:	$500
Number of awards:	4
Application deadline:	April 30
Total amount awarded:	$2,000

Contact:
Southwest Student Services Corporation
Attn: Community College Scholarship Committee
P.O. Box 41595
Mesa, AZ 85274
Fax: 480-461-6595
Web: www.sssc.com

SPIE - The International Society for Optical Engineering

SPIE Educational Scholarship in Optical Science and Engineering

Type of award: Scholarship, renewable.
Intended use: For full-time undergraduate, graduate or non-degree study in United States.
Basis for selection: Major/career interest in engineering; medical specialties/research; electronics or physics. Applicant must demonstrate seriousness of purpose.
Application requirements: Recommendations. Application, two sealed letters of recommendation. Must submit one original of all application documents and six copies, excluding sealed letters.
Additional information: Open to SPIE members; nonmembers may submit SPIE student membership application with scholarship application (dues must accompany to qualify). Applicant must be enrolled full-time in optics, photonics, imaging, optoelectronics or related program at accredited institution for year in which award will be used. Award amount varies. See Website for application.

Amount of award:	$1,000-$7,000
Application deadline:	January 28

Contact:
SPIE/Scholarship Committee
P.O. Box 10
Bellingham, WA 98227-0010
Phone: 360-676-3290 ext. 659
Fax: 360-647-1445
Web: www.spie.org/info/scholarships

Contact:
Scholarship Committee
4590 MacArthur Boulevard
Suite 250
Washington, DC 20007-4226
Phone: 202-944-3285
Fax: 202-944-3295
Web: www.sbaa.org

Spina Bifida Association of America

Spina Bifida Association of America Annual Scholarship

Type of award: Scholarship.
Intended use: For undergraduate study at postsecondary institution in United States.
Basis for selection: Applicant must demonstrate financial need and high academic achievement.
Application requirements: Recommendations, essay, transcript, proof of eligibility. Statement verifying disability from physician. Verification of high school diploma or GED, letter verifying acceptance at school/college. Financial aid forms.
Additional information: Open to all persons with spina bifida. Applicant must be high school graduate or GED recipient. Awards in $500 and $1,000 increments. The number of scholarship awards will be determined by the Scholarship Committee and is based on the total amount of funds available. Visit Website for more information.

Amount of award:	$500-$1,000
Application deadline:	April 1
Total amount awarded:	$10,000

Contact:
Scholarship Committee
4590 MacArthur Boulevard, NW
Suite 250
Washington, DC 20007-4226
Phone: 202-944-3285
Fax: 202-944-3295
Web: www.sbaa.org

Spina Bifida Association of America Four-Year Scholarship

Type of award: Scholarship, renewable.
Intended use: For full-time undergraduate or graduate study at 4-year institution.
Basis for selection: Applicant must demonstrate financial need, high academic achievement, leadership and service orientation.
Application requirements: Recommendations, essay, transcript. SAT/ACT scores. Statement verifying disability from physician. Verification of high school diploma or GED, letter verifying acceptance at school/college. Financial aid forms.
Additional information: Open to all persons with spina bifida. May be used for any postsecondary four-year study, vocational and specialized training.

Number of awards:	1
Application deadline:	February 15
Notification begins:	November 1
Total amount awarded:	$20,000

Spinsters Ink

Young Feminist Scholarship Program

Type of award: Scholarship.
Intended use: For freshman study.
Eligibility: Applicant must be female, high school senior. Applicant must be U.S. citizen or permanent resident.
Basis for selection: Competition/talent/interest in writing/journalism, based on best essay on feminism. Major/career interest in journalism or publishing.
Application requirements: Essay. Include typed application. Essay must be no longer than 1,200 words.
Additional information: Scholarship applicable to college of choice. Winner will also be invited to attend Norcroft: A Writing Retreat for Women for one week. Visit Website for application details.

Amount of award:	$1,000
Number of awards:	1
Application deadline:	December 31
Notification begins:	March 8

Contact:
Young Feminist Scholarship
Spinsters Ink
P.O. Box 22005
Denver, CO 80222
Web: www.spinsters-ink.com

State Council of Higher Education for Virginia

Eastern Shore Tuition Assistance Program

Type of award: Scholarship, renewable.
Intended use: For junior or senior study in United States. Designated institutions: University of Maryland-Eastern Shore or Salisbury State University.
Eligibility: Applicant must be U.S. citizen or permanent resident residing in Virginia.
Application requirements: Completed application. Applicant cannot hold any prior baccalaureate or higher degree.
Additional information: No more than two years of full-time awards or equivalent. Theology or divinity majors not eligible. Must be a commuter student. For residents of Accomack and Northampton counties. Amount of award varies.

Number of awards:	17,000
Application deadline:	July 31
Total amount awarded:	$41,000,000

Scholarships

Contact:
Eastern Shore Tuition Assistance Program
State Council of Higher Education for VA
James Monroe Building, 101 N. Fourteenth St.
Richmond, VA 23219
Phone: 804-225-2632
Fax: 804-225-2604
Web: www.schev.edu

Virginia Academic Common Market

Type of award: Scholarship.
Intended use: For full-time undergraduate or graduate study at 4-year or graduate institution. Designated institutions: Eligible public institutions outside of Virginia.
Eligibility: Applicant must be permanent resident residing in Virginia.
Application requirements: Application (available online). Applicant must be enrolled full-time at eligible institution.
Additional information: Awards Virginia residents in-state tuition at participating non-Virginia institutions in 13 states in the South. Institution must offer programs unavailable in Virginia public institutions.
Contact:
Academic Common Market/SCHEV
James Monroe Building
101 North Fourteenth Street
Richmond, VA 23219
Phone: 804-225-2632
Fax: 804-225-2638
Web: www.schev.edu

Virginia Tuition Assistance Grant

Type of award: Scholarship, renewable.
Intended use: For full-time undergraduate, master's, doctoral or first professional study at accredited postsecondary institution. Designated institutions: Private, nonprofit institutions in Virginia.
Eligibility: Applicant must be permanent resident residing in Virginia.
Application requirements: Proof of eligibility. Applicant must not be enrolled in program leading to second bachelor, graduate or professional degree.
Additional information: Non-need-based award. Applicant must be in eligible degree program in participating Virginia private college. Theology and divinity majors not eligible. If funding is insufficient, priority given first to renewals, then to new applicants who apply prior to July 31.

Number of awards:	17,000
Application deadline:	July 31
Total amount awarded:	$41,000,000

Contact:
Financial aid office of qualifying postsecondary institution.
Web: www.schev.edu

State of Alabama

Alabama Scholarship for Dependents of Blind Parents

Type of award: Scholarship, renewable.
Intended use: For undergraduate study at vocational, 2-year or 4-year institution. Designated institutions: Alabama public postsecondary institutions.

Eligibility: Parent must be visually impaired. Applicant must be U.S. citizen or permanent resident residing in Alabama.
Basis for selection: Applicant must demonstrate financial need.
Application requirements: Proof of eligibility. Applicant must be dependent of blind parent.
Additional information: Award waives instructional fees and tuition costs at Alabama public institutions of higher education and pays for books and supplies. Parent must be head of household and legally blind, and family income must be at or below 1.3% of federal poverty guidelines.

Amount of award:	Full tuition
Number of awards:	15

Contact:
Alabama Department of Rehabilitation Services
2129 East South Boulevard
Montgomery, AL 36116-2455
Phone: 334-613-2248
Fax: 334-613-3444

State of Maine-Department of Agriculture, Food and Rural Resources

Maine Rural Rehabilitation Fund Scholarship

Type of award: Scholarship, renewable.
Intended use: For full-time undergraduate or graduate study at accredited 2-year or 4-year institution in United States.
Eligibility: Applicant must be U.S. citizen or permanent resident residing in Maine.
Basis for selection: Major/career interest in agriculture; forestry; environmental science or agricultural education. Applicant must demonstrate financial need, high academic achievement and seriousness of purpose.
Application requirements: Transcript, proof of eligibility. Application form, financial aid forms, letter confirming school acceptance for first-time applicant.
Additional information: Applicant must be enrolled or accepted for enrollment at accredited college or university offering agricultural degree. Must demonstrate financial need. Minimum 2.7 GPA (cumulative) or 3.0 GPA in most recent semester. Contact sponsor for application or download from Website. Applications available from Maine Department of Agriculture.

Amount of award:	$800-$2,000
Number of awards:	14
Number of applicants:	14
Application deadline:	June 15
Total amount awarded:	$20,000

Contact:
Maine Rural Rehabilitation Fund Scholarship Committee
Dept. of Agriculture, Food and Rural Resource
28 State House Station
Augusta, ME 04333
Phone: 207-287-7628
Web: www.state.me.us/agriculture

Scholarships

449

Stephen T. Marchello Scholarship Foundation

Stephen T. Marchello Scholarship for Survivors of Childhood Cancer

Type of award: Scholarship, renewable.
Intended use: For undergraduate study at accredited vocational, 2-year or 4-year institution in United States.
Eligibility: Applicant must be survivor of childhood cancer. Applicant must be high school senior. Applicant must be U.S. citizen residing in Colorado or Arizona.
Application requirements: Interview, recommendations, essay, transcript, proof of eligibility. Submit SAT/ACT scores when available. Send SASE.
Additional information: Award is renewable each semester for up to four years. There is a one-time grant of $1000. Visit Website for more information. Submit application online or send SASE to address below. Number of awards varies.

Amount of award:	$1,000-$2,500
Number of awards:	4
Number of applicants:	21
Application deadline:	March 15
Total amount awarded:	$9,250

Contact:
Stephen T. Marchello Scholarship Foundation
1170 E. Long Place
Centennial, CO 80122
Phone: 303-886-5018
Web: www.stmfoundation.org

Student Pilot Network, Inc.

"SPN Flight Dreams" Scholarship Program

Type of award: Scholarship.
Intended use: For undergraduate or non-degree study. Designated institutions: Student Pilot Network participating institutions.
Eligibility: Applicant must be U.S. citizen.
Basis for selection: Major/career interest in aviation.
Application requirements: Essay. School-endorsed application certificate. Student should be active in a flight training program at SPN registered flight school.
Additional information: Applicant must register to become SPN member. Visit Website to search for SPN participating schools using SPN's Flight School Search Engine.

Amount of award:	$250-$1,000
Number of awards:	18
Number of applicants:	5
Application deadline:	November 30
Notification begins:	January 15

Contact:
Student Pilot Network
P.O. Box 854
West Chicago, IL 60186
Phone: 630-584-5424
Web: www.studentpilot.net

Sunkist Growers

A.W. Bodine Sunkist Memorial Scholarship

Type of award: Scholarship, renewable.
Intended use: For full-time undergraduate study at accredited 2-year or 4-year institution.
Eligibility: Applicant must be residing in California or Arizona.
Basis for selection: Applicant must demonstrate financial need, high academic achievement, depth of character, leadership, seriousness of purpose and service orientation.
Application requirements: Recommendations, essay, transcript, proof of eligibility. Tax return (or parent's tax return for applicants younger than 21). SAT/ACT scores.
Additional information: Applicant must have minimum 3.0 GPA. Applicant or someone in immediate family must have derived majority of income from California- or Arizona-based agriculture. All majors eligible. Award renewable up to four years based on annual review. Must maintain 2.7 GPA and carry 12 credits per semester to qualify for renewal.

Amount of award:	$2,000
Number of awards:	22
Number of applicants:	300

Contact:
A.W. Bodine Sunkist Memorial Scholarship
Sunkist Growers
P.O. Box 7888
Van Nuys, CA 91409-7888
Phone: 818-986-4800
Web: www.sunkist.com/about/bodine_scholarship.asp

Supreme Guardian Council, International Order of Job's Daughters

The Grottos Scholarships

Type of award: Scholarship.
Intended use: For full-time undergraduate study at 2-year or 4-year institution.
Eligibility: Applicant or parent must be member/participant of International Order of Job's Daughters. Applicant must be single, female, no older than 30.
Basis for selection: Major/career interest in dentistry. Applicant must demonstrate financial need, high academic achievement, depth of character, leadership and seriousness of purpose.
Application requirements: Recommendations, transcript, proof of eligibility. Photograph. Personal letter.
Additional information: Job's Daughters activities, applicant's financial self-help, and achievements outside of Job's Daughters are also factors in awarding scholarships. Applicants must be trained in the handicapped field. Visit Website for more information.

Amount of award:	$1,500
Application deadline:	April 30

Contact:
International Center for Job's Daughters
233 W. 6th Street
Papillion, NE 68046-2210
Phone: 402-592-7987
Fax: 402-592-2177
Web: www.iojd.org

Supreme Guardian Council, International Order of Job's Daughters Scholarship

Type of award: Scholarship.
Intended use: For undergraduate study at vocational, 2-year or 4-year institution.
Eligibility: Applicant or parent must be member/participant of International Order of Job's Daughters. Applicant must be single, female, no older than 30.
Basis for selection: Applicant must demonstrate financial need, high academic achievement, depth of character, leadership, seriousness of purpose and service orientation.
Application requirements: Recommendations, transcript, proof of eligibility. Photograph. Personal letter.
Additional information: High school seniors eligible to apply. Job's Daughters activities, applicant's financial self-help, and achievements outside of Job's Daughters are also factors evaluated in awarding scholarships. Visit Website for more information.

Amount of award:	$750
Number of applicants:	80
Application deadline:	April 30

Contact:
Supreme Guardian Council
International Order of Job's Daughters
233 West 6 Street
Papillion, NE 68046
Phone: 402-592-7987
Fax: 402-592-2177
Web: www.iojd.org

Susie Holmes Memorial Scholarship

Type of award: Scholarship.
Intended use: For full-time undergraduate study at 2-year or 4-year institution.
Eligibility: Applicant or parent must be member/participant of International Order of Job's Daughters. Applicant must be single, female, no older than 30.
Basis for selection: Applicant must demonstrate financial need, depth of character and seriousness of purpose.
Application requirements: Recommendations, transcript, proof of eligibility. Photograph. Personal letter.
Additional information: Applicant must be H.S. graduate with 2.5 GPA; dedicated, continuous, joyful service to Job's Daughters; regular attendance at Grand and/or Supreme Session with participation in competitions at Grand and/or Supreme Session; a Job's Daughter who promotes friendship within her Bethel and exhibits good character and integrity. Job's Daughter's activities, applicant's financial self-help, and achievements outside of Job's Daughters are also factors in awarding scholarships. Visit Website for more details.

Amount of award:	$1,000
Application deadline:	April 30

Contact:
International Center for Job's Daughters
233 W. 6th Street
Papillion, NE 68046-2210
Phone: 402-592-7987
Fax: 402-592-2177
Web: www.iojd.org

Swiss Benevolent Society of New York

Sonia Streuli Maguire Outstanding Scholastic Achievement Award

Type of award: Scholarship.
Intended use: For full-time senior, post-bachelor's certificate, master's, doctoral or first professional study at accredited 4-year or graduate institution in United States.
Eligibility: Applicant must be Swiss. Applicant must be permanent resident residing in New York, Connecticut, Delaware, New Jersey or Pennsylvania.
Basis for selection: Applicant must demonstrate high academic achievement.
Application requirements: Recommendations, transcript, proof of eligibility.
Additional information: Applicant or parent must be Swiss citizen. Must have minimum 3.8 GPA. See Website for application.

Amount of award:	$2,500-$5,000
Number of awards:	2
Application deadline:	March 31
Notification begins:	June 1
Total amount awarded:	$5,000

Contact:
Swiss Benevolent Society
608 Fifth Avenue
Room 309
New York, NY 10020
Web: www.swissbenevolentny.com

Swiss Benevolent Society Medicus Student Exchange

Type of award: Scholarship.
Intended use: For full-time junior, senior, post-bachelor's certificate, master's, doctoral or first professional study at accredited 4-year or graduate institution in Universities and Polytechnic institutes in Switzerland. Designated institutions: Institutions in Switzerland.
Eligibility: Applicant must be Swiss. Applicant must be U.S. citizen, permanent resident, international student or Swiss citizen.
Basis for selection: Competition/talent/interest in study abroad. Applicant must demonstrate high academic achievement.
Application requirements: Recommendations, transcript, proof of eligibility. Fluency in language of instruction.
Additional information: For U.S. students, applicant or one parent must be Swiss national. Minimum 3.7 GPA required.

Application deadline:	March 31
Notification begins:	June 1

Scholarships

Contact:
Swiss Benevolent Society
550 Fifth Avenue
Room 1800
New York, NY 10110
Phone: 212-246-0655
Fax: 212-246-1366
Web: www.swissbenevolentny.com/scholarships.htm

Swiss Benevolent Society Pellegrini Scholarship

Type of award: Scholarship, renewable.
Intended use: For undergraduate, graduate or non-degree study at accredited postsecondary institution in United States.
Eligibility: Applicant must be Swiss. Applicant must be permanent resident residing in New York, Connecticut, Delaware, New Jersey or Pennsylvania.
Basis for selection: Applicant must demonstrate financial need and high academic achievement.
Application requirements: Recommendations, transcript, proof of eligibility. Proof of Swiss parentage and tax return.
Additional information: Applicant or parent must be a Swiss national. Minimum 3.0 GPA required. Scholarship paid directly to school. See Website for application.

Amount of award:	$500-$4,000
Number of awards:	55
Number of applicants:	61
Application deadline:	March 31
Notification begins:	June 1
Total amount awarded:	$95,550

Contact:
Swiss Benevolent Society
608 Fifth Avenue
Room 309
New York, NY 10020
Web: www.swissbenevolentny.com

Technology Association of Georgia

Web Challenge Contest

Type of award: Scholarship.
Intended use: For full-time undergraduate study. Designated institutions: Georgia college or university.
Eligibility: Applicant must be enrolled in high school. Applicant must be U.S. citizen or permanent resident residing in Georgia.
Basis for selection: Competition/talent/interest in Web-site design, based on originality, creativity and sophistication in Website design. Major/career interest in computer/information sciences or computer graphics. Applicant must demonstrate seriousness of purpose.
Application requirements: Proof of eligibility. Registration form.
Additional information: Open to Georgia high school students. Applicants must assemble team of at least two participants to design and build a Website; team must be sponsored by faculty advisor. Registration is limited to first 100 schools. Total amount awarded varies. Visit Website for registration information, contest information and theme.

Total amount awarded:	$30,000

Contact:
Technology Association of Georgia
75 Fifth Street, NW
Suite 310
Atlanta, GA 30318
Phone: 404-817-3333
Web: www.webchallenge.org

Tennessee Student Assistance Corporation

Need-Based Supplement Award

Type of award: Scholarship.
Intended use: For full-time freshman or sophomore study. Designated institutions: Institutions accredited by the Southern Association of Colleges.
Eligibility: Applicant must be residing in Tennessee.
Application requirements: FAFSA. Entering freshman must have a minimum 19 ACT (890 SAT) or 3.0 GPA and complete college core and university track courses. Sophomores must complete 24 hours in first college year with minimum 2.75 GPA.
Additional information: Parent's or student's income must be $36,000 or less.

Amount of award:	$1,000
Application deadline:	May 1

Contact:
Tennessee Student Assistance Corporation
Parkway Towers, Suite 1950
404 James Robertson Parkway
Nashville, TN 37243-0820
Phone: 615-741-1346 or 800-342-1663
Fax: 615-741-6101
Web: www.state.tn.us/tsac

Tennessee Christa McAuliffe Scholarship

Type of award: Scholarship.
Intended use: For full-time senior study. Designated institutions: Eligible Tennessee school.
Eligibility: Applicant must be residing in Tennessee.
Basis for selection: Major/career interest in education, teacher; education; education, early childhood or education, special. Applicant must demonstrate high academic achievement, depth of character, leadership, seriousness of purpose and service orientation.
Application requirements: Transcript. Written statement of intent to teach in a Tennessee elementary or secondary school. Application must be postmarked by April 1.
Additional information: To be eligible, applicant must be enrolled full-time in a teacher education program in an accredited Tennessee postsecondary institution. Applicant must have completed the first semester of junior year with a cumulative GPA of 3.5 or higher and ACT or SAT score that meets or exceeds the national norm. Amount of award based on funding.

Amount of award:	$500
Number of awards:	1
Application deadline:	April 1
Total amount awarded:	$500

Contact:
Tennessee Student Assistance Corporation
Parkway Towers, Suite 1950
404 James Robertson Parkway
Nashville, TN 37243-0820
Phone: 615-741-1346 or 800-342-1663
Fax: 615-741-6101
Web: www.state.tn.us/tsac

Tennessee Dependent Children Scholarship

Type of award: Scholarship, renewable.
Intended use: For full-time undergraduate study at accredited postsecondary institution. Designated institutions: Accredited Tennessee schools.
Eligibility: Applicant must be single. Applicant must be U.S. citizen residing in Tennessee.
Basis for selection: Applicant must demonstrate financial need.
Application requirements: Proof of eligibility. FAFSA.
Additional information: Applicant must be enrolled full time in a degree-granting program. Applicant's parent must have been a Tennessee resident killed or disabled in work-related accident as law enforcement officer, fireman, or emergency medical technician. Award based on student's financial aid package.

Amount of award:	Full tuition
Number of awards:	5
Number of applicants:	5
Application deadline:	July 15
Total amount awarded:	$16,000

Contact:
Tennessee Student Assistance Corporation
Parkway Towers, Suite 1950
404 James Robertson Parkway
Nashville, TN 37243-0820
Phone: 615-741-1346 or 800-342-1663
Fax: 615-741-6101
Web: www.state.tn.us/tsac

Tennessee HOPE Access Grant

Type of award: Scholarship.
Intended use: For full-time freshman or sophomore study at 2-year or 4-year institution. Designated institutions: Institutions accredited by the Southern Association of Colleges.
Eligibility: Applicant must be residing in Tennessee.
Application requirements: Minimum 18 ACT, 860 SAT. FAFSA.
Additional information: Award amount varies; $2,000 for four-year institutions, $1,250 for two-year institutions. Minimum 2.75 GPA. Parent(s) adjusted gross income of $36,000 or less for dependent student or student (and spouse) for independent student.

Contact:
Tennessee Student Assistance Corporation
Parkway Towers, Suite 1950
404 James Robertson Parkway
Nashville, TN 37243-0820
Phone: 615-741-1346 or 800-342-1663
Fax: 615-741-6101
Web: www.state.tn.us/tsac

Tennessee HOPE Scholarship

Type of award: Scholarship.

Intended use: For full-time freshman study. Designated institutions: Tennessee institutions accredited by the Southern Assocation of Colleges.
Eligibility: Applicant must be residing in Tennessee.
Application requirements: FAFSA. Minimum 3.0 GPA. Minimum ACT 19.
Additional information: Award amount varies; $3,000 for four-year institutions, $1,500 for two-year institutions.

Amount of award:	$3,000

Contact:
Tennessee Student Assistance Corporation
Parkway Towers, Suite 1950
404 James Robertson Parkway
Nashville, TN 37243-0820
Phone: 615-741-1346 or 800-342-1663
Fax: 615-741-6101
Web: www.state.tn.us/tsac

Tennessee Ned McWherter Scholarship

Type of award: Scholarship, renewable.
Intended use: For full-time freshman study at accredited 2-year or 4-year institution. Designated institutions: Accredited Tennessee schools.
Eligibility: Applicant must be high school senior. Applicant must be U.S. citizen residing in Tennessee.
Basis for selection: Applicant must demonstrate leadership.
Application requirements: Transcript, proof of eligibility. Applicant must demonstrate high academic achievement.
Additional information: Applicant must score at 95th percentile on ACT/SAT. Minimum 3.5 GPA through seven semesters. Difficulty level of high school courses and leadership considered.

Amount of award:	$6,000
Number of awards:	50
Number of applicants:	902
Application deadline:	February 15
Total amount awarded:	$300,000

Contact:
Tennessee Student Assistance Corporation
Parkway Towers, Suite 1950
404 James Robertson Parkway
Nashville, TN 37243-0820
Phone: 615-741-1346 or 800-342-1663
Fax: 615-741-6101
Web: www.state.tn.us/tsac

Tennessee Robert C. Byrd Honors Scholarship

Type of award: Scholarship, renewable.
Intended use: For full-time freshman study at accredited vocational, 2-year or 4-year institution in United States.
Eligibility: Applicant must be high school senior. Applicant must be U.S. citizen or permanent resident residing in Tennessee.
Basis for selection: Random selection based on the three grand divisions of the state.
Application requirements: Transcript, proof of eligibility. Applications must be postmarked by 3/1.
Additional information: Minimum 3.5 GPA. May also qualify with 3.0 GPA and 24 ACT (1090 SAT). Score of 57 or above on GED is also accepted.

Amount of award:	$1,500
Number of awards:	125
Number of applicants:	3,500
Application deadline:	March 1
Total amount awarded:	$187,500

Contact:
Tennessee Student Assistance Corporation
Parkway Towers, Suite 1950
404 James Robertson Parkway
Nashville, TN 37243-0820
Phone: 615-741-1346 or 800-342-1663
Fax: 615-741-6101
Web: www.state.tn.us/tsac

Tennessee Student Assistance Award

Type of award: Scholarship, renewable.
Intended use: For undergraduate study. Designated institutions: Eligible Tennessee postsecondary institutions.
Eligibility: Applicant must be U.S. citizen or permanent resident residing in Tennessee.
Basis for selection: Applicant must demonstrate financial need.
Additional information: FAFSA must be processed by May 1. Applicant's expected family contribution must be less than $1,900. Award is up to $4,644 for private institutions; up to $2,322 for public, based on funding.

Amount of award:	$2,322-$4,644
Number of applicants:	165,000
Application deadline:	May 1

Contact:
Tennessee Student Assistance Corporation
Parkway Towers, Suite 1950
404 James Robertson Parkway
Nashville, TN 37243-0820
Phone: 615-741-1346 or 800-342-1663
Fax: 615-741-6101
Web: www.state.tn.us/tsac

Wilder-Naifeh Technical Skills Grant

Type of award: Scholarship.
Intended use: For full-time freshman or sophomore study at vocational institution. Designated institutions: Instiuitions accredited by the Southern Assocation of Colleges.
Eligibility: Applicant must be residing in Tennessee.
Application requirements: FAFSA.
Additional information: Applicant must be Tennessee resident attending a Tennessee Technology Center.

Amount of award:	$1,250
Application deadline:	May 1

Contact:
Tennessee Student Assistance Corporation
Parkway Towers, Suite 1950
404 James Robertson Parkway
Nashville, TN 37243-0820
Phone: 615-741-1346 or 800-342-1663
Fax: 615-741-6101
Web: www.state.tn.us/tsac

Tennessee Student Assitance Corporation

General Assembly Merit Scholarhsip

Type of award: Scholarship, renewable.
Intended use: For full-time freshman or sophomore study. Designated institutions: Tennessee institution accredited by the Southern Association of Colleges and Schools.
Eligibility: Applicant must be residing in Tennessee.
Application requirements: FAFSA. Entering freshman must have minimum 3.75 GPA, 29 ACT (1280 SAT), complete required college core and university track courses.
Additional information: Must meet Tennessee HOPE eligibility first year.

Amount of award:	$1,000
Application deadline:	May 1

Contact:
Tennessee Student Assitance Corporation
Parkway Towers, Suite 1950
404 James Robertson Parkway
Nashville, TN 37243-0820
Phone: 615-741-1346 or 800-342-1663
Fax: 614-741-6101
Web: www.state.tn.us/tsac

Texas Higher Education Coordinating Board

Educational Aide Exemption

Type of award: Scholarship.
Intended use: For undergraduate or graduate study at postsecondary institution in United States. Designated institutions: Public postsecondary institutions in Texas.
Eligibility: Applicant must be U.S. citizen or permanent resident residing in Texas.
Basis for selection: Applicant must demonstrate financial need.
Application requirements: Must be certified by Texas Board of Teacher Certification as a Certified Aide.
Additional information: Assists educational aides by exempting them from payment of tuition and fees. Applicant must have applied for financial aid through college of attendance, including filing FAFSA or qualifying based on income. Applicant must have worked with students in classroom for at least one year (includes library aides, computer lab aides and P.E. aides) out of the last five years. Applicant must also be working, in some capacity, in a Texas public school during semester for which exemption is applied and must be enrolled in classes toward teacher certification. Maintenance of good academic standing required. The deadlines for applying are: Fall - June 1 through February 1; Spring - November 1 through July 1; Summer - April 1 through October 1. Visit website or contact the Texas Higher Education Coordinating Board at 800-242-3062, ext. 6387 to obtain a current application.

Number of awards:	4,000

Contact:
Texas Higher Education Coordinating Board
Student Services Division
P. O. Box 12788
Austin, TX 78711-2788
Phone: 800-242-3062
Fax: 512-427-6420
Web: www.collegefortexans.com

Exemption for Peace Officers Disabled in the Line of Duty

Type of award: Scholarship.
Intended use: For undergraduate study at postsecondary institution in United States. Designated institutions: Texas public colleges and universities.
Eligibility: Applicant must be residing in Texas.
Application requirements: Proof of eligibility. Applicant must work directly with school registrar and submit satisfactory evidence of status as a disabled peace officer as required by that institution.
Additional information: Award for persons injured in the line of duty while serving as peace officers. Person must enroll in classes for which college receives tax support. Persons enrolled in master's and doctoral degree programs not eligible. Maximum award is exemption from payment of tuition and fees for not more than 12 semesters or sessions. Contact college for additional information.
　　Amount of award:　　　　　Full tuition
Contact:
Texas Higher Education Coordinating Board
Student Services Division
P. O. Box 12788
Austin, TX 78711-2788
Phone: 800-242-3062
Fax: 512-427-6420
Web: www.collegefortexans.com

Exemption for the Surviving Spouse and Dependent Children of Certain Deceased Public Servants (Employees)

Type of award: Scholarship.
Intended use: For full-time undergraduate study at postsecondary institution in United States. Designated institutions: Texas public colleges and universities.
Eligibility: Applicant must be residing in Texas.
Application requirements: Proof of eligibility.
Additional information: Exemption for surviving spouse and/or dependent children of certain public employees (defined by Texas Government Code 615.003) killed in the line of duty. Public employee must have died on or after September 1, 2000. Program provides free tuition and fees, free textbooks, and possibly free room and board. Contact registrar's office at college/university for information on claiming this exemption.
　　Amount of award:　　　　　Full tuition
Contact:
Texas Higher Education Coordinating Board
Student Services Division
P. O. Box 12788
Austin, TX 78711-2788
Phone: 800-242-3062
Fax: 512-427-6420
Web: www.collegefortexans.com

Reduction in Tuition Charges for Students Taking 15 or More Semester Credit Hours Per Term

Type of award: Scholarship.
Intended use: For full-time undergraduate study at postsecondary institution. Designated institutions: Texas public colleges and universities.
Eligibility: Applicant must be residing in Texas.
Application requirements: Proof of eligibility.
Additional information: Applicant must be enrolled in at least 15 credit hours at institution during semester/term for which reduction is offered. Must be enrolled in and making satisfactory progress toward completion of a degree program. Contact registrar's office at college/university to inquire whether the college offers reduction.
Contact:
Texas Higher Education Coordinating Board
Student Services Division
P. O. Box 12788
Austin, TX 78711-2788
Phone: 800-242-3062
Fax: 512-427-6420
Web: www.collegefortexans.com

Senior Citizen, 65 or Older, Free Tuition for 6 Credit Hours

Type of award: Scholarship.
Intended use: For half-time undergraduate or graduate study at 2-year or 4-year institution in United States. Designated institutions: Texas public colleges and universities honoring this program.
Eligibility: Applicant must be at least 65, returning adult student. Applicant must be U.S. citizen, permanent resident or international student residing in Texas.
Application requirements: Proof of eligibility.
Additional information: Program open to Texas residents, nonresidents, and foreign students. Applicants must enroll in courses at college or university offering program. Texas institutions not required to offer program; applicants should check with registrar. Classes must not already be filled with students paying at full price and must use tax support for some of their cost. Contact college for additional information.
　　Number of awards:　　　　　2,316
Contact:
Texas Higher Education Coordinating Board
Student Services Division
P. O. Box 12788
Austin, TX 78711-2788
Phone: 800-242-3062
Fax: 512-427-6420
Web: www.collegefortexans.com

TANF (Temporary Assistance to Needy Families) Exemption

Type of award: Scholarship.
Intended use: For undergraduate certificate or freshman study at accredited 2-year or 4-year institution in United States. Designated institutions: Texas public institutions.
Eligibility: Applicant must be no older than 22. Applicant must be U.S. citizen or permanent resident residing in Texas.
Application requirements: Proof of eligibility. Applicant must provide proof that a parent received TANF (Temporary Assistance to Needy Families) on their behalf for at least six

months of their senior year of high school. Graduated from a Texas public high school.

Additional information: Award includes tuition and fees for student's first academic year. Must have graduated from Texas public high school. Must have received financial assistance under Chapter 31 Human Resources Code (TANF) for not less than six months during senior year in high school. Must enroll within two years of high school graduation. Must enroll in classes for which college receives tax support. Contact financial aid office at college or university for more information.

    Number of awards: 204

Contact:
Contact college/university financial aid office to apply.
Phone: 800-242-3062
Fax: 512-427-6420
Web: www.collegefortexans.com

Texas Early High School Graduation Scholarship

Type of award: Scholarship, renewable.
Intended use: For undergraduate study in United States. Designated institutions: Public postsecondary institutions in Texas.
Eligibility: Applicant must be U.S. citizen or permanent resident residing in Texas.
Application requirements: Proof of eligibility.
Additional information: Average award $504. Applicant must have completed graduation requirements at a Texas public high school in less than 36 consecutive months. Applicants should contact Texas board for copy of letter submitted by their high school counselor. Contact college/university financial aid office for information on applying for this scholarship.
    Amount of award: $500-$2,000

Contact:
Contact college/university financial aid office to apply.
Phone: 800-242-3062
Fax: 512-427-6420
Web: www.collegefortexans.com

Texas Fifth-Year Accountancy Scholarship Program

Type of award: Scholarship.
Intended use: For senior, post-bachelor's certificate or master's study in United States. Designated institutions: Public nonprofit or independent institutions in Texas.
Basis for selection: Major/career interest in accounting. Applicant must demonstrate financial need.
Application requirements: Proof of eligibility. Signed statement of intent to take CPA exam in Texas.
Additional information: Must be enrolled as fifth-year accounting student who has completed at least 120 credit hours.
    Amount of award: $3,000
    Number of awards: 355
    Total amount awarded: $655,878

Contact:
Contact college financial aid office for application.
Phone: 800-242-3062
Web: www.collegefortexans.com

Texas Foster Care Students Exemption

Type of award: Scholarship, renewable.

Intended use: For undergraduate or graduate study at accredited vocational, 2-year or 4-year institution in United States. Designated institutions: Texas public institutions.
Eligibility: Applicant must be U.S. citizen or permanent resident residing in Texas.
Application requirements: Proof of eligibility. Must provide college registrar with written proof of eligibility from the Department of Protective and Regulatory Services.
Additional information: Applicants must have been either in the care or conservatorship of Texas Department of Protective and Regulatory Services on the day before their 18th birthday, the day of their graduation from high school, or the day of receipt of GED; or in the care or conservatorship of the TDPRS through 14th birthday and then adopted. Must enroll in college before third anniversary of discharge from foster care. Program awards tuition and fees; once a student has been determined eligible for the benefit, the benefit continues indefinitely. Contact college's financial aid office for application.
Contact:
Contact college/university financial aid office to apply.
Phone: 800-242-3062
Fax: 512-427-6420
Web: www.collegefortexans.com

Texas General Scholarship for Nursing Students

Type of award: Scholarship.
Intended use: For undergraduate or graduate study at accredited 2-year, 4-year or graduate institution. Designated institutions: Texas public, private, and non-profit institutions with vocational nursing programs.
Eligibility: Applicant must be U.S. citizen or permanent resident residing in Texas.
Basis for selection: Major/career interest in nursing or health-related professions. Applicant must demonstrate financial need.
Application requirements: Proof of eligibility. Must be enrolled in program leading to license as a Licensed Vocational Nurse or a degree in professional nursing. Register for the Selective Service or are exempt from this requirement. Must be enrolled at least half time.
Additional information: Degree students must not be licensed as a Licensed Vocational Nurse. Students with associate and bachelor's degrees in nursing must not be licensed to practice as a Registered Nurse. Can obtain application from institution's Financial Aid Office or by calling the Student Services Division at the Texas Higher Education Coordinating Board at 512-427-6340 (Austin area) or 800-242-3062 (outside Austin).
    Amount of award: $1,500

Contact:
Contact the college/university financial aid office to apply.
Phone: 800-242-3062
Fax: 512-427-6420
Web: www.collegefortexans.com

Texas Good Neighbor Scholarship

Type of award: Scholarship.
Intended use: For undergraduate or graduate study at accredited 2-year, 4-year or graduate institution in United States. Designated institutions: Texas public institutions.
Eligibility: Applicant must be international student or native-born citizen of any Western Hemisphere country other than Cuba. Applicant must be residing in Texas.

Application requirements: Proof of eligibility. Intended to return to eligible country upon completion of the program of study.

Additional information: Award is exemption from tuition for citizens of another country of the Americas. Must reside in Texas. Award amount is one year of tuition. Contact the Student Financial Aid Office or the International Student Affairs Office at institution for application.

Application deadline: March 15

Contact:
Contact college/university financial aid office/int'l student office.
Phone: 800-242-3062
Fax: 512-427-6420
Web: www.collegefortexans.com

TEXAS Grant (Toward EXcellence, Access, and Success)

Type of award: Scholarship, renewable.

Intended use: For undergraduate study at vocational, 2-year or 4-year institution. Designated institutions: Public and private non-profit colleges and universities in Texas.

Eligibility: Applicant must be U.S. citizen or permanent resident residing in Texas.

Basis for selection: Applicant must demonstrate financial need and high academic achievement.

Application requirements: Selective Service registration or exemption from requirement. FAFSA. 2.5 GPA.

Additional information: GED and home school students not eligible. Applicants must have graduated from a Texas public or accredited private high school in Fall 1998 or later. Applicant must have completed the Recommended or Advanced High School Curriculum. Applicant must enroll in college on at least a 3/4-time basis (unless granted hardship waiver). Applicant must receive first award within 16 months of high school graduation. Applicant must not have been convicted of felony or crime involving controlled substance. No awards given for more than student's need or public institution tuition and fees; maximum for private institution attendees is $1,570 per semester; maximum for community college attendees is $635 per semester; maximum for technical college attendees is $930 per semester. Applicants should contact the financial aid office at the college/university they plan to attend for application deadlines and procedures.

Number of awards: 18,162

Contact:
Financial aid office at college/university.
Phone: 800-242-3062
Fax: 512-427-6420
Web: www.collegefortexans.com

Texas Hazlewood Act Tuition Exemption: Veterans and Dependents

Type of award: Scholarship, renewable.

Intended use: For undergraduate or graduate study at accredited 2-year, 4-year or graduate institution. Designated institutions: Texas public institutions.

Eligibility: Applicant must be residing in Texas. Applicant must be veteran; or dependent of deceased veteran.

Application requirements: Proof of eligibility. Have served at least 181 days of active military duty, excluding basic training. Have received an honorable discharge or separation or a general discharge under honorable conditions. Have used up all his/her federal education benefits available for the semester for which he/she is enrolled (GI/Montgomery Bill and Federal Pell and SEOG Grants). Enroll in classes for which the college receives tax support.

Additional information: Must have tuition and fee charges that exceed all federal education benefits. Applicant or parent must have been resident of Texas prior to enlistment. Applicants should contact the financial aid office at the college/university they plan to attend for more information.

Contact:
Contact the college/university financial aid office to apply.
Phone: 800-242-3062
Fax: 512-427-6420
Web: www.collegefortexans.com

Texas Highest Ranking High School Graduate Tuition Exemption

Type of award: Scholarship.

Intended use: For freshman study at accredited 2-year or 4-year institution. Designated institutions: Public postsecondary Texas institutions.

Eligibility: Applicant must be U.S. citizen or permanent resident residing in Texas.

Basis for selection: Applicant must demonstrate high academic achievement.

Application requirements: Proof of eligibility. Applicant must prove he/she is high school valedictorian by presenting certificate issued by Texas Education Agency.

Additional information: Must be valedictorian of accredited Texas high school. Recipient is exempt from certain charges for first two semesters. Award covers tuition during both semesters of first regular session immediately following the student's high school graduation; fees not included. Deadline varies.

Contact:
Contact college/university financial aid office to apply.
Phone: 800-242-3062
Web: www.collegefortexans.com

Texas National Guard Tuition Assistance Program

Type of award: Scholarship.

Intended use: For undergraduate study at postsecondary institution in United States. Designated institutions: Texas public, private, or nonprofit colleges and universities.

Eligibility: Applicant must be residing in Texas.

Application requirements: Proof of eligibility.

Additional information: Program provides exemption from payment of tuition to certain members of Texas National Guard, Texas Air Guard, or State Guard. Applicant must be registered for Selective Service or exempt from this requirement. Awards at public colleges/universities are for student's tuition charges, up to 6 credit hours per semester. Awards for private or nonprofit institutions are based on public university tuition charges. For more information, visit Texas National Guard Website at www.agd.state.tx.us/education_office/state_tuition.htm. Applicants may also contact the unit commander of their National Air Guard or State Guard unit or the Education Officer, State Adjutant General's Office, P.O. Box 5218/AGTX-PAE, Austin TX 78763-5218 or at 512-465-5001. The Education Office will provide instructions.

Amount of award: Full tuition
Number of awards: 2,297

Contact:
Texas Higher Education Coordinating Board
Student Services Division
P. O. Box 12788
Austin, TX 78711-2788
Phone: 800-242-3062
Fax: 512-427-6420
Web: www.collegefortexans.com

Texas Public Student Incentive Grant - Leveraging Educational Assistance Partnership Program (PSIG-LEAP)

Type of award: Scholarship.
Intended use: For undergraduate or graduate study at accredited vocational, 2-year or 4-year institution. Designated institutions: Texas public colleges and universities.
Eligibility: Applicant must be U.S. citizen or permanent resident residing in Texas.
Basis for selection: Applicant must demonstrate financial need.
Application requirements: Proof of eligibility. FAFSA. Applicant must register for Selective Service or be exempt.
Additional information: Applicant must have received a grant through the PSIG program. Maximum award $2500. Average award $449. Award may not exceed student's financial need. Deadlines vary. Contact financial aid office at college/university for more information.

Number of awards:	2,675
Total amount awarded:	$827,732

Contact:
Contact financial aid office at college/university.
Phone: 800-242-3062 or 877-782-7322
Web: www.collegefortexans.com

Texas Robert C. Byrd Honors Scholarship

Type of award: Scholarship, renewable.
Intended use: For undergraduate study at vocational, 2-year or 4-year institution.
Eligibility: Applicant must be high school senior. Applicant must be U.S. citizen or permanent resident residing in Texas.
Basis for selection: Applicant must demonstrate high academic achievement.
Application requirements: Transcript, nomination by high school guidance counselor or GED center director.
Additional information: Average award $1,330. Must be high school senior or person completing GED to receive initial award. Must rank in top ten percent of class and have minimum 3.75 GPA. High school guidance officer or GED center director will submit applications of top candidates to Texas Higher Education Coordinating Board.

Amount of award:	$1,500
Number of awards:	3,955
Application deadline:	March 15

Contact:
High school guidance office or GED center director.
Phone: 800-242-3062
Fax: 512-427-6420
Web: www.collegefortexans.com

Texas Student Incentive Grant

Type of award: Scholarship.

Intended use: For undergraduate or graduate study at accredited 2-year or 4-year institution. Designated institutions: Texas public institutions.
Eligibility: Applicant must be residing in Texas.
Basis for selection: Applicant must demonstrate financial need.
Application requirements: Completed FAFSA.
Additional information: Award may not exceed student's financial need. Deadlines vary. Contact financial aid office at college or university for more information.

Amount of award:	$2,500
Number of awards:	2,675

Contact:
Apply through school's financial aid office.
Phone: 800-242-3062
Web: www.collegefortexans.com

Texas Tuition Exemption for Blind or Deaf Students

Type of award: Scholarship, renewable.
Intended use: For undergraduate or graduate study at accredited 2-year or 4-year institution in United States. Designated institutions: Public postsecondary institutions in Texas.
Eligibility: Applicant must be visually impaired or hearing impaired. Applicant must be U.S. citizen or permanent resident residing in Texas.
Basis for selection: Applicant must demonstrate depth of character.
Application requirements: Recommendations, transcript, proof of eligibility. Certification of disability. FAFSA. Written statement indicating which certificate, degree program, or professional enhancement applicant intends to pursue.
Additional information: Must be certified by relevant state vocational rehabilitation agency and have high school diploma or equivalent. Applicant must enroll in classes for which the college receives tax support. Award amount and deadlines vary. Contact financial aid office at college/university for more information.
Contact:
Financial aid office at college/university.
Phone: 800-242-3062
Fax: 512-427-6420
Web: www.collegefortexans.com

Tuition Equalization Grant (TEG)

Type of award: Scholarship.
Intended use: For undergraduate or graduate study at accredited 2-year or 4-year institution in United States. Designated institutions: Private, non-profit Texas colleges and universities.
Eligibility: Applicant must be U.S. citizen or permanent resident residing in Texas.
Basis for selection: Applicant must demonstrate financial need.
Application requirements: Proof of eligibility. Selective Service registration or exemption from requirement. FAFSA.
Additional information: Applicant must be Texas resident or non-resident National Merit finalist. Not open to religion/theology majors or to athletic scholarship recipients. Award covers difference between applicant's tuition at private institution and what applicant would pay at public institution. Students must be enrolled on at least a half-time basis. Applicants should contact the financial aid office at the Texas

private college/university they plan to attend for more information.

Number of awards: 25,875

Contact:
Financial aid office at college or university.
Phone: 800-242-3062
Web: www.collegefortexans.com

Tuition Exemption for Children of Disabled or Deceased Firefighters, Peace Officers, Game Wardens, and Employees of Correctional Institutions

Type of award: Scholarship, renewable.
Intended use: For undergraduate or graduate study at 2-year or 4-year institution in United States. Designated institutions: Public postsecondary institutions in Texas.
Eligibility: Applicant must be no older than 21. Applicant must be residing in Texas. Applicant's parent must have been killed or disabled in work-related accident as fire fighter, police officer or public safety officer.
Application requirements: Proof of eligibility. Completed Texas Higher Education Coordinating Board form.
Additional information: Applicant must be child of paid or volunteer firefighter; paid municipal, county or state peace officer; custodial employee of Department of Corrections; or game warden disabled or killed in the line of duty. Applicant must apply before 21st birthday. Persons eligible to participate in a school district's special education program under section 29.003 at age 22 may also apply. Applicant must enroll in courses that use tax support to cover some of their cost. Applicant must obtain form letter from Texas Higher Education Coordinating Board, have parent's former employer complete form, and submit form back to Texas Higher Education Coordinating Board. The Board will notify applicant's institution of eligibility. Students enrolling for the first time after 9/1/01 may be exempted from tuition and fees for the first 120 semester credits or at age 26, whichever comes first. Those enrolled in the program before 9/1/01 may be exempted for up to four years.

Contact:
Texas Higher Education Coordinating Board
Student Services Division
P O. Box 12788
Austin, TX 78711-2788
Phone: 800-242-3062
Web: www.collegefortexans.com

Tuition Exemption for Children of U.S. Military POW/MIAs

Type of award: Scholarship, renewable.
Intended use: For undergraduate study at accredited 2-year or 4-year institution. Designated institutions: Public postsecondary institutions in Texas.
Eligibility: Applicant must be no older than 25. Applicant must be U.S. citizen or permanent resident residing in Texas. Applicant must be dependent of POW/MIA.
Application requirements: Proof of eligibility. Documentation from Department of Defense that a parent, classified as Texas resident, is missing in action or a prisoner of war. Completed FAFSA.
Additional information: Applicants 22 to 25 years of age must receive most of their support from a parent. Applicant

must enroll in courses that use tax support to cover some of their cost. Maximum award is tuition and fees. Applicants should contact the registrar's at the college/university they plan to attend for more information.

Contact:
Financial aid office at college/university.
Phone: 800-242-3062
Web: www.collegefortexans.com

Tuition Rebate for Certain Undergraduates

Type of award: Scholarship.
Intended use: For freshman study at postsecondary institution in United States. Designated institutions: Texas public colleges or universities.
Eligibility: Applicant must be residing in Texas.
Application requirements: Student nust have attempted no more than three semester credit hours in excess of the minimum number of hours required for their degree.
Additional information: Program provides tuition rebates for students to prepare for university studies while completing high school work. Student must have taken all coursework at Texas public institutions of higher education, and have been entitled to pay in-state tuition at all times while pursuing degree. Students must apply for tuition rebate prior to receiving bachelor's degree. Contact business office at college/university for more information.

Amount of award: $1,000

Contact:
Texas Higher Education Coordinating Board
Student Services Division
P. O. Box 12788
Austin, TX 78711-2788
Phone: 800-242-3062
Fax: 512-427-6420
Web: www.collegefortexans.com

Third Marine Division Association

Third Marine Division Memorial Scholarship Fund

Type of award: Scholarship, renewable.
Intended use: For undergraduate study at accredited 2-year or 4-year institution in United States.
Eligibility: Applicant or parent must be member/participant of Third Marine Division Association. Applicant must be at least 16, no older than 24. Applicant must be U.S. citizen. Applicant must be dependent of active service person in the Marines. Must be dependent child of active duty Marines or Navy Corpsmen who are serving or who have served in Third Marine division.
Basis for selection: Applicant must demonstrate financial need.
Application requirements: Proof of eligibility. Financial aid form.
Additional information: Number of awards varies. Parent must be a member of Third Marine Division Association for at least two years. Eligible dependent children automatically receive renewal application forms upon submission of copies of grade reports. Must maintain 2.0 GPA.

Amount of award:	$500-$1,500
Application deadline:	April 15

Contact:
Third Marine Division Association
3111 Sundial Drive
Dallas, TX 75229-3757

Third Wave Foundation

Scholarship Program for Young Women

Type of award: Scholarship, renewable.
Intended use: For undergraduate or graduate study at accredited vocational, 2-year, 4-year or graduate institution in United States.
Eligibility: Applicant must be female, no older than 30.
Basis for selection: Applicant must demonstrate financial need and service orientation.
Application requirements: Recommendations, essay, transcript, proof of eligibility.
Additional information: Applicant should also be involved as activist, artist, or cultural worker working on issues such as racism, homophobia, sexism, or other forms of inequality. Visit Website for additional details and application.

Amount of award:	$500-$5,000
Number of awards:	17
Number of applicants:	400
Application deadline:	April 1, October 1
Total amount awarded:	$25,000

Contact:
Third Wave Foundation
511 West 25th St.
#301
New York, NY 10001
Phone: 212-675-0700
Fax: 212-255-6653
Web: www.thirdwavefoundation.org

Thurgood Marshall Scholarship Fund

Thurgood Marshall Scholarship Award

Type of award: Scholarship, renewable.
Intended use: For full-time undergraduate or graduate study at 4-year or graduate institution in United States. Designated institutions: One of 45 designated historically black public universities.
Eligibility: Applicant must be African American. Applicant must be high school senior. Applicant must be U.S. citizen.
Basis for selection: Applicant must demonstrate financial need, high academic achievement and service orientation.
Application requirements: Recommendations, essay, transcript. Minimum 1100/SAT or 25/ACT. Resume. Headshot or personal photograph.
Additional information: Must be admitted to one of 45 participating historically black colleges and universities before applying. Download list of institutions from Website. Must have high school GPA of 3.0 or higher; must maintain 3.0 GPA throughout duration of scholarship. Awards are made directly to applicant's university. Award is $2,200 per semester. Contact university's Thurgood Marshall Scholarship Fund campus coordinator directly for more information.

Amount of award:	$4,400
Number of awards:	1,000
Number of applicants:	3,000
Total amount awarded:	$2,500,000

Contact:
Thurgood Marshall Scholarship Fund,
60 East 42nd St.
Suite 833
New York, NY 10165
Phone: 212-573-8888
Web: www.thurgoodmarshallfund.org

Transportation Clubs International

Alice Glaisyer Warfield Memorial Scholarship

Type of award: Scholarship.
Intended use: For sophomore, junior, senior or graduate study at accredited postsecondary institution.
Basis for selection: Major/career interest in transportation. Applicant must demonstrate financial need, high academic achievement and depth of character.
Application requirements: Recommendations, essay, transcript. Three letters of recommendation, black-and-white photograph, 200-word essay explaining choice of career path and objectives.

Amount of award:	$1,000
Number of awards:	1
Application deadline:	April 30
Total amount awarded:	$1,000

Contact:
Transportation Clubs International, Attention: Gay Fielding
7031 Manchester Street
New Orleans, LA 70126-1751
Phone: 504-243-9825
Web: www.transportationclubsinternational.com

Charlotte Woods Memorial Scholarship

Type of award: Scholarship.
Intended use: For sophomore, junior, senior or graduate study.
Eligibility: Applicant or parent must be member/participant of Transportation Clubs International.
Basis for selection: Major/career interest in transportation. Applicant must demonstrate financial need, high academic achievement and depth of character.
Application requirements: Recommendations, essay, transcript. Three letters of recommendation, black and white photograph, 200 word essay explaining choice of career path and objectives.
Additional information: Student must be a member or a dependent of a member of the Transportation Clubs International.

Amount of award:	$1,000
Number of awards:	1
Application deadline:	April 30
Total amount awarded:	$1,000

Contact:
Transportation Clubs International, Attention: Gay Fielding
7031 Manchester Street
New Orleans, LA 70126-1751
Phone: 504-243-9825
Web: www.transportationclubsinternational.com

Denny Lydic Scholarship

Type of award: Scholarship.
Intended use: For sophomore, junior, senior or graduate study.
Basis for selection: Major/career interest in transportation. Applicant must demonstrate financial need, high academic achievement and depth of character.
Application requirements: Recommendations, essay, transcript. Three letters of recommendation, black and white photograph, 200 word essay explaining choice of career path and objectives.

Amount of award:	$500
Number of awards:	1
Application deadline:	April 30
Total amount awarded:	$500

Contact:
Transportation Clubs International, Attention: Gay Fielding
7031 Manchester Street
New Orleans, LA 70126-1751
Phone: 504-243-9825
Web: www.transportationclubsinternational.com

Ginger and Fred Deines Canada Scholarship

Type of award: Scholarship.
Intended use: For sophomore, junior, senior or graduate study in United States or Canada. Designated institutions: Institutions in U.S. or Canada.
Eligibility: Applicant must be international student or Canadian citizen.
Basis for selection: Major/career interest in transportation. Applicant must demonstrate financial need, high academic achievement and depth of character.
Application requirements: Recommendations, essay, transcript. Three letters of recommendation, black-and-white photograph, 200-word essay explaining choice of career path and objectives.
Additional information: For a student of Canadian nationality enrolled in Canadian or U.S. institution.

Amount of award:	$1,500
Number of awards:	1
Application deadline:	April 30
Total amount awarded:	$1,500

Contact:
Transportation Clubs International, Attention: Gay Fielding
7031 Manchester Street
New Orleans, LA 70126-1751
Phone: 504-243-9825
Web: www.transportationclubsinternational.com

Ginger and Fred Deines Mexico Scholarship

Type of award: Scholarship.

Intended use: For sophomore, junior, senior or graduate study. Designated institutions: Institutions in United States or Mexico.
Eligibility: Applicant must be international student.
Basis for selection: Major/career interest in transportation. Applicant must demonstrate financial need, high academic achievement and depth of character.
Application requirements: Recommendations, essay, transcript. Three letters of recommendation, black-and-white photograph, 200-word essay explaining choice of career path and objectives.
Additional information: For a student of Mexican nationality enrolled in Mexican or U.S. institution.

Amount of award:	$1,500
Number of awards:	1
Application deadline:	April 30
Total amount awarded:	$1,500

Contact:
Transportation Clubs International, Attention: Gay Fielding
7031 Manchester Street
New Orleans, LA 70126-1751
Phone: 504-243-9825
Web: www.transportationclubsinternational.com

Hooper Memorial Scholarship

Type of award: Scholarship.
Intended use: For sophomore, junior, senior or graduate study.
Basis for selection: Major/career interest in transportation. Applicant must demonstrate financial need, high academic achievement and depth of character.
Application requirements: Recommendations, essay, transcript. Three letters of recommendation, black and white photograph, 200 word essay explaining choice of career path and objectives.

Amount of award:	$1,500
Number of awards:	1
Application deadline:	April 30
Total amount awarded:	$1,500

Contact:
Transportation Clubs International, Attention: Gay Fielding
7031 Manchester Street
New Orleans, LA 70126-1751
Phone: 504-243-9825
Web: www.transportationclubsinternational.com

Texas Transportation Scholarship

Type of award: Scholarship.
Intended use: For sophomore, junior, senior or graduate study.
Basis for selection: Major/career interest in transportation. Applicant must demonstrate financial need, high academic achievement and depth of character.
Application requirements: Recommendations, essay, transcript. Three letters of recommendation, black-and-white photograph, 200-word essay explaining choice of career path and objectives.
Additional information: Applicant must have been enrolled in a Texas school for some phase of education (elementary through high school).

Amount of award:	$1,000
Number of awards:	1
Application deadline:	April 30
Total amount awarded:	$1,000

Contact:
Transportation Clubs International, Attention: Gay Fielding
7031 Manchester Street
New Orleans, LA 70126-1751
Phone: 504-243-9825
Web: www.transportationclubinternational.com

Travel and Tourism Research Association

J. Desmond Slattery Award: Student

Type of award: Scholarship.
Intended use: For undergraduate study at postsecondary institution.
Basis for selection: Competition/talent/interest in research paper, based on originality, creativity, quality of research, relationship to travel/tourism, usefulness/applicability, and quality of presentation. Major/career interest in tourism/travel.
Application requirements: Submit four copies of original research paper and 500- to 1,000-word abstract with completed application. Download application from Website.
Additional information: Only undergraduates enrolled in degree-granting program qualify. Winner also receives plaque, one-year student TTRA membership, $300 travel allowance and complimentary registration to TTRA annual conference. Winner notified end of May.

Amount of award:	$700
Application deadline:	March 31

Contact:
Travel and Tourism Research Association
P.O. Box 2133
Boise, ID 83701
Phone: 208-429-9511
Fax: 208-429-9512
Web: www.ttra.com

Travel Research Grant

Type of award: Research grant.
Intended use: For undergraduate, graduate or non-degree study.
Basis for selection: Based on ability to improve measurement, decrease costs, and improve information for better application and understanding. Project must show significant benefits to travel/tourism industry. Major/career interest in tourism/travel.
Application requirements: Research proposal. Download application from Website.
Additional information: Grant recipient has three years to complete project. Material must be submitted in English. Winner also receives plaque, $300 travel allowance, and complimentary registration to TTRA annual conference.

Amount of award:	$2,000
Number of awards:	1
Application deadline:	March 31

Contact:
Travel and Tourism Research Association
P.O. Box 2133
Boise, ID 83701
Phone: 208-429-9511
Fax: 208-429-9512
Web: www.ttra.com

Treacy Company

Treacy Company Scholarship

Type of award: Scholarship, renewable.
Intended use: For full-time freshman or sophomore study at postsecondary institution.
Eligibility: Applicant must be residing in South Dakota, Montana, Idaho or North Dakota.
Basis for selection: Applicant must demonstrate financial need, leadership, seriousness of purpose and service orientation.
Application requirements: Transcript. Application; letter stating reason for applying, including personal information.
Additional information: Student must be resident of North Dakota, South Dakota, Idaho, or Montana; student's school need not be in those states. Must write for application; applications available from January to end of May.

Amount of award:	$400
Number of awards:	70
Number of applicants:	350
Application deadline:	June 15
Notification begins:	July 31
Total amount awarded:	$28,000

Contact:
Treacy Company
P.O. Box 1479
Helena, MT 59624

Trinity Episcopal Church

Shannon Scholarship

Type of award: Scholarship, renewable.
Intended use: For undergraduate study.
Eligibility: Applicant must be female. Applicant must be Episcopal. Applicant must be residing in Pennsylvania.
Basis for selection: Applicant must demonstrate financial need.
Application requirements: Proof of eligibility. Application (available April 15).
Additional information: Only open to daughters of Episcopal clergy in state of Pennsylvania. Must apply for state and federal financial assistance first. Previous recipients may reapply. Number of awards varies. For more information, contact the Reverend Canon Charles Morris.

Amount of award:	$500-$5,000
Application deadline:	May 15

Contact:
Trinity Episcopal Church
200 South Second Street
Pottsville, PA 17901
Phone: 570-622-8720

Two Ten Footwear Foundation

Two Ten Footwear Design Scholarship

Type of award: Scholarship, renewable.
Intended use: For undergraduate study in United States.
Eligibility: Applicant must be U.S. citizen or permanent resident.
Basis for selection: Major/career interest in fashion/fashion design/modeling. Applicant must demonstrate financial need.
Application requirements: Recommendations, transcript, proof of eligibility.
Additional information: Rolling deadline. Must have footwear design as major or component of major.

    Amount of award: $3,000

Contact:
Two Ten Footwear Foundation
Scholarship Department
1466 Main Street
Waltham, MA 02451
Phone: 800-346-3210, ext. 1503
Web: www.twoten.org

Two/Ten International Footwear Foundation

Two/Ten International Footwear Foundation Scholarship

Type of award: Scholarship, renewable.
Intended use: For undergraduate study at accredited vocational, 2-year or 4-year institution.
Eligibility: Applicant or parent must be employed by Footwear/Leather Industry. Applicant must be U.S. citizen.
Basis for selection: Applicant must demonstrate financial need, high academic achievement, depth of character, leadership and seriousness of purpose.
Application requirements: Recommendations, essay, transcript, proof of eligibility.
Additional information: Must have worked 500 hours in footwear or leather industries, or have parent currently employed in this field for minimum of one year. Top-ranking applicant candidate for $15,000 super-scholarship, renewable up to four years. Additional information and application available on Website.

    Amount of award: $200-$3,000
    Number of awards: 942
    Application deadline: January 1
    Notification begins: June 15
    Total amount awarded: $646,260

Contact:
Two/Ten International Footwear Foundation
Attn: Scholarship Department
1466 Main Street
Waltham, MA 02451-1623
Phone: 800-346-3210
Web: www.twoten.org

Ukrainian Fraternal Association

Eugene and Elinor Kotur Scholarship

Type of award: Scholarship, renewable.
Intended use: For full-time sophomore, junior or senior study at accredited 4-year institution. Designated institutions: Contact sponsor for list of eligible institutions.
Eligibility: Applicant or parent must be member/participant of Ukrainian Fraternal Association. Applicant must be Ukrainian.
Basis for selection: Applicant must demonstrate financial need, high academic achievement and depth of character.
Application requirements: Essay, transcript, proof of eligibility. Autobiographical statement containing information regarding Ukrainian roots. Small photograph.
Additional information: Must have completed first year of undergraduate studies. Membership in the Ukrainian Fraternal Association is encouraged but not required for this scholarship.

    Amount of award: $1,000-$3,000
    Application deadline: May 1

Contact:
Ukrainian Fraternal Association Scholarship Coordinator
371 N. 9th Ave.
Scranton, PA 18504
Phone: 570-342-0937

Ukrainian Fraternal Association Scholarship

Type of award: Scholarship, renewable.
Intended use: For full-time sophomore, junior or senior study.
Eligibility: Applicant or parent must be member/participant of Ukrainian Fraternal Association. Applicant must be Ukrainian.
Basis for selection: Applicant must demonstrate financial need and high academic achievement.
Application requirements: Essay, transcript. Include photo and autobiography.
Additional information: Applicant must be member of Ukrainian Fraternal Association. Must have completed first year of undergraduate study.

    Amount of award: $300
    Application deadline: May 30

Contact:
Ukrainian Fraternal Association Scholarship Coordinator
371 N 9th Ave.
Scranton, PA 18504
Phone: 570-342-0937

Unico Foundation, Inc.

Alphonse A. Miele Scholarship

Type of award: Scholarship.
Intended use: For undergraduate study.
Eligibility: Applicant must be high school senior. Applicant must be Italian.
Basis for selection: Applicant must demonstrate financial need, high academic achievement, depth of character and leadership.

Application requirements: Recommendations, essay, transcript, proof of eligibility.

Additional information: Student must reside in the corporate limits of a city wherein an active chapter of Unico National is located. Award is for $1,500 per year for four years. Student does not have to be Italian.

Amount of award:	$6,000
Application deadline:	April 15

Contact:
Unico Foundation, Inc.
271 US Highway, 46 West
Suite A-108
Fairfield, NJ 07004
Phone: 973-748-9144

Major Don S. Gentile Scholarship

Type of award: Scholarship.
Intended use: For undergraduate study.
Eligibility: Applicant must be high school senior. Applicant must be Italian.
Basis for selection: Applicant must demonstrate financial need, high academic achievement, depth of character and leadership.
Application requirements: Recommendations, essay, transcript, proof of eligibility.
Additional information: Students must reside in corporate limits of a city wherein an active chapter of Unico National is located. Award is distributed in four annual installments of $1,500.

Amount of award:	$6,000
Application deadline:	April 15

Contact:
Unico Foundation, Inc.
271 US Highway 46 #A108
Fairfield, NJ 07004-2458
Phone: 973-748-9144

Theodore Mazza Scholarship

Type of award: Scholarship.
Intended use: For undergraduate study.
Eligibility: Applicant must be high school senior.
Basis for selection: Major/career interest in art/art history. Applicant must demonstrate financial need, high academic achievement, depth of character and leadership.
Application requirements: Recommendations, essay, transcript, proof of eligibility.
Additional information: Student must reside in the corporate limits of a city wherein an active chapter of Unico National is located. Award is distributed in four annual installments of $1,500.

Amount of award:	$6,000
Application deadline:	April 15

Contact:
Unico Foundation, Inc.
271 US Highway 46 #A108
Fairfield, NJ 07004-2458

William C. Davini Scholarship

Type of award: Scholarship.
Intended use: For undergraduate study.
Eligibility: Applicant must be high school senior. Applicant must be Italian.
Basis for selection: Applicant must demonstrate financial need, high academic achievement, depth of character and leadership.

Application requirements: Recommendations, essay, transcript, proof of eligibility.

Additional information: Students must reside in the corporate limits of a city wherein an active chapter of Unico National is located. Award is distributed in four annual installments of $1,500.

Amount of award:	$6,000
Application deadline:	April 15

Contact:
Unico Foundation, Inc.
271 US Highway 46 #A108
Fairfield, NJ 07004-2458

Unitarian Universalist Association

Stanfield and D'Orlando Art Scholarship

Type of award: Scholarship.
Intended use: For full-time undergraduate or first professional study in United States.
Eligibility: Applicant must be at least 16, returning adult student, high school senior. Applicant must be Unitarian Universalist.
Basis for selection: Major/career interest in arts, general. Applicant must demonstrate financial need, high academic achievement, depth of character and service orientation.
Application requirements: Portfolio, recommendations, essay, transcript, proof of eligibility.
Additional information: Must be active member in Unitarian Universalist Church. Number of awards varies. Application due February 15; supporting materials due March 1. Applicant must be preparing for fine arts career in fields such as painting, drawing, sculpture or photography. Performing arts majors not eligible. See Website for application and more information.

Application deadline:	February 15, March 1
Notification begins:	May 15

Contact:
Unitarian Universalist Funding Program
P.O. Box 1149
Jamaica Plain, MA 02130
Phone: 617-971-9600
Web: www.uua.org

United Food and Commercial Workers Union

United Food and Commercial Workers Union Scholarship Program

Type of award: Scholarship.
Intended use: For full-time undergraduate study at accredited 4-year institution.
Eligibility: Applicant or parent must be member/participant of United Food and Commerical Workers. Applicant must be high school senior.

Application requirements: Transcript. Complete biographical questionnaire. SAT/ACT scores (except Canadian applicants).
Additional information: Applicant or applicant's parent must be member of United Food and Commercial Workers Union for one year prior to application.

Amount of award:	$4,000
Number of awards:	7
Number of applicants:	4,000
Application deadline:	December 31, March 15
Total amount awarded:	$28,000

Contact:
United Food and Commercial Workers Union
1775 K Street, N.W.
Washington, DC 20006
Phone: 202-223-3111
Web: www.ufcw.org

United Methodist Church

United Methodist Bass Scholarship

Type of award: Scholarship, renewable.
Intended use: For full-time undergraduate study at postsecondary institution in United States.
Eligibility: Applicant must be United Methodist. Applicant must be U.S. citizen or permanent resident.
Basis for selection: Major/career interest in religion/theology. Applicant must demonstrate seriousness of purpose.
Additional information: Preference given to applicants preparing for ministry or other full-time religious work. Must be active member of United Methodist Church one year prior to application.

Application deadline:	June 1

Contact:
United Methodist Church/Board of Higher Education and Ministry
Office of Loans and Scholarships
P.O. Box 340007
Nashville, TN 37203-0007
Phone: 615-340-7344
Web: www.gbhem.org

United Methodist Church Conference Merit Award

Type of award: Scholarship, renewable.
Intended use: For undergraduate study at 2-year or 4-year institution. Designated institutions: Must be used at United Methodist affiliated college or university.
Eligibility: Applicant must be United Methodist. Applicant must be U.S. citizen or permanent resident.
Basis for selection: Applicant must demonstrate leadership.
Additional information: Must reside and participate in United Methodist Church Annual Conference. Must be full, active member of United Methodist Church one year prior to application. Amount of award and deadline varies. Application and additional information available at Annual Conference office where local church is member.

United Methodist Hana Scholarship

Type of award: Scholarship, renewable.
Intended use: For full-time junior, senior, master's, doctoral or first professional study at 4-year or graduate institution in United States.

Eligibility: Applicant must be Asian American, African American, Mexican American, Hispanic American, Puerto Rican or American Indian. Pacific Islander. At least one parent of applicant must be a minority. Applicant must be United Methodist. Applicant must be U.S. citizen or permanent resident.
Basis for selection: Applicant must demonstrate financial need, high academic achievement, leadership and service orientation.
Application requirements: Recommendations, transcript. Leadership development plan.
Additional information: Must be active member of United Methodist Church for three years prior to application. Above average scholarship expected.

Application deadline:	April 1

Contact:
United Methodist Church/Board of Higher Education and Ministry
Office of Loans and Scholarships
P.O. Box 340007
Nashville, TN 37203-0007
Phone: 615-340-7344
Web: www.gbhem.org

United Methodist J.A. Knowles Memorial Scholarship

Type of award: Scholarship, renewable.
Intended use: For undergraduate or graduate study. Designated institutions: One of the eight United Methodist affiliated institutions in Texas.
Eligibility: Applicant must be United Methodist. Applicant must be U.S. citizen or permanent resident residing in Texas.
Basis for selection: Applicant must demonstrate financial need.
Additional information: Must be active member of United Methodist Church one year prior to application. Recipients must attend one of eight United Methodist affiliated institutions in Texas.

Application deadline:	June 1

Contact:
United Methodist Church/Board of Higher Education and Ministry
Office of Loans and Scholarships
P.O. Box 340007
Nashville, TN 37203-0007
Phone: 615-340-7344
Web: www.gbhem.org

United Methodist Priscilla R. Morton Scholarship

Type of award: Scholarship, renewable.
Intended use: For full-time sophomore, junior or senior study at accredited 4-year institution in United States.
Eligibility: Applicant must be United Methodist. Applicant must be U.S. citizen or permanent resident.
Basis for selection: Applicant must demonstrate high academic achievement.
Additional information: Highly competitive academic scholarship. Must be active member of United Methodist Church one year prior to application. Minimum 3.5 college GPA required. Not open to high school seniors entering college. Must have completed at least one semester of college.

Application deadline:	June 1

Contact:
United Methodist Church/Board of Higher Education and Ministry
Office of Loans and Scholarships
P.O. Box 340007
Nashville, TN 37203-0007
Phone: 615-340-7344
Web: www.gbhem.org

United Methodist Scholarship

Type of award: Scholarship, renewable.
Intended use: For full-time freshman, sophomore, junior or senior study at 2-year or 4-year institution in United States. Designated institutions: United Methodist affiliated institutions.
Eligibility: Applicant must be United Methodist.
Basis for selection: Applicant must demonstrate financial need and high academic achievement.
Application requirements: Transcript.
Additional information: Available to undergraduate students attending United Methodist affiliated institutions who have been active members of United Methodist Church for one year prior to application. Must have minimum 3.0 GPA. Information and application available through institution's financial aid director.

United Methodist Communications

Leonard M. Perryman Communications Scholarship for Ethnic Minority Students

Type of award: Scholarship.
Intended use: For full-time junior or senior study at accredited 4-year institution in United States.
Eligibility: Applicant must be Alaskan native, Asian American, African American, Mexican American, Hispanic American, Puerto Rican or American Indian. Applicant must be Christian.
Basis for selection: Major/career interest in journalism; communications or radio/television/film. Applicant must demonstrate seriousness of purpose.
Application requirements: Portfolio, recommendations, essay, transcript. Three examples of journalistic work in any media; statement of interest in religious journalism and planned course of study; photograph (appropriate for publicity purposes).
Additional information: Must plan to pursue career in religious journalism or religious communication. Application forms available October 1 and may be downloaded from Website. One of two scholarships will be awarded to a United Methodist.

Amount of award:	$2,500
Number of awards:	2
Number of applicants:	6
Application deadline:	March 15
Total amount awarded:	$5,000

Contact:
United Methodist Communications
Scholarship Committee
P.O. Box 320
Nashville, TN 37202-0320
Phone: 615-742-5407
Web: www.umcom.org

United Negro College Fund

Alfred R. Chisholm Memorial Scholarship

Type of award: Scholarship, renewable.
Intended use: For full-time undergraduate study at accredited 4-year institution in United States. Designated institutions: UNCF member institutions.
Eligibility: Applicant must be African American. Applicant must be U.S. citizen or permanent resident residing in New Jersey.
Basis for selection: Major/career interest in computer/information sciences; engineering; chemistry or mathematics. Applicant must demonstrate high academic achievement and service orientation.
Application requirements: Recommendations, essay, transcript, proof of eligibility, nomination by financial aid office of designated institution. FAFSA, photographs.
Additional information: Minimum 3.0 GPA. Computer science majors also eligible.

Amount of award:	$5,000
Number of awards:	325,000
Application deadline:	November 16

Contact:
United Negro College Fund
8260 Willow Oaks Corporate Drive
P.O. Box 10444
Fairfax, VA 22031-8044
Phone: 800-331-2244
Web: www.uncf.org

Alton R. Higgins, MD, and Dorothy Higgins Scholarship

Type of award: Scholarship, renewable.
Intended use: For full-time junior, senior or first professional study at accredited 4-year or graduate institution in United States. Designated institutions: Dillard University, Fisk University, Morehouse College, Oakwood College, Spelman College, Talladega College, Tuskegee University, Xavier University.
Eligibility: Applicant must be African American. Applicant must be U.S. citizen or permanent resident.
Basis for selection: Major/career interest in medicine. Applicant must demonstrate financial need and high academic achievement.
Application requirements: Recommendations, essay, transcript, proof of eligibility, nomination by financial aid office of designated institution. FAFSA, photographs.
Additional information: Minimum GPA 3.0. Must be enrolled at UNCF member institution. Undergraduates eligible for $5,000 award, renewable in senior year. Graduate medical students must attend Morehouse. Graduate award is $10,000.

Amount of award:	$5,000-$10,000
Number of applicants:	13

Contact:
United Negro College Fund
8260 Willow Oaks Corporate Drive
P. O. Box 10444
Fairfax, VA 22031-8044
Phone: 800-331-2244
Web: www.uncf.org

American Home Products Wyeth Ayerst Scholarship

Type of award: Scholarship, renewable.
Intended use: For full-time undergraduate study in United States. Designated institutions: UNCF member schools, FAMU, Hampton, Howard and Texas Southern; it is also open to students attending Morehouse School of Medicine, Temple University, U of Toledo, UMBC, Meharry Medical College, and Charles R. Drew University of Medicine & Science.
Eligibility: Applicant must be U.S. citizen or permanent resident residing in New Jersey.
Basis for selection: Major/career interest in business/ management/administration; health-related professions; agricultural economics or veterinary medicine. Applicant must demonstrate financial need, high academic achievement and leadership.
Application requirements: Recommendations, essay, transcript, proof of eligibility, nomination by financial aid office of designated institution. FAFSA, photograph, resume, two letters of recommendation.
Additional information: Minimum 3.0 GPA. Scholarship includes the opportunity of a summer internship to students who are pursuing health-related or business administration fields who have unmet financial need as verified by the financial aid office.

Amount of award:	$5,000
Number of awards:	4
Application deadline:	February 6
Total amount awarded:	$20,000

Contact:
United Negro College Fund
8260 Willow Oaks Corporate Drive
P.O. Box 10444
Fairfax, VA 22031-8044
Phone: 800-331-2244
Web: www.uncf.org

Berbeco Senior Research Fellowship

Type of award: Scholarship.
Intended use: For full-time junior or senior study at accredited 4-year institution in United States. Designated institutions: UNCF member colleges and universities.
Eligibility: Applicant must be Alaskan native, Asian American, African American, Mexican American, Hispanic American, Puerto Rican or American Indian. Applicant must be U.S. citizen or permanent resident.
Basis for selection: Applicant must demonstrate financial need and high academic achievement.
Application requirements: Essay, proof of eligibility. One-page letter of intent outlining the research project and summer research objectives.
Additional information: The Berbeco Senior Research Fellowship is intended to encourage study abroad, through an established program or under the guidance of the faculty member at a foreign university. Minimum 2.5 GPA. Visit Website for additional information.

Application deadline:	November 3

Contact:
United Negro College Fund
8260 Willow Oaks Corporate Drive
P.O. Box 10444
Fairfax, VA 22031-8044
Phone: 800-331-2244
Web: www.uncf.org

Bigwood Memorial Fund

Type of award: Scholarship, renewable.
Intended use: For full-time undergraduate study in United States. Designated institutions: UNCF member institutions.
Eligibility: Applicant must be Alaskan native, Asian American, African American, Mexican American, Hispanic American, Puerto Rican or American Indian.
Basis for selection: Major/career interest in health-related professions. Applicant must demonstrate financial need and high academic achievement.
Application requirements: Recommendations, essay, transcript, proof of eligibility, nomination by Financial aid office of designated institution. FAFSA and photograph.
Additional information: Minimum 2.5 GPA. This fund was created in the memory of Mrs. Gertrude Bigwood. Need-based scholarship for students planning careers in health care. Visit Website for additional information. Contact financial aid office of member institution for application, deadlines, award amount and details.

Amount of award:	$1,000-$5,000

Contact:
United Negro College Fund
8260 Willow Oaks Corporate Drive
P.O. Box 10444
Fairfax, VA 22031-4511
Phone: 800-331-2244
Web: www.uncf.org

Cargill Scholarship Program

Type of award: Scholarship.
Intended use: For full-time freshman, sophomore or junior study at accredited 2-year or 4-year institution. Designated institutions: UNCF member institutions.
Eligibility: Applicant must be Alaskan native, Asian American, African American, Mexican American, Hispanic American, Puerto Rican or American Indian. Applicant must be U.S. citizen or permanent resident.
Basis for selection: Major/career interest in accounting; finance/banking; computer/information sciences; chemistry; biochemistry; microbiology; engineering, chemical or engineering, mechanical. Applicant must demonstrate financial need and high academic achievement.
Application requirements: Recommendations, essay, transcript by financial aid officer of eligible institution. FAFSA, resume, 250-word essay about applicant, selected major, career goals and how they might be fulfilled at Cargill.
Additional information: Minimum 3.0 GPA. Students are also eligible for this scholarship from the following institutions: University of Minnesota, Iowa State University, North Carolina A&T State University and University of Wisconsin-Madison. Internship opportunities may become available to students receiving this scholarship. Cargill wil also consider the following majors: agriculture, animal and food sciences.

Amount of award:	$5,000
Application deadline:	March 15

Contact:
United Negro College Fund Program Services
8260 Willow Oaks Corporate Drive
P.O. Box 10444
Fairfax, VA 22031-8044
Phone: 800-331-2244
Web: www.uncf.org

Chevron Texaco Scholars Program

Type of award: Scholarship, renewable.

Intended use: For full-time junior or senior study at accredited 4-year institution in United States. Designated institutions: Clark Atlanta University, Morehouse College, Morris Brown College, Spelman College, Tuskegee Universtiy, Florida A&M.
Eligibility: Applicant must be Alaskan native, Asian American, African American, Mexican American, Hispanic American, Puerto Rican or American Indian.
Basis for selection: Major/career interest in engineering. Applicant must demonstrate financial need and high academic achievement.
Application requirements: Recommendations, essay, transcript, nomination by financial aid office of designated institution. FAFSA, resume, two personal reference letters, one-page personal statement of career interest.
Additional information: Minimum 2.5 GPA. Residents of Texas, Florida or California preferred. Applicant must demonstrate community service and leadership activities. Applicants for this scholarship must major in civil, mechanical, or petroleum engineering. Funds from this scholarship may be used toward tuition and room/board, or to repay federal student loans.

Amount of award:	$3,000
Number of awards:	80
Application deadline:	December 8

Contact:
United Negro College Fund
8260 Willow Oaks Corporate Drive
P.O. Box 10444
Fairfax, VA 22031-8044
Phone: 800-331-2244
Web: www.uncf.org

Cisco/UNCF Scholars Program

Type of award: Scholarship, renewable.
Intended use: For full-time sophomore, junior or senior study at accredited 4-year institution in United States. Designated institutions: Claflin University, Clark Atlanta University, Dillard University, Jarvis Christian College, Johnson C. Smith University, Livingstone College, Morehouse College, Paul Quinn College, Rust College, Saint Augustine's College, Shaw University, Spelman College, Wiley College, Xavier University, Morgan State, North Carolina A&T, N.C. Central University, Massachusetts Institute of Technology, North Carolina State University, Grambling State University, University of California - Berkeley, Stanford University, Univ. San Luis Obispo, University of Illinois Champaign-Urbana, University of Michigan, Purdue University, University of Texas at Austin, Georgia Tech, Prairie View A&M University, San Jose State University.
Eligibility: Applicant must be Alaskan native, Asian American, African American, Mexican American, Hispanic American, Puerto Rican or American Indian. Applicant must be female. Applicant must be U.S. citizen or permanent resident.
Basis for selection: Major/career interest in computer/information sciences or engineering, electrical/electronic. Applicant must demonstrate financial need and high academic achievement.
Application requirements: Recommendations, essay, transcript, proof of eligibility, nomination by financial aid office of designated institution. Resume, financial need statement.
Additional information: Minimum 3.2 GPA. Application available online.

Amount of award:	$4,000
Number of awards:	10
Application deadline:	March 27

Contact:
United Negro College Fund
8260 Willow Oaks Corporate Drive
P.O. Box 10444
Fairfax, VA 22031-8044
Phone: 800-331-2244
Web: www.uncf.org

Earl & Patricia Armstrong Scholarship

Type of award: Scholarship.
Intended use: For full-time sophomore, junior or graduate study at accredited 4-year institution in United States. Designated institutions: UNCF member institutions.
Eligibility: Applicant must be Alaskan native, Asian American, African American, Mexican American, Hispanic American, Puerto Rican or American Indian. Applicant must be U.S. citizen or permanent resident.
Basis for selection: Major/career interest in medicine; biology or health sciences. Applicant must demonstrate financial need and high academic achievement.
Application requirements: Recommendations, essay, transcript, proof of eligibility, nomination by financial aid office of designated institution. FAFSA.
Additional information: Minimum 3.0 GPA. Visit Website for application.

Amount of award:	$3,000
Notification begins:	March 1

Contact:
United Negro College Fund
8260 Willow Oaks Corporate Drive
P.O. Box 10444
Fairfax, VA 22031-8044
Phone: 800-331-2244
Web: www.uncf.org

Gates Millennium Scholars Program

Type of award: Scholarship, renewable.
Intended use: For full-time undergraduate or graduate study at accredited 4-year or graduate institution.
Eligibility: Applicant must be Alaskan native, Asian American, African American, Mexican American, Hispanic American, Puerto Rican or American Indian.
Basis for selection: Major/career interest in mathematics; science, general; engineering; education or library science. Applicant must demonstrate financial need, high academic achievement, leadership and service orientation.
Application requirements: Recommendations, transcript, nomination by high school principal, teacher or counselor; or nomination by college president, professor or dean. Students are required to provide a completed Nominee Personal Information Form. FAFSA, GMS information sheet, admission letters.
Additional information: Must be Pell Grant eligible. Must participate in community service, volunteer work or extracurricular activities. Minimum 3.3 GPA required. Scholarship provides tuition, room, materials and board not covered by existing financial aid. Eliminates loans, work-study and outside jobs for scholarship recipients. All majors accepted for undergraduate scholarships; graduate students must be enrolled in degree program in engineering, mathematics, science, education or library science. Funded by Bill and Melinda Gates Foundation.

Number of awards: 4,000
Application deadline: March 15
Notification begins: May 1
Total amount awarded: $50,000,000
Contact:
United Negro College Fund Program Services
8260 Willow Oaks Corporate Drive
P. O. Box 10444
Fairfax, VA 22031-8044
Phone: 800-331-2244 or 877-690-4677
Web: www.uncf.org or www.gmsp.org

Janet Jackson Rhythm Nation Scholarships

Type of award: Scholarship, renewable.
Intended use: For full-time undergraduate study at accredited 4-year institution in United States. Designated institutions: UNCF member colleges and universities.
Eligibility: Applicant must be Alaskan native, Asian American, African American, Mexican American, Hispanic American, Puerto Rican or American Indian.
Basis for selection: Major/career interest in communications; performing arts; English or music.
Application requirements: Recommendations, essay, proof of eligibility, nomination by financial aid office of designated institution. FAFSA, resume, photograph, and SAR must be sent to school's financial aid office.
Additional information: Minimum 3.0 GPA. Fine arts majors also eligible. Awards funded by $395,000 endowment. Awards are made annually and may be used for tuition costs, room and board, or to repay federal student loans. For more information and application, see Website.
Amount of award: $2,000
Application deadline: November 26
Contact:
United Negro College Fund
8260 Willow Oaks Corporate Deive
P. O. Box 10444
Fairfax, VA 22031-8044
Phone: 800-331-2244
Web: www.uncf.org

John Lennon Scholarship Fund

Type of award: Scholarship, renewable.
Intended use: For full-time undergraduate study at accredited 4-year institution in United States. Designated institutions: UNCF member institution.
Eligibility: Applicant must be Alaskan native, Asian American, African American, Mexican American, Hispanic American, Puerto Rican or American Indian.
Basis for selection: Major/career interest in performing arts or communications. Applicant must demonstrate financial need and high academic achievement.
Application requirements: Recommendations, essay, transcript, proof of eligibility, nomination by financial aid office of designated institution. FAFSA and photograph.
Additional information: Minimum 2.5 GPA. $800,000 endowed scholarship fund established by Yoko Ono. Visit Website for additional information. Contact financial aid office of member institution for application and deadlines.
Amount of award: $5,000

Contact:
United Negro College Fund
8260 Willow Oaks Corporate Drive
P. O. Box 10444
Fairfax, VA 22031-8044
Phone: 800-331-2244
Web: www.uncf.org

John W. Anderson Foundation Scholarship

Type of award: Scholarship, renewable.
Intended use: For full-time undergraduate study at accredited 4-year institution in United States. Designated institutions: UNCF member institutions.
Eligibility: Applicant must be Alaskan native, Asian American, African American, Mexican American, Hispanic American, Puerto Rican or American Indian. Applicant must be U.S. citizen or permanent resident residing in Indiana.
Basis for selection: Applicant must demonstrate financial need and high academic achievement.
Application requirements: FAFSA.
Additional information: Minimum 2.5 GPA. Preference given to Indiana residents. See Website for more information.
Amount of award: $3,000
Contact:
United Negro College Fund
8260 Willow Oaks Corporate Drive
P.O. Box 10444
Fairfax, VA 22031-8044
Phone: 800-331-2244
Web: www.uncf.org

Malcolm X Scholarship for Exceptional Courage

Type of award: Scholarship, renewable.
Intended use: For full-time junior study at accredited 4-year institution in United States. Designated institutions: UNCF member institutions.
Eligibility: Applicant must be Alaskan native, Asian American, African American, Mexican American, Hispanic American, Puerto Rican or American Indian.
Basis for selection: Applicant must demonstrate financial need, high academic achievement, leadership and seriousness of purpose.
Application requirements: Recommendations, essay, transcript, proof of eligibility, nomination by academic dean or vice president for academic affairs of UNCF member institution. FAFSA and SAR must be sent to school's financial aid office.
Additional information: Minimum 2.5 GPA. Application and list of colleges available online. Renewable each year until graduation. Scholarship is awarded to students who demonstrate academic excellence, campus and community leadership, and exceptional courage. See Website for deadline.
Amount of award: $4,000
Contact:
United Negro College Fund Attn: William Dunham
8260 Willow Oaks Corporate Drive
P. O. Box 10444
Fairfax, VA 22031-8044
Phone: 800-331-2244
Web: www.uncf.org

Scholarships

Maya Angelou/Vivian Baxter Scholarhip

Type of award: Scholarship, renewable.
Intended use: For full-time undergraduate study at accredited 4-year institution in United States. Designated institutions: UNCF member institutions.
Eligibility: Applicant must be Alaskan native, Asian American, African American, Mexican American, Hispanic American, Puerto Rican or American Indian. Applicant must be residing in North Carolina.
Basis for selection: Applicant must demonstrate financial need, high academic achievement, leadership and service orientation.
Application requirements: FAFSA.
Additional information: Minimum 2.5 GPA.
   Amount of award: $2,500
Contact:
United Negro College Fund
8260 Willow Oaks Corporate Drive
P. O. Box 10444
Fairfax, VA 22031-8044
Phone: 800-331-2244
Web: www.uncf.org

Michael Jackson Scholarships

Type of award: Scholarship, renewable.
Intended use: For undergraduate study at accredited 4-year institution in United States. Designated institutions: UNCF member institutions.
Eligibility: Applicant must be Alaskan native, Asian American, African American, Mexican American, Hispanic American, Puerto Rican or American Indian.
Basis for selection: Major/career interest in performing arts; communications or English. Applicant must demonstrate financial need and high academic achievement.
Application requirements: Recommendations, essay, transcript, proof of eligibility, nomination by financial aid office of institution. FAFSA, photographs. SAR must be sent to school's financial aid office.
Additional information: Minimum 3.0 GPA. Funds may be used for tuition, room and board, and books, or to repay federal student loans. Awards funded by $1.5 million endowment.
   Amount of award: $4,000
   Application deadline: October 22
Contact:
United Negro College Fund
8260 Willow Oaks Corporate Drive
P. O. Box 10444
Fairfax, VA 22031-8044
Phone: 800-331-2244
Web: www.uncf.org

Reader's Digest Foundation Scholarship Program

Type of award: Scholarship, renewable.
Intended use: For full-time junior or senior study at accredited 4-year institution in United States. Designated institutions: UNCF member institutions.
Eligibility: Applicant must be Alaskan native, Asian American, African American, Mexican American, Hispanic American, Puerto Rican or American Indian.
Basis for selection: Major/career interest in journalism; communications or English. Applicant must demonstrate financial need and high academic achievement.

Application requirements: Recommendations, essay, transcript, proof of eligibility, nomination by financial aid director at eligible institution. Application, published writing sample, photograph, FAFSA, personal statement on background and career goals, recommendation from professor of journalism, communications or English.
Additional information: Minimum 3.0 GPA. Scholarship designed for students demonstrating interest in print journalism. Funds from this scholarship may be used for tuition, room/board, and books, or to repay a federal student loan. Renewable only if eligibility requirements met and funds available. Contact sponsor for application or visit Website.
   Amount of award: $5,000
   Number of awards: 6
   Application deadline: November 14
   Total amount awarded: $30,000
Contact:
United Negro College Fund Program Services
8260 Willow Oaks Corparate Drive
P.O. Box 10444
Fairfax, VA 22031-8044
Phone: 800-331-2244
Web: www.uncf.org

Sallie Mae Fund American Dream Scholarship

Type of award: Scholarship.
Intended use: For full-time undergraduate study at accredited 2-year or 4-year institution in United States. Designated institutions: Title IV accredited college or university.
Eligibility: Applicant must be African American. Applicant must be U.S. citizen or permanent resident.
Basis for selection: Applicant must demonstrate financial need and high academic achievement.
Application requirements: Recommendations, essay, transcript by financial aid office of institution. FAFSA, two letters of recommendation, essay describing "your dreams for the future and your plans for making your dreams a reality."
Additional information: Minimum 2.5 GPA. Visit Website for list of member colleges and universities.
   Amount of award: $500-$5,000
   Application deadline: April 15
Contact:
United Negro College Fund
8260 Willow Oaks Corporate Drive
P.O. Box 10444
Fairfax, VA 22031-8044
Phone: 800-331-2244
Web: www.uncf.org

UBS/Paine Webber Scholarships

Type of award: Scholarship, renewable.
Intended use: For full-time sophomore or junior study at accredited 4-year institution. Designated institutions: UNCF member colleges and universities.
Eligibility: Applicant must be Alaskan native, Asian American, African American, Mexican American, Hispanic American, Puerto Rican or American Indian.
Basis for selection: Major/career interest in business; economics; business/management/administration or finance/banking.
Application requirements: Recommendations, essay, transcript, proof of eligibility, nomination by financial aid office of institution. FAFSA and photograph.

Additional information: Minimum 3.0 GPA. Applicant with career interest in sales also eligible. Visit Website for additional information. Contact financial aid office of member institution for application, deadlines, award amount and details.

Amount of award: $8,000

Contact:
United Negro College Fund
8260 Willow Oaks Corporate Drive
P.O. Box 10444
Fairfax, VA 22031-8044
Phone: 800-331-2244
Web: www.uncf.org

Virginia Health and Human Services Fund

Type of award: Scholarship.
Intended use: For undergraduate study in United States. Designated institutions: UNCF member institutions.
Eligibility: Applicant must be Alaskan native, Asian American, African American, Mexican American, Hispanic American, Puerto Rican or American Indian. Applicant must be U.S. citizen or permanent resident residing in Virginia.
Basis for selection: Applicant must demonstrate financial need and high academic achievement.
Application requirements: Recommendations, essay, transcript, proof of eligibility, nomination by financial aid office of designated institution. FAFSA and photograph.
Additional information: Annual award offsets living expenses for students from Virginia. Minimum 2.0 GPA. Visit Website for additional information. Contact financial aid office of member institution for application, deadlines, award amount and details. Funds provided by Richmond, Virginia, United Way.

Total amount awarded: $100,000

Contact:
United Negro College Fund
8260 Willow Oaks Corporate Drive
P. O. Box 10444
Fairfax, VA 22031-8044
Phone: 800-331-2244
Web: www.uncf.org

United States Association of Blind Athletes

Arthur E. Copeland Scholarship for Males

Type of award: Scholarship.
Intended use: For full-time undergraduate study at postsecondary institution.
Eligibility: Applicant or parent must be member/participant of United States Association of Blind Athletes. Applicant must be visually impaired. Applicant must be male, high school senior. Applicant must be U.S. citizen.
Application requirements: Transcript, proof of eligibility. Autobiographical sketch outlining USABA involvement and academic goals. References.
Additional information: Applicants must be legally blind and a participant in USABA activities for at least two years. Must be current USABA member. Open to all majors.

Amount of award:	$500
Number of awards:	1
Application deadline:	October 1
Notification begins:	November 1

Contact:
USABA Scholarship Director
33 North Institute St.
West Hall
Colorado Springs, CO 80903
Web: www.usaba.org

Helen Copeland Scholarship for Females

Type of award: Scholarship.
Intended use: For undergraduate study.
Eligibility: Applicant must be visually impaired. Applicant must be female. Applicant must be U.S. citizen.
Application requirements: Transcript, proof of eligibility. Autobiographical sketch outlining USABA involvement, academic goals and objective for which scholarship funds will be used. Three references (a USABA reference, an academic reference and a personal reference).
Additional information: Applicants must be legally blind and a participant in USABA sports programs. Must be current USABA member.

Amount of award:	$500
Number of awards:	1
Application deadline:	October 1
Notification begins:	November 1
Total amount awarded:	$500

Contact:
U.S. Association of Blind Athletes
33 North Institute Street
Colorado Springs, CO 80903
Phone: 719-630-0422
Fax: 719-630-0616
Web: www.usaba.org

United States Institute of Peace

National Peace Essay Contest

Type of award: Scholarship.
Intended use: For undergraduate study.
Eligibility: Applicant must be enrolled in high school. Applicant must be U.S. citizen.
Basis for selection: Competition/talent/interest in Writing/journalism. Major/career interest in peace studies.
Application requirements: Student form and coordinator form must accompany essay submission.
Additional information: Applicant will write a three-part essay with a 1500-word limit on a topic chosen by the Institute. Applicant must submit essay to their contest coordinator in advance of the deadline; the coordinator will submit the essay to the Institute. Contest winners receive $1000 for their college or university studies. First-place state winners will also compete for national awards of $10,000, $5,000 and $2,500 for first, second, and third place, respectively. They are also invited to attend an awards dinner in Washington, DC. Visit Website for more information.

Number of awards:	1
Application deadline:	February 2

Contact:
United States Institute of Peace
1200 17th St. NW
Suite 200
Washington, DC 20036-3011
Phone: 202-429-3854
Fax: 202-429-6063
Web: www.usip.org/npec

United Transportation Union Insurance Association

United Transportation Union Insurance Association Scholarship

Type of award: Scholarship, renewable.
Intended use: For full-time undergraduate study at accredited vocational, 2-year or 4-year institution in or outside United States.
Eligibility: Applicant or parent must be member/participant of United Transportation Union. Applicant must be no older than 25. Applicant must be permanent resident.
Application requirements: Proof of eligibility.
Additional information: Applicant must be accepted to or enrolled in an eligible institution. Members and direct descendants of living or deceased members eligible. Members of the United Transportation Union Insurance Association also eligible. Scholarships awarded by lottery. Notification takes place prior to fall enrollment.

Amount of award:	$500
Number of awards:	50
Number of applicants:	1,700
Application deadline:	March 31

Contact:
United Transportation Union Insurance Association
14600 Detroit Ave.
Cleveland, OH 44107-4250
Phone: 216-228-9400
Web: www.utu.org

University Film and Video Association

Carole Fielding Video Grant

Type of award: Research grant.
Intended use: For undergraduate or graduate study at accredited 2-year or 4-year institution.
Basis for selection: Major/career interest in film/video.
Application requirements: Application form. Research/production proposal. Must have UFVA faculty sponsor.
Additional information: Project categories include narrative, documentary, experimental, multimedia/installation, animation, and research. Applicant must submit one-page resume, budget and summary proposal. Applicant must be sponsored by faculty member who is active member of University Film and Video Association. Number of awards varies. Send five collated and

stapled copies of completed application. Applicant must be enrolled in school's film or television program.

Amount of award:	$1,000-$4,000
Number of applicants:	86
Application deadline:	January 1
Notification begins:	March 31
Total amount awarded:	$5,000

Contact:
Professor Robert Johnson, Jr., Grants Chair
Framingham State College, Commun. Arts Dept.
100 State Street
Framingham, MA 01701
Phone: 508-626-4684
Web: www.ufva.org

UPS

UPS Earn and Learn Program Grant

Type of award: Scholarship, renewable.
Intended use: For undergraduate study at accredited vocational, 2-year or 4-year institution in United States.
Eligibility: Applicant or parent must be employed by United Parcel Service (UPS).
Application requirements: Proof of eligibility. Applicant must be UPS employee at participating location.
Additional information: Employees attending college part-time qualify for up to $1,500 per semester in tuition assistance. Visit Website for current list of participating locations and more information.

Contact:
UPS
55 Glenlake Parkway N.E.
Atlanta, GA 30328
Phone: 888-WORK-UPS
Web: www.upsjobs.com

U.S. Army Recruiting Command

Montgomery GI Bill (MGIB)

Type of award: Scholarship.
Intended use: For undergraduate or graduate study at accredited postsecondary institution in United States.
Eligibility: Applicant must be at least 18, no older than 34. Applicant must be U.S. citizen. Applicant must be in military service in the Army.
Basis for selection: Applicant must demonstrate depth of character, leadership, patriotism, seriousness of purpose and service orientation.
Application requirements: Interview. Armed Services Vocational Aptitude Battery required.
Additional information: Must enlist for a minimum active duty service of two years. Award amount varies. $28,800 for two-year enlistment. $35,460 for three-year or more enlistment.

Amount of award:	$26,352-$32,400
Number of awards:	63,908

Contact:
U.S. Army Recruiting Command
P.O. Box 3219
Warminster, PA 18974-9844
Phone: 800-USA-ARMY

Montgomery GI Bill Plus Army College Fund

Type of award: Scholarship.
Intended use: For undergraduate or graduate study at accredited postsecondary institution.
Eligibility: Applicant must be at least 18, no older than 34, returning adult student. Applicant must be U.S. citizen. Applicant must be in military service in the Army.
Basis for selection: Applicant must demonstrate depth of character, leadership, patriotism, seriousness of purpose and service orientation.
Application requirements: Interview. Minimum score of 50 on Armed Services Vocational Aptitude Battery. High school diploma or 15 college semester hours.
Additional information: Enlistment in active Army for two to six years for active duty service, in an eligible ACF Military Occupational Specialty. Enrollment in colleges outside United States must be approved by Veterans Administration.
>   **Amount of award:** $30,000-$50,000
>   **Number of awards:**   11,369

Contact:
U.S. Army Recruiting Command
P.O. Box 3219
Warminster, PA 18974-9844
Phone: 800-USA-ARMY

Selected Reserve Montgomery GI Bill

Type of award: Scholarship.
Intended use: For undergraduate or graduate study at accredited postsecondary institution.
Eligibility: Applicant must be at least 17, no older than 34. Applicant must be U.S. citizen. Applicant must be veteran who served in the Army or Reserves/National Guard.
Basis for selection: IADT. Applicant must demonstrate depth of character, leadership, patriotism, seriousness of purpose and service orientation.
Application requirements: Interview. Armed Services Vocational Aptitude Battery required.
Additional information: Have a six-year obligation to serve in the Selected Reserve signed after June 30, 1985. Officers must have agreed to serve six years in addition to original obligation. For some types of training, it is necessary to have a six-year commitment that begins after September 30, 1990. Must remain in good standing while serving. Award amount varies.
>   **Amount of award:** $10,152-$22,752
>   **Number of awards:**   23,135

Contact:
U.S. Army
P.O. Box 3219
Warminster, PA 18974-9844
Phone: 800-USA-ARMY

U.S. Army Reserve Officers Training Corps

U.S. Army ROTC-Nurse Scholarship

Type of award: Scholarship, renewable.
Intended use: For undergraduate study at accredited 4-year institution in United States.
Eligibility: Applicant must be U.S. citizen.
Basis for selection: Major/career interest in nursing. Applicant must demonstrate leadership and seriousness of purpose.
Additional information: Award may be renewed up to four years. Student will receive an additional monthly stipend between $250-400 and an annual book allowance of $600. Must have a minimum 3.0 GPA. Complete application on Website. Number of awards varies by region and year.
>   **Amount of award:** $17,000

Contact:
U.S. Army Reserve Officers Training Command and U.S. Army Nurse Corps
441 East Fordham Road
Faculty Memorial Hall, Room 130
Bronx, NY 10458-9993
Phone: 646-996-3092
Web: www.nycrotc.com/nurse

U.S. Bank Student Banking Division

U.S. Bank Internet Scholarship Program

Type of award: Scholarship.
Intended use: For full-time undergraduate study at accredited 2-year or 4-year institution in United States.
Eligibility: Applicant must be high school senior. Applicant must be U.S. citizen or permanent resident.
Basis for selection: Major/career interest in humanities/liberal arts. Applicant must demonstrate depth of character.
Application requirements: Must provide GPA. Must provide transcript if merit award; must provide signed letter from counselor on goals.
Additional information: Scholarship awarded based on a random drawing. Visit Website from October through February to apply.
>   **Amount of award:** $1,000
>   **Number of awards:**   30
>   **Total amount awarded:** $30,000

Contact:
See Website for online application and complete information.
Phone: 800-242-1200
Web: www.usbank.com/studentbanking

U.S. Department of Agriculture

USDA/1890 National Scholars Program

Type of award: Scholarship.
Intended use: For full-time undergraduate study at 4-year institution in United States. Designated institutions: One of the 1890 Historically Black Land-Grant Institutions: Alabama A&M University, Alcorn State University (MS), Delaware State University, Florida A&M University, Fort Valley State University (GA), Kentucky State University, Lincoln University (MO), Langston University (OK), North Carolina A&T University, Prairie View A&M University (TX), South Carolina State University, Southern University (LA), Tennessee State University, Tuskegee University (AL), University of Arkansas at Pine Bluff, University of Maryland at Eastern Shore, and Virginia State University.
Eligibility: Applicant must be high school senior. Applicant must be U.S. citizen.
Basis for selection: Major/career interest in agriculture; agribusiness; agricultural education; agricultural economics; food science/technology; computer/information sciences; veterinary medicine; biology or chemistry. Applicant must demonstrate high academic achievement, leadership and service orientation.
Application requirements: Recommendations, transcript. Must have minimum 1000 SAT/21 ACT and 3.0 GPA. Transcript with official school seal and signature.
Additional information: For entering freshman at designated universities who are seeking bachelor's degrees in any field of study in agriculture, food, natural resource sciences and other related disciplines. Scholarship covers full tuition and fees for four years. Upon completion of scholar's academic degree program, there is an obligation of one year of service to USDA for each year of financial support. Number of awards varies depending on funding.

> **Amount of award:** Full tuition
> **Application deadline:** January 15

Contact:
U.S. Department of Agriculture
USDA/1890 National Scholars Program Manager
STOP 9477, 1400 Independence Ave., S.W.
Washington, DC 20250
Phone: 202-401-3647
Fax: 202-720-5909
Web: 1890scholars.program.usda.gov

U.S. Department of Education

Federal Pell Grant Program

Type of award: Scholarship, renewable.
Intended use: For undergraduate study at 2-year or 4-year institution.
Eligibility: Applicant must be U.S. citizen or permanent resident.
Basis for selection: Applicant must demonstrate financial need.
Application requirements: Proof of eligibility. FAFSA.
Additional information: Federal Pell Grant does not have to be repaid. Grant based on financial need, costs to attend school, and enrollment status. Must not have previously earned baccalaureate or professional degree. Amount of award varies.

> **Application deadline:** June 30

Contact:
Federal Student Aid Programs
P.O. Box 84
Washington, DC 20044-0084
Phone: 800-4-FED-AID or 800-730-8913
Web: studentaid.ed.gov

Federal Supplemental Educational Opportunity Grant Program

Type of award: Scholarship, renewable.
Intended use: For undergraduate study at accredited vocational, 2-year or 4-year institution in United States.
Eligibility: Applicant must be U.S. citizen or permanent resident.
Basis for selection: Applicant must demonstrate financial need.
Application requirements: Proof of eligibility. FAFSA.
Additional information: Priority given to Federal Pell Grant recipients with exceptional financial need. Must not have defaulted on federal grant or educational loan. Awards not generally made to students enrolled less than half-time. Unlike Pell Grants, availability of FSEOG awards not federally guaranteed, but depends on availability of funds at student's institution.

> **Amount of award:** $100-$4,000
> **Application deadline:** June 30

Contact:
Federal Student Aid Programs
P.O. Box 84
Washington, DC 20044-0084
Phone: 800-4-FED-AID
Web: studentaid.ed.gov

Robert C. Byrd Honors Scholarship Program

Type of award: Scholarship, renewable.
Intended use: For undergraduate study at postsecondary institution in United States.
Eligibility: Applicant must be high school senior. Applicant must be U.S. citizen or permanent resident.
Basis for selection: Applicant must demonstrate high academic achievement.
Application requirements: Proof of eligibility.
Additional information: Merit-based. Renewable up to three years. Selections by state education agencies (SEAs) supervising public elementary/secondary schools. Awards made in all 50 states, District of Columbia, Puerto Rico and insular areas. Application deadlines are set forth by the respective SEA. Contact high school guidance counselor for details, or call number listed for contact information of appropriate SEA.

> **Amount of award:** $1,500

Contact:
Federal Student Aid Programs
P.O. Box 84
Washington, DC 20044
Phone: 800-4-FED-AID
Web: http://studentaid.ed.gov

U.S. Department of Educational Rehabilitation Services Administration

Vocational Rehabilitation Scholarship

Type of award: Scholarship, renewable.
Intended use: For undergraduate or graduate study at postsecondary institution in United States.
Eligibility: Applicant must be physically challenged.
Application requirements: Proof of eligibility.
Additional information: Program provides a wide range of services and job training to people with disabilities who want to work. Must have medically verifiable disability that constitutes substantial impediment to employment. Award may be used for programs of study leading to development of employment skills. Number of awards varies; amounts vary depending on state vocational rehabilitation agency. See Website for more information.
Contact:
Rehabilitation Services Administration
330 C Street, S.W.
Room 3028
Washington, DC 20202-2531
Web: www.ed.gov/offices/OSERS

U.S. Department of Health and Human Services

National Health Service Corps Scholarship

Type of award: Scholarship.
Intended use: For full-time undergraduate or graduate study at accredited 4-year or graduate institution in United States.
Eligibility: Applicant must be U.S. citizen.
Basis for selection: Major/career interest in dentistry; nursing or nurse practitioner. Applicant must demonstrate depth of character, seriousness of purpose and service orientation.
Application requirements: Interview, proof of eligibility. Submission of required documentation; personal interview.
Additional information: Scholarship is for students pursuing allopathic (MD) and osteopathic (DO) medicine; nurse midwifery; dentistry; family nurse practitioner; and physician assistant education. Doctorate nurse training ineligible; premedical students ineligible. Awardees commit to providing health-care services in underserved communities anywhere in the United States. One year of service owed for every year of scholarship support. Minimum service commitment is two years; maximum is four years. Monthly stipend payment is taxable. Must be in training program. Application deadline is last Friday in March.

Amount of award:	Full tuition
Number of awards:	316
Number of applicants:	1,500

Contact:
United States Department of Health and Human Services
c/o IQ Solutions
11300 Rockville Pike, Suite 901
Rockville, MD 20852
Phone: 800-638-0824
Web: nhsc.bhpr.hrsa.gov

U.S. Department of Interior-Bureau of Indian Affairs

Indians Higher Education Grant Program

Type of award: Scholarship.
Intended use: For full-time undergraduate study at accredited 2-year or 4-year institution.
Eligibility: Applicant must be Alaskan native or American Indian. Must be member (or at least one-quarter degree Indian blood descendant of member) of American Indian tribe eligible for special programs and services provided by United States through Bureau of Indian Affairs. Applicant must be U.S. citizen.
Basis for selection: Applicant must demonstrate financial need.
Application requirements: Proof of eligibility. Application.
Additional information: Deadlines vary. Contact education officer of affiliated tribe for application.
Contact:
U.S. Department of Interior-Bureau of Indian Affairs
Office of Education Programs MS 3512- MIB
1849 C Street, NW
Washington, DC 20240
Web: www.oiep.bia.edu

U.S. Dept. of Justice, Office of the Police Corps and Law Enforcement Education

Police Corps Scholarship

Type of award: Scholarship, renewable.
Intended use: For full-time undergraduate or graduate study at accredited 4-year or graduate institution. Designated institutions: Public or nonprofit institutions.
Eligibility: Applicant must be U.S. citizen or permanent resident.
Basis for selection: Major/career interest in criminal justice/law enforcement. Applicant must demonstrate high academic achievement, leadership and service orientation.
Application requirements: Interview, recommendations, essay, proof of eligibility. Each state has its own application form and requirements.
Additional information: Must be interested in law enforcement but may major in any subject. Program is active in 27 states. May apply to program in any state regardless of residency. Applicant must commit to serving as law enforcement officer ("street cop") after graduation for at least four years in the assigned department. Must undergo 16-24

Scholarships

475

weeks of training prior to police service. Must be chosen based on mental, physical and emotional criteria. Tuition reimbursement available for upperclassmen; transfer students from community colleges to four-year schools are eligible for scholarship/tuition reimbursement. Total of up to $15,000 may be awarded toward individual's degree. Visit Website for list of participating states, eligibility requirements and application information. Application accepting date varies by state.

Amount of award: $15,000
Number of awards: 1,100
Total amount awarded: $40,000,000
Contact:
Office of the Police Corps and Law Enforcement Education
U.S. Department of Justice
810 Seventh Street, NW
Washington, DC 20531
Phone: 800-421-6770 or 888-942-6777
Fax: 202-353-0598
Web: www.ojp.usdoj.gov/opclee

Police Corps Scholarships for Children of Officers Killed in the Line of Duty

Type of award: Scholarship.
Intended use: For undergraduate or graduate study.
Eligibility: Applicant's parent must have been killed or disabled in work-related accident as police officer.
Basis for selection: Applicant must demonstrate high academic achievement.
Application requirements: Proof of eligibility. To be considered "dependent," at time of parent's death student must be under 21 or be receiving more than half of financial support from parents. Each state has own application form.
Additional information: For dependent children of local, state or federal law enforcement officers killed in the line of duty after the state in which they served joined the Police Corps. Program is active in 27 states. Program must have been in existence in officer's state at time of death. A total of $15,000 may be awarded toward an individual's degree. Visit Website for list of participating states, eligibility requirements and application information.

Amount of award: $15,000
Contact:
Office of the Police Corps and Law Enforcement Education
U.S. Department of Justice
810 Seventh Street, NW
Washington, DC 20531
Phone: 800-421-6770 or 888-942-6777
Fax: 202-353-0598
Web: www.ojp.usdoj.gov/opclee

U.S. Environmental Protection Agency

EPA National Network for Environmental Management Studies Fellowship

Type of award: Research grant.
Intended use: For undergraduate or graduate study.

Eligibility: Applicant must be U.S. citizen or permanent resident.
Basis for selection: Major/career interest in environmental science; public relations; communications; computer/information sciences or law.
Application requirements: Recommendations, transcript. NNEMS application. One-page work plan proposal. Must submit letter of reference from faculty member or department head familiar with student's work and qualifications; letter must state how research project will benefit student's academic studies. Undergraduate students must: 1) be enrolled in academic program directly related to pollution control or environmental protection; 2) have cumulative 3.0 GPA; 3) have already completed four courses related to environmental field. Seniors who graduate prior to completion of advertised NNEMS fellowship period ineligible unless admitted to graduate school with submittable verification.
Additional information: Program provides undergraduate and graduate students with research opportunities and experience at EPA locations nationwide. NNEMS develops and distributes annual catalog listing available research opportunities for coming year. Selected students receive stipend for performing research project. Projects also available in environmental management/administration and environmental policy, regulation and law. Application generally due in January.

Amount of award: $6,000-$10,000
Number of awards: 65
Contact:
US Environmental Protection Agency NNEMS Fellowship Program
Office of Environmental Education
1200 Pennsylvania Avenue, NW (1704A)
Washington, DC 20460
Phone: 800-358-8769
Web: www.epa.gov/enviroed/students.html

Minority Academic Institutions Undergraduate Student Fellowships

Type of award: Scholarship.
Intended use: For full-time junior or senior study at accredited 4-year institution in United States. Designated institutions: Minority academic institutions, including Historically Black Colleges or Universities (HBCUs), Hispanic Serving Institutions (HSIs), Tribal Colleges (TCs), Native Hawaiian Serving Institutions (NHSIs), and Alaska Native Serving Institutions (ANSIs).
Eligibility: Applicant must be U.S. citizen or permanent resident.
Basis for selection: Major/career interest in life sciences; environmental science; engineering; social/behavioral sciences; physical sciences; mathematics; computer/information sciences; biology or chemistry. Applicant must demonstrate financial need, high academic achievement and seriousness of purpose.
Application requirements: Recommendations, essay, transcript, proof of eligibility. Preapplication form. Resident Aliens must include green card number. EPA may verify number with the Immigration and Naturalization Service.
Additional information: Fellowship provides up to $17,000 per year for two years. Recipient must complete summer internship at EPA facility between funded junior and senior years. Must be enrolled in environmental program at a minority academic institution. Applicants must submit pre-application form first; following a merit review, top-ranked applicants will be asked to submit formal application. See Website for details and a list of eligible schools. Applications available beginning in mid-August.

Number of awards: 20
Application deadline: November 20
Contact:
U.S. Environmental Protection Agency
Peer Review Division (8703R), Ariel Rios Bldg
1200 Pennsylvania Avenue, NW
Washington, DC 20460
Web: www.epa.gov/ncer

U.S. Navy Recruitment Officer

Immediate Selection Decision (ISD)

Type of award: Scholarship.
Intended use: For full-time senior study at 4-year institution in United States. Designated institutions: Colleges or universities hosting the NROTC Program or cross-enrolled with a host school.
Eligibility: Applicant or parent must be member/participant of Reserve Officers Training Corps (ROTC). Applicant must be at least 17, no older than 22. Applicant must be U.S. citizen.
Basis for selection: Applicant must demonstrate high academic achievement and leadership.
Application requirements: Proof of eligibility. SAT composite 1290 and SAT Math 650; ACT combined 57 and ACT Math 29.
Additional information: NROTC scholarships pay for college tuition, fees, book allowance, uniforms and a $250 monthly allowance, which increases annually. They do not pay for room and board.

Amount of award:	Full tuition
Number of awards:	81
Number of applicants:	81
Application deadline:	July 1, December 1

Contact:
Recruitment Officer
801 North Randolph
Arlington, VA 22203-9933
Phone: 800-USA-NAVY
Web: www.nrotc.navy.mil

U.S. Navy/Marine NROTC College Scholarship Program

ROTC/Navy Nurse Corps Scholarship Program

Type of award: Scholarship.
Intended use: For full-time undergraduate study at accredited 4-year institution in United States. Designated institutions: NJROTC approved nursing schools.
Eligibility: Applicant must be at least 17, no older than 23, high school senior. Applicant must be U.S. citizen.
Basis for selection: Must be medically qualified for the NROTC Scholarship Program. Major/career interest in nursing. Applicant must demonstrate high academic achievement and leadership.

Application requirements: Interview, transcript, proof of eligibility. SAT Verbal 530, Math 520; ACT English 22, Math 22. Participation in extracurricular activities, work experience, and evaluations from high school officials.
Additional information: Four-year NROTC scholarships are available to students interested in pursuing bachelor's degree in nursing (BSN). Scholarships pay for college tuition, fees, books and uniforms, and offer a $250 monthly allowance, which increases yearly. They do not pay for room and board. SAT or ACT scores must be received by December 31 and electronic application must be completed by January 15. Electronic application is first step in application process. Contact local recruiter for further details.

Amount of award:	Full tuition
Number of awards:	111
Number of applicants:	161
Application deadline:	January 15

Contact:
Recruitment Officer
801 North Randolph
Arlington, VA 22203-9933
Phone: 800-NAV-ROTC
Web: www.nrotc.navy.mil

ROTC/Navy/Marine Two or Four-Year Scholarship

Type of award: Scholarship.
Intended use: For freshman study at accredited 4-year institution in United States. Designated institutions: Colleges and universities hosting the NROTC Program.
Eligibility: Applicant must be at least 17, no older than 23, high school senior. Applicant must be U.S. citizen.
Basis for selection: Must be medically qualified for the NROTC Scholarship.
Application requirements: Interview, transcript. Participation in extracurricular activities, work experience, and evaluations from high school officials.
Additional information: Scholarships are highly competitive and based on individual merit. Provides full tuition, fees, book allowance and $250 monthy allowance, which increases annually. They do not pay for room and board. SAT and ACT scores must be received by December 31 and completed application must be received by January 31. Contact the nearest NROTC unit for more information or visit website.

Amount of award:	Full tuition
Number of awards:	2,314
Number of applicants:	4,123
Application deadline:	July 1, December 1

Contact:
United States Navy/Marine ROTC College Scholarship Program
801 North Randolph
Arlington, VA 22203-9933
Phone: 800-NAV-ROTC
Web: www.cnet.navy.mil

Utah Higher Education Assistance Authority (UHEAA)

UHEAA Scholarship

Type of award: Scholarship, renewable.

Intended use: For undergraduate or graduate study at 4-year or graduate institution in United States. Designated institutions: Eligible Utah institutions.
Eligibility: Applicant must be residing in Utah.
Basis for selection: Applicant must demonstrate financial need.
Application requirements: Nomination by financial aid director.
Additional information: Allotments are made to eligible schools. The schools' financial aid directors nominate recipients, and awards are made by UHEAA.

Amount of award:	$2,500-$4,000
Number of awards:	312
Total amount awarded:	$419,247

Contact:
Apply through nomination by school financial aid office.

Utah Centennial Opportunity Program for Education (UCOPE)

Type of award: Research grant, renewable.
Intended use: For undergraduate study. Designated institutions: Utah state institutions.
Eligibility: Applicant must be residing in Utah.
Basis for selection: Applicant must demonstrate financial need.
Application requirements: Submit FAFSA to campus financial aid office.
Additional information: Awards are made by individual institutions from allotments sent to them by UHEAA as part of campus-based financial packaging. Application available through school's financial aid office.

Amount of award:	$300-$5,000
Number of awards:	3,277
Total amount awarded:	$2,720,000

Contact:
Contact school's financial aid office.

Utah Higher Education Assistance Partnership

Leaveraging Educational Assistance Partnership (LEAP)

Type of award: Research grant, renewable.
Intended use: For undergraduate study in United States. Designated institutions: Utah state institutions.
Eligibility: Applicant must be residing in Utah.
Basis for selection: Applicant must demonstrate financial need.
Application requirements: Submit FAFSA to institution's financial aid office.
Additional information: Awards are made by individual institutions from allotments sent to them by UHEAA as part of campus-based financial packaging.

Amount of award:	$300-$2,500
Number of awards:	2,920
Total amount awarded:	$1,344,152

Contact:
Contact school's financial aid office.

Utah State Office of Education

Utah Robert C. Byrd Honors Scholarship

Type of award: Scholarship, renewable.
Intended use: For undergraduate study.
Eligibility: Applicant must be high school senior. Applicant must be permanent resident residing in Utah.
Basis for selection: Applicant must demonstrate high academic achievement.
Application requirements: Transcript. Should have high ACT scores.
Additional information: Contact high school counselor or financial aid adviser for application after January, or see Website at www.usoe.k12.ut.us/cert and click on "scholarships."

Amount of award:	$1,500
Number of awards:	62
Number of applicants:	500
Application deadline:	March 31
Notification begins:	May 15
Total amount awarded:	$384,000

Contact:
High school counselor or financial aid adviser for application.

The Vegetarian Resource Group

The Vegetarian Resource Group College Scholarships

Type of award: Scholarship.
Intended use: For freshman study at postsecondary institution in United States.
Eligibility: Applicant must be high school senior. Applicant must be U.S. citizen.
Basis for selection: Major/career interest in culinary arts or dietetics/nutrition.
Application requirements: Essay.
Additional information: Award for graduating high school students who have promoted vegetarianism or veganism in their schools or communities. Students will be judged on having shown compassion, courage and a strong commitment in promoting a peaceful world through a vegetarian or vegan diet/lifestyle. Visit Website for application information.

Amount of award:	$5,000
Number of awards:	2
Application deadline:	February 20
Total amount awarded:	$10,000

Contact:
The Vegetarian Resource Group
P.O. Box 1463
Baltimore, MD 21203
Phone: 410-366-8343
Web: www.vrg.org

Scholarships

Ventura County Japanese-American Citizens League

Ventura County Japanese-American Citizens League Scholarships

Type of award: Scholarship.
Intended use: For undergraduate study at vocational, 2-year or 4-year institution in United States.
Eligibility: Must be American of Japanese or part-Japanese ancestry residing or attending high school in Ventura County. Applicant must be high school senior. Applicant must be Japanese. Applicant must be U.S. citizen residing in California.
Application requirements: Recommendations, essay, transcript, proof of eligibility. SAT scores. One-page personal statement.
Additional information: Must be high school senior graduating from Ventura County school. Must also be of Japanese ancestry or a member of JACL to be eligible.

  Application deadline: April 1
Contact:
Ventura County JACL Scholarship Committee
P.O. Box 1092
Camarillo, CA 93011
Phone: 805-373-4536
Web: www.vcjacl.org/scholarship.htm

Vermont Golf Association Scholarship Fund, Inc.

Vermont Golf Association Scholarship

Type of award: Scholarship, renewable.
Intended use: For full-time undergraduate study at 2-year or 4-year institution.
Eligibility: Applicant must be high school senior. Applicant must be permanent resident residing in Vermont.
Application requirements: Interview, recommendations, transcript. FAFSA.
Additional information: Must be graduate of Vermont high school and in top 40 percent of class or have GPA of 3.0 and SAT of 1000. Students of Hanover High School, NH, and Grantville High School, NY, are also eligible. Applicant must have valid connection to golf. Can renew scholarship up to four years.

  Amount of award: $1,000
  Number of awards: 40
  Number of applicants: 40
  Application deadline: April 20
  Total amount awarded: $34,000
Contact:
Vermont Golf Association Scholarship Fund
P.O. Box 1612
Station A
Rutland, VT 05701
Web: www.vtga.org

Vermont Student Assistance Corporation

Vermont Incentive Grant

Type of award: Scholarship.
Intended use: For full-time undergraduate or graduate study in United States.
Eligibility: Applicant must be U.S. citizen or permanent resident residing in Vermont.
Basis for selection: Based on residency in Vermont, must be enrolled full-time at an approved postsecondary institution, and must meet needs test. Applicant must demonstrate financial need.
Application requirements: Proof of eligibility. Complete "Financial Aid Packet for Vermont Students," available from schools.
Additional information: Open to Vermont residents who plan to attend college full-time and who do not yet have bachelor's degree. Application may be completed online.

  Amount of award: $500-$9,100
  Number of awards: 8,961
  Number of applicants: 16,242
  Total amount awarded: $14,219,107
Contact:
Grant Department
Vermont Student Assistance Corporation
P.O. Box 2000
Winooski, VT 05404-2601
Phone: 802-655-9602; in-state 800-642-3177
Fax: 802-654-3765
Web: www.vsac.org

Vermont Non-Degree Program

Type of award: Scholarship.
Intended use: For non-degree study at postsecondary institution in United States.
Eligibility: Applicant must be permanent resident residing in Vermont.
Basis for selection: Applicant must demonstrate financial need.
Application requirements: Proof of eligibility. Must meet needs test.
Additional information: Maximum amount for this award is $715 for one course per semester. Available to any Vermont resident enrolled in non-degree course that will improve employability or encourage further study. Applications available at Vermont Department of Employment and Training offices, schools and vocation centers, and VSAC.

  Amount of award: $715
  Number of awards: 932
  Number of applicants: 1,551
  Total amount awarded: $663,815
Contact:
Grant Department
Vermont Student Assistance Coirporation
P.O. Box 2000
Winooski, VT 05404-2601
Phone: 802-655-9602; in-state 800-642-3765
Fax: 802-654-3765
Web: www.vsac.org

Vermont Part-Time Grant

Type of award: Scholarship.

Scholarships

479

Intended use: For half-time undergraduate study at vocational, 2-year or 4-year institution in or outside United States.
Eligibility: Applicant must be permanent resident residing in Vermont.
Basis for selection: Applicant must demonstrate financial need.
Application requirements: Proof of eligibility.
Additional information: Must be taking fewer than 12 credits and have not yet received bachelor's degree. Award amounts vary according to the number of credits the student is taking. Must be a Vermont resident.

Number of awards:	2,108
Number of applicants:	4,382
Total amount awarded:	$987,122

Contact:
Grant Department
Vermont Student Assistance Corporation
P.O. Box 2000
Winooski, VT 05404-2601
Phone: 802-655-9602
Fax: 802-654-3765
Web: www.vsac.org

Veterans of Foreign Wars

Voice of Democracy Scholarship

Type of award: Scholarship.
Intended use: For undergraduate or graduate study at postsecondary institution in United States.
Eligibility: Applicant must be no older than 19, enrolled in high school.
Basis for selection: Based on interpretation of assigned patriotic theme, content and presentation of recorded 3-5 minute audio-essay.
Application requirements: Essay. Audio cassette tape of essay. Participants are judged by cassette tape, not written essay script.
Additional information: Must apply through high school or local Veterans of Foreign Wars post. Any entry submitted to VFW National Headquarters will be returned to sender. Visit Website for additional information. This is a one-time award; it is non-renewable.

Amount of award:	$1,000-$25,000
Number of awards:	56
Number of applicants:	100,000
Application deadline:	November 1
Total amount awarded:	$140,500

Contact:
Veterans of Foreign Wars National Headquarters
Voice of Democracy Program
406 West 34 Street
Kansas City, MO 64111
Phone: 816-968-1117
Fax: 816-968-1149
Web: www.vfw.org

Virgin Islands Board of Education

Virgin Islands Leveraging Educational Assistance Partnership Program

Type of award: Scholarship, renewable.
Intended use: For full-time undergraduate study at postsecondary institution.
Eligibility: Applicant must be U.S. citizen or permanent resident residing in Virgin Islands.
Basis for selection: Applicant must demonstrate financial need and high academic achievement.
Application requirements: Transcript. Application, acceptance letter from institution for first-time applicants or transfer students. Must fill out profile (CSS code 0396).
Additional information: Minimum 2.0 GPA required. Number of awards and applicants varies.

Amount of award:	$500-$3,000

Contact:
Virgin Islands Board of Education-Financial Aid Office
P.O. Box 11900
St. Thomas, VI 801
Phone: 340-774-4546

Virgin Islands Music Scholarship

Type of award: Scholarship, renewable.
Intended use: For full-time undergraduate study at accredited 2-year or 4-year institution in United States.
Eligibility: Applicant must be high school senior. Applicant must be U.S. citizen or permanent resident residing in Virgin Islands.
Basis for selection: Major/career interest in music. Applicant must demonstrate financial need.
Application requirements: Transcript.
Additional information: Minimum 2.0 GPA. Number of awards varies.

Amount of award:	$2,000
Application deadline:	May 1

Contact:
Virgin Islands Board of Education - Financial Aid Office
P.O. Box 11900
St. Thomas, VI 00801
Phone: 340-774-4546

Virginia Department of Education

Virginia Lee-Jackson Scholarship

Type of award: Scholarship.
Intended use: For full-time freshman study at accredited 4-year institution in United States.
Eligibility: Applicant must be high school junior or senior. Applicant must be residing in Virginia.
Basis for selection: Competition/talent/interest in writing/journalism, based on essay demonstrating appreciation for virtues exemplified by General Robert E. Lee or General "Stonewall" Jackson.

Application requirements: Essay. Students must submit essay and application form to high school principal or guidance counselor.

Additional information: Three $1,000 awards in each of Virginia's eight public high school regions. Three $1,000 awards for best essays by private school or home-schooled students. Additional awards for exceptional essays. Application deadline is generally in December. See Website for more information.

Amount of award:	$1,000-$10,000

Contact:
High school guidance counselor or principal.
Phone: 434-977-1861
Web: www.lee-jackson.org

Virginia Robert C. Byrd Honor Scholarship

Type of award: Scholarship, renewable.
Intended use: For full-time undergraduate study at accredited postsecondary institution in United States.
Eligibility: Applicant must be high school senior. Applicant must be U.S. citizen or permanent resident residing in Virginia.
Basis for selection: Applicant must demonstrate high academic achievement and service orientation.
Application requirements: Recommendations, transcript by by high school. SAT/ACT scores. Application.
Additional information: Application and information sent to principals of public and private high schools in February. Number and amount of awards vary.

Contact:
High school principal or guidance counselor.
Web: www.pen.k12.va.us

Virginia Department of Health

Mary Marshall Nursing Scholarship

Type of award: Scholarship.
Intended use: For full-time undergraduate study. Designated institutions: Virginia nursing schools.
Eligibility: Applicant must be U.S. citizen or permanent resident residing in Virginia.
Basis for selection: Major/career interest in nursing. Applicant must demonstrate financial need.
Application requirements: Transcript. Application; financial aid forms (FAFSA).
Additional information: Minimum 3.0 GPA in required courses, not electives. Provides awards to students who agree to work in nursing profession in Virginia at rate of one month for every $100 of aid received. Must reside in Virginia at least one year prior to application. Recipient may reapply for succeeding years. Applications and guidelines available from dean or financial aid office at applicant's nursing school or from below address. Applications not accepted prior to April 30.

Amount of award:	$1,200-$2,000
Number of awards:	91
Application deadline:	June 30

Contact:
Virginia Dept. of Health Office of Health Policy and Planning
109 Governor St., 1016-East Offices
James Madison Bldg
Richmond, VA 23219
Phone: 804-864-7433

Virginia Museum of Fine Arts

Virginia Museum of Fine Arts Fellowship

Type of award: Scholarship, renewable.
Intended use: For full-time undergraduate or graduate study at accredited 4-year or graduate institution.
Eligibility: Applicant must be U.S. citizen residing in Virginia.
Basis for selection: Artistic merit. Major/career interest in arts, general; film/video or art/art history. Applicant must demonstrate financial need.
Application requirements: Portfolio, transcript.
Additional information: May apply in one of the following categories: crafts, drawing, sculpture, filmmaking, painting, photography, printmaking, video, on the graduate or undergraduate levels. Candidates in art history may apply on the graduate level only. Must submit either ten 35mm slides representing recent work or three of the following: 16mm or video format films, videos, research papers, or published articles. References required. Visit Website for guidelines and application.

Amount of award:	$4,000-$6,000
Number of awards:	18
Number of applicants:	600
Application deadline:	March 1
Notification begins:	May 15
Total amount awarded:	$80,000

Contact:
Virginia Museum of Fine Arts Fellowships
Education and Outreach Division
2800 Grove Avenue
Richmond, VA 23221-2466
Phone: 804-204-2661
Web: www.vmfa.state.va.us

Wal-Mart Foundation

Higher REACH Scholarship

Type of award: Scholarship.
Intended use: For undergraduate study.
Eligibility: Applicant or parent must be employed by Wal-Mart Stores, Inc.
Basis for selection: Applicant must demonstrate financial need.
Application requirements: Essay, transcript. Job performance appraisal.
Additional information: Awarded to nontraditional students who have been employed by Wal-Mart Stores, Inc. for at least one year. Award amount varies depending on part-time or full-time enrollment. Applicants must be out of high school for one

year in order to apply. Applications available in November from personnel office.

Application deadline:	February 1
Total amount awarded:	$2,000

Contact:
Wal-Mart Foundation
702 S.W. 8th St.
Bentonville, AR 72716-8071
Phone: 800-530-9925
Web: www.walmartfoundation.org

Sam Walton Community Scholarship

Type of award: Scholarship.
Intended use: For freshman study at postsecondary institution in United States. Designated institutions: Institutions approved by the Wal-Mart Foundation.
Basis for selection: Applicant must demonstrate financial need and high academic achievement.
Application requirements: Transcript. ACT/SAT scores, community/extracurricular involvement and work experience.
Additional information: Applicant must be graduating high school senior and must not be an employee of Wal-Mart Stores, Inc., or the child/dependent of an employee. Applications available first week of December at Wal-Mart and Sam's Club stores, and from high school counselor.

Amount of award:	$1,000
Number of awards:	4,617
Number of applicants:	42,564
Application deadline:	February 1

Contact:
Wal-Mart Foundation
702 SW 8 Street
Bentonville, AR 72716-0150
Phone: 800-530-9925
Web: www.walmartfoundation.org

Wal-Mart Associate Scholarship

Type of award: Scholarship.
Intended use: For full-time undergraduate study at accredited 2-year or 4-year institution in United States.
Eligibility: Applicant or parent must be employed by Wal-Mart Stores, Inc. Applicant must be high school senior.
Basis for selection: Applicant must demonstrate financial need and high academic achievement.
Application requirements: Transcript, proof of eligibility. SAT/ACT scores and financial data.
Additional information: Award for Wal-Mart employees and their dependents who are not eligible for the Walton Foundation Scholarship. Applications available starting November. Visit local store or contact Wal-Mart Foundation for application.

Amount of award:	$2,000
Application deadline:	February 1

Contact:
Wal-Mart Foundation
702 SW 8 Street
Bentonville, AR 72716-0150
Phone: 800-530-9925
Fax: 479-273-6850
Web: www.walmartfoundation.org

Walton Family Foundation Scholarship

Type of award: Scholarship.

Intended use: For full-time undergraduate study at accredited 2-year or 4-year institution.
Eligibility: Applicant or parent must be employed by Wal-Mart Stores, Inc. Applicant must be high school senior.
Basis for selection: Applicant must demonstrate financial need and high academic achievement.
Application requirements: Transcript, proof of eligibility. SAT/ACT scores and financial data. Applicant or parent must be full-time employee of Wal-Mart.
Additional information: $8,000 scholarship payable over four years. Applicant's parent or guardian must have been employed with Wal-Mart full-time (28 hrs/wk) at least one year as of March 1. Applicant must demonstrate both financial need and high academic achievement. Applications available in November from personnel office.

Amount of award:	$8,000
Number of awards:	120
Number of applicants:	2,000
Application deadline:	February 1
Total amount awarded:	$960,000

Contact:
Wal-Mart Foundation
702 SW 8 Street
Bentonville, AR 72716-0150
Phone: 800-530-9925
Fax: 479-273-6850
Web: www.walmartfoundation.org

Washington Crossing Foundation

Washington Crossing Foundation Scholarship

Type of award: Scholarship.
Intended use: For full-time undergraduate study at accredited 4-year institution.
Eligibility: Applicant must be high school senior. Applicant must be U.S. citizen.
Basis for selection: Major/career interest in political science/ government or public administration/service. Applicant must demonstrate high academic achievement, depth of character, leadership, patriotism, seriousness of purpose and service orientation.
Application requirements: Interview, recommendations, essay, transcript, proof of eligibility. SAT/ACT scores.
Additional information: Applicants must write essay on why they plan a career in government service, including any inspiration to be derived from Washington's famous crossing of the Delaware. Applicants must pursue course of study related to public service of any kind. Award is distributed over four years of study. One award is reserved for Pennsylvania's five southeastern counties; one for the state.

Amount of award:	$1,000-$20,000
Number of awards:	10
Number of applicants:	600
Application deadline:	January 15
Notification begins:	April 15
Total amount awarded:	$45,500

Contact:
Washington Crossing Foundation
Attn: Vice Chairman
P.O. Box 503
Levittown, PA 19058
Phone: 215-949-8841
Web: www.gwcf.org

Washington Gas

Washington Gas Scholarships

Type of award: Scholarship.
Intended use: For full-time freshman study at accredited postsecondary institution in United States.
Eligibility: Applicant must be high school senior. Applicant must be residing in District of Columbia.
Basis for selection: Major/career interest in business; science, general; mathematics; computer/information sciences; accounting; marketing or engineering. Applicant must demonstrate high academic achievement, depth of character, leadership, patriotism, seriousness of purpose and service orientation.
Application requirements: Recommendations, transcript. PSAT/SAT scores. Resume. Brief description of what student wishes to accomplish at school and after graduation. List of community work.
Additional information: Minimum 3.0 GPA. Students with any career interest may apply. Program may change; contact sponsor for updated information. Notification begins in May.

Amount of award:	$1,000
Number of awards:	16
Application deadline:	March 20

Contact:
Washington Gas DC Public Affairs
Attn. Scholarship Coordinator
1100 H Street, NW
Washington, DC 20080
Phone: 202-624-6697
Fax: 202-624-6010
Web: www.washgas.com

Washington State Higher Education Coordinating Board

Washington Promise Scholarship

Type of award: Scholarship, renewable.
Intended use: For freshman or sophomore study at accredited vocational, 2-year or 4-year institution.
Eligibility: Applicant must be high school senior. Applicant must be permanent resident residing in Washington.
Basis for selection: Applicant must demonstrate financial need and high academic achievement.
Application requirements: Nomination by Washington high school. Applicant must be in top 15 percent of WA high school senior class or have combined score of 1200 on the SAT or 27 on the ACT. Must meet certain income cutoffs.

Additional information: Contact guidance counselor for more information on nomination. Amount of individual award may be prorated, may not exceed community college tutition. Applicant must not pursue a degree in theology.

Number of awards:	6,600
Application deadline:	May 30
Total amount awarded:	$6,300,000

Contact:
Washington State Higher Education Coordinating Board
917 Lakeridge Way SW
P.O. Box 43430
Olympia, WA 98504-3430
Phone: 888-535-0747
Fax: 360-704-6220
Web: www.hecb.wa.gov

Washington State American Indian Endowed Scholarship

Type of award: Scholarship.
Intended use: For full-time undergraduate study at accredited vocational, 2-year, 4-year or graduate institution. Designated institutions: Postsecondary schools in the state of Washington.
Eligibility: Must have close social and cultural ties to American Indian community within Washington state. Applicant must be U.S. citizen residing in Washington.
Basis for selection: Applicant must demonstrate financial need, high academic achievement and service orientation.
Application requirements: Recommendations, essay, transcript, proof of eligibility. FAFSA, application form.
Additional information: Applicant must have strong commitment to return service to state's American Indian community.

Amount of award:	$1,000-$2,000
Number of awards:	20
Application deadline:	May 15

Contact:
Washington State Higher Education Coordinating Board
917 Lakeridge Way SW
P.O. Box 43430
Olympia, WA 98504-3430
Phone: 360-753-7843
Web: www.hecb.wa.gov

Washington State Educational Opportunity Grant

Type of award: Scholarship, renewable.
Intended use: For full-time junior or senior study at accredited 4-year institution. Designated institutions: Eligible postsecondary institutions in Washington.
Eligibility: Applicant must be U.S. citizen or permanent resident residing in Washington.
Basis for selection: Applicant must demonstrate financial need.
Application requirements: Essay, proof of eligibility. FAFSA.
Additional information: Must be "place-bound." Must be transfer students at junior or senior level. Application deadlines vary. Contact financial aid office of institution for details and to initiate an application. Deadline varies.

Amount of award:	$2,500
Number of awards:	400
Total amount awarded:	$1,500,000

Contact:
Washington State Higher Education Coordinating Board
917 Lakeridge Way SW
P.O. Box 43430
Olympia, WA 98504-3430
Phone: 360-753-7850
Web: www.hecb.wa.gov

Washington State Need Grant

Type of award: Scholarship, renewable.
Intended use: For undergraduate study at accredited vocational, 2-year or 4-year institution. Designated institutions: Eligible postsecondary institutions in Washington.
Eligibility: Applicant must be U.S. citizen or permanent resident residing in Washington.
Basis for selection: Applicant must demonstrate financial need.
Application requirements: Proof of eligibility. FAFSA.
Additional information: Contact institution's financial aid office for additional requirements and deadlines. Grants are only given to students from low-income families. Average grant in most recent year was $2,000. Must meet qualifications every year for renewal, up to five years. Contact institution for application deadline.

Number of awards:	53,000
Total amount awarded:	$104,000,000

Contact:
Washington State Higher Education Coordinating Board
917 Lakeridge Way SW
P.O. Box 43430
Olympia, WA 98504-3430
Phone: 360-753-7850
Fax: 360-753-7808
Web: www.hecb.wa.gov

Washington State Scholars Program

Type of award: Scholarship.
Intended use: For undergraduate study at accredited vocational, 2-year or 4-year institution. Designated institutions: Postsecondary institutions in Washington.
Eligibility: Applicant must be high school senior. Applicant must be U.S. citizen or permanent resident residing in Washington.
Basis for selection: Applicant must demonstrate high academic achievement, depth of character, leadership, seriousness of purpose and service orientation.
Application requirements: Nomination by Applicant must be nominated by high school principal or guidance counselor. SAT/ACT scores.
Additional information: Four-year award based on tuition, which may be prorated. Must rank in top one percent of class. May not defer enrollment. Eligible high school seniors should contact their high school counselors for more information.

Number of awards:	400
Total amount awarded:	$1,400,000

Contact:
Washington State Higher Education Coordinating Board
917 Lakeridge Way SW
P.O. Box 43430
Olympia, WA 98504-3430
Phone: 360-753-7843
Fax: 360-704-6243
Web: www.hecb.wa.gov

Washington State PTA Scholarship Foundation

Washington State PTA Scholarship

Type of award: Scholarship.
Intended use: For full-time freshman study at accredited vocational, 2-year or 4-year institution.
Eligibility: Applicant must be U.S. citizen or permanent resident residing in Washington.
Basis for selection: Applicant must demonstrate financial need, depth of character, leadership, seriousness of purpose and service orientation.
Application requirements: Recommendations, essay, transcript, proof of eligibility.
Additional information: Applicant must be graduate of Washington state public high school. Grant administered according to college's determination. Not transferable to another institution if already enrolled in classes. Applications available after December 1. Visit Website for additional information and application.

Amount of award:	$1,000-$2,000
Number of awards:	60
Number of applicants:	2,000
Application deadline:	March 1
Notification begins:	May 1
Total amount awarded:	$65,000

Contact:
Washington State PTA Scholarship Foundation
2003 65 Avenue West
Tacoma, WA 98466-6215
Phone: 253-565-2153
Fax: 253-565-7753
Web: www.wastatepta.org

Wells Fargo

CollegeSTEPS Program

Type of award: Scholarship.
Intended use: For undergraduate study.
Eligibility: Applicant must be high school senior. Applicant must be U.S. citizen or permanent resident.
Additional information: Tuition prizes and educational postcards on college-preparatory topics offered. Visit Website to apply. High school freshmen, sophomores, and juniors can also sign up to receive postcards. Employees of Wells Fargo Educational Financial Services and immediate family members not eligible for tuition prize.

Amount of award:	$1,000
Number of awards:	100
Total amount awarded:	$100,000

Contact:
Education Financial Services
Wells Fargo
P.O. Box 5185
Sioux Falls, SD 57117-5185
Phone: 800-658-3567
Fax: 800-456-0561
Web: www.wellsfargo.com/collegesteps

Welsh Society of Philadelphia

Welsh Heritage Scholarship

Type of award: Scholarship, renewable.
Intended use: For full-time undergraduate study at accredited postsecondary institution. Designated institutions: Must be located within 150 miles of Philadelphia, if applicant not resident of same area.
Eligibility: Applicant must be Welsh.
Basis for selection: Applicant must demonstrate high academic achievement and seriousness of purpose.
Application requirements: Recommendations, essay, transcript. Statement of purpose. SAT scores.
Additional information: Applicant must be a resident of Philadelphia, or attending college within 150 miles of city. Participation in Welsh organizations or events preferred.

Amount of award:	$1,000
Number of awards:	5
Number of applicants:	50
Application deadline:	March 1
Notification begins:	May 1
Total amount awarded:	$5,000

Contact:
Welsh Society of Philadelphia
Scholarship Committee Chairman
P.O. Box 7287
St. David's, PA 19087-7287

Wendt Memorial Scholarship Committee

Barry K. Wendt Commitment Award and Scholarship

Type of award: Scholarship.
Intended use: For full-time undergraduate study in United States. Designated institutions: Any engineering school.
Eligibility: Applicant must be U.S. citizen or permanent resident.
Basis for selection: Major/career interest in engineering. Applicant must demonstrate high academic achievement.
Application requirements: Recommendations, essay. Application. Recommendation from faculty adviser. Essay should be 300-500 words on applicant's plans for career in aggregate industry.
Additional information: Visit Website for details and application.

Amount of award:	$2,500
Number of awards:	1
Application deadline:	April 30

Contact:
Wendt Memorial Scholarship Committee
c/o NSSGA
2101 Wilson Blvd., Suite 100
Arlington, VA 22201
Phone: 703-525-8788 or 800-342-1415
Fax: 703-525-7782
Web: www.nssga.org/careers/scholarships.htm

West Pharmaceutical Services, Inc.

Herman O. West Scholarship

Type of award: Scholarship, renewable.
Intended use: For full-time undergraduate study at accredited 2-year or 4-year institution.
Eligibility: Applicant or parent must be employed by West Pharmaceutical Services, Inc. Applicant must be high school senior. Applicant must be U.S. citizen.
Basis for selection: Applicant must demonstrate high academic achievement.
Application requirements: Recommendations, essay, transcript, proof of eligibility. Extracurricular activity.
Additional information: Parent must be employee of West Pharmaceutical Services, Inc. Award is renewable annually for a maximum of four years.

Amount of award:	$2,500
Application deadline:	February 28
Notification begins:	May 1
Total amount awarded:	$50,000

Contact:
H.O. West Foundation
101 Gordon Drive
Lionville, PA 19341-0645
Phone: 610-594-2945

West Virginia Division of Veterans Affairs

West Virginia War Orphans Educational Assistance

Type of award: Scholarship, renewable.
Intended use: For undergraduate, graduate or non-degree study in United States. Designated institutions: West Virginia-supported colleges or universities.
Eligibility: Applicant must be at least 16, no older than 23. Applicant must be U.S. citizen residing in West Virginia. Applicant must be dependent of deceased veteran who served in the Army, Air Force, Marines, Navy, Coast Guard or Reserves/National Guard. Applicant's parent must be veteran who was killed while on active-duty during wartime or who died of injury or illness resulting from wartime service.
Application requirements: Proof of eligibility.
Additional information: Award is waiver of tuition and registration fees. Toll-free number for in-state calls: 888-838-2332.

Amount of award:	Full tuition
Number of awards:	23
Number of applicants:	23
Application deadline:	July 1, December 1
Notification begins:	July 15, December 15

Contact:
West Virginia Division of Veterans Affairs
1321 Plaza East-Suite 101
Charleston, WV 25301-1400
Phone: 304-558-3661
Fax: 304-558-3662
Web: www.state.wv.us

West Virginia Higher Education Policy Commission

West Virginia Engineering, Science and Technology Scholarship

Type of award: Scholarship, renewable.
Intended use: For full-time undergraduate study at postsecondary institution in United States. Designated institutions: Eligible West Virginia institutions.
Eligibility: Applicant must be U.S. citizen or permanent resident residing in West Virginia.
Basis for selection: Major/career interest in science, general; engineering; engineering, civil; engineering, computer; engineering, electrical/electronic; engineering, mechanical; computer/information sciences; life sciences; physical sciences or natural sciences. Applicant must demonstrate high academic achievement and seriousness of purpose.
Application requirements: Completed application. Interested high school students should apply through high school counselor; currently enrolled college/university students should apply through their institution. Minimum 3.0 GPA.
Additional information: The objective of this scholarship is for recipient to obtain a degree/certificate in engineering, science or technology and to commit to pursue a career in West Virginia. Recipient must, within one year after ceasing to be a full-time student, work full-time in engineering, science or technology field in West Virginia, or begin a program of community service relating to these fields in West Virginia for a duration of one year for each year scholarship was received. If work requirement fails to be met, recipient is responsible for repayment of scholarship plus interest and any required collection fees.

Amount of award:	$3,000
Number of awards:	290
Number of applicants:	350
Application deadline:	March 1
Total amount awarded:	$660,097

Contact:
West Virginia Higher Education Policy Commission
Engineering, Science and Technology Program
1018 Kanawha Boulevard East, Suite 700
Charleston, WV 25301-2827
Phone: 888-825-5707 or 304-558-4618
Fax: 304-558-4622
Web: www.hepc.wvnet.edu

West Virginia Higher Education Adult Part-time Student (HEAPS) Grant Program

Type of award: Scholarship, renewable.
Intended use: For half-time undergraduate study at postsecondary institution.
Eligibility: Applicant must be returning adult student. Applicant must be U.S. citizen or permanent resident residing in West Virginia.
Basis for selection: Applicant must demonstrate financial need.
Application requirements: FAFSA and any supplemental materials required by individual institutions. Must either be enrolled in college with cumulative 2.0 GPA (for renewal applicants), or be accepted for enrollment by intended institution (for first-time applicants); must have complied with Military Selective Service Act; must qualify as independent student according to federal financial aid criteria; must not be in default on higher education loan; and must not be incarcerated in correctional facility.
Additional information: Applicant must be out of high school for at least two years and plan to continue education on part-time basis. Must maintain a minimum 2.0 GPA. At public colleges/universities, award is actual amount of tuition and fees. At independent colleges/universities and vocational/technical schools, award is based upon average per credit/term hours tuition and fee charges assessed by all public undergraduate institutions. Contact school's financial aid office, or visit Website for additional information.

Amount of award:	Full tuition

Contact:
West Virginia Higher Education Policy Commission
Judy Kee
1018 Kanawha Boulevard, Suite 700
Charleston, WV 25301
Phone: 304-558-4618
Web: www.hepc.wvnet.edu

West Virginia Higher Education Grant

Type of award: Scholarship, renewable.
Intended use: For full-time undergraduate study at accredited 2-year or 4-year institution. Designated institutions: Public or private nonprofit degree-granting colleges/universities in West Virginia or Pennsylvania.
Eligibility: Applicant must be U.S. citizen residing in West Virginia.
Basis for selection: Based on certain academic standards. Applicant must demonstrate financial need and high academic achievement.
Application requirements: Transcript. FAFSA. ACT/SAT scores.
Additional information: Applicants must be resident of West Virginia for one year preceding date of application, but may attend school in public or private nonprofit institutions in West Virginia or Pennsylvania. Award restricted for payment of tuition and fees at nonprofit institutions or hospital schools of nursing. Applicants must fill out common application for state level financial aid programs.

Amount of award:	$350-$2,846
Number of awards:	10,800
Number of applicants:	60,833
Application deadline:	March 1
Notification begins:	May 1
Total amount awarded:	$20,500,000

Contact:
West Virginia Higher Education Grant Program
Office of Financial Aid and Outreach Services
1018 Kanawha Boulevard East, Suite 700
Charleston, WV 25301-2827
Phone: 888-825-5707 or 304-558-4614
Web: www.hepc.wvnet.edu

West Virginia Robert C. Byrd Honors Scholarship

Type of award: Scholarship, renewable.
Intended use: For full-time freshman study at vocational, 2-year or 4-year institution in United States.

Eligibility: Applicant must be high school senior. Applicant must be U.S. citizen or permanent resident residing in West Virginia.

Basis for selection: Applicant must demonstrate high academic achievement.

Application requirements: Transcript, proof of eligibility, nomination by high school. SAT or ACT.

Additional information: Because of limited funding, high schools with a senior class enrollment of 1-199 may submit one application for consideration and high schools with a senior class of 200+ may submit two applications for consideration. Applicants who are not residents of West Virginia must contact their State Department of Education in order to apply.

Amount of award:	$1,500
Number of awards:	35
Number of applicants:	164
Application deadline:	March 1
Notification begins:	April 1
Total amount awarded:	$226,500

Contact:
West Virginia Higher Education Policy Commission
Robert C. Byrd Honors Scholarship Program
1018 Kanawha Boulevard East, Suite 700
Charleston, WV 25301-2827
Phone: 304-558-4618
Fax: 304-558-4622
Web: www.hepc.wvnet.edu

Western District Scholarship Chairman

American Legion District Postsecondary Scholarship

Type of award: Scholarship.
Intended use: For undergraduate study at postsecondary institution.
Eligibility: Applicant must be high school senior. Applicant must be residing in Alaska.
Application requirements: GPA 2.0 to 3.0.
Additional information: $750 scholarship payable to school. Must be graduating senior and Alaska resident.

Amount of award:	$750
Application deadline:	February 15

Contact:
Western District Scholarship Chairman
1417 Lacey Street
Fairbanks, AK 99701
Phone: 907-456-3183
Fax: 907-456-3183

Western European Architecture Foundation

Gabriel Prize

Type of award: Research grant.
Intended use: For non-degree study.
Eligibility: Applicant must be U.S. citizen.

Basis for selection: Major/career interest in architecture. Applicant must demonstrate seriousness of purpose.

Application requirements: Portfolio, recommendations, research proposal. Resume. Send SASE for return of materials.

Additional information: To encourage personal investigative and critical studies of French architectural compositions completed between 1630 and 1830. Work is expected to be executed in France under supervision of foundation's European representative. Winner is required to begin studies in France by May 1, keep a traveling sketchbook, and prepare three large colored drawings within three months. Must use stipend for travel and study. Visit Website for deadlines and application.

Amount of award:	$15,000
Number of awards:	1
Number of applicants:	24
Application deadline:	December 1, January 15
Total amount awarded:	$15,000

Contact:
Western European Architecture Foundation
306 West Sunset Road, Suite 119
San Antonio, TX 78209
Phone: 210-829-4040
Web: www.gabrielprize.org

Western Golf Association/ Evans Scholars Foundation

Chick Evans Caddie Scholarship

Type of award: Scholarship, renewable.
Intended use: For full-time undergraduate study at accredited 4-year institution in United States.
Eligibility: Applicant must be high school senior.
Basis for selection: Competition/talent/interest in Athletics/ sports, based on consistent caddie record at Western Golf Association affiliated club. Applicant must demonstrate financial need, high academic achievement, depth of character and leadership.
Application requirements: Interview, recommendations, transcript, proof of eligibility. Tax returns and SAT/ACT scores required. Financial aid profile.
Additional information: Scholarship for full tuition plus housing. Must have caddied minimum two years at Western Golf Association affiliated club and rank in top 25 percent of class. Most recipients attend one of the 14 universities where Evans Scholars Foundation owns and operates chapter house. Approximately 225 new Evans Scholarships awarded each year. See Website for designated institutions.

Amount of award:	Full tuition
Number of awards:	825
Application deadline:	September 30

Contact:
Scholarship Committee
Western Golf Assoc./Evans Scholars Foundation
1 Briar Road
Golf, IL 60029
Phone: 847-724-4600
Web: www.evansscholarsfoundation.com

William Randolph Hearst Foundation

Hearst Journalism Award

Type of award: Scholarship.
Intended use: For freshman, sophomore, junior or senior study at accredited 4-year institution. Designated institutions: Institution must be accredited by Accrediting Council on Education in Journalism and Mass Communication.
Basis for selection: Competition/talent/interest in writing/journalism, based on newsworthiness, research, excellence of journalistic writing, photojournalism, or broadcast news. Major/career interest in journalism; radio/television/film or communications.
Application requirements: Entries must be submitted by journalism department. Student must be journalism major actively involved in campus media.
Additional information: Field of study may also include photojournalism or broadcast news. Applicants must submit work that has been published or aired to be considered. Competition consists of monthly contests and one championship. Scholarships are awarded to student winners with matching grants awarded to their departments of journalism. The program offers over $400,000 in awards, matching grants, and stipends. For additional information, applicants should contact journalism department chair or visit Website.

Amount of award:	$500-$2,000
Number of awards:	130

Contact:
Hearst Journalism Awards Program
90 New Montgomery Street
Suite 1212
San Francisco, CA 94105-4504
Phone: 415-543-6033
Fax: 415-348-0887
Web: www.hearstfdn.org

United States Senate Youth Program

Type of award: Scholarship.
Intended use: For freshman, sophomore, junior or senior study at accredited 2-year or 4-year institution in United States.
Eligibility: Applicant must be permanent resident and currently enrolled in public or private secondary school located in the state (including District of Columbia) in which parent or guardian legally resides. Applicant must be high school junior or senior. Applicant must be U.S. citizen or permanent resident.
Basis for selection: Applicant must demonstrate leadership and service orientation.
Application requirements: Nomination by high school principal based on merit and community service; final selection by state-level department of education. Application available from high school principal or visit Website for state-level selection administrator and further rules and information.
Additional information: Must be currently serving in elected capacity as student body officer, class officer, student council representative, or student representative to district, regional, or state-level civic or educational organization. Selection process managed by state-level department of education of each applicant. Scholarship includes all-expenses-paid week in Washington. Application deadline is in early fall for most states. Visit Website for more information.

Amount of award:	$5,000
Number of awards:	104
Total amount awarded:	$520,000

Contact:
Rita Almon, Program Director William Randolph Hearst Foundation
90 New Montgomery Street
Suite 1212
San Francisco, CA 94105-4504
Phone: 800-841-7048
Fax: 415-243-0760
Web: www.ussenateyouth.org

Wilson Ornithological Society

George A. Hall/Harold F. Mayfield Award

Type of award: Research grant.
Intended use: For non-degree study.
Basis for selection: Major/career interest in ornithology.
Application requirements: Recommendations, research proposal. Application (available online), budget. Research proposal must be no longer than three pages.
Additional information: Research grant for studies of birds. Award restricted to amateur researchers, including high school students, without access to funds and facilities of academic institutions or governmental agencies. Willingness to report research results as oral or poster paper is condition of award. Applicants whose first language is not English may submit proposal in their first language. See Website for contact information.

Amount of award:	$1,000
Number of awards:	1
Number of applicants:	3
Application deadline:	January 15
Total amount awarded:	$1,000

Contact:
Web: www.ummz.lsa.umich.edu/birds/wosawards.html

Paul A. Stewart Award

Type of award: Research grant.
Intended use: For undergraduate, master's, doctoral, postgraduate or non-degree study at graduate institution.
Basis for selection: Major/career interest in ornithology.
Application requirements: Recommendations, research proposal. Application (available online), research budget.
Additional information: Research grant for studies of birds. Preference given to proposals studying bird movements based on banding, analysis of recoveries and returns of banded birds, with an emphasis on economic ornithology. Willingness to report research results as oral or poster paper is condition of award. Multiple awards given annually. Applicants whose first language is not English may submit proposal in their first language. See Website for contact information.

Amount of award:	$500
Number of awards:	4
Application deadline:	January 15
Total amount awarded:	$2,000

Contact:
Web: www.ummz.lsa.umich.edu/birds/wosawards.html

Wisconsin Dental Foundation

Wisconsin Dental Foundation Scholarship

Type of award: Scholarship.
Intended use: For sophomore study at accredited postsecondary institution. Designated institutions: Marquette University and Wisconsin technical schools.
Eligibility: Applicant must be residing in Wisconsin.
Basis for selection: Major/career interest in dental hygiene or dentistry. Applicant must demonstrate financial need, high academic achievement, depth of character, leadership, seriousness of purpose and service orientation.
Application requirements: Recommendations, nomination by committees at each campus.
Additional information: Applicant must be attending participating school in Wisconsin.

Amount of award:	$500
Number of awards:	20
Total amount awarded:	$11,000

Contact:
Participating Wisconsin postsecondary institutions.
Phone: 414-276-4520
Fax: 414-276-8431

Wisconsin Department of Veterans Affairs

Wisconsin Veterans Affairs Part-Time Study Grant

Type of award: Scholarship.
Intended use: For half-time undergraduate study at accredited vocational, 2-year or 4-year institution. Designated institutions: Approved Wisconsin postsecondary schools.
Eligibility: Applicant must be residing in Wisconsin. Applicant must be veteran; or dependent of deceased veteran; or spouse of deceased veteran. Must have served two years of active duty during peacetime or 90 days of active duty during specified wartime period.
Application requirements: Proof of eligibility.
Additional information: Veterans may be reimbursed for up to 100 percent of tuition and fees (not to exceed cost at UW-Madison for the same number of undergraduate credits) after successfully completing part-time classroom or correspondence courses at most Wisconsin schools. Statutory combined income limit of $50,000. Limit increases by $1,000 for each dependent child in excess of two. Must carry 11 credits or less per semester. Part-time coursework must be related to the applicant's occupational, professional or employment objectives. Application deadline is 60 days after completion of semester/quarter.
Contact:
Wisconsin Department of Veterans Affairs
P.O. Box 7843
30 West Mifflin Street
Madison, WI 53703-7843
Phone: 800-947-8387
Web: http://dva.state.wi.us

Wisconsin Veterans Affairs Retraining Grant

Type of award: Scholarship.
Intended use: For undergraduate study at accredited vocational institution. Designated institutions: Wisconsin vocational institutions.
Eligibility: Applicant must be residing in Wisconsin. Applicant must be veteran. Must have served two years of continuous active duty during peacetime or 90 days of active duty during designated wartime period.
Basis for selection: Applicant must demonstrate financial need.
Application requirements: Must have been a resident of Wisconsin on entry into military service or a continuous resident of Wisconsin for at least five years after separation from military service.
Additional information: Applicant must be recently unemployed or underemployed veteran and registered for or enrolled in education program that will lead to reemployment and be completed within two years. Must have been employed for six consecutive months with same employer or in the same or similar occupation. Certification and counseling is provided at accredited Wisconsin schools. Training at other schools does not qualify. Apply year-round at local county Veterans Service Office to establish eligibility.

Amount of award:	$3,000

Contact:
Wisconsin Department of Veterans Affairs
P.O. Box 7843
30 West Mifflin Street
Madison, WI 53703-7843
Phone: 800-947-8387
Web: dva.state.wi.us

Wisconsin Veterans Affairs Tuition and Fee Reimbursement Grant

Type of award: Scholarship, renewable.
Intended use: For undergraduate study at postsecondary institution. Designated institutions: Approved Wisconsin postsecondary schools.
Eligibility: Applicant must be residing in Wisconsin. Applicant must be veteran.
Basis for selection: Applicant must demonstrate financial need.
Application requirements: Proof of eligibility. Federal tax return or proof of annual income.
Additional information: Family income limit of $50,000. Limit increases by $1,000 for each dependent child. Veterans may receive up to 85% reimbursement of cost of tuition and fees. May receive reimbursement for up to eight semesters of full-time study. Courses must be taken within 10 years of separation from active military service.
Contact:
Wisconsin Department of Veterans Affairs
P.O. Box 7843
30 West Mifflin Street
Madison, WI 53703-7843
Phone: 800-947-8387
Web: http://dva.state.wi.us

Scholarships

Wisconsin Higher Educational Aids Board

Wisconsin Academic Excellence Scholarship

Type of award: Scholarship, renewable.
Intended use: For full-time undergraduate study at vocational, 2-year or 4-year institution. Designated institutions: University of Wisconsin, Wisconsin Technical College, or independent institution in the state.
Eligibility: Applicant must be high school senior. Applicant must be residing in Wisconsin.
Basis for selection: Applicant must demonstrate high academic achievement.
Application requirements: Nomination by high school guidance counselor by February 15.
Additional information: Awarded to Wisconsin high school seniors who have the highest grade point average in each public and private high school throughout the State of Wisconsin. 3.0 GPA must be maintained for renewal. Awards range from $2,250 to full tuition and fees. Private school students eligible.

Amount of award:	$2,250
Number of awards:	2,670
Application deadline:	February 15
Total amount awarded:	$2,894,469

Contact:
Higher Education Aids Board
Attn: Alice Winters
131 West Wilson
Madison, WI 53707
Phone: 608-267-2213
Web: http://heab.state.wi.us/programs.html

Wisconsin Handicapped Student Grant

Type of award: Scholarship, renewable.
Intended use: For undergraduate study. Designated institutions: Wisconsin institutions.
Eligibility: Applicant must be visually impaired or hearing impaired. Applicant must be residing in Wisconsin.
Basis for selection: Applicant must demonstrate financial need.
Application requirements: Proof of eligibility. FAFSA and Hearing & Visually Handicapped Student Grant Application.

Amount of award:	$250-$1,800
Number of awards:	54
Total amount awarded:	$85,910

Contact:
Higher Educational Aids Board
Attn: Sandy Thomas
131 West Wilson
Madison, WI 53707-7885
Phone: 608-266-0888

Wisconsin Higher Education Grant

Type of award: Scholarship, renewable.
Intended use: For undergraduate study at vocational or 4-year institution. Designated institutions: University of Wisconsin and Wisconsin technical institutions.
Eligibility: Applicant must be residing in Wisconsin.
Basis for selection: Applicant must demonstrate financial need.

Application requirements: Proof of eligibility.
Additional information: Apply with FAFSA through high school guidance counselor or financial aid office of institution.

Amount of award:	$250-$2,500
Number of awards:	37,172
Total amount awarded:	$35,060,586

Contact:
Higher Educational Aids Board
Attn: Sandra Thomas
131 West Wilson
Madison, WI 53707
Phone: 608-267-0888

Wisconsin Indian Student Assistance Grant

Type of award: Scholarship, renewable.
Intended use: For undergraduate or graduate study. Designated institutions: Wisconsin institutions.
Eligibility: Applicant must be American Indian. Must be at least one-quarter Native American. Applicant must be residing in Wisconsin.
Basis for selection: Major/career interest in humanities/liberal arts. Applicant must demonstrate financial need.
Application requirements: Proof of eligibility. FAFSA, Indian Student Assistance Grant Application.

Amount of award:	$250-$1,100
Number of awards:	837
Total amount awarded:	$784,857

Contact:
Higher Educational Aids Board
Attn: Sandra Thomas
131 West Wilson
Madison, WI 53707
Phone: 608-267-2206

Wisconsin Minority Retention Grant

Type of award: Scholarship, renewable.
Intended use: For sophomore, junior or senior study at vocational, 2-year or 4-year institution. Designated institutions: Private and non-profit schools in Wisconsin.
Eligibility: Applicant must be Asian American, African American, Mexican American, Hispanic American, Puerto Rican or American Indian. Asian American applicants must be former citizens or children of former citizens of Laos, Vietnam, or Cambodia admitted to United States after 12/31/75. Applicant must be residing in Wisconsin.
Basis for selection: Applicant must demonstrate financial need.
Application requirements: FAFSA and nomination by Financial Aid Office.

Amount of award:	$250-$2,500
Number of awards:	613
Total amount awarded:	$687,596

Contact:
Higher Educational Aids Board
Attn: May Lou Kuzdas
131 West Wilson
Wisconsin, WI 53707
Phone: 608-267-2212

Wisconsin Talent Incentive Program Grant

Type of award: Scholarship, renewable.

Intended use: For freshman, sophomore, junior or senior study at postsecondary institution. Designated institutions: University of Wisconsin, Wisconsin Technical College, and independent institutions in the state.

Eligibility: Applicant must be residing in Wisconsin.

Basis for selection: Major/career interest in humanities/liberal arts. Applicant must demonstrate financial need.

Application requirements: Nomination by financial aid department or WEOP. FAFSA.

Additional information: First-time freshmen students are nominated for TIP Grant by school financial aid offices or by counselors of the Wisconsin Educational Opportunity Programs (WEOP). Eligibility cannot exceed ten semesters.

Amount of award:	$250-$1,800
Number of awards:	4,146
Total amount awarded:	$5,489,498

Contact:
Higher Educational Aids Board
Attn: John Whitt
131 West Wilson
Madison, WI 53707
Phone: 608-266-1665
Web: heab.state.wi.us/programs.html

Wisconsin Tuition Grant

Type of award: Scholarship, renewable.

Intended use: For undergraduate or post-bachelor's certificate study. Designated institutions: Independent, nonprofit institutions in Wisconsin.

Eligibility: Applicant must be residing in Wisconsin.

Basis for selection: Applicant must demonstrate financial need.

Application requirements: FAFSA.

Additional information: Applicant must be Wisconsin resident who will be attending a Wisconsin university, technical college or independent institution. Must be enrolled at least half time. Maximum award amount set annually by HEAB.

Amount of award:	$250
Number of awards:	12,343
Total amount awarded:	$23,247,820

Contact:
Higher Educational Aids Board
Attn: Mary Lou Kuzdas
131 West Wilson
Madison, WI 53707
Phone: 608-267-2212

Women Grocers of America

Mary Macey Scholarship

Type of award: Scholarship, renewable.

Intended use: For sophomore, junior, senior or graduate study at accredited 2-year, 4-year or graduate institution in United States.

Basis for selection: Major/career interest in food production/management/services.

Application requirements: Recommendations, essay, transcript.

Additional information: Must plan on a career in the independent sector of the grocery industry. Majors in public health and hotel management are not eligible. Minimum 2.0 GPA. Minimum of two awards each year.

Amount of award:	$1,000-$1,500
Number of awards:	7
Number of applicants:	18
Application deadline:	June 1
Notification begins:	July 1
Total amount awarded:	$7,000

Contact:
Women Grocers of America
1005 North Glebe Road
Suite 250
Arlington, VA 22201-5758
Phone: 703-516-0700
Fax: 703-516-0115
Web: www.nationalgrocers.org

Women of the Evangelical Lutheran Church in America

Laywomen Scholarships

Type of award: Scholarship.

Intended use: For undergraduate or graduate study.

Eligibility: Applicant must be female, at least 21, returning adult student. Applicant must be Lutheran. Applicant must be U.S. citizen.

Basis for selection: Applicant must demonstrate financial need, high academic achievement and service orientation.

Application requirements: Essay, transcript, proof of eligibility. Academic and personal references. Reference from pastor or, if pastor is a relative, from chairperson or vice-chairperson of congregation.

Additional information: Must be member of Evangelical Lutheran Church in America. Must have interrupted education since high school for at least two years. Must show clear educational goals. Cannot be studying for ordination, diaconate, or church-certified professions. Must be laywoman. Applicants may reapply and receive assistance for maximum of two years. Visit Website or write to address below for more information and to request application.

Amount of award:	$2,000
Number of applicants:	100
Application deadline:	February 15
Notification begins:	May 25

Contact:
Women of the ELCA Scholarship Program
8765 W. Higgins Road
Chicago, IL 60631-4189
Phone: 773-638-3522
Fax: 773-380-2419
Web: www.elca.org/wo/scholpro.html

Women's Western Golf Foundation

Women's Western Golf Foundation Scholarship

Type of award: Scholarship, renewable.

Intended use: For full-time freshman study at accredited 4-year institution in United States.
Eligibility: Applicant must be female, high school senior. Applicant must be U.S. citizen.
Basis for selection: Competition/talent/interest in athletics/sports. Applicant must demonstrate financial need, high academic achievement, depth of character, leadership and seriousness of purpose.
Application requirements: Essay, transcript, proof of eligibility. SAT/ACT scores, FAFSA. Personal recommendation required from high school teacher or counselor. List of high school activities.
Additional information: Must be in top 15 percent of class. 3.5 GPA is recommended. Must demonstrate involvement in sport of golf, but skill not criterion. Deadline to request application is March 1; SASE required. Must file FAFSA with U.S. government and provide copy with application. Awards renew for each of four years, assuming scholarship terms are fulfilled (financial need, GPA above 3.0). About 20 new awards each year, plus 50 renewals.

Amount of award:	$2,000
Number of awards:	70
Number of applicants:	500
Application deadline:	April 5
Total amount awarded:	$150,000

Contact:
Director of Scholarship
Women's Western Golf Foundation
393 Ramsay Road
Deerfield, IL 60015

Woodrow Wilson National Fellowship Foundation

Thomas R. Pickering Foreign Affairs Fellowship

Type of award: Scholarship.
Intended use: For full-time sophomore study at accredited 4-year or graduate institution in United States. Designated institutions: Graduate portion of fellowship must be used at institutions affiliated with Association of Professional Schools of International Affairs.
Eligibility: Applicant must be U.S. citizen.
Basis for selection: Major/career interest in international relations. Applicant must demonstrate financial need, high academic achievement, depth of character, leadership, seriousness of purpose and service orientation.
Application requirements: Recommendations, essay, transcript, proof of eligibility.
Additional information: Must have interest in career as Foreign Service officer. Number of fellowships determined by available funding. Finalists will attend interview session in Princeton, NJ, or Washington, DC; transportation to interview site paid. Orientation in Washington, D.C. Medical and security clearances required for program participation. Applicants must have minimum 3.2 GPA at time of application and maintain GPA throughout fellowship. Women and members of minority groups historically underrepresented in the Foreign Service encouraged to apply.

Amount of award:	Full tuition
Application deadline:	February 22

Contact:
Dr. Richard Hope, Director Foreign Affairs Fellowship Program
Woodrow Wilson National Fellowship Foundation
P.O. Box 2437
Princeton, NJ 08543-2437
Phone: 609-452-7007
Web: www.woodrow.org

Worcester County Horticultural Society

Worcester County Horticultural Society Scholarship

Type of award: Scholarship, renewable.
Intended use: For full-time sophomore, junior or graduate study at 4-year or graduate institution in United States.
Eligibility: Applicant must be residing in Vermont, New Hampshire, Connecticut, Maine, Massachusetts or Rhode Island.
Basis for selection: Major/career interest in horticulture or landscape architecture. Applicant must demonstrate financial need, high academic achievement and seriousness of purpose.
Application requirements: Recommendations, essay, transcript. Application.
Additional information: Applicant must reside in New England. Applicants are also eligible if only attending college in one of the listed states. Applications must be completed and postmarked no later than April 30. Number of scholarship awards varies. Contact for availability.

Amount of award:	$500-$2,000
Number of applicants:	60
Application deadline:	April 30
Notification begins:	June 15

Contact:
Scholarship Committee of the Worcester County Horticultural Society
Tower Hill Botanic Garden
11 French Drive, P.O. Box 598
Boylston, MA 01505-0598
Phone: 508-869-6111 ext. 24
Fax: 508-869-0314

Working in Support of Education (WISE)

Quality of Life Research Competition

Type of award: Scholarship.
Intended use: For undergraduate study.
Eligibility: Applicant must be high school sophomore, junior or senior. Applicant must be U.S. citizen or permanent resident residing in New York.
Basis for selection: Competition/talent/interest in Research paper, based on practicality, likely benefit to community, clarity of expression and breadth of vision.
Additional information: Applicant must reside in New York City. For competition, students must research, write and present scholarly proposals suggesting practical ways to improve the

quality of life in their community. Applicants must be high school sophomores, juniors or seniors. Research proposals due in March. Notification for semifinalists begins in April; prize winners notified in May.

Amount of award: $1,000-$15,000
Number of applicants: 1,000
Contact:
WISE
Quality of Life Competition
227 E. 56th Street, Suite 201
New York, NY 10022
Phone: 212-421-2700
Web: www.qlcompetition.org

World Studio Foundation

Indigenous Peoples Award

Type of award: Scholarship.
Intended use: For full-time undergraduate study at postsecondary institution in United States.
Eligibility: Applicant must be Alaskan native or American Indian. Applicant must be U.S. citizen or permanent resident.
Basis for selection: Major/career interest in art/art history; arts, general or design. Applicant must demonstrate financial need, high academic achievement and seriousness of purpose.
Application requirements: Essay.
Additional information: A special scholarship awarded to artists of Native American, Alaska Native/Inuit, or other indigenous tribes of the Americas. With an emphasis on artists, designers or craftspeople seeking to maintain traditional forms. Visit Website for more information.

Amount of award: $1,500-$5,000
Application deadline: March 19
Contact:
Worldstudio Foundation
200 Varick Street, Suite 507
New York, NY 10014
Phone: 212-366-1317 ext. 18
Fax: 212-807-0024
Web: www.worldstudio.org

Special Illustration & Animation Award

Type of award: Scholarship.
Intended use: For full-time undergraduate study at accredited 4-year institution in United States.
Eligibility: Applicant must be U.S. citizen.
Basis for selection: Competition/talent/interest in Visual arts, Quality of submitted work; financial need; minority status; academic record; recommendations; strength of written statement. Major/career interest in arts, general; arts management or computer graphics. Applicant must demonstrate financial need.
Application requirements: Portfolio, recommendations, essay, transcript. Complete financial need information on scholarship form must be signed by Financial Aid Officer.
Additional information: Only for students interested in Animation, Illustration and Cartooning. Award inlcudes an internship for the top 3 candidates. Minorities heavily encouraged to apply. Applicants must have a GPA of 2.0. Incoming students who are undecided must submit proof of acceptance from schools of choice.

Amount of award: $1,500
Number of awards: 25
Number of applicants: 250
Application deadline: March 19
Total amount awarded: $37,500
Contact:
Worldstudio Foundation
200 Varick Street, 5th Floor
New York, NY 10014
Phone: 212-366-1317 ext. 18
Fax: 212-807-0024
Web: www.worldstudio.org

World Studio Foundation Scholarship

Type of award: Scholarship.
Intended use: For full-time undergraduate study at postsecondary institution in United States.
Eligibility: Applicant must be Alaskan native, Asian American, African American, Mexican American, Hispanic American, Puerto Rican or American Indian. Applicant must be U.S. citizen.
Basis for selection: Demonstrated commitment to giving back to the larger community through artwork. Major/career interest in arts, general; architecture; advertising; film/video; design or urban planning. Applicant must demonstrate seriousness of purpose and service orientation.
Application requirements: Portfolio, recommendations, transcript. Portfolio must be in slide format. A short autobiography and a statement of purpose are also needed.
Additional information: The foundation's primary aim is to increase diversity in the creative professions and to foster social and environmental responsibility in the artists, designers and studios of tomorrow. Awards are paid directly to college or university to be applied toward student's tuition. Students studying photography, interior, furniture, product, fashion or textile design; and illustration encouraged to apply. Visit Website to download guidelines and application, or send SASE to receive application by mail.

Amount of award: $1,500-$5,000
Application deadline: March 19
Contact:
Worldstudio Foundation
200 Varick Street, 5th Floor
New York, NY 10014
Phone: 212-366-1317 ext. 18
Fax: 212-807-0024
Web: www.worldstudio.org

Xerox

Technical Minority Scholarship

Type of award: Scholarship.
Intended use: For undergraduate study in United States.
Eligibility: Applicant must be Alaskan native, Asian American, African American, Mexican American, Hispanic American, Puerto Rican or American Indian. Applicant must be U.S. citizen or permanent resident.
Basis for selection: Major/career interest in chemistry; engineering; science, general; information systems; physics or computer/information sciences. Applicant must demonstrate leadership, patriotism and seriousness of purpose.

Application requirements: Application, resume and cover letter. Minimum 3.0 GPA.
Additional information: Visit Website for application and more information.

Amount of award:	$1,000
Application deadline:	September 15

Contact:
Xerox
Xerox Technical Minority Scholarship Program
150 State St, 4th Floor
Rochester, NY 14614
Web: www.xerox.com

Yakama Nation Higher Education Program

Yakama Nation Tribal Scholarship

Type of award: Scholarship.
Intended use: For freshman, sophomore, junior, senior, master's or doctoral study at accredited 2-year, 4-year or graduate institution.
Eligibility: Applicant must be American Indian. Must be enrolled member of Yakama Indian Nation.
Application requirements: Transcript. Tribal ID number. Enrollment verification, high school transcript, FAFSA, college acceptance letter.
Additional information: There is a priority list for selection.

Amount of award:	$2,000
Number of awards:	255
Number of applicants:	364
Application deadline:	July 1
Notification begins:	August 1
Total amount awarded:	$394,000

Contact:
Yakama Nation Higher Education Program
P.O. Box 151
Toppenish, WA 98948
Phone: 509-865-5121
Fax: 509-865-6994

Yes I Can! Foundation for Exceptional Children

Stanley Edward Jackson Award for Gifted/Talented Students with Disabilities

Type of award: Scholarship.
Intended use: For full-time freshman study at postsecondary institution in United States.
Eligibility: Applicant must be physically challenged or learning disabled. Applicant must be high school senior. Applicant must be U.S. citizen.
Application requirements: Recommendations, essay, transcript, proof of eligibility. Appplication. Statement indicating financial need.
Additional information: Statement verifying disability from physician or school counselor, three letters of recommendation

and completed application required. Applicant must have demonstrated talent in any one of the following categories: general intellect, high academic aptitude, creativity, leadership or visual/performing arts.

Amount of award:	$500
Number of awards:	10
Number of applicants:	500
Application deadline:	February 1
Total amount awarded:	$2,000

Contact:
Stanley E. Jackson Award for Gifted/Talented Students w/Disabilities
Yes I Can! Foundation
1110 North Glebe Rd. Suite 300
Arlington, VA 22201
Phone: 800-224-6830
Web: http://yesican.sped.org

Stanley Edward Jackson Scholarship Award for Ethnic Minority Gifted/Talented Students with Disabilities

Type of award: Scholarship.
Intended use: For full-time freshman study at postsecondary institution in United States.
Eligibility: Applicant must be physically challenged or learning disabled. Applicant must be Alaskan native, Asian American, African American, Mexican American, Hispanic American, Puerto Rican or American Indian. Applicant must be high school senior. Applicant must be U.S. citizen or permanent resident.
Basis for selection: Applicant must demonstrate financial need and high academic achievement.
Application requirements: Recommendations, essay, transcript, proof of eligibility. Application. Statement indicating financial need.
Additional information: Statement verifying disability from physician or school counselor, three letters of recommendation and completed application required. Applicant must have demonstrated talent in any one of the following categories: general intellect, high academic aptitude, creativity, leadership or visual/performing arts.

Amount of award:	$500
Number of awards:	10
Number of applicants:	200
Application deadline:	February 1
Total amount awarded:	$4,000

Contact:
Stanley E. Jackson Award for G/T Minorities w/Disabilities
Yes I Can! Foundation
1110 North Glebe Rd. Suite 300
Arlington, VA 22201
Phone: 800-224-6830
Web: http://yesican.sped.org

Stanley Edward Jackson Scholarship Award for Ethnic Minority Students with Disabilities

Type of award: Scholarship.
Intended use: For full-time undergraduate study at vocational or 2-year institution in United States.
Eligibility: Applicant must be physically challenged or learning disabled. Applicant must be Alaskan native, Asian American, African American, Mexican American, Hispanic

American, Puerto Rican or American Indian. Applicant must be high school senior. Applicant must be U.S. citizen.

Basis for selection: Applicant must demonstrate financial need, depth of character and leadership.

Application requirements: Recommendations, essay, transcript, proof of eligibility. Application. Statement indicating financial need.

Additional information: Statement verifying disability from physician or school counselor.

Amount of award:	$500
Number of awards:	10
Number of applicants:	200
Application deadline:	February 1
Total amount awarded:	$2,000

Contact:
Stanley E. Jackson Award for Ethnic Minority Students w/Disabilities
Yes I Can! Foundation
1110 North Glebe Road, Suite 300
Arlington, VA 22201
Phone: 800-224-6830
Web: http://yesican.sped.org

Scholarships

Internships

Academy of Television Arts & Sciences Foundation

Academy of Television Arts & Sciences Foundation Student Internship Program

Type of award: Internship.
Intended use: For full-time undergraduate or graduate study in United States.
Eligibility: Applicant must be U.S. citizen or permanent resident.
Basis for selection: Major/career interest in film/video.
Application requirements: Recommendations, essay, transcript. Resume and cover letter. Three letters of recommendation.
Additional information: Designed to expose students to professional TV production facilities, techniques and practices. Opportunities available in many fields. See Website for categories and special requirements. Most internships start in late June and end eight weeks after start date. Interns responsible for housing, transportation and living expenses (housing stipend may be available). Interns must have car for transportation in Los Angeles.

Amount of award:	$4,000
Application deadline:	March 15

Contact:
Academy of Television Arts & Sciences Foundation
Internships
5220 Lankershim Boulevard
North Hollywood, CA 91601-3109
Phone: 818-754-2830
Web: www.emmys.tv/foundation

Accuracy in Media

Accuracy in Media Internships

Type of award: Internship.
Intended use: For undergraduate or graduate study.
Basis for selection: Major/career interest in marketing; English; journalism or graphic arts/design.
Application requirements: Application. Cover letter and resume. Two references. Writing sample, if applying for position with writing duties.
Additional information: Accuracy in Media is a nonprofit media watchdog group that reports on media bias. Internships open to applicants from all majors, though some positions require experience in a particular field. Internships pay $25 per day. High school students may apply, as well as recent college graduates. Applications are processed on rolling basis; for best chance, send early. Deadlines: March 31 for summer, August 15 for fall, November 15 for winter. See Website for application and more information.

Application deadline:	March 31, August 15

Contact:
Accuracy in Media
Internship Coordinator
4455 Connecticut Avenue, NW, Suite 330
Washington, DC 20008
Phone: 202-364-4401
Fax: 202-364-4098
Web: www.aim.org

Aeromet, Inc.

Atmospheric Science Internship

Type of award: Internship.
Intended use: For senior or graduate study at 4-year or graduate institution in United States.
Eligibility: Applicant must be single. Applicant must be U.S. citizen.
Basis for selection: Major/career interest in atmospheric sciences/meteorology. Applicant must demonstrate high academic achievement.
Application requirements: Transcript. Resume, three references.
Additional information: Should have completed two years of physics, two years of calculus, and four courses in atmospheric science or meteorology. Position from May 15 to September 1. Salary $9 to $11/hour, depending on experience. Visit Website or contact via e-mail (recruiting@aeromet.com) for additional information.

Amount of award:	$2,000
Number of awards:	2
Application deadline:	May 1

Contact:
Aeromet, Inc.
112 Beechcraft Drive
Jones River Airport
Tulsa, OK 74170-1767
Phone: 918-299-2621
Fax: 918-299-8211
Web: www.aeromet.com

Allstate

Allstate Internships

Type of award: Internship, renewable.
Intended use: For full-time undergraduate study at accredited 4-year institution.
Basis for selection: Major/career interest in insurance/actuarial science; accounting; marketing; business; business/management/administration; computer/information sciences or finance/banking. Applicant must demonstrate high academic achievement.

Application requirements: Resume, cover letter.
Additional information: In addition to salary and amenities of Illinois headquarters, eligible interns receive daily transportation and subsidized housing. Please respond directly to position as posted on website. Applications accepted on a rolling deadline basis.
Contact:
Allstate Insurance Company
2775 Sanders Rd., Suite A-1
Northbrook, IL 60062
Fax: 800-526-4831
Web: www.allstate.com/careers

American Association of Advertising Agencies

Multicultural Advertising Intern Program

Type of award: Internship, renewable.
Intended use: For full-time junior, senior or graduate study at accredited 4-year or graduate institution.
Eligibility: Applicant must be Asian American, African American, Mexican American, Hispanic American, Puerto Rican or American Indian. Applicant must be U.S. citizen or permanent resident.
Basis for selection: Major/career interest in advertising; communications; marketing or humanities/liberal arts.
Application requirements: Interview. Semi-finalists are interviewed by agency professionals before selection. Submission of Multicultural Advertising Intern Program application, also available under "Initiatives" section of Website.
Additional information: Must have completed junior year of college and have strong interest in advertising. Minimum 3.0 GPA required. Applicants with lower GPA (2.7-2.9) must complete an essay question on application. Students are placed in member agency offices for ten weeks during the summer. Salary minimum $350 per week. 60 percent of housing and travel costs (if applicable) are provided. Can apply for following departments: account management, creative, interactive technologies, media, production, traffic or strategic planning. See Website for more information.

Number of awards:	101
Application deadline:	February 1

Contact:
American Association of Advertising Agencies
Manager of Diversity Programs
405 Lexington Avenue, 18th Floor
New York, NY 10174-1801
Phone: 800-676-9333
Fax: 212-573-8968
Web: www.aaaa.org

American Bar Foundation

Law and Social Sciences Summer Research Fellowship for Minority Undergraduates

Type of award: Internship.
Intended use: For sophomore or junior study.
Eligibility: Applicant must be U.S. citizen or permanent resident.
Basis for selection: Major/career interest in law; social/behavioral sciences; criminal justice/law enforcement or public administration/service. Applicant must demonstrate high academic achievement.
Application requirements: Recommendations, essay, transcript. Minimum 3.0 GPA.
Additional information: Interns work ten 35-hour weeks as research assistants at American Bar Foundation in Chicago and receive $3,600 stipend. Fellowships are intended for, but not limited to, persons who are African American, Hispanic/Latino, Native American or Puerto Rican.

Amount of award:	$3,600
Number of awards:	4
Application deadline:	February 28
Notification begins:	April 6

Contact:
American Bar Foundation
750 North Lake Shore Drive, Fourth Floor
Chicago, IL 60611
Phone: 312-988-6580
Web: www.abf-sociolegal.org

American Conservatory Theater

American Conservatory Theater Production Internships

Type of award: Internship.
Intended use: For undergraduate or graduate study.
Eligibility: Applicant must be U.S. citizen.
Basis for selection: Major/career interest in performing arts; theater arts or theater/production/technical. Applicant must demonstrate high academic achievement.
Application requirements: $15 application fee. Interview, portfolio, recommendations, essay. Work permit. Internships intended for college students and graduates planning career in theater.
Additional information: Provides intern with practical experience in many areas of theater production. Departments include costume rentals, costume shop, lighting design, properties, sound design, stage management, technical design, wig construction/makeup, production. A small hourly wage is available for full-time seasonal internships. Must have valid work permit. Visit Website for more information.

Number of awards:	10
Number of applicants:	70
Application deadline:	April 15
Notification begins:	June 1

Internships

Contact:
American Conservatory Theater
Intern Coordinator
30 Grant Avenue, 6th Floor
San Francisco, CA 94108
Phone: 415-834-3200
Fax: 415-433-2711
Web: act-sf.org

Artistic and Administrative Internships

Type of award: Internship.
Intended use: For undergraduate or graduate study at 2-year, 4-year or graduate institution.
Eligibility: Applicant must be U.S. citizen.
Basis for selection: Major/career interest in theater arts; theater/production/technical; arts management; arts, general; public relations; marketing; English; English literature; literature or performing arts. Applicant must demonstrate high academic achievement.
Application requirements: $15 application fee. Interview, portfolio, recommendations, essay. Work permit.
Additional information: Provides intern with opportunity to work in artistic, literary/publications, management, development and markekting/public relations departments. Some internships require writing and art samples. A small hourly wage is available. If intern needs paying employment, ACT will adjust hours. Different departments have available positions at different times of year. Application deadlines are rolling. Visit Website for more information.

Number of awards:	6
Number of applicants:	75

Contact:
American Conservatory Theater
Intern Coordinator
30 Grant Avenue, 6th Floor
San Francisco, CA 94108
Phone: 415-834-3200
Fax: 415-834-3326
Web: www.act-sfbay.org

American Indian Science & Engineering Society

Bureau of Reclamation Scholarship and Internship

Type of award: Internship, renewable.
Intended use: For full-time undergraduate study in United States.
Eligibility: Applicant or parent must be member/participant of American Indian Science & Engineering Society. Applicant must be U.S. citizen or permanent resident.
Basis for selection: Major/career interest in engineering or environmental science. Applicant must demonstrate high academic achievement.
Application requirements: Recommendations, essay, transcript, proof of eligibility. Resume. Essay topic: How applicant will contribute their knowledge or experience to a Native American community.
Additional information: Minimum 2.5 GPA. Applicant must be seeking bachelor's degree in engineering or science, relating

to water resources or other environmental field. Recipient must agree to serve eight- to ten-week paid internship with Bureau of Reclamation before graduation. Membership and scholarship applications available on Website. Otherwise, send SASE with information or application requests.

Amount of award:	$5,000
Application deadline:	June 15

Contact:
AISES Scholarships
P.O. Box 9828
Albuquerque, NM 87119-9828
Phone: 505-765-1052
Web: www.aises.org

American Museum of Natural History

Research Experience for Undergraduates

Type of award: Internship.
Intended use: For undergraduate study at accredited 4-year institution in United States.
Eligibility: Applicant must be U.S. citizen.
Basis for selection: Major/career interest in science, general; biology or microbiology. Applicant must demonstrate high academic achievement and seriousness of purpose.
Application requirements: Recommendations, essay, research proposal. Scientific proposal.
Additional information: Internship in evolutionary biology at museum. Applicant must have a very strong scientific background, including, but not limited to, polymerase chain reactions, systematics and biodiversity, and conservation interests. Travel and research expenses reimbursed. Internship lasts for ten weeks. No applications will be accepted before January 1. Deadline for application varies but is usually at the beginning of March. Check Website in February for exact deadline.

Amount of award:	$3,500
Number of awards:	10
Total amount awarded:	$35,000

Contact:
American Museum of Natural History
Office of Grants and Fellowships
Central Park West at 79th Street
New York, NY 10024-5192
Web: www.amnh.org

American Society of International Law

American Society of International Law Internships

Type of award: Internship.
Intended use: For undergraduate or graduate study at accredited postsecondary institution.
Basis for selection: Major/career interest in law; international relations; public administration/service or journalism.

Application requirements: Cover letter, resume, writing samples and a list of three references with contact information.
Additional information: Positions require a minimum commitment of 15 hours per week during the fall and winter semesters, and 20 hours per week during summer semester. All internships are unpaid; students may arrange academic credit. Some positions for graduate students only. Deadlines: December 1 for spring semester, April 1 for summer semester, August 1 for fall semester. See Website for more information.
   Application deadline: December 1, April 1
Contact:
American Society of International Law
Internship Coordinator
2223 Massachusetts Avenue, NW
Washington, DC 20008
Fax: 202-797-7133
Web: www.asil.org

Applied Materials

Applied Materials Internships and Co-ops

Type of award: Internship.
Intended use: For undergraduate or graduate study.
Basis for selection: Major/career interest in engineering. Applicant must demonstrate high academic achievement.
Application requirements: Resume.
Additional information: Applicant should have interest in the semi-conductor industry and should be pursuing a degree. Paid internships and co-op positions based in Texas and California. Summer and year-round positions. Resumes can be sent via mail to the attention of Co-op/Intern Coordinator. Visit Website for additional addresses, to submit resume, and to find out when internship interviews will be held at college campuses.
   Number of awards: 400
Contact:
Applied Materials -- Attn: Co-op/Intern Coordinator
3195 Kifer Road
M/S 2963
Santa Clara, CA 95051
Web: www.appliedmaterials.com

Asian American Journalists Association

New Media Internship Grant

Type of award: Internship.
Intended use: For full-time at 4-year institution.
Eligibility: Applicant must be at least 18.
Basis for selection: Major/career interest in journalism. Applicant must demonstrate financial need.
Application requirements: Recommendations, essay, proof of eligibility. Three copies of essay, resume, proof of age, statement of financial need and internship verification.
Additional information: Grant for student with internship in new media. Applicant must have secured summer internship at online-related division of news-oriented organization, or at news division of online company.

Amount of award:	$2,500
Number of awards:	1
Number of applicants:	18
Application deadline:	April 16

Contact:
Asian American Journalists Association
1182 Market Street
Suite 320
San Francisco, CA 94102
Phone: 415-346-2051
Fax: 416-346-6343
Web: www.aaja.org

Siani Lee Broadcast Internship for Television

Type of award: Internship.
Intended use: For at postsecondary institution.
Eligibility: Applicant must be at least 18.
Basis for selection: Major/career interest in journalism.
Application requirements: Portfolio, essay, transcript, proof of eligibility. Three copies of essay, transcript and work samples. Minimum 2.7 GPA overall. Minimum 3.0 GPA in major courses.
Additional information: Summer internship at CBS affiliate KYW-TV in Philadelphia. Must be enrolled in postsecondary program that offers academic credit for internships. Stipend of $2,500 to help defray costs of travel and lodging. Qualified AAJA members are preferred.

Amount of award:	$2,500
Number of awards:	4
Number of applicants:	20
Application deadline:	March 5

Contact:
Asian American Journalists Association
1182 Market Street
San Francisco, CA 94102
Phone: 415-346-2051
Fax: 416-346-6343
Web: www.aaja.org

Stanford Chen Internship Grant

Type of award: Internship.
Intended use: For junior or senior study at 4-year institution.
Basis for selection: Major/career interest in journalism. Applicant must demonstrate financial need.
Application requirements: Recommendations, essay, proof of eligibility. Three copies of essay, resume, proof of age, statement of financial need and internship verification.
Additional information: Applicant must be an intern or have been accepted into a journalism internship program with a small-to-medium media company. Daily circulation for print companies must be under 100,000. For broadcast, markets must be 50 to 100. One of three grants will be awarded to a resident of the Pacific Northwest.

Amount of award:	$1,500
Number of awards:	3
Number of applicants:	25
Total amount awarded:	$4,500

Contact:
Asian American Journalists Association
1182 Market Street
Suite 320
San Francisco, CA 94102
Phone: 415-346-2051
Web: www.aaja.org

Baxter International Inc.

Baxter International Summer Internships

Type of award: Internship.
Intended use: For undergraduate or graduate study at accredited 2-year or 4-year institution.
Eligibility: Applicant must be U.S. citizen or permanent resident.
Basis for selection: Major/career interest in finance/banking; engineering; biochemistry; information systems; accounting; chemistry; human resources or marketing. Applicant must demonstrate high academic achievement.
Application requirements: Send resume via e-mail to internships@baxter.com.
Additional information: Paid three-month summer internship. Apply between January 1 to March 1. Visit Website for additional information.

    Application deadline: March 1
    Notification begins: April 28
Contact:
Baxter Healthcare Corporation
College Relations
One Baxter Parkway
Deerfield, IL 60015
Fax: 847-948-3642
Web: www.baxter.com

Bernstein-Rein Advertising

Advertising Internship (Summer Only)

Type of award: Internship.
Intended use: For junior or senior study.
Basis for selection: Major/career interest in advertising; journalism; marketing or communications.
Application requirements: Interview, recommendations, essay, proof of eligibility. Resume, cover letter, application, three reference names. Essay is one-page writing sample.
Additional information: Applicant must be second-semester junior or first-semester senior (will graduate in one to two semesters after summer). Pay is $8/hour.

    Number of awards: 9
    Number of applicants: 150
    Application deadline: February 1
    Total amount awarded: $27,000
Contact:
Bernstein-Rein Advertising
Human Resources
4600 Madison, Suite 1500
Kansas City, MO 64112
Phone: 816-756-0640
Fax: 816-531-5708
Web: www.bradv.com

Bethesda Lutheran Homes and Services, Inc.

Bethesda Lutheran Homes and Services Cooperative Program Internship

Type of award: Internship.
Intended use: For full-time junior or senior study at accredited postsecondary institution.
Eligibility: Applicant must be Lutheran.
Basis for selection: Major/career interest in social work; psychology; nursing or education. Applicant must demonstrate high academic achievement, depth of character, seriousness of purpose and service orientation.
Application requirements: Interview, recommendations.
Additional information: Minimum 3.0 GPA required. Housing is provided during 12-week summer internship. Salary is $7.50/hour, 40 hours a week. Applicants may also study public relations or chaplaincy.

    Amount of award: $3,600
    Number of awards: 8
    Application deadline: March 15
    Total amount awarded: $28,800
Contact:
Bethesda Lutheran Homes and Services, Inc.
Coordinator, Outreach Programs
600 Hoffmann Drive
Watertown, WI 53094
Phone: 800-369-4636 ext. 416
Fax: 920-262-6513
Web: www.blhs.org

Black & Veatch

Black & Veatch Internships, Co-op, and Summer Employment

Type of award: Internship.
Intended use: For full-time sophomore, junior or senior study in United States.
Eligibility: Applicant must be U.S. citizen or permanent resident.
Basis for selection: Major/career interest in engineering; construction or architecture. Applicant must demonstrate high academic achievement.
Application requirements: Transcript. Submit resume through Website; be sure to indicate GPA where requested.
Additional information: Internship compensation varies on discipline and major. Minimum 2.75 GPA. Majority of positions located in Kansas City, Missouri, area.
Contact:
Black & Veatch Job Code: CB00
College Relations Coordinator (PGA-1)
P.O. Box 8405
Kansas City, MO 64114-9859
Web: www.bv.com/careers

Internships

501

Blue Ridge Foundation New York

Blue Ridge Foundation New York Internship

Type of award: Internship.
Intended use: For undergraduate or graduate study.
Basis for selection: Major/career interest in education or philanthropy. Applicant must demonstrate seriousness of purpose and service orientation.
Application requirements: Cover letter and resume.
Additional information: Internship pays $1,500/month and is full-time. Application deadlines and program start date are flexible.
Contact:
Blue Ridge Foundation New York
150 Court Street
Second Floor
Brooklyn, NY 11210
Phone: 718-923-1400
Fax: 718-923-2869
Web: www.brfny.org

BMI Foundation, Inc. Linda Livingston

Pete Carpenter Fellowship

Type of award: Internship.
Intended use: For undergraduate, graduate or non-degree study at vocational, 2-year, 4-year or graduate institution.
Eligibility: Applicant must be no older than 34.
Basis for selection: Based on original one- to three-minute composition or selection from score appropriate for theme to theatrical or television film or series. Major/career interest in music or radio/television/film.
Application requirements: Application form and cassette tape of composition.
Additional information: Applicant must be under age of 35 at deadline. Winner of competition will work for one month in Los Angeles on day-to-day basis with distinguished television and theatrical film composers. Up to $2,000 for travel and living expenses to work with TV/film composer Mike Post in Los Angeles.
   Amount of award: $2,000
   Number of awards: 1
Contact:
BMI Foundation, Inc. Linda Livingston
320 W. 57th Street
New York, NY 10019
Web: www.bmi.com/bmifoundation

Board of Governors of the Federal Reserve System

Economic Research Divisions Internships

Type of award: Internship, renewable.
Intended use: For undergraduate or graduate study.
Basis for selection: Major/career interest in economics; information systems; finance/banking or mathematics. Applicant must demonstrate high academic achievement.
Application requirements: Recommendations, transcript. Resume and cover letter.
Additional information: For local applicants, work is during the school year so students can obtain credit. Summer internship programs last from June 1st to September 1st.
   Application deadline: April 1, July 31
Contact:
Board of Governors of the Federal Reserve System
Lori Carrington, Mail Stop 65
20th St. and Constitution Avenue, N.W.
Washington, DC 20551
Phone: 202-452-3374
Fax: 202-736-1919

Boeing Corporation

Boeing Internship Program

Type of award: Internship.
Intended use: For undergraduate or graduate study in United States. Designated institutions: Boeing sites in Seattle, WA; Arizona; Florida; Southern California; St. Louis, MO; Texas and Wichita, KS.
Eligibility: Applicant must be U.S. citizen.
Basis for selection: Major/career interest in aerospace; computer/information sciences; finance/banking; human resources; manufacturing; marketing; public relations; engineering or mathematics.
Application requirements: Recommendations, transcript, proof of eligibility. Resume.
Additional information: See Website for detailed information on available positions and to submit resume. Deadlines, eligiblity requirements and compensation vary from location to location; contact sponsor for more information. Applicant must apply online.
Contact:
Internship Coordinator
PO Box 516
Mailcode S2761740
St. Louis, MO 63166-0516
Phone: 314-232-0232
Web: www.boeing.com

Bok Tower Gardens

Bok Tower Gardens Internship

Type of award: Internship.

Intended use: For full-time undergraduate or graduate study at 4-year or graduate institution. Designated institutions: Bok Tower Gardens.

Basis for selection: Major/career interest in horticulture; landscape architecture or botany.

Application requirements: Interview, recommendations, transcript. Letter outlining interests. Resume. Three references necessary. Copies of transcript are acceptable.

Additional information: Major/interest in plant science also eligible. Preference given to students who will receive college credit for internship. Program offers on-the-job training in horticulture and conservation. Some experience in biological surveying, monitoring with a GPS unit, plant propagation, or working with Florida ecosystems is highly desirable. Good written and oral communication skills and good data collection abilities necessary. One one-year program, one six-month program. Intern receives $10/hr. Housing provided. Intern must have own vehicle and be willing to make field visits (mileage will be reimbursed). Other application deadlines: summer, April 1; winter, October 1. Write or call for application packet.

Application deadline: January 1, July 1

Contact:
Historic Bok Sanctuary
Attn: Human resources
1151 Tower Boulevard
Lake Wales, FL 33853-3412
Phone: 863-676-1408
Fax: 863-676-6770
Web: www.boktower.org

Boston Globe

Boston Globe One-Year Development Program

Type of award: Internship.
Intended use: For non-degree study.
Eligibility: Members of minority groups and candidates with unusual cultural backgrounds are strongly encouraged to apply.
Basis for selection: Major/career interest in journalism.
Application requirements: Resume, writing samples.
Additional information: Award provides one-year full-time employment at $751.53/week. Applicants must have six months newspaper experience. Applicants can apply for this program year-round.

Amount of award: $36,560
Number of awards: 1
Contact:
The Boston Globe
P.O. Box 2378
Boston, MA 02107-2378
Phone: 617-929-3120

Boston Globe Summer Internship

Type of award: Internship.
Intended use: For freshman, sophomore or junior study at 4-year institution.
Basis for selection: Major/career interest in journalism.
Application requirements: Interview, recommendations. Writing samples and clips.
Additional information: Award is for 12 weeks full-time summer employment at $600/week.

Amount of award: $6,900
Number of awards: 15
Application deadline: November 4
Notification begins: January 30
Contact:
The Boston Globe
P.O. Box 2378
Boston, MA 02107-2378
Phone: 617-929-3120

Bucks County Courier Times

Bucks County Courier Times Minority Internship

Type of award: Internship, renewable.
Intended use: For junior, senior or graduate study.
Eligibility: Applicant must be Alaskan native, Asian American, African American, Mexican American, Hispanic American, Puerto Rican or American Indian. Applicant must be U.S. citizen.
Basis for selection: Major/career interest in journalism; publishing; public relations; English or graphic arts/design.
Application requirements: Resume, clips, driver's license, and vehicle.
Additional information: Internship duration is 12 weeks. Applicant must have basic journalism skills. Interns work as news reporters, bureau reporters, copy desk assistants, photographers, graphic artists, sports writers, and feature writers.

Amount of award: $4,620
Number of awards: 5
Number of applicants: 100
Application deadline: February 1
Contact:
Bucks County Courier Times
Attn: Patricia S. Walker
8400 Route 13
Levittown, PA 19057

California Student Aid Commission

California State Work-Study Program

Type of award: Internship, renewable.
Intended use: For undergraduate or graduate study in United States. Designated institutions: Participating California postsecondary institutions.
Eligibility: Applicant must be U.S. citizen or permanent resident residing in California.
Basis for selection: Applicant must demonstrate financial need.
Application requirements: Applicants must apply through financial aid office at their school.
Additional information: Colleges identify jobs that relate to student's course of study, career goals, or exploration of

careers. Contact financial aid office at participating postsecondary institutions. Actual amount awarded varies based on financial need and individual institution's award policies.

Contact:
California Student Aid Commission
Specialized Programs
P.O. Box 419029
Rancho Cordova, CA 95741-9029
Phone: 916-526-7960 or 888-224-7268 # 3
Web: www.csac.ca.gov

Center for Defense Information

Center for Defense Information Internship

Type of award: Internship.
Intended use: For undergraduate or graduate study.
Basis for selection: Major/career interest in political science/government; military science; international relations; communications or computer/information sciences. Applicant must demonstrate high academic achievement, depth of character, leadership, seriousness of purpose and service orientation.
Application requirements: Recommendations, essay, transcript. Resume and cover letter stating interests and reasons for wanting to work at CDI. Writing sample.
Additional information: Intended for graduates and highly qualified undergraduates. Students must work full time for internship's duration (three to five months) to receive monthly stipend of $1,000. Deadline for summer application is March 1. Internships divided into three sections: research, television, and web design/software support. Deadlines are for the fall and spring semesters, respectively. Check Website for latest information.

Amount of award:	$3,000-$5,000
Number of awards:	12
Application deadline:	May 1, September 1
Notification begins:	July 22, November 7

Contact:
Center for Defense Information
1779 Massachusetts Avenue, NW
Washington, DC 20036
Phone: 202-332-0600
Fax: 202-462-4559
Web: www.cdi.org/aboutcdi/intern.cfm

Center for Investigative Reporting

Center for Investigative Reporting Internship

Type of award: Internship.
Intended use: For undergraduate or graduate study.
Basis for selection: Major/career interest in journalism or public administration/service.

Application requirements: Resume, cover letter, and writing samples.
Additional information: Part-time internships in San Francisco and Washington, DC, offer next generation of reporters a chance to build investigative reporting skills. Internships pay monthly stipend of $500 for minimum commitment of 15 to 20 hours per week, for approximately five months; housing is not provided. Winter/spring internship starts around February 1 (December 1 application deadline). Summer/fall internship starts around July 1 (May 1 application deadline).

Number of awards:	6
Application deadline:	December 1, May 1

Contact:
Center for Investigative Reporting
Internship Coordinator
131 Steuart Street, Suite 600
San Francisco, CA 94105
Phone: 415-543-1200
Fax: 415-543-8311
Web: www.muckraker.org

Chevron Texaco Corporation

Chevron Internship Program

Type of award: Internship.
Intended use: For full-time junior or senior study.
Eligibility: Applicant must be U.S. citizen, permanent resident, international student or a non-U.S. citizen qualified to work in the U.S.
Basis for selection: Major/career interest in science, general; engineering; finance/banking; information systems; computer/information sciences; human resources or business.
Application requirements: Transcript. Resume and cover letter.
Additional information: Paid full-time internships, terms vary. Openings available in many fields. Visit Website for more details and information about on-campus recruiting dates and special events. Attending a college recruiting event or national convention recruiting event is only acceptable means of application.
Contact:
See Website for college recruiting events and convention dates.
Web: www.chevrontexaco.com

City & Suburban Lifestyle Magazine

C&S Editorial Internships

Type of award: Internship.
Intended use: For junior or senior study at accredited 2-year or 4-year institution in United States. Designated institutions: Colleges and universities in White Plains, NY.
Eligibility: Applicant must be African American. Applicant must be U.S. citizen or permanent resident residing in New York.
Basis for selection: Major/career interest in English; publishing or advertising. Applicant must demonstrate seriousness of purpose.

Internships

Application requirements: Interview, portfolio. Sample writing clips from school newspaper or periodicals.
Additional information: Six- to twelve-week internships. Interns receive weekly stipend for travel expenses. African-American students residing and attending school in all boroughs of New York are welcome. Interns assist editors and advertising executives in all aspects of their work.

    Number of awards: 4
    Application deadline: April 15, January 15
Contact:
City & Suburban Lifestyle Magazine
307 West 38th Street 7th. Floor
7th Floor
New York, NY 10018
Phone: 212-967-5140
Web: www.citysuburbanmedia.com

Congressional Hispanic Caucus Institute

CHCI Summer Internship Program

Type of award: Internship.
Intended use: For full-time sophomore, junior or senior study at accredited 2-year or 4-year institution.
Eligibility: Applicant must be Mexican American, Hispanic American or Puerto Rican. Applicant must be U.S. citizen or permanent resident residing in District of Columbia.
Basis for selection: Applicant must demonstrate high academic achievement, depth of character, leadership, seriousness of purpose and service orientation.
Application requirements: Essay, transcript. Application, resume, GMAT and LSAT scores.
Additional information: Applicant must have completed one year of college by start of program, therefore college seniors graduating before the program begins are ineligible. Applicant will work 36 hours a week in Washington, D.C. congressional offices. Transportation, summer housing, and $2,000 stipend provided. Must have excellent writing and communications skills and an active interest in community affairs. Interns assigned to congressional offices regardless of political affiliation. Work experience is complemented by leadership development sessions. Minimum 3.0 GPA. Application available on Website.

    Application deadline: January 31
Contact:
Congressional Hispanic Caucus Institute Program Coordinator
504 C Street, NE
Washington, DC 20002
Phone: 202-543-1771
Fax: 202-546-2143
Web: www.chciyouth.org

Congressional Hispanic Caucus Institute Summer Internship Program

Type of award: Internship.
Intended use: For undergraduate study at postsecondary institution.
Eligibility: Applicant must be Mexican American or Hispanic American.

Additional information: Provides opportunity to spend two months in Washingon, DC, working for member of Congress, getting "behind the scenes" look at how US government functions. Stipend, roundtrip transportation and housing in university dormitory.
    Amount of award: $2,000
    Application deadline: January 31
Contact:
Congressional Hispanic Caucus Institute
911 2nd Street NE
Washington, DC 20002
Phone: 800-EXCEL-DC or 202-543-1771
Fax: 202-546-2143
Web: www.chciyouth.org

Congressional Institute, Inc.

Congressional Institute Internships

Type of award: Internship.
Intended use: For undergraduate study at accredited 2-year or 4-year institution in United States.
Eligibility: Applicant must be U.S. citizen.
Basis for selection: Major/career interest in political science/government; public administration/service; law or communications. Applicant must demonstrate high academic achievement.
Application requirements: Recommendations. Resume and writing samples.
Additional information: Paid internships available throughout the year on flexible terms. Must be undergraduate with interest in public policy or legislative policy issues. For application and additional information, visit Website.
Contact:
Congressional Institute, Inc.
401 Wythe Street, Suite 103
Alexandria, VA 22314-1172
Phone: 703-837-8812
Fax: 703-837-8817
Web: www.conginst.org

CORPORATEinterns, Inc.

CORPORATEinterns.com Student Placement

Type of award: Internship.
Intended use: For full-time undergraduate or graduate study at accredited 4-year institution.
Eligibility: Applicant must be U.S. citizen or permanent resident.
Basis for selection: Major/career interest in accounting; business/management/administration; finance/banking; computer/information sciences; communications or marketing. Applicant must demonstrate high academic achievement.
Application requirements: Visit Website to register.
Additional information: CORPORATEinterns, Inc. is a free-to-students (employer-paid) intern placement service. Positions available appropriate to most major fields of study. Wages are competitive. Most placements in Minnesota.

Contact:
CORPORATEinterns, Inc.
449 East Seventh Street
Suite 200
St. Paul, MN 55101
Phone: 888-875-3565
Fax: 651-224-6003
Web: www.corporateinterns.com

Creede Repertory Theatre

Creede Repertory Theatre Summer Internship

Type of award: Internship.
Intended use: For undergraduate, graduate or non-degree study at postsecondary institution.
Basis for selection: Major/career interest in business; design; humanities/liberal arts; performing arts; theater arts or theater/production/technical.
Application requirements: Audition, recommendations. Resume or application. Interview preferred, but not required.
Additional information: Mainly for students interested in theatre and business-related fields, but open to all majors. Offers internships in costumes, set building, box office, business management. High school seniors may apply, but must graduate by summer. Also hire actors, designers (set, costume, lights, etc.) and stage managers. Applicants awarded positions on basis of qualifications for particular jobs. Actors must audition. All others fill out internship application and/or send resume. We will consider any age/sex/race applicant. Housing is free, interns receive $175 a week.

   Application deadline: March 1
Contact:
Creede Repertory Theatre
Summer Internships
P.O. Box 269
Creede, CO 81130
Web: www.creederep.org

Cushman School

Cushman School Internship

Type of award: Internship, renewable.
Intended use: For undergraduate or graduate study. Designated institutions: Cushman School.
Eligibility: Applicant must be U.S. citizen, permanent resident, international student or International students must have J1 visa.
Basis for selection: Major/career interest in education. Applicant must demonstrate depth of character.
Application requirements: Resume, cover letter.
Additional information: 18-week internships on Cushman School campus for fall and spring semesters. Interns will assist teachers in classrooms. Internships are full-time, 8am-3pm, Monday to Friday. Stipend of $2,000 for U.S. students and $3,000 for international students awarded each semester. Students may also participate in Education Camp for six weeks during summer. For details, contact Anne Gorman at (305) 754-3729 after 7pm EST.

   Amount of award: $2,000-$3,000

Contact:
Cushman School
592 Northeast 60th St.
Miami, FL 33137
Phone: 305-754-3729 or 305-757-1966
Fax: 305-757-1632
Web: www.cushmanschool.org

Davis and Company

Employee Communication Internship

Type of award: Internship.
Intended use: For undergraduate or graduate study.
Eligibility: Applicant must be U.S. citizen or permanent resident.
Basis for selection: Major/career interest in communications; journalism or marketing. Applicant must demonstrate depth of character.
Application requirements: Interview. Resume.
Additional information: Six- to 12-week internship. Interns receive $10/hour for 40-hour work week. Interns assist account executives in all aspects of work.
Contact:
Davis and Company
11 Harristown Rd.
Glen Rock, NJ 07452
Web: www.davisandco.com

Deloitte and Touche

SELECT Internship Program

Type of award: Internship.
Intended use: For full-time sophomore, junior or senior study at accredited 4-year institution.
Eligibility: Applicant must be U.S. citizen, permanent resident, international student or students must be eligible to work in United States.
Basis for selection: Major/career interest in accounting; business/management/administration; engineering or finance/banking. Applicant must demonstrate high academic achievement, depth of character and seriousness of purpose.
Application requirements: Interview. Resume, cover letter.
Additional information: Internships in more than 40 offices nationwide. Interns also attend annual conference and receive a laptop computer for use during internship. Interns are required to complete two-day orientation. Visit Website to submit resume online. Check with school career center to find out when Deloitte & Touche will be visiting campus.
Contact:
Deloitte and Touche
SELECT Internship Program
1633 Broadway
New York, NY 10019-6754
Phone: 212-489-1600
Fax: 212-489-1687
Web: www.deloitte.com

Denver Rescue Mission

Denver Rescue Mission Center for Mission Studies Interns

Type of award: Internship.
Intended use: For undergraduate study in United States.
Basis for selection: Major/career interest in social work; religion/theology; ministry or nonprofit administration. Applicant must demonstrate service orientation.
Additional information: Work in full-service ministry to the needy in Colorado Front Range area, including work with homeless families and children. Applicant must have two years of postsecondary education or be at least 21 years old. Also offers a 10-week Summer Servant Corps. Check with sponsor for pay, college credit opportunity, current openings, and job qualifications.
Contact:
Denver Rescue Mission
P.O. Box 5206
Denver, CO 80217
Phone: 303-297-1815
Web: www.denverrescuemission.org/internships

Dow Jones Newspaper Fund

Business Reporting Intern Program

Type of award: Internship.
Intended use: For full-time sophomore or junior study at 2-year or 4-year institution.
Eligibility: Applicant must be Alaskan native, Asian American, African American, Mexican American, Hispanic American, Puerto Rican or American Indian. Applicant must be U.S. citizen.
Basis for selection: Major/career interest in journalism or business. Applicant must demonstrate high academic achievement and seriousness of purpose.
Application requirements: Essay, transcript, proof of eligibility. Must also take a reporting test.
Additional information: Applications available June 15 to October 20. Finalists notified mid-January. All applicants notified by January 31. Reporting test administered by designated professor on applicant's campus. Telephone interview required for finalists. Paid summer internships as business reporters at daily newspapers last ten to 12 weeks. Interns returning to school receive scholarship at end of summer to apply toward following year. All interns attend pre-internship training that lasts one week. Must submit resume and application form.

Amount of award:	$1,000
Number of awards:	12
Application deadline:	November 1
Total amount awarded:	$12,000

Contact:
Dow Jones Newspaper Fund
Business Reporting Intern Program
P.O. Box 300
Princeton, NJ 08543-0300
Web: newsfund@wsj.dowjones.com

Newspaper Editing Intern Program

Type of award: Internship.
Intended use: For full-time junior, senior or graduate study at 4-year or graduate institution in United States.
Eligibility: Applicant must be U.S. citizen.
Basis for selection: Major/career interest in journalism. Applicant must demonstrate high academic achievement and seriousness of purpose.
Application requirements: Essay, transcript. Resume, application form and editing test.
Additional information: Applications available June 15 to October 25. Finalists notified mid-December. All applicants notified by December 31. Editing test administered by designated professor on applicant's campus. Telephone interview required for finalists. Paid summer internships, as editors at daily newspapers, online newspapers or real-time financial news services, last ten to 12 weeks. Interns returning to school receive scholarship at end of summer to apply toward following year. All interns attend pre-internship training that lasts one to two weeks.

Amount of award:	$1,000
Number of awards:	100
Number of applicants:	600
Application deadline:	November 1

Contact:
Dow Jones Newspaper Fund
Newspaper Editing Intern Program
P.O. Box 300
Princeton, NJ 08543-0300
Web: djnewspaperfund.dowjones.com

E. I. du Pont de Nemours and Company

DuPont Cooperative Education Program

Type of award: Internship.
Intended use: For full-time sophomore, junior or senior study at accredited 4-year institution in United States. Designated institutions: DuPont company sites throughout the U.S.
Eligibility: Applicant must be U.S. citizen or permanent resident.
Basis for selection: Major/career interest in engineering, chemical; engineering, mechanical; engineering, electrical/electronic; science, general; biology; chemistry; information systems; business; accounting or materials science.
Application requirements: Resume and cover letter.
Additional information: Participants alternate work assignments and academic terms. Applicants can start no earlier than after completion of freshman year and work a minimum of three industrial work periods. Preference given to juniors and seniors. Must be registered with school's co-op office. Must have minimum 3.0 GPA. Non-U.S. citizens must have green card; temporary work authorization does not meet eligibility requirements. Contact school co-op office or visit Website to apply.

Contact:
DuPont Resume Processing Center
P.O. Box 540117
Waltham, MA 02453-0177
Fax: 800-978-9774
Web: www.dupont.com/careers

DuPont Internships

Type of award: Internship.
Intended use: For full-time junior or senior study at accredited 4-year institution in United States. Designated institutions: DuPont company sites throughout the United States.
Eligibility: Applicant must be U.S. citizen, permanent resident, international student or Non-U.S. citizens must have green card.
Basis for selection: Major/career interest in engineering, chemical; engineering, mechanical; engineering, electrical/electronic; science, general; biology; chemistry; information systems; business; accounting or computer/information sciences.
Application requirements: Resume and cover letter.
Additional information: Positions available for summer, fall and winter/spring. Preference given to juniors and seniors. May apply for extended internship (summer and fall semester). Must have minimum 3.0 GPA. Non-U.S. citizens must have green card; temporary work authorization does not meet eligibility requirements. Number and amount of awards vary. Visit Website to apply.
Contact:
Apply through Website only.
Web: www.dupont.com/careers

Eastman Kodak Company

Eastman Kodak Cooperative Internship Programs

Type of award: Internship.
Intended use: For full-time sophomore, junior, senior or graduate study.
Eligibility: Applicant must be U.S. citizen or permanent resident.
Basis for selection: Major/career interest in computer/information sciences; engineering; science, general; physics; mathematics; manufacturing or chemistry.
Application requirements: Resume and cover letter.
Additional information: Internship must be minimum of ten consecutive weeks anytime during year (most occur in the summer). Most positions are technical in nature. Internship includes competitive salary based upon discipline and education level, travel expenses, paid holidays and vacation. Assistance in locating housing, health benefits and life insurance available. Applicant must be drug screened as a condition of employment. Minimum GPA 2.8. E-mail resume and cover letter to: staffing@kodak.com (ASCII text only) or apply online at www.kodak.com/go/careers. Applications accepted year-round.
Contact:
Eastman Kodak Company
Staffing, Dept. Attn: CIP
343 State Street
Rochester, NY 14650-1139
Web: www.kodak.com

Eaton Corporation

Eaton Internships

Type of award: Internship.
Intended use: For full-time sophomore, junior or senior study at accredited 4-year institution in United States.
Eligibility: Applicant must be U.S. citizen or permanent resident.
Basis for selection: Major/career interest in engineering; computer/information sciences; information systems; finance/banking or accounting. Applicant must demonstrate high academic achievement.
Additional information: Paid internships available in many departments/locations. Visit Website for list of target schools and recruitment events. Terms vary, summer or year-round. Apply online; application deadline is rolling.
Contact:
Web: www.eatonjobs.com

Elizabeth Dow Ltd.

Elizabeth Dow Internship Program

Type of award: Internship.
Intended use: For undergraduate, graduate or non-degree study.
Eligibility: Applicant must be returning adult student.
Basis for selection: Major/career interest in interior design; arts, general; design or marketing. Applicant must demonstrate seriousness of purpose.
Application requirements: Interview, recommendations. Resume and cover letter.
Additional information: Duration of internship is flexible. Position available as unpaid or at $5.15 per hour minimum. Candidates should have ability to work independently and with others, oral communication skills, personal interest in the field, and self-motivation. Application deadline is rolling, but apply as early as possible for summer. Academic credit available. Current high school students also eligible. Visit Website for more information.

Number of awards:	45
Number of applicants:	450

Contact:
Elizabeth Dow Ltd. Attn: Xavier Santana
155 6th Avenue, 4th Floor
New York, NY 10013
Fax: 212-463-0824
Web: www.elizabethdow.com/internships.html

Elizabeth Glaser Pediatric AIDS Foundation

Elizabeth Glaser Pediatric AIDS Foundation Student Intern Award

Type of award: Internship.
Intended use: For undergraduate or graduate study.
Eligibility: Applicant must be high school senior.

Internships

Basis for selection: Major/career interest in medical specialties/research. Applicant must demonstrate seriousness of purpose.

Application requirements: Nomination by research sponsor. Sponsor (M.D., Ph.D., C.C.S.W.) must have pediatric HIV/AIDS research experience. Applicant must demonstrate seriousness of purpose in pediatric research.

Additional information: This program is to encourage students to choose career in pediatric HIV/AIDS research. Provides $2,000 for 320 hours of work. Students must work minimum of four hours per week. High school seniors, undergraduates, graduates and medical students are eligible. Applications available in January. See Website for applications and deadlines.

Amount of award:	$2,000
Number of awards:	50
Number of applicants:	91
Total amount awarded:	$100,000

Contact:
Elizabeth Glaser Pediatric AIDS Foundation
2950 31st Street
Suite 125
Santa Monica, CA 90405
Phone: 310-314-1459
Fax: 310-314-1469
Web: www.pedaids.org

EMC

EMC Summer Internship Program and Co-ops

Type of award: Internship.

Intended use: For full-time undergraduate study at accredited 4-year institution.

Eligibility: Applicant must be U.S. citizen or permanent resident.

Basis for selection: Major/career interest in accounting; engineering; finance/banking; human resources; manufacturing; marketing; computer/information sciences; computer/information sciences or engineering, computer. Applicant must demonstrate high academic achievement.

Application requirements: Send resume. Must be committed to the duration of the assignment. Minimum 3.0 GPA.

Additional information: Offering both co-op and summer internship positions, EMC's program is designed to provide a challenging learning experience. Three-, six- and eight-month co-op positions available throughout year for eligible students. Summer intern program begins in June and runs through August. Deadline for summer internships is April 1. Submit resume to university@emc.com. Visit Website for more information.

Contact:
EMC University Relations
176 South Street
Hopkinton, MA 01748
Phone: 508-435-1000
Web: www.emc.com

Entergy

Entergy Jumpstart Co-ops and Internships

Type of award: Internship, renewable.

Intended use: For full-time undergraduate or graduate study at accredited 4-year or graduate institution in United States.

Eligibility: Applicant must be U.S. citizen or permanent resident.

Basis for selection: Major/career interest in engineering; business; accounting; computer/information sciences; human resources; engineering, electrical/electronic; engineering, mechanical; engineering, nuclear; information systems or finance/banking. Applicant must demonstrate high academic achievement and depth of character.

Application requirements: Minimum 3.0 GPA.

Additional information: Visit Website for list of targeted campuses in the South, recruiting schedule and current openings. Undergraduate and graduate co-ops and internships available. Rolling application deadline. Apply online or e-mail resume to college@entergy.com.

Contact:
Phone: 800-368-3749
Web: www.entergy.com

Entertainment Weekly

Entertainment Weekly Internship

Type of award: Internship.

Intended use: For junior, senior or graduate study at postsecondary institution.

Basis for selection: Major/career interest in journalism or publishing. Applicant must demonstrate seriousness of purpose.

Application requirements: Resume, cover letter and four to five previously published clips.

Additional information: Opportunities to work in editorial, photo and design departments. Internship lasts 12-18 weeks and pays $10/hour. Overtime available. Summer deadline is February 15. Fall and spring internships for graduate students only. Summer internships open to rising seniors and recent graduates.

Number of awards:	5
Number of applicants:	400
Application deadline:	February 15, June 15

Contact:
Entertainment Weekly Internship Coordinator
1675 Broadway
New York, NY 10019
Phone: 212-522-5558
Fax: 212-522-6104

Internships

The Environmental Careers Organization

Hydrographic Systems and Technology Associate Internship

Type of award: Internship.
Intended use: For full-time sophomore, junior or senior study at 4-year institution.
Eligibility: Applicant must be U.S. citizen.
Basis for selection: Major/career interest in computer/ information sciences. Applicant must demonstrate seriousness of purpose.
Application requirements: GPA should be in upper one-third of class.
Additional information: Applicant must have a demonstrated technical background-not necessarily having "Computer Science" as a declared major. Applicant should have experience operating boats, navigating with charts, have knowledge of a programming language, preferably C, C++, or Python, and have an interest in organizing information. This is a full-time paid internship that lasts for 52 weeks. Possibility for travel to a NOAA hydrographic ship exists, but is not required. Visit Website for more information.

> **Amount of award:** $32,000
> **Application deadline:** December 20

Contact:
The Environmental Careers Organization
179 South Street
5th Floor
Boston, MA 02111
Phone: 617-426-4375
Fax: 617-423-0998
Web: www.eco.org

Remote Sensing Research Engineer Internship

Type of award: Internship.
Intended use: For full-time undergraduate certificate, sophomore, junior or senior study at 4-year institution.
Eligibility: Applicant must be U.S. citizen.
Basis for selection: Major/career interest in environmental science. Applicant must demonstrate seriousness of purpose.
Additional information: Applicant must have at least one year experience in the analysis of advanced remote sensing technologies. Visit Website for more information.

> **Amount of award:** $37,000
> **Application deadline:** February 28

Contact:
The Environemntal Careers Organization
179 South Street
5th Floor
Boston, MA 02111
Phone: 617-426-4375 xt. 131
Fax: 617-423-0998
Web: www.ego.org

ESPN Inc.

ESPN Internship

Type of award: Internship.
Intended use: For full-time junior or senior study.
Eligibility: Applicant must be U.S. citizen.
Basis for selection: Major/career interest in journalism; communications; radio/television/film; graphic arts/design; marketing; accounting; business; computer/information sciences or sports/sports administration. Applicant must demonstrate high academic achievement.
Application requirements: Resume and cover letter.
Additional information: Sports knowledge/interest/ participation highly desirable. ESPN will assist interns in finding housing. Interns receive $8 per hour. Application deadlines: March 1 for summer; June 1 for fall; November 1 for spring. Applicants should submit a resume and cover letter.

> **Number of awards:** 30
> **Number of applicants:** 1,000
> **Application deadline:** March 1

Contact:
ESPN Inc.
Program Manager of College Relations
935 Middle Street
Bristol, CT 06010
Phone: 860-766-2000

Essence Magazine

Essence Summer Internship

Type of award: Internship, renewable.
Intended use: For senior study at 2-year or 4-year institution in United States.
Eligibility: Applicant must be African American or Hispanic American. Applicant must be U.S. citizen.
Basis for selection: Major/career interest in publishing; literature; advertising or graphic arts/design. Applicant must demonstrate depth of character.
Application requirements: Interview.
Additional information: This six-week summer internship is open to college seniors. Interns receive training in one of several departments: sales and marketing, Essence.com, fashion and beauty, graphics, public relations or editorial. Interns responsible for their travel, housing, food and personal expenses. Visit Website for application and more information.

> **Application deadline:** December 27
> **Notification begins:** March 1

Contact:
Essence Magazine
1500 Broadway, Suite 600
New York, NY 10036
Phone: 212-642-0600
Web: www.essence.com

Internships

Federal Bureau of Investigation

Honors Internship Program

Type of award: Internship, renewable.
Intended use: For full-time junior, senior or graduate study at accredited 4-year or graduate institution in United States.
Eligibility: Applicant must be U.S. citizen.
Basis for selection: Major/career interest in criminal justice/ law enforcement. Applicant must demonstrate high academic achievement, depth of character, leadership and seriousness of purpose.
Application requirements: Interview, recommendations, essay, transcript, proof of eligibility. Application form and background survey. Two current professional photographs.
Additional information: Graduate students must be attending school full time. All students must be returning to their respective schools for at least one semester immediately following internship. Positions available in Washington, D.C., Virginia and Maryland. Deadline for application submission is November 1, but application process must start in July or August to complete necessary vetting. Individuals selected based on how their specific skills and educational background meet current FBI needs. Must have minumum 3.0 GPA. Must be able to pass extensive background check and drug test. Visit closest FBI field office for application packet or see Website for more information.
   Application deadline: November 1
Contact:
Federal Bureau of Investigation
J. Edgar Hoover Building
935 Pennsylvania Avenue, N.W.
Washington, DC 20535-0001
Phone: 202-324-3000
Web: www.fbi.gov

Federal Reserve Bank of New York

Federal Reserve Undergraduate Summer Analyst Program

Type of award: Internship.
Intended use: For full-time undergraduate study.
Eligibility: Applicant must be U.S. citizen, permanent resident, international student or legally authorized to work in the U.S. on a multi-year basis.
Basis for selection: Major/career interest in finance/banking; economics or business. Applicant must demonstrate high academic achievement.
Application requirements: Interview, transcript. Cover letter, resume, and writing sample.
Additional information: Paid internships begin in May/June. Applicants should have completed junior year of college before beginning internship. Opportunities available in bank supervision and regulation, domestic and international research, information technology services, markets, and operations. Applicants must be available for in-bank interviews in March/ April. Housing not provided.
   Application deadline: January 31

Contact:
Federal Reserve Bank of New York
Summer Internship Coordinator
33 Liberty Street, 26th Floor
New York, NY 10045
Phone: 212-720-5000
Web: www.ny.frb.org/careers/summerintern.html

Federated Department Stores, Inc.

Federated Department Stores Internships

Type of award: Internship, renewable.
Intended use: For full-time undergraduate study.
Basis for selection: Major/career interest in marketing; business or retailing/merchandising. Applicant must demonstrate high academic achievement.
Application requirements: Resume.
Additional information: May apply online. Visit Website for additional information and campus recruiting schedule.
Contact:
Federated Department Stores, Inc.
7 West Seventh Street
Cincinnatti, OH 45202
Phone: 212-695-4400
Web: www.retailology.com/internships

Feminist Majority Foundation

Feminist Web Internship

Type of award: Internship.
Intended use: For full-time undergraduate study.
Basis for selection: Major/career interest in women's studies; computer graphics; public administration/service or computer/ information sciences. Applicant must demonstrate leadership.
Application requirements: Resume and cover letter. Samples of writing and Web work. Two letters of recommendation.
Additional information: Full-time internships, which run for minimum of two months, are available year-round in Washington, DC, area. Part-time internships are also available during the spring and fall. Interns learn about online activism strategies and contribute to organization's online presence. Internships are unpaid, but students may have opportunity to earn small stipend in exchange for administrative work. Applicants with experience in women's issues and Website design or online activism preferred. People of color, people with disabilities and math/science majors encouraged to apply. Applications processed on rolling basis. Visit Website for more information.

Internships

Contact:
Feminist Majority Foundation
Information Technology Director
1600 Wilson Boulevard, Suite 801
Arlington, VA 22209
Phone: 703-522-2214
Fax: 703-522-2219
Web: www.feminist.org/intern

Internship in Feminism and Public Policy

Type of award: Internship.
Intended use: For full-time undergraduate study at accredited 4-year institution.
Basis for selection: Major/career interest in law; public relations; social/behavioral sciences; women's studies or political science/government. Applicant must demonstrate leadership.
Application requirements: Resume, cover letter, writing sample (three to five pages on topic pertinent to women's issues), two letters of recommendation.
Additional information: Full-time internships, which run for a minimum of two months, are available year-round in Washington, DC, area and Los Angeles. Part-time internships are also available during the spring and fall. Interns are given a wide variety of responsibilities, such as monitoring press conferences and public hearings, researching, writing, analyzing policies, and organizing events and demonstrations. Internships are unpaid, but students may have opportunity to earn small stipend in exchange for administrative work. Applicants with experience working on women's issues preferred. People of color, people with disabilities, and math/science majors encouraged to apply. Applications processed on rolling basis. See Website for more information.
Contact:
Feminist Majority Foundation
1600 Wilson Boulevard, Suite 801
Arlington, VA 22209
Phone: 703-522-2214
Fax: 703-522-2219
Web: www.feminist.org/intern

Filoli Center

Filoli Center Garden Internship

Type of award: Internship.
Intended use: For undergraduate, graduate or non-degree study. Designated institutions: Filoli Center.
Basis for selection: Major/career interest in horticulture; landscape architecture or botany. Applicant must demonstrate depth of character, leadership and seriousness of purpose.
Application requirements: Interview, recommendations, transcript. Cover letter outlining interests.
Additional information: Internships designed for students pursuing career in horticulture, public garden management, landscape maintenance or landscape architecture. Techniques of planting, watering, hedging, fertilizing, mowing and pruning; operation of power equipment; and use of hand tools taught. Interns required to learn garden and greenhouse plants, weeds and native plants. Students paid $8 per hour and may earn college credits for ten-week program. Applicants must have at least 15 units of horticulture classes, 3.0 GPA. Ability to work

well with public and work teams essential. Application deadline for summer internship is March 31.

Amount of award:	$3,200
Number of awards:	15
Application deadline:	July 16
Total amount awarded:	$48,000

Contact:
Filoli Center
Filoli Garden Internships
86 Cañada Road
Woodside, CA 94062
Phone: 650-364-8300 ext. 214
Web: www.filoli.org

Florida Department of Education

Florida Work Experience Program

Type of award: Internship, renewable.
Intended use: For undergraduate study at 2-year or 4-year institution. Designated institutions: Eligible Florida postsecondary institutions.
Eligibility: Applicant must be U.S. citizen or permanent resident residing in Florida.
Basis for selection: Applicant must demonstrate financial need.
Application requirements: Proof of eligibility. Submit FAFSA. Minimum 2.0 GPA.
Additional information: Provides students with opportunity to be employed off campus in jobs related to their academic major or area of career interest. Applications available from participating universities' financial aid offices. Amount of award determined by institution's financial aid office, and may not exceed student's financial need.
Contact:
Florida Department of Education
Office of Student Financial Assistance
1940 North Monroe Street, Suite 70
Tallahassee, FL 32303-4759
Phone: 888-827-2004
Web: www.FloridaStudentFinancialAid.org

Florida Power & Light Company

Florida Power & Light Co-op Program

Type of award: Internship, renewable.
Intended use: For full-time undergraduate or graduate study at accredited 4-year or graduate institution in United States.
Eligibility: Applicant must be U.S. citizen or permanent resident.
Basis for selection: Major/career interest in engineering; engineering, nuclear; engineering, mechanical; engineering, electrical/electronic or engineering, civil. Applicant must demonstrate high academic achievement.
Application requirements: Resume.

Additional information: Industrial Engineering majors also eligible. For more information contact designated institution's Cooperative Education Coordinator or write Florida Power & Light's Co-op Coordinator at sponsor address.
Contact:
Florida Power & Light Company
College Coordinator
P. O. Box 14000, HRR/JB
Juno Beach, FL 33408-0420
Phone: 561-694-6349
Fax: 561-694-4669
Web: www.fpl.com

Forbes Magazine

Forbes Internship

Type of award: Internship.
Intended use: For undergraduate or graduate study.
Eligibility: Applicant must be U.S. citizen.
Basis for selection: Major/career interest in business or journalism. Applicant must demonstrate depth of character.
Application requirements: Interview. Resume and cover letter.
Additional information: All applicants must be flexible. This is a floating internship program where interns have the opportunity to see different aspects of publishing. Interns rotate through different departments and seminars about publishing. Interns paid $8 to $10 per hour for 35-hour work week during summer. Applicants living in New York metro area preferred. Contact sponsor for further information.
   Application deadline: March 31
Contact:
Internship Coordinator
Forbes Magazine
60 Fifth Avenue
New York, NY 10011

Franklin D. Roosevelt Library

Franklin D. Roosevelt Library/ Roosevelt Summer Internship

Type of award: Internship.
Intended use: For undergraduate or graduate study.
Basis for selection: Major/career interest in computer/ information sciences; museum studies; history or political science/government.
Application requirements: Transcript. Application and resume required. Some familiarity with FDR presidency helpful.
Additional information: Interns work at FDR library with other interns and staff organizing archival materials, making indices, finding aids and databases, digitizing documents and photographs, and assisting with other projects. Internship can last six or seven weeks and must take place during summer break (mid-May through end of August). FDR Library is in Hyde Park, NY, 80 miles north of NYC. Housing not provided. Work Monday through Friday, 9 am to 5 pm. Stipend of $250/ week for summer interns, academic credit for fall and spring. Number of awards depends on funding.
   Application deadline: April 15
Contact:
Franklin D. Roosevelt Library
4079 Albany Post Road
Hyde Park, NY 12538
Phone: 845-486-7745
Fax: 845-486-1147

Gannett Company

Pulliam Journalism Fellowship

Type of award: Internship.
Intended use: For sophomore, junior or senior study at 4-year institution.
Basis for selection: Major/career interest in journalism. Applicant must demonstrate seriousness of purpose.
Additional information: The Pulliam Journalism Fellowship is a solid, 30-year-old program that boasts four Pulitzer Prize winners among its alumni. Fellows are assigned to The Indianapolis Star or The Arizona Republic in Pheonix for 10 weeks as staff reporters. Visit Website for more information.
   Number of awards: 20
   Application deadline: March 1, November 15
Contact:
Pulliam Journalism Fellowship Attn: Russell B. Pulliam, Director
P.O. Box 145
Indianapolis, IN 46206-0145
Phone: 317-444-6001
Fax: 317-444-6750
Web: http://www.indystar.com/pjf

Genentech, Inc.

Genentech Internship Program

Type of award: Internship, renewable.
Intended use: For full-time junior or senior study at accredited 4-year institution.
Eligibility: Applicant must be U.S. citizen, permanent resident, international student or Foreign students must be legally authorized to work in United States.
Basis for selection: Major/career interest in biology; chemistry; engineering, chemical; computer/information sciences or life sciences. Applicant must demonstrate high academic achievement.
Application requirements: Resume and cover letter.
Additional information: Internships paid by competitive monthly stipend and membership at health club. Students majoring in biochemical engineering also eligible. Apply online or send resume and cover letter by mail.
   Application deadline: February 14
Contact:
Genentech College Programs
1 DNA Way MS 39A
South San Francisco, CA 94080
Phone: 650-225-1000
Web: www.gene.com

General Mills

General Mills Summer Internship

Type of award: Internship, renewable.
Intended use: For sophomore, junior or senior study.
Eligibility: Applicant must be U.S. citizen.
Basis for selection: Major/career interest in marketing; advertising; food science/technology or engineering.
Application requirements: Interview. Resume.
Additional information: Visit Website for more information and to submit resume.
Contact:
Internship Coordinator
P.O. Box 1113
Minneapolis, MN 55440
Phone: 763-764-2505
Web: www.generalmills.com

General Motors North America

General Motors Corporation Talent Acquisition Internship

Type of award: Internship, renewable.
Intended use: For full-time sophomore, junior, senior or master's study at accredited 4-year or graduate institution.
Basis for selection: Major/career interest in engineering or business. Applicant must demonstrate high academic achievement and leadership.
Application requirements: Interview, transcript. Resume.
Additional information: Co-ops and paid internships available. Salary varies with job, skills and degree/program of study. Temporary, full-time positions during semester break, three months in summer. Visit Website for details or to submit resume. For Saturn Corp. and other GM divisions, see Website or contact sponsor. In most cases, applicant must have completed freshman year of study to be eligible.
Contact:
General Motors North America
200 Renaissance Center
MC: 482-BO9-D46
Detroit, MI 48265
Web: www.gm.com/careers

Georgia-Pacific Corporation

Georgia-Pacific Internships and Co-ops

Type of award: Internship, renewable.
Intended use: For undergraduate study in United States.
Eligibility: Applicant must be U.S. citizen or permanent resident.
Basis for selection: Major/career interest in accounting; computer/information sciences; communications; engineering; forestry; human resources or marketing. Applicant must demonstrate high academic achievement.

Application requirements: Transcript, proof of eligibility.
Additional information: Must have minimum 2.5 GPA, or minimum 3.0 GPA for accounting majors. Internships and co-ops are paid, and number awarded varies. Submit resume through Website form or by using "job search" feature.
Contact:
Georgia Pacific Corporation
Attn: College Relations
133 Peachtree Street, N.E.
Atlanta, GA 30303
Phone: 404-652-4000
Fax: 404-584-1481
Web: www.gp.com/careers

Hallmark Cards

Hallmark Internship Program

Type of award: Internship.
Intended use: For full-time senior or master's study.
Eligibility: Applicant must be permanent resident.
Basis for selection: Applicant must demonstrate high academic achievement, leadership experience and excellent interpersonal and communication skills. Applicant must demonstrate high academic achievement, depth of character and leadership.
Application requirements: Interview, recommendations, transcript. Resume and cover letter.
Additional information: Internships open to students entering final year of graduate or undergraduate program. Applicants must have experience and excellent interpersonal and communications skills. Open to all majors. Program seeks to create pool of qualified candidates to be considered for full-time employment.
  Number of awards: 30
  Application deadline: January 15
Contact:
Internship Coordinator
Mail Drop #112
P.O. Box 419580
Kansas City, MO 64141

Hannaford Bros Co.

Hannaford Internships

Type of award: Internship.
Intended use: For undergraduate study. Designated institutions: Albany College of Pharmacy, University of Connecticut, University of Rhode Island, Massachusetts College of Pharmacy, Northeastern University, Virginia College of Medicine, University of No. Carolina, Campbell University, Hampton University.
Eligibility: Applicant must be U.S. citizen, permanent resident, international student or Foreign students must be legally authorized to work in United States.
Basis for selection: Major/career interest in pharmacy/pharmaceutics/pharmacology; marketing; retailing/merchandising or accounting.
Application requirements: Submit cover letter and resume.
Additional information: Interns at Hannaford are exposed to a multicultural organization with support systems and training

Internships

opportunities. Internships available at Hannaford's corporate offices, retail locations and distribution facilities. Inquire at campus placement office to schedule recruiting interview or e-mail sponsor (working@hannaford.com) for additional information. Must be legally authorized to work in United States. Amount of payment or course credit awarded varies. Visit Website for additional information.

Application deadline: March 1
Contact:
Hannaford Brothers Company
P.O. Box 1000
Mail Sort #7700
Portland, ME 04104
Phone: 800-442-6049
Fax: 207-885-2859
Web: www.hannaford.com

Hartford Life

The Hartford Life Internship and Co-op Opportunities

Type of award: Internship.
Intended use: For full-time junior or senior study at accredited 4-year institution.
Basis for selection: Major/career interest in accounting; business; information systems; computer/information sciences; insurance/actuarial science or finance/banking. Applicant must demonstrate seriousness of purpose.
Application requirements: Interview. Resume and cover letter.
Additional information: Must have completed sophomore year, be enrolled in school's formal co-op or intern program, possess a 3.0 GPA. Paid, course credit. Co-op positions offered twice yearly in six-month assignments: January through June (recruiting starts in mid-October) and June through December (recruiting starts in mid-April). Summer internships run from late May through late August. Visit Website for schedules and to submit resume.
Contact:
Hartford Life
200 Hopmeadow Street
Simsbury, CT 06089
Web: www.thehartford.com

Hispanic Association of Colleges and Universities

HACU National Internship Program

Type of award: Internship.
Intended use: For sophomore, junior, senior or graduate study at 2-year, 4-year or graduate institution. Designated institutions: Institutions with significant numbers of Hispanic students.
Eligibility: Applicant must be Mexican American, Hispanic American or Puerto Rican. Applicant must be U.S. citizen or permanent resident.
Basis for selection: Applicant must demonstrate high academic achievement and service orientation.

Application requirements: Essay, transcript. Application, professional-level resume, certificate of enrollment and class level, minimum 3.0 GPA, 250-500 word essay.
Additional information: Paid internships provide opportunities for students from institutions with significant numbers of Hispanic students to explore potential careers with federal agencies and private corporations. Interns work in Washington, DC, area and field sites throughout country. Some internships require U.S. citizenship to participate. Applicants must have completed freshman year of college before internship begins. Weekly pay varies according to class level: $420 for sophomores and juniors, $450 for seniors and $520 for graduates. Must be active in college and community service. Fall and spring internships last 15 weeks; summer internships last ten weeks. Deadlines: November 7 for spring, February 27 for summer, June 11 for fall. Visit website for application and list of assignments.
Contact:
Hispanic Association of Colleges and Universities
One Dupont Circle, NW
Suite 605
Washington, DC 20036
Phone: 202-467-0893
Fax: 202-496-9177
Web: www.hnip.net

Hispanic Scholarship Fund

Partnership and Internship Programs

Type of award: Internship, renewable.
Intended use: For full-time undergraduate or graduate study at accredited 4-year or graduate institution in or outside United States.
Eligibility: Applicant must be Mexican American, Hispanic American or Puerto Rican. Applicants must be of Hispanic heritage (one parent fully Hispanic or each parent half Hispanic): Cuban, Caribbean, Central American, South American, Puerto Rican, Mexican American, Spanish. Applicant must be U.S. citizen or permanent resident.
Basis for selection: Applicant must demonstrate high academic achievement.
Application requirements: Recommendations, essay, transcript, proof of eligibility. Completed application. Copy of Permanent Resident card or passport stamped I-551. Student Aid Report (SAR), Financial Aid Award letter, Enrollment Verification (update applicants only).
Additional information: All applicants must have earned minimum of 12 undergraduate college credits in United States, Puerto Rico, or U.S. Virgin Islands. Minimum 3.0 GPA. Students enrolled in study-abroad program at U.S. accredited college or university also eligible. Numerous programs available; visit Website for more information.
Application deadline: October 31
Contact:
Hispanic Scholarship Fund
55 Second Street
Suite 1500
San Francisco, CA 94105
Phone: 877-HSF-INFO
Fax: 415-808-2302
Web: www.hsf.net

Internships

Hoffman-La Roche Inc.

Hoffman-La Roche Inc. Student Internship

Type of award: Internship.
Intended use: For full-time freshman, sophomore, junior or graduate study. Designated institutions: Carnegie Mellon, Fuqua, Johnson School, Rutgers, Yale.
Basis for selection: Major/career interest in pharmacy/pharmaceutics/pharmacology; engineering; computer/information sciences; science, general; business or business/management/administration.
Application requirements: Interview. Cover letter, resume.
Additional information: Applicant must be authorized to work in the United States. Internship fields, topics, and amount of awards vary. Inexpensive housing arranged through local college dormitory. Applicant must be attending one of Roche's target schools. Send materials to address provided. If deadline is missed, application will be considered after those students who have met deadline.

Application deadline:	February 15
Notification begins:	April 16

Contact:
University Relations Department Hoffman-La Roche, Inc.
340 Kingsland Street
Nutley, NJ 07110-1199
Phone: 973-235-5000
Web: www.rocheusa.com

IBM

IBM Employment Pathways for Interns and Co-ops Program

Type of award: Internship.
Intended use: For full-time sophomore, junior, senior or graduate study at accredited 4-year or graduate institution in United States.
Basis for selection: Revelant work or research experience, communication and team skills, high evaluation during interview process. Major/career interest in computer/information sciences; engineering, computer; engineering, electrical/electronic; information systems; accounting or finance/banking. Applicant must demonstrate high academic achievement and leadership.
Application requirements: Interview.
Additional information: IBM offers part-time internships for students near IBM facilities, 20 hours per week maximum. Multiple assignments may be available. Applicants chosen on competitive basis and hired on semester basis. Must submit resume via IBM Website.
Contact:
IBM EPIC Program
1DPA Source Code IBMNICSMR
3808 Six Forks Road
Raleigh, NC 27609
Web: www.ibm.com/careers/us

The Indianapolis Star, a Gannett Newspaper

Pulliam Journalism Fellowship

Type of award: Internship.
Intended use: For undergraduate or postgraduate study.
Basis for selection: Competition/talent/interest in writing/journalism. Major/career interest in humanities/liberal arts or journalism. Applicant must demonstrate high academic achievement, depth of character, leadership and seriousness of purpose.
Application requirements: Portfolio, recommendations, essay, transcript, proof of eligibility. Application. Writing samples. Photograph. Three letters of recommendation. 400- to 600-word editorial.
Additional information: Fellowship lasts ten weeks during summer. Ten recipients work for The Indianapolis Star, ten for The Arizona Republic in Phoenix. Applicants must be college students. Early deadline in November; final postmark deadline in March. Go to Website for application and more information.

Amount of award:	$6,500
Number of awards:	20
Number of applicants:	140
Application deadline:	March 1
Notification begins:	April 1

Contact:
Russell B. Pulliam, Director
The Pulliam Fellowship
P.O. Box 145
Indianapolis, IN 46206-0145
Phone: 317-444-6001
Web: www.starnews.com/pjf

INROADS, Inc.

INROADS Internship

Type of award: Internship, renewable.
Intended use: For full-time freshman or sophomore study.
Eligibility: Applicant must be Alaskan native, Asian American, African American, Mexican American, Hispanic American, Puerto Rican or American Indian.
Basis for selection: Major/career interest in engineering; business; computer/information sciences; communications; retailing/merchandising or health-related professions. Applicant must demonstrate high academic achievement, leadership and service orientation.
Application requirements: Interview, essay, transcript. Minimum high school 3.0 GPA or college 2.8 GPA; minimum 1000 SAT or 20 ACT. Resume, application required.
Additional information: Internship duration and compensation varies. Visit Website for additional information. Deadline varies according to local affiliate office.

Number of awards:	6,600
Number of applicants:	30,000

Contact:
INROADS, Inc.
10 S. Broadway
Suite 700
St. Louis, MO 63102
Phone: 314-241-7488
Fax: 314-241-9325
Web: www.inroads.org

Interns for Peace

Interns for Peace Internship

Type of award: Internship, renewable.
Intended use: For non-degree study in Israel.
Eligibility: Applicant must be Arab or Jewish.
Basis for selection: Competition/talent/interest in study abroad. Major/career interest in Middle Eastern studies or peace studies. Applicant must demonstrate depth of character, seriousness of purpose and service orientation.
Application requirements: Interview, recommendations, essay, proof of eligibility.
Additional information: Open to persons of either Arab or Jewish descent. Two-year internship on ethnic conflict resolution in assigned community in Israel for Jews, Israeli Arabs and Arabs. Must have knowledge of and commitment to furthering Jewish-Arab relations. Must have B.A., M.A. or equivalent; prior residence in Israel for six months; proficiency in advanced level Hebrew or Arabic; some previous work experience. Salary approximately $500 per month plus housing and health benefits. Internship begins in fall; applications accepted year-round. Travel expenses responsibility of intern.

Number of awards:	2
Number of applicants:	180

Contact:
Interns for Peace
475 Riverside Drive
2nd Floor
New York, NY 10115

J. Paul Getty Trust

Getty Multicultural Undergraduate Internships

Type of award: Internship.
Intended use: For full-time undergraduate study at 4-year institution.
Eligibility: Applicant must be Asian American, African American, Mexican American, Hispanic American, Puerto Rican or American Indian.
Basis for selection: Major/career interest in arts management; communications; humanities/liberal arts; architecture; museum studies/administration or art/art history.
Application requirements: Interview, recommendations, transcript. Application, which is available online or from Grant Program office.
Additional information: Ten-week internship in specific departments of Getty Museum and other programs located at the Getty Center in Los Angeles. Limited to students attending school in or residing in Los Angeles County. Intended for outstanding students who are members of groups currently underrepresented in museum professions and fields related to visual arts and humanities. Applicants must have completed at least one semester of college by June and not be graduating before December. Housing and transportation not included. Applications accepted in December, and applicants notified of acceptance in early May.

Amount of award:	$3,500
Number of awards:	16
Number of applicants:	124
Application deadline:	March 1

Contact:
The Getty Grant Program
Multicultural Undergraduate Internships
1200 Getty Center, Suite 800
Los Angeles, CA 90049-1685
Phone: (310) 440-7320
Fax: (310) 440-7703
Web: www.getty.edu/grants/education

Getty Multicultural Undergraduate Internships at Los Angeles Area Museums and Visual Arts Organizations

Type of award: Internship.
Intended use: For full-time undergraduate study at 4-year institution.
Eligibility: Applicant must be Asian American, African American, Mexican American, Hispanic American, Puerto Rican or American Indian.
Basis for selection: Major/career interest in art/art history; arts management; museum studies/administration; humanities/liberal arts; architecture; communications or parks/recreation.
Application requirements: Interview, recommendations, transcript. Apply directly to participating organizations for available positions.
Additional information: Ten-week internship at Los Angeles area museums and visual arts organizations. Applicant must be currently enrolled undergraduate who either resides in or attends college in Los Angeles County. Organizations will be seeking eligible interns for summer during April and May. Intended specifically for outstanding students who are members of groups currently underrepresented in museum professions and fields related to visual arts and humanities. Pacific Islanders also eligible. Applicants must have completed at least one semester of college by June and not be graduating before December. Housing and transportation not included. Finalists contacted in mid-April for in-person or telephone interviews. All applicants notified of Grant Program's decision in early May.

Amount of award:	$3,500

Contact:
The Getty Grant Program
1200 Getty Center Drive
Suite 800
Los Angeles, CA 90049-1685
Phone: 310-440-7320
Fax: 310-440-7703
Web: www.getty.edu/grants/education

Internships

Jeppesen Dataplan

Jeppesen Meteorology Internship

Type of award: Internship.
Intended use: For non-degree study.
Basis for selection: Major/career interest in atmospheric sciences/meteorology.
Application requirements: Resume.
Additional information: Meteorology internship available all year. Salary $8 to $10 per hour. Must be enrolled in accredited meteorology degree program. Ideally, applicant is a junior.

Number of awards: 1
Contact:
Jeppesen Dataplan
Attn: Judy Graun, Human Resources
121 Albright Way
Los Gatos, CA 95032
Phone: 408-866-7611
Web: judy_graun@jeppesen.com

Jeppesen Meterology Internship

Type of award: Internship.
Intended use: For full-time junior study at accredited 4-year institution.
Basis for selection: Major/career interest in geography; atmospheric sciences/meteorology or aviation.
Application requirements: Resume. 2.5 to 3.0 GPA.
Additional information: Part-time internship available all year, up to 20 hours per week. Salary $8 to $10 per hour. Must be enrolled in accredited degree program. Ideally, applicant is a junior. Number of awards granted varies.
Contact:
Jeppesen Dataplan
225 West Santa Clara Street
Suite 1600
San Jose, CA 95113
Phone: 408-961-2825
Web: www.jeppesen.com

John Deere

John Deere Student Training Programs

Type of award: Internship.
Intended use: For full-time undergraduate or graduate study at accredited 2-year, 4-year or graduate institution.
Eligibility: Applicant must be U.S. citizen or permanent resident.
Basis for selection: Major/career interest in accounting; finance/banking; human resources; health services administration; engineering; information systems or marketing. Applicant must demonstrate high academic achievement.
Application requirements: Recommendations.
Additional information: Deere and Company offers paid internships, course credit and academic scholarships through Student Training Program. Applicants may also be interested/majoring in supply management and credit. Open to all levels of undergraduates; graduate students may also be eligible. Apply through Career Section on Website. Co-op applicants must be enrolled undergraduates and meet academic

requirement. Number and amount of awards vary. For co-ops, students must apply through and be recommended by Cooperative Education Office at college/university.
Contact:
Recruitment Coordinator
Deere and Company
One John Deere Place
Moline, IL 61265
Phone: 309-765-8000
Web: www.deere.com

The John F. Kennedy Center for the Performing Arts

Vilar Institute for Arts Management Internship

Type of award: Internship.
Intended use: For junior, senior or post-bachelor's certificate study at accredited 4-year or graduate institution.
Basis for selection: Major/career interest in arts management.
Application requirements: Recommendations, transcript. Cover letter stating career goals. Two letters of recommendation. Resume and writing sample.
Additional information: Interns receive $800 stipend per month to defray housing and transportation costs. College credit may be available. Interns attend weekly sessions led by executives of Kennedy Center and other major arts institutions in Washington, D.C. Interns may attend performances, workshops, classes and courses presented by center, free of charge (space available), during their internship. Applicant must have a minimum of 830 on the SAT and 17 on the ACT. Application deadline for fall, June 15; winter/spring, November 1; summer, March 1. Visit Website for application and more information.

Number of awards: 40
Number of applicants: 800
Application deadline: June 15, November 1
Contact:
Vilar Institute for Arts Management/Internships
2700 F Street N.W
Washington, DC 20566
Phone: 202-416-8821
Fax: 202-416-8853
Web: www.kennedy-center.org/vilarinstitute/internships

John F. Kennedy Library Foundation

Kennedy Library Archival Internship

Type of award: Internship.
Intended use: For undergraduate or graduate study at 4-year or graduate institution.
Eligibility: Applicant must be U.S. citizen or permanent resident.
Basis for selection: Major/career interest in history; political science/government; library science; English; journalism;

Internships

communications or museum studies. Applicant must demonstrate high academic achievement.

Application requirements: Interview, recommendations, transcript.

Additional information: Minimum 12 hours per week, $11 per hour. Provides intern with opportunity to work on projects such as preservation of papers of Kennedy and his administration. Interns given career-relevant archival experience. Limited number of additional internships may open up during fall, winter and spring. Library considers proposals for unpaid internships, independent study, work-study and internships undertaken for academic credit. See Website for application and more information.

Application deadline:	February 28
Notification begins:	April 1

Contact:
Archival Internships c/o Intern Coordinator
John F. Kennedy Library
Columbia Point
Boston, MA 02125-3313
Phone: 617-514-1624
Fax: 617-514-1625
Web: www.jfklibrary.org

John Wiley and Sons, Inc.

John Wiley and Sons, Inc, Internship Program

Type of award: Internship.
Intended use: For junior or senior study at 4-year institution.
Basis for selection: Major/career interest in marketing; publishing; information systems or public relations.
Application requirements: Resume. Letter addressing why applicant would like to be selected for the program and his/her areas of interest.
Additional information: Internship programs available year-round. Summer program offers weekly stipend and runs from mid-June through mid-August. Summer internship applications due by February 15. Internships available in marketing, editorial, production, information technology, new media, customer service and publicity; based at corporate offices in Hoboken and Somerset in New Jersey; Indianapolis, Indiana; and San Francisco, California. Those interested in interning in Somerset should email cgagas@wiley.com; for San Francisco e-mail jobs@josseybass.com; for Hoboken or Indianapolis e-mail opportunities@wiley.com.

Application deadline:	February 15

Contact:
John Wiley and Sons, Inc. Internship Program
Human Resources Department
111 River Street
Hoboken, NJ 07030
Fax: 201-748-6049
Web: www.wiley.com

Johnson Controls

Johnson Controls Co-op and Internship Programs

Type of award: Internship, renewable.
Intended use: For full-time undergraduate or graduate study at accredited 4-year institution in United States.
Basis for selection: Major/career interest in engineering; law; business/management/administration; manufacturing or automotive technology. Applicant must demonstrate high academic achievement.
Application requirements: Proof of eligibility. Resume, cover letter.
Additional information: Johnson Controls offers several co-op and internship programs in locations throughout the U.S. and abroad. The Engineering Co-op Program develops and trains students in all aspects of the Automotive Systems Group at Johnson Controls. Over a period of two to five years, mechanical and design engineering students alternate between work terms at Johnson Controls and school terms at college or university. Paid summer internships and positions in most other company divisions also available. Visit Website for complete program descriptions.

Contact:
Johnson Controls Human Resources
P.O. Box 591
Milwaukee, WI 53201
Web: www.johnsoncontrols.com/hr/coops.htm

J.W. Saxe Memorial Fund

J.W. Saxe Memorial Prize

Type of award: Internship.
Intended use: For undergraduate or non-degree study.
Basis for selection: Major/career interest in public administration/service. Applicant must demonstrate financial need, depth of character, leadership, seriousness of purpose and service orientation.
Application requirements: Recommendations, essay. Resume, letter of support from faculty member, four recommendations and an essay on short- and long-term goals.
Additional information: Award enables public-service-minded college or university students to gain practical experience working no-pay or low-pay public service job or internship during summer or other term. Preference given to applicants who have already found public-service-oriented position, but require additional funds. Applicants must demonstrate financial need.

Amount of award:	$1,500
Number of applicants:	200
Application deadline:	March 15
Notification begins:	May 1
Total amount awarded:	$16,500

Contact:
J.W. Saxe Memorial Fund
1524 31 St. N.W.
Washington, DC 20007-3074
Web: www.jwsaxefund.org

Internships

519

Kentucky Higher Education Assistance Authority (KHEAA)

Kentucky Work-Study Program

Type of award: Internship, renewable.
Intended use: For undergraduate, master's, doctoral, first professional or postgraduate study at vocational, 2-year, 4-year or graduate institution. Designated institutions: Postsecondary institutions in Kentucky.
Eligibility: Applicant must be U.S. citizen residing in Kentucky.
Application requirements: Interview, proof of eligibility.
Additional information: Job must be related to major course of study. Work-study wage is at least federal minimum wage. May also be enrolled in technical schools. Cannot be enrolled in religion, theology or divinity program. Visit Website for additional information.

    Number of awards: 780
    Total amount awarded: $621,080
Contact:
Kentucky Higher Education Assistance Authority (KHEAA)
KHEAA Work-Study Program
1050 U.S. 127 South
Frankfort, KY 40601-4323
Phone: 800-928-8926
Fax: 502-695-7373
Web: www.kheaa.com

KIMT

KIMT Weather/News Internships

Type of award: Internship.
Intended use: For undergraduate study.
Basis for selection: Major/career interest in atmospheric sciences/meteorology; journalism; radio/television/film or sports/sports administration.
Application requirements: Interview. Resume.
Additional information: Only children of KIMT employees eligible for program. Ideally, student should have completed junior year, have valid driver's license, good driving record, computer experience and ability to shoot video. All internships for college credit only. Student must arrange to receive college credit. Internships available year-round. Hours are flexible.

    Number of awards: 6
Contact:
KIMT Weather/News Internships
112 North Pennsylvania
Mason City, IA 50401
Phone: 641-423-2540

Landscape Architecture Foundation

LAF/CLASS Fund Internship Program

Type of award: Internship.
Intended use: For full-time undergraduate study. Designated institutions: Cal Poly Pomona, Cal Poly San Luis Obispo, University of California at Davis.
Eligibility: Applicant must be residing in California.
Basis for selection: Major/career interest in landscape architecture or construction. Applicant must demonstrate financial need.
Application requirements: Recommendations, essay, transcript. Academic, community and professional involvement background. 300-word statement on the profession. 100-word statement on intended use of funds. Two faculty recommendation letters. One confidential department head recommendation, cover sheet and personal profile (details on Website). Faxed applications will not be accepted.
Additional information: Award given for internship consisting of employment for nine-week period during the summer in selected field within the green industry. $2,000 stipend for internship. Firm/office sponsoring internship provides participant with an additional $10 per hour.

    Amount of award: $2,000
    Number of awards: 2
    Application deadline: April 6
Contact:
Landscape Architecture Foundation
818 18th Street
Suite 810
Washington, DC 20006
Phone: (202) 331-7070
Web: www.laprofession.org/financial/scholarships.htm

Library of Congress

Library of Congress Hispanic Division Junior Fellows Internship

Type of award: Internship.
Intended use: For junior, senior or graduate study at accredited 4-year or graduate institution. Designated institutions: Library of Congress.
Eligibility: Applicant must be U.S. citizen or permanent resident.
Basis for selection: Fluency in Spanish or Portuguese. Major/career interest in library science or Latin american studies. Applicant must demonstrate seriousness of purpose.
Application requirements: Interview, recommendations, transcript. Cover letter with contact information and interview availability. Resume.
Additional information: Fellowships last approximately eight weeks during the summer, according to the needs and schedules of the Hispanic Division. Fellows will be required to work full time (40 hours per week). Women, minorities and people with disabilities encouraged to apply. Thorough knowledge of Spanish/Portuguese is required. Visit Website to download application. Fax completed applications to 202-707-2005.

Amount of award: $2,400
Number of awards: 2
Application deadline: April 20
Total amount awarded: $4,800
Contact:
Library of Congress
Chief of Hispanic Division
Washington, DC 20540-4850
Phone: 202-707-5400
Fax: 202-707-2005
Web: www.loc.gov/rr/hispanic

Los Angeles Times

Los Angeles Times Editorial Internship

Type of award: Internship.
Intended use: For junior, senior or graduate study at postsecondary institution.
Basis for selection: Major/career interest in journalism.
Application requirements: Resume and up to 12 samples of published work.
Additional information: Full-time paid internships available in summer. Applicants should have experience on campus newspaper or professional daily newspaper, preferably one with circulation of 100,000 or more.
Application deadline: January 1
Contact:
Editorial Internship Director
202 West 1st Street
Los Angeles, CA 90012
Phone: 800-LATIMES

Makovsky & Company Inc.

Public Relations Internship

Type of award: Internship.
Intended use: For junior or senior study at vocational institution in United States or Canada.
Basis for selection: Major/career interest in public relations. Applicant must demonstrate high academic achievement.
Application requirements: Interview. Resume, cover letter, writing sample.
Additional information: Two to three full-time or part-time paid positions offered in spring, summer and fall. Applicant must be responsible, diligent and energetic. Provides opportunity to receive hands-on experience in all facets of public relations under direction of forums staff. Deadlines: April 15 for summer; August 15 for fall; December 15 for spring. Submit resume at Website.
Number of awards: 3
Number of applicants: 150
Application deadline: August 15, December 15

Contact:
Makovsky & Company, Inc. Internship Coordinator
575 Lexington Ave.
15th Floor
New York, NY 10022
Phone: 212-508-9600
Fax: 212-751-9710
Web: www.makovsky.com

Maria Mitchell Observatory

Maria Mitchell Internships for Astronomical Research

Type of award: Internship.
Intended use: For undergraduate study at 4-year institution. Designated institutions: Maria Mitchell Observatory, Nantucket, MA.
Eligibility: Applicant must be U.S. citizen or permanent resident.
Basis for selection: Major/career interest in astronomy or physics. Applicant must demonstrate high academic achievement.
Application requirements: Recommendations, essay, transcript. Application (available on the Website).
Additional information: Positions provide chance for students to conduct independent research and to participate in common project. Students expected to develop their ability to communicate with the public. Furnished housing is available at no cost. Partial travel funds available. Internship runs from June through August, with $1,400 monthly stipend. Applicant must demonstrate motivation in research. Minimum of one year undergraduate physics required.
Number of awards: 6
Number of applicants: 100
Application deadline: February 15
Notification begins: March 1
Contact:
Maria Mitchell Observatory
Attn: Vladimir Strelnitski
4 Vestal Street
Nantucket, MA 02554
Phone: 508-228-9273
Fax: 508-228-1031
Web: www.mmo.org

Massachusetts Democratic Party

Paid Summer Internship: JFK Scholars Award

Type of award: Internship, renewable.
Intended use: For junior or senior study at accredited 4-year institution.
Eligibility: Applicant must be at least 18, no older than 23. Applicant must be U.S. citizen or permanent resident residing in Massachusetts.
Basis for selection: Major/career interest in political science/ government or public administration/service. Applicant must

521

demonstrate financial need, high academic achievement and seriousness of purpose.
Application requirements: Community service and political involvement.
Additional information: Preference given to registered Democrats and students with 3.0 GPA or higher. Two internships available, paying $1,500. Visit Website for more program information and important dates.

Amount of award:	$1,500
Number of awards:	2
Total amount awarded:	$5,000

Contact:
Massachusetts Democratic Party
DSC Office
10 Granite Street, 4th Floor
Quincy, MA 02169
Phone: 617-472-0637
Fax: 617-472-4391
Web: www.massdems.org

MCC Theater

MCC Theater Internships

Type of award: Internship.
Intended use: For undergraduate study at vocational institution.
Eligibility: Applicant must be residing in New York.
Basis for selection: Major/career interest in theater arts; theater/production/technical; performing arts; design; business/management/administration or arts management.
Application requirements: Resume.
Additional information: Rolling application deadlines, negotiable schedule. Internships available in general management/theater administration, development, marketing, and literary and arts education.

Contact:
MCC Theater
145 West 28th Street, 8th Floor
New York, NY 10001
Phone: 212-727-7722
Fax: 212-727-7780
Web: www.mcctheater.org/jobs

MERITS

Maine Research Internships for Teachers and Students

Type of award: Internship.
Intended use: For undergraduate study at 2-year or 4-year institution. Designated institutions: Maine colleges and universities.
Eligibility: Applicant must be U.S. citizen residing in Maine.
Basis for selection: Major/career interest in education, teacher.
Additional information: MERITS places students who are interested in the science and technology fields. Must be Maine resident or attending Maine college/university. Internships last throughout the summer and are in Maine field or laboratory settings.

Amount of award:	$2,400
Number of applicants:	15
Application deadline:	January 31
Total amount awarded:	$19,200

Contact:
MERITS
622 Old Portland Road
Brunswick, ME 04011
Phone: 207-725-7903
Web: www.fbr.org/edu/merits

Metropolitan Museum of Art

The Cloisters Summer Internship Program

Type of award: Internship.
Intended use: For undergraduate study. Designated institutions: Metropolitan Museum of Art: The Cloisters.
Basis for selection: Major/career interest in art/art history or history.
Application requirements: Recommendations, essay, transcript. Include resume and list of art history courses taken.
Additional information: Students with interest in medieval studies especially encouraged to apply. Nine-week, full-time internship from mid-June to mid-August. Five-day, 40-hour work week.

Amount of award:	$2,500
Number of awards:	8
Number of applicants:	300
Application deadline:	February 4
Notification begins:	April 15
Total amount awarded:	$20,000

Contact:
The Cloisters
College Internship Program
Fort Tryon Park
New York, NY 10040
Phone: 212-650-2280
Web: www.metmuseum.org/education/er_internship.asp

Six-Month Internship

Type of award: Internship.
Intended use: For senior, graduate or non-degree study at 4-year or graduate institution.
Eligibility: Applicant must be U.S. citizen, international student or or non U.S. citizen able to earn a stipend in U.S.
Basis for selection: Major/career interest in art/art history; museum studies or history.
Application requirements: Recommendations, essay, transcript, proof of eligibility. Resume. List of art history and other relevant courses taken and foreign languages spoken. 500-word essay describing career goals, interest in museum work, specific areas of interest within the museum, and reasons for applying to the program.
Additional information: Interns work full time from early June to early December and participate in summer orientation program. Application deadline is late January. Visit Website for more information.

Amount of award:	$10,000

Contact:
Metropolitan Museum of Art
1000 Fifth Avenue
New Yrok, NY 10028-0198
Phone: 212-570-3710
Web: www.metmuseum.org/education/er_internship.asp

Summer Internship for College Students

Type of award: Internship.
Intended use: For junior, senior, graduate or non-degree study at postsecondary institution.
Eligibility: Applicant must be U.S. citizen, international student or or non U.S. citizens with permission to work in U.S.
Basis for selection: Major/career interest in art/art history; arts management or museum studies/administration. Applicant must demonstrate seriousness of purpose.
Application requirements: No official application form. In typed paper, applicant should indicate desired internship and include name, home and school addresses and phone numbers. Resume. Two academic recommendations. Transcripts. Separate list with art history or relevant courses taken and knowledge of foreign languages. 500-word (maximum) essay describing career goals, interest in museum work, specific areas of interest within the museum, and reason for applying.
Additional information: Ten-week program for college students, recent college graduates who have not yet entered graduate school, and graduate students who have completed at least one year of graduate work in art history or related field. Interns work full-time. Applicants should have broad background in art history. Program begins in June with two-week orientation, ends in August, and includes $3,000 honorarium for college interns and recent graduates and $3,250 for graduate interns. Graduate students and other students showing special interest in museum careers also considered for Roswell L. Gilpatrick Internship but need not apply separately. Application deadline is mid-January. Visit Website for more information.

Amount of award:	$3,000-$3,250

Contact:
Attn: Internship Programs
Metropolitan Museum of Art
1000 Fifth Avenue
New York, NY 10028-0198
Phone: 212-570-3710
Web: www.metmuseum.org/education/er_internship.asp

Michigan Higher Education Assistance Authority

Michigan Work-Study Program

Type of award: Internship, renewable.
Intended use: For undergraduate or graduate study at 2-year, 4-year or graduate institution. Designated institutions: Michigan public or private nonprofit institutions.
Eligibility: Applicant must be U.S. citizen or permanent resident residing in Michigan.
Basis for selection: Applicant must demonstrate financial need.
Application requirements: Proof of eligibility. FAFSA.
Additional information: Program pays students with financial need to work in school-related jobs while enrolled.

Number of awards:	6,518
Number of applicants:	89,909
Total amount awarded:	$7,573,373

Contact:
College financial aid office
Web: www.michigan.gov/mistudentaid

Minnesota Higher Education Services Office

Minnesota Work-Study Program

Type of award: Internship.
Intended use: For undergraduate or graduate study at accredited vocational, 2-year, 4-year or graduate institution. Designated institutions: Minnesota institutions.
Eligibility: Applicant must be U.S. citizen or permanent resident residing in Minnesota.
Basis for selection: Applicant must demonstrate financial need.
Application requirements: Interview.
Additional information: This is a work-study program, but it may be applied to internships. Work placement must be approved by school or nonprofit agency. Must be used at Minnesota college or for internship with non-profit or private sector employer located in Minnesota. Apply to financial aid office of school.

Number of awards:	11,978
Total amount awarded:	$12,949,459

Contact:
MHESO
1450 Energy Park Drive, Suite 350
St. Paul, MN 55108-5227
Phone: 651-642-0567 or 800-657-3866
Web: www.mheso.state.mn.us

Mississippi Office of Student Financial Aid

Mississippi Psychology Apprenticeship Program

Type of award: Internship.
Intended use: For freshman, sophomore, junior or senior study. Designated institutions: Mississippi colleges and universities.
Eligibility: Applicant must be U.S. citizen or permanent resident residing in Mississippi.
Basis for selection: Major/career interest in psychology; health sciences; mental health/therapy; social/behavioral sciences; neuroscience or neurology.
Application requirements: Recommendations, proof of eligibility.
Additional information: Three-month apprenticeship program at a Veterans Affairs Medical Center. Stipend of $500 per month, not to exceed three months. Applicant must be full-time student at Mississippi college or university. Minimum 3.0 GPA.

Amount of award:	$500-$1,500
Application deadline:	March 31

Contact:
Mississippi Office of Student Financial Aid
3825 Ridgewood Road
Jackson, MS 39211-6453
Phone: 601-432-6997
Fax: 601-432-6527
Web: www.ihl.state.ms.us

Morris Arboretum of the University of Pennsylvania

Morris Arboretum Arboriculture Internship

Type of award: Internship.
Intended use: For undergraduate or graduate study.
Basis for selection: Major/career interest in horticulture.
Application requirements: Recommendations, transcript. Letter of intent, resume.
Additional information: Applicant should have interest in arboriculture. Internships train students in most up-to-date tree care techniques. Interns work 40 hrs/week at hourly rate of $8.16 for full year. Intern works with Chief Arborist in all aspects of tree care, including tree assessment, pruning, cabling and removal. Safety-conscious techniques are emphasized, and recent innovations in climbing and rigging are demonstrated and put into practice. Other opportunities include participation in the management of the arboretum's woodland and assisting with outreach activities including workshops and off-site consulting. Benefits include health insurance and dental plan. Must have solid academic background in arboriculture and horticulture. Tree climbing ability helpful. Driver's license required. Both semesters of program receive academic credit from U. Penn.
   Application deadline: February 15
Contact:
Morris Arboretum of the University of Pennsylvania
Internship Coordinator
9414 Meadowbrook Avenue
Philadelphia, PA 19118
Phone: 215-247-5777 ext. 156
Web: www.morrisarboretum.org

Morris Arboretum Education Internship

Type of award: Internship.
Intended use: For undergraduate or graduate study.
Basis for selection: Major/career interest in education; botany; horticulture; ecology or education, teacher.
Application requirements: Recommendations, transcript. Letter of intent, resume.
Additional information: Interns work 40 hours/week at hourly wage of $8.16 for full year. Interns develop workshops for experienced guides, training sessions for new guides, lead tours. Other responsibilities include supervising the school tour program, running special programs for the public, helping to prepare the adult education course brochure, and writing promotional copy including a newsletter for volunteer guides. Benefits include insurance, a dental plan, and tuition benefits. Academic background or experience in education or educational programming preferred. Knowledge of plant-related subjects

helpful. Strong writing and interpersonal skills essential. Both semesters of program receive academic credit from U. Penn.
   Application deadline: February 15
Contact:
Morris Arboretum of the University of Pennsylvania
Internship Coordinator
9414 Meadowbrook Avenue
Philadelphia, PA 19118
Phone: 215-247-5777 ext. 156
Web: www.morrisarboretum.org

Morris Arboretum Horticulture Internship

Type of award: Internship.
Intended use: For undergraduate or graduate study.
Basis for selection: Major/career interest in horticulture.
Application requirements: Recommendations, transcript. Letter of intent, resume.
Additional information: Intern assists in all phases of garden development and care of collections. Specific emphasis on refining practical horticultural skills. Supervisory skills are developed by directing activities of volunteers and part-time staff. Other activities include developing Integrated Pest Management skills, arboricultural techniques and the operation and maintenance of garden machinery. Special projects will be assigned to develop individual skills in garden planning and management. Must have strong academic background in horticulture or closely related field. Interns work 40 hours/week at hourly wage of $8.16 for full year. Benefits include health insurance, a dental plan, and tuition benefits. Some internships require travel. Driver's license is required. Both semesters of program receive academic credit from U. Penn.
   Application deadline: February 15
Contact:
Morris Arboretum of the University of Pennsylvania
Internship Coordinator
9414 Meadowbrook Avenue
Philadelphia, PA 19118
Phone: 215-247-5777 ext. 156
Web: www.morrisarboretum.org

Morris Arboretum Plant Propagation Internship

Type of award: Internship.
Intended use: For undergraduate or graduate study.
Basis for selection: Major/career interest in botany or horticulture.
Application requirements: Recommendations, transcript. Letter of intent, resume.
Additional information: Strong background in woody landscape plants, plant propagation, nursery management and plant physiology required. Interns work 40 hours/week at hourly rate of $8.16 for full year. Benefits include health insurance, a dental plan, and tuition benefits. Both semesters of program receive academic credit from U. Penn. Intern assists Propagator in the development of plant propagation and production schemes for arboretum. Emphasis is placed on the refinement of skills in traditional methods of plant propagation, nursery production and greenhouse management. Other duties include management of the field nursery and data collection for ongoing research projects.
   Application deadline: February 15

Internships

Contact:
Morris Arboretum of the University of Pennsylvania
Internship Coordinator
9414 Meadowbrook Avenue
Philadelphia, PA 19118
Phone: 215-247-5777 ext. 156
Web: www.morrisarboretum.org

Morris Arboretum Plant Protection Internship

Type of award: Internship.
Intended use: For undergraduate or graduate study.
Basis for selection: Major/career interest in horticulture; entomology or botany.
Application requirements: Recommendations, transcript. Letter of intent, resume.
Additional information: Interns work 40 hours/week at hourly wage of $8.16 for full year. Course work in entomology, mycology or plant pathology required. Intern assists arboretum's plant pathologist with the Integrated Pest Management program, which includes regular monitoring of the living collection and communicating information on pests and diseases to staff members. Related projects include establishing threshold levels for specific plant pests and evaluating the effectiveness of control measures. Modern laboratory facilities are available for identifying plant pests and pathogens. Intern also participates in Plant Clinic's daily operations, providing diagnostic services to the public about horticultural problems. Benefits include health insurance, a dental plan and tuition benefits. Strong writing skills essential. Both semesters of program receive academic credit from U. Penn.
  Application deadline: February 15
Contact:
Morris Arboretum of the University of Pennsylvania
Internship Coordinator
9414 Meadowbrook Avenue
Philadelphia, PA 19118
Phone: 215-247-5777 ext. 156
Web: www.morrisarboretum.org

Morris Arboretum Rose and Flower Garden Internship

Type of award: Internship.
Intended use: For undergraduate or graduate study.
Basis for selection: Major/career interest in horticulture. Applicant must demonstrate seriousness of purpose.
Application requirements: Recommendations, transcript. Resume. Letter of intent. Three letters of recommendation including one academic and one work reference.
Additional information: Intern assists rosarian in garden development, management and care of collections. Emphasis on mastering skills used in the culture of modern and antique roses, developing pest management skills and refining horticulture skills including formal garden maintenance. Other duties include plant record keeping, support for volunteer gardeners, operation of garden machinery and supervision of part-time staff. Interns work 40-hour week at hourly rate of $8.16 for full year. Benefits include health insurance and dental plan. Applicant should have strong academic background in horticulture with course work in herbaceous and woody landscape plants. Driver's license required.
  Application deadline: February 15

Contact:
Morris Arboretum of the University of Pennsylvania
Internship Coordinator
9414 Meadowbrook Avenue
Philadelphia, PA 19118
Phone: 215-247-5777 ext. 156
Web: www.morrisarboretum.org

Morris Arboretum Urban and Community Forestry Internship

Type of award: Internship.
Intended use: For undergraduate study.
Basis for selection: Major/career interest in forestry; horticulture; landscape architecture or ecology.
Application requirements: Recommendations, transcript. Letter of intent, resume.
Additional information: Intern will engage in natural resources programs and strategies for public gardens, government agencies, and educational and community organizations; learn and teach stewardship concepts and practical applications through riparian and woodland restoration projects; develop community partnership, urban vegetation analysis and management planning skills; and assist with outreach consulting services in arboriculture and design. Forty hours/week at hourly wage of $8.16 for full year. Benefits include health insurance, a dental plan and tuition benefits. Academic background in urban forestry, horticulture, landscape design or related field. Communication skills essential. Car required; mileage reimbursed. Both semesters of program receive academic credit from U. Penn.
  Application deadline: February 15
Contact:
Morris Arboretum of the University of Pennsylvania
Internship Coordinator
9414 Meadowbrook Avenue
Philadelphia, PA 19118
Phone: 215-247-5777 ext. 156
Web: www.morrisarboretum.org

Mother Jones

Mother Jones Magazine Editorial Internship

Type of award: Internship.
Intended use: For junior, senior, graduate or non-degree study.
Basis for selection: Major/career interest in political science/government; communications; journalism or publishing. Applicant must demonstrate high academic achievement.
Application requirements: Interview, recommendations. Send resume with cover letter and writing samples, if you have them.
Additional information: Deadlines are rolling. Internships run four months with $100/month stipend and health insurance. After four months, interns are reviewed for fellowship program which also runs four months with $1,381/month stipend. Hours vary according to magazine production schedule. No course credit offered. Reporting, writing and research skills preferred. More information at www.motherjones.com.
Contact:
Mother Jones
731 Market St., Suite 600
San Francisco, CA 94103
Web: www.motherjones.com

Internships

Mother Jones MoJo Wire Internship

Type of award: Internship.
Intended use: For junior, senior, graduate or non-degree study.
Basis for selection: Major/career interest in journalism or publishing. Applicant must demonstrate high academic achievement.
Application requirements: Interview, recommendations. Send resume with cover letter and writing samples.
Additional information: Deadlines are rolling. Internships are full-time, 35 hours/week, and run four months with $100/month stipend. After four months, interns are reviewed for fellowship program which runs eight months with $1,176/month stipend. Reporting and writing skills preferred. No course credit offered.
Contact:
Mother Jones
731 Market St., Suite 600
San Francisco, CA 94103
Fax: 415-665-6696
Web: www.motherjones.com

Museum of Modern Art

Museum of Modern Art Internship

Type of award: Internship.
Intended use: For junior, senior or graduate study.
Eligibility: Applicant must be U.S. citizen.
Basis for selection: Major/career interest in arts management; museum studies/administration; arts, general or art/art history.
Application requirements: Interview, essay, transcript. Application, resume and two recommendations.
Additional information: Course credit available. Fall, spring, summer and 12-month internships. Summer internship pays $2,500 depending on available funds. Twelve-month internships are paid, full-time programs for recent college graduates. Fields of study encompass broad spectrum of topics. Contact coordinator for specific information. Visit Website for complete list of departments, applications and deadline information.
   Number of awards: 90
   Number of applicants: 550
Contact:
The Museum of Modern Art
Internship Coordinator, Dept. of Education
11 W. 53rd St.
New York, NY 10019
Phone: 212-708-9893
Web: www.moma.org

NASA Arizona Space Grant Consortium

NASA Space Grant Arizona Undergraduate Research Internship

Type of award: Internship, renewable.
Intended use: For full-time sophomore, junior, senior or graduate study at accredited 2-year, 4-year or graduate institution in United States. Designated institutions: Arizona State University, Dine College, Embry-Riddle, Northern Arizona University, Pima Community College and University of Arizona; full-time graduate students must attend Arizona State University or University of Arizona.
Eligibility: Applicant must be U.S. citizen residing in Arizona.
Basis for selection: Major/career interest in aerospace; astronomy; engineering; physics; geology/earth sciences; science, general; journalism or education.
Additional information: Approximately 100 full-time undergraduate students will be employed for 10-20 hours per week, for the academic year in research programs, working alongside upper-level graduate students and practicing scientists. Hourly wage offered. Awardees must attend Arizona Space Grant Consortium member institution. Availability of internships varies. Current announcements/application posted on Website.
   Number of applicants: 350
Contact:
NASA Space Grant Arizona Space Grant Consortium
Lunar and Planetary Laboratory, Room 345
U of Arizona, 1629 E. University Blvd.
Tucson, AZ 85721-0092
Phone: 520-621-8556
Web: http://spacegrant.arizona.edu

NASA Hawaii Space Grant Consortium

NASA Hawaii Undergraduate Traineeship

Type of award: Internship.
Intended use: For freshman or sophomore study. Designated institutions: Must attend a Consortium member school in Hawaii.
Eligibility: Applicant must be U.S. citizen residing in Hawaii.
Basis for selection: Major/career interest in science, general; astronomy; geology/earth sciences; oceanography/marine studies or physics.
Additional information: This is a training program providing practical experience in any space-related field of science, engineering or math that covers one semester, plus up to $250 for travel and supplies. Student must have faculty mentor. Contact sponsor for application details. Women, minority and physically challenged students who have interest in space-related fields encouraged to apply.
   Amount of award: $1,000
   Application deadline: June 15, December 1
Contact:
Hawaii Space Grant College
University of Hawaii
1680 East West Road
Honolulu, HI 96822
Phone: 808-956-3138
Web: www.spacegrant.hawaii.edu

NASA Maine Space Grant Consortium

NASA Space Grant Maine Consortium Undergraduate Internship Program

Type of award: Internship.
Intended use: For undergraduate study at accredited 2-year or 4-year institution. Designated institutions: Maine two- and four-year colleges and universities.
Eligibility: Applicant must be U.S. citizen.
Basis for selection: Major/career interest in geology/earth sciences; astronomy; aerospace; engineering; biology or medicine.
Additional information: Applicant must be U.S. citizen attending Maine institution. Internships are conducted during the summer at Maine-based businesses and research institutions. Application requirements determined by MERITS (Maine Educational Research Internships for Teachers and Students). See Website for details.

Amount of award:	$2,400
Number of awards:	8
Number of applicants:	15
Application deadline:	January 31
Total amount awarded:	$19,200

Contact:
MERITS
622 Old Portland Road
Brunswick, ME 04011
Phone: 207-725-7903
Web: www.fbr.org/edu/merits

NASA Massachusetts Space Grant Consortium

NASA Space Grant Massachusetts Summer Jobs for Students

Type of award: Internship, renewable.
Intended use: For undergraduate or graduate study in United States. Designated institutions: Massachusetts Space Grant Consortium members: Boston University, Harvard University, Massachusetts Institute of Technology, Tufts University, University of Massachusetts, Wellesley College, Worcester Polytechnic Institute, The Five College Astronomy Department.
Eligibility: Applicant must be U.S. citizen or permanent resident residing in Massachusetts.
Basis for selection: Major/career interest in aerospace; astronomy; engineering or physics.
Application requirements: Interview. Application, resume.
Additional information: The Space Grant Summer Jobs program is designed to give college students a practical learning experience in industry. Each summer 20-30 students are placed in space-related technical positions. Must attend Massachusetts Space Grant Consortium member institution. Deadline in mid-December; call coordinator for exact date.

Contact:
NASA Space Grant Massachusetts Space Grant Consortium
MIT, Aeronautics & Astronautics
77 Massachusetts Ave., Bldg. 33, Rm. 208
Cambridge, MA 02139
Phone: 617-258-5546
Web: www.maspacegrant.org

NASA New Jersey Space Grant Consortium

Undergraduate Summer Fellowships in Engineering and Science

Type of award: Internship, renewable.
Intended use: For junior or senior study at accredited 4-year institution in United States. Designated institutions: New Jersey Institute of Technology, Princeton University, Rutgers University, Stevens Institute of Technology, University of Medicine and Dentistry of NJ.
Eligibility: Applicant must be U.S. citizen.
Basis for selection: Major/career interest in aerospace; biology; computer/information sciences; engineering, computer; engineering, chemical; engineering, electrical/electronic; engineering, mechanical; materials science; natural sciences or physical sciences.
Application requirements: Recommendations, essay. Biographical sketch, statement that describes career goals and what applicant hopes to accomplish as Space Grant Fellow, plan for immediate future and reference letter from faculty advisor.
Additional information: Applicants must have completed at least two, but preferably three, years of college. Award for ten week at $600 per week with additional $600 per student for laboratory supplies. Consortium actively encourages women, minority students, and physically challenged students to apply. Awardees must attend NJSPC member institution. Visit Website for important dates and additional information.

Number of awards:	12
Number of applicants:	30

Contact:
Program Director
New Jersey Space Grant Consortium
Stevens Institute of Technology
Hoboken, NJ 07030-5991
Phone: 201-216-8964
Fax: 201-216-8929
Web: www.njsgc.org

NASA Pennsylvania Space Grant Consortium

NASA Academy Internship

Type of award: Internship.
Intended use: For full-time junior, senior or graduate study at accredited 4-year or graduate institution in United States. Designated institutions: Pennsylvania colleges and universities.
Eligibility: Applicant must be U.S. citizen or permanent resident residing in Pennsylvania.

Basis for selection: Major/career interest in engineering; science, general or mathematics. Applicant must demonstrate high academic achievement.

Application requirements: Recommendations, essay, transcript.

Additional information: Awards are for ten-week internships at NASA Academy: Goddard Space Flight Center, Ames Research Center. Stipend, plus room and board and travel expenses. Applicants should be juniors, seniors, or first year graduate students. Awardees must attend Pennsylvania institution or be a full-time resident. Consortium actively encourages women, minority, and physically challenged students to apply. Visit the NASA Academy Website to download application.

Amount of award:	$4,000
Number of awards:	2
Application deadline:	January 31

Contact:
NASA Space Grant Pennsylvania Space Grant Consortium
Penn State, University Park
2217 Earth-Engineering Sciences Building
University Park, PA 16802
Phone: 814-863-5957
Web: www.nasa-academy.nasa.gov

National Association of Latino Elected and Appointed Officials (NALEO)

Ford Motor Company Fellows Program

Type of award: Internship.

Intended use: For junior, senior or graduate study at accredited 4-year or graduate institution in United States.

Eligibility: Applicant must be Mexican American, Hispanic American or Puerto Rican. Applicant must be of Latino background. Must possess sense of commitment to Latino community. Applicant must be at least 21. Applicant must be U.S. citizen or permanent resident residing in Michigan, California, Puerto Rico, Texas, Illinois or Florida.

Basis for selection: Major/career interest in social work; public administration/service; political science/government; sociology; psychology; public relations; urban planning or Latin american studies. Applicant must demonstrate high academic achievement, depth of character, leadership and service orientation.

Application requirements: Recommendations, essay, transcript. Completed application form, resume, and legislative analysis.

Additional information: Internship includes $1,200 stipend, plus airfare, housing and some meals. Visit Website for additional information. Fellows will attend NALEO Conference and five-week paid fellowship with elected or appointed official in Washington, D.C.

Amount of award:	$1,200
Application deadline:	March 11

Contact:
National Association of Latino Elected and Appointed Officials (NALEO)
Lourdes Ferrer Deputy Director
1122 Washington Blvd., 3rd Floor
Los Angeles, CA 90015
Phone: 213-747-7606 ext.127
Fax: 213-747-7994
Web: www.naleo.org

Shell Legislative Internship Program (SLIP)

Type of award: Internship.

Intended use: For sophomore, junior or senior study at accredited 4-year institution.

Eligibility: Applicant must be Mexican American, Hispanic American or Puerto Rican. Must possess sense of commitment to Latino community. Applicant must be U.S. citizen or permanent resident residing in California, New York, Texas, New Mexico, Colorado, Illinois, Arizona or Florida.

Basis for selection: Major/career interest in public administration/service; political science/government; urban planning or Latin american studies. Applicant must demonstrate depth of character, leadership and service orientation.

Application requirements: Recommendations, essay, transcript. Application form, transcripts, resume, two letters of recommendation, and state legislative analysis.

Additional information: Four-week internships (from end of June to August) in offices of elected or appointed Latino officials. A $1,500 stipend will be provided to participants in four installments. Program includes trip to NALEO annual conference, week in Washington, DC, and four-week paid internship with local official from applicant's hometown. Visit Website for more information. Award includes air travel, housing, and some meals.

Amount of award:	$1,500
Application deadline:	March 11

Contact:
National Association of Latino Elected and Appointed Officials (NALEO)
Lourdes Ferrer Deputy Director
1122 Washington Blvd. 3rd Fl.
Los Angeles, CA 90015
Phone: 213-747-7607 ext. 127
Fax: 213-747-7664
Web: www.naleo.org

National Basketball Association

NBA Internship Program

Type of award: Internship.

Intended use: For sophomore or junior study.

Basis for selection: Major/career interest in sports/sports administration; marketing; theater/production/technical; public relations; finance/banking or computer/information sciences.

Application requirements: Resume and cover letter.

Additional information: Internship opportunities are available in various areas including television production, broadcast operations, finance, NBA photos, global merchandising, international public relations, corporate communications, human resources, and events and attractions. Internships are for ten weeks, from June to August. For more information, visit Website and click on "Employment Opportunities" link.

Contact:
National Basketball Association
Internship Coordinator
645 Fifth Ave.
New York, NY 10022
Web: www.nba.com

National Credit Union Administration

National Credit Union Administration Student Intern Program

Type of award: Internship.
Intended use: For undergraduate or graduate study at accredited vocational, 2-year, 4-year or graduate institution in United States.
Eligibility: Applicant must be U.S. citizen.
Basis for selection: Major/career interest in accounting; finance/banking; business; marketing; human resources; computer/information sciences; law or business/management/ administration. Applicant must demonstrate depth of character, leadership, seriousness of purpose and service orientation.
Application requirements: Interview, recommendations, transcript, proof of eligibility.
Additional information: Paid and non-paid internships offered to students year-round.
Contact:
National Credit Union Administration
Attn: Recruitment Coordinator
1775 Duke Street
Alexandria, VA 22314
Phone: 703-518-6510
Fax: 703-518-6539
Web: www.ncua.gov

National Geographic Society

Geography Students Internship

Type of award: Internship.
Intended use: For junior, senior or master's study at 4-year or graduate institution in United States.
Basis for selection: Major/career interest in geography or cartography.
Application requirements: Recommendations, essay, transcript. Resume. Applicant must have a geography or cartography major.
Additional information: Spring, summer, and fall internships for 14 to 16 weeks in Washington, D.C., at $325/week. Emphasis on editorial and cartographic research. Students should contact their school's geography department chair or call internship hotline for more information.

Number of awards:	30
Number of applicants:	100

Contact:
National Geographic Society
Robert E. Dulli
1145 17 Street, NW
Washington, DC 20036-4688
Phone: 202-857-7134
Web: www.nationalgeographic.com

National Institutes of Health

NIH Summer Internship Program in Biomedical Research

Type of award: Internship, renewable.
Intended use: For undergraduate or graduate study in United States.
Eligibility: Applicant must be at least 16. Applicant must be U.S. citizen or permanent resident.
Basis for selection: Research experience. Major/career interest in science, general; medicine or medical specialties/research. Applicant must demonstrate high academic achievement.
Application requirements: Recommendations, transcript, proof of eligibility. Cover letter and resume. Applicant must be enrolled at least half-time in accredited U.S. high school, college or university.
Additional information: Program offers summer training in environment devoted totally to biomedical research. Includes Summer Lecture Series by leading NIH researchers and opportunity to participate in annual poster day for students for students in summer internship programs. Internships last eight to ten weeks, beginning in late May and ending in August. Candidates notified early April. Visit Website for online application.

Amount of award:	$1,200-$2,900
Application deadline:	March 1

Contact:
National Institutes of Health, Office of Education
Building 2, Room 2E06
2 Center Drive MSC 0240
Bethesda, MD 20892-0240
Phone: 800-445-8283
Fax: 301-402-0483
Web: www.training.nih.gov

National Museum of the American Indian

National Museum of the American Indian Internship

Type of award: Internship.
Intended use: For undergraduate, graduate or non-degree study.
Basis for selection: Professional and education goals of student, needs of museum. Major/career interest in museum studies.
Application requirements: Recommendations, transcript. Resume.

Additional information: Provides educational work/research experience for students in museum practice and related programming using resources of museum and other Smithsonian offices. Internships available at NMAI in Washington, DC, and New York City. Applicants must have minimum 3.0 GPA. Four 10-week internships, deadlines as follows: February 11 for summer; October 8 for winter; July 9 for fall; and November 19 for spring. Limited number of stipends targeted primarily at American Indian, Native Hawaiian and Alaskan Native students. Students receiving stipends must work full-time; other interns must work at least 20 hours/week. Visit Website or contact via e-mail (interns@nmai.si.edu) for more information.

Number of awards:	20
Number of applicants:	40

Contact:
Internship Program, National Museum of the American Indian
Community Services, Cultural Resource Center
4220 Silver Hill Road
Suitland, MD 20746-2863
Phone: 301-238-6624 ext. 6235
Fax: 301-238-3200
Web: www.si.edu/nmai

National Museum of Women in the Arts

Museum Coca-Cola Internship

Type of award: Internship.
Intended use: For junior, senior, graduate or non-degree study in United States. Designated institutions: National Museum of Women in the Arts.
Basis for selection: Major/career interest in public relations; advertising; library science; publishing; museum studies; art/art history; museum studies/administration; accounting; education or retailing/merchandising. Applicant must demonstrate high academic achievement and seriousness of purpose.
Application requirements: Recommendations, transcript. One personal and one academic recommendation. Resume, cover letter and writing sample of 1-2 pages in length.
Additional information: Internship lasts 12 weeks. Available to students interested in pursuing museum careers. Minimum 3.25 GPA. Application deadline for winter is October 15; summer is March 15; fall is June 15.

Amount of award:	$1,500
Number of awards:	1
Number of applicants:	50
Total amount awarded:	$1,500

Contact:
National Museum of Women in the Arts
1250 New York Ave. NW
Washington, DC 20005-3920
Phone: 202-783-7996
Web: www.nmwa.org

National Tourism Foundation

National Tourism Foundation Internship

Type of award: Internship.
Intended use: For full-time junior or senior study.
Basis for selection: Major/career interest in tourism/travel. Applicant must demonstrate service orientation.
Application requirements: Resume and application.
Additional information: Minimum 3.0 GPA. Must have excellent written, oral and interpersonal skills. Interns receive $3,000 stipend to offset travel and lodging expenses while in Lexington, Kentucky. Interns also travel to NTA Annual Convention, all expenses paid.

Amount of award:	$3,000
Number of awards:	2
Application deadline:	April 10
Total amount awarded:	$3,000

Contact:
National Tourism Foundation
546 East Main Street
Lexington, KY 40508
Phone: 800-682-8886
Fax: 859-226-4437
Web: www.ntfonline.org

Patrick Murphy Internship

Type of award: Internship.
Intended use: For junior or senior study. Designated institutions: Washington, DC.
Basis for selection: Major/career interest in tourism/travel or political science/government. Applicant must demonstrate high academic achievement.
Application requirements: Resume and application. Minimum 3.0 GPA.
Additional information: Two to three month internship. $1,000 stipend. Minimum 3.0 GPA. Must have excellent written, oral and interpersonal skills. Check Website for updated information.

Amount of award:	$2,000
Number of awards:	1
Application deadline:	April 10
Total amount awarded:	$2,000

Contact:
National Tourism Foundation
546 East Main Street
Lexington, KY 40508
Phone: 800-682-8886
Web: www.ntfonline.org

NationalJournal.com

NationalJournal.com Editorial Internship

Type of award: Internship.
Intended use: For full-time senior or graduate study at 4-year or graduate institution.

Internships

Basis for selection: Major/career interest in political science/ government; journalism or economics.
Application requirements: Samples of writing, resume.
Additional information: Paid internship. Deadline for summer internship is March 15. Deadline for fall internship is July 15. Deadline for spring internship is November 15. Good writing skills and strong interest in government and politics required. Applicants with previous editorial internships preferred. Recent grads may apply. Apply by e-mail to awagner@nationaljournal.com. No phone calls.

   Number of awards: 4
   Application deadline: March 15, November 15
Contact:
NationalJournal.com
1501 M Street, NW
Suite 3000
Washington, DC 20005
Web: www.nationaljournal.com

NCR Corporation

NCR Summer Internships

Type of award: Internship.
Intended use: For full-time undergraduate or graduate study at accredited 4-year institution.
Eligibility: Applicant must be residing in District of Columbia, California, South Carolina or Georgia.
Basis for selection: Major/career interest in computer/ information sciences; engineering, computer; engineering, electrical/electronic; information systems; finance/banking; accounting or human resources.
Application requirements: Proof of eligibility. Apply via NCR Career Website.
Additional information: Applicants must complete personal profile, including resume, on Website before applying for positions. Students then use stored profile to apply for individual internship opportunities posted online. Applicants encouraged to visit Website frequently during spring to review newly added offerings and important information.
Contact:
Visit Website for further information.
Web: www.ncr.com/careers

New Dramatists

New Dramatists Internship

Type of award: Internship.
Intended use: For undergraduate or graduate study.
Basis for selection: Major/career interest in theater arts; performing arts or arts management.
Application requirements: Interview.
Additional information: Must have passion for new plays and playwrights. Twelve- to twenty-week internships, three to four days per week, $25 per week stipend. Unpaid part-time internships available. College credit may be available. Computer and writing skills essential. See Website for application.

Contact:
New Dramatists
Internship Coordinator
424 West 44th Street
New York, NY 10036
Web: www.newdramatists.org

New Mexico Commission on Higher Education

New Mexico Work-Study Program

Type of award: Internship, renewable.
Intended use: For undergraduate or graduate study at postsecondary institution. Designated institutions: Public or approved private non-profit postsecondary institutions in New Mexico.
Eligibility: Applicant must be U.S. citizen or permanent resident residing in New Mexico.
Basis for selection: Applicant must demonstrate financial need.
Application requirements: FAFSA.
Additional information: Awards vary. Limit of 20 hrs/wk, on-campus or off-campus in federal, state or local public agency. New Mexico residents receive state portion of funding. Contact financial aid office of New Mexico public postsecondary institutions for information, deadlines and application.
Contact:
New Mexico Commission on Higher Education
Financial Aid and Student Services
1068 Cerrillos Road
Santa Fe, NM 87501
Phone: 800-279-9777
Web: www.nmche.org

The New Republic

The New Republic Internship

Type of award: Internship.
Intended use: For undergraduate, graduate or non-degree study.
Eligibility: Applicant must be U.S. citizen.
Basis for selection: Major/career interest in journalism. Applicant must demonstrate depth of character and seriousness of purpose.
Application requirements: Must submit resume, two writing samples (one showing reporting ability, other showing opinion writing ability), plus one 750-word critique of "Politics of the World" section of The New Republic.
Additional information: Year-long full-time internship for college graduates and soon-to-be college graduates with journalism experience. Payment is $300 per week plus health benefits. Provides intern with opportunity to gain editorial experience at leading opinion magazine. Must have excellent organizational skills, research ability, and experience writing news and opinion. Position starts in August or September.
   Application deadline: April 25

Internships

Contact:
The New Republic
1331 H Street NW
Suite 700
Washington, DC 20005
Phone: 202-508-4444
Web: www.tnr.com

New Stage Theatre

New Stage Theatre Internship

Type of award: Internship.
Intended use: For undergraduate or graduate study.
Basis for selection: Major/career interest in performing arts; theater/production/technical or theater arts. Applicant must demonstrate seriousness of purpose.
Application requirements: Interview, audition, portfolio, recommendations, proof of eligibility.
Additional information: Eight-month internships starting in September. Salary approximately $175 per week. Travel extensively in Mississippi.

Amount of award:	$7,000
Application deadline:	May 1

Contact:
New Stage Theatre
1100 Carlisle Street
Jackson, MS 39202-4792
Web: www.newstagetheatre.com

New York City Department of Education

Summer in the City Internships

Type of award: Internship.
Intended use: For half-time junior, senior or graduate study at 4-year institution in United States.
Eligibility: Applicant must be permanent resident residing in New York.
Basis for selection: Major/career interest in education; education, early childhood; education, special or education, teacher. Applicant must demonstrate seriousness of purpose.
Application requirements: Recommendations, essay, transcript, proof of eligibility. Application, work experience, completion minimum 60 hours of college coursework. Bilingual a plus.
Additional information: Applicants must attend New York State University institution. Program runs from June 30 to August 6 and offers field experience for college students considering teaching in New York City public schools. Housing is available in local dormitories for students who live outside of the metropolitan New York area. Credit may be awarded for this internship.

Amount of award:	$2,000
Number of awards:	500
Application deadline:	February 27
Total amount awarded:	$1,000,000

Contact:
Center for Recruitment and Professional Development
Attention: Pat Woerner
65 Court Street, Room 307A
Brooklyn, NY 11201
Phone: 718-935-4625
Fax: 718-935-4262
Web: www.teachny.com

New York State Assembly

New York State Assembly Session Internship Program

Type of award: Internship, renewable.
Intended use: For full-time junior, senior or graduate study.
Basis for selection: Applicant must demonstrate high academic achievement.
Application requirements: Recommendations, essay, transcript, proof of eligibility. Application. Writing sample. Letter from college endorsing candidate and outlining course credit arrangements.
Additional information: All majors eligible. Interns assigned to work with assembly members or assembly staff. Program runs from January to May. Applications accepted on an ongoing basis until deadline. Extensions granted upon request. Visit Website for deadline information.

Amount of award:	$3,500
Number of awards:	150
Application deadline:	November 1

Contact:
New York State Assembly
Assembly Intern Committee
Legislative Office Building, Room 104A
Albany, NY 12248
Phone: 518-455-4704
Fax: 518-455-4705
Web: www.assembly.state.ny.us

New York State Bar Association, Department of Media Services and Public Affairs

New York State Bar Association Summer Public Relations Internship

Type of award: Internship.
Intended use: For senior study at 4-year institution.
Eligibility: Applicant must be U.S. citizen.
Basis for selection: Major/career interest in public relations.
Application requirements: Interview. Send letter and three writing samples.
Additional information: For study in the field of public relations only. There is a two-hour writing test. There is no application per se. Interested students should send a letter detailing their interest and providing specific examples of work-related experience. Three writing samples required.

Amount of award: $2,800
Application deadline: April 1
Contact:
New York State Bar Association
One Elk Street
Albany, NY 12207
Phone: 518-463-3200
Fax: 518-463-4276
Web: www.nysba.org

New York Times

New York Times Summer Internship Program

Type of award: Internship.
Intended use: For junior, senior, graduate or non-degree study.
Basis for selection: Major/career interest in journalism. Applicant must demonstrate seriousness of purpose.
Application requirements: Portfolio. Resume, eight to ten writing samples.
Additional information: Program open to all applicants, regardless of race or ethnicity. Salary is $800 per week for 10 weeks, plus housing allowance. Applicants must have journalism experience. All queries by mail or e-mail (rulesh@nytimes.com).
Application deadline: November 15
Contact:
The New York Times
Sheila Rule, Senior Mgr. Reporter Recruiting
229 West 43rd Street
New York, NY 10036
Web: www.nytco.com/intern.html

North Carolina Arts Council

North Carolina Arts Council Community Arts Administration Internship

Type of award: Internship.
Intended use: For non-degree study.
Eligibility: Applicant must possess four-year college degree, have strong administrative and/or business capability, preferably demonstrated by work experience, and have close familiarity with the arts.
Basis for selection: Based on broad familiarity with the arts and business/administrative abilities. Major/career interest in business/management/administration or arts management.
Application requirements: Interview, recommendations, essay.
Additional information: Interns assigned to sponsoring North Carolina community arts council or cultural center for three months between September 1 and June 30. Out-of-state applicants eligible to apply. Preference given to North Carolina residents.

Amount of award: $4,000
Number of awards: 3
Number of applicants: 20
Application deadline: May 1
Total amount awarded: $12,000
Contact:
North Carolina Arts Council
Department of Cultural Resources
Mail Service Center #4632
Raleigh, NC 27699-4632
Phone: (919) 733-7597
Fax: (919) 715-8287
Web: www.ncarts.org

Oak Ridge Institute for Science and Education

Department of Commerce Internship for Postsecondary Students

Type of award: Internship.
Intended use: For undergraduate or graduate study at 4-year or graduate institution in United States. Designated institutions: Department of Commerce headquarters, division offices and field centers.
Eligibility: Applicant must be U.S. citizen.
Basis for selection: Major/career interest in computer/information sciences; engineering; life sciences; physical sciences or business.
Additional information: Provides opportunities to participate in hands-on education and training related to Department of Commerce mission. Ten-week internship in summer; 16-week internship for fall or spring semesters. Weekly stipend of $400; dislocation allowance of $100 per week based on appointment location; limited travel reimbursement; accidental medical expense coverage provided. Deadlines: February 26 for summer; July 30 for fall; December 31 for spring. Number of awards varies.
Contact:
Web: www.orau.gov/orise/educ.htm

Department of Energy Special Emphasis Program

Type of award: Internship.
Intended use: For undergraduate or graduate study at 2-year, 4-year or graduate institution in United States. Designated institutions: Germantown, Md., and participating facilities.
Eligibility: Applicant must be U.S. citizen.
Basis for selection: Major/career interest in computer/information sciences; economics; engineering; finance/banking; law; mathematics; business or science, general.
Additional information: Provides opportunities to participate in ongoing research and related activities at the U.S. Department of Energy Office of Science. Program lasts ten weeks. Weekly stipend of $500 to $550. Limited travel reimbursement (round-trip transportation expenses between facility and home or campus). Number of awards granted varies. Deadline third Tuesday in January. See Website for application and more information.
Contact:
Web: www.orau.gov/orise/educ.htm

Great Lakes Colleges Association/ Associated Colleges of the Midwest Oak Ridge Science Semester

Type of award: Internship.
Intended use: For full-time undergraduate study at accredited 4-year institution in United States. Designated institutions: Oak Ridge National Laboratory in Oak Ridge, TN.
Eligibility: Applicant must be U.S. citizen or permanent resident.
Basis for selection: Major/career interest in computer/ information sciences; engineering; life sciences; mathematics or physical sciences.
Application requirements: Must be undergraduate at institutions belonging to the Great Lakes Colleges Association or the Associated Colleges of the Midwest.
Additional information: Opportunities to join ongoing investigations at the Oak Ridge National Laboratory (ORNL) in research areas relating to energy production, use, conservation, and societal implications. Program is 16 weeks in the fall (late August through mid-December). See Website for application deadline, www.denison.edu/oakridge. Weekly stipend; limited travel reimbursement, housing, academic credit offered for combination of research, coursework, and seminar series.
Contact:
Web: www.orau.org

Great Lakes Colleges Association/ Associated Colleges of the Midwest Oak Ridge Science Semester

Type of award: Internship.
Intended use: For full-time junior or senior study at 4-year institution in United States. Designated institutions: Oak Ridge National Laboratory (Oak Ridge, TN).
Basis for selection: Major/career interest in computer/ information sciences; physical sciences; engineering; life sciences; mathematics or science, general.
Application requirements: Proof of eligibility.
Additional information: Minimum 3.0 GPA. For undergraduates at institutions belonging to the Great Lakes Colleges Association or the Associated Colleges of the Midwest. Internship lasts 16 weeks, from August to December. Weekly stipend, limited travel reimbursement, and housing offered. Academic credit also offered for combination of research, coursework and seminar series. Administered by Denison University and the Oak Ridge Institute for Science and Education. See Website for application and more information.
Contact:
Web: www.orau.gov/orise/educ.htm

Office of Biological and Environmental Research Global Change Education Program

Type of award: Internship, renewable.
Intended use: For junior, senior or graduate study in United States. Designated institutions: U.S. Department of Energy facilities (undergraduates); U.S. Department of Energy facilities and universities (graduates).
Eligibility: Applicant must be U.S. citizen.
Basis for selection: Major/career interest in ecology or atmospheric sciences/meteorology.
Additional information: Provides opportunities to participate in research areas related to global change. Disciplines include

atmospheric studies, ecology, global carbon cycles, climatology and terrestrial processes. Ten to 12 week summer program. Amount of award is $475 per week, plus travel expenses. For application and more information, see www.atmos.anl.gov/gcep.
   Application deadline: February 1
Contact:
Oak Ridge Institute for Science and Education
P.O. Box 117
Oak Ridge, TN 37831-0117
Phone: 865-576-9655
Web: www.orau.org

ORISE Community College Institute

Type of award: Internship.
Intended use: For undergraduate study at accredited 2-year or 4-year institution in United States. Designated institutions: Oak Ridge National Laboratory (Oak Ridge, TN).
Eligibility: Applicant must be at least 18. Applicant must be U.S. citizen or permanent resident.
Basis for selection: Major/career interest in computer/ information sciences; science, general; engineering; environmental science; life sciences; mathematics or physical sciences. Applicant must demonstrate high academic achievement.
Application requirements: Recommendations, transcript. Minimum 3.25 GPA.
Additional information: Applicant must be student at community college. Provides opportunities to participate in educational training and research relating to energy production, use, conservation and societal implications. Applicant must have passed at least 12 credit hours of coursework toward a degree (with at least six credit hours in science, math, engineering or technology courses) at community college. Ten-week summer internship. $400 weekly stipend. Limited travel reimbursement and limited housing allowance. Student must have health insurance. See Website for application and deadlines.
Contact:
Web: www.orau.gov/orise/educ.htm

ORISE Higher Education Research Experiences at Oak Ridge National Laboratory

Type of award: Internship.
Intended use: For undergraduate or graduate study in United States. Designated institutions: Oak Ridge National Laboratory (Oak Ridge, TN).
Eligibility: Applicant must be at least 18. Applicant must be U.S. citizen or permanent resident.
Basis for selection: Major/career interest in chemistry; environmental science; geology/earth sciences; hydrology; engineering, chemical; engineering, civil; engineering, environmental; engineering, mechanical or computer/ information sciences.
Application requirements: Recommendations. Two academic references.
Additional information: Provides opportunities to participate in energy-related research. Terms vary with academic level; full- or part-time positions available. Minimum 3.0 GPA. Weekly stipend varies with academic level. One round-trip travel reimbursement and housing allowance. Number of awards varies. Deadlines for undergraduates: February 1 for summer, June 1 for fall, and October 1 for spring. Deadline for

Internships

freshman is February 1. See Website for application and more information.
Contact:
Web: www.orau.gov/orise/educ.htm

ORISE National Library of Medicine Student Research Participation

Type of award: Internship.
Intended use: For undergraduate or graduate study at 4-year or graduate institution in United States. Designated institutions: National Library of Medicine (Bethesda, MD) and some on-campus appointments.
Eligibility: Applicant must be U.S. citizen.
Basis for selection: Major/career interest in computer/ information sciences; health-related professions or medicine. Applicant must demonstrate high academic achievement.
Additional information: Provides opportunities to participate in ongoing research and development programs. Program lasts from 10 weeks to 1 year. Stipend based on degree, research area and experience. Number of awards varies. Applications accepted on a year-round basis. See Website for application and more information.
Contact:
Web: www.orau.gov/orise/educ.htm

ORISE National Oceanic and Atmospheric Administration Student Research Participation

Type of award: Internship.
Intended use: For undergraduate or graduate study at 2-year, 4-year or graduate institution in United States. Designated institutions: NOAA headquarters and field centers.
Eligibility: Applicant must be U.S. citizen or permanent resident.
Basis for selection: Major/career interest in computer/ information sciences; health sciences; engineering; physical sciences; business or life sciences.
Additional information: Provides opportunities to participate in research and development relating to science, math, and engineering. Ten-week summer internship. Weekly stipend of $400 to $515, depending on academic classification; limited travel reimbursement (round-trip transportation expenses between facility and home or campus). Applications accepted on year-round basis. Number of internships varies.
Contact:
Web: www.orau.gov/orise/educ.htm

ORISE Professional Internship at Oak Ridge National Laboratory

Type of award: Internship.
Intended use: For undergraduate or graduate study at 2-year, 4-year or graduate institution in United States. Designated institutions: Oak Ridge National Laboratory (Oak Ridge, TN.) and sites of the Hazardous Waste Remedial Actions Program.
Eligibility: Applicant must be U.S. citizen or permanent resident.
Basis for selection: Major/career interest in chemistry; environmental science; geology/earth sciences; hydrology; engineering, chemical; engineering, civil; engineering, environmental; engineering, mechanical; computer/information sciences or science, general.

Additional information: Provides opportunities for students to participate in energy-related research. Weekly stipend varies with academic level. Term varies with academic level, full-time or part-time appointments. Number of awards varies. One round-trip travel reimbursement. Housing allowance. Last deadline is October 1.
　Application deadline:　　October 1, February 15
Contact:
Web: www.orau.gov/orise/educ.htm

ORISE Professional Internship at Savannah River Site

Type of award: Internship.
Intended use: For undergraduate or graduate study at 2-year, 4-year or graduate institution in United States. Designated institutions: Savannah River Site (Aiken, SC).
Eligibility: Applicant must be U.S. citizen or permanent resident.
Basis for selection: Major/career interest in environmental science; chemistry; engineering; geology/earth sciences; physics; science, general or computer/information sciences.
Additional information: Provides opportunities to participate in energy-related and environmental research. Three to 24 consecutive months; full-time or part-time appointments. Weekly stipend varies with academic level; limited travel reimbursement (round-trip transportation expenses between facility and home or campus). Additional deadlines June 1 and February 15. Funded by Westinghouse Savannah River Company.
　Application deadline:　　October 1, February 1
Contact:
Web: www.orau.gov/orise/educ.htm

ORISE Professional Internship Program for National Energy Technology Laboratory

Type of award: Internship, renewable.
Intended use: For undergraduate or graduate study at accredited 2-year, 4-year or graduate institution in United States. Designated institutions: National Energy Technology Laboratory (Pittsburgh, PA, and Morgantown, WV).
Eligibility: Applicant must be U.S. citizen.
Basis for selection: Major/career interest in chemistry; computer/information sciences; engineering; environmental science; geology/earth sciences; mathematics; physics; mathematics; geology/earth sciences or physics.
Additional information: Provides opportunities to participate in fossil energy-related research. Three to 24 consecutive months, full-time or part-time appointments. Weekly stipend. Limited travel reimbursement (round-trip transportation expenses between facility and home or campus). Off-campus tuition and fees if required by the home institution. Additional deadline June 1. Number of awards varies.
　Application deadline:　　October 1, February 15
Contact:
Web: www.orau.gov/orise/educ.htm

ORISE Student Environmental Management Participation at the U.S. Army Environmental Center

Type of award: Internship, renewable.
Intended use: For undergraduate or graduate study at 2-year, 4-year or graduate institution. Designated institutions: U.S.

Internships

Army Environmental Center (Aberdeen Proving Ground, Md.) and other approved locations.

Eligibility: Applicant must be U.S. citizen.

Basis for selection: Major/career interest in archaeology; biology; chemistry; computer/information sciences; zoology; ecology; engineering; entomology or environmental science.

Additional information: Provides opportunities to participate in research in environmental programs involving cultural and natural resources, restoration, compliance, conservation, pollution prevention, validation, demonstration, technology transfer, quality assurance and quality control, training, information management and reporting, and related programs. Three months to one year; full-time or part-time appointments. Stipend based on research area and academic classification. Applications accepted year-round. Number of awards varies.

Contact:
Web: www.orau.gov/orise/educ.htm

ORISE Student Internship at the Office of Water

Type of award: Internship, renewable.

Intended use: For undergraduate or graduate study in United States. Designated institutions: Office of Water (Cincinnati, Ohio, and Washingon, D.C.)

Eligibility: Applicant must be U.S. citizen.

Basis for selection: Major/career interest in engineering; environmental science or physical sciences.

Additional information: Provides opportunities to participate in studies related to development and implementation of drinking water regulations. Internships last one year. Number of awards vary. Stipend based on research area and academic classification; limited reimbursement for inbound travel and moving. Applications accepted year-round. See Website for application and more information.

Contact:
Web: www.orau.gov/orise/educ.htm

ORISE Student Internship at the U.S. Army Center for Health Promotion and Preventive Medicine

Type of award: Internship, renewable.

Intended use: For undergraduate or graduate study at accredited postsecondary institution in United States. Designated institutions: U.S. Army Center for Health Promotion and Preventive Medicine (Aberdeen Proving Ground, MD) and other approved locations.

Eligibility: Applicant must be U.S. citizen.

Basis for selection: Major/career interest in biology; chemistry; engineering; environmental science; physical sciences; science, general or health sciences.

Additional information: Provides opportunities to participate in applied clinical research in areas such as occupational and environmental health engineering, entomology, ionizing and nonionizing radiation, health promotion, industrial hygiene and worksite hazards, ergonomics, environmental sanitation and hygiene, laboratory science, chemistry, biology, toxicology, health physics, environmental health risk assessment and risk communication and related projects. Three months to one year; full-time or part-time appointments. Stipend based on research area(s) and academic classification. Number of awards varies. Applications accepted year-round.

Contact:
Web: www.orau.gov/orise/educ.htm

ORISE Student Research - National Center for Toxicological Research

Type of award: Internship, renewable.

Intended use: For undergraduate or graduate study at accredited 2-year, 4-year or graduate institution in United States. Designated institutions: National Center for Toxicological Research (Jefferson, AK).

Eligibility: Applicant must be U.S. citizen or permanent resident.

Basis for selection: Major/career interest in biology; chemistry; computer/information sciences; mathematics; pharmacy/pharmaceutics/pharmacology; science, general or medicine.

Additional information: Provides opportunities to participate in research on biological effects of potentially toxic chemicals and solutions to toxicology problems that have a major impact on human health and the environment. Ten weeks to one year; full-time or part-time appointments. Stipend based on research area(s) and academic classification. Summer deadline is March 1; applications accepted year-round for academic year appointments. Number of awards varies.

Application deadline: March 1

Contact:
Web: www.orau.gov/orise/educ.htm

ORISE Student Research at the Agency for Toxic Substances and Disease Registry

Type of award: Internship.

Intended use: For undergraduate or graduate study at accredited 2-year, 4-year or graduate institution in United States. Designated institutions: Agency for Toxic Substances and Disease Registry (Atlanta, GA).

Basis for selection: Major/career interest in biology; environmental science; public health; epidemiology; medicine; pharmacy/pharmaceutics/pharmacology; physical sciences; science, general or medical specialties/research.

Additional information: Provides opportunities to participate in research relating to exposure and disease registries, health investigations, public health assessments, toxicological profiles, emergency response and health education. Ten weeks to one year; full-time or part-time appointments. Stipend based on research area(s) and academic classification. Number of internships varies.

Application deadline: February 1

Contact:
Web: www.orau.gov/orise/educ.htm

ORISE Student Research at the Centers for Disease Control and Prevention

Type of award: Internship.

Intended use: For undergraduate or graduate study at accredited 2-year, 4-year or graduate institution in United States. Designated institutions: Centers for Disease Control and Prevention (Atlanta, GA, and Morgantown, WV).

Eligibility: Applicant must be U.S. citizen or permanent resident.

Basis for selection: Major/career interest in epidemiology; health sciences; environmental science; communications; economics; science, general; life sciences; medicine or physical sciences.

Internships

Additional information: Provides opportunities to participate in research on infectious diseases, environmental health, epidemiology, or occupational safety and health. One month to one year; full-time or part-time appointments. Stipend based on research area(s) and academic classification. Applications accepted year-round except at Division of Prevention Research and Analytic Methods; call for deadline.
Contact:
Web: www.orau.gov/orise/educ.htm

ORISE Student Research Participation at the U.S. Army Medical Research Institute of Chemical Defense

Type of award: Internship, renewable.
Intended use: For undergraduate or graduate study at 2-year, 4-year or graduate institution in United States. Designated institutions: U.S. Army Medical Research Institute of Chemical Defense (Aberdeen Proving Ground, MD) and other approved locations.
Eligibility: Applicant must be U.S. citizen.
Basis for selection: Major/career interest in biochemistry; biology; medicine or physical sciences.
Application requirements: Minimum 3.0 GPA.
Additional information: Provides opportunities to participate in development of medical countermeasures to chemical warfare agents. Internship lasts three months to one year; full- and part-time appointments available. Stipend based on research area and academic classification. Number of awards varies. Applications accepted year-round. See Website for application and more details.
Contact:
Web: www.orau.gov/orise/educ.htm

ORISE Student Research Participation at U.S. Army Facilities

Type of award: Internship.
Intended use: For undergraduate or graduate study at 2-year, 4-year or graduate institution in United States. Designated institutions: U.S. Army Research Laboratory (Aberdeen Proving Ground, MD); U.S. Army Center for Health Promotion and Preventative Medicine; U.S. Army Medical Research Institute of Chemical Defense; U.S. Army Environmental Center; Edgewood Chemical Biological Center.
Eligibility: Applicant must be U.S. citizen.
Basis for selection: Major/career interest in biology; medicine; physical sciences; computer/information sciences; materials science or engineering.
Application requirements: Application packet.
Additional information: Provides opportunities to participate in research and technology development in areas such as engineering, mechanics, chemistry, computational modeling, science and materials research related to enhancing the lethality and survivability of America's ground forces. Internship lasts three months to one year; up to a total of three years; full- or part-time appointments available. Stipend based on research area and classification. Number of awards varies. Applications accepted year-round. See Website for application packet. Recipients notified within one month of application.
Contact:
Web: www.orau.gov/orise/educ.htm

Pre-Service Teacher Internships

Type of award: Internship.
Intended use: For sophomore or graduate study. Designated institutions: Oak Ridge National Laboratory (Oak Ridge, TN).
Eligibility: Applicant must be at least 18. Applicant must be U.S. citizen or permanent resident.
Basis for selection: Major/career interest in science, general; mathematics or education. Applicant must demonstrate high academic achievement.
Application requirements: Recommendations, transcript. Minimum 3.0 GPA. List of courses.
Additional information: Provides opportunities to participate in educational training and research relating to preparation for teaching K-12 science, math and technology. Ten-week summer program. $400 weekly stipend with limited travel reimbursement and limited housing allowance. Must have health insurance and must have completed a minimum of two math classes above college algebra or at least two laboratory science classes. Application available online.
Contact:
Web: www.orau.gov/orise/educ.htm

Student Research Participation at the Federal Bureau of Investigation Counterterrorism/Forensic Science Research Unit

Type of award: Internship.
Intended use: For undergraduate or graduate study at accredited 2-year or 4-year institution in United States. Designated institutions: Federal Energy Technology Center (Pittsburgh, PA., and Morgantown, WV).
Eligibility: Applicant must be U.S. citizen.
Basis for selection: Major/career interest in forensics; chemistry or biology.
Additional information: Opportunities to participate in advancement of forensic science for the FBI Laboratory as well as federal, state, and local law enforcement agencies. Award number varies. Applications accepted on year-round basis. Stipend based on research area and academic classification. Appointments range from three months to one year.
   Number of awards: 5
Contact:
Web: www.orau.org

U.S. Department of Homeland Security Scholarship and Fellowship Program

Type of award: Internship.
Intended use: For full-time junior or senior study at accredited 4-year or graduate institution in United States.
Eligibility: Applicant must be U.S. citizen.
Basis for selection: Major/career interest in biology; engineering; social/behavioral sciences; physical sciences; mathematics or computer/information sciences.
Additional information: Opportunity to participate in an educational program intended to ensure a diverse and highly talented science and technology human resource base to meet the mission, goals, and objectives of the U.S. Department of Homeland Security. Appointments are for one year, with renewal for one additional year, given satisfactory progress. Application deadline is the first Friday in December.

Internships

Contact:
Web: www.orau.org

Owens Corning

Owens Corning Internships

Type of award: Internship.
Intended use: For full-time junior or senior study at accredited 4-year institution.
Eligibility: Applicant must be U.S. citizen, permanent resident, international student or Foreign students must be eligible to work in United States on full-time basis.
Basis for selection: Major/career interest in engineering; finance/banking; human resources; information systems; marketing or materials science. Applicant must demonstrate high academic achievement.
Application requirements: Proof of eligibility.
Additional information: Summer internship with housing assistance, competitive salary, access to credit union and fitness center. Summer program lasts from eight to ten weeks. Most majors considered. Most positions in Toledo, Ohio.
Contact:
Owens Corning
One Owens Corning Parkway
Toledo, OH 43659
Phone: 800-GET-PINK
Web: www.owenscorning.com/career

Pacific Gas and Electric Company

Pacific Gas and Electric Summer Intern Program

Type of award: Internship.
Intended use: For full-time undergraduate study in United States.
Eligibility: Applicant must be U.S. citizen or permanent resident residing in California.
Basis for selection: Major/career interest in accounting; business; communications; computer/information sciences; economics; engineering, mechanical; engineering, civil; engineering, electrical/electronic; mathematics or social/behavioral sciences. Applicant must demonstrate high academic achievement.
Application requirements: Resume, cover letter.
Additional information: Internships available throughout northern and central California, many in San Francisco. Students whose date of graduation is within six months of the May prior to start of internship are also eligible to apply. Deadline is rolling, but early applications are encouraged. Resume may be submitted online; format specifications available online. Visit Website or call sponsor for openings and campus recruitment dates. Must be eligible to work in the United States. Number and amount of awards vary. Most internships are summer only and typically last 10-12 weeks.

Contact:
Pacific Gas and Electric Company
College Relations/CHP
P.O. Box 770000, Mail Code N14G
San Francisco, CA 94177
Phone: 415-973-2798
Web: www.pge.com/jobs

PBS

Adult Learning Service Internship

Type of award: Internship.
Intended use: For sophomore, junior, senior or graduate study.
Basis for selection: Major/career interest in education; design or English.
Application requirements: Resume and cover letter.
Additional information: Applicant must have completed one year of undergraduate study. Program involves work for the ALS Web site. Knowledge of HTML and HTML editing programs preferred. Internships filled on rolling basis. Full- and part-time positions available; positions last from two to three months and pay $6 per hour. Located in Alexandria, VA. See Website for more information.
Contact:
PBS Internship Program
1320 Braddock Place
Alexandria, VA 22314
Phone: 703-739-5298
Web: www.pbs.org

Brand Management & Promotion Internship

Type of award: Internship.
Intended use: For sophomore, junior, senior or graduate study.
Basis for selection: Major/career interest in communications or marketing.
Application requirements: Resume and cover letter.
Additional information: Applicant must have completed one year of undergraduate study. Internship in Brand Management & Promotion department; applicant should have strong skills in writing, communication and project management. Internships filled on rolling basis. Full- and part-time positions available; positions last from two to three months and pay $6 per hour. Located in Alexandria, VA. Visit Website for more information.
Contact:
PBS Internship Program
1320 Braddock Place
Alexandria, VA 22314
Phone: 703-739-5298
Web: www.pbs.org

Cable & Satellite Strategy Internship

Type of award: Internship.
Intended use: For sophomore, junior, senior or graduate study.
Basis for selection: Major/career interest in public administration/service or computer/information sciences.
Application requirements: Resume and cover letter.
Additional information: Applicant must have completed one year of undergraduate study. Interns assist staff of cable and satellite office in drafting agreements with major cable

Internships

companies and researching and developing cable-and satellite-related projects. Requires excellent research and project-management skills. Internships filled on rolling basis. Full- and part-time positions available; positions last from two to three months and pay $6 per hour. Located in Alexandria, VA. Visit Website for more information.

Contact:
PBS Internship Program
1320 Braddock Place
Alexandria, VA 22314
Phone: 703-739-5298
Web: www.pbs.org

Children's Programming Services Internship

Type of award: Internship.
Intended use: For sophomore, junior, senior or graduate study.
Basis for selection: Major/career interest in education; film/video or English.
Application requirements: Resume and cover letter.
Additional information: Applicant must have completed one year of undergraduate study. Interns provide assistance to Children's Programming department. Internships filled on rolling basis. Full- and part-time positions available; positions last from two to three months and pay $6 per hour. Located in Alexandria, VA. Visit Website for more information.

Contact:
PBS Internship Program
1320 Braddock Place
Alexandria, VA 22314
Phone: 703-739-5298
Web: www.pbs.org

Creative Services Internship

Type of award: Internship.
Intended use: For sophomore, junior, senior or graduate study.
Basis for selection: Major/career interest in library science.
Application requirements: Resume and cover letter.
Additional information: Applicant must have completed one year of undergraduate study. Intern will assist in management of video promo library. Solid understanding of library systems and interest in film and broadcasting preferred. Internships filled on rolling basis. Full- and part-time positions available; positions last from two to three months and pay $6 per hour. Located in Alexandria, VA. See Website for more information.

Contact:
PBS Internship Program
1320 Braddock Place
Alexandria, VA 22314
Phone: 703-739-5298
Web: www.pbs.org

Engineering Internship

Type of award: Internship.
Intended use: For sophomore, junior, senior or graduate study.
Basis for selection: Major/career interest in engineering, electrical/electronic or computer/information sciences.
Application requirements: Resume and cover letter.
Additional information: Applicant must have completed one year of undergraduate study. Interns assist PBS systems engineers. Familiarity with AutoCad required; experience reading circuit diagrams and schematics highly desired. Internships filled on rolling basis. Full- and part-time positions available; positions last from two to three months and pay $6

per hour. Located in Alexandria, VA. Visit Website for more information.

Contact:
PBS Internship Program
1320 Braddock Place
Alexandria, VA 22314
Phone: 703-739-5298
Web: www.pbs.org

Human Resources Internship

Type of award: Internship.
Intended use: For sophomore, junior, senior or graduate study.
Basis for selection: Major/career interest in human resources; psychology or humanities/liberal arts.
Application requirements: Resume and cover letter.
Additional information: Applicant must have completed one year of undergraduate study. Graduate students in human resources encouraged to apply. Must have strong writing and customer service skills. Internships filled on rolling basis. Full- and part-time positions available; positions last two to three months and pay $6 per hour. Located in Alexandria, VA. Visit Website for more information.

Contact:
PBS Internship Program
1320 Braddock Place
Alexandria, VA 22314
Phone: 703-739-5298
Web: www.pbs.org

Interactive Internship

Type of award: Internship.
Intended use: For sophomore, junior, senior or graduate study.
Basis for selection: Major/career interest in education or humanities/liberal arts.
Application requirements: Resume and cover letter.
Additional information: Applicant must have completed one year of undergraduate study. Interns develop and produce content for PBS Web sites. Must have HTML skills and experience with Web page layout and design. Some editorial experience and work experience in educational setting preferred. Internships filled on rolling basis. Full- and part-time positions available; positions last from two to three months and pay $6 per hour. Located in Alexandria, VA. Visit Website for more information.

Contact:
PBS Internship Program
1320 Braddock Place
Alexandria, VA 22314
Phone: 703-739-5298
Web: www.pbs.org

Interconnection Replacement Office Internship

Type of award: Internship.
Intended use: For sophomore, junior, senior or graduate study.
Basis for selection: Major/career interest in engineering or computer/information sciences.
Application requirements: Resume and cover letter.
Additional information: Applicant must have completed one year of undergraduate study. Intern will manage assigned engineering/IT projects. Applicant must have proficiency with MS Office Suite and should be familiar with MS Project, Visio and AutoCAD. Internships filled on rolling basis. Full- and part-time positions available; positions last from two to three months

and pay $6 per hour. Located in Alexandria, VA. Visit Website for more information.

Contact:
PBS Internship Program
1320 Braddock Place
Alexandria, VA 22314
Phone: 703-739-5298
Web: www.pbs.org

Program Business Affairs Internship

Type of award: Internship.
Intended use: For junior study at 4-year institution.
Basis for selection: Major/career interest in law or business.
Application requirements: Resume and cover letter.
Additional information: Applicant must have completed one year of undergraduate study. Intern will gain basic knowledge of legal and business issues connected with the acquisition and production of PBS programming. All majors considered, although candidates interested in attending law school preferred. Internships filled on rolling basis. Full- and part-time positions available; positions last from two to three months and pay $6 per hour. Located in Alexandria, VA. Visit Website for more information.

Contact:
PBS Internship Program
1320 Braddock Place
Alexandria, VA 22314
Phone: 703-739-5298
Web: www.pbs.org

Program Development & Independent Film Internship

Type of award: Internship.
Intended use: For sophomore, junior, senior or graduate study.
Basis for selection: Major/career interest in communications or radio/television/film.
Application requirements: Resume and cover letter.
Additional information: Applicant must have completed one year of undergraduate study. Interns will support all functions of PBS Program Development and Independent Film department, including proposal log-in, documentation requests and data entry. Knowledge of Web applications required. Internships filled on rolling basis. Full- and part-time positions available; positions last from two to three months and pay $6 per hour. Located in Alexandria, VA. Visit Website for more information.

Contact:
PBS Internship Program
1320 Braddock Place
Alexandria, VA 22314
Phone: 703-739-5298
Web: www.pbs.org

Program Information & Special Events Internship

Type of award: Internship.
Intended use: For sophomore, junior, senior or graduate study.
Basis for selection: Major/career interest in communications; public relations or advertising.
Application requirements: Resume and cover letter.
Additional information: Applicant must have completed one year of undergraduate study. Intern will assist with media relations and promotions. Must have experience with HTML coding and excellent writing, proofreading and editing skills.

Internships filled on rolling basis. Full- and part-time positions available; positions last from two to three months and pay $6 per hour. Located in Alexandria, VA. Visit Website for more information.

Contact:
PBS Internship Program
1320 Braddock Place
Alexandria, VA 22314
Phone: 703-739-5298
Web: www.pbs.org

Program Management Internship

Type of award: Internship.
Intended use: For sophomore, junior, senior or graduate study.
Basis for selection: Major/career interest in communications.
Application requirements: Resume and cover letter.
Additional information: Applicant must have completed one year of undergraduate study. Interns will observe and assist with monthly live teleconference; screen and evaluate NPS and PLUS programs; and observe and train in AVID editing. Broadcast communications majors preferred. Internships filled on rolling basis. Full- and part-time positions available; positions last from two to three months and pay $6 per hour. Located in Alexandria, VA. Visit Website for more information.

Contact:
PBS Internship Program
1320 Braddock Place
Alexandria, VA 22314
Phone: 703-739-5298
Web: www.pbs.org

Video Operations Internship

Type of award: Internship.
Intended use: For sophomore, junior, senior or graduate study.
Basis for selection: Major/career interest in business/management/administration.
Application requirements: Resume and cover letter.
Additional information: Applicant must have completed one year of undergraduate study. Intern will assist with setup and maintenance of inventory database and work closely with purchasing, customer service and fulfillment warehouse to solve inventory discrepancies. Material management majors preferred. Internships filled on rolling basis. Full- and part-time positions available; positions last from two to three months and pay $6 per hour. Located in Alexandria, VA. Visit Website for more information.

Contact:
PBS Internship Program
1320 Braddock Place
Alexandria, VA 22314
Phone: 703-739-5298
Web: www.pbs.org

Pennsylvania Higher Education Assistance Agency

Pennsylvania Work-Study Program

Type of award: Internship, renewable.

Intended use: For full-time undergraduate, master's, doctoral or first professional study at accredited postsecondary institution. Designated institutions: PHEAA-approved institutions.

Eligibility: Applicant must be U.S. citizen or permanent resident residing in Pennsylvania.

Basis for selection: Applicant must demonstrate financial need.

Application requirements: Interview, proof of eligibility. State grant or subsidized Stafford loan.

Additional information: Student must demonstrate ability to benefit from career-related high-tech or community service work experience. Funds earned must be used to pay school costs at PHEAA-approved postsecondary institution. Amount and number of awards vary. Deadlines: Fall and entire year - Oct. 1; Spring - January 1; Summer - May 15.

    Number of applicants: 3,400
    Application deadline: October 1, January 1
Contact:
Pennsylvania Higher Education Assistance Agency
State Grant and Special Programs Division
1200 North Seventh Street
Harrisburg, PA 17102
Phone: 800-692-7392
Web: www.pheaa.org

PGA Tour

PGA Tour Diversity Internship Program

Type of award: Internship.
Intended use: For junior, senior or master's study.
Eligibility: Applicant must be Alaskan native, Asian American, African American, Mexican American, Hispanic American, Puerto Rican or American Indian. Applicant must be U.S. citizen.
Basis for selection: Major/career interest in marketing; business/management/administration; communications; information systems; journalism; radio/television/film; sports/ sports administration or public relations. Applicant must demonstrate high academic achievement, depth of character, leadership, seriousness of purpose and service orientation.
Application requirements: Interview, recommendations, essay, transcript.
Additional information: Internship lasts ten weeks at $360/ week with $120/month deducted for housing. Site locations include California, Florida, Georgia, Washington, Massachusettes, Michigan, and Texas. E-mail pgatdip@mail.pgatour.com for additional information.

    Amount of award: $3,600
    Number of applicants: 175
    Application deadline: February 13
    Notification begins: April 26
Contact:
PGA Tour Diversity Intern Program
Attn:Mike Cooney
100 PGA Tour Blvd.
Ponte Vedra Beach, FL 32082
Phone: 904-273-3520
Fax: 904-273-3588
Web: www.pgatour.com

Phipps Conservatory and Botanical Gardens

Phipps Conservatory and Botanical Gardens Internships

Type of award: Internship.
Intended use: For full-time junior, senior or graduate study at accredited postsecondary institution.
Eligibility: Applicant must be U.S. citizen.
Basis for selection: Major/career interest in horticulture; landscape architecture; environmental science; botany or education. Applicant must demonstrate high academic achievement.
Application requirements: Application.
Additional information: Contact sponsor or visit Website for more information.
Contact:
Human Resources
Phipps Conservatory and Botanical Gardens
1059 Shady Ave
Pittsburgh, PA 15232
Phone: 412-441-4442
Fax: 412-622-7363
Web: www.conservatory.org

Playhouse on the Square

Playhouse on the Square Internship

Type of award: Internship.
Intended use: For graduate or non-degree study.
Basis for selection: Major/career interest in performing arts; theater arts or theater/production/technical. Applicant must demonstrate depth of character, leadership, seriousness of purpose and service orientation.
Application requirements: Interview, audition, portfolio, recommendations, proof of eligibility. An audition is required as well.
Additional information: $100 per week, free housing. Internships are located in Memphis, TN, and last a full year. Write or visit Website for an application.

    Amount of award: $5,200
    Number of awards: 10
Contact:
Playhouse on the Square
51 South Cooper
Memphis, TN 38104
Phone: 901-725-0776
Fax: 901-272-7530
Web: www.playhouseonthesquare.org

Population Institute

Population Institute Fellowship

Type of award: Internship.
Intended use: For undergraduate study.
Eligibility: Applicant must be at least 21, no older than 25.

Internships

541

Basis for selection: Based on academic record, international travels, and foreign language. Major/career interest in social/behavioral sciences; foreign languages or international relations. Applicant must demonstrate high academic achievement, depth of character, leadership, seriousness of purpose and service orientation.

Application requirements: Interview, recommendations, transcript, proof of eligibility. Three letters of recommendation required, two of which must be academic. Resume and cover letter also required. Applicant must speak a foreign language.

Additional information: Fellowship pays $2,000 per month, one year long with 10 days paid vacation. Full medical and dental benefits start immediately. Funding used to train new generation of leaders for the Population Stabilization Movement. Applicant must be able to work in the U.S.

Amount of award:	$24,000
Number of awards:	8
Application deadline:	April 15

Contact:
The Population Institute
Fellowship Coordinator
107 2nd Street, NE
Washington, DC 20002
Fax: 202-544-0068
Web: www.populationinstitute.org

Princeton Plasma Physics Laboratory

Plasma Physics National Undergraduate Fellowship Program

Type of award: Internship.
Intended use: For junior study.
Eligibility: Applicant must be U.S. citizen or permanent resident.
Basis for selection: Major/career interest in engineering; physics; mathematics or computer/information sciences. Applicant must demonstrate high academic achievement, depth of character, leadership, seriousness of purpose and service orientation.
Application requirements: Recommendations, essay, transcript.
Additional information: Student must be U.S. citizen or permanent resident, and have a 3.5 GPA. Internship is ten weeks in the summer.

Amount of award:	$4,800
Number of awards:	25
Number of applicants:	100
Application deadline:	February 1
Notification begins:	March 15

Contact:
Princeton Plasma Physics Laboratory
P.O. Box 451, MS-40
Princeton, NJ 08543-0451
Phone: 609-243-2116
Web: www.pppl.gov

Pro-Found Software

Pro-Found Software Internship

Type of award: Internship.
Intended use: For junior, senior or graduate study.
Basis for selection: Major/career interest in computer/information sciences; engineering, computer or information systems. Applicant must demonstrate high academic achievement, depth of character, leadership, seriousness of purpose and service orientation.
Application requirements: Recommendations, transcript, proof of eligibility. Cover letter and resume.
Additional information: Must be studying in technical fields and be proficient in JAVA or C/C++. UNIX and Windows desirable. International students eligible. Year-round positions, $550-$800 per week, located in Teaneck, NJ. Interns work full life-cycle on real-world software development with professionals. Focus on component-based distributed systems, JAVA, Internet/Intranet. Relocation assistance and other benefits. Minutes from NYC.

Number of awards:	5

Contact:
Pro-Found Software
Glenpointe Centre West
500 Frank W. Burr Blvd.
Teaneck, NJ 07666
Phone: 201-928-0400
Web: www.pro-foundsoftware.com

Radio and Television News Directors Foundation

Capitol Hill Internship

Type of award: Internship.
Intended use: For graduate study.
Basis for selection: Major/career interest in journalism.
Application requirements: Essay, reference letter, resume.
Additional information: Interns must commit to minimum 40 hours a week. Summer and spring internships coincide with academic year. Application deadline for spring is January 5; for summer April 5.

Application deadline:	January 5, April 5

Contact:
Radio and Television News Directors Foundation
1600 K Street, NW
Suite 700
Washington, DC 20006
Web: www.rtndf.org

Random House

Random House Internship

Type of award: Internship.
Intended use: For senior study at 4-year institution.
Basis for selection: Major/career interest in publishing. Applicant must demonstrate seriousness of purpose.

Application requirements: Resume, cover letter. Apply in junior year for New York program; Westminster program open to all undergrads.

Additional information: Ten-week internship beginning in early June. All majors encouraged to apply. $300 per week stipend. Application accepted beginning January 1. If invited, applicant must travel to New York City or Westminster, Maryland, at own expense for interview in late February through mid-April. See Website for application and more information.

Application deadline: February 28

Contact:
Random House Internship Coordinator
Human Resources, 19th Floor
1745 Broadway
New York, NY 10019
Web: www.randomhouse.com/careers

Rhode Island State Government

Rhode Island Government Intern Program

Type of award: Internship, renewable.

Intended use: For junior, senior or graduate study in United States.

Eligibility: Applicant must be residing in Rhode Island.

Basis for selection: Major/career interest in public administration/service or governmental public relations.

Application requirements: Interview, recommendations. Cover letter.

Additional information: Interns are placed in various state offices. Students from other states may work for academic credit in unpaid internships.

Amount of award:	$100-$800
Number of awards:	180
Application deadline:	May 15

Contact:
Rhode Island Government Intern Program
Room 8AA, State House
Providence, RI 02903
Phone: 401-222-6782

Rhode Island State Government Internship Program

Type of award: Internship.

Intended use: For undergraduate or postgraduate study.

Eligibility: Applicant must be residing in Rhode Island.

Basis for selection: Major/career interest in governmental public relations or public administration/service. Applicant must demonstrate high academic achievement, depth of character, leadership, seriousness of purpose and service orientation.

Application requirements: Interview, recommendations, transcript, proof of eligibility. Writing sample required for law students only.

Additional information: Minimum 2.5 GPA. Summer program lasts eight weeks; spring and fall programs last entire semester. Fall application deadline is rolling. Compensation for summer interns only, at $100 per week. Spring and fall interns earn academic credit or work-study, if eligible. All placements in Rhode Island.

Application deadline: May 15, November 15

Contact:
Rhode Island State Government
State Capitol, Rm. 8AA
Providence, RI 02903
Phone: 401-222-6782
Fax: 401-222-4447

Seventeen Magazine

Seventeen Magazine Journalism Internship

Type of award: Internship.

Intended use: For undergraduate or graduate study at postsecondary institution.

Basis for selection: Major/career interest in journalism or design.

Application requirements: Portfolio, recommendations. Resume, cover letter, writing samples.

Additional information: Non-paying internship. Course credit is necessary. Spring deadline is mid-November. Summer deadline is mid-January. Fall deadline is late May. Applicants with interest in photography also encouraged to apply. Please mail all resumes.

Number of applicants:	1,000
Application deadline:	March 1, July 1

Contact:
Seventeen Magazine
Internship Coordinator
1440 Broadway, 13th floor
New York, NY 10018

SGI (Silicon Graphics)

SGI (Silicon Graphics) Internship/ Co-op Program

Type of award: Internship.

Intended use: For undergraduate or graduate study.

Basis for selection: Major/career interest in computer/ information sciences; engineering, computer; engineering, electrical/electronic; mathematics; information systems; human resources; business or marketing.

Application requirements: Resume and cover letter.

Additional information: Positions, locations, and awards vary. Visit Website for internship descriptions and application deadlines, and to submit resume. Programs run for 10-12 weeks, from May to August or from June to September. Undergraduate and postgraduate students in computer science/ computer engineering, electrical engineering, math, MIS, human resources, and business (analysis, marketing, development) preferred.

Contact:
SGI (Silicon Graphics)
Internship Program
1600 Amphiteatre Parkway
Mountain View, CA 94043
Web: www.sgi.com/employment

Simon and Schuster Inc.

Simon and Schuster Summer Internship Program

Type of award: Internship, renewable.
Intended use: For full-time junior or senior study at accredited vocational or 4-year institution.
Basis for selection: Major/career interest in publishing. Applicant must demonstrate high academic achievement.
Application requirements: Interview. Resume. Cover letter. Letter of interest.
Additional information: This is an eight-week, full-time paid program. It runs from early June through early August and is designed to train and recruit a diverse group of students interested in exploring careers in publishing. Applicants must have well-rounded extracurricular interests and work experience. This company also offers fall/spring internships for college credit only.
Contact:
Simon and Schuster, Inc.
Internship Coordinator
1230 Avenue of the Americas
New York, NY 10020
Web: www.simonandschuster.com

Smithsonian Environmental Research Center

Smithsonian Environmental Research Center Internship Program

Type of award: Internship, renewable.
Intended use: For undergraduate or graduate study at 4-year or graduate institution. Designated institutions: Smithsonian Environmental Research Center in Edgewater, Maryland.
Basis for selection: Major/career interest in biology; chemistry; environmental science or engineering, environmental. Applicant must demonstrate seriousness of purpose.
Application requirements: Recommendations, essay, transcript. Formal application, academic credentials, relevant experience and the congruence of the student's expressed goals with those of the Internship Program.
Additional information: Stipends are $350 per week and are available during spring and summer months. Projects are 40 hours per week, lasting from 10 to 16 weeks. Dorm space is available for $60 per week on a limited basis. Several application deadlines: Spring, November 15; Summer, February 1; Fall, June 1.

Number of awards:	25
Number of applicants:	250
Notification begins:	March 15, December 15
Total amount awarded:	$60,000

Contact:
Smithsonian Environmental Research Center
Internship Program
P.O. Box 28
Edgewater, MD 21037-0028
Phone: 443-428-2217
Fax: 443-428-2380
Web: www.serc.si.edu/internship/index.htm

Smithsonian Institution

James E. Webb Internship Program for Minority Undergraduate Seniors and Graduate Students in Business and Public Administration

Type of award: Internship.
Intended use: For senior or graduate study at 4-year or graduate institution. Designated institutions: Smithsonian Institution.
Eligibility: Applicant must be African American, Puerto Rican or American Indian. Applicant must be member of minority group underrepresented in management of non-profit scientific and cultural organizations. Applicant must be U.S. citizen.
Basis for selection: Based on relevance of internship at the Smithsonian to student's academic and career goals. Major/career interest in business/management/administration or public administration/service. Applicant must demonstrate high academic achievement.
Application requirements: Recommendations, essay, transcript. Include resume with completed application. Minimum 3.0 GPA.
Additional information: Applicant must be minority student enrolled as undergraduate senior or graduate student in business or public administration program. Applicants who have completed their degree within the past four months also eligible. Internships are full-time, 40 hours per week for ten weeks during the summer. Stipend is $400/week, with additional travel allowances offered in some cases. Contact sponsor or visit Website for more information and application.

Amount of award:	$4,000
Application deadline:	February 1
Notification begins:	April 15

Contact:
Office of Fellowships Smithsonian Institution
750 9th Street, NW, Suite 9300
P.O. Box 37012
Washington, DC 20013-7012
Phone: 202-275-0655
Fax: 202-275-0489
Web: www.si.edu/research+study

Smithsonian Minority Internship

Type of award: Internship.
Intended use: For undergraduate or graduate study. Designated institutions: Smithsonian Institution.
Basis for selection: Major/career interest in anthropology; archaeology; ecology; environmental science or art/art history.
Application requirements: Applicants must have major/career interest in research or museum-related activity pursued by the Smithsonian Institution. Contact Office of Fellowships for application procedures.
Additional information: Research internships at Smithsonian Institution in anthropology/archaeology; astrophysics; earth sciences/paleontology; ecology; environmental, behavioral (tropical animals), evolutionary and systematic biology; history of science and technology; history of art (including American contemporary, African, Asian); 20th-century American crafts; social and cultural history and folk life of America. Stipend of $350 a week for ten weeks. February 1 deadline for summer session; June 15 deadline for fall; October 15 deadline for spring. Minority students encouraged to apply.

Amount of award: $3,500
Application deadline: February 1, October 15
Contact:
Smithsonian Institution Office of Fellowships
750 9th Street, NW, Suite 9300 MRC 902
P.O. Box 37012
Washington, DC 20013-7012
Phone: 202-275-0655
Web: www.si.edu/research+study

Smithsonian Native American Internship

Type of award: Internship.
Intended use: For undergraduate or graduate study. Designated institutions: Smithsonian Institution.
Eligibility: Applicant must be American Indian.
Basis for selection: Major/career interest in Native American studies.
Application requirements: Contact Office of Fellowships for application procedures.
Additional information: Internship at Smithsonian Institution in research or museum activities related to Native American studies. Stipend of $350 a week for ten weeks. Deadline for summer is February 1; fall is June 1; spring is October 1. American Indian students encouraged to apply.
Amount of award: $3,500
Application deadline: June 1, October 1
Contact:
Smithsonian Institution Office of Fellowships
750 9th St, NW, Ste 9300 MRC902
P.O. Box 37012
W ashington, DC 20013-7012
Phone: 202-275-0655
Web: www.si.edu/research+study

Society of Physics Students

Society of Physics Students Summer Internship Program

Type of award: Internship.
Intended use: For full-time undergraduate study.
Eligibility: Applicant or parent must be member/participant of Society of Physics Students.
Basis for selection: Major/career interest in physics. Applicant must demonstrate high academic achievement.
Application requirements: Recommendations, transcript. Application. Resume and cover letter.Two letters of recommendation (one should be written by SPS advisor).
Additional information: Offers eight-week internships in science policy and research for undergraduate physics majors. Internships include $3,000 stipend, paid housing and transportation supplement. Internships are based in Washington, DC. Applicants must be active SPS members with excellent scholastic record and experience in science outreach events or science research. See Website for application and deadline.
Amount of award: $2,500
Contact:
SPS Summer Internship Program
One Physics Ellipse
College Park, MD 20740
Phone: 301-209-3034
Web: www.spsnational.org/programs/interns.htm

Solomon R. Guggenheim Museum

Guggenheim Museum Internship

Type of award: Internship.
Intended use: For junior, senior or graduate study.
Eligibility: Applicant must be U.S. citizen, permanent resident, international student or International students must have J-1 visa.
Basis for selection: Major/career interest in arts management; art/art history; arts, general; film/video; museum studies or museum studies/administration. Applicant must demonstrate high academic achievement.
Application requirements: Interview, recommendations, essay, transcript. Cover letter, resume. Separate list of relevant coursework and foreign languages. All official academic transcripts with official seal of universities. A 500-word typed, double-spaced essay indicating interest in program and museum work, with reason for applying.
Additional information: Applicant must have taken at least one modern art course. Summer application deadline is February 15. Fall deadline is May 1. Spring deadline is November 1. Spring and fall internships are full or part time, with a minimum commitment of 15 hours/week for six months. Summer internships are full time. See Website for list of individual programs and departments. A related internship program gives preference to minority students from New York City area.
Number of applicants: 300
Contact:
Solomon R. Guggenheim Museum
Internship Coordinator
1071 Fifth Avenue
New York, NY 10128
Phone: 212-423-3526
Web: www.guggenheim.org

Peggy Guggenheim Internship

Type of award: Internship.
Intended use: For undergraduate or graduate study.
Basis for selection: Major/career interest in arts, general; art/art history or museum studies. Applicant must demonstrate high academic achievement, depth of character, leadership and seriousness of purpose.
Application requirements: Recommendations, essay, transcript. List of relevant coursework, resume, cover letter, academic writing sample.
Additional information: One- to three-month internship at Peggy Guggenheim Collection in Venice, Italy. Must be fluent in English with knowledge of spoken Italian. Interns receive a monthly stipend. Request futher information and application forms from the Peggy Guggenheim Collection. Visit Website for details.
Number of awards: 139
Number of applicants: 800
Contact:
Peggy Guggenheim Collection Internship Coodinator
Palazzo Venier dei Leoni
701 Dorsoduro, 30123 Venice, Italy
Phone: 39-041-2405-401
Web: www.guggenheim.org

Sony Music Entertainment

Sony Credited Internship

Type of award: Internship.
Intended use: For undergraduate or graduate study at accredited postsecondary institution.
Basis for selection: Major/career interest in business; accounting; finance/banking; computer/information sciences; law; music or music management.
Application requirements: Interview, transcript, proof of eligibility. Resume and cover letter.
Additional information: Nonpaid internship. Applicant must be available to work at least two full days a week. Deadlines for spring and fall are rolling. Summer session deadline is March 31. Must be enrolled at accredited university and provide verification of course credit. Interns are placed in various departments throughout company. Send resume and cover letter in envelope clearly marked Sony Credited Internship.
Contact:
Sony Music Entertainment
Credited Internship Program
550 Madison Avenue, 2nd Floor
New York, NY 10022-3211
Phone: 212-833-7980
Web: www.sonymusic.com

Sony Summer Minority Internship

Type of award: Internship.
Intended use: For full-time undergraduate study at postsecondary institution in United States.
Eligibility: Applicant must be Asian American, African American, Mexican American, Hispanic American, Puerto Rican or American Indian.
Basis for selection: Major/career interest in business; music; recording arts or music management.
Application requirements: Interview. Resume and cover letter. Minimum 3.0 GPA. Applicant must be returning to school in the fall.
Additional information: Ten-week paid internship. Most interns are placed in New York offices; opportunities in sales and distribution offices in Los Angeles, Atlanta, New York and Chicago. Indicate preferred geographic location in cover letter and on outside of envelope; interns outside of New York will need a car. Record industry experience is preferred.
Application deadline: March 31
Contact:
Sony Music Entertainment
Minority Internship Program
550 Madison Avenue
New York, NY 10022-3211
Phone: 212-833-7980
Web: www.sonymusic.com

Southern Progress Corporation

Southern Progress Corporation Internship Program

Type of award: Internship.
Intended use: For junior, senior or graduate study.
Basis for selection: Major/career interest in journalism, graphic arts/design, marketing, landscape horticulture, or advertising. Major/career interest in journalism; graphic arts/design; marketing; advertising; accounting; information systems; landscape architecture or horticulture.
Application requirements: Recommendations, transcript. Cover letter, resume and writing/design samples.
Additional information: Three- to five-month internships in editorial, graphic design, market research, advertising and accounting departments. Internship available at Birmingham location only. Summer application deadline: February 15; fall deadline: June 15; spring deadline: September 15. Salary is $10/hour. Minimum 3.0 GPA. Recent graduates who received their bachelor's degree no more than six months prior to beginning of internship also eligible. Visit Website for details.

Number of awards:	30
Number of applicants:	500
Application deadline:	June 15, September 15

Contact:
Holly Goff, Internship Coordinator
P.O. Box 2581
Birmingham, AL 35202
Web: www.southernprogress.com

Southface Energy Institute

Southface Internship

Type of award: Internship.
Intended use: For undergraduate or graduate study at accredited 2-year, 4-year or graduate institution in United States.
Eligibility: Applicant must be U.S. citizen, permanent resident, international student or Foreign students must be eligible to work in United States.
Basis for selection: Major/career interest in architecture; environmental science; engineering, environmental; urban planning; horticulture; business/management/administration or landscape architecture. Applicant must demonstrate high academic achievement.
Application requirements: Application. Statement of intent. Names of references with contact information.
Additional information: Southface is an educationally focused non-profit working in the "green building" field. Internships cover variety of interests; sustainable building, community design, water-efficient landscaping, smart growth, enviromental event planning, energy policy and tech assistance, non-profit marketing and public relations. Three- to six-month positions available, with preference to six-month positions. Students work 40 hours per week; monthly tiered stipend begins at $335. Shared housing is available if space permits. Transportation assistance available. Some part-time positions may be available. Applications accepted year-round.

Contact:
Southface Energy Institute
241 Pine Street, NE
Atlanta, GA 30308
Phone: 404-872-3549
Fax: 404-872-5009
Web: www.southface.org

Spoleto Festival USA

Spoleto Festival Apprenticeship Program

Type of award: Internship, renewable.
Intended use: For undergraduate, graduate or non-degree study in United States. Designated institutions: Spoleto Festival U.S.A.
Basis for selection: Major/career interest in arts management; arts, general; music; public relations or theater/production/technical. Applicant must demonstrate seriousness of purpose.
Application requirements: Application, resume, and two letters of recommendation. Media relations applicants submit two writing samples.
Additional information: Interested students should visit Website for application. Four-week apprenticeship with arts professionals producing and operating international arts festival. Posts available in media relations, development, finance, box office, production, housing, general administration, merchandising, orchestra management, chamber music and rehearsals. Weekly stipend, housing and travel allowance provided.

Number of awards:	45
Application deadline:	February 1

Contact:
Spoleto Festival USA
P.O. Box 100, Apprentice Program
Charleston, SC 29402
Web: www.spoletousa.org

Spoleto Festival Production Internship

Type of award: Internship, renewable.
Intended use: For full-time undergraduate, graduate or non-degree study in United States. Designated institutions: Spoleto Festival U.S.A.
Eligibility: Applicant must be U.S. citizen.
Basis for selection: Major/career interest in performing arts; electronics or construction. Applicant must demonstrate seriousness of purpose.
Application requirements: Application, resume, two letters of recommendation.
Additional information: Interested students should visit Website for application. Four to six-week apprenticeship with arts professionals producing and operating international arts festival. Posts available for stage carpenters; stage electricians; production administrators; and sound, properties, wardrobe, wigs and makeup assistants. Must have related experience in technical theater. Weekly stipend of $250 and housing included.

Amount of award:	$250-$1,500
Number of awards:	30
Application deadline:	February 1

Contact:
Spoleto Festival USA
P.O. Box 100, Apprentice Program
Charleston, SC 29402
Web: www.spoletousa.org

Student Conservation Association

SCA Conservation Internships

Type of award: Internship, renewable.
Intended use: For undergraduate or graduate study at accredited postsecondary institution in United States.
Eligibility: Applicant must be U.S. citizen.
Basis for selection: Major/career interest in archaeology; ecology; forestry; natural resources/conservation; history; education; wildlife/fisheries; biology or communications.
Application requirements: Interview, recommendations.
Additional information: Internships include expenses such as food, travel, housing, and insurance. Positions at various locations in United States. Five deadlines yearly: January 5, March 1, June 1, August 15, November 1. Applications are accepted on a rolling basis; apply early for best chance. Applications received on or before February 1 may be considered for early selection. Applicants with interest in environmental education, interpretation, marine biology, and wilderness preservation also eligible. See Website for application.

Amount of award:	$4,725

Contact:
Recruiting Department Student Conservation Association
P.O. Box 550
Charlestown, NH 03603
Phone: 603-543-1700
Fax: 603-543-1828
Web: www.thesca.org

Sun Microsystems

Sun Microsystems Student Intern and Co-op Program

Type of award: Internship.
Intended use: For full-time sophomore, junior, senior or graduate study at accredited 4-year or graduate institution in United States.
Eligibility: Applicant must be U.S. citizen, permanent resident, international student or Foreign student must have unrestricted permission to work in United States.
Basis for selection: Major/career interest in computer/information sciences; engineering, electrical/electronic; engineering, computer; engineering, mechanical; information systems; marketing; finance/banking; human resources or business/management/administration. Applicant must demonstrate high academic achievement.
Additional information: Only open to full-time students. Students enrolled in industrial engineering degree program also eligible to apply. Must maintain 3.0 GPA or higher. Visit Website to submit resume and sign up to search for current

openings. Best-qualified students contacted within two weeks. Most internships take place in San Francisco Bay Area (Broomfield and Burlington campuses) and in San Diego, Los Angeles and Austin. Occasional positions elsewhere in United States.

Contact:
Apply through Website.
M/S UPAL01-471
Web: www.sun.com/studentzone

Texas Higher Education Coordinating Board

Texas College Work-Study Program

Type of award: Internship.
Intended use: For undergraduate, graduate or non-degree study at accredited 2-year, 4-year or graduate institution. Designated institutions: Public, private, and non-profit postsecondary institutions in Texas.
Eligibility: Applicant must be U.S. citizen or permanent resident residing in Texas.
Basis for selection: Applicant must demonstrate financial need.
Application requirements: Completed FAFSA. Register for the Selective Service or sign a statement that they are exempt from this requirement.
Additional information: Candidate must be enrolled at least half time. Award amount based on financial need. Not available at proprietary schools. Number of hours of part-time work based on need. May reapply. Contact financial aid office at college or university for more information.

> **Number of awards:** 2,970
> **Total amount awarded:** $2,547,719

Contact:
Phone: 800-242-3062
Fax: 512-427-6420
Web: www.collegefortexans.com

Twentieth Century Fox

Twentieth Century Fox Internship

Type of award: Internship.
Intended use: For full-time undergraduate or master's study at 4-year or graduate institution in United States.
Eligibility: Applicant must be U.S. citizen, permanent resident, international student or Non-citizens must be eligible to work in United States.
Basis for selection: Major/career interest in theater/production/technical; communications or film/video.
Application requirements: Resume and cover letter that includes areas of interest.
Additional information: Ten-week summer internships in many divisions of Fox Filmed Entertainment. These internships only offer college credit. Applicants must apply via Website.

Contact:
Twentieth Century Fox
Personnel Dept.
P.O. Box 900
Beverly Hills, CA 90123
Web: www.foxcareers.com

Tyson Foods, Inc.

Tyson Foods Intern Program

Type of award: Internship.
Intended use: For full-time undergraduate study at accredited vocational, 2-year or 4-year institution.
Basis for selection: Major/career interest in computer/information sciences; food science/technology or engineering, agricultural. Applicant must demonstrate high academic achievement.
Application requirements: Proof of eligibility. Resume, cover letter.
Additional information: Paid summer internships in computer programming, industrial engineering, livestock (pork) procurement, quality control. Program locations in South Dakota, Iowa and elsewhere. Must be eligible to work in the U.S. Visit Website for job descriptions, list of campus recruiting events, or to submit resume and cover letter.

> **Application deadline:** November 15

Contact:
College Relations Representative
Tyson Foods, Inc. World Headquarters
800 Stevens Port Drive-Suite 818
Dakota Dunes, SD 57049
Fax: 605-235-2025
Web: www.tysonfoodsinc.com

United Negro College Fund

Dell Corporate Scholars Program

Type of award: Internship.
Intended use: For full-time junior, senior or graduate study at 4-year institution in United States. Designated institutions: UNCF member colleges and universities; selected HBCUs (Historically Black Colleges and Universities) and majority institutions.
Eligibility: Applicant must be Alaskan native, African American, Mexican American, Hispanic American, Puerto Rican or American Indian. Applicant must be residing in Texas.
Basis for selection: Major/career interest in computer/information sciences; human resources; engineering, electrical/electronic; engineering, mechanical; engineering, computer; business or finance/banking. Applicant must demonstrate financial need and high academic achievement.
Application requirements: Recommendations, essay, transcript. FASFA, 3.0 GPA, resume, personal statement of career interest, and financial need statement or award letter.
Additional information: As part of this award, scholars will receive up to a $10,000 scholarship (based on successful internship performance), a paid summer internship salary, housing accomodations in Austin, TX, and round-trip transportation to Austin. Students must submit completed applications to UNCF for a preliminary screening. A team of

Internships

Dell representatives will interview the finalists and select 15 scholar recipients. See Website below for application and brochure. See www.dell.com for further information.

Amount of award:	$10,000
Number of awards:	15
Application deadline:	January 31

Contact:
Dell Corporate Scholars Program United Negro College Fund
P.O. Box 1435
Alexandria, VA 22313-9998
Phone: 866-671-7237
Web: www.uncf.org

Oracle Scholars Internship Program

Type of award: Internship.

Intended use: For sophomore or junior study at 4-year institution in United States. Designated institutions: UNCF member colleges or universities; HBCU schools.

Eligibility: Applicant must be African American. Applicant must be residing in Virginia or California.

Basis for selection: Major/career interest in business; marketing; finance/banking; engineering; human resources; computer/information sciences or accounting. Applicant must demonstrate high academic achievement.

Application requirements: Recommendations, transcript. Application, resume, personal statement of career interest, and financial need statement (available on Website).

Additional information: Applicants must have a minimum 3.0 GPA. Award is an 8-week paid summer internship at an Oracle location, which includes a $4,000 monthly salary; housing accomodations or monthly housing allowance; and round-trip transportation from school to internship location and local transportation to and from internship site. There is also a $10,000 scholarship available upon successful completion of the internship. Completed applications with all supporting documentation should be forwarded to UNCF/Oracle Scholars Internship Program. Once applications are submitted, UNCF will identify the top-ranked candidates; these candidates will be sent to Oracle for review and final selection.

Application deadline:	March 15

Contact:
UNCF/Oracle Scholarship Interns Program Attn: Marquis Miller
8260 Willow Oaks Corporate Drive
P.O. Box 1044
Fairfax, VA 22031-8044
Phone: 800-331-2244
Web: www.uncf.org

United Negro College Fund/ Pfizer Inc

UNCF/Pfizer Corporate Scholars Program

Type of award: Internship.

Intended use: For full-time sophomore, junior or graduate study at 4-year or graduate institution in United States. Designated institutions: UNCF schools and targeted institutions.

Eligibility: Applicant must be African American.

Basis for selection: Major/career interest in chemistry; animal sciences; business; human resources; finance/banking; biology; law or veterinary medicine. Applicant must demonstrate financial need and high academic achievement.

Application requirements: Recommendations, transcript. Resume, 3.0 GPA, completed UNCF application form, 2 recommendation letters, personal statement of career interest, financial need statement. Must be matriculated in one of the following degree programs: BS in Chemistry (organic or analytical), Pre-Vet, Microbiology, Animal Science; BS, BA in Supply Chain Management, Logistics, Operations Mnagement, Business; BA in Human Resources, Organizational Development; MS in Chemistry (organic or analytical); MBA in Finance, Human Resources, Organizational Development.

Additional information: This program is an 8-10 week paid internship at a Pfizer location. To determine eligibility, students must submit completed application form to UNCF for preliminary screening. A team of Pfizer representatives will interview the finalists and select ten scholars. For more information, visit www.pfizer.com. See uncf.org for deadlines, application and brochure.

Amount of award:	$15,000
Number of awards:	10
Application deadline:	January 31

Contact:
Pfizer/UNCF Corporate Scholars Program
P.O. Box 1435
Alexandria, VA 22313-9998
Phone: 866-671-7237
Fax: 703-205-3574
Web: www.uncf.org

United States Holocaust Memorial Museum

United States Holocaust Memorial Museum Internship

Type of award: Internship, renewable.

Intended use: For undergraduate or graduate study.

Eligibility: Applicant must be U.S. citizen, permanent resident, international student or Foreign students must be qualified to work in the United States.

Basis for selection: Major/career interest in museum studies/administration; history; English; foreign languages; communications; geography; graphic arts/design; communications or law.

Application requirements: Interview, recommendations, transcript. Resume, brief personal statement, cover letter, application.

Additional information: Semester-long internships available during summer, fall and spring in Holocaust research and museum studies. Not all positions paid. Applicants interested in German or Eastern European studies also eligible. Award amount is $1,000-$1,500 per month. Apllication deadline March 15 for summer; June 15 for fall; October 15 for spring. Applicant must complete phone interview, have two letters of recommendation, resume, and complete the application available online at www.ushmm.org, keyword "intern".

Amount of award:	$1,000-$1,500

Contact:
Internship Coordinator, Office of Volunteer and Intern Services
United States Holocaust Memorial Museum
100 Raoul Wallenburg Place, SW
Washington, DC 20024-2150
Phone: 202-479-9738
Fax: 202-488-6568
Web: www.ushmm.org

United States Senate

United States Senate Member Internships

Type of award: Internship.
Intended use: For full-time undergraduate study at accredited 4-year institution.
Eligibility: Applicant must be U.S. citizen or permanent resident.
Basis for selection: Major/career interest in political science/government; law; communications; public relations; public administration/service or economics. Applicant must demonstrate high academic achievement.
Application requirements: Will vary by individual progam. Generally include resume, cover letter, and writing sample.
Additional information: Senators administer their own internship programs complete with unique and more specific guidelines. Senate member interns generally reside or attend college in senator's state. Positions available in Washington, D.C., or member's state. Internships may be unpaid or (less frequently) paid, but generally offer assistance obtaining college credit. Term of service, eligibility vary. Some internships restricted to upper-level undergraduates. Contact individual senator's office directly. Visit Website for complete links to member sites, e-mail addresses and telephone contact numbers.
Contact:
Office of (Name of Senator)
United States Senate
Washington, DC 20510
Web: www.senate.gov

U.S. Department of Agriculture

USDA Summer Intern Program

Type of award: Internship.
Intended use: For undergraduate study.
Eligibility: Applicant must be high school senior. Applicant must be U.S. citizen.
Basis for selection: Major/career interest in public administration/service; political science/government; science, general or business/management/administration.
Application requirements: Recommendations, transcript. Resume, cover letter, U.S. government forms.
Additional information: Internships last approximately four months (May - August). Stipends are based on level of education, prior experience and position. Open to undergraduates and high school graduates entering college.

Applications available in January. All majors encouraged to apply. Deadline varies. See Website for additional information.
    Application deadline: March 1
    Notification begins: May 31
Contact:
United States Department of Agriculture Summer Intern Program Manager
1400 Independence Ave., SW
Rm 316-W, Jaimie L. Whitten Federal Building
Washington, DC 20250-9600
Phone: 202-720-7168
Web: www.usda.gov

U.S. Department of Education

Federal Work-Study Program

Type of award: Internship.
Intended use: For undergraduate or graduate study at accredited postsecondary institution in United States.
Eligibility: Applicant must be U.S. citizen or permanent resident.
Basis for selection: Applicant must demonstrate financial need.
Application requirements: Proof of eligibility. FAFSA.
Additional information: Part-time on-campus and off-campus jobs based on class schedule and academic progress. Students earn at least minimum wage.
    Application deadline: June 30
Contact:
Federal Student Aid Programs
P.O. Box 84
Washington, DC 20044-0084
Phone: 800-4-FED-AID
Web: http://studentaid.ed.gov

U.S. Department of Energy

ORISE U.S. Nuclear Regulatory Commission Historically Black Colleges and Universities Student Research Participation

Type of award: Internship.
Intended use: For undergraduate or graduate study at accredited postsecondary institution in United States.
Designated institutions: Laboratories where NRC research is being conducted; some appointments on HBCU campuses; some appointments at host universities under the guidance of principal investigators who have NRC research grant.
Eligibility: Applicant must attend historically black college or university. Applicant must be U.S. citizen or permanent resident.
Basis for selection: Major/career interest in computer/information sciences; engineering; biology; mathematics; geophysics; physics; materials science; physical sciences or health sciences.

Internships

Additional information: Provides opportunities for students from historically black colleges to participate in ongoing NRC research and development. Ten to 12 weeks during the summer; some part-time appointments of one year. Weekly stipend of $500 to $600. Limited travel reimbursement (round-trip transportation expenses between facility and home or campus). Funded by U.S. Nuclear Regulatory Commission through cooperative agreement with U.S. Department of Energy. Application deadline is third Tuesday in January.

Application deadline: February 20
Contact:
Web: www.orau.gov/orise/educ.htm

Student Research at the U.S. Army Edgewood Chemical Biological Center

Type of award: Internship, renewable.
Intended use: For undergraduate or graduate study at accredited 4-year or graduate institution in United States. Designated institutions: U.S. Army Edgewood Chemical Biological Center (Aberdeen Proving Ground, Md.) and other approved locations.
Eligibility: Applicant must be U.S. citizen.
Basis for selection: Major/career interest in biology; computer/information sciences; engineering; environmental science; physical sciences or science, general.
Additional information: Provides opportunities to participate in research and development in support of military missions. Three months to one year; full-time or part-time appointments. Stipend based on research area(s) and academic classification. Applications accepted year-round. Funded by U.S. Army Edgewood Chemical Biological Center through interagency agreement with U.S. Department of Energy.
Contact:
Web: www.orau.gov/orise/educ.htm

U.S. Department of State

U.S. Department of State Internship

Type of award: Internship.
Intended use: For junior, senior or graduate study at 4-year or graduate institution.
Eligibility: Applicant must be U.S. citizen.
Basis for selection: Major/career interest in political science/government; foreign languages; governmental public relations; business; public administration/service; social work; economics; information systems; journalism or science, general. Applicant must demonstrate high academic achievement.
Application requirements: Transcript. Application. Statement of interest.
Additional information: Applicant must be continuing student. Provides opportunities working in varied administrative branches of the Department of State, both abroad and in Washington, D.C. Internships are generally unpaid, but many institutions provide academic credit and/or financial assistance for overseas assignments. Paid internships primarily granted to students in financial need. Must be able to work a minimum of ten weeks. Selected students must undergo background investigation to receive security clearance. Deadlines: November 1 for summer, March 1 for fall, July 1 for spring. Contact intern coordinator or visit Website for further details.
Application deadline: March 1, July 1

Contact:
Intern Coordinator
U.S. Department of State
2401 E Street, NW, Room H518
Washington, DC 20522
Web: www.state.gov

U.S. House of Representatives

House Member Internships

Type of award: Internship, renewable.
Intended use: For full-time undergraduate study.
Eligibility: Applicant must be U.S. citizen or permanent resident.
Basis for selection: Major/career interest in political science/government; public administration/service; public relations or communications. Applicant must demonstrate high academic achievement.
Additional information: Members of the United Stated House of Representatives use undergraduate interns for a variety of jobs including constituent contact, research and correspondence. Positions are based in Congressional District Offices and in Washington, DC. Internships generally facilitate course credit, but offer no stipend. Some paid internships are funded through private nonprofit organizations. Information about the individual House member intern programs can usually be found online. A complete set of links to representatives' sites is available at www.house.gov. In general, applicants residing in the member's home district and enrolled in the same political party are favored. Typically, many Washington, D.C.-based internships are filled by students from outside the member district. Applicants may also be interested in working for congressperson serving on committee (i.e. Agriculture, Financial Services) relevant to their major. Interested parties should contact the representative with whom they are interested in working.
Contact:
U.S. House of Representatives
Washington, DC 20515
Phone: 202-224-3121
Web: www.house.gov/house/MemberWWW.html

U.S. National Arboretum

U.S. National Arboretum Internship

Type of award: Internship.
Intended use: For sophomore, junior, senior or graduate study at postsecondary institution.
Eligibility: Applicant must be U.S. citizen.
Basis for selection: Major/career interest in horticulture; botany; agriculture or forestry.
Application requirements: Application form. Resume and cover letter.
Additional information: Internships pay stipend of $9.24/hr. Average workday for most interns: Monday through Friday, 7 a.m. to 3:30 p.m.. Provides opportunity to gain experience in plant research in premier horticultural collection. Applicants need to have completed coursework or have acquired practical

experience in horticulture or related field. Basic gardening or laboratory skills, interest in plants, strong communication skills and ability to work independently preferred. Course credit may be arranged. See Website for deadlines, application requirements, and more information.

Number of awards: 15
Number of applicants: 30
Contact:
Internship Coordinator
U.S. National Arboretum
3501 New York Avenue, NE
Washington, DC 20002-1958
Phone: 202-245-4521
Fax: 202-245-4575
Web: www.usna.usda.gov

Wachovia

Finance Undergraduate Internships

Type of award: Internship.
Intended use: For full-time sophomore or junior study at accredited 4-year institution.
Eligibility: Applicant must be U.S. citizen or permanent resident.
Basis for selection: Major/career interest in finance/banking; accounting; business/management/administration or economics. Applicant must demonstrate high academic achievement.
Application requirements: 3.0 GPA, resume and cover letter.
Additional information: Ten-week program that consists of work assignments and professional development opportunities. Annual start date is on or around June 1. Number of awards varies; most positions located in Charlotte, North Carolina. Visit Website to apply online. Graduate program also offered.
Contact:
Apply through Wachovia Website.
Web: www.wachovia.com/college

Wall Street Journal

Wall Street Journal Internship

Type of award: Internship.
Intended use: For undergraduate or graduate study.
Basis for selection: Major/career interest in journalism.
Application requirements: Cover letter, resume and 12 bylined clips (letter- or legal-sized).
Additional information: Full-time summer internship lasts ten weeks. Previous journalism or college newspaper experience required. Interns paid $700 a week. All majors encouraged to apply.

Number of awards: 18
Application deadline: November 1
Notification begins: February 28
Contact:
WSJ Intern Application Cathy Panagoulias Asst. Managing Editor
The Wall Street Journal
200 Liberty Street
New York, NY 10281

Walt Disney World

Walt Disney World Horticulture Summer Internship

Type of award: Internship.
Intended use: For junior or senior study in United States. Designated institutions: Walt Disney World.
Basis for selection: Major/career interest in landscape architecture; horticulture or entomology. Applicant must demonstrate high academic achievement, seriousness of purpose and service orientation.
Application requirements: Interview, transcript. Resume and cover letter. College Program application.
Additional information: Please visit Website for more information and application deadline.

Number of awards: 30
Contact:
Walt Disney World
Horticulture Creative Services
P.O. Box 10000
Lake Buena Vista, FL 32830-1000
Web: www.wdwcollegeprogram.com

Walt Disney World Co.

Walt Disney World College Program

Type of award: Internship.
Intended use: For undergraduate study.
Eligibility: Applicant must be U.S. citizen or permanent resident.
Application requirements: Interview, recommendations. Application. Minimum 2.0 GPA.
Additional information: Applicant must have completed one semester at college or university. Must attend Walt Disney World College Program presentation to interview for program. Students guaranteed 30 hours per week with a maximum of 45 hours per week. Starting pay rate is $6/hour. See Website for application and more information.
Contact:
Walt Disney World
P.O. Box 10090
Lake Buena Vista, FL 32830
Web: www.wdwcollegeprogram.com

Washington Internships for Students of Engineering

Washington Internships for Students of Engineering

Type of award: Internship.
Intended use: For senior study.
Eligibility: Applicant must be U.S. citizen.
Basis for selection: Major/career interest in engineering.
Application requirements: Recommendations, transcript. Application and reference forms.

Additional information: Ten-week summer internship available to students who have completed three years of study. Interns write required research paper as part of process. Fare card for Washington metro system supplied. Lodging expenses covered. If seeking sponsorship by ANS, ASCE, ASME, or IEEE, student must be member. IEEE will sponsor computer science majors.

Amount of award:	$1,800
Number of awards:	15
Application deadline:	December 1

Contact:
Washington Internships for Students of Engineering
Attn: Allian Pratt, ASME
1828 L St. NW Suite 906
Washington, DC 20036
Phone: 202-785-3756
Fax: 202-429-9417
Web: www.wise-intern.org

The Weather Channel

The Weather Channel Meteorology Minority Summer Internship

Type of award: Internship.
Intended use: For senior study at accredited 4-year institution.
Eligibility: Applicant must be Alaskan native, Asian American, African American, Mexican American, Hispanic American, Puerto Rican or American Indian.
Basis for selection: Major/career interest in atmospheric sciences/meteorology.
Application requirements: Recommendations, transcript. Include cover letter and resume. Applicant can be from any minority group.
Additional information: Meteorologist intern. Preference given to those who have taken several atmospheric science/ meteorology courses, are highly computer literate and have interest in operational forecast career. Salary approximately $12 per hour, 40 hr/wk. Intern trained and incorporated into daily behind-the-scenes forecast, graphical and production work (not on-camera).

Number of awards:	1
Application deadline:	March 15

Contact:
The Weather Channel
Attn: Kathy Strebe, Dir. Weather Graphics
300 Interstate North Parkway
Atlanta, GA 30339

The Weather Channel Meteorology Summer Internship

Type of award: Internship.
Intended use: For senior study in United States.
Basis for selection: Major/career interest in atmospheric sciences/meteorology.
Application requirements: Recommendations, transcript. Include cover letter and resume.
Additional information: Meteorologist intern. Preference given to those who have taken several atmospheric science/ meteorology courses, are highly computer literate and have interest in operational forecast career. Salary approximately $12 per hour, 40 hr/wk. Intern trained and incorporated into daily behind-the-scenes forecast, graphical and production work (not on-camera).

Number of awards:	1
Application deadline:	March 15

Contact:
The Weather Channel
Attn: Kathy Strebe, Dir. Weather Graphics
300 Interstate North Parkway
Atlanta, GA 30339

Wilhelmina Models

Wilhelmina Models Internship

Type of award: Internship.
Intended use: For undergraduate or graduate study.
Eligibility: Applicant must be U.S. citizen or permanent resident.
Basis for selection: Major/career interest in fashion/fashion design/modeling. Applicant must demonstrate seriousness of purpose and service orientation.
Application requirements: Recommendations. Resume.
Additional information: Internships available in New York City. Stipend of $35 a day to cover lunch and travel expenses. High school graduates, undergraduates, recent college graduates and graduate students eligible. High school graduates and college graduates of any age are also eligible to work at New York City office only. Interns assist booking agents in men's, women's, children's, and marketing divisions.

Number of awards:	8
Number of applicants:	1,000

Contact:
Internship Coordinator
Cassi Caesar
300 Park Ave. S.
New York, NY 10010
Web: www.wilhelmina.com

Wolf Trap Foundation for the Performing Arts

Wolf Trap Foundation for the Performing Arts Internship

Type of award: Internship.
Intended use: For sophomore, junior, senior or graduate study in United States.
Eligibility: Applicant must be U.S. citizen, permanent resident, international student or Mus be able to meet INS I-9 requirement.
Basis for selection: Major/career interest in performing arts or arts management. Applicant must demonstrate seriousness of purpose.
Application requirements: Recommendations, essay. Cover letter with internship interest, outlining career goals and specification of departmental internship desired, resume, two letters of recommendation. Two writing samples (except technical, scenic painting, costuming, stage management, accounting, graphic design, photography, or information

553

systems applicant). Graphic design applicants must submit three design samples.

Additional information: March 1 deadline for full-time summer internships; July 1 deadline for part-time fall internships; November 1 deadline for part-time spring internships. Stipend: up to $210 per week in summer and $126 per week in fall and spring. College credit available. Applicant must have own means of transportation. Internships available in the following areas: Opera (Directing, Administrative, Stage Management, Technical); Education; Development; Special Projects; Communications and Marketing (Advertising/Marketing, Graphic Design, Publications, Media Relations, Photography); Human Resources; Accounting; Special Events; Food & Beverage Events Catering. Notification begins approximately one month following application deadline.

Amount of award:	$8,400
Number of awards:	40
Application deadline:	March 1, November 1

Contact:
Wolf Trap Foundation for the Performing Arts
Internship Program
1645 Trap Road
Vienna, VA 22182
Phone: 703-255-1933 or 800-404-8461
Fax: 703-255-1924
Web: www.wolftrap.org

Women's Sports Foundation

Jackie Joyner Kersee/Minority Internship

Type of award: Internship, renewable.
Intended use: For full-time undergraduate or graduate study in United States.
Eligibility: Applicant must be Alaskan native, Asian American, African American, Mexican American, Hispanic American, Puerto Rican or American Indian. Applicant must be female.
Basis for selection: Applicant must demonstrate high academic achievement.
Application requirements: Application, resume, and two letters of recommendation, as well as a phone or in-person interview.
Additional information: Internship set up to increase women of color in sports leadership posts. Open to students or women in career change. Applicants must have interest in sports, although the internship is open to a broad range of majors. Stipend is $1,000/month, with a minimum three-month term. Other internships available with base $450/month stipend. Download application form from Website. Internships available throughout the year.

Amount of award:	$3,000-$12,000
Number of awards:	6
Number of applicants:	50
Total amount awarded:	$12,000

Contact:
Women's Sports Foundation
Eisenhower Park
East Meadow, NY 11554
Phone: 800-227-3988
Web: www.womenssportsfoundation.org

Y.E.S. To Jobs

Youth Entertainment Summer

Type of award: Internship.
Intended use: For undergraduate study.
Eligibility: Applicant must be Alaskan native, Asian American, African American, Mexican American, Hispanic American, Puerto Rican or American Indian. Applicant must be at least 16, no older than 18, high school junior or senior. Applicant must be U.S. citizen residing in Michigan, New York, Tennessee, Texas, Florida, Georgia, District of Columbia, California or Illinois.
Basis for selection: Major/career interest in film/video; law; business or computer/information sciences.
Application requirements: Interview, recommendations, essay, transcript. Resume.
Additional information: Provides summer employment in various aspects of entertainment industry. Must be resident of Los Angeles, San Francisco Bay area, Dallas, Nashville, Chicago, Detroit, New York, Washington, D.C., Miami, or Atlanta. Application deadline 3/1 for Los Angeles; 3/15 for Atlanta, Miami, Nashville, New York City and Washington, DC.

Number of awards:	250
Number of applicants:	1,300

Contact:
Program Coordinator, Y.E.S. To Jobs
P.O. Box 3390
Los Angeles, CA 90078-3390
Web: www.yestojobs.org

Internships

Loans

Alaska Commission on Postsecondary Education

Alaska Family Education Loan

Type of award: Loan, renewable.
Intended use: For full-time undergraduate or graduate study at postsecondary institution. Designated institutions: Must be approved by U.S. Department of Education or Alaska Commission on Postsecondary Education.
Eligibility: Applicant must be U.S. citizen or permanent resident residing in Alaska.
Basis for selection: Applicant must demonstrate financial need.
Application requirements: Proof of eligibility. Must be a U.S. citizen and a permanent resident of Alaska.
Additional information: Low interest loan for family member of student to assist with student's educational costs. Must reapply each year. Recipients not eligible for Alaska Student Loan. Amount of awards: $9,500 graduates, $8,500 undergraduates.

Amount of award:	$8,500-$9,500

Contact:
Alaska Commission on Postsecondary Education
Alaska Student Loan
3030 Vintage Boulevard
Juneau, AK 99801-7100
Phone: 800-441-2962

Alaska Teacher Education Loan

Type of award: Loan, renewable.
Intended use: For full-time undergraduate or post-bachelor's certificate study at 4-year institution. Designated institutions: Must be approved by U.S. Department of Education or Alaska Commission on Postsecondary Education.
Eligibility: Applicant must be U.S. citizen or permanent resident residing in Alaska.
Basis for selection: Major/career interest in education, teacher; education, early childhood or education, special.
Application requirements: Recommendations, proof of eligibility, nomination by rural school districts (pop. under 5,500 and not on road or rail route to Fairbanks or Anchorage or pop. under 1,500 and on road or rail route). Applicant must be Alaska high school graduate. Must be enrolled or plan to be enrolled in bachelor's degree program in elementary or secondary teacher education, or in a teacher certificate program.
Additional information: Loan forgiveness possible for teaching in rural Alaskan school district. May not borrow more than $37,500 in total. Must reapply each year. Minimum GPA of 2.0 required.

Amount of award:	$7,500
Number of awards:	100
Application deadline:	July 1
Notification begins:	June 1

Contact:
Alaska Commission on Postsecondary Education
Alaska Teacher Education Loan
3030 Vintage Boulevard
Juneau, AK 99801-7100
Phone: 800-441-2962

Alaska Winn Brindle Memorial Education Loan Program

Type of award: Loan, renewable.
Intended use: For full-time undergraduate or graduate study at postsecondary institution. Designated institutions: Must be approved by U.S. Department of Education or Alaska Commission on Postsecondary Education.
Eligibility: Applicant must be U.S. citizen or permanent resident residing in Alaska.
Basis for selection: Major/career interest in wildlife/fisheries or food science/technology.
Application requirements: Proof of eligibility. Must be a U.S. citizen and a permanent resident of Alaska.
Additional information: Applicants with recommendation from an Alaskan fisheries business may be given priority. Minimum GPA of 2.0 required. Amount of loans based on budget. Contact office for more information.

Number of awards:	49
Application deadline:	May 15
Notification begins:	June 30
Total amount awarded:	$510,391

Contact:
Alaska Commission on Postsecondary Education
Winn Brindle Memorial Education Loan
3030 Vintage Boulevard
Juneau, AK 99801-7100
Phone: 800-441-2962

American Legion Kentucky Auxiliary

Mary Barrett Marshall Student Loan Fund

Type of award: Loan, renewable.
Intended use: For undergraduate study at vocational, 2-year or 4-year institution. Designated institutions: Eligible postsecondary institutions in Kentucky.
Eligibility: Applicant must be female. Applicant must be residing in Kentucky. Applicant must be descendant of veteran; or dependent of veteran; or spouse of veteran or deceased veteran.
Basis for selection: Applicant must demonstrate financial need.
Additional information: Maximum $800 per year, payable monthly, without interest after graduation or upon securing employment; 6% interest after five years. Daughters, wives, sisters, widows, and granddaughters of veterans eligible.

Amount of award: $800
Application deadline: April 1
Contact:
American Legion Auxiliary, Department of Kentucky
Chairman: Velma Greenleaf
1448 Leafdale Rd.
Hodgenville, KY 42748-9379
Phone: 720-358-3341

Contact:
American Legion Wisconsin Auxiliary, Department Secretary
2930 American Legion Drive
P.O. Box 140
Portage, WI 53901-0140
Phone: 608-745-0124
Fax: 608-745-1947
Web: www.amlegionauxwi.org

American Legion South Dakota

American Legion South Dakota Educational Loan

Type of award: Loan, renewable.
Intended use: For undergraduate study at vocational, 2-year or 4-year institution. Designated institutions: South Dakota vocational schools or colleges.
Eligibility: Applicant must be residing in South Dakota. Applicant must be dependent of veteran.
Additional information: Up to $1,500 per year, $3,000 maximum.
Amount of award: $1,500-$3,000
Application deadline: December 15, June 15
Contact:
American Legion South Dakota
Department Adjutant
P.O. Box 67
Watertown, SD 57201-0067
Phone: 605-886-3604

American Legion Wisconsin Auxiliary, Department Secretary

M. Louise Wilson Educational Loan Fund

Type of award: Loan.
Intended use: For undergraduate study.
Eligibility: Applicant must be female. Applicant must be residing in Wisconsin. Applicant must be veteran; or dependent of veteran; or spouse of veteran during Grenada conflict, Korean War, Lebanon conflict, Panama conflict, Persian Gulf War, WW I, WW II or Vietnam.
Basis for selection: Applicant must demonstrate financial need and high academic achievement.
Additional information: Minimum 3.2 GPA. $400 annually up to five years, but must reapply each year if grades are acceptable. No interest. Repayments begin three months after graduation at minimum of $35 per month.
Amount of award: $400-$2,000
Application deadline: March 15

American Society of Mechanical Engineers

ASME Student Loan Program

Type of award: Loan, renewable.
Intended use: For full-time undergraduate or graduate study in United States or Canada.
Eligibility: Applicant or parent must be member/participant of American Society of Mechanical Engineers.
Basis for selection: Major/career interest in engineering, mechanical. Applicant must demonstrate financial need.
Application requirements: Recommendations. Minimum 2.2 GPA for undergraduates; minimum 3.2 GPA for graduates.
Additional information: Applicant must be member of ASME in United States, Canada or Mexico, and enrolled in mechanical engineering or mechanical engineering technology program/courses. Award is $3,000 per year; $9,000 maximum for undergraduate degree.
Amount of award: $3,000
Application deadline: October 15, April 15
Contact:
American Society of Mechanical Engineers
Three Park Avenue
New York, NY 10016-5990
Phone: 212-591-8131
Fax: 212-591-7143
Web: www.asme.org/education/enged/aid

American Society of Mechanical Engineers Auxiliary

ASME Auxiliary Student Loan

Type of award: Loan.
Intended use: For junior, senior or graduate study at accredited 4-year or graduate institution in United States. Designated institutions: Must be enrolled in ABET-accredited mechanical engineering department.
Eligibility: Applicant or parent must be member/participant of American Society of Mechanical Engineers. Applicant must be U.S. citizen.
Basis for selection: Major/career interest in engineering, mechanical. Applicant must demonstrate financial need, high academic achievement and depth of character.
Application requirements: Recommendations.
Additional information: These loans are interest-free until graduation. There is no application deadline. Visit Website for

information and to download application or send SASE to address.

Amount of award: $3,000

Contact:
Janet Watson
623 N. Valley Forge Road
Devon, PA 19333-1241
Phone: 610-688-4826
Web: www.asme.org/education/enged/aid

Arkansas Department of Higher Education

Arkansas Minority Teachers Loan

Type of award: Loan, renewable.
Intended use: For full-time junior or senior study at accredited 4-year institution. Designated institutions: Arkansas institutions.
Eligibility: Applicant must be Asian American, African American, Mexican American, Hispanic American, Puerto Rican or American Indian. Applicant must be U.S. citizen or permanent resident residing in Arkansas.
Basis for selection: Major/career interest in education, teacher.
Application requirements: Transcript. 2.5 GPA.
Additional information: Applicant must pursue course of study for teacher education and have completed at least 60 credit hours. Loan forgiveness for teaching five years in Arkansas public schools or three years in Arkansas teacher shortage area. Visit website or call (501) 371-2050 or (800) 54-STUDY for an application.

Amount of award: $5,000
Number of awards: 100
Application deadline: June 1
Total amount awarded: $500,000

Contact:
Arkansas Department of Higher Education
114 E. Capitol Street
Little Rock, AR 72201-3818
Phone: 800-547-8839
Web: www.arkansashighered.com

California Student Aid Commission

California Assumption Program Loans for Education

Type of award: Loan, renewable.
Intended use: For junior, senior or post-bachelor's certificate study at accredited postsecondary institution. Designated institutions: Any California postsecondary institution with Commision on Teacher Credentialing approved program.
Eligibility: Applicant must be U.S. citizen residing in California.
Basis for selection: Major/career interest in education, teacher. Applicant must demonstrate financial need and high academic achievement.
Application requirements: Interview, recommendations, transcript, proof of eligibility, nomination by each participating institution. Loan indebtedness; must not hold an initial teaching

credential. Applicants must be pursuing teaching credentials to teach K-12.
Additional information: Must have outstanding educational loans in good status. Participants receive awards after providing eligible teaching service in a designated shortage area. Loans assumed for up to four years: up to $2,000 for first year and up to $3,000 for second, third and fourth years of consecutive eligible teaching service. Bonus amounts for teaching in the areas of mathematics, science, special education, and at low-performing schools.

Amount of award: $19,000
Number of awards: 6,500
Application deadline: June 15
Notification begins: September 1

Contact:
California Student Aid Commission
Specialized Programs
P.O. Box 419027
Rancho Cordova, CA 95741-9027
Phone: 888-224-7268
Fax: 916-526-7977
Web: www.csac.ca.gov

Connecticut Higher Education Supplemental Loan Authority

Connecticut Family Education Loan Program (CT FELP)

Type of award: Loan.
Intended use: For undergraduate or graduate study in United States. Designated institutions: Connecticut residents may attend any non-profit institution in the United States. Non-residents must attend non-profit Connecticut institution to be eligible.
Eligibility: Applicant must be residing in Connecticut.
Application requirements: Non-citizens must have alien registration receipt card (I-151 or I-551).

Amount of award: $2,000
Total amount awarded: $16,970,000

Contact:
Connecticut Higher Education Supplemental Loan Authority (CHESLA)
342 North Main Street
Suite 202
West Hartford, CT 06117
Phone: 800-252-FELP (in CT) 860-236-1400 (out of state)
Web: www.chesla.org

Delaware Higher Education Commission

Delaware Christa McAuliffe Teacher Scholarship Loan

Type of award: Loan, renewable.

Loans

Intended use: For full-time freshman, sophomore, junior or senior study at accredited 4-year institution. Designated institutions: Delaware schools.
Eligibility: Applicant must be permanent resident residing in Delaware.
Basis for selection: Major/career interest in education, teacher. Applicant must demonstrate high academic achievement.
Application requirements: Essay, transcript, proof of eligibility. Application. Must be Delaware resident.
Additional information: Recipient must be Delaware resident enrolled in Delaware college in program leading to teacher certification. Applicant must be high school senior with minimum 1050 on SAT/25 on ACT and rank in top half of class, or undergraduate with minimum 2.75 GPA. Loan-forgiveness provisions.

Amount of award:	$5,000
Number of awards:	68
Application deadline:	March 31
Notification begins:	July 1
Total amount awarded:	$280,000

Contact:
Delaware Higher Education Commission
820 North French Street
Wilmington, DE 19801
Phone: 302-577-3240
Fax: 302-577-6765
Web: www.doe.state.de.us/high-ed

Delaware Nursing Incentive Program

Type of award: Loan, renewable.
Intended use: For full-time undergraduate or non-degree study at vocational, 2-year or 4-year institution in United States.
Eligibility: Applicant must be permanent resident residing in Delaware.
Basis for selection: Major/career interest in nursing. Applicant must demonstrate high academic achievement.
Application requirements: Essay, transcript, proof of eligibility. Application. Must be Delaware resident.
Additional information: Must be Delaware resident. Minimum 2.5 GPA required. Recipient must be enrolled in full-time nursing program. Loan-forgiveness for practicing nursing at state-owned hospital, one year for each year of financial assistance.

Amount of award:	$5,000
Number of awards:	25
Application deadline:	March 31
Notification begins:	May 1
Total amount awarded:	$54,000

Contact:
Delaware Higher Education Commission
820 North French Street
Wilmington, DE 19801
Phone: 302-577-3240
Fax: 302-577-6765
Web: www.doe.state.de.us/high-ed

Delta Gamma Foundation

Delta Gamma Student Loan

Type of award: Loan.
Intended use: For undergraduate or graduate study in or outside United States.
Eligibility: Applicant or parent must be member/participant of Delta Gamma.
Basis for selection: Applicant must demonstrate financial need.
Application requirements: Recommendations, transcript.
Additional information: Applicant must be member, or sister son/daughter of member, of Delta Gamma. Loan must be applied towards cost of tuition, books, or other specific educational purposes.

Amount of award:	$1,000-$2,000

Contact:
Delta Gamma Foundation
3250 Riverside Drive
P.O. Box 21397
Columbus, OH 43221-0397
Phone: 614-481-8169

Florida Department of Education

Critical Occupational Therapist or Physical Therapist Shortage Loan Program

Type of award: Loan, renewable.
Intended use: For undergraduate or graduate study.
Eligibility: Applicant must be residing in Florida.
Basis for selection: Major/career interest in occupational therapy or physical therapy.
Application requirements: Florida Financial Aid Application by April 15; certification from the chairperson or director of the therapist program by April 15 to the Office of Student Financial Assistance ensuring that applicant is enrolled in eligible program; Critical Occupational Therapist or Physical Therapist Shortage Scholarship Loan Program Promissory Note to the Office of Student Financial Aid by date specified in cover letter.
Additional information: Annual amount of the award will be the cost of education, minus other student financial aid, up to a maximum annual award of $4,000. Awards are for licensed therapists with valid temporary permit who have worked full-time in Florida public schools for one year and who intend to be employed in Florida public schools for minimum of three years. Priority given to renewal applicants.

Amount of award:	$4,000

Contact:
Florida Department of Education
Office of Student Financial Assistance
1940 North Monroe Street, Suite 70
Tallahassee, FL 32303-4759
Phone: 888-827-2004
Web: www.FloridaStudentFinancialAid.org

Loans

Critical Occupational/Physical Therapist Scholarship Loan Program

Type of award: Loan, renewable.
Intended use: For full-time undergraduate or graduate study at graduate institution. Designated institutions: Florida institutions.
Eligibility: Applicant must be residing in Florida.
Basis for selection: Major/career interest in physical therapy or occupational therapy.
Application requirements: Proof of eligibility. Florida Financial Aid Application.
Additional information: Applicant must be enrolled in therapist assistant program, or upper division or graduate level therapist program for a minimum of twelve credits of undergraduate study or nine credits of graduate study for each academic term in which aid is received. Must declare intent to be employed for a minimum of three years as a licensed therapist in public schools, and must do so upon graduation or else loan will have to be repaid. Must have minimum 2.0 GPA for undergraduates and 3.0 GPA for graduates who are renewing.

    Amount of award: $4,000
    Application deadline: April 15
Contact:
Florida Department of Education
Bureau of Instructional Support/Com. Services
601 Turlington Bldg.- 325 West Gaines Street
Tallahassee, FL 32399-0400
Phone: 888-827-2004
Web: www.FloridaStudentFinancialAid.org

Critical Teacher Shortage Student Loan Forgiveness Program

Type of award: Loan, renewable.
Intended use: For undergraduate certificate or post-bachelor's certificate study at 4-year or graduate institution in United States.
Eligibility: Applicant must be U.S. citizen or permanent resident residing in Florida.
Basis for selection: Major/career interest in education, teacher; education, special or education.
Application requirements: Must be full-time teacher in critical teacher shortage subject area in Florida public or developmental research school.
Additional information: Must have graduated from undergraduate or graduate teacher preparation program and have been certified in critical teacher shortage subject area. Applicants must apply within 12 months of certification and teach full-time in critical subject area for at least 90 days. Loan must be repaid by teaching in Florida public school or in cash. Applications may be obtained from Critical Teacher Shortage contact person at public school district where applicant is employed, or Florida Department of Education, Office of Student Financial Assistance.

    Amount of award: $2,500-$10,000
    Application deadline: July 15
Contact:
Florida Department of Education
Office of Student Financial Assistance
1940 North Monroe Street, Suite 70
Tallahassee, FL 32303-4759
Phone: 888-827-2004
Web: www.FloridaStudentFinancialAid.org

Florida Teacher Scholarship and Forgivable Loan Program

Type of award: Loan, renewable.
Intended use: For full-time undergraduate or graduate study at accredited 4-year institution. Designated institutions: Eligible Florida postsecondary institutions.
Eligibility: Applicant must be high school senior. Applicant must be U.S. citizen or permanent resident residing in Florida.
Basis for selection: Major/career interest in education, teacher; education or education, special. Applicant must demonstrate high academic achievement and seriousness of purpose.
Application requirements: Proof of eligibility, nomination by by high school (for high school students only). SAT/ACT scores. Principal or dean must review application before submitting to Office of Student Financial Assistance by April 1.
Additional information: High school applicant must be member of future teaching organization (if high school has one), be in top 25 percent of class during school's seventh semester, have 3.0 unweighted cumulative GPA and intend to teach in Florida. Award given to one student from each public high school and proportionate number from all private high schools. Undergraduates must have 2.5 GPA and intend to teach in Florida schools. Graduates must have 3.0 GPA. Renewal applicant must have minimum cumulative GPA of 2.5. Fifteen percent of scholarships reserved for minorities.

    Application deadline: March 15
Contact:
Florida Department of Education
Office of Student Financial Assistance
1940 North Monroe Street, Suite 70
Tallahassee, FL 32303-4759
Phone: 888-827-2004
Web: www.FloridaStudentFinancialAid.org

Franklin Lindsay Student Aid Fund

Franklin Lindsay Student Aid Loan

Type of award: Loan, renewable.
Intended use: For full-time sophomore, junior, senior or graduate study at accredited postsecondary institution in United States. Designated institutions: Must be used at institutions approved by Southern Association of Accredited Schools in state of Texas.
Eligibility: Applicant must be U.S. citizen residing in Texas.
Basis for selection: Applicant must demonstrate financial need, depth of character, seriousness of purpose and service orientation.
Application requirements: Interview. Loan package must be completed and must have a co-signer other than spouse.
Additional information: Must have a GPA of 2.0 for undergraduates and 3.0 for graduates. Full-time study requires 12 credit hours undergraduate, nine credit hours graduate. Must have completed 24 credits before applying. Upon graduation or termination from school, loan goes to repayment structure at six percent, with maximum payment term of seven years.

    Amount of award: $5,000
    Application deadline: July 1
    Notification begins: June 1

Loans

Contact:
Franklin Lindsay Student Aid Fund
Bank One Private Client Services
P.O. Box 901057-TX1-1315
Fort Worth, TX 76101-2057
Phone: 800-765-8338 x5111
Web: www.franklinlindsay.org

Georgia Student Finance Commission

Georgia Promise Teacher Scholarship

Type of award: Loan, renewable.
Intended use: For junior or senior study at accredited 4-year institution. Designated institutions: Public or private colleges/universities in Georgia offering teacher-education programs approved by Georgia Professional Standards Commission.
Eligibility: Applicant must be U.S. citizen or permanent resident residing in Georgia.
Basis for selection: Major/career interest in education, teacher or education. Applicant must demonstrate high academic achievement and seriousness of purpose.
Application requirements: Transcript, proof of eligibility.
Additional information: Provides cancelable loans. Recipient must commit to teach one year in Georgia public school for each $1,500 awarded. Must teach at preschool, elementary, middle or secondary level. Out-of-state residents attending accredited Georgia teacher-education programs also eligible. Applicant must have minimum 3.0 GPA; be academically classified as junior; have declared education as major and/or be accepted for enrollment into teacher-education program leading to initial certification. Must obtain signatures from institution's Department of Education teacher-certification official and financial aid office.

Amount of award:	$1,500-$6,000
Number of awards:	1,626
Total amount awarded:	$4,435,823

Contact:
Scholarship Committee
2082 East Exchange Place
Suite 100
Tucker, GA 30084
Phone: 800-776-6878
Fax: 770-724-9031
Web: www.gsfc.org

Georgia Scholarship for Engineering Education

Type of award: Loan, renewable.
Intended use: For full-time undergraduate study at accredited postsecondary institution in United States. Designated institutions: GSFA-approved postsecondary private schools offering programs of study accredited by the Engineering Accreditation Commission.
Eligibility: Applicant must be U.S. citizen or permanent resident residing in Georgia.
Basis for selection: Major/career interest in engineering; engineering, civil or engineering, construction.
Application requirements: Transcript. Include signed promissory note.

Additional information: Sophomores, juniors and seniors must maintain 2.5 GPA. Must work in Georgia in engineering field one year for each $3,500 received or repay within six years.

Amount of award:	$3,500
Number of awards:	199
Total amount awarded:	$666,373

Contact:
Georgia Student Finance Commission
2082 East Exchange Place
Suite 100
Tucker, GA 30084
Phone: 800-546-4673
Fax: 770-724-9031
Web: www.gsfc.org

Grand Encampment of Knights Templar of the USA

Knights Templar Educational Foundation Loan

Type of award: Loan, renewable.
Intended use: For junior, senior, master's, doctoral, first professional or postgraduate study at accredited vocational, 4-year or graduate institution in United States.
Eligibility: Applicant must be U.S. citizen.
Basis for selection: Major/career interest in history or religion/theology. Applicant must demonstrate high academic achievement and depth of character.
Application requirements: Recommendations.
Additional information: Applicant must be referred by a Sir. Knight. Student should request application from Grand Encampment of Knights Templar of U.S.A. in state of residence. Personal dependability important. Send SASE for application.

Amount of award:	$3,000

Contact:
Grand Encampment of Knights Templar of the USA
5097 North Elston Avenue
Suite 101
Chicago, IL 60630-2460
Phone: 773-777-3300

Hattie M. Strong Foundation

Strong Foundation Interest-Free Student Loan

Type of award: Loan.
Intended use: For full-time senior or graduate study at accredited 4-year or graduate institution.
Eligibility: Applicant must be U.S. citizen or permanent resident.
Basis for selection: Major/career interest in humanities/liberal arts. Applicant must demonstrate financial need, high academic

Loans

achievement, depth of character, leadership, seriousness of purpose and service orientation.

Application requirements: Recommendations, proof of eligibility. SASE.

Additional information: Must be entering final year of baccalaureate or graduate degree program. Terms of repayment are based upon monthly income after graduation. Students should write between January 1 and March 31, giving brief personal history and identification of educational institution attended, the subject studied, date expected to complete studies and amount of funds needed. Enclose SASE with application.

Amount of award:	$5,000
Application deadline:	March 31

Contact:
Hattie M. Strong Foundation
1620 Eye Street, NW
Suite 700
Washington, DC 20006-4005
Phone: 202-331-1619
Fax: 202-466-2894
Web: www.hmstrongfoundation.org

Idaho State Board of Education

Idaho Education Incentive Loan Forgiveness Program

Type of award: Loan, renewable.
Intended use: For full-time undergraduate study. Designated institutions: Idaho postsecondary schools.
Eligibility: Applicant must be residing in Idaho.
Basis for selection: Major/career interest in education, teacher or nursing.
Application requirements: Must have graduated from Idaho secondary school within last two years.
Additional information: Loan forgiveness for teaching or nursing service in Idaho. Minimum 3.0 GPA or rank within top 15 percent of high school graduating class. Contact financial aid office of postsecondary Idaho public institutions for application materials and information.
Contact:
Financial aid office at designated institution
Web: www.idahoboardofed.org/scholarships/loan.asp

Jewish Family and Children's Services (JFCS)

Anna and Charles Stockwitz Children and Youth Fund

Type of award: Scholarship.
Intended use: For undergraduate study.
Eligibility: Jewish. Applicant must be high school senior. Applicant must be Jewish. Applicant must be residing in California.
Basis for selection: Applicant must demonstrate financial need and high academic achievement.
Application requirements: Minimum 3.0 GPA for grants.

Additional information: Up to $3,000 for grant and up to $6,000 for loan. Applicant must be 26 or younger to receive grant; no age limit for loan. Grant/scholarship applicant must be resident for at least one year of one of the following counties: San Francisco, Marin, Sonoma, San Mateo, or northern Santa Clara. Loan applicant must be resident for at least one year of any Bay Area county and must provide qualified local guarantor.

Amount of award:	$1,000-$6,000
Number of awards:	39
Application deadline:	September 1

Contact:
Jewish Family and Children's Services
Attn: Eric Singer
2150 Post Street
San Francisco, CA 94115
Phone: 415-449-1226
Fax: 415-449-1229

Kentucky Higher Education Assistance Authority (KHEAA)

Kentucky Teacher Scholarship

Type of award: Loan, renewable.
Intended use: For full-time undergraduate or graduate study at 2-year, 4-year or graduate institution. Designated institutions: Postsecondary institutions in Kentucky.
Eligibility: Applicant must be U.S. citizen residing in Kentucky.
Basis for selection: Major/career interest in education, teacher; education, early childhood or education, special. Applicant must demonstrate financial need.
Application requirements: Proof of eligibility. FAFSA, separate application (May 1 deadline).
Additional information: Must enroll in course of study leading to Kentucky teacher certification. Loan forgiveness for teaching in Kentucky schools: one semester for each semester of financial assistance, two semesters if service is in teacher shortage area. Cannot be enrolled in a program that leads to degree, diploma or certificate in religion, divinity or theology. Visit Website for additional information.

Amount of award:	$100-$5,000
Number of awards:	647
Number of applicants:	1,523
Application deadline:	May 1
Notification begins:	May 30
Total amount awarded:	$2,148,500

Contact:
Kentucky Higher Education Assistance Authority (KHEAA)
Teacher Scholarship Program
1050 U.S. 127 South
Frankfort, KY 40601-4323
Phone: 800-928-8926
Fax: 502-695-7373
Web: www.kheaa.com

Loans

Maine Education Loan Authority

Maine Loan

Type of award: Loan.
Intended use: For undergraduate or graduate study at accredited vocational, 2-year, 4-year or graduate institution in United States or Canada.
Eligibility: Applicant must reside in Maine or attend school in Maine. Applicant must be residing in Maine.
Application requirements: Proof of eligibility. Income information/credit analysis.
Additional information: Loans available to Maine residents for school of their choice. Out-of-state students attending Maine schools also eligible. May borrow full cost of education minus other financial aid. Loans are not forgivable. Amount of loan varies. Minimum amount $1,000.

Amount of award:	$1,000
Number of awards:	715
Number of applicants:	1,092
Total amount awarded:	$5,932,000

Contact:
Maine Educational Loan Authority
One City Center, 11th Floor
Portland, ME 04101
Phone: 800-922-6352
Web: www.mela.net

Maryland Higher Education Commission Office of Student Financial Assistance

Janet L. Hoffman Loan Assistance Repayment Program

Type of award: Loan, renewable.
Intended use: For undergraduate study. Designated institutions: Maryland schools.
Eligibility: Applicant must be U.S. citizen residing in Maryland.
Basis for selection: Applicant must demonstrate financial need.
Additional information: Loan repayment program for graduates who received degree from Maryland institution or a law school and are working for state or local government or nonprofit sector in Maryland. Priority given to current critical shortage fields. Applications available June through September. Funds may not be available to all eligible applicants.

Amount of award:	$7,500
Number of awards:	365
Application deadline:	September 30
Notification begins:	October 31
Total amount awarded:	$981,636

Contact:
Maryland Higher Ed. Commission Office of Student Financial Assistance
Loan Assistance Repayment Program
839 Bestgate Road, Suite 400
Annapolis, MD 21401-3013
Phone: 410-260-4565 or 800-974-1024
Fax: 410-260-3200
Web: www.mhec.state.md.us

Massachusetts Board of Higher Education

Massachusetts No Interest Loan

Type of award: Loan.
Intended use: For full-time undergraduate study at accredited vocational, 2-year or 4-year institution. Designated institutions: Massachusetts institutions.
Eligibility: Applicant must be U.S. citizen or permanent resident residing in Massachusetts.
Basis for selection: Applicant must demonstrate financial need.
Application requirements: Submit FAFSA.
Additional information: No Interest Loan (NIL) Program offers no interest loans to those who meet requirements; students have 10 years to repay NIL loans and a borrowing limit of $20,000.

Amount of award:	$1,000-$4,000
Number of applicants:	5,000
Application deadline:	May 1
Total amount awarded:	$9,200,000

Contact:
Office of Student Financial Assistance
Massachusetts Board of Higher Education
454 Broadway, Suite 200
Revere, MA 02151
Phone: 617-727-9420
Fax: 617-727-0667
Web: www.osfa.mass.edu

Michigan Higher Education Student Loan Authority

Michigan Alternative Student Loan (MI-LOAN)

Type of award: Loan.
Intended use: For undergraduate or graduate study. Designated institutions: Degree-granting colleges and universities in Michigan.
Eligibility: Applicant must be U.S. citizen or permanent resident residing in Michigan.
Basis for selection: Applicant must demonstrate financial need.
Application requirements: Proof of eligibility. Must be accepted for enrollment at a Michigan school or attending one currently. Applicant can be under 18 if emancipated minor. Applicant cannot be in default of any student loans. Cosigner may be required.

Loans

Additional information: MI-LOAN consists of two programs: Creditworthy Loan Program and Credit Ready Loan Program. Creditworthy Loan Program applicants must meet all credit standards. Credit Ready Loan Program applicants must attend eligible schools, but income, expenses and employment history not reviewed. Students or parents/guardians may apply; student may be emancipated minor. Students can be attending less than half time. Repayment terms: 25 years with maximum of 5 years of forbearance of either principal only or principal and interest. Applications accepted up to five months prior to loan period and deadline up to last day of loan period.

Amount of award:	$500-$125,000
Number of applicants:	19,134
Total amount awarded:	$110,357,093

Contact:
Michigan Higher Education Student Loan Authority
MI-LOAN Program
P.O. Box 30051
Lansing, MI 48909
Phone: 888-643-7521
Fax: 517-335-6699
Web: www.michigan.gov/mistudentaid

Military Officers Association of America

MOAA Interest-Free Loan and Grant Program

Type of award: Loan, renewable.
Intended use: For full-time undergraduate study at accredited 2-year or 4-year institution in United States.
Eligibility: Applicant must be no older than 24. Applicant must be U.S. citizen. Applicant must be dependent of deceased veteran. Applicant must be child of MOAA member or active-duty, Reserve, National Guard, or retired enlisted military personnel.
Basis for selection: Applicant must demonstrate financial need, high academic achievement, depth of character, leadership, patriotism, seriousness of purpose and service orientation.
Application requirements: Transcript, proof of eligibility. 3.0 GPA. Parent must sign promissory note before funds can be disbursed.
Additional information: Applicant must child of MOAA member and/or child of active-duty or retired enlisted personnel. Must be under 24; however, if applicant served in Uniformed Service before completing college, maximum age for eligibility increases by number of years served, up to five years. Application available on Website.

Amount of award:	$3,750
Number of applicants:	2,000
Application deadline:	March 1
Notification begins:	June 1

Contact:
MOAA Scholarship Fund
Educational Assistance Program
201 North Washington Street
Alexandria, VA 22314-2529
Phone: 800-245-8762
Fax: 703-838-5819
Web: www.moaa.org/education

Minnesota Higher Education Services Office

Minnesota Student Educational Loan Fund (SELF)

Type of award: Loan.
Intended use: For undergraduate or graduate study at vocational, 2-year, 4-year or graduate institution. Designated institutions: Minnesota or eligible out-of-state institutions.
Eligibility: Applicant must be residing in Minnesota.
Additional information: Applicant must be enrolled at least half-time in an eligible Minnesota school, or be a resident of Minnesota enrolled in an eligible school outside Minnesota. Must seek aid from certain other sources before applying, except federal unsubsidized & subsidized Stafford loans, National Direct Student loans, HEAL loans, other private loans. Institution must approve application. Maximum eligibility for freshmen and sophomores $4,500; juniors, seniors, and fifth-year students $6,000; graduate students $9,000. Must have a creditworthy cosigner.

Amount of award:	$500-$9,000
Number of awards:	28,571
Total amount awarded:	$103,937,897

Contact:
MHESO
1450 Energy Park Drive, Suite 350
St. Paul, MN 55108-5227
Phone: 651-642-0567 or 800-657-3866
Web: www.selfloan.org

Mississippi Office of Student Financial Aid

Critical Needs Teacher Loan/ Scholarship

Type of award: Loan, renewable.
Intended use: For undergraduate study at 4-year institution in United States. Designated institutions: Mississippi colleges and universities.
Eligibility: Applicant must be U.S. citizen residing in Mississippi.
Basis for selection: Major/career interest in education, teacher.
Application requirements: Application. Applicants must have minimum 2.5 GPA on college coursework. Must have passed Praxis I or have minimum composite score of 21 on ACT with minimum of 18 on all subscores. Must be enrolled in program of study leading to Class "A" teacher educator license.
Additional information: Applicant must agree to employment, upon completion of degree, as a full-time classroom teacher in a Mississippi public school located in critical teacher shortage or subject area. Must attend on-site entrance counseling session. Award is tuition and required fees plus average cost of room and meals and $500 book allowance. Students at private institutions receive award equivalent to costs at nearest comparable public institution. Recipients must maintain 2.5 GPA to renew loan. Interested non-Mississippi residents may apply if they have been accepted to Mississippi school.

Application deadline:	March 31

Loans

Contact:
Mississippi Student Financial Aid
3825 Ridgewood Road
Jackson, MS 39211-6453
Phone: 601-432-6997
Web: www.mississippiuniversities.com

Mississippi Health Care Professional Loan/Scholarship

Type of award: Loan, renewable.
Intended use: For full-time junior, senior or graduate study at accredited postsecondary institution. Designated institutions: Mississippi public institutions.
Eligibility: Applicant must be residing in Mississippi.
Basis for selection: Major/career interest in occupational therapy; speech pathology/audiology or psychology. Applicant must demonstrate high academic achievement.
Application requirements: Proof of eligibility.
Additional information: Must be enrolled in accredited training program of critical need in Mississippi public institution. Undergrads receive up to $1500, while graduate students receive up to $3000. Loan forgiveness for service in Mississippi health care institution: one year for each year of financial assistance, with a maximum of two years.

Amount of award:	$1,500-$3,000
Application deadline:	March 31
Notification begins:	August 1

Contact:
Mississippi Office of Student Financial Aid
3825 Ridgewood Road
Jackson, MS 39211-6453
Phone: 601-432-6997
Fax: 601-432-6527
Web: www.ihl.state.ms.us

Mississippi Nursing Education Loan/Scholarship

Type of award: Loan, renewable.
Intended use: For undergraduate, master's or doctoral study at accredited 4-year or graduate institution. Designated institutions: Mississippi public or pivate schools.
Eligibility: Applicant must be U.S. citizen residing in Mississippi.
Basis for selection: Major/career interest in nursing; nurse practitioner; pediatric nurse practitioner; health education or health-related professions. Applicant must demonstrate high academic achievement.
Application requirements: Proof of eligibility.
Additional information: Loan forgiveness for nursing service in Mississippi, one year for each year of financial assistance, for a maximum of two years. Undergraduate awards for RN to BSN and BSN study.

Amount of award:	$4,000-$10,000
Application deadline:	March 31
Notification begins:	August 1

Contact:
Mississippi Office of Student Financial Aid
3825 Ridgewood Road
Jackson, MS 39211-6453
Phone: 601-432-6997
Fax: 601-432-6527
Web: www.ihl.state.ms.us

Mississippi William Winter Teacher Scholar Loan Program

Type of award: Loan, renewable.
Intended use: For full-time undergraduate study at postsecondary institution. Designated institutions: Mississippi schools.
Eligibility: Applicant must be U.S. citizen residing in Mississippi.
Basis for selection: Major/career interest in education, teacher. Applicant must demonstrate high academic achievement.
Application requirements: Proof of eligibility.
Additional information: Undergraduate applicants must have 2.5 GPA. Loan forgiveness for teaching service in Mississippi public school or public school district: one year for each year of financial assistance, for a maximum of two years. See also www.mississippiuniversities.com.

Amount of award:	$4,000
Application deadline:	March 31
Notification begins:	August 1
Total amount awarded:	$3,416,831

Contact:
Mississippi Student Financial Aid
3825 Ridgewood Road
Jackson, MS 39211-6453
Phone: 601-432-6997
Fax: 601-432-6527
Web: www.ihl.state.ms.us

Navy-Marine Corps Relief Society

Vice Admiral E.P. Travers Loan

Type of award: Loan, renewable.
Intended use: For full-time undergraduate study.
Eligibility: Applicant must be U.S. citizen. Applicant must be dependent of active service person; or spouse of active service person in the Marines or Navy.
Basis for selection: Applicant must demonstrate financial need.
Application requirements: Proof of eligibility. Current military ID required for both applicant and service member.
Additional information: Loan must be repaid in allotments over 24-month period (minimum monthly repayment is $50). Must reapply to renew. Minimum 2.0 GPA. Applicant must be the dependent child of an active duty or retired service member who serves or served in the Navy or Marine Corps. The applicant may also be the spouse of an active duty sailor or Marine.

Amount of award:	$500-$3,000
Application deadline:	March 1

Contact:
Navy-Marine Corps Relief Society
801 North Randolph Street
Room 1228
Arlington, VA 22203

New Hampshire Higher Education Loan Corporation

TREE, The Resource for Education Expenses

Type of award: Loan, renewable.
Intended use: For undergraduate or graduate study at postsecondary institution.
Eligibility: Applicant must be at least 18. Applicant must be residing in New Hampshire.
Application requirements: Must be creditworthy.
Additional information: Must be New Hampshire resident enrolled in U.S. institution or non-resident enrolled in New Hampshire institution. Fee of four to eight percent of principal borrowed charged upon disbursement. Interest rate adjusted quarterly. Award ranges from $500 to entire cost less financial aid received.

  Amount of award: $500-$10,000
Contact:
New Hampshire Higher Education Loan Corporation
4 Barrell Court
P.O. Box 2097
Concord, NH 03302
Phone: 800-525-2577
Fax: 603-224-2581
Web: www.nhheaf.org

New Jersey Higher Education Student Assistance Authority

New Jersey Class Loan Program

Type of award: Loan.
Intended use: For undergraduate or graduate study at accredited vocational, 2-year, 4-year or graduate institution in United States. Designated institutions: Approved institutions. Proprietary institutions also eligible.
Eligibility: Applicant must be U.S. citizen, permanent resident, international student or Out-of-state students attending approved NJ school are eligible. Applicant must be residing in New Jersey.
Application requirements: Proof of eligibility.
Additional information: Must demonstrate credit-worthiness or provide co-signer. Parent or other eligible family member may borrow on behalf of student, or student may borrow. Must have filed all financial information required by the school to determine eligibility for Federal Stafford Loan or W.D. Ford Federal Direct Loan. Maximum loan amount varies, may not exceed education cost (less all other financial aid). Minimum loan amount $500. No interest rate loans available for graduate students. Apply year-round. Three percent administrative fee deducted from gross loan amount.
Contact:
New Jersey Higher Education Student Assistance Authority
4 Quakerbridge Plaza, P.O. Box 540
Trenton, NJ 08625-0540
Phone: 800-792-8670
Web: www.hesaa.org

New Jersey Higher Education Student Assistance Authority Federal Family Education Loan Program

Type of award: Loan.
Intended use: For half-time undergraduate study at postsecondary institution in United States. Designated institutions: Participating postsecondary institutions.
Eligibility: Applicant must be residing in New Jersey.
Application requirements: FAFSA.
Additional information: Program offers highly affordable loans available to students and their parents. Student loans require guarantor. Application and more information can be obtained on Website.
Contact:
NJ Higher Education Student Assistance Authority
P.O. Box 540
Trenton, NY 08625
Phone: 800-792-8670
Web: www.hesaa.org

New Mexico Commission on Higher Education

New Mexico Allied Health Student Loan-for-Service Program

Type of award: Loan, renewable.
Intended use: For undergraduate or graduate study at accredited postsecondary institution. Designated institutions: Public New Mexico postsecondary institutions.
Eligibility: Applicant must be U.S. citizen or permanent resident residing in New Mexico.
Basis for selection: Major/career interest in health-related professions; occupational therapy; mental health/therapy; physical therapy; pharmacy/pharmaceutics/pharmacology or dietetics/nutrition. Applicant must demonstrate financial need.
Application requirements: FAFSA.
Additional information: Loan forgiveness offered to those who practice in medically underserved areas in New Mexico. Must be accepted by or enrolled in following allied health programs at accredited New Mexico public postsecondary institution: physical therapy, occupational therapy, speech-language pathology, audiology, pharmacy, nutrition, respiratory care, laboratory technology, radiologic technology, mental health services, emergency medical services, or licensed or certified health profession as defined by Commission. Call sponsor number or visit Website for application.
  Amount of award: $12,000
  Application deadline: July 1
Contact:
New Mexico Commission on Higher Education
Financial Aid and Student Services
1068 Cerrillos Road
Santa Fe, NM 87501
Phone: 800-279-9777
Web: www.nmche.org

Loans

New Mexico Medical Student Loan-for-Service

Type of award: Loan, renewable.
Intended use: For undergraduate or first professional study in United States. Designated institutions: Accredited public schools of medicine.
Eligibility: Applicant must be U.S. citizen or permanent resident residing in New Mexico.
Basis for selection: Major/career interest in medicine or physician assistant. Applicant must demonstrate financial need.
Application requirements: FAFSA.
Additional information: Loan forgiveness for New Mexico residents to practice in medically underserved areas in New Mexico. Part-time students eligible for prorated awards. Preference given to students accepted for enrollment at the UNM School of Medicine. Number of awards and total dollar amount cover (cumulatively) New Mexico's higher education loan programs.

    Amount of award: $12,000
    Application deadline: July 1
Contact:
New Mexico Commission on Higher Education
Financial Aid and Student Services
1068 Cerrillos Road
Santa Fe, NM 87501
Phone: 800-279-9777
Web: www.nmche.org

New Mexico Nursing Student Loan-for-Service

Type of award: Loan, renewable.
Intended use: For undergraduate or graduate study at accredited 2-year or 4-year institution. Designated institutions: New Mexico postsecondary institutions.
Eligibility: Applicant must be U.S. citizen or permanent resident residing in New Mexico.
Basis for selection: Major/career interest in nursing. Applicant must demonstrate financial need.
Application requirements: FAFSA.
Additional information: Loan forgiveness to New Mexico resident for practice in medically underserved areas in New Mexico. Number of awards and total dollar amount cover (cumulatively) New Mexico's higher education loan programs.

    Amount of award: $12,000
    Application deadline: July 1
Contact:
New Mexico Commission on Higher Education
Financial Aid and Student Services
1068 Cerillos Road
Santa Fe, NM 87501
Phone: 800-279-9777
Web: www.nmche.org

New Mexico Teacher's Loan-for-Service

Type of award: Loan.
Intended use: For undergraduate or post-bachelor's certificate study at accredited postsecondary institution. Designated institutions: Regionally accredited New Mexico postsecondary institutions.
Eligibility: Applicant must be U.S. citizen or permanent resident residing in New Mexico.

Basis for selection: Major/career interest in education, teacher. Applicant must demonstrate financial need.
Application requirements: FAFSA.
Additional information: New Mexico residents enrolled in or accepted by undergraduate, graduate, or alternative licensure teacher preparation program approved by NM State Board of Education.

    Amount of award: $4,000
    Application deadline: July 1
Contact:
New Mexico Commission on Higher Education
Financial Aid and Student Services
1068 Cerrillos Road
Santa Fe, NM 87505
Phone: 800-279-9777
Web: www.nmche.org

New York State Grange

Grange Student Loan Fund

Type of award: Loan, renewable.
Intended use: For full-time undergraduate or graduate study at postsecondary institution.
Eligibility: Applicant or parent must be member/participant of New York State Grange. Applicant must be residing in New York.
Basis for selection: Applicant must demonstrate financial need.
Additional information: Must send SASE for application.

    Amount of award: $2,000
    Number of awards: 11
    Number of applicants: 11
    Application deadline: April 15
    Notification begins: June 15
    Total amount awarded: $22,000
Contact:
New York State Grange
100 Grange Place
Cortland, NY 13045
Phone: 607-756-7553

North Carolina Department of Community Colleges

Community College Grant & Loan

Type of award: Loan.
Intended use: For undergraduate study at 2-year institution. Designated institutions: North Carolina community colleges.
Eligibility: Applicant must be residing in North Carolina.
Application requirements: FAFSA. Must be enrolled for minimum six credit hours per semester in curriculum programs.
Additional information: Value of grants and loans vary. Students in Non-Pell eligible programs may receive NC Community College grants. NC Community loans may be given to students who will qualify for the federal Hope Scholarship tax credits or the Life Time Learning tax credit.

Contact:
North Carolina Department of Community Colleges
200 West Jones St.
Raleigh, NC 27603
Phone: 919-733-7051 ext. 440
Fax: 919-733-0680

North Carolina State Education Assistance Authority

North Carolina Nurse Education Scholarship Loan

Type of award: Loan.
Intended use: For undergraduate study at accredited 2-year or 4-year institution. Designated institutions: Designated North Carolina institutions.
Eligibility: Applicant must be U.S. citizen residing in North Carolina.
Basis for selection: Major/career interest in nursing. Applicant must demonstrate financial need and service orientation.
Application requirements: Proof of eligibility.
Additional information: Must attend specific participating North Carolina institutions. Applicant must be a resident of North Carolina for tuition purposes. Recipient agrees to work for one year as a full-time nurse in North Carolina for each year of NESLP funding. Nontraditional students, including older individuals, ethnic minorities, males and individuals with previous careers and/or degree encouraged to apply.

Amount of award:	$400-$5,000
Number of awards:	973
Total amount awarded:	$1,055,000

Contact:
NCSEAA-HEW
P.O. Box 14223
Research Triangle Park, NC 27709-4223
Phone: 1800-700-1775 ext. 624
Web: www.cfnc.org

North Carolina Nurse Scholars Program

Type of award: Loan, renewable.
Intended use: For full-time undergraduate study at accredited postsecondary institution. Designated institutions: North Carolina schools.
Eligibility: Applicant must be U.S. citizen residing in North Carolina.
Basis for selection: Major/career interest in nursing. Applicant must demonstrate high academic achievement, leadership and service orientation.
Application requirements: Recommendations, essay, transcript, proof of eligibility.
Additional information: Applicant must be a resident of North Carolina for tuition purposes. Minimum 3.0 GPA required for undergraduate applicants. Loan forgiveness for nursing service in North Carolina.

Amount of award:	$3,000-$5,000
Number of awards:	450

Contact:
North Carolina Nurse Scholars Program
P.O. Box 14223
Research Triangle Park, NC 27709-4223
Phone: 1-800-700-1775, ext. 624
Web: www.cfnc.org cfnc.org

North Carolina Student Loans for Health/Science/Mathematics

Type of award: Loan, renewable.
Intended use: For full-time junior, senior or graduate study at accredited postsecondary institution in United States. Designated institutions: North Carolina postsecondary institutions or eligible out-of-state schools.
Eligibility: Applicant must be U.S. citizen residing in North Carolina.
Basis for selection: Major/career interest in health-related professions; mathematics; science, general; dentistry; optometry/ophthalmology; social work or nursing. Applicant must demonstrate financial need.
Application requirements: Transcript, proof of eligibility. FAFSA. Signed promissory note endorsed by two or more co-signers.
Additional information: Loan obligation may be forgiven through approved employment within the state of North Carolina, provided the recipient works in the field for which he/she was funded. Students should request application as soon as possible after January 15 from the North Carolina Student Loan Program for Health, Science and Mathematics.

Amount of award:	$3,000-$8,000
Application deadline:	June 1

Contact:
North Carolina Student Loan Program
Health, Science and Mathematics
P.O. Box 14223
Research Triangle Park, NC 27709-4223
Phone: 1800-700-1775, ext. 624
Web: www.cfnc.org

Ohio Board of Regents

Ohio Nurse Education Assistance Loan Program

Type of award: Loan, renewable.
Intended use: For freshman, sophomore, junior, senior, post-bachelor's certificate or master's study. Designated institutions: Eligible Ohio institutions.
Eligibility: Applicant must be U.S. citizen or permanent resident residing in Ohio.
Basis for selection: Major/career interest in nursing. Applicant must demonstrate financial need and high academic achievement.
Application requirements: Proof of eligibility.
Additional information: Must be accepted to or enrolled in an approved pre- or post-licensure licensed practical nurse or registered nursing education program. Debt cancellation at rate of 20 percent per year (for maximum of five years) if borrower is employed in clinical practice of nursing in Ohio after graduation. Applications are available from high school guidance offices, nursing education programs, vocational schools, and the Ohio Board of Education.

Loans

Amount of award: $3,000
Application deadline: June 1, November 1
Notification begins: July 15, December 15
Contact:
State Grants and Scholarships Department
Ohio Board of Regents
P.O. Box 182452
Columbus, OH 43218-2452
Phone: 888-833-1133
Fax: 614-752-5903

Pickett and Hatcher Educational Fund, Inc.

Pickett and Hatcher Educational Loan

Type of award: Loan, renewable.
Intended use: For full-time freshman, sophomore, junior or senior study at 4-year institution. Designated institutions: Four-year institutions in Alabama, Florida, Georgia, Kentucky, Mississippi, North Carolina, South Carolina, Tennessee, and Virginia.
Eligibility: Applicant must be high school senior. Applicant must be U.S. citizen residing in Tennessee, South Carolina, Georgia, Florida, Virginia, Mississippi, Alabama, Kentucky or North Carolina.
Basis for selection: Applicant must demonstrate financial need and high academic achievement.
Additional information: First-time applicants must be entering freshmen. Not available to law, medicine, or ministry students. Loans renewed up to $22,000.
Amount of award: $1,000-$5,500
Number of awards: 393
Number of applicants: 610
Application deadline: January 1
Total amount awarded: $1,952,041
Contact:
Pickett and Hatcher Educational Fund, Inc.
Loan Program
P.O. Box 8169
Columbus, GA 31908-8169
Phone: 706-327-6586
Fax: 706-324-6788
Web: www.phef.org

Presbyterian Church (USA)

Presbyterian Undergraduate and Graduate Loan

Type of award: Loan, renewable.
Intended use: For full-time undergraduate or graduate study at accredited 2-year, 4-year or graduate institution in United States.
Eligibility: Applicant must be Presbyterian. Applicant must be U.S. citizen or permanent resident.
Basis for selection: Applicant must demonstrate financial need and high academic achievement.

Additional information: Must establish and maintain minimum 2.0 GPA. Contact office for current interest rates and deferment policies. Must give evidence of financial reliability. Undergraduates and graduates can apply for up to $15,000 spread out over undergraduate and graduate studies. If student is in the last year of study and has not yet applied for these loans, student can apply for the full amount.
Amount of award: $200-$15,000
Contact:
Presbyterian Church (USA)
Financial Aid for Studies
100 Witherspoon Street, M065
Louisville, KY 40202-1396
Phone: 888-728-7228 ext. 5735
Fax: 502-569-8766
Web: www.pcusa.org/financialaid

South Carolina Student Loan Corporation

South Carolina Teacher Loans

Type of award: Loan, renewable.
Intended use: For undergraduate or graduate study at accredited 2-year, 4-year or graduate institution. Designated institutions: South Carolina institutions.
Eligibility: Applicant must be U.S. citizen residing in South Carolina.
Basis for selection: Major/career interest in education. Applicant must demonstrate high academic achievement.
Application requirements: Teacher Loan Application Form.
Additional information: Freshmen and sophomores may borrow up to $2,500 per year; juniors, seniors and graduate students may borrow up to $5,000 per year. Graduate study eligible only if required for initial teacher certification. Entering freshman must have minimum SAT score of 994 (ACT 19.2) and rank in top 40 percent of high school class. Undergraduate and entering graduate applicants must have 2.75 GPA and have passed Education Entrance Examination. Graduate applicant must have 3.5 GPA. Loan forgiveness for service in teacher shortage area in South Carolina public schools: 20 percent for each year of service, 33 percent if service in geographic and subject shortage area.
Amount of award: $2,500-$5,000
Number of awards: 1,597
Application deadline: June 1
Notification begins: July 15
Total amount awarded: $5,556,496
Contact:
South Carolina Student Loan Corporation
P.O. Box 21487
Columbia, SC 29221
Phone: 803-798-0916
Web: www.scstudentloan.org

Student Aid Foundation

Student Aid Foundation Loan

Type of award: Loan, renewable.

Intended use: For full-time undergraduate, master's, doctoral or first professional study at accredited vocational, 2-year, 4-year or graduate institution in United States.
Eligibility: Applicant must be female. Applicant must be U.S. citizen residing in Georgia.
Basis for selection: Applicant must demonstrate financial need, high academic achievement and seriousness of purpose.
Application requirements: Essay, transcript. References required.
Additional information: Non-Georgia residents attending Georgia institutions can qualify. Loan not forgivable. Must have financially responsible endorser. Minimum 2.5 GPA. Send SASE with request for application, or download it from Website.

Amount of award:	$3,500-$5,000
Number of awards:	40
Application deadline:	April 15
Notification begins:	June 1

Contact:
Student Aid Foundation
2520 East Piedmont Road
Suite F, PMB 180
Marietta, GA 30062
Phone: 770-973-7077
Fax: 770-973-2220
Web: www.studentaidfoundation.org

Tennessee Student Assistance Corporation

Tennessee Minority Teaching Fellows Program

Type of award: Loan, renewable.
Intended use: For full-time freshman, sophomore, junior or senior study at accredited 2-year or 4-year institution. Designated institutions: Accredited Tennessee schools.
Eligibility: Applicant must be Alaskan native, Asian American, African American, Mexican American, Hispanic American, Puerto Rican or American Indian. Applicant must be U.S. citizen residing in Tennessee.
Basis for selection: Selection based on applicant's GPA, ACT/SAT, rank, quality of essay and extra-curricular activities. Applicant must demonstrate academic achievement.
Application requirements: Recommendations, essay, transcript. Include extracurricular list. Application must be postmarked by 4/15.
Additional information: Entering freshmen applicants have priority and must have a minimum 2.75 GPA, rank in top 25 percent of class, or score at least 18 on ACT (780 SAT). Undergraduate applicants must have a minimum 2.5 college GPA. Must make commitment to teaching. Loan can be forgiven by teaching in Tennessee public K-12 schools, one year for each year of funding.

Amount of award:	$5,000
Number of awards:	29
Number of applicants:	200
Application deadline:	April 15
Total amount awarded:	$145,000

Contact:
Tennessee Student Assistance Corporation
Parkway Towers, Suite 1950
404 James Robertson Parkway
Nashville, TN 37243-0820
Phone: 615-741-1346 or 800-342-1663
Fax: 615-741-6101
Web: www.state.tn.us/tsac

Tennessee Teaching Scholarship

Type of award: Loan, renewable.
Intended use: For junior, senior, post-bachelor's certificate or master's study at accredited graduate institution. Designated institutions: Accredited Tennessee schools.
Eligibility: Applicant must be U.S. citizen residing in Tennessee.
Basis for selection: Major/career interest in education; education, teacher; education, special or education, early childhood. Applicant must demonstrate high academic achievement.
Application requirements: Recommendations, transcript, proof of eligibility. Must provide verification of standardized test score and be accepted into Teacher Licensure Program.
Additional information: Loan can be forgiven for teaching in Tennessee public schools, K-12. Minimum 2.75 cumulative GPA and a standardized test score adequate for admission to the Teacher Education Program in Tennessee schools. Amount of award based on funding.

Amount of award:	$4,500
Number of awards:	195
Number of applicants:	300
Application deadline:	April 15
Total amount awarded:	$500,000

Contact:
Tennessee Student Assistance Corporation
Parkway Towers, Suite 1950
404 James Robertson Parkway
Nashville, TN 37243-0820
Phone: 615-741-1346 or 800-342-1663
Fax: 615-741-6101
Web: www.state.tn.us/tsac

Texas Higher Education Coordinating Board

Hinson-Hazlewood College Access Loan (CAL)

Type of award: Loan.
Intended use: For undergraduate or graduate study at 2-year, 4-year or graduate institution in United States. Designated institutions: Public and private non-profit postsecondary institutions in Texas.
Eligibility: Applicant must be U.S. citizen or permanent resident residing in Texas.
Additional information: Texas colleges and universities have a limited number of CAL loans. Applicants need not show financial need. The loan may be used to cover the family's expected contribution (EFC). Cosigners must have good credit and meet other program criteria. Total amount available for loan is $10,000 per academic year or lifetime total of $45,000. Applicants should contact their college/university financial aid office for more information and to request application packet.

Loans

569

Amount of award: $10,000
Contact:
Texas Higher Education Coordinating Board
Student Services Division
P. O. Box 12788
Austin, TX 12788-2788
Phone: 800-242-3062
Fax: 512-427-6420
Web: www.collegefortexans.com

Teach for Texas Conditional Grant Program

Type of award: Loan.
Intended use: For junior or senior study at 4-year institution. Designated institutions: Texas colleges and universities offering degree programs leading to teacher certification.
Eligibility: Applicant must be residing in Texas.
Application requirements: Minimum 2.5 GPA. Application for financial aid. Are enrolled at least 3/4 time in an approved educator certification program as: a junior, a senior, a renewal recipient in the final fifth year required by some institutions in order to be recommended for certification, or a post-baccalaureate student enrolled for the first time in a traditional educator certification program. Have no conviction for a felony or an offense under Chapter 481, Health and Safety Code (Texas Controlled Substances Act), or under the law of another jurisdiction involving a controlled substance as defined in Chapter 481, Health and Safety Code, (unless other applicable eligibility requirements set forth in rule have been met.
Additional information: Student loan with cancellation provisions for teaching. Must be enrolled in a teaching field designated as having a critical shortage of teachers or agree to teach in Texas community with certified critical shortage of teachers. Amount award varies.
Contact:
Texas Higher Education Coordinating Board
Student Services Division
P. O. Box 12788
Austin, TX 78711-2788
Phone: 800-242-3062
Fax: 512-427-6420
Web: www.thecb.state.tx.us

United Methodist Church

United Methodist Loan Program

Type of award: Loan, renewable.
Intended use: For undergraduate or graduate study at accredited postsecondary institution in United States.
Eligibility: Applicant must be United Methodist. Applicant must be U.S. citizen or permanent resident.
Additional information: Must be active member of United Methodist Church one year prior to application. Must maintain "C" average. May reapply for loan to maximum of $15,000. Interest rate 6%; cosigner required. Ten years permitted to repay loan after graduation or withdrawal from school. Qualified applicants are chosen on a first come, first served basis.
Amount of award: $2,500

Contact:
United Methodist Church/ Board of Higher Education and Ministry
Office of Loans and Scholarships
P.O. Box 340007
Nashville, TN 37203-0007
Phone: 615-340-7346
Web: www.gbhem.org

UPS

United Parcel Service Earn & Learn Program Loans

Type of award: Loan.
Intended use: For undergraduate study at accredited vocational, 2-year or 4-year institution in United States.
Eligibility: Applicant or parent must be employed by United Parcel Service (UPS).
Application requirements: Proof of eligibility. Must be UPS employee at participating location.
Additional information: Award is $2,000 per year in forgivable student loans. UPS pays back percentage of loan as long as student remains employed by UPS. Visit Website for specifics.
Contact:
UPS
55 Glenlake Parkway N.E.
Atlanta, GA 30328
Phone: 888-WORK-UPS
Web: www.upsjobs.com

U.S. Department of Education

Federal Direct Stafford Loans

Type of award: Loan, renewable.
Intended use: For undergraduate or graduate study at postsecondary institution.
Eligibility: Applicant must be U.S. citizen or permanent resident.
Basis for selection: Applicant must demonstrate financial need.
Application requirements: Proof of eligibility. Send FAFSA, loan application and promissory note.
Additional information: Maximum interest rate 8.25 percent. Some loans subsidized, based on need eligibilty. Loan amount depends on grade level in school and student type. Telecommunications Device for the Deaf at 800-730-8913. FAFSA available online.
Amount of award: $2,625-$18,500
Application deadline: June 30
Contact:
Federal Student Aid Programs
P.O. Box 84
Washington, DC 20044-0084
Phone: 800-4-FED-AID
Web: http://studentaid.ed.gov

Loans

Federal Family Education Loan Program (FFEL)

Type of award: Loan, renewable.
Intended use: For undergraduate or graduate study at accredited postsecondary institution in or outside United States or Canada. Designated institutions: Schools approved by the U.S. Department of Education.
Eligibility: Applicant must be U.S. citizen or permanent resident.
Basis for selection: Applicant must demonstrate financial need.
Application requirements: Proof of eligibility. Send FAFSA.
Additional information: Subsidized and unsubsidized loans. If school participates in FFEL program, private lender provides funds for loan, although federal government guarantees loan funds. First-year undergraduates eligible for up to $2,625. Maximum interest rate 8.25 percent.
  Application deadline: June 30
Contact:
Federal Student Aid Programs
P.O. Box 84
Washington, DC 20044-0084
Phone: 800-4-FED-AID
Web: http://studentaid.ed.gov

Federal Perkins Loan

Type of award: Loan, renewable.
Intended use: For undergraduate or graduate study at accredited postsecondary institution in United States.
Eligibility: Applicant must be U.S. citizen or permanent resident.
Basis for selection: Applicant must demonstrate financial need.
Application requirements: Proof of eligibility. Send FAFSA.
Additional information: Maximum annual loan amount: $4,000 for undergraduates, $6,000 for graduates. Five percent interest rate. Applicant must demonstrate exceptional financial need. Repayment begins nine months after graduation, leaving school, or dropping below half-time status.
  Application deadline: June 30
Contact:
Federal Student Aid Programs
P.O. Box 84
Washington, DC 20044-0084
Phone: 800-4-FED AID
Web: http://studentaid.ed.gov

Federal Plus Loan

Type of award: Loan.
Intended use: For undergraduate or graduate study at accredited postsecondary institution in or outside United States or Canada. Designated institutions: Schools approved by the U.S. Department of Education.
Eligibility: Applicant must be U.S. citizen or permanent resident.
Basis for selection: Applicant must demonstrate financial need.
Application requirements: Must pass credit check. Must file PLUS loan application and sign promissory note. FAFSA. Student must be dependent enrolled at least half-time.
Additional information: Unsubsidized loans for parents of student. Interest rate is flexible, but capped at nine percent annually. Award amount varies. Loan is equal to cost of attendance minus any other financial aid. Generally, repayment must begin 60 days after the loan is fully disbursed.
  Application deadline: June 30
Contact:
Federal Student Aid Programs
P.O. Box 84
Washington, DC 20044-0084
Phone: 800-4-FED-AID
Web: http://studentaid.ed.gov

Utah State Office of Education

Utah Career Teaching Scholarship/ T.H. Bell Teaching Incentive Loan

Type of award: Loan, renewable.
Intended use: For full-time undergraduate study at accredited postsecondary institution. Designated institutions: Utah schools.
Eligibility: Applicant must be high school senior. Applicant must be U.S. citizen residing in Utah.
Basis for selection: Major/career interest in education, teacher; education; education, early childhood or education, special.
Application requirements: Transcript. SAT/ACT scores.
Additional information: Provides tuition waiver with additional awards to limited number of qualified recipients. Loan forgiveness for teaching in Utah public schools. Application available after January 15.
  Amount of award: Full tuition
  Number of awards: 25
  Number of applicants: 320
  Application deadline: March 31
  Notification begins: May 15
Contact:
High school counselor or financial aid officer.

Vermont Student Assistance Corporation

VSAC Advantage Loan

Type of award: Loan.
Intended use: For undergraduate or graduate study at vocational, 2-year, 4-year or graduate institution in United States.
Eligibility: Applicant must be U.S. citizen residing in Vermont.
Basis for selection: Applicant must demonstrate financial need.
Additional information: Applicant must be eligible for federal aid and borrowing maximum for Stafford Loan. Must be enrolled or reenrolling at least half-time at an eligible postsecondary school. Interest rate changes quarterly.
Contact:
Vermont Student Assistance Corporation
Education Loan Finance Department
P.O. Box 2000
Winooski, VT 05404
Phone: 800-798-8722
Web: www.vsac.org

Virgin Islands Board of Education

Virgin Islands Territorial Grants/ Loans Program

Type of award: Loan, renewable.
Intended use: For full-time undergraduate or graduate study at accredited postsecondary institution.
Eligibility: Applicant must be high school senior. Applicant must be U.S. citizen or permanent resident residing in Virgin Islands.
Basis for selection: Applicant must demonstrate financial need.
Application requirements: Transcript. Application. Acceptance letter from institution for first-time applicants or transfer students.
Additional information: Combined loan and grant program to assist Virgin Islands residents. Minimum 2.0 GPA. Must agree to accept employment in Virgin Islands government one year for every year of award upon completion of studies. Number and amount of awards vary. 6% interest on repayment, additional 2% if delinquent.

 Amount of award: $500-$2,500
 Application deadline: May 1
Contact:
Scholarship Committee
Virgin Islands Board of Education
P.O. Box 11900
St. Thomas, VI 801
Phone: 340-774-4546

West Virginia Higher Education Policy Commission

West Virginia Underwood-Smith Teacher Scholarship

Type of award: Loan, renewable.
Intended use: For full-time junior, senior or graduate study at 4-year or graduate institution. Designated institutions: West Virginia institutions.
Eligibility: Applicant must be U.S. citizen or permanent resident residing in West Virginia.
Basis for selection: Major/career interest in education, teacher. Applicant must demonstrate high academic achievement.
Application requirements: Essay, proof of eligibility. Must be enrolled at a West Virginia instituiton of higher education as a full-time student in a course of study leading to certification as a teacher. Must have cumulative 3.25 GPA.
Additional information: Must rank in top 10 percent of class. Must be permanent resident of West Virginia. Undergraduate applicants must be juniors or seniors already majoring in education. Number of applicants varies. Recipients must agree to teach at the public school level in West Virginia for 2 years for each year the scholarship was received or be willing to repay the scholarship on a pro rata basis.

 Amount of award: $5,000
 Number of awards: 54
 Application deadline: March 1
 Notification begins: July 1
 Total amount awarded: $258,470
Contact:
West Virginia Higher Education Policy Commission
Underwood-Smith Teacher Scholarship Program
1018 Kanawha Boulevard East, Suite 700
Charleston, WV 25301-2827
Phone: 304-558-4618 or 888-825-5707
Fax: 304-558-4622
Web: www.hepc.wvnet.edu

Wisconsin Department of Veterans Affairs

Wisconsin Veterans Affairs Personal Loan Program

Type of award: Loan.
Intended use: For undergraduate or graduate study at postsecondary institution in United States.
Eligibility: Applicant must be residing in Wisconsin. Applicant must be veteran; or dependent of veteran or deceased veteran; or spouse of veteran or deceased veteran. Must meet WDVA service requirements. Must have 90 days of active duty during wartime and/or two years of continuous active duty.
Application requirements: Applicant must have been a resident of Wisconsin on entry into military service or a continuous resident of Wisconsin for at least one year immediately preceding the application date. Must be current Wisconsin resident.
Additional information: Loan amount up to $25,000 annually. Subsidized annual interest rate varies; loan has ten-year term. Apply to local county veterans service officer to establish eligibility.
Contact:
Wisconsin Department of Veterans Affairs
P.O. Box 7843
30 West Mifflin Street
Madison, WI 53703-7843
Phone: 800-947-8387
Web: http://dva.state.wi.us

Wisconsin Higher Educational Aids Board

Wisconsin Minority Teacher Loan Program

Type of award: Loan, renewable.
Intended use: For junior or senior study at accredited 4-year institution.
Eligibility: Applicant must be Asian American, African American, Mexican American, Hispanic American, Puerto Rican or American Indian. Asian American applicants must be either former citizens or descendants of former citizens of Laos,

Vietnam, or Cambodia admitted to the U.S. after 12/31/1975. Applicant must be residing in Wisconsin.

Basis for selection: Major/career interest in education; education, special or education, teacher. Applicant must demonstrate financial need.

Application requirements: Nomination by Student Financial Aid Department. FAFSA.

Additional information: Recipient must agree to teach in Wisconsin school district where minority students constitute at least 29% of enrollment or in school district participating in the inter-district pupil transfer (Chapter 220) program. For each year student teaches in eligible district, 25% of loan is forgiven; otherwise loan must be repaid at interest rate of 5%.

Amount of award: $250-$2,500
Number of awards: 109
Total amount awarded: $238,662
Contact:
Higher Educational Aids Board
Attn: Mary Lou Kuzdas
131 West Wilson
Madison, WI 53707
Phone: 608-267-2212

Loans

Sponsor Index

Sponsor Index

579

Sponsor Index

Program Index

Program Index

2004–2005 SAT Program Test Calendar

Test Dates	Oct. 9*	Nov. 6	Dec. 4	Jan. 22*	Mar. 12* New SAT	May 7 New SAT	June 4 New SAT
Registration Deadlines							
Regular	Sept. 7	Oct. 1	Oct. 29	Dec. 20	Feb. 7	Mar. 25	Apr. 29
Late	Sept. 11	Oct. 13	Nov. 10	Dec. 29	Feb. 16	Apr. 6	May 11
SAT Reasoning Test	■	■	■	■	■	■	■
SAT Subject Tests							
Writing	■	■	■	■			
Literature	■	■	■	■		■	■
United States (U.S.) History	■	■	■	■		■	■
World History				■			■
Math Level 1	■	■	■	■		■	■
Math Level 2	■	■	■	■		■	■
Biology E/M (Ecological/Molecular)	■	■	■	■		■	■
Chemistry	■	■	■	■		■	■
Physics	■	■	■	■		■	■
Languages: Reading Only							
French	■		■	■		■	■
German							■
Modern Hebrew							■
Italian				■			
Latin				■			■
Spanish	■		■	■		■	■
Languages: Reading and Listening							
Chinese		■					
French		■					
German		■					
Japanese		■					
Korean		■					
Spanish		■					
ELPT™		■		■			

* Question-and-Answer Service available.
†Calculator required
NOTE: Sunday test dates follow each Saturday test date for students who cannot test on Saturday because of a religious observance.

SERVICES FOR STUDENTS WITH DISABILITIES

Students may receive accommodations (extended time, large print, etc.) on College Board exams if they submit an eligibility form and meet the Eligibility Requirements. **Students must: 1)** have a disability that requires testing accommodations; **2)** have documentation on file that supports the need for accommodations; **3)** receive and use the requested accommodations for school-based tests. (See program material regarding the Guidelines for Documentation, and for exceptions to the above requirements.)

Contacts
Voice   609 771-7137
TTY   609 882-4118
Fax   609 771-7944
E-mail   sat.ssd@ets.org